Houghton
Mifflin
Harcourt

collections

GRADE 10

Program Consultants:

Kylene Beers

Martha Hougen

Carol Jago

William L. McBride

Erik Palmer

Lydia Stack

HISTORY

Cover, Title Page Photo Credits: © Pulse/Corbis

Printed in the U.S.A.

ISBN 978-0-544-08713-2

2 3 4 5 6 7 8 9 10 0914 22 21 20 19 18 17 16 15 14 13

4500432003   A B C D E F G

collections

Houghton Mifflin Harcourt

Teacher's Edition Table of Contents

Kylene Beers Nationally known lecturer and author on Reading and Literacy; 2011 recipient of the Conference on English Leadership Exemplary Leader Award; coauthor of *Notice and Note: Strategies for Close Reading*; former President of the National Council of Teachers of English. Dr. Beers is the nationally known author of *When Kids Can't Read: What Teachers Can Do* and coeditor of *Adolescent Literacy: Turning Promise into Practice*, as well as articles in the *Journal of Adolescent and Adult Literacy*. Former editor of *Voices from the Middle*, she is the 2001 recipient of NCTE's Richard W. Halley Award, given for outstanding contributions to middle-school literacy. She recently served as Senior Reading Researcher at the Comer School Development Program at Yale University as well as Senior Reading Advisor to Secondary Schools for the Reading and Writing Project at Teachers College.

Martha Hougen National consultant, presenter, researcher, and author. Areas of expertise include differentiating instruction for students with learning difficulties, including those with learning disabilities and dyslexia; and teacher and leader preparation improvement. Dr. Hougen has taught at the middle school through graduate levels. Recently her focus has been on working with teacher educators to enhance teacher and leader preparation to better meet the needs of all students. Currently she is working with the University of Florida at the Collaboration for Effective Educator Development, Accountability, and Reform Center (CEEDAR Center) to improve the achievement of students with disabilities by reforming teacher and leader licensure, evaluation, and preparation. She has led similar efforts in Texas with the Higher Education Collaborative and the College & Career Readiness Initiative Faculty Collaboratives. In addition to peer-reviewed articles, curricular documents, and presentations, Dr. Hougen has published two college textbooks: *The Fundamentals of Literacy Assessment and Instruction Pre-K–6* (2012) and *The Fundamentals of Literacy Assessment and Instruction 6–12* (2014).

Carol Jago Teacher of English with 32 years of experience at Santa Monica High School in California; author and nationally known lecturer; and Past President of the National Council of Teachers of English. Currently serves as Associate Director of the California Reading and Literature Project at UCLA. With expertise in standards assessment and secondary education, Ms. Jago is the author of numerous books on education, including *With Rigor for All* and *Papers, Papers, Papers*, and is active with the California Association of Teachers of English, editing its scholarly journal *California English* since 1996. Ms. Jago also served on the planning committee for the 2009 NAEP Framework and the 2011 NAEP Writing Framework.

William L. McBride Curriculum Specialist. Dr. McBride is a nationally known speaker, educator, and author who now trains teachers in instructional methodologies. He is coauthor of *What's Happening*, an innovative, high-interest text for middle-grade readers, and author of *If They Can Argue Well, They Can Write Well*. A former reading specialist, English teacher, and social studies teacher, he holds a master's degree in reading and a doctorate in curriculum and instruction from the University of North Carolina at Chapel Hill. Dr. McBride has contributed to the development of textbook series in language arts, social studies, science, and vocabulary. He is also known for his novel *Entertaining an Elephant*, which tells the story of a veteran teacher who becomes reinspired with both his profession and his life.

Erik Palmer Veteran teacher and education consultant based in Denver, Colorado. Author of *Well Spoken: Teaching Speaking to All Students* and *Digitally Speaking: How to Improve Student Presentations*. His areas of focus include improving oral communication, promoting technology in classroom presentations, and updating instruction through the use of digital tools. He holds a bachelor's degree from Oberlin College and a master's degree in curriculum and instruction from the University of Colorado.

Lydia Stack International ESL consultant. Director of the Screening and Assessment Center in the San Francisco Unified School District. Her areas of expertise are English language teaching strategies, ESL standards for students and teachers, and curriculum writing. Her teaching experience includes 25 years as an elementary and high school ESL teacher. She is past president of TESOL. Her awards include the James E. Alatis Award for Service to TESOL and the San Francisco STAR Teacher Award. Her publications include *On Our Way to English*; *Wordways*; *Games for Language Learning*; and *Visions: Language, Literature, Content*.

Additional thanks to the following Program Reviewers:

Rosemary Asquino
Sylvia B. Bennett
Yvonne Bradley
Leslie Brown
Haley Carroll
Caitlin Chalmers
Emily Colley-King
Stacy Collins
Denise DeBonis
Courtney Dickerson
Sarah Easley
Phyllis J. Everette
Peter J. Foy Sr.

Carol M. Gibby
Angie Gill
Mary K. Goff
Saira Haas
Lisa M. Janeway
Robert V. Kidd Jr.
Kim Lilley
John C. Lowe
Taryn Curtis MacGee
Meredith S. Maddox
Cynthia Martin
Kelli M. McDonough
Megan Pankiewicz

Linda Beck Pieplow
Molly Pieplow
Mary-Sarah Proctor
Jessica A. Stith
Peter Swartley
Pamela Thomas
Linda A. Tobias
Rachel Ukleja
Lauren Vint
Heather Lynn York
Leigh Ann Zerr

Collections offers maximum **flexibility** for planning instruction.

Teacher Dashboard

Log onto the Teacher Dashboard and *my*SmartPlanner. Use these **versatile** and fully **searchable** tools to **customize** lessons that engage students and achieve your instructional goals.

Text Complexity Rubrics

help you identify dimensions of complex text.

COLLECTION 1 INSTRUCTIONAL OVERVIEW   PLAN

Collection 1 Lessons	Key Learning Objective	Performance Task	Vocabulary Strategy	Language and Style	Student Instructional Support	CLOSE READER Selection
ANCHOR TEXT Argument by Anna Quindlen *"A Quilt of a Country,"* p. 000 — Lexile 1260	The student will be able to... analyze an author's claim and delineate and evaluate an argument	Writing Activity: Argument	Patterns of Word Changes	Noun Clauses	**Scaffolding for ELL Students:** Understand Cultural References **When Students Struggle:** Summarize (label not in TE)	Blog by Eboo Patel *"Making the Future Better, Together,"* p. 000 — Lexile 0000
ANCHOR TEXT Short Story by Nadine Gordimer *"Once Upon a Time,"* p. 000 — Lexile 1390	The student will be able to... analyze author's choices concerning the structure of a text and determine and make inferences about the theme of a work of fiction	Speaking Activity: Fairy Tale	Words from Latin	Prepositional Phrases	**Scaffolding for ELL Students:** Language: Dialect **When Students Struggle:** • Theme • Words from Latin **To Challenge Students:** Write from Author's Perspective	Short Story by Lisa Fugard *"Night Calls,"* p. 000 — Lexile 0000
Essay by Kimberly M. Blaeser from *"Rituals of Memory,"* p. 000 — Lexile 1380	The student will be able to... determine a central idea and analyze its development over the course of a text	Speaking Activity: Discussion	Denotations and Connotations		**Scaffolding for ELL Students:** Analyze Language **When Students Struggle:** Main Idea and Supporting Details	
Speech by Abraham Lincoln *"The Gettysburg Address,"* p. 000 — Lexile 1170	The student will be able to... analyze an author's purpose and the use of rhetorical devices in a seminal U.S. document	Speaking Activity: Presentation	Multiple-Meaning Words	Parallel Structure	**Scaffolding for ELL Students:** Analyze Language **When Students Struggle:** Comprehension **To Challenge Students:** Tone and Structure	Speech by Bill Clinton *"Oklahoma Bombing Memorial Address,"* p. 000 — Lexile 0000
Photo Essay *"Views of the Wall,"* p. 000 Poem by Alberto Rios *"The Vietnam Wall,"* p. 000	The student will be able to... analyze the representation of a subject in two separate mediums	Media Activity: Reflection			**Scaffolding for ELL Students:** Build Background **When Students Struggle:** Compare Text and Photos	

COLLECTION 1 DIGITAL OVERVIEW

mySmartPlanner | **eBook** | **myNotebook** | **my WriteSmart** | **fyi**

Collection 1 Lessons	Media	Teach and Practice		Assess	
Student Edition | eBook	▶ Video Links	**Close Reading and Evidence Tracking**		Performance Task	Online Assessment
ANCHOR TEXT Argument by Anna Quindlen *"A Quilt of a Country"*	🔊 Audio *"A Quilt of a Country"*	**Close Read Screencasts** • Modeled Discussion 1 (lines 22-28) • Modeled Discussion 2 (lines 72-79) • Close Read application pdf (lines 00-000)	**Strategies for Annotation** • Delineate and Evaluate an Argument • Patterns of Word Change	Writing Activity: Argument	Selection Test
CLOSE READER Blog by Eboo Patel *"Making the Future Better, Together"*	🔊 Audio *"Making the Future Better, Together"*				
ANCHOR TEXT Short Story by Nadine Gordimer *"Once Upon a Time"*	🔊 Audio *"Once Upon a Time"*	**Close Read Screencasts** • Modeled Discussion 1 (lines 1-10) • Modeled Discussion 2 (lines 121-130) • Close Read application pdf (lines 000-000)	**Strategies for Annotation** • Analyze Author's Choices: Text Structure	Speaking Activity: Fairy Tale	Selection Test
CLOSE READER Short Story by Lisa Fugard *"Night Calls"*	🔊 Audio *"Night Calls"*				
Essay by Kimberly M. Blaeser from *"Rituals of Memory"*	🔊 Audio from *"Rituals of Memory"*		**Strategies for Annotation** • Determine Central Idea • Denotation and Connotation	Speaking Activity: Discussion	Selection Test
Speech by Abraham Lincoln *"The Gettysburg Address"*	▶ Video HISTORY *"The Gettysburg Address: A New Declaration of Independence"* 🔊 Audio *"The Gettysburg Address"*		**Strategies for Annotation** • Analyze Seminal U.S. Documents	Speaking Activity: Presentation	Selection Test
CLOSE READER Speech by Bill Clinton *"Oklahoma Bombing Memorial Address"*	🔊 Audio *"Oklahoma Bombing Memorial Address"*				
Photo Essay *Views of the Wall* Poem by Alberto Rios *"The Vietnam Wall"*	▶ Video HISTORY *"Remembering Fallen Friends"* 🔊 Audio *"The Vietnam Wall"*		**Strategies for Annotation** • Analyze Representations in Different Mediums	Media Activity: Reflection	Selection Test
Collection 1 Performance Tasks: A Presparing a Speech B Writing an Analytical Essay	**fyi** hmhfyi.com	**Interactive Lessons** A Writing Arguments A Giving a Presentation	B Writing Informative Texts B Using Textual Evidence	A Preparing a Speech B Writing an Analytical Essay	Collection Test

Print planning pages show the integrated Table of Contents and all assets in the **Student Edition** and the **Close Reader.**

For Systematic Coverage of Writing and Speaking & Listening Standards	**Interactive Lessons** Writing as a Process Participating in Collaborative Discussions	**Lesson Assessments** Writing as a Process Participating in Collaborative Discussions

Digital natives?   Media enthusiasts?   Writers?

Collections engages learners with today's digital tools.

Voices and images from **A&E®, bio.®,** and **HISTORY®** transport students to different times and places.

Online Tools allow students to annotate critical passages for discussion and writing, by using **highlighting, underlining,** and **notes.**

***my*Notebook** stores students' annotations and notes for use in **Performance Tasks.**

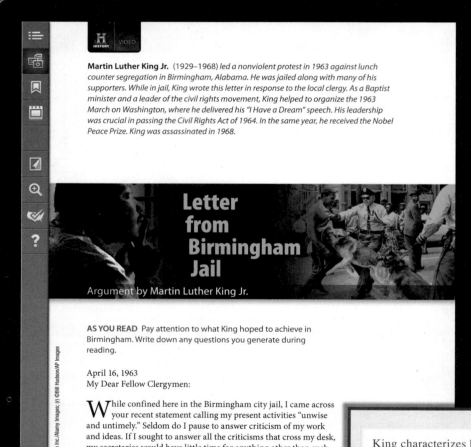

Martin Luther King Jr. (1929–1968) *led a nonviolent protest in 1963 against lunch counter segregation in Birmingham, Alabama. He was jailed along with many of his supporters. While in jail, King wrote this letter in response to the local clergy. As a Baptist minister and a leader of the civil rights movement, King helped to organize the 1963 March on Washington, where he delivered his "I Have a Dream" speech. His leadership was crucial in passing the Civil Rights Act of 1964. In the same year, he received the Nobel Peace Prize. King was assassinated in 1968.*

Letter from Birmingham Jail

Argument by Martin Luther King Jr.

AS YOU READ Pay attention to what King hoped to achieve in Birmingham. Write down any questions you generate during reading.

April 16, 1963
My Dear Fellow Clergymen:

While confined here in the Birmingham city jail, I came across your recent statement calling my present activities "unwise and untimely." Seldom do I pause to answer criticism of my work and ideas. If I sought to answer all the criticisms that cross my desk, my secretaries would have little time for anything other than such correspondence in the course of the day, and I would have no time for constructive work. But since I feel that you are men of genuine good will and that your criticisms are sincerely set forth, I want to t... ur statement in what I hope will be patient and reasonable terms.

I think I should indicate why I am here in Birmingham, since you have been influenced by the view which argues against "outsiders coming in." I have the honor of serving as president of ... hristian Leadership Conference, an organization

Letter from Birmingham Jail **319**

Student Note ✕

King characterizes his critics as "men of good-will" to suggest that an understanding can be reached with them.

✓ **Save to Notebook**   **Delete**   **Save**

*my*Notebook

King characterizes his critics as "men of good-will" to suggest that an understanding can be reached with them.

Informational text

on **fyi** is linked to each collection topic and is **curated** and **updated** monthly.

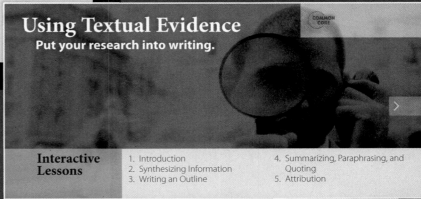

Available in Your eBook

Digital Collections

for **writing, speaking,** and **listening** provide opportunities for in-depth instruction and practice in key 21st-century skills.

Available in Your eBook

Media Lessons

prompt students to read **news reports, literary adaptations, ads,** and **websites** as complex texts.

Close reading strategies? Conversations about text?

Collections prepares students for rigorous expectations.

Background *The Hmong (hmông) are an ethnic group from southern China, Laos, Vietnam, and Thailand. In the 1970s, war and conflict caused many of the Hmong people in Laos to flee to refugee camps in Thailand. Author* **Kao Kalia Yang** *(b. 1980) was born in one of these camps. She moved with her family, including her older sister Dawb, to Minnesota in 1987. Four other siblings were born in the United States, where all the Yang children received their educations.*

from
The Latehomecomer

Memoir by Kao Kalia Yang

SETTING A PURPOSE As you read, notice the challenges and the opportunities that life in a new country presents Kao Kalia Yang and her family. How does Yang react to her situation?

We had been in America for almost ten years. I was nearly fifteen, and Dawb had just gotten her driver's license. The children were growing up. We needed a new home—the apartment was too small. There was hardly room to breathe when the scent of jasmine rice and fish steamed with ginger mingled heavily with the scent of freshly baked pepperoni pizza—Dawb's favorite food. We had been looking for a new house for nearly six months.

It was in a poor neighborhood with houses that were
10 ready to collapse—wooden planks falli[ng] away, sloping porches—and huge, old tr[ees.] realty sign in the front yard, a small pat[ch] of the white house. It was one story, wit[h] and a single wide window framed by bla[ck] black door. There was a short driveway [...]

(c) ©Houghton Mifflin Harcourt; (t) ©Der Yang

Anchor Texts
drive each collection and have related selections in the **Close Reader.**

Close Reading Screencasts
provide **modeled conversations** about text at point of use in your **eBook.**

I was feeling a strong push to reinvent myself. Without my realizing, by the time high school began, I had a feeling in the pit of my stomach that I had been on simmer for too long. I wanted to bubble over the top and douse the confusing fire that burned in my belly. Or else I wanted to turn the stove off. I wanted to sit cool on the burners of life, lid on, and steady. I was ready for change, but there was so little in my life that I could adjust. So life took a blurry seat.

These images give the impression the narrator is uncomfortable.

Background *A member of the Standing Rock Sioux,* **Susan Power** *was born in 1961 and grew up in Chicago. She spent her childhood listening to her mother tell stories about their American Indian heritage. These stories later served as inspiration for Power's writing. As a young girl, Power made frequent visits with her mother to local museums—trips that inspired her memoir "Museum Indians."*

Museum Indians

Memoir by Susan Power

© Houghton Mifflin Harcourt Publishing Company • Image Credits: ©Sophie Bassouls/Sygma/Corbis; © Werner Forman/Universal Images Group/Getty Images

1. **READ ▶** As you read lines 1–16, begin to cite text evidence.

- Underline a metaphor in the first paragraph that describes the mother's braid.
- Underline a metaphor in the second paragraph that describes the mother's braid differently.
- In the margin, note the adjectives the narrator uses to describe the braid.

CLOSE READ
Notes

A snake coils in my mother's dresser drawer; it is thick and black, glossy as sequins. My mother cut her hair several years ago, before I was born, but she kept one heavy braid. It is the <u>three-foot snake</u> I lift from its nest and handle as if it were alive.

"Mom, why did you cut your hair?" I ask. I am a little girl lifting a <u>sleek black river</u> into the light that streams through the kitchen window. Mom turns to me.

"It gave me headaches. Now put that away and wash your hands for lunch."

10 "You won't cut *my* hair, will you?" I'm sure this is a whi[...]

"No, just a little trim now and then to even the e[...]

I return the dark snake to its nest among[...]

arranging it so that its thin tail hide[...]

thick
black
glossy

Close Reader

allows students to apply standards and practice close reading strategies in a consumable **print** or **digital** format.

Image Credits: ©dboystudio/Shutterstock

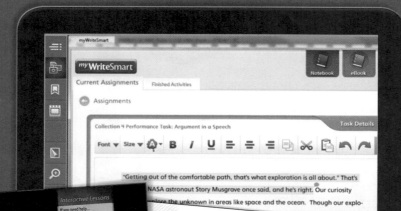

myWriteSmart

Current Assignments   Finished Activities

Assignments

Collection 4 Performance Task: Argument in a Speech   Task Details

Font ▾ Size ▾ A ▾ B i U

"Getting out of the comfortable path, that's what exploration is all about." That's
NASA astronaut Story Musgrave once said, and he's right. Our curiosity
explore the unknown in areas like space and the ocean. Though our explo-
advances in medicine

Interactive Lessons
If you need help...
• Writing Arguments
• Using Textual Evidence

COLLECTION 1
PERFORMANCE TASK

Write an Argument

This collection focuses on how and why Europeans came to the Americas and what happened as they settled in unfamiliar environments. Relocating to the Americas dramatically changed settlers' lives. In turn, the settlers changed the Americas through their interaction with its land and its native populations. Look back at the anchor text, "Of Plymouth Plantation," and at other texts you have read in this collection. Synthesize your ideas about them by writing an argument. Your argument should persuade readers to agree with your claim about how immigration changed America, and how America changes those who come here.

COMMON CORE

W 1a–e Write arguments to support claims in an analysis of substantive topics or texts, using valid reasoning and relevant and sufficient evidence.
W 9 Draw evidence form literary or informational texts to support analysis, reflection, and research.

An effective argument

- identifies a central issue or question
- states a precise claim in response to the question
- develops the claim with valid reasons and relevant evidence, such as examples and quotations from the texts
- anticipates opposing claims and counters them with well-supported counterclaims
- establishes clear, logical connections among claims, counterclaims, reasons, and evidence
- includes an introduction, a logically structured body including transitions, and a conclusion
- maintains an appropriate tone based on its audience and context
- follows the conventions of written English

PLAN

*my*Notebook

Analyze the Text Think about the following questions as they relate to the anchor text, "Of Plymouth Plantation":

- Why did European settlers come to the New World?
- When settlers came to explore and settle the Americas, how did it change their lives?
- What changes did these settlers bring to the Americas?

Choose one question to address in your argument. Then, select three texts from this collection—including "Of Plymouth Plantation"—that provide evidence for your position. These texts might present similar or different views from each other.

ACADEMIC VOCABULARY

As you share your ideas about the role of immigration in American society, be sure to use these words.

adapt
coherent
device
displace
dynamic

Collection Performance Task   **103**

COLLECTION 6   **TASK A**
ARGUMENT

Ideas and Evidence	Organization	Language
ADVANCED • The introduction is memorable and persuasive; the claim clearly states a position on a substantive topic. • Valid reasons and relevant evidence from the texts convincingly support the writer's claim. • Counterclaims are anticipated and effectively addressed with counterarguments. • The concluding section effectively summarizes the claim.	• The reasons and textual evidence are organized consistently and logically throughout the argument. • Varied transitions logically connect reasons and textual evidence to the writer's claim.	• The writing reflects a formal style and an objective, or controlled, tone. • Sentence beginnings, lengths, and structures vary and have a rhythmic flow. • Spelling, capitalization, and punctuation are correct. • Grammar and usage are correct.
COMPETENT • The introduction could do more to capture the reader's attention; the claim states a position on an issue. • Most reasons and evidence from the texts support the writer's claim, but they could be more convincing. • Counterclaims are anticipated, but the counterarguments need to be developed more. • The concluding section restates the claim.	• The organization of reasons and textual evidence is confusing in a few places. • A few more transitions are needed to connect reasons and textual evidence to the writer's claim.	• The style is informal in a few places, and the tone is defensive at times. • Sentence beginnings, lengths, and structures vary somewhat. • Several spelling and capitalization mistakes occur, and punctuation is inconsistent. • Some grammatical and usage errors are repeated in the argument.
• The introduction is ordinary; the claim identifies an issue, but the writer's position is not clearly stated. • The reasons and evidence from the texts are not always logical or relevant. • Counterclaims are anticipated but not addressed logically. • The concluding section includes an incomplete summary of the claim.	• The organization of reasons and textual evidence is logical in some places, but it often doesn't follow a pattern. • Many more transitions are needed to connect reasons and textual evidence to the writer's position.	• The style becomes informal in many places, and the tone is often dismissive of other viewpoints. • Sentence structures barely vary, and some fragments or run-on sentences are present. • Spelling, capitalization, and punctuation are often incorrect but do not make reading the argument difficult. • Grammar and usage are incorrect in many places, but the writer's ideas are still clear.
The introduction is missing. Significant supporting reasons and evidence from the texts are missing. Counterclaims are neither anticipated nor addressed. The concluding section is missing.	• An organizational strategy is not used; reasons and textual evidence are presented randomly. • Transitions are not used, making the argument difficult to understand.	• The style is inappropriate, and the tone is disrespectful. • Repetitive sentence structure, fragments, and run-on sentences make the writing monotonous and hard to follow. • Spelling and capitalization are often incorrect, and punctuation is missing. • Many grammatical and usage errors change the meaning of the writer's ideas.

604   Collection 6

T10 Grade 10

Common Core Assessment

print and **online** resources provide instruction in three steps: **Analyze the Model, Practice the Task,** and **Perform the Task.**

STEP 2 PRACTICE THE TASK

Should a business have the right to ban teenagers?

You will read:

▶ A NEWSPAPER AD
Munchy's Promise

▶ A BUSINESS ANALYSIS
Munchy's Patrons in July–October

▶ A STUDENT BLOG
Munchy's Bans Students!

▶ A NEWSPAPER EDITORIAL
A Smart Idea Can Save a Business

You will write:

▶ AN ARGUMENTATIVE ESSAY
Should a business have the right to ban teenagers?

Unit 1: Argumentative Essay **9**

Mr. Jones,
Here is the analysis of
July vs. October data.
Your Accountant,
Hector Ramirez, CPA

Munchy's Patrons in October

■ minors
■ adults

73%

Monthly Sales

■ minors
■ adults

September   October

...hart.

...wn in the graph?

...wo forms of data.

Unit 1: Argumentative Essay **11**

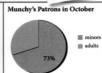

...ty studies on sleep deprivation have ...nly thing that might improve. An ...ositively affect a student's mood ...says that when he was in school, ...nd were better rested. With ...hers and students would get along

...agers should take affirmative ...therwise adjust to the reality of ...m to research done in the 1990s, ...nd wake patterns in adolescents ...xperts talked, and California ...stened. She introduced House ..., the "ZZZ's to A's Act," to ...earlier than 8:30 A.M.

...g again. It's 7:00 A.M. You say to ...nd I've got plenty of time to get ...e a huge difference in your mood

...ool should start later? If so, which data was the most

You use an effective transition to create cohesion and signal the introduction of another reason. Your language is formal and non-combative. You remain focused on your purpose.

You anticipated and addressed an opposing claim that is likely to occur to your audience. Your answer to the opposing claim is well-supported with valid evidence.

Smooth flow from beginning to end. Clear conclusion restates your claim. Your evidence is convincing. Excellent use of conventions of English. Good job!

Unit 1: Argumentative Essay **7**

Graphics

enhance instruction making **Common Core Assessment** unique and effective.

Common Core Enrichment App

provides instant feedback for **close reading practice** with appeal for today's students.

COLLECTION 1
Ourselves and Others

Collection Overviews

Each collection suggests different starting points, as well as overviews of digital resources and instructional topics for selections.

COLLECTION PERFORMANCE TASKS

Image Credits: ©Henry Balanay/Houghton Mifflin Harcourt

Annotated Student Edition Table of Contents

Topical Organization

Each collection reflects an engaging topic that connects selections for discussion and analysis, so students can explore several dimensions of the topic.

COMMON CORE

COLLECTION **1**

Ourselves and Others

KEY LEARNING OBJECTIVES
Support inferences about theme.
Analyze character motivations.
Analyze impact of word choice on tone.
Analyze how author creates tension through pacing.
Analyze impact of cultural background on point of view.

Cite text evidence to support inferences.
Analyze order of ideas.
Determine purpose and point of view.
Analyze seminal U.S. documents.

Close Reader

Image Credits: ©Henry Blakney/Houghton Mifflin Harcourt

eBook *Explore It!*

 Video Links 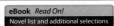 HISTORY A+E

 eBook *Read On!* Novel list and additional selections

fyi **Visit hmhfyi.com** for current articles and informational texts.

Common Core State Standards

Each collection addresses a range of **Common Core State Standards,** ensuring coverage of the Reading Literature and Reading Informational Texts standards.

Close Reader

The **Close Reader** provides selections related to the collection topic for additional practice and application of close reading skills and annotation strategies.

Student Edition + Close Reader

In each collection, the collection topic is explored in both the **Student Edition** and **Close Reader** selections. This page shows how the two components are integrated.

Annotated Student Edition Table of Contents

Anchor Texts

Complex and challenging, the anchor texts provide a cornerstone for exploring the collection topic, while also being integral to the Collection Performance Task. Close Reader selections relate to the Student Edition anchor texts.

Text-Dependent Questions

Both the Student Edition and the Close Reader include text-dependent questions that ask students to re-enter the text and cite textual evidence to support their claims.

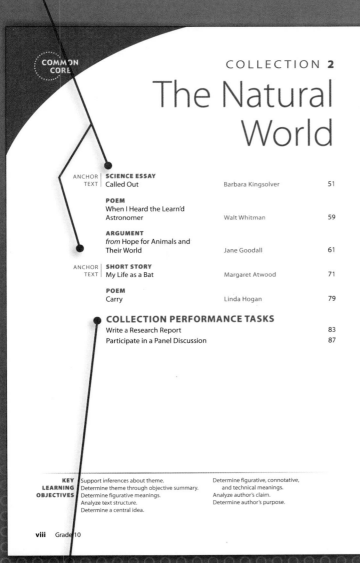

COMMON CORE

COLLECTION 2

The Natural World

KEY LEARNING OBJECTIVES

Support inferences about theme.
Determine theme through objective summary.
Determine figurative meanings.
Analyze text structure.
Determine a central idea.

Determine figurative, connotative, and technical meanings.
Analyze author's claim.
Determine author's purpose.

Close Reader

eBook *Explore It!*

  Video Links  eBook *Read On!* Novel list and additional selections Visit hmhfyi.com for current articles and informational texts.

Image Credits: ©Carlos Sanchez Pereyra/JAI/Corbis

Collection Performance Tasks

Collection Performance Tasks present a cumulative task for students. To develop writing or speaking products, students draw on their reading and analysis of the collection's selections, as well as additional research.

COLLECTION **3**
Responses to Change

Contemporary Selections

Selections by contemporary writers promote new insights into classic selections, enriching students' understanding of both classic and recent texts.

Image Credits: ©Dennis Novak/Photographer's Choice/Getty Images

Compare Texts

To enrich the analysis and discussion of each text, students compare and contrast selections, exploring how the writers' choices affect meaning.

COMMON CORE

COLLECTION **3**

Responses to Change

Close Reader

Image Credits: ©Dennis Novak/Photographer's Choice/Getty Images

eBook *Explore It!*

 Video Links  **eBook** *Read On!* Novel list and additional selections **Visit hmhfyi.com** for current articles and informational texts.

KEY LEARNING OBJECTIVES
Cite text evidence to support inferences.
Support inferences about theme.
Analyze representations in different mediums.
Analyze cause-and-effect order.
Determine technical meanings.
Analyze development of ideas.

Media Anchor

Like a print anchor, a media anchor provides a focus for the collection and is central to the Collection Performance Task.

eBook

The eBook, both Student Edition and Teacher's Edition, is the entryway to a full complement of digital resources.

INTEGRATED PROGRAM CONTENTS

Themes Across Time

Classic and contemporary selections illustrate how themes and topics transcend time and remain relevant to today's readers.

Image Credits: ©Mark Grenier/Shutterstock

COMMON CORE

COLLECTION **4**

How We See Things

Close Reader

eBook *Explore It!*

 Video Links HISTORY A&E

 eBook *Read On!*
Novel list and additional selections

 Visit hmhfyi.com
for current articles and
informational texts.

Image Credits: ©Mark Grenier/Shutterstock

KEY LEARNING OBJECTIVES
Paraphrase and summarize ideas.
Analyze poetic structure.
Analyze representations in different mediums.
Cite text evidence to support analysis.

Analyze development of ideas.
Understand scientific words and ideas.
Analyze effects of author's choices about structure.

COLLECTION 5
Absolute Power

Acclaimed Writers

Selections by acclaimed writers expose students to the very best in literary and nonfiction texts.

Annotated Student Edition Table of Contents

Media Analysis

Lessons based on media provide opportunities for students to apply analysis and techniques of close reading to other kinds of texts.

Variety of Genres

Both the Student Edition and the Close Reader include a variety of genres of literary texts, informational texts, and media. The genre of each selection is clearly labeled.

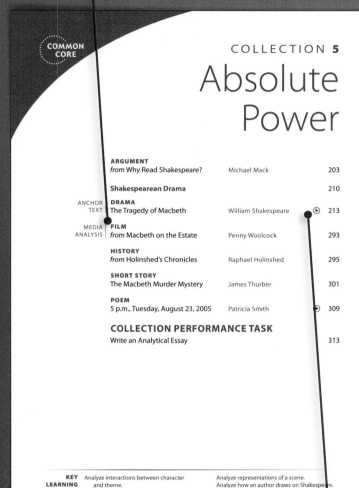

COMMON CORE

COLLECTION **5**

Absolute Power

KEY LEARNING OBJECTIVES	Analyze interactions between character and theme.	Analyze representations of a scene.
	Support inferences about how word choice affects tone.	Analyze how an author draws on Shakespeare.
		Analyze historical text.
		Analyze use of rhetoric in an argument.

Close Reader

DRAMA
from The Tragedy of Macbeth, Act I   William Shakespeare

Image Credits: ©Ruthven Carstairs/Alamy Images

eBook *Explore It!*

▶ **Video Links**   HISTORY   A&E   **eBook** *Read On!* Novel list and additional selections   **fyi** hmhfyi.com   **Visit hmhfyi.com** for current articles and informational texts.

Supplemental Video

▶ This icon indicates supplementary video that accompanies selections.

Adding the images and voices that make selections come alive, these video assets are available at point of use in the eBook.

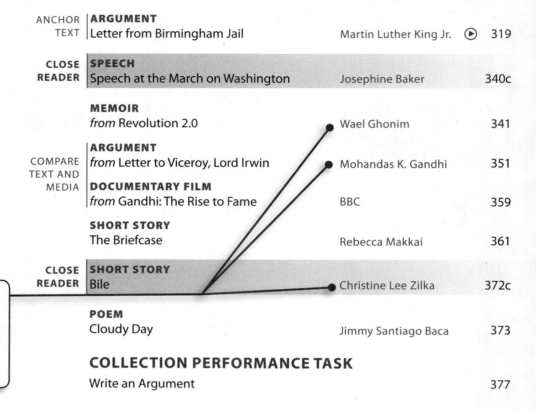

Cultural Diversity

To enrich students' perspectives, both the Student Edition and the Close Reader include selections by writers from diverse cultures.

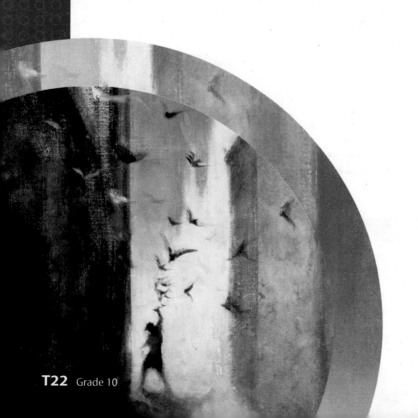

Annotated Student Edition Table of Contents

COMMON CORE

COLLECTION **6**

Hard-Won Liberty

Close Reader

Image Credits: Calle II, 2008 (oil on canvas) ©Bill Jacklin/Private Collection/The Bridgeman Art Library

eBook *Explore It!*

 Video Links   HISTORY   A&E

eBook *Read On!*
Novel list and additional selections

 Visit hmhfyi.com for current articles and informational texts.

KEY LEARNING OBJECTIVES
Analyze how tone contributes to theme.
Analyze interactions between character and theme.
Analyze evidence and ideas in a functional document.

Analyze use of rhetoric in an argument.
Analyze accounts of a subject in different mediums.
Analyze argument in a seminal document.

Student Resources

Information, Please

When students have questions, they can turn to Student Resources for answers. This section includes information about performance tasks; the nature of argument; vocabulary and spelling; and grammar, usage, and mechanics.

Word Knowledge

The Glossaries provide definitions for selection, academic, and domain-specific vocabulary, conveniently compiled in a single location.

Connecting to Your World

Every time you read something, view something, write to someone, or react to what you've read or seen, you're participating in a world of ideas. You do this every day, inside the classroom and out. These skills will serve you not only at home and at school, but eventually (if you can think that far ahead!), in your career.

The digital tools in this program will tap into the skills you already use and help you sharpen those skills for the future.

Start your exploration at my.hrw.com

Start with the Dashboard

Get one-stop access to the complete digital program for *collections*, as well as management and assessment tools.

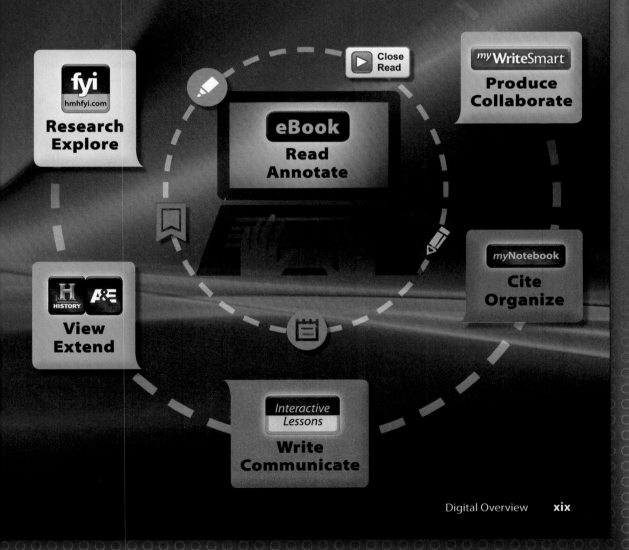

COMMON CORE

Writing and Speaking & Listening

Communication in today's world requires quite a variety of skills. To express yourself and win people over, you have to be able to write for print, for online media, and for spoken presentations. To collaborate, you have to work with people who might be sitting right next to you or at the other end of an Internet connection.

Comprehensive Standards Coverage

Twelve digital collections provide thorough coverage of all Writing and Speaking and Listening Common Core State Standards.

Available Only in Your eBook

Interactive Lessons

The interactive lessons in these collections will help you master the skills needed to become an expert communicator.

What Does a Strong Argument Look Like?

Read this argument and answer the questions about how the writer states and supports his position.

Tip

Pitching Perfect Pitch
by José Alvarez

Did you know that when you are listening to your favorite vocalist, you might be hearing a computer-generated pitch? Many record companies use pitch-correction software to ensure that their performers are pitch-perfect. While perfectionism is an admirable goal, there is a fine line between using technology to enhance music and using it to make performers into something they're not. Whether recording in the studio or playing a live performance, musicians should not use pitch-correction software. ●

Music production has become a digital experience. Producers use software to cut and paste pieces of music together, just like you cut and paste words together in your word-processing software. ○ When editing these different things together digitally, slight imperfections can occur where the pieces are joined. Enter the correction software. What began as a method to streamline the digital editing process has turned into an almost industry-wide standard of altering a musician"s work. "Think of it like plastic surgery," says a Grammy-winning recording engineer.

What is the writer's position, or **claim**, on the use of pitch-correction software?

☐ Musicians should learn to live with their imperfections.

☑ Musicians should never use the software.

☐ Musicians should use the software to enhance live performances only.

xx   Grade 10

Writing Arguments
Master the art of proving your point.

COMMON CORE W 1, W 10

Interactive Lessons

1. Introduction
2. What Is a Claim?
3. Support: Reasons and Evidence
4. Building Effective Support
5. Creating a Coherent Argument
6. Persuasive Techniques
7. Formal Style
8. Concluding Your Argument

Student-Directed Lessons

Though primarily intended for individual student use, these interactive lessons also offer opportunities for whole-class and small-group instruction and practice.

Writing Informative Texts
Shed light on complex ideas and topics.

COMMON CORE W 2, W 10

Interactive Lessons

1. Introduction
2. Developing a Topic
3. Organizing Ideas
4. Introductions and Conclusions
5. Elaboration
6. Using Graphics and Multimedia
7. Precise Language and Vocabulary
8. Formal Style

Writing Narratives
A good storyteller can always capture an audience.

COMMON CORE W 3, W 10

Interactive Lessons

1. Introduction
2. Narrative Context
3. Point of View and Characters
4. Narrative Structure
5. Narrative Techniques
6. The Language of Narrative

Writing as a Process

COMMON CORE W 4, W 5, W 10

Get from the first twinkle of an idea to a sparkling final draft.

Interactive Lessons

1. Introduction
2. Task, Purpose, and Audience
3. Planning and Drafting
4. Revising and Editing
5. Trying a New Approach

Teacher Support

Each collection in your teacher eBook includes

- support for English language learners and less-proficient writers
- instructional and management tips for every screen
- a rubric
- additional writing applications

Producing and Publishing with Technology

COMMON CORE W 6

Learn how to write for an online audience.

Interactive Lessons

1. Introduction
2. Writing for the Internet
3. Interacting with Your Online Audience
4. Using Technology to Collaborate

Conducting Research

COMMON CORE W 6, W 7, W 8

There's a world of information out there. How do you find it?

Interactive Lessons

1. Introduction
2. Starting Your Research
3. Types of Sources
4. Using the Library for Research
5. Conducting Field Research
6. Using the Internet for Research
7. Taking Notes
8. Refocusing Your Inquiry

Evaluating Sources

Approach all sources with a critical eye.

COMMON CORE **W 8**

| **Interactive Lessons** | **1.** Introduction | **3.** Evaluating Sources for Reliability |
| | **2.** Evaluating Sources for Usefulness | |

Using Textual Evidence

Put your research into writing.

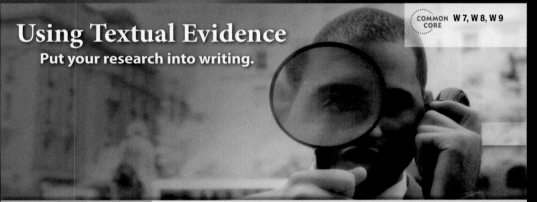

COMMON CORE **W 7, W 8, W 9**

Interactive Lessons	**1.** Introduction	**4.** Summarizing, Paraphrasing, and Quoting
	2. Synthesizing Information	**5.** Attribution
	3. Writing an Outline	

Participating in Collaborative Discussions

There's power in putting your heads together.

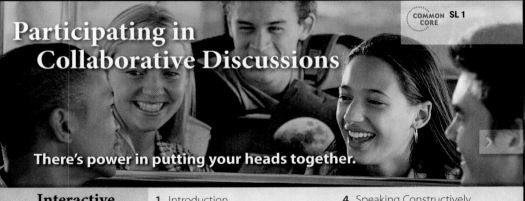

COMMON CORE **SL 1**

Interactive Lessons	**1.** Introduction	**4.** Speaking Constructively
	2. Preparing for Discussion	**5.** Listening and Responding
	3. Establishing and Following Procedure	**6.** Wrapping Up Your Discussion

Analyzing and Evaluating Presentations

Is there substance behind the style?

COMMON CORE SL 2, SL 3, SL 6

Interactive Lessons	1. Introduction	4. Tracing a Speaker's Argument
	2. Analyzing a Presentation	5. Rhetoric and Delivery
	3. Evaluating a Speaker's Reliability	6. Synthesizing Media Sources

Assessments in *my*WriteSmart

Test students' mastery of the standards covered in each digital collection by assigning the accompanying assessment in *my*WriteSmart.

Giving a Presentation

Learn how to talk to a roomful of people.

COMMON CORE SL 4, SL 6

Interactive Lessons	1. Introduction	3. The Content of Your Presentation
	2. Knowing Your Audience	4. Style in Presentation
		5. Delivering Your Presentation

Using Media in a Presentation

If a picture is worth a thousand words, just think what you can do with a video.

COMMON CORE SL 5

| **Interactive Lessons** | 1. Introduction | 3. Using Presentation Software |
| | 2. Types of Media: Audio, Video, and Images | 4. Practicing Your Presentation |

DIGITAL SPOTLIGHT

eBook | myNotebook | fyi hmhfyi.com | my WriteSmart

Supporting Close Reading, Research, and Writing

Understanding complex texts is hard work, even for experienced readers. It often takes multiple close readings to understand and write about an author's choices and meanings. The dynamic digital tools in this program will give you opportunities to learn and practice this critical skill of close reading—and help you integrate the text evidence you find into your writing.

Integrated Digital Suite

The digital resources and tools in *collections* are designed to support students in grappling with complex text and formulating interpretations from text evidence.

▶ Close Read

Learn How to Do a Close Read

An effective close read is all about the details; you have to examine the language and ideas a writer includes. See how it's done by accessing the **Close Read Screencasts** in your eBook. Hear modeled conversations about anchor texts.

Close Read Screencasts

For each anchor text, students can access modeled conversations in which readers analyze and annotate key passages.

of the birds, how they soared and glided overhead. He pointed out the slow, graceful sweep of their wings as they beat the air steadily, without fluttering. Soon Icarus was sure that he, too, could fly and, raising his arms up and down, skirted over the white sand and even out over the waves, letting his feet touch the snowy foam as the water thundered and broke over the sharp rocks. Daedalus watched him proudly but

Soon Icarus was sure that he, too, could fly and, raising his arms up and down, skirted over the white sand and even out over the waves, letting his feet touch the snowy foam as the water thundered and broke over the sharp rocks.

> There might be a sense of danger here.

Daedalus watched him proudly but with misgivings. He called Icarus to his side and, putting his arm round the boy's shoulders, said, 'Icarus, my son, we are about to make our flight. No human being has ever traveled through the air before, and I want you to listen carefully to my instructions.

Annotate the Texts

Practice close reading by utilizing the powerful annotation tools in your eBook. Mark up key ideas and observations using highlighters and sticky notes.

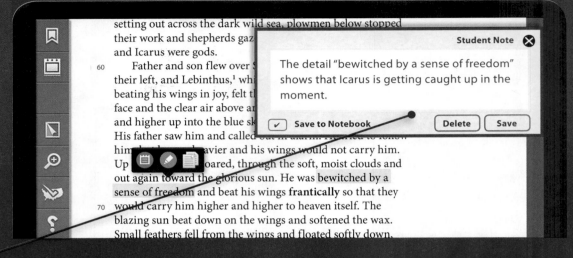

Digital Tools for Close Reading

Annotation tools allow students to note central ideas and details about an author's craft. Students can save their annotations to *my*Notebook, tagging them to particular performance tasks.

*my*Notebook

Collect Text Evidence

Save your annotations to your notebook. Gathering and organizing this text evidence will help you complete performance tasks and other writing assignments.

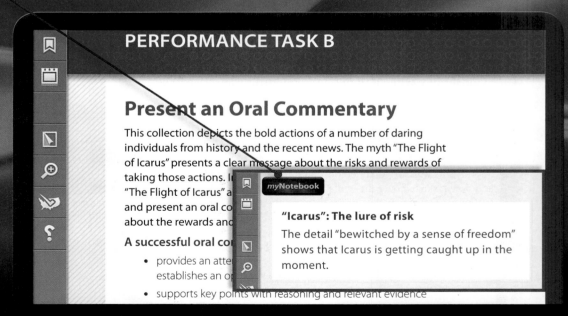

Find More Text Evidence on the Web

hmhfyi.com

Tap into the *FYI* website for links to high-interest informational texts about collection topics. Capture text evidence from any Web source by including it in your notebook.

High-Interest Informational Text

Updated monthly, *FYI* features links to reputable sources of informational text.

Integrate Text Evidence into Your Writing

Use the evidence you've gathered to formulate interpretations, draw conclusions, and offer insights. Integrate the best of your text evidence into your writing.

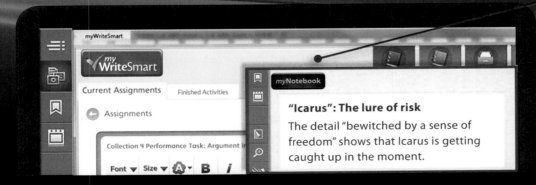

Tools for Writing

Assign and manage performance tasks in *my*WriteSmart. Students can use the annotations they've gathered and tools for writing and collaboration to complete each task.

Correlation of *Collections*, Grade 10, to the English Language Arts Common Core State Standards

The grade 10 standards on the following pages define what students should understand and be able to do by the end of each grade. They correspond to the College and Career Readiness (CCR) anchor standards below by number. The CCR and grade-specific standards are necessary complements—the former providing broad standards, the latter providing additional specificity—that together define the skills and understandings that all students must demonstrate.

College and Career Readiness Anchor Standards for Reading

Common Core State Standards
KEY IDEAS AND DETAILS
1. Read closely to determine what the text says explicitly and to make logical inferences from it; cite specific textual evidence when writing or speaking to support conclusions drawn from the text.
2. Determine central ideas or themes of a text and analyze their development; summarize the key supporting details and ideas.
3. Analyze how and why individuals, events, and ideas develop and interact over the course of a text.
CRAFT AND STRUCTURE
4. Interpret words and phrases as they are used in a text, including determining technical, connotative, and figurative meanings, and analyze how specific word choices shape meaning or tone.
5. Analyze the structure of texts, including how specific sentences, paragraphs, and larger portions of the text (e.g., a section, chapter, scene, or stanza) relate to each other and the whole.
6. Assess how point of view or purpose shapes the content and style of a text.
INTEGRATION OF KNOWLEDGE AND IDEAS
7. Integrate and evaluate content presented in diverse formats and media, including visually and quantitatively, as well as in words.
8. Delineate and evaluate the argument and specific claims in a text, including the validity of the reasoning as well as the relevance and sufficiency of the evidence.
9. Analyze how two or more texts address similar themes or topics in order to build knowledge or to compare the approaches the authors take.
RANGE OF READING AND LEVEL OF COMPLEXITY
10. Read and comprehend complex literary and informational texts independently and proficiently.

Reading Standards for Literature

Common Core State Standard	Student/Teacher's Edition

KEY IDEAS AND DETAILS

1. Cite strong and thorough textual evidence to support analysis of what the text says explicitly as well as inferences drawn from the text.

Student Edition
10, 36, 40, 76, 81, 82, 106, 126, 139, 158, 159, 180, 181, 244, 260, 277, 291, 307, 311, 312, 371, 375

Teacher's Edition
3, 4, 5, 6, 8, 10, 25, 36, 39, 40, 40a, 40b, 59, 60, 71, 72, 74, 76, 79, 80, 81, 82, 82b, 93, 94, 95, 96, 97, 98, 99, 100, 102, 104, 105, 106, 106a, 109, 111, 113, 114, 117, 118, 119, 120, 121, 122, 125, 126, 137, 138, 139, 140a, 156, 157, 158, 159, 160a, 171, 172, 176, 179, 180, 181, 182a, 190, 191, 192, 222, 224, 230, 231, 232, 233, 234, 236, 238, 239, 241, 244, 246, 249, 260, 261, 262, 263, 264, 265, 266, 267, 268, 269, 270, 271, 272, 273, 274, 275, 276, 277, 282, 291, 298, 301, 307, 311, 312, 312b, 361, 362, 363, 364, 365, 366, 367, 368, 369, 371, 373, 374, 375

2. Determine a theme or central idea of a text and analyze in detail its development over the course of the text, including how it emerges and is shaped by specific details; provide an objective summary of the text.

Student Edition
10, 36, 40, 60, 76, 81, 82, 106, 126, 139, 158, 159, 181, 192, 244, 290, 291, 294, 312, 370, 371, 375

Teacher's Edition
10, 27, 32, 36, 39, 40, 40b, 59, 60, 60a, 74, 76, 79, 80, 81, 82, 82b, 93, 94, 96, 98, 100, 101, 103, 106, 110, 111, 113, 115, 116, 125, 126, 137, 139, 140a, 156, 157, 158, 159, 181, 192, 192a, 215, 217, 218, 220, 221, 222, 223, 226, 227, 229, 230, 231, 233, 235, 236, 239, 240, 242, 244, 246, 256, 258, 259, 260, 261, 262, 263, 264, 265, 266, 268, 269, 270, 271, 274, 275, 276, 278, 279, 280, 281, 283, 285, 286, 287, 288, 289, 290, 291, 292a, 294, 312, 362, 364, 365, 366, 367, 368, 369, 370, 371, 372a, 374, 375, 376b

3. Analyze how complex characters (e.g., those with multiple or conflicting motivations) develop over the course of a text, interact with other characters, and advance the plot or develop the theme.

Student Edition
9, 10, 40, 76, 82, 106, 181, 210, 231, 244, 260, 277, 290, 291, 370, 371, 375

Teacher's Edition
3, 4, 5, 6, 7, 8, 9, 10, 26, 30, 31, 40, 71, 76, 82, 94, 96, 97, 100, 102, 104, 105, 106, 106a, 109, 112, 113, 117, 121, 122, 125, 126, 181, 210, 216, 217, 219, 220, 221, 222, 223, 224, 225, 228, 231, 233, 235, 236, 239, 240, 241, 242, 244, 245, 246, 250, 258, 260, 261, 262, 263, 264, 265, 266, 267, 268, 269, 270, 271, 272, 274, 275, 276, 277, 278, 279, 280, 281, 283, 284, 285, 286, 287, 288, 289, 290, 291, 292a, 312, 312a, 361, 362, 363, 364, 365, 366, 367, 368, 369, 370, 371, 372a, 374, 375

Common Core State Standard	Student/Teacher's Edition
CRAFT AND STRUCTURE	
4. Determine the meaning of words and phrases as they are used in the text, including figurative and connotative meanings; analyze the cumulative impact of specific word choices on meaning and tone (e.g., how the language evokes a sense of time and place; how it sets a formal or informal tone).	**Student Edition** 12, 35, 36, 60, 75, 76, 82, 181, 211, 231, 244, 260, 307, 311, 312, 371, 375 **Teacher's Edition** 11, 12, 25, 27, 29, 35, 36, 39, 40, 40a, 40b, 59, 60, 72, 73, 75, 76, 82, 82a, 96, 98, 99, 101, 111, 112, 114, 122, 126, 137, 138, 159, 160a, 181, 211, 215, 225, 226, 229, 231, 234, 236, 237, 238, 239, 243, 244, 245, 248, 251, 252, 253, 257, 258, 260, 267, 269, 271, 272, 273, 278, 280, 282, 286, 290, 303, 307, 310, 311, 312, 312b, 361, 367, 371, 372a, 373, 374, 375, 376b
5. Analyze how an author's choices concerning how to structure a text, order events within it (e.g., parallel plots), and manipulate time (e.g., pacing, flashbacks) create such effects as mystery, tension, or surprise.	**Student Edition** 10, 35, 36, 75, 76, 82, 106, 126, 158, 159, 180, 181, 210, 231, 244, 277, 291, 312, 371, 375 **Teacher's Edition** 7, 10, 12a, 28, 31, 32, 33, 34, 35, 36, 39, 59, 60, 60a, 71, 73, 74, 75, 76, 78a, 80, 82, 93, 95, 98, 106, 119, 126, 156, 157, 158, 159, 160a, 171, 172, 173, 174, 175, 177, 178, 179, 180, 181, 192b, 210, 214, 219, 227, 231, 232, 234, 235, 236, 237, 238, 239, 244, 247, 252, 254, 255, 260, 268, 274, 277, 282, 284, 291, 312, 312b, 371, 375, 376a
6. Analyze a particular point of view or cultural experience reflected in a work of literature from outside the United States, drawing on a wide reading of world literature.	**Student Edition** 9, 10, 106, 181 **Teacher's Edition** 4, 5, 8, 9, 10, 12a, 40b, 101, 106, 181, 182a, 190, 191, 300a
INTEGRATION OF KNOWLEDGE AND IDEAS	
7. Analyze the representation of a subject or a key scene in two different artistic mediums, including what is emphasized or absent in each treatment (e.g., Auden's "Musée des Beaux Arts" and Breughel's Landscape with the Fall of Icarus).	**Student Edition** 126, 192, 294 **Teacher's Edition** 40b, 107, 108, 109, 113, 114, 115, 116, 117, 118, 119, 120, 123, 124, 125, 126, 128a, 190, 191, 192, 192b, 293, 294, 294a

Common Core State Standard	Student/Teacher's Edition
8. (Not applicable to literature)	
9. Analyze how an author draws on and transforms source material in a specific work (e.g., how Shakespeare treats a theme or topic from Ovid or the Bible or how a later author draws on a play by Shakespeare).	**Student Edition** 126, 298, 306, 307 **Teacher's Edition** 108, 125, 126, 295, 296, 297, 298, 301, 302, 303, 304, 305, 306, 307, 308a

RANGE OF READING AND LEVEL OF TEXT COMPLEXITY

10. By the end of grade 10, read and comprehend literature, including stories, dramas, and poems, at the high end of the grades 9–10 text complexity band independently and proficiently.	**Student Edition** 25–36, 93–106, 156–159, 171–181, 214–291, 310–312 **Teacher's Edition** 25A, 25–36, 93A, 93–106, 155A, 156–159, 171A, 171–181, 210A, 214–291, 309A, 310–312

Reading Standards for Informational Text

Common Core State Standard	Student/Teacher's Edition

KEY IDEAS AND DETAILS

1. Cite strong and thorough textual evidence to support analysis of what the text says explicitly as well as inferences drawn from the text.

Student Edition
21, 56, 134, 144, 168, 208, 298, 338, 348, 357, 360

Teacher's Edition
13, 14, 14a, 15, 16, 17, 18, 19, 20, 21, 22, 24a, 40b, 51, 52, 54, 56, 61, 62, 63, 64, 65, 66, 68, 129, 132, 133, 134, 136a, 144, 163, 164, 165, 168, 183, 184, 185, 208, 295, 296, 297, 298, 300a, 328, 333, 336, 338, 342, 343, 344, 347, 348, 350a, 352, 353, 354, 355, 357, 359, 360

2. Determine a central idea of a text and analyze its development over the course of the text, including how it emerges and is shaped and refined by specific details; provide an objective summary of the text.

Student Edition
55, 56, 142–143, 144, 167, 168, 187, 298, 338, 360

Teacher's Edition
14, 15, 17, 24a, 51, 52, 53, 54, 55, 56, 58a, 61, 63, 68, 129, 141, 142–143, 144, 144a, 161, 162, 163, 164, 165, 166, 167, 168, 170a, 183, 187, 188a, 296, 298, 338, 360

3. Analyze how the author unfolds an analysis or series of ideas or events, including the order in which the points are made, how they are introduced and developed, and the connections that are drawn between them.

Student Edition
14, 68, 133, 134, 142–143, 144, 167, 187, 298, 348, 357, 360

Teacher's Edition
13, 14, 15, 17, 22, 63, 64, 65, 66, 68, 129, 130, 131, 132, 133, 134, 136a, 141, 142–143, 144, 144a, 161, 163, 164, 165, 166, 167, 168, 184, 185, 186, 187, 298, 348, 357, 360

CRAFT AND STRUCTURE

4. Determine the meaning of words and phrases as they are used in a text, including figurative, connotative, and technical meanings; analyze the cumulative impact of specific word choices on meaning and tone (e.g., how the language of a court opinion differs from that of a newspaper).

Student Edition
17, 21, 22, 55, 56, 57, 68, 133, 134, 135, 168, 187, 208, 348, 357, 358, 360

Teacher's Edition
17, 18, 19, 21, 22, 40b, 51, 53, 54, 55, 56, 57, 58a, 62, 68, 70a, 129, 132, 133, 134, 135, 164, 168, 169, 183, 184, 185, 187, 188a, 205, 206, 208, 299, 322, 326, 330, 331, 348, 357, 358, 360

5. Analyze in detail how an author's ideas or claims are developed and refined by particular sentences, paragraphs, or larger portions of a text (e.g., a section or chapter).

Student Edition
67, 68, 134, 144, 168, 187, 208, 348, 357

Teacher's Edition
17, 56, 61, 62, 63, 65, 66, 67, 68, 70a, 129, 130, 131, 132, 133, 134, 136a, 144, 168, 170a, 184, 185, 186, 187, 188a, 208, 321, 327, 341, 342, 343, 344, 345, 346, 347, 348, 350a, 357

Common Core State Standard	Student/Teacher's Edition
6. Determine an author's point of view or purpose in a text and analyze how an author uses rhetoric to advance that point of view or purpose.	**Student Edition** 14, 22, 67, 68, 168, 208, 298, 348, 356, 357, 360, R16–R22 **Teacher's Edition** 13, 14, 14a, 22, 40b, 52, 58a, 61, 62, 63, 64, 65, 66, 67, 68, 70a, 162, 168, 203, 204, 208, 209a, 296, 298, 322, 323, 326, 330, 331, 334, 348, 352, 353, 354, 355, 356, 357, 360, R16–R22

INTEGRATION OF KNOWLEDGE AND IDEAS

Common Core State Standard	Student/Teacher's Edition
7. Analyze various accounts of a subject told in different mediums (e.g., a person's life story in both print and multimedia), determining which details are emphasized in each account.	**Student Edition** 213, 319, 360 **Teacher's Edition** 40b, 213, 319, 359, 360, 360a
8. Delineate and evaluate the argument and specific claims in a text, assessing whether the reasoning is valid and the evidence is relevant and sufficient; identify false statements and fallacious reasoning.	**Student Edition** 17, 22, 208, 337, 338, 356, 357, 360 **Teacher's Edition** 17, 20, 22, 66, 203, 207, 208, 209a, 319, 320, 321, 324, 325, 326, 327, 328, 329, 332, 333, 334, 335, 336, 337, 338, 340a, 352, 353, 356, 357, 360
9. Analyze seminal U.S. documents of historical and literary significance (e.g., Washington's Farewell Address, the Gettysburg Address, Roosevelt's Four Freedoms speech, King's "Letter from Birmingham Jail"), including how they address related themes and concepts.	**Student Edition** 17, 337, 338, R22 **Teacher's Edition** 15, 16, 17, 24a, 319, 320, 324, 325, 326, 328, 329, 332, 333, 335, 336, 337, 338, 340a, R22

RANGE OF READING AND LEVEL OF TEXT COMPLEXITY

Common Core State Standard	Student/Teacher's Edition
10. By the end of grade 10, read and comprehend literary nonfiction at the high end of the grades 9–10 text complexity band independently and proficiently.	**Student Edition** 61–68, 161–168, 183–187, 319–338, 352–357 **Teacher's Edition** 61A, 61–68, 161A, 161–168, 183A, 183–187, 319A, 319–338, 351A, 352–357

College and Career Readiness Anchor Standards for Writing

Common Core State Standards

TEXT TYPES AND PURPOSES

1. Write arguments to support claims in an analysis of substantive topics or texts, using valid reasoning and relevant and sufficient evidence.

2. Write informative/explanatory texts to examine and convey complex ideas and information clearly and accurately through the effective selection, organization, and analysis of content.

3. Write narratives to develop real or imagined experiences or events using effective technique, well-chosen details, and well-structured event sequences.

PRODUCTION AND DISTRIBUTION OF WRITING

4. Produce clear and coherent writing in which the development, organization, and style are appropriate to task, purpose, and audience.

5. Develop and strengthen writing as needed by planning, revising, editing, rewriting, or trying a new approach.

6. Use technology, including the Internet, to produce and publish writing and to interact and collaborate with others.

RESEARCH TO BUILD AND PRESENT KNOWLEDGE

7. Conduct short as well as more sustained research projects based on focused questions, demonstrating understanding of the subject under investigation.

8. Gather relevant information from multiple print and digital sources, assess the credibility and accuracy of each source, and integrate the information while avoiding plagiarism.

9. Draw evidence from literary or informational texts to support analysis, reflection, and research.

RANGE OF WRITING

10. Write routinely over extended time frames (time for research, reflection, and revision) and shorter time frames (a single sitting or a day or two) for a range of tasks, purposes, and audiences.

Writing Standards

Common Core State Standard	Student/Teacher's Edition	Digital Collection/Lesson
TEXT TYPES AND PURPOSES		
1. Write arguments to support claims in an analysis of substantive topics or texts, using valid reasoning and relevant and sufficient evidence.	**Student Edition** 14, 36, 139, 149–152, 208, 291, 377–380, R2–R3 **Teacher's Edition** 14, 36, 139, 149–152, 181, 208, 291, 377–380, R2–R3	**Writing Arguments** • Introduction • What Is a Claim? • Support: Reasons and Evidence • Building Effective Support • Creating a Coherent Argument • Persuasive Techniques • Formal Style • Concluding Your Argument
a. Introduce precise claim(s), distinguish the claim(s) from alternate or opposing claims, and create an organization that establishes clear relationships among claim(s), counterclaims, reasons, and evidence.	**Student Edition** 149–152, 377–380, R2–R3 **Teacher's Edition** 149–152, 377–380, R2–R3	**Writing Arguments** • What Is a Claim? • Creating a Coherent Argument
b. Develop claim(s) and counterclaims fairly, supplying evidence for each while pointing out the strengths and limitations of both in a manner that anticipates the audience's knowledge level and concerns.	**Student Edition** 149–152, 377–380, R2–R3 **Teacher's Edition** 149–152, 377–380, R2–R3	**Writing Arguments** • Support: Reasons and Evidence • Building Effective Support
c. Use words, phrases, and clauses to link the major sections of the text, create cohesion, and clarify the relationships between claim(s) and reasons, between reasons and evidence, and between claim(s) and counterclaims.	**Student Edition** 149–152, 377–380, R2–R3 **Teacher's Edition** 149–152, 377–380, R2–R3	**Writing Arguments** • Creating a Coherent Argument
d. Establish and maintain a formal style and objective tone while attending to the norms and conventions of the discipline in which they are writing.	**Student Edition** 149–152, 377–380, R2–R3 **Teacher's Edition** 38a, 149–152, 377–380, R2–R3	**Writing Arguments** • Formal Style
e. Provide a concluding statement or section that follows from and supports the argument presented.	**Student Edition** 149–152, 377–380, R2–R3 **Teacher's Edition** 149–152, 377–380, R2–R3	**Writing Arguments** • Concluding Your Argument

Common Core State Standard	Student/Teacher's Edition	Digital Collection/Lesson
2. Write informative/explanatory texts to examine and convey complex ideas, concepts, and information clearly and accurately through the effective selection, organization, and analysis of content.	**Student Edition** 45–48, 60, 68, 83–86, 134, 159, 181, 231, 260, 313–316, 357, R4–R5 **Teacher's Edition** 45–48, 56, 60, 68, 83–86, 134, 159, 181, 231, 260, 312a, 313–316, 357, R4–R5	**Writing Informative Texts** • Introduction • Developing a Topic • Organizing Ideas • Introductions and Conclusions • Elaboration • Using Graphics and Multimedia • Precise Language and Vocabulary • Formal Style **Using Textual Evidence** • Writing an Outline
a. Introduce a topic; organize complex ideas, concepts, and information to make important connections and distinctions; include formatting (e.g., headings), graphics (e.g., figures, tables), and multimedia when useful to aiding comprehension.	**Student Edition** 45–48, 83–86, 134, 313–316, R4–R5 **Teacher's Edition** 45–48, 83–86, 134, 188a, 313–316, R4–R5	**Writing Informative Texts** • Developing a Topic • Organizing Ideas • Introductions and Conclusions • Using Graphics and Multimedia
b. Develop the topic with well-chosen, relevant, and sufficient facts, extended definitions, concrete details, quotations, or other information and examples appropriate to the audience's knowledge of the topic.	**Student Edition** 17, 45–48, 83–86, 313–316, R4–R5 **Teacher's Edition** 17, 45–48, 83–86, 313–316, R4–R5	**Writing Informative Texts** • Elaboration
c. Use appropriate and varied transitions to link the major sections of the text, create cohesion, and clarify the relationships among complex ideas and concepts.	**Student Edition** 83–86, 136, 313–316, R4–R5 **Teacher's Edition** 83–86, 134, 136, 188a, 313–316, R4–R5	**Writing Informative Texts** • Organizing Ideas
d. Use precise language and domain-specific vocabulary to manage the complexity of the topic.	**Student Edition** 313–316, R4–R5 **Teacher's Edition** 134, 136a, 313–316, R4–R5	**Writing Informative Texts** • Precise Language and Vocabulary
e. Establish and maintain a formal style and objective tone while attending to the norms and conventions of the discipline in which they are writing.	**Student Edition** 45–48, 83–86, 313–316, R4–R5 **Teacher's Edition** 45–48, 83–86, 313–316, R4–R5	**Writing Informative Texts** • Formal Style

Common Core State Standard	Student/Teacher's Edition	Digital Collection/Lesson
f. Provide a concluding statement or section that follows from and supports the information or explanation presented (e.g., articulating implications or the significance of the topic).	**Student Edition** 45–48, 83–86, 313–316, R4–R5 **Teacher's Edition** 45–48, 83–86, 313–316, R4–R5	**Writing Informative Texts** • Introductions and Conclusions
3. Write narratives to develop real or imagined experiences or events using effective technique, well-chosen details, and well-structured event sequences.	**Student Edition** 40, 197–200, 307, R6–R7 **Teacher's Edition** 40, 197–200, 307, R6–R7	**Writing Narratives** • Introductions • Narrative Context • Point of View and Characters • Narrative Structure • Narrative Techniques • The Language of Narrative
a. Engage and orient the reader by setting out a problem, situation, or observation, establishing one or multiple point(s) of view, and introducing a narrator and/or characters; create a smooth progression of experiences or events.	**Student Edition** 40, 197–200, R6–R7 **Teacher's Edition** 40, 197–200, 308a, R6–R7	**Writing Narratives** • Narrative Context • Point of View and Characters • Narrative Structure
b. Use narrative techniques, such as dialogue, pacing, description, reflection, and multiple plot lines, to develop experiences, events, and/or characters.	**Student Edition** 40, 197–200, R6–R7 **Teacher's Edition** 40, 197–200, R6–R7	**Writing Narratives** • Narrative Structure • Narrative Techniques • The Language of Narrative
c. Use a variety of techniques to sequence events so that they build on one another to create a coherent whole.	**Student Edition** 197–200, R6–R7 **Teacher's Edition** 40, 197–200, R6–R7	**Writing Narratives** • Narrative Structure
d. Use precise words and phrases, telling details, and sensory language to convey a vivid picture of the experiences, events, setting, and/or characters.	**Student Edition** 197–200, R6–R7 **Teacher's Edition** 197–200, R6–R7	**Writing Narratives** • The Language of Narrative

Common Core State Standard	Student/Teacher's Edition	Digital Collection/Lesson
e. Provide a conclusion that follows from and reflects on what is experienced, observed, or resolved over the course of the narrative.	**Student Edition** 40, 197–200, R6–R7 **Teacher's Edition** 40, 197–200, R6–R7	**Writing Narratives** • Narrative Structure

PRODUCTION AND DISTRIBUTION OF WRITING

Common Core State Standard	Student/Teacher's Edition	Digital Collection/Lesson
4. Produce clear and coherent writing in which the development, organization, and style are appropriate to task, purpose, and audience. (Grade-specific expectations for writing types are defined in standards 1–3 above.)	**Student Edition** 45–48, 82, 83–86, 149–152, 197–200, 313–316, 371, 377–380 **Teacher's Edition** 45–48, 59, 60, 68, 82, 82b, 83–86, 106, 126, 128, 149–152, 197–200, 244, 260, 313–316, 371, 377–380	**Writing as a Process** • Task, Purpose, and Audience
5. Develop and strengthen writing as needed by planning, revising, editing, rewriting, or trying a new approach, focusing on addressing what is most significant for a specific purpose and audience. (Editing for conventions should demonstrate command of Language standards 1–3 up to and including grades 9–10.)	**Student Edition** 45–48, 83–86, 128, 149–152, 170, 182, 197–200, 313–316, 340, 377–380 **Teacher's Edition** 45–48, 83–86, 149–152, 170, 182, 197–200, 313–316, 340, 377–380	**Writing as a Process** • Introduction • Task, Purpose, and Audience • Planning and Drafting • Revising and Editing • Trying a New Approach
6. Use technology, including the Internet, to produce, publish, and update individual or shared writing products, taking advantage of technology's capacity to link to other information and to display information flexibly and dynamically.	**Student Edition** 45–48, 83–86, 149–152, 197–200, 313–316, 377–380 **Teacher's Edition** 45–48, 83–86, 149–152, 197–200, 313–316, 377–380	**Producing and Publishing with Technology** • Introduction • Writing for the Internet • Interacting with Your Online Audience • Using Technology to Collaborate

RESEARCH TO BUILD AND PRESENT KNOWLEDGE

Common Core State Standard	Student/Teacher's Edition	Digital Collection/Lesson
7. Conduct short as well as more sustained research projects to answer a question (including a self-generated question) or solve a problem; narrow or broaden the inquiry when appropriate; synthesize multiple sources on the subject, demonstrating understanding of the subject under investigation.	**Student Edition** 76, 83–86, 187, 348, R8 **Teacher's Edition** 22, 76, 78a, 83–86, 187, 348, 360a, R8	**Conducting Research** • Introduction • Starting Your Research • Refocusing Your Inquiry **Using Textual Evidence** • Synthesizing Information

Common Core State Standard	Student/Teacher's Edition	Digital Collection/Lesson
8. Gather relevant information from multiple authoritative print and digital sources, using advanced searches effectively; assess the usefulness of each source in answering the research question; integrate information into the text selectively to maintain the flow of ideas, avoiding plagiarism and following a standard format for citation.	**Student Edition** 83–86, 348, R8–R11 **Teacher's Edition** 83–86, 348, R8–R11	**Conducting Research** • Types of Sources • Using the Library for Research • Using the Internet for Research **Evaluating Sources** • Introduction • Evaluating Sources for Usefulness • Evaluating Sources for Reliability **Using Textual Evidence** • Summarizing, Paraphrasing, and Quoting • Attribution
9. Draw evidence from literary or informational texts to support analysis, reflection, and research.	**Student Edition** 45–48, 83–86, 313–316, 357 **Teacher's Edition** 14a, 45–48, 76, 83–86, 192, 313–316, 357	**Writing Informative Texts** • Elaboration **Conducting Research** • Taking Notes **Using Textual Evidence** • Introduction • Synthesizing Information • Summarizing, Paraphrasing, and Quoting
a. Apply *grades 9–10 Reading standards* to literature (e.g., "Analyze how an author draws on and transforms source material in a specific work [e.g., how Shakespeare treats a theme or topic from Ovid or the Bible or how a later author draws on a play by Shakespeare]").	**Student Edition** 145–148, 149–152, 193–196, 313–316, 377–380 **Teacher's Edition** 145–148, 149–152, 193–196, 312a, 313–316, 377–380	
b. Apply *grades 9–10 Reading standards* to literary nonfiction (e.g. "Delineate and evaluate the argument and specific claims in a text, assessing whether the reasoning is valid and the evidence is relevant and sufficient; identify false statements and fallacious reasoning").	**Student Edition** 145–148, 149–152, 193–196, 313–316, 338, 377–380 **Teacher's Edition** 145–148, 149–152, 193–196, 313–316, 338, 377–380	

RANGE OF WRITING

10. Write routinely over extended time frames (time for research, reflection, and revision) and shorter time frames (a single sitting or a day or two) for a range of tasks, purposes, and audiences.	**Student Edition** 45–48, 83–86, 149–152, 197–200, 313–316, 338, 377–380 **Teacher's Edition** 10, 45–48, 76, 83–86, 149–152, 197–200, 313–316, 338, 377–380	**Writing as a Process** • Task, Purpose, and Audience **Writing Arguments** **Writing Informative Texts** **Writing Narratives** **Using Textual Evidence**

College and Career Readiness Anchor Standards for Speaking and Listening

Common Core State Standards

COMPREHENSION AND COLLABORATION

1. Prepare for and participate effectively in a range of conversations and collaborations with diverse partners, building on others' ideas and expressing their own clearly and persuasively.

2. Integrate and evaluate information presented in diverse media and formats, including visually, quantitatively, and orally.

3. Evaluate a speaker's point of view, reasoning, and use of evidence and rhetoric.

PRESENTATION OF KNOWLEDGE AND IDEAS

4. Present information, findings, and supporting evidence such that listeners can follow the line of reasoning and the organization, development, and style are appropriate to task, purpose, and audience.

5. Make strategic use of digital media and visual displays of data to express information and enhance understanding of presentations.

6. Adapt speech to a variety of contexts and communicative tasks, demonstrating command of formal English when indicated or appropriate.

Speaking and Listening Standards

Common Core State Standard	Student/Teacher's Edition	Digital Collection/Lesson
COMPREHENSION AND COLLABORATION		
1. Initiate and participate effectively in a range of collaborative discussions (one-on-one, in groups, and teacher-led) with diverse partners on *grades 9–10 topics, texts, and issues,* building on others' ideas and expressing their own clearly and persuasively.	**Student Edition** 10, 56, 82, 87–90, 106, 145–148, 168, 244, 277, 298, 360, 375, R12–R13, R14–R15 **Teacher's Edition** 10, 40, 40a, 40b, 56, 59, 82, 87–90, 106, 126, 128, 134, 145–148, 160a, 168, 244, 277, 298, 360, 375, R12–R13, R14–R15	**Participating in Collaborative Discussions** • Introduction • Preparing for Discussion • Establishing and Following Procedure • Speaking Constructively • Listening and Responding • Wrapping Up Your Discussion
a. Come to discussions prepared, having read and researched material under study; explicitly draw on that preparation by referring to evidence from texts and other research on the topic or issue to stimulate a thoughtful, well-reasoned exchange of ideas.	**Student Edition** 10, 56, 82, 87–90, 145–148, 168, 277, 298, 375, R12–R13, R14–R15 **Teacher's Edition** 10, 40a, 56, 82, 87–90, 126, 134, 145–148, 168, 277, 298, 375, R12–R13, R14–R15	**Participating in Collaborative Discussions** • Preparing for Discussion • Speaking Constructively
b. Work with peers to set rules for collegial discussions and decision-making (e.g., informal consensus, taking votes on key issues, presentation of alternate views), clear goals and deadlines, and individual roles as needed.	**Student Edition** 87–90, 145–148, R12–R13, R14–R15 **Teacher's Edition** 40, 87–90, 145–148, 277, R12–R13, R14–R15	**Participating in Collaborative Discussions** • Establishing and Following Procedure
c. Propel conversations by posing and responding to questions that relate the current discussion to broader themes or larger ideas; actively incorporate others into the discussion; and clarify, verify, or challenge ideas and conclusions.	**Student Edition** 87–90, 145–148, 277, R12–R13, R14–R15 **Teacher's Edition** 82a, 87–90, 145–148, 186, 277, 298, 376b, R12–R13, R14–R15	**Participating in Collaborative Discussions** • Speaking Constructively • Listening and Responding

Common Core State Standard	Student/Teacher's Edition	Digital Collection/Lesson
d. Respond thoughtfully to diverse perspectives, summarize points of agreement and disagreement, and, when warranted, qualify or justify their own views and understanding and make new connections in light of the evidence and reasoning presented.	**Student Edition** 56, 87–90, 145–148, 277, R12–R13, R14–R15 **Teacher's Edition** 40a, 56, 58a, 87–90, 145–148, 277, 298, 376b, R12–R13, R14–R15	**Participating in Collaborative Discussions** • Listening and Responding • Wrapping Up Your Discussion
2. Integrate multiple sources of information presented in diverse media or formats (e.g., visually, quantitatively, orally) evaluating the credibility and accuracy of each source.	**Student Edition** 83–86, 348 **Teacher's Edition** 40b, 76, 83–86, 312a, 348, 350a	**Analyzing and Evaluating Presentations** • Introduction • Evaluating a Speaker's Reliability • Synthesizing Media Sources
3. Evaluate a speaker's point of view, reasoning, and use of evidence and rhetoric, identifying any fallacious reasoning or exaggerated or distorted evidence.	**Student Edition** 145–148, R14–R15 **Teacher's Edition** 40, 40a, 40b, 145–148, 192a, R14–R15	**Analyzing and Evaluating Presentations** • Tracing a Speaker's Argument • Rhetoric and Delivery

PRESENTATION OF KNOWLEDGE AND IDEAS

Common Core State Standard	Student/Teacher's Edition	Digital Collection/Lesson
4. Present information, findings, and supporting evidence clearly, concisely, and logically such that listeners can follow the line of reasoning and the organization, development, substance, and style are appropriate to purpose, audience, and task.	**Student Edition** 14, 41–44, 76, 126, 192, 193–196, 208, 294, 348 **Teacher's Edition** 14, 22, 40, 40a, 40b, 41–44, 76, 126, 128a, 192, 193–196, 208, 294, 348	**Giving a Presentation** • Introduction • Knowing Your Audience • The Content of Your Presentation • Style in Presentation
5. Make strategic use of digital media (e.g., textual, graphical, audio, visual, and interactive elements) in presentations to enhance understanding of findings, reasoning, and evidence and to add interest.	**Student Edition** 41–44, 144 **Teacher's Edition** 41–44, 144, 144a, 294a	**Using Media in a Presentation** • Introduction • Types of Media: Audio, Video, and Images • Using Presentation Software • Building and Practicing Your Presentation
6. Adapt speech to a variety of contexts and tasks, demonstrating command of formal English when indicated or appropriate. (See grades 9–10 Language standards 1 and 3 for specific expectations.)	**Student Edition** 40, 42, 43, 312 **Teacher's Edition** 40, 40a, 42, 43, 294, 312	**Participating in Collaborative Discussions** • Speaking Constructively **Giving a Presentation** • Style in Presentation

College and Career Readiness Anchor Standards for Language

Common Core State Standards

CONVENTIONS OF STANDARD ENGLISH

1. Demonstrate command of the conventions of standard English grammar and usage when writing or speaking.

2. Demonstrate command of the conventions of standard English capitalization, punctuation, and spelling when writing.

KNOWLEDGE OF LANGUAGE

3. Apply knowledge of language to understand how language functions in different contexts, to make effective choices for meaning or style, and to comprehend more fully when reading or listening.

VOCABULARY ACQUISITION AND USE

4. Determine or clarify the meaning of unknown and multiple-meaning words and phrases by using context clues, analyzing meaningful word parts, and consulting general and specialized reference materials, as appropriate.

5. Demonstrate understanding of figurative language, word relationships, and nuances in word meanings.

6. Acquire and use accurately a range of general academic and domain-specific words and phrases sufficient for reading, writing, speaking, and listening at the college and career readiness level; demonstrate independence in gathering vocabulary knowledge when considering a word or phrase important to comprehension or expression.

Language Standards

Common Core State Standard	Student/Teacher's Editions
CONVENTIONS OF STANDARD ENGLISH	
1. Demonstrate command of the conventions of standard English grammar and usage when writing or speaking.	**Student Edition** 24, 42, 44, 45, 46, 47, 48, 58, 60, 70, 85, 86, 128, 140, 152, 160, 170, 182, 193, 196, 200, 300, 316, 340, 376, 377, 379, 380, R23–R25, R30–R49 **Teacher's Edition** 24, 40, 40a, 42, 44, 45, 46, 47, 48, 58, 60, 70, 85, 86, 128, 134, 140, 152, 160, 170, 182, 193, 196, 200, 300, 316, 340, 376, 377, 379, 380, R23–R25, R30–R49
a. Use parallel structure.	**Student Edition** 60, 170, 340 **Teacher's Edition** 40a, 60, 170, 323, 340
b. Use various types of phrases (noun, verb, adjectival, adverbial, participial, prepositional, absolute) and clauses (independent, dependent; noun, relative, adverbial) to convey specific meanings and add variety and interest to writing or presentations.	**Student Edition** 24, 58, 70, 128, 140, 182, 300, 376, R23, R39–R44 **Teacher's Edition** 24, 40a, 58, 70, 128, 140, 140a, 182, 295, 300, 376, R23, R39–R44
2. Demonstrate command of the conventions of standard English capitalization, punctuation, and spelling when writing.	**Student Edition** 48, 78, 86, 152, 160, 200, 316, 350, 372, 380, R23, R26–R29, R50, R55–R58 **Teacher's Edition** 48, 78, 86, 152, 160, 200, 316, 350, 372, 380, R23, R26–R29, R50, R55–R58
a. Use a semicolon (and perhaps a conjunctive adverb) to link two or more closely related independent clauses.	**Student Edition** 372, R23, R26–R27 **Teacher's Edition** 372, R23, R26–R27

Common Core State Standard	Student/Teacher's Editions
b. Use a colon to introduce a list or quotation.	**Student Edition** 78, 350, R23, R27 **Teacher's Edition** 78, 350, R23, R27
c. Spell correctly.	**Student Edition** 48, 86, 152, 200, 316, 380, R50, R55–R58 **Teacher's Edition** 48, 86, 152, 200, 316, 380, R50, R55–R58

KNOWLEDGE OF LANGUAGE

3. Apply knowledge of language to understand how language functions in different contexts, to make effective choices for meaning or style, and to comprehend more fully when reading or listening.	**Student Edition** 38, 209, 292, 299, R23, R25, R30–R49, R50–R54 **Teacher's Edition** 12, 26, 29, 38, 40a, 209, 249, 292, 292a, 299, R23, R25, R30–R49, R50–R54
a. Write and edit work so that it conforms to the guidelines in a style manual (e.g., *MLA Handbook*, Turabian's *Manual for Writers*) appropriate for the discipline and writing type.	**Student Edition** 84, R9–R11 **Teacher's Edition** 84, 360a, R9–R11

VOCABULARY ACQUISITION AND USE

4. Determine or clarify the meaning of unknown and multiple-meaning words and phrases based on *grades 9–10 reading and content*, choosing flexibly from a range of strategies.	**Student Edition** 11, 23, 69, 77, 127, 133, 169, 188, 299, 308, 339, 349, R50–R55 **Teacher's Edition** 11, 23, 69, 77, 127, 129, 133, 169, 181, 183, 185, 188, 188a, 299, 308, 339, 349, R50–R55

Common Core State Standard	Student/Teacher's Editions
a. Use context (e.g., the overall meaning of a sentence, paragraph, or text; a word's position or function in a sentence) as a clue to the meaning of a word or phrase.	**Student Edition** 11, 133, 339, R50 **Teacher's Edition** 11, 28, 127, 129, 132, 133, 183, 185, 188a, 299, 339, R50
b. Identify and correctly use patterns of word changes that indicate different meanings or parts of speech (e.g., *analyze, analysis, analytical; advocate, advocacy*).	**Student Edition** 23, 69, 133, 188, 308, R50, R51–R52 **Teacher's Edition** 23, 69, 133, 188, 308, R50, R51–R52
c. Consult general and specialized reference materials (e.g., dictionaries, glossaries, thesauruses), both print and digital, to find the pronunciation of a word or determine or clarify its precise meaning, its part of speech, or its etymology.	**Student Edition** 77, 133, 169, 308, R52–R53, R54–R55 **Teacher's Edition** 77, 127, 133, 169, 183, 185, 188a, 299, 308, R52–R53, R54–R55
d. Verify the preliminary determination of the meaning of a word or phrase (e.g., by checking the inferred meaning in context or in a dictionary).	**Student Edition** 127, 133, 349, R50, R52 **Teacher's Edition** 11, 127, 133, 183, 185, 299, 339, 349, R50, R52
5. Demonstrate understanding of figurative language, word relationships, and nuances in word meanings.	**Student Edition** 37, 55, 56, 75, 76, 81, 135, 159, 231, 311, 358 **Teacher's Edition** 37, 55, 56, 75, 76, 81, 135, 159, 205, 231, 248, 250, 251, 252, 280, 311, 358

Common Core State Standard	Student/Teacher's Editions
a. Interpret figures of speech (e.g., euphemism, oxymoron) in context and analyze their role in the text.	**Student Edition** 55, 56, 75, 76, 81, 135, 231, 311 **Teacher's Edition** 53, 55, 56, 75, 76, 81, 135, 231, 311
b. Analyze nuances in the meaning of words with similar denotations.	**Student Edition** 37, 55, 56, 311, 358 **Teacher's Edition** 33, 37, 38a, 55, 56, 82a, 253, 311, 339, 358, 376a
6. Acquire and use accurately general academic and domain-specific words and phrases, sufficient for reading, writing, speaking, and listening at the college and career readiness level; demonstrate independence in gathering vocabulary knowledge when considering a word or phrase important to comprehension or expression.	**Student Edition** 2, 41, 45, 50, 57, 83, 87, 92, 145, 149, 154, 193, 197, 202, 313, 318, 349, 377, R50–R55 **Teacher's Edition** 2, 41, 45, 50, 57, 83, 87, 92, 145, 149, 154, 193, 197, 202, 313, 318, 349, 377, R50–R55

Navigating Complex Texts

By Carol Jago

Reading complex literature and nonfiction doesn't need to be painful.

But to enjoy great poetry and prose you are going to have to do more than skim and scan. You will need to develop the habit of paying attention to the particular words on the page closely, systematically, even lovingly. Just because a text isn't easy doesn't mean there is something wrong with it or something wrong with you. Understanding complex text takes effort and focused attention. Do you sometimes wish writers would just say what they have to say more simply or with fewer words? I assure you that writers don't use long sentences and unfamiliar words to annoy their readers or make readers feel dumb. They employ complex syntax and rich language because they have complex ideas about complex issues that they want to communicate. Simple language and structures just aren't up to the task.

Excellent literature and nonfiction—the kind you will be reading over the course of the year—challenge readers in many ways. Sometimes the background of a story or the content of an essay is so unfamiliar that it can be difficult to understand why characters are behaving as they do or to follow the argument a writer is making. By persevering—reading like a detective and following clues in the text—you will find that your store of background knowledge grows. As a result, the next time you read about this subject, the text won't seem nearly as hard. Navigating a terrain you have been over once before never seems quite as rugged the second time through. The more you read, the better reader you become.

Good readers aren't scared off by challenging text. When the going gets rough, they know what to do. Let's take vocabulary, a common measure of text complexity, as an example. Learning new words is the business of a lifetime. Rather than shutting down when you meet a word you don't know, take a moment to think about the word. Is any part of the word familiar to you? Is there something in the context of the sentence or paragraph that can help you figure out its meaning? Is there someone or something that can provide you with a definition? When we read literature or nonfiction from a time period other than our own, the text is often full of words we don't know.

Each time you meet those words in succeeding readings you will be adding to your understanding of the word and its use. Your brain is a natural word-learning machine. The more you feed it complex text, the larger vocabulary you'll have and as a result, the easier navigating the next book will be.

Have you ever been reading a long, complicated sentence and discovered that by the time you reached the end you had forgotten the beginning? Unlike the sentences we speak or dash off in a note to a friend, complex text is often full of sentences that are not only lengthy but also constructed in intricate ways. Such sentences require readers to slow down and figure out how phrases relate to one another as well as who is doing what to whom. Remember, rereading isn't cheating. It is exactly what experienced readers know to do when they meet dense text on the page. On the pages that follow you will find stories and articles that challenge you at a sentence level. Don't be intimidated. By paying careful attention to how those sentences are constructed, you will see their meanings unfold before your eyes.

Another way text can be complex is in terms of the density of ideas. Sometimes a writer piles on so much information that you find even if your eyes continue to move down the page, your brain has stopped taking in anything. At times like this, turning to a peer and discussing particular lines or concepts can help you pay closer attention and begin to unpack the text. Sharing questions and ideas, exploring a difficult passage together, makes it possible to tease out the meaning of even the most difficult text.

> **"Your brain is a natural word-learning machine. The more you feed it complex text, the larger vocabulary you'll have."**

Poetry is by its nature particularly dense and for that reason poses particular challenges for casual readers. Don't ever assume that once through a poem is enough. Often, seemingly simple poems in terms of word choice and length—for example an Emily Dickinson, Mary Oliver, or W.H. Auden poem—express extremely complex feelings and insights. Poets also often make reference to mythological and Biblical allusions which contemporary readers are not always familiar with. Skipping over such references robs your reading of the richness the poet intended. Look up that bird. Check out the note on the page. Ask your teacher.

You will notice a range of complexity within each collection of readings. This spectrum reflects the range of texts that surround us: some easy, some hard, some seemingly easy but hard, some seemingly hard but easy. Navigating this sea of texts should stretch you as a reader and a thinker. How could it be otherwise when your journey is in the realms of gold? Please accept this invitation to an intellectual voyage I think you will enjoy.

Understanding the Common Core State Standards

What are the English Language Arts Common Core State Standards?

The Common Core State Standards for English Language Arts indicate what you should know and be able to do by the end of your grade level. These understandings and skills will help you be better prepared for future classes, college courses, and a career. For this reason, the standards for each strand in English Language Arts (such as reading informational text or writing) directly relate to the College and Career Readiness Anchor Standards for each strand. The Anchor Standards broadly outline the understandings and skills you should master by the end of high school so that you are well-prepared for college or for a career.

How do I learn the English Language Arts Common Core State Standards?

Your textbook is closely aligned to the English Language Arts Common Core State Standards. Every time you learn a concept or practice a skill, you are working on mastery of one of the standards. Each collection, each selection, and each performance task in your textbook connects to one or more of the standards for English Language Arts listed on the following pages.

The English Language Arts Common Core State Standards are divided into five strands: Reading Literature, Reading Informational Text, Writing, Speaking and Listening, and Language.

Strand	What It Means to You
Reading Literature (RL)	This strand concerns the literary texts you will read at this grade level: stories, drama, and poetry. The Common Core State Standards stress that you should read a range of texts of increasing complexity as you progress through high school.
Reading Informational Text (RI)	Informational text includes a broad range of literary nonfiction, including exposition, argument, and functional text, in such genres as personal essays, speeches, opinion pieces, memoirs, and historical and scientific accounts. The Common Core State Standards stress that you will read a range of informational texts of increasing complexity as you progress from grade to grade.
Writing (W)	The Writing strand focuses on your generating three types of texts—arguments, informative or explanatory texts, and narratives—while using the writing process and technology to develop and share your writing. The Common Core State Standards also emphasize research and specify that you should write routinely for both short and extended time frames.
Speaking and Listening (SL)	The Common Core State Standards focus on comprehending information presented in a variety of media and formats, on participating in collaborative discussions, and on presenting knowledge and ideas clearly.
Language (L)	The standards in the Language strand address the conventions of standard English grammar, usage, and mechanics; knowledge of language; and vocabulary acquisition and use.

Common Core Code Decoder

The codes you find on the pages of your textbook identify the specific knowledge or skill for the standard addressed in the text.

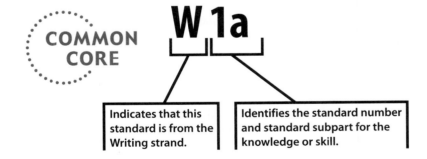

Indicates that this standard is from the Writing strand.	Identifies the standard number and standard subpart for the knowledge or skill.

English Language Arts
Common Core State Standards

Listed below are the English Language Arts Common Core State Standards that you are required to master by the end of grade 10. We have provided a summary of the concepts you will learn on your way to mastering each standard. The CCR anchor standards and high school grade-specific standards for each strand work together to define college and career readiness expectations—the former providing broad standards, the latter providing additional specificity.

College and Career Readiness Anchor Standards for Reading

Common Core State Standards

KEY IDEAS AND DETAILS

1. Read closely to determine what the text says explicitly and to make logical inferences from it; cite specific textual evidence when writing or speaking to support conclusions drawn from the text.

2. Determine central ideas or themes of a text and analyze their development; summarize the key supporting details and ideas.

3. Analyze how and why individuals, events, and ideas develop and interact over the course of a text.

CRAFT AND STRUCTURE

4. Interpret words and phrases as they are used in a text, including determining technical, connotative, and figurative meanings, and analyze how specific word choices shape meaning or tone.

5. Analyze the structure of texts, including how specific sentences, paragraphs, and larger portions of the text (e.g., a section, chapter, scene, or stanza) relate to each other and the whole.

6. Assess how point of view or purpose shapes the content and style of a text.

INTEGRATION OF KNOWLEDGE AND IDEAS

7. Integrate and evaluate content presented in diverse formats and media, including visually and quantitatively, as well as in words.

8. Delineate and evaluate the argument and specific claims in a text, including the validity of the reasoning as well as the relevance and sufficiency of the evidence.

9. Analyze how two or more texts address similar themes or topics in order to build knowledge or to compare the approaches the authors take.

RANGE OF READING AND LEVEL OF TEXT COMPLEXITY

10. Read and comprehend complex literary and informational texts independently and proficiently.

Reading Standards for Literature, Grades 9–10 Students

The College and Career Readiness Anchor Standards for Reading apply to both literature and informational text.

Common Core State Standards	What it Means to You
KEY IDEAS AND DETAILS	
1. Cite strong and thorough textual evidence to support analysis of what the text says explicitly as well as inferences drawn from the text.	You will use details and information from the text to support your understanding of its main ideas—both those that are stated directly and those that are suggested.
2. Determine a theme or central idea of a text and analyze in detail its development over the course of the text, including how it emerges and is shaped and refined by specific details; provide an objective summary of the text.	You will analyze the development of a text's main ideas and themes by showing how they progress throughout the text. You will also summarize the main idea of the text as a whole without adding your own ideas or opinions.
3. Analyze how complex characters (e.g., those with multiple or conflicting motivations) develop over the course of a text, interact with other characters, and advance the plot or develop the theme.	You will analyze the development of a text's characters and how their actions, thoughts, and words contribute to the story's plot or themes.
CRAFT AND STRUCTURE	
4. Determine the meaning of words and phrases as they are used in the text, including figurative and connotative meanings; analyze the cumulative impact of specific word choices on meaning and tone (e.g., how the language evokes a sense of time and place; how it sets a formal or informal tone).	You will analyze specific words and phrases in the text to determine both what they mean individually as well as how they contribute to the text's tone and meaning as a whole.
5. Analyze how an author's choices concerning how to structure a text, order events within it (e.g., parallel plots), and manipulate time (e.g., pacing, flashbacks) create such effects as mystery, tension, or surprise.	You will analyze the ways in which the author has chosen to structure and order the text and determine how those choices affect the text's mood or tone.
6. Analyze a particular point of view or cultural experience reflected in a work of literature from outside the United States, drawing on a wide reading of world literature.	You will analyze the point of view or cultural experience of a work of literature from outside the United States.

Common Core State Standards	What it Means to You
INTEGRATION OF KNOWLEDGE AND IDEAS	
7. Analyze the representation of a subject or a key scene in two different artistic mediums, including what is emphasized or absent in each treatment (e.g., Auden's "Musée des Beaux Arts" and Breughel's Landscape with the Fall of Icarus).	You will compare and contrast how events and information are presented in visual and non-visual texts.
8. (Not applicable to literature)	
9. Analyze how an author draws on and transforms source material in a specific work (e.g., how Shakespeare treats a theme or topic from Ovid or the Bible or how a later author draws on a play by Shakespeare).	You will recognize and analyze how an author draws from and uses source material from other texts or other types of sources.
RANGE OF READING AND LEVEL OF TEXT COMPLEXITY	
10. By the end of grade 10, read and comprehend literature, including stories, dramas, and poems, at the high end of the grades 9–10 text complexity band independently and proficiently.	You will demonstrate the ability to read and understand grade-level appropriate literary texts by the end of grade 10.

Reading Standards for Informational Text, Grades 9–10 Students

Common Core State Standards	What it Means to You
KEY IDEAS AND DETAILS	
1. Cite strong and thorough textual evidence to support analysis of what the text says explicitly as well as inferences drawn from the text.	You will use details and information from the text to support your understanding of its main ideas—both those that are stated directly and those that are suggested.
2. Determine a central idea of a text and analyze its development over the course of the text, including how it emerges and is shaped and refined by specific details; provide an objective summary of the text.	You will analyze the development of a text's main ideas and themes by showing how they progress throughout the text. You will also summarize the main idea of the text as a whole without adding your own ideas or opinions.

Common Core State Standards	What it Means to You
3. Analyze how the author unfolds an analysis or series of ideas or events, including the order in which the points are made, how they are introduced and developed, and the connections that are drawn between them.	You will analyze the ways in which the author has chosen to structure and order the text and determine how those choices affect the text's central ideas.

CRAFT AND STRUCTURE

Common Core State Standards	What it Means to You
4. Determine the meaning of words and phrases as they are used in a text, including figurative, connotative, and technical meanings; analyze the cumulative impact of specific word choices on meaning and tone (e.g., how the language of a court opinion differs from that of a newspaper).	You will analyze specific words and phrases in the text to determine both what they mean individually as well as how they contribute to the text's tone and meaning as a whole.
5. Analyze in detail how an author's ideas or claims are developed and refined by particular sentences, paragraphs, or larger portions of a text (e.g., a section or chapter).	You will examine specific portions of the text (sentences, paragraphs, or larger sections) to understand how they develop the author's ideas and claims.
6. Determine an author's point of view or purpose in a text and analyze how an author uses rhetoric to advance that point of view or purpose.	You will understand the author's purpose and analyze how the author uses language to effectively communicate that purpose.

INTEGRATION OF KNOWLEDGE AND IDEAS

Common Core State Standards	What it Means to You
7. Analyze various accounts of a subject told in different mediums (e.g., a person's life story in both print and multimedia), determining which details are emphasized in each account.	You will compare and contrast the ways in which various media, such as newspapers, television, documentaries, blogs, and the Internet, portray the same events.
8. Delineate and evaluate the argument and specific claims in a text, assessing whether the reasoning is valid and the evidence is relevant and sufficient; identify false statements and fallacious reasoning.	You will evaluate the strength of the author's claims by examining the supporting details and reasoning and identifying any faults or weaknesses in them.
9. Analyze seminal U.S. documents of historical and literary significance (e.g., Washington's Farewell Address, the Gettysburg Address, Roosevelt's Four Freedoms speech, King's "Letter from Birmingham Jail"), including how they address related themes and concepts.	You will read and analyze influential documents and explain how they address important themes related to United States history and culture.

Common Core State Standards	What it Means to You
RANGE OF READING AND LEVEL OF TEXT COMPLEXITY	
10. By the end of grade 10, read and comprehend literary nonfiction at the high end of the grades 9–10 text complexity band independently and proficiently.	You will demonstrate the ability to read and understand grade-level appropriate literary nonfiction texts by the end of grade 10.

College and Career Readiness Anchor Standards for Writing

Common Core State Standards
TEXT TYPES AND PURPOSES
1. Write arguments to support claims in an analysis of substantive topics or texts, using valid reasoning and relevant and sufficient evidence.
2. Write informative/explanatory texts to examine and convey complex ideas and information clearly and accurately through the effective selection, organization, and analysis of content.
3. Write narratives to develop real or imagined experiences or events using effective technique, well-chosen details, and well-structured event sequences.
PRODUCTION AND DISTRIBUTION OF WRITING
4. Produce clear and coherent writing in which the development, organization, and style are appropriate to task, purpose, and audience.
5. Develop and strengthen writing as needed by planning, revising, editing, rewriting, or trying a new approach.
6. Use technology, including the Internet, to produce and publish writing and to interact and collaborate with others.
RESEARCH TO BUILD AND PRESENT KNOWLEDGE
7. Conduct short as well as more sustained research projects based on focused questions, demonstrating understanding of the subject under investigation.
8. Gather relevant information from multiple print and digital sources, assess the credibility and accuracy of each source, and integrate the information while avoiding plagiarism.
9. Draw evidence from literary or informational texts to support analysis, reflection, and research.
RANGE OF WRITING
10. Write routinely over extended time frames (time for research, reflection, and revision) and shorter time frames (a single sitting or a day or two) for a range of tasks, purposes, and audiences.

Writing Standards, Grades 9–10 Students

Common Core State Standards	What it Means to You
TEXT TYPES AND PURPOSES	
1. Write arguments to support claims in an analysis of substantive topics or texts, using valid reasoning and relevant and sufficient evidence.	You will write and develop arguments with strong evidence and valid reasoning that include
a. Introduce precise claim(s), distinguish the claim(s) from alternate or opposing claims, and create an organization that establishes clear relationships among claim(s), counterclaims, reasons, and evidence.	a. a clear organization of precise claims and counterclaims
b. Develop claim(s) and counterclaims fairly, supplying evidence for each while pointing out the strengths and limitations of both in a manner that anticipates the audience's knowledge level and concerns.	b. relevant and unbiased support for claims
c. Use words, phrases, and clauses to link the major sections of the text, create cohesion, and clarify the relationships between claim(s) and reasons, between reasons and evidence, and between claim(s) and counterclaims.	c. use of transitional words, phrases, and clauses to link information
d. Establish and maintain a formal style and objective tone while attending to the norms and conventions of the discipline in which they are writing.	d. a tone and style appropriate to the task
e. Provide a concluding statement or section that follows from and supports the argument presented.	e. a strong concluding statement or section that summarizes the evidence presented
2. Write informative/explanatory texts to examine and convey complex ideas, concepts, and information clearly and accurately through the effective selection, organization, and analysis of content.	You will write clear, well-organized, and thoughtful informative and explanatory texts with
a. Introduce a topic; organize complex ideas, concepts, and information to make important connections and distinctions; include formatting (e.g., headings), graphics (e.g., figures, tables), and multimedia when useful to aiding comprehension.	a. a clear introduction and organization, including headings and graphic organizers (when appropriate)

Common Core State Standards	What it Means to You
b. Develop the topic with well-chosen, relevant, and sufficient facts, extended definitions, concrete details, quotations, or other information and examples appropriate to the audience's knowledge of the topic.	**b.** sufficient supporting details and background information
c. Use appropriate and varied transitions to link the major sections of the text, create cohesion, and clarify the relationships among complex ideas and concepts.	**c.** appropriate transitions
d. Use precise language and domain-specific vocabulary to manage the complexity of the topic.	**d.** precise language and relevant vocabulary
e. Establish and maintain a formal style and objective tone while attending to the norms and conventions of the discipline in which they are writing.	**e.** a tone and style appropriate to the task
f. Provide a concluding statement or section that follows from and supports the information or explanation presented (e.g., articulating implications or the significance of the topic).	**f.** a strong concluding statement or section that restates the importance or relevance of the topic
3. Write narratives to develop real or imagined experiences or events using effective technique, well-chosen details, and well-structured event sequences.	You will write clear, well-structured, detailed narrative texts that
a. Engage and orient the reader by setting out a problem, situation, or observation, establishing one or multiple point(s) of view, and introducing a narrator and/or characters; create a smooth progression of experiences or events.	**a.** draw your readers in with a clear topic and an interesting progression of events or ideas
b. Use narrative techniques, such as dialogue, pacing, description, reflection, and multiple plot lines, to develop experiences, events, and/or characters.	**b.** use literary techniques to develop and expand on events and/or characters
c. Use a variety of techniques to sequence events so that they build on one another to create a coherent whole.	**c.** have a coherent sequence and structure
d. Use precise words and phrases, telling details, and sensory language to convey a vivid picture of the experiences, events, setting, and/or characters.	**d.** use precise words and sensory details that keep readers interested
e. Provide a conclusion that follows from and reflects on what is experienced, observed, or resolved over the course of the narrative.	**e.** have a strong conclusion that reflects on the topic

Common Core State Standards	What it Means to You

PRODUCTION AND DISTRIBUTION OF WRITING

Common Core State Standards	What it Means to You
4. Produce clear and coherent writing in which the development, organization, and style are appropriate to task, purpose, and audience. (Grade-specific expectations for writing types are defined in standards 1–3 above.)	You will produce writing that is appropriate to the task, purpose, and audience for whom you are writing.
5. Develop and strengthen writing as needed by planning, revising, editing, rewriting, or trying a new approach, focusing on addressing what is most significant for a specific purpose and audience. (Editing for conventions should demonstrate command of Language standards 1–3 up to and including grades 9–10.)	You will revise and refine your writing to address what is most important for your purpose and audience.
6. Use technology, including the Internet, to produce, publish, and update individual or shared writing products, taking advantage of technology's capacity to link to other information and to display information flexibly and dynamically.	You will use technology to share your writing and to provide links to other relevant information.

RESEARCH TO BUILD AND PRESENT KNOWLEDGE

Common Core State Standards	What it Means to You
7. Conduct short as well as more sustained research projects to answer a question (including a self-generated question) or solve a problem; narrow or broaden the inquiry when appropriate; synthesize multiple sources on the subject, demonstrating understanding of the subject under investigation.	You will engage in short and more complex research tasks that include answering a question or solving a problem by using multiple sources. The product of your research will demonstrate your understanding of the subject.
8. Gather relevant information from multiple authoritative print and digital sources, using advanced searches effectively; assess the usefulness of each source in answering the research question; integrate information into the text selectively to maintain the flow of ideas, avoiding plagiarism and following a standard format for citation.	You will effectively conduct searches to gather information from different sources and assess the relevance of each source, following a standard format for citation.
9. Draw evidence from literary or informational texts to support analysis, reflection, and research. a. Apply grades 9–10 Reading standards to literature (e.g., "Analyze how an author draws on and trans-forms source material in a specific work [e.g., how Shakespeare treats a theme or topic from Ovid or the Bible or how a later author draws on a play by Shakespeare]").	You will paraphrase, summarize, quote, and cite primary and secondary sources, using both literary and informational texts, to support your analysis, reflection, and research.

Common Core State Standards	What it Means to You
b. Apply grades 9–10 Reading standards to literary nonfiction (e.g., "Delineate and evaluate the argument and specific claims in a text, assessing whether the reasoning is valid and the evidence is relevant and sufficient; identify false statements and fallacious reasoning").	

RANGE OF WRITING

Common Core State Standards	What it Means to You
10. Write routinely over extended time frames (time for research, reflection, and revision) and shorter time frames (a single sitting or a day or two) for a range of tasks, purposes, and audiences.	You will write for many different purposes and audiences both over short and extended periods of time.

College and Career Readiness Anchor Standards for Speaking and Listening

Common Core State Standards
COMPREHENSION AND COLLABORATION
1. Prepare for and participate effectively in a range of conversations and collaborations with diverse partners, building on others' ideas and expressing their own clearly and persuasively.
2. Integrate and evaluate information presented in diverse media and formats, including visually, quantitatively, and orally.
3. Evaluate a speaker's point of view, reasoning, and use of evidence and rhetoric.
PRESENTATION OF KNOWLEDGE AND IDEAS
4. Present information, findings, and supporting evidence such that listeners can follow the line of reasoning and the organization, development, and style are appropriate to task, purpose, and audience.
5. Make strategic use of digital media and visual displays of data to express information and enhance understanding of presentations.
6. Adapt speech to a variety of contexts and communicative tasks, demonstrating command of formal English when indicated or appropriate.

Speaking and Listening Standards, Grades 9–10 Students

Common Core State Standards	What it Means to You
COMPREHENSION AND COLLABORATION	
1. Initiate and participate effectively in a range of collaborative discussions (one-on-one, in groups, and teacher-led) with diverse partners on grades 9–10 topics, texts, and issues, building on others' ideas and expressing their own clearly and persuasively.	You will actively participate in a variety of discussions in which you
a. Come to discussions prepared, having read and researched material under study; explicitly draw on that preparation by referring to evidence from texts and other research on the topic or issue to stimulate a thoughtful, well-reasoned exchange of ideas.	a. have read any relevant material beforehand and have come to the discussion prepared
b. Work with peers to set rules for collegial discussions and decision-making (e.g., informal consensus, taking votes on key issues, presentation of alternate views), clear goals and deadlines, and individual roles as needed.	b. work with others to establish goals and processes within the group
c. Propel conversations by posing and responding to questions that relate the current discussion to broader themes or larger ideas; actively incorporate others into the discussion; and clarify, verify, or challenge ideas and conclusions.	c. initiate dialogue by asking and responding to questions and by relating the current topic to other relevant information
d. Respond thoughtfully to diverse perspectives, summarize points of agreement and disagreement, and, when warranted, qualify or justify their own views and understanding and make new connections in light of the evidence and reasoning presented.	d. respond to different perspectives and summarize points of agreement or disagreement when needed
2. Integrate multiple sources of information presented in diverse media or formats (e.g., visually, quantitatively, orally) evaluating the credibility and accuracy of each source.	You will integrate multiple sources of information, assessing the credibility and accuracy of each source.
3. Evaluate a speaker's point of view, reasoning, and use of evidence and rhetoric, identifying any fallacious reasoning or exaggerated or distorted evidence.	You will evaluate a speaker's argument and identify any false reasoning or evidence.

Common Core State Standards	What it Means to You
PRESENTATION OF KNOWLEDGE AND IDEAS	
4. Present information, findings, and supporting evidence clearly, concisely, and logically such that listeners can follow the line of reasoning and the organization, development, substance, and style are appropriate to purpose, audience, and task.	You will organize and present information to your listeners in a logical sequence and style that are appropriate to your task and audience.
5. Make strategic use of digital media (e.g., textual, graphical, audio, visual, and interactive elements) in presentations to enhance understanding of findings, reasoning, and evidence and to add interest.	You will use digital media to enhance and add interest to presentations.
6. Adapt speech to a variety of contexts and tasks, demonstrating command of formal English when indicated or appropriate. (See grades 9–10 Language standards 1 and 3 for specific expectations.)	You will adapt the formality of your speech appropriately, depending on its context and purpose.

College and Career Readiness Anchor Standards for Language

Common Core State Standards
CONVENTIONS OF STANDARD ENGLISH
1. Demonstrate command of the conventions of standard English grammar and usage when writing or speaking.
2. Demonstrate command of the conventions of standard English capitalization, punctuation, and spelling when writing.
KNOWLEDGE OF LANGUAGE
3. Apply knowledge of language to understand how language functions in different contexts, to make effective choices for meaning or style, and to comprehend more fully when reading or listening.
VOCABULARY ACQUISITION AND USE
4. Determine or clarify the meaning of unknown and multiple-meaning words and phrases by using context clues, analyzing meaningful word parts, and consulting general and specialized reference materials, as appropriate.
5. Demonstrate understanding of word relationships and nuances in word meanings.
6. Acquire and use accurately a range of general academic and domain-specific words and phrases sufficient for reading, writing, speaking, and listening at the college and career readiness level; demonstrate independence in gathering vocabulary knowledge when considering a word or phrase important to comprehension or expression.

Language Standards, Grades 9–10 Students

Common Core State Standards	What it Means to You
CONVENTIONS OF STANDARD ENGLISH	
1. Demonstrate command of the conventions of standard English grammar and usage when writing or speaking.	You will correctly use the conventions of English grammar and usage, including
a. Use parallel structure.	**a.** parallel structure
b. Use various types of phrases (noun, verb, adjectival, adverbial, participial, prepositional, absolute) and clauses (independent, dependent; noun, relative, adverbial) to convey specific meanings and add variety and interest to writing or presentations.	**b.** phrases and clauses
2. Demonstrate command of the conventions of standard English capitalization, punctuation, and spelling when writing.	You will correctly use the conventions of English capitalization, punctuation, and spelling, including
a. Use a semicolon (and perhaps a conjunctive adverb) to link two or more closely related independent clauses.	**a.** semicolons
b. Use a colon to introduce a list or quotation.	**b.** colons
c. Spell correctly.	**c.** spelling
KNOWLEDGE OF LANGUAGE	
3. Apply knowledge of language to understand how language functions in different contexts, to make effective choices for meaning or style, and to comprehend more fully when reading or listening.	You will apply your knowledge of language in different contexts, including
a. Write and edit work so that it conforms to the guidelines in a style manual (e.g., *MLA Handbook*, Turabian's *Manual for Writers*) appropriate for the discipline and writing type.	**a.** conforming to a style manual when writing and editing

Common Core State Standards	What it Means to You
VOCABULARY ACQUISITION AND USE	
4. Determine or clarify the meaning of unknown and multiple-meaning words and phrases based on grades 9–10 reading and content, choosing flexibly from a range of strategies.	You will understand the meaning of grade-level appropriate words and phrases by
a. Use context (e.g., the overall meaning of a sentence, paragraph, or text; a word's position or function in a sentence) as a clue to the meaning of a word or phrase.	**a.** using context clues
b. Identify and correctly use patterns of word changes that indicate different meanings or parts of speech (e.g., *analyze, analysis, analytical; advocate, advocacy*).	**b.** recognizing and adapting root words according to meaning or part of speech
c. Consult general and specialized reference materials (e.g., dictionaries, glossaries, thesauruses), both print and digital, to find the pronunciation of a word or determine or clarify its precise meaning, its part of speech, or its etymology.	**c.** using reference materials
d. Verify the preliminary determination of the meaning of a word or phrase (e.g., by checking the inferred meaning in context or in a dictionary).	**d.** inferring and verifying the meanings of words in context
5. Demonstrate understanding of figurative language, word relationships, and nuances in word meanings.	You will understand figurative language, word relationships, and slight differences in word meanings by
a. Interpret figures of speech (e.g., euphemism, oxymoron) in context and analyze their role in the text.	**a.** interpreting figures of speech in context
b. Analyze nuances in the meaning of words with similar denotations.	**b.** analyzing slight differences in the meanings of similar words
6. Acquire and use accurately general academic and domain-specific words and phrases, sufficient for reading, writing, speaking, and listening at the college and career readiness level; demonstrate independence in gathering vocabulary knowledge when considering a word or phrase important to comprehension or expression.	You will develop vocabulary knowledge at the college and career readiness level and demonstrate confidence in using it appropriately.

Ourselves and Others

CONNECTING WORD AND IMAGE

ASK STUDENTS to discuss how the collection opener image and the collection quotation work together to create a connection.

PERFORMANCE TASK PREVIEW

Point out to students that they will complete two performance tasks at the end of the collection. The performance tasks will require them to further analyze the selections in the collection and to synthesize ideas about these analyses. They will present their findings in a variety of products.

ACADEMIC VOCABULARY

> ▶ **View It!**
> Professional Development Podcast:
> **Academic Vocabulary**

Students can acquire facility with the academic vocabulary words through frequent, repeated exposure as they analyze and discuss the selections in the collection. Academic vocabulary can be used in the following instructional contexts. This will enable students to incorporate the academic vocabulary words into their working vocabulary.

- Collaborative Discussion at the end of each selection
- Analyzing the Text questions for each selection
- Selection-level Performance Task
- Vocabulary instruction (for Critical Vocabulary and/or for Vocabulary Strategy)
- Language and Style
- End-of-collection Performance Task for all selections in the collection

ASK STUDENTS to review the academic vocabulary word list for this collection. You may wish to pronounce each word aloud, so students hear the correct pronunciation. Then discuss the definitions and the related forms for each word. Remind students that they will encounter these five academic vocabulary words throughout the collection.

Ourselves and Others

This collection explores how we interact with other people— family, enemies, neighbors, strangers, and those with whom we disagree.

hmhfyi.com

COLLECTION
PERFORMANCE TASK Preview

At the end of this collection, you will have the opportunity to complete two tasks:

- Deliver a speech about how people's relationships with others shape who they are.

- Write an essay about how the texts in this collection do or do not support the idea that people must accept others who are different from themselves.

ACADEMIC VOCABULARY

Study the words and their definitions in the chart below. You will use these words as you discuss and write about the texts in this collection.

Word	Definition	Related Forms
discriminate (dĭ-skrĭm´ə-nāt´) *v.*	to note clear differences; to separate into categories	discrimination, discriminatory
diverse (dĭ-vûrs´) *adj.*	made up of elements that are different from each other	diversify, diversity
inhibit (ĭn-hĭb´ĭt) *v.*	to hold back or prevent from acting	inhibition
intervene (ĭn´tər-vēn´) *v.*	to come between two things, persons, or events	intervention
rational (răsh´ə-nəl) *adj.*	based on logic or sound reasoning	rationale, rationalize, irrational

2

Image Credits: ©Gluey Batuay/Houghton Mifflin Harcourt

USING COLLECTIONS YOUR WAY

Use the following information, along with the charts on the following pages, to help you decide how you want to introduce the collection. Based on your teaching style, your students' interests, or your instructional goals, you may want to structure this collection in various ways. You may choose different entry points each time you teach the collection.

"I love to concentrate on contemporary literature."

This story offers a modern take on the theme of making wishes, showing how wishes granted by a magic fish give insights about what people believe will make their lives happier.

Background *The Jewish people were expelled from their homeland, Israel, in the first century. In the late 1800s, Jews from Europe, Asia, Africa, and the Americas began returning to the region; World War II and the Holocaust drastically increased this immigration. Israel became an independent nation in 1948, but tensions with its Arab neighbors and its Arab citizens have led to conflict. With the collapse of the Soviet Union in 1991, many Russian Jews were finally able to move to Israel and make their own mark on the nation's culture. In this story, Israeli writer* **Etgar Keret** *(b. 1967) explores the hopes and dreams of people in this diverse society.*

What, of This Goldfish, Would You Wish?

Short Story by Etgar Keret   Translated by Nathan Englander

AS YOU READ Think about the kinds of things people wish for to make their lives happier. In particular, look for clues to what Sergei Goralick wants from life. Note any questions you have as you read.

Yonatan had a brilliant idea for a documentary. He'd knock on doors. Just him. No camera crew, no nonsense. Just Yonatan, on his own, a small camera in hand, asking, "If you found a talking goldfish that granted you three wishes, what would you wish for?" Folks would give their answers, and Yoni would edit them down and make clips of the more surprising responses. Before every set of answers, you'd see the person standing stock-still in the entrance to his house. Onto this shot he'd superimpose¹ the subject's name, family situation, monthly income, and maybe even the party he'd voted for in the last election. All that, combined with the three wishes, and maybe he'd end up with a **poignant** piece of social commentary, a testament to the massive rift between our dreams and the often compromised reality in which we live.

poignant
(poin'yənt) *adj.* emotionally moving or stimulating.

¹ **superimpose:** place one thing on top of another so that both remain visible.

What, of This Goldfish, Would You Wish?   **3**

"I like to teach by comparing texts."

This court opinion asserts how the Constitution's First Amendment principles of freedom of expression can be applied to present-day situations like flag burning, and the editorial offers one person's point of view about the Court's ruling.

COMPARE ANCHOR TEXTS

Background *At the 1984 Republican National Convention in Dallas, Texas, protesters marched, held signs, and chanted slogans opposing the policies of then-President Ronald Reagan. One of the protesters, Gregory Lee Johnson, set an American flag on fire. He was punished with a fine and a jail term for breaking a state law banning flag desecration. He appealed, and the case was sent to the Supreme Court to decide whether flag burning is a form of expression protected by the Constitution. The Court delivered its ruling in 1989.* **William J. Brennan** *(1906–1997), who served on the Supreme Court from 1956 to 1990, wrote the majority opinion in the case. His staunch defense of First Amendment rights influenced many significant Court decisions.*

from
Texas v. Johnson Majority Opinion
Court Opinion by William J. Brennan

American Flag Stands for Tolerance
Newspaper Editorial by Ronald J. Allen

from
Texas v. Johnson Majority Opinion

Court Opinion by William J. Brennan

AS YOU READ Pay attention to the details that explain the Court's reasons for its decision. Note any questions you have as you read.

We decline, therefore, to create for the flag an exception to the joust¹ of principles protected by the First Amendment. . . .²
To say that the government has an interest in encouraging proper treatment of the flag, however, is not to say that it may criminally punish a person for burning a flag as a means of political protest.

¹ **joust:** competition.
² **First Amendment:** the part of the Bill of Rights added to the U.S. Constitution that deals with freedom of speech, among other freedoms.

Compare Anchor Texts   **15**

"I stress the importance of language and style."

The author establishes a peaceful tone in a small town and then slowly builds suspense, leading up to an unexpected ending that shows what happens when characters unquestioningly accept and blindly follow conventions.

Shirley Jackson *(1919–1965) said about her writing, "It's great fun and I love it." Although some of her works humorously chronicle her life with her husband and four children, she is best known for exploring the darker side of human nature. Her story "The Lottery" ignited controversy when it was published in The New Yorker in 1948. Readers cancelled their subscriptions and sent hundreds of letters expressing their outrage over the tale. Her novel The Haunting of Hill House, considered by many to be the "greatest haunted house story ever written," and the gothic horror tale We Have Always Lived in the Castle have been adapted for film and stage and are still widely read.*

The Lottery

Short Story by Shirley Jackson

AS YOU READ Pay attention to details that reveal the purpose of the lottery and the villagers' reactions to it. Note any questions you have.

The morning of June 27th was clear and sunny, with the fresh warmth of a full-summer day; the flowers were blossoming **profusely** and the grass was richly green. The people of the village began to gather in the square, between the post office and the bank, around ten o'clock; in some towns there were so many people that the lottery took two days and had to be started on June 26th, but in this village, where there were only about three hundred people, the whole lottery took less than two hours, so it could begin at ten o'clock in the morning and still be through in time to allow the villagers to get home for noon dinner.
The children assembled first, of course. School was recently over for the summer, and the feeling of liberty sat uneasily on most of them; they tended to gather together quietly for a while before they broke into boisterous play, and their talk was still of the classroom and the teacher, of books and reprimands. Bobby Martin had already stuffed his pockets full of stones, and the other boys soon followed his example, selecting the smoothest and roundest stones; Bobby and Harry Jones and Dickie Delacroix—the villagers

profusely
(prə-fyoōs'lē) *adv.* plentifully, in a freely available way.

The Lottery   **25**

*my*SmartPlanner | eBook | *my*Notebook | *my* WriteSmart | fyi hmhfyi.com

Collection 1 Lessons	Media	Teach and Practice
Student Edition | eBook	▶ Video Links	**Close Reading and Evidence Tracking**
ANCHOR TEXT — Short Story by Etgar Keret / Translated by Nathan Englander "What, of This Goldfish, Would You Wish?"	🔊 **Audio** "What, of This Goldfish, Would You Wish?"	**Close Read Screencasts** • Modeled Discussion 1 (lines 10–20) • Modeled Discussion 2 (lines 116–130) **Strategies for Annotation** • Analyze Character: Motivations • Using Context Clues
CLOSE READER — Short Story by Ursula LeGuin "The Wife's Story"	🔊 **Audio** "The Wife's Story"	
Movie Trailer from a Film directed by Lisa Gossels "My So-Called Enemy"	🔊 **Audio** "My So-Called Enemy"	
ANCHOR TEXT — Court Opinion by William J. Brennan from *Texas v. Johnson Majority Opinion* Editorial by Ronald J. Allen "American Flag Stands for Tolerance"	🔊 **Audio** from *Texas v. Johnson Majority Opinion* 🔊 **Audio** "American Flag Stands for Tolerance"	**Close Read Screencasts** • Modeled Discussion 1 (lines 1–12) • Modeled Discussion 2 (lines 31–39) • Modeled Discussion 3 (lines 22–32) • Modeled Discussion 4 (lines 64–68) **Strategies for Annotation** • Analyze Impact of Word Choice: Compare Tone • Words from Latin
CLOSE READER — from *The Universal Declaration of Human Rights* by the UN Commission on Human Rights from *Towards a True Refuge* by Aung San Suu Kyi	🔊 **Audio** from *The Universal Declaration of Human Rights* 🔊 **Audio** from *Towards a True Refuge*	
Short Story by Shirley Jackson "The Lottery"	🔊 **Audio** "The Lottery"	**Strategies for Annotation** • Analyze Author's Choices: Tension and Surprise
Poem by Diane Glancey "Without Title"	▶ **Video HISTORY** *AMERICA The Story of Us: American Buffalo* 🔊 **Audio** "Without Title"	
Collection 1 Performance Tasks: **A** Present a Speech **B** Write an Analytical Essay	fyi **hmhfyi.com**	**Interactive Lessons** **A** Giving a Presentation **A** Using Textual Evidence **B** Writing Informative Texts **B** Using Textual Evidence

	For Systematic Coverage of Writing and Speaking & Listening Standards	Interactive Lessons Writing as a Process Participating in Collaborative Discussions	Lesson Assessments Writing as a Process Participating in Collaborative Discussions

Assess		Extend	Reteach
Performance Task	**Online Assessment**	**Teacher eBook**	**Teacher eBook**
Speaking Activity: Discussion	Selection Test	**Analyze How Authors Use Time**	**Analyze Point of View > Level Up Tutorial >** Historical and Cultural Context
Speaking Activity: Argument	Selection Test	**Support Inferences > Interactive Whiteboard Lesson >** Making Inferences	**Determine Point of View > Level Up Tutorial** > Author's Purpose
Writing Activity: Comparison Writing Activity: Analysis	Selection Test	**Analyze Themes in Seminal U.S. Documents**	**Cite Evidence > Level Up Tutorial** > Evidence
Writing Activity: Letter	Selection Test	**Attend to Conventions of Letter Writing > Interactive Whiteboard Lesson >** Maintaining a Formal Style and Objective Tone	**Vocabulary Strategy: Denotation and Connotation > Wordsharp: Interactive Vocabulary Tutorial >** Denotative and Connotative Meanings
Speaking Activity: Oral Narrative	Selection Test	**Adapting Speech to Contexts Analyzing the Impact of Word Choices > Level Up Tutorial >** Elements of Poetry **Evaluating Media Sources**	**Support Inferences About Theme > Level Up Tutorial >** Theme
A Present a Speech **B** Write an Analytical Essay	Collection Test		

Collection 1 Lessons	COMMON CORE Key Learning Objective	Performance Task
ANCHOR TEXT **Short Story by Etgar Keret** **Lexile 900** **Translated by Nathan Englander** **"What, of This Goldfish, Would You Wish?," p. 3A**	**The student will be able to…** analyze the impact of cultural background on point of view	Speaking Activity: Discussion
ANCHOR TEXT **Lexile 1420** **Court Opinion by William J. Brennan** from *Texas v. Johnson Majority Opinion,* p. 15A **Editorial by Ronald J. Allen** **Lexile 1170** **"American Flag Stands for Tolerance," p. 18A**	**The student will be able to…** analyze a Supreme Court opinion, cite evidence used to make inferences in an editorial, and compare tone in two texts by analyzing the impact of word choice	Writing Activity: Comparison Writing Activity: Analysis
Movie Trailer from a Film directed by Lisa Gossels **"My So-Called Enemy," p. 13A**	**The student will be able to…** analyze how a director unfolds a series of ideas to advance a purpose and a point of view	Speaking Activity: Argument
Short Story by Shirley Jackson **Lexile 1140** **"The Lottery," p. 25A**	**The student will be able to…** analyze a writer's choices in terms of pacing, word choice, tone, and mood	Writing Activity: Letter
Poem by Diane Glancey **"Without Title," p. 39A**	**The student will be able to…** support inferences about theme	Speaking Activity: Oral Narrative

Collection 1 Performance Tasks:
A Present a Speech
B Write an Analytical Essay

Vocabulary Strategy	Language and Style	Student Instructional Support	CLOSE READER Selection
Context Clues	Formal vs Informal Tone	**Scaffolding for ELL Students:** • Analyze Idioms • Language: Conversational Patterns **When Students Struggle:** Sequence of Events and Inferences	Short Story by Ursula LeGuin "The Wife's Story," p. 12b **Lexile 880**
Words from Latin	Noun Clauses	**Scaffolding for ELL Students:** • Analyze Seminal U.S. Documents • Cite Evidence	Public Document by the UN Commission on Human Rights from "The Universal Declaration of Human Rights," p. 24b **Lexile 3260** Speech by Aung San Suu Kyi from "Towards a True Refuge," p. 24b **Lexile 1490**
		Scaffolding for ELL Students: Determine Purpose and Point of View	
Denotation and Connotation	Colloquialisms	**Scaffolding for ELL Students:** • Make Inferences • Identify Symbols and Theme • Analyze Language **When Students Struggle:** • Keeping Track of Characters • Understanding Critical Vocabulary **To Challenge Students:** Dialogue, Characterization, and Mood/Tone	
		Scaffolding for ELL Students: Support Inferences About Theme	

ANCHOR TEXT

What, of This Goldfish, Would You Wish?

Short Story by Etgar Keret   Translated by Nathan Englander

Why This Text?

Students often read fictional short stories starring complex characters who develop over the course of the narrative. In this story, Etgar Keret explores people's dreams and their reality of living in a land where people from many cultures often struggle to coexist.

View It!

Professional Development Podcast:

Text Complexity

Key Learning Objective: The student will be able to analyze the impact of cultural background on point of view.

For practice and application:

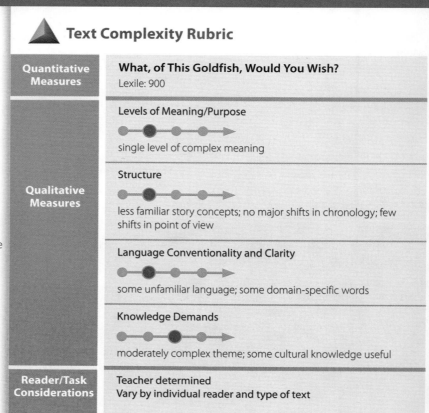

The Wife's Story

Close Reader selection
"The Wife's Story"
a short story by Ursula LeGuin

COMMON CORE
Common Core Standards

RL 1 Cite textual evidence.

RL 2 Determine a theme and analyze its development.

RL 3 Analyze how complex characters develop, interact, and advance the plot.

RL 4 Determine the meaning of words and phrases.

RL 5 Analyze how an author's choices create mystery, tension, or surprise.

RL 6 Analyze a particular point of view from outside the United States.

SL 1a Come to discussions prepared, refer to evidence from texts to stimulate ideas.

L 3 Apply language in different contexts to make choices for style, and to comprehend more fully.

L 4a Use context as a clue to the meaning of a word.

▲ Text Complexity Rubric

Quantitative Measures	**What, of This Goldfish, Would You Wish?** Lexile: 900
Qualitative Measures	**Levels of Meaning/Purpose** single level of complex meaning
	Structure less familiar story concepts; no major shifts in chronology; few shifts in point of view
	Language Conventionality and Clarity some unfamiliar language; some domain-specific words
	Knowledge Demands moderately complex theme; some cultural knowledge useful
Reader/Task Considerations	Teacher determined Vary by individual reader and type of text

Background Have students read the background and information about the author. Tell students that various groups still clash over the internal boundaries of Israel and which government controls which portions of land. Yonatan would have no trouble visiting cities located outside of the hotly contested West Bank area, such as Tel Aviv and Ashdod. Within that area, however, which is surrounded by a protective wall, he would have more difficulty interviewing people living in Palestinian-controlled cities, such as Hebron.

AS YOU READ Direct students to use the As You Read question to focus their reading.

Analyze Character (LINES 1–13) RL 1, RL 3

Explain to students that they should consider the things a character thinks, says, and does to understand his or her personality. Have them think about Yoni's plan to create a documentary and the question he plans to ask. Then ask them to draw a conclusion about the kind of person he is. *(He thinks his idea is brilliant, and he wants to make the film on his own, using no camera crew and "no nonsense." He hopes his question and the answers will lead to a poignant social commentary. This shows that he has a high opinion of his work and a dream of making a documentary that matters.)*

Ⓐ CITE TEXT EVIDENCE Have students read the first two paragraphs and summarize what they know so far about Yoni's project. *(He is planning to make a documentary about people's wishes. He wants to show the difference between what people think and want and the way they actually live.)*

CRITICAL VOCABULARY

Poignant: Yoni plans to create a poignant documentary by contrasting images and facts about each person's life with information about his or her wishes.

ASK STUDENTS how the film Yoni plans to create might be poignant. *(Hearing about what people wish for while seeing their real lives could be very emotional for the viewer.)*

Background *The Jewish people were expelled from their homeland, Israel, in the first century. In the late 1800s, Jews from Europe, Asia, Africa, and the Americas began returning to the region; World War II and the Holocaust drastically increased this immigration. Israel became an independent nation in 1948, but tensions with its Arab neighbors and its Arab citizens have led to conflict. With the collapse of the Soviet Union in 1991, many Russian Jews were finally able to move to Israel and make their own mark on the nation's culture. In this story, Israeli writer* **Etgar Keret** *(b. 1967) explores the hopes and dreams of people in this diverse society.*

What, of This Goldfish, Would You Wish?

Short Story by Etgar Keret   Translated by Nathan Englander

AS YOU READ Think about the kinds of things people wish for to make their lives happier. In particular, look for clues to what Sergei Goralick wants from life. Note any questions you have as you read.

Image Credits: (t) ©Marco Secchi/Corbis; (cr) ©Eddie Gerald/Alamy Images; (c) ©Mike Kemp/Rubberball/Alamy Images

Ⓐ Yonatan had a brilliant idea for a documentary. He'd knock on doors. Just him. No camera crew, no nonsense. Just Yonatan, on his own, a small camera in hand, asking, "If you found a talking goldfish that granted you three wishes, what would you wish for?"

Folks would give their answers, and Yoni would edit them down and make clips of the more surprising responses. Before every set of answers, you'd see the person standing stock-still in the entrance to his house. Onto this shot he'd superimpose[1] the subject's name, family situation, monthly income, and maybe even 10 the party he'd voted for in the last election. All that, combined with the three wishes, and maybe he'd end up with a **poignant** piece of social commentary, a testament to the massive rift between our dreams and the often compromised reality in which we live.

poignant
(poin´yənt) *adj.*
emotionally moving
or stimulating.

---

[1] **superimpose:** place one thing on top of another so that both remain visible.

What, of This Goldfish, Would You Wish?   **3**

Close Read Screencasts ▶ View It!

Modeled Discussions

Have students click the *Close Read* icons in their eBooks to access the screencast in which readers discuss and annotate the key passage that describes how Yoni pictures his project (lines 10–20).

As a class, view and discuss this video. Then have students pair up to do an independent close read of an additional passage—the exchange that fleshes out the relationship and conflict between Sergei and the goldfish (lines 116–130).

Analyze Character

COMMON CORE **RL 1, RL 3**

(LINES 14–26)

Explain that an author develops a character by providing the reader with additional details that deepen a reader's initial impression of the character and may change a reader's opinion about the character.

B **CITE TEXT EVIDENCE** Have students cite the details that help them more fully understand Yoni's character and intentions. *(Yoni now thinks that if his project isn't genius, at least it is "cheap" [line 14]. He begins to think about how easy it will be to sell his work as a film or a commercial [lines 16–24].)* Then ask students to evaluate the line, "No prep, no plotting, natural as can be..." *(Yoni believes that he is shooting naturally, with no planning, but in truth he has thought a great deal about his project.)*

Point of View (LINES 31–47)

COMMON CORE **RL1, RL 6**

Explain to students that by setting this story in Israel, the author has the opportunity to populate it with characters of many different cultural backgrounds and points of view, or ways of looking at the world and life.

C **CITE TEXT EVIDENCE** Have students read the last three paragraphs and identify cultural backgrounds of some of the characters. *(The Holocaust survivor came from Europe. Yoni also plans to interview Arabs, Ethiopians, and Americans.)*

CRITICAL VOCABULARY

wizened: The woman Yoni meets is old and wizened, and wishes for a child she can no longer have.

ASK STUDENTS why the old lady is described as wizened. *(Her skin is probably saggy and wrinkled.)*

beleaguered: Yoni imagines meeting a beleaguered Arab living in Hebron, who's seen much violence in his life.

ASK STUDENTS why the beleaguered man might wish for peace. *(Peace would be a blessing after the problems he faces being an Arab living in Israel.)*

B It was genius, Yoni was sure. And, if not, at least it was cheap. All he needed was a door to knock on and a heart beating on the other side. With a little decent footage, he was sure he'd be able to sell it to Channel 8 or Discovery in a flash, either as a film or as a bunch of vignettes,[2] little cinematic corners, each with that singular soul standing in a doorway, followed by three killer wishes, 20 precious, every one.

Even better, maybe he'd cash out, package it with a slogan and sell it to a bank or cellular phone company. Maybe tag it with something like "Different dreams, different wishes, one bank." Or "The bank that makes dreams come true."

No prep, no plotting, natural as can be, Yoni grabbed his camera and went out knocking on doors. In the first neighborhood he went to, the kindly folk that took part generally requested the foreseeable things: health, money, bigger apartments, either to shave off a couple of years or a couple of pounds. But there were 30 also powerful moments. One drawn, **wizened** old lady asked simply for a child. A Holocaust survivor with a number on his arm asked **C** very slowly, in a quiet voice—as if he'd been waiting for Yoni to come, as if it wasn't an exercise at all—he'd been wondering (if this fish didn't mind), would it be possible for all the Nazis left living in the world to be held accountable for their crimes? A cocky, broad-shouldered lady-killer put out his cigarette and, as if the camera wasn't there, wished he were a girl. "Just for a night," he added, holding a single finger right up to the lens.

And these were wishes from just one short block in one 40 small, sleepy suburb of Tel Aviv. Yonatan could hardly imagine what people were dreaming of in the development towns and the collectives[3] along the northern border, in the West Bank settlements and Arab villages, the immigrant absorption centers full of broken trailers and tired people left to broil out in the desert sun.

Yonatan knew that if the project was going to have any weight, he'd have to get to everyone, to the unemployed, to the ultrareligious, to the Arabs and Ethiopians and American expats.[4] He began to plan a shooting schedule for the coming days: Jaffa, Dimona, Ashdod, Sderot, Taibe, Talpiot. Maybe Hebron, even. 50 If he could sneak past the wall, Hebron would be great. Maybe somewhere in that city some **beleaguered** Arab man would stand in his doorway and, looking through Yonatan and his camera, looking out into nothingness, just pause for a minute, nod his head, and wish for peace—that would be something to see.

wizened
(wĭz´ənd) *adj.* shrunken and wrinkled.

beleaguered
(bĭ-lē´gərd) *adj.* troubled with many problems.

---

[2] **vignettes**: small scenes or images.

[3] **collectives**: cooperative businesses or enterprises.

[4] **expats**: expatriates, people living in a foreign country.

SCAFFOLDING FOR ELL STUDENTS

Analyze Idioms Using a whiteboard, project lines 21–24. Underline the phrase "cash out." Explain that this phrase is an idiom, or a phrase with a meaning that is different than the literal meaning of the words. Note that students can use context clues in the sentences to help them figure out an idiom's meaning.

ASK STUDENTS What does the phrase "cash out" mean here? *(to take what money you can get for something)* How does this idiom contribute to the passage? *(It shows how Yoni is just as tempted to make money from his film as he is to make a work of art.)*

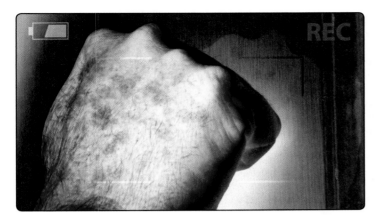

Sergei Goralick doesn't much like strangers banging on his door. Especially when those strangers are asking him questions. In Russia, when Sergei was young, it happened plenty. The KGB felt right at home knocking on his door. His father had been a Zionist,[5] which was pretty much an invitation for them to drop by any old time.

60   When Sergei got to Israel and then moved to Jaffa, his family couldn't wrap their heads around it. They'd ask him, What are you looking to find in a place like that? There's no one there but addicts and Arabs and pensioners.[6] But what is most excellent about addicts and Arabs and pensioners is that they don't come around knocking on Sergei's door. That way Sergei can get his sleep, and get up when it's still dark. He can take his little boat out into the sea and fish until he's done fishing. By himself. In silence. The way it should be. The way it was.

Until one day some kid with a ring in his ear . . . comes
70   knocking. Hard like that—rapping at his door. Just the way Sergei doesn't like. And he says, this kid, that he has some questions he wants to put on the TV.

Sergei tells the boy, tells him in what he thinks is a straightforward manner, that he doesn't want it. Not interested. Sergei gives the camera a shove, to help make it clear. But the earring boy is stubborn. He says all kinds of things, fast things. And it's hard for Sergei to follow; his Hebrew isn't so good.

The boy slows down, tells Sergei he has a strong face, a nice face, and that he simply has to have him for this movie picture.
80   Sergei can also slow down, he can also make clear. He tells the kid to shove off. But the kid is slippery, and somehow between saying

[5] **Zionist:** supporter of a separate state for Jewish people.
[6] **pensioners:** people living on modest retirement payments.

What, of This Goldfish, Would You Wish?   **5**

CLOSE READ

Analyze Character   COMMON CORE RL 3
(LINES 60–72)

Explain to students that the way an author describes what characters think and want can make it easier to understand why they behave and interact with each other in certain ways.

D ASK STUDENTS what Sergei wants from life. *(All Sergei wants is to be left alone in silence.)* Have students reread the sentences, "Until one day some kid with a ring in his ear…comes knocking. Hard like that—rapping at his door." Ask how the description of Yoni and the use of the words *knocking* and *rapping* help the reader understand the effect Yoni has when entering Sergei's life. *(Yoni breaks into Sergei's peaceful, quiet existence by knocking on his door. The language imitates the sound of something breaking the silence; the description shows how different the two characters are.)*

Point of View (LINES 73–77)   COMMON CORE RL 1, RL 6

Remind students to continue looking for information about the cultural background of various characters. Note that these details can help them understand why the characters relate to one another in certain ways.

E CITE TEXT EVIDENCE Have students consider whether Yoni and Sergei are communicating well with one another and cite text to support their view. *(The two men are not able to communicate well because Yoni is speaking Hebrew very fast and Sergei, who comes from Russia, cannot speak this language very well.)*

APPLYING ACADEMIC VOCABULARY

diverse	rational

As you discuss this short story, incorporate the following Collection 1 academic vocabulary words: *diverse* and *rational*. To appreciate the different backgrounds and histories of the people living in Israel, ask students to describe some examples from the text of the **diverse** characters who make their homes there. As you read about Sergei's actions when Yoni comes to his door and the goldfish's counsel about what Sergei should do next, ask students to evaluate how **rational** each character's reaction to the situation is.

Analyze Character

COMMON CORE **RL 3**

(LINES 83–100)

Explain to students that sometimes an author develops a character by contrasting two actions or by juxtaposing one character's impression with another character's actions.

F **ASK STUDENTS** what Sergei's actions tell them about his personality. *(He is untrusting and impulsive.)* How do Sergei's actions contrast with Yoni's first impression of Sergei? What is the effect? *(Yoni says Sergei's face is tender, so Sergei's sudden brutal action comes as a surprise to the reader.)* As they continue to read, tell students to look for clues that will help them decide if Yoni's initial impression is ultimately correct or incorrect.

Analyze Character

COMMON CORE **RL 1, RL 3**

(LINES 104–107)

Tell students that authors can create humor through the use of understatement, or creating emphasis by making something seem less significant. An author's use of understatement can help readers better understand a character's personality.

G **CITE TEXT EVIDENCE** Have students identify an example of understatement. *(Sergei thinks that taking Yoni to the hospital will "complicate things" [line 101], which understates the possibility of being arrested for murder. Then he calls the burner "'Only a little thing… It's not even that hard.'"[lines 110–111].)* Ask students to explain what this tells them about Sergei's character. *(Sometimes he tries to deal with unpleasant things by making them seem less important or less serious than they are.)*

CRITICAL VOCABULARY

fluent: The goldfish is fluent in all languages because he is magic.

ASK STUDENTS how being fluent in Hebrew makes the goldfish's reaction to Yoni different from Sergei's reaction. *(Unlike Sergei, the goldfish understands exactly what Yoni wants to do.)*

F no and pushing the door closed, Sergei finds that the kid is in his house. He's already making his movie, running his camera without any permission, and from behind the camera he's still telling Sergei about his face, that it's full of feeling, that it's tender. Suddenly the kid spots Sergei's goldfish flitting around in its big glass jar in his kitchen.

The kid with the earring starts screaming, "Goldfish, goldfish," he's so excited. And this, this really pressures Sergei, who tells
90 the kid, it's nothing, just a regular goldfish, stop filming it. Just a goldfish, Sergei tells him, just something he found flapping around in the net, a deep-sea goldfish. But the boy isn't listening. He's still filming and getting closer and saying something about talking and fish and a magic wish.

Sergei doesn't like this, doesn't like that the boy is almost at it, already reaching for the jar. In this instant Sergei understands the boy didn't come for television, what he came for, specifically, is to snatch Sergei's fish, to steal it away. Before the mind of Sergei Goralick really understands what it is his body has done, he seems
100 to have taken the burner off the stove and hit the boy in the head. The boy falls. The camera falls with him. The camera breaks open on the floor, along with the boy's skull. There's a lot of blood coming out of the head, and Sergei really doesn't know what to do.

G That is, he knows exactly what to do, but it really would complicate things. Because if he takes this kid to the hospital, people are going to ask what happened, and it would take things in a direction Sergei doesn't want to go.

"No reason to take him to the hospital anyway," says the goldfish, in Russian. "That one's already dead."
110 "He can't be dead," Sergei says, with a moan. "I barely touched him. It's only a burner. Only a little thing." Sergei holds it up to the fish, taps it against his own skull to prove it. "It's not even that hard."

"Maybe not," says the fish. "But, apparently, it's harder than that kid's head."

"He wanted to take you from me," Sergei says, almost crying.

"Nonsense," the fish says. "He was only here to make a little something for TV."

"But he said . . . "
120 "He said," says the fish, interrupting, "exactly what he was doing. But you didn't get it. Honestly, your Hebrew, it's terrible."

"Yours is better?" Sergei says. "Yours is so great?"

"Yes. Mine's supergreat," the goldfish says, sounding impatient.
H "I'm a magic fish. I'm **fluent** in everything." All the while the puddle of blood from the earring kid's head is getting bigger

fluent
(flōō'ənt) *adj.*
able to express
oneself clearly and
easily.

and bigger and Sergei is on his toes, up against the kitchen wall, desperate not to step in it, not to get blood on his feet.

"You do have one wish left," the fish reminds Sergei. He says it easy like that, as if Sergei doesn't know—as if either of them ever
130 loses count.

"No," Sergei says. He's shaking his head from side to side. "I can't," he says. "I've been saving it. Saving it for something."

"For what?" the fish says.

But Sergei won't answer.

"You do have **one** wish left."

That first wish, Sergei used up when they discovered a cancer in his sister. A lung cancer, the kind you don't get better from. The fish undid it in an instant—the words barely out of Sergei's mouth. The second wish Sergei used up five years ago, on Sveta's boy. The kid was still small then, barely three, but the doctors already knew
140 something in her son's head wasn't right. He was going to grow big but not in the brain. Three was about as smart as he'd get. Sveta cried to Sergei in bed all night. Sergei walked home along the beach when the sun came up, and he called to the fish, asked the goldfish to fix it as soon as he'd crossed through the door. He never told Sveta. And a few months later she left him for some cop, a Moroccan with a shiny Honda. In his heart, Sergei kept telling himself it wasn't for Sveta that he'd done it, that he'd wished his wish purely for the boy. In his mind, he was less sure, and all kinds of thoughts about other things he could have done with that wish
150 continued to gnaw at him, half driving him mad. The third wish, Sergei hadn't yet wished for.

"I can restore him," says the goldfish. "I can bring him back to life."

SCAFFOLDING FOR ELL STUDENTS

Language: Conversational Patterns Explain to students that some sentences are missing words or use unusual word order. For example, lines 135–136 can be rewritten as, "Sergei used up that first wish when they discovered his sister had cancer. It was the kind of lung cancer that you do not get better from."

ASK STUDENTS to work together in mixed language-ability Jigsaw groups. Assign each group a passage, and have them look for sentences that they find confusing. Have them work together to fill in the missing words or to rearrange the phrases to make the meaning more clear. Then discuss with students why the author used the unusual word order.

CLOSE READ

Analyze Character RL 3
(LINES 126–150)

Explain to students that paying close attention to a character's actions can tell them things about his or her personality that are not directly stated by the author.

H **ASK STUDENTS** to reread lines 124–127 and explain what new information is revealed about Sergei's character. *(He does not want to get the blood on him because he does not want to face the consequences of his actions.)*

I **ASK STUDENTS** what Sergei's first two wishes reveal about his character. How are these wishes like his reaction when Yoni looks at his goldfish? How are the wishes different from his reaction? *(He is impulsive. He used his first two wishes almost without thinking, in order to heal his sister and Sveta's boy. Just as when he hits Yoni, he has acted on impulse to protect something (the goldfish) or someone (his family) he cared about. His wishes were selfless, but hitting Yoni is selfish because he does not want to lose the magic goldfish.)*

Analyze Author's Choice RL 5
(LINES 135-144)

Explain to students that authors choose different techniques in order to create specific effects. For example, they may want to create mystery, tension, or even surprise.

J **ASK STUDENTS** what technique the author uses to tell us about Sergei's wishes. *(flashback)* What effect does this have? *(It increases the tension while providing information about Sergei.)*

Analyze Character

COMMON CORE RL 1, RL 3

(LINES 159–166)

Explain to students that authors can reveal information about characters by describing the observations other characters make about them.

 CITE TEXT EVIDENCE Have students cite evidence from the text that reveals the type of relationship Sergei and the goldfish have. What does this say about Sergei? *(They know each other well, which means they have been together for a long time. Sergei knows the fish is excited at the prospect of being set free because it swishes its tail back and forth [lines 159–161]. The fish knows that Sergei has a good heart and is not a murderer. The fish is so sure that Sergei will do the right thing and use his last wish to save Yoni that he holds his head steady even when Sergei is trying to come up with another plan to clean up the mess [lines 164–166]. The passage shows that Sergei is willing to consider anything to avoid being alone.)*

Point of View (LINES 176–181)

COMMON CORE RL 1, RL 6

Have students review what they have learned so far in this story about the various cultural backgrounds of people living in Israel.

L ASK STUDENTS why Yoni thinks the Arab he finds is perfect for his film. *(Because Jews and Arabs have had so many conflicts over sharing the land in Israel, Yoni thinks viewers will be emotionally moved by an Arab who only wishes for peace.)*

COLLABORATIVE DISCUSSION In pairs, have students review the text to identify where Sergei and the fish discuss using the third wish. Have students consider what they believe Sergei is saving his wish for based on his background, thoughts, and actions, as well as what he says. Invite them to share their ideas with the class.

ASK STUDENTS to share any questions they generated in the course of reading and discussing the selection.

"No one's asking," Sergei says.

"I can bring him back to the moment before," the goldfish says. "To before he knocks on your door. I can put him back to right there. I can do it. All you need to do is ask."

"To wish my wish," Sergei says. "My last."

K 160 The fish swishes his fish tail back and forth in the water, the way he does, Sergei knows, when he's truly excited. The goldfish can already taste freedom. Sergei can see it on him.

After the last wish, Sergei won't have a choice. He'll have to let the goldfish go. His magic goldfish. His friend.

"Fixable," Sergei says. "I'll just mop up the blood. A good sponge and it'll be like it never was."

That tail just goes back and forth, the fish's head steady.

Sergei takes a deep breath. He steps out into the middle of the kitchen, out into the puddle. "When I'm fishing, while it's dark and the world's asleep," he says, half to himself and half to the fish, "I'll 170 tie the kid to a rock and dump him in the sea. Not a chance, not in a million years, will anyone ever find him."

"You killed him, Sergei," the goldfish says. "You murdered someone—but you're not a murderer." The goldfish stops swishing his tail. "If, on this, you won't waste a wish, then tell me, Sergei, what is it good for?"

L It was in Bethlehem, actually, that Yonatan found his Arab, a handsome man who used his first wish for peace. His name was Munir; he was fat with a big white mustache. Superphotogenic.[7] It 180 was moving, the way he said it. Perfect, the way in which Munir wished his wish. Yoni knew even as he was filming that this guy would be his promo for sure.

Either him or that Russian. The one with the faded tattoos that Yoni had met in Jaffa. The one that looked straight into the camera and said, if he ever found a talking goldfish he wouldn't ask of it a single thing. He'd just stick it on a shelf in a big glass jar and talk to him all day, it didn't matter about what. Maybe sports, maybe politics, whatever a goldfish was interested in chatting about.

Anything, the Russian said, not to be alone.

COLLABORATIVE DISCUSSION Why does Sergei save his third wish for so long? With a partner, discuss the reasons for his behavior. Cite specific evidence from the text to support your answer.

---

[7] **superphotogenic:** looking extremely good in photos or on film.

WHEN STUDENTS STRUGGLE . . .

To guide students' comprehension of the final events of the story, have students work in pairs to fill out a sequence of events graphic organizer. Direct students to reread lines 167–175 and then lines 176–188. Have them discuss what is happening in the first passage and fill in the first space on the graphic organizer. Then have them discuss what is happening in the second passage and fill in the final space. Finally, have students work together to infer and describe what must have taken place between these two events. Depending on your students' needs, you may have to review how to make an inference by combining what you have just read with what you already know.

Analyze Character: Motivations

   COMMON CORE RL 3

A good fictional character is complex, just like a real person. A character develops over the course of a story as his or her unique personality is revealed by the author. To analyze the complex character of Sergei Goralick, find clues about his traits and consider his **motivations,** the reasons behind his actions.

Character Traits	Character Motivations
Authors provide numerous clues about character traits: • **What does the character say?** A character's words can reveal whether he or she is polite or rude, shy or bold, caring or cruel. Dialogue can also reveal a character's relationships with other characters. • **How does the character act?** The actions of characters move a story's plot forward. They also show what the characters want and how they respond to the world around them. • **What does the character think?** A character's thoughts, if revealed, provide deeper insight into what he or she is truly like. • **How does he or she interact with other characters?** Observe how well—or badly—the character gets along with others. Both personality and life history will affect relationships.	You understand a character when you can explain the motivations behind his or her actions. A character might even have two conflicting motivations for the same action. For example, Yoni makes his video thinking of commercial gain. But at the same time, he hopes to create a serious documentary. Consider these questions: • What does the character value? • What does the character want? Does he or she want conflicting things? • What does the character believe? • What does the character fear?

Analyze Point of View: Cultural Background

COMMON CORE RL 6

This story is set in Tel Aviv, Israel. Each character's experience in Israel's complex society shapes his or her point of view. The majority of Israelis are Jews, but their backgrounds are diverse. Immigrants brought with them the cultures of the many countries in which they had lived. Russian Jews were among the last to arrive, but they now make up about 15 percent of the population. They have tended to settle in neighborhoods with other Russians and to speak Russian, not Hebrew. The experiences of Israel's Arab population add another dimension to this story's cultural context. Arabs are full citizens, but ethnic and religious differences—as well as disputes over territory—have often led to conflict with their Jewish neighbors.

 What, of This Goldfish, Would You Wish? **9**

 TEACH

CLOSE READ

Analyze Character: Motivations

COMMON CORE RL 3

Once students have identified examples of things Sergei Goralick says, does, and thinks as he interacts with other characters, have them consider and answer the questions in the Character Motivations column. *(Sergei values the goldfish because he considers it his friend; having the goldfish keeps him from feeling alone. He wants to be left alone, but he wants the goldfish for company. He believes he needs to save his third wish for something special, but he is actually saving it so he does not have to set the goldfish free. He fears being all alone.)*

Analyze Point of View: Cultural Background

 COMMON CORE RL 6

Help students understand how the cultural background of a character influences his or her actions, thoughts, and motivations. Have them identify Sergei's background, and explain how it plays a part in the story. *(Although Jewish, like many other Israeli people, Sergei is originally from Russia. When he was growing up in Russia, the KGB regularly came to his home to question his family. These constant intrusions made him not want to be bothered by anyone, so he selected a place in Israel where he could live without people trying to get to know him. Another way he is set apart from many Israelis is that his Hebrew is not very good. He and the goldfish speak Russian together.)*

Strategies for Annotation  *Annotate it!*

Analyze Character: Motivations

COMMON CORE RL 3

Have students use their eBook annotation tools to analyze the text. Ask them to do the following:

• Highlight in yellow the dialogue that reveals information about a character's motivations.

• Highlight in blue the text that describes the way a character acts and reveals information about the reasons for those actions.

• Highlight in pink the text that reveals a character's thoughts.

Sergei doesn't like this, doesn't like that the boy is almost at it, already reaching for the jar. In this instant Sergei understands the boy didn't come for the television, what he came for, specifically, is to snatch Sergei's fish, to steal it away. Before the mind of Sergei Goralick really understands what it is his body has done, he seems to have taken the burner off the stove and hit the boy in the head.

 What, of This Goldfish, Would You Wish? **9**

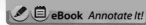
PRACTICE & APPLY

Analyzing the Text

COMMON CORE RL 1, RL 2, RL 3, RL 5, RL 6

Possible answers:

1. *Sergei acts suspicious and unfriendly and tries to shove the camera away. He has no reason to suspect that Yoni is not there to ask him a question for TV, so his response does not seem rational. Sergei is from Russia, where he was used to the KGB knocking on his door to investigate his Zionist father. This explains why he is suspicious when someone knocks on his door.*

2. *The dialogue shows that Sergei and the fish know each other well. The fish knows Sergei has a good heart and tells him he is not really a murderer.*

3. *Sergei cares about other people more than himself because he uses his first two wishes to save the lives of his sister and his girlfriend's little boy.*

4. *The fish and Sergei are in conflict because the fish wants Sergei to use his last wish so the fish can be free. The fish swishes his tail in excitement when he thinks Sergei is about to use his last wish. Their relationship cannot truly be called a friendship, however, because even if the fish really does like Sergei, the fish is not there by choice.*

5. *If Sergei uses his last wish to save Yoni's life, he will lose the fish, who Sergei feels is his only friend, and then he will be alone. If Sergei does not use his last wish, however, he will be a murderer.*

6. *This is an effective structure because it creates suspense, since the reader doesn't know how Sergei finally makes his decision. The reader has enough clues from the rest of the story to understand and believe that Sergei is willing to condemn himself to loneliness to save someone else's life. The last paragraph reveals that Yoni was correct to think Sergei was a good man.*

7. *The story conveys the theme that wishes cannot buy happiness and that sometimes doing the right thing means making sacrifices and being selfless. Sergei was happier when he had the goldfish for company, but at the same time, he had to let the goldfish go because he could not have lived with himself or with the goldfish if he was willing to murder someone out of his own selfishness.*

Analyzing the Text

COMMON CORE RL 1, RL 2, RL 3, RL 5, RL 6, SL 1a

Cite Text Evidence Support your responses with evidence from the selection.

1. **Analyze** Consider how Sergei reacts when Yoni comes to his door. Does his response seem rational (reasonable) or not? How does Sergei's cultural experience help explain his reaction?

2. **Analyze** What does the dialogue between Sergei and the goldfish reveal about their relationship?

3. **Infer** When you **infer**, you use details in a text to draw a conclusion about something that the author does not state directly. What can you infer about Sergei's character based on the way he uses his first two wishes?

4. **Draw Conclusions** Sergei considers the goldfish to be his friend. What details in the story reveal their conflict with each other? Can their relationship truly be called a friendship? Explain.

5. **Analyze** When Sergei realizes that Yoni is dead, he must make a decision. What conflicting motivations must he sort out before he can decide whether or not to use his last wish?

6. **Evaluate** The last section of the story is a flash forward. Readers must infer what happens in the intervening time between Sergei's conversation with the fish and Yoni's final report on his video. Is this structure effective, or would it have been better to know the details about Sergei's decision? Explain.

7. **Analyze** A **theme** is an important idea about life or human nature expressed through a story's characters and events. What theme about happiness does this story convey through Sergei's situation and actions and the outcome of events?

PERFORMANCE TASK

Speaking Activity: Discussion "What, of This Goldfish, Would You Wish?" provides a modern twist on the "three wishes" structure used in many folk tales. Explore this aspect of the story with a small group.

- Each group member should research one folk tale involving three wishes. Retell your folk tale to the rest of the group. Discuss similarities and differences between the tales. What happens to the characters, and why?

- Then, discuss how Etgar Keret's story fits in with the others. What elements are similar? What makes it unique?
- Write a summary of your group's conclusions about Keret's story and other tales of three wishes.

Assign this performance task.

PERFORMANCE TASK

COMMON CORE SL 1a

Speaking Activity: Discussion Have students work in small groups. Provide suggestions for folk tales to research, such as "The Three Wishes" by the Brothers Grimm. Suggest that students use compare-contrast charts to keep track of similarities and differences between the tales, such as where the wishes come from, how each wish is used, and what lesson the characters learn. Then have students use a Venn diagram to compare the tales with Keret's story.

Critical Vocabulary

  L 4a

poignant   wizened   beleaguered   fluent

Practice and Apply Answer these questions to demonstrate your understanding of each Critical Vocabulary word.

1. You have just read a **poignant** blog post. Will you still be thinking about it tomorrow, or will you forget it immediately? Explain.

2. The flowers you received last week appear **wizened.** What will you do with them? Why?

3. Maria feels **beleaguered** on the first day of school. Does her facial expression show confidence or panic? Why?

4. Doug is **fluent** in French. Does he need to pack a French dictionary when he travels to France? Explain.

Vocabulary Strategy: Context Clues

If you come across an unfamiliar word while reading, you can use **context clues,** or information in the surrounding text, to figure out the word's meaning. For example, the word *fluent* appears in the context of a conversation about Sergei's poor understanding of the Hebrew language. The goldfish says, "Mine's supergreat. . . . I'm fluent in everything." The contrast between Sergei's poor Hebrew and the fish's fluent Hebrew helps you guess that *fluent* means "able to express oneself clearly and easily."

Practice and Apply Find these words in the story: *testament* (line 12), *foreseeable* (line 28), *accountable* (line 35), *promo* (line 181). Working with a partner, use context clues to determine each word's meaning as it is used in the story.

1. Determine the word's function in the sentence. Does it function as a noun, adjective, verb, or adverb? How might the word fit into the overall meaning of the sentence?

2. If the sentence does not provide enough information, read the paragraph in which the word appears and consider the larger context of the story. How might the word fit with what you know about the characters or the plot?

3. Write down your definition and the clues you used to determine the meaning of each word.

PRACTICE & APPLY

Critical Vocabulary

COMMON CORE L 4a

Possible answers:

1. *Yes, I will still be thinking about it because if it is poignant, I probably had an emotional response to it.*

2. *I will compost them because they are old and dried out.*

3. *Her expression shows panic, because she is troubled about starting school.*

4. *He does not need to pack a dictionary because he speaks and understands the language very well.*

Vocabulary Strategy: Context Clues

COMMON CORE RL 4, L 4a

Possible answers:

- Testament *functions as a noun and names the kind of film Yoni is making: a social commentary. It is something written or spoken that communicates or proves an idea. Clue: the film will be a commentary on the situation in Israel.*

- Foreseeable *functions as an adjective that describes the things the people would wish for. It means "predictable" because the things the people are wishing for are things that people commonly desire.*

- Accountable *functions as an adjective that describes how he wants the Nazis to be treated based on their actions. It means "answerable." Clue: Nazis have committed crimes that a Holocaust survivor would most likely want them to be punished for.*

- Promo *functions as a noun that describes the way Yoni will use the footage. It means "something that catches people's interest." Clues: Yoni wants to attract viewers; this man is described as "superphotogenic;" Yoni dreams of finding such an Arab because that would make his film "something to see."*

 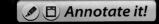

Using Context Clues

COMMON CORE L 4a

Have students locate the sentences containing *testament, foreseeable, accountable,* and *promo* in the story. Encourage them to use their eBook annotation tools to do the following:

- Highlight each vocabulary word in yellow.
- Reread the surrounding sentences, looking for clues to the word's meaning. Underline any clues they find, such as examples, synonyms, or antonyms.
- Review the annotations and try to infer the word's meaning.

> All that, combined with the three wishes, and maybe he'd end up with a <u>poignant piece of social commentary</u>, a testament to the massive rift between our dreams and the often compromised reality in which we live.

PRACTICE & APPLY

Language and Style: Formal Versus Informal Tone

Tell students that the examples on this page are just a few instances where Keret uses language to create an informal tone. Invite volunteers to scan the text, identify some other examples, discuss how each one is informal rather than formal, and explain what effect this language has on the overall tone of that part of the story.

To prepare students to write their two paragraphs, work with them to list characteristics of informal and formal language. For example, formal language usually uses longer, more sophisticated sentence structures, while informal language might use shorter, incomplete sentence structures. Informal language uses idioms, contractions, and exclamation points, and might start sentences with conjunctions such as *and* or *but*. Formal language uses standard grammar and spelling and avoids the use of run-on sentences or fragments.

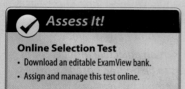

Assess It!

Online Selection Test
- Download an editable ExamView bank.
- Assign and manage this test online.

Language and Style: Formal Versus Informal Tone

An author's word choices and sentence structures express a particular **tone**, or attitude, toward characters and events. The tone may also reflect the personality of one or more characters. Etgar Keret's writing uses techniques such as slang and incomplete sentences to create an informal tone. Read this passage from the story.

> Yonatan had a brilliant idea for a documentary. He'd knock on doors. Just him. No camera crew, no nonsense. Just Yonatan, on his own, a small camera in hand, asking, "If you found a talking goldfish that granted you three wishes, what would you wish for?"

The author could have used more formal language, like this:

> Yonatan had a brilliantly simple idea for a documentary. He would do all the filming himself, without a camera crew. Knocking on people's doors with a small hand-held camera, he would inquire of each person, "If you found a talking goldfish that granted you three wishes, what would you wish for?"

The informal language sets a tone that is better suited to Yoni's youthful enthusiasm and his spirit of adventure.

Here are some other examples of language from the story and how they contribute to the informal tone:

Example	How It Affects Tone
"three killer wishes"	*Killer* is slang for "excellent." Slang is the language of casual, everyday speech.
"When Sergei got to Israel and then moved to Jaffa, his family couldn't wrap their heads around it."	The expression *wrap their heads around* ("understand") is an idiom that people use in conversation but not in formal writing or speech.
"But the earring boy is stubborn."	Calling Yoni "the earring boy" reflects Sergei's private thoughts. The humor in this mild insult fits the informal tone of the story.

Practice and Apply Write two versions of a paragraph describing an experience you have had. Choose words, phrases, and sentence structures that create a formal tone in the first version and an informal tone in the second. Identify which version best fits the event your writing describes.

Analyze How Authors Manipulate Time

COMMON CORE

RL 5

TEACH

In creating his narrative, Etgar Keret had to make choices about how his story would unfold in time. Keret used chronological order to tell some parts of his story; he used flashbacks and flash forwards to relate other parts of the narrative. Provide students with the following information:

- A **flashback** is an account of a conversation or an event that has taken place before the beginning of the story. Flashbacks are often used to reveal information about a character or to provide background information about a setting or an event. Flashbacks may also be used to create tension by pausing the action at a crucial point in the story.
- A **flash forward** is the opposite of a flashback. It takes the reader out of the current time and into a future one. A flash forward allows a writer to skip the action that took place in the intervening time period and forces the reader to make inferences about what happened. Flash forwards allow a writer to speed up the pace of a narrative; they may also create surprise when juxtaposed with an event occurring at a different point in time.

PRACTICE AND APPLY

Display lines 135–145 of the story on the board or on a device. Have students point out one or two examples of flashback. Then ask them to explain what effect the flashback has on the story. *(Lines 135–137; "That first wish, Sergei used up when they discovered a cancer in his sister. A lung cancer, the kind you don't get better from. The fish undid it in an instant—the words barely out of Sergei's mouth."; Line 138; "The second wish Sergei used up five years ago, on Sveta's boy". The flashbacks give the reader insight into Sergei's character and also increases the tension in the story. The action is suspended with Sergei trying to avoid Yoni's blood while telling the fish he can't use his last wish.)*

Display lines 172–188 of the story. Have students point out the example of a flash forward and explain its effect on the story. *(Lines 176–177; "It was in Bethlehem, actually, that Yonatan found his Arab, a handsome man who used his first wish for peace." The flash forward allows the writer to jump forward in time to show Yoni alive and oblivious to the fact that his documentary has had a devastating effect on Sergei's life.)*

Analyze Point of View: Cultural Background

COMMON CORE

RL 6

RETEACH

Review how a person or character's cultural background affects the way he or she lives and interacts with others.

- Have students reread the Background note from SE page 3 and the information about Israel on SE page 9, and then summarize what they know about the backgrounds of the groups of people living in Israel.
- Have students consider the characters in the story, review what they know about each one, and analyze how the background of each character (major or minor) might influence his or her point of view. *(Sample answer: The Holocaust survivor's wish is influenced by his past experiences with the Nazis. Sergei is suspicious of people coming to his door because of his past experiences in Russia with the KGB.)*

 LEVEL UP TUTORIALS Assign the following *Level Up* tutorial: **Historical and Cultural Context**

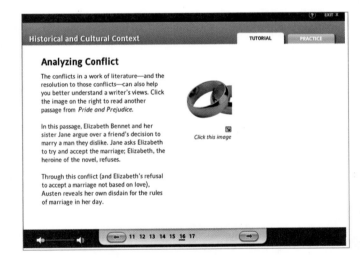

CLOSE READING APPLICATION

Have students work independently to read a different story from a world culture other than their own, particularly modern Israel, and think about the background of the writer and the characters in the story. Ask: How did the past experiences of the characters in this story affect their points of view? How did their points of view then influence the actions they took in the story and their motivations for taking these actions?

The Wife's Story

Short Story by Ursula Le Guin

Why This Text

Students are familiar with straightforward narratives, but may have difficulty understanding plot twists or ironies in literature. Ursula Le Guin's story sets up a reader's expectations and then turns them upside down. With the help of the close-reading questions, students will analyze how the author structures the story and develops the characters. This close reading will lead students to develop a deep understanding of the innovative plot of the story.

Background Have students read the background and information about the author. Point out that her quote invites readers into the process of creating literature; after all, the author knows what will happen in the world she has created, while the reader discovers and explores that world. Introduce the selection by explaining that Ursula Le Guin is known for seeing things from an alternative viewpoint.

AS YOU READ Ask students to pay attention to how the characters' feelings and actions change, advancing the plot. When do they realize that all is not as it seems?

 Common Core Support

- cite strong and thorough textual evidence

- analyze how complex characters develop, interact with others, and advance the plot

- analyze how an author's choices to structure a text create mystery

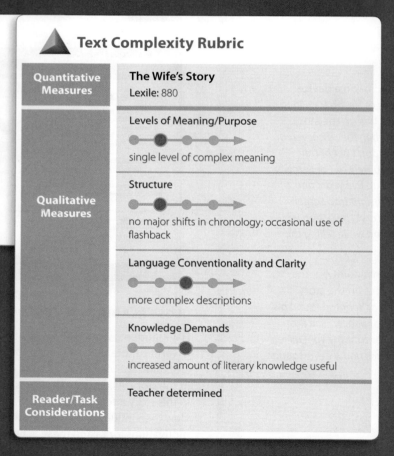

Text Complexity Rubric

Quantitative Measures	**The Wife's Story** Lexile: 880
Qualitative Measures	**Levels of Meaning/Purpose** single level of complex meaning
	Structure no major shifts in chronology; occasional use of flashback
	Language Conventionality and Clarity more complex descriptions
	Knowledge Demands increased amount of literary knowledge useful
Reader/Task Considerations	Teacher determined

Strategies for CLOSE READING

Analyze Character: Motivations

Students should read this story carefully all the way through. Close-reading questions at the bottom of the page will help them focus on a thorough analysis of the characters' motivations and interactions. As they read, students should jot down comments or questions about the text in the margins.

WHEN STUDENTS STRUGGLE . . .

To help students analyze the characters in "The Wife's Story," have them work in small groups to fill out a chart like the one shown below.

CITE TEXT EVIDENCE For practice in analyzing and understanding a character's traits and motivations, ask students to cite text evidence for each point in the chart.

	Husband	Wife
At the start		
How do they act?	kind and hard-working	happy and in love
How do they interact?	good to his wife	appreciates her husband
What motivates them?	family, hard work	family, optimism
At the end		
How do they act?	acts strangely, is disturbed	frightened and confused
How do they interact?	tries to harm his wife and children	"mother anger" toward him
What motivates them?	is under a curse	defends family

Background *Best known for her fantasy works The Books of Earthseas series,* **Ursula Le Guin** *has been writing most of her life. She has written in a variety of genres, including science fiction and poetry. Growing up in Berkeley, California, Le Guin was inspired by her father, who was a writer himself. For Le Guin, writers and readers, working together, make literature meaningful: "Readers, after all, are making the world with you. You give them the material, but it's the readers who build that world in their own minds."*

The Wife's Story

Short Story by Ursula Le Guin

CLOSE READ
Notes

1. **READD** As you read lines 1–31, begin to collect and cite text evidence.

- Underline text that describes the husband.
- Circle language that hints that something bad is going to happen.
- In the margin, list the events in the narrator's story in the order in which they occur.

He was a good husband, a good father. I don't understand it. I don't believe in it. I don't believe that it happened. I saw it happen but it isn't true. It can't be. He was always gentle. If you'd have seen him playing with the children, anybody who saw him with the children would have known that there wasn't any bad in him, not one mean bone. When I first met him he was still living with his mother, over near Spring Lake, and I used to see them together, the mother and the sons, and think that any young fellow that was that nice with his family must be one worth knowing. Then one time when I was walking in the woods I met him by himself
10 coming back from a hunting trip. He hadn't got any game at all, not so much as a field mouse, but he wasn't cast down about it. He was just larking along enjoying the morning air. That's one of the things I first loved about him. He didn't take things hard, he didn't grouch and whine when things didn't go his way. So we got to talking that day. And I guess things moved

A B

1. met him in the woods when he was living with his mother

3

---

1. **READ AND CITE TEXT EVIDENCE** Explain that descriptions of a character include more than physical descriptions. Words that explain how a character acts in different situations, what skills he or she has, and what he or she says can be used to describe the character as well as words that show what he or she looks like.

Ⓐ **ASK STUDENTS** to cite specific text evidence in which the narrator describes her husband in lines 1–31. *Responses may include text in which the narrator describes him with "the children" (line 5), his attitude (lines 13–14), his looks (line 24), and his voice (line 26).*

2. parents had moved out

3. sister moves out

4. he moves in

right along after that, because pretty soon he was over here pretty near all the time. And my sister said—see, my parents had moved out the year before and gone south, leaving us the place—my sister said, kind of teasing but serious, "Well! If he's going to be here every day and half the night, I guess there isn't room for me!" And she moved out—just down the way.

20 We've always been real close, her and me. That's the sort of thing doesn't ever change. I couldn't ever have got through this bad time without my sis.

Well, so he come to live here. And all I can say is, it was the happy year of my life. He was just purely good to me. A hard worker and never lazy, and so big and fine-looking. Everybody looked up to him, you know, young as he was. Lodge Meeting nights, more and more often they had him to lead the singing. He had such a beautiful voice, and he'd lead off strong, and the others following and joining in, high voices and low. It brings the shivers on me now to think of it, hearing it, nights when I'd stayed home from meeting when the children was babies—the singing coming up through the trees

30 there, and the moonlight, summer nights, the full moon shining. I'll never hear anything so beautiful. I'll never know a joy like that again.

It was the moon, that's what they say. It's the moon's fault, and the blood. It was in his father's blood. I never knew his father, and now I wonder what become of him. He was from up Whitewater way, and had no kin around here. I always thought he went back there, but now I don't know. There was some talk about him, tales, that come out after what happened to my husband. It's something runs in the blood, they say, and it may never come out, but if it does, it's the change of the moon that does it. Always it happens in the dark of the moon. When everybody's home and asleep.

40 Something comes over the one that's got the curse in his blood, they say,

2. **REREAD** Reread lines 1–16, and think about how the narrator describes her husband. What do you learn about her character? Support your answer with explicit textual evidence.

She loved her husband, valued hard work, and respected family ties.

3. **READ** As you read lines 32–58, continue to cite textual evidence.

• Underline text that hints that something bad is going to happen.
• Circle text that describes changes in the husband's behavior.
• In the margin, note what the narrator experiences directly.

> *Always it happens in the dark of the moon.*

and he gets up because he can't sleep, and goes out into the glaring sun, and goes off all alone—drawn to find those like him.

And it may be so, because my husband would do that. I'd half **rouse** and say, "Where you going to?" and he'd say, "Oh, hunting, be back this evening," and it wasn't like him, even his voice was different. But I'd be so sleepy, and not wanting to wake the kids, and he was so good and responsible, it was no call of mine to go asking "Why?" and "Where?" and all like that.

So it happened that way maybe three times or four. He'd come back

50 late, and worn out, and pretty near cross for one so sweet-tempered—not wanting to talk about it. I figured everybody got to bust out now and then, and nagging never helped anything. But it did begin to worry me. Not so much that he went, but that he come back so tired and strange. Even, he smelled strange. It made my hair stand up on end. I could not endure it and I said, "What is that—those smells on you? All over you!" And he said, "I don't know," real short, and made like he was sleeping. But he went down when he thought I wasn't noticing, and washed and washed himself. But those smells stayed in his hair, and in our bed, for days.

And then the awful thing. I don't find it easy to tell about this. I want to

60 cry when I have to bring it to my mind. Our youngest, the little one, my baby, she turned from her father. Just overnight. He come in and she got scared-looking, stiff, with her eyes wide, and then she begun to cry and try to hide behind me. She didn't yet talk plain but she was saying over and over, "Make it go away! Make it go away!"

rouse:
awaken

She see changes in her husband's behavior: he stays out late and returns tired and acting—and—smelling strange. He washes and washes.

4. **REREAD** Reread lines 43–58. How has the narrator's relationship with her husband changed? Support your answer with explicit textual evidence.

She notices he goes hunting and comes back late and tired. His voice changes and he "smelled strange."

2. **REREAD AND CITE TEXT EVIDENCE** Point out that the narrator does not say much about herself in lines 1–16, but what she says about her husband reveals her character.

B **ASK STUDENTS** to cite text evidence that lets them know what the narrator values. *Students should refer to text that shows the narrator appreciates goodness (line 5), respects family ties (line 8), and values optimism and good nature (lines 4 and 13).*

3. **READ AND CITE TEXT EVIDENCE** Discuss with students why an author uses foreshadowing—suggesting an event before it happens—in a story. *Students should realize that it creates atmosphere, tension, and anticipation.*

C **ASK STUDENTS** to cite specific examples of foreshadowing that mention the moon. (lines 32–33 and lines 38–39)

4. **REREAD AND CITE TEXT EVIDENCE**

D **ASK STUDENTS** what specific examples of his behavior have caused the narrator's relationship with her husband to change. *Students should point out that the narrator starts to worry about her husband when he returns late, worn out, and cross, and that his smell repels her.*

Critical Vocabulary: rouse (line 43) Have students share their definitions of *rouse*. Point out that the verb can be transitive or intransitive; people can *rouse* others from sleep, or can themselves rouse. Have students use the verb in both forms.

FOR ELL STUDENTS Point out to ELL students that the sentence "Where you going to?" is, in fact, incorrect because it is missing an active verb. Explain that the correct sentence would be "Where are you going?" Explain that the author is using colloquial language to make her dialogue realistic.

The child **E** wants the father to go away. He looks at the child strangely. The narrator scolds the child to stop crying.

Her husband is turning into some kind of monster.

The look in his eyes, just for one moment, when he heard that. That's what I don't want ever to remember. That's what I can't forget. The look in his eyes looking at his own child.

I said to the child, "Shame on you, what's got into you!"—scolding, but keeping her right up close to me at the same time, because I was frightened too. Frightened to shaking.

He looked away then and said something like, "Guess she just waked up dreaming." and passed it off that way. Or tried to. And so did I. And I got real mad with my baby when she kept on acting crazy scared of her own dad. But she couldn't help it and I couldn't change it.

He kept away that whole day. Because he knew, I guess. It was just beginning dark of the moon.

It was hot and close inside, and dark, and we'd all been asleep some while, when something woke me up. He wasn't there beside me. I heard a little stir in the passage, when I listened. So I got up, because I could bear it no longer. I went out into the passage, and it was light there, hard sunlight coming in from the door. And I saw him standing just outside, in the tall grass by the entrance. His head was hanging. Presently he sat down, like he felt weary, and looked down at his feet. I held still, inside, and watched—I didn't know what for.

And I saw what he saw. I saw the changing. In his feet, it was, first. **They got long, each foot got longer, stretching out, the toes stretching out and the foot getting long, and fleshy, and white. And no hair on them.**

The hair begun to come away all over his body. It was like his hair fried away in the sunlight and was gone. **He was white all over,** then, like a worm's skin. And he turned his face. It was changing while I looked. **It got flatter and flatter, the mouth flat and wide, and the teeth grinning flat and dull, and the nose just a knob of flesh with nostril holes, and the ears gone, and the eyes gone blue—blue, with white rims around the blue—staring at me out of that flat, soft, white face.**

5. **READ** ▶ Read lines 59–70. In the margin, explain what happens between the father and the child. Why does the narrator scold her child?

6. **READ** ▶ As you read lines 71–100, continue to cite textual evidence.
• Underline the unexpected events the narrator witnesses.
• In the margin, write what you think is happening to the narrator's husband.

G He stood up then on two legs. I saw him, I had to see him, my own dear love, turned into the hateful one.

I couldn't move, but as I crouched there in the passage staring out into the day I was trembling and shaking with a growl that burst out into a crazy, awful howling. A grief howl and a terror howl and a calling howl. And the others heard it, even sleeping, and woke up.

H It stared and peered, that thing my husband had turned into, and shoved its face up to the entrance of our house. I was still bound by mortal fear, but behind me the children had waked up, and the baby was whimpering. The mother anger come into me then, and I snarled and crept forward.

The man thing looked around. It had no gun, like the ones from the man places do. But it picked up a heavy fallen tree branch in its long white foot, and shoved the end of that down into our house, at me. I snapped the end of it in my teeth and started to force my way out, because I knew the man would kill our children if it could. But my sister was already coming. I saw her running at the man with her head low and her mane high and her eyes yellow as the winter sun. It turned on her and raised up that branch to hit her. But I come out of the doorway, mad with the mother anger, and the others all were coming answering my call, the whole pack gathering, there in that blind glare and heat of the sun at noon.

The man looked round at us and yelled out loud, and **brandished** the branch it held. Then it broke and ran, heading for the cleared fields and lowlands, down the mountainside. It ran, on two legs, leaping and weaving, and we followed it.

brandished: waved in a threatening manner

7. ◀ **REREAD** Reread lines 88–100. What transformation has taken place? What assumptions had you made about the characters that had to be changed? Support your answer with explicit textual evidence.

At first I thought all the characters were humans, but now I realize that the characters are wolves and that the narrator's husband is a kind of reverse werewolf. Instead of a man turning into a wolf at the full moon, a wolf turns into a man.

8. **READ** ▶ As you read lines 101–131, underline text that describes changes in the narrator's feelings toward her husband.

---

5. **READ AND CITE TEXT EVIDENCE**

E ASK STUDENTS to compare their margin notes explaining their understanding of why the narrator scolds her child. _Students should realize that the narrator is angry at the child, but her anger is more widespread—she, too, is frightened of her husband, and cannot balance her emotions of fright and love._

6. **READ AND CITE TEXT EVIDENCE**

F ASK STUDENTS to compare their interpretations of what is happening. Encourage students to visualize the changes taking place—hair disappearing, face flattening, and so on—to create an image of what the husband originally looked like.

7. **REREAD AND CITE TEXT EVIDENCE** Students have made inferences about the narrator's husband as he changes; they should now compare those inferences with what they had previously assumed about the characters.

G ASK STUDENTS to cite text evidence supporting the change in their assumptions. _Students should understand that the "hateful one" the husband changes into is actually a man. They should cite evidence describing the transformation from wolf to man in lines 88, 89, 90–92, and 95._

8. **READ AND CITE TEXT EVIDENCE**

H ASK STUDENTS to identify text where the narrator describes her husband differently. _Students should cite evidence from lines 101–102._

Critical Vocabulary: brandished (line 116) Have students give examples of things they might _brandish_.

The Wife's Story **12e**

120   I was last, because love still bound the anger and the fear in me. I was
running when I saw them pull it down. My sister's teeth were in its throat. I
got there and it was dead. The others were drawing back from the kill,
because of the taste of the blood, and the smell. The younger ones were
cowering and some crying, and my sister rubbed her mouth against her
forelegs over and over to get rid of the taste. I went up close because I
thought if the thing was dead the spell, the curse must be done, and my
husband could come back—alive, or even dead, if I could only see him, my
true love, in his true form, beautiful. But only the dead man lay there white
and bloody. We drew back and back from it, and turned and ran, back up
130   into the hills, back to the woods of the shadows and the twilight and the
blessed dark.

9.   **◄ REREAD AND DISCUSS** Reread lines 120–131. With a small group,
discuss why the wolves killed "the man thing." Do you think this was the
right thing to do? Support your opinion with details from the story.

SHORT RESPONSE

Cite Text Evidence Le Guin purposely misleads her reader as to the true
identity of the narrator. How does this technique help the reader
understand the motivation behind the narrator's actions? **Cite text
evidence** in your response.

> At the beginning, the narrator seems to be a human female, with a
> normal husband, which helps the reader sympathize with her. Le Guin
> describes the community in human terms; they value hard work and
> respect, and hold "Lodge Meetings." By the time she describes the
> sister as having a "mane" and "yellow eyes," it is clear that the
> narrator is a wolf. By making the husband's transformation seem
> frightening, the reader is more sympathetic to the wife's efforts to
> protect her family.

8

TO CHALLENGE STUDENTS . . .

For more context for "The Wife's Story"—and to deepen students'
understanding of its irony—have students research other
werewolf stories and myths.

ASK STUDENTS to find common aspects in the werewolf
stories they research. They should recognize that these stories
rely on people's natural discomfort with animal transformation
and shapeshifting. Suggest that students research the history of
werewolf legends. They will find that stories about werewolves
existed in ancient Greek literature. They were common in
medieval times, they bloomed in the nineteenth century, and
they flourished in the twentieth century. In some modern
appearances, werewolves are presented as misunderstood and
blameless, whereas traditionally they were presented as evil and
repugnant.

9.   REREAD AND DISCUSS USING TEXT EVIDENCE

  ASK STUDENTS to assign a reporter for each group to
present the opinions of each group. Encourage students to
analyze how the text supports the conclusion they reach. They
will probably point to examples of the author presenting
sympathetic characters who are understandably repulsed by the
monster among them.

SHORT RESPONSE

Cite Text Evidence   Students' responses should include text
evidence that supports their positions. They should:

- explain how the author leads the reader into making assumptions
  about the characters.
- show how the author reveals the true nature of the characters.
- use text evidence to justify the reader's empathy with the narrator
  and her pack.

DIG DEEPER

1. With the class, return to Question 7, Reread. Have students share their responses to the question.

   ASK STUDENTS about the transformations that take place in lines 88–100.

   - Have students describe what happens to the husband— first to the parts of his body, and then to the way he carries himself. What can students infer about the way he used to look, and the way he used to stand?
   - Ask students about the transformation in the wife, in lines 97–100. Have them explain the changes in the wife's behavior, and ask them to interpret what a "grief howl and a terror howl and a calling howl" mean. What causes the wife to make these three distinct sounds?
   - Have students describe the husband and wife as they now know them to be, and to compare them with what they had previously assumed.

2. With the class, return to Question 9, Reread and Discuss. Have students share the results of their discussion.

   ASK STUDENTS the main reasons they had for deciding whether or not the wolves were right in killing "the man thing."

   - Have students tell whether it made a difference to their conclusions that the animal the wolves killed is a man, rather than—as in a traditional werewolf story—a wolf being killed by men.
   - Have groups balance the evidence they collected supporting a decision that it was right to kill "the man thing." Groups should include text evidence in which the wolves are shown as sympathetic creatures while the monster is unnatural and appears disgusting to them, and text evidence showing that the monster threatens the wolves and that they act in self-defense.
   - If groups determined that killing "the man thing" was not right, they might present evidence showing that the husband has always been a good and honorable character who is cursed through no fault of his own.

   ASK STUDENTS to return to their Short Response answer and revise it based on the class discussion.

CLOSE READING NOTES

Trailer for *My So-Called Enemy*

Film directed by Lisa Gossels

Why This Text?

Students regularly view films and videos on the Internet, on television, and in movie theaters. These media often have a purpose and a point of view conveyed by the director's choices. This lesson explores the choices a film director made to convey how discord and the violence of war shaped the lives of six teenagers on both sides of the Israeli-Palestinian conflict.

Key Learning Objective: The student will be able to analyze how a director unfolds a series of ideas to advance a purpose and a point of view.

COMMON CORE   Common Core Standards

RI 1 Cite textual evidence.
RI 3 Analyze how the author unfolds ideas or events.
RI 6 Determine an author's point of view and analyze how an author uses rhetoric.
W 1 Write arguments using valid reasoning and relevant evidence.
SL 4 Present information clearly so that the development and style are appropriate to purpose, audience, and task.

Text Complexity Rubric

Quantitative Measures	**Trailer for *My So-Called Enemy*** Lexile N/A
Qualitative Measures	**Levels of Meaning/Purpose** single level of complex meaning
	Structure organization of main ideas and details complex, but clearly stated and generally sequential
	Language Conventionality and Clarity mainly conversational language
	Knowledge Demands somewhat complex social studies concepts
Reader/Task Considerations	Teacher determined Vary by individual reader and type of text

Background Have students read the background. Explain that after World War II the United Nations partitioned Palestine to create the state of Israel as a homeland for the Jews. Neighboring Arab nations did not agree with the partitioning, and quickly invaded the area. Fighting commenced. Some Palestinians living in the new state fled; others were forced out. At the same time, Jews from around the world immigrated to Israel. Fighting continues.

AS YOU VIEW Direct students to the As You View note. Remind students to write down any questions they generate as they watch the trailer.

Analyze Order: Structure and Juxtaposition (1–29 SECONDS)
COMMON CORE RI 1, RI 3

Explain that a trailer shows what the full-length film is about. A director gets the point of the film across using **structure**, or arrangement of film clips, on-screen text, and audio. Another important element that communicates the director's message is **juxtaposition**, or the placement of elements near each other.

Ⓐ CITE TEXT EVIDENCE Have students view the first 29 seconds of the trailer again and identify elements that set the time and place. (*Clips of a peaceful urban setting are followed by footage of bombing in Israel and Palestine.*)

Determine Purpose and Point of View (1–1:05 MINUTES)
COMMON CORE RI 1, RI 6

Explain that the overall purpose of a trailer is to persuade viewers to watch the full-length film. Point out that a film director's arrangement of shots and use of media features reflect a specific purpose or point of view.

Ⓑ ASK STUDENTS to view the first 1:05 minutes of the trailer again and identify the director's purpose. (*Possible answer: The purpose is to show that people from both sides of the Israeli-Palestinian conflict can help one another understand the issues and emotions of the conflict.*)

COLLABORATIVE DISCUSSION Have students pair up, discuss their impressions, and share with the class.

ASK STUDENTS to share any questions they generated in the course of viewing and discussing the trailer.

Background *Conflict between Israeli Jews and Palestinians dates back to even before 1948, when the state of Israel was established to give Jews a homeland following the horrors of the Holocaust. The decades since have been marked by numerous outbreaks of violence interspersed with attempts to broker peace agreements. The documentary film My So-Called Enemy, by Emmy-award winning director Lisa Gossels, follows a group of teenagers from the two sides of the conflict for seven years. These teens were first brought together in the United States by a leadership group called Building Bridges for Peace in an attempt to sow peace one friendship at a time.*

MEDIA ANALYSIS

Trailer for
My So-Called Enemy

Film directed by Lisa Gossels

AS YOU VIEW Consider the choices the director makes about arranging shots and including media features such as music and on-screen text. Note any questions you generate during viewing.

COLLABORATIVE DISCUSSION With a partner, discuss the overall feeling or impression you take from the trailer. Identify how the director created this overall impression, citing specific shots or media techniques to support your ideas.

My So-Called Enemy **13**

SCAFFOLDING FOR ELL STUDENTS

Determine Purpose and Point of View Pair English learners with proficient English speakers in order to view the trailer multiple times. Then ask partners to discuss any details and elements the English learner finds confusing. Next, explain that the information presented in a trailer is related to the director's reason for making the full-length film. Directors make films to explain, entertain, inform, or persuade. Have partners discuss the director's reason for making the documentary film and the message expressed in the trailer.

PRACTICE & APPLY

Analyze Order: Structure and Juxtaposition RI 3

Help students understand the meaning of the terms. Point out that the three boxes in the chart further explain the structure of a work. Juxtaposition is a tool used to create structure. Have students cite examples from the trailer of how juxtaposition of elements presents a contrast between events or ideas. *(Examples include footage of a peaceful setting contrasted with footage of bombs; Gal's explanation of why Jews need to live in Israel contrasted with Hanin's view that Palestinians should not be forced out; and the girls' discussions contrasted with them having fun together.)*

Determine Purpose and Point of View RI 6

Encourage students to think about how the structure and juxtaposition of events and ideas in the trailer affect their understanding of the girls and their lives.

Analyzing the Media 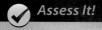 RI 1, RI 3, RI 6, SL 4

Possible answers

1. *Students may identify shots or scenes that present the conflict or the people affected. Have students explain why those shots and scenes are so powerful.*

2. *Media techniques include news footage; interviews; contrasting scenes, images, and audio; on-screen text; and music. Students should explain how each technique achieves the director's purpose.*

3. *The shots show the girls riding together in a paddle boat, cooperating in a trust exercise, and playfully squirting each other with water. These shots show that the girls' strong feelings about the Israeli-Palestinian conflict do not prevent them from being friends and that these friendships may improve relations between Israelis and Palestinians.*

Analyze Order: Structure and Juxtaposition RI 3

Both writers and film directors craft their work to increase the impact of their ideas and messages. They make choices such as these about how to **structure** or arrange the interviews, facts, and other diverse sources of material:

Order of events or ideas, including how to set the scene and where to place the most important points	How ideas are introduced and developed, moving from basic information to deeper or more significant points about the ideas	How to show connections among events and ideas and add meaning through **juxtaposition**, placing key elements close to each other in the piece

Determine Purpose and Point of View RI 6

Even when documenting a factual subject, writers and filmmakers have a point of view or purpose. Directors choose events, music, voiceovers, and on-screen text to advance a particular point of view. Note what you feel while reading or viewing a factual work, and identify how that effect was achieved. Understanding the choices a writer or director makes can help you identify his or her purpose.

Analyzing the Media RI 1, RI 3, RI 6, SL 4

Cite Text Evidence   Support your responses with evidence from the selection.

1. **Interpret** Identify the ways the conflict and people are introduced and developed in the trailer. Which shots or scenes most help you understand the situation the girls face? Why?

2. **Evaluate** List examples of media techniques used in the trailer, including news reports, music, and on-screen text. Which technique or example do you find most effective in achieving the director's purpose? Why?

3. **Analyze** Describe the shots that immediately follow Inas explaining her conflicted feelings about Jews. What is the effect of these shots, and how does this juxtaposition serve the director's purpose?

PERFORMANCE TASK

Speaking Activity: Argument Do you think that face-to-face interactions can help resolve conflicts? Express your view in a short speech.

- Review the trailer, noting evidence that supports your ideas. Add ideas from your experiences to your notes.

- Write a one-page argument expressing and supporting your ideas. Then, deliver the argument as a speech.

Assign this performance task.

PERFORMANCE TASK  W 1, SL 4

Speaking Activity: Argument Explain to students that the one-page argument should state a claim, or position, about using face-to-face interactions to resolve conflicts. Students should support their claims with reasons, or statements to explain their beliefs, and with evidence, such as facts, statistics, or examples.

Support Inferences

TEACH

Define an **inference** as an educated guess, a conclusion we draw about something based on available evidence. Remind students that we make countless inferences throughout the day, often without thinking about how or why we reach a certain conclusion about the people and events we witness. Explain that we can learn and grow by examining our inferences.

Tell students they will make and examine inferences as they view *My So-Called Enemy* again.

PRACTICE AND APPLY

Direct students to make a two-column chart to record inferences they make during a guided viewing:

Evidence	Inferences

Run the trailer. Stop it at 29 seconds and have students record the onscreen text in the left column of their charts:

> GAL: how are u?
>
> REZAN: doomed (lol)

Ask students to jot inferences about Gal and Rezan in the right column, opposite the text exchange. Have students share their inferences with the class. *(Gal and Rezan are students, they are both young, they are friends, they are familiar with the language of texting, and Rezan has a dark sense of humor—from her use of lol.)*

Ask students if they recognize the flags to the left of each texter's name. *(The flag of Israel is beside Gal's name; the flag of Palestine, beside Rezan's.)* In the left column, have students record the flag that goes with each name. In the right column, they will record the inferences they make from the pairing of names and flags. *(One texter is an Israeli and the other a Palestinian; they are on opposite sides of a long, complex conflict.)*

Run the remainder of the trailer. Stop at 2:43, just before headlines appear on a white screen, and again at 3:00, just after the second screen with headlines. Each time ask students to jot evidence and inferences on their charts. Discuss. Close by reminding students to regularly examine the inferences they make as they observe and read.

 For further instruction and practice, use this *Interactive Whiteboard Lesson:* **Making Inferences**

Determine Purpose and Point of View

RETEACH

Review that writers and filmmakers have a main **purpose**, or reason, for creating a work. The purpose may be to inform or explain, to share ideas, to persuade, or to entertain.

Have students chart clues about the director's purpose for making the trailer. Then have them state the director's purpose.

Inform/Explain	Share ideas	Persuade	Entertain

Explain that in addition to a purpose, writers and filmmakers may convey a **point of view**, or perspective, through their work. A point of view is a combination of ideas, values, feelings, and beliefs that shape the way the writer or filmmaker looks at a topic. Ask students to list elements in the trailer that hint at the director's point of view. Then have students state the director's point of view.

 LEVEL UP TUTORIALS Assign the following *Level Up* tutorial: **Author's Purpose**

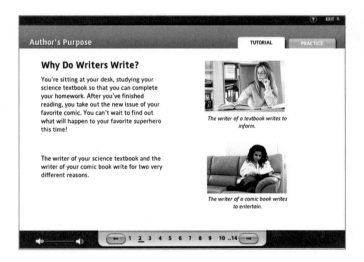

CLOSE VIEWING APPLICATION

Students can apply the skill to a trailer of another documentary film. Have them work independently to view another trailer. Then they can chart the clues and list the elements that show the director's purpose and point of view.

ANCHOR TEXT

from Texas v. Johnson Majority Opinion

ANCHOR TEXT

American Flag Stands for Tolerance

Court Opinion by William J. Brennan

Newspaper Editorial by Ronald J. Allen

Why These Texts?

Students often encounter multiple texts related to the same topic. This lesson explores and compares the ideas in a historical Supreme Court decision and an editorial defending that decision.

▶ **View It!**

Professional Development Podcast:

Text-Dependent Analysis

Key Learning Objective: The student will be able to analyze a Supreme Court opinion, cite evidence used to make inferences in an editorial, and compare tone in two texts by analyzing the impact of word choice.

For practice and application:

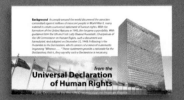

Close Reader selection
from "The Universal Declaration of Human Rights"
public document from the UN Commission on Human Rights

For practice and application:

Close Reader selection
"*from* Towards a True Refuge"
speech by Aung San Suu Kyi

COMMON CORE ## Common Core Standards

RI 1 Cite textual evidence.
RI 2 Determine a central idea and analyze its development.
RI 3 Analyze how the author unfolds ideas or events.
RI 4 Determine the meaning of words and phrases.
RI 5 Analyze how an author's ideas are developed by particular sentences or paragraphs.
RI 8 Delineate and evaluate the argument and specific claims in a text; identify false statements.
RI 9 Analyze seminal U.S. documents of historical and literary significance.
W 2b Develop the topic with well-chosen facts, extended definitions, concrete details, and quotations.
W 7 Conduct short research projects to answer a question.
L 1b Use various types of phrases and clauses to convey specific meanings.
L 4b Identify and use patterns of word changes that indicate different meanings.

 ## Text Complexity Rubric

	from Texas v. Johnson Majority Opinion Lexile: 1420L	American Flag Stands for Tolerance Lexile: 1170L
Quantitative Measures		
Qualitative Measures	**Levels of Meaning/Purpose** more than one purpose; implied but easy to infer	**Levels of Meaning/Purpose** purpose implied; easily identified from context
	Structure more than one text structure	**Structure** organization of main ideas and details complex but mostly explicit
	Language Conventionality and Clarity many unfamiliar, high academic, and complex domain-specific words; complex and varied sentence structure	**Language Conventionality and Clarity** increased unfamiliar words; more complex sentence structure
	Knowledge Demands complex civics concepts	**Knowledge Demands** somewhat complex civics concepts
Reader/Task Considerations	Teacher determined Vary by individual reader and type of text	Teacher determined Vary by individual reader and type of text

CLOSE READ

Background Have students read the background and information about Justice Brennan. Tell students that Johnson's case went to the Supreme Court after the Texas Court of Criminal Appeals reversed Johnson's conviction, saying that Johnson's actions were symbolic speech that is protected by the First Amendment. The Supreme Court ruled on two issues: (1) Whether burning of the flag was a form of expressive conduct, permitting him to invoke the First Amendment; and (2) whether Texas's interest in preserving the flag as a symbol of the United States justified Johnson's conviction.

AS YOU READ Direct students to the As You Read note to focus their reading.

Analyze Seminal U.S. Documents (LINES 1–6)

COMMON CORE **RI 1, RI 3, RI 9**

Explain to students that court decisions are written in a formal language that includes rich vocabulary and lengthy, complex sentences. Suggest that students reread and **paraphrase**, or restate in their own words, sentences as needed for comprehension.

(A) ASK STUDENTS to restate the first paragraph in their own words. *(Possible answer: The Court will not say that our First Amendment rights are protected except when it comes to the treatment of the flag.)*

Explain to students that a sentence's meaning can often change, depending on the placement of a few key words.

(B) CITE TEXT EVIDENCE Have students reread the second paragraph. Then ask them to identify the phrase that indicates that the Court does not think *encouraging* proper treatment of the flag is the same as legally *requiring* proper treatment of the flag. *("is not to say")*

Background *At the 1984 Republican National Convention in Dallas, Texas, protesters marched, held signs, and chanted slogans opposing the policies of then-President Ronald Reagan. One of the protesters, Gregory Lee Johnson, set an American flag on fire. He was punished with a fine and a jail term for breaking a state law banning flag desecration. He appealed, and the case was sent to the Supreme Court to decide whether flag burning is a form of expression protected by the Constitution. The Court delivered its ruling in 1989.*
William J. Brennan *(1906–1997), who served on the Supreme Court from 1956 to 1990, wrote the majority opinion in the case. His staunch defense of First Amendment rights influenced many significant Court decisions.*

from
Texas v. Johnson Majority Opinion

American Flag Stands for Tolerance

Court Opinion by William J. Brennan

Newspaper Editorial by Ronald J. Allen

from
Texas v. Johnson Majority Opinion

Court Opinion by William J. Brennan

AS YOU READ Pay attention to the details that explain the Court's reasons for its decision. Note any questions you have as you read.

(A) We decline, therefore, to create for the flag an exception to the joust[1] of principles protected by the First Amendment. . . . [2]
(B) To say that the government has an interest in encouraging proper treatment of the flag, however, is not to say that it may criminally punish a person for burning a flag as a means of political protest.

Image Credits: ©Guy Jarvis/Houghton Mifflin Harcourt

---

[1] **joust:** competition.
[2] **First Amendment:** the part of the Bill of Rights added to the U.S. Constitution that deals with freedom of speech, among other freedoms.

Compare Anchor Texts **15**

Close Read Screencasts   ▶ **View It!**

Modeled Discussions

Have students click the *Close Read* icons in their eBooks to access a screencast in which readers discuss and annotate the following key passage:

- the Court's statement of the issues it has considered (lines 1–12)

As a class, view and discuss the video. Then have students pair up to do an independent close read of an additional passage—the Court's explanation of the flag's symbolism (lines 31–39).

Analyze Seminal U.S. Documents (LINES 17–24)

COMMON CORE RI 1, RI 9

Explain that lines 17–19 refer to *Abrams v. United States*, a freedom-of-speech case from 1919. Justice Oliver Wendell Holmes wrote the dissenting opinion. Holmes said the government did not prove that the defendants' actions presented a danger to the nation.

C **CITE TEXT EVIDENCE** Have students cite the lines in which Justice Brennan applies Holmes's idea to the current case. *(lines 20–24)*

> #### CRITICAL VOCABULARY
>
> **compulsion**: Justice Brennan cites a previous Court case that questioned whether the Constitution allows children to be forced to pledge allegiance to the flag. **ASK STUDENTS** to explain the compulsion regarding the flag in *Texas v. Johnson*. *(Texas tried to force its citizens to treat the flag properly by banning the burning of the flag in protest.)*
>
> **implicit**: The Texas statute implies that society is offended by mistreatment of the flag. **ASK STUDENTS** how Brennan uses the state's implicit assumption to support his argument. *(The flag must be special if disrespect of it offends people.)*
>
> **reaffirmation**: Justice Brennan says that the Court's opinion endorses the principles that the flag symbolizes. **ASK STUDENTS** why Justice Brennan makes this reaffirmation. *(The Court agrees with the principles the flag stands for and has made its decision based on them.)*
>
> **resilience**: Justice Brennan says that Texas and the Court agree that one of the nation's strengths is its ability to return to normal after a disturbing event. **ASK STUDENTS** to explain Justice Brennan's use of the word "resilience" in "and it is that resilience that we reassert" (line 35). *(The Court's decision confirms that the U.S. is a resilient nation.)*

COLLABORATIVE DISCUSSION Have partners discuss the Court's decision and the reasons for it. Then ask them to share their conclusions with the class.

ASK STUDENTS to share any questions they generated in the course of reading and discussing the selection.

National unity as an end which officials may foster by persuasion and example is not in question. The problem is whether, under our Constitution, **compulsion** as here employed is a permissible means for its achievement.

[Barnette, 319 U.S. at 640.]

compulsion
(kəm-pŭl´shən) *n.*
forced obligation.

We are fortified in today's conclusion by our conviction that forbidding criminal punishment for conduct such as Johnson's will not endanger the special role played by our flag or the feelings it inspires. To paraphrase Justice Holmes, we submit that nobody can suppose that this one gesture of an unknown man will change our Nation's attitude towards its flag [*Abrams v. United States*]. Indeed, Texas' argument that the burning of an American flag "is an act having a high likelihood to cause a breach of the peace," and its statute's **implicit** assumption that physical mistreatment of the flag will lead to "serious offense," tend to confirm that the flag's special role is not in danger; if it were, no one would riot or take offense because a flag had been burned.

implicit
(ĭm-plĭs´ĭt) *adj.*
understood, but not expressed.

We are tempted to say, in fact, that the flag's deservedly cherished place in our community will be strengthened, not weakened, by our holding today. Our decision is a **reaffirmation** of the principles of freedom and inclusiveness that the flag best reflects, and of the conviction that our toleration of criticism such as Johnson's is a sign and source of our strength. Indeed, one of the proudest images of our flag, the one immortalized in our own national anthem, is of the bombardment it survived at Fort McHenry.[3] It is the Nation's **resilience**, not its rigidity, that Texas sees reflected in the flag—and it is that resilience that we reassert today.

reaffirmation
(rē´ə-fûr mā´shən) *n.*
the act of verifying or endorsing again.

resilience
(rĭ-zĭl´yəns) *n.*
ability to return to a normal state after a change or an injury.

The way to preserve the flag's special role is not to punish those who feel differently about these matters. It is to persuade them that they are wrong.

COLLABORATIVE DISCUSSION With a partner, discuss what the Court decided and why. Cite specific textual evidence from the opinion to support your ideas.

---

[3] **Fort McHenry:** War of 1812 battle site in Baltimore. In 1814, poet Francis Scott Key, being held prisoner on a ship nearby, was elated to see the American flag flying there and wrote "The Star-Spangled Banner" to celebrate this American victory over the British.

SCAFFOLDING FOR ELL STUDENTS

Analyze Seminal U.S. Documents Group English learners with one or two English speakers. Have the groups define important information in the last two paragraphs of the majority opinion. Suggest that each group review lines 26–39, discuss the details, and clarify any ideas anyone in the group finds confusing. Then have groups write a list of the important points from the passage. If students list six or more points, tell them to review the list and cross out half of the points so that only the most important ideas remain. Then have groups compare their lists with another group to see whether they identified the same points, to discuss any differences, and to explain how they identified what was important in the passage.

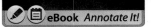
Analyze Seminal U.S. Documents

 COMMON CORE RI 9

Seminal means "creative, original, and having great influence on what follows." A **seminal document**, then, is one that establishes or defines principles that shape the way others think or act. The *Texas* v. *Johnson* opinion is a seminal document. It sets forth a rational interpretation of the First Amendment that includes protection of "symbolic speech," such as flag burning. This decision set a precedent for rulings in later cases, and it increased understanding of how First Amendment principles apply to contemporary situations.

Analyzing the Text

COMMON CORE RI 1, RI 3, RI 4, RI 5, RI 9, W 2b

 Support your responses with evidence from the selection.

1. **Connect** What earlier points of law does Justice Brennan use to support the Court's opinion in this case?

2. **Compare** In its argument to make flag burning a criminal offense, what events did Texas predict might happen? How does the Court interpret the significance of these possible events?

3. **Cite Evidence** How does Justice Brennan support the idea that "the flag's deservedly cherished place in our community will be strengthened, not weakened" by the ruling?

4. **Analyze** How is the image of the flag flying over Fort McHenry related to the central idea of the opinion?

5. **Analyze** What does Justice Brennan's repetition of the word *resilience* to refer to the nation suggest about his view of the Constitution?

PERFORMANCE TASK

Writing Activity: Comparison The Supreme Court determines whether official actions follow the Constitution. In *Texas* v. *Johnson*, the Court's ruling centered on the First Amendment. Compare ideas in the decision and the amendment:

> **First Amendment** *Congress shall make no law respecting an establishment of religion, or prohibiting the free exercise thereof; or abridging the freedom of speech, or of the press; or the right of the people peaceably to assemble, and to petition the Government for a redress of grievances.*

- Identify concepts that are discussed in both documents. How does each document address them?

- In a paragraph, compare the two documents. Support your points with examples from both texts.

Compare Texts **17**

Assign this performance task.

PERFORMANCE TASK

COMMON CORE W 2b

Writing Activity: Comparison Pair students to identify and take notes about the concepts discussed in both documents and how those concepts are developed. Then have students work individually to write the one-paragraph comparison of the two documents, supporting their ideas with examples from their notes.

PRACTICE & APPLY

Analyze Seminal U.S. Documents

COMMON CORE RI 9

Help students understand the meaning of the terms *seminal* and *seminal document* as well as any unfamiliar words. Ask students to provide two examples of seminal U.S. documents. *(Examples include the U.S. Constitution and Martin Luther King Jr.'s "I Have a Dream" speech.)*

To help students understand how seminal U.S. documents relate to contemporary situations, ask students to explain how the Court's opinion in *Texas v. Johnson* has or could affect our lives today. *(Responses should describe situations today in which First Amendment rights are at issue.)*

Analyzing the Text

COMMON CORE RI 1, RI 3, RI 4, RI 5, RI 9, W 2b

Possible answers:

1. *Students may identify Barnette, 319 U.S. at 640 or Abrams v. United States.*

2. *Texas argued that flag burning would cause rioting and the loss of the flag's special role in our culture. The Court points out that the flag's special role is not in danger, because if it were, no one would care that it was being burned.*

3. *Justice Brennan says that the Court's decision reaffirms the principles of free speech, specifically freedom and inclusiveness, which are the very principles the flag represents (lines 28–32).*

4. *The flag flying after the bombardment of Fort McHenry strengthened people's pride in the nation. Similarly, the Court believes its ruling will increase people's pride in the principles the flag represents.*

5. *Justice Brennan's repetition of* resilience *suggests that he sees the nation and Constitution as strong because they are flexible.*

CLOSE READ

AS YOU READ Direct students to use the As You Read note to focus their reading. Remind them to write down any questions they generate during reading.

Analyze Impact of Word Choice (LINES 4–15)

COMMON CORE RI 1, RI 4

Explain to students that we make associations with words. For example, *controversy* and *firestorm* both refer to a discussion involving opposing views. However, *firestorm* has stronger emotional associations, suggesting a more contentious, or argumentative, discussion. **Connotative** meanings relate to the attitudes or feelings associated with words. Writers choose words with particular connotations to reflect their tone, or attitude, toward the subject of their writing.

 ASK STUDENTS how Allen's use of *slaughtered* instead of *killed* reveals his attitude toward the subject. (*The more negative connotation of "slaughtered" suggests he finds the Chinese government's actions horrifying.*)

> #### CRITICAL VOCABULARY
>
> **orthodoxy:** Allen is suggesting, for the sake of argument, that banning flag burning is not the same thing as forcing government beliefs on people.
>
> **ASK STUDENTS** why banning flag burning might be considered governmental orthodoxy. (*Possible answer: Making it illegal to burn the American flag would force on all people the government's belief that the flag must be respected.*)
>
> **sanctity:** Allen feels that what separates our nation from other nations is Americans' belief that freedom is of the utmost importance.
>
> **ASK STUDENTS** to give an example of how Americans demonstrate their belief in the sanctity of the human conscience. (*Possible answer: A person can pass out literature or express opinions in public without fear of being arrested.*)

American Flag Stands for Tolerance

Newspaper Editorial by Ronald J. Allen

AS YOU READ Pay attention to words and details that communicate the author's opinion on his topic.

In a controversial decision, the Supreme Court, by the closest possible margin of a 5-to-4 vote, held that a person has a right to express disagreement with governmental policies by burning the American flag. In a decision at least as controversial, the leadership of the People's Republic of China decided that citizens who peacefully express disagreement with government policies may be slaughtered.[1] On the surface, these two events may seem to bear little relationship to one another, but deep and fundamental lessons can be drawn from their comparison.

10 The American flag is a cherished symbol of our national aspirations. It is the closest object to a national icon,[2] rivaled only by the Constitution and the Declaration of Independence. Given the widespread and deeply felt reverence for this symbol of what we perceive to be the best of our civilization, what is the harm in insisting upon a modicum[3] of respect for it? After all, no one can seriously equate a prohibition on flag burning with the imposition of governmental **orthodoxy** in political speech. Any messages that burning the flag might convey easily can be communicated in other ways. Those are powerful points, deserving the greatest respect. If

20 not rebutted,[4] they compel the conclusion that the Supreme Court was wrong in its decision.

The Supreme Court was not wrong. Indeed, a decision contrary to the one reached would have been a definitive step away from our national aspirations. A commitment to the intertwined freedoms of conscience and expression is at the core of those aspirations. What most distinguishes our civilization from both its predecessors and its contemporary competitors is a belief in the **sanctity** of the human conscience. Each individual is to have the freedom to develop by his or her own lights, and not by the command of

orthodoxy
(ôr′thə-dŏk sē) *n.* traditionally accepted codes and customs.

sanctity
(săngk′tĭ-tē) *n.* sacredness or ultimate importance.

---

[1] **People's Republic of China . . . slaughtered:** In June 1989, government tanks fired on citizens who had gathered in Beijing's Tiananmen Square to demand democratic reforms. Hundreds were killed.
[2] **icon:** symbol of deeply held values.
[3] **modicum:** small amount offered as a symbol or gesture.
[4] **rebutted:** opposed using reasons and evidence.

Close Read Screencasts   **▶ View It!**

Modeled Discussions

Have students click the *Close Read* icons in their eBooks to access a screencast in which readers discuss and annotate the following key passage:

- Allen's argument supporting the Supreme Court's decision (lines 22–32)

As a class, view and discuss the video. Then have students pair up to do an independent close read of an additional passage—Allen's beliefs about what the American flag symbolizes (lines 64–68).

Dallas police arrest Gregory Lee Johnson for burning an American flag outside the 1984 Republican National Convention.

30 officialdom. That requires not just the right to be let alone, but also the right to communicate with, to learn from and test views in conversations.

B It is, thus, no surprise that the First Amendment is where it is in the Bill of Rights, for it is first in importance. A concomitant of the commitment to freedom of conscience, in a sense its mirror image, is that no one has better access to truth than anyone else. Official **dogma** is not better (perhaps no worse) than the beliefs of private citizens.

40 The **dissenters** in the flag-burning case and their supporters might at this juncture note an irony in my argument. My point is that freedom of conscience and expression is at the core of our self-conception and that commitment to it requires the rejection of official dogma. But how is that admittedly dogmatic belief different from any other dogma, such as the one inferring that freedom of expression stops at the border of the flag?

C The crucial distinction is that the commitment to freedom of conscience and expression states the simplest and least self-contradictory principle that seems to capture our aspirations.

50 Any other principle is hopelessly at odds with our commitment to freedom of conscience. The controversy surrounding the flag-burning case makes the case well.

The controversy will rage precisely because burning the flag is such a powerful form of communication. Were it not, who

dogma
(dôg′mə) *n.*
principles or beliefs that an authority insists are true.

dissenter
(dĭ-sĕn′tər) *n.*
one who disagrees or refuses to accept.

SCAFFOLDING FOR ELL STUDENTS

Cause and Effect Using a whiteboard, project lines 33–34. Explain that sometimes a writer uses cause (what makes something happens) and effect (what happens) to make a point. Read aloud lines 33–34. Then have students work together to highlight in green the words that indicate a cause and effect. Help students verbalize the cause (importance of freedom of speech) and effect (part of the First Amendment).

It is, thus, no surprise that the First Amendment is where it is

in the Bill of Rights, for it is first in importance. A concomitant of

CLOSE READ

Image Credits: ©David Leeson/Image Works/Time & Life Pictures/Getty Images

Cite Evidence (LINES 33–38)   **RI 1**

Explain that writers use facts, statistics, examples, and expert opinions as evidence to support their arguments. Understanding how writers use this evidence is crucial when analyzing a text.

B **CITE TEXT EVIDENCE** Have students cite the evidence Allen uses to support his argument that freedom of conscience is of profound importance to Americans. *(Allen points out how the First Amendment, which lists citizens' freedoms, is at the beginning of the Bill of Rights because it is "first in importance," lines 33–34.)*

Analyze Impact of Word Choice (LINES 46–51)   **RI 1, RI 4**

Explain that **context** is the situation for which a writer creates a piece of writing. In the context of an editorial, for example, a writer often uses emotional language to express his or her opinions and attitudes toward a subject.

C **CITE TEXT EVIDENCE** Have students reread lines 46–51 and identify the emotional language Allen uses to help make his point. *(hopelessly at odds, line 49)*

CRITICAL VOCABULARY

dogma: Allen feels that the beliefs and opinions of private citizens are just as legitimate as the established beliefs and opinions of the government. No individual, group, or institution has the right to impose those beliefs and opinions on another. **ASK STUDENTS** to consider the possible dangers in following dogma. *(Possible answer: More relevant and helpful ideas may be possible; the beliefs of one group might conflict with the beliefs of another group and lead to dangerous conflict.)*

dissenters: Allen understands that those who disagree with the flag-burning decision might see a contradiction in his argument. **ASK STUDENTS** to explain how the dissenters of the case might find Allen's opinion ironic. *(Possible answer: By saying we should reject dogma, Allen is, in fact, being dogmatic.)*

Cite Evidence (LINES 69–76) COMMON CORE RI 1, RI 8

Explain that readers use text evidence and personal experience to make **inferences** about the implied meaning in a text.

D **CITE TEXT EVIDENCE** Ask students what inference they can make after reading lines 69–76. (*Allen believes controversy is important to freedom.*) Then have students identify text evidence that supports their inference. (*"With controversy comes debate, enlightenment, and renewed commitment," lines 72–73; and "After all, it is in robust debate that we are most true to ourselves," lines 75–76.*)

Tell students that a **fallacy** is a deceptive, misleading, or false idea or belief. A writer will employ a fallacy to make a statement sound reasonable.

E **ASK STUDENTS** whether any of Allen's statements in the last paragraph are examples of fallacy, and have them explain why. (*Possible answer: Allen's statements are not examples of fallacy because he has provided evidence to support his view that the controversy of flag burning is part of our commitment to freedom of conscience and expression.*)

COLLABORATIVE DISCUSSION Have students pair up and discuss Allen's opinion about the Supreme Court's ruling. Have them identify the reasons, evidence, and word choices Allen uses to advance his argument. Then have partners share their conclusions with the class as a whole. Accept all reasonable responses.

ASK STUDENTS to share any questions they generated in the course of reading and discussing the selection.

---

would care? Thus were we to embrace a prohibition on such communication, we would be saying that the First Amendment protects expression only when no one is offended. That would mean that this aspect of the First Amendment would be of virtually no consequence. It would protect a person only when no protection was needed. Thus, we do have one official dogma—each
60 American may think and express anything he wants. The exception is expression that involves the risk of injury to others and the destruction of someone else's property. Neither was present in this case.

At the core of what the flag symbolizes, then, is tolerance. More than anything else, the flag stands for free expression of ideas, no matter how distasteful. The ultimate irony would have been to punish views expressed by burning the flag that stands for the right to those expressions.

. . . Perhaps, though, there is another way to look at it—to
70 acknowledge that not even such a fundamental value as the commitment to freedom of conscience should be free from controversy. With controversy comes debate, enlightenment and renewed commitment. Perhaps, then, we are in the court's debt for not treating the flag-burning case like the simple case it is. Let the controversy rage. After all, it is in robust debate that we are most true to ourselves.

COLLABORATIVE DISCUSSION Does the author agree or disagree with the Court's ruling? With a partner, discuss the author's opinion and attitude toward the decision. Cite specific textual evidence to support your ideas.

APPLYING ACADEMIC VOCABULARY

diverse	rational

As you discuss Allen's editorial, incorporate the following Collection 1 academic vocabulary words: *diverse* and *rational*. Ask students to explain how Allen's caution against dogma is important to a country of people with **diverse** ideas. As you evaluate the effectiveness of his argument, have students indicate the **rational** points Allen makes in the editorial.

Cite Evidence

COMMON CORE **RI 1**

Editorial writers express opinions on current issues and events, supporting their ideas with reasons and evidence, including facts, examples, and expert views. To decide whether you agree with the writer's argument, you must be sure you understand both the **explicit meaning**—the ideas stated directly in the text—and the ideas that are implied. To make **inferences**, or logical assumptions, about the writer's implied meaning you must identify text evidence as well as consider what you already know.

Analyze Impact of Word Choice: Compare Tone

COMMON CORE **RI 4**

Tone reflects a writer's attitude toward the subject, audience, and context for writing. The **context,** or situation for which a piece of writing is created, often determines both its form and its tone.

A Supreme Court ruling is written in a serious and thoughtful context; it must use precise language and reasoning because it represents the law of the land and may be cited in future decisions as a **precedent**—the legal basis of other rulings with far-reaching effects. A newspaper editorial, on the other hand, is written in a more immediate and emotional context; it expresses the writer's current thinking about a controversial topic.

Compare the tone and meaning expressed in the following passages from Brennan's and Allen's writing:

Brennan	Allen
To say that the government has an interest in encouraging proper treatment of the flag, however, is not to say that it may criminally punish a person for burning a flag as a means of political protest.	The ultimate irony would have been to punish views expressed by burning the flag that stands for the right to those expressions.

When you compare the language the two writers use, consider the cumulative impact of their word choices. In this example, Brennan's precise word choices and careful sentence construction add up to a deliberate, careful, painstaking tone. In contrast, Allen's word choices are more evocative and his sentence structure more free. His tone is more that of a fiery speech than of the law of the land.

CLOSE READ

Cite Evidence

COMMON CORE **RI 1**

Review with the class the difference between explicit and implicit meaning. Then have partners explain Allen's arguments and decide whether they agree or disagree with his opinion. Encourage students to discuss any inferences they made and the text evidence they used to make those inferences.

Analyze Impact of Word Choice: Compare Tone

COMMON CORE **RI 4**

Review the terms *tone* and *context* with the class. To help students compare the tone of Brennan's and Allen's writing, make sure they understand the importance of word choice in establishing tone:

- Explain that pieces written for a serious context—such as a court ruling—use words for their explicit meanings. Point out *criminally punish* in Brennan's example, and explain how this word choice is more precise than saying only *punish*.
- Explain that writers of editorials are expressing opinions and so their word choice is more evocative and less formal than a Supreme Court decision. Point out *ultimate irony* in Allen's example as an illustration of a less formal tone.

Strategies for Annotation 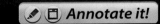 *Annotate it!*

Analyze Impact of Word Choice: Compare Tone

COMMON CORE **RI 1, RI 4**

Share these strategies for guided or independent analysis:

- Highlight in green some of Brennan's word choices that show his attitude toward the subject. On a note, analyze how his choices establish meaning and tone.
- Highlight in blue some of Allen's word choices that show his attitude toward the subject. On a note, analyze how his choices establish meaning and tone.

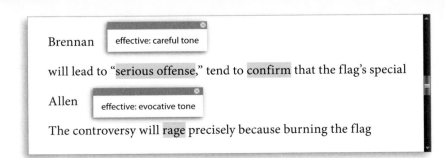

Brennan   effective: careful tone

will lead to "serious offense," tend to confirm that the flag's special

Allen   effective: evocative tone

The controversy will rage precisely because burning the flag

PRACTICE & APPLY

Analyzing the Text COMMON CORE RI 1, RI 3, RI 4, RI 8

Possible answers:

1. *The words "cherished," "aspirations," "reverence," "best," and "deserving the greatest respect" show Allen's feelings toward the flag. Understanding his attitude toward the flag makes his argument stronger because it's clear that he has great respect for the flag, yet he thinks it's important to our belief in freedom that people should be allowed to burn the flag in protest if they wish.*

2. *Both "sanctity of the human conscience" and the "enlightenment" have strongly positive connotations, which convey a positive attitude, or tone, toward the freedoms we share and the commitment to keep them.*

3. *Both texts are about how people should be allowed to burn the flag in protest without being criminally punished. Allen's use of emotional language makes his argument more convincing because it makes his ideas more personal for readers.*

4. *The statement is a fallacy because it makes an assumption based on a personal interpretation of what the First Amendment means. The statement ignores the fact that the Supreme Court makes rulings based on its interpretation of the Constitution, including its amendments. Such a statement would contradict much of what Allen said in his editorial, and it would have weakened, if not negated, the rest of his argument.*

5. *Allen points out that the First Amendment protects freedom of expression, even when that expression is offensive, as long as it does not cause risk of injury or destruction of someone else's property. He further says that "the flag stands for free expression of ideas, no matter how distasteful."*

Analyzing the Text COMMON CORE RI 1, RI 3, RI 4, RI 8, W 7

Cite Text Evidence   Support your responses with evidence from the selection.

1. **Infer** What words in the second paragraph convey Allen's feelings toward the flag? Does understanding his attitude make you feel that his argument is stronger or weaker? Why?

2. **Analyze** In his editorial, Allen talks about the "sanctity of the human conscience" and the "enlightenment" that comes from debate. Explain how the connotations of these words convey his tone.

3. **Compare** What ideas are expressed in both the editorial and the court opinion? Which argument do you find more convincing? Why?

4. **Evaluate** A **fallacy** is an error in reasoning. Suppose Allen had included this sentence in his editorial: *Anyone who wants to throw flag burners in jail is obviously not a supporter of the Constitution.* In what way is this statement a fallacy? What would have been the effect of this sentence on Allen's argument?

5. **Analyze** Allen discriminates, or distinguishes, between what people *should* do and what they *should be allowed* to do. How does he reconcile this apparent contradiction in his argument?

PERFORMANCE TASK

Writing Activity: Analysis Beginning with the examples on the previous page, analyze the differences in meaning and tone between the *Texas* v. *Johnson* court opinion and the newspaper editorial discussing the decision.

- Using photocopies or sticky notes, identify word choices and sentences in both texts that strongly contribute to the overall tone of each.

- Write a one-page analysis of the differences in tone between the two texts. Conclude your analysis by explaining how the tone of each text fits the context for which it was written.

Assign this performance task.

PERFORMANCE TASK   COMMON CORE W 7

Writing Activity: Analysis Have students work in pairs or small groups. Then direct them to reread both texts, looking for examples of word choice that convey each writer's tone. Remind students to consider the context of each text and how context influences tone.

Critical Vocabulary

compulsion	implicit	reaffirmation	resilience
orthodoxy	sanctity	dogma	dissenter

Practice and Apply Answer each question by incorporating the meanings of both Critical Vocabulary words.

1. Which is more flexible, **orthodoxy** or **dogma?**

2. When might a **dissenter** show **resilience?**

3. What is a situation in which a **compulsion** might be **implicit?**

4. How might the **sanctity** of something need **reaffirmation?**

Vocabulary Strategy: Words from Latin

The Critical Vocabulary words *compulsion, implicit, reaffirmation, resilience, sanctity,* and *dissenter* all have Latin roots. Knowing the meaning of a root helps you define the various words derived from it. This chart defines several Latin roots and shows English words that derive from them:

Latin Root and Its Meaning	Related Words
sanctus means "sacred"	sanctity, sanctuary
firmus means "strong"	reaffirmation, firmament
resilire means "to leap back"	resilience, resilient
sentire means "to feel"	dissenter, sentiment

Practice and Apply For each row of the chart, identify one new word that belongs to the word family. (You may use a dictionary if needed.) For each word you choose, follow these steps:

1. Write a definition that incorporates the meaning of the Latin root.

2. Identify the part of speech.

3. Use the word in a sentence that reflects its meaning.

PRACTICE & APPLY

Critical Vocabulary

Possible answers:

1. *Orthodoxy is more flexible than dogma because dogma is instilled by an authority, which may have a vested interest in maintaining the status quo. On the other hand, orthodoxy is a set of traditional beliefs and customs which can change over time as societal attitudes change.*

2. *A dissenter could show resilience by trying to understand the other side of the issue. If the person still dissents, he or she could accept the decision while further contemplating his or her own opinion.*

3. *You may feel a compulsion to attend an event, such as a relative's birthday party. No one may have said you had to go, but the assumption of your attendance is implicit.*

4. *The sanctity of freedom may need reaffirmation if people start taking it for granted or start taking freedoms away.*

Vocabulary Strategy: Words from Latin

Possible answers:

sanctus: *sanctify; to make sacred; verb; The priest will sanctify the marriage during the wedding ceremony.*

firmus: *firm; something that is strongly fixed in place; adjective; She took a firm stand against allowing her friends to be bullied.*

resilire: *resile; verb; to leap back to a previous position; I will resile on this issue if my conditions are not met.*

sentire: *sentient; adjective; to be able to feel or perceive; Many people disagree on whether animals are sentient beings.*

Strategies for Annotation 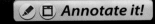 *Annotate it!*

Words from Latin

Have students locate the sentences containing *compulsion, implicit, reaffirmation, resilience, sanctity,* and *dissenter* in either the Supreme Court ruling or the newspaper editorial. Encourage them to use their eBook annotation tools to do the following:

- Highlight each vocabulary word.
- Underline the Latin root.
- Reread the sentence to determine the part of speech of the word and its meaning in the sentence.

What most distinguishes our civilization from both its predecessors and its contemporary competitors is a belief in the sanctity of the human conscience. Each individual is to have the freedom

Language and Style: Noun Clauses

COMMON CORE L 1b

Read through the examples in the chart. Then have students work with a partner to write a paragraph that includes a noun clause for each function. Upon completion, have pairs exchange papers and identify the noun clause and function in each example.

Possible answers:

Students' paragraphs will vary. Check that each paragraph includes noun clauses that act as subject, indirect object, predicate nominative, and object of a preposition.

Assess It!

Online Selection Test
- Download an editable ExamView bank.
- Assign and manage this test online.

Language and Style: Noun Clauses

COMMON CORE L 1b

An **independent clause** is a group of words with a subject and a verb that can stand alone as a complete sentence. By contrast, a **dependent** or **subordinate clause** also contains a subject and a verb, but it cannot stand alone as a sentence.

> **Independent clause:** I ran

> **Dependent or subordinate clause:** While I was running

Subordinate clauses help writers express complex and specific ideas while also adding variety and interest to their writing style. A **noun clause** is a type of subordinate clause that takes the place of a noun in a sentence.

The author of "American Flag Stands for Tolerance" uses noun clauses frequently to convey important information. Read this sentence from the editorial:

> In a controversial decision, the Supreme Court, by the closest possible margin of a 5-to-4 vote, held <u>that a person has a right to express disagreement with governmental policies by burning the American flag.</u>

In this sentence, the noun clause acts as the direct object of the verb *held*. It states an idea that could not be summed up in one or two words without sacrificing clarity and meaning. It is introduced by the pronoun *that* and contains its own subject (*person*) and verb (*has*).

Many words besides *that* can introduce noun clauses. In this chart, note the various introductory words and the way each noun clause functions in the example sentence.

Uses of Noun Clauses	
Function	**Example**
subject	**Why he wakes so early in the morning** is a mystery to his parents.
indirect object	I gave **whoever asked first** the prize.
predicate nominative	The fair is **what we wait for all year.**
object of a preposition	I wrote about **how we conducted the experiment.**

Practice and Apply Work with a partner to write a paragraph expressing your own thoughts about the ruling on flag burning. Include noun clauses that serve each of the four functions listed in the chart.

Analyze Themes in Seminal U.S. Documents

COMMON CORE

RI 1, RI 2, RI 9

TEACH

Explain that the Court's majority opinion *Texas v. Johnson* is a seminal U.S. document because it has helped establish and define the principles of our nation and our current way of life. Point out to students that these seminal documents are important not only because of their influence on later thought or actions, but also because of the themes, or topics, they address. Explain that seminal U.S. documents may address similar political concepts or national concerns.

- In order to determine theme, tell students to ask themselves what general message emerges from reading the document.
- Remind students that they can find clues to a document's theme by paying attention to supporting evidence in the text. In a document such as a court opinion, that evidence might take the form of court precedents, statutes, or the Constitution as well as the ideas the writer includes to explain why the evidence applies in the case.
- Tell students that repetition of terms or symbols often indicates emphasis and may help them determine the theme. Remind students that in *Texas v. Johnson*, the flag is discussed as a symbol for our country's values.

PRACTICE AND APPLY

Have students identify the themes in *Texas v. Johnson* and Roosevelt's "Four Freedoms" address on page R22. *(Texas v. Johnson: Freedom of speech and tolerance are two of our key principles; our strength comes from flexibility, not rigidity; the importance of persuasion over compulsion. "Four Freedoms": the four freedoms; importance of cooperation.)*

Display lines 26–36 of *Texas v. Johnson* on the board or a device. Have students identify any repeated terms or symbols. Ask them why Brennan emphasizes what the flag symbolizes. *(resilience; the flag; to show that it stands for our principles of freedom and inclusiveness)*

Have students reread the first five paragraphs of Roosevelt's speech and identify any terms that are repeated. Ask students what effect the repetition has. *(freedom; everywhere in the world; anywhere in the world; repetition clearly points out Roosevelt's theme of freedom)*

Finally, have students identify themes that are common to both documents. *(freedom of speech; tolerance and cooperation)*

Cite Evidence

COMMON CORE

RI 1

RETEACH

Remind students that writers express ideas both explicitly and implicitly. Review how writers use facts, statistics, examples, and expert opinions to support their arguments. Then review that readers make inferences by combining information in a text with personal knowledge or experience.

- Have students find examples of evidence used by both Brennan and Allen. *(Possible answers: Brennan refers to Abrams v. United States in lines 17–19; Allen points out how our freedoms are protected in the First Amendment in lines 33–34.)*
- Provide students with the following inference based on Brennan's opinion paper: *Brennan respects the opinion of Justice Holmes.* Ask: What text evidence can you cite to support this inference? *(Possible answer: When Brennan paraphrases Justice Holmes in lines 17–19, I can infer that Brennan respects Justice Holmes.)*

 LEVEL UP TUTORIALS Assign the following *Level Up* tutorial: **Evidence**

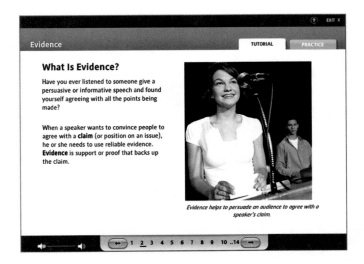

CLOSE READING APPLICATION

Students can apply the skill to a current magazine or newspaper editorial. Have them work independently to decide whether they agree with the writer's argument. Tell them to identify inferences they draw from the text, citing textual evidence that supports their inferences. Ask: Does the writer include enough evidence to make a strong argument? What makes me agree or disagree with the writer's argument?

from the Universal Declaration of Human Rights

Public Document by the UN Commission on Human Rights

Why This Text

The Universal Declaration of Human Rights is a landmark document in human history. The writing style, however, may be unfamiliar to students at any level of proficiency, as it is replete with legal jargon, rhetorical flourishes, and archaic turns of phrase. With the help of the close-reading questions, students will be able to unpack the content of this seminal document and examine its meaning, which is undeniably clear.

Background Have students read the background information about this document. Point out that the drafting committee included members from many nations and religious groups. As one member, Hernán Santa Cruz from Chile, reported, "a consensus was reached on the supreme value of a human person"—a value that was not based on the decision of a worldly power, but on the simple fact of a person's existence.

AS YOU READ Ask students to note the use of "*Whereas*" to introduce each point. Is there a substitute word or phrase they can use as they read to keep them focused on the meaning?

Common Core Support

- cite strong and thorough textual evidence
- determine a central idea of a text
- analyze the impact of specific word choices
- analyze a seminal document

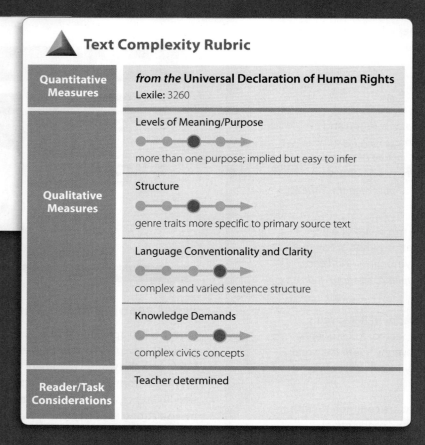

Text Complexity Rubric

Quantitative Measures	*from the* Universal Declaration of Human Rights Lexile: 3260
Qualitative Measures	**Levels of Meaning/Purpose** more than one purpose; implied but easy to infer
	Structure genre traits more specific to primary source text
	Language Conventionality and Clarity complex and varied sentence structure
	Knowledge Demands complex civics concepts
Reader/Task Considerations	Teacher determined

Analyze a Seminal Document

Students should read the document carefully all the way through. Close-reading questions at the bottom of the page will help them analyze the text. As they read, students should jot down comments or questions about the text in the margins.

WHEN STUDENTS STRUGGLE . . .

To help students analyze the text, have them work in small groups to fill out a chart like the one shown below.

CITE TEXT EVIDENCE For practice in analyzing a seminal document, have students paraphrase each section of text.

Text	Paraphrase
"Whereas recognition of the inherent dignity and of the equal and inalienable rights of all members of the human family . . ."	Everyone has the right to be treated with dignity, and no one can take these rights away.
"Whereas disregard and contempt for human rights have resulted in barbarous acts which have outraged the conscience of mankind . . ."	Human rights have been ignored, resulting in acts of violence that have shocked the world.
"Whereas . . . freedom of speech and belief and freedom from fear and want has been proclaimed as the highest aspiration of the common people . . . "	We all have the right to say and think what we choose, to live without fear, to have what we need in order to live.
"Whereas it is essential if man is not to be compelled to have recourse, as a last resort, to rebellion against tyranny and oppression, that human rights should be protected by the rule of law . . . "	We must protect human rights so that oppressed people won't have to resort to violent rebellion.

Background As people around the world discovered the atrocities committed against millions of innocent people in World War II, many wanted to create a universal statement of human rights. With the formation of the United Nations in 1945, this became a possibility. With guidance from the UN and First Lady Eleanor Roosevelt, Chairperson of the UN Commission on Human Rights, such a document was formulated, and adopted on December 10, 1948. Following is the Preamble to the Declaration, which consists of a series of statements beginning "Whereas . . . ." These statements provide a rationale for the Declaration; that is, they say why such a Declaration is necessary.

from the
Universal Declaration of Human Rights
Public Document by the UN Commission on Human Rights

CLOSE READ
Notes

1. **READ ▶** As you read lines 1–13, begin to collect and cite text evidence.
   - Underline what conditions are necessary for "freedom, justice, and peace."
   - Circle the text that describes the biggest goal of the people of the world.

Ⓐ Whereas recognition of the inherent dignity and of the equal and inalienable rights of all members of the human family is the foundation of freedom, justice and peace in the world,

Whereas disregard and contempt for human rights have resulted in barbarous acts which have outraged the conscience of mankind, and the advent of a world in which human beings shall enjoy freedom of speech and belief and freedom from fear and want has been proclaimed as the highest aspiration of the common people,

Ⓑ Whereas it is essential, if man is not to be compelled to have recourse, as a last resort, to rebellion against tyranny and oppression, that human rights should be protected by the rule of law,

Whereas it is essential to promote the development of friendly relations between nations,

inalienable:
not to be taken or given away

There will be rebellion, which can be violent.

2. **◀ REREAD** Reread lines 9–11. In the margin, explain what will happen without protection of human rights.

9

---

1. **READ AND CITE TEXT EVIDENCE**

Ⓐ **ASK STUDENTS** to count the references to all humankind in lines 1–13. What do these references suggest about the goals of the drafters? *They were aware that human rights for all was a new idea, and certain language had to be emphasized.*

2. **REREAD AND CITE TEXT EVIDENCE**

Ⓑ **ASK STUDENTS** what the word *compelled* (line 9) suggests about those who rebel against oppression. *An oppressed people—unless they have legal protection—have no other choice but to rebel against their oppressors.*

Critical Vocabulary: inalienable (line 2) Have students share their definitions of *inalienable*. What rights do they think should be inalienable under the law?

Whereas the people of the United Nations have in the Charter underline[reaffirmed their faith] in fundamental human rights, in the dignity and worth of the human person and in the equal rights of men and women and have determined to promote social progress and better standards of life in larger freedom,

20   Whereas Member States have pledged themselves to achieve, in co-operation with the United Nations, the promotion of universal respect for and observance of human rights and fundamental freedoms,

Whereas a common understanding of these rights and freedoms is of the greatest importance for the full realization of this pledge,

C D   Now, Therefore, THE GENERAL ASSEMBLY proclaims THIS UNIVERSAL DECLARATION OF HUMAN RIGHTS as a common standard of achievement for all people and all nations, to the end that every individual and every organ of society, keeping this Declaration constantly in mind, shall strive by teaching and education to promote respect for these rights and freedoms and by progressive measures, national and

30   international, to secure their universal and effective recognition and observance, both among the peoples of Member States themselves and among the peoples of territories under their **jurisdiction**.

jurisdiction:
the power to apply the law

3. **READ ▶** As you read lines 14–32, continue to cite textual evidence. Underline the values and goals of this document.

4. **◀ REREAD AND DISCUSS** Reread lines 24–32. With a small group, discuss the "call to action" in this paragraph. How might World War II have influenced the writers of this document?

SHORT RESPONSE

Cite Text Evidence A seminal document establishes or defines principles that shape the way others think or act. Why do you think the Preamble from the Universal Declaration of Human Rights is considered a seminal document? **Cite text evidence** from the document to support your claim.

It is a seminal document because it provides basic human rights to all people in all nations that are a part of the United Nations and under their jurisdiction. It also pledges to create a worldwide standard for human rights and respect in the aftermath of World War II.

10

TO CHALLENGE STUDENTS . . .

For more context and to deepen their understanding of the document, students can visit the Youth For Human Rights website. This organization seeks to teach young people about human rights—specifically the UN Declaration of Human Rights—both in the classroom and in nontraditional settings.

The website links to the Youth For Human Rights Videos, where students will find 30 human rights identified and put in the form of a bulleted list. The rights, which range from *We are all born free and equal* (Number 1), to *No one can take away your human rights* (Number 30) are pared down and reader-friendly. Then, each point links to a short video that captures the essence of that particular idea.

ASK STUDENTS to watch one of the videos and write a summary of the story, emphasizing the human right it represents.

---

3. **READ AND CITE TEXT EVIDENCE**

C ASK STUDENTS what *Therefore* (line 24) refers to and how it fits into rest of the document. *"Whereas . . ." is the first part of a complete thought; "therefore . . ." is the second part.*

4. **REREAD AND DISCUSS USING TEXT EVIDENCE**

D ASK STUDENTS to consider the way people felt after World War II. *They wanted to prevent a reoccurrence of such a war.*

Critical Vocabulary: jurisdiction (line 32) Have students use the word *jurisdiction* in sentences.

SHORT RESPONSE

Cite Text Evidence Students should:

- analyze the central idea of the Preamble.
- cite evidence of inclusiveness and universal appeal.

DIG DEEPER

With the class, return to Question 4, Reread and Discuss. Have students share the results of their discussion.

ASK STUDENTS to consider the last section of the document, which contains its central message.

- Have students discuss the fact that the document was written more than half a century ago, when the world was a very different place. What might the Declaration look like if it were written today?
- Have groups analyze the language in this section of text. What is meant by a "common standard of achievement"? How does one keep the "Declaration constantly in mind"? What are "progressive measures?"
- Have groups analyze the effectiveness of this document. Has it achieved its goal? If not, why not? Is there any document that can end human rights abuses worldwide?
- Have each group take one section of text and write a paraphrase, which can be the basis of an original document.
- Have students work collaboratively to update the document, adding points or altering content to make it more relevant to the challenges of today.

ASK STUDENTS to return to their Short Response answer and revise it based on the class discussion.

CLOSE READING NOTES

from **Towards a True Refuge**

Speech by Aung San Suu Kyi

Why This Text

Students may read or hear a speech without a complete understanding of the argument or ideas in the text. This speech by Aung San Suu Kyi uses difficult language and complex reasoning that becomes clear only by close analysis. Guide students to see that writers who express opinions about current political issues or events need to support their ideas with reasons and evidence. With the help of the close-reading questions, students will develop an understanding of Suu Kyi's argument about the need for justice and tolerance, security and peace.

Background Have students read the background and biographical information about Aung San Suu Kyi. Tell students that Suu Kyi had returned to Burma from overseas in 1988 to look after her dying mother. The country was controlled by a military junta—a group of military officers ruling a country—which put down any protests with extreme violence. Once Suu Kyi began speaking out, the junta quickly arrested her.

AS YOU READ Ask students to pay attention to the reasons, some directly stated, others implied, that Suu Kyi cites to support her position about the human desire for a "secure refuge." How soon into the speech can students begin to identify her position about the "greatest threats to global security"?

 Common Core Support

- cite strong and thorough textual evidence
- support inferences drawn from the text
- analyze the impact of specific word choices on meaning and tone

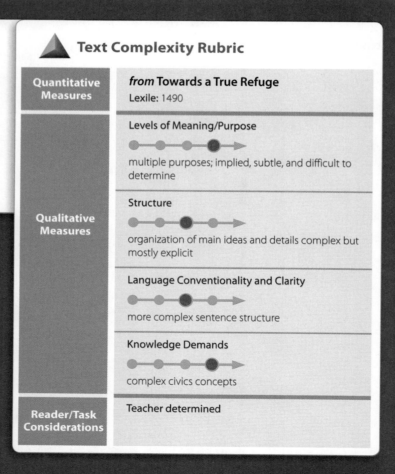

Text Complexity Rubric

Quantitative Measures	*from* **Towards a True Refuge** Lexile: 1490
Qualitative Measures	**Levels of Meaning/Purpose** multiple purposes; implied, subtle, and difficult to determine
	Structure organization of main ideas and details complex but mostly explicit
	Language Conventionality and Clarity more complex sentence structure
	Knowledge Demands complex civics concepts
Reader/Task Considerations	Teacher determined

Strategies for CLOSE READING

Cite Textual Evidence

Students should read this speech carefully all the way through. Close-reading questions at the bottom of the page will help them focus on a thorough analysis of the argument and on the evidence, including details, facts, examples, quotations, and expert opinions that support them. As they read, students should record comments or questions about the text in the side margins.

WHEN STUDENTS STRUGGLE . . .

To help students follow the reasons Aung San Suu Kyi cites to support her claim that a "true refuge" is a society ruled by reason and justice, have students work in a small group to fill out a chart such as the one shown below as they analyze the textual evidence in her speech.

CITE TEXT EVIDENCE For practice in tracing an argument, ask students to cite the evidence Suu Kyi uses to support each reason. Point out that in order for students to understand the implied meaning in her argument, they will need to identify textual evidence and combine it with their own prior knowledge and experience.

CLAIM: The greatest threat to global security is not economics but unfair, authoritarian governments.

SUPPORT:

Reason 1: Political dissensions and partisan interests, not economic deficiencies, account for human-made disasters.

Reason 2: There is no link between economic success and greater global security and peace.

Reason 3: No amount of material goods will buy peace, stability, unity, security, justice, and tolerance.

Reason 4: The drive for economic progress needs to be tempered with a society ruled by kindness, humanity, reason, and justice in order to promote a "true refuge."

Background Aung San Suu Kyi *is the chairperson of the National League for Democracy in Myanmar (formerly known as Burma). She was placed under house arrest for opposing the military government shortly before she received a majority of votes in Myanmar's 1990 general election. In 1991, she won the Nobel Peace Prize for her commitment to nonviolence, but was unable to accept the prize until 2012, after spending 15 years under house arrest. In 2012, Aung San Suu Kyi topped the Foreign Policy list of the Top 100 Global Thinkers. The following excerpt is from a speech she wrote during her time as a political prisoner.*

from Towards a True Refuge

Speech by Aung San Suu Kyi

CLOSE READ
Notes

1. **READk▶** As you read lines 1–16, begin to collect and cite text evidence.
   - Underline Suu Kyi's idea of the "greatest threats to global security."
   - Circle words describing things that do <u>not</u> lead to global security, or "true refuge."

It is perfectly natural that all people should wish for a secure refuge. It is unfortunate that in spite of strong evidence to the contrary, so many still act as though security would be guaranteed if they fortified themselves with an abundance of material possessions. The greatest threats to global security today come not from the economic deficiencies of the poorest nations but from religious, racial (or tribal) and political **dissensions** raging in those regions where principles and practices which could reconcile the diverse instincts and aspirations of mankind have been ignored, repressed or distorted. Man-made disasters are made by dominant individuals and

10 cliques which refuse to move beyond the autistic¹ confines of **partisan** interest. An eminent development economist has observed that the best defense against famine is an accountable government. It makes little political or economic sense to give aid without trying to address the circumstances that render aid ineffectual. No amount of material goods

¹ **autistic:** in this context, "self-centered."

dissensions:
differences of opinion

partisan:
factional; biased

11

---

1. **READ AND CITE TEXT EVIDENCE**

Ⓐ **ASK STUDENTS** to determine how Suu Kyi first identifies the "greatest threats to global security." *Suu Kyi identifies what the greatest threats to global security are not—they are not from economic shortcomings.*

Critical Vocabulary: dissensions (line 6) Have students share their definitions of *dissensions*. Ask how *dissensions* fits in with Suu Kyi's discussion of the "greatest threats to global security." *Suu Kyi believes that political differences of opinion are the outgrowth of governmental practices that have ignored human hopes.*

Critical Vocabulary: partisan (line 10) Ask students to explain *partisan* as Suu Kyi uses it here. Have them give examples of partisan politics they have witnessed. *Students should be able to point to blockages in Congress caused by one party's attempt to hinder the opposing party's legislation.*

CLOSE READ
Notes

You can't throw money at a problem that is rooted in human irresponsibility and expect it to get better.

and technological know how will compensate for human irresponsibility and viciousness.

(C) Developed and developing nations alike suffer as a result of policies removed from a framework of values which uphold minimum standards of justice and tolerance. The rapidity with which the old Soviet Union splintered into new states, many of them stamped with a fierce racial assertiveness, illustrates that decades of authoritarian rule may have achieved uniformity and obedience but could not achieve long-term harmony or stability. Nor did the material benefits enjoyed under the relatively successful post-totalitarian state of Yugoslavia succeed in dissipating the psychological impress of brooding historical experience that has now led to some of the worst religious and ethnic violence the Balkans have ever witnessed. Peace, stability and unity cannot be bought or coerced; they have to be nurtured by promoting a sensitivity to human needs and respect for the rights and opinions of others. Diversity and dissent need not inhibit the emergence of strong, stable societies, but inflexibility, narrowness and unadulterated materialism can prevent healthy growth. And when attitudes have been allowed to harden to the point that otherness becomes a sufficient reason for nullifying a person's claim to be treated as a fellow human being, the trappings of modern civilization crumble with frightening speed.

(D) In the most troubled areas of the world reserves of tolerance and compassion disappear, security becomes nonexistent and creature comforts are reduced to a minimum—but stockpiles of weapons abound. As a system of values this is totally mad. By the time it is accepted that the only way out of an impasse of hate, bloodshed and social and economic chaos created by men is for those men to get together to find a peaceful solution through dialogue and compromise, it is usually no longer easy to restore sanity. Those who have been conditioned by systems which make a mockery of the law by legalizing injustices and which attack the very foundations of harmony by perpetuating social, political and economic imbalances cannot adjust quickly—if at all—to the concept of a fair settlement which places general well-being and justice above partisan advantage.

2. **◄ REREAD** Reread lines 1–16. In the margin, paraphrase Suu Kyi's position in these lines.

3. **READ ►** As you read lines 17–47, continue to cite textual evidence.

• Underline the claims that Suu Kyi makes.
• Circle the evidence presented to support those claims.

12

During the Cold War the iniquities of ruthless governments and armed groups were condoned for ideological reasons. The results have been far from happy. Although there is greater emphasis on justice and human rights today, there are still ardent advocates in favor of giving priority to political and economic **expediency**—increasingly the latter. It is the old argument: achieve economic success and all else will follow. But even long-affluent societies are plagued by formidable social ills which have provoked deep anxieties about the future. And newly rich nations appear to be spending a significant portion of their wealth on arms and armies.

(E) Clearly there is no inherent link between greater prosperity and greater security and peace—or even the expectation of greater peace. Both prosperity and peace are necessary for the happiness of mankind, the one to alleviate suffering, the other to promote tranquility. Only policies that place equal importance on both will make a truly richer world, one in which men can enjoy *chantha*[2] of the body and of the mind. The drive for economic progress needs to be tempered with an awareness of the dangers of greed and selfishness which so easily lead to narrowness and inhumanity. If peoples and nations cultivate a generous spirit which welcomes the happiness of others as an enhancement of the happiness of the self, many seemingly insoluble problems would prove less **intractable**.

Those who have worked with refugees are in the best position to know that when people have been stripped of all their material supports, there only remain to sustain them the values of their cultural and spiritual inheritance. A tradition of sharing instilled by age-old beliefs in the joy of giving and the sanctity of compassion will move a homeless destitute to press a portion of his meager ration on strangers with all the grace and delight of one who has ample riches to dispense. On the other hand, predatory traits honed by a long-established habit of yielding to "every urge

[2] *chantha*: prosperity and general happiness.

expediency:
the use of means to bring about a desired result, often without regard to what is fair or right

intractable:
not easily relieved or cured

4. **◄ REREAD** Reread lines 36–47. Think about Suu Kyi's choice of words here. How would you describe her tone in this paragraph?

Suu Kyi's tone is impassioned; her choice of words show her frustration with the way things work in troubled areas of the world. She says that restoring sanity where there are so many weapons and injustice has been legalized cannot happen easily or quickly.

5. **READ ►** As you read lines 48–92, underline sentences in which the author both presents solutions and provides evidence.

13

---

2. **REREAD AND CITE TEXT EVIDENCE**

(B) ASK STUDENTS to explain Suu Kyi's point about what others claim to be threatening global security. *She doesn't view the threats as being economic but sees them as the result of unfair governments that have ignored or suppressed people's hopes and dreams.*

3. **READ AND CITE TEXT EVIDENCE** Suu Kyi claims that nations that are unjust and intolerant must find a peaceful solution through dialogue and compromise.

(C) ASK STUDENTS to locate specific examples she presents in the text that support her claims. *Students should cite specific examples from lines 19–20, 23–24, 32, and 36–38.*

FOR ELL STUDENTS Explain that *rule, point, claim, mad,* and *general* are multiple-meaning words. Ask students to give two meanings for each of the words. Then have them use both meanings of each word in one or more sentences.

4. **REREAD AND CITE TEXT EVIDENCE**

(D) ASK STUDENTS to think about Suu Kyi's word choice and how it influences the tone of the speech. *Students should cite evidence such as "totally mad" (line 39) and "restore sanity" (line 42).*

5. **READ AND CITE TEXT EVIDENCE**

(E) ASK STUDENTS to cite the solutions Suu Kyi presents and the textual evidence she provides to support them. *Students should cite specific references to lines 58–60, 65–67, 71–74, and 81–92.*

Critical Vocabulary: expediency (line 52) Encourage students to share their definitions of *expediency* and to cite things they have done for the sake of expediency.

Critical Vocabulary: intractable (line 67) Ask students to explain *intractable* as Suu Kyi uses it here. *She uses it to describe problems that can be difficult to treat or solve.*

of nature which made self-serving the essence of human life" will lead men to plunder fellow sufferers of their last pathetic possessions.

And of course the great majority of the world's refugees are seeking

dearth:
scarcity; lack

sanctuary from situations rendered untenable by a **dearth** of humanity

80 and wisdom.

F **G** The dream of a society ruled by loving kindness, reason and justice is a dream as old as civilized man. Does it have to be an impossible dream? Karl Popper,[3] explaining his abiding optimism in so troubled a world as ours, said that the darkness had always been there but the light was new. Because it is new it has to be tended with care and diligence. It is true that even the smallest light cannot be extinguished by all the darkness in the world because darkness is wholly negative. It is merely an absence of light. But a small light cannot dispel acres of encircling gloom. It needs to grow stronger, to shed its brightness further and further. And people need to

90 accustom their eyes to the light to see it as a benediction[4] rather than a pain, to learn to love it. We are so much in need of a brighter world which will offer adequate refuge to all its inhabitants.

[3] **Karl Popper** (1902–1994): a Viennese-born philosopher who became a British subject.
[4] **benediction:** blessing.

6. **READID** ▶ Read lines 81–92 and underline Suu Kyi's hopes for the future.

7. ◀ **REREAD AND DISCUSS** Reread lines 81–92. With a small group, discuss Suu Kyi's conclusion. What does the word *light* mean in her conclusion? How can light grow enough to overcome darkness?

SHORT RESPONSE

Cite Text Evidence What is Aung San Suu Kyi arguing for and against? How does her word choice and tone affect her overall meaning? Review your reading notes and **cite text evidence** in your response.

Suu Kyi argues in favor of governments guided by values such as "the joy of giving and the sanctity of compassion." She argues against over-valuing economic success, as well as partisan interests, authoritarian rule, and legalized injustices. Her language is symbolic, and inspiring, such as her use of the word light. She inspires her listeners to "learn to love it," suggesting that she is not offering a vague comfort, but a noble challenge.

14

---

6. READ AND CITE TEXT EVIDENCE

F **ASK STUDENTS** to explain what Suu Kyi hopes for. *She hopes for a society governed by "loving kindness, reason and justice."*

7. REREAD AND DISCUSS USING TEXT EVIDENCE

G **ASK STUDENTS** to appoint a reporter for each group to explain its conclusion. *Students should cite evidence from lines 81–92—Suu Kyi defines darkness as an "absence of light."*

Critical Vocabulary: dearth (line 79) How does *dearth* fit into Suu Kyi's discussion of refugees seeking sanctuary?

SHORT RESPONSE

Cite Text Evidence Students should:

- explain what Suu Kyi is arguing for and against.
- describe how word choice and tone affect the overall meaning.
- cite specific evidence from the text.

TO CHALLENGE STUDENTS . . .

For more context, have students research Suu Kyi and the country of Myanmar (formerly known as Burma).

ASK STUDENTS why Suu Kyi, an opposition political leader, might be in recent headlines. *Students should recognize that Aung San Suu Kyi is a national hero of Myanmar and is recognized all over the world as a leader of freedom and democracy.*

DIG DEEPER

With the class, return to Question 7, Reread and Discuss. Have students share the results of their discussion.

ASK STUDENTS whether they were satisfied with the outcome of their small-group discussions. Have each group share what they discussed about Suu Kyi's use of the term *light* in her conclusion. What evidence did the groups cite from lines 81–92 to support their opinion?

- What reasons does Suu Kyi give for optimism about light in the world? *She explains that the light is new. Even though it may be small, it is not in danger from darkness, which is merely an absence of light.*

- What does Suu Kyi say should be done with the light we have? *She says that we should nourish it and make it grow. We should revel in the light and love it.*

- How does the word *brighter* convey different levels of meaning in Suu Kyi's conclusion? *It relates to the light that she has been using as a metaphor. It also suggests that the brighter things are, the less room there is to hide inhumanity. The word bright is often used to describe a happy disposition or mood.*

ASK STUDENTS to return to their Short Response answer to revise it based on the class discussion.

The Lottery

Short Story by Shirley Jackson

Why This Text?

Students regularly encounter literature and nonfiction in which the writer creates tone and meaning through word choice and style. This lesson gives students an opportunity to evaluate how a writer's word choices create a specific tone.

View It!

Professional Development Podcast:

Text-Dependent Analysis

Key Learning Objective: The student will be able to analyze a writer's choices in terms of pacing, word choice, tone, and mood.

Common Core Standards

RL 1 Cite textual evidence.
RL 2 Determine a theme and analyze its development.
RL 3 Analyze how complex characters develop, interact, and advance the plot.
RL 4 Determine the meaning of words and phrases.
RL 5 Analyze how an author's choices create mystery, tension, or surprise.
W 1 Write arguments using valid reasoning and relevant evidence.
W 1d Establish and maintain a formal style and objective tone.
L 3 Apply language in different contexts to make choices for style, and to comprehend more fully.
L 4a Use context as a clue to the meaning of a word.
L 5b Analyze nuances in words with similar denotations.

Text Complexity Rubric

Quantitative Measures	**The Lottery** Lexile: 1140L
Qualitative Measures	**Levels of Meaning/Purpose** multiple levels of meaning (multiple themes)
	Structure conventional story structure
	Language Conventionality and Clarity some figurative language
	Knowledge Demands experience includes unfamiliar aspects
Reader/Task Considerations	Teacher determined Vary by individual reader and type of text

Shirley Jackson Have students read the information about the author. Tell students that Jackson lived in and raised her family in a village similar to the one she portrays in her story. On the day she wrote "The Lottery," she had wheeled her toddler in a stroller through the village to complete a number of errands. After pushing the stroller up a hill to her home, Jackson sat down and wrote the story in two hours. About that day, Jackson said, "Perhaps the effort of that last fifty yards up the hill put an edge on the story. It was a warm morning, and the hill was steep."

AS YOU READ Direct students to use the As You Read directions to focus their reading. Remind students to note any questions they have as they read.

Make Inferences (LINES 1–10) COMMON CORE **RL 1**

Explain that readers can draw conclusions about setting, characters, and plot based on information and details in the text. Tell students they can make inferences by evaluating words and phrases in the selection.

 ASK STUDENTS to reread the first paragraph and explain what they can infer about the village and its people. *(The village is small and people likely know one another. Life will continue as normal after the lottery.)*

CRITICAL VOCABULARY

profusely: Jackson describes a lush summer day. **ASK STUDENTS** to explain how the presence of profusely blooming flowers affects their expectations of what might happen in the story. *(The presence of many flowers in bloom suggests a beautiful place where good things happen.)*

Analyze Impact of Word Choice: Tone (LINES 1–18) COMMON CORE **RL 4**

Explain that tone is the attitude of the narrator toward setting, characters, and the action of the story. Examples of tone include sarcastic, formal, informal, indifferent, sentimental, reverent, irreverent, serious, and humorous. Ask students to note the narrator's attitude as they read.

 ASK STUDENTS to describe the tone on page 25. *(The tone is calm and factual. The narrator describes the setting and people in a distant and removed manner.)*

Shirley Jackson (1919–1965) *said about her writing, "It's great fun and I love it." Although some of her works humorously chronicle her life with her husband and four children, she is best known for exploring the darker side of human nature. Her story "The Lottery" ignited controversy when it was published in* The New Yorker *in 1948. Readers cancelled their subscriptions and sent hundreds of letters expressing their outrage over the tale. Her novel* The Haunting of Hill House, *considered by many to be the "greatest haunted house story ever written," and the gothic horror tale* We Have Always Lived in the Castle *have been adapted for film and stage and are still widely read.*

The Lottery
Short Story by Shirley Jackson

AS YOU READ Pay attention to details that reveal the purpose of the lottery and the villagers' reactions to it. Note any questions you have.

The morning of June 27th was clear and sunny, with the fresh warmth of a full-summer day; the flowers were blossoming **profusely** and the grass was richly green. The people of the village began to gather in the square, between the post office and the bank, around ten o'clock; in some towns there were so many people that the lottery took two days and had to be started on June 26th, but in this village, where there were only about three hundred people, the whole lottery look less than two hours, so it could begin at ten o'clock in the morning and still be through in time to allow the villagers to get home for noon dinner.

10 The children assembled first, of course. School was recently over for the summer, and the feeling of liberty sat uneasily on most of them; they tended to gather together quietly for a while before they broke into boisterous play, and their talk was still of the classroom and the teacher, of books and reprimands. Bobby Martin had already stuffed his pockets full of stones, and the other boys soon followed his example, selecting the smoothest and roundest stones; Bobby and Harry Jones and Dickie Delacroix—the villagers

profusely
(prə-fyōōs′ lē) *adv.* plentifully, in a freely available way.

SCAFFOLDING FOR ELL STUDENTS

Make Inferences Using a whiteboard, project the first paragraph of the story. Have students mark up the first paragraph.

- Underline details about the setting.
- Highlight in yellow the details about the villagers.
- Highlight in green the details about the lottery itself.

ASK STUDENTS What can you infer about the lottery and why?

> began to gather in the square, between the post office and the bank,
>
> around ten o'clock; in some towns there were so many people that

Analyze Language   COMMON CORE **L 3**

(LINES 38–40)

Point out the use of the passive voice in the first sentence of this paragraph. Explain that the passive voice is often used to remove the connection between the doer of the action and the action itself.

C **ASK STUDENTS** why the author might have chosen to write this sentence in passive voice. *(Perhaps the author wanted to suggest that the lottery is more important than the person who conducts it.)*

Analyze Character Development (LINES 40–53) COMMON CORE **RL 3**

Guide students in a discussion of the different ways that writers develop characters (through dialogue, direct description, interactions with other characters).

D **ASK STUDENTS** to describe Mr. Summers based on his responsibilities and the way that others react to him. *(He is a leader in the community, and while people are not eager to see him in this capacity, they follow his direction.)*

pronounced this name "Dellacroy"—eventually made a great

20 pile of stones in one corner of the square and guarded it against the raids of the other boys. The girls stood aside, talking among themselves, looking over their shoulders at the boys, and the very small children rolled in the dust or clung to the hands of their older brothers or sisters.

Soon the men began to gather, surveying their own children, speaking of planting and rain, tractors and taxes. They stood together, away from the pile of stones in the corner, and their jokes were quiet and they smiled rather than laughed. The women, wearing faded house dresses and sweaters, came shortly after

30 their menfolk. They greeted one another and exchanged bits of gossip as they went to join their husbands. Soon the women, standing by their husbands, began to call to their children, and the children came reluctantly, having to be called four or five times. Bobby Martin ducked under his mother's grasping hand and ran, laughing, back to the pile of stones. His father spoke up sharply, and Bobby came quickly and took his place between his father and his oldest brother.

C The lottery was conducted—as were the square dances, the teenage club, the Halloween program—by Mr. Summers, who had

D 40 time and energy to devote to civic activities. He was a round-faced, jovial man and he ran the coal business, and people were sorry for him, because he had no children and his wife was a scold. When he arrived in the square, carrying the black wooden box, there was a murmur of conversation among the villagers, and he waved and called, "Little late today, folks." The postmaster, Mr. Graves, followed him, carrying a three-legged stool, and the stool was put in the center of the square and Mr. Summers set the black box down on it. The villagers kept their distance, leaving a space between themselves and the stool, and when Mr. Summers said, "Some of

50 you fellows want to give me a hand?" there was a hesitation before two men, Mr. Martin and his oldest son, Baxter, came forward to hold the box steady on the stool while Mr. Summers stirred up the papers inside it.

The original paraphernalia[1] for the lottery had been lost long ago, and the black box now resting on the stool had been put into use even before Old Man Warner, the oldest man in town, was born. Mr. Summers spoke frequently to the villagers about making a new box, but no one liked to upset even as much tradition as was represented by the black box. There was a story that the present box **F**

E 60 had been made with some pieces of the box that had preceded it, the one that had been constructed when the first people settled down

---

[1] **paraphernalia:** necessary items and equipment for a particular activity.

APPLYING ACADEMIC VOCABULARY

discriminate

As you discuss Jackson's short story, incorporate the following Collection 1 academic vocabulary word: *discriminate*. To develop an understanding of the characters as they first gather, ask students to describe how the writer uses the actions of the men, women, boys, and girls to **discriminate** among the groups.

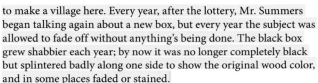

to make a village here. Every year, after the lottery, Mr. Summers began talking again about a new box, but every year the subject was allowed to fade off without anything's being done. The black box grew shabbier each year; by now it was no longer completely black but splintered badly along one side to show the original wood color, and in some places faded or stained.

Mr. Martin and his oldest son, Baxter, held the black box securely on the stool until Mr. Summers had stirred the papers
70 thoroughly with his hand. Because so much of the ritual had been forgotten or discarded, Mr. Summers had been successful in having slips of paper substituted for the chips of wood that had been used for generations. Chips of wood, Mr. Summers had argued, had been all very well when the village was tiny, but now that the population was more than three hundred and likely to keep on growing, it was necessary to use something that would fit more easily into the black box. The night before the lottery, Mr. Summers and Mr. Graves made up the slips of paper and put them in the box, and it was then taken to the safe of Mr. Summers' coal company and locked up

Analyze Impact of Word Choice: Tone (LINES 59–79)
COMMON CORE RL 4

Tell students that writers often make deliberate word choices when describing characters, setting, and events in order to create a tone that carries throughout an entire piece.

E **ASK STUDENTS** to explain the tone, or attitude, expressed in lines 59–79. (*The tone is neutral or detached with actions described in a factual and nonjudgmental manner. The narrator states that the subject of a new box "was allowed to fade off" rather than describe the villagers' reactions to the idea. Details of preparing the box are reported without revealing whether the narrator approves or disapproves.*)

Identify Symbols and Theme (LINES 59–67)
COMMON CORE RL 2

Explain that a symbol is something that represents something else, such as an idea or theme. Sometimes writers use symbols to develop the main idea or theme of a story.

F **CITE TEXT EVIDENCE** Have students discuss what the box might symbolize and cite evidence from the passage for support. Then have students suggest an unspoken message that Jackson wants to convey to the reader about the lottery. (*The box represents the past itself, the people's need to stay connected to their past. The text states that the box has grown shabbier each year and that it has not been replaced or refinished. The poor condition of the box suggests that the villagers may have mixed feelings about the lottery.*)

SCAFFOLDING FOR ELL STUDENTS

Identify Symbols and Theme Help students tell the meaning of each phrase in lines 62–64. Explain that this will help them understand a message that Jackson wants to convey about the lottery by writing about the box.

- Every year, *(how often the event occurs)*
- after the lottery, *(when the lottery is over)*
- Mr. Summers began talking again about a new box, *(event continues to happen)*
- but every year the subject was allowed to fade off *(the cause of what results from Mr. Summers talking about a new box; "to fade off" means to gradually end)*
- without anything's being done. *(This is the result: nothing changed.)*

CLOSE READ

Analyze Author's Choices: Tension and Surprise

 COMMON CORE RL 5

(LINES 85–104)

Explain that the pacing of a story is how quickly or slowly the author moves the action along. Changes in pacing affect the story's mood.

G **ASK STUDENTS** to reread the paragraph and discuss the pacing and its overall effect on the story. *(This section slows the story down by interrupting the flow of events with details about conducting the lottery and Mr. Summers. It creates suspense because the reader knows the lottery is important but doesn't know the point of the lottery.)*

Use Context Clues

COMMON CORE L 4a

(LINES 100–104)

Describe how words and phrases surrounding a word can be used to determine the meaning of a word. Point out that while there may be enough information within a sentence, sometimes the reader needs to look at a larger context, such as a paragraph or section of text.

H **ASK STUDENTS** to read lines 100–106 and then explain what it means to talk *interminably*. *(To talk interminably means to talk endlessly. The phrase "finally left off talking" is a clue to the word's meaning.)*

CRITICAL VOCABULARY

perfunctory: The writer describes lottery rituals that occurred in the past.

ASK STUDENTS what a "perfunctory chant" might suggest about past lotteries. *(People participate because they have to; there is little interest in the ceremonial aspects of it.)*

---

80 until Mr. Summers was ready to take it to the square next morning. The rest of the year, the box was put away, sometimes one place, sometimes another; it had spent one year in Mr. Graves's barn and another year underfoot in the post office, and sometimes it was set on a shelf in the Martin grocery and left there.

G There was a great deal of fussing to be done before Mr. Summers declared the lottery open. There were the lists to make up—of heads of families, heads of households in each family, members of each household in each family. There was the proper swearing-in of Mr. Summers by the postmaster, as the official of 90 the lottery; at one time, some people remembered, there had been a recital of some sort, performed by the official of the lottery, a **perfunctory**, tuneless chant that had been rattled off duly each year; some people believed that the official of the lottery used to stand just so when he said or sang it, others believed that he was supposed to walk among the people, but years and years ago this part of the ritual had been allowed to lapse. There had been, also, a ritual salute, which the official of the lottery had had to use in addressing each person who came up to draw from the box, but this also had changed with time, until now it was felt necessary only for 100 the official to speak to each person approaching. Mr. Summers was very good at all this; in his clean white shirt and blue jeans, with one hand resting carelessly on the black box, he seemed very proper and important as he talked interminably to Mr. Graves and the **H** Martins.

Just as Mr. Summers finally left off talking and turned to the assembled villagers, Mrs. Hutchinson came hurriedly along the path to the square, her sweater thrown over her shoulders, and slid into place in the back of the crowd. "Clean forgot what day it was," **I** she said to Mrs. Delacroix, who stood next to her, and they both 110 laughed softly. "Thought my old man was out back stacking wood," Mrs. Hutchinson went on, "and then I looked out the window and the kids was gone, and then I remembered it was the twenty-seventh and came a-running." She dried her hands on her apron, and Mrs. Delacroix said. "You're in time, though. They're still talking away up there."

Mrs. Hutchinson craned her neck to see through the crowd and found her husband and children standing near the front. She tapped Mrs. Delacroix on the arm as a farewell and began to make her way through the crowd. The people separated good-humoredly 120 to let her through; two or three people said, in voices just loud enough to be heard across the crowd, "Here comes your Missus, Hutchinson," and "Bill, she made it after all." Mrs. Hutchinson reached her husband, and Mr. Summers, who had been waiting, said cheerfully, "Thought we were going to have to get on without

perfunctory
(pər-fŭngk´tə-rē)
adj. done mechanically and without enthusiasm.

Strategies for Annotation    *Annotate it!*

Analyze Author's Choices: Tension and Surprise

COMMON CORE RL 5

Have students use their eBook annotation tools to analyze the text. Ask them to do the following:

- Highlight in blue the paragraph that begins with line 85.
- Underline dialogue or sentences written in active voice.
- Write a note explaining how the paragraph affects the pace of the story.

you, Tessie." Mrs. Hutchinson said, grinning, "Wouldn't have me leave m'dishes in the sink, now, would you, Joe?," and soft laughter ran through the crowd as the people stirred back into position after Mrs. Hutchinson's arrival.

"Well, now," Mr. Summers said soberly, "guess we better get
130 started, get this over with, so's we can go back to work. Anybody ain't here?"

"Dunbar," several people said. "Dunbar, Dunbar."

Mr. Summers consulted his list. "Clyde Dunbar," he said. "That's right. He's broke his leg, hasn't he? Who's drawing for him?"

"Me, I guess," a woman said, and Mr. Summers turned to look at her. "Wife draws for her husband," Mr. Summers said. "Don't you have a grown boy to do it for you, Janey?" Although Mr. Summers and everyone else in the village knew the answer perfectly well, it was the business of the official of the lottery to ask such questions
140 formally. Mr. Summers waited with an expression of polite interest while Mrs. Dunbar answered.

"Horace's not but sixteen yet," Mrs. Dunbar said regretfully. "Guess I gotta fill in for the old man this year."

"Right," Mr. Summers said. He made a note on the list he was holding. Then he asked, "Watson boy drawing this year?"

A tall boy in the crowd raised his hand. "Here," he said. "I'm drawing for m'mother and me." He blinked his eyes nervously and ducked his head as several voices in the crowd said things like "Good fellow, Jack," and "Glad to see your mother's got a man to
150 do it."

"Well," Mr. Summers said, "guess that's everyone. Old Man Warner make it?"

"Here," a voice said, and Mr. Summers nodded.

A sudden hush fell on the crowd as Mr. Summers cleared his throat and looked at the list. "All ready?" he called. "Now, I'll read the names—heads of families first—and the men come up and take a paper out of the box. Keep the paper folded in your hand without looking at it until everyone has had a turn. Everything clear?"

The people had done it so many times that they only half
160 listened to the directions; most of them were quiet, wetting their lips, not looking around. Then Mr. Summers raised one hand high and said, "Adams." A man disengaged himself from the crowd and came forward. "Hi, Steve," Mr. Summers said, and Mr. Adams said, "Hi, Joe." They grinned at one another humorlessly and nervously. Then Mr. Adams reached into the black box and took out a folded paper. He held it firmly by one corner as he turned and went hastily back to his place in the crowd, where he stood a little apart from his family, not looking down at his hand.

"Allen," Mr. Summers said. "Anderson. . . . Bentham."

The Lottery   29

CLOSE READ

Language and Style: Colloquialisms (LINES 105–115)

COMMON CORE **L 3**

Point out that writers use colloquialisms in dialogue to develop characters. Explain that colloquialisms are regional expressions that sometimes are not standard English.

ASK STUDENTS to point out examples of colloquialisms in lines 105–115 and explain what they tell the reader about the characters in the story. *(Colloquialisms include "clean forgot," "old man," "came a-running." They help to place the characters in a small village.)*

Analyze Impact of Word Choice: Tone (LINES 159–168)

COMMON CORE **RL 4**

Point out that the words an author uses to describe characters and action often help to set the tone of a story. Point out that what an author chooses not to include can also help to set the tone.

CITE TEXT EVIDENCE Have students re-read lines 159–168 and have them describe the tone. *(calm, factual, unsympathetic)* Then have them cite words that led them to that conclusion. *(The tone is calm and matter of fact. Instead of using words with a lot of connotation, the narrator uses spare, neutral language, as if deliberately withholding judgment about what is happening: "most of them were quiet"; "man disengaged himself"; "went hastily"; "stood apart".)*

There was a great deal of fussing to be done before Mr. Summers declared the lottery open. There were the lists to make up—of heads of families, heads of households in each family, members of each household in each family. There was the proper swearing-in of Mr. Summers by the postmaster, as the official of the lottery; at one time, some people remembered, there had been

Nothing is underlined because there are no sentences written in active voice or dialogue. This slows the pace of the story.

Analyze Details in the Text (LINES 191–204)

COMMON CORE RL 3

Explain that the views of the characters may reveal the writer's own viewpoint, possibly in support of the characters or by showing some sort of flaw in the characters' views.

K CITE TEXT EVIDENCE Have students cite text evidence that shows how Old Man Warner feels about the lottery. *(He thinks it is important to keep the lottery going because "There has always been a lottery" [line 200]. He thinks that giving up the lottery and "listening to young folks" in the north village will cause their society to decline [lines 195–199].)* As students read and learn more about the lottery, have them think back to this dialogue as they analyze the writer's viewpoint.

170   "Seems like there's no time at all between lotteries any more," Mrs. Delacroix said to Mrs. Graves in the back row. "Seems like we got through with the last one only last week."

"Time sure goes fast," Mrs. Graves said.

"Clark. . . . Delacroix."

"There goes my old man," Mrs. Delacroix said. She held her breath while her husband went forward.

"Dunbar," Mr. Summers said, and Mrs. Dunbar went steadily to the box while one of the women said, "Go on, Janey," and another said, "There she goes."

180   "We're next," Mrs. Graves said. She watched while Mr. Graves came around from the side of the box, greeted Mr. Summers gravely, and selected a slip of paper from the box. By now, all through the crowd there were men holding the small folded papers in their large hands, turning them over and over nervously. Mrs. Dunbar and her two sons stood together, Mrs. Dunbar holding the slip of paper.

"Harburt. . . . Hutchinson."

"Get up there, Bill," Mrs. Hutchinson said, and the people near her laughed.

190   "Jones."

"They do say," Mr. Adams said to Old Man Warner, who stood next to him, "that over in the north village they're talking of giving up the lottery."

WHEN STUDENTS STRUGGLE . . .

Students may have trouble keeping track of the characters, particularly in cases where characters are referred to by different names. To guide students in keeping track, have them create a chart like the one shown and complete it as they read.

K Old Man Warner snorted. "Pack of crazy fools," he said. "Listening to the young folks, nothing's good enough for *them*. Next thing you know, they'll be wanting to go back to living in caves, nobody work any more, live *that* way for a while. Used to be a saying about 'Lottery in June, corn be heavy soon.' First thing you know, we'd all be eating stewed chickweed and acorns.

200 There's *always* been a lottery," he added **petulantly**. "Bad enough to see young Joe Summers up there joking with everybody."

"Some places have already quit lotteries," Mrs. Adams said.

"Nothing but trouble in *that*," Old Man Warner said stoutly. "Pack of young fools."

"Martin." And Bobby Martin watched his father go forward. "Overdyke. . . . Percy."

"I wish they'd hurry," Mrs. Dunbar said to her older son. "I wish they'd hurry."

"They're almost through," her son said.

210 "You get ready to run tell Dad," Mrs. Dunbar said.

Mr. Summers called his own name and then stepped forward precisely and selected a slip from the box. Then he called, "Warner."

"Seventy-seventh year I been in the lottery," Old Man Warner said as he went through the crowd. "Seventy-seventh time."

"Watson." The tall boy came awkwardly through the crowd. Someone said, "Don't be nervous, Jack," and Mr. Summers said, "Take your time, son."

"Zanini."

After that, there was a long pause, a breathless pause, until **L**

220 Mr. Summers, holding his slip of paper in the air, said, "All right, fellows." For a minute, no one moved, and then all the slips of paper were opened. Suddenly, all the women began to speak at once, saying, "Who is it?," "Who's got it?," "Is it the Dunbars?," "Is it the Watsons?" Then the voices began to say, "It's Hutchinson. It's Bill," "Bill Hutchinson's got it."

"Go tell your father," Mrs. Dunbar said to her older son. People began to look around to see the Hutchinsons. Bill Hutchinson was standing quiet, staring down at the paper in his hand. Suddenly, Tessie Hutchinson shouted to Mr. Summers, "You didn't give him

M 230 time enough to take any paper he wanted. I saw you. It wasn't fair!"

"Be a good sport, Tessie," Mrs. Delacroix called, and Mrs. Graves said, "All of us took the same chance."

"Shut up, Tessie," Bill Hutchinson said.

"Well, everyone," Mr. Summers said, "that was done pretty fast, and now we've got to be hurrying a little more to get done in time." He consulted his next list. "Bill," he said, "you draw

petulantly
(pĕch´ə-lənt-lē) *adv.* in a grouchy or bad-tempered way.

The Lottery **31**

Character Name(s)	Description	Additional Details
Mr. Summers	runs the lottery	a leader; people respect him
Hutchinson, Bill, Mr. Hutchinson	tells his wife to stop complaining	is very matter-of-fact about what is happening
Tessie, Mrs. Hutchinson	"wins" the lottery	is fearful, blames others

CLOSE READ

Analyze Author's Choices: Tension and Surprise
COMMON CORE RL 5

(LINES 219–225)

Tell students that a story's pacing affects the reader's experience. For example, as the action picks up pace, the reader may become more excited or eager to read more quickly.

L **CITE TEXT EVIDENCE** Have students cite words or phrases that change the story's pacing. *(In lines 219–221, the pace is slow. Evidence: "long pause," "breathless pause," "For a minute, no one moved." The pace quickens at line 222 when the women begin to speak at once.)*

Analyze Character Development (LINES 228–243)
COMMON CORE RL 3

Explain that one way to evaluate characters in a story is to note how the author develops the character and how the character's actions develop the theme.

M **ASK STUDENTS** to describe Mrs. Hutchinson's behavior and the reaction from the other villagers. Then have students compare their observations with their earlier perceptions of the characters. *(Mrs. Hutchinson is upset and shouts out that the drawing wasn't fair. Others act as if they want matters to proceed as in previous lotteries. Even her husband tells her to shut up. People don't seem as friendly as they did earlier.)*

CRITICAL VOCABULARY

petulantly: Old Man Warner is clearly upset about the idea of making changes to the lottery.

ASK STUDENTS to read Old Man Warner's dialogue aloud, using tone and inflection to demonstrate what it means to speak *petulantly*.

CLOSE READ

Determine Central Idea and Details

COMMON CORE **RL 2**

(LINES 237–249)

Writers often use precise details to develop a work's theme.

** ASK STUDENTS** to examine the discussion of households and families in lines 237–249. Then ask them to explain what Mr. Summers means when he distinguishes between family and household. *(The family is a person's entire lineage, but the household refers to the people who live together.)* Then ask students to explain why Jackson chose to include this information. *(Jackson wants the reader to understand exactly how the lottery works. It's an old-fashioned notion that women go to live with their husbands' families, and Jackson may want the reader to have that in mind while reading the rest of the story.)*

Analyze Author's Choices: Tension and Surprise

COMMON CORE **RL 5**

(LINES 237–287)

Explain that one way a writer creates tension is to withhold information about the significance of events or characters' actions.

CITE TEXT EVIDENCE Have students cite examples where Jackson doesn't explain the action or what characters say and do. *(Tessie is upset [line 243] and repeats that the drawing isn't fair [lines 259–260]; the Hutchinson household's papers are collected and put back in the box [lines 261–262]; each member of the household draws another slip [lines 271–287].)*

---

for the Hutchinson family. You got any other households in the Hutchinsons?"

"There's Don and Eva," Mrs. Hutchinson yelled. "Make *them* 240 take their chance!"

"Daughters draw with their husbands' families, Tessie," Mr. Summers said gently. "You know that as well as anyone else."

"It wasn't *fair*," Tessie said.

"I guess not, Joe," Bill Hutchinson said regretfully. "My daughter draws with her husband's family, that's only fair. And I've got no other family except the kids."

"Then, as far as drawing for families is concerned, it's you," Mr. Summers said in explanation, "and as far as drawing for households is concerned, that's you, too. Right?"

250 "Right," Bill Hutchinson said.

"How many kids, Bill?" Mr. Summers asked formally.

''Three," Bill Hutchinson said. "There's Bill, Jr., and Nancy, and little Dave. And Tessie and me."

"All right, then," Mr. Summers said. "Harry, you got their tickets back?"

Mr. Graves nodded and held up the slips of paper. "Put them in the box, then," Mr. Summers directed. "Take Bill's and put it in."

"I think we ought to start over," Mrs. Hutchinson said, as quietly as she could. "I tell you it wasn't *fair*. You didn't give him 260 time enough to choose. *Every*body saw that."

Mr. Graves had selected the five slips and put them in the box, and he dropped all the papers but those onto the ground, where the breeze caught them and lifted them off.

"Listen, everybody," Mrs. Hutchinson was saying to the people around her.

"Ready, Bill?" Mr. Summers asked, and Bill Hutchinson, with one quick glance around at his wife and children, nodded.

"Remember," Mr. Summers said, "take the slips and keep them folded until each person has taken one. Harry, you help little Dave."

270 Mr. Graves took the hand of the little boy, who came willingly with him up to the box. "Take a paper out of the box, Davy," Mr. Summers said. Davy put his hand into the box and laughed. "Take just *one* paper," Mr. Summers said. "Harry, you hold it for him." Mr. Graves took the child's hand and removed the folded paper from the tight fist and held it while little Dave stood next to him and looked up at him wonderingly.

"Nancy next," Mr. Summers said. Nancy was twelve and her school friends breathed heavily as she went forward, switching her skirt, and took a slip daintily from the box. "Bill, Jr.," Mr. Summers 280 said, and Billy, his face red and his feet overlarge, nearly knocked the box over as he got a paper out. "Tessie," Mr. Summers said. She

---

SCAFFOLDING FOR ELL

Analyze Language Explain to students that *family* and *household* are examples of collective nouns, or nouns that refer to a group as one singular unit. Both *family* and *household* can refer to a group made up of one or more individuals. Have students divide into groups to help them understand the differentiation between *families* and *households* in the text. Have one group of students represent the Dunbars. Have another group represent the Hutchinsons. Have a third group represent the Hutchinson's daughter and her husband.

I tell you it wasn't *fair*.

hesitated for a minute, looking around **defiantly**, and then set her lips and went up to the box. She snatched a paper out and held it behind her.

"Bill," Mr. Summers said, and Bill Hutchinson reached into the box and felt around, bringing his hand out at last with the slip of paper in it.

The crowd was quiet. A girl whispered, "I hope it's not Nancy," and the sound of the whisper reached the edges of the crowd.

290 "It's not the way it used to be," Old Man Warner said clearly. "People ain't the way they used to be."

"All right," Mr. Summers said. "Open the papers. Harry, you open little Dave's."

Mr. Graves opened the slip of paper and there was a general sigh through the crowd as he held it up and everyone could see that it was blank. Nancy and Bill, Jr., opened theirs at the same time, and both beamed and laughed, turning around to the crowd and holding their slips of paper above their heads.

"Tessie," Mr. Summers said. There was a pause, and then Mr. 300 Summers looked at Bill Hutchinson, and Bill unfolded his paper and showed it. It was blank.

"It's Tessie," Mr. Summers said, and his voice was hushed. "Show us her paper, Bill."

Bill Hutchinson went over to his wife and forced the slip of paper out of her hand. It had a black spot on it, the black spot Mr. Summers had made the night before with the heavy pencil in the

defiantly
(dĭ-fī´ənt-lē) *adv.*
boldly, rebelliously.

The Lottery **33**

Image Credits: ©Houghton Mifflin Harcourt

TO CHALLENGE STUDENTS . . .

Ask students to reread this page. Have students form small groups and re-examine the dialogue and the action. Suggest that students take turns reading the dialogue to each other. Ask them to change the inflection and tone of their voices to match how they imagine each character would speak based on what they have read about that character or how the character is portrayed in context of the action on the page. Then ask students to discuss how Jackson uses the dialogue and action on this page to create mystery and tension.

Analyze Author's Choices: COMMON CORE RL 5
Tension and Surprise
(LINES 285-306)

Tell students that changing the **pacing** of the story can create tension or change the overall **mood**.

P **ASK STUDENTS** to describe the pacing on this page and how it affects the mood. (*The pacing of the story speeds up. There is no lengthy dialogue or description, and the plot actions are happening quickly. The mood changes to a feeling of tension and a sense that something is about to happen.*)

> **CRITICAL VOCABULARY**
>
> **defiantly**: Tessie is angry with the villagers and shows her emotions by her actions.
>
> **ASK STUDENTS** to list other ways Tessie could have behaved defiantly in this situation. (*She could have walked away from the square, refused to take a slip of paper, or refused to unfold her paper.*)

Denotation and COMMON CORE L 5b
Connotation (LINES 300–306)

Tell students that an author's specific choice of words and the feelings associated with them can affect how readers understand setting, characters, and events.

Q **CITE TEXT EVIDENCE** Ask students to examine lines 300–306 and find words with connotations that affect how the reader sees or understands an element of the story. (*The words "his wife" remind the reader that Tessie is Bill's wife and not just another villager. The word "forced" shows that Bill takes the paper roughly instead of trying to reason with his wife. Jackson may have wanted the reader to see Bill's reaction as symbolic of all the villagers—they are accustomed to how lottery "winners" react.*)

Analyze Author's Choices: Tension and Surprise

COMMON CORE **RL 5**

(LINES 310–321)

Explain that **situational irony** is the difference between what a reader expects to happen and what actually happens.

® **ASK STUDENTS** to explain what expectation the reader might have had about the lottery at the beginning of the story. *(The reader could expect that the lottery is a family-oriented, friendly event that results in a prizewinner.)* Ask students what part of the story changed that expectation. *(When Tessie begins to act fearfully, the reader suspects that there is something about the lottery that has not yet been revealed.)* Finally, ask students to cite the lines in the story that confirm suspicions that winning the lottery is not good. *(In lines 311–316, it is explained that the villagers remember to use stones.)*

COLLABORATIVE DISCUSSION Have students work in pairs to discuss specific choices that Jackson made concerning words and structure that affected their response to the story. Then have students share their ideas with the class. Accept all reasonable responses.

ASK STUDENTS to share any questions they generated in the course of reading and discussing the selection.

---

coal-company office. Bill Hutchinson held it up, and there was a stir in the crowd.

"All right, folks," Mr. Summers said. "Let's finish quickly."

310   Although the villagers had forgotten the ritual and lost the original black box, they still remembered to use stones. The pile of stones the boys had made earlier was ready; there were stones on the ground with the blowing scraps of paper that had come out of the box. Mrs. Delacroix selected a stone so large she had to pick it up with both hands and turned to Mrs. Dunbar. "Come on," she said. "Hurry up."

Mrs. Dunbar had small stones in both hands, and she said, gasping for breath, "I can't run at all. You'll have to go ahead and I'll catch up with you."

320   The children had stones already, and someone gave little Davy Hutchinson a few pebbles.

Tessie Hutchinson was in the center of a cleared space by now, and she held her hands out desperately as the villagers moved in on her. "It isn't fair," she said. A stone hit her on the side of the head.

Old Man Warner was saying, "Come on, come on, everyone." Steve Adams was in the front of the crowd of villagers, with Mrs. Graves beside him.

"It isn't fair, it isn't right," Mrs. Hutchinson screamed, and then they were upon her.

COLLABORATIVE DISCUSSION At what point did you realize the purpose of the lottery? With a partner, discuss how the villagers' reactions affected your own response. Cite specific textual evidence from the story to support your ideas.

APPLYING ACADEMIC VOCABULARY

intervene	rational

As students discuss the ending of the story, incorporate the following Collection 1 academic vocabulary words: *intervene* and *rational*. Ask students whether the villagers act in a **rational** manner. Ask students to explain why they think no one would **intervene** on behalf of Mrs. Hutchinson.

Analyze Impact of Word Choice: Tone

COMMON CORE RL 4

In a fictional story such as "The Lottery," the narrator's **tone** or attitude influences how readers see and understand the setting, characters, and events. Over the course of a story, the specific words an author chooses to use work together to create a tone. The tone of a story may evoke a sense of time and place to help readers more fully experience the setting. It may also point toward the underlying theme, or message, of the story.

Shirley Jackson evokes a timeless, small-town setting with her word choices. In these examples, note how the tone would change if Jackson had chosen a different word.

Jackson's words	Synonyms
village	town, community
noon dinner	lunch, the midday meal
gossip	news, information

Analyze Author's Choices: Tension and Surprise

COMMON CORE RL 5

An author uses the structure of a story as well as narrative and literary devices to create a certain **mood** or feeling in readers. Jackson relies on the following elements to generate a mood of horror and surprise.

Irony	Foreshadowing	Pacing
Situational irony is the contrast between what is expected and what actually happens. This type of irony can be used to surprise readers. For example, "The Lottery" takes place on a beautiful June day. The peaceful setting lulls readers into thinking that nothing bad will happen, making later events more startling.	**Foreshadowing** is a writer's use of clues to hint at events that will occur later in the story. Jackson uses foreshadowing to add **suspense,** or tension, and to hold readers' interest as they wonder what the characters are doing and why.	**Pacing** is the way in which the writer moves the action along. Pacing helps to create mood. For example, a deceptively peaceful mood is developed by the slow pace of the narrator's detailed descriptions in the first part of the story. By speeding up the pacing in the second part of the story, the author also changes the mood.

CLOSE READ

Analyze Impact of Word Choice: Tone

COMMON CORE RL 4

To help students understand the importance of word choice, make sure they understand that the connotation of words or word groups throughout a piece can create tone. One way to see how word choices can affect a story is to think about how synonyms would change the tone of a passage. Point out that it can be helpful to analyze word choices in smaller contexts and throughout the entire story.

Help students analyze the words in the chart. Ask them to describe what the writer might evoke by using words that create an image or sense of a small-town setting. (*a setting that is old-fashioned, peaceful, or homey*)

Analyze Author's Choices: Tension and Surprise

COMMON CORE RL 5

Review with students the literary elements described in the chart. Have students identify an example of each in the story. (*Situational irony: A lottery is usually a drawing for a prize; the winner of this lottery was stoned to death. Foreshadowing: As the lottery drawing progresses (lines 129–169), villagers become anxious instead of excited; Suspense: the writer withholds information about the true nature of the lottery until the very end; Pacing: The pace slows when Jackson describes the history and details of the lottery (lines 38–104) and the drawing (lines 155–218). As the lottery's function is revealed, the action speeds to the story's conclusion.*)

Strategies for Annotation   ✎ 🖫 *Annotate it!*

Analyze Author's Choices: Tension and Surprise

COMMON CORE RL 5

Have students use their eBook annotation tools to analyze the text. Ask them to do the following:

- Highlight in blue actions that are surprising.
- Highlight in yellow actions that are not surprising.
- On a note, explain the overall effect of the surprising actions in this passage.

The children had stones already, and someone gave little Davy Hutchinson a few pebbles.

Tessie Hutchinson was in the center of a cleared space by now, and she held her hands out desperately as the villagers moved in on her. "It isn't fair," she said. A stone hit her on the side of the head.

PRACTICE & APPLY

Analyzing the Text COMMON CORE RL 1, RL 2, RL 4, RL 5

Possible answers:

1. *The boys had been gathering stones and making a pile. As people gather, they do not stand near the pile of stones. The people talk quietly and do not laugh. It takes a while for someone to respond when Mr. Summers asks for help.*

2. *By not including the year or details about the village, the reader might infer the story takes place in any town at any time, including the present.*

3. *The word* ritual *might make people feel as if they should not question such a long-held tradition or go against it since they feel powerless to change it.*

4. *Jackson creates tension and suspense by waiting until the end to reveal the conflict. The story would lose impact if the reader couldn't experience horror by realizing that the winner is stoned to death.*

5. *At the beginning of the story, Mrs. Delacroix and Mrs. Hutchinson were behaving friendly toward each other. By Mrs. Delacroix's selecting a large stone, Jackson suggests that the ritual of the lottery is stronger than any feeling of empathy the villagers might have toward one another and that seemingly ordinary people are capable of brutal behavior.*

6. *Dialogue in the second half of the story increases the pacing. An anxious mood is developed by the quicker pace of dialogue that conveys excitement, nervousness, and fear.*

7. *At the beginning, the narrator refers to "the lottery" (line 8) without words that show disapproval. Even when the true nature of the lottery comes to light (lines 310–316), the narrator reserves judgment and maintains a distant tone.*

8. *Students may express shock that a story about ritual murder could be written with such removal and dispassion. Students may suggest that the theme is about how people freely participate in cruelty and injustice until they themselves become the target.*

Analyzing the Text COMMON CORE RL 1, RL 2, RL 4, RL 5, W 1

Cite Text Evidence   Support your responses with evidence from the selection.

1. **Cite Evidence** How does the author use foreshadowing to increase suspense in the first four paragraphs of the story? Provide specific examples and explain their connection to the story's outcome.

2. **Infer** The author does not include the year in which the story takes place or the name of the village. Why are these details of setting omitted?

3. **Infer** The word *ritual* is used four times to describe the lottery. Why might viewing the lottery as a ritual inhibit the villagers' possible objections to it?

4. **Evaluate** Explain why Jackson waits until the end of the story to reveal the **conflict**—the purpose of the lottery. How would the story be less effective if the conflict were revealed earlier?

5. **Analyze** At the end of the story, Mrs. Delacroix selects a huge stone and urges Mrs. Dunbar to hurry. Explain why this is **ironic** or unexpected. What important idea is brought out by this instance of irony?

6. **Analyze** In the first part of the story, readers learn about characters, setting, and plot through the narrator's exposition. The second part of the story depends mostly on dialogue to advance the plot. How does this change affect the pacing and mood of this part of the story?

7. **Infer** How would you describe the narrator's tone throughout the story? Identify words that convey this tone to readers.

8. **Evaluate** Do you find the narrator's tone strange, or even shocking? Why? What theme about cruelty or injustice does this tone help communicate?

PERFORMANCE TASK

Writing Activity: Letter The publication of "The Lottery" in *The New Yorker* prompted many readers to write letters expressing their feelings about it. What would you say to the magazine's editors about the story's events and its overall meaning? Write your own letter, following these steps.

1. Support your explanation of your reaction and interpretation with specific evidence from the story.

2. Conclude by relating what you have discussed to the broader issue of whether the story should have been published.

Assign this performance task.

PERFORMANCE TASK COMMON CORE W 1

Writing Activity: Letter Have students write a sentence that describes their interpretation of the story. Then have them review the text to locate evidence that supports this interpretation and include it in their letters.

Critical Vocabulary

profusely   perfunctory   petulantly   defiantly

Practice and Apply Write the Critical Vocabulary word that most accurately answers each question. Explain the reason for your choice.

1. Which word is associated with a challenge? Why?

2. Which word goes with daily routines? Why?

3. Which word goes with an unhappy child? Why?

4. Which word is associated with excessive growth? Why?

Vocabulary Strategy: Denotation and Connotation

The **denotation** of a word is the meaning found in a dictionary. The **connotation** of a word refers to the feelings or ideas associated with it. In writing "The Lottery," Shirley Jackson chose words for both their denotations and their connotations. In this sentence, she describes Old Man Warner as speaking petulantly: "'There's always been a lottery,' he added petulantly." The denotation of *petulantly* is "irritably." But by choosing *petulantly*, Jackson suggests that Old Man Warner is whiny, unreasonable, and childish as well. This chart shows the connotations and denotations of the remaining Critical Vocabulary words:

Word	Denotation	Connotation
profusely	plentifully	over the top; overly generous
perfunctory	done with little interest	done carelessly
defiantly	resistantly	rebelliously or angrily

Practice and Apply Work with a partner to brainstorm at least two synonyms for these words from the story. Note the connotation of each original word, and discuss how the connotation of each synonym changes the meaning of the original sentence.

1. assembled (line 11)

2. stained (line 67)

3. thrown (line 107)

WHEN STUDENTS STRUGGLE...

Help students develop their own understanding of the critical vocabulary words by having them work with partners to answer or discuss the following:

- Is there ever a time when people should act *defiantly*? If so, when?
- Name two tasks that can be performed in a *perfunctory* way.
- What other than growing things can occur *profusely*?
- How do people generally respond when someone complains *petulantly*?

PRACTICE & APPLY

Critical Vocabulary

Answers: 1. defiantly, *this adverb describes the bold manner in which a person, when challenged, stands up to someone or something;* **2.** perfunctory, *a daily routine is often performed without any feeling;* **3.** petulantly, *an unhappy child is likely to be grouchy or ill-tempered;* **4.** profusely, *if something grows excessively there will be a lot of it.*

Vocabulary Strategy: Denotation and Connotation

Original Word	Connotation	Synonyms	How the synonym's connotation changes the meaning of the sentence
assembled	came together formally or for an official event	gathered	suggests an informal event
		met	suggesting more casual than "gathered"; a planned or chance meeting
stained	impurity or that the villagers didn't take care of the box	discolored	neutral word suggesting age or exposure rather than neglect
		blotchy	natural appearance not caused by neglect
thrown	sweater is lying on her shoulders in a disheveled manner, suggesting having been put on in a hurry	tossed	similar meaning—put on in a hurry
		wrapped	taken great care in getting dressed

Language and Style: Colloquialisms

 COMMON CORE L 3

Tell students that colloquialisms are unique to a particular region or group of people. Point out that an author's use of colloquialisms in dialogue is a deliberate choice that will give meaning about the characters and setting. Add that students should notice when colloquialisms are used in descriptions that are not part of the dialogue. In these cases, the colloquialisms give information about the narrator.

Possible answers:

Examples of colloquial language in "The Lottery":
so's we, m'mother, my old man, talking away, your Missus.

Sample dialogue:

Man 1: I hear your Missus is going to bake apple pie again this year for the county fair.

Man 2: She sure is! I told m'wife that her pies are better'n m'mother's! Know what m'wife said? She said, "My old man had better say that!"

Man 1: Here we are talking away. We better get back to plowin' so's we can finish before sundown.

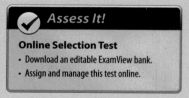

✓ Assess It!

Online Selection Test
- Download an editable ExamView bank.
- Assign and manage this test online.

Language and Style: Colloquialisms

 COMMON CORE L 3

Colloquialisms are words or expressions used in everyday speech in a particular region. In "The Lottery," although the narrator uses formal English, the villagers speak colloquially to each other. This use of colloquial language results in dialogue that flows naturally and sounds authentic for the characters.

Read this line of dialogue from the story.

> **"Horace's not but sixteen yet . . . Guess I gotta fill in for the old man this year."**

Jackson captures a small-town feel through informal grammatical structures ("Horace's"; "not but"; "Guess I") and slang expressions ("gotta"; "fill in"; "old man"). Now look at how the replacement of colloquial language with more standard wording changes the flow of the dialogue as well as your impression of the character:

> **"Horace is only sixteen. I suppose I'll have to take my husband's place this year."**

With standard English dialogue, readers lose the sense of character and setting so crucial to Jackson's story.

This chart includes some of the characteristics of the colloquial language used in the story.

Characteristic	Example
implied subject rather than stated	"Seems like there's no time at all . . ."
nonstandard verb forms	"The kids was gone . . . I . . . came a-running"
use of idioms and slang	"Some of you fellows want to give me a hand?" "People ain't the way they used to be."

Practice and Apply List additional examples of the colloquial language in "The Lottery." Then, incorporate your examples into a three- or four-sentence dialogue. Share your conversation with a partner and evaluate each other's use of colloquialisms. In particular, note how the colloquialisms create a mood or sense of setting in each dialogue.

Attend to Conventions of Letter Writing

COMMON CORE

W 1d

TEACH

Remind students that their Performance Task for "The Lottery" is to write a **business letter** to the editors of *The New Yorker,* which originally published this Shirley Jackson story. Review with students the parts of a business letter—sender's address, date, inside address, salutation, body, closing, and signature. A quick web search for images of business letters will produce dozens of excellent examples, with each part labeled.

Next, conduct a brief discussion of the differences between **informal** (e-mail and texting) and **formal English** (a college application essay). Students will use formal English in their business letters.

 For further instruction in formal style, use this *Interactive Whiteboard Lesson:* **Maintaining a Formal Style and Objective Tone**

PRACTICE AND APPLY

Help students develop and organize their letters: have them make a two-column chart with space beneath for a summary activity.

Message	My Opinion

For the **first column,** conduct a class brainstorm on the story's message, or what it says about human nature. (Ideas will vary but might include: Humans are unquestioning slaves of tradition; humans can be brutal to one another; humans irrationally direct their aggressions at innocent targets.)

Ask students to circle or underline the words and phrases in the first column that best represent their understanding of the story's message. In the space remaining in this column, ask students to **list three actions or events** in "The Lottery" that illustrate the message they've identified.

Have students use the **second column** to state and briefly explain their opinion of the message stated in the first column.

Finally, beneath the chart, ask students to state whether the story should have been published and briefly defend their answer.

Direct students to write a **letter in three parts,** with a paragraph for each part of their charts. Remind them to follow business letter form and use formal English.

Vocabulary Strategy: Denotation and Connotation

COMMON CORE

L 5b

RETEACH

Review the terms *denotation* and *connotation*. Display the following sentence: The <u>people</u> <u>walked</u> up the steps of the courthouse, <u>carrying</u> <u>signs</u> and <u>stating</u> their <u>ideas</u>. Then ask students to replace the underlined words in this sentence with synonyms that have different connotations and create a mood for the reader. Have volunteers read aloud the sentences they wrote with the replacement words and discuss the difference in connotation of the synonyms. Then have students discuss how the replaced words affect the meaning of the sentence. **Sample sentence:** *The <u>mob</u> <u>marched</u> up the steps of the courthouse, <u>waving</u> <u>placards</u> and <u>shouting</u> their <u>protests</u>.*

 Assign the following *WordSharp: Interactive Vocabulary* tutorial: **Denotative and Connotative Meanings**

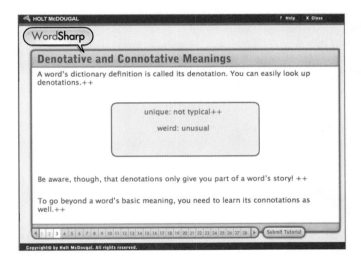

CLOSE READING APPLICATION

Students can apply the skill to other works of fiction. Have them work independently to list about 5–10 words from a short story or novel that they are reading. Students should indicate the denotation and connotation of each word.

Without Title

Poem by Diane Glancy

Why This Text?

Like all people, students want to belong to a larger group. Being accepted into a group means they have been assimilated, or absorbed, by the group. Both the student and the group often change with assimilation, through an exchange of ideas, beliefs, and attitudes. This lesson explores such a relationship through a poem by Diane Glancy, whose father is part Cherokee.

Key Learning Objective: The student will support inferences about theme.

Common Core Standards

RL 1   Cite textual evidence.

RL 2   Determine a theme and analyze its development.

RL 4   Determine the meaning of words and phrases.

RL 5   Analyze how an author's choices create mystery, tension, or surprise.

W 3   Write narratives using effective technique, details, and event sequences.

SL 1   Participate in collaborative discussions with diverse partners.

SL 3   Evaluate a speaker's point of view, reasoning, and use of evidence.

SL 4   Present information clearly so that the development and style are appropriate to purpose, audience, and task.

SL 6   Adapt speech to a variety of contexts, demonstrating formal English.

L 1   Demonstrate standard English grammar and usage.

Text Complexity Rubric

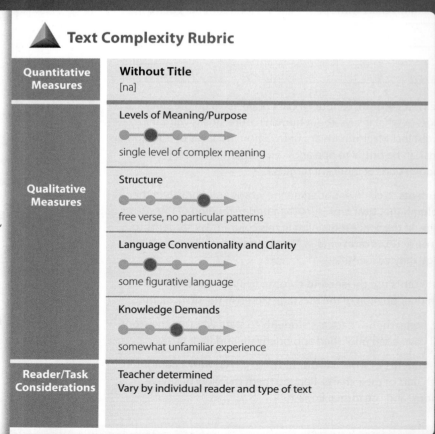

Quantitative Measures	**Without Title** [na]
Qualitative Measures	**Levels of Meaning/Purpose** — single level of complex meaning
	Structure — free verse, no particular patterns
	Language Conventionality and Clarity — some figurative language
	Knowledge Demands — somewhat unfamiliar experience
Reader/Task Considerations	Teacher determined — Vary by individual reader and type of text

CLOSE READ

For more context and historical background, students can view the video "American Buffalo" in their eBooks.

Background Explain that, after World War II, the U.S. government's Urban Relocation Program promised Native Americans better jobs if they moved to cities and tried to join mainstream society. In "Without Title," the speaker's father moved from the land and life he loved to the city.

AS YOU READ Direct students to the As You Read question to focus their reading. Have students write down any questions they generate during reading.

Support Inferences About Theme
COMMON CORE **RL 1, RL 2, RL 4, RL 5**

Explain to students that some poems state the theme directly, but many poems have an **implied theme** that is revealed bit by bit throughout the poem.

Ⓐ CITE TEXT EVIDENCE Have students identify details in the title and subtitle that may provide clues to the theme. (*The subtitle reveals the poem is about the speaker's father; "lived without ceremony" may mean he was common and ordinary; "Without Title" may suggest an identity theme, or the lack or loss of identity.*)

Analyze Language (LINES 1–22)
COMMON CORE **RL 1, RL 4, RL 5**

Tell students that Glancy uses **repetition,** or repeated sounds, words, phrases, or lines, to emphasize an important idea and create unity in the poem.

Ⓑ CITE TEXT EVIDENCE Have students identify the repetition and explain what it may suggest about the theme. (*Repetition of the word* buffalo *may suggest that, like the buffalo, the Native American culture so important to his identity is close to extinction.*)

COLLABORATIVE DISCUSSION Have students pair up to discuss the meaning of the subtitle and what is missing from the father's life, then share their ideas with the class.

ASK STUDENTS to share any questions they generated in the course of reading and discussing the selection.

Ⓐ **Without Title**
for my Father who lived without ceremony

Poem by Diane Glancy

AS YOU READ Think about how Diane Glancy, a poet of Native American descent, portrays the life of the speaker's father. In what ways is it different from the traditional life of his people?

> It's hard you know without the buffalo, Ⓑ
> the shaman,[1] the arrow,
> but my father went out each day to hunt
> as though he had them.
> 5 He worked in the stockyards.
> All his life he brought us meat.
> No one marked his first kill,
> no one sang his buffalo song.
> Without a vision[2] he had migrated to the city
> 10 and went to work in the packing house.
> When he brought home his horns and hides
> my mother said
> get rid of them.
> I remember the animal tracks of his car
> 15 backing out the drive in snow and mud,
> the aerial[3] on his old car waving
> like a bow string.
> I remember the silence of his lost power,
> the red buffalo painted on his chest.
> 20 Oh, I couldn't see it
> but it was there, and in the night I heard
> his buffalo grunts like a snore.

COLLABORATIVE DISCUSSION What is the meaning of the subtitle, "for my Father who lived without ceremony"? With a partner, discuss what is missing from the father's life, citing evidence from the poem.

[1] **shaman:** a person who interacts with the spiritual world.
[2] **vision:** a guiding experience that often comes in a dream or a trance.
[3] **aerial:** a thin, metal antenna.

Image Credits: ©Richard Wear/Design Pics/Corbis

Without Title **39**

SCAFFOLDING FOR ELL STUDENTS

Support Inferences About Theme English learners may be unfamiliar with terms used in this poem. Using a whiteboard, project the poem and discuss the vocabulary footnoted at the bottom of the student page, underlining those words in the poem. Ask volunteers to underline other unfamiliar words in the poem and help students define them, using context clues when possible. Then read aloud the poem, occasionally stopping for questions, discussion, or explanation.

ASK STUDENTS to use the underlined words in the poem to retell the most important ideas and details of the poem.

PRACTICE & APPLY

Support Inferences About Theme COMMON CORE RL 1, RL 2, RL 4

Help students understand the meaning of the terms **theme** and **infer** and then examine the steps for determining theme in a poem. Have students compile important details from the poem in a T-chart.

Analyzing the Text COMMON CORE RL 1, RL 2

Possible answers:

1. *Contrasts include "hunting" in the stockyards vs. hunting buffalo; a waving aerial on his car vs. a bow string; buffalo grunts vs. a snore.*

2. *Details such as "It's hard you know," "no one marked his first kill," "without a vision," and the repetition of "buffalo" and "I remember" suggest the speaker understands how hard it was for her father to take a job in the city. Students may say the speaker didn't intervene because she was caught between two cultures.*

3. *Theme: Personal identity is strong when a person feels connected to community, family, and traditions. Summary: The speaker remembers her father who left his Native American homeland to work at a stockyard packing house in a city to provide for his family. One day the speaker's mother tells her husband to get rid of the horns and hides he brought home. The father storms out feeling diminished and powerless. Details: The repetition of "buffalo" and "I remember"; comparisons between the original culture in which the father had a strong identity and the city culture in which he had little sense of identity; and the phrase "the silence of his lost power" all develop the theme.*

Assess It!

Online Selection Test
- Download an editable ExamView bank.
- Assign and manage this test online.

Support Inferences About Theme COMMON CORE RL 1, RL 2

The **theme** of a poem is a message about life or about human nature that the poet wishes to communicate to readers. Usually, the theme is not stated directly. Readers must **infer** the theme, or draw a conclusion based on details in the text. A theme can be stated in a sentence, such as "Honesty is the sign of a true friendship."

Follow these steps to determine theme in a poem:

- Develop an objective summary of the poem. In a sentence or two, state the most important ideas and details that the poet presents.
- Ask yourself what message about life or about people the poem conveys. A poem may have more than one theme, but all themes must be supported by textual evidence.
- Write a sentence that states the theme. Check to make sure there are enough details in the poem to support your theme. The evidence must be both strong and thorough.

Analyzing the Text COMMON CORE RL 1, RL 2, RL 3, W 3a–b, e, SL 1

Cite Text Evidence   Support your responses with evidence from the selection.

1. **Identify** What details does the speaker use to contrast life in her father's original culture and life in the city?

2. **Infer** What can you infer about the speaker's feelings toward her father? Why doesn't she try to intervene in the conflict between her parents? Cite evidence from the text to support your answer.

3. **Analyze** What theme about tradition and community does this poem convey? Draft an objective summary, and then cite key details that help develop the theme over the course of the poem.

PERFORMANCE TASK

Speaking Activity: Oral Narrative Plan and present a spoken narrative about one day in the life of the speaker's family.

- Decide who will be the narrator: the speaker, the speaker's father or mother, or a third-person narrator outside the poem.
- Describe the events of one day through your narrator's voice, incorporating details from the poem.
- Make sure your narrative builds to a logical conclusion that reflects what the characters experience in the poem.
- Speak using conventions of English that are appropriate to the narrator and context.

Assign this performance task.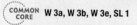

PERFORMANCE TASK COMMON CORE W 3a, W 3b, W 3e, SL 1

Speaking Activity: Oral Narrative Have students plan their narratives individually, but pair students to rehearse their spoken narratives. Partners should comment on the effectiveness of the narrator's voice in conveying details from the poem, whether the narrative builds to a logical conclusion that reflects the characters' experiences in the poem, and if the conventions of standard English are appropriate to the narrator and context.

Adapting Speech to Contexts

COMMON CORE

SL 1,
SL 1a,
SL 1d,
SL 3, SL 4,
SL 6,
L 1a-b, L 3

TEACH

Before students present the oral narrative of the Performance Task, have them take time to reflect on the narrator and plot they have chosen, review textual evidence from the poem to support their choices, and rehearse their presentation.

- **Get into character.** Develop a way of speaking that is true to the narrator's personality and physical characteristics as well as his or her personal and cultural history. Consider how the narrator feels and thinks about other characters and events and add those emotions to the narrator's voice.
- Make the narrator real by adding various **verbal techniques** that match the character's language, personality, and meaning in the context of the plot. For example, experiment with voice modulation, speaking rate, pitch, and volume and use language conventions, such as parallel structure and various types of phrases and clauses.
- Use **nonverbal techniques,** or body language, appropriate to the narrator. Make eye contact with the audience the way the narrator's character would. Incorporate posture and gestures that the narrator would use.

PRACTICE AND APPLY

Have students rehearse their oral narrative. First, encourage students to practice by themselves the first few times to become comfortable with the timing of the narrator's language as well as the verbal and nonverbal techniques they have chosen.

Then, ask students to practice the presentation in front of a classmate, who will offer suggestions for improving the effectiveness of delivery. Partners should comment on how well the narrative incorporates details from the poem and reflects the narrator's and other characters' experiences in the poem, citing textual evidence in support.

Finally, students should incorporate the suggested changes they agree upon and rehearse the presentation once more before delivering the oral narrative to a larger group.

Analyzing the Impact of Word Choices

COMMON CORE

RL 1,
RL 4

TEACH

Poets choose and arrange words in a precise way to create specific effects, to suggest a sense of time and place, and to set a **tone**, or attitude a speaker has toward a subject. Imagery, figurative language, and sound devices are techniques writers use to create meaning.

 LEVEL UP TUTORIALS Assign the following *Level Up* tutorial: **Elements of Poetry.** Have students focus on screens 16–21 to review the impact of word choice, including imagery and figurative language.

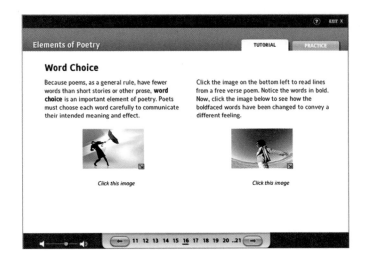

PRACTICE AND APPLY

Display the poem on the board or on a device. Have students find imagery, including figurative language, in the poem by asking them what senses the poem appeals to most. *(sight and hearing)*

Have volunteers circle the words or phrases that triggered those senses. (*Sight*: buffalo, shaman, arrow, stockyards, horns and hides, animal tracks on his car, snow and mud, aerial waving like a bow string, red buffalo painted on his chest; *hearing*: sang his buffalo song, silence of his lost power, buffalo grunts like a snore)

Next, have students point out repetition in the poem. *(The word buffalo is repeated in lines 1, 8, 19, and 22; the words I remember are repeated in lines 14 and 18.)*

Ask students to explain any important ideas conveyed through imagery and repetition. *(Accept reasonable responses that are supported by text evidence, such as the following: Native American images and repetition suggest a tone of sadness over the loss of a culture's way of life.)*

Evaluating Media Sources

RL 1, RL 4,
RL 6, RL 7,
RI 1, RI 4,
RI 6, RI 7,
SL 1, SL 2,
SL 3, SL 4

TEACH

Students gather information every day from various types of **media**. Each type of media presents information in a way that affects the audience differently, and often the information and messages themselves include the viewpoints, beliefs, and biases of the people who created them. Readers, viewers, and listeners need to think critically and evaluate the credibility and accuracy of each source.

To evaluate media sources, students should ask questions like the following:

- Who compiled the information or created this message? What viewpoints, beliefs, or biases are conveyed and how do they affect the message?
- For what purpose is the information presented or the message created?
- What type of language is used in the message? Is it persuasive? Is it informative?
- Who is the intended audience?
- Does the message include symbols representing ideas that will impact the audience?
- Does the message convey a culture and values?
- Does the medium contain design elements, techniques, or special effects to help create a reaction from the audience?

PRACTICE AND APPLY

The poem "Without Title" describes how the changing Native American culture affected the speaker's family. Have students conduct a mini-research project to learn more about the changing Native American culture. Direct students to gather information from at least three media sources, including the poem "Without Title," a History Video such as "Revisiting Sacred Ground," and one source of their choice. Students should evaluate the credibility and accuracy of information in each source and then integrate the information in a brief report presented to a small group of students.

Students may want to view the following History Video: **Revisiting Sacred Ground**

Support Inferences About Theme

RL 1, RL 2

RETEACH

Review that the **theme** of a poem is a message about life that the poet communicates to readers. Sometimes the theme is stated directly in the poem. Most frequently the theme is implied, and readers have to **infer**, or guess, the meaning from details in the poem. Clues to a theme may be conveyed through **repetition** of words, phrases, or lines and **images** that appeal to the senses. A historical or cultural context may also influence the theme of a poem.

Display a chart like this one on the board or a device. Ask students to fill in the chart with details from the poem.

Repetition	Images	Cultural Context	Speaker's Feelings
Theme:			

 LEVEL UP TUTORIALS Assign the following *Level Up* tutorial: **Theme**

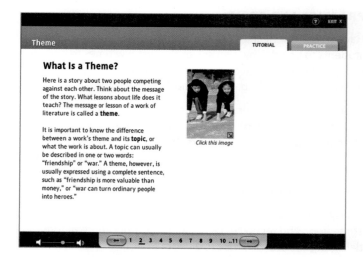

CLOSE READING APPLICATION

Students can apply the skill to a poem of their choice. Have them work independently to write a one- or two-sentence summary of the poem. Then have students identify details in the poem that suggest a theme, including devices such as repetition, images, historical or cultural context, and speaker's feelings. Finally, have students ask themselves what message about life the details suggest and write a sentence that states the theme.

Present a Speech

This collection explores the significance of our relationships with others, both individuals and groups. Look back at the texts you have read, including the anchor text "What, of This Goldfish, Would You Wish?" and synthesize your ideas about them. Based on these texts and your own experience, make a generalization about how our relationships with others help define who we are. Share your ideas in a speech.

COMMON CORE

SL 4 Present information, findings, and supporting evidence clearly, concisely, and logically.

SL 6 Adapt speech to a variety of contexts and tasks.

An effective speech

- presents a clear, logical, and well-defended generalization
- provides quotations or examples from the texts that illustrate the generalization
- includes an introduction, a logically structured body including transitions, and a conclusion
- incorporates appropriate images, music, and other media to enhance meaning and maintain audience interest
- engages listeners with appropriate and clear use of language, emphasis, volume, and gestures

PLAN

Analyze the Texts Choose three texts from this collection, including "What, of This Goldfish, Would You Wish?" Identify the key relationship represented in each text.

- Make notes about each relationship.
- Think about how the relationships define who the people or characters are.
- Pay attention to specific examples and quotations from the texts that provide insights into the relationships.

Evaluate Your Own Experience Think about your own relationships with either individuals or groups. How do these relationships help to define who you are? Which author, if any, shares your own view about the role of relationships in shaping a person's identity?

- Make notes about your own view on the role of relationships.
- Provide evidence from your own experience that supports your view.

*my*Notebook

Use the annotation tools in your eBook to find evidence that supports your ideas. Save each piece of evidence to your notebook.

ACADEMIC VOCABULARY

As you share your ideas about the role of relationships for an individual, be sure to use these words.

discriminate
diverse
inhibit
intervene
rational

COMMON CORE SL 4, SL 6

PRESENT A SPEECH

Introduce students to the Performance Task by reading the introductory paragraph with them and reviewing the criteria for what makes an effective speech. Remind students that a speech needs to be written well, in the same way that an essay does, but that the delivery of the speech is of equal importance.

PLAN

ANALYZE THE TEXT

▶ **View It!**

Professional Development Podcast:
Performance Task

Remind students that their speeches must contain not only their own experiences but also specific evidence from the texts to support their main ideas about relationships. Review the types of evidence they should include in their speeches:

- Examples: specific details or events from the texts
- Quotations: specific words, phrases and sentences presented word-for-word from the texts and attributed to the author
- Summaries: important information from the texts summed up in their own words.

PERFORMANCE TASK A

PRODUCE

GET ORGANIZED

Suggest to students that they organize their evidence into categories—for instance, which supporting idea a piece of evidence illustrates or which text is its source. Then they can decide what order of categories will be most effective in supporting the generalization on which the speech centers.

PRODUCE

WRITE YOUR SPEECH

As students draft their speeches, remind them that listeners must understand ideas the first time, since they cannot go back and reread a confusing sentence. For this reason, students must use transitions to signal shifts or connections between ideas and draft clearly worded and concisely structured sentences.

- Explain why you agree or disagree with the authors of your three chosen texts.

Make a Generalization Based on these texts and your own experience, make a generalization about how our relationships with others help determine who we are. When you make a **generalization**, you draw a broad, rational conclusion that is true most of the time. You should focus on the main elements of the texts and your own experience, not the specific details. Draft a logical and clearly worded generalization to serve as the basis for your speech.

Get Organized Organize your notes in an outline to make sure the connections among your ideas will be clear for your audience.

- Write your generalization in the introduction section of your outline.
- List your main ideas about the role our relationships play in defining who we are. These ideas will form the body of your speech.
- Note the examples and quotations from the texts that you will use to support each main idea.
- In the conclusion section of your speech, restate your generalization and summarize your strongest support for it.

PRODUCE

Write Your Speech Use your notes to write a clearly organized speech with an introduction, body, and conclusion. Keep your focus on providing support for your generalization with evidence from the texts. Remember to include

- transitions between the main sections of your speech
- quotations and examples from the texts and from your own experience that support your generalization
- media elements, such as photos, music, and video clips, that enhance or illustrate your ideas and appeal to your audience
- language that is appropriately formal for an oral presentation
- a variety of grammatical structures to keep your audience interested in your ideas

myWriteSmart

Write your rough draft in myWriteSmart. Focus on getting your ideas down, rather than perfecting your choice of language.

REVISE

Fine Tune Unlike readers of an essay, your listening audience will not be able to go back and review any parts that are unclear to them. Revise your draft to make sure your audience will understand all of your ideas the first time. Your goal is to clearly and concisely present your ideas about how relationships help define who we are. Use the chart on the following page to review the characteristics of an effective speech. Then, read the rough draft of your speech, ensuring that your listeners will be able to

- follow your reasoning, organization, and development of ideas
- understand specific meanings conveyed by your choice of words and phrases
- see how your ideas, examples, and evidence are connected to each other

my WriteSmart

Have your partner or a group of peers review your draft in *my*WriteSmart. Ask your reviewers to note any details that do not support the generalization.

PRESENT

Practice Before presenting to the class, practice with a partner.

- Mark your text to show where you will use your voice or a gesture to emphasize a point. Think about when you might want to stress a particular word or phrase, pause for effect, or change your pace to speak more quickly or slowly.
- Speak at an appropriate volume and pace so that your audience can hear you clearly.
- Set up and practice using any media elements in your speech. Make sure that the equipment you need will be available and working, and practice using it several times to be sure you can continue speaking smoothly while operating, introducing, or responding to media elements.
- Ask your partner to give you feedback so that you can improve your speech before presenting it to the whole class.

Deliver Your Speech As you present your speech, keep your audience in mind and remember to speak loudly and clearly at an appropriate pace. If you feel nervous, you may find yourself talking too fast. Take a deep breath and slow down. When your speech is over, ask your audience for constructive feedback to help you improve your next presentation.

PERFORMANCE TASK A

REVISE

FINE TUNE

Suggest to students that they complete their drafts a day ahead of their scheduled speech to allow time for practice and revision. Whether they practice in front of a mirror or with a partner, they should evaluate both content and delivery and practice using media elements as a smooth part of the presentation.

PRESENT

PRACTICE

Suggest that students set up and test any media elements ahead of time. If time allows, before the speech ask each student to speak briefly to ensure that a classmate or teacher at the back of the room can easily understand the speech. Remind students to look at the audience often to monitor whether they can hear the speech.

LANGUAGE

Have students look at the chart and identify how they did on the Performance Task in the Language category. Ask students if the language in their speech was more formal or informal. If students answer informal, have them practice rephrasing the language using formal English.

COLLECTION 1 **TASK A**
SPEECH

	Ideas and Evidence	Organization	Language
ADVANCED	• The speaker presents relevant examples from all of the chosen texts and media sources to support a logical generalization. • The speech effectively synthesizes analysis of the texts and personal experience to strengthen the generalization. • Media choices effectively illustrate and expand on ideas. • The conclusion reinforces the generalization and summarizes key ideas.	• The speech's organization helps listeners identify the generalization and the supporting ideas and evidence. • Ideas are presented in a logical order with effective transitions to show the connections between ideas.	• The speaker uses appropriately formal English to discuss the texts and ideas. • The speaker consistently quotes accurately from the texts to support ideas. • The speaker is easy to understand and adapts volume and pacing to audience needs.
COMPETENT	• The speaker states a generalization and supports it with relevant ideas and evidence from the texts and personal experience. • The speech synthesizes ideas from texts and experience. • Media choices are clearly linked to the speaker's ideas. • The speaker concludes with a statement that reinforces the generalization.	• The organization makes clear the generalization, supporting ideas, and evidence. • Ideas are presented in a logical order and linked with transitions.	• The speaker mostly uses formal English to discuss literature and ideas. • The speaker mostly quotes accurately from the texts to support ideas. • The speaker is generally easy to understand and uses appropriate volume and pacing.
LIMITED	• The speaker states a generalization but may support it with only limited evidence. • Common themes or connections among texts may not be clear to listeners. • Media choices lack a clear connection to the speaker's ideas. • The conclusion does little to reinforce the generalization.	• The organization may make it difficult to identify the speaker's generalization, supporting ideas, or evidence. • Ideas may seem disorganized and the speech may lack some needed transitions.	• The speaker inconsistently uses formal English to discuss the texts and ideas. • The speaker may misquote one or more examples. • The speaker is occasionally difficult to understand.
EMERGING	• The speaker's generalization is unclear; ideas and evidence are not coherent. • No attempt is made to synthesize ideas from multiple texts. • Media choices are absent or distracting. • The speech lacks any kind of conclusion or summary.	• The organization fails to distinguish among a generalization, support, and evidence. • Ideas are presented in a disorganized way with no transitions.	• The speaker uses informal English and/or slang, resulting in ideas that are not clearly expressed. • The speaker's frequently misquotes the texts. • The speaker is often difficult to understand.

Write an Analytical Essay

COMMON CORE

W 2 Write informative/explanatory texts to examine and convey complex ideas, concepts, and information.
W 9 Draw evidence from literary or informational texts to support analysis, reflection, and research.

This collection focuses on the way we relate to and interact with others, both individuals and groups. Look back at the texts you have read—particularly the anchor selections on burning the American flag—in the context of the collection-opening quotation from Barbara Jordan. Synthesize your ideas about how the texts explore the idea of accepting others by writing an analytical essay.

An effective analytical essay

- makes logical connections between the quotation and texts
- clearly and accurately analyzes the content and themes of the chosen texts
- provides quotations or examples from the texts that support and elaborate on the analysis
- has an introduction, a logically structured body including transitions, and a conclusion
- follows the conventions of written English

PLAN

Analyze the Texts Think back to the quotation from Barbara Jordan that opened this collection: "We, as human beings, must be willing to accept people who are different from ourselves." How does the quotation play out in the selections you have read?

- Choose three texts from this collection, including either "*Texas* v. *Johnson* Majority Opinion" or "American Flag Stands for Tolerance."
- Identify the specific differences between people that are explored in each text.
- Make notes about how people either do or do not show acceptance in each text. If they discriminate against others, what are their reasons?
- Compare and contrast the authors' views. Do the authors present a common view about acceptance, or do they differ? Explain.

*my*Notebook

Use the annotation tools in your eBook to find evidence that supports your ideas. Save each piece of evidence to your notebook.

ACADEMIC VOCABULARY

As you share your ideas about the role of individuals in society, be sure to use these words.

discriminate
diverse
inhibit
intervene
rational

WRITE AN ANALYTICAL ESSAY

COMMON CORE   **W 2, W 9**

Point out to students the qualities of an effective analytical essay. Note that their completed essays should reflect accurate analysis, sufficient textual evidence to support their ideas, a clear organizational structure, and correct use of language conventions.

PLAN

ANALYZE THE TEXT

View It!

Professional Development Podcast:

Writing from Sources

Remind students that their analyses must center on the quotation from Barbara Jordan. They may find it useful to skim through all of the texts in the collection to make notes on why accepting others is both difficult and necessary. They should choose the three texts (including at least one anchor) in which they note the strongest evidence.

Collection Performance Task B   **45**

PERFORMANCE TASK B

PLAN

GET ORGANIZED

As students outline or organize ideas, ask them to highlight quotations or examples from the chosen texts in each body paragraph and underline the explanations of how each quotation or example relates to the quotation from Barbara Jordan. Any paragraph plan lacking either highlighting or underlining will need to be developed more.

PRODUCE

WRITE A DRAFT

Suggest to students that they read their essays aloud to a partner to ensure that they have effectively used transitions to link ideas. If a listener cannot easily follow the connections between Barbara Jordan's quotation and text evidence, students should use words, phrases, or sentences to strengthen connections among ideas.

Get Organized Organize your notes in an outline. Begin your outline with a statement about accepting those who are different. This statement will form the basis of your introduction.

In the body of your essay, each paragraph should

- present and support a main idea
- discuss the idea of acceptance presented in one of the texts
- provide quotations or examples from the text to illustrate the main idea
- explain how the quotation or examples support the main idea

Your conclusion should

- make a concluding statement that reiterates or supports your main ideas
- make a more general or universal conclusion about the concept of acceptance in our society

> **PRODUCE**

*my*WriteSmart

Write your rough draft in *my*WriteSmart.

Write a Draft Use your outline to write an essay that analyzes how the quotation plays out in each selection, explains the differences expressed in each text, and shows how people either do or do not show acceptance.

Remember to

- provide a clear and cohesive introduction, body, and conclusion
- support your main points with evidence from the text
- explain how the evidence supports your ideas
- use language that is appropriate for your audience
- include transitions to link the major sections of the text

As you draft your analytical essay, remember that this kind of writing requires formal language and a respectful tone. Essays that analyze texts are expected to be appropriate for an academic context. If you find that considering language and tone at this stage inhibits the flow of ideas, be sure to revise for language and tone later.

Improve Your Draft You should now have a rough draft that analyzes the concept of acceptance in each of your chosen texts. Use the chart on the following page to review the characteristics of a well-written analytical essay. Then, review and revise your draft to make sure your ideas are clear and coherent. As you read your first draft, ensure that it

my **WriteSmart**

Have your partner or a group of peers review your draft in *my*WriteSmart.

- makes logical connections between the collection quotation and each of the texts you chose
- has sufficient evidence to support these connections
- has a clearly developed introduction, body, and conclusion
- follows the conventions of standard written English

Then write a new draft of your essay, making sure to incorporate any changes.

PRESENT

Exchange Essays When your final draft is completed, exchange essays with a partner. Read your partner's essay and provide feedback. Reread the criteria for an effective analytical essay and answer the following questions:

- What did your partner do well in the essay?
- How could your partner's essay be improved?

PERFORMANCE TASK B

REVISE

IMPROVE YOUR DRAFT

Suggest to students that they read their drafts critically while reviewing the criteria on page 48. For each bullet point in the chart, have them identify where their work would fall. They should then focus revisions on the two or three lowest-ranking bullet points.

PRESENT

EXCHANGE ESSAYS

Provide students with other options for presenting their essays, such as posting in the classroom or on a school blog or website. Having an authentic audience will help students to develop more effective essays.

PERFORMANCE TASK B

ORGANIZATION

Have students look at the chart and identify how they did on the Performance Task in the Organization category. Ask students to review their introduction and conclusion. Have students work in pairs to evaluate and improve each other's introductions and conclusions.

COLLECTION 1 TASK B
ANALYTICAL ESSAY

	Ideas and Evidence	Organization	Language
ADVANCED	• The introduction is intriguing and informative. • The topic is strongly developed with relevant facts, concrete details, interesting quotations, and examples from the texts. • The writer makes logical assertions about the texts and synthesizes ideas from the texts with the quotation in an insightful way. • The concluding section capably follows from and supports the ideas presented.	• The organization of body paragraphs is effective and logical throughout the essay. • Transitions successfully connect related ideas.	• The writing reflects a formal style and an objective, knowledgeable tone. • The writing demonstrates strong command of the conventions of standard English writing, including spelling, capitalization, punctuation, grammar, and usage.
COMPETENT	• The introduction clearly states the topic of the essay. • One or two key points could use additional support in the form of relevant facts, details, quotations, and examples from the texts. • The writer accurately identifies ways in which the chosen texts relate to the quotation. • The concluding section mostly follows from and supports the ideas presented.	• The organization of body paragraphs is generally clear. • Transitions usually connect related ideas.	• The style is generally formal, though the tone is subjective at times. • Minor errors in spelling, capitalization, punctuation grammar, or usage occur but do not hinder communication.
LIMITED	• A brief introduction may identify the topic. • Most key points need additional support in the form of relevant facts, details, quotations, and examples from the texts. • The writer identifies how only one text relates to the quotation, or makes illogical connections. • The concluding section may simply restate the topic or fail to follow from the ideas presented.	• The organization of body paragraphs is confusing. • More transitions are needed throughout to connect related ideas.	• The style is too informal; the tone is subjective. • Spelling, capitalization, and punctuation are often incorrect and in some cases cause confusion. • Grammar and usage are incorrect in many places, making some of the writer's ideas unclear.
EMERGING	• Facts, details, quotations, and examples from the texts are missing. • The writer fails to identify connections between the chosen texts and the quotation. • Introduction and/or conclusion may be absent.	• A logical organization is not used; information is presented randomly. • Transitions are not used, making the essay difficult to understand.	• The style and tone are inappropriate for the essay. • Spelling, capitalization, and punctuation are incorrect throughout. • Many grammatical and usage errors hinder the meaning of the writer's ideas.

Image Credits: ©Carlos Sanchez Pereyra/JAI/Corbis

The Natural World

❝Wildness reminds us what it means to be human, what we are connected to rather than what we are separate from.❞

—Terry Tempest Williams

We are intertwined with nature: We affect it as much as it affects us.

hmhfyi.com

CONNECTING WORD AND IMAGE

ASK STUDENTS to discuss how the collection opener image and the collection quotation work together to create a connection.

PERFORMANCE TASK PREVIEW

Point out to students that they will complete two performance tasks at the end of the collection. The performance tasks will require them to further analyze the selections in the collection and to synthesize ideas about these analyses. They will present their findings in a variety of products.

ACADEMIC VOCABULARY

View It!
Professional Development Podcast:
Academic Vocabulary

Students can acquire facility with the academic vocabulary words through frequent, repeated exposure as they analyze and discuss the selections in the collection. Academic vocabulary can be used in the following instructional contexts. This will enable students to incorporate the academic vocabulary words into their working vocabulary.

- Collaborative Discussion at the end of each selection
- Analyzing the Text questions for each selection
- Selection-level Performance Task
- Vocabulary instruction (for Critical Vocabulary and/or for Vocabulary Strategy)
- Language and Style
- End-of-collection Performance Task for all selections in the collection

ASK STUDENTS to review the academic vocabulary word list for this collection. You may wish to pronounce each word aloud, so students hear the correct pronunciation. Then discuss the definitions and the related forms for each word. Remind students that they will encounter these five academic vocabulary words throughout the collection.

COLLECTION
PERFORMANCE TASK Preview

At the end of this collection, you will have the opportunity to complete two tasks:

- Write a research report about an interaction between humans and nature.
- Participate in a panel discussion exploring what we learn about ourselves through nature.

ACADEMIC VOCABULARY

Study the words and their definitions in the chart below. You will use these words as you discuss and write about the texts in this collection.

Word	Definition	Related Forms
advocate (ăd´və-kāt´) v.	to argue for or plead in favor of	advocacy, advocator
discrete (dĭ-skrēt´) adj.	made up of separate or distinct things or parts	discretely, discreteness
domain (dō-mān´) n.	a sphere of activity	dominion
enhance (ĕn-hăns´) tr.v.	to make better, or add to the value or effectiveness	enhancement, enhancer
scope (skōp) n.	the size or extent of the activity or subject that is involved	scope out

50

USING COLLECTIONS YOUR WAY

Use the following information, along with the charts on the following pages, to help you decide how you want to introduce the collection. Based on your teaching style, your students' interests, or your instructional goals, you may want to structure the collection in various ways. You may choose different entry points each time you teach the collection.

"I emphasize building vocabulary."

This essay uses technical vocabulary, figurative language, and scientific details to offer an informed description of desert plant life, including explanations about how certain plant species can endure severe desert conditions.

Background Desert plants have both beauty and clever mechanisms for survival. Despite extreme temperatures and scarce rain, they have thrived and adapted, ensuring that the desert will continue to bloom far into the future.

Barbara Kingsolver (b. 1955) was awarded the National Humanities Medal in 2000 for service to the United States through her writing. Writer's Digest named Kingsolver one of the 20th century's most influential writers. Much of her writing focuses on humans' relationship with the natural world.

Called Out

Science Essay by Barbara Kingsolver   Written with Steven Hopp

AS YOU READ Pay attention to how the author describes a series of events to show how desert plants adapt, survive, and thrive in the harsh desert environment. Note any questions you have as you read.

The spring of 1998 was the Halley's Comet[1] of desert wildflower years. While nearly everyone else on the planet was cursing the soggy consequences of El Niño's[2] downpours, here in southern Arizona we were cheering for the show: Our desert hills and valleys were colorized in wild schemes of maroon, indigo, tangerine, and some hues that Crayola hasn't named yet. Our mountains wore mantles of yellow brittlebush on their rocky shoulders, as fully transformed as eastern forests in their colorful autumn foliage. Abandoned cotton fields—flat, salinized ground long since left for dead—rose again, wearing brocade. Even highway medians were so crowded with lupines and poppies that they looked like the seed-packet promises come true: that every one came up. For weeks, each

[1] **Halley's Comet:** an orbiting comet that is only visible from Earth once every 76 years.
[2] **El Niño (ĕl nēn'yō):** a temporary change in climate caused by currents in the eastern Pacific Ocean.

Called Out **51**

Jane Goodall (b. 1934) watched wild chimpanzees shaping twigs to dig for termites while on a field study in Africa at age 26. It was the first recorded observation of nonhumans making and using tools, and it rocked the scientific world. Since then, Goodall has become the world's leading expert on chimpanzees and an advocate for wildlife conservation. She spends much of her time giving lectures and writing about animals and the environment. Her books, including In the Shadow of Man and The Chimpanzee Family Book, have inspired readers around the world.

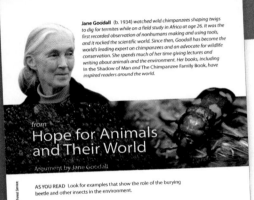

from
Hope for Animals and Their World

Argument by Jane Goodall

AS YOU READ Look for examples that show the role of the burying beetle and other insects in the environment.

American Burying Beetle
(Nicrophorus americanus)

The American burying beetle is but one of the millions of insects and other invertebrates[1] that play such a major, though seldom acknowledged, role in the maintenance of habitats and ecosystems. Most people simply lump them all into the category "creepy-crawlies" or "bugs." Some, such as butterflies, are admired and loved for their beauty (though people tend to be less interested in or even repelled by their caterpillars). Others, such as spiders, are the inadvertent cause of fear—even terror. Cockroaches are **loathed.** Hundreds of species are persecuted for the role they play in damaging our food—such as the desert locust, which ravages crops across huge areas. And there are countless species such as

loathe
(lōth) v.
to hate or despise.

[1] **invertebrates:** animals without backbones or spinal columns.

Hope for Animals and Their World **61**

"I emphasize informational texts."

Jane Goodall is a British anthropologist with many years of experience studying animals and the environment, and her argument provides information about how certain insects benefit the environment.

"I want to challenge my students to the utmost."

This short story uses humor, exaggeration, and an unconventional narrative structure to defend bats and contrast them with humans, while also including many details about how bats live.

Margaret Atwood (b. 1939) has published more than fifty works of fiction, poetry, and nonfiction. This Canadian author uses her keen intellect and sharp wit to explore ideas about nature, science, the search for identity, social criticism, and human rights. Her award-winning novels include The Handmaid's Tale, which was made into a movie, Cat's Eye, Alias Grace, and Oryx and Crake.

My Life as a Bat

Short Story by Margaret Atwood

AS YOU READ Think about the narrator's attitudes toward bats and toward humans. Pay attention to clues that show which species the narrator thinks is superior. Note any questions you have as you read.

1. Reincarnation

In my previous life I was a bat.

If you find previous lives amusing or unlikely, you are not a serious person. Consider: a great many people believe in them, and if sanity is a general **consensus** about the content of reality, who are you to disagree?

Consider also: previous lives have entered the world of commerce. Money can be made from them. You were Cleopatra,[1] you were a Flemish duke, you were a Druid priestess, and money changes hands. If the stock market exists, so must previous lives.

In the previous-life market, there is not such a great demand for Peruvian ditch-diggers as there is for Cleopatra; or for Indian latrine-cleaners, or for 1952 housewives living in California split-levels. Similarly, not many of us choose to remember our lives as vultures, spiders, or rodents, but some of us do. The fortunate few. Conventional wisdom has it that reincarnation as an animal is a

consensus
(kən-sĕn'səs) n.
agreement.

[1] **Cleopatra:** Queen of Egypt in the first century b.c.

My Life as a Bat **71**

COLLECTION 2 DIGITAL OVERVIEW

mySmartPlanner | **eBook** | *my*Notebook | *my* **WriteSmart** | **fyi** hmhfyi.com

Collection 2 Lessons	Media	Teach and Practice
Student Edition | eBook	▶ Video Links 🅷 A&E	**Close Reading and Evidence Tracking**
ANCHOR TEXT Essay by Barbara Kingsolver **"Called Out"**	🔊 **Audio** "Called Out"	**Close Read Screencasts** • Modeled Discussion 1 (lines 26–36) • Modeled Discussion 2 (lines 50–56) **Strategies for Annotation** • Determine Word Meanings • Scientific Terms
CLOSE READER Essay by Barbara Hurd **"Sea Stars"** Poem by Lorna Dee Cervantes **"Starfish"**	🔊 **Audio** "Sea Stars" 🔊 **Audio** "Starfish"	
Poem by Walt Whitman **"When I Heard the Learn'd Astronomer"**	🔊 **Audio** "When I Heard the Learn'd Astronomer"	
Argument by Jane Goodall from *Hope for Animals and Their World*	🔊 **Audio** from *Hope for Animals and Their World*	**Strategies for Annotation** • Analyze Author's Claim and Determine Purpose • Patterns of Word Changes
CLOSE READER Blog Post by Andrew C. Revkin **"Emma Marris: In Defense of Everglade Pythons"**	🔊 **Audio** "Emma Marris: In Defense of Everglade Pythons"	
ANCHOR TEXT Short Story by Margaret Atwood **"My Life as a Bat"**	🔊 **Audio** "My Life as a Bat"	**Close Read Screencasts** • Modeled Discussion 1 (lines 21–29) • Modeled Discussion 2 (lines 106–114) **Strategies for Annotation** • Determine Figurative Meanings • Using Reference Sources
CLOSE READER Short Story by Haruki Murakami **"The Seventh Man"**	🔊 **Audio** "The Seventh Man"	
Poem by Linda Hogan **"Carry"**	🔊 **Audio** "Carry"	**Strategies for Annotation** • Support Inferences About Theme
Collection 2 Performance Tasks **A** Write a Research Report **B** Participate in a Panel Discussion	**fyi** hmhfyi.com hmhfyi.com	**Interactive Lessons** **A** Conducting Research and Evaluating Sources **A** Writing Informative Texts **B** Participating in Collaborative Discussions **B** Using Textual Evidence

		Interactive Lessons Writing an Argument Analyzing and Evaluating Presentations	Lesson Assessments Writing an Argument Analyzing and Evaluating Presentations
For Systematic Coverage of Writing and Speaking & Listening Standards			

Assess		Extend	Reteach
Performance Task	**Online Assessment**	**Teacher eBook**	**Teacher eBook**
Speaking Activity: Analysis	Selection Test	**Respond Thoughtfully in Discussions**	**Determine Central Idea > Level Up Tutorial** > Main Idea and Supporting Details
Writing Activity: Comparison	Selection Test	**Interactive Whiteboard Lesson >** Analyze Text Structure	**Determine Theme Through Objective Summary > Level Up Tutorial >** Universal and Recurring Themes
Writing Activity: Analysis	Selection Test	**Analyze Impact of Word Choice on Tone**	**Analyze Author's Claim and Determine Purpose > Level Up Tutorial >** Elements of an Argument
Speaking Activity: Research	Selection Test	**Conducting Research on the Web**	**Analyze Author's Choices: Text Structure > Level Up Tutorial >** Plot: Sequence of Events
Speaking Activity: Discussion	Selection Test	**Pose and Respond to Questions** **Analyze Figurative Meanings** **Interactive Whiteboard Lesson >** Figurative Language and Imagery	**Support Inferences About Theme > Level Up Tutorial >** Imagery
A Write a Research Report **B** Participate in a Panel Discussion	Collection Test		

Collection 2 Lessons	COMMON CORE Key Learning Objective	Performance Task
ANCHOR TEXT **Essay by Barbara Kingsolver** **Lexile 1180** **"Called Out," p. 51A**	**The student will be able to...** determine a central idea in an essay and figurative, connotative, and technical meanings of words and phrases	Speaking Activity: Analysis
Poem by Walt Whitman **"When I Heard the Learn'd Astronomer" p. 59A**	**The student will be able to...** identify the theme of a poem through writing an objective summary that states the key events and ideas in the poem	Writing Activity: Comparison
Argument by Jane Goodall **Lexile 1300** **from *Hope for Animals and Their World,* p. 61A**	**The student will be able to...** analyze an author's claim and purpose	Writing Activity: Analysis
ANCHOR TEXT **Short Story by Margaret Atwood** **Lexile 1020** **"My Life as a Bat," p. 71A**	**The student will be able to...** analyze a writer's choices in terms of text structure, figurative meaning, and tone	Speaking Activity: Research
Poem by Linda Hogan **"Carry" p. 79A**	**The student will be able to...** support inferences about theme	Speaking Activity: Discussion

Collection 2 Performance Tasks:
A Write a Research Report
B Participate in a Panel Discussion

Vocabulary Strategy	Language and Style	Student Instructional Support	CLOSE READER Selection
Scientific Terms	Participial Phrases	**Scaffolding for ELL Students:** Vocabulary Support: Idioms **When Students Struggle:** Language Support: Participial Phrases	Essay by Barbara Hurd "Sea Stars," p. 58b **Lexile 1210** Poem by Lorna Dee Cervantes "Starfish," p. 58b
		Scaffolding for ELL Students: Analyze Language	
Patterns of Word Changes	Relative Clauses	**Scaffolding for ELL Students:** • Determine Purpose • Analyze Language **When Students Struggle:** Comprehension of Claims and Supporting Evidence **To Challenge Students:** Make Connections	Blog Post by Andrew C. Revkin "Emma Marris: In Defense of Everglade Pythons," p. 70b **Lexile 1360**
Using Reference Sources	Colons and Dashes	**Scaffolding for ELL Students:** Determine Figurative Meanings **When Students Struggle:** Identifying Theme	Short Story by Haruki Murakami "The Seventh Man," p. 78b **Lexile 910**
		Scaffolding for ELL Students: Pronoun Referents	

ANCHOR TEXT # Called Out

Science Essay by Barbara Kingsolver

Why This Text?

Students regularly encounter nonfiction writing in textbooks, in periodicals, and on the Internet. This lesson explores a science essay in which Barbara Kingsolver uses figurative and connotative language along with technical words and phrases to create an essay that is both informative and emotionally engaging.

Key Learning Objective: Determine a central idea in an essay and figurative, connotative, and technical meanings of words and phrases.

For practice and application:

Writing About the Sea

Close Reader selection
"Sea Stars," an essay by Barbara Hurd

Close Reader selection
"Starfish," a poem by Lorna Dee Cervantes

COMMON CORE Common Core Standards

RI 1 Cite textual evidence.

RI 2 Determine a central idea and analyze its development.

RI 4 Determine the meaning of words and phrases.

RI 5 Analyze how an author's ideas are developed by particular sentences or paragraphs.

RI 6 Determine an author's point of view and analyze how an author uses rhetoric.

SL 1 Participate in collaborative discussions with diverse partners.

SL 1d Respond thoughtfully to diverse perspectives, make new connections based on evidence.

L 1b Use various types of phrases and clauses to convey specific meanings.

L 5 Demonstrate understanding of figurative language.

L 6 Acquire and use general academic words and phrases.

▲ Text Complexity Rubric

Quantitative Measures	**Called Out** Lexile: L1180
Qualitative Measures	**Levels of Meaning/Purpose** more than one purpose; implied, easily identified from context
	Structure organization of main ideas and details complex but explicit
	Language Conventionality and Clarity some unfamiliar, academic, or domain-specific words
	Knowledge Demands some specialized knowledge required; difficult science concepts
Reader/Task Considerations	Teacher determined Vary by individual reader and type of text

CLOSE READ

Background Have students read the background and information about the author. Tell students that the Sonoran Desert, about which Kingsolver writes, may receive as little as eight inches of rain per year. Some plants have adapted to this condition by developing deep roots that tap into groundwater.

Barbara Kingsolver is well known for writing fiction, as well as nonfiction. Explain to students that she uses many of the techniques of fiction writing to make her science writing more interesting to readers. In 1998, Kingsolver established the PEN/Bellwether Prize for Socially Engaged Fiction, which is awarded to previously unpublished authors who address issues of social change in their work.

AS YOU READ Direct students to use the As You Read activity to focus their reading. Remind students to note any questions they have as they read.

Determine Central Idea <small>COMMON CORE</small> RI 2
(LINES 1–15)

Explain that writers often use an opening paragraph to gain their readers' attention. Kingsolver uses her opening paragraph to excite readers about her topic and to introduce them to a fascinating process in nature.

Ⓐ ASK STUDENTS to read the opening paragraph. Have them identify the idea Kingsolver will explore and its significance. *(Kingsolver will discuss the blooming of desert wildflowers in 1998. This blooming produced an abundance of wildflowers, as well as unfamiliar species.)*

Determine Word Meanings <small>COMMON CORE</small> RI 1, RI 4
(LINES 2–8)

Explain to students that writers use **connotative meanings**—the emotions and ideas associated with specific words—to create an emotional response in their readers. Kingsolver uses this type of language to engage her readers.

Ⓑ CITE TEXT EVIDENCE Have students reread lines 2–8 and find examples of connotative language. How do these words affect the reader? *(Connotative words: cursing, cheering, colorized, wild, transformed. These words make the description more vivid; they help the reader understand how people felt about the desert blooming.)*

Background *Desert plants have both beauty and clever mechanisms for survival. Despite extreme temperatures and scarce rain, they have thrived and adapted, ensuring that the desert will continue to bloom far into the future.*

Barbara Kingsolver *(b. 1955) was awarded the National Humanities Medal in 2000 for service to the United States through her writing. Writer's Digest named Kingsolver one of the 20th century's most influential writers. Much of her writing focuses on humans' relationship with the natural world.*

Called Out

Science Essay by Barbara Kingsolver   Written with Steven Hopp

AS YOU READ Pay attention to how the author describes a series of events to show how desert plants adapt, survive, and thrive in the harsh desert environment. Note any questions you have as you read.

Ⓐ The spring of 1998 was the Halley's Comet[1] of desert wildflower years. While nearly everyone else on the planet was cursing the soggy consequences of El Niño's[2] downpours, here in southern Arizona we were cheering for the show: Our desert hills and valleys were colorized in wild schemes of maroon, indigo, tangerine, and some hues that Crayola hasn't named yet. Our mountains wore mantles of yellow brittlebush on their rocky shoulders, as fully transformed as eastern forests in their colorful autumn foliage.
10 Abandoned cotton fields—flat, salinized ground long since left for dead—rose again, wearing brocade. Even highway medians were so crowded with lupines and poppies that they looked like the seed-packet promises come true: that every one came up. For weeks, each Ⓑ

---

[1] **Halley's Comet:** an orbiting comet that is only visible from Earth once every 76 years.
[2] **El Niño (ĕl nēn´ yō):** a temporary change in climate caused by currents in the eastern Pacific Ocean.

Image Credits: (t) ©AP Images; (c) ©Susie Mccaffrey/Garden Picture Library/Getty Images; (b) ©Kitch Bain/Shutterstock

---

Close Read Screencasts ▶ View It!

Modeled Discussions

Have students click the *Close Read* icons in their eBooks to access the screencast in which readers discuss and annotate the following key passage:

- explaining the blooming desert to outsiders (lines 26–36).

As a class, view and discuss this video. Then have students pair up to do an independent close read of an additional passage—the difference between knowledge and experiencing something firsthand (lines 50–56).

CLOSE READ

Determine Central Idea

COMMON CORE RI 1, RI 2

(LINES 16–49)

Point out to students that Kingsolver calls the flowering of the desert "a kind of miracle" (lines 16–18).

 CITE TEXT EVIDENCE Have students cite other examples of nonscientific reasons for the desert's flowering. ("God" [line 42];" higher power" [line 48]) How do these references help shape Kingsolver's central idea? (*The flowering of the desert seems mysterious because it is highly unpredictable and in some ways, unexplainable.*)

Analyze Language

COMMON CORE RI 6

(LINES 26–42)

Explain that writers may vary the kind of language they use to create a specific tone. In this passage, Kingsolver uses dialogue within a scientific essay.

D **ASK STUDENTS** how Kingsolver's use of dialogue advances her purpose and affects the reader. (*Even though the essay's topic is a scientific one, the use of dialogue makes the passage accessible to the reader.*)

CRITICAL VOCABULARY

botanical: Kingsolver describes leaving the house as a "botanical treasure hunt." **ASK STUDENTS** to identify the treasure she is hunting. (*She is looking for plants that have bloomed.*)

climes: Kingsolver explains that people from other climate areas don't understand why everyone is excited about the desert blooming. **ASK STUDENTS** why Kingsolver uses the word climes instead of a word such as region. (*Outsiders don't understand how the climate of the desert affects life there, and Kingsolver probably wants to call attention to the unique desert climate.*)

prognosticating: Kingsolver says people who live in the desert spend a lot of time predicting what plants will bloom in the spring. **ASK STUDENTS** why it is difficult for desert dwellers to prognosticate the arrival of spring foliage. (*Too many factors, such as temperature and rainfall, affect what plants will bloom.*)

 A day's walk to the mailbox became a **botanical** treasure hunt, as our attention caught first on new colors, then on whole new species in this terrain we thought we had already cataloged.

The first warm days of March appear to call out a kind of miracle here: the explosion of nearly half our desert's flowering species, all stirred suddenly into a brief cycle of bloom and death.
20 Actually, though, the call begins subtly, much earlier, with winter rains and gradually climbing temperatures. The intensity of the floral outcome varies a great deal from one spring to another; that much is obvious to anyone who ventures outdoors at the right time of year and pays attention. But even couch potatoes could not have missed the fact that 1998 was special: Full-color wildflower photos made the front page of every major newspaper in the Southwest.

Our friends from other **climes** couldn't quite make out what the fuss was about. Many people aren't aware that the desert blooms at all, even in a normal year, and few would guess how much effort we devote to waiting and **prognosticating**. "Is this something like
30 Punxsutawney Phil on Groundhog Day?"[3] asked a friend from the East.

"Something like that. Or the fall color in New England. All winter the experts take measurements and make forecasts. This year they predicted gold, but it's already gone platinum. In a spot where you'd expect a hundred flowers, we've got a thousand. More kinds than anybody alive has ever seen at once."

"But these are annual flowers?"

"Right."

"Well, then. . . ." Our nonbiologist friend struggled to frame her
40 question: "If they weren't there *last* year, and this year they *are*, then who planted them?"

One of us blurted, "*God* planted them!"

We glanced at each other nervously: A picturesque response indeed, from scientifically trained types like ourselves. Yet it seemed more compelling than any pedestrian lecture on life cycles and latency periods.[4] Where *had* they all come from? Had these seeds just been lying around in the dirt for decades? And how was it that, at the behest of some higher power than the calendar, all at once there came a crowd?
50 The answers to these questions tell a tale as complex as a Beethoven symphony. Before a concert, you could look at a lot of sheet music and try to prepare yourself mentally for the piece it inscribed, but you'd still be knocked out when you heard it performed. With wildflowers, as in a concert, the magic is in the

botanical
(bə-tăn´ĭ-kəl) *adj.*
related to plants.

C

clime
(klīm) *n.*
climate area.

prognosticate
(prŏg-nŏs´tĭ-kāt´) *v.*
to forecast or predict.

C

C

---

[3] **Punxsutawney Phil on Groundhog Day:** the "official" Pennsylvania animal whose shadow or lack thereof on February 2 forecasts the duration of winter.
[4] **latency periods:** times when growth stops or pauses.

SCAFFOLDING FOR ELL STUDENTS

Vocabulary Support: Idioms Pair English learners with proficient English speakers. Explain to students that an **idiom** is an expression whose accepted meaning is different from its literal meaning. If students cannot guess the idiom's meaning from context and word meaning, they can try looking up the full expression, enclosed in quotation marks, in an online source. Ask the proficient English speaker in each pair to elaborate on the definition and provide additional examples of the idiom's usage.

ASK STUDENTS what they think "couch potatoes" refers to. (*People who are too lazy to get off the couch.*) Have students work in small groups to find other examples of idioms and present their findings to the class. (***Possible answer:*** *"knocked out," line 53.*)

timing, the subtle combinations—and, most important, the extent of the preparations.

For a species, the bloom is just the means to an end. The flower show is really about making seeds, and the object of the game is persistence through hell or high water, both of which are features of the Sonoran Desert. In winter, when snow is falling on much of North America, we get slow, drizzly rains that can last for days and soak the whole region to its core. The Navajo call these female rains, as opposed to the "male rains" of late summer—those rowdy thunderstorms that briefly disrupt the hot afternoons, drenching one small plot of ground while the next hill over remains parched. It's the female rains that affect spring flowering, and in some years, such as 1998, the **benefaction** trails steadily from winter on into spring. In others, after a lick and a promise, the weather dries up for good.

Challenging conditions for an **ephemeral**, these are. If a little seed begins to grow at the first promise of rain, and that promise gets broken, that right there is the end of its little life. If the same thing happened to every seed in the bank, it would mean the end of the species. But it *doesn't* happen that way. Desert wildflowers have had millennia in which to come to terms with their inconstant mother. Once the plant has rushed through growth and flowering, its seeds wait in the soil—and not just until the next time conditions permit germination,[5] but often longer. In any given year, a subset of a species's seeds don't germinate, because they're programmed for a longer dormancy. This seed bank is the plant's

benefaction
(bĕn´ə-făk´shən) *n.*
a gift or assistance.

ephemeral
(ĭ-fĕm´ər-əl) *n.*
a short-lived plant.

---

[5] **germination:** the process in which plants emerge from seeds.

APPLYING ACADEMIC VOCABULARY

scope	enhance

As you discuss Kingsolver's essay, incorporate the following Collection 2 academic vocabulary words: *scope* and *enhance*. When you explore Kingsolver's central idea and supporting details, consider how she shapes the **scope** of her essay. As you examine her writing, ask students to explain how Kingsolver uses language to **enhance** the tone of her essay.

CLOSE READ

Determine Word Meanings (LINES 57–69)

COMMON CORE · RI 1, RI 4, RI 5, RI 6, L 5a

Explain that Kingsolver uses **figurative language,** language not meant to be taken literally, to describe inanimate objects as having human characteristics.

E CITE TEXT EVIDENCE Have students find examples of this kind of figurative language, personification, in the first paragraph. *(Flowers are described as persistent [line 59]; rains are male and female [lines 62–63]; male rains are "rowdy" [line 63].)* How does this language affect how the reader perceives this information? *(It makes the natural world seem more alive.)*

Determine Central Idea

COMMON CORE · RI 1, RI 2, RL 2, RL 4

(LINES 70–80)

Point out to students that Kingsolver's tone changes somewhat in this section. Have them read this page with that idea in mind.

F CITE TEXT EVIDENCE Have students explain how Kingsolver's tone shifts in this paragraph. *(She uses more technical terms.)* Have them cite examples of **scientific language.** *("ephemeral" [line 70]; "bank" [line 73]; "millennia" [line 75]; "germination" [line 78]; "dormancy" [line 80])* Have them identify the main idea of this paragraph. *(Seed banks—and wildflowers—have developed methods they can use to protect themselves and survive.)*

CRITICAL VOCABULARY

benefaction: Kingsolver describes the "female rains" as a gift to the seeds of the Sonoran Desert. **ASK STUDENTS** what the seeds need to bloom. *(water)* How are the "female rains" a gift to the seeds? *(They give seeds what they need to bloom.)*

ephemeral: Kingsolver discusses how weather conditions affect short-lived plants. **ASK STUDENTS** to describe one way ephemerals have adapted to their environment. *(Seeds of the same species have different germination periods so they don't all grow at the same time.)*

Determine Central Idea RI 1, RI 2

(LINES 89–107)

Remind students that they can determine the main idea by examining specific details. Identifying main ideas can help them discover a text's central idea.

G CITE TEXT EVIDENCE Have students cite specific strategies desert ephemerals use to survive. (*Vary schedules for germination, flowering, and seed-set; vary seed size.*) Have students use the evidence to determine the main idea. (*Variation reduces competition within species and invasion by annuals.*)

Determine Word Meanings (LINES 108–118)   COMMON CORE RI 1, RI 4, RI 5, RI 6

Remind students that Kingsolver often uses **figurative language** to make her descriptions vivid for her readers.

H CITE TEXT EVIDENCE Have students cite examples of figurative language in the final paragraph. (*"captive to the calendar" [line 100]; "magic show" [line 111]; "smile" [line 115]*) How is this language different from that in the previous paragraph? (*That language is more scientific.*) Why might Kingsolver choose to end on this note? (*to suggest that understanding nature doesn't remove the mystery*)

COLLABORATIVE DISCUSSION Have students pair up and discuss the scientific process that explains how the plants bloom and then discuss the vivid effect of such a bloom, citing textual evidence for them both. Then have students share their conclusions with the class as a whole. Accept all reasonable responses.

ASK STUDENTS to share any questions they generated in the course of reading and discussing this selection.

---

protection against a beckoning rain followed by drought. If any kind of wildflower ever existed whose seeds all sprouted and died before following through to seed-set, then that species perished long ago. This is what natural selection is about. The species that have made it this far have encoded genetic smarts enough to outwit every peril. They produce seeds with different latency periods: Some germinate quickly, and some lie in wait, not just loitering there but loading the soil with many separate futures.

90   Scientists at the University of Arizona have spent years examining the intricacies of seed banks. Desert ephemerals, they've learned, use a surprising variety of strategies to fine-tune their own cycles to a climate whose cycles are not predictable—or at least, not predictable given the relatively short span of human observation. Even in a year as wet as 1998, when photo-ops and seed production exploded, the natives were not just seizing the moment; they were stashing away future seasons of success by varying, among and within species, their genetic schedules for germination, flowering, and seed-set. This variation reduces the intense competition that would result if every seed germinated at once. Some species
100   even vary seed size: Larger seeds make more resilient sprouts, and smaller ones are less costly to produce; either morph may be programmed for delayed germination, depending on the particular strategy of the species. As a consequence of these sophisticated adaptations, desert natives can often hold their own against potential invasion by annual plants introduced from greener, more predictable pastures. You have to get up awfully early in the morning to outwit a native on its home turf.

The scientific term for these remarkable plants, "ephemeral annuals," suggests something that's as fragile as a poppy petal, a
110   captive to the calendar. That is our misapprehension, along with our notion of this floral magic show—now you see it, now you don't—as a thing we can predict and possess like a garden. In spite of our determination to contain what we see in neat, annual packages, the blazing field of blues and golds is neither a beginning nor an end. It's just a blink, or maybe a smile, in the long life of a species whose blueprint for perseverance must outdistance all our record books. The flowers will go on mystifying us, answering to a clock that ticks so slowly we won't live long enough to hear it.

COLLABORATIVE DISCUSSION In what way is the desert bloom even more impressive when viewed with an awareness of the underlying science? With a partner, discuss the complex ways desert plants ensure their survival. Cite specific textual evidence to support your ideas.

WHEN STUDENTS STRUGGLE. . .

Comprehension Support Students may find Kingsolver's writing difficult to follow because of the length of her sentences. To guide their comprehension, have them break up her longer sentences into shorter sentences that are easier to understand. Demonstrate how to break up a long sentence using the complete sentence in lines 90–93. Then have students work in pairs to create an edited version of the paragraph, using sentences that are easier to follow.

Determine Central Idea

Barbara Kingsolver uses many specific details to shape her **central idea** in "Called Out." By analyzing these details, you can better understand how Kingsolver develops her central idea over the course of the essay. A graphic organizer can help you analyze details and determine a central idea. You can then use this information to write an **objective summary** of the text, one that captures the main ideas and most important details but does not express your opinions.

Detail: Some seeds are "programmed for a longer dormancy." (lines 79–80)

Detail: Seeds have different latency periods: "some germinate quickly" while others "lie in wait." (lines 86–87)

Central Idea: _____

Detail: Desert plant species vary their "genetic schedules for germination" to reduce competition. (lines 96–99)

Detail: "Some species even vary seed size: Larger seeds make more resilient sprouts. . . ." (lines 99–100)

Determine Word Meanings

COMMON CORE RI 4

An author chooses words carefully to enhance the overall meaning and **tone**, or attitude, of a text. Kingsolver skillfully integrates figurative, connotative, and technical language to help convey her sense of wonder at the adaptability of desert plants.

Figurative	Connotative	Technical
Figurative meanings go beyond the literal to make a striking comparison. If a word doesn't make sense at first, consider its figurative meanings. For example, when Kingsolver describes fields as "wearing brocade," you can determine that the fields are not covered in elaborate fabric; this figurative use creates a vivid picture of how the fields look.	**Connotative language** is a writer's use of the feelings suggested by words to prompt an emotional response. Kingsolver uses connotative language to suggest awe at the ability of plants to survive in the desert. For example, describing the plants as "fragile" not only expresses their physical state but may make readers appreciate and want to protect them.	**Technical words and phrases** precisely describe complicated ideas or processes. Particularly in science writing, you may encounter unfamiliar words or technical meanings of familiar words, such as "banks" in line 90. Use footnotes or a dictionary as you read to be sure you understand technical meanings.

TEACH

CLOSE READ

Determine Central Idea
COMMON CORE RI 2

Make sure that students understand the difference between *objective* and *subjective* writing. Objective writing seeks to present facts without personal point of view or bias. This is different from a personal response, which requires a point of view.

Have students determine the central idea based on the details provided in the graphic organizer. *(Desert plants use a variety of strategies to ensure their survival in a harsh environment.)*

Determine Word Meanings
COMMON CORE RI 4

Point out that Kingsolver often uses figurative language, connotative language, and technical words and phrases in the same paragraph. Have students reread lines 89–107. Have them cite examples of each kind of language. *(Figurative: seizing the moment [line 95], stashing away [line 96]; connotative: exploded [line 95], invasion [line 105]; technical: genetic, germination [line 97].)* How does the combination of different kinds of language affect her tone? *(It brings personality and playfulness to a scientific essay.)*

Strategies for Annotation   ✎ 🖥 *Annotate it!*

Determine Word Meanings
COMMON CORE RI 4

Encourage students to use their eBook annotation tools to indicate different styles of language Kingsolver uses in her essay. Have them:

- Highlight in yellow figurative language
- Highlight in blue connotative language
- Highlight in green technical words
- Write a note for each highlighted word or phrase. Classify it as figurative, connotative, or technical. Note the tone or impression it brings. Explain how that type of language enhanced the essay.

Our mountains wore mantles of yellow brittlebush on their rocky shoulders, as fully transformed as eastern forests in their colorful autumn foliage. Abandoned cotton fields—flat, salinized ground long since left for dead—rose again, wearing brocade. Even highway medians were so crowded with lupines and poppies that they looked like the seedpacket promises come true: that every one came up.

PRACTICE & APPLY

Analyzing the Text COMMON CORE RI 1, RI 2, RI 4, RI 5, SL 1

Possible answers:

1. *The author describes the flowering of the desert as a "show" and says residents were "cheering" (line 4). She compares the flowers to rich clothing, such as "mantles" (line 7) and "brocade" (line 10). She calls the desert's blooming a "miracle" (line 17). This language all describes the desert as a magical place.*

2. *In lines 26–49, Kingsolver develops the central idea that the flowering of the desert can't be fully explained. She tells us that many people don't know the desert blooms at all, and compares the predictions to Punxsutawney Phil, the groundhog that "predicts" the end of winter. Even though she and her friends are scientifically trained, one points to God as the source of the beauty. Despite the best efforts of the experts to make predictions, everyone is surprised when the desert blooms.*

3. *In lines 58–59, Kingsolver says the "object of the game is persistence," as if the plants are competing directly against each other. Plants "outwit every peril" and "lie in wait" (lines 85–87). Desert plants can "hold their own" against "invasion" by outsiders. These word choices work together to create a sense of desert plants as competitive, sentient beings.*

4. *"Female rains" are slow, persistent rains that fall in winter and soak the desert completely. "Male rains" are the thunderstorms of summer. They drench some land but leave other plots dry (lines 60–67). Plants depend on the soaking of female rains for the water they need to germinate and grow. Male rains are too inconsistent to benefit plant life.*

5. *In the second half of the essay, Kingsolver uses technical terms, such as "germination" (line 78), "seed bank" (line 80), and "latency periods" (line 86) to provide detailed information about how desert plants survive. The first half of the essay takes a more emotional approach to desert life. By providing technical details, Kingsolver gives the reader a scientific basis for the sense of beauty and wonder she has infused in her writing.*

6. *In the final paragraph, Kingsolver returns to the writing style used in her opening. Even though experts understand the science behind the flowering of desert plants, there are too many variables for them to accurately predict when they will bloom. Science can't overcome the mystery of life.*

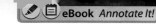

Analyzing the Text COMMON CORE RI 1, RI 2, RI 4, RI 5, SL 1

Cite Text Evidence Support your responses with evidence from the selection.

1. **Cite Evidence** How does the author use figurative language to establish a tone of wonder in the first two paragraphs of the essay? Provide specific examples and explain how they provide the reader with a unique sense of the desert.

2. **Summarize** Reread lines 26–49. How does this passage help develop a central idea of Kingsolver's essay? Explain that central idea in an objective summary.

3. **Cite Evidence** Throughout the essay, the author uses connotative words and phrases such as "treasure hunt" (line 13) that suggest a contest or competition is taking place in the desert. Find several other examples of language that suggests competition. Explain how these discrete, or separate, word choices work together to shape the overall meaning and tone of the essay.

4. **Compare** What is the difference between the "female rains" and the "male rains"? What are the effects of each type of rain on the desert, and why is this difference significant?

5. **Analyze** In the second half of the essay, the author uses technical words and phrases to provide a more scientific description of how plant seeds survive in the desert. Find some examples, and explain how this technical language helps refine, or sharpen, her ideas about desert seeds.

6. **Draw Conclusions** Reread the last paragraph of the essay. Why does the author conclude by stating that the "flowers will go on mystifying us"?

PERFORMANCE TASK

Speaking Activity: Analysis Kingsolver's essay uses figurative, connotative, and technical language to give readers new perspectives on the desert ecosystem. Which kind of language is most effective in communicating scientific information to a general audience? Discuss this topic with a small group of classmates.

1. Working with a partner, review the text to find especially good examples of figurative, connotative, and technical language.

2. Form a small group to discuss the examples you have identified. Why is each one effective?

3. When you have discussed all the examples, take a vote on which kind of language best communicates information.

4. Write a summary of your group's discussion that includes your conclusion, the reasons for it, and some examples from the text.

Assign this performance task.

PERFORMANCE TASK COMMON CORE RI 1, RI 4

Speaking Activity: Analysis Have students in each group assign everyone a role in creating the summary. Each group member has one of the following roles: state the group's conclusion, explain reasons for this conclusion, cite examples from the text. As groups discuss examples of figurative, connotative, and technical language and decide which is most effective, group members can take notes to complete their portion of the group summary.

Critical Vocabulary

botanical   clime   prognosticate   benefaction   ephemeral

Practice and Apply Complete each sentence stem so that your addition reflects the meaning of the Critical Vocabulary word.

1. To **prognosticate** the next big desert bloom is difficult because . . .

2. In the desert, rain is considered a **benefaction** because . . .

3. Kingsolver's essay could be called a **botanical** essay because . . .

4. It would be hard to plan a trip to see a particular desert **ephemeral** in bloom because . . .

5. People in a different **clime** might be surprised that the desert spring is so colorful because . . .

Vocabulary Strategy: Scientific Terms

Knowing the meanings of the scientific words and phrases used in Kingsolver's essay is essential for understanding her central ideas. For instance, Kingsolver uses the Critical Vocabulary word *ephemeral* several times in the second half of her essay. This word is more commonly used as an adjective meaning "lasting a short time." However, readers need to understand its scientific meaning as a very specific kind of desert plant to appreciate her discussion of these plants' survival mechanisms. The chart shows another example.

Word	Example of Usage from Text	Significance
botanical	"For weeks, each day's walk to the mailbox became a *botanical* treasure hunt, as our attention caught first on new colors, then on whole new species in this terrain we thought we had already cataloged."	The meaning of *botanical* ("relating to plants") clarifies that the new colors and species are those of plants that have bloomed in the yard.

Practice and Apply With a partner, review the text and identify three other scientific terms in Kingsolver's essay. With each word you choose, follow these steps:

1. Define each term. Use classroom and online resources for help, but write the definition in your own words.

2. Provide an example of how the term is used in the essay and explain its significance to Kingsolver's central ideas and her purpose for writing.

3. Use each word you chose in a sentence.

Critical Vocabulary

Possible answers:

1. *. . . there are too many variables to make an accurate prediction.*

2. *. . . it benefits the seeds waiting in the earth.*

3. *. . . it explains how plants survive in the desert.*

4. *. . . these plants only live for a short period of time.*

5. *. . . they are unfamiliar with the climate in the desert.*

Vocabulary Strategy: Scientific Terms

Sample answer:

1. *Dormancy: a time of inaction*

2. *In the essay, Kingsolver says some seeds don't sprout because they are designed for longer dormancy. This is one way desert plants survive.*

3. *Animals go through a period of dormancy when they hibernate.*

Strategies for Annotation   ✎ 🖺 *Annotate it!*

Scientific Terms

Have students locate the sentences containing the scientific terms *dormancy, germination, latency,* and *seed bank* in Kingsolver's essay. Encourage them to use their eBook annotation tools to explore how these words are used in the context of the essay. Have students:

- Highlight in yellow each scientific term or phrase.
- Reread the surrounding sentences, underlining any words and phrases that explain or deepen the meaning of the term.
- Review their annotations to determine the significance of the terms.

of the species. But it *doesn't* happen that way. Desert  wildflowers have had millennia in which to come to terms with their inconstant mother. Once the plant has rushed through growth and flowering, its seeds wait in the soil—and not just until the next time conditions permit germination, but often longer. In any given

PRACTICE & APPLY

Language and Style: Participial Phrases

 COMMON CORE L 1b

Remind students that not every verb form indicates a participial phrase. Instruct them that, when looking for participial phrases, they should look for the noun or pronoun that the phrase modifies.

Possible answers:

1. *"Abandoned cotton fields—flat, salinized ground long since left for dead—rose again, wearing brocade."* The phrase *"wearing brocade"* describes how the cotton fields suddenly broke out in color. *"The first warm days of March appear to call out a kind of miracle here: the explosion of nearly half our desert's flowering species, all stirred suddenly into a brief cycle of bloom and death."* The phrase *"stirred suddenly into a brief cycle of bloom and death"* gives a vivid description of the fast and violent cycle of flowers in the desert. *"The Navajo call these female rains, as opposed to the "male rains" of late summer— those rowdy thunderstorms that briefly disrupt the hot afternoons, drenching one small plot of ground while the next hill over remains parched."* The phrase *"drenching one small plot of ground while the next hill over remains parched"* gives more character to the "male rains," and shows how they are "rowdy."

2. *Answers will vary. When students' paragraphs are complete, they should be able to point to two participial phrases.*

 Assess It!

Online Selection Test
- Download an editable ExamView bank.
- Assign and manage this test online.

Language and Style: Participial Phrases

 L 1b

A **participle** is a verb form that functions like an adjective, modifying nouns and pronouns. Typically, a participle uses a present-tense verb form ending in -*ing* or a past-tense verb form ending in -*ed* or -*en*. Kingsolver uses participles to add vibrancy and specificity to her descriptions, as in *"flowering* species" (lines 17–18).

Participial phrases are made up of participles and their modifiers and complements. An example from Kingsolver's essay is *"ground long since left for dead"* (lines 9–10). In this example, the participle is *left*, and words that modify it are *long since* and *for dead*. The entire participial phrase modifies the noun *ground*.

Read the following sentence from the essay:

> Some germinate quickly, and some lie in wait, not just loitering there but loading the soil with many separate futures.

Kingsolver could have expressed this idea using two separate sentences:

> Some germinate quickly, and some lie in wait. These seeds do not just loiter there but load the soil with many separate futures.

While this version communicates the same idea, the wording is less engaging and creates a pause between linked ideas. The use of the participial phrase, *not just loitering there but loading the soil with many separate futures,* in the original version conveys a relationship more quickly and holds the reader's interest.

Practice and Apply Understand and use participial phrases by following these steps:

1. Working with a partner, identify three additional participial phrases in "Called Out" and discuss how these phrases add to your understanding of the topic.

2. Then on your own, write a short paragraph on a topic of your choice. In your paragraph, include two sentences that contain participial phrases. Trade your paragraph with your partner. Identify the participial phrases in your partner's paragraph while your partner identifies the participial phrases in your paragraph.

WHEN STUDENTS STRUGGLE...

Language Support: Participial Phrases Use the sentences below to help guide students' understanding of participial phrases.

The *happy* **woman** walked through the *flowering* **desert**.

Sheilded from the sun by a wide-brimmed hat, **she** approached the *blooming* **flowers**.

The **flowers**, *sparkling with dew,* made **her** smile.

Have students identify the nouns and pronouns in the sentences (boldfaced). Review that adjectives modify, or describe, nouns and pronouns. Point out the adjective in the first sentence. Finally, demonstrate how participial phrases act as adjectives. Help students find the participles and participial phrases in the rest of the sentences.

Respond Thoughtfully in Discussions

COMMON CORE
SL 1d,
RI 4,
RI 6

TEACH

Before students begin work on this selection's Performance Task, review good practices for participating in collaborative discussions.

- **Consider different ideas** because other students participating in the discussion may have different opinions. It's important to listen to them and consider what they have to say. Understanding their ideas and opinions may clarify your own.
- **Summarize** points of agreement or disagreement in a discussion to build on them.
- **Respond thoughtfully** to others' opinions. Build on their ideas and express your own clearly and persuasively.

Review the different types of language students encountered in this selection.

- **Figurative language** compares two unlike things to create an effect. For example, Kingsolver compares the spring bloom of 1998 to Halley's Comet because it was a rare event.
- **Connotative language** uses the feelings evoked by a word to create an emotional response. Kingsolver says ephemerals are "captive" to the calendar.
- **Technical words and phrases** describe complicated ideas or processes with precision. Kingsolver uses terms that are specific to botany, such as *germination*.

COLLABORATIVE DISCUSSION

Have students work in groups to determine strategies for identifying word choice. For example, they may choose to use a three-column chart to list examples of figurative, connotative, and technical language.

Remind students to review the descriptions of different types of language on page 55 when determining word meanings. Encourage them to provide evidence to explain why they understand a word or phrase as they do. Remind them that figurative and connotative language may be interpreted in more than one way. Encourage them to listen to the opinions of others and find common ground.

Determine Central Idea

COMMON CORE
RI 2

RETEACH

Remind students that the purpose of informative writing is to present a central idea. Readers can determine the central idea by analyzing details.

Explain to students that paragraphs also have central ideas that are normally referred to as main ideas. The main ideas of individual paragraphs may serve as supporting details for the central idea of the larger work.

Have students review lines 70–88 in Kingsolver's essay. Ask volunteers to suggest important details from this paragraph. *(The desert presents challenging conditions; seeds lie dormant in the soil; seeds from the same plant have different latency periods.)* From these details, ask students to determine the main idea of the paragraph. *(In order to survive, desert plants have adapted to uncertain rainfall followed by drought.*

 LEVEL UP TUTORIALS Assign the following *Level Up* tutorial: **Main Idea and Supporting Details**

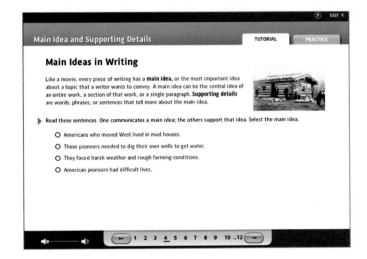

CLOSE READING APPLICATION

Students can apply the skill to another informative text. Have students work independently to read an article from a magazine, newspaper, or website. Have them analyze details, including the main ideas of individual paragraphs, to determine the central idea. Suggest they use a graphic organizer to help them keep track of details and determine the central idea. Have them use their analysis to write an objective summary of the article.

Writing About the Sea

Starfish

Poem by Lorna Dee Cervantes

Sea Stars

Essay by Barbara Hurd

Why These Texts

Students often read the text of a poem or essay without a complete grasp of the text's central idea. Poetry and literary nonfiction may use figurative language to contribute to a central idea. Analyzing the authors' use of figurative language will help students understand the central ideas of the poem and essay. With the help of the close-reading questions, students will analyze the authors' descriptions and comparisons. This close reading will lead students to a deeper understanding of the authors' central ideas.

Background Have students read the background and the information about the authors. Introduce the selections by telling students that they will read a poem and an essay that have the same topic: starfish. There are about 1,500 species of starfish. Both authors have written about starfish that are washed up by the sea onto the shore. Tell students to look for the larger message about life each author is trying to convey.

AS YOU READ Ask students to pay attention to details that are clues to the authors' central ideas. How soon into the texts can they begin to identify the authors' central ideas?

 COMMON CORE

Common Core Support

- cite strong and thorough textual evidence
- analyze the development of a central idea, including how it is shaped and refined by specific details
- analyze the impact of word choices on meaning

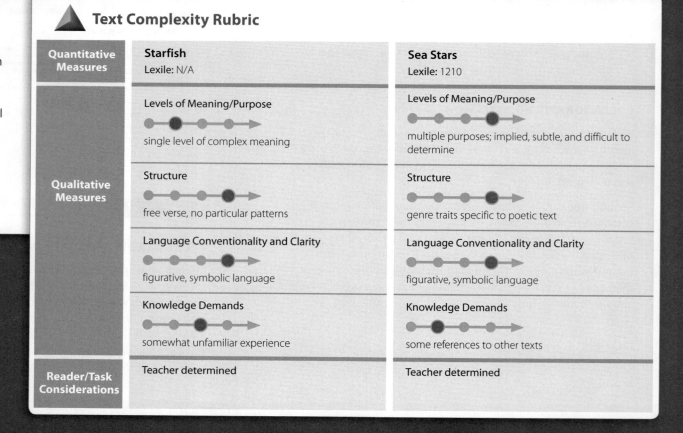

Text Complexity Rubric

	Starfish	Sea Stars
Quantitative Measures	Lexile: N/A	Lexile: 1210
Qualitative Measures	**Levels of Meaning/Purpose** single level of complex meaning	**Levels of Meaning/Purpose** multiple purposes; implied, subtle, and difficult to determine
	Structure free verse, no particular patterns	**Structure** genre traits specific to poetic text
	Language Conventionality and Clarity figurative, symbolic language	**Language Conventionality and Clarity** figurative, symbolic language
	Knowledge Demands somewhat unfamiliar experience	**Knowledge Demands** some references to other texts
Reader/Task Considerations	Teacher determined	Teacher determined

Strategies for CLOSE READING

Determine Central Idea

Students should read the texts carefully all the way through. Close-reading questions at the bottom of the page will help them focus on a thorough analysis of the poem and the essay. As they read, students should jot down comments or questions about the texts in the side margins.

WHEN STUDENTS STRUGGLE . . .

To help students determine the central ideas of the poem and the essay, have them work in small groups to fill out charts like the ones shown below as they analyze the texts.

CITE TEXT EVIDENCE For practice in determining central ideas, ask students to cite details that contribute to each author's central idea.

Starfish
Central Idea
We see comparisons between the lives of starfish and our own lives. Life is both beautiful and tragic.

Detail _Cervantes describes starfish surroundings as terrariums._	**Detail** _Fragile words like "soft" and "pliant" describe their bodies, highlighting their vulnerability._
Detail _Cervantes calls the starfish "little martyrs."_	**Detail** _The phrase "five-fingered specimen" gives starfish human qualities._

Sea Stars
Central Idea
Sea stars and humans are connected by the cycle of life.

Detail _Like sea stars, humans look for things to cling to._	**Detail** _Like stars, "things that seem to disappear often have not," such as phantom limbs._
Detail _Sea stars hold onto rocks to escape "the way the world grinds the living into debris."_	**Detail** _People look for an "encounter ... that can beckon what lies broken and hungry inside us all."_

Background _The following two selections are examples of writing about the sea—in particular, the creatures known as sea stars, or starfish. The word_ starfish _is misleading. Starfish are not actually fish but echinoderms, animals with spiny skeletons. Although starfish come in a wide range of sizes, most species are between eight and twelve inches in diameter and have five arms. Their colors range from brown to various shades of yellow, orange, and pink. Starfish are flexible and move by using the tube feet on the undersides of their arms._

Writing About the Sea

Starfish	Poem by Lorna Dee Cervantes
Sea Stars	Essay by Barbara Hurd

Lorna Dee Cervantes _Growing up in San Jose, California, Lorna Dee Cervantes discovered literature by reading the books in the houses that her mother cleaned for a living. Cervantes completed her first collection of poetry when she was fifteen. Writing gave Cervantes, who is of Mexican and American Indian ancestry, a sense of freedom: "When you grow up as I did, a Chican-India in a barrio in a Mexican neighborhood in California . . . you're ignored . . . And you're not expected to speak, much less write."_

Barbara Hurd _is a writer who specializes in creative nonfiction nature writing. She explains, "I'm interested in landscapes, both the physical—swamps and caves—and the psychological, that are marked by multiplicities and contradictions, pocked with secrets, laced with what can't be immediately seen, but, which properly pressed by imagination and language, have the power to transform experience into something sculpted and meaningful. . . . I'm after form, in other words, which leaves the reader and me at least knee-deep in this world, aware of and almost weaker than the wish to resist."_

17

CLOSE READ Notes

1. **READ** ▶ As you read lines 1–15 of "Starfish," begin to cite text evidence.

- Underline examples of figurative language.
- Circle text used to describe the starfish's body.
- In the margin, explain the actions of the speaker.

Starfish
Lorna Dee Cervantes

They were lovely in the quartz and jasper sand
As if they had created terrariums¹ with their bodies
On purpose; adding sprigs of seaweed, seashells,
White feathers, eel bones, miniature
5   Mussels, a fish jaw. Hundreds; no—
Ⓐ Thousands of baby stars. We touched them,
Surprised to find them soft, pliant almost
Living in their attitudes. We would dry them, arrange them,
Form seascapes, geodesics² . . . We gathered what we could
10 In the approaching darkness. Then we left hundreds of
Thousands of flawless five-fingered specimens sprawled
Along the beach as far as we could see, all massed
Ⓑ Together: little martyrs, soldiers, artless suicides
In lifelong liberation from the sea. So many
15 Splayed hands, the tide shoveled in.

_____
¹ **terrarium:** small enclosure or container that houses plants or animals.
² **geodesic:** interlocking, repeating pattern.

pliant:
easily bent

*She found
and
collected
starfish on
the beach.*

2. **◀ REREAD** Reread lines 1–15. How does the description of the "approaching darkness" change the tone of the poem? What happens to the starfish the speaker leaves behind? Support your answer with explicit text evidence.

Before the phrase "approaching darkness," the poet has marveled
at the starfish strewn along the beach and the patterns they create
with their surroundings. Following the phrase, the figurative
language becomes darker. The thousands of starfish carried by the
tide will die, stranded on the beach.

18

CLOSE READ Notes

SHORT RESPONSE

Cite Text Evidence   How does the poet's use of figurative language contribute to her central idea? **Cite text evidence** to support your response.

Cervantes uses figurative language to describe the beauty of the
starfish, describing their surroundings as "terrariums." She uses
fragile words like "soft" and "pliant" to describe their bodies,
highlighting their vulnerability. The author also gives the starfish
human qualities, calling them "little martyrs" and referring to them
as "five-fingered specimen." We empathize with the starfish, seeing
the comparisons between the lives of these creatures and our own
lives. Life is both beautiful and tragic.

19

---

1. READ AND CITE TEXT EVIDENCE

Ⓐ **ASK STUDENTS** to cite text evidence to support their descriptions of the speaker's actions. *Students should cite line 6, "We touched them," and line 9, "We gathered what we could."*

2. REREAD AND CITE TEXT EVIDENCE

Ⓑ **ASK STUDENTS** to read their answer aloud to a partner. Have partners discuss and then rewrite their responses, including explicit textual evidence from line 13 ("martyrs, soldiers, artless suicides,") to show that the thousands of startish carried by the tide will die, stranded on the beach. *Students should recognize that the tone becomes darker.*

Critical Vocabulary: pliant (line 7) Have students determine the meaning of *pliant* as it is used in the text. Ask them how this word choice impacts meaning and tone in the poem.

FOR ELL STUDENTS Explain that *quartz* and *jasper* are minerals.

SHORT RESPONSE

Cite Text Evidence   Student responses will vary, but they should cite evidence from the poem to support their analysis. Students should:

- provide a text-based analysis of how Cervantes' use of figurative language contributed to her central idea.
- cite specific textual evidence of the starfish's beauty and vulnerability.
- state the central idea of the poem.

CLOSE READ
Notes

1. **READ ▶** As you read lines 1–12 of "Sea Stars," begin to cite text evidence.
   - Underline words and phrases used to describe the sky, the moon, and the stars.
   - Circle text that gives the sea stars human qualities.
   - In the margin, explain the comparison the author makes.

Sea Stars
Barbara Hurd

At night, the sea stars would have looked like a constellation of stars on earth.

The sky is pink this morning and on the shore a whole host[1] of sea stars has been stranded.

I know from the charts the moon was full last night, the midnight tide higher than usual. Were the skies clear? Were the stars out? I'd like to have seen these creatures then: stars in the dark overhead and here a spiny constellation draped over the rocks.

One of the largest, a northern sea star, now lies upside down in the palm of my hand. Almost a foot across, its orangy body glistens wet in the dawn light. Hundreds of slender tubes wriggle like antennae, only these aren't sense organs; they're feet, and what they're searching for isn't food or enemy or mate, but something to cling to, any firm surface that can anchor them and end this **futile** flailing at the air.

Of its five arms, three remain, five or six inches long. I've read that most sea stars lose their limbs to other sea stars' hunger. Traveling in slow-motion swarms, the lead **contingent** feasts on oysters and clams, depleting the supply for those in the rear, who resort to the nearest neighbor's arm.

futile: ineffective

contingent: part of a group

[1] **host:** an army, group or formation.

2. **◀ REREAD** Reread lines 1–12. In your own words, explain the central idea of these lines.

Hurd notes that the sea stars have been "stranded" and imagines what they would have looked like at night. Her description of the sea star in her hand emphasizes the animal's vulnerability. Her central idea might be that sea stars are both beautiful and needy.

3. **READ ▶** As you read lines 13–26, continue to cite text evidence.
   - Underline facts about the life cycle of the sea star.
   - Circle emotions that humans are "burdened" with.
   - In the margin, explain the physical feeling that both amputees and people born without a limb may have in common.

20

The sea star, of course, can regenerate[2] when the food supply increases, grow back the missing limb, and continue unburdened by notions of heroism or sacrifice, even consciousness.

We, in contrast, have to live with those burdens, made heavier by loss and the sensation that often emanates from what's missing. Amputees[3] call it phantom pain, those sensations—tingling or sharp stabs—by which something absent makes its presence known. Even those born without a limb sometimes feel what was never there and experience, physically, what others of us know psychologically—a need to confirm what we feel but can't see.

When its third arm begins to wriggle, I turn the sea star over and carry it back to the water. Oblivious to patience or my unreliable intentions, it knows only the dangers of drying out set against the dangers of being washed out to sea. I try to imagine that twice-daily rhythm, sun on its baking back, tube feet squishing as it inches along among drying seaweed and barnacles. And then the fierce holding on as the tide comes in and wave after wave crashes on top of delicate tissues.

Were the stars out last night? Silly question, really. They're always out. In the daytime too. Where do we think they'd go? I try to remember this: the obscuring effect of clouds and of sunlight, how things that seem to disappear often have not. Up in the daytime sky, the whirling constellations—Cassiopeia, Orion, Big Dipper—may be invisible to us, but stage a noontime solar eclipse and there they are, as always, reminders of other worlds we'll probably never see. And here, underfoot, half a dozen sea

They both feel loss and the presence of something no longer or never there.

The stars are always out, but we often forget this.

[2] **regenerate:** to replace a lost or damaged part by forming new tissue.
[3] **amputee:** a person who has had one or more limbs removed.

4. **◀ REREAD** Reread lines 13–26. What point is the author making by comparing a sea star missing an arm to a human missing a limb?

The author makes the comparison to show the adaptability of the sea star—it is able to regenerate an arm. Humans, lacking this ability, are burdened by "notions of heroism, or sacrifice, even consciousness" if we lose a limb. Humans are aware of what we lose.

5. **READ ▶** As you read lines 27–58, continue to cite text evidence.
   - Underline the "twice-daily rhythm" the author describes in lines 30–33.
   - Circle the idea the author tries to remember.
   - In the margin, explain the author's answers to the questions she poses in lines 34–35.

21

CLOSE READ
Notes

---

1. **READ AND CITE TEXT EVIDENCE**

C ASK STUDENTS to cite text evidence to support their explanations. *Students should cite evidence in lines 5–6.*

2. **REREAD AND CITE TEXT EVIDENCE**

D ASK STUDENTS to discuss their response and evidence with a partner, then rewrite it.

3. **READ AND CITE TEXT EVIDENCE**

E ASK STUDENTS to cite text evidence to support their explanation of physical feelings in people missing limbs. *Students should cite evidence from lines 21–24.*

Critical Vocabulary: futile (line 12) Have students determine the meaning of *futile* as it is used here.

Critical Vocabulary: contingent (line 15) Have students share their definitions of the word *contingent*.

4. **REREAD AND CITE TEXT EVIDENCE**

F ASK STUDENTS to cite specific text evidence to support their answer. *Students should cite the adaptability of the sea star, its ability to regenerate a limb (lines 17–18), and cite the byproducts of a human sense of loss, "heroism," "sacrifice," and "consciousness," that may result from the absence of the ability to regenerate a lost limb (lines 18–19).*

5. **READ AND CITE TEXT EVIDENCE**

G ASK STUDENTS to cite text evidence to support their explanation of the idea the author evokes by asking questions in lines 34–35. *The author wants to remember that things that are lost to our sensual experience, such as seeing the stars, are not truly evidence of the absence of the objects themselves (lines 34–40).*

FOR ELL STUDENTS Point out the word *unreliable* (line 28). Ask a volunteer to identify the base word (*reliable*) and its meaning. Then ask another volunteer to guess the meaning of *unreliable*.

CLOSE READ
Notes

If Ahab had not been so set on revenge, he would have accepted his reality and the truth about loss and wanting.

elusive: difficult to define

stars, about to disappear underwater where they'll go on too, misshapen maybe and less visible, doing what they've always done: making their slow way through a galaxy spread out at our feet.

Foaming and inching its lunar way up the beach, the sea polishes small stones, sloshes into and out of the tiny whorled and bivalved⁴ shells somersaulting in the undercurl of its waves. I take it as a given we can't escape the way the world grinds the living into debris. But before it does, there's a chance for the lucky encounter with someone or something—a painting or poem, a place—that can beckon to what lies broken and hungry inside us all. I believe it's what most of us long for.

50 Oh Ahab,⁵ I often think, if you could have hunted with less vengeance and fewer absolutes, might the whale have someday returned to you what it took so long ago, so violently? Not literally, no leg, of course. Not even in a story would anyone believe a human could do what a sea star can. But something else, something **elusive** that retreats in the onslaught of high drama and fierce truths, that survives between the layers of the said and the felt, and makes itself known to us only by the ghostly presence of its wanting.

⁴ **bivalve:** a class of mollusks characterized by a hinged shell.
⁵ **Ahab:** the main character from Herman Melville's *Moby Dick*, whose main purpose in life is to seek out and destroy the giant whale that bit off his leg.

6. **◄ REREAD** Reread lines 27–58. In the margin, explain what the author wants to say to Ahab in lines 51–58.

SHORT RESPONSE

Cite Text Evidence In what ways does the author's use of figurative language contribute to her central idea? **Cite text evidence** to support your response.

The author uses figurative language to make connections between sea stars and humans. She brings in facts about the sea star's abilities: to regenerate, to cling fiercely to rocks, and compares them to our lack of such talents. She reminds us that the stars are always out, whether we see them or not and "things that seem to disappear often have not." Just as sea stars look for something to hold onto, to escape "the way the world grinds the living into debris," she suggests we look for an "encounter with someone or something . . . that can beckon what lies broken and hungry inside us all."

22

TO CHALLENGE STUDENTS . . .

Remind students that Hurd used a natural landscape to explore an aspect of human psychology: the pain of loss. Creative nonfiction is a genre that uses accuracy and facts to make its point. Hurd references the science of regeneration and the process of renewal and restoration that would allow a sea star to grow back a lost limb. He suggests this process as a counterpoint to the human experience of loss.

ASK STUDENTS to choose an area to research from the following: regeneration, prosthetics, the psychology of grief. Have students share the results of their research.

---

6. **REREAD AND CITE TEXT EVIDENCE**

H **ASK STUDENTS** to cite text evidence to support their explanation of what the author wants to say to Ahab in lines 51–58. *Ahab was set on revenge (line 51) and if he had been more accepting (line 52), he might have been able to grasp a truth about the human condition, loss, and wanting—a truth that "retreats in the onslaught of high drama and fierce truths" (lines 54–58).*

Critical Vocabulary: elusive (line 55) Ask students to explain how *elusive* contributes to the tone here.

SHORT RESPONSE

Cite Text Evidence Students should:

- state Hurd's central idea.
- analyze Hurd's use of figurative language.
- cite textual evidence of how Hurd uses sea stars to make a point about the human experience.

DIG DEEPER

1. With the class, return to Question 2 in "Starfish." Have students share their responses.

ASK STUDENTS to cite the text evidence that supports their analysis of tone in the poem.

- Ask students to cite text evidence of beauty at the beginning of the poem. *Students might point out the adjective "lovely" and the imagery "quartz and jasper sand" in line 1, or or the allusion to art: "created" in line 2.*

- Have students cite evidence of vulnerability from lines 6–9. *Students may cite the author's choice of the word "baby" (line 6), or the choice of the words "soft" and "pliant" in line 7. They might see evidence of vulnerability in the phrases "We touched them," "We would dry them," and "We gathered what we could," in lines 6, 8, and 9.*

- Then, ask students to cite evidence of a change in tone in lines 10–15. *Students may cite phrases such as "the approaching darkness" (line 10), "We left…sprawled" (lines 10–11), and in line 13 "little martyrs, soldiers, artless suicides," as evidence that the starfish carried by the tide will die.*

- Ask students how the poet alluded to a connection between the starfish and humans. *Students may cite phrases such as "On purpose" (line 3), "baby" (line 6), or "little martyrs, soldiers, artless suicides," in line 13.*

ASK STUDENTS to return to their Short Response on page 19, and revise it based on the class discussion.

2. Now, return to Question 6 in "Sea Stars." Have students share their responses.

ASK STUDENTS to cite text evidence that supports their explanation of Hurd's reference to Captain Ahab.

- Invite volunteers to summarize *Moby Dick,* and explain the reference to Ahab. If they are not familiar with Melville's novel, allow time for research.

- Review Hurd's references to human desire. *Students might cite the desire to contextualize loss suggested by the phrase "heroism, or sacrifice, even consciousness" in line 19, the "need to confirm what we feel but can't see," in lines 25–26, and Hurd's assertion about what "most of us long for," in lines 48–50: the desire for someone or something to touch what "lies broken and hungry inside us all."*

- Discuss what Hurd means by that which "lies broken and hungry inside us all." Why does she choose to express this figuratively rather than saying it straight out?

ASK STUDENTS to return to their Short Response answer on page 22, and revise it based on the class discussion.

CLOSE READING NOTES

When I Heard the Learn'd Astronomer

Poem by Walt Whitman

Why This Text?

Students regularly encounter themes or ideas about life as they read various works of literature. Poetry is a major literary genre, and many modern critics consider Walt Whitman's writings to be distinctly representative of messages about democratic values and American life.

Key Learning Objective: The student will be able to identify the theme of a poem through writing an objective summary that states the key events and ideas in the poem.

Common Core Standards

RL 1 Cite textual evidence.
RL 2 Determine a theme and analyze its development.
RL 4 Determine the meaning of words and phrases.
RL 5 Analyze how an author's choices create mystery, tension, or surprise.
W 4 Produce writing in which the organization and style are appropriate to task, purpose, and audience.
SL 1 Participate in collaborative discussions with diverse partners.

Text Complexity Rubric

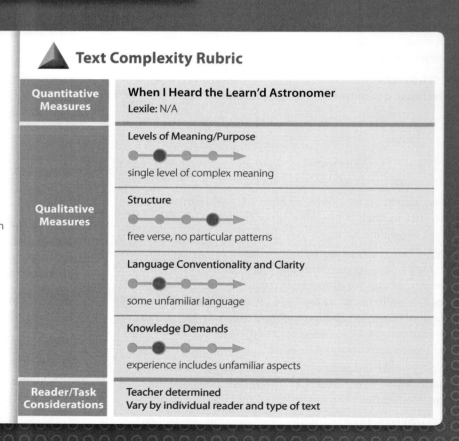

Quantitative Measures

When I Heard the Learn'd Astronomer
Lexile: N/A

Qualitative Measures

Levels of Meaning/Purpose
single level of complex meaning

Structure
free verse, no particular patterns

Language Conventionality and Clarity
some unfamiliar language

Knowledge Demands
experience includes unfamiliar aspects

Reader/Task Considerations
Teacher determined
Vary by individual reader and type of text

TEACH

CLOSE READ

Walt Whitman Have students read the background and information about the author. Tell them that in 1855, *Leaves of Grass* consisted of twelve untitled poems. The 1891–92 edition contains 293 poems.

AS YOU READ Direct students to use the As You Read prompt to focus their reading.

Analyze Language (LINES 1–8)   COMMON CORE   RL 4, RL 5

Remind students that poetry differs from prose in its structure, word choice, use of grammar and spelling, and use of rhythm and rhyme. Emphasize to students that the poet makes deliberate choices when crafting a poem and presents ideas and images to create a specific effect.

(A) CITE TEXT EVIDENCE Ask students to point out and explain Whitman's use of structure, words, and phrases that are examples of poetic language. *(He uses unusual word order ["I sitting heard" and "out I wander'd"] and contractions [the "learn'd astronomer," "I wander'd," and "Look'd"] to contrast how the speaker's physical presence changed from passive ["sitting"] to active ["wander'd," "Look'd"], but the "learn'd" astronomer's did not.)*

Determine Theme Through Objective Summary (LINES 1–8)   COMMON CORE   RL 1, RL 2, W 4, SL 1

Explain to students that poets convey ideas about life through the events, words, structure, and images in their poems. Analyzing these details, and not their personal reactions, can help students identify a poem's theme.

(B) ASK STUDENTS to focus on the speaker's actions and the motivations for them in three lines 4– 6 and indirectly summarize and determine theme. *(Possible answer: The speaker becomes sick and leaves the lecture to look at the stars, rejecting the astronomer's way of seeing the universe. The theme could be that science contributes less to our understanding of nature than experiencing it.)*

COLLABORATIVE DISCUSSION Have students work with a partner to discuss the specific attributes or qualities that caused the images to contrast with each other.

ASK STUDENTS to share any questions they generated in the course of reading and discussing the selection.

Walt Whitman *(1819–1892) ended his formal schooling and went to work at age 11. Apprenticing for a local newspaper, he discovered that he loved putting words to paper. In the 1840s he began writing poems for his masterpiece, Leaves of Grass. Because no publisher would accept his unorthodox poems, Whitman self-published his collection in 1855. He continued to revise and add to it for the rest of his life. Many modern critics view Whitman's poems as distinctly American, marked by democratic values, a love of nature, and optimism for the future.*

When I Heard the Learn'd Astronomer

Poem by Walt Whitman

AS YOU READ Pay attention to contrasts in the poem. Jot down specific images that you find striking or interesting. Also, write down any questions you generate during reading.

When I heard the learn'd astronomer,
When the proofs,[1] the figures, were ranged in columns before me,
When I was shown the charts and diagrams, to add, divide, and
    measure them,
When I sitting heard the astronomer where he lectured with much
    applause in the lecture-room,
5 How soon unaccountable I became tired and sick,
Till rising and gliding out I wander'd off by myself,
In the mystical moist night air, and from time to time,
Look'd up in perfect silence at the stars.

COLLABORATIVE DISCUSSION With a partner, discuss the images you jotted down. Which images contrast with each other?

Image Credits: (tl) Library of Congress Prints & Photographs Division); (cl) NASA; (cr) ©Jim Ballard/Photographer's Choice/Getty Images

---

[1] **proofs:** formal scientific statements of evidence.

SCAFFOLDING FOR ELL STUDENTS

Analyze Language Remind students that the simple past tense of regular verbs is formed by adding *-ed*. Ask them to highlight regular past tense verbs in the poem. Then point out *wander'd* and *look'd*. Explain that these are not typical examples of English contractions and that Whitman has left out the letter *e* for effect. Have mixed proficiency groups identify two examples of words in the regular past tense where Whitman does not omit the letter *e*. *("ranged" and "lectured")* Have students say Whitman's contracted verbs and then the uncontracted ones. Ask them to note that when read aloud the contracted forms do not affect the pronunciation of the verbs.

ASK STUDENTS to explain why Whitman chose not to change the spelling of *ranged* and *lectured*.

Determine Theme Through Objective Summary

 COMMON CORE RL 2

To help students understand objective summary, tell them that objective information does not include personal opinions or connections but instead must be based on:

- what is read in written formats.
- what is seen in visual formats.
- what is heard in auditory formats.

Analyzing the Text

 COMMON CORE RL 1, RL 2, RL 4, RL 5, W 4

Possible answers:

1. *Lines 1–4 all begin with the subordinating conjunction "When." Lines 2–3 contain lists. This suggests that the astronomer's lecture was dull because it droned facts in a repetitious manner.*

2. *The learn'd astronomer used figures and diagrams to lecture about the universe and received applause for his information. The speaker became "tired and sick" of the facts and "wander'd" out into the night air to look silently up at the stars.*

3. *Whitman uses a repetitive structure in lines 1–4, droning about how science sees nature. The speaker dislikes reducing the observation of stars to impersonal facts. In lines 5–8, Whitman uses contrasting language in more personal images ("rising and gliding") and alliteration ("mystical moist") as the speaker leaves the lecture. This supports the theme that the science of nature does not capture or express the wonder of experiencing it.*

4. *The speaker, who is the only one not enjoying the lecture, disapproves of the others. Instead of joining in their applause, he distances himself by going outside to look at the stars.*

 Assess It!

Online Selection Test
- Download an editable ExamView bank.
- Assign and manage this test online.

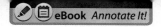 eBook *Annotate It!*

Determine Theme Through Objective Summary

 COMMON CORE RL 2

The **theme** of a literary work is a message about life that the writer wants readers to understand. Because Whitman, like most poets, does not directly state his theme, readers must infer it from details in the poem. The poem's images, structure, symbolism, and other poetic devices can serve as clues. Sometimes, writing an **objective summary**—a brief statement of the most important events or ideas in the poem—can be a good starting point in determining the poem's theme. Once you have identified the key events and ideas, you can consider what deeper meaning the poet may be trying to convey. As you analyze Whitman's poem, consider how the speaker responds to the lecture and what changes occur by the end of the poem.

Analyzing the Text

 COMMON CORE RL 1, RL 2, RL 4, RL 5, W 4

Cite Text Evidence   Support your responses with evidence from the poem.

1. **Analyze** Whitman uses **parallelism**, the repetition of a grammatical structure, in lines 1–4. Describe what is parallel in these lines. What impression of the astronomer's lecture does the parallelism create?

2. **Summarize** Write a two-sentence objective summary of the poem. Summarize what happens or what is stated directly, without including any of your own opinions or interpretations.

3. **Contrast** How does Whitman's language describing the domain of science in lines 1–4 contrast with his language in lines 5–8? How does this contrast express a theme in the poem?

4. **Draw Conclusions** The speaker notes that the astronomer's lecture is greeted "with much applause in the lecture-room." What **tone**, or attitude, does the speaker have toward the other people in the room?

 **WriteSmart**

PERFORMANCE TASK

Writing Activity: Comparison Whitman's poem contrasts two different ways of viewing the natural world. Write a paragraph that similarly contrasts two ways of looking at something in your world.

1. Think of a place, event, or idea that people view in different ways. Create a T-chart to brainstorm details about the opposing views of your subject.

2. Write a paragraph that explores contrasting views of your subject, describing the view you hold last.

3. Share your paragraph with the class, and explain how it does or does not mirror Whitman's theme.

 Assign this performance task. **WriteSmart**

PERFORMANCE TASK

COMMON CORE W 4

Writing Activity: Comparison Before Step 1, have the class brainstorm places, events, or ideas that can be viewed differently. Pair students who select the same place, event, or idea to complete the T-chart. Have individuals write their paragraphs for Step 2. Then bring pairs together again before Step 3. Have students compare how their paragraphs differ. Have individuals present their paragraphs and explain how they do or do not mirror Whitman's theme.

INTERACTIVE WHITEBOARD LESSON

Analyze Text Structure

COMMON CORE

RL 5

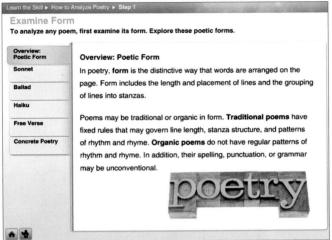

Learn the Skill ▶ How to Analyze Poetry ▶ Step 1

Examine Form

To analyze any poem, first examine its form. Explore these poetic forms.

Overview:
Poetic Form

Sonnet

Ballad

Haiku

Free Verse

Concrete Poetry

Overview: Poetic Form

In poetry, **form** is the distinctive way that words are arranged on the page. Form includes the length and placement of lines and the grouping of lines into stanzas.

Poems may be traditional or organic in form. **Traditional poems** have fixed rules that may govern line length, stanza structure, and patterns of rhythm and rhyme. **Organic poems** do not have regular patterns of rhythm and rhyme. In addition, their spelling, punctuation, or grammar may be unconventional.

TEACH

Use Step 1, Overview: Poetic Form and Free Verse from the Interactive Whiteboard lesson. Explain that poets choose a poem's structure in the same way that they choose specific words. Reinforce the steps for analyzing the structure of a poem:

- **Step 1: Examine Form—Overview: Poetic Form** Point out that form, or the arrangement and grouping of lines, is one aspect of a poem's structure. Other structures, such as rhyme and rhythm, appear within the lines and might be more evident when the poem is read aloud. Discuss the differences between traditional and organic poems.

- **Step 1: Examine Form—Free Verse** Point out that "When I Heard the Learn'd Astronomer" is written in free verse. That is, it has no prescribed rhyme or meter and does not follow other restrictions characteristic of traditional poems. Whitman's poem is organic—its structure grows naturally from the subject matter to create an integrated whole. Display "A Noiseless Patient Spider" and have students point out what makes its structure organic.

PRACTICE AND APPLY

Display the poem and ask a volunteer to read it aloud. Ask what makes it organic. *(sounds like speech, lacks rhyme, doesn't have identifiable stanzas)* Challenge students to identify and explain an aspect of the poem's structure that is bound to its meaning. *(In lines 2–3, the speaker lists the astronomer's proofs in long, monotonous lines of facts, but when the speaker tells of leaving the lecture [lines 6–8], the lines become shorter and more poetic.)*

Determine Theme Through Objective Summary

COMMON CORE

RL 2

RETEACH

Remind students that an **objective summary** is a brief statement of the most important events or ideas in a work. Review that **theme** is a message about life that the writer wants readers to understand. Explain that since the writer might want to convey the message to all readers, the themes should be universal, or relating to the breadth of human experience.

- Ask students to note important details about what happens in the poem and then use them to write a summary that does not include their personal thoughts and feelings.

- Then ask students to look beyond what happens in the poem to see what universal meaning about life the poet might want readers to understand. Have students share their objective summaries by reading them aloud or exchanging them with partners. Guide a discussion about the most important ideas in the poem and whether students' objective summaries support a universal theme.

LEVEL UP TUTORIALS Assign the following *Level Up* tutorial: **Universal and Recurring Themes**

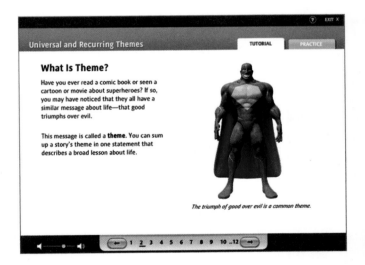

Universal and Recurring Themes

TUTORIAL   PRACTICE

What Is Theme?

Have you ever read a comic book or seen a cartoon or movie about superheroes? If so, you may have noticed that they all have a similar message about life—that good triumphs over evil.

This message is called a **theme**. You can sum up a story's theme in one statement that describes a broad lesson about life.

The triumph of good over evil is a common theme.

1 **2** 3 4 5 6 7 8 9   10 ..12

CLOSE READING APPLICATION

Students can apply the skill to another poem of their choice. Have them select a poem, write a brief objective summary, and determine the poem's theme. Ask: What are the most important events or ideas? What universal theme is conveyed by the writer?

from Hope for Animals and Their World

Argument by Jane Goodall

Why This Text?

Students regularly encounter debate regarding the importance of human needs versus environmental needs. This lesson explores Goodall's argument about the value of the American burying beetle to people and the environment.

▶ *View It!*
Professional Development Podcast:
Teaching Argument

Key Learning Objective: The student will be able to analyze an author's claim and purpose.

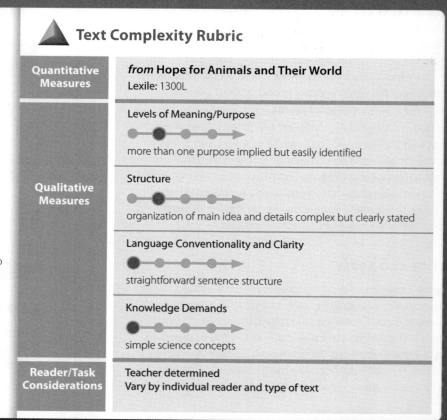

COMMON CORE · Common Core Standards

RI 1 Cite textual evidence.
RI 2 Determine a central idea and analyze its development.
RI 3 Analyze how the author unfolds ideas or events.
RI 4 Determine the meaning of words and phrases.
RI 5 Analyze how an author's ideas are developed by particular sentences or paragraphs.
RI 6 Determine an author's point of view and analyze how an author uses rhetoric.
W 2 Write informative texts to convey complex ideas, concepts, and information.
L 1b Use various types of phrases and clauses to convey specific meanings.
L 4b Identify and use patterns of word changes that indicate different meanings.

▲ Text Complexity Rubric

Quantitative Measures	**_from_ Hope for Animals and Their World** Lexile: 1300L
Qualitative Measures	**Levels of Meaning/Purpose** more than one purpose implied but easily identified
	Structure organization of main idea and details complex but clearly stated
	Language Conventionality and Clarity straightforward sentence structure
	Knowledge Demands simple science concepts
Reader/Task Considerations	Teacher determined Vary by individual reader and type of text

CLOSE READ

Jane Goodall Have students read the information about the author. Tell students that Goodall's first study of African chimpanzees was encouraged by the anthropologist Louis S. B. Leakey. Prior to her observations, only humans were thought to have the ability to make tools.

AS YOU READ Direct students to use the As You Read statement to focus their reading. Remind students to write down any questions they generate during reading.

Analyze Author's Claim (LINES 1–4)

COMMON CORE RI 2, RI 5

Explain to students that when writing an **argument,** an author sets forth a **claim,** or position on a specific issue, and supports it with reasons and evidence. Often, this claim is stated in the opening paragraph of an argument.

A **ASK STUDENTS** to identify the topic of Goodall's argument and her opinion of it. *(Possible answer: Insects and other small, seldom-seen animals play a major role in maintaining the health of the environment. Goodall is passionate about her topic.)*

Determine Purpose

COMMON CORE RI 1, RI 6

(LINES 4–13)

Inform students that an author carefully decides how to present information in an argument. One effective strategy is to create a connection with the audience.

B **CITE TEXT EVIDENCE** Ask students to identify the feelings the author acknowledges. *(fear and hatred of insects)* How does the author connect with the audience? *(uses first-person pronouns; keys into audience emotions and experiences)* How does this language engage readers? *(It allows them to relate to the author.)*

CRITICAL VOCABULARY

loathe: Goodall explains that humans have strong negative feelings about some insects.

ASK STUDENTS to explain why many people loathe cockroaches. *(They are large insects whose moving body parts are easy to see.)*

Jane Goodall (b. 1934) *watched wild chimpanzees shaping twigs to dig for termites while on a field study in Africa at age 26. It was the first recorded observation of nonhumans making and using tools, and it rocked the scientific world. Since then, Goodall has become the world's leading expert on chimpanzees and an advocate for wildlife conservation. She spends much of her time giving lectures and writing about animals and the environment. Her books, including* In the Shadow of Man *and* The Chimpanzee Family Book, *have inspired readers around the world.*

from

Hope for Animals and Their World

Argument by Jane Goodall

AS YOU READ Look for examples that show the role of the burying beetle and other insects in the environment.

American Burying Beetle
(Nicrophorus americanus)

Image Credits: (tl) ©Tim Wimborne/Reuters/Landov; (cr) Gary Chancey/U.S. Dept of Agriculture/Forest Service; (cl) ©Fenton/Shutterstock.

B **A** The American burying beetle is but one of the millions of insects and other invertebrates[1] that play such a major, though seldom acknowledged, role in the maintenance of habitats and ecosystems. Most people simply lump them all into the category "creepy-crawlies" or "bugs." Some, such as butterflies, are admired and loved for their beauty (though people tend to be less interested in or even repelled by their caterpillars). Others, such as spiders, are the inadvertent cause of fear—even terror. Cockroaches are **loathed.** Hundreds of species are persecuted for the role they play
10 in damaging our food—such as the desert locust, which ravages crops across huge areas. And there are countless species such as

loathe
(lōth) v.
to hate or despise.

---

[1] **invertebrates:** animals without backbones or spinal columns.

Hope for Animals and Their World **61**

SCAFFOLDING FOR ELL STUDENTS

Determine Purpose Using a whiteboard, project the first paragraph of Goodall's argument. Invite volunteers to mark up lines 5–13.

- Highlight in yellow words that tell about human feelings.

ASK STUDENTS to complete this sentence frame: Goodall thinks readers may not agree with her claim because they _____. *(are afraid of insects)*

> are the inadvertent cause of fear—even terror. Cockroaches are
>
> **loathed.** Hundreds of species are persecuted for the role they play

Analyze Rhetoric
COMMON CORE RI 1, RI 4, RI 6

(LINES 44–51)

Explain that an author writes an argument to support a claim based on a specific **point of view,** or perspective, on an issue. To support the claim and convey his or her point of view, the author carefully selects each word in the argument. Tell students that this point of view is revealed through **rhetoric,** the art of using language to persuade an audience. Continue the lesson by explaining that **connotation** is the positive or negative association the audience makes with a word.

C **CITE TEXT EVIDENCE** Direct students to identify the words that have positive connotations. *("perfect," "passionately," "loved," "understanding," "supportive," "fascination")* What does this language tell us about Goodall's point of view regarding Lou Perrotti? *(She admires him and the work he does.)*

Analyze Author's Claim
COMMON CORE RI 1, RI 5

(LINES 52–54)

Explain that Goodall has stated her claim. Now she will continue her argument by supporting her claim.

D **CITE TEXT EVIDENCE** Ask students to identify how Goodall, on this page, supports her claim. *(She introduces experts who share her opinion.)* On what lines does Goodall show the reader that Lou clearly agrees with her claim? *(lines 52–54)*

CRITICAL VOCABULARY

pollinate: Goodall explains that while many insects are destructive, others provide benefits. For example, bees pollinate, or fertilize, food crops.

ASK STUDENTS to explain how bees help humans when they pollinate food crops. *(Pollination is a necessary step in plant reproduction. Therefore, when bees pollinate crops, they ensure the continued growth of foods such as grains, fruits, and vegetables.)*

B mosquitoes, tsetse flies, fleas, and ticks that carry diseases that can devastate other creatures, including ourselves.

It is for these reasons that they have been attacked by farmers, gardeners, and governments. Unfortunately the weapons of choice have been chemical pesticides—and this has led to horrific damage of all too many ecosystems, either through directly killing countless life-forms in addition to the intended targets, or when poisoned insects are eaten by creatures higher up the food chain.

20   Yet for every species that harms us or our food, there are countless others that work away, sometimes unseen, for the good of the environment where they live. I first became aware of this when I was a small child, picking up every earthworm I found stranded on the road (as did Dr. Albert Schweitzer,[2] by the way), and then learning about the valuable contribution they make to soil health. Millions of invertebrates provide food for species—including our own—higher up the food chain.

In many places people feast on termites, locusts, and beetle larvae—even I have tasted these things! Bees **pollinate** the vast
30   majority of our food crops, and the current devastation of hives in North America and Europe is causing real anxiety.

And what about the American burying beetle? What role, if any, does it play in our environment? This is what I learned about when, on March 18, 2007, I met with Lou Perrotti and Jack Mulvena of the Roger Williams Park Zoo in Providence, Rhode Island. Back in 1989, they told me, biologists had realized that the American burying beetle was fast declining, and it became one of just a few insect species to be listed under the Endangered Species Act. Then in 1993, the Roger Williams Park Zoo started a breeding program
40   for the US Fish and Wildlife Service; in 2006, this beetle became the first insect species to be assigned a Species Survival Plan. Lou is currently the coordinator for the American burying beetle for the Association of Zoos and Aquariums.

C As he began talking about the beetles, it was immediately apparent that they had the perfect spokesman! He is a man passionately interested in insects and, he told me, has "loved all things creepy-crawly" since he was a child. Like so many of the other people I have talked to while gathering information for this book, Lou had parents who were understanding and supportive of
50   his fascination with invertebrates. (And other creatures, too—they allowed him to breed boa constrictors when he was nine years old!)

While we talked, Lou became increasingly animated. "Somebody needs to be out there saving these critters [the burying beetles]," he said. And that is just what he is doing. Let me share some of what I **D**

pollinate
(pŏl´ə-nāt´) *v.*
to fertilize.

---

[2] **Dr. Albert Schweitzer:** (1875–1965) Australian physician and writer who operated a hospital in Africa.

APPLYING ACADEMIC VOCABULARY

advocate	enhance

As you discuss Goodall's argument, incorporate the following Collection 2 academic vocabulary words: *advocate* and *enhance*. To help students understand Goodall's point of view toward Lou Perrotti, ask students to explain how he **advocates** for the preservation of the American burying beetle by **enhancing** the public's knowledge of the insect's importance.

> ## " Would the loss of the American burying beetle matter? "

learned from him about these remarkable beetles. Most people have no idea how fascinating they are. Certainly I hadn't.

    The American burying beetle is the largest member of its genus[3] in North America—it is sometimes called the "giant carrion beetle." Once these beetles lived in forest and scrub grassland
60 habitats—anyplace where there was carrion of a suitable size and soil suitable for burying it—in thirty-five states throughout temperate eastern North America. But by 1920, populations in the East had largely disappeared. By 1970 populations had also disappeared from Ontario, Kentucky, Ohio, and Missouri. And during the 1980s, the beetle declined rapidly throughout the American Midwest.

    Today there are only seven places where they are known to exist— Block Island (Rhode Island), a single county in eastern Oklahoma, scattered populations in Arkansas, Nebraska, South Dakota, Kansas,
70 and a recently discovered population on a military installation in Texas. One reason for the species' **precipitous** decline across its historical range, in addition to habitat loss and fragmentation, is possibly connected with the extinction of the passenger pigeon and the greatly reduced number of black-footed ferrets and prairie chickens, all of which provided carrion of ideal size.

precipitous
(prĭ-sĭp´ĭ-təs) *adj.*
sudden and rapid.

Why We Need the Burying Beetle

    Let me return to the question I asked earlier—would the loss of the American burying beetle matter? The answer, stressed by Lou and Jack, is an emphatic *yes.* They feed on carrion—the flesh of dead animals. Lou calls them "nature's most efficient recyclers"
80 because they are responsible for recycling decaying animals back into the ecosystem. This returns nutrients to the earth, which stimulates the growth of plants. And by burying carcasses underground, this industrious beetle helps keep flies and ants from reaching epidemic proportions.

    Lou explained how these beetles find their meals. They can "smell" carrion from as far away as two miles, by means of sensors

---

[3] **genus:** a category or group of species.

WHEN STUDENTS STRUGGLE . . .

To guide students' comprehension of Goodall's claim and her supporting reasons and evidence, pair students to complete graphic organizers. Begin by referring students to lines 76–84. Have each pair fill in their organizers. Then have them compare and discuss their organizers with other pairs.

Claim	We need burying beetles.
Reason	They control pest populations.
Evidence	Beetles bury dead animals and keep flies and ants away from them.

CLOSE READ

Analyze Rhetoric

COMMON CORE RI 1, RI 3, RI 6

(LINES 76–84)

Tell students that an author may use a **rhetorical question**, a question that does not require an answer, to make a point. An author uses this device to engage the audience's attention or thought.

E **ASK STUDENTS** to identify the rhetorical question in lines 76–84. *(Would the loss of the American burying beetle matter?)* What point does Goodall make with this question and the answer that follows? *(She restates her claim.)* Point out that Lou and Jack provide the answer for this rhetorical question, and as experts they agree with Goodall's claim.

Analyze Author's Claim

COMMON CORE RI 1, RI 2, RI 3, RI 5

(LINES 79–84)

Point out that an author may use headings as guides to help an audience understand his or her argument.

F **CITE TEXT EVIDENCE** Direct students to the heading and ask them to identify its purpose. *(to alert readers that reasons why the burying beetle matters will follow)* Then have students reread this section and identify the reasons Goodall gives to support her claim. *(The beetle recycles decaying animals back into the ecosystem, which returns nutrients to the soil and controls fly and ant populations.)*

CRITICAL VOCABULARY

precipitous: Goodall explains the reasons for the beetle population's precipitous, or sudden and rapid, decline.

ASK STUDENTS to identify the causes of this precipitous decline in the beetle population. *(habitat loss and fragmentation; extinction of passenger pigeons and reduced numbers of black-footed ferrets and prairie chickens, which provided carrion for the beetles and their young to feed upon)*

Determine Purpose

COMMON CORE RI 1, RI 3, RI 6

(LINES 85–116)

Review with students an author's purposes for writing: to inform, to persuade, to entertain, to explain, or to describe.

G **ASK STUDENTS** to reread lines 85–107 and identify the author's purpose for writing these paragraphs. *(to describe how the beetles recycle decayed animals)* What does the language and level of detail reveal about the author's point of view toward the beetles? *(The author is amazed or impressed by the beetles.)*

Remind students that Goodall begins this argument by connecting to her audience, acknowledging people's fears regarding insects. Now she makes another connection by describing a familiar relationship, one between a parent and a child.

H **CITE TEXT EVIDENCE** Have students identify how the beetle parents are similar to human parents. *(Beetle parents work together to care for their young, as human parents do.)* Ask students why Goodall suggests this comparison between the beetles and humans. *(If readers find common links with the beetles, such as the parent-child relationship, they may be persuaded to agree with Goodall's claim.)*

CRITICAL VOCABULARY

sate: After two weeks of feeding, the beetle larvae are full.

ASK STUDENTS to explain how the parent beetles create sated young despite competition from flies. *(They carry on their bodies tiny orange mites that feed on the fly eggs and maggots.)*

G on their antennae. Flying noisily through the dusk, a male usually reaches the carcass he has located soon after dark. Then he— and any other males who have also discovered the feast—emits
90 pheromones that are irresistible to females of the species. Thus, you'll likely find a number of beetles gathered around any one corpse. It seems they form pairs, and there may be a good deal of fighting until one couple claims the prize. They then cooperate to bury it. This can be hard work: A carcass the size of a blue jay will take about twelve hours to bury.

Beetle Co-Parenting

Once the carcass is safely underground, the beetles strip it of feathers or hair and then coat it with . . . secretions, which help to preserve the flesh that will serve as food for their young. Next, the couple consummates their pairing, and within a day the female
100 lays the fertilized eggs in a small chamber that they have dug out close to the carcass. Here both parents wait for their eggs to hatch, which will be in two or three days. Both mother and father carry **H** the larvae to their "larder." And then—and this really blew my mind away—the young beetles will stroke the mandibles of their parents to entice feeding, and the adults will regurgitate food for their young. How absolutely amazing—an insect species in which mother and father care for their young together!

Usually, by the time the carcass is safely underground, flies have already laid their eggs on it. These hatch quickly into hungry
110 competitors for the young beetles. But help is close by: Riding on the bodies of the adult beetles are tiny orange mites that quickly climb onto the carcass, where they feed on fly eggs and maggots. In about two weeks, the **sated** beetle larvae burrow into the soil to pupate,[4] and the parents move on. As they do so, the orange mites hop back on board. The young beetles will emerge about forty-five days later.

Lou and his team have been very successful with their captive breeding program—by the end of 2006, more than three thousand beetles had been reared and released into the wild on Nantucket
120 Island. The captive-bred females (each paired with a genetically suitable mate) are transported to the release site in plastic containers. These are placed in an Igloo cooler, since the beetles cannot survive undue heat. A second cooler is used to transport dead quail, which the beetles will use as the carrion for their young. With a chuckle, Lou told us, "I can be traveling on a ferry during the height of tourist season and will still have room around me due to the terrible smell coming from the coolers."

sate (sāt) *v.* to fully feed or satisfy an appetite.

---
[4] **pupate:** grow from a larva to the next development stage.

SCAFFOLDING FOR ELL STUDENTS

Analyze Language Refer to the idiom ("blew my mind away") in the sentence in lines 103–106. Explain that an idiom is an expression with a meaning other than its literal meaning. The idiom "blew my mind away" means something was amazing or surprising. Goodall's use of this idiom relates to her point of view—she approaches the animal world with a sense of wonder and a desire to learn. Provide one or two other examples of how this idiom may be used in conversation, such as, "Did you see that incredible show last night?" "Yes, it blew my mind away." Then provide other idioms that express amazement: knock my socks off; stop dead in my tracks; took my breath away. Have students work in pairs to create a dialogue that uses one or more of these idioms correctly.

At the release site, holes have been pre-dug for the beetles. The dead quail are placed into the holes with floss tied to their feet and
130 attached to a small orange flag to assist the recovery team with finding the buried carcasses at a later date. The beetles are then released into the hole, where ideally they will realize that they have a jump start on the reproduction process! Lou said that Nantucket was chosen as a release site because, as with Block Island, there are no mammalian competitors present. After a while, though, birds such as crows and seagulls began to recognize that an orange flag represented a food source, and began to dig up the beetles' carrion, so the recovery team is now also placing a mesh screen over each brood to protect it.

140 Lou told me that he really enjoys teaching children about insects. We agreed that it does not take much to trigger their interest—children are naturally curious. And "creepy-crawlies," although they may elicit fear and horror, hold a real fascination for them. I told Lou I had spent hours as a child watching spiders, dragonflies, bumblebees, and the like. My son was fascinated as a little boy to watch ants as they set out in an orderly column to raid a termite nest, and returned each bearing an unfortunate victim in its mandibles. And my sister's three-year-old grandson, after

Image Credits: Gary Chancey/U.S. Dept of Agriculture/Forest Service

Hope for Animals and Their World **65**

APPLYING ACADEMIC VOCABULARY

scope	domain

As you discuss Goodall's argument, incorporate the following Collection 2 academic vocabulary words: *scope* and *domain*. To help students understand Lou's beetle breeding program, discuss why the **scope** of the project is limited to places such as Nantucket and Block Islands. Discuss why curiosity about the natural world is often the **domain** of children.

Determine Purpose
COMMON CORE RI 3, RI 6
(LINES 128–139)

Tell students that graphic elements such as photographs, charts, or diagrams can support an author's purpose for writing.

Ⓘ ASK STUDENTS to identify the author's purpose for writing the first paragraph on page 65. *(to explain the steps of Lou's breeding program)* How does the photograph support the ideas she presents in the paragraph? *(The photo clearly shows the first three steps in the process: the hole, the dead quail, and the beetle release. The photo also shows the relative sizes of the beetle and quail.)* How does the photograph relate to the author's point of view? *(The photo shows that the beetle is being handled gently, carefully, and respectfully. This is in line with how Goodall approaches all topics related to animals and the environment, including the burying beetle.)*

Analyze Author's Claim
COMMON CORE RI 1, RI 3, RI 5, RI 6
(LINES 144–152)

Tell students that in order to engage readers and support a claim, an author must provide sufficient and credible reasons. To further engage and persuade the reader, Goodall discusses her appreciation of the natural curiosity of children.

Ⓙ CITE TEXT EVIDENCE Have students describe the evidence Goodall uses to show the reader that she appreciates the curiosity of children. *(In lines 144–152, she provides three anecdotes from her experience with children's curiosity.)* How might Goodall hope that readers will respond to these anecdotes? *(She hopes that readers will remember their own positive experiences with the natural world.)* At what other point in the argument does Goodall ask readers to identify with the beetles? *(when she discusses co-parenting)* If readers make these connections with the natural world and the beetles, how might they respond to Goodall's overall claim about the importance of the American burying beetle? *(They may be persuaded to agree with Goodall's claim.)*

Determine Purpose

COMMON CORE RI 1, RI 3, RI 6

(LINES 156–157)

Explain that when an author presents a point of view, he or she generally includes not only facts but also opinions. **Facts** can be proven true through reliable sources. **Opinions** are statements of belief, which an author might signal with words such as *could, would, should, think, believe, best,* or *worst.* Point out Goodall's opinion in lines 156–157.

K **ASK STUDENTS** how this opinion relates to Goodall's point of view. *(The opinion reflects Goodall's point of view. That is, she is curious about nature, takes time to observe it, and appreciates its wonders. These attributes have enriched her life and in her opinion, they would enrich the lives of others.)*

Analyze Author's Claim

COMMON CORE RI 1, RI 3, RI 5

(LINES 163–166)

Point out that Goodall ends her argument, not with a restatement of her claim or a directive to readers, but with a personal statement regarding a gift from Lou.

L **CITE TEXT EVIDENCE** Ask students to identify why the print from Lou is special to Goodall. *(It reminds her of all the magic or wonder of the natural world.)* How does this reminder relate to Goodall's claim? *(The burying beetle and its behaviors are part of the magic and wonder of the natural world.)* If the reader connects to Goodall's personal statement at the end of the text, what is he or she likely to agree with? *(Goodall's claim)*

COLLABORATIVE DISCUSSION Have students work with partners to identify the author's claim and supporting reasons and evidence. Then ask them to discuss whether they are persuaded by Goodall's argument and explain why or why not. Have them share their evaluations with the class. Accept all reasonable responses.

ASK STUDENTS to share any questions they have generated during the course of reading and discussing the selection.

---

150 watching a snail crawling over the ground, suddenly placed it on the windowpane and rushed indoors to look through the glass, clearly fascinated and curious about the mechanism that enabled the creature to glide forward, as if by magic.

Unfortunately, Lou finds it much harder to interest adults in the efforts being made to save the American burying beetle. "So often the first question," he told me, "is 'Will it eat my garden?'" If only people would take the time to listen, retain the curiosity and wonder of childhood, how much richer their lives would be.

Certainly during my short early-morning meeting with Lou and Jack, I had been transported to a different and utterly fascinating 160 world, where giant insects nurture their young and tiny mites, in exchange for a free meal and a ride to the restaurant, rid their benefactors of their competitors.

After our visit, Lou sent me a beautiful print of an American burying beetle, its orange and black colors vivid and glowing. It is propped against the wall as I write, reminding me of all the magic of the natural world.

COLLABORATIVE DISCUSSION What have you learned about the burying beetle and other insects? With a partner, discuss how the author makes a case for the burying beetle's importance to the environment. Cite specific evidence from the text to support your ideas.

TO CHALLENGE STUDENTS . . .

Make Connections Today, we often hear stories about the struggle to find balance between human needs and wants and environmental needs. Challenge students to think of a current event that focuses on this issue and decide which position they support. After they have selected a topic and formulated a claim, have them write an argument in the form of a blog entry. Remind students to support the claim with reasons and evidence. Enourage them to use rhetoric effectively throughout the argument.

Analyze Author's Claim and Determine Purpose RI 5, RI 6

In any kind of text, the author's **purpose** is his or her reason for writing. An **argument** is a particular kind of writing in which the author states a **claim**, or a position on an issue, and then supports it with reasons and evidence. If the argument is well reasoned and provides sufficient evidence, readers are likely to accept the claim made by the author.

Some arguments begin with a clear statement of the author's claim. Others develop a claim over the course of the argument through the presentation of information and through **rhetoric**, the art of using language effectively to appeal to an audience. When you read or listen to an argument, consider these two ways of developing a claim:

Information in each section that contributes to an overall picture of the issue

Consider:
- In what order does Goodall present information about the beetles? How does this order build reader empathy for them?
- How does each section or subheading of the text contribute to Goodall's larger claim about the beetles' importance?

Rhetoric that advances the author's point of view on the issue

Consider:
- What words does Goodall choose when writing about the work done by the American burying beetle? Do her words suggest a positive or negative perspective on the beetles?
- Why do you think Goodall emphasizes the beetles as parents? What words link beetle parents to human parents?

The author of any argument bases his or her claim on a specific **point of view,** or perspective. If that point of view isn't clear from the start, you will need to watch for clues as you read.

Keep in mind that the writer's point of view drives both the information provided and the rhetoric used. For example, Jane Goodall has been concerned about animals and the environment throughout her life. Her passion for these issues gives her a particular point of view on every topic she writes about. However, what kinds of information and rhetoric would you expect in an argument about endangered beetles written from the point of view of a real-estate developer? Read with an awareness that the scope and substance of any argument depends on the writer's perspective; this strategy will help you carefully evaluate the argument.

TEACH

CLOSE READ

Analyze Author's Claim and Determine Purpose RI 5, RI 6

Make sure students understand each term by asking them to relate the terms to Goodall's argument. Ask students about the **purpose** of Goodall's argument. What is her **claim**? How does she use **rhetoric**? What is her **point of view**? *(The purpose of this argument is to persuade readers of the claim that the American burying beetle is important to the environment. The writer uses rhetoric through effective word choice, such as "remarkable" and "fascinating" when describing the beetle. The author writes from the point of view of someone who supports wildlife conservation.)*

To help students analyze the author's claim and determine purpose, divide the class into four expert groups. Provide each group with chart paper and markers. Assign each group one of the four bulleted questions on this page. Instruct each group to write its assigned question at the top of the chart paper. Then tell students to record their responses to the questions. They should support and explain their responses by citing evidence from the text. Have each group present its completed chart to the class.

Strategies for Annotation    Annotate it!

Analyze Author's Claim and Determine Purpose   RI 5, RI 6

Have students use their eBook annotation tools as they analyze the text. Ask them to do the following:

- Highlight in yellow Goodall's claim.
- Write a note that states Goodall's purpose for writing.
- Highlight in blue the reasons that support Goodall's claim.
- Underline examples of rhetoric.

Let me return to the question I asked earlier—would the loss of the American burying beetle matter? The answer, stressed by Lou and Jack, is an emphatic *yes*. They feed on carrion—the flesh of dead animals. Lou calls them "nature's most efficient recyclers" because they are responsible for recycling decaying animals back into the

> Goodall's purpose is to persuade.

PRACTICE & APPLY

Analyzing the Text
COMMON CORE RI 1, RI 2, RI 4, RI 5, RI 6, W 2

Possible answers:

1. *If Goodall quickly shows she understands her readers, they may be more receptive to her point of view.*

2. *Goodall chooses negative words. Examples include: "attacked," "weapons," "horrific," and "poisoned."*

3. *Goodall uses a question to stimulate thinking in her readers.*

4. *Goodall describes her own enthusiasm as she learns about the beetle from the experts Lou and Jack. She uses positive rhetoric such as "perfect spokesman," "blew my mind away," and "very successful."*

5. *Goodall feels that the American burying beetle is an interesting, amazing creature, and serves a purpose in maintaining a healthy environment. Goodall wants to persuade readers to think of these creatures in ways they may not have so that they can share her appreciation of them and understand their importance in the environment. Word choices in lines 79, 83, and 159 provide evidence for her claim.*

6. *The female beetle lays eggs near a food source. When the eggs hatch in a few days, both parents help feed the larvae. In two weeks, the beetle larvae burrow into the soil to pupate, and only then do the parents leave. These details show that both parents care for their young, and this behavior may help persuade readers to support Goodall's claim.*

7. *Goodall supports her claim by explaining how the beetles recycle nutrients (lines 76–82) and control pests (lines 82–84). Her claim may be restated as: The American burying beetle is important to the health of ecosystems and should be appreciated and protected.*

Analyzing the Text
COMMON CORE RI 1, RI 2, RI 4, RI 5, RI 6, W 2

Cite Text Evidence   Support your responses with evidence from the selection.

1. **Analyze** Why does Goodall begin her argument by acknowledging that many people dislike insects? How does this order of ideas help her develop her claim?

2. **Cite Evidence** Identifying persuasive rhetoric can help readers understand an author's point of view. In the second paragraph, how does the author use word choice to show her point of view on the use of pesticides against insects? Provide specific examples of word choice from the text to support your answer.

3. **Identify** In line 32, the discussion of insects returns to a focus on the American burying beetle. What rhetorical device does Goodall use to shift the discussion? How does this device help engage readers in her argument?

4. **Evaluate** Describe the importance of using Lou Perrotti and Jack Mulvena to tell the story of the American burying beetle. How does Goodall invite the reader to share her enthusiasm for the beetle? Describe the rhetoric she uses to persuade the reader.

5. **Draw Conclusions** What is Goodall's point of view on insects generally and on the American burying beetle in particular? Given the way she expresses this point of view, what is her purpose for writing the selection? Give specific textual evidence to support your answer.

6. **Infer** Summarize the life cycle of the American burying beetle. Why does the author offer so much detail about the beetle's life cycle? How does the information cited about the beetle support the author's purpose?

7. **Analyze** Reread the first sentence of the selection and think of it as the "rough draft" of Goodall's claim. What facts and reasons does she use to develop this claim throughout the text? After reading the entire selection, how would you state her claim in your own words?

PERFORMANCE TASK

Writing Activity: Analysis A key aspect of Goodall's writing style is her enthusiastic tone. In two paragraphs, analyze how she creates this tone and what effect it has on her argument.

1. Review the text, noting word choices, punctuation, and other examples that contribute to Goodall's tone. Summarize these techniques in your first paragraph.

2. Reflect on your response to Goodall's tone as you read. Did her tone make you more or less receptive to her claim about the importance of the American burying beetle? Discuss this effect in your second paragraph.

Assign this performance task.

PERFORMANCE TASK
COMMON CORE RI 1, RI 4, RI 5, W 2

Writing Activity: Analysis Have students work in pairs to gather examples of word choices, punctuation, and other strategies that show Goodall's enthusiasm for the beetles. You may want to provide students with the following sentence frames to begin each paragraph: 1) Goodall uses _____ to show her enthusiasm for the beetles. For example, _____ . 2) Goodall's enthusiastic tone makes me feel _____ toward the beetles because _____ .

Critical Vocabulary

loathe   pollinate   precipitous   sate

Practice and Apply   Answer each question with the appropriate Critical Vocabulary word and an explanation of why you chose the word you did.

1. Which Critical Vocabulary word goes with a cliff? Why?

2. Which Critical Vocabulary word goes with flowering plants? Why?

3. Which Critical Vocabulary word goes with a big meal? Why?

4. Which Critical Vocabulary word goes with something disgusting? Why?

Vocabulary Strategy: Patterns of Word Changes

Identifying patterns in the way a root word changes meaning when various word parts are added to it will help you clarify the meaning of unknown words. The Critical Vocabulary word *precipitous*, for example, is an adjective formed by adding the suffix -*ous*, meaning "full of," to the root *praecipit*, meaning "headlong or extremely steep." Various suffixes indicate different meanings or parts of speech when paired with the same root. Note the underlined suffixes in the chart and how they affect the meaning and part of speech.

Noun Suffix + Meaning	Verb Suffix + Meaning	Adjective Suffix + Meaning
precipitous<u>ness</u>, precipit<u>ation</u>, precipit<u>ator</u> -*ness*: state, quality -*ion*: state, condition; action, process -*or*: one that performs a specified action	precipit<u>ate</u> -*ate*: to act upon or become	precipit<u>ous</u> -*ous*: possessing, full of

Practice and Apply   Refer to both the chart above and a dictionary as needed to complete the following steps:

1. Choose two other words from the text that include suffixes. Identify and define the root—that is, the main word part without the suffix—for each word.

2. Combine each root word with a noun, verb, or adjective suffix to produce a new word. Write definitions for the words you produce.

3. Identify the parts of speech for the original words you selected from the text and the new words you created. Then, write an original sentence for each of the words, the two original words and the new words.

Critical Vocabulary

Possible answers:

1. *precipitous, because a cliff is sudden or steep*

2. *pollinate, because flowering plants must be fertilized*

3. *sate, because a big meal satisfies an appetite*

4. *loathe, because something disgusting might be hated*

Vocabulary Strategy: Patterns of Word Changes

Possible answers:

1. countless: count *means "to list or name one by one in order to find the total"*
   devastation: devastate *means "to ravage or lay waste, as by war or natural disaster"*

2. countable *means "able to be listed or named"*
   devastating *means "ravaging or destroying"*

3. countless *(adj.);* countable *(adj.);* devastation *(n.);* devastating *(adj.)*
   Countless ants marched along the picnic table. There are a countable number of salt shakers on the shelf. The earthquake caused devastation in the city. The flood was devastating to the local economy.

Strategies for Annotation   Annotate it!

Patterns of Word Changes

Have students use their eBook annotation tools to analyze the text. Ask them to do the following:

- Examine a passage that contains at least three words with suffixes.
- Highlight in yellow each base word.
- Highlight in blue each suffix.
- For each base word, write a note that includes the word with a new suffix. Write the part of speech and meaning of the new word.

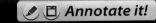

If only people would take the time to listen, retain the curiosity and wonder of childhood, how much richer their lives would be.

richest (adj.) having the greatest value

PRACTICE & APPLY

Language and Style: Relative Clauses

Be sure students understand in the example how the relative clause "that are irresistible to females of the species" makes a clear connection between the noun, *pheromones*, and the information that modifies the noun. Review the other examples in the chart. Explain when to use the relative pronoun *who* versus *that* when signaling a relative clause. *Who* is used when referring to a person; *that* is used when referring to things, including animals.

Possible answers: *Answers will vary because of the unique writing done by each student. When students have completed the exercise, they should be able to point to at least two examples of relative clauses.*

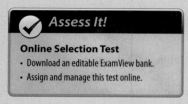

Assess It!

Online Selection Test
- Download an editable ExamView bank.
- Assign and manage this test online.

Language and Style: Relative Clauses

A **relative clause** is sometimes called an adjective clause because it can be used to describe a noun or pronoun. A writer's use of relative clauses can help readers better understand complex ideas. Relative clauses convey specific meanings and add variety and interest to writing. They are a type of **subordinate clause** because they cannot stand alone as sentences even though they include a subject and verb. In "Hope for Animals and Their World," Jane Goodall frequently links ideas by using relative clauses.

Read the following sentence from the selection. The relative clause is underlined.

> **Then he . . . emits pheromones <u>that are irresistible to females of the species.</u>**

The author could instead have expressed the same ideas this way:

> **Then he emits pheromones. The pheromones are irresistible to females of the species.**

Notice how the first example expresses the idea more clearly. Use of the relative clause allows the reader to more easily connect the noun, *pheromones*, with its modifying information: the fact that these pheromones are irresistible to female beetles.

Relative clauses can be signaled by **relative pronouns**, most often *who, which, that, whose,* or *whom*, and by **relative adverbs,** such as *where, when,* and *why*. The following chart shows examples of relative clauses from the selection:

	Identifying Relative Clauses	
Signal Word	**Relative Clause (underlined)**	**Word Modified**
who	Lou had parents <u>who were understanding and supportive of his fascination with invertebrates.</u>	parents
where	Today there are only seven places <u>where they are known to exist</u> . . .	places
that	. . . within a day the female lays the fertilized eggs in a small chamber <u>that they have dug out close to the carcass.</u>	chamber

Practice and Apply Look back at the paragraphs you wrote for this selection's Performance Task. Find two places to add relative clauses to more clearly express your ideas. Trade papers with a partner and evaluate the clarity of each other's sentences before and after revision.

Analyze Impact of Word Choice on Tone

COMMON CORE

RI 4

TEACH

Review with students that many words have **connotations** or associations that readers make with them. These associations may be positive or negative. Explain that an author's tone is his or her attitude toward the subject. Often, an author reveals **tone** through word choice. Words with positive connotations, such as *honest* and *brilliant*, reveal a positive tone; words with negative connotations, such as *tricky* and *dull*, reveal a negative tone. Lead students to compare and contrast the author's tone in the following examples:

- "Unfortunately the weapons of choice have been chemical pesticides—and this has led to horrific damage of all too many ecosystems . . ." (lines 15–17)
- "Let me share some of what I learned from him about these remarkable beetles. Most people have no idea how fascinating they are." (lines 54–56)

For each example, ask the following questions:
- What is the subject?
- What words does the author use to discuss the subject?
- Do these words have positive or negative connotations?
- What is the author's tone?

PRACTICE AND APPLY

Display lines 163–166 on the board or on a device. Ask students what the subject of this passage is. *(the American burying beetle)* Have volunteers take turns pointing out words the author uses to describe the American burying beetle *(beautiful, vivid, glowing, magic).*

Ask whether these words have positive or negative connotations. *(positive)* What is the author's tone or attitude toward the American burying beetle? *(She admires the beetle.)* Suppose the author described the beetle as *ugly, muted, dull,* and *ordinary.* How would that change the author's tone? *(These words have negative connotations. They would suggest that the author disapproves of the beetle.)*

Analyze Author's Claim and Determine Purpose

COMMON CORE

RI 5, RI 6

RETEACH

Review the terms *purpose, argument, claim, rhetoric,* and *point of view.* Then ask a volunteer to give an example of a claim for a specific argument, such as "Coyotes, bears, and other wildlife that enter urban areas should be removed without being harmed."

- Ask students to provide a purpose and a point of view of a writer that is consistent with the claim. *(Possible answers: The purpose is to persuade. The point of view is from a wildlife biologist.)* Record these items on a whiteboard.
- Then lead students to define an audience, such as the citizens of a city, for a potential written argument that makes the claim noted above. Record this information.
- Discuss possible rhetoric they might use to persuade the defined audience. Examples include *humane, parents,* and *natural.* Add these items to the whiteboard.

 LEVEL UP TUTORIALS Assign the following *Level Up* tutorial: **Elements of an Argument**

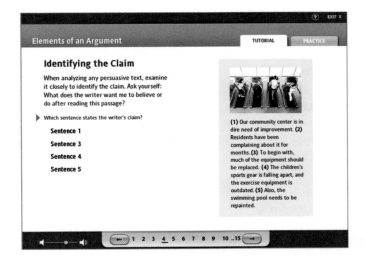

CLOSE READING APPLICATION

Students can apply the skill to a print or online newspaper or magazine editorial. Have them work independently to identify the claim, purpose, point of view, and rhetorical strategies of the argument. Ask students if they are persuaded to agree with the author's claim. Why or why not? Make sure they cite text evidence to support evaluations.

Emma Marris: In Defense of Everglades Pythons

Blog by Andrew C. Revkin

Why This Text

Students may read the text of an argument without a thorough understanding of the writer's claims or ideas, evidence, or point of view. Arguments such as the one cited in this blog entry may use complex reasoning that becomes clear only with careful study. With the help of the close-reading questions, students will analyze how Marris develops and refines her claim about the Everglades pythons in particular sentences, paragraphs, and larger portions of the text.

Background Have students read the background. Introduce the selection as a blog entry by Andrew C. Revkin, who writes the Dot Earth blog for *The New York Times*. In his blog, he provides commentary written by Emma Marris, a science writer whom Revkin admires. An expert on the environment, Marris's popular book—*Rambunctious Garden: Saving Nature in a Post-Wild World*—argues convincingly that human activity is disrupting ecology but that it is time for us to adapt to the inevitable changes.

AS YOU READ Ask students to pay close attention to the reasons Marris gives to support her defense of Everglades pythons. How soon into Marris's response can they begin to identify her point of view?

 COMMON CORE

Common Core Support

- cite multiple pieces of textual evidence

- analyze how an author's ideas or claims are developed and refined by particular sentences, paragraphs, or larger portions of a text

- assess an author's claims and reasoning

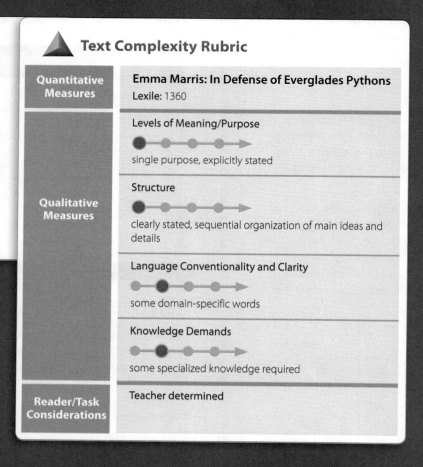

Text Complexity Rubric

Quantitative Measures	**Emma Marris: In Defense of Everglades Pythons** Lexile: 1360
Qualitative Measures	**Levels of Meaning/Purpose** single purpose, explicitly stated
	Structure clearly stated, sequential organization of main ideas and details
	Language Conventionality and Clarity some domain-specific words
	Knowledge Demands some specialized knowledge required
Reader/Task Considerations	Teacher determined

Strategies for CLOSE READING

Analyze an Author's Claims

Students should read this blog carefully all the way through. Close-reading questions at the bottom of the page will help students focus on a thorough analysis of Marris's claim and on how it is developed and refined. As they read, students should record comments or questions about the text in the margins.

WHEN STUDENTS STRUGGLE . . .

To help students follow the evidence Marris cites to support her claim, have students work in small groups to fill out a chart such as the one shown below.

CITE TEXT EVIDENCE For practice in analyzing an author's claims and in tracing how an author develops and refines those claims, ask students to cite the sentences and paragraphs Marris uses to support and refine her claims.

CLAIM: Pythons should be allowed to stay in the Everglades since humans introduced them into this environment, and it is not their fault that they are harming this ecosystem.

SUPPORT:

Lines 20–22: " . . . these snakes . . . are just doing what they evolved to do as they pig out on the native fauna . . ."

Lines 22–23: "It's the blame-the-invasive species narrative . . . "

Line 25: "But it isn't the pythons' fault. It is our fault for introducing them."

Lines 26–29: " . . . insofar as they threaten species in the Everglades, I wish we could undo that mistake and remove them all. But it ain't gonna happen. And so, I suggest, we might try to learn to love the pythons rather than revile them."

Lines 35–46: "The pythons came up at this June's Aspen Environment Forum. . . .I suggested that the pythons were likely here to stay no matter how hard we tried . . . I rejoined that . . . I fought for Nature as a dynamic and mutable thing. . . ."

Lines 53–57: "If the choice is to fight for a pure Everglades and lose, or to work with nature as it changes and adapts to what we humans have done to planet Earth . . . I vote for the latter."

Background *The Everglades are a natural region of wetlands located in southern Florida. For nearly 100 years, scientists and environmental activists have been focused on saving this "River of Grass" from investors eager to drain it for land development. Today, however, there is a new threat to the Everglades— the human introduction of nonnative predators, such as the Burmese python, to this fragile ecosystem. In this follow-up to a post he had written for the Dot Earth blog of The New York Times, environmental reporter* **Andrew C. Revkin** *presents enviromental author Emma Marris's response to the issue.*

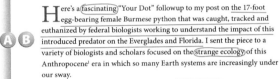

Emma Marris:
In Defense of Everglade Pythons
Blog by Andrew C. Revkin

CLOSE READ
Notes

1. **READ ▶** As you read lines 1–11, begin to collect and cite text evidence.
   - Underline information in the first paragraph that summarizes Revkin's first post about the python.
   - Circle persuasive language that Revkin uses to convince readers that the response to his post is interesting.
   - In the margin, explain how the use of the word *plight* in line 10 expresses Revkin's point of view.

(A) (B)

Here's a fascinating "Your Dot" followup to my post on the 17-foot egg-bearing female Burmese python that was caught, tracked and euthanized by federal biologists working to understand the impact of this introduced predator on the Everglades and Florida. I sent the piece to a variety of biologists and scholars focused on the strange ecology of this Anthropocene[1] era in which so many Earth systems are increasingly under our sway.

Emma Marris, the author of one of my favorite books of the last few years, "Rambunctious Garden: Saving Nature in a Post-Wild World," sent
10 this provocative reflection on the plight of the python, which—because of humans' penchant for exotic pets—has become such a "movable beast":

> *"Plight" implies that the pythons faced a difficult, unfortunate journey.*

[1] **Anthropocene:** an informal name for a new geologic era referred to as the Age of Man. This new era is defined by the impact of human activities on Earth's ecosystems.

23

---

1. **READ AND CITE TEXT EVIDENCE** Explain that Revkin's first post was about a 17-foot Burmese python that had been tracked and killed in the Everglades by agents from the United States Geological Survey.

(A) ASK STUDENTS why Revkin sent his blog to several biologists and scholars. *Revkin probably wanted to get a consensus about the killing of this invasive species from professionals who are studying the impact of human activity on the environment.*

FOR ELL STUDENTS Clarify the meaning of the technical term *blog.* Explain that it is a blended word made up of two words: *web + log = blog.* Have students define this word. *It is an online journal of someone's opinions, comments, or experiences.*

ASK STUDENTS to find other examples of technical language and cite them in the margin.

* * *

I think that the pythons in the Everglades fascinate us not only because enormous pythons are intrinsically mesmerizing, but because they echo the old biblical story of the serpent in Eden, a nasty outsider **defiling** paradise

D and ruining everything. Of course, the notion of the Everglades as a paradise is relatively new. We used to think of the place as a "worthless **morass**," as Michael Grunwald put it in his book on the history of the Everglades. The idea that marshes and swamps are places of natural beauty is less than 100 years old.

C 20 But now that the Everglades has become an international treasure, these snakes, which are just doing what they evolved to do as they pig out on the native fauna, have been painted as evil and despicable. It's the blame-the-invasive species narrative that's been in fashion for a few decades now, here helped out by the fact that many people have a visceral ick or eek reaction to snakes. But it isn't the pythons' fault. It is our fault for introducing them.

Yes, insofar as they threaten native species in the Everglades, I wish we could undo that mistake and remove them all. But it ain't gonna happen. And so, I suggest, we might try to learn to love the pythons rather than **revile** them. They are really impressive beasts. This doesn't mean we

30 shouldn't necessarily try to control their numbers as part of an overall management strategy, but it might mean that if you are touring the

defile:
to make impure

morass:
a swamp

Humans introduced pythons to the swamp.

revile:
to hate or speak badly of

---

2. **◄ REREAD** Reread lines 1–7. What is the author's attitude toward human activity and its impact on the environment? Support your answer with explicit textual evidence.

The author is trying to point out that many elements of ecology are "increasingly under our sway." The python was tracked and later euthanized while scientists studied its impact on the Everglades, it did not die a natural death.

3. **READ ►** As you read lines 12–25, continue to cite text evidence.

- Underline the reason Marris gives for our fascination with pythons in the Everglades.
- Underline the claim Marris makes in lines 20–25 and paraphrase it in the margin.
- Circle the phrase in lines 20–25 that Marris uses to describe the situation.

"But it isn't the pythons' fault. It is our fault for introducing them."

Everglades and you see one, you might consider yourself lucky, rather than grimacing and feeling that the purity of your experience was somehow tainted.

The pythons came up at this June's Aspen Environment Forum. I got into a debate with E. O. Wilson about the Everglades [*during this session*].

E He believes (more or less) that we should be going in there guns blazing, get every last python out, and keep the River of Grass "pure." I suggested that the pythons were likely here to stay no matter how hard we tried and that

40 the effort would likely be wasted, since the Everglades will probably be underwater in a few generations anyway, thanks to climate-change induced sea level rise. I said we should focus on protecting areas uphill so the species we like in the marsh have somewhere to go. He then suggested I was carrying around a white flag of surrender, and I rejoined that I never enlisted in the war for "purity" as defined by the world as it was in 1492, that rather I fought for Nature as a dynamic and mutable thing. And then the buzzer sounded and we both went back to our corners to get toweled off.

Wilson thinks we should kill all the pythons in the Everglades.

---

4. **◄ REREAD** Reread lines 12–19. What evidence does Marris use to support her claim that the "notion of the Everglades as a paradise is relatively new"?

Marris cites a quote from a book on the history of the Everglades by Michael Grunwald. She explains that only in the past hundred years have we begun to think of swamps as "places of natural beauty."

5. **READ ►** Read lines 26–57 and continue to cite evidence.

- Underline Marris's counterarguments to E.O. Wilson.
- In the margin, restate Wilson's viewpoints.

---

2. **REREAD AND CITE TEXT EVIDENCE**

B **ASK STUDENTS** to cite evidence that shows Revkin's point of view about the impact of human activity on Earth's ecosystems. What rhetoric does he use to advance his point of view? *His use of the loaded phrase "strange ecology" (line 5) and the sentence that includes it (lines 4–7) suggests that he recognizes that the python's death is part of the larger issue of human-disrupted ecology.*

3. **READ AND CITE TEXT EVIDENCE** Marris's claim is that the pythons can't be blamed for harming the Everglades since humans introduced this nonnative species.

C **ASK STUDENTS** to find and cite specific textual evidence to support Marris's claim. *Students should cite examples in lines 20–25.*

Critical Vocabulary: defile (line 14), **morass** (line 17), and **revile** (line 29) Have students share their definitions of these three words and use each in a sentence.

4. **REREAD AND CITE TEXT EVIDENCE**

D **ASK STUDENTS** to evaluate the effectiveness of the sentences Marris uses to develop, support, and refine her claim. *Students should cite evidence from lines 15–19, including Marris's explicit statement that "the notion of the Everglades as a paradise is relatively new" (lines 15–16); Grunwald's statement in his history of the Everglades, which Marris cites as support for her claim: "We used to think of the place as a 'worthless morass'" (lines 16–17); and Marris's refinement: "The idea that marshes and swamps are places of natural beauty is less than 100 years old" (lines 18–19).*

5. **READ AND CITE TEXT EVIDENCE**

E **ASK STUDENTS** to read their margin notes to a partner and write one response that best states Wilson's opposing viewpoint in lines 37–38 and 43–46, citing textual evidence. *Students should note that Wilson's viewpoint, the opposite of Marris's, is that we should kill the pythons in the Everglades to keep it "pure."*

It is possible that I am being too accepting of change here. This is the Everglades we are talking about, and there are so many people who have
50 fallen in love with the particular constellation of species that were there when Europeans first came to this continent, that it might be worth fighting very hard to keep it that way. Maybe I am going overboard on my "learn to love the inevitable changes" mantra. But it is really how I feel. If the choice is to fight for a pure Everglades and lose, or to work with nature as it changes and adapts to what we humans have done to planet Earth, respecting its dynamism and resilience as it shifts to new states, I vote for the latter. Just don't call me a python hugger. That sounds painful.

F

6. ◀ **REREAD** Reread lines 35–57. In your own words, restate Marris's opinions about change.

Nature can adapt to human-disrupted ecology; changes are
inevitable, and humans must respect them.

SHORT RESPONSE

Cite Text Evidence Did Marris convince you that the pythons should be allowed to stay in the Everglades? Explain, **citing text evidence** in your response.

Marris claims that pythons should be allowed to remain in the
Everglades since it is not their fault that the ecosystem is being
harmed by them. She also points out that "the Everglades will probably
be underwater in a few generations anyway." The support for her
claim is reasonable, and the evidence she offers has merit, including
the probability that pythons probably cannot be removed at this point.
She concludes that change is inevitable and must be respected.

26

---

6. **REREAD AND CITE TEXT EVIDENCE** Marris refines her position in the last paragraph.

F **ASK STUDENTS** to cite textual evidence that shows how Marris appeals to the reader's emotion in her idea about accepting the "inevitable changes." _By citing her opinion in lines 53–57 that it is preferable to work with nature as it changes, she uses an emotional appeal to ask her audience to be accepting of change. She refines her argument and concludes her response._

SHORT RESPONSE

Cite Text Evidence Students should:

- explain whether or not they were convinced by Marris's argument.
- give reasons for their point of view.
- cite specific evidence from the text to support their reasons.

TO CHALLENGE STUDENTS . . .

For more context about the pythons in the Everglades, students can view the video "Giant Killer Snakes," from the program MonsterQuest, in their eBooks.

ASK STUDENTS to look back at lines 38–47 to read Marris's counterargument to Wilson's claim in which she expresses her opinion that no matter how hard people may work to rid the Everglades of its pythons, they are here to stay. _Students should compare and contrast her views with those presented in the video about the Everglades pythons._

DIG DEEPER

With the class, return to Question 6, Reread. Have students share their restatement of Marris's opinion about the acceptance of change that she makes in her last paragraph.

ASK STUDENTS to work with a small group to assess each student's restatement (or paraphrase) of Marris's claim in her last paragraph. Ask groups to design a peer-assessment rubric and to choose one group member to offer student feedback. Some questions on the rubric might be:

Did the student . . .

- paraphrase Marris's opinion correctly?
- understand the point Marris is making?
- use his or her own words to restate Marris's point of view?
- begin with a clear, brief statement of Marris's position?
- use as few words as possible, being careful not to change Marris's ideas?
- use accurate quotations from the text?
- use specific textual evidence?
- speak loudly and clearly?

Have students explain if everyone in the group agreed on the student's content and presentation. How did the group resolve any conflicts or disagreements?

ASK STUDENTS to return to their Short Response answer and revise it based on the class restatements and discussion.

ANCHOR TEXT My Life as a Bat

Short Story by Margaret Atwood

Why This Text?

Students are accustomed to reading stories with a traditional text structure. This lesson presents a short story that includes traditional elements framed within a nontraditional text structure.

▶ **View It!**

Professional Development Podcast:

Text-Dependent Analysis

For practice and application:

Close Reader selection
"The Seventh Man"
short story by Haruki Murakami

Key Learning Objective: The student will be able to analyze a writer's choices in terms of text structure, figurative meaning, and tone.

COMMON CORE Common Core Standards

RL 1 Cite textual evidence.

RL 2 Determine a theme and analyze its development.

RL 3 Analyze how complex characters develop, interact, and advance the plot.

RL 4 Determine the meaning of words and phrases.

RL 5 Analyze how an author's choices create mystery, tension, or surprise.

W 7 Conduct short research projects to answer a question.

W 9 Draw evidence from texts to support analysis, reflection, and research.

W 10 Write over extended and shorter time frames for a range of tasks, purposes, and audiences.

SL 2 Integrate multiple sources of information presented in diverse media or formats.

SL 4 Present information clearly so that the development and style are appropriate to purpose, audience, and task.

L 2b Use a colon to introduce a list or quotation.

L 4c Consult reference materials to find a pronunciation or clarify meaning.

▲ Text Complexity Rubric

Quantitative Measures	**My Life as a Bat** Lexile: 1020L
Qualitative Measures	**Levels of Meaning/Purpose** multiple levels of meaning (multiple themes)
	Structure unconventional story structure
	Language Conventionality and Clarity some figurative language
	Knowledge Demands single perspective with unfamiliar aspects; some cultural and literary knowledge useful
Reader/Task Considerations	Teacher determined Vary by individual reader and type of text

Margaret Atwood Have students read about the author. Tell students that Atwood was born in Ottawa in the Province of Ontario, Canada. Atwood is a strong proponent of technology as it relates to writing and publishing. She co-invented a device that enables authors to remotely attend their own book signings, and she participates in social media and online writing communities.

AS YOU READ Direct students to use the As You Read statement to focus their reading. Remind students to note any questions they have as they read.

Analyze Author's Choices: Text Structure (LINES 1–17)
COMMON CORE **RL 5**

Explain that a traditional structure for a short story is paragraph form. The story usually begins with an **exposition** that introduces the characters and setting.

 ASK STUDENTS to scan the first page and explain how this story's structure is similar to a traditional one and how it is different. *(Like traditional stories, a character is introduced. Unlike stories, paragraphs are written in sections under numbered heads as in an article or essay.)*

Analyze Characters
COMMON CORE **RL 1, RL 3**

(LINES 1–17)

Explain that authors choose how to develop their characters. They might give detailed descriptions about them or reveal information slowly as the plot develops.

B **CITE TEXT EVIDENCE** Ask students to cite text evidence that tells about the characters. *(The first line is the only mention of a character. The only character so far is the narrator.)* Guide students to understand that the narrator is human. Ask them to point out text evidence. *(In lines 13–14, the narrator uses "us" and "our lives" to distinguish humans from different animals.)*

CRITICAL VOCABULARY

consensus: The narrator tries to convince the reader about the validity of believing in past lives.

ASK STUDENTS why the narrator believes readers who do not believe in reincarnation are not serious people. *(Since there is a general consensus about reincarnation, readers should agree with the majority.)*

Margaret Atwood (b. 1939) *has published more than fifty works of fiction, poetry, and nonfiction. This Canadian author uses her keen intellect and sharp wit to explore ideas about nature, science, the search for identity, social criticism, and human rights. Her award-winning novels include* The Handmaid's Tale, *which was made into a movie,* Cat's Eye, Alias Grace, *and* Oryx and Crake.

My Life as a Bat

Short Story by Margaret Atwood

AS YOU READ Think about the narrator's attitudes toward bats and toward humans. Pay attention to clues that show which species the narrator thinks is superior. Note any questions you have as you read.

1. Reincarnation

A In my previous life I was a bat. **B**

If you find previous lives amusing or unlikely, you are not a serious person. Consider: a great many people believe in them, and if sanity is a general **consensus** about the content of reality, who are you to disagree?

Consider also: previous lives have entered the world of commerce. Money can be made from them. *You were Cleopatra,*[1] *you were a Flemish duke, you were a Druid priestess,* and money changes hands. If the stock market exists, so must previous lives.

10 In the previous-life market, there is not such a great demand for Peruvian ditch-diggers as there is for Cleopatra; or for Indian latrine-cleaners, or for 1952 housewives living in California split-levels. Similarly, not many of us choose to remember our lives as **B** vultures, spiders, or rodents, but some of us do. The fortunate few. Conventional wisdom has it that reincarnation as an animal is a

---

[1] **Cleopatra:** Queen of Egypt in the first century B.C.

Image Credits: (t) ©Christopher Wahl/Contour by Getty Images

Close Read Screencasts   ▶ View It!

Modeled Discussions

Have students click the Close Read icons in their eBooks to access a screencast in which readers discuss and annotate the following key passage:

- a description of the narrator's nightmare about a man launching an attack with a tennis racket (lines 21–29)

As a class, view and discuss the video. Then have students pair up to do an independent close read of an additional passage:

- a description of the narrator's longing to return to life as a bat (lines 106–114).

Determine Figurative Meanings (LINES 18–29)

 RL 1, RL 4

Explain that writers often use comparisons between two dissimilar objects or ideas to express meaning. Two types of figurative comparisons include **similes**, explicit comparisons using *like* or *as*, and **metaphors**, implied comparisons.

C **CITE TEXT EVIDENCE** Ask students to read lines 18–29 and identify one simile and one metaphor and explain their meanings. *(Simile: "man's face . . . rising up like a marine float" suggests a large bobbing object, which is how the man's face appears to the bat above him. Metaphor: "curse of pity" suggests that feeling pity is an act of superiority.)*

Explain that figurative language also includes detailed descriptions that writers use to create images in the mind of the reader for a desired effect.

D **CITE TEXT EVIDENCE** Ask students to examine lines 38–46 for detailed imagery. Have students identify images that the writer uses and their effects. *(The writer uses images such as "water trickling" and "glistening hush." The images allow the reader to sense the safety and comfort of the home that the bat is anticipating.)*

---

punishment for past sins, but perhaps it is a reward instead. At least a resting place. An interlude[2] of grace.

Bats have a few things to put up with, but they do not inflict. When they kill, they kill without mercy, but without hate. They are 20 immune from the curse of pity. They never gloat.

2. Nightmares

I have recurring nightmares.

In one of them, I am clinging to the ceiling of a summer cottage while a red-faced man in white shorts and a white V-necked T-shirt jumps up and down, hitting at me with a tennis racket. There are cedar rafters up here, and sticky flypapers attached with tacks, dangling like toxic seaweeds. I look down at the man's face, foreshortened and sweating, the eyes bulging and blue, the mouth emitting furious noise, rising up like a marine float, sinking again, rising as if on a swell of air.

30 The air itself is muggy, the sun is sinking; there will be a thunderstorm. A woman is shrieking, "My hair! My hair!" and someone else is calling, "Anthea! Bring the stepladder!" All I want is to get out through the hole in the screen, but that will take some concentration and it's hard in this din of voices, they interfere with my sonar.[3] There is a smell of dirty bathmats—it's his breath, the breath that comes out from every pore, the breath of the monster. I will be lucky to get out of this alive.

In another nightmare I am winging my way—flittering, I suppose you'd call it—through the clean-washed demilight before 40 dawn. This is a desert. The yuccas are in bloom, and I have been gorging myself on their juices and pollen. I'm heading to my home, to my home cave, where it will be cool during the burnout of day and there will be the sound of water trickling through limestone, coating the rock with a glistening hush, with the moistness of new mushrooms, and the other bats will chirp and rustle and doze until night unfurls again and makes the hot sky tender for us.

But when I reach the entrance to the cave, it is sealed over. It's blocked in. Who can have done this?

I vibrate my wings, sniffing blind as a dazzled moth over the 50 hard surface. In a short time the sun will rise like a balloon on fire and I will be blasted with its glare, shriveled to a few small bones.

Whoever said that light was life and darkness nothing?

For some of us, the mythologies are different.

---

[2] **interlude:** an intermission or time of rest.
[3] **sonar:** a system for identifying objects with reflected sound.

SCAFFOLDING FOR ELL STUDENTS

Determine Figurative Meanings Using a whiteboard, project lines 22–29. Ask volunteers to identify similes by doing the following:

- Underline sentences that contain the word *like*.
- Highlight in green the word *like*.

ASK STUDENTS to tell which two things are being compared in each simile.

> There are cedar rafters up here, and sticky flypapers attached with tacks, dangling like toxic seaweeds. I look down at the man's face,

3. Vampire Films

I became aware of the nature of my previous life gradually, not only through dreams but through scraps of memory, through hints, through odd moments of recognition.

There was my preference for the **subtleties** of dawn and dusk, as opposed to the vulgar blaring hour of high noon. There was my déjà vu[4] experience in the Carlsbad Caverns—surely I had been there before, long before, before they put in the pastel spotlights and the cute names for stalactites and the underground restaurant where you can combine claustrophobia and indigestion and then take the elevator to get back out.

There was also my dislike for headfuls of human hair, so like nets or the tendrils of poisonous jellyfish: I feared entanglements. No real bat would ever suck the blood of necks. The neck is too near the hair. Even the vampire bat will target a hairless extremity—by choice a toe, resembling as it does the teat of a cow.

Vampire films have always seemed ludicrous to me, for this reason but also for the idiocy of their bats—huge rubbery bats, with red Christmas-light eyes and fangs like a sabertoothed tiger's, flown in on strings, their puppet wings flapped sluggishly like those of an overweight and degenerate bird. I screamed at these filmic moments, but not with fear; rather with outraged laughter, at the insult to bats.

O Dracula, unlikely hero! . . . Why was it given to you by whoever stole your soul to transform yourself into bat and wolf, and only those? Why not a vampire chipmunk, a duck, a gerbil? Why not a vampire turtle? Now that would be a plot.

4. The Bat as Deadly Weapon

During the Second World War they did experiments with bats. Thousands of bats were to be released over German cities, at the hour of noon. Each was to have a small **incendiary** device strapped onto it, with a timer. The bats would have headed for darkness, as is their habit. They would have crawled into holes in walls, or secreted themselves under the eaves of houses, relieved to have found safety. At a preordained moment they would have exploded, and the cities would have gone up in flames.

That was the plan. Death by flaming bat. The bats too would have died, of course. Acceptable megadeaths.

The cities went up in flames anyway, but not with the aid of bats. The atom bomb had been invented, and the fiery bat was no longer thought necessary.

---

[4] **déjà vu:** a sense of having already experienced a present condition or event.

subtleties
(sŭt´l-tēz) *n.* fine details or nuances.

incendiary
(ĭn-sĕn´dē-ĕr´ē) *adj.* intended to cause fire; flammable.

APPLYING ACADEMIC VOCABULARY

discrete	advocate

As you discuss the short story, incorporate the following Collection 2 academic vocabulary words: *discrete* and *advocate*. Ask students what position they think the narrator is trying to **advocate**. As you talk about which species is superior, bats or humans, cite text evidence of **discrete** differences between the two.

CLOSE READ

Analyze Author's Choices: Text Structure (LINES 54-79) COMMON CORE RL 5

Remind students to continue to take note of the nontraditional structure of the story.

E **ASK STUDENTS** to look back at sections 1 and 2 and identify the information presented in them. Have them explain why the writer chose to tell the story in this order. *(The case for reincarnation in section 1 progresses to experiences as a bat in section 2, which introduces the contrast between bats and humans. Section 3 reinforces the possibility of the narrator's previous life as a bat through "moments of recognition" [line 56] and the conventions of vampire films. It seems as if the writer is building up to an important revelation.)*

> **CRITICAL VOCABULARY**
>
> **subtleties:** The narrator distinguishes between the loudness of noon and the quiet of dawn and dusk.
>
> **ASK STUDENTS** to explain how the narrator's preference for dawn and dusk over noon supports the narrator being a bat. *(Just as bats, the author prefers darkness and is more active at night.)*

Determine Figurative Meanings (LINES 80–93) COMMON CORE RL 4

Remind students to continue to notice the use and meaning of figurative language.

F **CITE TEXT EVIDENCE** Ask students to identify and explain the writer's use of detailed descriptions that reveal the narrator's tone toward humans in lines lines 80–93. *("Preordained moment" [line 86] suggests humans act in a god-like manner. "Acceptable" and "megadeaths" [line 89] suggests a disregard for life.)*

> **CRITICAL VOCABULARY**
>
> **incendiary:** The narrator describes a plan in which bats are exploited to cause mass destruction.
>
> **ASK STUDENTS** to explain why the narrator thinks bats were used for this experiment. *(Incendiary devices are used as a means of assault during wars.)*

Determine Figurative Meanings (LINES 106–119)

 COMMON CORE RL 1, RL 4

Remind students that writers make specific word choices when creating figurative language.

G **CITE TEXT EVIDENCE** Ask students to identify examples of figurative language in lines 106–119 that, in combination, help to support the idea that the narrator believes bats and their lives are beautiful. *(These images combine to support the idea: "plunge into the nectars of crepuscular flowers," "hovering in the infrared of night," "bodies rounded and soft as furred plums," "anticipations of the tongue," and "beauty of slippery wings and sharp white canines and shining eyes.")*

Determine Theme

 COMMON CORE RL 1, RL 2

(LINES 100–125)

Remind students that the message a writer wants to convey can be stated as a **theme**.

H **CITE TEXT EVIDENCE** Ask students to state a theme of the story and to cite textual evidence that supports their response. *(One theme is that humans are destructive creatures who could look to examples in nature for redemption. In lines 101–102, the narrator suggests that perhaps the mission as a reincarnated human is to "save and redeem my own folk.")*

> **CRITICAL VOCABULARY**
>
> **denizen**: The narrator explains that the bat's unusual face makes it look like an alien from Pluto.
>
> **ASK STUDENTS** to explain the characteristics that denizens of a bat colony would have. *(Denizens of a bat colony would be a species of bat.)*

COLLABORATIVE DISCUSSION Have students work in pairs. Ask them to identify the narrator's statements about bats and humans and write notes about their opinions of the narrator's views. Remind students to cite text evidence for support.

ASK STUDENTS to share questions they generated in the course of reading and discussion of the selection.

If the bats had been used after all, would there have been a war memorial to them? It isn't likely.

If you ask a human being what makes his flesh creep more, a bat or a bomb, he will say the bat. It is difficult to experience loathing for something merely metal, however ominous. We save these sensations for those with skin and flesh: a skin, a flesh, unlike our own.

5. Beauty

100 Perhaps it isn't my life as a bat that was the interlude. Perhaps it is this life. Perhaps I have been sent into human form as if on a dangerous mission, to save and redeem my own folk. When I have gained a small success, or died in the attempt—for failure, in such a task and against such odds, is more likely—I will be born again, back into that other form, that other world where I truly belong. **H**

More and more, I think of this event with longing. The quickness of heartbeat, the vivid plunge into the nectars of crepuscular flowers, hovering in the infrared of night; the dank lazy half-sleep of daytime, with bodies rounded and soft as furred

110 plums clustering around me, the mothers licking the tiny amazed faces of the newborn; the swift love of what will come next, the anticipations of the tongue and of the infurled, corrugated and scrolled nose, nose like a dead leaf, nose like a radiator grille, nose of a **denizen** of Pluto.

And in the evening, the supersonic hymn of praise to our Creator, the Creator of bats, who appears to us in the form of a bat and who gave us all things: water and the liquid stone of caves, the woody refuge of attics, petals and fruit and juicy insects, and the beauty of slippery wings and sharp white canines and shining eyes.

120 What do we pray for? We pray for food as all do, and for health and for the increase of our kind; and for deliverance from evil, which cannot be explained by us, which is hair-headed and walks in the night with a single white unseeing eye, and stinks of half-digested meat, and has two legs.

Goddess of caves and grottoes: bless your children.

denizen
(dĕn´ĭ-zən) *n.* a resident.

COLLABORATIVE DISCUSSION With a partner, discuss whether you do or do not agree with the narrator's views of bats and humans. Cite specific evidence from the text to support your answer.

WHEN STUDENTS STRUGGLE . . .

To guide students' ability to identify a theme, have students work in pairs. Direct them to lines 95–99. Ask them to reread this passage and to explain who is doing the loathing and what it is that they loathe. Then ask them to connect this passage to other statements in the story that tell how humans think and act toward bats.

Determine Figurative Meanings

Writers often make imaginative comparisons between two dissimilar things to create vivid images and to convey specific meanings. **Similes** are comparisons that use the word *like* or *as*; **metaphors** are comparisons that are implied, rather than stated. To analyze the figurative meanings of the comparisons that Margaret Atwood uses in "My Life as a Bat," form a mental image of the two things that are being compared. Then ask yourself questions such as the ones in the following examples.

- **Simile:** "flypapers . . . dangling like toxic seaweeds." In what way are the items being compared similar? What feeling does the word *toxic* convey?
- **Metaphor:** "his breath, . . . the breath of the monster." Is the man really a monster? What does this comparison suggest about him or his likely actions? What is the narrator's **tone**, or attitude, toward him?

Analyze Author's Choices: Text Structure

COMMON CORE RL 5

Most stories follow a structure of exposition, rising action, climax, falling action, and resolution.

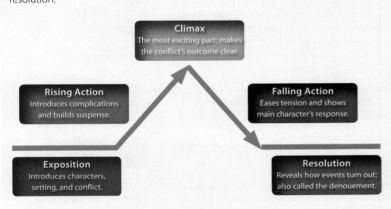

Climax
The most exciting part; makes the conflict's outcome clear.

Rising Action
Introduces complications and builds suspense.

Falling Action
Eases tension and shows main character's response.

Exposition
Introduces characters, setting, and conflict.

Resolution
Reveals how events turn out; also called the denouement.

In this story, Atwood dispenses with traditional narrative structure. Instead, she arranges events, conflicts, and reflections using an informative essay format, with numbered heads. Readers must piece together the narrative to determine the order and significance of events. As you read a story such as this one that uses an unusual narrative structure, consider the effect of the author's choices: How does the structure work to maintain reader interest and communicate theme?

CLOSE READ

Determine Figurative Meanings

COMMON CORE RL 4

Make sure students understand the difference between **simile** and **metaphor** and understand **tone**.

- Point out that **similes** have explicit structures (use of *like* or *as*) that are easily identifiable.
- Explain that **metaphors** can be more difficult to identify. To help students understand the difference, have them turn the example of a simile into a metaphor. *(Flypapers are toxic seaweeds.)*
- Remind students that the nature of the images can convey the **tone** of the narrator. Rather than state explicitly that the narrator feels, for example, kinship or animosity toward a subject, Atwood uses images that suggest kinship or animosity.

Analyze Author's Choices: Text Structure

COMMON CORE RL 5

Tell students that the text structure of Atwood's story may not be traditional, but it still includes the traditional elements of a story. Ask students to identify the exposition, rising action, climax, resolution, and to explain their reasoning. Due to the nonlinear structure of the story, students may not agree on which passages align with each element. Make sure students' reasoning supports their assertions.

Strategies for Annotation ✎ 🗖 *Annotate it!*

Determine Figurative Meanings

COMMON CORE RL 4

Have students use their eBook annotation tools to analyze the text. Ask them to do the following:

- Highlight similes in green. Underline the two items being compared.
- Highlight metaphors in blue. Use the note tool to annotate what the metaphor refers to and the tone of the narrator.

Lazy half-sleep of daytime, with bodies rounded and soft as furred plums clustering around me, the mothers licking the tiny amazed

Whoever said that light was life and darkness nothing?

PRACTICE & APPLY

Analyzing the Text  RL 1, RL 2, RL 3, RL 4, RL 5, W 9, W 10

Possible answers:

1. The narrator's evidence for believing in previous lives is that "a great many people believe in them" (line 3) and that people pay ("the world of commerce" [line 6–7]) to hear who they were in past lives. The narrator uses logic: Since many people believe in previous lives, and there is a "general consensus about the content of reality" (line 4), previous lives must exist, as does the stock market (line 9).

2. The narrator uses a humorous example to comment that there isn't a great demand in the previous-life market for "Peruvian ditch-diggers" or "Indian latrine-cleaners" (lines 11–12). Knowing that the narrator has a wry sense of humor will make the reader look for levels of meaning in the narrator's comments.

3. To the nocturnal bat, the sun is something that burns ("the burnout of the day" [line 43]) instead of giving warmth. The balloon may blast her with its glare, causing her to shrivel.

4. The narrator contrasts the beauty of bats ("bodies rounded and soft as furred plums" [lines 109–110) with the hideousness of humans (lines 26–28 and 121–124). The morality of bats and humans are contrasted: Bats "kill without mercy, but without hate"; they do not pity nor gloat (lines 19–20). It is implied that humans do all these things. The stories about humans using bats as incendiary devices (lines 80–87), the man swatting at the narrator with a tennis racket (lines 21–37), and the nightmare about the sealed cave (lines 38–51) all show humans as evil aggressors (lines 121–124) who the narrator may be on a mission to redeem (line 102). These contrasts develop a theme suggesting that humans are not as advanced a species as they think they are.

5. Sensory details include images of the cave in lines 42–46 ("water trickling through limestone," "moistness of new mushrooms,") and lines 106–119 ("vivid plunge," hovering in the infrared of night," "tiny amazed faces of the newborn"). The details create a tone of reverence toward bats.

6. Examples of figurative language using unexpected combinations of images include "dangling like toxic seaweeds" (line 26) and "supersonic hymn of praise" (line 115). These images surprise the reader with unlikely comparisons.

7. "Beauty" works best as the last section because it sums up the narrator's dual connection to bats and humans. After having the narrator relate experiences with humans and living as a bat in prior sections, the writer leaves the reader with a final embrace of the beauty of bats and a compelling prayer for continued life and deliverance from evil.

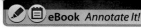 **eBook** *Annotate It!*

Analyzing the Text  RL 1, RL 2, RL 3, RL 4, RL 5, W 9, W 10

Cite Text Evidence Support your responses with evidence from the selection.

1. **Cite Evidence** What evidence does the narrator offer for believing in a past life as a bat? What device or method does the author use to provide this evidence?

2. **Analyze** Throughout the story, the author uses wry humor in the form of exaggeration and irony. Give an example of humor from the text. How does the humor develop the character of the narrator?

3. **Interpret** The narrator, as a bat, describes the sun rising "like a balloon on fire" (line 50). What meaning is conveyed by this simile in the context of the flashback?

4. **Compare** What are some of the main contrasts the narrator makes between humans and bats? Cite specific statements as well as stories that imply the differences. What theme about people is developed through these contrasts?

5. **Evaluate** Details that appeal to the senses can create positive or negative feelings. What sensory details does the narrator use to describe the bat's domain and tell what it feels like to be a bat? What tone toward bats do the sensory details create?

6. **Analyze** Some of Atwood's figurative language involves unexpected combinations of sensory images. For example, the narrator imagines water in a cave "coating the rock with a glistening hush" (line 44). *Glistening* means "shiny" and *hush* means "silence," appealing to both sight and hearing at once. Find other examples of this kind of figurative language in the text. What is the overall effect of these descriptions on readers?

7. **Evaluate** The last section of the story is called "Beauty." Why did the author choose to place this section last in the structure of the story? Would any other section have worked as well as the conclusion to the story?

PERFORMANCE TASK

Speaking Activity: Research "My Life as a Bat" includes many details about how bats live. Examine these details to determine whether the story details are factually accurate.

1. With a partner, list details about bats from the story, such as where they live, how they behave, what they eat, what they look like.

2. Research facts about these aspects of bats.

3. Create a chart or a Venn diagram to compare the story details with the facts.

4. Write and present your findings in a brief oral report in which you evaluate the author's use of factual material.

 Assign this performance task.

PERFORMANCE TASK  SL 2, SL 4

Speaking Activity: Research Explain to students that they must use sources that are reliable and valid. Tell students they may use their Venn diagrams during their oral reports if the diagrams help clarify the details they present.

Critical Vocabulary

COMMON CORE L 4c

consensus   subtleties   incendiary   denizen

Practice and Apply Answer the questions to demonstrate your understanding of each Critical Vocabulary word.

1. What **consensus** do humans hold about bats?

2. What are some of the **subtleties** of life inside a bat colony?

3. Why might military strategists choose to use bats as **incendiary** weapons?

4. What environments can a bat be considered a **denizen** of?

Vocabulary Strategy: Using Reference Sources

If you come across an unfamiliar word while reading, look first for a footnote on the page. If one is not provided, you can use the context—the words and sentences around the unfamiliar word—to help you determine the meaning. If context is not helpful, turn to a reference source, such as a glossary, dictionary, or thesaurus.

Glossary	Dictionary	Thesaurus
• **Where it is found:** at the back of the book in which the word is used	• **Where it is found:** library; Internet; print and digital versions	• **Where it is found:** library; Internet; print and digital versions
• **What it includes:** pronunciation; definition as it is used in the text	• **What it includes:** part of speech; syllable division; pronunciation; definitions; synonyms; etymology	• **What it includes:** synonyms; shades of meaning

Practice and Apply Use reference sources to find the specified information about each of the Critical Vocabulary words. Write your answers and explain which reference source you used and why.

1. Write three synonyms for **consensus**.

2. Write the pronunciation for **subtleties**.

3. Write the etymology, or origin, of the word **incendiary**.

4. Write the part of speech and syllable division for **denizen**.

PRACTICE & APPLY

Critical Vocabulary

COMMON CORE L 4c

Possible answers:

1. *Humans hold the consensus that a bat makes their flesh creep more than a bomb does.*

2. *Some of the subtleties in a bat colony include the chirping and rustling in the clusters of bats and the tender care of newborns by mothers.*

3. *The narrator states that bats released at noon would seek dark places such as under eaves or in holes in walls. The incendiary devices attached to the bats would create fires when detonated.*

4. *Bats are denizens of caves and dark places.*

Vocabulary Strategy: Using Reference Sources

Possible answers:

1. *accord, agreement, unanimity. A thesaurus was used because it is a source for synonyms.*

2. *(sŭt´l-tēz). A dictionary was used because entries include the pronunciation.*

3. *Middle English, from Latin* incendiārius, *from* incendium, *fire, from* incendere, *to set on fire. A dictionary was used because entries include word etymologies.*

4. *(den·i·zen) n. A dictionary was used because entries include part of speech and syllable division.*

Strategies for Annotation   *Annotate it!*

Using Reference Sources

COMMON CORE L 4c

Have students locate three words in the text they are not familiar with. Ask them to arrive at a definition for each based on context clues in the text. Encourage them to use their eBook annotation tools to do the following:

- Highlight in yellow the three unfamiliar words.
- Underline context clues.
- Use the note tool to write a note for each that confirms or provides the meaning they determined based on the word's entry in a reference source.

quickness of heartbeat, the vivid plunge into the nectars of **crepuscular** flowers, hovering in the infrared of night; the dank

crepuscular: occurring or active during twilight

PRACTICE & APPLY

Language and Style: Colons and Dashes

Explain to students that skillful writers use marks of punctuation with an eye toward enhancing emphasis and meaning. Point out that these punctuation marks should be used only as described in the instruction. The overuse of colons and dashes interrupts the structure and flow of sentences.

Possible answers:

Answers will vary because of the unique writing done by each student. When students have completed the exercise, invite volunteers to explain why they chose the sentences they revised.

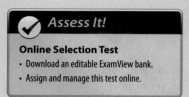

Assess It!

Online Selection Test
- Download an editable ExamView bank.
- Assign and manage this test online.

Language and Style: Colons and Dashes

A writer's use of punctuation helps clarify meaning for the reader by showing places of emphasis or change of tone. In "My Life as a Bat," Margaret Atwood uses colons and dashes not only for meaning but also to create an engaging style.

Colons are used to introduce lists, as in the following passage from the story:

> **And in the evening, the supersonic hymn of praise to our Creator, the Creator of bats, who appears to us in the form of a bat and who gave us all things: water and the liquid stone of caves, the woody refuge of attics, petals and fruit and juicy insects, and the beauty of slippery wings and sharp white canines and shining eyes.**

Colons can also be used to introduce direct quotations, as in this example:

> **Atwood suggests that humans could learn from animals' lives: "When they kill, they kill without mercy, but without hate. They are immune from the curse of pity. They never gloat."**

Just as readers naturally pause at a colon to prepare for what comes after it, they also pause at a dash. A dash or pair of dashes is used to set off or emphasize ideas. Here are some common uses of dashes:

Uses of Dashes	
Purpose	**Example from the Text**
set off a definition or explanation	In another nightmare I am winging my way—flittering, I suppose you'd call it—through the clean-washed demilight before dawn.
show a sudden break in thought in a sentence	When I have gained a small success, or died in the attempt—for failure, in such a task and against such odds, is more likely—I will be born again, back into that other form, that other world where I more truly belong.
emphasize a word, a series of words, a phrase, or a clause	There is a smell of dirty bathmats—it's his breath, the breath that comes out from every pore, the breath of the monster.

Practice and Apply Look back at the presentation you created for this selection's Performance Task. Revise your written presentation to include at least one colon and one dash or set of dashes. Then, discuss with a partner how each punctuation mark you added clarifies or enhances the meaning of your ideas.

Conducting Research on the Web

COMMON CORE

W 7

TEACH

Before students research bats in order to complete the Performance Task, review the steps for conducting a Web search.

- **Step 1: Formulate Research Questions** Tell partners that they will use their lists of details about bats in the story to form research questions, such as "How do bats communicate?"
- **Step 2: Start Your Search** Tell partners that in addition to a keyword search in a search engine, they might search the Web sites of prominent zoos or national parks for facts about bats. Keywords, such as *bats, nocturnal animals,* and *bat behavior,* can also be searched in school and public library online catalogues.
- **Step 3: Refine Your Search** Use *AND, NOT,* or *OR* between keywords and phrases to narrow your search.
- **Step 4: Analyze the Results** Evaluate results of your keyword search and choose the most relevant and credible sites. Check for the most current information and whether the source is an authority on the subject. Verify information by cross-referencing it with other reliable sources.

COLLABORATIVE DISCUSSION

Direct students to work in pairs to conduct their research on bats using the strategies you presented. Have pairs complete their Venn diagrams to compare the story details with facts. Then have students write and present their oral reports, evaluating the author's use of factual information.

Analyze Author's Choices: Text Structure

COMMON CORE

RL 5

RETEACH

Ask students to reread the story, paying particular attention to each individual section. Divide the class into four groups.

- Display the sequence of a traditional story structure: exposition, rising action, climax, and resolution. Give each group an index card with a different story element at the top.
- Tell students to work together to identify their assigned element in the selection. Have them note section numbers and list lines where the element is found. Explain that since the story has a nontraditional sequence and structure, they might identify some elements in more than one section.
- To help guide students, ask questions such as: Where do you read about character and setting? What is the main character's conflict? In which section is the conflict revealed? In which section is it resolved?
- Ask students to explain why the writer chose to write this particular story using a nontraditional structure.

 LEVEL UP TUTORIALS Assign the following *Level Up* tutorial: **Plot: Sequence of Events**

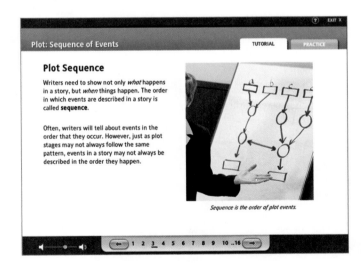

CLOSE READING APPLICATION

Students can apply the skill to another short story with a nontraditional structure. Have them work independently to identify traditional structure elements within the nontraditional structure. Ask: Does the writer make effective use of the nontraditional structure?

The Seventh Man

Short Story by Haruki Murakami   translated by Jay Rubin

Why This Text

Students may have difficulty understanding a frame story (a story within a story). In "The Seventh Man," the author rejects standard narrative form, blending realistic and fantastical elements. With the help of the close-reading questions, students will piece together the events into a coherent narrative and examine how the structure works to underscore the story's theme.

Background Have students read the background and information about the author. Point out that Murakami is known for his eclectic style and unique vision. Explain that as in his other work, "The Seventh Man" draws upon American realism as well as Japanese surrealism, with elements of comedy thrown in. As students read this deceptively simple tale, have them note the way the author uses language to make his wild imaginings seem utterly believable.

AS YOU READ Ask students to pay attention to the way the author uses figurative language and imagery to bring his descriptions to life.

Common Core Support

- cite strong and thorough textual evidence
- determine figurative meanings of words and phrases
- analyze an author's choices concerning how to structure a text

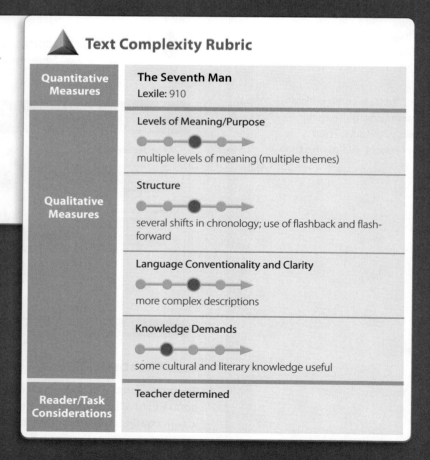

Text Complexity Rubric

Quantitative Measures	**The Seventh Man** Lexile: 910
Qualitative Measures	**Levels of Meaning/Purpose** multiple levels of meaning (multiple themes)
	Structure several shifts in chronology; use of flashback and flash-forward
	Language Conventionality and Clarity more complex descriptions
	Knowledge Demands some cultural and literary knowledge useful
Reader/Task Considerations	Teacher determined

Strategies for CLOSE READING

Determine Figurative Meanings

Students should read this story carefully all the way through. Close-reading questions at the bottom of the page will help them analyze how the author uses figurative language to add meaning to the text. As they read, students should jot down comments or questions about the text in the margins.

WHEN STUDENTS STRUGGLE . . .

To help students determine meanings of figurative language in "The Seventh Man," have students work in small groups to fill out a chart like the one shown below.

CITE TEXT EVIDENCE For practice in recognizing how the author's use of figurative language adds meaning to the text, have them find examples of each type in the chart below.

Figurative Language	Text Evidence
Simile	"Every once in a while, the house would creak and shudder as if a huge hand were shaking it" (lines 79–80) "The whole, huge space felt like a room without furniture" (line 132)
Metaphor	". . it was just a great big circus" (line 68)
Personification	"It just barely missed me, but in my place it swallowed everything that mattered most to me" (lines 12–13) "The storm's great 'eye' seemed to be up there, fixing its cold stare on all of us below" (lines 104–105)
Sensory image	But something ominous about them—something like the touch of a reptile's skin—had sent a chill down my spine" (lines 153–154)

Background As a boy, Haruki Murakami *preferred reading American paperbacks to studying traditional Japanese literature. He went on to become a novelist and short-story writer known for unique and whimsical works that break away from typical Japanese forms. Murakami combines mystery, comedy, and fantasy in his work, while keeping his messages practical, profound, and believable.*

The Seventh Man

Short Story by Haruki Murakami   translated by Jay Rubin

CLOSE READ
Notes

1. **READD** As you read lines 1–30, begin to collect and cite text evidence.

- Circle text in lines 1–15 that creates a mood. In the margin, describe that mood.
- Underline examples of figurative language: personification, simile, and metaphor.
- In lines 16–30, circle text that makes the seventh man seem mysterious.

"A huge wave nearly swept me away," said the seventh man, almost whispering.

"It happened one September afternoon when I was ten years old."

The man was the last one to tell his story that night. The hands of the clock had moved past ten. The small group that huddled in a circle could hear the wind tearing through the darkness outside, heading west. It shook the trees, set the windows to rattling, and moved past the house with one final whistle.

"It was the biggest wave I had ever seen in my life," he said. "A strange
10 wave. An absolute giant."

He paused.

Ⓐ "It just barely missed me, but in my place it swallowed everything that mattered most to me and swept it off to another world. I took years to find it again to recover from the experience—precious years that can never be replaced."

The mood is eerie and threatening.

27

---

1. **READ AND CITE TEXT EVIDENCE** Remind students that figurative language is used to create imaginative comparisons that add meaning to the text. Here, the author uses *personification*—or, the attribution of human characteristics to a nonhuman entity—to create vivid images that spring to life on the page.

Ⓐ **ASK STUDENTS** to explain how the word "swallowed" (line 12) helps them "see" the wave. What comparison is the author making by using this word? How does it help describe the actions of the wave? *The author uses* swallowed *to describe the devastating effects of the wave—how it seemed to "eat up" everything in its path.*

The seventh man appeared to be in his mid-fifties. He was a thin man, tall, with a moustache, and next to his right eye he had a short but deep-looking scar that could have been made by the stab of a small blade. Stiff, bristly patches of white marked his short hair. His face had the look you see on people when they can't quite find the words they need. In his case, though, the expression seemed to have been there from long before, as though it were part of him. The man wore a simple blue shirt under a grey tweed coat, and every now and then he would bring his hand to his collar. None of those assembled there knew his name or what he did for a living.

He cleared his throat, and for a moment or two his words were lost in silence. The others waited for him to go on.

B "In my case, it was a wave," he said. "There's no way for me to tell, of course, what it will be for each of you. But in my case it just happened to take the form of a gigantic wave. It presented itself to me all of a sudden one day, without warning. And it was devastating."

C I grew up in a seaside town in the Province of S. It was such a small town, I doubt that any of you would recognize the name if I were to mention it. My father was the local doctor, and so I led a rather comfortable childhood. Ever since I could remember, my best friend was a boy I'll call K. His house was close to ours, and he was a grade behind me in school. We were like brothers, walking to and from school together, and always playing together when we got home. We never once fought during our long

A flashback starts here. The seventh man becomes the narrator.

2. ◄ REREAD Reread lines 16–30. Explain what the wave might symbolize to Murakami.

The wave could be a symbol for change or loss.

_____

_____

_____

_____

_____

3. READ ► As you read lines 31–58, continue to cite text evidence.

- In the margin, explain how the structure of the story changes in line 31.
- Underline text that describes the narrator's relationship with K.

28

friendship. I did have a brother, six years older, but what with the age difference and differences in our personalities, we were never very close. My real brotherly affection went to my friend K.

K. was a frail, skinny little thing, with a pale complexion and a face almost pretty enough to be a girl's. He had some kind of speech **impediment**, though, which might have made him seem retarded to anyone who didn't know him. And because he was so frail, I always played his protector, whether at school or at home. I was kind of big and athletic, and the other kids all looked up to me. But the main reason I enjoyed spending time with K. was that he was such a sweet, pure-hearted boy. He was not the least bit retarded, but because of his impediment, he didn't do too well at school. In most subjects, he could barely keep up. In art class, though, he was great. Just give him a pencil or paints and he would make pictures that were so full of life that even the teacher was amazed. He won prizes in one contest after another, and I'm sure he would have become a famous painter if he had continued with his art into adulthood. He liked to do seascapes. He'd go out to the shore for hours, painting. I would often sit beside him, watching the swift, precise movements of his brush, wondering how, in a few seconds, he could possibly create such lively shapes and colors where, until then, there had been only blank white paper. I realize now that it was a matter of pure talent.

One year, in September, a huge typhoon hit our area. The radio said it was going to be the worst in ten years. The schools were closed, and all the shops in town lowered their shutters in preparation for the storm. Starting early in the morning, my father and brother went around the house nailing shut all the storm doors, while my mother spent the day in the kitchen cooking emergency provisions. We filled bottles and canteens with water, and packed our most important possessions in rucksacks for possible evacuation. To the adults, typhoons were an annoyance and a threat they had to face almost annually, but to the kids, removed as we were from such practical concerns, it was just a great big circus, a wonderful source of excitement.

D Just after noon the color of the sky began to change all of a sudden. There was something strange and unreal about it. I stayed outside on the porch, watching the sky, until the wind began to howl and the rain began to

impediment:
defect

The author first compares the storm to a circus and then to a beast with the word "howl."

4. READ ► As you read lines 59–118, continue to cite text evidence.

- Underline figurative language, including similes, metaphors, personification, and idioms.
- In the margin, explain the images this language evokes.

29

---

2. **REREAD AND CITE TEXT EVIDENCE** Tell students that the seventh man is telling the story about the most tragic event in his life.

B **ASK STUDENTS** to cite text evidence that explains the importance of the wave to the author. *In lines 27–30, the seventh man explains that a wave has nearly devastated him and refers to "what it will be for each of you" (line 28). He is about to tell a story of a tragic event caused by a wave. The wave symbolizes tragedy, change, or loss.*

3. **READ AND CITE TEXT EVIDENCE** Have students note the sudden shift in the text starting in line 31.

C **ASK STUDENTS** to identify this new subject. *The seventh man is talking about his childhood.* When did the events he describes happen? *They happened in the past.* When does the story start out? *It starts out in the present.*

4. **READ AND CITE TEXT EVIDENCE** Have students note the circus metaphor used to describe the approaching storm (line 68).

D **ASK STUDENTS** to explain why the storm was like a circus to the children. *Both the storm and the circus are fun and exciting but with an air of danger; they represent a departure from normal routine.* What did the adults think of the storm? *To them it was "an annoyance, a threat they had to face annually" (lines 66–67).*

Critical Vocabulary: impediment (line 43) Have students explain the meaning of *impediment*, and ask them how K.'s speech impediment affected the way others perceived him. *It made him seem "slow."*

FOR ELL STUDENTS Help ELL students find out what the word *seascapes* means from context clues. Point out that the author is talking about painting, and that he describes K. going to the shore to paint. Encourage students to "connect the dots."

Personifying
the storm
through this
simile makes
its destruction
intentional,
and more
cruel.

beat against the house with a weird dry sound, like handfuls of sand. Then
we closed the last storm door and gathered together in one room of the
darkened house, listening to the radio. This particular storm did not have a
great deal of rain, it said, but the winds were doing a lot of damage, blowing
roofs off houses and capsizing ships. Many people had been killed or
injured by flying debris. Over and over again, they warned people against
leaving their homes. Every once in a while, the house would creak and
80 shudder as if a huge hand were shaking it, and sometimes there would be a
great crash of some heavy-sounding object against a storm door. My father
guessed that these were tiles blowing off the neighbors' houses. For lunch
we ate the rice and omelettes my mother had cooked, waiting for the
typhoon to blow past.

But the typhoon gave no sign of blowing past. The radio said it had lost
momentum almost as soon as it came ashore at S. Province, and now it was
moving north-east at the pace of a slow runner. The wind kept up its savage
howling as it tried to uproot everything that stood on land.

Perhaps an hour had gone by with the wind at its worst like this when
90 a hush fell over everything. All of a sudden it was so quiet, we could hear
a bird crying in the distance. My father opened the storm door a crack
and looked outside. The wind had stopped, and the rain had ceased to
fall. Thick, grey clouds edged across the sky, and patches of blue showed
here and there. The trees in the yard were still dripping their heavy burden
of rainwater.

"We're in the eye of the storm," my father told me. "It'll stay quiet like
this for a while, maybe fifteen, twenty minutes, kind of like an intermission.
Then the wind'll come back the way it was before."

The idiom
"eye of the
storm" makes
the typhoon
seem powerful
and human, or
god-like.

I asked him if I could go outside. He said I could walk around a little if I
100 didn't go far. "But I want you to come right back here at the first sign of
wind."

I went out and started to explore. It was hard to believe that a wild
storm had been blowing there until a few minutes before. I looked up at the
sky. The storm's great "eye" seemed to be up there, fixing its cold stare on
all of us below. No such "eye" existed, of course: we were just in that
momentary quiet spot at the center of the pool of whirling air.

While the grown-ups checked for damage to the house, I went down to
the beach. The road was littered with broken tree branches, some of them
thick pine boughs that would have been too heavy for an adult to lift alone.
110 There were shattered roof tiles everywhere, cars with cracked windshields,

and even a doghouse that had tumbled into the middle of the street. A big
hand might have swung down from the sky and flattened everything in its
path.

K. saw me walking down the road and came outside.
"Where are you going?" he asked.
"Just down to look at the beach," I said.
Without a word, he came along with me. He had a little white dog that
followed after us.
"The minute we get any wind, though, we're going straight back home,"
120 I said, and K. gave me a silent nod.
The shore was a 200-yard walk from my house. It was lined with a
concrete breakwater—a big **dyke** that stood as high as I was tall in those
days. We had to climb a short flight of steps to reach the water's edge. This
was where we came to play almost every day, so there was no part of it we
didn't know well. In the eye of the typhoon, though, it all looked different:
the color of the sky and of the sea, the sound of the waves, the smell of the
tide, the whole expanse of the shore. We sat atop the breakwater for a time,
taking in the view without a word to each other. We were supposedly in the
middle of a great typhoon, and yet the waves were strangely hushed. And
130 the point where they washed against the beach was much farther away than
usual, even at low tide. The white sand stretched out before us as far as we
could see. The whole, huge space felt like a room without furniture, except
for the band of **flotsam** that lined the beach.

The storm
seems to have
intentionally
destroyed
things.

dyke:
a wall
constructed to
control water

flotsam:
floating
wreckage of a
ship or its
cargo

5. **◀ REREAD** Reread lines 96–118. How does the author foreshadow the
danger to come? Support your answer with explicit textual evidence.

We already know a huge wave is coming. The strength of the storm,
the fact that people have been killed, and the father's warning that
"the wind'll come back the way it was before" all foreshadow that
something bad will happen.

6. **READ ▶** As you read lines 119–159, continue to cite text evidence.
   - Circle references to soundlessness.
   - Continue to underline figurative language: idioms, similes, metaphors,
     personification.
   - In the margin, explain the impact of the figurative language the author
     uses.

FOR ELL STUDENTS You may want to clarify that this part of the
selection is talking about a *typhoon*, a kind of severe storm. Then
point out words and phrases that are related to the storm or its
damage: *capsizing ships, flying debris, eye of the storm, shattered,
cracked, flattened, tumbled,* and so on.

5. **REREAD AND CITE TEXT EVIDENCE**

E **ASK STUDENTS** to cite examples of personification in lines
96–118 that imply dangerous intent. *The storm's "great eye" (line
104), "A big hand might have swung down from the sky" (lines
111–112).*

6. **READ AND CITE TEXT EVIDENCE**

F **ASK STUDENTS** to identify the simile in lines 138–139.
What two things are being compared? *To the narrator, the rubble
on the beach looks like a "candy store."*

Critical Vocabulary: dyke (line 122) What does the use of this
word say about the boy's familiarity with his surroundings? *He is
very familiar with his surroundings.*

Critical Vocabulary: flotsam (line 133) Have students share
definitions and use the word in a sentence.

> *The sea had suddenly stretched its long, smooth tonuge out to where I stood on the beach.*

this simile brings innocence to mind

F We stepped down to the other side of the breakwater and walked along the broad beach, examining the things that had come to rest there. Plastic toys, sandals, chunks of wood that had probably once been parts of furniture, pieces of clothing, unusual bottles, broken crates with foreign writing on them, and other, less recognizable items: it was like a big candy store. The storm must have carried these things from very far away.

140 Whenever something unusual caught our attention, we would pick it up and look at it every which way, and when we were done, K.'s dog would come over and give it a good sniff.

We couldn't have been doing this more than five minutes when I realized that the waves had come up right next to me. Without any sound or other warning, the sea had suddenly stretched its long, smooth tongue out to where I stood on the beach. I had never seen anything like it before. Child though I was, I had grown up on the shore and knew how frightening the ocean could be—the savagery with which it could strike unannounced.

And so I had taken care to keep well back from the waterline. In spite of

150 that, the waves had slid up to within inches of where I stood. And then, just as soundlessly, the water drew back—and stayed back. The waves that had approached me were as unthreatening as waves can be—a gentle washing of the sandy beach. But something ominous about them—something like the

G touch of a reptile's skin—had sent a chill down my spine. My fear was totally groundless—and totally real. I knew instinctively that they were alive. They knew I was here and they were planning to grab me. I felt as if some huge, man-eating beast were lying somewhere on a grassy plain, dreaming of the moment it would pounce and tear me to pieces with its sharp teeth. I had to run away.

Describing the ocean as having a tongue and "a reptile's skin" makes it seem like an animal or monster.

160 "I'm getting out of here!" I yelled to K. He was maybe ten yards down
H the beach, squatting with his back to me, and looking at something. I was sure I had yelled loud enough, but my voice did not seem to have reached him. He might have been so absorbed in whatever it was he had found that my call made no impression on him. K. was like that. He would get involved with things to the point of forgetting everything else. Or possibly I had not yelled as loudly as I had thought. I do recall that my voice sounded strange to me, as though it belonged to someone else.

Then I heard a deep rumbling sound. It seemed to shake the earth. Actually, before I heard the rumble I heard another sound, a weird gurgling

170 as though a lot of water was surging up through a hole in the ground. It continued for a while, then stopped, after which I heard the strange rumbling. Even that was not enough to make K. look up. He was still squatting, looking down at something at his feet, in deep concentration. He probably did not hear the rumbling. How he could have missed such an earth-shaking sound, I don't know. This may seem odd, but it might have been a sound that only I could hear—some special kind of sound. Not even K.'s dog seemed to notice it, and you know how sensitive dogs are to sound.

I told myself to run over to K., grab hold of him, and get out of there. It was the only thing to do. I *knew* that the wave was coming, and K. didn't

180 know. As clearly as I knew what I ought to be doing, I found myself running the other way—running full speed toward the dyke, alone. What made me do this, I'm sure, was fear, a fear so overpowering it took my voice away and set my legs to running on their own. I ran stumbling along the soft sand beach to the breakwater, where I turned and shouted to K.

---

7. ◀ **REREAD AND DISCUSS** Reread lines 149–159. With a small group, discuss what the narrator means when he says he "knew" that the waves were alive.

8. **READ** ▶ As you read lines 160–205, continue to cite text evidence.
   • Circle meaningful references to sound or soundlessness.
   • In the margin, explain what happens to K.

FOR ELL STUDENTS Explain that often people refer to a *candy store* as a fun place where you can get your pick of a variety of things. Ask a volunteer to explain why the author may compare the beach to a candy store.

7. **REREAD AND DISCUSS USING TEXT EVIDENCE**

G **ASK STUDENTS** to note lines 154–155: "My fear was totally groundless—and totally real." Have students discuss this contradiction. *The narrator knows his fears have no logic, yet he is so scared he can feel it.*

8. **READ AND CITE TEXT EVIDENCE** In this section the narrator describes the experience as if it were a dream.

H **ASK STUDENTS** to identify images that seem to come straight out a nightmare. What examples can they find in the text? *Examples include: "I was sure I had yelled loud enough, but my voice did not seem to have reached him" and "my voice sounded strange to me, as though it belonged to someone else."*

"Hurry, K.! Get out of there! The wave is coming!" This time my voice worked fine. The rumbling had stopped, I realized, and now, finally, K. heard my shouting and looked up. But it was too late. A wave like a huge snake with its head held high, poised to strike, was racing towards the shore. I had never seen anything like it in my life. It had to be as tall as a three-story building. Soundlessly (in my memory, at least, the image is soundless), it rose up behind K. to block out the sky. K. looked at me for a few seconds, uncomprehending. Then, as if sensing something, he turned towards the wave. He tried to run, but now there was no time to run. In the next instant, the wave had swallowed him.

The wave crashed on to the beach, shattering into a million leaping waves that flew through the air and plunged over the dyke where I stood. I was able to dodge its impact by ducking behind the breakwater. The spray wet my clothes, nothing more. I scrambled back up on to the wall and scanned the shore. By then the wave had turned and, with a wild cry, it was rushing back out to sea. It looked like part of a gigantic rug that had been yanked by someone at the other end of the earth. Nowhere on the shore could I find any trace of K., or of his dog. There was only the empty beach.

K. is "swallowed" by the wave.

9. ◀ **REREAD** Reread lines 160–205. Why do you think the narrator fails to rescue K? What else does the narrator have problems doing?

The narrator is too afraid to save K., and his fear makes him run away. He also seems to have problems speaking or being heard.

The receding wave had now pulled so much water out from the shore that it seemed to expose the entire ocean bottom. I stood along on the breakwater, frozen in place.

The silence came over everything again—a desperate silence, as though sound itself had been ripped from the earth. The wave had swallowed K. and disappeared into the far distance. I stood there, wondering what to do. Should I go down to the beach? K. might be down there somewhere, buried in the sand . . . But I decided not to leave the dyke. I knew from experience that big waves often came in twos and threes.

I'm not sure how much time went by—maybe ten or twenty seconds of eerie emptiness—when, just as I had guessed, the next wave came. Another gigantic roar shook the beach, and again, after the sound had faded, another huge wave raised its head to strike. It towered before me, blocking out the sky, like a deadly cliff. This time, though, I didn't run. I stood rooted to the sea wall, entranced, waiting for it to attack. What good would it do to run, I thought, now that K. had been taken? Or perhaps I simply froze, overcome with fear. I can't be sure what it was that kept me standing there.

The second wave was just as big as the first—maybe even bigger. From far above my head it began to fall, losing its shape, like a brick wall slowly

Another giant wave comes but the narrator doesn't move.

The wave begins to fall, and then stops.

10. **READ ▶** As you read lines 206–247, continue to cite text evidence.
- Circle mentions of silence or soundlessness.
- Underline text where the narrator expresses doubt about what to do.
- In the margin, briefly note the events that happen.

34

35

9. **REREAD AND CITE TEXT EVIDENCE**

Ⓘ ASK STUDENTS to cite evidence about the problems the narrator is having. *Students should cite evidence in lines 161–167 that the narrator was not sure if he "had yelled loud enough." In lines 180–184, the narrator finds himself running in the opposite direction, away from K.*

FOR ELL STUDENTS Clarify the meaning of the words *dodge* and *ducking* (line 197). Explain that *to dodge* means "to avoid," and that *ducking* means "lowering your head and/or body to avoid being hit."

10. **READ AND CITE TEXT EVIDENCE** Have students note the author's use of sensory language in this section.

Ⓙ ASK STUDENTS to find examples of words and phrases that appeal to the senses. *Examples include: "The silence came over everything again . . . as though sound itself had been ripped from the earth" and "The wave had swallowed K" (lines 206–207).*

crumbling. It was so huge that it no longer looked like a real wave. It was like something from another, far-off world, that just happened to assume the shape of a wave. I readied myself for the moment the darkness would take me. I didn't even close my eyes. I remember hearing my heart pound with incredible clarity.

The moment the wave came before me, however, it stopped. All at once it seemed to run out of energy, to lose its forward motion and simply hover 230 there, in space, crumbling in stillness. And in its crest, inside its cruel, transparent tongue, what I saw was K.

Some of you may find this impossible to believe, and if so, I don't blame you. I myself have trouble accepting it even now. I can't explain what I saw any better than you can, but I know it was no illusion, no hallucination. I am telling you as honestly as I can what happened at that moment—what K really happened. In the tip of the wave, as if enclosed in some kind of transparent capsule, floated K.'s body, reclining on its side. But that is not all. K. was looking straight at me, smiling. There, right in front of me, so close that I could have reached out and touched him, was my friend, my 240 friend K. who, only moments before, had been swallowed by the wave. And he was smiling at me. Not with an ordinary smile—it was a big, wide-open grin that literally stretched from ear to ear. His cold, frozen eyes were locked on mine. He was no longer the K. I knew. And his right arm was stretched out in my direction, as if he were trying to grab my hand and pull me into that other world where he was now. A little closer, and his hand would have caught mine. But, having missed, K. then smiled at me one more time, his grin wider than ever.

I seem to have lost consciousness at that point. The next thing I knew, I was in bed in my father's clinic. As soon as I awoke the nurse went to call 250 my father, who came running. He took my pulse, studied my pupils, and

The narrator sees K. inside the wave, reaching out to him.

11. **◀ REREAD** Reread lines 206–247. Why do you think the narrator has trouble remembering what happened? How does this affect the believability of his story?

The narrator can't remember because it was a long time ago, or maybe he's been so affected by this event that his memory of this time is shaky. His inability to remember specifics makes the story more mysterious but perhaps more believable.

36

> One way or another, though, I managed to recover ... But my life would never be the same again.

put his hand on my forehead. I tried to move my arm, but couldn't lift it. I was burning with fever, and my mind was clouded. I had been wrestling with a high fever for some time, apparently. "You've been asleep for three days," my father said to me. A neighbor who had seen the whole thing had L picked me up and carried me home. They had not been able to find K. I wanted to say something to my father. I *had* to say something to him. But my numb and swollen tongue could not form words. I felt as if some kind of creature had taken up residence in my mouth. My father asked me to tell him my name, but before I could remember what it was, I lost consciousness 260 again, sinking into darkness.

Altogether, I stayed in bed for a week on a liquid diet. I vomited several times, and had bouts of delirium. My father told me afterwards that I was so bad that he had been afraid that I might suffer permanent **neurological** damage from the shock and high fever. One way or another, though, I managed to recover—physically, at least. But my life would never be the same again.

Feeling a creature in his mouth ties him to the wave, like something living inside of him.

neurological: *relating to the nervous system*

12. **READ ▶** As you read lines 248–289, continue to cite text evidence.

• Underline the example of figurative language in lines 257–258, and analyze it in the margin.

• In the margin, explain the narrator's belief about K.'s death (lines 267–289).

37

---

11. **REREAD AND CITE TEXT EVIDENCE**

K **ASK STUDENTS** to cite examples in lines 206–247 that show that the narrator is unsure exactly what happened. *Students should cite examples such as "I'm not sure how much time went by" (line 212); "Some of you may find this impossible to believe" (line 232); "I am telling you as honestly as I can . . ." (lines 234–235).*

FOR ELL STUDENTS Some of your Spanish-speaking students may recognize the word *hallucination* from its Spanish cognate *alucinación.*

12. **READ AND CITE TEXT EVIDENCE**

L **ASK STUDENTS** to cite evidence in the text that supports the narrator's conclusions about K.'s death. *Students should cite lines 267–270 that explain that bodies usually washed up, but K.'s body was never found.*

Critical Vocabulary: neurological (line 263) Have students share their definitions. What does the narrator's father think could have caused neurological damage? *The father thinks the shock and fever might have caused neurological damage.*

The narrator believes he could have saved K. from a horrible, terrifying death.

They never found K.'s body. They never found his dog, either. Usually when someone drowned in that area, the body would wash up a few days later on the shore of a small inlet to the east. K.'s body never did. The big waves probably carried it far out to sea—too far for it to reach the shore. It must have sunk to the ocean bottom to be eaten by the fish. The search went on for a very long time, thanks to the cooperation of the local fishermen, but eventually it petered out[1]. Without a body, there was never any funeral. Half crazed, K.'s parents would wander up and down the beach every day, or they would shut themselves up at home, chanting sutras.[2]

As great a blow as this had been for them, though, K.'s parents never chided me for having taken their son down to the shore in the midst of a typhoon. They knew how I had always loved and protected K. as if he had been my own little brother. My parents, too, made a point of never mentioning the incident in my presence. But I knew the truth. I knew that I could have saved K. if I had tried. I probably could have run over and dragged him out of the reach of the wave. It would have been close, but as I went over the timing of the events in my memory, it always seemed to me that I could have made it. As I said before, though, overcome with fear, I abandoned him there and saved only myself. It pained me all the more that K.'s parents failed to blame me and that everyone else was so careful never to say anything to me about what had happened. It took me a long time to

[1] **petered out:** came to an end.
[2] **sutras:** short Buddhist texts.

13. **◀ REREAD** Reread lines 261–289. Compare and contrast K.'s parents' reaction to their loss with the narrator's reaction. Support your answer with explicit textual evidence.

For both, the loss is deeply felt. However, K.'s parents do not feel the guilt the narrator feels. Their agony has an external expression. They are "half crazed" and "wander up and down the beach." They have the support of their religion, "chanting sutras," whereas the narrator seems alone in his agony. He withdraws, does not eat, and spends days "in bed, staring at the ceiling."

38

recover from the emotional shock. I stayed away from school for weeks. I hardly ate a thing, and spent each day in bed, staring at the ceiling.

K. was always there, lying in the wave tip, grinning at me, his hand outstretched, beckoning. I couldn't get that picture out of my mind. And when I managed to sleep, it was there in my dreams—except that, in my dreams, K. would hop out of his capsule in the wave and grab my wrist to drag me back inside with him.

And then there was another dream I had. I'm swimming in the ocean. It's a beautiful summer afternoon, and I'm doing an easy breaststroke far from shore. The sun is beating down on my back, and the water feels good. Then, all of a sudden, someone grabs my right leg. I feel an ice-cold grip on my ankle. It's strong, too strong to shake off. I'm being dragged down under the surface. I see K.'s face there. He has the same huge grin, split from ear to ear, his eyes locked on mine. I try to scream, but my voice will not come. I swallow water, and my lungs start to fill.

I wake up in the darkness, screaming, breathless, drenched in sweat.

At the end of the year I pleaded with my parents to let me move to another town. I couldn't go on living in sight of the beach where K. had been swept away, and my nightmares wouldn't stop. If I didn't get out of there, I'd go crazy. My parents understood and made arrangements for me to live elsewhere. I moved to Nagano Province in January to live with my father's family in a mountain village near Komoro. I finished elementary school in Nagano and stayed on through junior and senior high school there. I never went home, even for holidays. My parents came to visit me now and then.

I live in Nagano to this day. I graduated from a college of engineering in the City of Nagano and went to work for a precision toolmaker in the area. I still work for them. I live like anybody else. As you can see, there's nothing unusual about me. I'm not very sociable, but I have a few friends I go mountain climbing with. Once I got away from my hometown, I stopped having nightmares all the time. They remained a part of my life, though. They would come to me now and then, like debt collectors at the door. It happened when I was on the verge of forgetting. And it was always the same dream, down to the smallest detail. I would wake up screaming, my sheets soaked with sweat.

14. **READ ▶** As you read lines 290–335, continue to cite text evidence.
• In the margin, describe in your own words the seventh man's dreams.
• Underline text explaining how the seventh man tries to get rid of his memories of K.'s death.

K. pulls him into the wave.

He is swimming and K. pulls him under the water.

39

---

13. **REREAD AND CITE TEXT EVIDENCE**

M ASK STUDENTS to describe the behavior of the narrator's parents and K.'s parents following the event. *Neither the narrator's parents nor K.'s parents mention the incident.* How does this make the narrator feel? Why does he feel this way? *He feels terribly guilty because he thinks he could have saved his friend.*

14. **READ AND CITE TEXT EVIDENCE**

N ASK STUDENTS to find images in the narrator's dreams that come from his story about the wave. *Students may cite lines 300–302: "He has has the same huge grin, split from ear to ear, his eyes locked on mine. I try to scream, but my voice will not come." The dreams feature waves and K. reaching out for the narrator.*

That is probably why I never married. I didn't want to wake someone sleeping next to me with my screams in the middle of the night. I've been in love with several women over the years, but I never spent a night with any of them. The terror was in my bones. It was something I could never share with another person.

I stayed away from my hometown for over forty years. I never went near that seashore—or any other. I was afraid that if I did, my dream might happen in reality. I had always enjoyed swimming, but after that day I never even went to swim in a pool. I wouldn't go near deep rivers or lakes. I avoided boats and wouldn't take a plane to go abroad. Despite all these precautions, I couldn't get rid of the image of myself drowning. Like K.'s cold hand, this dark premonition caught hold of my mind and refused to let go.

Then, last spring, I finally revisited the beach where K. had been taken by the wave.

My father had died of cancer the year before, and my brother had sold the old house. In going through the storage shed, he had found a cardboard carton crammed with childhood things of mine, which he sent to me in Nagano. Most of it was useless junk, but there was one bundle of pictures that K. had painted and given to me. My parents had probably put them away for me as a keepsake of K., but the pictures did nothing but reawaken the old terror. They made me feel as if K.'s spirit would spring back to life from them, and so I quickly returned them to their paper wrapping, intending to throw them away. I couldn't make myself do it, though. After several days of indecision, I opened the bundle again and forced myself to take a long, hard look at K.'s watercolors.

15. ◀ **REREAD** Reread lines 290–335. Explain how the incident with K. haunts the narrator throughout his life.

The narrator never got married, and left his hometown, so he has no regular, close connections with people. He lost the activity that he enjoyed, swimming, because he never went near water. He is still haunted by the image of K.'s drowning.

16. **READ** ▶ As you read lines 336–384, continue to cite text evidence.

- Circle evidence that the narrator has changed.
- In the margin, summarize the sequence of events that occur when the seventh man receives K.'s watercolors.

40

Most of them were landscapes, pictures of the familiar stretch of ocean and sand beach and pine woods and the town, and all done with that special clarity and coloration I knew so well from K.'s hand. They were still amazingly vivid despite the years, and had been executed with even greater skill than I recalled. As I leafed through the bundle, I found myself steeped in warm memories. The deep feelings of the boy K. were there in his pictures—the way his eyes were opened on the world. The things we did together, the places we went together began to come back to me with great intensity. And I realized that his eyes were my eyes, that I myself had looked upon the world back then with the same lively, unclouded vision as the boy who had walked by my side.

I made a habit after that of studying one of K.'s pictures at my desk each day when I got home from work. I could sit there for hours with one painting. In each I found another of those soft landscapes of childhood that I had shut out of my memory for so long. I had a sense, whenever I looked at one of K.'s works, that something was permeating my very flesh.

Perhaps a week had gone by like this when the thought suddenly struck me one evening: I might have been making a terrible mistake all those years. As he lay there in the tip of the wave, surely K. had not been looking at me with hatred or resentment; he had not been trying to take me away with him. And that terrible grin he had fixed me with: that, too, could have been an accident of angle or light and shadow, not a conscious act on K.'s part. He had probably already lost consciousness, or perhaps he had been giving me a gentle smile of eternal parting. The intense look of hatred I thought I saw on his face had been nothing but a reflection of the profound terror that had taken control of me for the moment.

The more I studied K.'s watercolor that evening, the greater the conviction with which I began to believe these new thoughts of mine. For no matter how long I continued to look at the picture, I could find nothing in it but a boy's gentle, innocent spirit.

I went on sitting at my desk for a very long time. There was nothing else I could do. The sun went down, and the pale darkness of evening began to envelop the room. Then came the deep silence of night, which seemed to go on forever. At last, the scales tipped, and dark gave way to dawn. The new day's sun tinged the sky with pink.

It was then I knew I must go back.

17. ◀ **REREAD AND DISCUSS** Reread lines 365–384. In a small group, discuss why you think the narrator decided he must go back to his hometown.

41

At first, the seventh man plans to throw away the watercolors. Instead, he forces himself to look at them. Then, he finds himself flooded with "warm memories," and his beliefs about the disaster shift.

---

15. **REREAD AND CITE TEXT EVIDENCE** Point out the words the narrator uses to describe the "premonition" (lines 333–335).

O **ASK STUDENTS** what the premonition feels like to the narrator. When did the premonition start? *The premonition "caught hold of my mind and refused to let go." The premonition began when the narrator saw K. in the wave.*

16. **READ AND CITE TEXT EVIDENCE**

P **ASK STUDENTS** to cite an event in the narrator's life that might have changed him. *Students may suggest: "My father had died of cancer the year before, and my brother had sold the old house" (lines 338–339).*

17. **REREAD AND DISCUSS USING TEXT EVIDENCE**

Q **ASK STUDENTS** to describe the narrator's "terrible mistake" and tell what he now understands that he didn't before. *Students may say he misinterpreted the boy's grin, and now understands that his friend was saying goodbye.*

I threw a few things in a bag, called the company to say I would not be in, and boarded a train for my old hometown.

(R) I did not find the same quiet, little seaside town that I remembered. An industrial city had sprung up nearby during the rapid development of the Sixties, bringing great changes to the landscape. The one little gift shop by
390 the station had grown into a mall, and the town's only movie theater had been turned into a supermarket. My house was no longer there. It had been demolished some months before, leaving only a scrape on the earth. The trees in the yard had all been cut down, and patches of weeds dotted the black stretch of ground. K.'s old house had disappeared as well, having been replaced by a concrete parking lot full of commuters' cars and vans. Not that I was overcome by **sentiment.** The town had ceased to be mine long before.

I walked down to the shore and climbed the steps of the breakwater. On
400 the other side, as always, the ocean stretched off into the distance, unobstructed, huge, the horizon a single straight line. The shoreline, too, looked the same as it had before: the long beach, the lapping waves, people strolling at the water's edge. The time was after four o'clock, and the soft sun of late afternoon embraced everything below as it began its long, almost meditative descent to the west. I lowered my bag to the sand and sat down next to it in silent appreciation of the gentle seascape. Looking at this scene, it was impossible to imagine that a great typhoon had once raged here, that a massive wave had swallowed my best friend in all the world. There was almost no one left now, surely, who remembered those terrible events. It began to seem as if the whole thing were an illusion that I had dreamed up
410 in vivid detail.

And then I realized that the deep darkness inside me had vanished. Suddenly. As suddenly as it had come. I raised myself from the sand, and, without bothering to take off my shoes or roll up my cuffs, walked into the surf and let the waves lap at my ankles.

sentiment:
*feeling;
emotion*

18. **READ ▶** As you read lines 385–449, continue to cite evidence.
Continue to circle text that shows the narrator has changed.

Almost in **reconciliation,** it seemed, the same waves that had washed up on the beach when I was a boy were now fondly washing my feet, soaking black my shoes and pant cuffs. There would be one slow-moving wave, then a long pause, and then another wave would come and go. The people passing by gave me odd looks, but I didn't care.
420 I looked up at the sky. A few grey cotton chunks of cloud hung there, motionless. They seemed to be there for me, though I'm not sure why I felt that way. I remembered having looked up at the sky like this in search of the "eye" of the typhoon. And then, inside me, the axis of time gave one great heave. Forty long years collapsed like a dilapidated house, mixing old time and new time together in a single swirling mass. All sounds faded, and the light around me shuddered. I lost my balance and fell into the waves. My heart throbbed at the back of my throat, and my arms and legs lost all sensation. I lay that way for a long time, face in the water, unable to stand. But I was not afraid. No, not at all. There was no longer anything for me to
430 fear. Those days were gone.

I stopped having my terrible nightmares. I no longer wake up screaming in the middle of the night. And I am trying now to start life over again. No, I know it's probably too late to start again. I may not have much time left to live. But even if it comes too late, I am grateful that, in the end, I was able to attain a kind of salvation, to effect some sort of recovery. Yes, grateful: I could have come to the end of my life unsaved, still screaming in the dark, afraid.

reconciliation:
*a settlement;
resolution*

42

43

---

18. **READ AND CITE TEXT EVIDENCE** In lines 387–397 the narrator describes how the town of his youth had changed.

(R) **ASK STUDENTS** to cite examples of this change. How did the narrator respond to these changes? *There was a new mall and supermarket, his house was gone, they had cut down the trees, and K.'s house was a parking lot. The narrator says that he does not feel sentimental: "The town had ceased to be mine long before."*

Critical Vocabulary: sentiment (line 396) Have students share their definitions. What does the narrator's tone reveal when he says he was "not overcome by sentiment?" *He describes his feelings in a flat, disaffected way, as if the memory meant very little.*

FOR ELL STUDENTS The word *concrete* can be confused by some Spanish-speaking students with its false cognate *concreto* ("specific"). Explain that here, it is a material used for construction.

The seventh man fell silent and turned his gaze upon each of the others. No one spoke or moved or even seemed to breathe. All were waiting for the rest of his story. Outside, the wind had fallen, and nothing stirred. The seventh man brought his hand to his collar once again, as if in search for words.

440

"They tell us that the only thing we have to fear is fear itself; but I don't believe that," he said. Then, a moment later, he added: "Oh, the fear is there, all right. It comes to us in many different forms, at different times, and overwhelms us. But the most frightening thing we can do at such times is to turn our backs on it, to close our eyes. For then we take the most precious thing inside us and surrender it to something else. In my case, that something was the wave."

19. ◀ **REREAD** Reread lines 438–449. What does the narrator think is more frightening than fear itself?

The seventh man believes it's more frightening to run away from your fears.

SHORT RESPONSE

Cite Text Evidence What theme, or central idea, about fear does Murakami explore in "The Seventh Man." How does his use of figurative language help him advance his theme? Review your reading notes, and be sure to **cite evidence** from the story in your response.

The central idea that Murakami explores in his story is that unless you confront fear, it will take over your life. Even though he survived the tsunami that killed his best friend, the seventh man's entire life was affected. Murakami's use of figurative language lets the reader see how the fear the seventh man had was almost tangible and monster-like. This fear stays with the seventh man until he is an adult. Only when he returns to the village of his youth and faces the sea again is he able to let go of his fear and try to restart his life.

44

---

19. ⬤ **REREAD AND CITE TEXT EVIDENCE** Have students review the last lines of the story in which the narrator, referring to fear, says that "the most frightening thing we can do at such times is to turn our backs on it, to close our eyes" (lines 446–447).

Ⓢ **ASK STUDENTS** when the narrator had "turned his back" before. What were the consequences? *The narrator had turned his back on his friend; his friend had been swallowed up by the wave.*

SHORT RESPONSE

Cite Text Evidence Students should:

- explain how the author's use of figurative language adds meaning to the text.
- determine the story's theme, or central idea.
- cite text evidence in their response.

TO CHALLENGE STUDENTS . . .

Students are probably familiar enough with horror movies to see how well this story might translate onto a big screen.

ASK STUDENTS to write a proposal, or "pitch," for a blockbuster movie based on the story.

- Each proposal should include a plot summary, suggestions for a musical score and special effects, ideas about a director, names of actors who'd be "right" for various roles, ideas about locations, and a proposed budget. Explain that the goal of the pitch is to persuade others to fund the project.

- Have students brainstorm ideas about their movie project. Remind them that they can take liberties with the plot: they can change or add details, or present it as a parody or thriller. Groups may decide to use CGI for the dream sequences, or have fewer special effects.

- After the proposals have been written, each group can present their pitch to a committee of their peers for evaluation. "Committee members" can then comment on each idea and tell whether they think it will work.

DIG DEEPER

1. With the class, return to Question 7, Reread and Discuss. Have students share the results of their discussion.

> **ASK STUDENTS** how they came up with their ideas about the boy "knowing" the waves were alive and how this knowledge affected his decision to flee.
>
> - Have students cite examples in which the boy experiences otherwordly occurrences, or those that have no rational explanation.
> - Students may include text evidence that shows examples of the narrator's feeling of helplessness and his inability to control the powerful force he has been thrust into.
> - Students may point out that the narrator's survival instinct kicks in at this point and proves to be a stronger force than his desire to help his friend.

2. ASK STUDENTS to return to Question 11, Reread. Have students share their responses.

> - Have students cite evidence of the narrator's state of mind during the episode.
> - Students may point out that the narrator's symptoms following the episode are similar to those of other victims of life-altering catastrophes. How do his symptoms mirror those of victims of post-traumatic shock?
> - Have students evaluate the believability of the narrator's account. Is there a rational explanation for what happened to him?

3. ASK STUDENTS to return to Question 19, Reread. Have students share their responses.

> - Have students cite evidence of ways the narrator's life was affected by fear.
> - Have students analyze why they think the narrator was afraid. What images haunted him? Was his fear rational?
> - Have students cite evidence that shows how the narrator was able to free himself from the fear.

CLOSE READING NOTES

Carry

Poem by Linda Hogan

Why This Text?

Students will regularly encounter figurative language as they read various written works. The presence of figurative language can assist students in determining the theme of a work. Hogan's work demonstrates how figurative language conveys an idea about life.

Key Learning Objective The student will be able to support inferences about theme.

Common Core Standards

RL 1 Cite textual evidence.
RL 2 Determine a theme and analyze its development.
RL 3 Analyze how complex characters develop, interact, and advance the plot.
RL 4 Determine the meaning of words and phrases.
RL 5 Analyze how an author's choices create mystery, tension, or surprise.
W 4 Produce writing in which the organization and style are appropriate to task, purpose, and audience.
SL 1 Participate in collaborative discussions with diverse partners.
SL 1a Come to discussions prepared, refer to evidence from texts to stimulate ideas.
SL 1c Propel conversations with questions that relate the current discussion to broader themes.
L 5b Analyze nuances in words.

Text Complexity Rubric

Quantitative Measures	**Carry** Lexile: N/A
Qualitative Measures	**Levels of Meaning/Purpose**  multiple levels of meaning (multiple themes)
	Structure/Rhyme Scheme  free verse, no particular patterns
	Language Conventionality and Clarity  figurative, symbolic language; sophisticated descriptions
	Knowledge Demands somewhat unfamiliar perspective
Reader/Task Considerations	Teacher determined Vary by individual reader and type of text

TEACH

CLOSE READ

Background Have students read the information about the author. Tell students that in 2007, Hogan was recognized for her writing accomplishments by becoming part of the Chickasaw Nation Hall of Fame.

AS YOU READ Direct students to use the As You Read statement to focus their reading.

Support Inferences About Theme (LINES 1–15)

COMMON CORE RL 1, RL 2

Tell students that an **inference** is a logical conclusion that is based on clues in the text and on a reader's own experience.

Ⓐ CITE TEXT EVIDENCE Ask students to reread lines 2–6 of the poem and infer what has happened, citing evidence from the text to support their inference. *(When the fish was pulled out of the water, something besides the fish came out as well because the poem states that "there was more" than just fish.)*

Support Inferences About Theme (LINE 1, LINES 6–14)

COMMON CORE RL 2

Explain to students that poets often use **figurative language**, or language that carries meaning beyond the literal meaning of the words, in order to convey **themes,** or underlying messages. Point out the **simile**, a comparison that uses *like* or *as* in line 12.

Ⓑ ASK STUDENTS to identify the event that is described by the use of the simile. *(The hawk is now "like a ghost" because it drowned while trying to catch the fish.)* Then explain the idea the simile suggests. *(death)*

Linda Hogan (b. 1947) *grew up in Oklahoma and Colorado. A member of the Chickasaw Nation, Hogan has received many awards and honors for her writing. She is a strong advocate for preserving endangered species, and her work reflects her deep interest in environmental issues, native cultures, and spirituality. Hogan says of her writing: "It takes perseverance. I will do it over and over again until I get it right." Her poetry collections include* The Book of Medicines *and* Rounding the Human Corners. *Her first novel,* Mean Spirit, *was a finalist for the Pulitzer Prize.*

Carry

Poem by Linda Hogan

AS YOU READ Think about what the images in the poem reveal about the cycle of nature. Write down any questions you generate during reading.

Image Credits: (t) ©Christopher Felver/Corbis; (c) ©Jeff Hornbaker/Water Rights/age fotostock

> From water's broken mirror
> we pulled it,
> Ⓐ alive and shining,
> gasping the painful other element of air.
> 5　It was not just fish.
> There was more.
> It was hawk, once wild with
> hunger, sharp talons
> locked into the dying twist
> 10　and scale of fish,
> its long bones
> trailing like a ghost　Ⓑ
> behind fins
> through the dark, cold water.

SCAFFOLDING FOR ELL STUDENTS

Pronoun Referents Explain that every pronoun stands in for a noun. If you look around the pronoun, you can usually find out what noun it replaces. Most of the time, the noun comes first, before the pronoun. Sometimes, like in this poem, the noun comes after the pronoun. For example: "From water's broken mirror / we pulled it, / alive and shining, / gasping the painful other element of air. / It was not just fish." Have students discuss how they discovered that the pronoun *it* referred to a fish.

Have students work with a partner to review the rest of the poem for pronouns, circle each pronoun, and underline the noun it replaces.

Support Inferences About Theme (LINE 22) COMMON CORE RL 2

Explain that **personification,** giving human attributes or qualities to an object or idea, is another type of figurative language.

C **ASK STUDENTS** to reread line 22 and explain why the line is an example of personification. *(Water does not have the ability to be lonely, but humans do. Since the ability to be lonely is a human attribute, line 22 is an example of personification.)* Based on this personification, what can we infer about the theme? *(Water, and nature, is a powerful and unpredictable force.)*

Analyze Author's Choice (LINE 15–32) COMMON CORE RL 1, RL 5

Explain that authors choose their words carefully to create a tone or mood. Authors may use imagery, description, and rhythm to do this.

D **CITE TEXT EVIDENCE** Ask students what two ways water is being described. *(soft and calm, versus rough and strong)* Have students cite examples of descriptive words or phrases for the water and contrast them. *("beautiful," "calm," "soft," "rough hands," "absence," "carry you down," "never knew or dreamed," "something stronger, older, deeper.")* Ask what effect this has on the mood of the poem. *(It creates a mysterious mood, by getting us to think of the water in two different ways.)*

COLLABORATIVE DISCUSSION Have students work in small groups to discuss what the hawk's fate reflects about nature. Then have each group share its ideas and supporting evidence from the text with the class as a whole.

ASK STUDENTS to share any questions they generated in the course of reading and discussing the selection.

---

15 It was beautiful, that water,
   like a silver coin stretched thin
   enough to feed us all,
   smooth as skin before anyone knew
   the undertow's[1] rough hands
20 lived inside it, working everything down
   to its absence,
   and water is never lonely, **C**
   it holds so many.
   It says, come close, you who want to swallow me;
25 already I am part of you.
   Come near. I will shape myself around you
   so soft, so calm
   I will carry you
   down to a world you never knew or dreamed,
30 I will gather you
   into the hands of something stronger,
   older, deeper.

COLLABORATIVE DISCUSSION What does the hawk's fate reflect about nature, if anything? Discuss your ideas with a partner. Cite specific evidence from the text to support your ideas.

---

[1] **undertow:** a strong current below the surface of water.

APPLYING ACADEMIC VOCABULARY

enhance	domain

As you discuss the Hogan poem, incorporate the following Collection 2 academic vocabulary words: *enhance* and *domain*. Ask students to indicate how the author is able to **enhance** the poem through the use of details and figurative language. As you determine the poem's theme, ask students to explain what the message about life communicates about the **domain** of nature.

Support Inferences About Theme

COMMON CORE RL 1, RL 2

The **theme** of a work is the message about life that the writer wants to communicate. Because readers make inferences to discover theme, a work may reveal different meanings to different readers. Your interpretation of theme will be valid if you base it on evidence from the text.

To determine themes in "Carry," look for clues in the poem's images and descriptive details, and think about the writer's use of symbols and repetition. Pay attention to how the writer uses details to shape and refine particular themes throughout the poem. This chart can help guide your analysis.

Text Evidence to Consider	Examples	Analysis and Questions
metaphors that create strong images	"water's broken mirror"	• This image is attractive, but somewhat unsettling. • Is water used as a symbol throughout the poem? If so, what might it represent?
similes that create strong images	"its long bones / trailing like a ghost / behind fins"	• This striking image depicts the opposite of the expected predator/ prey outcome. • What message is intended here? Do other images of death appear in the poem?
descriptive details that create a mood or feeling	"like a silver coin stretched thin / enough to feed us all"	• This simile creates an image of water as nourishing force, counterbalancing the image of water as an agent of death. • What broad idea does the water represent?
personification that conveys feelings or emotions	"and water is never lonely"	• Here, certain character traits are associated with water. • What does this depiction of water add to its symbolic meaning within the context of the entire poem?
title	"Carry"	• The title is a clue to the writer's broader message about the force of nature.

To make sure you understand what the poet is saying explicitly, draft an objective summary that provides the basic facts of the poem. Your final step in determining theme will be to synthesize your summary and your analysis of text evidence into a theme statement that expresses the poet's message.

TEACH

CLOSE READ

Support Inferences About Theme

COMMON CORE RL 1, RL 2

To help students use the text to make and support inferences about theme, conduct a small-group activity.

• Place students into three groups. One group will consider metaphors, one group will consider similes, and one group will consider personification.

• Ask groups to use the information from the chart on this page to find additional examples of their assigned forms of figurative language in the poem. Encourage them to discuss the questions in column 3 of the chart in their groups.

• Have groups focus on how each example conveys a **mood**, or feeling.

• Have groups share their findings and, as a class, work together to determine the poet's message.

Strategies for Annotation   *Annotate it!*

Support Inferences About Theme   COMMON CORE RL 1, RL 2

Share these strategies for guided or independent analysis:

• Highlight metaphors in blue.
• Highlight similes in yellow.
• Highlight examples of personification in green.
• On a note, record any feelings or emotions associated with the descriptive details.

smooth as skin before anyone knew

the undertow's rough hands

lived inside it, working everything down

to its absence,

Analyzing Text

COMMON CORE · RL 1, RL 2, RL 3, RL 4, RL 5, SL 1a, W 4

Possible answers:

1. *A live fish was pulled from the water. A dead hawk was attached to the fish and its body trailed behind the fish as the fish was pulled from the water. The image in these lines creates a somber, heavy mood for the poem.*

2. *The hawk was pulled down into the water's undertow and drowned while trying to catch the fish. This is unexpected because a weaker prey like a fish is often killed by a strong predator like a hawk. In this poem, the prey survives instead of the predator.*

3. *Sensory details: beautiful, that water; silver coin; feed us all; smooth as skin; rough hands; water is never lonely; it holds so many. These details give the reader the sense that the water is a living, vibrant thing.*

4. *The water is not empty and many things can be found beneath its surface, like the fish and the hawk. Line 20 also mentions "working everything down," which suggests that many things are under the water's surface.*

5. *The water wants those who would swallow it to come to it. The water offers to calmly and softly carry those who want to swallow it to a deeper, older, stronger world that is not known or dreamed about by those above the water's surface.*

6. *Water acts as a symbol of nature—both nature's life-giving abundance and its ability to deal out death—throughout the poem.*

7. *All living things are part of nature. We are sustained by nature and ultimately ended by it. Nature provided the fish as life-sustaining food for the hawk, yet the fish ultimately led the hawk to its death.*

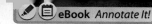 eBook *Annotate It!*

Analyzing the Text

COMMON CORE · RL 1, RL 2, RL 3, RL 4, RL 5, SL 1a, W 4

Cite Text Evidence   Support your responses with evidence from the selection.

1. **Summarize** Review what is stated explicitly in lines 1–14 and write a brief summary of what the speaker describes. How does the image created in these lines affect the **mood,** or emotion, of the poem?

2. **Infer** Use clues from the text to infer what happened to the hawk. Why is this unexpected?

3. **Analyze** Words and phrases that describe how things look, feel, sound, taste, or smell are called **sensory details.** Write down sensory details from lines 15–23. How do these details help engage readers in the poem?

4. **Interpret** Explain what is meant by lines 22–23: "and water is never lonely, / it holds so many." Support your interpretation with evidence from other lines.

5. **Analyze** Review the water's plea and promise at the end of the poem (lines 24–32). What does the water want? What does it offer?

6. **Interpret** A **symbol** is something that stands for or represents something beyond itself. Review the descriptions of water in the poem. What does the water symbolize?

7. **Cite Evidence** What theme about our connection with nature does this poem convey? Support your theme statement with evidence from the poem.

PERFORMANCE TASK

Speaking Activity: Discussion In "Carry," descriptions of water are central to the poem's meaning. Discuss the choices the poet made in her use of water imagery.

- Form a small group of three or four students to analyze the descriptions of water throughout the poem.

- For each image of water in the poem, ask questions about what feelings or ideas the author wanted to convey. For example, why did the poet choose to use a "broken mirror" as an image?

- Consider how the images of water develop throughout the poem, from an inanimate object to a powerful living force.

- Write a brief summary that includes the most important insights from the discussion.

Assign this performance task.

PERFORMANCE TASK

COMMON CORE · SL 1, W 4

Speaking Activity: Discussion Encourage group members to share all insights about the poem in a respectful manner. Ask students to include insights that compare and contrast with each other so that every member's interpretations and thoughts are represented in each group's written summary.

Pose and Respond to Questions

TEACH

Point out that when students are engaging with a work to determine theme, analyze figurative language, evaluate the use of symbols, or interact with text in another way, posing or responding to questions can help them to organize information such as textual evidence or their own inferences and interpretations about a piece of literature.

Explain that questions can include a wide range of topics, such as:

- What is this example of figurative language telling me?
- How does my interpretation of textual evidence help show that my theme statement is valid?
- Why is the author using this person, place, or object as a symbol?

PRACTICE AND APPLY

Ask students to work with their Performance Task group members to review the summaries created during that activity. Have students reread the poem and then reread the summaries that they wrote.

Have each group write one new question about water imagery that they did not ask when students first wrote their summaries and one question that each group thinks is not answered in its summary.

Ask students to work in their groups to locate and discuss the information that will answer their new question. Tell students they do not have to rewrite the summaries, but they should add both the additional question and answer to what has previously been written.

Bring the class together as a whole. Invite a volunteer from each group to share one or both questions that were posed and responded to during the activity.

ASK STUDENTS How did asking questions affect or change the way you approached the poem and your summaries when you read them this time? *(Accept all reasonable responses.)*

Analyze Figurative Meanings

TEACH

Remind students that **figurative language,** such as metaphors, similes, and personification, consists of words or phrases that emphasize or illustrate an idea in a creative way.

Tell students figurative language can be **nuanced**, or have different degrees of meaning or feeling. Mention that the simile *like a silver coin stretched thin* brings to mind that the water is described as having a beautiful silver color, but the additional nuance of the meaning is that the water is also delicate since it is stretched thin.

Point out that figurative language can illustrate an idea through a **symbol**, or one thing that stands for something else. For example, the symbol of water in the poem is one of both a nourishing and deadly force.

PRACTICE AND APPLY

Review with students the examples of figurative language from the poem listed below. Have students work in pairs or small groups to record the nuances and symbols about the poem's figurative language in a chart like this one.

Figurative Language	Symbol	Nuance
water's broken mirror	mirror	reflective, smooth
long bones trailing like a ghost	ghost	death, impermanent
undertow's rough hands	hands	powerful, strong

Figurative Language and Imagery

 COMMON CORE

RL 1,
RL 4,
W 4

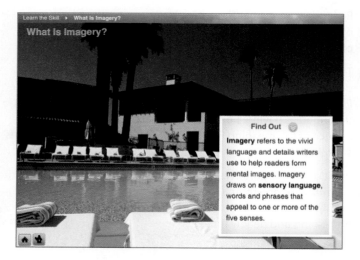

TEACH

Tell students that they will write another version of "Carry."

- Begin the lesson with the "What Is Imagery?" screen. Point out the definition of sensory language.
- Skip to "Types of Figurative Language." Focus on simile, metaphor, and personification.
- Move to the "Identify Figurative Language" screen that includes the poem "The Taxi." Have students work in pairs or small groups to identify examples of figurative language in this poem and in the Shakespeare poem on the "Analyze Figurative Language in Poetry" screen.

Ask students to write another version of "Carry" that focuses on description and imagery that relates to the hawk, the fish, or the speaker, and not the water as Hogan did. Point out that the outcome of the poem should remain the same, and students should include at least one example of a simile, a metaphor, and personification in their poems. Direct students to also write theme statements that express the messages of their poems.

COLLABORATIVE DISCUSSION

Place students in discussion groups based on whether they are focusing on the hawk, the fish, or the speaker. Remind them that they can discuss descriptions and images with each other, but they must each write an individual poem. Then have the members of each discussion group share their poems with the class as a whole.

Support Inferences About Theme

COMMON CORE

RL 1,
RL 2,
RL 4

RETEACH

Review the term **theme**, or universal message from the author. Explain that an **inference** is an educated guess about the meaning of something, based on details and your own experiences or knowledge. **Imagery** uses words and phrases that create mental pictures. Readers can use the imagery in a poem as details to infer the poem's theme. When thinking about a poem's imagery, students should ask themselves:

- What do I picture when I read this?
- How are the images related to each other and the poem as a whole?
- What ideas do they express?
- What do I already know about these ideas?
- What clues does this give me about the poem's theme?

Read aloud lines 19–21. Encourage students to close their eyes and listen. Then have students work with a partner to answer the questions above. Discuss the answers as a class.

 LEVEL UP TUTORIALS Assign the following *Level Up* tutorial: **Imagery**

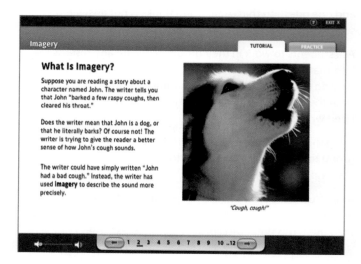

CLOSE READING APPLICATION

Have students work independently to select a poem and identify examples of imagery. Then have students use this information to determine the poem's theme. Ask: *What do you see, hear, touch, and smell when you read this poem? What clues does this give you about the author's message about life?*

Write a Research Report

The texts in this collection examine nature through a variety of viewpoints and genres. Choose three of the texts you have read, including the anchor text "Called Out," that illustrate ways in which humans interact with the natural world. Identify one aspect of the interaction between humans and nature represented in the three chosen texts, and conduct additional research about it. Write a report that develops your central finding about our relationship with nature.

Your research report should include

- a clear central idea, supported by examples from all three of the chosen texts and additional information from research

- an introduction, a logically structured body including transitions, and a conclusion

- smoothly integrated source information that avoids plagiarism, with correctly cited sources

- precise use of language with appropriate tone and style for a formal report

COMMON CORE

W 2 Write informative/explanatory texts.
W 4 Produce clear and coherent writing.
W 7 Conduct research projects.
W 8 Gather relevant information from multiple sources.
W 9 Draw evidence from texts.

PLAN

Analyze the Texts Reread "Called Out," and identify how Barbara Kingsolver illustrates an interaction between humans and nature. Make notes about specific details and evidence from the text. Then, review your other two chosen texts and note any relevant details about interactions between humans and nature. Be sure to identify only *one* aspect of our relationship with nature that appears in all three texts. This will be the central idea in your research report.

Research Once you have established your central idea and have sufficient evidence from the three texts, you will gather additional evidence to support this idea from other print or online resources.

- Locate information on your topic by searching in books, in magazines, or on the Internet. If you are using the Internet, be sure to use reliable resources such as well-known publications or government sites. Avoid personal websites or blogs, which may advocate a particular point of view.

myNotebook

Use the annotation tools in your eBook to find evidence that supports your ideas. Save each piece of evidence, along with information from your research, to your notebook.

ACADEMIC VOCABULARY

As you write your research report, be sure to use these words.

advocate
discrete
domain
enhance
scope

WRITE A RESEARCH REPORT

COMMON CORE W 2, W 4, W 7, W 8, W 9

Introduce students to the Performance Task by reading the introductory paragraph with them and reviewing the criteria for what makes a well-developed research report. Remind students that such a report should be focused clearly on one topic (or research question) and contain only examples and evidence that provide relevant information about that particular topic.

PLAN

ANALYZE THE TEXT

View It!

Professional Development Podcast:
Writing from Sources

Explain to students that although they might be tempted to dive right into writing their papers, they must do research first to help them narrow down their topic to a manageable size and figure out how best to support their ideas with evidence. At the same time, some students may be worried if they do not have their central idea fully fleshed out before they start their research. Assure students that it is a normal part of the research process to discover, refine, or even change a main idea as you collect and examine more evidence. Encourage them not to be afraid to develop their understanding of what aspect of the interaction between humans and nature they will write about as they learn more about their subject by conducting research.

PLAN

GET ORGANIZED

As students organize the information they have collected, have them keep in mind what their central topic is and why this topic is important and interesting for others to read about. Keeping this focus will help them select the best plan for presenting their ideas and evidence. If the first method they use does not seem to be working, they should not be afraid to scrap this first attempt and play with moving blocks of information around to see if there might be a more effective way to order the points they are making.

PRODUCE

DRAFT YOUR REPORT

Although students should use their outline as a guide for writing, they should also be open to rearranging sections and taking their paper in a different direction if, in the middle of drafting, they discover a more effective way to make their key points or a more logical way to order and transition between them. Add that although each key point should be supported by sources, the main emphasis of each section should always be on the point itself, not on how many sources, quotes, or extraneous bits of trivia students can fit into that section.

- Make note of any important details or quotations on index cards. Include reference information on your card. You will need this later when you cite the text.

Get Organized Organize your details and evidence in an outline.

- Decide what organizational pattern you will use for your report. Will you support your central idea by presenting the evidence text by text? Or, will you provide reasons that support your thesis followed by specific references to your chosen texts and additional research?
- Decide which textual and research evidence most effectively supports and enhances the key points expressed in your central idea.
- Use your organizational pattern to sort your textual evidence and research information into a logical order.
- Select an interesting quotation or detail to introduce your research report.
- Jot down some ideas for your concluding section.

PRODUCE

Draft Your Report Write a draft of your report, following your outline.

- Introduce the topic of your central idea. You can begin your report with a broad statement and narrow the scope of your topic as you develop your report.
- Present your details, facts, quotations, and examples from the texts in logically ordered paragraphs. Include appropriate citations for any facts or quotations.
- Use headings to indicate a transition to a new section.
- Write a concluding section that summarizes your research findings. End your report with a universal closing statement about the relationship between humans and nature based on the information presented in your report.
- Create a reference page or Works Cited list. You will need to include each author's last and first name; the title of the book, magazine, or website; the year of publication; the publisher; and other details. Your teacher will guide you in organizing the information on the reference page.

my **WriteSmart**

Write your rough draft in *my*WriteSmart. Focus on getting your ideas down rather than perfecting your choice of language.

Improve Your Draft Revise your draft to make sure it is clear, coherent, and engaging. Use the chart on the following page to review the characteristics of an effective research report. Ask yourself these questions as you revise:

- Have I introduced my central idea clearly? Does my introduction engage the reader?
- Have I presented relevant evidence from the texts and outside resources to support the discrete points of my central idea?
- Is my report logically organized? Are facts and quotations relevant to the central idea? Do I need to incorporate additional transitions?
- Have I maintained a formal style, avoiding slang and nonstandard English?
- Does my conclusion follow logically from the body and provide a satisfying ending?

my WriteSmart

Have a partner or a group of peers review your draft in *my*WriteSmart.

PRESENT

Present Your Report When your final draft is completed, take turns sharing your reports in a small group. Take notes while your classmates are presenting, and be prepared to ask and respond to questions.

REVISE

IMPROVE YOUR DRAFT

Have students set their first drafts aside for a time before revising them so that they can see their work through fresh eyes. To reduce wasted effort, instruct students to revise large-scale issues before smaller-scale ones. In order, students can:

- Check that they have included a clear introduction, logical transitions between each section, and a strong conclusion. Remind students to compare their introduction to their conclusion to make sure that they have maintained the same focus throughout the whole report.
- Check that all key points are adequately supported and any extraneous material has been deleted.
- Check the organization of each paragraph in turn, making sure each one includes a clear topic sentence, a logical sequence of ideas, and good transitions between sentences.
- Check the grammar, punctuation, and spelling of each sentence.
- Read the paper aloud to a friend as a final check to make sure everything is written correctly and flows smoothly.

PRESENT

PRESENT YOUR REPORT

Because a research report is so long, students must keep their audience in mind while reading it aloud to prevent their listeners from becoming lost or bored. For example, suggest that students pause briefly after each section and read each new heading with special emphasis to signal that they are transitioning from one part of their paper to another.

PERFORMANCE TASK A

IDEAS AND EVIDENCE

Have students look at the chart and identify how they did on the Performance Task in the Ideas and Evidence category. Have them evaluate the evidence and sources cited in their report for relevancy and accuracy. Ask them to devise a plan for how they could raise their performance in this area to the next level for their next writing project.

COLLECTION 2 TASK A
RESEARCH REPORT

	Ideas and Evidence	Organization	Language
ADVANCED	• The introduction is compelling and informative; the controlling idea clearly identifies a research question. • Sufficient, well-chosen evidence from the texts and from reliable sources provides strong support. • The writer cites information from multiple authoritative sources. • The concluding section effectively summarizes the answer to the research question and makes a thoughtful observation.	• The organization of key points and supporting evidence is effective; ideas are arranged logically. • Varied, well-crafted transitions effectively connect ideas.	• The writing has a formal style and a knowledgeable, objective tone. • Precise language is skillfully used. • Sentence beginnings, lengths, and structures vary and have a rhythmic flow. • Spelling, capitalization, and punctuation are correct. • Grammar and usage are correct. • All sources are completely and correctly identified in a Works Cited list.
COMPETENT	• The introduction is adequate; the controlling idea identifies a research question. • Evidence from the texts and reliable sources supports key points. • Additional authoritative sources would strengthen the key ideas. • The concluding section summarizes the answer to the research question.	• The organization of key points and supporting evidence is generally clear. • Transitions usually connect ideas.	• The style generally formal, though the tone is sometimes opinionated. • Most language is precise. • Sentence beginnings, lengths, and structures vary somewhat. • Minor spelling, capitalization, and punctuation mistakes occur. • Some grammatical and usage errors occur but do not hinder understanding. • A few formatting errors appear in the Works Cited list.
LIMITED	• The introduction is partially informative; the controlling idea does not clearly identify the research question. • Evidence from the texts and from sources supports some key points but is often too general. • Many cited sources are not authoritative or reliable. • The concluding section gives an incomplete summary of the answer to the research question.	• The organization of key points and supporting evidence is logical in some places, but some noticeable gaps in logic occur. • More transitions are needed throughout to connect ideas.	• The style is often informal, and the tone communicates a superficial understanding of the topic. • Language is vague or general at times. • Sentence structures barely vary; some fragments or run-on sentences occur. • Many spelling, capitalization, and punctuation mistakes occur. • Grammar and usage are incorrect in many places, but ideas are mostly clear. • One or two sources are missing from the Works Cited list.
EMERGING	• The appropriate elements of an introduction are missing. • Evidence from the texts and sources is irrelevant or missing. • Sources are unreliable or not cited. • The paper lacks an identifiable concluding section.	• An organizational strategy is not used; information is presented randomly. • Transitions are not used, making the paper difficult to understand.	• The style and tone are inappropriate for a research paper. • Language is vague and repetitive. • Repetitive sentence structure, fragments, and run-on sentences occur. • Spelling and capitalization are often incorrect, and punctuation is missing. • Many grammatical and usage errors hinder the writer's ideas. • The Works Cited list is missing.

Participate in a Panel Discussion

COMMON CORE

SL 1a–d Initiate and participate effectively in a range of collaborative discussions with diverse partners, building on others' ideas and expressing their own clearly and persuasively.

This collection examines nature through a variety of viewpoints and genres. Look back at the texts and consider what we learn about ourselves through our experience with nature. Then choose three texts from this collection, including the anchor text "My Life as a Bat." Identify the ideas expressed about human nature by each of the three writers. What similarities and differences do you find? Explore these connections in a panel discussion with two or three classmates.

Your contribution to the panel discussion should include

- clear, logical, and well-defended connections among the three texts' views of how humans experience nature

- quotations or examples from the three texts you chose that illustrate your points

- reasonable responses to the ideas of others in your group, adapting or expanding upon your own ideas or politely challenging others' assertions if you disagree with them

- attention to fairness and engagement, taking turns and asking questions to ensure participation of all group members

PLAN

myNotebook

Use the annotation tools in your eBook to find evidence that supports your ideas. Save each piece of evidence to your notebook.

Get Organized Work with your classmates to prepare for the discussion.

- Select one student to be the moderator for the discussion.

- Create a format for your discussion—a schedule that shows the order in which members of the panel will speak and for how many minutes. It will be the moderator's job to keep the discussion moving along on schedule.

- Set rules regarding the appropriate time for either the moderator or other panel members to ask the speaker questions.

- Get together with your team and choose three texts from this collection, including "My Life as a Bat," that you will use to compare and contrast ideas about humans and nature.

- Work individually to analyze the texts and gather evidence for the discussion. During this time, the moderator should review the same texts and make a list of discrete points to be addressed during the discussion.

ACADEMIC VOCABULARY

As you prepare for your panel discussion, be sure to use these words.

> advocate
> discrete
> domain
> enhance
> scope

PARTICIPATE IN A PANEL DISCUSSION

 COMMON CORE **SL 1a-d**

Review with students the characteristics of a useful contribution to a panel discussion. Emphasize to students that, unlike the purpose of a debate, the main aim of a panel discussion is to educate the audience about a subject. Fellow panelists should work together to try to understand and build upon each other's positions, not focus on scoring points, contradicting one another's ideas, or solely defending their own views.

PLAN

GET ORGANIZED

 **View It!**

Professional Development Podcast:

Performance Task

When organizing their panel and selecting the texts to be discussed, groups should keep in mind what aspects of their subject might be the most important to present and explain to their audience. Remind the moderator to write discussion points and questions that will provoke more sophisticated responses than a simple yes or no.

PERFORMANCE TASK B

PLAN

ANALYZE THE TEXTS

Remind students that they will not have time during the panel discussion to be flipping through the texts to collect information. Suggest that they be as thorough as possible in gathering evidence now so as to be prepared for any topics of conversation that might come up logically during the panel discussion. They will also not have time to present every piece of support for their ideas, so they should use only the facts or examples that best help them to make their points persuasively and concisely.

PRODUCE

CREATE AN OUTLINE

Point out to students that their outline must serve two main purposes: 1) it must provide structure and support for the comparison the student will be making and 2) it must include a collection of material from which the student can draw to address any questions or objections that they anticipate coming from the audience, other panelists, or moderator. Note that this outline should act only as a general road map to guide what the student will say, not be a detailed statement that will be read aloud word for word.

REVISE

PRACTICE FOR THE DISCUSSION

Practicing their panel discussion ahead of time will reduce the chance of panelists being caught off-guard with nothing to contribute about a point. If students have strong disagreements about a point, now is the time to talk through their positions and try either to come to a mutual understanding or to prepare how to present their opposing views in a civil manner.

Analyze the Texts Work individually to review the chosen texts. Reread "My Life as a Bat" and take notes about how Margaret Atwood expresses her central idea about how humans interact with nature. Gather evidence from the text and note any specific details, quotations, or examples. Then, review your two other chosen texts, taking notes on the writers' view of humans and nature as well. Pay attention to similarities and differences in views as you review the texts.

> **PRODUCE**

Create an Outline Organize your details and evidence in an outline.

- Introduce the topic of your comparison. Be sure that your identified idea(s) about what humans can learn from nature is expressed in all three chosen texts.

- Choose how you will organize your ideas. Will you first outline all of the similarities, followed by a section illustrating the differences? Or, will you discuss each selection separately?

- Sort through the evidence you have collected from "My Life as a Bat" and the other texts. Match each piece of evidence with the similarity or difference it most clearly supports.

- Think of questions the moderator or your panel members may ask you, and be prepared to answer them.

- Draft a closing statement regarding how humans interact with nature that you will make when it is your last turn to speak.

my **WriteSmart**

Write your rough draft in *my*WriteSmart. Focus on getting your ideas down rather than perfecting your choice of language.

> **REVISE**

Practice for the Discussion A discussion is more than a series of prepared statements read aloud. Participants listen closely to what all speakers say so that they can respond appropriately and ask relevant questions. Use the chart that follows this task to review the characteristics of an effective panel discussion. Then, join the other members of your panel discussion to practice for a lively exchange of ideas.

my **WriteSmart**

Have your partner or a group of peers review your draft in *my*WriteSmart.

- Decide whether certain panel members will focus on presenting the similarities between the texts and others on the differences or present one selection at a time.

- Take turns speaking in a format similar to the one you have planned for the real discussion.

- The first speaker should clearly state an idea about what humans learn about themselves through nature and give evidence from the three texts to support the idea. Subsequent speakers should either provide additional support for the first speaker's idea or introduce new ideas on the topic.

- Pay attention to what each speaker says, and be prepared to modify your own ideas to respond to your panel members' analysis of the texts.

- Each panel member should have an opportunity to summarize his or her ideas based on evidence from the texts as well as ideas from the panel discussion.

- When your practice discussion is over, evaluate each other's ideas and use of evidence. Discuss how you can improve your performance in the actual discussion.

PRESENT

Have the Discussion With guidance from your moderator, carry out the format you agreed on. Remember to maintain a respectful tone toward your fellow panel members, even when you disagree with their ideas. When the discussion is over, talk about the reasons and evidence that you found most compelling and why. Summarize how holding a panel discussion enhanced your perspective on the topic.

PRESENT

HAVE THE DISCUSSION

When presenting, panelists should speak loudly and clearly and remember to maintain eye contact with the moderator, other panelists, and audience members when addressing each in turn. When not speaking, panelists should model good listening behavior and direct their attention to whoever is talking. While answering questions and addressing comments in as much detail as they can, panelists should not continue on if they have nothing left to contribute to a subject.

PERFORMANCE TASK B

LANGUAGE

Have students look at the chart and identify how they did on the Performance Task in the Language category. Ask them to think about how well they used formal English, incorporated quotes from the texts, and maintained a thoughtful tone during the discussion. Have students isolate one item that they believe they could improve on and make a plan for the next panel discussion.

	Ideas and Evidence	Organization	Language
ADVANCED	• The panelist clearly states a valid generalization and supports it with strong, relevant ideas and well-chosen evidence from the texts and personal experience. • The panelist carefully evaluates others' evidence and reasoning and responds with insightful comments and questions. • The panelist synthesizes the analysis of the texts to help listeners understand the generalization.	• The panelist's remarks are based on a well-organized outline or notes that clearly identify the supporting ideas and evidence. • Ideas are presented in a logical order with effective transitions to show connections. • The panelist concludes by reinforcing the generalization and noting key ideas from the discussion.	• The panelist adapts speech to the context of the discussion, using appropriately formal English to discuss the texts and ideas. • The panelist consistently quotes accurately from the texts to support ideas. • The panelist consistently maintains a polite and thoughtful tone throughout the discussion.
COMPETENT	• The panelist states a generalization and supports it with ideas and evidence from the texts and personal experience. • The panelist evaluates others' evidence and reasoning and responds with appropriate comments and questions. • The panelist synthesizes some ideas and links to the generalization.	• The panelist's remarks are based on an outline or notes that organize ideas and evidence. • Ideas are presented in a logical order and linked with transitions. • The panelist concludes with a statement that reinforces the generalization.	• The panelist mostly uses formal English to discuss literature and ideas. • The panelist mostly quotes accurately from the texts to support ideas. • The panelist generally maintains a polite tone.
LIMITED	• The panelist states a generalization and supports it with some evidence. • The panelist's response to others' comments shows limited evaluation of the evidence and reasoning. • The panelist's conclusion does not synthesize but simply repeats the generalization in a vague way.	• The panelist's remarks may reflect the use of notes. • Ideas are somewhat disorganized and need more transitions. • The panelist concludes by restating the generalization.	• The panelist uses some informal English to discuss the texts and ideas. • The panelist's quotations and examples sometimes do not accurately reflect the texts. • The panelist occasionally forgets to maintain a polite tone when responding to others' comments and questions.
EMERGING	• The panelist's generalization is unclear; ideas and evidence are not coherent. • The panelist does not evaluate others' evidence and reasoning. • The panelist does not synthesize.	• The panelist does not follow an outline or notes that organize ideas and evidence. • Ideas are presented in a disorganized way with no transitions. • The panelist's remarks lack any kind of conclusion or summary.	• The panelist uses informal English and/or slang, resulting in ideas that are not clearly expressed. • The panelist's quotations and examples do not accurately reflect the texts. • The panelist does not maintain a polite tone when responding to others' comments and questions.

Image Credits: ©Dennis Novak/Photographer's Choice/Getty Images

Responses to Change

❝ When the wind of change blows, some build walls
while others build windmills. ❞

—Chinese proverb

CONNECTING WORD AND IMAGE

ASK STUDENTS to discuss how the collection opener image and the collection quotation work together to create a connection.

PERFORMANCE TASK PREVIEW

Point out to students that they will complete two performance tasks at the end of the collection. The performance tasks will require them to further analyze the selections in the collection and to synthesize ideas about these analyses. They will present their findings in a variety of products.

ACADEMIC VOCABULARY

View It!
Professional Development Podcast:
Academic Vocabulary

Students can acquire facility with the academic vocabulary words through frequent, repeated exposure as they analyze and discuss the selections in the collection. Academic vocabulary can be used in the following instructional contexts. This will enable students to incorporate the academic vocabulary words into their working vocabulary.

- Collaborative Discussion at the end of each selection
- Analyzing the Text questions for each selection
- Selection-level Performance Task
- Vocabulary instruction (for Critical Vocabulary and/or for Vocabulary Strategy)
- Language and Style
- End-of-collection Performance Task for all selections in the collection

ASK STUDENTS to review the academic vocabulary word list for this collection. You may wish to pronounce each word aloud, so students hear the correct pronunciation. Then discuss the definitions and the related forms for each word. Remind students that they will encounter these five academic vocabulary words throughout the collection.

Change is inevitable; how we respond to it reveals who we are.

hmhfyi.com

COLLECTION
PERFORMANCE TASK Preview

At the end of this collection, you will have the opportunity to complete two tasks:

- Participate in a panel discussion about the ways in which people either do or do not adapt to change.
- Write an argument about the positive and negative aspects of change.

ACADEMIC VOCABULARY

Study the words and their definitions in the chart below. You will use these words as you discuss and write about the texts in this collection.

Word	Definition	Related Forms
abstract (ăb-străkt´) *adj.*	apart from physical existence; theoretical rather than concrete	abstraction, abstractly
evolve (ĭ-vŏlv´) *v.*	to change or develop gradually over time	evolution
explicit (ĭk-splĭs´ĭt) *adj.*	clearly stated or expressed	explicitly, explicitness
facilitate (fə-sĭl´ĭ-tāt´) *v.*	to make something easier	facility, facilitator
infer (ĭn-fûr´) *v.*	to deduce from evidence or reason	inference, inferential

USING COLLECTIONS YOUR WAY

Use the following information, along with the charts on the following pages, to help you decide how you want to introduce the collection. Based on your teaching style, your students' interests, or your instructional goals, you may want to structure the collection in various ways. You may choose different entry points each time you teach the collection.

"I rely heavily on novels and longer works."

This novella excerpt tells the surreal tale of Gregor Samsa—who wakes up in his bedroom one morning to find that he has been changed into an insect—and builds suspense as other characters knock with concern at his bedroom door.

COMPARE ANCHOR TEXTS

Franz Kafka (1883–1924) was born in Prague and overcame emotional, physical, and financial struggles to become a leading twentieth-century writer. His innovative fiction has been compared to Shakespeare's works for its literary importance. Kafka even has a literary term named after him—Kafkaesque, which means "a twisted reality that is foreboding and oppressive." After a long illness, Kafka died before many of his works were published. His influence spread with the wide translation of his works.

from
The Metamorphosis

Novella by Franz Kafka   Graphic Novel by Peter Kuper

from **The Metamorphosis**
Novella by Franz Kafka
Translated by David Wyllie

AS YOU READ Pay attention to how details and pacing help the story evolve. Write down any questions you generate during reading.

One morning, when Gregor Samsa woke from troubled dreams, he found himself transformed in his bed into a horrible **vermin**. He lay on his armor-like back, and if he lifted his head a little he could see his brown belly, slightly domed and divided by arches into stiff sections. The bedding was hardly able to cover it and seemed ready to slide off any moment. His many legs, pitifully thin compared with the size of the rest of him, waved about helplessly as he looked.

"What's happened to me?" he thought. It wasn't a dream.
10   His room, a proper human room although a little too small, lay peacefully between its four familiar walls. A collection of textile

vermin
[vûr´mĭn] *n.*
creatures that are considered destructive, annoying, or repulsive; pests.

Compare Anchor Texts   **93**

Background Although individual circumstances differ, immigrants share the experience of adapting to a new and unfamiliar environment. They must learn new behaviors and languages while keeping alive the traditions and original cultures of their original cultures. Poet **Cathy Song** was born in Honolulu in 1955. Her grandfather came to Hawaii from China; her grandmother arrived from Korea in an arranged marriage. Their experiences inform many of Song's poems.

Magic Island
Poem by Cathy Song

AS YOU READ Look for clues that explain the meaning of the poem's title, "Magic Island." Write down any questions you generate during reading.

A collar of water
surrounds the park peninsula
at noon.
Voices are lost
5   in waves of wind
that catches a kite
and keeps it there
in the air above the trees.
If the day has one color,
10   it is this:
the blue immersion of horizons,
the sea taking the sky like a swimmer.

Magic Island   **137**

"I stress the importance of language and style."

This poem uses colorful language to create imagery and provide details that enhance the poet's message about the special moment that makes the island seem magical.

MEDIA ANALYSIS

from
Rivers and Tides
Documentary Film by Thomas Riedelsheimer

AS YOU VIEW Pay attention to the settings shown in the film clip and how they affect your perception of the artist's work. Write down any questions you generate during viewing.

COLLABORATIVE DISCUSSION In a small group, discuss how the settings in the film clip interact with and become a part of Andy Goldsworthy's work. What changes within the settings are important to the art?

Rivers and Tides   **141**

"I like to use digital product as a starting point."

This documentary clip shows the changes of rivers and tides in fast-motion sequences, providing a visual element that reveals the extent and result of these changes over time.

mySmartPlanner | eBook | myNotebook | WriteSmart | fyi hmhfyi.com

Collection 3 Lessons	Media	Teach and Practice
**Student Edition	eBook**	▶ Video Links HISTORY A&E	**Close Reading and Evidence Tracking**
ANCHOR TEXT Novella by Franz Kafka Translated by David Wyllie from *The Metamorphosis*	◀) **Audio** from *The Metamorphosis*	**Close Read Screencasts** • Modeled Discussion 1 (lines 18–27) • Modeled Discussion 2 (lines 207–220) / **Strategies for Annotation** • Support Inferences
ANCHOR TEXT Graphic Novel by Peter Kuper from *The Metamorphosis*	◀) **Audio** from *The Metamorphosis*	**Close Read Screencasts** • Modeled Discussion 1 (page 111) / **Strategies for Annotation** • Analyze Representations in Different Mediums • Verifying Word Meanings
CLOSE READER Poem by Anne Sexton "The Starry Night" Painting by Vincent Van Gogh *The Starry Night*	◀) **Audio** "The Starry Night"	
Science Writing by Jeffrey Kluger from *Simplexity*	◀) **Audio** from *Simplexity*	**Strategies for Annotation** • Analyze Author's Order: Cause and Effect • Figurative Meanings
Poem by Cathy Song "Magic Island"	◀) **Audio** "Magic Island" ▶ **Video HISTORY** *Angel Island: Ellis Island of the West*	**Strategies for Annotation** • Support Inferences About Theme
Documentary Film by Thomas Riedelsheimer from *Rivers and Tides*	◀) **Audio** from *Rivers and Tides*	
CLOSE READER Science Writing by Dolores Vasquez *Life After People*	◀) **Audio** from *Life After People*	
Collection 3 Performance Tasks: **A** Participate in a Panel Discussion **B** Write an Argument	fyi hmhfyi.com	**Interactive Lessons** **A** Participating in Collaborative Discussions **A** Using Textual Evidence / **B** Writing Arguments **B** Using Textual Evidence

	For Systematic Coverage of Writing and Speaking & Listening Standards	**Interactive Lessons** Conducting Research Evaluating Sources	**Lesson Assessments** Conducting Research Evaluating Sources

Assess		Extend	Reteach
Performance Task	**Online Assessment**	**Teacher eBook**	**Teacher eBook**
Speaking Activity: Discussion	Selection Test	**Interactive Whiteboard Lesson >** Analyze Complex Characters	**Support Inferences > Level Up Tutorial >** Making Inferences About Characters
Speaking Activity: Comparison	Selection Test	**Presenting Findings > Interactive Lesson >** Giving a Presentation	**Analyze Representations in Different Mediums > Level Up Tutorial >** Characters and Conflict
Writing Activity: Analysis	Selection Test	**Use Precise Language**	**Analyze Author's Order: Cause and Effect > Level Up Tutorial >** Cause-and-Effect Organization
Writing Activity: Argument	Selection Test	**Use Various Types of Phrases**	**Support Inferences About Theme > Level Up Tutorial >** Theme
Media Activity: Reflection	Selection Test	**Interactive Whiteboard Lesson >** Using Media in Presentations	**Analyze Development of Ideas > Level Up Tutorial >** Main Idea and Supporting Details
A Participate in a Panel Discussion **B** Write an Argument	Collection Test		

Collection 3 Lessons	COMMON CORE Key Learning Objective	Performance Task
ANCHOR TEXT **Novella by Franz Kafka** **Translated by David Wyllie** **from *The Metamorphosis*, p. 93A** Lexile 1110	**The student will be able to...** cite text evidence to support inferences	Speaking Activity: Discussion
ANCHOR TEXT **Graphic Novel by Peter Kuper** **from *The Metamorphosis*, p. 107A**	**The student will be able to...** analyze representations in different mediums	Speaking Activity: Comparison
Science Writing by Jeffrey Kluger **from *Simplexity*, p. 129A** Lexile 1490	**The student will be able to...** use cause-and-effect relationships to make connections between ideas and events	Writing Activity: Analysis
Poem by Cathy Song **"Magic Island," p. 137A**	**The student will be able to...** analyze language and make inferences about the theme of a poem	Writing Activity: Argument
Documentary Film by Thomas Riedelsheimer **from *Rivers and Tides*, p. 141A**	**The student will be able to...** analyze the development of ideas in a documentary	Media Activity: Reflection

Collection 3 Performance Tasks:
A Participate in a Panel Discussion
B Write an Argument

Vocabulary Strategy	Language and Style	Student Instructional Support	CLOSE READER Selection
		Scaffolding for ELL Students: Idioms **When Students Struggle:** • Character Interaction and Plot • Understanding Character Development • Reading with Expression **To Challenge Students:** • Theme • Tone	
Verifying Word Meanings	Prepositional, Adjectival, and Adverbial Phrases	**Scaffolding for ELL Students:** • Analyze How an Author Draws on Source Material • Analyze Idioms • Analyze Word Choice **When Students Struggle:** • Understanding Fragmented Language • False Cognates • Sequence of Events and Illustrations • Multiple Meaning Words • Unfamiliar Words • Onomatopoeia • Understanding Characters • Understanding How Images Tell a Story **To Challenge Students:** Compare Story Pacing in Different Genres	Poem by Anne Sexton ""The Starry Night," p.128b Painting by Vincent Van Gogh *The Starry Night,* p. 128b
Figurative Meanings	Transitional Words and Phrases	**Scaffolding for ELL Students:** • Analyze Author's Order: Cause and Effect • Language and Style: Transitional Words and Phrases **When Students Struggle:** Comprehension **To Challenge Students:** Debate the Issue	
	Noun Phrases and Verb Phrases	**Scaffolding for ELL Students:** Support Inferences About Theme **When Students Struggle:** Differentiating Between Metaphors and Similes	
		Scaffolding for ELL Students: Analyzing the Media **When Students Struggle:** Strategies for Describing Abstract Images and Text	Science Writing by Dolores Vasquez *Life After People,* p. 144b **Lexile 970**

ANCHOR TEXT EXEMPLAR

from The Metamorphosis

Novella by Franz Kafka, Translated by David Wyllie

Why This Text?

Students are regularly expected to read narratives and make inferences in order to analyze the text's meaning. This lesson explores the first part of Franz Kafka's novella, *The Metamorphosis*.

Key Learning Objective: The student will be able to cite text evidence to support inferences.

For practice and application:

Close Reader selection
The Starry Night
poem by Anne Sexton and painting by Vincent Van Gogh.

Common Core Standards

RL 1 Cite textual evidence.
RL 2 Determine a theme and analyze its development.
RL 3 Analyze how complex characters develop, interact, and advance the plot.
RL 4 Determine the meaning of words and phrases.
RL 5 Analyze how an author's choices create mystery, tension, or surprise.
RL 6 Analyze a particular point of view from outside the United States.
W 4 Produce writing in which the organization and style are appropriate to task, purpose, and audience.
SL 1 Participate in collaborative discussions with diverse partners.

Text Complexity Rubric

Quantitative Measures	***from* The Metamorphosis** Lexile: L1110
Qualitative Measures	**Levels of Meaning/Purpose** multiple levels of meaning (multiple themes) **Structure** less familiar story concepts; no major shifts in chronology **Language Conventionality and Clarity** increased unfamiliar language; more complex sentence structure **Knowledge Demands** situation includes unfamiliar aspects; some cultural and literary knowledge useful
Reader/Task Considerations	Teacher determined Vary by individual reader and type of text

CLOSE READ

Biography Although Kafka had a passion for writing, he earned a law degree from the German University in Prague and worked for an insurance company where he got a first-hand look at how bureaucracies and big businesses often dehumanized people. Much of his writing focuses on the way the government and large corporations manipulated, insulated, and intimidated individuals. While his works had little impact during his lifetime, his themes of fear and isolation in the modern world became influential and relevant after World War II.

AS YOU READ Direct students to use the As You Read note to focus their reading.

Analyze Author's Choices: Text Structure (LINES 1–8)   COMMON CORE RL 1, RL 5

Explain that authors make decisions about all aspects of a story, including where best to begin. In *The Metamorphosis,* Kafka sets up a situation that hooks readers and makes them want to continue reading.

 CITE TEXT EVIDENCE Ask students what Kafka reveals about the main character in the first paragraph. *(Gregor has been transformed overnight into an insect.)* What expectations does this set for readers? *(that this story has unusual, fantastical elements)*

CRITICAL VOCABULARY

vermin: Kafka describes Gregor's newly transformed body as "horrible" and describes how his body looks.

ASK STUDENTS to explain why people consider vermin to be disgusting. *(Vermin may carry germs and disease.)*

Analyze Theme (LINES 10–11)   COMMON CORE RL 2

Tell students that authors often include multiple themes in a literary work. In *The Metamorphosis,* Kafka includes several themes, one of which is that being dehumanized by society leads to immense isolation.

 CITE TEXT EVIDENCE Have students cite evidence that introduces this theme. *(lines 10–11: "His room, a proper human room although a little too small, lay peacefully between its four familiar walls.")*

Franz Kafka (1883–1924) *was born in Prague and overcame emotional, physical, and financial struggles to become a leading twentieth-century writer. His innovative fiction has been compared to Shakespeare's works for its literary importance. Kafka even has a literary term named after him—* Kafkaesque, *which means "a twisted reality that is foreboding and oppressive." After a long illness, Kafka died before many of his works were published. His influence spread with the wide translation of his works.*

from
The Metamorphosis

Novella by Franz Kafka   Graphic Novel by Peter Kuper

from **The Metamorphosis**

Novella by Franz Kafka
Translated by David Wyllie

AS YOU READ Pay attention to how details and pacing help the story evolve. Write down any questions you generate during reading.

One morning, when Gregor Samsa woke from troubled dreams, he found himself transformed in his bed into a horrible **vermin**. He lay on his armor-like back, and if he lifted his head a little he could see his brown belly, slightly domed and divided by arches into stiff sections. The bedding was hardly able to cover it and seemed ready to slide off any moment. His many legs, pitifully thin compared with the size of the rest of him, waved about helplessly as he looked.

"What's happened to me?" he thought. It wasn't a dream.
10 His room, a proper human room although a little too small, lay peacefully between its four familiar walls. A collection of textile

> **vermin**
> (vûr´mĭn) *n.* creatures that are considered destructive, annoying, or repulsive; pests.

Image Credits: (t) ©Hulton Archive/Getty Images; (c) ©Edward Holub/Photodisc/Getty Images

Close Read Screencasts   ▶ *View It!*

Modeled Discussion

Have students click the *Close Read* icons in their eBooks to access two screencasts in which readers discuss and annotate the following passages:

- Gregor's initial experiences with his new body (lines 18–27)
- Gregor's frustration with working for a company that did not trust its employees (lines 207–220)

As a class, view and discuss at least one of these videos. Then have students pair up to do an independent close read of an additional passage—Gregor's increased skill at using his new body (lines 374–384).

CLOSE READ

Analyze Theme (LINES 28–40)   COMMON CORE RL 2

Explain that authors reveal a theme throughout a text, shaping and refining it with specific details.

C **CITE TEXT EVIDENCE** Remind students that one of Kafka's themes is isolation. Have students cite details that support this theme. *(lines 32–34: "contact with different people all the time so that you can never get to know anyone or become friendly with them")*

Support Inferences   COMMON CORE RL 1
(LINES 20–48)

Explain that readers use text evidence and personal experience to make **inferences**, or logical conclusions.

D **CITE TEXT EVIDENCE** How does Gregor initially react to his situation? *(He wants to go back to sleep and forget his problems, but he can't because he cannot roll over. [lines 20-24] He then complains about how he dislikes his job. [lines 28-34])* Ask students what they can infer about his character and feelings based on lines 29–48. *(He is just as disgusted with his life as a human as he is with being an insect.)*

Analyze Characters   COMMON CORE RL 3
(LINES 41–53)

Explain that understanding a character's **motivations**, or reasons for doing things, helps readers better understand a character.

E **ASK STUDENTS** what motivates Gregor to keep his job. *(In lines 48–50, he says he stays because of his parents.)* Then ask students what this reveals about his values and character. *(He loves his parents and feels responsible for them.)*

CRITICAL VOCABULARY

subordinate: Gregor's boss does not have a good opinion of the people who work for him.

ASK STUDENTS to list at least three examples of subordinates to the school principal. *(teachers, office assistants, maintenance staff)*

---

samples lay spread out on the table—Samsa was a traveling salesman—and above it there hung a picture that he had recently cut out of an illustrated magazine and housed in a nice, gilded frame. It showed a lady fitted out with a fur hat and fur boa who sat upright, raising a heavy fur muff[1] that covered the whole of her lower arm towards the viewer.

20 Gregor then turned to look out the window at the dull weather. Drops of rain could be heard hitting the pane, which made him feel quite sad. "How about if I sleep a little bit longer and forget all this nonsense," he thought, but that was something he was unable to do because he was used to sleeping on his right, and in his present state couldn't get into that position. However hard he threw himself onto his right, he always rolled back to where he was. He must have tried it a hundred times, shut his eyes so that he wouldn't have to look at the floundering legs, and only stopped when he began to feel a mild, dull pain there that he had never felt before.   **D**

C 30 "Oh, God," he thought, "what a strenuous career it is that I've chosen! Traveling day in and day out. Doing business like this takes much more effort than doing your own business at home, and on top of that there's the curse of traveling, worries about making train connections, bad and irregular food, contact with different people all the time so that you can never get to know anyone or become friendly with them. It can all go to Hell!" He felt a slight itch up on his belly; pushed himself slowly up on his back towards the headboard so that he could lift his head better; found where the itch was, and saw that it was covered with lots of little white spots which he didn't know what to make of; and when he tried to feel the place with one of his legs he drew it quickly back because as soon as he 40 touched it he was overcome by a cold shudder.   **D**

E He slid back into his former position. "Getting up early all the time," he thought, "it makes you stupid. You've got to get enough sleep. Other traveling salesmen live a life of luxury. For instance, whenever I go back to the guest house during the morning to copy out the contract, these gentlemen are always still sitting there eating their breakfasts. I ought to just try that with my boss; I'd get kicked out on the spot. But who knows, maybe that would be the best thing for me. If I didn't have my parents to think about I'd have given in my notice a long time ago, I'd have gone up to the boss and told 50 him just what I think, tell him everything I would, let him know just what I feel. He'd fall right off his desk! And it's a funny sort of business to be sitting up there at your desk, talking down at your **subordinates** from up there, especially when you have to go right   **D**

subordinate
(sə-bôr´dn-ĭt) *n.* a person of a lesser rank or under another's authority.

---

[1] **boa . . . muff:** A boa is a long, thin piece of women's clothing that is worn around the neck. A muff is a short, soft tube into which people put their hands for warmth.

94   Collection 3

SCAFFOLDING FOR ELL STUDENTS

Idioms Explain that an idiom is a phrase whose meaning is different from the literal meaning of the words. Idioms are examples of local speech because their meanings have been established through usage. Point out the sentence "It can all go to Hell!" in line 35 and the phrase "talking down" in line 53.

ASK STUDENTS what the sentence means. *(He hates his job and boss and wishes he could quit.)* Then ask what the phrase means. *(to speak to someone in a way that shows you do not think he or she is very smart or important)* How does this idiom contribute to the passage? *(It shows what kind of character Gregor's boss is and what Gregor thinks of him and his job.)*

"I've got to get up, my train leaves at five."

up close because the boss is hard of hearing. Well, there's still some hope; once I've got the money together to pay off my parents' debt to him—another five or six years I suppose—that's definitely what I'll do. That's when I'll make the big change. First of all though, I've got to get up, my train leaves at five."

60   And he looked over at the alarm clock, ticking on the chest of drawers. "God in Heaven!" he thought. It was half past six and the hands were quietly moving forwards, it was even later than half past, more like quarter to seven. Had the alarm clock not rung? He could see from the bed that it had been set for four o'clock as it should have been; it certainly must have rung. Yes, but was it possible to quietly sleep through that furniture-rattling noise? True, he had not slept peacefully, but probably all the more deeply because of that. What should he do now? The next train went at seven; if he were to catch that he would have to rush like mad and the collection of samples was still not packed, and he did not at all

70   feel particularly fresh and lively. And even if he did catch the train he would not avoid his boss's anger as the office assistant would have been there to see the five o'clock train go, he would have put in his report about Gregor's not being there a long time ago. The office assistant was the boss's man, spineless, and with no understanding. What about if he reported sick? But that would be extremely strained and suspicious as in fifteen years of service Gregor had never once yet been ill. His boss would certainly come round with

The Metamorphosis   **95**

©Edward Holub/Photodisc/Getty Images

Analyze Author's Choices: Tension and Surprise

 COMMON CORE **RL 1, RL 5**

(LINES 57–73)

Explain that authors manipulate time in a text through **pacing**. Alternating the pace in a narrative is an effective way to build tension or suspense.

F **CITE TEXT EVIDENCE** Ask students how Kafka uses pacing to create a sense of panic. *(Gregor says he must get up and ready in order to catch the five o'clock train, but when he looks at the clock, he sees it's already half-past six, and even later than that, almost a quarter to seven. By moving time quickly forward in just one sentence, Kafka instills in the reader the sense of panic Gregor feels.)*

Analyze Word Choice

COMMON CORE RL 3, RL 4

(LINES 100–115)

Explain that an author's choice of words can effectively convey characters' feelings and their relationships.

G **CITE TEXT EVIDENCE** Ask students what the father does when Gregor oversleeps. *(He knocks on Gregor's door, calls his name, and asks if something is wrong.)* Have students identify the words Kafka uses to suggest the way the father feels. *(In line 104, Kafka uses the word fist, and in line 105, Gregor's father speaks with "warning deepness.")* What do these words help you understand about Gregor's relationship with his family? *(It seems strained because they expect certain things from him, and he is afraid to tell the truth or disappoint them.)*

Support Inferences

COMMON CORE RL 1, RL 2, RL 3

(LINES 112–115)

Tell students readers often use details to infer how a character's actions help develop the central idea.

H **CITE TEXT EVIDENCE** Ask students what inference they can make about the theme based on Gregor's actions. Have students identify text evidence that supports their inference. *(In lines 112–115, Gregor locks his bedroom door when he is home. I can infer that he does not feel safe or comfortable even when he is at home, which supports and develops the central idea of isolation.)*

CRITICAL VOCABULARY

plaintively: Gregor's sister is upset by the fact that he has not yet left his room.

ASK STUDENTS how someone's voice might sound if he or she was making a plaintive request. *(pleading, whiny)*

enunciate: Gregor knows his new voice makes it hard to be understood, so he speaks slowly and clearly.

ASK STUDENTS how enunciating makes someone's speech easier to understand. *(When you enunciate, you pronounce your words clearly and slowly.)*

---

the doctor from the medical insurance company, accuse his parents of having a lazy son, and accept the doctor's recommendation not
80 to make any claim as the doctor believed that no one was ever ill but that many were workshy.[2] And what's more, would he have been entirely wrong in this case? Gregor did in fact, apart from excessive sleepiness after sleeping for so long, feel completely well and even felt much hungrier than usual.

He was still hurriedly thinking all this through, unable to decide to get out of the bed, when the clock struck quarter to seven. There was a cautious knock at the door near his head. "Gregor," somebody called—it was his mother—"it's quarter to seven. Didn't you want to go somewhere?" That gentle voice! Gregor was
90 shocked when he heard his own voice answering, it could hardly be recognized as the voice he had had before. As if from deep inside him, there was a painful and uncontrollable squeaking mixed in with it, the words could be made out at first but then there was a sort of echo which made them unclear, leaving the hearer unsure whether he had heard properly or not. Gregor had wanted to give a full answer and explain everything, but in the circumstances contented himself with saying: "Yes, mother, yes, thank you, I'm getting up now." The change in Gregor's voice probably could not be noticed outside through the wooden door, as his mother was
100 satisfied with this explanation and shuffled away. But this short conversation made the other members of the family aware that Gregor, against their expectations, was still at home, and soon his father came knocking at one of the side doors, gently, but with his fist. "Gregor, Gregor," he called, "what's wrong?" And after a short while he called again with a warning deepness in his voice: "Gregor! Gregor!" At the other side door his sister came **plaintively**: "Gregor? Aren't you well? Do you need anything?" Gregor answered to both sides: "I'm ready, now," making an effort to remove all the strangeness from his voice by **enunciating** very carefully and
110 putting long pauses between each individual word. His father went back to his breakfast, but his sister whispered: "Gregor, open the door, I beg of you." Gregor, however, had no thought of opening the door, and instead congratulated himself for his cautious habit, acquired from his traveling, of locking all doors at night even when he was at home.

The first thing he wanted to do was to get up in peace without being disturbed, to get dressed, and most of all to have his breakfast. Only then would he consider what to do next, as he was well aware that he would not bring his thoughts to any sensible
120 conclusions by lying in bed. He remembered that he had often felt a

plaintively
(plān´tĭv-lē) *adv.*
sadly or wistfully.

enunciate
(ĭ-nŭn´sē-āt´) *v.*
to articulate or
pronounce clearly.

---

[2] **workshy:** lazy; unwilling to perform labor.

WHEN STUDENTS STRUGGLE...

After students read lines 85–115, have volunteers summarize each family member's reaction toward Gregor's oversleeping. Discuss how the family's concern might be more for themselves than for Gregor. *(Kafka revealed earlier that Gregor is unhappy at his job, but he can't leave because he must pay off the family's debt. Gregor's family is likely worried that he may lose his job if he doesn't go to work soon, which will be a problem for them.)* Ask students to explain how this interaction advances the plot.

slight pain in bed, perhaps caused by lying awkwardly, but that had always turned out to be pure imagination and he wondered how his imaginings would slowly resolve themselves today. He did not have the slightest doubt that the change in his voice was nothing more than the first sign of a serious cold, which was an occupational hazard for traveling salesmen.

It was a simple matter to throw off the covers; he only had to blow himself up a little and they fell off by themselves. But it became difficult after that, especially as he was so exceptionally
130 broad. He would have used his arms and his hands to push himself up; but instead of them he only had all those little legs continuously moving in different directions, and which he was moreover unable to control. If he wanted to bend one of them, then that was the first one that would stretch itself out; and if he finally managed to do what he wanted with that leg, all the others seemed to be set free

Image Credits: ©Irene Lamprakou/Flickr/Getty Images

CLOSE READ

Support Inferences

COMMON CORE **RL 1, RL 3**

(LINES 121–135)

Remind students to look for details to help them make inferences about characters and events. Making inferences will help them better relate to the characters and understand the plot. Review how, in the first paragraph, Gregor easily accepted that he was not dreaming, even though his body was no longer human.

CITE TEXT EVIDENCE Ask students what they can infer about Gregor based on lines 121–126. *(He does not want to believe he has become an insect, so he tries to tell himself that he is only imagining things, just like he has done before.)* What can you infer about his character when he tries to get out of bed? Use evidence to support your response. *(In lines 130–131 he realizes he cannot use his hands and arms like he normally would, but he refuses to panic or give up. In lines 133–135 he is frustrated that he cannot move his little legs the way he wants to, but he doesn't stop trying. He is very determined, probably because he is so concerned about getting to work in order to please his family.)*

APPLYING ACADEMIC VOCABULARY

evolve	explicit	infer

As you discuss Kafka's narrative, incorporate the following Collection 3 academic vocabulary words: *evolve, explicit,* and *infer.* As you discuss the plot events, ask students to explain how Gregor's ideas about his situation are **evolving.** As you analyze the meaning of the text, ask them to note which ideas are **explicitly** stated and which must be **inferred.**

Analyze Author's Choice: Tension and Surprise

COMMON CORE **RL 1, RL 5**

(LINES 149–154)

Tell students authors use details to build tension.

J **CITE TEXT EVIDENCE** Ask students what details Kafka includes to build tension. (*Kafka carefully describes how Gregor is finally able to sit up and what Gregor thinks once he finally has his head up. Gregor immediately worries about falling and knocking himself unconscious, which he says he must avoid "at any price." His fear makes the reader feel sorry for Gregor and worry that he might get hurt or never get out of bed.*)

Analyze Impact of Word Choice: Tone

COMMON CORE **RL 1, RL 2, RL 4**

(LINES 156–158)

Explain that the author's choice of words, details, and sentence structure often communicate the tone.

K **CITE TEXT EVIDENCE** Ask students what the tone of the story is. (*informal; removed and disconnected*) Then have them identify phrases that helped them determine the tone. (*"watching his legs as they struggled against each other," [lines 156–157] The narrator's description of the absurd situation is straightforward and unemotional.*) How does the tone of the narrative reflect the theme? (*The detached tone creates a separation between the events and emotions, which supports the theme of isolation.*)

Support Inferences

COMMON CORE **RL 1**

(LINES 172–175)

Remind students that their inferences, or conclusions, must be supported by textual evidence.

L **CITE TEXT EVIDENCE** Ask students what inference they can make about Gregor's employer. (*He does not trust his employees.*) Have students identify text evidence that supports their inference. (*Gregor knows that as soon as his absence is noted, his employer will send someone to his house to see where he is.*)

---

and would move about painfully. "This is something that can't be done in bed," Gregor said to himself, "so don't keep trying to do it."

The first thing he wanted to do was get the lower part of his body out of the bed, but he had never seen this lower part, and
140 could not imagine what it looked like; it turned out to be too hard to move; it went so slowly; and finally, almost in a frenzy, when he carelessly shoved himself forwards with all the force he could gather, he chose the wrong direction, hit hard against the lower bedpost, and learned from the burning pain he felt that the lower part of his body might well, at present, be the most sensitive.

So then he tried to get the top part of his body out of the bed first, carefully turning his head to the side. This he managed quite easily, and despite its breadth and its weight, the bulk of his body eventually followed slowly in the direction of the head. But when
150 he had at last got his head out of the bed and into the fresh air it occurred to him that if he let himself fall it would be a miracle if his head were not injured, so he became afraid to carry on pushing himself forward the same way. And he could not knock himself out now at any price; better to stay in bed than lose consciousness.

It took just as much effort to get back to where he had been earlier, but when he lay there sighing, and was once more watching his legs as they struggled against each other even harder than before, if that was possible, he could think of no way of bringing peace and order to this chaos. He told himself once more that it was
160 not possible for him to stay in bed and that the most sensible thing to do would be to get free of it in whatever way he could at whatever sacrifice. At the same time, though, he did not forget to remind himself that calm consideration was much better than rushing to desperate conclusions. At times like this he would direct his eyes to the window and look out as clearly as he could, but unfortunately, even the other side of the narrow street was enveloped in morning fog and the view had little confidence or cheer to offer him. "Seven o'clock, already," he said to himself when the clock struck again, "seven o'clock, and there's still a fog like this." And he lay there
170 quietly a while longer, breathing lightly as if he perhaps expected the total stillness to bring things back to their real and natural state.

But then he said to himself: "Before it strikes quarter past seven I'll definitely have to have got properly out of bed. And by then somebody will have come round from work to ask what's happened to me as well, as they open up at work before seven o'clock." And so he set himself to the task of swinging the entire length of his body out of the bed all at the same time. If he succeeded in falling out of bed in this way and kept his head raised as he did so he could probably avoid injuring it. His back seemed to be quite hard, and
180 probably nothing would happen to it falling onto the carpet. His

98 Collection 3

SCAFFOLDING FOR ELL STUDENTS

Idioms Remind students that the meaning of an idiom is different from the literal meaning of the words. Point out the phrase "at any price" in line 154.

ASK STUDENTS what this phrase means. (*to do whatever it takes to avoid something from happening*) How does this idiom contribute to your understanding of Gregor? (*It shows how Gregor is concerned with needing to stay awake and in control of the situation.*)

main concern was for the loud noise he was bound to make, and which even through all the doors would probably raise concern if not alarm. But it was something that had to be risked.

When Gregor was already sticking half way out of the bed—the new method was more of a game than an effort, all he had to do was rock back and forth—it occurred to him how simple everything would be if somebody came to help him. Two strong people—he had his father and the maid in mind—would have been more than enough; they would only have to push their arms under the dome of his back, peel him away from the bed, bend down with the load and then be patient and careful as he swang over onto the floor, where, hopefully, the little legs would find a use. Should he really call for help though, even apart from the fact that all the doors were locked? Despite all the difficulty he was in, he could not suppress a smile at this thought.

After a while he had already moved so far across that it would have been hard for him to keep his balance if he rocked too hard. The time was now ten past seven and he would have to make a final decision very soon. Then there was a ring at the door of the flat. "That'll be someone from work," he said to himself, and froze very still, although his little legs only became all the more lively as they danced around. For a moment everything remained quiet. "They're not opening the door," Gregor said to himself, caught in some nonsensical hope. But then of course, the maid's firm steps went to the door as ever and opened it. Gregor only needed to hear the visitor's first words of greeting and he knew who it was—the chief clerk himself. Why did Gregor have to be the only one condemned to work for a company where they immediately became highly suspicious at the slightest shortcoming? Were all employees, every one of them, louts, was there not one of them who was faithful and devoted who would go so mad with pangs of conscience that he couldn't get out of bed if he didn't spend at least a couple of hours in the morning on company business? Was it really not enough to let one of the trainees make enquiries—assuming enquiries were even necessary—did the chief clerk have to come himself, and did they have to show the whole, innocent family that this was so suspicious that only the chief clerk could be trusted to have the wisdom to investigate it? And more because these thoughts had made him upset than through any proper decision, he swang himself with all his force out of the bed. There was a loud thump, but it wasn't really a loud noise. His fall was softened a little by the carpet, and Gregor's back was also more elastic than he had thought, which made the sound muffled and not too noticeable. He had not held his head carefully enough, though, and hit it as he fell; annoyed and in pain, he turned it and rubbed it against the carpet.

CLOSE READ

Determine Word Meanings (LINES 199–220)

COMMON CORE RL 1, RL 4

Explain that **connotation** is the negative or positive feelings or ideas a word evokes. Authors choose words to create specific feelings or convey certain ideas. Authors can also use words in a figurative way.

M ASK STUDENTS to reread lines 199–205. What does *nonsensical* in line 204 mean? *(an idea that is contrary to good sense)* What is the effect when Kafka pairs *nonsensical* with hope? *(It changes the meaning of* hope, *making the situation hopeless since having hope in this situation does not make sense.)* Have students reread lines 206–220 and identify words with negative and positive connotations. *(negative: condemned, highly suspicious, shortcoming, louts; positive: faithful, devoted, innocent)* How does Kafka use words with traditionally positive connotations to express negative thoughts? What is the effect? *(He is using these words sarcastically to highlight the way Gregor feels about his company and his coworkers.)*

CLOSE READ

Support Inferences

COMMON CORE RL 1, RL 3

(LINES 226–235)

Remind students that complex characters change throughout the story and often have conflicting feelings and motivations. Students often have to make inferences about a complex character based on his or her thoughts, words, and actions.

N CITE TEXT EVIDENCE Ask students to explain whether Gregor thinks his situation is unique to him. *(He thinks it can happen to anyone.)* Have students cite text evidence to support their response. *(When wondering if what happened to him could happen to the chief clerk, Gregor thinks how "you had to concede that it was possible," line 229.)* Given the strangeness of the situation, what can you infer about Gregor and the type of person he is? *(He is not overly emotional and is more concerned about his job than he is about himself.)*

Explain that readers can make inferences about a character's personality by noting how he or she interacts with other characters.

O CITE TEXT EVIDENCE Ask students what they can infer about the relationship between Gregor and his sister. *(They get along well; she tries to look out for him.)* Have students cite text evidence to support their responses. *("Gregor's sister whispered to him to let him know: 'Gregor, the chief clerk is here,'" lines 232–233.)*

Analyze Theme

COMMON CORE RL 2

(LINES 241–248)

Remind students to continue looking for evidence that develops or reinforces the theme.

P CITE TEXT EVIDENCE Have students reread lines 241–248. Then have students cite details that reinforce the theme. *(In lines 244–248, the father says Gregor only thinks about work and explains to the clerk how Gregor rarely goes out in the evenings, which reinforces the theme that corporations and their demands on workers have caused people to become isolated and unsocial.)*

"Something's fallen down in there," said the chief clerk in the room on the left. Gregor tried to imagine whether something of the sort that had happened to him today could ever happen to the chief clerk too; you had to concede that it was possible. But as if in gruff
230 reply to this question, the chief clerk's firm footsteps in his highly polished boots could now be heard in the adjoining room. From the room on his right, Gregor's sister whispered to him to let him know: "Gregor, the chief clerk is here." "Yes, I know," said Gregor to himself; but without daring to raise his voice loud enough for his sister to hear him.

"He isn't well, he said this morning that he is, but he isn't."

"Gregor," said his father now from the room to his left, "the chief clerk has come round and wants to know why you didn't leave on the early train. We don't know what to say to him. And anyway, he wants to speak to you personally. So please open up this door. I'm
240 sure he'll be good enough to forgive the untidiness of your room." Then the chief clerk called, "Good morning, Mr. Samsa." "He isn't well," said his mother to the chief clerk, while his father continued to speak through the door. "He isn't well, please believe me. Why else would Gregor have missed a train! The lad only ever thinks about the business. It nearly makes me cross the way he never goes out in the evenings; he's been in town for a week now but stayed home every evening. He sits with us in the kitchen and just reads the paper or studies train timetables. His idea of relaxation is working with his fretsaw.[3] He's made a little frame, for instance, it only took him two

---

[3] **fretsaw:** a saw used to cut delicate curves in wood.

WHEN STUDENTS STRUGGLE...

To guide students' understanding of the characters' development, have them work in pairs. Tell them to review lines 87–115, where Gregor's family members first make an appearance, and lines 226–264. Have partners choose one character and fill out a chart like the one shown. Then have them use the chart to discuss the following questions:

- What does the character value?
- What does the character believe?
- What does the character fear?

or three evenings, you'll be amazed how nice it is; it's hanging up in his room; you'll see it as soon as Gregor opens the door. Anyway, I'm glad you're here; we wouldn't have been able to get Gregor to open the door by ourselves; he's so stubborn; and I'm sure he isn't well, he said this morning that he is, but he isn't." "I'll be there in a moment," said Gregor slowly and thoughtfully, but without moving so that he would not miss any word of the conversation. "Well I can't think of any other way of explaining it, Mrs. Samsa," said the chief clerk, "I hope it's nothing serious. But on the other hand, I must say that if we people in commerce ever become slightly unwell then, fortunately or unfortunately as you like, we simply have to overcome it because of business considerations." "Can the chief clerk come in to see you now then?" asked his father impatiently, knocking at the door again. "No," said Gregor. In the room on his right there followed a painful silence; in the room on his left his sister began to cry.

So why did his sister not go and join the others? She had probably only just got up and had not even begun to get dressed. And why was she crying? Was it because he had not got up, and had not let the chief clerk in, because he was in danger of losing his job and if that happened his boss would once more pursue their parents with the same demands as before? There was no need to worry about things like that yet. Gregor was still there and had not the slightest intention of abandoning his family. For the time being he just lay there on the carpet, and no one who knew the condition he was in would seriously have expected him to let the chief clerk in. It was only a minor discourtesy, and a suitable excuse could easily be found for it later on, it was not something for which Gregor could be sacked on the spot. And it seemed to Gregor much more sensible to leave him now in peace instead of disturbing him with talking at him and crying. But the others didn't know what was happening, they were worried, that would excuse their behavior.

The chief clerk now raised his voice, "Mr. Samsa," he called to him, "what is wrong? You barricade yourself in your room, give us no more than yes or no for an answer, you are causing serious and unnecessary concern to your parents and you fail—and I mention this just by the way—you fail to carry out your business duties in a way that is quite unheard of. I'm speaking here on behalf of your parents and of your employer, and really must request a clear and immediate explanation. I am astonished, quite astonished. I thought I knew you as a calm and sensible person, and now you suddenly seem to be showing off with peculiar whims. This morning, your employer did suggest a possible reason for your failure to appear, it's true—it had to do with the money that was recently entrusted to you—but I came near to giving him my word of honor that that could not be the right explanation. But now that

TEACH

CLOSE READ

Analyze Point of View: Cultural Background

COMMON CORE **RL 2, RL 4, RL 6**

(LINES 256-264)

Explain that authors can express the cultural background of a place through the opinions and actions of characters. By doing this, authors reveal what the society of a particular place—and often a particular time—value. An author's point of view, or attitude toward the subject, supports and develops a theme or message about society and human nature. Throughout the narrative, Kafka has shown Gregor's anxiety about being late for work and the possible consequences of that action.

Q **CITE TEXT EVIDENCE** Ask students to explain what Kafka is revealing to readers about society's opinion of workers. *(A worker's comfort and health is second to production of work.)* How do these revelations help develop the theme? *(Kafka is trying to warn people about how modern corporations have affected society and demeaned workers.)* Then have students identify text evidence that supports their inference. *(The chief clerk's words in lines 256–261.)*

Character: Gregor's sister

Character's Words/Thoughts	Character's Actions	Character's Interactions
"Gregor! Aren't you well? Do you need anything?" line 107	She cries when Gregor won't let anyone into his room, line 264	She warns Gregor that the chief clerk is at the house, line 233

Analyze Character

COMMON CORE RL 1, RL 3

(LINES 304–321)

Explain that authors sometimes use **dialogue**, or the conversation between characters, to build tension in a narrative. Dialogue can also reveal motivations and the way characters think and feel.

(R) **ASK STUDENTS** to explain the feeling Gregor's dialogue in lines 304–321 evokes. *(alarm, anxiety, desperation)* What words or techniques does Kafka use to create this feeling? *(Kafka repeats the word "please" and the phrases "just a moment" and "quite all right" to show Gregor's desperation and anxiety. Such a long, uninterrupted dialogue filled with excuses creates a sense of panic and helps readers understand just how worried Gregor is about losing his job and how desperately he wants the clerk to believe him.)*

Support Inferences

COMMON CORE RL 1, RL 3

(LINES 315–321)

Remind students that authors do not always explicitly reveal a character's feelings and motivations, or reasons for acting a certain way. Readers must use information in the text to make an inference about what is not stated directly.

(S) **CITE TEXT EVIDENCE** Ask students what inference they can make about the reason Gregor is so worried. *(He thinks he will lose his job, which will negatively impact his family and affect how others view him.)* Then have students identify text evidence that supports their inference. *(Gregor tells the chief clerk "there's no basis for the accusations you're making," lines 315–316; and that he has several new contracts, line 317.)*

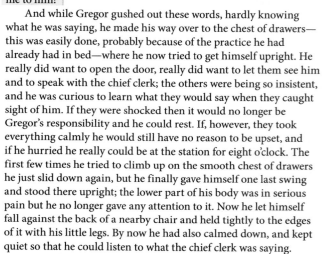

I see your incomprehensible stubbornness I no longer feel any wish whatsoever to intercede on your behalf. And nor is your position all that secure. I had originally intended to say all this to you in private, but since you cause me to waste my time here for no good reason I don't see why your parents should not also learn of it. Your
300 turnover has been very unsatisfactory of late; I grant you that it's not the time of year to do especially good business, we recognize that; but there simply is no time of year to do no business at all, Mr. Samsa, we cannot allow there to be."

"But Sir," called Gregor, beside himself and forgetting all else in the excitement, "I'll open up immediately, just a moment. I'm slightly unwell, an attack of dizziness, I haven't been able to get up. I'm still in bed now. I'm quite fresh again now, though. I'm just getting out of bed. Just a moment. Be patient! It's not quite as easy as I'd thought. I'm quite all right now, though. It's shocking, what
310 can suddenly happen to a person! I was quite all right last night, my parents know about it, perhaps better than me, I had a small symptom of it last night already. They must have noticed it. I don't know why I didn't let you know at work! But you always think you can get over an illness without staying at home. Please, don't make my parents suffer! There's no basis for any of the accusations you're making; nobody's ever said a word to me about any of these things. Maybe you haven't read the latest contracts I sent in. I'll set off with the eight o'clock train, as well, these few hours of rest have given me strength. You don't need to wait, sir; I'll be in the office soon after
320 you, and please be so good as to tell that to the boss and recommend me to him!"

And while Gregor gushed out these words, hardly knowing what he was saying, he made his way over to the chest of drawers—this was easily done, probably because of the practice he had already had in bed—where he now tried to get himself upright. He really did want to open the door, really did want to let them see him and to speak with the chief clerk; the others were being so insistent, and he was curious to learn what they would say when they caught sight of him. If they were shocked then it would no longer be
330 Gregor's responsibility and he could rest. If, however, they took everything calmly he would still have no reason to be upset, and if he hurried he really could be at the station for eight o'clock. The first few times he tried to climb up on the smooth chest of drawers he just slid down again, but he finally gave himself one last swing and stood there upright; the lower part of his body was in serious pain but he no longer gave any attention to it. Now he let himself fall against the back of a nearby chair and held tightly to the edges of it with his little legs. By now he had also calmed down, and kept quiet so that he could listen to what the chief clerk was saying.

102 Collection 3

WHEN STUDENTS STRUGGLE...

Explain that reading with prosody means reading with expression. Remind students that, in the scene in lines 304–321, Gregor is anxious about his job and desperate for the chief clerk to believe him. Discuss how people who are anxious and desperate speak. Read aloud Gregor's first few lines to model reading with prosody. Then, have students work in mixed-ability groups to practice reading with prosody.

340   "Did you understand a word of all that?" the chief clerk asked his parents, "surely he's not trying to make fools of us." "Oh, God!" called his mother, who was already in tears, "he could be seriously ill and we're making him suffer. Grete! Grete!" she then cried. "Mother?" his sister called from the other side. They communicated across Gregor's room. "You'll have to go for the doctor straight away. Gregor is ill. Quick, get the doctor. Did you hear the way Gregor spoke just now?" "That was the voice of an animal," said the chief clerk, with a calmness that was in contrast with his mother's screams. "Anna! Anna!" his father called into the kitchen through

350 the entrance hall, clapping his hands, "get a locksmith here, now!" And the two girls, their skirts swishing, immediately ran out through the hall, wrenching open the front door of the flat as they went. How had his sister managed to get dressed so quickly? There was no sound of the door banging shut again; they must have left it open; people often do in homes where something awful has happened.

   Gregor, in contrast, had become much calmer. So they couldn't understand his words any more, although they seemed clear enough to him, clearer than before—perhaps his ears had become used to

360 the sound. They had realized, though, that there was something wrong with him, and were ready to help. The first response to his situation had been confident and wise, and that made him feel better. He felt that he had been drawn back in among people, and from the doctor and the locksmith he expected great and surprising achievements—although he did not really distinguish one from the other. Whatever was said next would be crucial, so, in order to make his voice as clear as possible, he coughed a little, but taking care to do this not too loudly as even this might well sound different from the way that a human coughs and he was no longer sure he could

370 judge this for himself. Meanwhile, it had become very quiet in the next room. Perhaps his parents were sat at the table whispering with the chief clerk, or perhaps they were all pressed against the door and listening.

   Gregor slowly pushed his way over to the door with the chair. Once there he let go of it and threw himself onto the door, holding himself upright against it using the adhesive on the tips of his legs. He rested there a little while to recover from the effort involved and then set himself to the task of turning the key in the lock with his mouth. He seemed, unfortunately, to have no proper teeth—how

380 was he, then, to grasp the key?—but the lack of teeth was, of course, made up for with a very strong jaw; using the jaw, he really was able to start the key turning, ignoring the fact that he must have been causing some kind of damage as a brown fluid came from his mouth, flowed over the key and dripped onto the floor. "Listen,"

The Metamorphosis   **103**

CLOSE READ

Analyze Theme

COMMON CORE   **RL 2**

(LINES 357–373)

Remind students that a story's theme is the overall message the author wants to share. Themes are perceptions about human nature or society the author wants the reader to understand. Themes are usually unstated and must be inferred based on the way the character deals with and resolves (or does not resolve) the conflict.

T   **CITE TEXT EVIDENCE** Have students reread lines 357–373. Then have them cite details that shape and refine the story's theme. *(lines 363–366, when Gregor thinks he has been drawn back to people because of their concern)*

TO CHALLENGE STUDENTS...

Theme Explain that authors often include multiple themes in a literary work. Often, these themes build on one another to create a complex story. Have students identify the various themes in *The Metamorphosis*, such as:

- corporations are dehumanizing workers, thereby creating a sense of isolation in the modern world;
- communication is essential for any relationship and for society; or
- change is important and one person's transformation can affect others.

Tell them to find how two of the themes are developed and support each other. Then have students write a paragraph or two explaining their analysis.

Support Inferences

COMMON CORE RL 1, RL 3

(LINES 385–391)

Tell students that authors provide clues throughout a text about a character's development, and readers use those clues to infer information about the character.

 CITE TEXT EVIDENCE Ask students to review what they have learned about Gregor's personality. *(Gregor has a strong sense of family duty, he feels isolated from his family and society, and he is more concerned about others than he is about himself.)* Then ask students what they can infer about Gregor after reading lines 385–391, and cite information in the text that supports their inferences. *(Gregor thinks his parents should be congratulating him for figuring out how to turn the key, considering the limitations of his new body, which suggests he wants to feel appreciated and valued.)*

said the chief clerk in the next room, "he's turning the key." Gregor was greatly encouraged by this; but they all should have been calling to him, his father and his mother too: "Well done, Gregor," they should have cried, "keep at it, keep hold of the lock!" And with the idea that they were all excitedly following his efforts, he bit on
390 the key with all his strength, paying no attention to the pain he was causing himself. As the key turned round he turned around the lock with it, only holding himself upright with his mouth, and hung onto the key or pushed it down again with the whole weight of his body as needed. The clear sound of the lock as it snapped back was Gregor's sign that he could break his concentration, and as he regained his breath he said to himself: "So, I didn't need the locksmith after all." Then he lay his head on the handle of the door to open it completely.

Because he had to open the door in this way, it was already wide
400 open before he could be seen. He had first to slowly turn himself around one of the double doors, and he had to do it very carefully if he did not want to fall flat on his back before entering the room.

104 Collection 3

Image Credits: ©Alexandre Fundone/Flickr/Getty Images

APPLYING ACADEMIC VOCABULARY

abstract	evolve	facilitate

As you discuss Kafka's narrative, incorporate the following Collection 3 academic vocabulary words: *abstract* and *facilitate*. As you discuss Gregor's situation, ask students to explain how Kafka has kept Gregor's actual appearance **abstract**. Have students explain what details Kafka uses to **facilitate** the reader's understanding of how Gregor has **evolved**.

He was still occupied with this difficult movement, unable to pay attention to anything else, when he heard the chief clerk exclaim a loud "Oh!" which sounded like the soughing[4] of the wind. Now he also saw him—he was the nearest to the door—his hand pressed against his open mouth and slowly retreating as if driven by a steady and invisible force. Gregor's mother, her hair still disheveled from bed despite the chief clerk's being there, looked at his father. Then she unfolded her arms, took two steps forward towards Gregor and sank down onto the floor into her skirts that spread themselves out around her as her head disappeared down onto her breast. His father looked hostile, and clenched his fists as if wanting to knock Gregor back into his room. Then he looked uncertainly round the living room, covered his eyes with his hands and wept so that his powerful chest shook.

COLLABORATIVE DISCUSSION What elements of this novella distort the reader's sense of reality, while at the same time make Gregor Samsa's situation feel very real? In a small group, discuss textual evidence that supports your responses.

---
[4] **soughing (souˊĭng):** a soft moaning or whistling sound.

CLOSE READ

Support Inferences
(LINES 403–408)

COMMON CORE **RL 1, RL3**

Tell students that making inferences is important to help them understand and relate to the characters and recognize how certain actions advance the plot.

CITE TEXT EVIDENCE Ask students what inferences they can make about the way the chief clerk, his mother, and his father react after seeing Gregor. Why do you think each character acts this way? How might their feelings and interactions with Gregor advance the plot? (*Once the clerk sees Gregor he is afraid, the mother falls to the floor and sobs, and the father becomes angry and then sad. Based on their reactions I can infer that they will further isolate Gregor, leaving Gregor alone to resolve the conflict.*) Then have students identify text evidence that supports their inference. (*The chief clerk covers his mouth and starts slowly backing away from Gregor.*)

COLLABORATIVE DISCUSSION Have students work in small groups to discuss specific examples from the text that show how Kafka created a surreal situation for Gregor Samsa while still managing to have his situation feel realistic. Then have them consider the effect of this structure and share their conclusions with the class. Accept all reasonable responses.

ASK STUDENTS to share any questions they generated in the course of reading and discussing the selection.

TO CHALLENGE STUDENTS...

Tone Remind students that tone is the narrator's attitude toward the subject, and in *The Metamorphosis* Kafka uses a detached tone to tell Gregor's story. Have students find examples that reveal Kafka's tone. Then ask students why Kafka may have adopted this tone and how it supports his theme. Finally, have students infer what happens next. Have students work in pairs to anticipate the next scene in the narrative. Have partners write the scene using a similar tone.

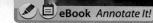
PRACTICE & APPLY

Support Inferences
 COMMON CORE RL 1

Help students understand that an inference is a conclusion they draw about the characters, events, or themes, based on details in the text. Have students discuss any inferences they made and the evidence they used to make them.

Support Inferences
 COMMON CORE RL 1

An **inference** is a conclusion based on facts. When analyzing literature, skilled readers make inferences drawn from the text. For instance, in the first paragraph of "The Metamorphosis," Franz Kafka writes that when Gregor Samsa woke up, "he found himself transformed in his bed into a horrible vermin." Based on this statement and the descriptive details that follow in the first paragraph, you might infer that Gregor actually was turned into an insect; or perhaps you might infer that he was just dreaming. As you read on, you'll make other inferences based on the evidence you encounter. You may also revise your earlier inferences and even discard them, based on further analysis of the text.

Analyzing the Text
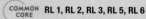 COMMON CORE RL 1, RL 2, RL 3, RL 5, RL 6

Possible answers:

1. *Kafka creates tension by following Gregor's worry about missing the train with the family's sudden appearance and insistence that he open the bedroom door. The pace in this section (lines 87–115) is fast and tense, with first one family member, then another, asking why he's still in bed. Kafka slows the pace a little by describing internal thoughts. Kafka continues to increase the tension by pointing out the passage of time and increasing the consequences for Gregor's lateness.*

2. *Gregor is not close to his parents. When his mother goes to check on him, she asks, "Didn't you want to go somewhere" (line 89) instead of pointing out that he's late for work. This suggests that their relationship is not strong enough for her to make an honest observation. Gregor's father points out how his son "sits with us in the kitchen and just reads the paper or studies train timetables" (lines 247–248), showing how Gregor does not interact with his family.*

3. *One theme is how the individual is less important than his duty to family and work. Gregor's metamorphosis might symbolize his insignificance and dehumanization. When Gregor finds himself transformed into an insect, his main concern is being late to work. Gregor dislikes his job and boss, but must continue because he has to pay off his family's debt. He stays in his room, trying to avoid upsetting his family. When the chief clerk arrives, Gregor panics and finally makes an effort to leave his room to prove that he is fit to work.*

4. *Kafka shows us how in the early 1900s in Europe, the worker was not highly regarded. In lines 77–81, Gregor assumes his boss will send the doctor, not out of concern for his health, but because his boss will think Gregor is being lazy. In lines 258–261, the chief clerk notes how people in their business need to keep working, even when they are sick.*

Analyzing the Text
 COMMON CORE RL 1, RL 2, RL 3, RL 5, RL 6, SL 1

Cite Text Evidence Support your responses with evidence from the selection.

1. **Analyze** An author makes choices about how to structure and pace events to achieve a purpose. In lines 59–84, Gregor suddenly starts to worry about missing the train. From this point onward, how does Kafka manipulate time to create tension? Consider how the pacing creates a sense of urgency and panic.

2. **Infer** Kafka provides many details about how Gregor interacts with his parents. Based on these details, what can you infer about Gregor's relationship with his mother and father? Use text evidence to support your inferences.

3. **Summarize** What theme emerges in the story? Consider what Gregor's changing into an insect might symbolize. Summarize the plot to explain how the theme evolves through the responses of Gregor and others to his condition.

4. **Connect** Franz Kafka wrote this story in 1912 in what is now the Czech Republic. What insights into European culture in the early 1900s does the text provide? Cite evidence from the text to support your ideas.

 my **WriteSmart**

PERFORMANCE TASK

Speaking Activity: Discussion What can you infer about the kind of person Gregor is based on how he responds to the change he has undergone?

- Make notes about the progression of Gregor's thoughts and actions in this selection. Use your notes to make inferences about Gregor's character, and jot down at least two adjectives that describe his personality.

- Use your notes to respond to this question in a group discussion: Does being changed into "a horrible vermin" really change Gregor? Why or why not? Write a summary of your group's answer.

Assign this performance task.  my **WriteSmart**

PERFORMANCE TASK
 COMMON CORE W 4, SL 1

Speaking Activity Have students review the narrative, taking notes about Gregor's thoughts, words, and actions to make inferences about what he values, wants, believes, and fears. Tell students to synthesize their findings to come up with two adjectives about Gregor's personality. Then have them form groups to discuss the question, summarizing the group's thoughts in writing.

INTERACTIVE WHITEBOARD LESSON
Analyze Complex Characters

COMMON CORE

RL 1, RL 3

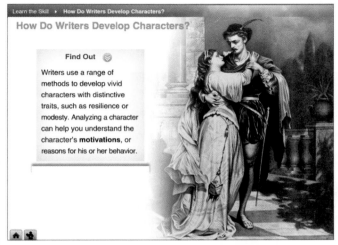

Learn the Skill ▸ How Do Writers Develop Characters?

How Do Writers Develop Characters?

Find Out

Writers use a range of methods to develop vivid characters with distinctive traits, such as resilience or modesty. Analyzing a character can help you understand the character's **motivations**, or reasons for his or her behavior.

TEACH

Before having students begin the discussion outlined in the Performance Task, review these methods of characterization:

- **Step 1: Identify Key Details** Record specific thoughts, words, or actions Gregor has regarding his present situation. For example, how does he react when he sees his body's transformation? When he is late for work? When the family insists that he open his door? When the chief clerk arrives?

- **Step 2: Infer Traits** Identify any conclusions you can make about Gregor's personality based on the details you identified in Step 1. What do his thoughts, words, and actions say about him?

- **Step 3: Infer Motivations** Analyze the motivations, or reasons, behind Gregor's thoughts, words, and actions. For example, how does Gregor's sense of duty to his family affect his reactions?

COLLABORATIVE DISCUSSION

Direct students to work individually to take notes, following the three steps for characterization you presented. Have students come together in small groups to compare their notes.

Support Inferences

COMMON CORE

RL 1

RETEACH

Review that authors do not always explicitly tell you what is happening in a text. Often, readers must make inferences about what the author means. An **inference** is a logical guess or conclusion based on information presented in a text.

- Ask students what kind of inference they might make from the following text: Isa pressed herself against the wall as the hall flooded with students. She clutched her thick chemistry book against her chest, took a deep breath, and joined the throng of students. (**Possible Answers:** *Isa is nervous; Isa does not like crowds; Isa is new to the school.*)

- Have students explain what information from the text they used to make their inferences. (**Possible Answers:** *"pressed herself against the wall"; "clutched her thick chemistry book against her chest"; "took a deep breath"*)

 LEVEL UP TUTORIALS Assign the following *Level Up* tutorial: **Making Inferences About Characters**

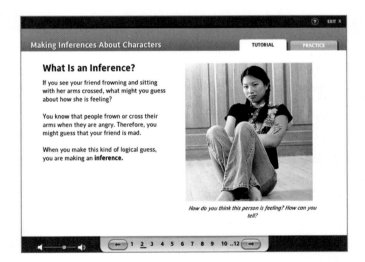

Making Inferences About Characters | TUTORIAL | PRACTICE

What Is an Inference?

If you see your friend frowning and sitting with her arms crossed, what might you guess about how she is feeling?

You know that people frown or cross their arms when they are angry. Therefore, you might guess that your friend is mad.

When you make this kind of logical guess, you are making an **inference.**

How do you think this person is feeling? How can you tell?

CLOSE READING APPLICATION

Students can apply the skill to another narrative. Assign small groups sections of a narrative. Tell students to read the section individually, noting at least three inferences they make while reading. Have group members come together. Ask: What inferences did you make? What evidence supports your inferences? What personal experiences or knowledge did you use to help make the inferences?

ANCHOR TEXT *from* **The Metamorphosis**

Graphic Novel by Peter Kuper

Why This Text?

Students regularly encounter adaptations in visual media and text materials. This lesson explores how the first part of Franz Kafka's novella, *The Metamorphosis,* is adapted as a graphic novel.

▶ View It!
Professional Development Podcast:
Text Complexity

Key Learning Objective: The student will be able to analyze representations in different mediums.

For practice and application:

The Starry Night

Close Reader selections
"The Starry Night"
*poem by Anne Sexton and
painting by Vincent Van Gogh*

COMMON CORE Common Core Standards

RL 1	Cite textual evidence.
RL 2	Determine a theme and analyze its development.
RL 3	Analyze how complex characters develop, interact, and advance the plot.
RL 4	Determine the meaning of words and phrases.
RL 5	Analyze how an author's choices create mystery, tension, or surprise.
RL 7	Analyze a subject or a key scene in two different artistic mediums.
RL 9	Analyze how an author draws on source material.
W 4	Produce writing in which the organization and style are appropriate to task, purpose, and audience.
SL 1–1a	Participate in collaborative discussions with diverse partners.
SL 4	Present information clearly so that the development and style are appropriate to purpose, audience, and task.
L 1b	Use various types of phrases and clauses to convey specific meanings.
L 4a–d	Determine the meaning of unknown and multiple-meaning words.

▲ Text Complexity Rubric

	from **The Metamorphosis**
Quantitative Measures	Lexile: N/A
Qualitative Measures	**Levels of Meaning/Purpose** single level of complex meaning
	Structure some unconventional story structure elements
	Language Conventionality and Clarity some unfamiliar language
	Knowledge Demands adapted from the original print source
Reader/Task Considerations	Teacher determined Vary by individual reader and type of text

Biography Peter Kuper is a teacher and illustrator whose work has appeared in many well-known magazines. He has written several graphic novels, including adaptations of other Franz Kafka works. Some of Kuper's works are "wordless," graphic novels, in which he relies solely on visual elements to tell a story.

AS YOU READ Direct the students to use the As You Read note to focus their reading.

Analyze Representations in Different Mediums RL 7

Explain to students that when writers and artists adapt a work, though they aim to stay true to the original work, they often make creative choices on what to include, and may sometimes choose to take a different approach to a scene. Have students read the first sentence of Kafka's novella, and then study this page.

Ⓐ **ASK STUDENTS** to explain how Kuper's opening differs from Kafka's. (*The very first sentence of Kafka's novella establishes that Gregor has turned into an insect. In the graphic novel, Kuper makes the reader turn the page before revealing what happens to Gregor.*) **How does Kuper use visual elements to accomplish this?** (*The page is all back, except for the few lines of text in the center. The text reveals only that Gregor has been transformed into something, but does not say to what. The effect is to create suspense for the reader.*)

After students turn to the next page, ask them how the change from this page to the next mimics waking up, as Gregor does. (*On p. 107, everything is black, because Gregor's eyes are still closed. After turning the page, the room is revealed. Gregor's transformed body is revealed to him and the reader at the same time.*)

---

from **The Metamorphosis**
Graphic Novel by Peter Kuper

AS YOU READ Pay attention to the text and graphic details that show what the main character is experiencing. Write down any questions you generate during reading.

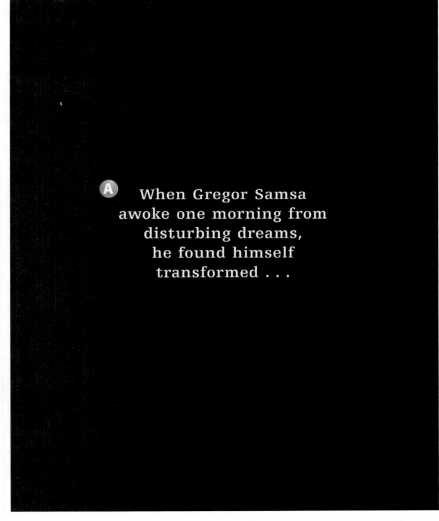

Ⓐ When Gregor Samsa awoke one morning from disturbing dreams, he found himself transformed . . .

Close Read Screencasts ▶ **View It!**

Modeled Discussions

Have students click the *Close Read* icons in their eBooks to access a screencast in which readers discuss and annotate the following key passage:

- Gregor recalling his early rising and long days (page 111)

As a class, view and discuss this video. Then have students pair up to do an independent close read of an additional passage—Gregor's struggle to get out of bed as time ticks away (page 119).

Analyze How an Author Draws on Source Material

COMMON CORE RL 9

Explain that when a writer adapts source material into a different medium, the emphasis on what happens can shift or be changed altogether.

B CITE TEXT EVIDENCE Have students revisit the first two paragraphs of the novella excerpt (lines 1–17). Then have them look at the text and images on this page. Ask students how Gregor's reaction differs from his reaction in the beginning of the novella. Then ask them to cite text evidence. (*Students may note that in the novella, Gregor sounds confused but not too surprised. In the graphic novel, his first reaction is one of shock, which is evident in the surprised look on his face and in the way he stutters in the thought balloon.*)

Analyze Representations in Different Mediums

COMMON CORE RL 7

Point out that when adapting a text to a visual medium, such as a graphic novel, the graphic novelist creates images of key scenes in the plot to show what the writer created through words.

C ASK STUDENTS whether Kuper does an effective job of depicting Gregor's room as "a proper human room" that "lays peacefully between its four familiar walls." Ask students to use details from the image to support their responses. (*Possible answer: The dresser, bookcase, curtains and decorations make it look like a person's bedroom.*) Ask whether the room is as peaceful as Kafka describes it, or does it create a different tone. Have students explain, using evidence from the text. (*Possible answer: The room is neat and orderly, which could suggest it's peaceful; but it's also very dark, which creates a serious tone.*)

108   Collection 3

SCAFFOLDING FOR ELL STUDENTS

Analyze How an Author Draws on Source Material Using a whiteboard, project the first page of the graphic novel. Ask a volunteer to circle the thought balloon. Ask volunteers to explain what Gregor is feeling and to tell how they know. (*Gregor is upset. He stutters in his thoughts. Instead of thinking "What," he thinks "W-what's..."*)

ASK STUDENTS to explain why Kuper chose to change this from the original. (*Because this is a graphic novel, Kuper wanted to show that Gregor was upset and not just tell about it.*)

But that was out of the question. Gregor was used to sleeping on his right side and in his present condition it was impossible to get into that position.

CLOSE READ

Support Inferences About Character

 COMMON CORE **RL 1, RL 3**

Remind students that an inference is a conclusion a reader draws from evidence in the text.

D **CITE TEXT EVIDENCE** Ask students to reread the thought balloon at the top of the page. Tell them to consider what Gregor's thought says about Gregor's character. Ask them what they can infer about how Gregor deals with difficult issues in his life and to cite text evidence. *(Possible answer: Gregor prefers to hide from his problems and avoid confronting them. In the first panel on this page, Gregor decides to go back to sleep and hopes his problem goes away.)*

Analyze Representations in Different Mediums

COMMON CORE **RL 7**

Tell students that a graphic novelist uses different methods to differentiate among dialogue, characters' thoughts, and narrative description.

E **ASK STUDENTS** to look at the different ways text is presented on this page. Ask them how they can tell the difference between information in Kuper's general narrative description and what he attributes to Gregor. *(Gregor's thoughts are shown in thought balloons. Narrative description is presented as white text on a black background.)* Ask students to explain what the narrative description on this page adds to their understanding of the story. *(Possible answer: The narrative description explains the eight panels that show Gregor trying to reposition himself in bed.)*

WHEN STUDENTS STRUGGLE . . .

To help students understand the often fragmented language used in speech and thought balloons in the graphic novel, read aloud the last two thought balloons on the page ("What an exhausting job …") and have students repeat after you. Explain to students that Gregor is using an uncommon sentence structure to express his thought. Guide students to identify the subject of this sentence. *("Being a traveling salesman")* Then have students rewrite the sentence in a more conventional pattern where the subject is expressed first. *(Possible response: Being a traveling salesman is an exhausting job.)*

Summarize a Text

COMMON CORE RL 2

Tell students that summarizing parts of a text not only helps them understand what they're reading, but it can also help them understand larger ideas the author might be trying to express.

 ASK STUDENTS to summarize what is happening on this page. *(Gregor is recalling how his job consumes his life, and day after day it is the exact same experience of stress and alienation.)*

Support Inferences About Theme

COMMON CORE RL 2

Remind students that a theme in a story is often a message about life or human nature that an author tries to convey.

G **ASK STUDENTS** to study the page, think about their summary, and state what theme the author may be trying to establish. Ask them to pay particular attention to how the graphic elements contribute to this theme. *(Possible answer: The daily stress of life can leave a person feeling alienated, or disconnected from people. Gregor's daily life has him increasingly feeling cut off from the rest of humanity.* Then ask students to explain how the graphic elements contribute to this theme. *(Possible answer: The frames show Gregor frantic or sad; two of the frames show him alone; in the only frame with another person, that person is clearly not happy to see Gregor. The individual frames are separated, which shows a lack of connection that reflects Gregor's lack of connection to people and his life.)*

WHEN STUDENTS STRUGGLE . . .

Help Spanish-speaking ELL students understand the word *parade*. Explain that this is a false cognate. In Spanish, the word *parada* means "a scheduled stop," as in a bus stop. Explain that this is very different from the idea Kuper is expressing.

ASK STUDENTS to explain what the word *parade* means as used here. Ask them to use clues from the page to support their answers. *(Here, "parade" means a line of things that go by. It refers to the faces that pass by Gregor every day. Gregor sees the faces but makes no connection with the people he constantly meets in his job.)* Have students verify their definition in a dictionary.

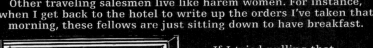

The Metamorphosis **111**

Determine the Meaning of Words

COMMON CORE **RL 4**

Point out the word *predicament* in the last thought balloon. Remind students that readers can determine the meaning of an unknown word by examining the context in which the word appears.

 ASK STUDENTS what the word *predicament* means and which clues on the page help them determine the meaning. *("Predicament" means "a difficult situation." Gregor's thoughts state that he'd have "quit long ago" if not for his parents' predicament, so it must mean a problem. It possibly involves money, and that would explain Gregor continuing to work at a job he dislikes so much.)*

Support Inferences About Theme

COMMON CORE **RL 1, RL 2**

Remind students that writers develop themes over the course of a piece of work.

 CITE TEXT EVIDENCE Have students think about the theme they inferred when responding on page 110. Tell them to think about how this page supports that theme. Then ask them to tell how Kuper uses graphic elements here to further support that theme and to cite evidence on the page. *(Possible answer: The theme that the daily stress of life can leave a person feeling alienated, or disconnected from people, is continued on this page. In the middle frame, Gregor climbs the stairs alone and in darkness. He is not interacting with the two laughing men who look comfortable in the brightly lit room.)*

WHEN STUDENTS STRUGGLE . . .

Students may find the structure of the frames on these two pages challenging and might struggle with the brief backward shift in time. Ask them to identify the character in the hat. *(Gregor, before he became an insect)* Ask students when the scene in the middle panel happened and to cite evidence on the page. *(It must have happened at a previous time because in the story Gregor has already been transformed. The panel shows Gregor as a human.)*

CLOSE READ

Analyze Word Choice
COMMON CORE RL 3, RL 4

Remind students that writers choose words to convey specific information about characters and setting.

J **ASK STUDENTS** to read the bottom panel and focus on the word *marched*. Ask students to consider why Kuper chose that word instead of another option, such as *walked* or *strolled*. Ask students to explain how the word *marched* reflects Gregor's feelings at this point. *("Marched" has a strong connotation, suggesting someone is walking swiftly and with a specific purpose. This reflects how Gregor imagines confronting his boss.)* Have students explain what Kuper wants the reader to understand about Gregor in this panel. *(Possible answer: Kuper wants the reader to know that Gregor might imagine marching up to his boss and wagging his finger in his boss's face, but he is too meek to stand up for himself or even get out of bed.)*

Analyze Idioms
COMMON CORE RL 4

Remind students that idioms are nonliteral expressions; that is, the meaning of the expression doesn't match the combined dictionary definitions of the words. Explain that idioms might be common to an entire language or particular to a specific geographic region. Explain that readers can use context to figure out the meaning of an idiom.

K **ASK STUDENTS** to explain the idioms *a piece of my mind* and *from the bottom of my heart*. *(To give someone a piece of your mind means to tell them exactly what you are thinking. To say something from the bottom of your heart means you are speaking sincerely.)* Ask students to point to clues in the panel that helped them with the meanings of the idioms. *(Gregor is shown towering over his tiny boss. He is pointing his left index finger and waving his arm at his boss. His mouth is open and he is yelling. He is holding his right hand near his heart.)*

SCAFFOLDING FOR ELL STUDENTS

Analyze Idioms Point out the phrase *talks down to*. Explain that while the image shows this can be read literally, the phrase also has a figurative meaning. Tell students to use context to figure out the meaning of this phrase.

ASK STUDENTS what the phrase *talks down to* means. *(If you talk down to someone, you are treating them like they are lower, or less important, than you.)* Ask students to explain how knowing the meaning helps them understand Gregor's relationship with his boss. *(Gregor's boss does not have any respect for Gregor or the other employees and treats them as inferiors.)* Have students verify their definition in a dictionary or idiom dictionary.

CLOSE READ

Analyze Representations in Different Mediums

COMMON CORE RL 1, RL 7

Remind students that writers make choices depending on the medium they are working with.

L **CITE TEXT EVIDENCE** Ask students to read lines 53–57 in the novella and then compare Kafka's prose to Kuper's text and image in the first half of this page. Have students explain whether the image on this page supports Gregor's claim in the novella that he still has hope. Ask them to cite evidence on the page. *(Possible answer: The image contrasts with Gregor's hope; it shows him barely keeping his head above the mass of dollars as they slip through the hourglass.)*

Support Inferences About Theme

COMMON CORE RL 1, RL 2

Remind students that they have already begun to discuss one theme of the story. Tell them that a story can have multiple themes.

M **ASK STUDENTS** to examine the images and text and consider another theme in the graphic novel. First, ask students to think about what is featured in the two panels. *(A time-keeping device is featured in each panel: The top shows an hourglass and the bottom shows a clock.)* Then ask how Gregor's reaction in each panel suggests a theme. *(Possible answer: The images suggest that people are at the mercy of time.)*

Analyze Characters

COMMON CORE RL 1, RL 3

Tell students that examining details in the images, in addition to examining what characters think and say, can help readers understand characters' traits.

N **CITE TEXT EVIDENCE** Ask students to cite text evidence about what the hourglass tells about Gregor. *(Possible answer: Gregor is shown almost drowning in the hourglass. He is as helpless in the image as he is lying in bed with time passing. In fact, time has run out in the bottom panel. According to the clock, Gregor is almost two hours late for his 5 A.M. train.)*

CLOSE READ

Determine Figurative Meanings

COMMON CORE RL 1, RL 4

Remind students that figurative language includes similes (comparisons using *like* or *as*) and metaphors (direct comparisons, which do not use *like* or *as*).

O **CITE TEXT EVIDENCE** Ask students to find an example of a simile and a metaphor on the page. Ask students to explain the meaning of the two phrases and how they enhance their understanding. *("Ear-splitting ringing" is a metaphor. It suggests that the ringing of the alarm clock is extremely loud—loud enough to split an ear. This phrase shows that Gregor was sleeping so deeply that even a loud alarm couldn't wake him. "Run like mad" is a simile. It means to run in a panicked or frantic manner. This phrase makes the reader imagine Gregor running frantically for the train, which he can hardly do in his transformed state.)*

Analyze Representations in Different Mediums

COMMON CORE RL 7

Remind students that Kuper's work graphically depicts Kafka's novella while exhibiting choices about what to include and how to move the action along.

P **ASK STUDENTS** to reread (lines 59–70) of Kafka's novella. Ask students to explain how Kuper expresses Gregor's thoughts from the novella through graphic elements on this page. *(Possible answer: Kuper puts Gregor's thoughts into sentences, each placed into a separate box. This creates the effect of Gregor's thoughts coming to him in isolated bursts.)* Ask students to explain the presence of the clock and what it represents. *(Possible answer: Kuper included the clock as a symbol of oppression for Gregor. It is looming over Gregor with bold circles coming out of it, as if it's trying to compel him to get up.)*

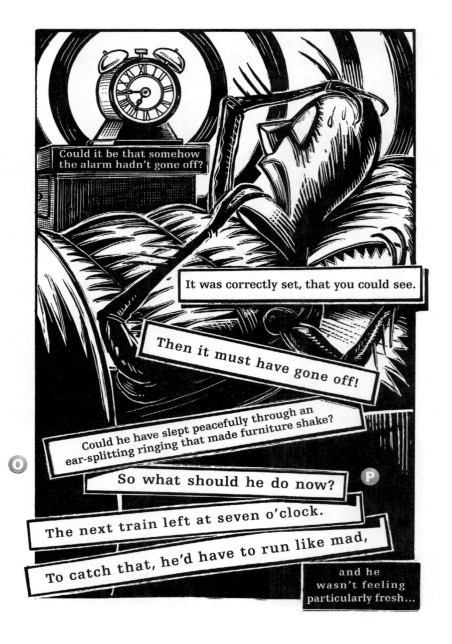

WHEN STUDENTS STRUGGLE . . .

To help students with multiple-meaning words, point out *fresh* at the bottom of this page. They may think of fresh as it relates to food, meaning food that is not stale or rotten.

ASK STUDENTS to explain what *fresh* means here and how the context supports this meaning. *(Here it means "rested" or "full of energy." Gregor is saying he couldn't catch the train because he's not feeling energetic enough.)* Have students verify their definition in a dictionary.

What if he were to call in sick?

But that would be quite awkward and suspicious,

since Gregor had not been ill even once in the last five years on the job.

The boss would no doubt show up with a health-insurance doctor, and use his diagnosis to dismiss all excuses and blame Gregor's parents for their son's laziness!

GREGOR?

The Metamorphosis **115**

CLOSE READ

Analyze Representations in Different Mediums

 COMMON CORE **RL 7**

Remind students that a prose piece and a graphic novel each has its own strengths.

Q **ASK STUDENTS** to reread lines 75–81 of Kafka's novella and this page. Then have students describe the strengths of both mediums in portraying Gregor's worries about calling in sick. *(Possible answer: Kafka's prose lays out Gregor's thought process about why calling in sick would be a bad idea. It is simple, straightforward, and unambiguous. Kuper uses almost the same language, but he enhances it with graphic elements. He formats key ideas on the page in different sizes, using large text when presenting Gregor's logical thoughts and small text when presenting thoughts that don't make sense. This suggests that Gregor isn't thinking rationally. Kuper's formatting of text around the clock face and his depiction of Gregor running clockwise inside are powerful images suggesting Gregor's struggle to keep up in his job.)*

Support Inferences About Theme

 COMMON CORE **RL 2**

Ask students to continue to look for events and ideas that suggest a theme or themes.

R **ASK STUDENTS** whether the image of the clock face here supports the theme that they suggested when they discussed the image of the hourglass on page 113. *(Possible answer: The image of Gregor running around the clock face supports the idea that people are at the mercy of time.)*

WHEN STUDENTS STRUGGLE . . .

To help students with unfamiliar words, point out the word *laziness* on the page. Have students determine the word's meaning by using context clues and looking for a familiar root in the word.

ASK STUDENTS how they determined the word's meaning. *(Possible answer: "Laziness" means "not willing to do work." Knowing the word "lazy" helped to determine the meaning. The context of the boss suggesting Gregor is faking being sick supports the definition.)* Have students verify their definition in a dictionary.

Analyze Representations in Different Mediums

COMMON CORE RL 7

Remind students that Kuper's graphic novel presents speech and thoughts in ways other than inside quotation marks.

S **ASK STUDENTS** to examine the speech balloons for each character and what each character says. Ask students to explain how Kuper graphically uses the speech balloons. *(The mother's dialogue balloon has gentle, decorative swirls, which reflects her gentle speaking. She must be speaking softly because Kuper uses small type for her words. Gregor's dialogue balloon has very uneven, jagged edges, and his words are written in jagged type, which reflects how shaky and shrill he must sound.)*

Support Inferences About Theme

COMMON CORE RL 2

Remind students that writers often convey a message about life in the themes they develop.

T **ASK STUDENTS** to recall the theme they discussed on pages 110 and 111, that the daily stress of life can leave a person feeling alienated or disconnected from people. Ask students to explain whether this page supports that theme. *(Possible answer: The thick, white diagonal line separating Gregor from his mother supports the theme of people being alienated from other human beings.)*

WHEN STUDENTS STRUGGLE...

Students may be unfamiliar with the word *garbled*. Explain that knowing what this word means is important to understanding what Gregor's voice sounds like to others. Tell students that the word is an example of onomatopoeia. Explain that onomatopoeia refers to words that reflect the sounds associated with them. For example, *boom* and *buzz* both sound like what they represent. Have students share the meaning of *garbled* and explain how it relates to Gregor's speech.

The change in Gregor's voice must have been muffled by the wooden door because his mother was reassured and shuffled off. However, their little exchange made his father and sister aware that Gregor had not, as they assumed, left for work.

GREGOR, GREGOR— what's going on?

GREGOR!

Gregor, it's Grete, are you alright?

Do you need anything?

Please, Gregor, open the door.

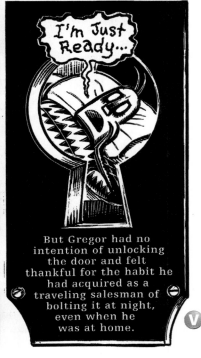

I'm Just Ready...

But Gregor had no intention of unlocking the door and felt thankful for the habit he had acquired as a traveling salesman of bolting it at night, even when he was at home.

The Metamorphosis **117**

Analyze Characters

COMMON CORE RL 3, RL 7

Tell students to notice what characters do and say as a way of understanding their relationships to other characters.

U **ASK STUDENTS** to explain the difference between how Gregor's father and sister interact with him and what graphic elements Kuper uses to reflect the difference. (*The father pounds on the door and demands to know what is going on; Kuper uses bold print and all caps and a thick jagged border for his speech balloon, reflecting his loudness and aggression. Gregor's sister asks if Gregor is well and asks him to please open the door. Kuper uses normal print and a dotted border for her speech balloon, reflecting her concern and softer tone.*)

Support Inferences About Characters

COMMON CORE RL 1, RL 3

Remind students to continue to make inferences about characters based on their actions and how they interact with others.

V **CITE TEXT EVIDENCE** Ask students to make an inference about how Gregor feels about his family based on information in the text. (*Possible answer: Gregor doesn't entirely trust his family because he bolts his door every night and "even . . . at home."*)

CLOSE READ

Analyze Representations in Different Mediums

COMMON CORE RL 1, RL 7

Remind students to continue to notice the differences in treatment of the same story, such as how the writers depict point of view.

W ASK STUDENTS to explain the point of view of Kafka's novella. *(It is written in third-person limited point of view. This means that the reader knows only what Gregor himself knows.)* Ask students to explain what advantage readers might have when reading Kuper's graphic novel that they might not have when reading Kafka's novella. Ask students to use a specific detail from this page for support. *(Possible answer: Kafka says that Gregor does not know what the lower part of his body looks like [lines 139–140]. Kuper has drawn Gregor's body, so the reader can clearly see what it looks like and can more clearly understand why Gregor is struggling.)*

Remind students that the novella and the graphic novel treat identical scenes differently and thereby achieve different effects.

X CITE TEXT EVIDENCE Direct students to lines 138–171 of the novella. Ask students to explain how Kuper's depiction of Gregor's efforts to get out of bed compares to Kafka's description. Ask students to cite text evidence. *(Possible answer: Kafka shows Gregor's struggles in a lengthy description of how Gregor tries to first move his lower body [lines 138–145] and then his upper body [lines 146–154] out of bed. Kuper focuses on the strongest details from Kafka's description to show Gregor's pain and awkwardness as he tries to get each end of his body out of bed. Kuper does an effective job using a minimum of text and three key drawings that show Gregor grimacing in pain, teetering on the edge of his bed, and back where he started—on his back.)*

WHEN STUDENTS STRUGGLE . . .

To understand Gregor's character, it's important to understand his motivations and how he faces conflict or difficult circumstances. Point out how Gregor thinks his problem might be that he's getting a bad cold, and that things might improve if he just gets up and has a good breakfast. Ask students what this says about how Gregor is dealing with his problem. *(He isn't dealing with it; he's denying what has happened to him.)* Have students find another example on this page that supports the idea that Gregor is not dealing well with his problem. *("Back where he started, he lay there expecting, perhaps, that everything would return to normal.")*

The Metamorphosis **119**

CLOSE READ

Analyze Author's Choices: RL 5
Tension and Suspense

Explain that writers can create mood in a number of ways, including the pacing of events. Writers can speed up or slow down the action to create a desired effect.

Y **ASK STUDENTS** to explain the action on this page and how the pacing affects the mood. *(There is little text on the page and almost no action. Gregor is lying in one position, thinking he should get up, but he doesn't move. Kuper has slowed the pacing with images of an immobilized Gregor. This creates tension and suspense about whether Gregor is going to be able to get up.)*

Analyze Representations COMMON CORE RL 1, RL 7
in Different Mediums

Explain to students that when a writer adapts a work, he or she might place greater or lesser emphasis on scenes or aspects of the original story.

Z **CITE TEXT EVIDENCE** Direct students to line 199 in the novella. Ask students to explain which writer placed greater emphasis on the arrival of the chief clerk and how this was achieved. Have students cite text evidence. *(Kuper places greater emphasis on the chief clerk's arrival. Kafka states it matter-of-factly: "Then there was a ring at the door of the flat." Kuper depicts a slowly paced scene suddenly interrupted by "RING" in all caps and jagged type in a speech balloon at the bottom corner of the page.)*

Analyze Representations in Different Mediums

COMMON CORE RL 1, RL 7

Ask students to continue to notice differences between how the story is treated in different mediums.

A2 ASK STUDENTS to reread Kafka's description of Gregor's reaction to the chief clerk's presence (lines 207–218). Ask students to explain how Kuper adapts this scene and whether it is more or less effective than the novella. *(Possible answer: Kuper replaces Kafka's lengthy description of Gregor's reaction with drawings of the chief clerk and Gregor worrying in bed. Kuper is effective at portraying the chief clerk as a man of importance. He is neatly dressed in a suit and hat and carries a briefcase and cane.)* Ask students to point out a graphic element, one that could not have been used in Kafka's novella, that gives a clue about the chief clerk. *(The chief clerk's speech balloon is a square with plain, neat type. This suggests he's an orderly man.)*

Ask students to continue to notice how an adaptation places greater or lesser emphasis on aspects of the original story.

B2 CITE TEXT EVIDENCE Ask students to reread lines 218–225 of the novella. Have them compare its effectiveness to the comparable scene on this page and to cite text evidence. *(Possible answer: Kafka states, "There was a loud thump, but it wasn't really a loud noise." The scene continues from Gregor's point of view. Kuper makes the moment more dramatic by shifting the point of view away from Gregor to the action at the apartment door, where the chief clerk is introducing himself to Gregor's mother. Kuper shows a large "THUMP!" in capital letters at the corner of the panel. The chief clerk's introduction is cut off mid-sentence by the sound. Motion lines around Gregor's mother's head suggest she rapidly turns her head at the sound. This scene is more effective than Kafka's description.)*

120 Collection 3

CLOSE READ

Analyze Characters

COMMON CORE RL 1, RL 3

Ask students to continue to examine what characters say, do, and how they are drawn in order to gain insight to them.

C2 **CITE TEXT EVIDENCE** Ask students to explain what they can learn about Gregor through his response to the chief clerk's request that he open the door. Have students cite text evidence from either the novella or the graphic novel. *(Possible answer: Gregor has not shown much inclination to challenge authority, but he replies "No" to a request from the chief clerk. Since Gregor was in a position from which he could not open the door, he could have replied, "I can't." Instead, he's shown to be defiant. It could be that both Kafka and Kuper want to show that Gregor has decided to stand up to authority after all.)*

WHEN STUDENTS STRUGGLE . . .

Remind students that in a graphic novel, the images are as important to telling a story and sharing information as the text. Have students look at the two top panels and examine each character's face. Then, relying only on the images, have them write a brief explanation of what the chief clerk, Gregor's sister, and Gregor's mother are feeling in this scene. Remind them to cite text evidence. *(The chief clerk is frustrated and impatient. His lips are closed tight in the first panel and then his mouth is open with an angry look as he pounds the door and calls to Gregor. Gregor's sister looks concerned and worried. Her eyes look sad and her hand is at her mouth. Gregor's mother looks afraid and worried. Her eyes are wide, and she looks frightened with her hand up to her mouth).*

CLOSE READ

Analyze Word Choice

COMMON CORE RL 4

Ask students to notice Kuper's word choices and treatments and how they affect the reader's understanding.

D2 **ASK STUDENTS** to point out the words that are emphasized in this panel, how Kuper emphasized them, and why he chose these particular words for special treatment. *(Kuper emphasizes "shocking" and "astonished." Kuper repeats them in capital letters immediately after they appear in regular type. Kuper may have wanted to show that the chief clerk can't believe that Gregor refuses to open the door and come to work.)* Ask students to explain how these words help to develop the character of the chief clerk. *(Possible answer: The chief clerk is "astonished" and finds Gregor's behavior "shocking" because he is clearly accustomed to having his requests immediately obeyed.)*

Support Inferences About Characters

COMMON CORE RL 1, RL 3

Remind students they can make inferences about characters based on how they look, how they act, and the way they interact with other characters.

E2 **CITE TEXT EVIDENCE** Ask students to make an inference about how the men and the women feel about Gregor based on details in the panel. Have students cite text evidence. *(Possible response: The women seem to be more caring and concerned. Gregor's sister is crying, and his mother is clutching her hands together, showing anguish over her son's behavior. The men appear angry and impatient. Gregor's father's face is distorted and sweating. His teeth and fist are clenched. The chief clerk is open-mouthed as he yells through the door. The fact that he is pounding when Gregor could actually be sick shows a lack of concern for Gregor's well-being.)*

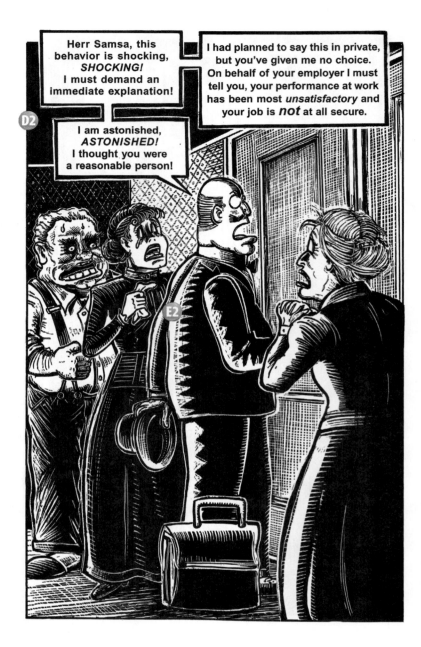

SCAFFOLDING FOR ELL STUDENTS

Analyze Word Choice Using a whiteboard, project page 122 of the graphic novel. Invite volunteers to underline the word *unsatisfactory*.

ASK STUDENTS what the word *satisfactory* means. *("acceptable")* Then ask what the prefix *un-* means. *("not")* Then ask students to tell what the word *unsatisfactory* means. *("not acceptable")* Then have students discuss why this is an appropriate word to describe how Gregor's employer views him. *(The chief clerk states that Gregor's job is not secure. The reason he gives is that Gregor's performance at work has not been acceptable.)* Have students verify their definition in a dictionary.

CLOSE READ

Analyze Representations in Different Mediums

COMMON CORE RL 7

Explain that in a prose medium, such as a novella, an author can provide deep insight into a character by telling the character's thoughts. A graphic novelist usually does not include as much text, so there may be limited sharing of a character's thoughts.

F2 **ASK STUDENTS** to reread lines 322–332 of the novella. Ask students what is happening in this passage. *(Gregor is having an interior monologue, or a silent discussion with himself.)* Have students compare the scene in the novella with the scene on this page. Ask students to tell whether they get insight into Gregor's feelings or state of mind. *(Possible answer: Other than the look of concern, maybe even fear on Gregor's face, the reader does not get the detailed insight that Kafka provides. In the novella, we see that Gregor really wants to open the door, but that is not apparent in Kuper's work.)* Ask students to explain how the difference in these scenes changes their experience as readers. *(Possible answer: You see Gregor differently in each work. Kafka's Gregor wants to open the door and get it over with. Kuper's Gregor is still avoiding facing his problems. Readers might feel more sympathetic toward Kafka's Gregor at this point.)*

WHEN STUDENTS STRUGGLE . . .

To help students understand the phrase *felt off,* ask them to look for context clues on the page.

ASK STUDENTS to explain the phrase *felt off* and cite which clues on the page helped them understand its meaning. *(The phrase "felt off" means "did not feel well." Gregor says he "just had a bit of a dizzy spell," which is a sick feeling.)* Have students explain what Gregor is telling the chief clerk to do. *(Gregor is trying to convince the chief clerk to tell his boss that he was feeling sick yesterday, but now he is fine and will catch the eight-o'clock train for work.)*

CLOSE READ

Analyze Representations in Different Mediums

COMMON CORE RL 7

Remind students that in a prose piece, such as a novella, the writer represents speech in lines of dialogue. Characters are identified by name, and what they say is placed inside quotation marks. This practice helps readers keep track of what each character says, especially in scenes involving three or more characters. Explain that graphic novelists might treat speech differently.

G2 **ASK STUDENTS** to tell how many characters and speakers are on this page and where they are located. *(Gregor is shown inside his room. He isn't speaking since his speech balloon shows only his thoughts. Three speakers are on the other side of the door.)* Ask students to identify the characters speaking from the other side of the door by panel and to explain how they know. *(Clockwise from top left, speakers are the chief clerk, Gregor's father, Gregor thinking, and Gregor's mother. Kuper has already established different types and borders for each character's speech balloon, so the type of speech balloons here let the reader know which characters are speaking.)*

TO CHALLENGE STUDENTS . . .

Have students compare this page to the comparable scenes in the novella (lines 340–384). Tell them to consider how the pacing in this sequence differs between the novella and the graphic novel. Have them write a short essay explaining which representation they feel is stronger and better suits the story. Remind them to use details from each selection in their writing. As an added challenge, have the students adapt Kuper's depiction to text form, trying to capture the much quicker pacing in the graphic novel's sequence.

COLLABORATIVE DISCUSSION With a partner, discuss the text and graphic details that help you infer Gregor's state of mind. Cite specific textual and visual evidence from the story to support your ideas.

CLOSE READ

Analyze How an Author Draws on Source Material
COMMON CORE RL 3, RL 9

Ask students to continue to notice how Kuper has treated source material from Kafka.

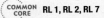 **ASK STUDENTS** to compare the scene in lines 385–391 of the novella to pages 124 and 125 of the graphic novel. Ask students to explain Kuper's treatment. *(Kafka and Kuper both capture how painful it is for Gregor to open the door. In the novella, Gregor keeps turning the key even though it injures his mouth. The narration states that Gregor keeps trying because he believes that his family understands his difficulty and supports his endeavor. Readers don't get this insight in the graphic novel. Gregor is shown turning the key and opening the door. Kuper might not have wanted the reader to be concerned with Gregor's motivations. Kuper might have been more concerned with moving the story along by revealing Gregor's transformed state to the characters on the other side of the door.)*

Support Inferences About Theme
COMMON CORE RL 1, RL 2, RL 7

Remind students that writers convey messages about life with the themes they develop in a work.

I2 **CITE TEXT EVIDENCE** Ask students to recall the theme they inferred earlier (the daily stress of life can leave a person feeling alienated from others). Ask them to explain and cite text evidence to support whether the characters' reaction to Gregor in both mediums supports or contradicts this theme. *(Their reaction supports this theme in both mediums. In the novella, the characters move away from Gregor "as if driven by a steady and invisible force." In the graphic novel, we see the characters recoiling in horror instead of moving forward to help. In both works, the door and Gregor's transformed state are symbols of alienation.)*

COLLABORATIVE DISCUSSION Have partners share the text evidence that helped them make their inference about Gregor's state of mind.

ASK STUDENTS to share questions they generated in the course of reading and discussions.

PRACTICE & APPLY

Analyze Representations in Different Mediums RL 7

Provide students with examples of how different artists use their mediums to present ideas. A writer uses description to give insight into a character's thoughts. A graphic artist relies heavily on images, text treatment, layout, color, and shades to create their stories.

Analyzing the Text RL 1, RL 2, RL 3, RL 4, RL 5, RL 7, RL 9

Possible answers:

1. *In depicting how Gregor's boss interacts with Gregor, Kuper draws the size of the characters in proportion to the forcefulness of their actions. To show the boss "talking down" to his employees, Kuper draws him as a giant, making him look mean and aggressive as he points a finger at tiny Gregor's chest. To show Gregor imagining a confrontation with his boss, the sizes change—Gregor becomes the giant, wagging a finger at his tiny, cowering boss.*

2. *Students may claim that Kuper does a good job transforming Kafka's work into a new medium. He uses less language but includes key events and distills dialogue and description to their essence. His graphic treatment is effective, capturing Kafka's lengthy descriptions in a frame or two.*

3. *Students should note that the novella and graphic novel both take place over the course of a morning, but the pacing is different. Kafka uses lengthy descriptions of Gregor's thoughts and what happens in and around the room, whereas Kuper picks up the pace at key points (just before Gregor opens the door), depicting events quickly. Each selection shares the theme that while people try to control time with clocks and hourglasses and train timetables, people are at time's mercy.*

4. *Kuper's graphic novel is Kafkaesque. Gregor's room is shown as very dark; the characters' faces are often shown in emotional anguish; the image of Gregor being sucked through the hourglass shows he has no control; visuals such as the enlarged boss and Gregor running around a clock face show a distorted sense of reality.*

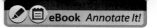

Analyze Representations in Different Mediums RL 7

The graphic artist Peter Kuper and the writer Franz Kafka use the strengths of different **mediums**, or forms, to convey similar ideas. For instance, early in the graphic novel eight small panels show Gregor's struggles to get into a comfortable position. In his novella, Kafka conveys this scene in paragraph three, stating that Gregor "must have tried it a hundred times" ("it" being Gregor's attempts to find a comfortable position). The medium of writing allows us to understand Gregor's thoughts at this moment in ways that a visual medium could not. On the other hand, even Kafka's powers of description cannot give readers the clear visual image of Gregor's struggle that a few frames of Kuper's graphic novel can. As you compare these representations, keep in mind the strengths of both mediums.

Analyzing the Text  RL 1, RL 2, RL 7, SL 4

Cite Text Evidence Support your responses with evidence from the selections.

1. **Compare** Reread paragraph five of Kafka's story, and then consider Kuper's depiction of Gregor's interaction with his boss. How does Kuper transform Gregor's thoughts about the boss into images? In your response, use evidence to support your ideas about the strengths of each medium.

2. **Evaluate** Sometimes, Kuper uses Kafka's exact words, but often he leaves out the words in the novella. Using details from both works, explain whether Kuper's use of language is effective in transforming the novella into a new work. Consider Kuper's graphic treatment of words in your explanation.

3. **Compare** Like Kafka, Kuper manipulates time to create tension. How are the graphic novel and story alike and different in their treatment of time? How does the idea of time figure into the story's theme in both works?

4. **Critique** The literary term *Kafkaesque* describes a distorted and oppressive sense of reality. Based on your careful reading of both works, is Kuper's graphic novel Kafkaesque? Use evidence from both works to support your ideas.

PERFORMANCE TASK

Speaking Activity: Comparison How does the graphic novel expand on the ideas in Kafka's version of "The Metamorphosis"? Choose one page of the graphic novel to compare with the source text in a short speech.

- Identify the page of the graphic novel that is closest to or furthest from what you visualized as you read the novella. Complete a Venn diagram comparing the page you chose with the same part of the written story.

- In a speech, explain how Kuper interprets an idea from Kafka's story and evaluate how effectively the page you chose communicates Kafka's ideas. Show the page to facilitate your explanation.

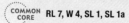

Assign this performance task.

PERFORMANCE TASK RL 7, W 4, SL 1, SL 1a

Speaking Activity: Comparison Have students work in pairs or small groups. Encourage them to consider a scene from the graphic novel that includes experimental elements, or one that may provide a noticeably different interpretation of Kafka's comparable scene.

Critical Vocabulary

vermin   subordinate   plaintively   enunciate

Practice and Apply Create a semantic map for each of the Critical Vocabulary words listed above. Use a dictionary or thesaurus as needed. The example is for a word appearing on line 164 of the novella.

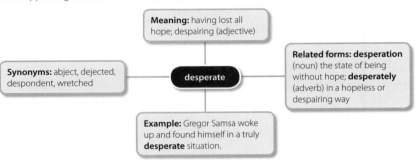

Meaning: having lost all hope; despairing (adjective)

Synonyms: abject, dejected, despondent, wretched

desperate

Related forms: desperation (noun) the state of being without hope; **desperately** (adverb) in a hopeless or despairing way

Example: Gregor Samsa woke up and found himself in a truly **desperate** situation.

Vocabulary Strategy: Verifying Word Meanings

When you encounter an unfamiliar word in your reading, you can often make an inference or educated guess about the word's meaning using context clues from the text. For example, in the first paragraph of the novella, the author uses the Critical Vocabulary word *vermin*. As you read, you can use context clues such as "stiff sections" and "many legs" to infer that *vermin* may refer to an insect. Since this word is so central to understanding Gregor's situation, you might want to verify that inferred meaning by reading further or by checking a dictionary.

Practice and Apply Practice this strategy by choosing three unfamiliar words from "The Metamorphosis." Verify their meanings using both context clues from the story and a reference source. For each word, follow these steps:

1. Copy the sentence in which the word is used.

2. Using only the context of that sentence, write down what you think the word means in your own words. (Do not use a dictionary at this point.)

3. Return to the story and find context clues in the surrounding sentences that support your inferred meaning. List them under your definition. If you find clues that suggest the word may have a different meaning, list those as well. Then, revise your definition as needed.

4. Finally, use a dictionary to verify the meaning of the word. How similar was your definition to the dictionary definition?

Critical Vocabulary

vermin
meaning: *creatures considered destructive, annoying, or repulsive; pests (noun);* **related forms:** *none;* **example:** *Too much garbage in the alley attracts vermin.* **synonyms:** *pests, rats, insects*

subordinate
meaning: *a person of lesser rank or under another's authority (noun);* **related forms:** *subordinately, subordination;* **example:** *Gregor's boss expected his subordinates to do whatever they were told.* **synonyms:** *inferior*

plaintively
meaning: *sadly or wistfully (adverb);* **related forms:** *plaintive, plaintiveness;* **example:** *Gregor's sister spoke plaintively because she was so worried about him.* **synonyms:** *achingly, sorrowfully*

enunciate
meaning: *to articulate or pronounce clearly (verb);* **related forms:** *enunciation;* **example:** *To make sure he was understood, Gregor enunciated each word as he spoke.* **synonyms:** *pronounce*

Vocabulary Strategy: Verifying Word Meanings

Students' answers will vary depending on the words they choose from the selection. An example of a word students might use is "strenuous" (line 28).

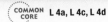

Verifying Word Meanings

Have students locate the three unfamiliar words in Kafka's text. Encourage them to use their eBook annotation tools to do the following:

- Highlight each unfamiliar word.
- Using a note, add what you think the word means.
- Reread the surrounding sentences, looking for clues to the word's meaning. Underline any clues you find, such as examples, synonyms, or antonyms.
- Add an additional note with the dictionary meaning.

"Oh, God," he thought, "what a strenuous career it is that I've chosen! Traveling day in and day out. Doing business like this takes much more effort than doing your own business at home, and on top of that there's the curse of traveling, worries about making train connections, bad and irregular food, contact with different people

PRACTICE & APPLY

Language and Style: Prepositional, Adjectival, and Adverbial Phrases

COMMON CORE   W 4, SL 1, L 1b

Explain to students that by using variety in their writing, they keep the writing from sounding repetitive, improve the flow of the language, and engage and maintain their listeners' and readers' attention. Using a variety of prepositional phrases is one way to connect and clarify ideas.

Students' revised comparison speeches should include three prepositional phrases, with at least one being adjectival and one being adverbial. They should be able to identify each phrase and explain what type of phrase it is.

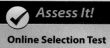

Assess It!

Online Selection Test
- Download an editable ExamView bank.
- Assign and manage this test online.

Language and Style: Prepositional, Adjectival, and Adverbial Phrases

COMMON CORE   W 4, SL 1, L 1b

Using a variety of phrases in your writing helps convey ideas and hold readers' interest. For example, prepositional phrases show readers the connections between key words in a sentence, clarifying *what kind, how many,* or *which one.* They can also tell *where, when,* and *how* something took place. In "The Metamorphosis," Franz Kafka uses prepositional phrases to help create a mood of tension and despair.

In the following sentence from the selection, the prepositional phrase tells *where* Gregor slid:

> He slid back <u>into his former position</u>.

Without the specificity this prepositional phrase adds, readers might be confused as to what is happening:

> He slid back.

By including the prepositional phrase *into his former position*, Kafka conveys the character's desperate situation.

A prepositional phrase used to modify a noun is called an **adjectival phrase;** one that modifies a verb is called an **adverbial phrase:**

Type of Phrase	Example of Usage
Adjectival Phrase—is a prepositional phrase that modifies a noun or pronoun. In the example to the right, *in the graphic novel* is the adjectival phrase because it modifies the noun *depiction.*	Gregor Samsa's depiction *in the graphic novel* is very haunting.
Adverbial Phrase—is a prepositional phrase that modifies a verb, adjective, or adverb. In the example, *in the very first paragraph* is the adverbial phrase because it modifies the verb *revealed.*	Is Gregor Samsa's true character revealed *in the very first paragraph*?

Practice and Apply Revisit the speech you wrote comparing the novella with the graphic novel in this selection's Performance Task. Add or change at least three prepositional phrases. Be sure to include at least one adjectival phrase and one adverbial phrase. In a small group, present your revised speech and discuss how each added or revised phrase improved the specificity and variety of your sentences.

Present Findings

TEACH

Before having students present their Performance Task speeches, discuss what's involved in creating and delivering a strong presentation. Tell them that when they present findings to an audience, they need to consider *how* they're presenting the information and *who* they're presenting to.

- **Structure:** Explain that there are a variety of organizational structures a presenter can use. Some of the more frequently used structures include Problem/Solution; Compare/Contrast; and Sequence. The key is determining which structure best fits the information to be presented.
- **Organization:** Have students determine how best to organize the information within the structure they choose. They might use a time sequence to show how something developed, or they might decide to organize the information in order of importance.
- **Style and Tone:** Students should consider whom they are addressing and what the audience knows. This determines how much background they will need to explain. Their audience also determines whether a formal or informal style is more appropriate.

PRACTICE AND APPLY

Tell students they will now determine how best to present the information in their Performance Task speech. They should start by identifying their task and to whom they are presenting the information. Then have them consider the following:

- *What structure is most appropriate for the information?*
- *How should I organize my information within that structure?*
- *How much does the audience know about the topic? How much background do I need to provide?*
- *Does the speech require a formal or informal style?*

Have students work in groups to practice their presentations. Listeners should take notes on how easy the presentation is to follow, what is clear and what needs more explanation, and how appropriate the style is to the content and the audience.

 INTERACTIVE LESSON Have students complete the tutorials in this lesson: **Giving a Presentation**

Analyze Representations in Different Mediums

RETEACH

Explain that when writers adapt works into a different medium, they decide how to retell the story. Ask students to point out how Kuper adapts Kafka's characters and conflict into a new medium.

- Have students compare the scenes in which the chief clerk arrives. Ask students to explain Kuper's depiction of the scene. *(Kafka presents the scene matter-of-factly. Gregor does not seem stunned at the accusation of taking money. Kuper uses graphic elements to show that this is an intrusion [the bold, jagged "RING!"], and Gregor seems more upset than in the novella. Kuper might have illustrated the chief clerk's arrival to heighten the drama of the story.)*
- Ask students how Kuper's graphic novel emphasizes a central idea. *(Kuper's images of clocks [pages 113–115] emphasize the idea that time is ruling Gregor's life.)*

 LEVEL UP TUTORIALS Assign the following *Level Up* tutorial: **Characters and Conflict**

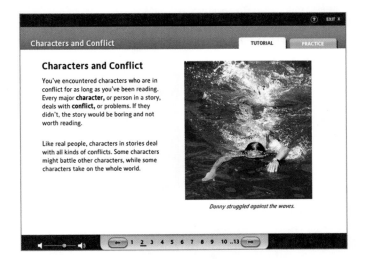

CLOSE READING APPLICATION

Have students apply the skill to other visual adaptations. Group students who have all read and then seen a film adaptation of the same book or story. Have groups list and discuss elements in which the film differs significantly from the original. Then have students work independently to write an explanation about how and why the screenwriter changed one or two scenes for the film.

The Starry Night

Painting by Vincent van Gogh

The Starry Night

Poem by Anne Sexton

Why These Texts

Students may view paintings without realizing that these, too, are texts that can be "read." Students may have difficulty analyzing the same subject or scene represented in two artistic mediums, such as in the painting *Starry Night* by Vincent van Gogh and the poem of the same name by Anne Sexton. Explain that what is emphasized or absent in each may be a clue to the meaning of the texts. With the help of the close-reading questions, students can draw inferences to compare the similarities and differences between the painting and the poem.

Background Have students read the background and the biographies of the artist Vincent van Gogh and the poet Anne Sexton. Introduce the two texts by telling students that Van Gogh is considered by art historians to be one of the most important modern painters and that today his paintings at auction would likely sell for more than 100 million dollars, as evidenced by the sale of his painting, *Portrait of Dr. Gachet*, that sold at auction for 82 million dollars in 1990.

AS YOU READ Ask students to pay close attention to the representation of the "starry night" scene in both the painting and the poem. After students read the poem, have them study the painting again.

Common Core Support

- cite textual evidence to support inferences
- analyze the representation of a subject or a key scene in two different artistic mediums

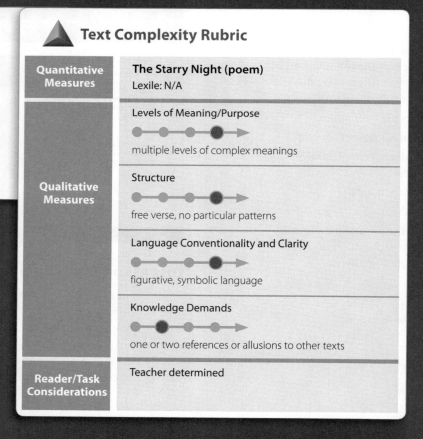

▲ Text Complexity Rubric

Quantitative Measures	**The Starry Night (poem)** Lexile: N/A
Qualitative Measures	Levels of Meaning/Purpose multiple levels of complex meanings
	Structure free verse, no particular patterns
	Language Conventionality and Clarity figurative, symbolic language
	Knowledge Demands one or two references or allusions to other texts
Reader/Task Considerations	Teacher determined

Strategies for CLOSE READING

Analyze Representation in Different Mediums

Students should view the painting closely and read the poem carefully all the way through. Close-reading questions at the bottom of the page will help them analyze the two representations of "The Starry Night." As they look at the painting and read the poem, students should record comments or questions in the side margins.

WHEN STUDENTS STRUGGLE . . .

To help students analyze the two representations in different mediums, have them work in small groups to complete a chart like the one shown below.

CITE TEXT EVIDENCE For practice in analyzing representation, ask students to cite specific evidence about what is emphasized or absent in each representation.

"Starry Night"	
Painting	*Poem*
The painting emphasizes the stars in the sky.	"Oh starry starry night!" (lines 8 and 14) "The night boils with eleven stars." (line 7) "They are all alive." (line 10)
In the painting, the village and trees are dark and subdued. The painting shows a whirling mass of colors and brightness in the sky, one that invokes awe.	"The town does not exist." (line 1) "The town is silent." (line 7) The poet compare the sky to a "rushing beast" (line 16) and a "great dragon." (line 17)

Background *In June 1889, Vincent van Gogh painted The Starry Night during a stay at an asylum in Saint-Remy, in southern France. The painting is of the view outside of his window, although the depiction of the village comes partly from van Gogh's imagination. The church spire resembles the architecture of the Netherlands, van Gogh's home. The Starry Night has been part of the permanent collection of the Museum of Modern Art in New York City since 1941. Almost a century later, Anne Sexton wrote her poem "The Starry Night" (based on van Gogh's painting). The poem opens with a quote from a letter from van Gogh to his brother Theo.*

The Starry Night

The Starry Night (painting) . . . . Vincent van Gogh
The Starry Night (poem) . . . . Anne Sexton

Vincent van Gogh *(1853–1890) was a Dutch impressionist artist. His first profession was as an art dealer, but he soon turned to making his own art. Between November 1881 and July 1890, van Gogh painted almost 900 paintings. He sold only one painting in the course of his life, but became one of the most famous and influential artists in history. Van Gogh suffered from mental illness and anxiety frequently throughout his life. At the age of 37, he died from a gunshot wound that most think was self-inflicted, although a gun was never found.*

Anne Sexton *(1928–1974) was an American poet born in Massachusetts. Married at 20, she worked for a time as a fashion model, gave birth to two children, and then, at age twenty-eight, began writing poetry. Known for her personal, confessional style, Sexton won the Pulitzer Prize for poetry in 1967. Like van Gogh, she spent time in several mental hospitals, and her poems often display a storm of emotions. Describing her own work, Sexton said, "Poetry should almost hurt."*

1. **READ** ▶ As you view the painting,

- write notes in the margin about what your eyes are drawn to first in the painting.
- locate the following images: cypress trees, stars, the moon, the village.

The Starry Night
by Vincent Van Gogh

The sky and the stars take over the village and seem to be in constant motion.

The Starry Night
Vincent van Gogh (Dutch, 1853–1890)
Saint Rémy, June 1889. Oil on canvas, 29 x 36 1/4" (73.7 x 92.1 cm).
Acquired through the Lillie P. Bliss Bequest

2. **◀ REREAD** Study the painting again. Then, consider this quote from van Gogh to his brother Theo: "Looking at the stars always makes me dream. Why, I ask myself, shouldn't the shining dots of the sky be as accessible as the black dots on the map of France?" In what ways does van Gogh make the stars accessible? In what ways do the stars contrast with the village?

The painting illustrates the energy of the stars in the sky, making them seem full of life. In contrast, the village seems quiet and still, and is dominated by the night sky. There is much more energy in the night sky than in the sleepy village.

48

3. **READ** ▶ As you read the poem, collect and cite text evidence.

- Underline imagery that relates to the stars and moon.
- Circle language that refers to the town.
- In the margin, make an inference about the night based on the language Sexton uses.

The Starry Night
by Anne Sexton

That does not keep me from having a terrible need of—I shall say the word—religion. Then I go out at night to paint the stars.
—Vincent Van Gogh in a letter to his brother

The town does not exist
5 except where one black-haired tree slips
up like a drowned woman into the hot sky.
The town is silent. The night boils with eleven stars.
Oh starry starry night! This is how
I want to die.

10 It moves. They are all alive.
Even the moon bulges in its orange irons
to push children, like a god, from its eye.
The old unseen serpent swallows up the stars.
Oh starry starry night! This is how
15 I want to die:

into that rushing beast of the night.
sucked up by that great dragon, to split
from my life with no flag,
no belly,
20 no cry.

The night is a "serpent," a "beast," a "dragon." The night is all-consuming and entices the speaker.

49

---

1. **READ AND CITE TEXT EVIDENCE**

A **ASK STUDENTS** to read and discuss their margin notes with a partner. *Students should support the idea that the whirling clouds and shining stars in the swirling sky create movement, drawing one's eyes to the top half of the painting first. The bright blue and yellow also draw one's eyes to the top half, where the energy in terms of composition is greatest.*

2. **REREAD AND CITE TEXT EVIDENCE**

B **ASK STUDENTS** to look at the painting in its entirety. Have them consider how the balance in form and color is achieved, and ask them to describe the painting based on their own impressions of it. *Students may say that the lighter colors at the top of the painting are anchored by the darkness below them; the wild sky is balanced by the unmoving landscape; the land and the sky are united by the cypress tree. Students may find the painting peaceful despite its action, or they may find it violent and forbidding.*

3. **READ AND CITE TEXT EVIDENCE** Sexton begins her poem with a passage from Van Gogh's letter to his brother, to show that her poem is based on his painting.

C **ASK STUDENTS** to share their margin notes with a partner. *Students should draw inferences from the text to suggest that Sexton is comparing the night that "boils" (line 7) to a "serpent" (line 13), a "beast" (line 16), and a "great dragon" (line 17), producing images of the night as a devouring creature.*

FOR ELL STUDENTS Explain that *its* (lines 11, 12) is often mistaken for *it's*, a contraction for "it is." Ask students if they know what *its* means, and if they know to what it is referring in the poem. *Students should recognize that* its *is a possessive pronoun that shows ownership, and is referring to the moon.*

4. **◀ REREAD** Reread the poem. How does Sexton contrast the sky and the town? Support your answer with explicit textual evidence.

She says the town is "silent" while the stars are "alive." For her, the town doesn't exist when she looks at the painting, except for the tree that looks like a "drowned woman."

SHORT RESPONSE

Cite Text Evidence In what ways does Sexton's poem evoke the painting? What parts of the painting does she emphasize? Review your reading notes, and be sure to **cite text evidence** from the poem and the painting in your response.

In the poem and the painting, the night sky is the major focal point. Sexton writes, "The town does not exist." Van Gogh paints the town and tree in dark colors, and makes the town smaller than the stars. The viewer's eye is drawn to the giant stars, the brightest and largest part of the painting. While van Gogh seems to have painted "Starry Night" with religion in mind, Sexton emphasizes a feeling of terror, calling the sky a "serpent" and a "beast," while the night "boils." Sexton's speaker says that she wants to die in that wild night; perhaps both Sexton and van Gogh found the spirit of the night irresistible.

50

4. REREAD AND CITE TEXT EVIDENCE

D ASK STUDENTS to cite evidence to support their response. *Students should cite specific text evidence from the poem, noting that Sexton uses "silent" (line 7) to describe the town and "alive" (line 10) to depict the stars. Students should also recognize that for Sexton, the town is nonexistent (line 4), except for a tree that she compares to a "drowned woman" (lines 5–6).*

SHORT RESPONSE

Cite Text Evidence Students should:

- explain how the poem evokes the painting.
- cite specific evidence from the poem and the painting to support their response.

TO CHALLENGE STUDENTS . . .

For more context about Van Gogh's life and work, students can view the video *Vincent Van Gogh: A Stroke of Genius* in their eBooks.

ASK STUDENTS how the contributions to the video by other artists and biographers, and excerpts from Van Gogh's writing, helped them get a fuller understanding of the artist and his work. *Students should see the influence that Van Gogh has on other artists and on painting in general. The facts about his life and work show how driven he was to express his ideas on canvas, despite his lack of commercial success.* What impression did you get about Van Gogh's place in the history of art? *His works are regarded as some of the greatest paintings of all time.*

DIG DEEPER

With the class, return to Question 4, Reread. Have students work in small groups to discuss how Sexton contrasts the sky and the town. What parts of Van Gogh's painting does she emphasize? How is her poem similar to, yet different from, Van Gogh's *Starry Night*? Then have groups share the results of their discussion.

ASK STUDENTS whether they were satisfied with the outcome of their small-group discussions. Have each group share what the majority opinion was of the group concerning how Sexton's poem evokes Van Gogh's painting by emphasizing certain parts of it in her words and images.

- Encourage students to tell whether there was any compelling evidence cited by group members holding a different opinion. If so, why wasn't the textual evidence strong enough to sway the group?
- Have partners explain how they decided whether or not they had found sufficient evidence to support their opinion. Did everyone in the group agree as to what made the evidence sufficient? How did the group resolve any differences of opinion?
- After groups have shared the results of their discussion, ask whether another group's findings convinced them that a viewpoint different from theirs had merit.

ASK STUDENTS to return to their Short Response answer and to revise it based on the class discussion.

from Simplexity

Science Writing by Jeffrey Kluger

Why This Text?

Some students may wonder why schools conduct fire, disaster, or emergency drills. This lesson explores how a simple fire evacuation can quickly become complex as factors such as obstacles and human behavior become involved.

View It!

Professional Development Podcast:

Text-Dependent Analysis

Key Learning Objective: The student will be able to use cause-and-effect relationships to make connections between ideas and events.

COMMON CORE · Common Core Standards

RI 1 Cite textual evidence.
RI 2 Determine a central idea and analyze its development.
RI 3 Analyze how the author unfolds ideas or events.
RI 4 Determine the meaning of words and phrases.
RI 5 Analyze how an author's ideas are developed by particular sentences or paragraphs.
W 2 Write informative texts to convey complex ideas, concepts, and information.
SL 1 Participate in collaborative discussions with diverse partners.
L 1 Demonstrate standard English grammar and usage.
L 4 Determine the meaning of unknown and multiple-meaning words.
L 5 Demonstrate understanding of figurative language.

Text Complexity Rubric

Quantitative Measures	*from* Simplexity Lexile: 1490L
Qualitative Measures	**Levels of Meaning/Purpose** implied; easily identified from context
	Structure organization of main ideas and details complex but mostly explicit
	Language Conventionality and Clarity increased domain-specific words; more complex sentence structure
	Knowledge Demands some specialized knowledge required
Considerations	Teacher determined Vary by individual reader and type of text

CLOSE READ

Background Have students read the background and information about the author. Tell them that the term *simplexity* is formed from the words *simplicity* and *complexity*. Explain that ideas about what is simple and what is complex can be surprising. Jeffrey Kluger has compared a star with a guppy to make this point. The star, though massive, is relatively simple—a ball of hot gases. A guppy, on the other hand, though tiny, is a set of complex systems that form a functioning organism.

AS YOU READ Direct students to the As You Read note to focus their reading. Remind students to write down any questions they generate during reading.

Analyze Author's Order: Cause and Effect (LINES 1–7)

COMMON CORE RI 1, RI 2, RI 3, RI 5

Explain to students that science writers often use a cause-and-effect organization to explain the relationships between events and ideas. Successful cause-and-effect writing grabs the reader's attention and clearly states the cause-and-effect relationships.

A **CITE TEXT EVIDENCE** Have students read the first paragraph and identify the thesis, or main point of the writing, that states the cause-and-effect relationship. *(The effect of many people not escaping the twin towers was caused by the hijackers who crashed the planes, as well as by the many variables that affected people's movements inside the buildings [lines 1–7].)*

Determine Technical Meanings (LINES 7–11)

COMMON CORE RI 4, L 4, L 4a

Tell students that science writers use terms that have **technical meanings** appropriate to the topic. A reader can often determine technical meanings by looking for clues in context and in related words.

B **ASK STUDENTS** to determine what role fluid dynamics (line 9) plays in people's movements. *(We know that a fluid is a liquid or a gas, and that something dynamic is moving, changing, or energetic. So fluid dynamics is the study of how fluids move, and it may play a role in understanding how people move when evacuating a building.)*

Background *Following the attacks on September 11, 2001, more than 13,000 people safely evacuated the World Trade Center towers before the two buildings collapsed. These survivors reacted in different ways. Some rushed directly to emergency exits. Some first saved their work and shut down their computers. Others paused to change their shoes or to visit the restroom.* **Jeffrey Kluger** *(b. 1954), author of several books on science topics and senior editor at* Time *magazine, explains how differences in behavior can make a simple process like evacuating a building very complex.*

from
Simplexity

Science Writing by Jeffrey Kluger

AS YOU READ Notice the role that human behavior plays when a large crowd exits a building.

A The people who stayed behind in both towers on September 11, 2001—or waited too long before trying to leave—bore no responsibility for what happened to them that morning. They were, instead, twice victimized—once by the men who hijacked the planes and took so many lives; and once by the impossibly complex interplay of luck, guesswork, psychology, architecture, and more that is at play in any such mass movement of people. Fear plays a role, so does bravado, so does desperation. But so do ergonomics,[1] fluid dynamics, engineering, even physics—all combining to **B**
10 determine which individuals get where they're going, which ones don't, and which survive the journey at all. Ultimately, we're misled by our most basic instincts—the belief that we know where the danger is and how best to respond to keep ourselves alive, when in fact we sometimes have no idea at all. It's the job of the people who think about such matters to tease all these things apart and put them back together in buildings and vehicles that keep their

---
[1] **ergonomics:** the science of maximizing workplace efficiency.

Image Credits: (t) ©Saez Pascal/SIPA/NewsCom

SCAFFOLDING FOR ELL STUDENTS

Analyze Author's Order: Cause and Effect Using a whiteboard, project lines 1–7. Reread the text and invite volunteers to mark the cause(s) and effect(s):

- A cause answers the question "Why did it happen?" Highlight each cause in green.
- An effect answers the question "What happened?" Highlight each effect in yellow.

ASK STUDENTS to explain the author's thesis in their own words.

responsibility for what happened to them that morning. They were, instead, twice victimized—once by the men who hijacked the planes and took so many lives; and once by the impossibly complex

CLOSE READ

Analyze Author's Order: Cause and Effect (LINES 41–50)

 COMMON CORE RI 3, RI 5

Point out to students that in lines 41–50 the author uses a chain of cause-and-effect relationships to explain how to control the flow of people exiting a building. Tell them to notice how an effect in one cause/effect relationship becomes the cause of another cause/effect relationship.

C **CITE TEXT EVIDENCE** Have students identify the causes and effects in this relationship. *(cause: obstacle in path to exit; cause/effect: turbulence staggers people's arrival at exit; effect: controlled flow allows people to escape)*

CRITICAL VOCABULARY

chaotically: Kluger explains that air molecules fill an available space by moving randomly in all directions.

ASK STUDENTS why Kluger compares air molecules to people working in a large building. *(Like the air molecules, people going about their business move chaotically in all directions, filling the space fairly uniformly.)*

reallocate: In lines 38–42, Kluger states that obstacles reallocate energy and the resulting "chaos can be a very good thing" when people are fleeing a building.

ASK STUDENTS to explain how creating chaos with an obstacle and thus reallocating people's energy can be helpful during an evacuation. *(Putting an obstacle in the path of people rushing to an exit will cause them to move to avoid the obstacle, slowing them down and staggering their arrival at the exit.)*

turbulence: In line 51, Kluger uses the word *turbulence* to further explain how creating chaos can be good for people fleeing a building.

ASK STUDENTS to give an example from the text of one way designers of interior spaces create turbulence and help people escape. *(Designers use a post positioned along the people's path to create turbulence.)*

---

occupants alive. It's the job of those occupants to learn enough about the systems so that they have the sense to use them.

To scientists studying complex systems, evacuees[2] abandoning a building or city or disabled airplane are not so much humans engaged in mortal flight as data points on the complexity arc. On an ordinary day, twenty thousand people working in a skyscraper or half a million people in a coastal city occupy the same spot on the complexity spectrum as air molecules filling a room—moving randomly and **chaotically** in all directions, filling all the available space more or less uniformly. They're very active, but also very simple and disordered. Send the same people on a stampede down stairways or onto highways and things quickly grow overloaded and grind to a halt, jumping to the other end of the complexity arc—robust, unchanging, frozen in place, but every bit as simple as the ever-shifting air molecules. It's in the middle of the arc, where the molecules just begin to take some shape or the people in the tower just begin to move to the exits, that true complexity begins to emerge.

The best way to understand the elaborate manner in which people move en masse[3] may be to understand the equally complex way water does the same, particularly how it navigates around obstacles or breakwaters. A foundered boat or a tumbled boulder in the middle of a rushing river turns even the most powerful current chaotic, **reallocating** its energy into increased swirling and churning and decreased velocity. When people are fleeing a building, a similar kind of chaos can be a very good thing. Designers of interior spaces have found that a perfectly useless post positioned along the path to a fire exit may actually help people escape. Give evacuees storming toward a doorway a little something to avoid and you stagger their arrival slightly, allowing them to stream through the opening in a reasonably controlled flow, rather than colliding there at once and causing a pileup. The obstacle keeps you at the top of the complexity arc, preventing you from plunging headlong to the frozen end.

"You create a little **turbulence**," says Santa Fe Institute economist John Miller, who specializes in complex adaptive social systems. "By adding a little noise to the system you produce coherence in the flow."

The problem with the human-beings-as-water-particles idea is that it takes you only so far. Early fluid-based computer models that designers relied on to simulate crowd flow had a troubling habit of producing results that were simply too tidy. Put a single exit

chaotically
(kā-ŏt´ĭk-lē) *adv.* disorderedly and unpredictably.

reallocate
(rē-ăl´ə-kāt´) *v.* to distribute or apportion again; reassign.

turbulence
(tûr´byə-ləns) *n.* violent, disordered movement.

---

[2] **evacuees:** people who have been relocated from a dangerous place.

[3] **en masse (ŏn măs´):** together as one.

APPLYING ACADEMIC VOCABULARY

infer	abstract

As you discuss the excerpt from *Simplexity,* incorporate the following Collection 3 academic vocabulary words: *infer* and *abstract.* After discussing how chaos and turbulence can help people fleeing a building, ask students what they can **infer** from the author's use of air molecules and flowing water to explain **abstract** concepts.

in an office and the computerized evacuees would flow through
it at a particular rate of speed. Open a second exit somewhere else
and the people would respond appropriately, with half of them
choosing that new option and the flow at both doors adjusting itself
commensurately.[4] Put a breakwater somewhere along the route and
things smoothed out even more. Certainly, the programmers weren't
fools. They would correct for things like accessibility and **proximity**
of the exits—with more of the simulated evacuees choosing the
closer, more convenient egresses. But after that, the software assumed, the people would behave sensibly. This, of course, was
nonsense.

For one thing, people have different levels of decision-making
skills, with some inevitably behaving more rationally than others.
For another, all of us have a tendency to believe that the rest of
the group knows what it's doing, and thus will gravitate toward a
more popular exit simply because other people have chosen it, even
if the alternative is perfectly safe and much less congested. Every
additional person who chooses the more popular exit only makes
it likelier that the next person will select that one too. Finally,
information tends to get distributed unevenly, with some people
learning about an emergency first and acting before the others.
Once all of this was written into the fluid-based programs, the
simulations ran amok. "A fluid particle cannot experience fear or
pain," writes David Low, a civil engineer who studies evacuations
at Hariot-Watt University in Edinburgh, Scotland. "It cannot have
a preferred direction of motion, cannot make decisions, cannot
stumble or fall." Humans do all of those things and, in the process,
make a mess of most models.

In response to such problems, evacuation software has gotten
a lot more sophisticated. Programs with such evocative names
as EGRESS, EESCAPE, and EXODUS take into consideration
everything from the nature of an emergency (fire, bomb scare,
blackout) to the season in which it occurs (cold weather causing
more problems since people have to collect their coats, which is not
only time-consuming but space-consuming once the bulkily clad
occupants of the building crowd into the stairwells) to the time of
day (fewer people being in the building at lunchtime, for example,
than at ten-thirty in the morning, meaning that the midday
evacuations will be quicker and smoother).

Of course, computers can't model the existential terror that
comes along with any evacuation and programs like EGRESS are
thus limited by their very nature. One place those limitations show
themselves is in the evacuation stairway. Once frightened people

60

70

80

90

100

proximity
(prŏk-sĭm´ĭ-tē) *n.*
nearness.

---

[4] **commensurately:** in a corresponding or equivalent manner.

Simplexity **131**

CLOSE READ

Analyze Author's Order: Cause and Effect (LINES 70–86)

 COMMON CORE RI 3, RI 5

Explain to students that writers often use transitional words and phrases to signal and help explain a cause-and-effect relationship. These transitions include *as a result, because, cause, consequently, due to, for this reason, had the effect, if … then, since, so, so that, then, therefore,* and *thus.*

D ASK STUDENTS to look for words that signal causes and effects in the second paragraph (lines 70–86). *(For one thing; thus; because; only; with; once; in the process)* Then ask them to identify two of the cause-and-effect relationships. *(Possible answers: cause: People have different decision-making skills; effect: Some people behave more rationally than others. cause: People believe the group knows best; effect: People follow the crowd. cause: Additional people choose an exit; effect: Other people are likely to choose the same exit.)*

CRITICAL VOCABULARY

proximity: Kluger explains that programmers of early fluid-based computer models made corrections to the programs to account for how accessible an exit was and how close it was to the evacuees.

ASK STUDENTS how programmers may have adjusted the programs to account for the proximity of exits. *(The programmers figured that people would choose the closest exit and so adjusted their models to account for this.)*

WHEN STUDENTS STRUGGLE...

In one lengthy sentence, the author describes how evacuation software has become more sophisticated (lines 88–97). To guide students' comprehension of the sentence, point out the author's use of parentheses. Discuss how the parentheses set off words that define or explain another word or phrase.

ASK STUDENTS to use the Cluster Diagram Interactive Graphic Organizer to clarify the explanation of how evacuation software has become more sophisticated. In the center oval of the diagram, have students write "Sophisticated Evacuation Software." In the secondary ovals, have students list the factors that the software now takes into consideration. In the remaining ovals, have students write the parenthetical examples for each factor.

CLOSE READ

Determine Technical Meanings (LINES 109–111)

COMMON CORE RI 4, L 4a

Kluger uses the term *pure speed* twice to explain the science behind stairway evacuations.

E **ASK STUDENTS** to determine the meaning of *pure speed.* ("*Pure*" *means "unmixed with other matter";* speed *means "the rate of motion." In the context of the paragraph, the term means how quickly people can move down the stairway when no other factors but their ability to move their legs and bodies are involved.*)

Analyze Author's Order: Cause and Effect (LINES 112–125)

COMMON CORE RI 1, RI 3, RI 5

The author explains why people in Tower Two were instructed to stay at their desks.

F **CITE TEXT EVIDENCE** Have students identify two assumed cause-and-effect relationships in lines 112–125 that resulted in the announcement. (*1. cause: improbability of two buildings collapsing; effect/cause: decision for sheltering in place; effect: people at desks should be safe; 2. cause: presence of fireproof doors and sprinklers; effect/cause: people are safe on unaffected floors; effect: stairwells used only by people in danger*)

> **CRITICAL VOCABULARY**
>
> **propagate**: Kluger says that it doesn't take much to create turbulence in a stream of evacuees, because the delay propagates like ripples through water.
>
> **ASK STUDENTS** to cite one factor that would propagate a delay in the stream of evacuees. (*People entering the stairway on the middle floors would be cutting in line and slowing people immediately behind them in the stairway, creating a ripple-effect slowdown higher in the stairway.*)

COLLABORATIVE DISCUSSION Have partners support their ideas with specific cause-and-effect relationships and share their ideas with the class.

ASK STUDENTS to share any questions they generated in the course of reading and discussing the selection.

---

reach the stairways that should take them to safety, things ought to get easier. To complexity scientists, emergency stairways are nothing more than what are known as relaxation pathways, outlets that allow pressure or an imbalance to be relieved—in this case, the pressure of a mass of people trying to descend from higher floors to lower floors and then spill out of the building altogether. Given that, the only thing that ought to count in a stairway evacuation is pure speed; anything short of a stampede that will get the building
110 emptied in a hurry is a good thing. But pure speed is hard to maintain.

Much has been made in the years since September 11 about the announcement in Tower Two that instructed workers to stay at their desks—something that undoubtedly contributed to some of the deaths that day even though that was precisely the correct thing to do as far as anyone at the moment knew. The improbability of one building suffering the kind of violence that was done to the towers that day—to say nothing of two—called not for a wholesale evacuation, but for a so-called sheltering in place, taking cover
120 precisely where you are and thus staying safe from the chaos and debris on the street below. What's more, ordinary fires don't spread instantly across multiple floors and aren't fed by thousands of gallons of jet fuel. Fireproof doors and localized sprinklers are designed to keep people on unaffected floors safe so that they don't crowd the stairwells and slow the people who are in real danger.

Even in an unexceptional emergency, however, it doesn't take much for a smooth stream of downward-flowing evacuees to turn turbulent. For one thing, people from middle floors who enter the stairwell somewhere in mid-current can cause things to slow or
130 stop. The delay flows back along the queue the same way a ripple **propagates** through water, or cars entering a highway briefly slow the ones closest to the on-ramp, causing a wave of tapped brake lights that may radiate miles back. Sequential evacuation is the best way to handle this problem, with people on lower floors leaving the building first and each higher floor following successively. But again, nobody pretends that people fearing for their lives would wait patiently at their desks until their floor was called, nor would it be wise in a situation like the September 11 attacks, when the towers themselves turned into ticking clocks, and people higher up
140 needed every minute of evacuation time they could get before the buildings collapsed on top of them.

propagate
(prŏp´ə-gāt´) *v.* to reproduce or extend in quantity.

COLLABORATIVE DISCUSSION Were you surprised by the difficulties of planning a building evacuation? With a partner, discuss the many factors involved in creating a successful building evacuation plan. Cite specific textual evidence to support your ideas.

TO CHALLENGE STUDENTS . . .

Debate the Issue Should complexity theory be relied on to design evacuation routes for people in high-rise buildings? Have students debate the issue with a partner or in a small group. Each student should begin by taking a side and stating a position. Debates should

- focus on the issue;
- present a clear position supported by text evidence;
- demonstrate understanding of technical language;
- reflect effective organization of ideas;
- include effective logical, emotional, and ethical appeals.

Analyze Author's Order: Cause and Effect

COMMON CORE RI 3

Physics and other fields of science seek to explain the causes and effects of events in the natural world. A **cause** is an event that leads another event to happen; the **effect** is the event that results from the cause. In *Simplexity*, Jeffrey Kluger describes the movement of people evacuating a building by drawing on scientific concepts. He breaks down complex scientific ideas into a series of simpler cause-and-effect relationships. Events are presented in the order in which they occur, and readers can infer that they are connected as causes and effects.

One way to analyze cause-and-effect organization in a piece of writing is to map out the events in a flow chart. Notice how an event, such as "Everyone heads for the stairway at once," is also the cause of the next event, thereby creating a chain of events.

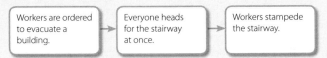

| Workers are ordered to evacuate a building. | → | Everyone heads for the stairway at once. | → | Workers stampede the stairway. |

Determine Technical Meanings

COMMON CORE RI 4

Science writing includes many **technical terms**—words with precise meanings in a particular field of study. Some of these terms may look familiar, but readers must determine their meanings as used in the text to understand exactly what the author means. For example, the word *particle* often means "speck" or "small bit of something." However, David Low's statement that "a fluid particle cannot experience fear or pain" (lines 81–82) uses the technical meaning of *particle*. In physics, a particle is a body, such as a water molecule, considered as a unit without regard to its internal structure.

When you encounter unfamiliar technical terms, try first to use context and other clues to determine their meanings. Sometimes, you may recognize a related word or word part. For instance, the author writes about "computer models that designers relied on to simulate crowd flow" (lines 56–57). The word *simulate* sounds a lot like *similar*, meaning "nearly the same or alike." The verb suffix *–ate* means "to act upon or become." The context discusses the use of computer models; we know that models represent images or ideas. Therefore, *simulate* means "to create a representation or model of."

If context alone won't help you determine a technical meaning, think about resources you can consult. Check the back of the book in which the word appears for a glossary of terms, or look online for a specialized dictionary devoted to the field of study. Note that a regular classroom dictionary may not include a word's technical meaning.

CLOSE READ

Analyze Author's Order: Cause and Effect

COMMON CORE RI 3

Help students understand the terms *cause* and *effect* and apply the terms to the details in the flow chart. Be sure students understand why some details may be labeled both as a cause and an effect. Have students determine whether the first detail in the flow chart, "Workers are ordered to evacuate a building," is a cause, an effect, or both, and to explain their reasoning. (*Possible answer: The detail is both a cause and an effect because something happened to cause this event and the event causes another event.*) Then have students suggest the effect for the last box shown in the chain of events. (*Possible answer: Some workers fall.*)

Determine Technical Meanings

COMMON CORE RI 4

Guide students in understanding that technical terms are specific to a field of study but that the terms may also have more general meanings. Ask students to explain the difference between the general meaning and technical meaning of the word *particle*. (*In general, a particle is a tiny portion or piece of something; in physics a particle is a tiny component of matter.*) The writer cites *molecule* to exemplify the technical meaning of *particle*. Have students provide another example of the technical meaning. (*Possible answers: atom, proton, electron*)

Strategies for Annotation

 *Annotate it!*

Analyze Author's Order: Cause and Effect

COMMON CORE RI 1, RI 4, RI 5

Share these strategies for guided or independent analysis:

- Highlight in yellow the events that are causes only.
- Highlight in green the events that are effects only.
- Underline events that are both a cause and an effect.

habit of producing results that were simply too tidy. Put a single exit in an office and the computerized evacuees would flow through it at a particular rate of speed. Open a second exit somewhere else and the people would respond appropriately, with half of them choosing that new option and the flow at both doors adjusting itself

Analyzing the Text COMMON CORE RI 1, RI 3, RI 4, RI 5

Possible answers:

1. *Kluger links the "complex interplay of luck, guesswork, psychology, architecture, and more" (lines 5–7), to a complex system—in this case, the evacuation of a building. Kluger may have used the historic reference because his audience is familiar with the events of that day and can relate them to the abstract scientific concept.*

2. *Both ends of a complexity arc represent simplicity, with one end having highly active but disordered particles and the other end having highly ordered but inactive particles. The middle of the arc represents complexity, having active and ordered particles just beginning to take shape.*

3. *Kluger uses the movement of water around an obstacle to explain how building designers can help people moving en masse to escape. "A tumbled boulder" in a river causes the rushing water to change direction, "swirling and churning" and slowing down (lines 38–41). Similarly a "perfectly useless post" (line 43) in the path of people rushing toward an exit causes people to change direction slightly, slowing them and staggering their arrival.*

4. *Kluger describes the sophistication of evacuation software as it considers variables such as type of emergency, season, and time of day (lines 89–95). He points out that programs are limited by their inability to consider variables such as people's fear (lines 98–100), a large volume of jet fuel (lines 122–123), and unpredictable behaviors (lines 136–137).*

5. *Cause: people enter the stairway on the middle floors; cause/effect: people immediately above them in the stairway slow down; effect: a ripple effect slows people all the way up the stairway (lines 128–130).*

6. *Kluger references events related to the attacks throughout the article, citing "evacuees abandoning a building" (lines 19–20), "people working in a skyscraper" (line 22), "storming toward a doorway" (line 45), "existential terror" (line 98), people descending "from higher floors" (line 106), "jet fuel" (line 123), and "September 11 attacks" (line 138).*

 **eBook** *Annotate It!*

Analyzing the Text COMMON CORE RI 1, RI 3, RI 4, RI 5, W 2

Cite Text Evidence Support your responses with evidence from the selection.

1. **Analyze** The author begins by referring to the destruction of the World Trade Center towers that occurred on September 11, 2001. What specific ideas does the author introduce to tie the events of September 11th to the scientific study of complex systems? Why might the author have decided to explain a scientific concept using a reference to a historic event?

2. **Infer** Using context clues in lines 19–34, determine the technical meaning of *complexity arc* as it is used in the text.

3. **Connect** In lines 35–50, how does the author develop his ideas about "the elaborate manner in which people move en masse"? Use evidence from the text to draw connections between the movement of people and the movement of water.

4. **Summarize** How does the author present his analysis of evacuation software such as EGRESS, EESCAPE, and EXODUS? In your response, note the order in which points are introduced and developed.

5. **Cause/Effect** Consider the problems that can cause "a smooth stream of downward-flowing evacuees to turn turbulent" (lines 126–128). Describe the causes and effects in this sequence of events.

6. **Analyze** The destruction of the World Trade Center towers happened when terrorists flew planes into the sides of the twin towers, setting off fiery explosions that eventually brought the towers down. Aside from his introduction, in what ways does the author keep the events of September 11th in the minds of readers throughout the article?

PERFORMANCE TASK

 *my* **WriteSmart**

Writing Activity: Analysis What does Kluger's analysis of responses during an evacuation tell you about human nature? Write an analysis using evidence from the text as well as your own experience.

- Reread *Simplexity*, making notes about how humans behave in crisis situations and why.
- Add to your notes your own thoughts about how you might react as well as evidence from other real-life events.
- Use your notes to draft a one-page analysis of why people act as they do during a crisis.
- Organize your ideas in cause-and-effect order to make your points clear to readers.

PERFORMANCE TASK COMMON CORE W 2, W 2a, W 2c, W 2d, SL 1, L 1

Assign this performance task.  *my* **WriteSmart**

Writing Activity: Analysis Have students work in pairs to reread *Simplexity*, looking for and recording details about human behavior in crisis situations. Encourage partners to share their thoughts as they reread and make notes about their own possible or real reactions in a crisis situation. Students' one-page analysis of why people react as they do during a crisis should

- hook the reader's interest with a strong introduction;
- include a thesis statement;
- use a logical order to cite evidence from the text as well as their own experiences;
- show clear connections between causes and effects;
- include transitional words to signal cause-and-effect relationships;
- use language appropriate to the audience.

Critical Vocabulary

COMMON CORE RI 4, L 5a

chaotically   reallocate   turbulence   proximity   propagate

Practice and Apply Explain which Critical Vocabulary word listed above is most closely associated with each idea or situation.

1. Which word goes with whitewater rafting? Why?

2. Which word goes with students leaving the building on the last day of school? Why?

3. Which word goes with a next-door neighbor? Why?

4. Which word goes with farming? Why?

5. Which word goes with the movement of resources? Why?

Vocabulary Strategy: Figurative Meanings

In **figurative language**, words and phrases have meanings beyond the literal definitions of the words. In some cases, a word with a concrete meaning is used to describe an abstract idea or process. For example, the Critical Vocabulary word *turbulence* is defined in line 53 as "adding a little noise to the system." The most common meaning of *noise* is "sound." However, *noise* can be used to mean "a disturbance that interrupts a steady flow." This definition acts as a **metaphor**, a figure of speech that makes a comparison between two unlike things. Turbulence disrupts a calm flow of water in the same way that noise disrupts a radio broadcast.

Consider the effect of the metaphor in lines 138–141, in which the author refers to

> a situation like the September 11 attacks, when the towers themselves turned into ticking clocks, and people higher up needed every minute of evacuation time they could get before the buildings collapsed on top of them.

The towers did not literally turn into ticking clocks, but the metaphor conveys the urgency of the situation for the people in the buildings.

Practice and Apply Kluger uses an **extended metaphor**, one that continues through a long section of text, to compare people evacuating a building to water flowing in a stream. Trace the extended metaphor by following these steps.

1. Identify where the author introduces the metaphor. Where is the first mention of flowing water?

2. Review the text to find additional comparisons between people and water. Look for places where the author explains the similarities, and for places where he uses a term normally applied to water to describe a moving crowd of people.

3. Explain whether this extended metaphor effectively communicates the author's ideas. Does it help you understand the scientific concepts the author is presenting? Why?

Simplexity **135**

PRACTICE & APPLY

Critical Vocabulary

COMMON CORE RI 4, L 5a

Answers:

1. *turbulence; Whitewater rafting is done in turbulent, or violent and swirling, water.* **2.** *chaotically; Students often leave the building quickly in a disordered way.* **3.** *proximity; A next-door neighbor is one that is nearby.* **4.** *propagate; A farmer reproduces crops and extends the food supply.* **5.** *reallocate; The movement of resources may include distributing them.*

Vocabulary Strategy: Figurative Meanings

Possible answers:

1. *Kluger introduces the flowing water metaphor in lines 35–38: "The best way to understand the elaborate manner in which people move en masse may be to understand the equally complex way water does the same, particularly how it navigates around obstacles or breakwaters."*

2. *Kluger extends the metaphor in the following: "stream through the opening in a reasonably controlled flow" (lines 46–47); "coherence in the flow" (line 54); "the human-beings-as-water particles idea" (line 55); "evacuees would flow" (line 59); "put a breakwater somewhere along the route" (line 63); "fluid-based programs" and "fluid particle" (lines 80–81); "a smooth stream of downward-flowing evacuees" (line 127); "mid-current" (line 129); "same way a ripple propagates through water" (lines 130–131); and "causing a wave" (line 132).*

3. *The metaphor is helpful because I have experience with how water flows and can relate it to the movement of people en masse.*

Figurative Meanings

COMMON CORE RI 4, L 5a

Have students locate the sentences in the selection that contain the comparison of people evacuating a building to water flowing in a stream:

- Highlight in pink references to people evacuating a building.
- Highlight in blue references to water flowing in a stream.
- Review your annotations to determine the connection between the movement of water and the movement of people.

The best way to understand the elaborate manner in which people move en masse may be to understand the equally complex way water does the same, particularly how it navigates around obstacles or breakwaters. A foundered boat or a tumbled boulder in the middle of a rushing river turns even the most powerful current

Simplexity **135**

Language and Style: Transitional Words and Phrases

COMMON CORE **W 2c**

Review with students the passages with and without transitions. Point out how the use of transitions connects ideas and makes them easier to understand. Also point out that the use of transitions in the last sentence prevents the need to repeat the phrase "to keep ourselves alive."

Answers:

Students' revised essays should include varied transitional words and phrases that create cohesion and link ideas. Transitions should be appropriate to the purpose of the specific idea, such as to show comparison and contrast, cause and effect, sequence, location, emphasis, and examples.

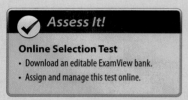

Language and Style: Transitional Words and Phrases

COMMON CORE **W 2c**

Transitional words and phrases connect ideas, making them easier to understand. Well-placed transitions act as stepping stones, guiding the reader from point to point, linking major sections of text from introduction to conclusion. The effect creates cohesion and clarifies the relationships among complex ideas and concepts. In *Simplexity*, Jeffrey Kluger uses transitional words and phrases to explain causes and effects in a complex process.

Note the underlined transitional words in this passage:

> **Ultimately, we're misled by our most basic instincts—the belief that we know where the danger is and how best to respond to keep ourselves alive, when in fact we sometimes have no idea at all.**

Without transitions, the writing would be difficult to follow and less meaningful:

> **We're misled by our most basic instincts. We believe we know where the danger is and how best to respond to keep ourselves alive. We have no idea at all how to keep ourselves alive.**

Notice how the transitions are used for different purposes: *ultimately* is used for emphasis; *when* and *sometimes* indicate time; *in fact* signals a contrast. Here are some other common transitions and their uses:

Transitions	
Word or Phrase	**Purpose**
again, and, also, equally, likewise, moreover, too, what's more	to show comparison
but, even so, however, in fact, not only, on the other hand, or, rather than, yet	to show contrast
after, before, during, finally, later, when, while	to show sequence or time
above, below, here, there, under	to show location
certainly, in fact, indeed, ultimately	to show emphasis
for example, in this case, like, such as, that is	to show examples

Practice and Apply Reread the selection, noting transitional words and phrases. Then, look back at the analysis you wrote for this selection's Performance Task. Revise it to add at least three transitional words or phrases that reflect your cause-and-effect order. Discuss with a partner how each added transition improves the meaning, flow, and cohesion of your work.

SCAFFOLDING FOR ELL STUDENTS

Language and Style: Transitional Words and Phrases Pair English learners with proficient English speakers to add transitions to the analyses they wrote for the Performance Task. Students should work together to:

- clarify the difference in purpose of the transitions listed in the Transitions chart on page 136;
- reread their analyses to identify cause-and-effect relationships;
- reread their analyses to identify other ideas that would flow better by adding transitional words and phrases.

ASK STUDENTS to revise their analyses, adding at least three transitional words and phrases to clarify relationships, meaning, and the flow of ideas.

Use Precise Language

COMMON CORE

RI 5, W 2d

TEACH

Explain that the use of precise language is important in writing, or writing about, any scientific text. Before students begin work on this selection's Performance Task, review good practices for using precise language.

- **Choose words carefully.** Explain that using precise language means choosing words carefully so that they convey the meaning you intend as exactly, or precisely, as possible.
- **Know definitions.** Point out that in order to use words to convey a precise meaning, you have to know exactly what they mean. For example, refer to the word *molecules* in line 24. Have students look up the definition of *molecule*. Ask for other, less precise, substitutions for this word. *(particle, bit)* Explain that these terms can mean different things to different people, and if used, might confuse the meaning of the text.
- **Make sure words cannot be misunderstood.** Explain that the more precise you can be in your language, the less chance you will be misunderstood. Refer to the word *stagger* in line 46. Discuss how this verb clearly describes the motion of people reaching a place at alternating times. Discuss how a less precise word, such as *change*, could mean many things and be misunderstood in the context of the passage.

PRACTICE AND APPLY

Display lines 3–11 on the board or on a device. Underline or highlight the following terms from the passage: *interplay, mass movement, bravado, desperation,* and *fluid dynamics.* Have students discuss how each term is an example of precise language—how each term conveys the intended meaning and how other terms might not convey that same meaning.

Display lines 126–128. Ask students how the use of the word *unexceptional* provides the intended meaning of the sentence. *(The evacuation of a building can easily become chaotic even in an emergency that is much more common than that experienced during the attack on the Twin Towers.)*

Analyze Author's Order: Cause and Effect

COMMON CORE

RI 1, RI 3, RI 5

RETEACH

Explain that cause and effect is one text structure authors use to maintain order for the ideas in their writing.

- Give students an example of a cause-and-effect relationship, such as "The snow fell all day and all night (cause), so school was cancelled the next day (effect)."
- Explain that writers use transitional words and phrases to alert readers to causes and effects. Some of those transitions include *as a result, because, due to, so, then, if . . . then, consequently, for this reason, since,* and *thus.*
- Place the cause-and-effect example in a flow chart so that students relate a cause to an effect. Then have them identify the cause and effect. Ask: What transitional word or phrase alerts you to a cause-effect relationship? *(so)*
- Have students add at least two more sections to the flow chart to create a cause-and-effect chain. Have them read the chart using transitional words or phrases.

 LEVEL UP TUTORIALS Assign the following *Level Up* tutorial: **Cause-and-Effect Organization**

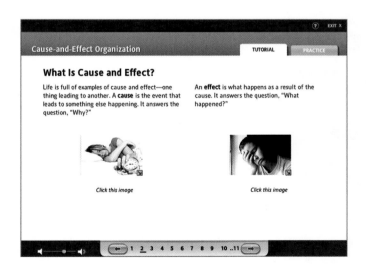

CLOSE READING APPLICATION

Students can apply the skill to a current print or digital news story. Have them create cause-and-effect flow charts. Ask students to decide whether the writer provides adequate transitional signals for readers and to support their opinions with text evidence.

Magic Island

Poem by Cathy Song

Why This Text?

Students regularly encounter poetry in which the writer uses imagery and figurative language to convey meaning and theme. This lesson gives students an opportunity to evaluate sensory language and infer meaning.

Key Learning Objective: The student will be able to analyze language and make inferences about the theme of a poem.

COMMON CORE Common Core Standards

RL 1 Cite textual evidence.
RL 2 Determine a theme and analyze its development.
RL 4 Determining the meaning of words and phrases.
W 1 Write arguments using valid reasoning and relevant evidence.
L 1b Use various types of phrases and clauses to convey specific meanings.

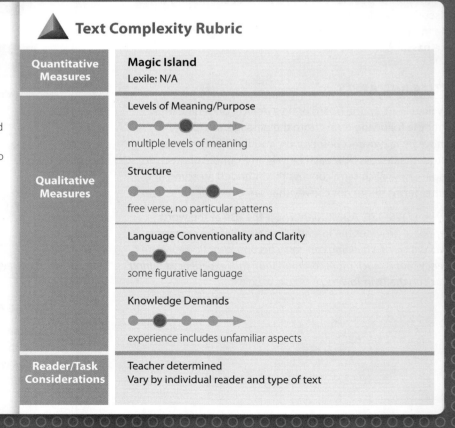

▲ Text Complexity Rubric

Quantitative Measures	**Magic Island** Lexile: N/A
Qualitative Measures	**Levels of Meaning/Purpose** ●—●—●—●—▶ multiple levels of meaning
	Structure ●—●—●—●—▶ free verse, no particular patterns
	Language Conventionality and Clarity ●—●—●—●—▶ some figurative language
	Knowledge Demands ●—●—●—●—▶ experience includes unfamiliar aspects
Reader/Task Considerations	Teacher determined Vary by individual reader and type of text

CLOSE READ

 For more context and historical background, students can view the video "Angel Island: Ellis Island of the West."

Background Have students read the background information about the author. Tell students that during the time when Song's grandparents lived, certain United States laws forbade interracial marriage. Consequently, many immigrant men from Asia found, through the exchange of family letters and pictures, brides willing to travel to the United States to enter into arranged marriages.

AS YOU READ Direct students to use the As You Read note to focus their reading.

Determine Figurative Meanings (LINES 11–12)

COMMON CORE RL 1, RL 4

Explain to students that a simile directly compares two things using the words *like* or *as*. Poets often use similes to create images in the reader's mind.

A **CITE TEXT EVIDENCE** Have students cite the line that contains a simile and identify what is being compared. *(Line 12: The poet compares the sky to a swimmer.)* What image does this simile create in your mind? *(Possible answer: the sea and sky blending into each other at the horizon)*

Support Inferences About Theme (LINES 1–12)

COMMON CORE RL 1, RL 2

Tell students that readers can make inferences about a theme, or message, based on details found in the text. One way writers convey theme is by using imagery, or language that helps create pictures in the reader's mind.

B **ASK STUDENTS** to reread lines 1–12. Then have them describe the park's setting. *(surrounded by water; windy; a kite flies above trees; water and sky are blue)*

 HISTORY | VIDEO

Background *Although individual circumstances differ, immigrants share the experience of adapting to a new and unfamiliar environment. They must learn new behaviors and languages while keeping alive the traditions and values of their original cultures. Poet* **Cathy Song** *was born in Honolulu in 1955. Her grandfather came to Hawaii from China; her grandmother arrived from Korea in an arranged marriage. Their experiences inform many of Song's poems.*

Magic Island

Poem by Cathy Song

AS YOU READ Look for clues that explain the meaning of the poem's title, "Magic Island." Write down any questions you generate during reading.

A collar of water
surrounds the park peninsula
at noon.   **B**
Voices are lost
5 in waves of wind
that catches a kite
and keeps it there
in the air above the trees.
If the day has one color,
10 it is this:
the blue immersion of horizons,   **A**
the sea taking the sky like a swimmer.

Image Credits: (bl) ©Jack Flash/Digital Vision/Getty Images; (br) ©Jolanta Dabrowska/Alamy Images

Magic Island **137**

SCAFFOLDING FOR ELL STUDENTS

Support Inferences About Theme Some students may have difficulty isolating or interpreting meaning from the text. Pair English language learners with students fluent in English. Have pairs work together to restate in their own words the following lines:

Lines 1–2: *(Water is all around the park.)*

Lines 4–5: *(Voices cannot be heard in the wind.)*

Lines 5–8: *(Wind blows a kite that flies above the trees.)*

Determine Figurative Meanings (LINES 35–47)

 COMMON CORE RL 1, RL 4

Explain to students that a metaphor directly compares two things without using the words *like* or *as*. Explain that similes and metaphors are forms of figurative language; that is, words or phrases that appeal to a reader's senses, evoke emotions, or imply alternate meanings.

C **CITE TEXT EVIDENCE** Have students identify the metaphor in lines 35–36. *(the sun sifting through the leaves in panes of light)* Ask to what the light is being compared? *(window panes)* Then have students identify similes in lines 38–48. *(Lines 40–41: "as if the child were a treasured sack of rice" and Lines 46–47: "a black umbrella, blooming like an ancient flower")* Does the poet use these examples of figurative language successfully? Explain with examples from the text. *(Possible answer: The figurative language is successful because it uses familiar objects and concepts to create images in my mind. For example, the word "treasured" makes me understand how the mother is holding the infant. The phrase "blooming like an ancient flower" lets me picture the opened umbrella.)*

Support Inferences About Theme (LINES 28–50)

COMMON CORE RL 1, RL 4

Explain that readers can make inferences based on information and details provided in the text.

D **ASK STUDENTS** to reread this part of the poem and explain what they can infer about the way the immigrants feel. *(The words "joy" [line 32], "bit of luck" [line 33], and "happiness" [line 42] indicate contentment; "suspicious" and "keep expecting rain" [lines 49–50] indicate caution in this new place.)*

COLLABORATIVE DISCUSSION Have pairs discuss specific words or phrases from the poem that help explain the title. Then have pairs draw conclusions about the poem's title and share with the class.

ASK STUDENTS to share any questions they generated in the course of reading and discussing the selection.

The picnickers have come
to rest their bicycles
15 in the sprawling shade.
Under each tree, a stillness
of small pleasures:
a boy, half in sunlight,
naps with his dog;
20 a woman of forty
squints up from her book
to bite into an apple.

It is a day an immigrant
and his family might remember,
25 the husband taking off his shirt
to sit like an Indian
before the hot grill.
He would not in his own language
call it work, to cook
30 the sticks of marinated meat
for his son circling a yarn
of joy around the chosen tree.
A bit of luck has made him generous.
At this moment in his life,
35 with the sun sifting through
the leaves in panes of light,
he can easily say he loves his wife. **C**
She lifts an infant
onto her left shoulder
40 as if the child
were a treasured sack of rice.
He cannot see her happiness,
hidden in a thicket of blanket
and shining hair.
45 On the grass beside their straw mat,
a black umbrella,
blooming like an ancient flower,
betrays their recent arrival.
Suspicious of so much sunshine,
50 they keep expecting rain.

COLLABORATIVE DISCUSSION With a partner, discuss what clues point to an explanation of the poem's title. Cite evidence from the text to support your ideas.

WHEN STUDENTS STRUGGLE . . .

Students may have trouble differentiating between metaphors and similes. To help guide in understanding metaphors, direct students to lines 35–36. Ask what two things are being compared? *(light to panes)* Explain that a pane is a piece or section, in this case, a section of a glass window. Point out that this comparison does not use the words *like* or *as*. Then direct students to the similes in lines 40–41 and 46–47. Discuss the comparisons and point out each instance of the use of *like* or *as*.

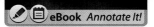

Support Inferences About Theme

COMMON CORE RL 1, RL 2

"Magic Island" uses language in powerful ways to create pictures in readers' minds and to convey meaning. By analyzing the language, you can infer themes that the poet wants to communicate. A **theme** is a message about life or people that emerges from details in the text.

This chart can guide your analysis of "Magic Island."

What Text Says Directly	Inferences Drawn from Text	Theme
Note what the characters in the poem do, say, and think. Look for **imagery**, or language that appeals to the senses. Use the imagery to form pictures in your mind of the poem's setting.	What inferences can you draw from details in the poem? Look for clues in the character's actions that allow you to guess more about them. Interpret any **symbols**, or objects that have meaning beyond the literal.	What message about life is the poet trying to communicate? Review the details you have noted and the inferences you have drawn, and think about the deeper meaning they suggest.

Analyzing the Text

 RL 1, RL 2, W 1

Cite Text Evidence   Support your responses with evidence from the selection.

1. **Analyze** Review lines 1–32. What images are the most striking? What **mood**, or feeling, do these images create?

2. **Interpret** Beginning in line 46, Song writes of "a black umbrella, / blooming like an ancient flower." What does the umbrella **symbolize**, or represent?

3. **Infer** Use your observations about the poem to summarize its meaning, or **theme**.

PERFORMANCE TASK

Writing Activity: Argument Consider the Chinese proverb, "When the wind of change blows, some build walls while others build windmills." Which does the family in this poem do? Explore your ideas in a written argument.

- Consider what "wind of change" has affected the family. Then make a two-column chart listing examples of their metaphorically building walls and windmills. Identify which column contains more or stronger examples.

- Write a paragraph in which you make your case for whether the family builds walls or windmills. Cite evidence from your chart to support your ideas.

Magic Island   **139**

Assign this performance task. **WriteSmart**

PERFORMANCE TASK

COMMON CORE W 1

Writing Activity: Argument Guide students in their thinking by discussing the functions of a wall and a windmill. Have students make a two-column chart and review the poem to find and record details from the text. Then have students write a paragraph that clearly states their position and cites evidence from the text that supports their argument.

PRACTICE & APPLY

Support Inferences About Theme

COMMON CORE RL 1, RL 2

Help students understand the terms. Clarify that **imagery** is language that appeals to a reader's senses—sight, sound, smell, taste, and touch. Explain that a **symbol** is something that represents something else, such as an idea, and that a **theme** is a message about life or people that comes from details in the text. Guide students in analyzing the poem by using the steps from the chart:

- Have students summarize what the text directly states. *(The setting is a sunny day at a park and the focus is on the actions of an immigrant family.)* Help students identify examples of imagery used in the text. *(For example, line 1: "collar of water;" lines 14–15: "rest their bicycles in the sprawling shade;" line 43: "hidden in a thicket of blanket")*

- Next, have students use details from the poem to make inferences about the characters. For example, discuss the actions of the husband at the grill or the significance of the black umbrella. *(The man's actions and point of view may suggest an effort to merge his cultural ways into a new environment. The presence of the black umbrella may reveal the family's cautious approach to their life in a new country.)*

- Discuss possible themes the poem conveys. Remind students to cite details from the poem to support their ideas.

Analyzing the Text

COMMON CORE RL 1, RL 2

Possible answers:

1. *Images include a windy day at the shore; a boy napping with his dog; the woman looking up from her book; the husband sitting before the grill. The imagery creates a mood of peace, contentment, happiness, and hope.*

2. *The umbrella symbolizes the cautious approach the couple takes as they adapt to their new surroundings.*

3. *The theme is that, while living in a new country may bring happiness, it is not without its challenges*

Magic Island   **139**

Language and Style: Noun Phrases and Verb Phrases COMMON CORE L 1b

Point out that in the noun phrase "A collar of water," "collar" modifies, or describes, "water." The use of this noun phrase adds imagery to the poem. Then point out that in the verb phrase "naps with his dog," "with his dog" modifies "nap." Have students work in pairs to identify other noun and verb phrases used in the poem. Then ask students to review and revise their paragraphs from the Performance Task to clarify and enrich their writing. Invite volunteers to share with the class their original and revised paragraphs.

Answers:

Students' revised paragraphs should include several noun phrases and verb phrases, improving on the detail and richness of their original paragraphs.

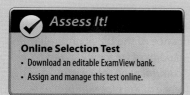

Assess It!

Online Selection Test
- Download an editable ExamView bank.
- Assign and manage this test online.

Language and Style: Noun Phrases and Verb Phrases

 COMMON CORE L 1b

A **phrase** is a group of related words that functions in a sentence as a single part of speech. A **noun phrase** contains a noun and any words that modify it. A **verb phrase** contains a verb plus any words that modify or complement the verb. Noun and verb phrases help a writer convey specific meanings because the modifiers add richness and detail to the noun or verb at the heart of each phrase.

In "Magic Island," Cathy Song uses many noun and verb phrases to evoke mood and meaning. This chart shows some of the phrases used in the first two stanzas of "Magic Island."

Noun Phrases	Verb Phrases
"A collar of water"	"surrounds the park peninsula / at noon"
"the air above the trees"	"are lost / in waves of wind"
"the blue immersion of horizons"	"have come / to rest their bicycles / in the sprawling shade"
"a stillness / of small pleasures"	"naps with his dog"
"a woman of forty"	"squints up from her book / to bite into an apple"

Consider how lines 13–22 might read without the noun and verb phrases Song has crafted to include modifying details:

The picnickers have come.

Under each tree, a stillness:

a boy naps;

a woman squints up.

This simplified version gives the basic facts of the scene, but it provides few details to help readers imagine it. The description is abstract and vague rather than concrete and specific. In your own writing, think about when it is appropriate to elaborate on your nouns and verbs with modifiers that will show readers your exact meaning.

Practice and Apply Look back at the paragraph you wrote for this selection's Performance Task. Circle any noun phrases and underline any verb phrases you used. Revise your paragraph by adding more explicit details to existing phrases or by adding modifying words to build phrases around nouns and verbs. Discuss with a partner how your revisions improve the original paragraph.

Use Various Types of Phrases

COMMON CORE
L 1b

TEACH

Song uses various types of phrases to add descriptive details throughout her poem. Provide students with the following definitions of some of the types of phrases.

- A **noun phrase** does the work of a noun in a sentence and includes both a noun or pronoun and any modifiers that tell more about it.
- A **verb phrase** does the work of a verb in a sentence and includes both the verb and any direct or indirect object.
- A **prepositional phrase** helps the reader understand the relationship between a noun or pronoun and the rest of the sentence, often explaining the object's location in time or space. The phrase begins with a preposition and includes an object and any other words that modify the object.
- An **adjectival phrase** is a group of words that work together to describe a noun or pronoun.
- An **adverbial phrase** is a group of words that work together to modify a verb or explain how something is done.
- A **participial phrase** is a phrase that begins with a participle, which is a verbal that does the work of an adjective in describing a noun or pronoun.
- An **absolute phrase** is a type of noun phrase that modifies an entire sentence, providing more information about one part of a whole.

PRACTICE AND APPLY

Display parts of the poem and have students identify an example of each type of phrase.

- Display lines 1–12 and have students identify a noun phrase (*a collar of water*), a verb phrase (*surrounds the park peninsula at noon*), a prepositional phrase (*at noon*), an adjectival phrase (*of water*), and a participial phrase (*taking the sky like a swimmer*).
- Display lines 13–22 and have students identify an absolute phrase (*under each tree, a stillness of small pleasures*) and an adverbial phrase (*up from her book*).

Then have partners work together to find other examples of different kinds of phrases in the poem.

Support Inferences About Theme

COMMON CORE
RL 1,
RL 2

RETEACH

Review the term *theme*. Then provide an example of a possible theme from the poem "Magic Island," such as "Moving to a new country can be frightening but also exciting and hopeful."

- Ask students how they can tell if this theme is appropriate. *(Reread the poem and think about what is stated as well as what is inferred. Then summarize these thoughts to see if the stated theme makes sense.)*
- On the board, draw two columns labeled "What Poem Says Directly" and "Inferences Drawn from Poem." Work with students to fill in the chart. In the first column, focus on imagery that the words evoke. In the second column, focus on symbols that have meaning beyond the literal. Then have students synthesize the information in the columns to determine if the stated theme makes sense.

 LEVEL UP TUTORIALS Assign the following *Level Up* tutorial: **Theme**

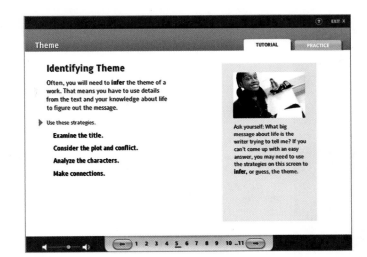

CLOSE READING APPLICATION

Students can apply the skill to other poems. Have them work independently to read a poem and identify uses of figurative language that support the students' inferences and ideas about the poem's theme.

from Rivers and Tides

Documentary Film by Thomas Riedelsheimer

Why This Text?

Students regularly view documentaries about significant events, people, and places. In this lesson, students will view a documentary about the artist Andy Goldsworthy, in order to explore the effect of the filmmaker's choice of setting and visuals.

Key Learning Objective: The student will analyze the development of ideas in a documentary.

For practice and application:

Close Reader selection
Life After People

COMMON CORE Common Core Standards

RI 1 Cite textual evidence.
RI 2 Determine a central idea and analyze its development.
RI 3 Analyze how the author unfolds ideas or events.
RI 5 Analyze how an author's ideas are developed by particular sentences or paragraphs.
RI 7 Analyze various accounts of a subject told in different mediums.
SL 5 Make use of digital media to enhance understanding of findings, reasoning, and evidence.

▲ Text Complexity Rubric

Quantitative Measures	***from* Rivers and Tides** Lexile: n/a
Qualitative Measures	**Levels of Meaning/Purpose** multiple levels of meaning
	Structure organization of main ideas, details complex but largely explicit
	Language Conventionality and Clarity mainly conversational language
	Knowledge Demands situation includes unfamiliar aspects
Reader/Task Considerations	Teacher determined Vary by individual reader and type of text

Background Tell students that Andy Goldsworthy is a British artist who creates sculptures from items found in nature. Unlike most sculptors, Goldsworthy creates work that he knows will be destroyed by nature relatively quickly. Goldsworthy has photographed many of his works and has held exhibits primarily featuring photographs of his sculptures.

AS YOU VIEW Direct students to think about why the director chose the settings featured in the film and how those settings create tone, mood, and affect the overall message of the documentary. Remind students to write down any questions they generate as they watch the video.

Analyze Development of Ideas

 RI 2, RI 3

Explain that a documentary film presents a factual account of a specific topic. At the same time, many documentaries also present a particular view of the topic.

 ASK STUDENTS to describe something they learn from the film. *(The artist makes artwork that he places in the outdoors, where natural forces will destroy or obstruct the works from view in a short period of time. Andy Goldsworthy sees his work as symbolizing life's challenges.)* Then have students discuss what they think director Thomas Riedelsheimer thinks of the work and tell how he develops that idea. *(Riedelsheimer seems to be fascinated by Goldsworthy and his work, and he wants to show what happens to Goldsworthy's creations over time. Because nature takes some time to have an impact on Goldsworthy's artwork, a viewer would normally not be able to experience the full effect of the art. This idea is developed through the way that the film helps to show how Goldsworthy creates his art and how nature eventually overcomes or changes it. The idea is also developed through the inclusion of the spoken words of Goldsworthy himself in the film.)*

COLLABORATIVE DISCUSSION Have students discuss how the settings shown in the film help develop an introduction to Goldsworthy's art. Have them discuss how the natural settings become a key part of the artist's work.

ASK STUDENTS to share any questions they generated while viewing and discussing the film.

MEDIA ANALYSIS

from
Rivers and Tides

Documentary Film by Thomas Riedelsheimer

AS YOU VIEW Pay attention to the settings shown in the film clip and how they affect your perception of the artist's work. Write down any questions you generate during viewing.

Image Credits: ©Sam Chrysanthou/All Canada Photos/Corbis; (b) ©Celluliod Dreams

COLLABORATIVE DISCUSSION In a small group, discuss how the settings in the film clip interact with and become a part of Andy Goldsworthy's work. What changes within the settings are important to the art?

APPLYING ACADEMIC VOCABULARY

abstract	evolve

As you discuss the film, incorporate the following Collection 3 academic vocabulary words: *abstract* and *evolve*. As students discuss the ideas of the film, ask them to explain how the ideas **evolve** over the course of the clip. Then have students discuss how both the film clip and Goldsworthy's art are **abstract** in nature.

CLOSE READ

Analyze Development of Ideas **RI 2, RI 3**

Help students understand the terms *central idea* and *supporting details*. After students view the film, discuss the central idea and supporting details expressed in the excerpt from *Rivers and Tides*. *(The central idea is the importance of natural forces in Andy Goldsworthy's work and how these forces change and affect the art itself. Supporting details are provided by images showing the ocean tide coming in to surround and then engulf Goldsworthy's rock sculpture and time-lapse visuals of plants in a meadow seeming to swallow up another of his sculptures.)*

To help students analyze the ideas and determine the supporting details in a film, make sure they understand the elements a filmmaker uses:

- Explain each of the elements listed, giving examples from this film and other videos students have seen.

- Use the examples you mentioned and have students determine the effect of each example on the development of ideas.

- Explain that one way to analyze the effect of visuals shown in a film is to think about how a director could have shown images differently. Choose a specific example from *Rivers and Tides* and have students explain how the director could have shown the events differently. Ask students to describe how that change would have affected the overall presentation of ideas.

Analyze Development of Ideas **RI 2, RI 3**

Rivers and Tides is a documentary film about the British artist Andy Goldsworthy. In this film, director Thomas Riedelsheimer documents the artist's process of creation.

Like a writer, a filmmaker works to develop ideas in a logical fashion. The **central idea** is the most important idea about a topic that a film conveys. **Supporting details** are the images and words that tell more about the central idea. A central idea will sometimes be shown or stated directly, but more often it will be implied by the supporting details. In order to appreciate and understand the central idea, the viewer needs to consider the order of and connections between images.

Filmmakers use a combination of elements to help them express a central idea.

- **Visual elements:** Film elements such as these help the filmmaker convey connections among ideas:
  camera shot—a single, continuous view taken by a camera
  camera angle—the angle at which the camera is positioned during the recording of a shot or image
  In *Rivers and Tides*, the filmmaker films the subject in different settings and then combines the images to show connections.

- **Sound elements:** Music, voice-over, and sound effects may be included in a film to give additional information and to set a mood or tone for a scene. For example, Andy Goldsworthy's monologue expresses what he thinks about his art pieces.

- **Special effects:** Special effects are manipulated video images. These can include
  speed—fast- or slow-motion sequences can heighten drama and create a tense or calm mood
  lighting—unusually bright or dim lighting can create a specific mood, and changes in lighting can communicate a shift in mood
  time-lapse—starting and stopping filming to connect images from one time period to the same images in another time period

- **Setting:** The locations in which a film is shot are its setting. In *Rivers and Tides*, the various settings are an integral part of how the filmmaker conveys the central idea.

SCAFFOLDING FOR ELL STUDENTS

Analyzing the Media Have students create a glossary of elements that filmmakers use to express ideas. Students should list each element, describe the element, and include an example of each element that is familiar to them. The examples can come from video clips, movies, or television programs or commercials. Tell students to use their glossaries to help them as they analyze the way that the director uses the elements to present the central idea and supporting details.

ASK STUDENTS to describe an example of each element from the film. You may name an element and ask for an example or name something from the film and have students identify the element.

- **Mood:** The mood is the atmosphere that the visual and sound elements in a film create for the viewer. Lighting, music, and sound effects all play a role in creating the mood. Mood helps support the central idea by reinforcing what the viewer is seeing.

- **Sequence:** A filmmaker presents images in a logical order. Sometimes this is a chronological order, but at other times, the images or scenes are shown in an order that helps the viewer relate the ideas being shown.

As you view the clip from *Rivers and Tides*, think about what central idea the director communicates through images, sounds, and **juxtaposition**, or side-by-side placement of key elements. If you were to summarize the clip for someone who had not seen it, what ideas and images would you emphasize? Developing an answer to that question is the beginning of media analysis.

Image Credits: ©Celluliod Dreams

Rivers and Tides **143**

Analyze Development of Ideas

Explain that when directors use juxtaposition, it is often a way of showing that they want to compare or contrast two ideas.

Have students work with a partner to discuss juxtaposition in the film excerpt. Partners should address the following in their discussions:

- Identify an example of elements that are juxtaposed in the film clip. *(the scene of the stone sculpture in the meadow and the scene of the stone sculpture in the ocean)*

- Explain how this juxtaposition helps the director create meaning or present an idea. *(The juxtaposition makes it clear to the viewer that these are two important ways of viewing the interaction of nature and the sculptures. The scenes are similar in that the water and the plants both seem to swallow up the artwork. They are different as well because the plants in the meadow would grow much more slowly than the tide would come in.)*

WHEN STUDENTS STRUGGLE . . .

Students may have difficulty describing the video clip because it is not a traditional film that shows a series of events from beginning to end. Provide students with a strategy for describing literary or visual works that are abstract:

- Think about the main scenes. Tell what seems to be most important in those scenes and why you think the writer or filmmaker chose to feature them.

- Describe how the different scenes, sounds, and details included work together.

ASK STUDENTS to work with partners and use these strategies to describe the film clip to one another.

PRACTICE & APPLY

Analyzing the Media
COMMON CORE RI 1, RI 2, RI 3, RI 5, RI 7

Possible answers:

1. *The filmmaker shows a rock sculpture being covered by the water of a rising tide. This is similar to the way the story builds in the film. The story is eventually revealed by images showing the artist creating the works and through visuals showing how nature interacts with the finished pieces.*

2. *The close-up images show how the sculptures were built and how they have meaning in a very personal way. The shots taken from farther away might show how the art has less impact as the memory of it fades. This might also show how the art is only temporary.*

3. *The central idea is that time is powerful and can cause permanent change. Evidence of this in the film is the video of the growing meadow that eventually envelops a sculpture. The meadow changes dramatically over time and the sculpture seems to disappear. Another example is shown in the way the ocean swallows up the sculpture constructed on the coast. In this case, the ocean does not seem to change, but the sculpture again disappears. Time seems to remove the art.*

4. *The music helps to create a sense of time elapsing. There is a long section with no voice-overs, only music. This helps to move the film along. The music is also soft and creates a serious mood. The voice-over provides a way for the artist to present his ideas about the work.*

5. *The special effect the filmmaker uses to show the passing of time and changes over time is time-lapse imagery. The film shows shots of the meadow as it grows, skipping from one time period to another.*

6. *The film shows how the artwork is constructed and how time and nature affect it. It is more of an extension of the way that Goldsworthy views nature. The photographs allow people to see the sculptures they would not otherwise be able to enjoy, but the film allows viewers to see how the art is modified by nature over a period of time.*

7. *The art symbolizes some of the effects that major challenges have on people. Sometimes the challenges seem to swallow a person up. Other times, the challenges change a person and the person becomes stronger.*

Analyzing the Media
COMMON CORE RI 1, RI 2, RI 3, RI 5, SL 5

Cite Text Evidence   Support your responses with evidence from the selection.

1. **Connect** What visual elements does the filmmaker use in the clip to make a connection between the flow of the film and the rivers and tides of the title?

2. **Compare** What effect does the filmmaker's use of close-up shots of the artist's work and shots taken from farther away have on your understanding of the connections between the sculptures?

3. **Summarize** This film with director Thomas Riedelsheimer and Andy Goldsworthy evolved over a long period of time. What central idea about time does the film convey? Support your answer with descriptions of details from the film.

4. **Identify Patterns** How do the sound elements, such as music, background sounds, and voice-over, facilitate connections between the images in the film and the central idea? Cite specific evidence from the film.

5. **Analyze** What special effect does the film use to help the viewer link the sculptures to the idea of time and changes over time?

6. **Connect** Andy Goldsworthy sculpts in ice, stone, leaves, and other natural materials. He usually takes photographs of his sculptures because many of them are ephemeral and last for only a short period of time. He says this is his way to "talk" about his sculptures. What is the role of this film in bringing Goldsworthy's art to the public? How is that role different from the role of the photographs of Goldsworthy's sculptures?

7. **Synthesize** During the interview, Goldsworthy trails off when attempting to connect his art with major changes in people's lives. How would you complete his thought, based on images and ideas in the film as well as your own knowledge and experience?

PERFORMANCE TASK

Media Activity: Reflection What connections can you make between changes you see in nature or your community and the kinds of major life changes people experience? Share your ideas in a media presentation.

- Take photographs, make video recordings, or organize a collection of existing images of a meaningful change. (Be sure any images made by others are copyright free or allowed for classroom use.)

- Record an audio track to accompany your visuals that tells what change they show and how that change is a good metaphor for a specific life change—moving, changing schools, growing up, etc.

Assign this performance task.

PERFORMANCE TASK
COMMON CORE SL 5

Media Activity: Reflection Have students work with partners to discuss different examples of meaningful life changes and how these might be shown in a visual presentation. Then have students work independently to create a visual representation of the change. Allow students to give their presentations to the class.

INTERACTIVE WHITEBOARD LESSON
Using Media in Presentations

COMMON CORE
SL 5

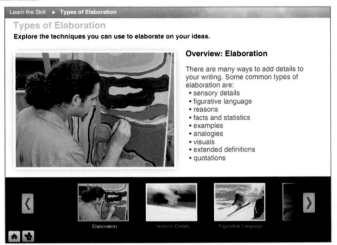

Learn the Skill ▶ Types of Elaboration

Types of Elaboration

Explore the techniques you can use to elaborate on your ideas.

Overview: Elaboration

There are many ways to add details to your writing. Some common types of elaboration are:
- sensory details
- figurative language
- reasons
- facts and statistics
- examples
- analogies
- visuals
- extended definitions
- quotations

Elaboration Sensory Details Figurative Language

TEACH

Before students begin planning their media presentations, explain that developing ideas in film is similar to developing ideas in writing. It is important to begin by determining the overall idea.

Once students have determined their central idea, they will need to decide what they will include in their media presentation. Discuss different methods of developing ideas:

- **Still Images and Action Scenes** Using still photographs or showing characters in action can help students paint a visual picture of an event, a person, or even an abstract idea.
- **Narration and Dialogue** One way to express ideas through language in a video is to have characters talk to one another or have a narrator speak.
- **Background Sounds** The background sound in a presentation can be music, nature sounds, or even the noise in a crowded airport. Sounds should contribute to the overall meaning, develop mood, or have another specific purpose.
- **Charts or Diagrams** These visual aids can be included to support factual information by using graphics.

COLLABORATIVE DISCUSSION

Have students discuss how the different aspects of a media presentation can help them present their idea about the connection between changes in nature and life changes. Students should list examples of each method that they could use in their presentations. Have groups compare the results of their searches.

Analyze Development of Ideas

COMMON CORE
RI 2, RI 3

RETEACH

Tell students that a central idea is the main idea of a work and the supporting details are the parts of the work that help to reveal that central idea. Explain that a video or film allows a filmmaker to reveal a main idea differently than in a written work, but the central idea is still the main or most important idea. Because video has the ability to present ideas through more than words or spoken dialogue, the main idea may be presented without including any words at all. Or it may be presented by using spoken language and other sound elements.

In order to analyze a video, it is important to consider all of the different aspects of the work, including the visual and auditory material. Of course, a filmmaker has many different tools that can help him present important sounds and sights in a film.

 LEVEL UP TUTORIALS Assign the following *Level Up* tutorial: **Main Idea and Supporting Details**

CLOSE READING APPLICATION

Have students work in groups to discuss their immediate reaction to the different things they saw and heard in the film clip. Allow students to view and review the film in order to facilitate this discussion. Tell students to take notes about the different reactions group members had. Students should also discuss the effect the filmmaker was trying to create in different parts of the film, by setting different elements or techniques. Finally, have the groups decide which elements they think were the most effective or powerful in creating the central idea.

Life After People

Science Writing by Dolores Vasquez

Why This Text

Students may not leave the text of a science article with a clear understanding of how the author develops his or her central ideas. In this article, students will read the text and view the pictures to understand the ideas the author makes about the future. With the help of the close-reading questions, students will analyze how the author describes a series of events in a speculative future. This close reading will lead students to understand the article's central idea.

Background Have students read the background information about the article. Enumerate some of the ways that humans have "marked" the planet: huge cities, vast transportation networks, agriculture to feed billions of people, massive mining operations, and, of course, the resulting air, soil, and water pollution. Point out that 200,000 years sounds like a long time, but it amounts to only about 4 thousandths of 1 percent of Earth's history.

AS YOU READ Ask students to pay attention to how the author develops the series of events in the future. How do these events lead to her conclusion?

 COMMON CORE

Common Core Support

- cite strong and thorough textual evidence
- determine a central idea of a text
- provide a summary of the text
- analyze how an author unfolds and develops a series of events

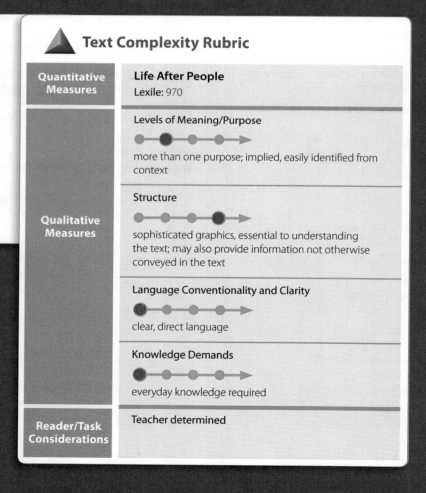

Text Complexity Rubric

	Life After People
Quantitative Measures	**Life After People** Lexile: 970
Qualitative Measures	**Levels of Meaning/Purpose** more than one purpose; implied, easily identified from context
	Structure sophisticated graphics, essential to understanding the text; may also provide information not otherwise conveyed in the text
	Language Conventionality and Clarity clear, direct language
	Knowledge Demands everyday knowledge required
Reader/Task Considerations	Teacher determined

Strategies for CLOSE READING

Analyze Development of Ideas

Students should read this article carefully all the way through. Close-reading questions at the bottom of the page will help them focus on a thorough analysis of the article's ideas. As they read, students should jot down comments or questions about the text in the margins.

WHEN STUDENTS STRUGGLE . . .

To help students analyze the development of ideas in "Life After People," have them work in small groups to fill out a chart like the one shown below.

CITE TEXT EVIDENCE For practice in analyzing the development of ideas in an article, ask students to cite text evidence for some of the cause-and-effect relationships that the author describes to present her ideas.

Time Period	Cause	Effect
within hours	power plants stop	gas tanks heat and leak gases, leading to fires
within days	treatment facilities at standstill	sewage poisons rivers and lakes
end of first week	pets run out of food	large dogs form packs
within weeks	cooling ponds of nuclear plants boil away	radiation leaks and spreads, killing plants and animals
over 15 years	roads overgrown, roofs of buildings collapse	animals make their homes in urban areas
in 50 to 100 years	packs of dogs roam	dog breeds disappear; dogs look like wolves
after 250 years	vegetation takes over cities; forests regrow	signs of humans disappear

Background *Human beings are a fairly recent arrival on Earth. In fact, many archaeologists estimate that Homo sapiens have been here for about 200,000 years, a fraction of the lifetime of Earth—approximately 4.6 billion years. In those 200,000 years, human beings have left their mark on the planet. But what would happen if we suddenly disappeared? The article below, accompanied by photographs from HISTORY's television show "Life After People," illustrates what a planet without people might look like.*

Life After People

Article by Dolores Vasquez

CLOSE READ
Notes

1. **READ ▶** As you read lines 1–12, begin to collect and cite text evidence.
   - Circle the question at the beginning of the article.
   - In the margin, paraphrase the central idea in lines 2–4, and underline the details that support it.
   - In the margin, explain the central idea in lines 5–12.

(W)hat would the world be like if people suddenly disappeared?
Imagine the immediate consequences: wrecks from driverless cars and planes; saucepans boiling over; startled dogs dragging their leashes down deserted streets. But what happens later?

Without people to fuel them, power plants stop providing electricity—within hours. We use electricity to make toast and to power TVs and computers, but the absence of electric energy has huge effects on an Earth void of human population. Without electricity, gas tanks are not kept cold; gases such as chlorine and natural gas heat up and escape the tanks into the
10 air. Animals die from the freed chlorine fumes, and the natural gas causes explosions and uncontrolled fires. Within days, treatment facilities are at a standstill and sewage begins to poison rivers and lakes.

Life without people might cause accidents and harm to animals.

Without people, the Earth's environment and its animals will be jeopardized.

51

---

1. **READ AND CITE TEXT EVIDENCE** Tell students that Vasquez opens the essay with a simple but surprising question that captures the reader's attention.

(A) ASK STUDENTS to think about the way the opening question affects the reader. *Students should realize that this ominous beginning raises a compelling question—what happens next?* Students should cite evidence from lines 2–4 to support the central idea that a life without people would immediately cause accidents and confusion.

After one year, plants and shrubs begin to overrun the highway system in Los Angeles.

After 200 years of neglect, the rusted skeleton of the Chrysler Building in New York finally collapses.

The author uses chronological order and a cause-and-effect pattern to show the results of particular events over time.

C By the end of the first week, pets that have run out of food in their homes must escape and try to survive in the new environment. The larger dogs form packs and prey on smaller animals. Dairy cattle die of thirst in their pens, and their bodies may provide food for scavenging dogs. Cows that were raised as food, however, will eventually establish huge herds on the plains, reinterpreting the lifestyle of the buffalo in the 1800s. Zoo animals that had been restrained by electric fences wander city streets. But
20 within weeks, many animals leave the cities to the mice, rats, and squirrels.
D Meanwhile, at nuclear power plants, the cooling ponds for spent fuel rods get hotter and hotter. Soon the water boils away, and the rods cause fires and release radiation into the air, where it is carried by the wind. Plants and animals in affected areas die.

E After several months, the radiation in the air is no longer a danger, and those animals that have survived begin to follow their new lives. And by the end of a year, rains have washed the radioactive pollution from the surface of the land.
Over the next fifteen years, the roads get overgrown and cracked. Yards
30 and gardens grow wild, and some animals make their homes in urban areas. Packs of dogs still roam the cities and countryside. Some sports stadiums become giant bat caves. As time passes, the roofs of buildings cave in, and trees and other plants grow in what used to be the indoors. Windows fall, paint is eroded, and concrete cracks. Plants begin to blanket the cities. Pet parrots—whose life span can be 60 years—may form flocks, still speaking the words they had been taught by their human owners.

Time-order words signal the order of events; the author uses cause-and-effect to develop the connection among events over time.

2. **◀ REREAD** Reread lines 1–12. Then, write a summary of the text so far, including essential supporting details.

If people suddenly disappeared from Earth, cars and planes would crash and fires would start. Pets would be ownerless. Within hours, power plants would stop producing electricity, and harmful gases would poison animals and cause explosions and fires.

3. **READ ▶** As you read lines 13–24, continue to cite textual evidence.
- Circle time-order words or phrases that introduce chronological events.
- In the margin, explain how the author develops her ideas and shows a relationship between events.

52

4. **◀ REREAD** Reread lines 13–24. List several cause-and-effect relationships to show a connection between events.

Pets run out of food, so they escape to a new environment. Dairy cattle die of thirst, and their bodies provide food for scavenging dogs. Water in nuclear power plants cooling ponds boils away, and the rods cause fires and release radiation into the air.

5. **READ ▶** As you read lines 25–48, continue to cite textual evidence.
- Circle each time-order word or phrase that introduces an event in chronological order.
- In the margin, explain how the author develops her ideas and shows a relationship among events.

53

2. **REREAD AND CITE TEXT EVIDENCE**

B **ASK STUDENTS** to describe one chain of events that would occur in the first week. *There are no people working in power plants, so the plants stop making electricity, which means that gas tanks get too hot and start to leak. Some of the leaked gases kill animals; others create fires. Without electricity, sewage treatment plants stop operating, so raw sewage flows into lakes and rivers.*

3. **READ AND CITE TEXT EVIDENCE**

C **ASK STUDENTS** what happens to animals that depend on people. *Pets are no longer fed, so they find new ways to survive. Big dogs join together to hunt small animals and scavenge. Cattle stuck in pens die of thirst, but cattle on ranch land can take over the plains.*

FOR ELL STUDENTS Students may confuse the meaning of the verbs *wander* (line 19) and *wonder*. Clarify that *to wander* is to walk without a specific purpose, and *to wonder* is to think about something or to be amazed by something.

4. **REREAD AND CITE TEXT EVIDENCE**

D **ASK STUDENTS** to name some of the consequences of the disappearance of operators at nuclear power plants. *Students should mention that cooling ponds will overheat, so the water will boil away. Then the fuel rods will become too hot, starting fires and leaking radiation. The radiation will kill some plants and animals.*

5. **READ AND CITE TEXT EVIDENCE**

E **ASK STUDENTS** why the author used so many time-order words and phrases. *The author wants to explore a possible future in chronological order. The process plays out over time, with some events occurring at various time periods. The author needs to use time-order words and phrases as guideposts that lead the reader through her ideas.*

CLOSE READ
Notes

As time passes, cities crumble, plants blanket cities, and animals adapt to their new environment.

F ⟨Between 50 and 100 years after⟩ the disappearance of human beings, skyscrapers begin to tumble. Bridges fall. The hulks of cars and buses start to disintegrate. The packs of dogs have reverted to their origins—they are

40 no longer German shepherds and Dobermans, but a single species more like a wolf. In cooler climates, the mighty cockroach meets its end; it cannot survive in unheated buildings.

⟨After 250 years⟩ the Statue of Liberty loses its torch. Old stone buildings have outlasted the toppled glass skyscrapers, especially as acid rain is no longer eroding them. But they are hidden under a mass of vegetation. Forests cover the eastern states, and ⟨over the next 250 years⟩ they return almost to the way they were ten thousand years ago.

It looks as though we had never been here.

6. **◀ REREAD** Reread lines 37–42. Determine the central ideas of this paragraph, and note it in the margin.

SHORT RESPONSE

Cite Text Evidence Use the central idea of the article and its development over the course of the article to write an objective summary of the text. Review your reading notes and **cite text evidence** in your response.

If people suddenly disappeared from Earth, there would be immediate and prolonged consequences. In the short term, animals would run out of food and would need to find ways to get food and adapt to their new environment. In the long term, the stoppage of work in power plants and sewage treatment plants would have a harmful effect on the environment and on living things, causing many plants and animals to die. With the passage of time, cities would crumble, plants would grow wild, some animals would revert to their origins, and much of Earth might look as if humans had never lived on the planet.

54

---

6. **REREAD AND DISCUSS USING TEXT EVIDENCE**

F **ASK STUDENTS** to summarize what happens to the physical remains of civilization during this period. *Bridges and buildings fall down, while vehicles begin to fall apart.* Have students summarize what happens to animals. *Dogs revert to a wolf-like breed, and cockroaches die out in cold places.*

SHORT RESPONSE

Cite Text Evidence Students' responses should include text evidence that supports their positions. They should:

- provide an objective summary of the article.
- give examples of some of the cause-and-effect relationships described in the article.
- state the author's central idea.

TO CHALLENGE STUDENTS . . .

The images in this selection are from the History Channel's *Life After People*. Students can see more images at http://www.history.com/shows/life-after-people/photos. For more examples of what would happen if people disappeared, they can also research the series *Life After People* online.

ASK STUDENTS to summarize what they learned from one of the videos. *Students should outline the chronology shown in the video, using time-order words and phrases to explain when key events in the subject's demise take place. They should explain the cause-and-effect relationships described in the video.*

DIG DEEPER

With the class, return to Question 4, Reread. Have students share their responses to the question.

ASK STUDENTS to discuss what happens in this period, from the end of the first week to several months later.

- Ask students to name other pets that would run out of food and explain how might they respond. *Cats, fish, hamsters, horses, and birds would run out of food. Pets that are locked in cages or stalls or are stuck indoors will starve or die of thirst. Pets that can get outside might be able to find other sources of food and survive.*

- Have students explain how cattle raised for food might repopulate the plains. *These cattle must live outdoors in fields. Many would die. But some would have enough food and water in their fields to survive. Eventually, fences around the fields would fall down, and the cattle could form herds.*

- Have students infer how nuclear power plants work. *They have fuel rods that get hot, so that heat must be used to produce electricity. When the fuel rods are spent, or used up, they stay hot because they have to be placed in cooling ponds.*

ASK STUDENTS to return to their Short Response answer and revise it based on the class discussion.

Participate in a Panel Discussion

COMMON CORE

W 9a–b Draw evidence from literary or informational texts.
SL 1a–d Initiate and participate effectively in a range of collaborative discussions.
SL 3 Evaluate a speaker's point of view, reasoning, and use of evidence and rhetoric.
SL 6 Adapt speech to a variety of contexts and tasks.

This collection explores the concept of change and how people respond to it. Recall the anchor text *The Metamorphosis* (both versions) and the other texts you have read. Synthesize your ideas about them by making a generalization about the ways in which people adapt to a major change. Then make your case in a panel discussion, citing evidence from the texts to support your points.

An effective participant in a panel discussion

- makes a clear, logical, and well-defended generalization about the ways people adapt to change

- uses quotations and examples from *The Metamorphosis* and two other texts to illustrate his or her ideas

- synthesizes ideas from all three texts with his or her own experiences

- responds thoughtfully and politely to the ideas of others on the panel

- evaluates other panel members' contributions, including the use of valid reasoning and sound evidence

PLAN

Get Organized Work with your classmates to prepare for the discussion.

- Join a small group and select one student to be the moderator for your discussion. The rest of your classmates will be the audience when you hold the discussion.

- Create a format for your discussion—a schedule that shows the order in which members of the panel will speak and for how many minutes. It will be the moderator's job to keep the discussion moving along on schedule.

- Set rules regarding the appropriate times for either the moderator or the audience to ask the panel members questions.

- Get together with your group and choose three texts from this collection, including a version of *The Metamorphosis,* that you will use to discuss change and adaptation.

myNotebook

Use the annotation tools in your eBook to find evidence that supports your ideas. Save each piece of evidence to your notebook.

ACADEMIC VOCABULARY

As you participate in your panel discussion, try to use these words.

> abstract
> evolve
> explicit
> facilitate
> infer

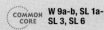
PARTICIPATE IN A PANEL DISCUSSION

COMMON CORE W 9a-b, SL 1a-d, SL 3, SL 6

Introduce students to the Performance Task by reading the introductory paragraph with them and reviewing the criteria for how to present and defend a generalization as part of a panel discussion. Remind students that the purpose of a panel discussion is to allow different speakers to share and explore their ideas about a topic and to educate an audience about the chosen subject.

PERFORMANCE TASK A

PLAN

GATHER EVIDENCE

View It!

Professional Development Podcast:
Performance Task

Because students will be collecting many different kinds of evidence from several different texts, suggest they record each bit of information on a separate index card and then use color-coding to sort the cards into groups based on what each fact or example illustrates about various ways people adapt or do not adapt to change. Once all the cards are sorted, students can begin making their generalizations or using the evidence in each pile to decide what they think is usually true about people in such situations.

PRODUCE

WRITE AND PRACTICE

Emphasize to students that their main ideas should relate both to their own experiences and to specific situations found in the texts. Encourage them to use the allotted practice time to try out various methods of communicating their points. Note that although they should not ramble on during their actual presentations, now is the time to experiment freely and figure out what works best by talking without fear of being cut off by a moderator or set time limit.

Gather Evidence Work individually to analyze *The Metamorphosis* and two other texts from the collection, gathering evidence about how people adapt (or don't adapt) to major change. Consider both concrete, easy-to-see changes and abstract changes as you read. Note specific details, examples, or quotations that illustrate responses to change. Then, think about your own experiences. Ask yourself these questions as you take notes:

- What are some different ways in which people can respond to change? What works, and what doesn't?

- Why do some people adapt easily while others do not? Is it a result of individual personalities, does it depend on the type of change, or both?

- What **generalization**, or broad conclusion, can you make about people's responses to major changes?

During this time, the moderator should review the same texts and make a list of relevant questions to be asked during the discussion.

PRODUCE

Write and Practice Outline your ideas and practice with a partner.

- State a clear generalization about the ways people respond to a major life change.

- Write several main ideas that support your generalization. Each idea should relate your generalization to a text or to your own experiences.

- Sort through the evidence you have collected and match each piece of evidence with the main idea it most clearly supports. Provide explicit examples.

- Present your ideas to a partner. Your partner will play the role of moderator, asking questions about your ideas and examples. This will prepare you to "think on your feet" during the real discussion.

- If you are the moderator, use this time to decide how you will introduce and conclude the panel discussion. Write a statement that tells the audience the topic of the discussion and its format. Write notes for a concluding statement, but be prepared to modify your remarks based on new ideas that emerge from the discussion.

my **WriteSmart**

Write your rough draft in *my*WriteSmart. Focus on getting your ideas down rather than perfecting your choice of language.

REVISE

Reinforce Your Ideas Based on your practice session with your partner, make changes to your outline. Use the chart on the following page to review the characteristics of an effective panel discussion. Consider the following questions:

- Were you able to defend your generalization? If not, revise your generalization statement so that it better reflects your textual evidence and your ideas.
- Were you able to answer your partner's questions clearly and without hesitation? If not, you may need to reorganize your outline so that you can find the information you need quickly and easily.
- Did your partner's questions help you see one of the texts in a new light? If so, add new evidence to your outline that you can share during the panel discussion.

my WriteSmart

Have your partner or a group of peers review your draft in myWriteSmart.

PRESENT

Have the Discussion You are now ready to participate in a lively exchange of ideas. Have your outline and/or notes handy for reference during the discussion.

- Begin by having the moderator introduce the topic, the panelists, and the basic format for the discussion. The moderator will then ask the first question and continue to facilitate the discussion in the agreed-upon format.
- Use your outline to remind you of your main points, but try to speak directly to the panel and to the audience. Don't just read from your paper.
- Listen closely to what all speakers say so that you can respond appropriately.
- Maintain a respectful tone toward your fellow panel members, even when you disagree with their ideas.
- When all the panelists have made their statements and discussed ideas among themselves, the moderator should invite audience members to ask questions.
- Conclude by having the moderator summarize the discussion. He or she should also thank the panelists for their participation.

Summarize Write a summary of the main points from the discussion. Then explain whether the discussion made you rethink your generalization, and why.

REVISE

REINFORCE YOUR IDEAS

Students should keep in mind that they will have a limited amount of time during their panel presentation in which to make their points. Using the feedback from their partners, they should attempt to simplify their explanation of each main idea so that it is expressed as clearly and concisely as possible. Along with strong bits of evidence from the texts, speakers can also plan ahead to use vivid language and interesting turns of phrase when presenting each idea to make it more memorable for the audience.

PRESENT

HAVE THE DISCUSSION

To capture the audience's attention and interest, students can keep some tips for effective public speaking in mind:

- Even if students feel nervous, they should take deep breaths to calm down and then speak with confidence.
- Students should make sure they do not speak too softly to be heard or too quickly to be understood.
- Students may want to use a few hand gestures to punctuate points.
- Although students may need to glance down at their notes to orient themselves from time to time, they should attempt to maintain good eye contact with whomever they are addressing.

PERFORMANCE TASK A

LANGUAGE

Have students look at the chart and identify how they did on the Performance Task in the Language category. Ask them to think about how formal or informal their language was during the discussion. If it was too informal, have students point out phrases that could be improved with formal English. Also, have them list the quotes and examples cited during the discussion and evaluate their accuracy.

PANEL DISCUSSION

	Ideas and Evidence	Organization	Language
ADVANCED	• Panelist clearly states a generalization and supports it with strong, relevant ideas and well-chosen evidence from the texts and personal experience. • Panelist carefully evaluates others' evidence and reasoning and responds with insightful comments and questions. • Panelist concludes remarks in a way that synthesizes analysis of the texts and helps listeners understand the generalization.	• Panelist's remarks are based on a well-organized outline of supporting ideas and evidence. • Ideas are presented in a logical order with effective transitions to clearly link ideas. • Panelist concludes with a statement that reinforces the generalization and takes into account the ideas that have emerged from the discussion.	• Panelist adapts speech to the context of the discussion, using appropriately formal English to discuss literature and ideas. • Panelist quotes accurately from the texts to support ideas. • Panelist maintains a polite and thoughtful tone throughout the discussion.
COMPETENT	• Panelist states a generalization and supports it with evidence from the texts and personal experience. • Panelist evaluates others' evidence and responds with appropriate comments and questions. • Panelist's concluding remark shows some synthesis of ideas and relates back to the generalization.	• Panelist's remarks are based on notes that identify supporting ideas and evidence. • Ideas are presented clearly and linked with transitions. • Panelist concludes with a statement that reinforces the generalization.	• Panelist mostly uses formal English to discuss literature and ideas. • Panelist usually quotes accurately from the texts to support ideas. • Panelist generally uses a polite and thoughtful tone.
LIMITED	• Panelist states a generalization and attempts to support it. • Panelist's response to others' comments shows limited evaluation of the evidence and reasoning. • Panelist's concluding remarks may simply repeat the generalization in a vague way.	• Panelist's remarks reflect notes but do not organize ideas and evidence well. • Ideas are presented in a disorganized way with few transitions. • Panelist concludes by restating the generalization.	• Panelist uses some informal English to discuss literature and ideas. • Panelist's quotations and examples sometimes do not accurately reflect the texts. • Panelist occasionally forgets to maintain a polite tone when responding to others' comments and questions.
EMERGING	• Panelist's generalization is unclear; ideas and evidence are not coherent. • Panelist does not evaluate others' evidence and reasoning. • Panelist does not provide a concluding remark.	• Panelist does not generate an outline or notes that organize ideas and evidence. • Ideas are presented in a disorganized way with no transitions. • Panelist's remarks lack a conclusion or summary.	• Panelist uses informal English and/or slang, resulting in ideas that are not clearly expressed. • Panelist's quotations and examples do not accurately reflect the texts. • Panelist does not maintain a polite tone when responding to others' comments and questions.

Write an Argument

COMMON CORE

W 1a–e Write arguments to support claims in an analysis of substantive topics or texts.

W 9a–b Draw evidence from literary or informational texts.

This collection focuses on change and our response to it. Look back at the anchor media selection *Rivers and Tides* and other selections you have read in the collection. In each selection, is change viewed as mostly positive, mostly negative, or a combination of the two? Synthesize your ideas by writing an argumentative essay.

An effective argument

- includes a clear claim about how change is viewed in *Rivers and Tides* and two other texts

- begins by engaging the reader with an interesting observation, quotation, or detail from one of the selections

- organizes central ideas in a logically structured body that clearly supports and elaborates on the claim

- uses transitions to create cohesion among sections of the text

- includes quotations or examples from the texts to illustrate central ideas

- has a concluding section that follows logically from the body of the essay and expresses the writer's own viewpoint on change

PLAN

Analyze the Texts Watch the clip from *Rivers and Tides* again, making notes on ideas about change. Is Andy Goldsworthy's view of change positive, negative, or neutral? Decide what you can infer beyond what is stated explicitly. Then, choose two other texts in the collection and ask the same question about change. In your notes, list details and examples that support your conclusions.

Clarify Your Own View Which text reflects your own view about change? Or, do you have a different perspective on change that is not portrayed in this collection?

- Make notes about your own view on change.

- Provide evidence from the texts or your own experience that supports your view.

- Explain why you agree or disagree with how change is portrayed in the texts.

my **Notebook**

Use the annotation tools in your eBook to find evidence that supports your ideas. Save each piece of evidence to your notebook.

ACADEMIC VOCABULARY

As you share your ideas about perspectives on change, be sure to use these words.

> *abstract*
> *evolve*
> *explicit*
> *facilitate*
> *infer*

WRITE AN ARGUMENT

COMMON CORE W 1a-e, W 9a-b

Review with students the characteristics of an effective argumentative essay. Explain that to write a successful argument, it is not enough just to state one's thoughts and opinions about an issue. One must both compose a clear and specific thesis statement and support this idea with concrete evidence and examples from several sources.

PLAN

ANALYZE THE TEXTS

View It!

Professional Development Podcast:

Performance Task

When fleshing out their position on a topic, students should clarify their view by examining the topic from various angles. They may find as they do additional research and ponder the issue in more depth that their original opinion might change and they may end up choosing to write from a totally different perspective.

Get Organized Organize your details and evidence in an outline.

- Write a clear thesis statement about how change is viewed in the video clip and in the texts.

- Choose an organizational pattern for your essay. You might discuss all of the positive portrayals of change in one section and all of the negative portrayals in another, or you might examine each text one after the other. How you organize ideas may also depend on whether your claim focuses on a single view of change or if it presents a mixed perspective.

- Use your organizational pattern to sort the evidence you have gathered from the selections into a logical order.

- Search for an interesting quotation or detail to complement your thesis statement.

- Write down some ideas for your conclusion that reflect your own perspective on change, including textual or personal evidence that supports your ideas.

PRODUCE

GET ORGANIZED

As students write, they can strengthen their argument by imagining what someone who disagrees with their claims might say. Once they have identified any valid counterarguments, they can include additional evidence to refute them. Explain to students that they must present these counterarguments fairly, however, and not include any "strawman" arguments, or intentionally weak opinions that are easily disproved and that no one would actually hold.

PRODUCE

Draft Your Essay Write a draft of your essay, following your outline.

- Introduce your claim, the foundation for your entire argument. Be as explicit and clear as possible so that readers will immediately understand your point of view on the topic.

- Present your details, quotations, and examples from the selections in logically ordered paragraphs. Each paragraph should have a central idea related to your thesis with evidence to support it. Explain how each piece of evidence supports the central idea.

- Use transitions to link sections of the text and to clarify the relationships among your ideas.

- Write a conclusion that follows logically from the body of the essay. Make a statement about your own perspective on change and provide supporting evidence.

*my*WriteSmart

Write your rough draft in *my*WriteSmart. Focus on getting your ideas down rather than perfecting your choice of language.

Improve Your Draft Revise your draft to make sure it is clear, coherent, and engaging. Use the chart on the following page to review the characteristics of an effective argument. Ask yourself these questions as you revise:

*my*WriteSmart

Have your partner or a group of peers review your draft in *my*WriteSmart. Ask your reviewers to note any reasons that do not support the claim or lack sufficient evidence.

- Does my introduction present my claim clearly? Will my readers want to continue reading?
- Are the titles and authors of the selections accurately identified in my introduction?
- Have I provided sufficient and relevant textual evidence to support my central ideas?
- Do my ideas develop logically? Are transitions smooth and coherent?
- Have I maintained an appropriate style of English for a formal argument? Does my choice of words convey a knowledgeable and confident tone, or attitude, toward the topic?
- Does my conclusion state my own perspective on change and provide a satisfying ending?

PRESENT

Exchange Essays When your final draft is completed, exchange essays with a partner. Read your partner's essay and provide feedback.

- Which aspects of your partner's essay are particularly strong?
- Did any sections of the essay confuse you? If so, how could they be clarified?

Publish Online If your school has a website where you can post your writing, work with your classmates to publish your collection of essays online. First, review your own essay and look for places to add links to other online sources that readers may find helpful. Then, as a group, create a front page that introduces the collection and invites readers to explore the individual essays. You might also consider setting up a blog to allow readers to share their own perspectives on change.

PERFORMANCE TASK B

REVISE

IMPROVE YOUR DRAFT

When revising, students should examine and fix larger issues such as organization and transitions first and then focus on smaller issues such as grammar and word choice. When fine-tuning the order in which they present evidence, students should prioritize their facts and take out any superfluous details that might distract the reader's attention from the main focus of the argument. Note that students can also strengthen the force of their arguments by deleting emotional phrases such as "I feel" or "I think" and just stating their opinions outright.

PRESENT

EXCHANGE ESSAYS

When selecting online sources for their links, students should consider the reliability and reputation of each site. When composing the introduction page for their collection, students should consider how best to group and order their essays. Can they classify them by the positions taken by each student or would it make more sense to organize them based on the additional collection texts that each essay analyzes? If students are unable to use a school website to publish their work, have them print out their individual essays and introduction page and bind them together as a class book.

PERFORMANCE TASK B

ARGUMENTATIVE ESSAY

Have students look at the chart and identify how they did on the Performance Task in each of the three main categories. Then have them examine how well their argument meets the characteristics of the highest level of proficiency and make a short list of things they could do during the composition of their next argumentative essay to strengthen their claim and its presentation to an audience.

COLLECTION 3 TASK B
ARGUMENTATIVE ESSAY

	Ideas and Evidence	Organization	Language
ADVANCED	• An eloquent introduction includes the titles and authors of the selections; the claim describes the view of change presented in three selections. • Specific, relevant details support the claim. • A satisfying concluding section synthesizes the ideas, summarizes the argument, and offers the writer's unique insight on change.	• Central ideas and supporting evidence are organized effectively and logically throughout the essay. • Varied transitions successfully show the relationships between ideas.	• The analysis has an appropriately formal style and a knowledgeable, objective tone. • Language is precise and captures the writer's thoughts with originality. • Sentence beginnings, lengths, and structures vary and have a rhythmic flow. • Spelling, capitalization, and punctuation are correct. • Grammar and usage are correct.
COMPETENT	• The introduction identifies the titles and authors of the selections but could be more engaging; the claim is stated clearly. • One or two central ideas need more support. • The concluding section synthesizes most of the ideas and summarizes most of the argument, but it doesn't provide an original insight on change.	• The organization of central ideas and supporting evidence is mostly clear. • Transitions generally clarify the relationships between ideas.	• The style is usually formal, and the tone at times communicates confidence. • Most language is precise. • Sentence beginnings, lengths, and structures vary somewhat. • Some spelling, capitalization, and punctuation mistakes occur. • Some grammar and usage errors appear but do not interfere with the writer's message.
LIMITED	• The introduction identifies the titles and the authors of the selections; the claim only hints at the main idea of the argument. • Details support some central ideas but are often too general. • The concluding section gives an incomplete summary of the argument and merely restates the thesis.	• Most central ideas are organized logically, but many supporting details are out of place. • More transitions are needed throughout the essay to connect ideas.	• The style is informal in many places, and the tone reflects a superficial understanding of the selections. • Language is repetitive or vague at times. • Sentence structures barely vary, and some fragments or run-on sentences are present. • Spelling, capitalization, and punctuation are often incorrect. • Grammar and usage are incorrect in many places.
EMERGING	• The appropriate elements of an introduction are missing. • Details and evidence are irrelevant or missing. • The argument lacks a concluding section.	• A logical organization is not used; ideas are presented randomly. • Transitions are not used, making the essay difficult to understand.	• The style and tone are inappropriate. • Language is inaccurate, repetitive, and vague. • Repetitive sentence structure, fragments, and run-on sentences make the writing difficult to follow. • Spelling, capitalization, and punctuation are incorrect throughout. • Many grammatical and usage errors make ideas difficult to understand.

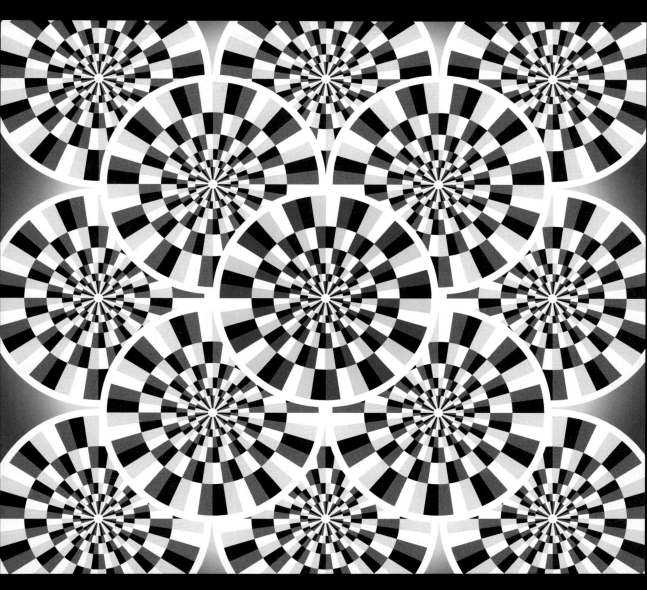

How We See Things

❝The question is not what you look at, but what you see.**❞**

—Henry David Thoreau

How We See Things

Our view of the world depends not only on our five senses but also on technology and surprising insights.

CONNECTING WORD AND IMAGE

ASK STUDENTS to discuss how the collection opener image and the collection quotation work together to create a connection.

PERFORMANCE TASK PREVIEW

Point out to students that they will complete two performance tasks at the end of the collection. The performance tasks will require them to further analyze the selections in the collection and to synthesize ideas about these analyses. They will present their findings in a variety of products.

ACADEMIC VOCABULARY

> **▶ View It!**
>
> Professional Development Podcast:
> **Academic Vocabulary**

Students can acquire facility with the academic vocabulary words through frequent, repeated exposure as they analyze and discuss the selections in the collection. Academic vocabulary can be used in the following instructional contexts. This will enable students to incorporate the academic vocabulary words into their working vocabulary.

- Collaborative Discussion at the end of each selection
- Analyzing the Text questions for each selection
- Selection-level Performance Task
- Vocabulary instruction (for Critical Vocabulary and/or for Vocabulary Strategy)
- Language and Style
- End-of-collection Performance Task for all selections in the collection

ASK STUDENTS to review the academic vocabulary word list for this collection. You may wish to pronounce each word aloud, so students hear the correct pronunciation. Then, discuss the definitions and the related forms for each word. Remind students that they will encounter these five academic vocabulary words throughout the collection.

COLLECTION

PERFORMANCE TASK Preview

At the end of this collection, you will have the opportunity to complete two tasks:

- Deliver a speech about how we perceive things.
- Write a short story using techniques employed by authors in this collection.

ACADEMIC VOCABULARY

Study the words and their definitions in the chart below. You will use these words as you discuss and write about the texts in this collection.

Word	Definition	Related Forms
differentiate (dĭf´ə-rĕn´shē-āt´) v.	to distinguish or demonstrate the individual qualities of	differentiation, undifferentiated
incorporate (ĭn-kôr´pə-rāt´) v.	to absorb or make part of a whole	incorporation, incorporated
mode (mōd) n.	a way or means for expressing or doing something	modus operandi
orient (ôr´ē-ĕnt´) v.	to place or align in relation to something else	orientation, disoriented
perspective (pər-spĕk´tĭv) n.	a viewpoint from a particular position; an outlook or standpoint	perspectival, perspicacious

154

USING COLLECTIONS YOUR WAY

Use the following information, along with the charts on the following pages, to help you decide how you want to introduce the collection. Based on your teaching style, your students' interests, or your instructional goals, you may want to structure the collection in various ways. You may choose different entry points each time you teach the collection.

"I love teaching traditional literature."

These poems from the 19th century—written by **Emily Dickinson**, who had sensitivity to light—appeal to the sense of sight by using metaphors and imagery related to eyes and light.

COMPARE ANCHOR TEXTS

We grow accustomed to the Dark
Before I got my eye put out

Poems by Emily Dickinson

Emily Dickinson *(1830–1886) had only a handful of her poems published during her lifetime. Nevertheless, those poems and the many published after her death earned her a place as a leading nineteenth-century American poet. Dickinson was born and spent her life—except for one year spent at a nearby seminary—in Amherst, Massachusetts. She adored her stern and principled father, but had a complicated relationship with her mother. She was very close to her older brother, Austin, and her younger sister, Vinnie.*

As an adult, Dickinson was known for her reclusiveness. During one of her last journeys away from Amherst, she saw an ophthalmologist in Boston for aches in her eyes and sensitivity to light. Her poems "We grow accustomed to the Dark" and "Before I got my eye put out" use imagery related to sight and light.

After Dickinson's death, her sister carried out the poet's wishes, burning all of her letters from family and friends. However, she rescued a little box filled with poems. Since her late teens or early twenties, Emily Dickinson had been writing poetry—on scraps of paper, old recipes, and the backs of envelopes. Though she wrote 1,775 poems, Dickinson published only seven, anonymously, during her lifetime. The private poet left the world pondering her untold secrets.

Compare Anchor Texts **155**

Julio Cortázar *(1914–1984) was an Argentine teacher, novelist, and short-story writer. A vocal opponent of the Argentinian government, Cortázar fled to Paris in 1951, where he remained until his death. He is best known for deftly weaving fantasy, hallucinations, and dreams into his fiction, as he does in "The Night Face Up." The Aztec sacrifice alluded to in this work was an important part of Aztec religious life. Human victims were usually prisoners of war or slaves; their sacrifice was thought to appease the gods and make them stronger.*

The Night Face Up

Short Story by Julio Cortázar   Translated by Paul Blackburn

AS YOU READ Notice the two separate stories that unfold at the same time. Write down any questions you generate during reading.

And at certain periods they went out to hunt enemies; they called it the war of the blossom.

Halfway down the long hotel vestibule,[1] he thought that probably he was going to be late, and hurried on into the street to get out his motorcycle from the corner where the next-door superintendent let him keep it. On the jewelry store at the corner he read that it was ten to nine; he had time to spare. The sun filtered through the tall downtown buildings, and he—because for himself, for just going along thinking, he did not have a name—he swung onto the machine, savoring the idea of the ride. The motor whirred between his legs, and a cool wind whipped his pantslegs.

[1] The war of the blossom was the name the Aztecs gave to a ritual war in which they took prisoners for sacrifice. It is metaphysics to say that the gods see men as flowers, to be so uprooted, trampled, cut down. –Ed. [Cortázar's note]
[1] **vestibule:** a hall or entryway next to a building's exterior door.

The Night Face Up **171**

"I want to challenge my students to the utmost."

This short story is structured to include two separate, parallel plots—one depicting the character's reality and one depicting the character's dream state—that serve to mirror each other.

"I like to teach by comparing texts."

Different aspects of the same topic, the Greek myth of Icarus, are explored in two different media—a 16th-century painting and a 20th-century poem that was inspired by the painting.

COMPARE TEXT AND MEDIA

Musée des Beaux Arts
Landscape with the Fall of Icarus

Poem by W. H. Auden   Painting by Pieter Breughel the Elder

Background *According to a Greek myth, King Minos imprisoned the architect and inventor Daedalus and his son Icarus on the isle of Crete. In order to escape, Daedalus built two pairs of wings with feathers and wax. Before fleeing the island, he warned his son to not fly too high, lest the warm sunlight melt the wax and destroy the wings. Once airborne, however, Icarus became exhilarated with the joy and freedom of flight. Higher and higher he flew, until the wax on his wings did indeed begin to soften. The feathers separated, and the young man fell and drowned in a part of the Aegean called the Icarian Sea.*

The story of Icarus shows the danger of upsetting the natural order, either through artifice or ambition. It has fascinated visual artists from ancient sculptors through Rubens and Matisse. Writers and poets, too, have expanded on the legend; the Roman poet Ovid published a particularly influential version in AD 8. Over the centuries, painters and poets have consistently informed and alluded to each others' work on the subject.

Ovid's tale inspired perhaps the best known Icarus painting, a work once attributed to Pieter Breughel the Elder (1525–1569). We know little about the life of the great Flemish painter, who became famous for his finely detailed, allegorical landscapes. Breughel began and ended his career in what is now Belgium, but he was greatly influenced by Italian art and spent several years painting in Italy.

Breughel's Landscape with the Fall of Icarus inspired a major 20th-century poet, W. H. Auden (1907–1973) first viewed the painting in a Brussels museum in 1938, shortly before war broke out in Europe. In 1939 he moved from his native England to New York City. "Musée des Beaux Arts" appeared in 1940. Auden taught at universities and wrote plays, prose, music lyrics, and over a dozen books of poems. His poetry, which features keen observation and direct, accessible language, had a profound influence on a generation of modern poets.

Compare Text and Media **189**

mySmartPlanner | **eBook** | **myNotebook** | **myWriteSmart** | **fyi** hmhfyi.com

Collection 4 Lessons	Media	Teach and Practice
Student Edition | eBook	▶ Video Links **H** HISTORY **A&E**	**Close Reading and Evidence Tracking**
ANCHOR TEXT Poems by Emily Dickinson "We grow accustomed to the Dark" "Before I got my eye put out"	◉ **Audio** "We grow accustomed to the Dark" "Before I got my eye put out"	**Close Read Screencasts** • Modeled Discussion 1 (lines 1–4) • Modeled Discussion 2 (lines 1–4) **Strategies for Annotation** • Analyze Author's Choices: Poetic Structure
CLOSE READER Essay by Billy Collins "The Trouble with Poetry Today"	◉ **Audio** "The Trouble with Poetry Today"	
ANCHOR TEXT Science Essay by Neil de Grasse Tyson "Coming to Our Senses"	◉ **Audio** "Coming to Our Senses"	**Close Read Screencasts** • Modeled Discussion 1 (lines 26–38) **Strategies for Annotation** • Determine a Theme and Analyze its Development • Understanding Context
CLOSE READER Book Review by Matilda Batters by "Every Second Counts"	◉ **Audio** "Every Second Counts"	
Short Story by Julio Cortázar Translated by Paul Blackburn "The Night Face Up"	◉ **Audio** "The Night Face Up" ▶ **Video HISTORY** Culture of Art and Death ▶ **Video BIOGRAPHY** Julio Cortázar	**Strategies for Annotation** • Analyze Author's Choices: Parallel Plots and Tension • Language and Style: Adverbial Clauses
ANCHOR TEXT Math Essay by Keith Devlin "The Math Instinct"	◉ **Audio** "The Math Instinct"	**Strategies for Annotation** • Prefixes
CLOSE READER News Article from *ScienceDaily* "Whale Sharks Use Geometry to Avoid Sinking"	◉ **Audio** "Whale Sharks Use Geometry to Avoid Sinking"	
Poem by W. H. Auden "Musée des Beaux Arts" Painting by Pieter Breughel the Elder *Landscape with the Fall of Icarus*	◉ **Audio** "Musée des Beaux Arts"	**Strategies for Annotation** • Analyzing Representations in Different Mediums
Collection 4 Performance Tasks: **A** Present a Speech **B** Write a Short Story	**fyi** hmhfyi.com	**Interactive Lessons** **A** Giving a Presentation **B** Writing Narratives **A** Using Textual Evidence **B** Writing as a Process

For Systematic Coverage of Writing and Speaking & Listening Standards	Interactive Lessons Using Textual Evidence Using Media in a Presentation	Lesson Assessments Using Textual Evidence Using Media in a Presentation

Assess		Extend	Reteach
Performance Task	**Online Assessment**	**Teacher eBook**	**Teacher eBook**
Writing Activity: Essay	Selection Test	**Interactive Whiteboard Lesson >** **Determine Figurative Meanings**	**Analyze Author's Choices: Poetic Structure** **> Level Up Tutorial >** Elements of Poetry
Speaking Activity: Discussion	Selection Test	**Analyze How Authors Develop Ideas**	**Analyze Development of Ideas** **Interactive Graphic Organizer >** Main Idea and Details Chart
Writing Activity: Analysis	Selection Test	**Analyze Point of View: Background > Level** **Up Tutorial >** Conducting Research	**Cite Textual Evidence > Level Up Tutorial >** Reading for Details
Writing Activity: Research	Selection Test	**Organize Ideas in Writing**	**Determine Meaning and Analyze ideas >** **Level Up Tutorial >** Main Idea and Supporting Details
Speaking Activity: Comparison	Selection Test	**Evaluate a Speaker** **Determine a Theme** **Interactive Whiteboard Lesson >** Form in Poetry	**Analyzing Representations in Different** **Mediums > Level Up Tutorial >** Universal and Recurring Themes
A Present a Speech **B** Write a Short Story	Collection Test		

Collection 4 Lessons	COMMON CORE Key Learning Objective	Performance Task
ANCHOR TEXT **Poems by Emily Dickinson** **"We grow accustomed to the Dark," p. 156** **"Before I got my eye put out," p. 157A**	**The student will be able to…** identify and compare poetic structure across two poems as well as paraphrase and summarize ideas	Writing Activity: Essay
ANCHOR TEXT **Lexile 1310** **Science Essay by Neil de Grasse Tyson** **"Coming to Our Senses," p. 161A**	**The student will be able to…** analyze the development of ideas in nonfiction	Speaking Activity: Discussion
ANCHOR TEXT **Lexile 1210** **Math Essay by Keith Devlin** **"The Math Instinct," p. 183A**	**The student will be able to…** determine meaning and analyze ideas	Writing Activity: Research
Short Story by Julio Cortázar **Translated by Paul Blackburn** **"The Night Face Up," p. 171A** **Lexile 1210**	**The student will be able to…** cite textual evidence and analyze how an author uses parallel plots, tone, pace, and foreshadowing to create tension	Writing Activity: Analysis
Poem by W. H. Auden **"Musée des Beaux Arts," p. 190A** **Painting by Pieter Breughel the Elder** *Landscape with the Fall of Icarus,* **p. 191A**	**The student will be able to…** analyze representations in different mediums	Speaking Activity: Comparison

Collection 4 Performance Tasks:
A Present a Speech
B Write a Short Story

Vocabulary Strategy	Language and Style	Student Instructional Support	CLOSE READER Selection
	Writing Conventions	**Scaffolding for ELL Students:** Analyzing Author's Choices: Poetic Structure **When Students Struggle:** Figurative Language **To Challenge Students:** Language Skills: Explore Poetic Form	Essay by Billy Collins "The Trouble with Poetry Today," p. 160b
Using Reference Sources	Parallel Structure	**Scaffolding for ELL Students:** Analyze Language **When Students Struggle:** • Comprehension • Analogy • Parallel Structure **To Challenge Students:** Extend and Develop a Concept	Book Review by Matilda Battersby "Every Second Counts," p. 170b **Lexile 1090**
Prefixes		**Scaffolding for ELL Students:** Determine Meaning **When Students Struggle:** Analyze Ideas **To Challenge Students:** Comprehension	News Article from *ScienceDaily* "Whale Sharks Use Geometry to Avoid Sinking," p. 188b **Lexile 1530**
	Adverbial Clauses	**Scaffolding for ELL Students:** • Analyze Author's Choices: Parallel Plots and Tension • Analyze Author's Choices: Parallel Plots • Analyze Author's Choices: Tension **When Students Struggle:** • Sensory Details • Comprehension • Descriptive Language **To Challenge Students:** • Character Perspectives • Story Maps	
		Scaffolding for ELL Students: Punctuation and Comprehension **When Students Struggle:** Analyzing a Painting	

ANCHOR TEXT EXEMPLAR

We grow accustomed to the Dark

 ANCHOR TEXT

Before I got my eye put out

Poems by Emily Dickinson

Why These Texts?

Students encounter increasingly complex poems in text material. This lesson explores how Emily Dickinson creates meaning through word choice and structure in two related selections.

Key Learning Objective: The student will be able to identify and compare poetic structure across two poems as well as paraphrase and summarize ideas.

For practice and application:

Close Reader selection
"The Trouble with Poetry Today"
essay by Billy Collins

COMMON CORE — Common Core Standards

RL 1 Cite textual evidence.

RL 2 Determine a theme and analyze its development.

RL 4 Determine the meaning of words and phrases.

RL 5 Analyze an author's choices concerning how to structure a text.

W 1 Write arguments using valid reasoning and relevant evidence.

SL 1 Participate in collaborative discussions with diverse partners.

L 1 Demonstrate standard English grammar and usage.

L 2 Demonstrate standard English capitalization, punctuation, and spelling.

▲ Text Complexity Rubric

	We grow accustomed to the Dark	Before I got my eye put out
Quantitative Measures	Lexile: N/A	Lexile: N/A
Qualitative Measures	**Levels of Meaning/Purpose** multiple levels of meaning (multiple themes)	**Levels of Meaning/Purpose** multiple levels of meaning (multiple themes)
	Structure regular stanzas with some liberties taken	**Structure** regular stanzas with some liberties taken
	Language Conventionality and Clarity ambiguous language requiring inferences	**Language Conventionality and Clarity** ambiguous language requiring inferences
	Knowledge Demands moderately complex theme	**Knowledge Demands** moderately complex theme
Reader/Task Considerations	Teacher determined Vary by individual reader and type of text	Teacher determined Vary by individual reader and type of text

TEACH

CLOSE READ

Emily Dickinson was a contemporary of early American poets such as Edgar Allan Poe, Henry Wadsworth Longfellow, and Walt Whitman. Dickinson was likely discouraged from reading Whitman's poems due to their scandalous reputation, but her work shares a similar openness of expression and disregard for conventional style.

Though Dickinson published only seven poems during her lifetime, she shared many others with friends and family. In 1862, she sent a selection of poems to Thomas Wentworth Higginson, a well-known writer of the time. Higginson did not encourage Dickinson to publish, but they struck up a correspondence that lasted the rest of her life. After her death, Higginson helped edit two volumes of her poems.

Early editions of Emily Dickinson's poems were heavily edited, with changes to her punctuation and some of her rhymes. Many poems that dealt with death and loss were omitted from collections. Despite the popularity of Dickinson's poetry, a complete collection of her works was not published until 1955.

Many lines from Emily Dickinson's poems have become a part of common usage. A few are listed below:

"Hope is the thing with feathers."

"Success is counted sweetest by those who ne'er succeed."

"After great pain, a formal feeling comes."

"Tell the truth, but tell it slant."

"A word is dead when it is said, some say. I say it just begins to live that day."

"Because I could not stop for death, He kindly stopped for me."

"That it shall never come again is what makes life so sweet."

We grow accustomed to the Dark
Before I got my eye put out

Poems by Emily Dickinson

Emily Dickinson (1830–1886) *had only a handful of her poems published during her lifetime. Nevertheless, those poems and the many published after her death earned her a place as a leading nineteenth-century American poet. Dickinson was born and spent her life—except for one year spent at a nearby seminary—in Amherst, Massachusetts. She adored her stern and principled father, but had a complicated relationship with her mother. She was very close to her older brother, Austin, and her younger sister, Vinnie.*

As an adult, Dickinson was known for her reclusiveness. During one of her last journeys away from Amherst, she saw an ophthalmologist in Boston for aches in her eyes and sensitivity to light. Her poems "We grow accustomed to the Dark" and "Before I got my eye put out" use imagery related to sight and light.

After Dickinson's death, her sister carried out the poet's wishes, burning all of her letters from family and friends. However, she rescued a little box filled with poems. Since her late teens or early twenties, Emily Dickinson had been writing poetry—on scraps of paper, old recipes, and the backs of envelopes. Though she wrote 1,775 poems, Dickinson published only seven, anonymously, during her lifetime. The private poet left the world pondering her untold secrets.

Compare Anchor Texts **155**

Close Read Screencasts   ▶ **View It!**

Modeled Discussions

Have students click the *Close Read* icons in their eBooks to access two screencasts in which readers discuss and annotate the following key passages:

- opening stanza of "We grow accustomed to the Dark" (lines 1–4)
- opening stanza of "Before I got my eye put out" (lines 1–4)

As a class, view and discuss at least one of these videos. Then have students pair up to do an independent close read of two additional passages—lines 9–16 of "We grow accustomed to the Dark" and lines 18–21 of "Before I got my eye put out."

AS YOU READ Direct students to use the As You Read statement to focus their reading.

Analyze Author's Choices: Poetic Structure (LINES 1–20)

COMMON CORE RL 5

Explain the following poetic structures: Most poems consist of groups of lines called **stanzas. Meter** is the repeated pattern, or rhythm, of stressed and unstressed syllables in each line. A combination of two or three syllables is a metrical **foot,** or one unit of rhythm. An **iamb** is a metrical foot consisting of an unstressed syllable followed by a stressed syllable. The number of feet per line determines meter. Write these examples on the board: a line with three metrical feet is a trimeter; with four metrical feet, a tetrameter; and with five metrical feet, a pentameter. Explain that a poet's choice of words controls the meter and rhyme of a poem.

 ASK STUDENTS to silently read the first line of "We grow accustomed to the Dark" and note the pattern of unstressed and stressed syllables. Then ask them to divide the line into feet and tell the meter of the line. *(tetrameter)* Ask students to examine the meter in the other lines in the stanza and tell whether the meter is consistent. *(No. The second and fourth lines each have three feet.)* Ask students how rhythm creates impact with one-syllable words such as "*Dark*" and "*Lamp*." *(The rhythm emphasizes those words.)* Have students continue to identify the meter in the remaining lines and point out words that are emphasized by the rhythm.

Cite Evidence: Paraphrase and Summary (LINES 16–20)

COMMON CORE RL 1, RL 2

Explain to students that a **paraphrase** is a rephrasing of a text using one's own words.

 CITE TEXT EVIDENCE Have students paraphrase lines 16–20 of the poem. *(As people's eyes grow used to the dark, there's a change. Either the night turns out to be less dark, or their vision adapts to the darkness. In either case, everything seems normal.)*

AS YOU READ Jot down references Dickinson makes in both poems to seeing. Write down any questions you generate during reading.

We grow accustomed to the Dark

We grow accustomed to the Dark –
When Light is put away –
As when the Neighbor holds the Lamp
To witness her Goodbye –

5 A Moment – We uncertain step
For newness of the night –
Then – fit our Vision to the Dark –
And meet the Road – erect –

And so of larger – Darknesses –
10 Those Evenings of the Brain –
When not a Moon disclose a sign –
Or Star – come out – within –

The Bravest – grope a little –
And sometimes hit a Tree
15 Directly in the Forehead –
But as they learn to see –

Either the Darkness alters –
Or something in the sight
Adjusts itself to Midnight –
20 And Life steps almost straight.

SCAFFOLDING FOR ELL STUDENTS

Analyzing Author's Choices: Poetic Structure Using a whiteboard, project the first stanza of the poem. Read aloud the first line of the poem, exaggerating each stressed syllable. Explain that "We grow" is one unit, or **foot,** made of two syllables with "We" being unstressed and "grow" being stressed. Explain that a foot with one unstressed syllable followed by one stressed syllable is called an **iamb.** Point out that a foot can be comprised of syllables from one or more word. Invite volunteers to read aloud lines from the first stanza, exaggerating the stressed syllables in order to mark up each foot. Then have students work in small groups to mark up the feet and practice reading aloud the rest of the poem. Conclude the activity by asking students to discuss how identifying the feet in the poem helps them understand meter.

Before I got my eye put out

Before I got my eye put out
I liked as well to see –
As other Creatures, that have Eyes
And know no other way –

5   But were it told to me – Today –
That I might have the sky
For mine – I tell you that my Heart
Would split, for size of me –

The Meadows – mine –
10 The Mountains – mine –
All Forests – Stintless[1] Stars –
As much of Noon as I could take
Between my finite eyes –

The Motions of the Dipping Birds –
15 The Morning's Amber Road –
For mine – to look at when I liked –
The News would strike me dead –

So safer – guess – with just my soul
Upon the Window pane –
20 Where other Creatures put their eyes –
Incautious – of the Sun –

COLLABORATIVE DISCUSSION Why are seeing and vision important in these poems? With a partner, discuss the references you noted in both poems to eyesight, seeing, or vision. Cite specific textual evidence from the poems to support your ideas.

---

[1] **Stintless:** without limit or restraint.

WHEN STUDENTS STRUGGLE . . .

Much of the sense of Dickinson's poem is carried by her use of figurative language. Explain to students that Dickinson uses language to paint a picture of the action of the poem. Read aloud "Before I got my eye put out" and ask students to echo your reading. As you read, pose questions about the images in the poem.

Ask students to identify the "Creatures" in line 3. *(people)* Then ask why people are referred to as creatures. *(because they are unthinking)* Why are birds described as "dipping" in line 14? *(They're swooping down to earth.)* Why is the road amber in line 15? *(It's yellow from the sunrise.)* Ask similar questions about other images in the poem.

CLOSE READ

Analyze Author's Choices: RL 5
Poetic Structure

(LINES 1–8, 14–17)

Explain that Dickinson uses rhyme in an atypical way, often using **assonance** (repetition of vowel sounds) and **consonance** (repetition of end consonant sounds). She also uses internal rhyme within stanzas.

C **CITE TEXT EVIDENCE** Ask students which words rhyme in the first line. *("I," "my", and "eye")* Ask which word is emphasized with this rhyme. *("eye")* Have students cite other words that repeat the "i" sound in the first two stanzas. *("liked," "might," mine," and "size")*

D **CITE TEXT EVIDENCE** Ask students to read the fourth stanza aloud. Have them cite an example of consonance. *("Dipping" and "Morning's," lines 14–15)* Ask which words are examples of assonance in lines 14 and 15. *("Motions," and "Road"; "Birds" and "Amber")*

Cite Evidence: Paraphrase RL 1, RL 2
and Summary (LINES 18–21)

Reiterate that a **paraphrase** is a restatement using one's own words and retaining most of the ideas. A **summary** is a short description of main ideas.

E **CITE TEXT EVIDENCE** Ask students to write a paraphrase of the final stanza of this poem. *(Possible answer: I guess it is safer to look out the window just using my memory, unlike other people who recklessly look at everything around them.)* Ask students what word they might use to replace "soul" in line 18. *(memory; thoughts)* Ask what word might replace "Creatures" in line 20 *(people)* and what word might replace "Incautious" in line 21. *(reckless)* Then have students write a summary of the same stanza. *(Possible answer: Using my imagination to see things is better than actually seeing them.)*

COLLABORATIVE DISCUSSION Have students pair up and discuss the references to sight in both poems, citing text evidence. Then have students share their ideas with the class as a whole.

ASK STUDENTS to share any questions they generated in the course of reading and discussing this selection.

CLOSE READ

Cite Evidence: Paraphrase and Summary RL 1, RL 2

Make sure that students understand the difference between a **paraphrase** and a **summary.** Explain that because Dickinson's work uses so few words to express meaning, a paraphrase of her verse is often longer than the original.

Have students paraphrase and write a summary of the first stanza of "Before I got my eye put out." Have them refer to the examples as a basis for their writing. *(Possible answers: Paraphrase: Before I lost my vision, I enjoyed seeing the world as much as other people who take their ability to see for granted. Summary: When I could see I never thought twice about it.)*

Analyze Author's Choices: Poetic Structure RL 5

Explain that line placement, stanzas, meter, and rhyme all contribute to a poem's structure. **Stanzas** consist of two or more lines with a pattern. Point out that both poems use four-line stanzas. Have students review "Before I got my eye put out." Explain that the first line of this poem has four **feet,** or units of rhythm. Ask students if that is true of all lines. *(No; alternating lines have three feet.)* Ask students to read the poem aloud and note the rhythmic patterns within each line and stanza. Add that while the placement and length of lines create a strong visual impact, meter and rhyme create a strong auditory impact.

Cite Evidence: Paraphrase and Summary RL 1, RL 2

One way to approach reading and understanding poetry is to paraphrase or summarize parts of the poem as you read. A **paraphrase** is a restatement in your own words. A **summary** is a brief statement of the central ideas in a piece of writing. Notice the differences in the following examples.

"We grow accustomed to the Dark," Stanza 1	
Paraphrase—Our eyes adjust to the darkness when a light is taken away, as when someone we are visiting says goodbye and steps away from the door with the lamp.	**Summary**—We get used to the darkness when there is no light.

Although paraphrases and summaries do not incorporate all the detail or style of the original, they draw closely on the wording and ideas of the text. Thinking about details and imagery as you read will help you identify themes and summarize or paraphrase poems to check your understanding.

Analyze Author's Choices: Poetic Structure RL 5

When you first read a poem, you will notice its **structure**, or the way the words are arranged on the page. The main structural components of a poem are the length and placement of the **lines**, and the way the lines are placed into groups called **stanzas**. In "We grow accustomed to the Dark," Dickinson uses quatrains, or four-line stanzas. Other key structural elements of poetry include meter and rhyme.

Meter	Rhyme
• **Meter**, the rhythmic pattern in a line of poetry, is based on the number of syllables and the stresses on them. • Meter is classified by the number of **feet**—units of rhythm—in a line. A common foot is an iamb, which has an unstressed syllable followed by a stressed one. "Before I got my eye put out" is an example of iambic tetrameter because it has four iambs. • Meter can vary within a poem to create striking effects.	• **Rhyme** is the repetition of similar ending sounds in poetry as in *dark* and *lark*. • **Slant rhyme**, or **consonance**, is the repetition of end consonant sounds preceded by different vowels, as in *heart* and *hurt*. • **Assonance** is the repetition of similar vowel sounds followed by different consonant sounds, as in *grow*, *holds*, and *close*. • Rhyme can be used at the ends of lines or within lines.

Strategies for Annotation 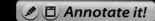 Annotate it!

Analyze Author's Choices: Poetic Structure RL 5

Encourage students to use their eBook annotation tools to trace poetic structure in Dickinson's poems. Have students do the following:

• Highlight **rhyming** words in yellow.
• Highlight **consonance** in blue.
• Highlight **assonance** in green.
• Underline stressed syllables.

The Motions of the Dipping Birds –

The Morning's Amber Road –

For mine – to look at when I liked –

The News would strike me dead –

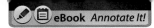 **eBook** *Annotate It!*

Analyzing the Text

COMMON CORE RL 1, RL 2, RL 5, W 1

Cite Text Evidence Support your responses with evidence from the selections.

1. **Interpret** Paraphrase stanza 2 of "We grow accustomed to the Dark." What is the central idea of this stanza?

2. **Infer** What does Dickinson mean beyond the literal meanings of the words when she says "We grow accustomed to the Dark"? With this interpretation in mind, consider the lines "And so of larger – Darknesses – / Those Evenings of the Brain – ": To what might these lines refer?

3. **Compare** Dickinson uses images of eyes and sight in both poems. Explain whether she uses these images for the same purpose in both poems.

4. **Analyze** Analyze the meter of "Before I got my eye put out." What pattern do most stanzas follow? What effect does the poet achieve by changing the meter?

5. **Identify Patterns** Review "Before I got my eye put out" and identify the number of lines in each stanza. Which stanza does not fit the pattern? What is the effect of this variation on Dickinson's meaning and tone?

6. **Synthesize** Write a summary of the conclusion the speaker comes to at the end of each poem. How and why do they differ? Cite lines from each poem to support your explanation.

PERFORMANCE TASK

Writing Activity: Essay Both of these poems are metaphorical—that is, they are not only about the literal loss of sight or physically stumbling in the darkness. Explore the metaphor of sight in Dickinson's poems by writing an analytical essay.

1. Identify what the speaker loses in "Before I got my eye put out" and explain the speaker's reaction to that loss. Would the speaker in "We grow accustomed to the Dark" react differently to the same loss?

2. In your essay, explain your interpretation of the attitude of each speaker toward sight.

3. Cite evidence from each poem to support your ideas, and use the conventions of standard English.

Assign this performance task.

PERFORMANCE TASK

COMMON CORE RL 1, RL 4, W 1

Writing Activity: Essay Explain that the speaker in a poem is not usually the author. A speaker can be a persona, or character, who reveals his or her thoughts and feelings. Explain that poems often have a meaning beyond their literal meaning. Lead a brief discussion about possible multiple meanings of words from the poem such as "Dark," "Vision," "darkness," and "sight." Remind students to use proper essay format and cite examples that support their ideas.

PRACTICE & APPLY

Analyzing the Text

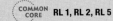

COMMON CORE RL 1, RL 2, RL 5

Possible answers:

1. *We don't rush out into the dark. We walk slowly at first, until we get used to the night. Then, as our eyes adjust to the dark, we walk more confidently. The central idea is that we walk slowly until we are used to the darkness.*

2. *Darkness is uncertainty. Darkness is always present, and one must learn how to navigate it. "Those Evenings of the Brain" might refer to dark thoughts or depression. It is possible to navigate emotional darkness. In lines 13–16, Dickinson explains that those who are brave learn to "grope" through darkness. In line 20, "Life seems almost straight" could refer to adjusting to a way of life.*

3. *In "We grow accustomed to the Dark," the concept of sight is figurative; people can eventually see through the dark. In line 7, our eyes get used to the dark, and in line 16, we learn to see. In "Before I got my eye put out," the idea of sight is literal; being able to see again is overwhelming. If the speaker regained her sight, her heart "Would split" (lines 7–8), and news of being able to regain her sight would strike her dead (line 17).*

4. *In "Before I got my eye put out" Dickinson alternates lines of four feet with lines of three feet. In lines 5, 9, and 10, she breaks the meter by separating out a word. This makes the reader stop, and highlights the importance of those words ("Today" in line 5 and "mine" in lines 9 and 10).*

5. *The third stanza of "Before I got my eye put out" has five lines instead of four. The first two lines (9–10) are short and repeat almost the same words. This makes them stand out. The stanza illustrates the wonder of the speaker as she imagines being able to see the meadows, mountains, forests, and stars again.*

6. *In "We grow accustomed to the Dark," the speaker comes to the conclusion that we can eventually see through Darkness as our surroundings adjust or we adjust to them. In "Before I got my eye put out," the speaker has accepted blindness and reveals that it is safer to rely on imagination than to actually see. These are opposite conclusions. In the first poem, the speaker wants to see. Either something changes about the darkness (line 17) or something changes in the viewer (lines 18–19); but the result is that life seems normal again. In the second poem, the speaker believes it is safer to depend on imagination (line 18), as "Creatures" who can see are "incautious," or described as having no restraint (line 21).*

Language and Style: Writing Conventions

 COMMON CORE L 1, L 2

Remind students that writing conventions such as capitalization or punctuation can serve different purposes within a poem. Project "Before I got my eye put out" onto a whiteboard. Circle the words Dickinson capitalizes. Do not include words that start lines or the pronoun *I*. Lead students in a discussion about why Dickinson may have chosen to capitalize some words, while not capitalizing others. For example, why does she capitalize *"Eyes"* in line 3, but not *"eye"* in line 1? *(Line 1 refers to her eye, while line 3 refers to all eyes.)* Repeat this exercise, examining how Dickinson uses punctuation.

Possible answer:

Students' answers will vary. Before students begin this activity, remind them that they are not writing a paraphrase and so should use Dickinson's language as much as possible. When students have completed the activity, have them share their versions of the revised stanza and discuss how standard conventions affect the tone and meaning of the original version.

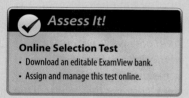

✓ Assess It!

Online Selection Test
- Download an editable ExamView bank.
- Assign and manage this test online.

Language and Style: Writing Conventions

 COMMON CORE L 1, L 2

Emily Dickinson uses writing conventions such as capitalization and punctuation to achieve specific purposes.

Read the following line from "Before I got my eye put out."

As other Creatures, that have Eyes

Note that Dickinson capitalizes *Creatures* and *Eyes*. Dickinson often uses capitalization for emphasis. Scan this poem for other capitalized words. You'll find *Today, Meadows, Mountains, Forests, Stintless Stars, Noon, Motions, Dipping Birds, Morning's Amber Road, News, Window,* and *Sun.* In some cases, these words make something simple seem more important, while at other times the emphasis helps draw out patterns. Scan for capitalized words in "We grow accustomed to the Dark" and see what kinds of words you find.

In addition to capitalization, punctuation is another convention that Dickinson varies for effect. Look again at "Before I got my eye put out," and you'll see that there are very few periods or commas, but there are many dashes. Dashes are used in the place of commas, periods, parentheses, colons, and semicolons in her poems. Look at some of the reasons Dickinson uses dashes.

Use of Dashes	
Purpose	**Example**
Connect ideas	"The Meadows – mine – The Mountains – mine –"
Set off an idea as parenthetical	"But were it told to me – Today –"
Create a pause	"Adjusts itself to Midnight – And Life steps almost straight."
Create open-endedness	"Incautious – of the Sun –"

Dickinson often chooses not to use standard English conventions. These are not errors but rather careful choices that help set pace, emphasize ideas, and create meaning in her poems.

Practice and Apply Choose a stanza from either of Dickinson's poems. Rewrite the stanza using standard conventions of capitalization and punctuation. (Remember that some ideas continue into the next stanza, so you may need to rewrite more than your chosen stanza to come to the end of a sentence.) Compare your version to Dickinson's version. How does the use of standard conventions affect tone or meaning?

TO CHALLENGE STUDENTS . . .

Language Skills: Explore Poetic Form As an opportunity to experience poetic form first hand, have students write a poem using Emily Dickinson's style of poetic structure. Before students begin, review how Dickinson structures her poems, reminding students that she generally writes in four-line stanzas and that the meter alternates between three and four iambs per line. Review her use of rhyme and writing conventions.

When students are done writing, have them meet in small groups to read their poetry. Encourage students to respond to one another's poems. Ask student volunteers to share their poems with the class.

INTERACTIVE WHITEBOARD LESSON
Determine Figurative Meanings

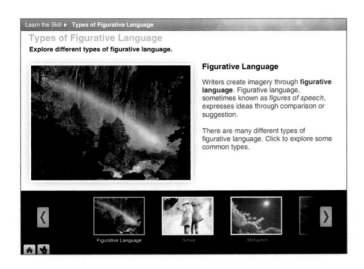

Learn the Skill ▶ Types of Figurative Language

Types of Figurative Language
Explore different types of figurative language.

Figurative Language

Writers create imagery through **figurative language**. Figurative language, sometimes known as *figures of speech*, expresses ideas through comparison or suggestion.

There are many different types of figurative language. Click to explore some common types.

Figurative Language   Simile   Metaphor

TEACH

Before students begin work on the Performance Task, review the types of figurative language Dickinson uses in her poems. Remind students of the difference between figurative and literal language. Explain that writers use literal language to describe something in detail. They use figurative language to appeal to the readers' senses or create an emotional response.

- A **metaphor** is a comparison between two unlike things. An **extended metaphor** compares two unlike things over several lines or an entire work. Both of these poems use vision as a metaphor.
- **Personification** gives human characteristics to a thing that is not human.
- **Synecdoche** uses a part to refer to the whole of something.

Point out "Evenings of the Brain" in line 10 of "We grow accustomed to the Dark." Explain that it is a metaphor for "Darkness" in line 9. Point out that darkness and evenings are alike because they both suggest the absence of light. "Evenings of the Brain" is a poetic way of renaming the time when your brain is deprived of vision. Point out that Dickinson's metaphor carries all that meaning in just four words.

COLLABORATIVE DISCUSSION

After students have finished their essays, have them work in groups. Have each student present his or her analysis of the poems to the group. Tell students to pay attention to ideas that are similar and ideas that are not. Ask them to discuss why students have different interpretations of the poems.

Analyze Author's Choices: Poetic Structure

RETEACH

Review the elements of poetic structure. Remind students that poems are composed of **lines** that are grouped together into **stanzas.** Each line of poetry has a rhythmic pattern called **meter.** Meter consists of a series of stressed and unstressed syllables that make up **feet,** or units of rhythm. Emily Dickinson wrote in **iambs,** which are common in English verse.

Read aloud the first two lines of "We grow accustomed to the Dark." Explain that the meter uses one unstressed syllable followed by a stressed syllable. Have students tap their desks on the stressed syllables. Ask students which syllables are accented in the first two lines (*Grow, -cus-, to, Dark, Light, put, -way*). Read the remainder of the stanza and discuss how the rhythm highlights certain words. Then have students pair up to analyze the meter of the remaining stanzas.

LEVEL UP TUTORIALS Assign the following *Level Up* tutorial: **Elements of Poetry**

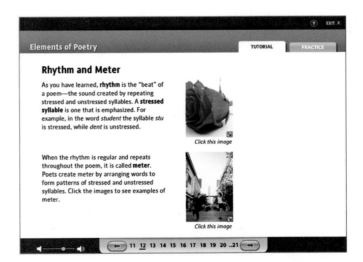

⑦ EXIT X

Elements of Poetry   TUTORIAL   PRACTICE

Rhythm and Meter

As you have learned, **rhythm** is the "beat" of a poem—the sound created by repeating stressed and unstressed syllables. A **stressed syllable** is one that is emphasized. For example, in the word *student* the syllable *stu* is stressed, while *dent* is unstressed.

Click this image

When the rhythm is regular and repeats throughout the poem, it is called **meter.** Poets create meter by arranging words to form patterns of stressed and unstressed syllables. Click the images to see examples of meter.

Click this image

11 **12** 13 14 15 16 17 18 19 20 ..21

CLOSE READING APPLICATION

Students can apply the skill to another poem. Have them work independently to read a poem you assign, and then analyze the structure of the poem according to the number of lines and their meter. Tell student to look for rhyme in the poem, even examples of slant rhyme. Ask students how the structure of the poem contributes to its meaning.

The Trouble with Poetry | Today

Why These Texts

Students may have difficulty understanding how a poet develops a theme in a poem. With the help of the close-reading questions in these selections, students will paraphrase and summarize different parts of the poems. The results of their close reading will help students understand each poem's theme and how the poet develops his ideas about these themes.

Background Have students read the background and the information about Billy Collins. Explain that one of the duties of the U.S. Poet Laureate is to promote poetry to the public. Toward this end, Billy Collins traveled throughout the country, reading his poems and talking about poetry and why poetry is important. The focus of his Poetry 180 program is a collection of 180 poems by different poets—one for each day of the school year. These poems can be printed without charge from the Poetry 180 website.

AS YOU READ Tell students to think about what the poet is writing about in each poem and to think about how they might express the poet's thoughts in their own words.

Common Core Support

- cite strong and thorough textual evidence
- determine a theme or central idea of a text
- provide a summary of a text
- analyze how an author's choices structure a text

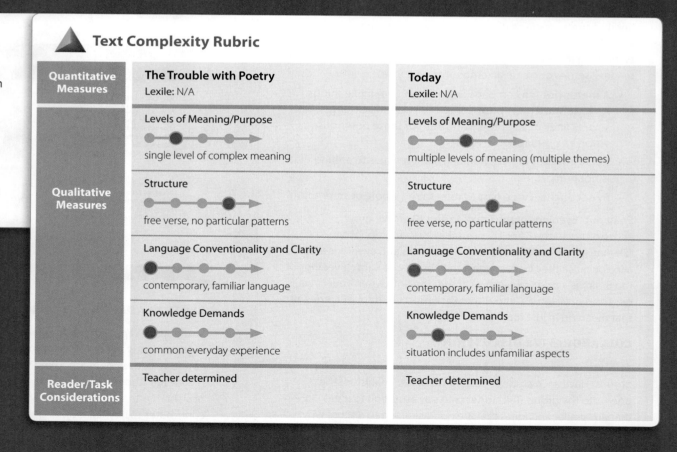

Text Complexity Rubric

Quantitative Measures	The Trouble with Poetry Lexile: N/A	Today Lexile: N/A
Qualitative Measures	**Levels of Meaning/Purpose** single level of complex meaning	**Levels of Meaning/Purpose** multiple levels of meaning (multiple themes)
	Structure free verse, no particular patterns	**Structure** free verse, no particular patterns
	Language Conventionality and Clarity contemporary, familiar language	**Language Conventionality and Clarity** contemporary, familiar language
	Knowledge Demands common everyday experience	**Knowledge Demands** situation includes unfamiliar aspects
Reader/Task Considerations	Teacher determined	Teacher determined

Strategies for CLOSE READING

Cite Evidence: Paraphrase and Summarize

Students should read the poems carefully, thinking about what the poet says about the subject. Close-reading questions at the bottom of the page will help students collect and cite text evidence to better paraphrase and summarize what the poet says. As they read, students should jot down in the margin comments and responses to each poem.

WHEN STUDENTS STRUGGLE . . .

To help students paraphrase and summarize ideas in the two poems by Billy Collins, have them work in small groups to fill out a chart like the one shown below for each poem.

CITE TEXT EVIDENCE For practice paraphrasing and summarizing, ask students to write in their own words what they think these lines from "The Trouble with Poetry" mean.

Lines from the Poem	What I Think the Lines Mean
"the trouble with poetry is that it encourages the writing of more poetry, more guppies crowding the fish tank" (lines 5–7)	Writing poetry is a problem because you just want to write more and more poems until you have too many poems, like fish crowded in a tank.
"Poetry fills me with joy and I rise like a feather in the wind. Poetry fills me with sorrow and I sink like a chain flung from a bridge." (lines 17–20)	When poems make me happy, I feel like a feather floating in the air. When they make me sad, I feel like a heavy chain sinking in a river.

Background Sometimes it's best to read more than one poem by an author to get a feel for his or her style. Read these poems more than once. Who knows? "The Trouble with Poetry" might just inspire you to write your own poem, using ideas from the other poems that you have read. "Today" might force you to look out the window.

Poems by
Billy Collins

Billy Collins has been called "the most popular poet in America" for his witty, and often funny poems. He served two terms as U.S. Poet Laureate, during which time he created a poetry program called Poetry 180 to get more high school students to read poetry each day during the 180-day school year.

Speaking about his writing process, Collins has said: "I have one reader in mind, someone who is in the room with me, and who I'm talking to, and I want to make sure I don't talk too fast, or too glibly. Usually I try to create a hospitable tone at the beginning of a poem. Stepping from the title to the first lines is like stepping into a canoe. A lot of things can go wrong."

57

1. **READ ▷** As you read lines 1–27 of "The Trouble with Poetry," begin to collect and cite evidence.

- Underline repeating phrases.
- Circle what "the trouble with poetry" is.
- In the margin, paraphrase lines 1–16.

The Trouble with Poetry

Ⓐ The trouble with poetry, I realized
as I walked along a beach one night—
cold Florida sand under my bare feet,
a show of stars in the sky—

5 the trouble with poetry is
that it encourages the writing of more poetry,
more guppies crowding the fish tank,
more baby rabbits
hopping out of their mothers into the dewy grass.

10 And how will it ever end?
unless the day finally arrives
when we have compared everything in the world
to everything else in the world,

and there is nothing left to do
15 but quietly close our notebooks
and sit with our hands folded on our desks.

Poetry fills me with joy
and I rise like a feather in the wind.
Poetry fills me with sorrow
20 and I sink like a chain flung from a bridge.

Ⓑ But mostly poetry fills me
with the urge to write poetry,
to sit in the dark and wait for a little flame
to appear at the tip of my pencil.

Margin note (left): While walking barefoot along a Florida beach one night with the stars in the sky, I understood that the problem with poetry is that it inspires more poetry. How will it end? Not until everything in the world is compared to everything else and then we will have nothing to do but close our books and sit quietly.

25 And along with that, the longing to steal,
to break into the poems of others
with a flashlight and a ski mask.

And what an unmerry band of thieves we are,
cut-purses, common shoplifters,
30 I thought to myself
Ⓒ as a cold wave swirled around my feet
and the lighthouse moved its megaphone over the sea,
Ⓓ which is an image I stole directly
from Lawrence Ferlinghetti[1]—
35 to be perfectly honest for a moment—

the bicycling poet of San Francisco
whose little amusement park of a book
I carried in a side pocket of my uniform
up and down the treacherous halls of high school.

Margin note (right): Collins uses just one sentence. This speeds up the flow of the poem and gives the impression of a single thought.

[1] **Lawrence Ferlinghetti:** American poet and founder of City Lights Bookstore in San Francisco. His poem "To the Oracle at Delphi" contains the lines "as a lighthouse moves its megaphone / over the sea" which Collins references here.

2. **◁ REREAD** Reread lines 1–27. What does the poet mean by "the trouble with poetry"? Cite evidence from the poem.

He is saying that poetry is a compulsion. The "urge to write poetry" consumes him as he waits "for a little flame to appear at the tip of my pencil." He's even compelled to steal from other poets.

3. **READ ▷** As you read lines 28–39, continue to cite textual evidence.

- In the margin, explain how many sentences the poet uses in these lines, and what effect that has on the reader.
- Underline the lines that explain how he uses another poet's words and where he first encountered his work.

58

59

---

1. **READ AND CITE TEXT EVIDENCE** Explain to students that repeated phrases in a poem are often clues to the poem's central idea.

Ⓐ **ASK STUDENTS** to name the comparisons the poet makes between poetry and other things in lines 1–27. *Students can cite "guppies crowding the fish tank" (line 7), "baby rabbits / hopping out of their mothers" (lines 8–9).*

FOR ELL STUDENTS You may need to explain to students that the word *flung* is the past tense and past participle of the irregular verb *fling*, meaning to "throw hard, or with violence."

2. **REREAD AND CITE TEXT EVIDENCE** Remind students that the repeated phrase "the trouble with poetry" is also the poem's title.

Ⓑ **ASK STUDENTS** to find details in lines 21–27 that further explain what the poet thinks the trouble with poetry is. *Students may cite the speaker's "urge to write poetry . . . to . . . wait for a little flame to appear at the tip of my pencil" (lines 22–24) and "the longing to steal, to break into the poems of others" (lines 25–26).*

3. **READ AND CITE TEXT EVIDENCE** Explain to students that paying attention to the structure of a poem can help them read it with appropriate feeling and at an appropriate speed.

Ⓒ **ASK STUDENTS** to describe how they would read aloud lines 28–39. *Possible response: quickly, without stopping* Then have students identify the lines containing details that describe the way the speaker uses the poems by Ferlinghetti. *lines 32–34; 37–39*

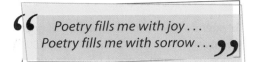

> Poetry fills me with joy . . .
> Poetry fills me with sorrow . . .

4. ◀ **REREAD** Reread lines 28–39. Explain what Collins says about the poet Lawrence Ferlinghetti.

Collins has "stolen" one of Ferlinghetti's images, and he implies that even in "the treacherous halls of high school" he loved the "amusement park of a book" that Ferlinghetti had written.

SHORT RESPONSE

Cite Text Evidence In your own words, write a summary of "The Trouble with Poetry." Then, think about what you left out. Which lines or phrases are the most difficult to say in other words? **Cite text evidence** in your response.

Collins writes about the effects poetry has on him. It encourages him to write more poetry, to wait for inspiration. The "trouble with poetry" he believes, is that if poetry inspires more poetry, one day everything will be compared to everything else and there will be nothing else to write. The most difficult line to express in other words is "The trouble with poetry..." perhaps because it is the most unique of the poet's ideas.

1. **READ ▶** As you read lines 1–18 of "Today," begin to collect evidence.
   - Underline actions that a spring day might inspire.
   - Write in the margin where the poet is, and circle the detail(s) that support your conclusion.
   - Circle the punctuation at the end of each line.

Today

If ever there were a spring day so perfect,
so uplifted by a warm **intermittent** breeze

E that it made you want to throw
open all the windows in the house

5 and unlatch the door to the canary's cage,
indeed, rip the little door from its jamb,

a day when the cool brick paths
and the garden bursting with peonies

seemed so **etched** in sunlight
10 that you felt like taking

a hammer to the glass paperweight
on the living room end table,

releasing the inhabitants
from their snow-covered cottage

15 so they could walk out,
holding hands and squinting

into this larger dome of blue and white,
well, today is just that kind of day.

intermittent:
stopping and starting again

inside on a beautiful spring day

etched:
engraved

4. **REREAD AND CITE TEXT EVIDENCE** Tell students to read the footnote about the poet Lawrence Ferlinghetti.

D **ASK STUDENTS** to cite the text evidence they underlined as they explain what Collins says about Ferlinghetti. *Students should cite lines 32–39.*

SHORT RESPONSE

Cite Text Evidence Students' responses will vary, but they should cite evidence from the text to support their summaries. Students should:

- identify the subject of the poem as "the trouble with poetry."
- tell in their own words what the poet believes that trouble to be, or what the effects of poetry are on him.
- identify parts of the poem that they find difficult to paraphrase.

1. **READ AND CITE TEXT EVIDENCE**

E **ASK STUDENTS** how they can identify throughout the poem the things the poet wants to do. *Many of the phrases begin with the word* you *or with a verb, such as* unlatch *or* rip.

Critical Vocabulary: intermittent (line 2) Have students share their definitions of *intermittent*. Then, ask what other things might be described as intermittent. *Possible response: periods of actual rain on a cloudy day, moments of sharp pain when a person has a toothache.*

Critical Vocabulary: etched (line 9) Discuss with students how Collins uses the word *etched* in his poem. What might a garden "etched in sunlight" look like? *Possible response: All the trees and flowers would be very brightly lit by the sunlight.*

Billy Collins reads his poetry at the grand opening of Poets House in New York City, 2009.

2. **◄ REREAD** Reread the poem. How does the poem's structure of run-on lines within and between the couplets echo the poet's feelings?

The poem is one long sentence, which when read outloud, mirrors the breathless excitement the poet feels about the beauty of today.

SHORT RESPONSE

Cite Text Evidence How is the poet like the canary and the paperweight's inhabitants? Review your reading notes, and be sure to **cite evidence** from the text in your response.

The poet, the canary, and the figures in the paperweight are all confined inside. The canary cannot get out of its cage unless "you" "unlatch the door," or "rip" it from the jamb. The paperweight's inhabitants need to be released by use of a "hammer." The poet is indoors, observing the perfect spring day. Smashing the paperweight to free its "inhabitants" and letting the bird out of its cage are actions the poet compares to his own desire to get outside.

62

TO CHALLENGE STUDENTS . . .

To extend students' understanding of poetic structure, have them read poems from Billy Collins's Poetry 180 program—a collection of poems by various poets housed online at the Library of Congress. Students should choose two poems and compare the structure (stanzas, rhyme, punctuation) in each.

ASK STUDENTS to compare the structure of the two poems they have chosen.

- Are they written in stanzas? Are the stanzas all of the same length or of different lengths? What effect does the stanza structure have on the poem?

- Is rhyme used in either of the poems? If so, what effect does the rhyme have?

- How are the poems punctuated? Remind students that their examination of the punctuation used in "Today" helped them know how to read the poem aloud.

Finally, have volunteers read aloud their favorite poems from the site.

---

2. **REREAD AND CITE TEXT EVIDENCE** Remind students that they have circled the punctuation at the end of those lines that end with punctuation.

ASK STUDENTS how they think the poem should be read aloud. *The poem should be read quickly without stopping, pausing only where there are commas.*

SHORT RESPONSE

Cite Text Evidence Students' responses will vary but should include evidence from the text that supports their answers. Students should:

- explain what the poet, the canary, and the figures in the paperweight have in common.
- explain what is similar about their predicaments.
- cite text evidence to support their ideas.

DIG DEEPER

With the class, return to Question 4, Reread, on page 60. Have students share and discuss their responses.

ASK STUDENTS what their responses have in common. Most students will probably have mentioned that Collins has stolen an image from one of Ferlinghetti's poems to use in his own poem and that Collins used to carry a book of Ferlinghetti's poems around in high school. You might have students read Ferlinghetti's poem "To the Oracle at Delphi" to give greater context to Collins's allusions to Ferlinghetti's poetry.

- Have students explain what the details from the text and their own ideas about them tell them about Collins's feelings about Ferlinghetti's work. *Collins obviously likes Ferlinghetti's poems enough to "steal" a line from one and use it in his own poem. He also obviously cared enough about Ferlinghetti in high school to carry a copy of his book around with him.*

- Then direct students' attention to the last three lines of the poem. Ask students why the poet might have used the word *treacherous* to describe the halls of his high school. *Students might mention that the hallways between classes and during lunch can be threatening. Students might infer that Collins did not enjoy high school.*

ASK STUDENTS to return to their response to Question 4 and revise it based on their discussion.

CLOSE READING NOTES

ANCHOR TEXT

Coming to Our Senses

Science Essay by Neil deGrasse Tyson

Why This Text?

In this essay, the importance of science in modern life is key. The role of observation and the understanding that our senses have limits help to enhance our understanding of our world. Scientifically literate citizens need to be able to analyze research and evaluate conclusions.

▶ **View It!**

Professional Development Podcast:

Informational Text

Key Learning Objective: The student will be able to analyze the development of ideas in nonfiction.

For practice and application:

Every Second Counts

Book Review by Matilda Battersby

Close Reader selection:
"Every Second Counts"
book review by Matilda Battersby

COMMON CORE | Common Core Standards

RI 1 Cite textual evidence.

RI 2 Determine a central idea and analyze its development.

RI 3 Analyze how the author unfolds ideas or events.

RI 4 Determine the meaning of words and phrases.

RI 5 Analyze how an author's ideas are developed by particular sentences or paragraphs.

RI 6 Determine an author's point of view and analyze how an author uses rhetoric.

W 5 Strengthen writing by planning, revising, editing, rewriting, or trying a new approach.

SL 1a Come to discussions prepared, refer to evidence from text to stimulate ideas.

L 1a Use parallel structure.

L 4a Use context as a clue to the meaning of a word.

L 4c Consult reference materials to find pronunciation or clarify meaning.

▲ Text Complexity Rubric

Quantitative Measures	**Coming to Our Senses** Lexile: 1310L
Qualitative Measures	**Levels of Meaning/Purpose** more than one purpose; implied
	Structure organization of main ideas and details complex, but sequential
	Language Conventionality and Clarity increased domain-specific words
	Knowledge Demands somewhat complex science concepts
Reader/Task Considerations	Teacher determined Vary by individual reader and type of text

TEACH

CLOSE READ

Background Have students read Tyson's biography and explain to them that one of his goals as a scientist is to engage young people in the study of science. He was instrumental in "demoting" Pluto from full planet status to dwarf planet. This caused many elementary school children to write him letters of protest, defending Pluto's planetary status.

AS YOU READ Direct students to use the As You Read prompt to focus their reading. Tell them to write down any questions they generate as they read.

Analyze Development of Ideas (LINES 1–13)

Ask a student volunteer to read the quote at the beginning of this selection. Explain that writers often use a quotation from an expert to grab the readers' attention and set the tone for their writing.

Ⓐ ASK STUDENTS to sumarize the main idea of this paragraph. *(Possible answer: Sight is the most important sense because it allows us to observe the world around us.)* How does the quote from Hubble support this idea? *(Hubble explains that our senses, including sight, allow us to explore and better understand the universe.)*

CRITICAL VOCABULARY

acuity: Tyson explains that when humans use all of their senses at the same time, they gain an increased perceptiveness and awareness of the world around them.

ASK STUDENTS to explain how using all five of our senses can result in increased acuity. *(By observing, listening, touching, tasting, and smelling the world around us, we are more aware of each small part of the universe.)*

Neil deGrasse Tyson (b. 1958) *is an American astrophysicist and the director of the Hayden Planetarium at the American Museum of Natural History. But he is best known for helping to explain science to the public through his many books and television appearances. Tyson is the author of* The Pluto Files: The Rise and Fall of America's Favorite Planet *and* Death by Black Hole and Other Cosmic Quandaries. *In addition, he has hosted the PBS miniseries* Origins *and* NOVA ScienceNOW *and has appeared on* The Colbert Report *and* The Daily Show.

Coming to Our Senses

Science Essay by Neil deGrasse Tyson

AS YOU READ Pay attention to the details the author provides about humans' five senses. Write down any questions you generate during reading.

> *Equipped with his five senses, man explores the universe around him and calls the adventure science.*
> —Edwin P. Hubble (1889–1953),
> *The Nature of Science*

Ⓐ

Among our five senses, sight is the most special to us. Our eyes allow us to register information not only from across the room but also from across the universe. Without vision, the science of astronomy would never have been born and our capacity to measure our place in the universe would have been hopelessly stunted. Think of bats. Whatever bat secrets get passed from one generation to the next, you can bet that none of them is based on the appearance of the night sky.

When thought of as an ensemble of experimental tools, our senses enjoy an astonishing **acuity** and range of sensitivity. Our ears can register the thunderous launch of the space shuttle, yet they can also hear a mosquito buzzing a foot away from our head. Our sense

acuity
(ə-kyōō´ĭ-tē) *n.* critical perceptiveness; awareness.

Image Credits: (t) ©Richard Drew/AP Images; (cl) University of Arizona/JPL-Caltech/NASA; (cr) ©Bo Valentino/Shutterstock

Coming to Our Senses **161**

Close Read Screencasts ▶ View It!

Modeled Discussions

Have students click the *Close Read* icon in their eBooks to access the screencast in which readers discuss and annotate the following key passage:

- explanation of how changes in sensory input are not easily detectible by humans because they are logarithmic, not linear (lines 26–38)

As a class, view and discuss this video. Then have students pair up to do an independent close read of an additional passage—Tyson's restatement of his central idea (lines 170–177).

Analyze Author's Use of Rhetoric (LINES 39–49)

 COMMON CORE RI 2, RI 6

Discuss the fact that Tyson begins this passage by posing **rhetorical questions.** Explain that although the author phrases these ideas as questions, no reply is expected. Rather, the author uses this technique to engage the reader's attention or thought.

B **ASK STUDENTS** what central idea Tyson is highlighting with these rhetorical questions. *(Tyson is making the point that humans can learn more about their environment than simply what their senses can tell them, and that using scientific tools can help them learn more.)*

CRITICAL VOCABULARY

stimuli: Tyson uses the word *stimuli* to refer to things that we notice and react to with our senses.

ASK STUDENTS to identify the stimuli Tyson discusses in this selection. *(a change in light, such as a solar eclipse, or a change in volume, such as the increase in decibels of music)*

propensity: Tyson explains that humans have a tendency to behave in a certain way because of our biology.

CITE EVIDENCE Ask students to cite one example from the text of a human's propensity for experiencing stimuli. *(As humans, we only see a change in the sky during an eclipse after the sun is covered 90%.)*

transcend: Tyson explains that our knowledge goes beyond what we experience with our senses due to the use of tools and machines that can be used for scientific investigation.

ASK STUDENTS to name one "tool of science" that allows us to transcend our sense of sight. *(microscope, telescope)*

---

of touch allows us to feel the magnitude of a bowling ball dropped on our big toe, just as we can tell when a one-milligram bug crawls
20 along our arm. Some people enjoy munching on habañero peppers while sensitive tongues can identify the presence of food flavors to the level of parts per million. And our eyes can register the bright sandy terrain on a sunny beach, yet these same eyes have no trouble spotting a lone match, freshly lit, hundreds of feet across a darkened auditorium.

But before we get carried away in praise of ourselves, note that what we gain in breadth we lose in precision: we register the world's **stimuli** in logarithmic[1] rather than linear increments. For example, if you increase the energy of a sound's volume by a factor
30 of 10, your ears will judge this change to be rather small. Increase it by a factor of 2 and you will barely notice. The same holds for our capacity to measure light. If you have ever viewed a total solar eclipse you may have noticed that the Sun's disk must be at least 90 percent covered by the Moon before anybody comments that the sky has darkened. The stellar magnitude scale of brightness, the well-known acoustic decibel scale, and the seismic scale for earthquake severity[2] are each logarithmic, in part because of our biological **propensity** to see, hear, and feel the world that way.

What, if anything, lies beyond our senses? Does there exist a way
40 of knowing that **transcends** our biological interfaces with the environment?

Consider that the human machine, while good at decoding the basics of our immediate environment—like when it's day or night or when a creature is about to eat us—has very little talent for decoding how the rest of nature works without the tools of science. **B** If we want to know what's out there then we require detectors other than the ones we are born with. In nearly every case, the job of scientific apparatus is to transcend the breadth and depth of our senses.
50 Some people boast of having a sixth sense, where they profess to know or see things that others cannot. Fortune-tellers, mind readers, and mystics are at the top of the list of those who lay claim to mysterious powers. In doing so, they instill widespread fascination in others, especially book publishers and television producers. The questionable field of parapsychology[3] is founded

stimuli
(stĭm´yə-lī´) *n.* things that cause a response or reaction.

propensity
(prə-pĕn´sĭ-tē) *n.* a tendency to behave in a certain way.

transcend
(trăn-sĕnd´) *v.* to go beyond or rise above.

---

[1] **logarithmic:** capable of being raised by repeated multiplication of itself; exponential.

[2] **stellar magnitude scale . . . acoustic decibel scale . . . seismic scale:** systems of measurement for the brightness of starlight, the loudness of sounds, and the intensity of earthquakes.

[3] **parapsychology:** the study of unexplainable or supernatural mental phenomena.

162 Collection 4

SCAFFOLDING FOR ELL STUDENTS

Analyze Language Explain that writers often use different words for the same thing to provide variety for the reader. This practice may be confusing for some students. Give students time to read lines 42–49 silently, and then read it aloud to them. Point out the phrases "tools of science" and "scientific apparatus" and explain how these two phrases are similar in meaning.

ASK STUDENTS to offer another word that could replace "decoding" in line 42 or 45. Encourage students to refer to a dictionary or thesaurus for help.

on the expectation that at least some people actually harbor such talents. To me, the biggest mystery of them all is why so many fortune-telling psychics choose to work the phones on TV hotlines instead of becoming insanely wealthy trading futures contracts
60 on Wall Street.[4] And here's a news headline none of us has seen, "Psychic Wins the Lottery."

Quite independent of this mystery, the persistent failures of controlled, double-blind experiments to support the claims of parapsychology suggest that what's going on is nonsense rather than sixth sense.

On the other hand, modern science wields dozens of senses. And scientists do not claim these to be the expression of special powers, just special hardware. In the end, of course, the hardware converts the information gleaned from these extra senses into
70 simple tables, charts, diagrams, or images that our inborn senses can interpret. In the original *Star Trek* sci-fi series, the crew that beamed down from their starship to the uncharted planet always brought with them a tricorder—a handheld device that could analyze anything they encountered, living or inanimate, for its basic properties. As the tricorder was waved over the object in question, it made an audible spacey sound that was interpreted by the user.

Suppose a glowing blob of some unknown substance were parked right in front of us. Without some diagnostic tool like
80 a tricorder to help, we would be clueless to the blob's chemical or nuclear composition. Nor could we know whether it has an electromagnetic field, or whether it emits strongly in gamma rays, x-rays, ultraviolet, microwaves, or radio waves. Nor could we

---

[4] **trading futures contracts on Wall Street:** a form of speculative investment in which someone agrees to pay a fixed price for an item at a future date. The success of the investment is measured by the difference between the agreed-upon price and the actual market price on that future date.

APPLYING ACADEMIC VOCABULARY

differentiate	incorporate

As you discuss Neil deGrasse Tyson's science essay, use the following Collection 4 academic vocabulary words: *differentiate* and *incorporate*. To understand Tyson's central idea, ask students to **differentiate** between the information provided by human senses and the information offered from scientific technology. Then ask students to **incorporate** specific examples of each in their discussions.

CLOSE READ

Analyze Development of Ideas (LINES 62–77)

COMMON CORE RI 1, RI 2, RI 3

Tell students that writers develop their central ideas with key points and examples.

Direct students to look at Tyson's key point and example regarding parapsychology. Explain to students that a double-blind experiment is one that takes place when neither the scientist nor the subject knows who is getting the test treatment. Double-blind experiments often produce the most reliable results.

C **ASK STUDENTS** to explain what it means if parapsychology claims are not held up in double-blind experiments. *(It means that those claims are unlikely to be based in science, and that humans probably do not have a sixth sense.)* How does this example develop Tyson's central idea? *(He is illustrating that human senses are limited. While they can help us gain some knowledge, we need scientific tools to measure and prove theories and facts.)*

Encourage students to continue to look for key points and examples that support Tyson's central idea.

D **CITE TEXT EVIDENCE** Ask students to name the device Tyson is describing in this passage and explain what the device does. *(a tricorder, a fictional device used to analyze anything it is held near)* How does using this example further Tyson's central idea? *(By using this example, Tyson is again highlighting the fact that our senses are limited and that even in science fiction stories, we have to rely on scientific tools in order to gain a solid understanding of the world around us. He continues to support his central idea by pointing out that even fictional portrayals of future generations clearly recognize the limits of human senses.)*

Analyze Impact of Word Choice: Tone (LINES 90–94)

COMMON CORE RI 4

Tell students that some authors use humor to grab the readers' attention and make a key point. When used properly, this technique can be more effective than serious explanations.

 CITE TEXT EVIDENCE Have students identify humorous phrases in this paragraph. *("lick the stuff," "'Captain, it's a blob'")* Then ask them to explain how these phrases make a valid point. *(Tyson is showing that by using only our senses (taste) we would not be able to analyze many elements of our world. In order to identify and understand our universe, we need to use scientific tools.)*

Analyze the Development of Ideas (LINES 95–116)

COMMON CORE RI 1, RI 2, RI 3

Remind students that writers often develop and support their central idea by using evidence and specific details. Direct their attention to the quotation on this page and ask for a student volunteer to read it aloud.

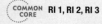 **CITE TEXT EVIDENCE** Ask students to identify the central idea in these lines. *(We cannot only use human senses to fully understand the world around us.)* Then have students reread lines 102–116 and identify the key point. *(Our perception of the world would be different if we had enhanced senses.)* Ask them to find the details Tyson uses to support this idea. *(If we had enhanced vision, we could see radio waves, the Milky Way, microwaves, x-rays, and gamma rays with our naked eyes. Each of these things would help us better understand and navigate the world around us.)*

determine the blob's cellular or crystalline structure. If the blob were far out in space, appearing as an unresolved point of light in the sky, our five senses would offer us no insight to its distance, velocity through space, or its rate of rotation. We further would have no capacity to see the spectrum of colors that compose its emitted light, nor could we know whether the light is polarized.

90   Without hardware to help our analysis, and without a particular urge to lick the stuff, all we can report back to the starship is, "Captain, it's a blob." Apologies to Edwin P. Hubble, the quote that opens this chapter, while poignant and poetic, should have instead been:

> *Equipped with our five senses, along with telescopes and microscopes and mass spectrometers and seismographs and magnetometers and particle accelerators and detectors across the electromagnetic*
> 100   *spectrum, we explore the universe around us and call the adventure science.*

Think of how much richer the world would appear to us and how much earlier the nature of the universe would have been discovered if we were born with high-precision, tunable eyeballs. Dial up the radio-wave part of the spectrum and the daytime sky becomes as dark as night. Dotting that sky would be bright and famous sources of radio waves, such as the center of the Milky Way, located behind some of the principal stars of the constellation Sagittarius. Tune into microwaves and the entire cosmos glows
110   with a remnant from the early universe, a wall of light set forth 380,000 years after the big bang. Tune into x-rays and you immediately spot the locations of black holes, with matter spiraling into them. Tune into gamma rays and see titanic explosions scattered throughout the universe at a rate of about one per day. Watch the effect of the explosion on the surrounding material as it heats up and glows in other bands of light.

If we were born with magnetic detectors, the compass would never have been invented because we wouldn't ever need one. Just tune into Earth's magnetic field lines and the direction of magnetic
120   north looms like Oz[5] beyond the horizon. If we had spectrum analyzers within our retinas, we would not have to wonder what we were breathing. We could just look at the register and know whether the air contained sufficient oxygen to sustain human life. And we would have learned thousands of years ago that the stars

---

[5] **Oz:** the magical city and destination for characters in L. Frank Baum's *The Wonderful Wizard of Oz.*

WHEN STUDENTS STRUGGLE . . .

Remind students that in his essay, Tyson is guiding readers through his thought process. Explain that the ideas build upon one another. Ask struggling students to read aloud the sentence beginning on line 102, "Think of how much . . . ." To check for comprehension, have students explain their understanding of what the phrase "tunable eyeballs" means. A clear understanding of this phrase will make comprehension of the rest of this paragraph clearer for struggling students.

ASK STUDENTS to talk with a partner about how their life would be different if they had "high-precision, tunable eyeballs." Ask students to compare Tyson's examples of what life would be like with their own. Move around the classroom and listen as students discuss to ensure their comprehension.

and nebulae in the Milky Way galaxy contain the same chemical elements found here on Earth.

And if we were born with big eyes and built-in Doppler motion detectors, we would have seen immediately, even as grunting troglodytes,[6] that the entire universe is expanding—with distant
130 galaxies all receding from us.

If our eyes had the resolution of high-performance microscopes, nobody would have ever blamed the plague and other sicknesses on divine wrath. The bacteria and viruses that made us sick would be in plain view as they crawled on our food or as they slid through open wounds in our skin. With simple experiments, we could easily tell which of these bugs were bad and which were good. And of course postoperative infection problems would have been identified and solved hundreds of years earlier.

If we could detect high-energy particles, we would spot
140 radioactive substances from great distances. No Geiger counters necessary. We could even watch radon gas seep through the basement floor of homes and not have to pay somebody to tell us about it.

The honing of our senses from birth through childhood allows us, as adults, to pass judgment on events and phenomena in our

___

[6] **troglodyte:** a primitive creature or a cave dweller.

Image Credits: ©Paramount/Everett Collection, Inc.

Coming to Our Senses **165**

CLOSE READ

Determine Central Idea   COMMON CORE RI 2
(LINES 146–149)

Guide students to understand that the conclusion of an essay allows the author to summarize his or her central idea.

 ASK STUDENTS to summarize the central idea of lines 146–149 in their own words. *(During the last 100 years, scientific discoveries have relied on math and technology to make new discoveries.)*

Analyze Development of Ideas   COMMON CORE RI 2, RI 3
(LINES 162–168)

Read the quote by Max Planck aloud.

ASK STUDENTS to summarize Planck's quotation in their own words. *(In modern physics, we can see that reality exists beyond what we can perceive through our senses.)* Ask students to explain how this relates to Tyson's main idea. *(Planck's quote supports Tyson's idea because it reinforces the concept that our senses are inadequate on their own; he too is saying we need to use tools and modern science to gain an indepth understanding of the universe around us.)*

CRITICAL VOCABULARY

precarious: Tyson is telling us that we can put ourselves in an unsafe situation if we only rely on our five senses to detect trouble.

ASK STUDENTS to think of a time or a situation where they used technology to avoid or prevent a precarious situation. *(Possible answers: Seeing the check engine light or tire pressure light come on in a car, hearing a smoke detector, reading or hearing severe weather alerts on smartphones or television.)*

---

lives, declaring whether they "make sense." Problem is, hardly any scientific discoveries of the past century flowed from the direct application of our five senses. They flowed instead from the direct application of sense-transcendent mathematics and hardware. This

150 simple fact is entirely responsible for why, to the average person, relativity, particle physics, and 10-dimensional string theory make no sense. Include in the list black holes, wormholes, and the big bang. Actually, these ideas don't make much sense to scientists either, or at least not until we have explored the universe for a long time, with all the senses that are technologically available. What emerges, eventually, is a newer and higher level of "common sense" that enables a scientist to think creatively and to pass judgment in the unfamiliar underworld of the atom or in the mind-bending domain of higher-dimensional space. The twentieth-century

160 German physicist Max Planck made a similar observation about the discovery of quantum mechanics:

> *Modern Physics impresses us particularly with the truth of the old doctrine which teaches that there are realities existing apart from our sense-perceptions, and that there are problems and conflicts where these realities are of greater value for us than the richest treasures of the world of experience.*
> (1931, p. 107)

170   Our five senses even interfere with sensible answers to stupid metaphysical questions like, "If a tree falls in the forest and nobody is around to hear it, does it make a sound?" My best answer is, "How do you know it fell?" But that just gets people angry. So I offer a senseless analogy, "Q: If you can't smell the carbon monoxide, then how do you know it's there? A: You drop dead." In modern times, if the sole measure of what's out there flows from your five senses then a **precarious** life awaits you.
        Discovering new ways of knowing has always heralded new windows on the universe that tap into our growing list of

180 nonbiological senses. Whenever this happens, a new level of majesty and complexity in the universe reveals itself to us, as though we were technologically evolving into supersentient beings, always coming to our senses.

precarious
(prĭ-kâr′ē-əs) *adj.*
unsafe or insecure.

COLLABORATIVE DISCUSSION   What details does the author use to discuss humans' five senses? With a partner, discuss these details and how they make the essay more interesting.

WHEN STUDENTS STRUGGLE . . .

Explain that an **analogy is** a technique writers use to compare two things that are usually thought to be different. Direct students to reread lines 170–178. Then tell them that in this section, Tyson is using an analogy to support his point about the importance of using tools to understand our world.

ASK STUDENTS to explain how using the sense of hearing to know if a tree falls is not nearly as useful as using a tool such as a detector to recognize the presence of carbon monoxide.

Analyze Development of Ideas

The central idea of a nonfiction selection is usually developed through several key points, each of which is supported by details.

- The **central idea** is the main point the writer wants to make about the topic, or subject of the writing. In a nonfiction selection, a writer may state a central idea outright, but more often the reader needs to infer it by putting together key points and details presented in the selection. Think about the central idea to which all of the key points and details add up in "Coming to Our Senses."

- In developing a central idea, the author presents a series of **key points** in an order that helps expand the topic and draws connections between them. Like building a brick wall, where each layer of bricks acts as a support for the next layer, so an author builds an essay by laying down one key idea and then building on it with the next. In "Coming to Our Senses," the central idea emerges with the support of key points and details about the senses that humans use. In this way, the author moves readers from one idea to the next, shaping the support for his central ideas.

- While the key points create a kind of outline, **details and examples** complete those ideas, developing and refining each by answering *who, what, when, where, why,* and *how* questions to support the central idea. Details and examples make a nonfiction selection meaningful and interesting to readers.

- To understand a nonfiction selection, readers can create an objective summary of the text. A **summary** of the text explains the central idea and the key points, as well as the most important details. Use a graphic organizer like this one to help you identify the information that you need for a summary.

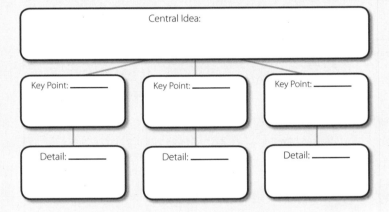

Central Idea:

Key Point: _____   Key Point: _____   Key Point: _____

Detail: _____   Detail: _____   Detail: _____

Analyze Development of Ideas

Project the graphic organizer and write the following terms on the board: **central idea, key points, details and examples,** and **summary.** After reviewing the definition of each term, have students copy the graphic organizer in their notebooks. Divide students into small groups and ask them to complete the graphic organizer by providing examples from the text. Then have groups summarize the purpose of Tyson's essay. When they have finished, have each group share their answers with the class.

To reinforce students' understanding of idea development, ask them to draw another copy of the graphic organizer in their notebooks. Then tell them to imagine that they are going to write a nonfiction essay on something they are knowledgeable about, such as the importance of playing a team sport or the need to listen to music while studying. Have each student complete the graphic organizer with key points, details, and examples that would support his or her central idea.

Strategies for Annotation 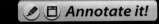 *Annotate it!*

Determine Central Idea and Analyze Its Development

Remind students that Tyson uses examples to develop his central idea. He repeats the central idea throughout the text to stress its importance. Have students use the eBook annotation tools to analyze Tyson's writing.

- Highlight phrases where the central idea is stated in yellow.
- Underline the key points.
- Highlight details and examples that support the central idea in green.

Suppose a glowing blob of some unknown substance were parked right in front of us. Without some diagnostic tool like a tricorder to help, we would be clueless to the blob's chemical or nuclear composition. Nor could we know whether it has an electromagnetic field, or whether it emits strongly in gamma rays,

PRACTICE & APPLY

Analyzing the Text

COMMON CORE RI 1, RI 2, RI 3, RI 4, RI 5, RI 6

Possible answers:

1. *The central idea of the essay is that we cannot rely only on our five senses; we have to use scientific tools to understand what is beyond our senses. For example, in lines 117–124, Tyson explains that magnetic detectors and spectrum analyzers are tools we need to understand what is beyond our senses.*

2. *Tyson says that the world is full of things that we cannot understand simply by observing or touching them. He claims that only using our five senses is inadequate. In lines 131–133, he explains that if our eyes functioned like high-performance microscopes, humans could have easily understood the cause of the plague.*

3. *He means that differences in sensory stimuli are less noticeable because they occur logarithmically, or exponentially. If the differences were linear, we would pick up on them more easily.*

4. *He compares parapsychology to real science, and finds that there is no way to find or confirm the infamous sixth sense, but that in real science, there exists many tools for measuring what our senses cannot perceive. This discussion supports his claim that we need scientific tools to truly understand the world around us.*

5. *Hubble's quotation claims that the five senses are the basis for science, and Tyson revises the quote to include modern equipment in order to illustrate that we have to rely on technology to help us understand the world we cannot sense.*

6. *He means that the five senses are not enough to fully perceive our surroundings, so if you don't use scientific tools, you may be putting yourself in a dangerous situation.*

7. *Using words such as* majesty *and* complexity *create a sense of wonder and amazement. Tyson's words elevate the topic of understanding of the universe to one of high honor (majesty).*

8. *"Coming to our senses" usually means acknowledging what's in front of us or what is really happening. Tyson is using it as a play on words to show us that we need technology to really sense what is in the world.*

Analyzing the Text

COMMON CORE RI 1, RI 3, RI 4, RI 5, RI 6, SL 1a

Cite Text Evidence   Support your responses with evidence from the selection.

1. **Identify** What is the central idea that the author develops throughout this essay? What key points support that central idea?

2. **Summarize** Why is using our five senses to understand the more complicated aspects of the world around us a problem, according to the author?

3. **Interpret** The author says, "we register the world's stimuli in logarithmic rather than linear increments." In your own words, explain what he means.

4. **Analyze** The author provides a brief explanation and discussion of parapsychology. Although it may seem like a digression, it serves his larger purpose. What function does this discussion serve?

5. **Synthesize** Why does the author begin the essay with a quotation by Edwin P. Hubble and then later suggest a revision of the quotation? How do the two versions of the quotation help shape and refine the essay's central idea?

6. **Interpret** Tyson writes, "In modern times, if the sole measure of what's out there flows from your five senses, then a precarious life awaits you." Explain what he means by this statement.

7. **Evaluate** Toward the end of the essay, Tyson asserts that as we develop more scientific tools with which to see and understand the universe, "a new level of majesty and complexity in the universe reveals itself to us." What is the impact of the author's word choice on the tone of this passage? How does the author's word choice help you understand his perspective?

8. **Analyze** What does the phrase "coming to our senses" usually mean? How does this usual meaning relate to Tyson's central idea?

PERFORMANCE TASK

Speaking Activity: Discussion In lines 102–143, Tyson imagines how our world and our history might be different if we had been born with the super senses that scientific tools now give us. Review this section. Then, explore the author's technique through this task.

1. In a small group, discuss how the author presents this idea, inviting the reader to imagine life with super senses. Discuss how this technique helps shape the author's central idea.

2. Write a one-page summary of the discussion, including all relevant points. Be sure to organize ideas in a clear and coherent way and use the conventions of standard English.

Assign this performance task.

PERFORMANCE TASK

COMMON CORE SL 1a

Speaking Activity: Discussion Encourage students in their discussion groups to allow their imaginations free reign. Encourage students to move through the senses one by one, imagining what life would be like with super senses. Explain that guiding the discussion this way will help them organize their thoughts when they write the one-page summary.

Critical Vocabulary

COMMON CORE L 4a, L 4c

acuity   stimuli   propensity   transcend   precarious

Practice and Apply Demonstrate an understanding of each Critical Vocabulary word by explaining your answer.

1. If you possessed **acuity** of vision, would you be more or less likely to need prescription glasses? Why?

2. Which of these **stimuli** is more likely to bring about a reaction from you: the sound of a ringing telephone or the smell escaping from a bakery? Why?

3. If you have a **propensity** for organization, is your closet messy or tidy? Explain.

4. If a singer's songs **transcend** musical genres, can you classify them as either country or rock? Why?

5. If your job was **precarious**, would you look for a new one? Explain.

Vocabulary Strategy: Using Reference Sources

The author of the essay incorporates pop culture, historical, and scientific references into the text. Though you may be able to discern the central idea without knowing what these references are, understanding them will enhance your comprehension. For example, if you didn't know the meaning of the Critical Vocabulary word *stimuli*, you would misunderstand the author's message about how we perceive the world through our senses.

To determine the meaning of an unknown word, name, or reference, consult general and specialized reference material, both print and digital. These may include dictionaries for defining specific words; encyclopedias for providing an explanation of places, events, and people; and a search engine for leading you to specialized online resources that will help identify more obscure references.

Practice and Apply Use print or digital resource materials to define or explain each reference from the essay.

1. Edwin P. Hubble

2. double-blind experiment

3. the *Star Trek* sci-fi series

4. Geiger counters

PRACTICE & APPLY

Critical Vocabulary

COMMON CORE RI 4, L 4a, L 4c

Possible answers:

1. *I would less likely need glasses because my vision would be finely tuned and sharp.*

2. *A ringing phone would bring more of a reaction because I am conditioned to answer the phone when it rings. The smell of freshly baked cakes or breads might encourage me to walk in the bakery.*

3. *My closet would be tidy. The word* propensity *means "an inclination to do something," so a propensity for organization would result in an organized closet.*

4. *Neither, because* transcend *means that the music goes beyond genres and does not fit into one category.*

5. *If I like danger and risk, I may not look for a new job.*

Vocabulary Strategy

Possible answers:

1. *American astronomer who lived in the first part of the 20th century; the Hubble telescope was named after him.*

2. *An experiment in which the identity of those subjects receiving the test treatment is concealed from both the subjects and those administering the experiment. These are supposed to be less biased than other kinds of experiments.*

3. *A popular American science-fiction TV series that began in 1966 and has had several different adaptations on TV, and in movies and books.*

4. *Measures the amount of nuclear radiation in the atmosphere; a particle detector that measures ionizing radiation.*

Strategies for Annotation 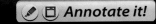 *Annotate it!*

Understanding Context

COMMON CORE RI 1, RI 4

Have students find the following references in the essay: Edwin Hubble, double-blind experiment, the *Star Trek* sci-fi series, and Geiger counters. Have students use the eBook Annotation tools to:

- Highlight each reference in yellow.
- On a note, write the definition or explanation of the reference.
- Reread the passage that surrounds the reference for enhanced understanding.

Equipped with his five senses, man explores the universe around him and calls the adventure science.

—Edwin P. Hubble (1889–1953),

The Nature of Science

> American astronomer who was very influential; Hubble telescope named after him.

Language and Style: Parallel Structure

COMMON CORE W 5, L 1a

As you discuss the concept of **parallel structure** with students, reinforce the idea that this technique uses similar grammatical construction to express related ideas. Discuss how his use of parallel structure enhances the experience of reading. Then invite volunteers to find an additional example of parallel structure in Tyson's essay. *("Without hardware to help our analysis, and without a particular urge to lick the stuff . . . ." [lines 90-91])* Discuss how this use of parallel structure enhances the reader's experience.

To continue the lesson, write the following terms on the board: *reading, swim,* and *dance.* Ask students to create an original sentence using parallel structure with these words. *(Over the summer, Rachel enjoys reading, swimming, and dancing.)* After students share their writing, discuss how verb forms contribute to parallel structure.

Encourage students to refer back to the examples they have worked with during this lesson as they revise their summaries. After they have finished this activity, invite students to discuss how their revisions have improved their writing.

Possible answer:

Answers will vary. When students finish the activity, they should be able to point to two examples of parallel structure with their revised summaries. Invite students to discuss how their revisions improved their writing.

Assess It!

Online Selection Test
- Download an editable ExamView bank.
- Assign and manage this test online.

Language and Style: Parallel Structure

COMMON CORE W 5, L 1a

Parallel structure is the repetition of a pattern of words or phrases within a sentence or passage to signify that two or more events or ideas have the same level of importance. Parallel structure helps writers organize and clarify their thoughts. It can also affect the meaning and tone of a sentence or passage.

> Read this sentence from the text:
>
> **Our eyes allow us to register information not only from across the room but also from across the universe.**

The author repeats the words *across the,* giving equal weight to the eyes' ability to register information that originates from locations that are quite different. Consider that he could have written the sentence like this:

> **Our eyes allow us to register information from different locations.**

This sentence does not emphasize the eyes' far-ranging abilities the way the first sentence does. It also lacks the strong rhythm that parallel structure creates.

Writers can use parallel structure not only within sentences but also within a passage. For example, Tyson begins two paragraphs similarly:

> **If we were born with magnetic detectors, . . .**
>
> **And if we were born with big eyes and built-in Doppler motion detectors, . . .**

By beginning the paragraphs as he does, the author emphasizes the conditional nature of his point ("*If* we were born with . . .") and gives both points equal weight and importance. The parallel structure also adds continuity to the passage, making the author's points easier to follow. In addition, the author's repetition is rhythmic, making it more memorable and enjoyable to read.

Practice and Apply   Look back at the summary of the discussion you created in response to this selection's Performance Task. Revise the summary to add at least two examples of parallel structure within a sentence or between paragraphs. Then, discuss with a partner how each use of parallel structure improves your meaning or tone.

WHEN STUDENTS STRUGGLE . . .

If students are struggling with parallel structure and its use in the essay, review the definition of this technique. Then explain that there are hints that can help them identify the use of parallel structure. Tell them to look for places where two elements are joined with *and, but,* or *or;* there is a list created with prepositions or infinitives; comparisions are made by linking verbs; and elements are joined by *either/or* and *not only/but also.*

ASK STUDENTS to work with a partner to write original sentences that use an example of each of these parallel structure techniques. Circulate around the room while students are working to check for understanding.

Analyze How Authors Develop Ideas

COMMON CORE

RI 5

EXTEND

Explain to students that writers develop their main idea by using sentences and paragraphs as building blocks. One technique writers often use is to begin with simple, easy to understand ideas and build to more complex conclusions. Look at the first paragraph of this essay as an example of this concept.

In the first sentence of the essay, Tyson states that our sense of sight is the most special. He explains in the next sentence that we see things across a room and across the universe. In this example, Tyson is taking us from a familiar, easier reference (seeing something across the room) to a more complex idea (seeing stars across our universe).

COLLABORATIVE DISCUSSION

Have students work in small groups to identify and discuss other examples of this strategy by Tyson in paragraphs 1–3, where the author moves from the amazing aspects of human senses to their limitations.

Analyze Development of Ideas

COMMON CORE

RI 2, RI 5

RETEACH

Review the terms *central idea, key points, details and examples,* and *summary.*

Explain to students that authors carefully organize their thoughts and ideas in order to effectively develop their central ideas. Each paragraph is written in order to build upon one another to create a cohesive piece of writing.

Tell students that one way to analyze how an author develops his or her central idea is to identify the topic sentence and the supporting details in each paragraph. By identifying these elements, a reader can see how the sections begin to fit together to support the central idea.

Use the first paragraph of Tyson's essay as a model for students:

- Ask a student volunteer to read aloud the first paragraph.
- Then have a different student identify the topic sentence. *("Among our five senses, sight is the most special to us.")* As a class, identify the ideas and details that support this topic sentence. *(Our eyes allow us to register information; without vision, we wouldn't have the science of astronomy; we wouldn't be able to measure our place in the universe without our eyesight.)*

PRACTICE AND APPLY

Divide the class into small groups and assign each group one of the following sections of text: lines 1–38; lines 38–65; lines 66–101; lines 102–143; lines 144–169; lines 170–183. Have the groups repeat this activity with their assigned text. When they have finished, allow time for groups to compare their identification of topic sentences and details with one another.

 INTERACTIVE GRAPHIC ORGANIZERS Have students use the interactive graphic organizer Main Idea and Details Chart to help them identify the main idea and supporting details of Tyson's essay.

Every Second Counts

Book Review by Matilda Battersby

Background Have students read the background and information about time and Claudia Hammond's book. Introduce the book review by pointing out that most human endeavors are limited by considerations of time. Hunting and gathering societies have to keep track of animal migrations. Agricultural peoples must know when to plant and harvest their crops. Today's industrial economies are run by the clock, from hurried breakfasts to executive board meetings.

AS YOU READ Ask students to pay attention to the central idea of the book review. How does the author develop these ideas?

Common Core Support

- cite strong and thorough textual evidence
- determine a central idea and how it is developed
- analyze how an author unfolds a series of ideas
- determine the meaning of words

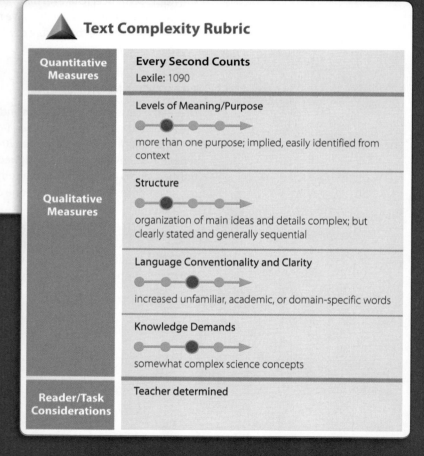

Text Complexity Rubric

Quantitative Measures	**Every Second Counts** Lexile: 1090
Qualitative Measures	**Levels of Meaning/Purpose** more than one purpose; implied, easily identified from context
	Structure organization of main ideas and details complex; but clearly stated and generally sequential
	Language Conventionality and Clarity increased unfamiliar, academic, or domain-specific words
	Knowledge Demands somewhat complex science concepts
Reader/Task Considerations	Teacher determined

Strategies for CLOSE READING

Analyze Development of Ideas

Students should read this review carefully all the way through. Close-reading questions at the bottom of the page will help them focus on a thorough analysis of the central ideas. As they read, students should jot down comments or questions about the text in the margins.

WHEN STUDENTS STRUGGLE . . .

To help students analyze the development of central ideas in "Every Second Counts," have them work in small groups to fill out a chart like the one shown below.

CITE TEXT EVIDENCE For practice in analyzing the development of ideas in a text, ask students to cite text evidence for each box in the chart.

Central Idea
People have notions that time is elastic.

Key Point
There are many time-based platitudes about time's inconstancy.

Key Point
Our perceptions of time are indeed elastic.

Detail
Time flies when you're having fun.

Detail
Time seems to stretch out when we're waiting for a holiday.

Detail
We obsess about timekeeping and time-saving.

Background *Everyone has noticed that sometimes time seems to fly and sometimes it seems to crawl. Our perception of time is a result of brain processes that have to do with memory and attention. Really, it isn't time that we perceive, but changes or events in time. British writer, broadcaster, and lecturer Claudia Hammond wrote the book TimeWarped to examine "the way we actively construct this experience of time in our minds." Find out more in this book review.*

Every Second Counts

Book Review by Matilda Battersby

CLOSE READ
Notes

1. **READ ▶** As you read lines 1–15, begin to cite evidence.
   - Underline three commonly used sayings in lines 1–9.
   - In the margin, explain what Battersby means when she says "time is elastic" in line 6.
   - Circle the question she asks in lines 10–15.

A Time is of the essence. Time heals all wounds. Time flies when you're having fun . . . Such time-based **platitudes** are neverending. In fact, time is the most-used noun in the English language, so concerned are we by our position in it, our grasp of it—and its power over us.

B The platitudes exist because they represent broad, if scientifically unproven, notions that time is elastic. Time does seem to fly by when we're having fun. Likewise, it stretches out ad infinitum when we're willing it to zip past and deliver us with birthdays, Christmas Day or that longed-for holiday.

10 But how often do we examine the many nuances of our relationship with time? It is a construct, after all. If I were a member of the Amazon's Amondawa tribe I would have no word for time, no clocks and no calendar to chart months or years passing. But that doesn't mean my past, present or future would be fundamentally any different. Yet we rely on (and obsess about) timekeeping, time-saving and the rate at which we gobble it up.

platitude:
a flat, dull, or trite remark

Time is flexible and stretches and contracts.

63

---

1. **READ AND CITE TEXT EVIDENCE** Note that the author begins the review by citing common expressions about time.

A **ASK STUDENTS** to discuss the sayings in lines 1–2. What idea(s) do these sayings support? *Students should understand that the sayings are examples of our never-ending concern about time—and "its power over us."*

Critical Vocabulary: platitude (line 2) Have students share their definitions of *platitude*, and ask volunteers to use the noun in sentences about time. *One of my favorite platitudes is "No time like the present."*

FOR ELL STUDENTS Explain that the phrase *gobble it up* means "to eat up" a lot of food very quickly. Point out that the author uses the phrase figuratively here.

There have been endless studies into time perception, whether or not time ticks away faster at altitude or whether there is any physical basis for the universal conclusion that time moves more slowly when we are children and speeds up as we grow older. Nobody knows the amount of time they 20 will live in their lives and yet we claim time as our own, demand more, and feel cheated when we lose it.

Claudia Hammond, the psychology lecturer, broadcaster, and writer, has a better understanding than most of the ways that our perspectives on time can be morphed, manipulated and played with.

C Her new book, *Time Warped*, examines the myriad ways that time seems to change gear. She also looks at our sense of time aesthetically and discovered that people visualize time in offbeat ways. Some see it as curling around like a Slinky or a roll of wallpaper; others may view days of the week as rectangles. To some, Monday is the color red (though it is yellow to me).

30 The puzzles of time, the tricks it plays and the ways we unconsciously amend our relationship with it are explored in detail by Hammond. She has **D** come up with the "holiday paradox," a description of the way that when we're relaxing on holiday, we feel that time cannot go faster. It whizzes by as we pack it full of new experiences. But when we look back afterwards, it feels as if we've been away for ages.

F Here she explains (or disproves) other mysteries of time.

Time is determined by the body's circadian rhythms FALSE

E The circadian rhythms[1] affect only our 24-hour day/night cycle. They have nothing else to do with our perception of time from moment to 40 moment. It's a myth that they affect time. We do, however, run an automatic body clock. This can go out of sync, which is known as "free running." This is common particularly in blind people, who are isolated

[1] **circadian rhythm:** a biological rhythmic activity cycle taking place within the span of a 24-hour day.

---

2. **◀ REREAD** Reread lines 1–9. What is the central idea in these lines? What details support this idea?

The central idea is that we have common, but faulty, ideas about time being elastic. Supporting details include common sayings about how time moves and our own perceptions of time slowing down.

3. **READ ▶** As you read lines 16–35, continue to cite evidence.
   • Underline the key points the author makes.
   • Summarize lines 22–35 in the margin.

64

Claudia Hammond's book examines how time seems to change gear. She also explores the tricks time plays on us.

---

from environmental time cues. In most of us, however, the circadian oscillations correct themselves using daylight.

Time speeds up as we get older FALSE

People think that time speeds up when we get older. But it's not true that time at any one moment (ie second by second) gets faster. It's our experiences over days, weeks, months and years that seem to condense. There's no biological basis for the sensation that it speeds up. It's simply to 50 do with our judgments on time **prospectively** and **retrospectively**. Looking back, time seems to go faster, but it can also be strangely elastic.

Time is money TRUE

Social psychologist Robert Levine measured three things in 31 countries around the world to determine the tempo of life: the time taken to buy a stamp, average walking speed of pedestrians during rush hour, and the accuracy of clocks on the walls of banks. It followed that places such as London and New York had the fastest times and that there was a correlation (though this was pre-recession) between the pace of life and gross domestic product. This suggests a connection between time and money, though it 60 isn't known which came first—the culture of rushing around or the buoyant economy.

We can mentally time-travel TRUE

We are the one animal able completely, at will, to throw ourselves backwards into the past or forwards into the future. The ability to conceive events that haven't happened yet is a crucial basis for our imagination. The reason our memories are so bad and let us down actually allows us mentally to time-travel into the future. The unreliability of memory is actually an indication of this sophistication. The mind uses our sense of space and memories to create a sense of the future. Amnesia sufferers lose the ability 70 to imagine the future, as well as their ability to recall who they are or what's happened to them.

Time feels slower when you want something done fast TRUE

Psychologists Chen-Bo Zhong and Sanford DeVoe conducted experiments that revealed that exposure to fast food, both visual symbols and actual food, increases feelings of impatience. We associate fast food with being in a hurry or a rush. This anxiety makes us feel time is going

---

4. **◀ REREAD AND DISCUSS** Reread lines 30–35. With a small group, discuss what Hammond means by the "holiday paradox."

5. **READ ▶** Read lines 36–85. Circle the boldfaced headings and underline the key points in each paragraph.

65

prospectively; retrospectively:
looking forward; looking backward

---

2. **REREAD AND CITE TEXT EVIDENCE**

B **ASK STUDENTS** how they determined the central idea of lines 1–9. *Line 5 explains that the platitudes listed in the first paragraph exist because of "broad . . . notions" that time is elastic. The word* because *indicates a reason—something that explains the platitudes.*

3. **READ AND CITE TEXT EVIDENCE**

C **ASK STUDENTS** to explain what Hammond writes about in her book. *Hammond examines the ways that time seems to change speed. She looks at our sense of time aesthetically. She explores the puzzles of time, the tricks it plays on us, and the ways we fix our relationship to it.*

4. **REREAD AND DISCUSS USING TEXT EVIDENCE**

D **ASK STUDENTS** from each group to discuss their conclusions about the meaning of the "holiday paradox." *While people are enjoying themselves on vacation, they generally relax and take it easy. But their perception of time speeds up—it feels as though time "whizzes by." The author explains this by pointing out that people on vacation have many new experiences, which leads to the impression that time is speeding up.*

5. **READ AND CITE TEXT EVIDENCE**

E **ASK STUDENTS** how they can determine the key points in each paragraph. *The key points are those that present the evidence that supports or disproves each boldfaced heading.*

Critical Vocabulary: prospectively; retrospectively (line 50) Have students share their definitions of *prospectively* and *retrospectively,* and ask volunteers to use the words in sentences.

more slowly. Research shows people felt they had been waiting for far longer than they actually had.

Our sense of time can be affected by biological conditions TRUE

80   A high temperature (a fever, not just wearing too many jumpers²) makes our perception of time change so it feels slower. American psychologist Hudson Hoagland's wife was lying in bed with bad flu and she allowed him to conduct time tests on her. Hoagland asked her to say when a minute had passed 30 times over a day. When her temperature reached 103°F, she felt a minute was up after just 34 seconds.

² **jumpers:** British term for sweaters.

6. ◀ REREAD Reread lines 36–85. What structure does the author use to discuss key points? In what way are they introduced and developed?

The author selects six common perceptions of time and discusses each one to show whether they are true or false. Headings introduce the topics. The topics are developed with details of studies or other facts.

SHORT RESPONSE

Cite Text Evidence Write an objective summary of this book review. Analyze the way in which key points are introduced and developed. **Cite evidence** from the text in your response.

The author introduces the topic by describing common perceptions and sayings about time. For example, time does seem to fly when we're having fun. Then, she explains that Claudia Hammond, a psychology lecturer and writer, has written a book that examines "the puzzles of time, the tricks it plays and the ways we unconsciously amend our relationship with it." Battersby then introduces six common perceptions about time and explains whether each one is true or false. These examples might make the reader want to read the book to learn more.

66

---

6. REREAD AND CITE TEXT EVIDENCE

F **ASK STUDENTS** why the reviewer might have structured her review this way. *Students should recognize that by organizing her writing in this way, the reviewer is able to present a great deal of information clearly and succinctly. In just a couple of pages, Battersby confirms or refutes six common "mysteries of time."*

SHORT RESPONSE

Cite Text Evidence Students' responses should include text evidence that supports their positions. Students should:

- summarize the book review.
- give examples of the review's key points.
- explain how key points are developed and supported.

TO CHALLENGE STUDENTS . . .

For more context and deeper understanding, students can research idioms about time online. Suggest the following examples before students research other idioms: *beat the clock; a race against time; turn back the hands of time; behind the times; watch the clock; the sands of time; time will tell.*

ASK STUDENTS to analyze these idioms. What does each idiom mean? Are some of the idioms more "timely," or contemporary, than others? *Students might suggest an explanation such as that turning back the hands of time means "going back to the past." This idiom relies on the image of the hands of a clock, but most clocks are digital now, so this is not timely. The sands of time refers to time's passing, and relies on the image of a sand timer or hourglass, neither of which is very timely.*

DIG DEEPER

With the class, return to Question 5, Read. Have students share their responses to the question.

ASK STUDENTS to discuss the relationship between the boldfaced headings and the subsequent paragraphs.

- What role do the headings play? *Students should understand that each heading is a topic, or thesis, sentence. Students may also compare the headings to scientific hypotheses that can be proven or disproven.*
- What information does the reviewer present in each paragraph? *Battersby first tells whether the claim in the heading is true or false and then explains why. Sometimes she simply summarizes the reasons. Other times, she gives a quick description of a relevant experiment or study. She also provides some details that make the paragraph interesting.*
- How would you describe this structure? *It's like a pyramid. The central idea, or thesis, is at the top. Under the central idea are some key points. And the bottom layer is made of details that support the key points.*

ASK STUDENTS to return to their Short Response answer and revise it based on the class discussion.

The Night Face Up

Short Story by Julio Cortázar Translated by Paul Blackburn

Why This Text?

Tension is a device that can engage readers and encourage them to keep reading. This lesson enables students to explore how an author creates tension through the use of parallel plots, foreshadowing, pace, and tone.

View It!

Professional Development Podcast:

Text-Dependent Analysis

Key Learning Objective: The student will be able to cite textual evidence and analyze how an author uses parallel plots, tone, pace, and foreshadowing to create tension.

COMMON CORE — Common Core Standards

RL 1 Cite textual evidence.

RL 3 Analyze how complex characters develop, interact, and advance the plot.

RL 4 Determine the meaning of words and phrases.

RL 5 Analyze how an author's choices create mystery, tension, or surprise.

RL 6 Analyze a particular point of view from outside the United States.

W 1 Write arguments using valid reasoning and relevant evidence.

L 1b Use various types of phrases and clauses to convey specific meanings.

L 4 Determine the meaning of unknown and multiple-meaning words.

Text Complexity Rubric

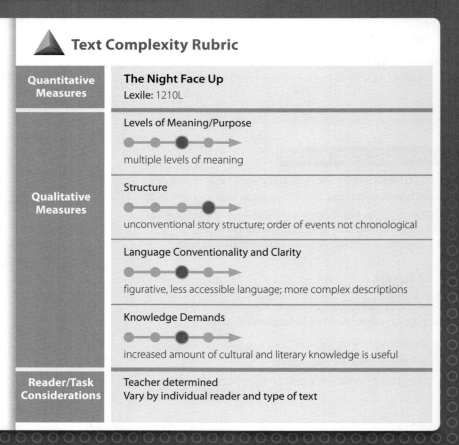

Quantitative Measures	**The Night Face Up** Lexile: 1210L
Qualitative Measures	**Levels of Meaning/Purpose** multiple levels of meaning
	Structure unconventional story structure; order of events not chronological
	Language Conventionality and Clarity figurative, less accessible language; more complex descriptions
	Knowledge Demands increased amount of cultural and literary knowledge is useful
Reader/Task Considerations	Teacher determined Vary by individual reader and type of text

Background Have students read the background and information about the author. Tell students Julio Cortázar also wrote under the pseudonym Julio Denis. He was a citizen of both Argentina and France. Explain that Cortázar's interest in fantasy and the supernatural was nurtured when he was a child and first read stories by Edgar Allan Poe.

AS YOU READ Direct students to use the As You Read statement to focus their reading.

Cite Textual Evidence

COMMON CORE RL 1

(LINES 1–11)

Explain to students that details from the text are known as **textual evidence**. Tell them they will use textual evidence to analyze what the text says explicitly, make inferences, and understand what is happening in the story's two plots.

A **CITE TEXT EVIDENCE** Point out the As You Read note, indicating that it refers to two separate stories. Ask students if two stories are unfolding on this page and to cite their evidence. *(Only one story is unfolding so far because the text is describing one scene and one plot.)* What is happening in the story now? *(A man is riding a motorcycle down a city street, enjoying the sunshine and cool breeze of the day.)*

Analyze Author's Choices: Parallel Plots and Tension

COMMON CORE RL 1, RL 5

Point out to students that writers often create tension in a story through the use of **foreshadowing.** This is when an author gives hints and clues as to what will happen later in the story.

B **CITE TEXT EVIDENCE** Have students cite a clue on this page that foreshadows events to come. *(The reference to the Aztec ritual war of the blossom foreshadows a violent incident.)*

and short-story writer. A vocal opponent of the Argentinian government, Cortázar fled to Paris in 1951, where he remained until his death. He is best known for deftly weaving fantasy, hallucinations, and dreams into his fiction, as he does in "The Night Face Up." The Aztec sacrifice alluded to in this work was an important part of Aztec religious life. Human victims were usually prisoners of war or slaves; their sacrifice was thought to appease the gods and make them stronger.

The Night Face Up

Short Story by Julio Cortázar   Translated by Paul Blackburn

AS YOU READ Notice the two separate stories that unfold at the same time. Write down any questions you generate during reading.

> *And at certain periods they went out to hunt enemies; they called it the war of the blossom.*

A Halfway down the long hotel vestibule,[1] he thought that probably he was going to be late, and hurried on into the street to get out his motorcycle from the corner where the next-door superintendent let him keep it. On the jewelry store at the corner he read that it was ten to nine; he had time to spare. The sun filtered through the tall downtown buildings, and he—because for himself, for just going along thinking, he did not have a name—he swung 10 onto the machine, savoring the idea of the ride. The motor whirred between his legs, and a cool wind whipped his pantslegs.

Image Credits: (t) ©Ulf Andersen/Getty Images; (bg) ©Sergey Dubrovskiy/E+/Getty Images; (c) ©Arville/Getty Images; (cr) ©Bildarchiv Steffens/AKG Images

---

* The war of the blossom was the name the Aztecs gave to a ritual war in which they took prisoners for sacrifice. It is metaphysics to say that the gods see men as flowers, to be so uprooted, trampled, cut down. –Ed. [Cortázar's note]
[1] **vestibule:** a hall or entryway next to a building's exterior door.

SCAFFOLDING FOR ELL STUDENTS

Analyze Author's Choices: Parallel Plots and Tension Pair English learners with proficient English speakers. Use a whiteboard to project the story's first page or have copies of the pages available. Invite a volunteer to do the following on this page and all subsequent pages of the story.

- Highlight in yellow the first line of text when events take place during the time of the Aztecs.
- Highlight in blue the first line of text when events take place during modern times.

ASK STUDENTS what items or places mentioned on the first page of the story show that these events take place during modern times. *(hotel, motorcycle, jewelry store, downtown buildings, machine, motor)*

Analyze Author's Choices: RL 5
Tension (LINES 12–30)

Tell students that **tension** in a story makes a reader want to keep reading to find out what will happen next.

C **ASK STUDENTS** to identify an event in this section of the story and explain how that event creates tension. (*The woman screamed as the man tried to avoid hitting her. This creates tension because at this point in the story, the reader does not know what happened to the woman after she screamed.*)

Cite Textual Evidence RL 1
(LINES 27–32)

Remind students that they should be able to cite details in a text that support not only what the text says explicitly, but also **inferences,** or logical assumptions they can make from the text.

D **CITE TEXT EVIDENCE** Have students infer whether the man was completely well or a bit groggy when others first lifted him at the site of the accident. Tell students to cite the evidence for their inference. (*He was groggy because the "voices . . . did not seem to belong to the faces hanging above him" [lines 30–31].*)

CRITICAL VOCABULARY

solace: The man felt relieved and took comfort in knowing that the light had been green for him when the woman rushed into the crosswalk.

ASK STUDENTS why the man might have been comforted by hearing that the light had been green at the time of the accident. (*The green light showed that the man had been obeying traffic laws and was not the cause of the accident; he had done nothing wrong.*)

lucid: The man was able to think clearly after the accident even though he knew he wasn't completely well.

ASK STUDENTS what information about the man's health can be learned from the fact that he was able to think rationally and clearly. (*He did not have a serious injury.*)

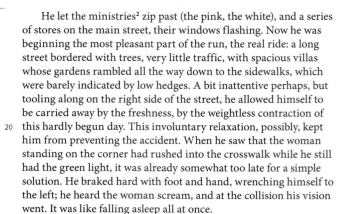

He let the ministries[2] zip past (the pink, the white), and a series of stores on the main street, their windows flashing. Now he was beginning the most pleasant part of the run, the real ride: a long street bordered with trees, very little traffic, with spacious villas whose gardens rambled all the way down to the sidewalks, which were barely indicated by low hedges. A bit inattentive perhaps, but tooling along on the right side of the street, he allowed himself to be carried away by the freshness, by the weightless contraction of this hardly begun day. This involuntary relaxation, possibly, kept him from preventing the accident. When he saw that the woman standing on the corner had rushed into the crosswalk while he still had the green light, it was already somewhat too late for a simple solution. He braked hard with foot and hand, wrenching himself to the left; he heard the woman scream, and at the collision his vision went. It was like falling asleep all at once.

He came to abruptly. Four or five young men were getting him out from under the cycle. He felt the taste of salt and blood, one knee hurt, and when they hoisted him up he yelped, he couldn't bear the pressure on his right arm. Voices which did not seem to belong to the faces hanging above him encouraged him cheerfully with jokes and assurances. His single **solace** was to hear someone else confirm that the lights indeed had been in his favor. He asked about the woman, trying to keep down the nausea which was edging up into his throat. While they carried him face up to a nearby pharmacy, he learned that the cause of the accident had gotten only a few scrapes on the legs, "Nah, you barely got her at all, but when ya hit, the impact made the machine jump and flop on its side . . ." Opinions, recollections of other smashups, take it easy, work him in shoulders first, there, that's fine, and someone in a dust coat giving him a swallow of something soothing in the shadowy interior of the small local pharmacy.

Within five minutes the police ambulance arrived, and they lifted him onto a cushioned stretcher. It was a relief for him to be able to lie out flat. Completely **lucid,** but realizing that he was suffering the effects of a terrible shock, he gave his information to the officer riding in the ambulance with him. The arm almost didn't hurt; blood dripped down from a cut over the eyebrow all over his face. He licked his lips once or twice to drink it. He felt pretty good, it had been an accident, tough luck; stay quiet a few weeks, nothing worse. The guard said that the motorcycle didn't seem badly racked up, "Why should it," he replied. "It all landed on top of me." They both laughed, and when they got to the hospital, the guard shook his hand and wished him luck. Now the nausea

solace
(sŏl´ĭs) *n.* source of relief and comfort.

lucid
(lōō´sĭd) *adj.* thinking rationally and clearly.

---
[2] **ministries:** government offices.

TO CHALLENGE STUDENTS . . .

Character Perspectives What might the woman or one of the young men who helped the crash victim have thought about the events that happened? How would their description and retelling of the accident be the same or different from that of the man? Explain that each character in a story has a **perspective,** or point of view, about the events and the other characters in a story. Challenge students to create a short monologue in which they describe and retell the events surrounding the accident from another character's perspective.

Alternatively, have students work in small groups to develop a skit in which each student, acting as a different character, describes the accident from that character's point of view.

was coming back little by little; meanwhile they were pushing him on a wheeled stretcher toward a pavilion further back, rolling along under trees full of birds, he shut his eyes and wished he were asleep or chloroformed.[3] But they kept him for a good while in a room with that hospital smell, filling out a form, getting his clothes off,
60 and dressing him in a stiff, grayish smock. They moved his arm carefully, it didn't hurt him. The nurses were constantly making wisecracks, and if it hadn't been for the stomach contractions he would have felt fine, almost happy.

They got him over to X-ray, and twenty minutes later, with the still-damp negative lying on his chest like a black tombstone, they pushed him into surgery. Someone tall and thin in white came over and began to look at the X-rays. A woman's hands were arranging his head, he felt that they were moving him from one stretcher to another. The man in white came over to him again, smiling,
70 something gleamed in his right hand. He patted his cheek and made a sign to someone stationed behind.

It was unusual as a dream because it was full of smells, and he never dreamt smells. First a marshy smell, there to the left of the trail the swamps began already, the quaking bogs from which no one ever returned. But the reek lifted, and instead there came a dark, fresh composite fragrance, like the night under which he moved, in flight from the Aztecs. And it was all so natural, he had to run from the Aztecs who had set out on their manhunt, and his sole chance was to find a place to hide in the deepest part of the
80 forest, taking care not to lose the narrow trail which only they, the Motecas, knew.

What tormented him the most was the odor, as though, notwithstanding the absolute acceptance of the dream, there was something which resisted that which was not habitual, which until that point had not participated in the game. "It smells of war," he thought, his hand going instinctively to the stone knife which was tucked at an angle into his girdle of woven wool. An unexpected sound made him crouch suddenly stock-still and shaking. To be afraid was nothing strange, there was plenty of fear in his dreams.
90 He waited, covered by the branches of a shrub and the starless night. Far off, probably on the other side of the big lake, they'd be lighting the bivouac[4] fires; that part of the sky had a reddish glare. The sound was not repeated. It had been like a broken limb. Maybe an animal that, like himself, was escaping from the smell of war. He stood erect slowly, sniffing the air. Not a sound could be heard, but the fear was still following, as was the smell, that cloying incense of the war of the blossom. He had to press forward, to stay out of the

---
[3] **chloroformed:** made unconscious by inhaling an anesthetic.
[4] **bivouac:** a temporary camp.

The Night Face Up **173**

Analyze Author's Choices: Parallel Plots and Tension (LINES 72–97)

COMMON CORE RL 1, RL 5

Have students reread the second full paragraph (lines 72–81). Explain that at this point in the story, Cortázar begins to use **parallel plots,** which share equal importance and, generally, equal space in a story.

E CITE TEXT EVIDENCE Have students work in pairs to locate examples of textual evidence that show the story has moved from one plot to the other. *(The setting has moved from an indoor hospital to an outdoor trail that is located near swamps. There are also mentions of the Aztecs and Motecas, a manhunt, the "game," the smell of war, a stone knife, a big lake, bivouac fires, and the "war of the blossom.")*

Point out to students that this parallel plot set in an ancient Aztec manhunt has its own tension building.

F CITE TEXT EVIDENCE Ask students what words and phrases communicate the tension in this parallel plot. *("swamps . . . ever returned" [lines 74–75]; "in flight from the Aztecs" [line 77]; "sole chance" [line 79]; "tormented" [line 82]; "his hand going . . . to the stone knife" [ine 86]; "escaping from the smell of war" [line 94])* Then ask students what sense the author focuses on in this parallel plot. *(smell)* Why is this sense noteworthy in this part of the story? *(The man had never dreamt smells.)* Have students pair up and discuss any possible significance of this fact.

WHEN STUDENTS STRUGGLE . . .

All students can benefit from the Scaffolding for ELL Students activity on page 171. Have students mark the text accordingly.

Then, to help students understand the context of the Aztec manhunt, have them reread the Background note and the italicized note and footnote about the war of the blossom that appear on the first page of the selection. Encourage students to visualize the setting of the manhunt. Then ask volunteers to describe the setting using as many senses as possible. Ask: What emotions or feelings about the manhunt are developed by the sensory details?

Analyze Author's Choices: Parallel Plots

COMMON CORE RL 1, RL 5

(LINES 105 and 139, 98–140)

Remind students that the plots switch back and forth.

 CITE TEXT EVIDENCE Have students identify the two places where the plots shift. *(lines 105 and 139)* Ask students to indicate the direction the plots shift in each instance. *(line 105: from the war of the blossom to the hospital; line 139: from the hospital to the war of the blossom)*

Explain that **tone** is the writer's attitude toward a character, place, or event. Tone is often countered in parallel plots so that the tone of one plot is the opposite of the other. Have students compare the tone in the two plots. *(The plot that takes place in the hospital has a calm tone, but the plot that takes place during the war of the blossom is tense.)*

H **CITE TEXT EVIDENCE** Ask students to work in pairs to create a two-column "tone chart," with one column headed *Calm* and the other headed *Tense.* Have pairs list words or phrases from this page that illustrate each type of tone. *(Calm: "enjoying the pleasure of keeping awake" [lines 115–116]; "the fever went along dragging him down softly" [lines 123–124]; "marvelous golden broth" [line 129]; " arm hardly hurt" [line 132]; "sigh of bliss" [line 137] Tense: "groping uncertainly" [line 98]; "horrible blast of that foul smell" [line 103]; "leaped forward desparately" [lines 103–104]; "confusion" [line 139])*

bogs and get to the heart of the forest. Groping uncertainly through the dark, stooping every other moment to touch the packed earth of the trail, he took a few steps. He would have liked to have broken into a run, but the gurgling fens[5] lapped on either side of him. On the path and in darkness, he took his bearings. Then he caught a horrible blast of that foul smell he was most afraid of, and leaped forward desperately.

"You're going to fall off the bed," said the patient next to him. "Stop bouncing around, old buddy."

He opened his eyes and it was afternoon, the sun already low in the oversized windows of the long ward. While trying to smile at his neighbor, he detached himself almost physically from the final scene of the nightmare. His arm, in a plaster cast, hung suspended from an apparatus with weights and pulleys. He felt thirsty, as though he'd been running for miles, but they didn't want to give him much water, barely enough to moisten his lips and make a mouthful. The fever was winning slowly and he would have been able to sleep again, but he was enjoying the pleasure of keeping awake, eyes half-closed, listening to the other patients' conversation, answering a question from time to time. He saw a little white pushcart come up beside the bed, a blond nurse rubbed the front of his thigh with alcohol and stuck him with a fat needle connected to a tube which ran up to a bottle filled with a milky, opalescent liquid. A young intern arrived with some metal and leather apparatus which he adjusted to fit onto the good arm to check something or other. Night fell, and the fever went along dragging him down softly to a state in which things seemed embossed as through opera glasses,[6] they were real and soft and, at the same time, vaguely distasteful; like sitting in a boring movie and thinking that, well, still, it'd be worse out in the street, and staying.

A cup of a marvelous golden broth came, smelling of leeks, celery, and parsley. A small hunk of bread, more precious than a whole banquet, found itself crumbling little by little. His arm hardly hurt him at all, and only in the eyebrow where they'd taken stitches a quick, hot pain sizzled occasionally. When the big windows across the way turned to smudges of dark blue, he thought it would not be difficult for him to sleep. Still on his back so a little uncomfortable, running his tongue out over his hot, too-dry lips, he tasted the broth still, and with a sigh of bliss, he let himself drift off.

First there was a confusion, as of one drawing all his sensations, for that moment blunted or muddled, into himself. He realized

---

[5] **fens:** wet, swampy land.
[6] **opera glasses:** small binoculars.

SCAFFOLDING FOR ELL STUDENTS

Analyze Author's Choices: Parallel Plots Pair English language learners with students fluent in English to create the "tone charts" described in the teacher's note in the side column. Encourage students in each pair to take turns reading aloud the words and phrases that illustrate each type of tone—calm or tense. Have them speak in a voice that reflects the tone. For example, they might speak soothingly and in a drawn out voice when saying "enjoying the pleasure of keeping awake." When saying "horrible blast of that foul smell" they might speak bruskly in a clipped voice. Encourage students to use facial expressions when speaking as well.

"He heard the cries and leaped up, knife in hand."

that he was running in pitch darkness, although, above, the sky criss-crossed with treetops was less black than the rest. "The trail," he thought, "I've gotten off the trail." His feet sank into a bed of leaves and mud, and then he couldn't take a step that the branches of shrubs did not whiplash against his ribs and legs. Out of breath, knowing despite the darkness and silence that he was surrounded, he crouched down to listen. Maybe the trail was very near, with the first daylight he would be able to see it again. Nothing now could help him to find it. The hand that had unconsciously gripped the

150 haft of the dagger climbed like a fen scorpion up to his neck where the protecting amulet[7] hung. Barely moving his lips, he mumbled the supplication of the corn which brings about the **beneficent** moons, and the prayer to Her Very Highness, to the distributor of all Motecan possessions. At the same time he felt his ankles sinking deeper into the mud, and the waiting in the darkness of the obscure grove of live oak grew intolerable to him. The war of the blossom had started at the beginning of the moon and had been going on for three days and three nights now. If he managed to hide in the depths of the forest, getting off the trail further up past the marsh

160 country, perhaps the warriors wouldn't follow his track. He thought of the many prisoners they'd already taken. But the number didn't count, only the **consecrated** period. The hunt would continue until the priests gave the sign to return. Everything had its number and its limit, and it was within the sacred period, and he on the other side from the hunters.

He heard the cries and leaped up, knife in hand. As if the sky were aflame on the horizon, he saw torches moving among the branches, very near him. The smell of war was unbearable, and when the first enemy jumped him, leaped at his throat, he felt an

---

beneficent
(bə-něf´ĭ-sənt) *adj.*
beneficial; producing good.

consecrate
(kŏn´sĭ-krāt´) *v.* to make or define as sacred.

---

[7] **amulet:** a charm or necklace believed to have protective powers.

The Night Face Up **175**

CLOSE READ

Analyze Author's Choices: Tension (LINES 143–146)
COMMON CORE RL 5

Remind students that one way Cortázar creates tension in the story is through his use of **foreshadowing,** giving hints and clues as to what will happen later in the story.

ASK STUDENTS to choose an example of foreshadowing on this page and explain why it is foreshadowing. *(The man knew that he had gotten off the trail and was surrounded by Aztec warriors. This gives a hint as to what will happen later in the story because it seems likely that the man will be caught and captured by the Aztecs—and surrounded by them again before his death.)*

CRITICAL VOCABULARY

beneficent: The man mumbled words that he hoped would bring about the moons that would be beneficial to him.

ASK STUDENTS to identify another situation when the Motecans would ask for these good moons. *(when they wanted corn crops to grow well)*

consecrated: The manhunt could only take place during the period that was defined as sacred.

ASK STUDENTS to explain why the number of prisoners taken didn't matter. *(It wasn't the number of prisoners that determined when the war of the blossom would end; it was only the time period. Prisoners were taken as long as it was within the consecrated time, as determined by the priests.)*

WHEN STUDENTS STRUGGLE . . .

To support students' comprehension of the story, ask pairs to do an oral reading activity. One student should read while the other listens.

Have the first student read lines 141–154 (as well as the first two words of the sentence at the end of line 140). Ask the second student to read from that point to the end of line 165. Then have both students read (either orally or silently) line 166 to the sentence that ends in the middle of line 168.

After each reading, have students discuss the events that happened in their particular passage, including the choices the man made, why students believe he made those choices, and whether or not they think the man could (or should) have made different choices.

Analyze Author's Choices: RL 1
Parallel Plots and Tension

(LINES 170–176, 206–212)

Explain that the author doesn't switch from one parallel plot to another randomly; instead, he includes a connector between plot lines so that the narration flows smoothly.

 ASK STUDENTS to describe the connection between the plot lines that switch near the top of the page. *(In one plot, the man is violently trying to fight off his captors. In the other plot, another hospital patient notices the man fighting in his sleep and assures him that his restlessness is just a result of fever.)*

Now have students consider the plot lines that switch again near the bottom of the page.

K **ASK STUDENTS** to describe this connection between the plots. *(Sleep once again takes over the man, and the lamp gets dimmer and dimmer. He finds himself once again in the world of the Aztecs.)*

170 almost-pleasure in sinking the stone blade flat to the haft into his chest. The lights were already around him, the happy cries. He managed to cut the air once or twice, then a rope snared him from behind.

"It's the fever," the man in the next bed said. "The same thing happened to me when they operated on my duodenum.[8] Take some water, you'll see, you'll sleep all right."

Laid next to the night from which he came back, the tepid shadow of the ward seemed delicious to him. A violet lamp kept watch high on the far wall like a guardian eye. You could hear
180 coughing, deep breathing, once in a while a conversation in whispers. Everything was pleasant and secure, without the chase, no . . . But he didn't want to go on thinking about the nightmare. There were lots of things to amuse himself with. He began to look at the cast on his arm, and the pulleys that held it so comfortably in the air. They'd left a bottle of mineral water on the night table beside him. He put the neck of the bottle to his mouth and drank it like a precious liqueur. He could now make out the different shapes in the ward, the thirty beds, the closets with glass doors. He guessed that his fever was down, his face felt cool. The cut
190 over the eyebrow barely hurt at all, like a recollection. He saw himself leaving the hotel again, wheeling out the cycle. Who'd have thought that it would end like this? He tried to fix the moment of the accident exactly, and it got him very angry to notice that there was a void there, an emptiness he could not manage to fill. Between the impact and the moment that they picked him up off the pavement, the passing out or what went on, there was nothing he could see. And at the same time he had the feeling that this void, this nothingness, had lasted an eternity. No, not even time, more as if, in this void, he had passed across something, or had run
200 back immense distances. The shock, the brutal dashing against the pavement. Anyway, he had felt an immense relief in coming out of the black pit while the people were lifting him off the ground. With pain in the broken arm, blood from the split eyebrow, contusion on the knee; with all that, a relief in returning to daylight, to the day, and to feel sustained and attended. That was weird. Someday he'd ask the doctor at the office about that. Now sleep began to take over again, to pull him slowly down. The pillow was so soft, and the coolness of the mineral water in his fevered throat. The violet light of the lamp up there was beginning to get dimmer and dimmer.
210 As he was sleeping on his back, the position in which he came to did not surprise him, but on the other hand the damp smell, the smell of oozing rock, blocked his throat and forced him to

---

[8] **duodenum** (do͞o′ə-dē′nəm): part of the small intestine.

TO CHALLENGE STUDENTS . . .

Story Maps How can students visually show the connections between parallel plots? Compare the connections between the plots to bridges that connect two parallel roads at various points along the routes. Challenge students to use this comparison to create a visual story map of the two plots and the connections between them. Have students go back through the previous pages of the story to find the transitions between the plots and map them. Maps might include parallel lines for the hospital and the Aztec plots. Bridges between the lines might indicate plot switches and include a phrase on either side of the bridge to show how the action or dialogue creates a transition. Have students present their story maps to the class and explain the configuration. They can continue building the maps as the story progresses.

understand. Open the eyes and look in all directions, hopeless. He was surrounded by an absolute darkness. Tried to get up and felt ropes pinning his wrists and ankles. He was staked to the ground on a floor of dank, icy stone slabs. The cold bit into his naked back, his legs. Dully, he tried to touch the amulet with his chin and found they had stripped him of it. Now he was lost, no prayer could save him from the final . . . From afar off, as though filtering through
220 the rock of the dungeon, he heard the great kettledrums of the feast. They had carried him to the temple, he was in the underground cells of Teocalli[9] itself, awaiting his turn.

He heard a yell, a hoarse yell that rocked off the walls. Another yell, ending in a moan. It was he who was screaming in the darkness, he was screaming because he was alive, his whole body with that cry fended off what was coming, the inevitable end. He thought of his friends filling up the other dungeons, and of those already walking up the stairs of the sacrifice. He uttered another choked cry, he could barely open his mouth, his jaws were
230 twisted back as if with a rope and a stick, and once in a while they would open slowly with an endless exertion, as if they were made of rubber. The creaking of the wooden latches jolted him like a whip. Rent, writhing, he fought to rid himself of the cords sinking into his flesh. His right arm, the strongest, strained until the pain became unbearable and he had to give up. He watched the double door open, and the smell of the torches reached him before the light did. Barely girdled by the ceremonial loincloths, the priests' acolytes[10] moved in his direction, looking at him with contempt. Lights reflected off the sweaty torsos and off the black hair dressed
240 with feathers. The cords went slack, and in their place the grappling of hot hands, hard as bronze; he felt himself lifted, still face up, and jerked along by the four acolytes who carried him down the passageway. The torchbearers went ahead, indistinctly lighting up the corridor with its dripping walls and a ceiling so low that the acolytes had to duck their heads. Now they were taking him out, taking him out, it was the end. Face up, under a mile of living rock which, for a succession of moments, was lit up by a glimmer of torchlight. When the stars came out up there instead of the roof and the great terraced steps rose before him, on fire with cries and
250 dances, it would be the end. The passage was never going to end, but now it was beginning to end, he would see suddenly the open sky full of stars, but not yet, they trundled him along endlessly in the reddish shadow, hauling him roughly along and he did not want that, but how to stop it if they had torn off the amulet, his real heart, the life-center.

---

[9] **Teocalli** (tē´ə-käl´ē): an ancient Mexican terraced pyramid and temple.
[10] **acolytes:** people who assist in religious services.

CLOSE READ

Analyze Author's Choices: Tension (LINES 213–246)

COMMON CORE RL 5

Point out to students that the **pace** is the rate or speed at which a story progresses. Various techniques can be used to vary pace. For example, an author might use shorter sentences, brief descriptions, and more action to create a fast pace. Conversely, the author could use longer sentences, longer descriptions, and less action to create a slower pace. Explain that as a story advances to its climax, or point of ultimate dramatic tension, the pace often quickens, with shorter amounts of time between events.

L ASK STUDENTS to work in pairs and use textual evidence to summarize events and analyze the strategies the author uses to speed up the pace. *(The man discovered that he was being held in the underground cells of Teocalli, and that his amulet had been stripped from him. He yelled and tried to free himself from the cords and wooden latches, but could not do so and gave up. The acolytes came, lifted him, and carried him down the passageway that led outside. The pace of the story is increasing because these events all happen on the same page. Shorter and sometimes incomplete sentences are also used in the section, which allows the section to be read faster, reflecting the increased pace of the plot.)*

SCAFFOLDING FOR ELL STUDENTS

Analyze Author's Choices: Tension Help students recognize and appreciate the author's use of pace to create tension. Read aloud each of the following passages and have students retell it in their own words.

- Lines 213–216 *(man finds himself in cold dark place unable to move)*
- Lines 223–228 *(man screams and thinks of friends being sacrificed)*
- Lines 232–237 *(doors open and people approach the struggling man)*
- Lines 240–246 *(man is carried down a passageway)*

ASK STUDENTS if they think the pace is fast or slow in these passages.

Analyze Author's Choices: Parallel Plots

COMMON CORE **RL 1, RL 5**

(LINES 256–258, 262–278)

Remind students of the connectors or bridges that authors use between plot lines so that the narration flows smoothly.

Ⓜ CITE TEXT EVIDENCE Ask students to reread lines 256–258 and identify the phrase that serves as the bridge. (*"In a single jump" [line 256]*) Then ask students how this phrase could be interpreted in two different ways. (*"A single jump" could refer to the transition between the two plots. The phrase could also be interpreted as the man attempting to escape from the danger of being sacrificed by the Aztecs to the safety of being in the hospital.*)

Have students work in pairs to reread the text, beginning with the sentence at the end of line 262 and finishing with the sentence that ends at the beginning of line 278.

Point out that these lines mention that the man was sure the night nurse would answer if he rang and that it would soon be daybreak. The text also indicates the man is face up as he is being carried out into the night ("a waning moon fell on a face whose eyes wanted not to see it") and that the man wanted to somehow find the "bare, protecting ceiling of the ward."

Ⓝ ASK STUDENTS how this passage shows the relationship between the two plots and the title of the story. (*It is night in the hospital because the night nurse is on duty, and it will soon be daybreak. The man is being carried out into the night face up because he can see the moon. The man wants to find the ceiling of the hospital ward again. To see the ceiling, he would be lying face up. The man is in "the night face up" in both plots.*)

CRITICAL VOCABULARY

translucent: The bottle of water on the night table makes a semi-transparent and indistinct figure. **ASK STUDENTS** how the figure of the bottle of water contrasts with the shadow of the windows. (*The shadow is dark; the bottle of water allows some light to show through it.*)

Aztec sacrificial knife

In a single jump he came out into the hospital night, to the high, gentle, bare ceiling, to the soft shadow wrapping him round. He thought he must have cried out, but his neighbors were peacefully snoring. The water in the bottle on the night table was
260 somewhat bubbly, a **translucent** shape against the dark azure shadow of the windows. He panted, looking for some relief for his lungs, oblivion for those images still glued to his eyelids. Each time he shut his eyes he saw them take shape instantly, and he sat up, completely wrung out, but savoring at the same time the surety that now he was awake, that the night nurse would answer if he rang, that soon it would be daybreak, with the good, deep sleep he usually had at that hour, no images, no nothing . . . It was difficult to keep his eyes open, the drowsiness was more powerful than he. He made one last effort, he sketched a gesture toward the bottle of water with
270 his good hand and did not manage to reach it, his fingers closed again on a black emptiness, and the passageway went on endlessly, rock after rock, with momentary ruddy flares, and face up he choked out a dull moan because the roof was about to end, it rose, was opening like a mouth of shadow, and the acolytes straightened up, and from on high a waning moon fell on a face whose eyes wanted not to see it, were closing and opening desperately, trying to pass to the other side, to find again the bare, protecting ceiling of the ward. And every time they opened, it was night and the moon, while they climbed the great terraced steps, his head hanging down
280 backward now, and up at the top were the bonfires, red columns of perfumed smoke, and suddenly he saw the red stone, shiny with

translucent
(trăns-loo′sənt) *adj.*
semi-transparent;
indistinct.

WHEN STUDENTS STRUGGLE . . .

To support students' understanding of descriptive language, discuss Cortázar's use of phrases such as *ruddy flares*. Demonstrate how to use a dictionary to locate the meaning of the word *ruddy*. Inform students that *ruddy* refers to the color red. Ask student to explain why the flares could be described as ruddy. (*The flares were lit with fire, which may contain some red, especially when seen at night.*)

Have students use dictionaries and work in pairs to locate the meanings of the descriptive words in phrases such as *waning moon, terraced steps,* and *perfumed smoke.* Then have each pair use the definitions and context clues to explain why each phrase is appropriate in the story. Accept all reasonable responses.

Image Credits: ©Bildarchiv Steffens/AKG Images

the blood dripping off it, and the spinning arcs cut by the feet of the victim whom they pulled off to throw him rolling down the north steps. With a last hope he shut his lids tightly, moaning to wake up. For a second he thought he had gotten there, because once more he was immobile in the bed, except that his head was hanging down off it, swinging. But he smelled death, and when he opened his eyes he saw the blood-soaked figure of the executioner-priest coming toward him with the stone knife in his hand. He managed
290 to close his eyelids again, although he knew now he was not going to wake up, that he was awake, that the marvelous dream had been the other, absurd as all dreams are—a dream in which he was going through the strange avenues of an astonishing city, with green and red lights that burned without fire or smoke, on an enormous metal insect that whirred away between his legs. In the infinite lie of the dream, they had also picked him off the ground, someone had approached him also with a knife in his hand, approached him who was lying face up, face up with his eyes closed between the bonfires on the steps.

COLLABORATIVE DISCUSSION With a partner, discuss the ending of the story. Is it clear which of the two plots was "real"? Why or why not?

APPLYING ACADEMIC VOCABULARY

orient	differentiate

As you discuss Cortázar's short story, incorporate the Collection 4 academic vocabulary words *orient* and *differentiate*. Having separate plots requires readers to **orient** themselves several times throughout the story. Time and place are two elements that can be used to **differentiate** each plot.

CLOSE READ

Analyze Author's Choices: Parallel Plots and Tension

COMMON CORE **RL 1, RL 5**

(LINES 289–299)

Tell students the two plots converge in the story's final scene. But what is that final scene: dream or reality? Explain that the narrator offers clues to the answer but some of the clues may be unreliable.

O CITE TEXT EVIDENCE Have students go back to page 178 and reread lines 262–267. Ask: Which plot is this? *(hospital plot)* What evidence shows that this plot is the reality? *(The man savors the "surety that now he was awake.")* Point out, however, that this is what is going through the man's mind at the time. It may or may not be reality. Next, refer students back to the beginning of the story. Point out that the man uses the correct vocabulary for modern objects, such as "motorcycle," "jewelry store," and "downtown." However, at the end of the story, the man doesn't know this vocabulary ("an enormous metal insect that whirred away between his legs"). Ask: What does this suggest about which plot is the dream and which is reality? *(The writer chooses to let the audience decide which plot represents reality and which represents a dream.)*

Have students turn back to page 173 and reread the sentence on lines 72–73. Then have them compare that sentence to the last sentence of the story.

P ASK STUDENTS what might the author mean by the "lie of the dream" in the last sentence. *(What the man thought was the dream could be the reality or vice versa.)* How does the author maintain tension even in the final scene of the story. *(Readers are left uncertain as to which story is the dream and which one is reality.)*

COLLABORATIVE DISCUSSION Have students pair up to discuss their thoughts about how the story ends, as well as which plot was the dream and which was reality. Then have them share their views with the class as a whole. Accept all reasonable responses.

ASK STUDENTS to share any questions they generated in the course of reading and discussing the selection.

CLOSE READ

Cite Textual Evidence **RL 1**

Summarize that details from the text can be used as evidence to support an analysis of the text. Tell students they can identify textual evidence in a story by looking for words, phrases, and sentences that:

- tell what events happen in the story
- show when these events occur
- identify who is present or which character is performing an action during each event
- describe the people, places, actions, and events in the story

In lines 32–33, ask students what textual evidence indicates that the man did nothing to deserve his fate? *(He was assured that the traffic lights had been green and he didn't break any laws.)*

Analyze Author's Choices: **RL 5**
Parallel Plots and Tension

Have students provide examples of tone, pace, and foreshadowing from the story:

- How does the **tone** of the story change? *(The tone switches between calm and soothing and anxious and fearful.)*
- How does the **pace** change? *(The pace becomes faster, almost frantic, as the story progresses.)*
- What is one of the most effective uses of **foreshadowing** in the story? *(The man says he never dreamt smells, line 73.)*

Cite Textual Evidence **RL 1**

Readers must be able to cite **textual evidence**, or details from the text, to support an analysis of what the text says explicitly as well as their inferences about the text. To analyze what the text says explicitly, readers look at words and phrases and think about the author's meaning. To understand what is happening in "The Night Face Up," a reader must develop a clear picture of both worlds in which the main character finds himself—and be able to differentiate the two—based on the details Cortázar provides. When a story's setting or events are unfamiliar to you, take the time to note key details, and go back and re-read for evidence to make sure you understand what the author is communicating.

Analyze Author's Choices: **RL 5**
Parallel Plots and Tension

To communicate their ideas and to make a story exciting, writers make specific stylistic and structural choices. In "The Night Face Up," Cortázar uses **parallel plots** that develop alongside each other to create **tension,** a sense of anxious anticipation. The story moves back and forth between the plots. You can analyze the author's choices in this short story by examining both of these elements.

Parallel Plots	Tension
When two plots share equal time and importance in a story, they are called parallel plots. Parallel plots often counter each other in **tone** and in **pace**. For example, in "The Night Face Up," the author creates one plot that involves a man recuperating from an accident and another involving a manhunt by Aztec warriors. The two plots unwind at different paces, jumping from one plot to another, increasing the tension the reader feels. Each plot has its own tone, developed through specific word choices. To make parallel plots work effectively, the author includes a bridge or connector that orients each plot so that the narration flows smoothly from one plot line to the other. The two plots eventually converge in a final scene.	Tension or suspense in a story makes a reader want to keep reading to find out what will happen next. Cortázar creates tension through pacing, with progressively shorter amounts of time in the calm hospital setting as the story advances to its climax. The author adds to the tension with **foreshadowing**, or hints and clues as to what will happen later in the story. The first use of foreshadowing comes when the reader learns that the protagonist never dreams smells. The reader must determine what this fact foreshadows. The author then builds on this tension, using carefully chosen words and phrases to develop scenes as the narration switches back and forth between the parallel plots.

Strategies for Annotation  *Annotate it!*

Analyze Author's Choices: **RL 5**
Parallel Plots and Tension

Share these strategies for guided or independent analysis:

- Highlight in yellow words, phrases, and sentences that indicate tone.
- Highlight in green words, phrases, and sentences that indicate foreshadowing.

What tormented him the most was the odor, as though, notwithstanding the absolute acceptance of the dream, there was something which resisted that which was not habitual, which until that point had not participated in the game. "It smells of war," he thought, his hand going instinctively to the stone knife which was

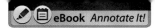

Analyzing the Text

COMMON CORE RL 1, RL 3, RL 4, RL 5, RL 6, W 1, L 4

Cite Text Evidence   Support your responses with evidence from the selection.

1. **Analyze** Cortázar begins the narrative with the plot concerning the motorcycle accident rather than the one about the manhunt. Why is this choice an effective way to structure the story?

2. **Interpret** In lines 201–202, the author writes, "Anyway, he had felt an immense relief in coming out of the black pit while the people were lifting him off the ground." What does the black pit represent? How is the main character's relief ultimately ironic, or different from what was expected?

3. **Compare** In both plots, the author refers frequently to smells. Explain how the descriptions of smells differ in each plot. How do these differences affect the tone of each plot?

4. **Connect** The author, Julio Cortázar, is from Argentina. What details from the story might reflect his perspective as a South American writer?

5. **Analyze** The **protagonist**, or main character, is never named, but his reality and his ongoing dream make up the parallel plots of the story. How does the reader's perception of the protagonist change throughout the story? Cite text evidence to support your ideas.

6. **Identify Patterns** The author structures the story so that the parallel plots mirror each other. For example, the author describes a scene in which the protagonist is x-rayed, taken to surgery, and approached by a doctor. Where in the second plot does the author echo this scene? What is the effect of this mode of narration?

7. **Evaluate** The author mentions time frequently, beginning in the first paragraph. Look back at the story. How does the protagonist's perception of time change throughout the story? What effect does the author's treatment of time have on the story?

PERFORMANCE TASK

Writing Activity: Analysis A central message or idea that an author wants to communicate through a story is its **theme**. The theme is usually something universal about human nature or the human experience. Usually, the theme of a story is not explicitly stated; it is the reader's job to infer the theme through an analysis of characters, plot, setting, tone, and imagery. Think about "The Night Face Up." Write a one-page analysis of the story in which you consider the following points:

- the theme of the story
- how the characters, plot, imagery, tone, and setting help convey the theme

Support your discussion of the story's theme with evidence from the text, and write using the conventions of standard English.

Assign this performance task.

PERFORMANCE TASK

COMMON CORE RL 1, RL 3, RL 4, RL 5, RL 6, W 1, L 4

Writing Activity: Analysis Work with students to brainstorm four or five broad statements about the human experience that might apply to this story, such as "Life can be mysterious and unpredictable" or "Dreams can take us to amazing, but sometimes frightening places" or "What is and isn't real?" Then have students form groups for each statement and discuss relevant elements from the story that could become part of their analyses. Encourage students to take notes during their discussions. Discuss the groups' findings as a class.

PRACTICE & APPLY

Analyzing the Text

COMMON CORE RL 1, RL 3, RL 4, RL 5, RL 6, L 4

Possible answers:

1. *Beginning the narrative with the plot about the motorcycle accident provides a modern world setting, which leads the reader to think that this plot is the reality and not the dream. This heightens the surprise a reader may feel at the end of the story.*

2. *The black pit (line 202) represents the underground cell of Teocalli. The main character's relief is different from what was expected because the man was lifted and carried to receive help in the accident plot. In the reality of the manhunt plot, however, the man was lifted and carried off to become a human sacrifice.*

3. *In the manhunt plot, the smells refer to odor, war, and oozing rock (line 212), which are unpleasant. In the motorcycle accident plot, the smells are pleasing, such as the leeks in the broth (line 129). The difference in smells affects the tone of each plot by making the accident plot seem comforting and safe and the manhunt seem foreboding and dangerous.*

4. *Details include the mention of government ministries (line 12) instead of offices or departments, the topic of the war of the blossom and how the manhunt involved the Aztecs and Motecans, and the specific mention of Teocalli, identifying the temple as terraced (line 249).*

5. *At the beginning of the story, the protagonist is in control as he rides his motorcycle. He becomes injured and no longer has as much control as he did, but the reader still perceives him to be safe. As the story moves forward, the protagonist is revealed to be hunted and less safe. By the end of the story, the reader perceives the protagonist has no control and is about to lose his life.*

6. *Cortázar echoes this scene in the second plot when the priest approaches the man with a knife in his hand (line 289), just before the reader assumes the priest kills the man. The effect of this mode of narration ties the two plots together so they relate to each other in some way, even though the plots may not seem similar.*

7. *The protagonist's perception of time moves from very specific to more general as the story progresses. The intervals between events or experiences also become briefer for the protagonist. The author's treatment of time varies the pace of the story, builds suspense, and adds to the unexpected nature of its ending.*

PRACTICE & APPLY

Critical Vocabulary

Possible answers:

1. *I visited my grandmother's grave. I consider that place consecrated, or sacred.*

2. *I always seek solace from my dog when I feel sad or bad about something. My dog gives me comfort.*

3. *I usually can tell someone is not completely lucid if the person yells and says things that don't make sense. Those are signs the person isn't thinking clearly.*

4. *I behaved in a beneficent manner when I agreed to mow my neighbor's lawn without pay.*

5. *Translucent glass might be used in the windows of a bathroom, allowing light in but not allowing someone outside to see distinct figures inside.*

Language and Style: Adverbial Clauses

Students' analyses will vary. Check that students have shown variety in choice of subordinating conjunctions and that the adverbial clauses are used correctly.

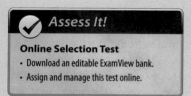

✓ Assess It!

Online Selection Test
- Download an editable ExamView bank.
- Assign and manage this test online.

Critical Vocabulary

solace   lucid   beneficent   consecrate   translucent

Practice and Apply Answer each question in a complete sentence that demonstrates your understanding of the meaning of each Critical Vocabulary word.

1. What **consecrated** place have you visited? Explain.

2. When have you ever sought **solace**? Why?

3. How can you tell someone is not completely **lucid**? Explain.

4. When did you behave in a **beneficent** manner? Explain.

5. Where might a **translucent** material be used in your home? Why?

Language and Style: Adverbial Clauses

Adverbial clauses modify verbs, adjectives, or adverbs. They help convey meaning by answering the questions *when, where, why, how,* or *to what degree.* They typically appear at the beginning or end of a sentence.

This sentence from "The Night Face Up" contains an adverbial clause:

> **As if the sky were aflame on the horizon,** he saw torches moving among the branches, very near him.

The adverbial clause begins with a **subordinating conjunction,** *as if,* and includes a subject and a verb. The clause gives more information about the main verb *saw.* Cortázar incorporates adverbial clauses to add interest and variety to his writing.

This chart shows some common subordinating conjunctions and the questions they answer about the main verb of the sentence.

Subordinating Conjunctions	Question They Answer
after, since, when, before, once, while	When?
where, wherever	Where?
because, since, so	Why?
as though, as if	How?
than	To what degree?

Practice and Apply Look back at the theme analysis you wrote for this selection's Performance Task. Revise your analysis to add at least two adverbial clauses. Try to use two different subordinating conjunctions in order to add variety to your writing.

Strategies for Annotation   ✏ 🗐 *Annotate it!*

Language and Style: Adverbial Clauses

Encourage students to use their eBook annotation tools to analyze the text. Have them do the following:

- Underline each adverbial clause.
- Highlight each subordinating conjunction in pink.
- Highlight the verb, adjective, or adverb the clause modifies in blue.
- On a note, write the question that is answered by each adverbial clause.

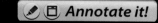

edging up into his throat. While they carried him face up to a nearby pharmacy, he learned that the cause of the accident had gotten only a few scrapes on the legs, "Nah, you barely got her at all, but when ya hit, the impact made the machine jump and flop

when

Analyze Point of View: Cultural Background

COMMON CORE

RL 6

TEACH

Refer students to the background of Cortázar at the beginning of the selection. Share or remind students of the additional background information provided in the teacher's notes.

Explain that "The Night Face Up" is an example of world literature. It was written by an author from another country and is about a topic involving experiences from another culture. By exploring the cultural background, experiences, and views of the author and by learning about the topic, the reader can more easily understand the author's point of view, or how he or she approaches the topic of the writing.

Elicit several questions from students regarding Cortázar's background as it relates to this story. Invite other questions about Aztec culture, especially as it relates to religious life and the war of the blossom. List students' questions on the board or on a device.

Have students work in pairs to research and answer the questions. Some pairs can focus on Cortázar while others focus on the Aztecs. Encourage students to take notes on information that will help explain the author's point of view on the story's topic.

 INTERACTIVE LESSON Have students complete the tutorials in this lesson: **Conducting Research.**

COLLABORATIVE DISCUSSION

Invite student pairs to report their findings to the class. Discuss not only the answers to students' previous questions but also other information that contributes to an understanding of Cortázar and of Aztec traditions.

Cite Textual Evidence

COMMON CORE

RL 1

RETEACH

Review the definition of *textual evidence* as details from the text that support analysis of the text. Discuss the meaning of the word *evidence*. Compare the concept to evidence that is gathered in a criminal case *(fingerprints, footprints, weapon, photographs, DNA, etc.)*. Apply evidence in a criminal case to textual evidence. Be sure students understand the following:

- Textual evidence can often answer one-word questions, such as *Who? What? When? Where?* and *How?*
- Textural evidence might be explicit, or clearly stated. For example, in the plot about the motorcycle accident, the detailed description of the accident is explicit evidence of the accident—what happened, when it happened, where it happened, how it happened, and who was involved. Textual evidence might also be used to make inferences, or logical assumptions. For example, the night of the manhunt is described as "starless" (line 90). This textual evidence can be used to infer that the night was cloudy.

 LEVEL UP TUTORIALS Assign the following *Level Up* tutorial: **Reading for Details**

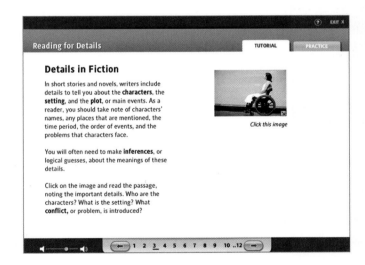

CLOSE READING APPLICATION

Students can apply the skill to another short story. Have them work independently to answer the questions *Who? What? When? Where?* and *How?* Then ask students to identify the answers that are explicitly stated in the text and those that are inferences. Have students cite textual evidence for the inferences.

Math Essay by Keith Devlin

Why This Text?

Students may feel that the subjects of math and science are foreign to their daily lives. This text suggests a new way of looking at such subjects—as instincts. This lesson explores how the author develops this idea.

▶ View It!
Professional Development Podcast:
Informational Text

For practice and application:

Whale Sharks Use Geometry to Avoid Sinking
Article from *Science Daily*

Close Reader selection
"Whale Sharks Use Geometry to Avoid Sinking"
news article from ScienceDaily

Key Learning Objective: The student will be able to determine meaning and analyze ideas.

COMMON CORE Common Core Standards

RI 1 Cite textual evidence.

RI 2 Determine central idea and analyze its development.

RI 3 Analyze how the author unfolds ideas.

RI 4 Determine the meaning of words and phrases.

RI 5 Analyze how an author's ideas are developed by particular sentences or paragraphs.

W 2a Introduce a topic; organize ideas, concepts, and information to make important connections.

W 2c Link sections of the text and clarify the relationships among complex ideas.

W 7 Conduct short research projects to answer a question.

SL 1c Propel conversations with questions that relate current discussion to broader themes.

L 4a Use context as a clue to the meaning of a word.

L 4b Identify and use patterns of word changes that indicate different meanings.

L 4c Consult reference materials to find pronunciation or clarify meaning.

L 4d Verify the preliminary determination of the meaning of a word.

▲ Text Complexity Rubric

Quantitative Measures	**The Math Instinct** Lexile: 1210L
Qualitative Measures	**Levels of Meaning/Purpose** more than one purpose; implied but easy to infer
	Structure organization of main ideas and details complex, but clearly stated and generally sequential
	Language Conventionality and Clarity increased unfamiliar, academic, or domain-specific words
	Knowledge Demands somewhat complex science concepts
Reader/Task Considerations	Teacher determined Vary by individual reader and type of text

CLOSE READ

AS YOU READ Direct students to use the As You Read statement to focus their reading. Remind students to note any questions they have as they read.

Determine Central Idea
COMMON CORE RI 1, RI 2

(LINES 1–13)

Explain that writers develop an idea throughout a text.

A CITE TEXT EVIDENCE Ask students to identify what the author finds "remarkable" about Ahmed. *(Ahmed finds his food by going in "one direction, then another." However, he is able to return to his home not by "retracing his steps," but by setting "off in a straight line.")*

CRITICAL VOCABULARY

obliterate: Devlin explains that Ahmed cannot retrace his steps because they were erased completely.

ASK STUDENTS to identify what may have obliterated Ahmed's footprints in the sand. *(wind)*

Determine Meaning
COMMON CORE RI 1, RI 4, L 4a, L 4c, L 4d

(LINES 17–29)

Explain to students that the spellings and meanings of words can change over time and according to context. Writers may share these details in order for readers to better understand the meanings of words.

B CITE TEXT EVIDENCE Ask students to cite the original term for "dead reckoning," look up the meaning of the individual words in the original term, and then explain the concept in their own words. *(The original term was "deductive reckoning" [line 18]. "Deductive" means "based on reasoning or using available facts." "Reckoning" is the process of calculating. "Dead reckoning" is a method of calculating your position by moving in straight lines and keeping track of speed and time of travel in order to determine the exact distance traveled and position of the starting point [lines 21–29].)*

The Math Instinct

Math Essay by Keith Devlin

AS YOU READ Pay attention to the way the writer, an award-winning author of numerous popular mathematics books, explains the idea of a math instinct in ants and humans. Note any questions you generate during reading.

Where Am I and Where Am I Going?

A Ahmed, who was the subject of a research paper published in 1981 by scholars R. Wehner and M. V. Srinivasan, lives in the Tunisian desert, on the northern edge of the Sahara. He has had no formal education, and everything he knows he has picked up by experience. Each day, Ahmed leaves his desert home and travels large distances in search of food. In his hunt, he heads first in one direction, then another, then another. He keeps going until he is successful, whereupon he does something very remarkable. Instead of retracing his steps—which may have been **obliterated**
10 by the wind blowing across the sands—he faces directly toward his home and sets off in a straight line, not stopping until he gets there, seemingly knowing in advance, to within a few paces, how far he has to go.

Ahmed has been unable to tell researchers how he performs this remarkable feat of navigation, nor how he acquired this ability. But the only known method is to use a technique known as "dead reckoning." Developed by the ancient mariners of long ago, the method was called "deductive reckoning" by British sailors, who abbreviated the name to "ded. reckoning," a term that in due course
20 acquired an incorrect spelling as "dead reckoning." In using this method, the traveler always moves in straight lines, with occasional sharp turns, keeping constant track of the direction in which he is heading, and keeping track too of his speed and the time that has elapsed since the last change of direction, or since setting off. From **B**

obliterate
(ə-blĭt´ə-rāt´) *v.*
erase completely.

Image Credits: ©Jason Edwards/National Geographic/Getty Images

---

SCAFFOLDING FOR ELL STUDENTS

Determine Meaning Using a whiteboard, project lines 20–29. Read the passage aloud and highlight or underline the key details related to dead reckoning. Invite volunteers to take turns creating a map to help them understand the concept. Have students:

- Mark a starting point and a distant ending point.
- Draw a path away from the starting point using straight, solid lines that change direction randomly.
- After connecting to the ending point, draw a dotted line that indicates the path that Ahmed would follow using dead reckoning.

Remind students that in addition to distance and direction, a traveler must keep track of speed and time to return to the starting point.

TEACH

CLOSE READ

Determine Meaning and Analyze Ideas (LINES 42–51)

COMMON CORE RI 1, RI 4, RI 5

Remind students that writers develop their ideas with words, phrases, sentences, and paragraphs.

C CITE TEXT EVIDENCE Ask students what word the author uses to describe Ahmed. *(remarkable)* How does the author develop the idea that Ahmed is remarkable in this paragraph? *(The author reveals that Ahmed is a "Tunisian desert ant," with "none of the aids that mariners and lunar astronauts" have.)*

CRITICAL VOCABULARY

impetus: Sailors' use of dead reckoning was the motivating force for developing accurate clocks.

ASK STUDENTS to explain why the use of dead reckoning led to the development of accurate clocks. *(Dead reckoning requires precise measurement of time in order to calculate distance traveled and position relative to a starting point.)*

Analyze Ideas (LINES 52–67)

COMMON CORE RI 1, RI 3, RI 5

A writer may structure paragraphs to show how ideas relate. For example, an author may use **comparison** and **contrast** to show similarities and differences.

D CITE TEXT EVIDENCE Have students reread lines 52–57 and identify the subjects that the author compares and contrasts and the word that signals the comparison. *(The navigational strategies of other kinds of ants are compared and contrasted with Tunisian desert ants. The signal word is Not.)*

A writer may develop an idea with an **anecdote,** or a brief story that illustrates a point.

E ASK STUDENTS to explain how Devlin supports the idea that desert ants use dead reckoning. *(He uses an anecdote [lines 58–67] about an ant that finds food and is then moved to another location by researchers. The ant becomes confused only after it has traveled the distance it thought it should to return home.)*

---

knowledge of the speed and the time of travel, the traveler can calculate the exact distance covered in any straight segment of the journey. And by knowing the starting point and the exact direction of travel, it is possible to calculate the exact position at the end of each segment.

30 Dead reckoning requires the accurate use of arithmetic and trigonometry,[1] reliable ways to measure speed, time and direction, and good record-keeping. When seamen navigated by dead reckoning they used charts, tables, various measuring instruments, and a considerable amount of mathematics. (The main **impetus** to develop accurate clocks came from the needs of sailors who used dead reckoning to navigate vast tracts of featureless ocean.) Until the arrival of navigation by the Global Positioning System (GPS) in the mid 1970s, sailors and airline pilots used dead reckoning to navigate the globe, and in the 1960s and 1970s, NASA's Apollo 40 astronauts used dead reckoning to find their way to the moon and back.

Yet Ahmed has none of the aids that mariners and lunar astronauts made use of. How does he do it? Clearly, this particular Tunisian is a remarkable individual. Remarkable indeed. For Ahmed measures little more than half a centimeter in length. He is not a person but an ant—a Tunisian desert ant, to be precise. Every day, this tiny creature wanders across the desert sands for a distance of up to fifty meters (165 feet) until it stumbles across the remains of a dead insect, whereupon it bites off a piece and takes 50 it directly back to its nest, a hole no more than one millimeter in diameter. How does he navigate?

Many kinds of ant find their way to their destination by following scents and chemical trails laid down by themselves or by other members of the colony. Not so the Tunisian desert ant. Observations carried out by Wehner and Srinivasan, the researchers mentioned above, leave little room for doubt. The only way Ahmed can perform this daily feat is by using dead reckoning.

Wehner and Srinivasan found that, if they moved one of these desert ants immediately after it had found its food, it would head 60 off in exactly the direction it *should* have taken to find its nest if it had not been moved, and, moreover, when it had covered the precise distance that should have brought it back home, it would stop and start a bewildered search for its nest. In other words, it knew the precise direction in which it should head in order to return home, and exactly how far in that direction it should travel, even though that straight-line path was nothing like the apparently random zigzag it had followed in its search for food.

[1] **trigonometry:** mathematical discipline that deals with the angles and sides of triangles.

impetus
(ĭm′pĭ-təs) *n.* motivating force or incentive.

APPLYING ACADEMIC VOCABULARY

| orient | incorporate |

As you discuss the essay, incorporate the Collection 4 academic vocabulary words *orient* and *incorporate*. To help students understand dead reckoning, ask them to describe the data that is **incorporated** in the brains of Tunisian desert ants in order for them to **orient** themselves for desert travel away from and toward home.

"Just because something comes naturally or without conscious awareness does not mean it is trivial."

A recent study has shown that the desert ant measures distance by counting steps. It "knows" the length of an individual step, so it can calculate the distance traveled in any straight-line direction by multiplying that distance by the total number of steps.

Of course, no one is suggesting that this tiny creature is carrying out multiplications the way a human would, or that it finds its way by going through exactly the same mental processes that, say, Neil Armstrong did on his way to the moon in *Apollo 11*. Like all human navigators, the Apollo astronauts had to go to school to learn how to operate the relevant equipment and how to perform the necessary computations. The Tunisian desert ant simply does what comes naturally—it follows its instincts, which are the result of hundreds of thousands of years of evolution.

In terms of today's computer technology, evolution has provided Ahmed with a brain that amounts to a highly sophisticated, highly specific computer, honed over many generations to perform precisely the measurements and computations necessary to navigate by dead reckoning. Ahmed no more has to *think* about any of those measurements or computations than we have to think about the measurements and computations required to control our muscles in order to run or jump. In fact, in Ahmed's case, it is not at all clear that he is capable of anything we would normally call conscious mental activity.

But just because something comes naturally or without conscious awareness does not mean it is trivial. After all, almost fifty years of intensive research in computer science and

The Math Instinct **185**

TO CHALLENGE STUDENTS . . .

Tell students that instinctual behavior is inborn, unlearned, and often triggered by environmental stimuli, such as when Ahmed finds food and heads for home. Learned behavior is determined by experience. Ask student groups to explore and discuss the differences between instinctual behavior and learned behavior in both animals and humans. Have groups conduct quick Web searches to provide examples of each type of behavior in both humans and a few animals. Ask students to explain what purpose the specific instinctual behaviors and learned behaviors serve. Then challenge students to identify an instinct or a learned behavior that humans and animals share.

CLOSE READ

Analyze Ideas (LINES 73–91)   COMMON CORE RI 1, RI 3, RI 5

Point out that a writer may develop an idea over several paragraphs.

F CITE TEXT EVIDENCE Ask students to compare the way humans and Tunisian ants learn to carry out mathematical navigation. Have students cite text to support their responses. *(Humans go to school to learn how to operate relevant equipment and perform necessary computations. Tunisian ants follow their instincts, which are based on "hundreds of thousands of years of evolution" [lines 76–81].)* Have partners discuss how this contrast helps them understand the idea of a math instinct.

G ASK STUDENTS to reread lines 82–91. Ask them to identify the familiar modern-day object Devlin compares with Ahmed's brain. *(a computer)* Ask students what human ability Devlin compares with Ahmed's actions. *(the ability to run or jump without thinking about how to control the body systems involved)* Have partners discuss how these comparisons help them understand the idea of a math instinct.

Determine Meaning   COMMON CORE RI 1, RI 4, L 4a, L 4c, L 4d
(LINES 92–103)

Remind students that when they encounter an unfamiliar word, they can look for clues to its meaning in the surrounding text. Point out that context clues might include comparisons such as synonyms and contrasts such as antonyms.

H CITE TEXT EVIDENCE Ask students to point out text where Devlin gives clues to the meaning of *trivial* and to explain what kind of clue it is. *(In lines 91–92, Devlin uses contrast. He contrasts "trivial" with something that "comes naturally or without conscious awareness.")* Then ask students to define *trivial*, using a dictionary as needed. *(having little value or importance; insignificant)*

CLOSE READ

Analyze Ideas (LINES 104–112) 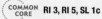 **RI 3, RI 5, SL 1c**

Tell students that writers often restate previous ideas in the conclusion. Remind students that earlier in the article Devlin states that instincts are not trivial or unimportant. In the conclusion he states why.

CITE TEXT EVIDENCE Ask students why the desert ant's navigational instinct is not trivial. *(The desert ant's ability to use dead reckoning "ensures the desert ant's survival.")*

> **CRITICAL VOCABULARY**
>
> **repertoire:** The author suggests that the Tunisian ant's brain may have a limited set of abilities.
>
> **ASK STUDENTS** to name the abilities that are probably not part of the Tunisian ant's set of skills. *(unable to learn anything new, unable to think about its own existence)*

COLLABORATIVE DISCUSSION Have students pair up and discuss their reactions to Devlin's revelation that Ahmed is an ant. Ask why Devlin delayed this information. Then have them discuss the author's focus on skills rather than species. Have them consider the following questions: What skill do both an ant and a human possess? How is the development of this skill different in the two species? How do the differences in development help you understand the importance of instinct? Have students take notes during their discussion. Invite volunteers to share their ideas with the class.

ASK STUDENTS to share any questions they generate during the course of reading and discussing the selection.

---

engineering has failed to produce a robot that can walk as well as a toddler can manage a few days after taking its first faltering steps. Instead, what all that research has shown is how complicated are the mathematics and the engineering required to achieve that feat. Few adults ever master that level of consciously performed mathematics—let alone a small child that runs with perfect bodily
100 control for the candy aisle in the supermarket. Rather, the ability to carry out the required computations for walking comes, as it were, hardwired in the human brain.

So too with the Tunisian desert ant. Its tiny brain might have a very limited **repertoire**. It may well be incapable of learning anything new, or of reflecting consciously on its own existence. But one thing it can do extremely well—indeed far better than the unaided human brain, as far as we know—is carry out the particular mathematical computation we call dead reckoning. That ability does not make the desert ant a "mathematician," of course,
110 but that one computation is enough to ensure the desert ant's survival.

repertoire
(rĕp´ər-twär´) *n.* a set of skills, abilities or functions.

COLLABORATIVE DISCUSSION Discuss your response to learning that Ahmed is an ant. How does focusing on skills, not species, help the author to make a point about navigation?

WHEN STUDENTS STRUGGLE...

Analyze Ideas Using a whiteboard, display and read aloud these sentence frames to help students connect Devlin's ideas.

- Humans need tools and _____ to navigate. *(math [lines 30–34])*
- A desert ant's brain allows it to _____ after finding food. *(return home [lines 47–51])*
- Desert ants use _____ to carry out dead reckoning. *(instinct [lines 73–81])*
- Desert ants are different from humans because ants cannot _____ and _____. *(learn; think [lines 104–106])*
- Desert ants use dead reckoning for _____. *(survival [lines 107–112])*

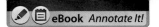
Determine Meaning and Analyze Ideas

 COMMON CORE **RI 4, RI 5**

In an informational essay, a writer may explain an unknown concept to the audience by beginning with more familiar ideas. The new information a reader must take in may range from words and phrases to sentences to entire paragraphs.

Words and phrases	Watch for **technical meanings**, words and phrases specific to a particular field of study. In this essay, Devlin uses mathematical terms and measurements, but he introduces them with familiar examples. In some cases, a word familiar to you may be used with an unfamiliar technical meaning.
Sentences	The mental processes required to navigate by dead reckoning are complicated; Devlin expresses *how* complicated by using a sentence that makes a comparison with the Apollo astronauts.
Paragraphs	Devlin defines dead reckoning for readers not only through the example of Ahmed's movements but also through an entire paragraph discussing how sailors once used this technique.

Analyzing the Text

COMMON CORE **RI 2, RI 3, RI 5, W 7**

Cite Text Evidence Support your responses with evidence from the selection.

1. **Evaluate** Why does Devlin structure his explanation as he does? Would the essay be more or less effective in explaining the concept of dead reckoning if you knew from the beginning that Ahmed is an ant? Explain.

2. **Analyze** How does Devlin's description of Ahmed's calculations help the reader differentiate between an instinctual act and an act of conscious mental activity as discussed in lines 85–90?

3. **Infer** What claim is Devlin supporting through his essay? Cite specific words and phrases in your explanation.

 **my WriteSmart**

PERFORMANCE TASK

Writing Activity: Research Conduct research on the use of dead reckoning, and summarize your findings in a one-page essay.

1. Research how dead reckoning was used to navigate before the invention of GPS. How were sailors able to orient a ship correctly?

2. Compare the usefulness and accuracy of dead reckoning with GPS.

3. End with a conclusion that explains the pros and cons of each way of navigating.

4. List your sources at the end of the essay.

The Math Instinct **187**

 Assign this performance task. **my WriteSmart**

PERFORMANCE TASK

COMMON CORE **W 7**

Writing Activity: Research Have students prepare three-column research charts by listing research questions in the first column, answers in the second, and sources in the third. Suggest the following research questions: How did ancient sailors use dead reckoning to navigate? What is GPS? How accurate were ancient sailor's calculations? GPS calculations? What are the benefits and drawbacks of each?

Determine Meaning and Analyze Ideas

COMMON CORE **RI 4, RI 5**

Have students work with partners to locate a text example of each of the following items: a technical vocabulary word introduced with a familiar example or a familiar word with an unfamiliar technical meaning; a sentence that compares or contrasts two items; and a paragraph that provides an example for one of the author's ideas. *(Answers will vary.)*

Analyzing the Text

COMMON CORE **RI 2, RI 3, RI 5**

Possible answers:

1. *Devlin structures his essay as he does to have readers focus on the skill rather than the species. The essay might be less effective if readers knew from the beginning that Ahmed is an ant because readers may be less impressed with Ahmed's abilities.*

2. *Devlin points out that Ahmed's ability to navigate is not a conscious mental process. His brain has evolved to be able to carry out the calculations necessary to navigate back home without thinking about them. His comparison to how humans "run or jump" without calculating how to move muscles helps the reader distinguish instinctual behavior from conscious mental activity.*

3. *Devlin supports the claim that some mathematical concepts are instinctual. He supports his claim with examples of a desert ant that navigates using dead reckoning. Devlin explains how Ahmed, the desert ant, doesn't retrace his steps after finding food. Instead, he heads in a straight line, directly to its home. Ahmed "has none of the aids that mariners and lunar astronauts made use of." Devlin also refers to research by Wehner and Srinivasan that showed when an ant was moved after finding food, it would still "head off in exactly the direction it should." In addition, another study found that desert ants counts their steps and calculate distance traveled "in any straight-line direction" using multiplication.*

PRACTICE & APPLY

Critical Vocabulary

COMMON CORE L 4b

Possible answers:

1. *b. The wrong answer is completely destroyed.*

2. *a. The push is a force that propels the go-cart.*

3. *b. All the songs are the total songs the piano player can play, including favorites.*

Vocabulary Strategy: Prefixes

Possible answers:

*in- (not)—**inaccurate:** Accurate means "free of mistakes" and in- means "not"; inaccurate means "not free of mistakes" or "having mistakes." Inaccurate tax forms will be returned.*

***invisible:** Visible means "able to be seen" and in- means "not"; invisible means "not able to be seen." The street sign was invisible in the fog.*

*im- (not)—**impossible:** Possible means "capable of being done" and im- means "not"; impossible means "not capable of being done." Getting 100% on the Algebra test seemed impossible.*

***impassable:** Passable means "capable of being crossed" and im- means "not"; impassable means "not capable of being crossed." The bridge was impassable after the mudslide.*

*il- (not)—**illegible:** Legible means "able to be read" and il- means "not"; illegible means "not able to be read." The scrawled signature was illegible.*

***illiterate:** Literate means "able to read and write" and il- means "not"; illiterate means "not able to read and write." Because my grandfather did not attend school, he is illiterate.*

*ir- (not)—**irrevocable:** Revocable means "can be taken back" and ir- means "not"; irrevocable means "not capable of being taken back." The lifetime membership was irrevocable.*

***irresponsible:** Responsible means "having a sense of responsibility" and ir- means "not"; irresponsible means "not having a sense of responsibility." The irresponsible student left her backpack out in the rain.*

Critical Vocabulary

COMMON CORE L 4b

obliterate   impetus   repertoire

Practice and Apply For each Critical Vocabulary word, choose which of the two situations best fits the word's meaning, and explain why your choice is the best response.

1. **obliterate**
   a. erasing an incorrect answer on a test paper
   b. scribbling out a wrong answer and shredding the paper

2. **impetus**
   a. the push sending a go-cart downhill
   b. the preparations made for a race

3. **repertoire**
   a. a piano player's favorite songs
   b. all the songs a piano player knows

Vocabulary Strategy: Prefixes

The Critical Vocabulary word *impetus* contains the Latin prefix *im–*, which is a variation of the prefix *in–*. This prefix means "in, into, or within." It can also mean "not." Before the consonant *l*, *in–* is usually spelled *il–* and before *r* it is spelled *ir–*. With the consonants *b*, *m*, and *p*, the spelling changes to *im–* as in *impetus*. This prefix is used in many English words. To understand the meaning of words with the prefix *in–*, use your knowledge of the base word as well as your knowledge of the prefix.

in–	im–	il–	ir–
instinct	impervious	illegal	irrational
individual	implausible	illogical	irrefutable

Practice and Apply Use a dictionary or other resource to identify two additional words that use each version of the prefix shown in the chart—that is, two new words beginning with *in–*, two beginning with *im–*, and so on. For each word you identify, use the steps below.

1. Define the prefix and the base word separately.

2. Explain how the meanings of the prefix and base word combine to create the word's overall meaning.

3. Use the word in a sentence that accurately reflects its meaning.

Strategies for Annotation 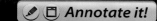 **Annotate it!**

Prefixes

COMMON CORE L 4b

Have students locate words in the essay that contain the prefixes *in-, im-, il-,* or *ir-*. Encourage them to use their eBook annotation tools to do the following:

- Highlight the prefix in yellow.
- Highlight the base word in blue.
- Write a note to define each prefix, base word, and combined word.

reckoning. Developed by the ancient mariners of long ago, the method was called "deductive reckoning" by British sailors, who abbreviated the name to "ded. reckoning," a term that in due course acquired an incorrect spelling as "dead reckoning." In using

incorrect:
"in" means "not";
"correct" means "right";
"incorrect" means "not right"

Organize Ideas in Writing

COMMON CORE

W 2a, W 2c

TEACH

This selection's Performance Tasks asks students to conduct research in order to compare the navigational methods of dead reckoning and GPS. To help students organize their research findings in a comparison-contrast structure, provide the following steps:

1. First, identify points of comparison—usefulness and accuracy.

2. Then explain each point by answering these questions: How useful is dead reckoning? How accurate is dead reckoning? How useful is GPS? How accurate is GPS?

3. Note the similarities and differences between the explanations.

4. Decide how you will organize the comparison portion of your essay. You may organize by subject, addressing first one subject and then the next, or you may organize by points of comparison, addressing both subjects while explaining a particular point.

5. Use comparison-and-contrast transition words and phrases to show the relationships among ideas.

| Comparison | *also, in the same way, likewise, similarly* |
| Contrast | *but, however, in contrast, yet* |

PRACTICE AND APPLY

Once students have completed their research, have them utilize the steps above to organize their research findings. When students reach Step 4, guide them in creating an outline that organizes their ideas either subject-by-subject or point-by-point.

Determine Meaning and Analyze Ideas

COMMON CORE

RI 2, RI 4, RI 5, L 4a, L 4c

RETEACH

Remind students that authors use different techniques, such as word choice, examples, and structure, to develop their ideas. Authors of technical texts must explain unknown terms and ideas to help readers understand the information.

- Tell students to look for context clues around technical terms to help determine their meanings. They can also consult a print dictionary or an online specialty dictionary.

- Have students identify the selection's central idea and the details the author uses to support that central idea. Remind students that the details can be words and phrases, sentences, or entire paragraphs.

 INTERACTIVE GRAPHIC ORGANIZERS Have students use the interactive graphic organizer Main Idea and Details Chart to help them identify the main idea and supporting details of Devlin's essay.

 LEVEL UP TUTORIALS Assign the following *Level Up* tutorial: **Main Idea and Supporting Details**

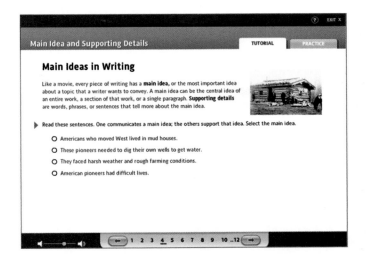

CLOSE READING APPLICATION

Students can apply the skills to another scientific article . Have them work independently to locate and define technical words and phrases. Then have them work with a partner to analyze how the author develops his or her central idea throughout the article. Have partners complete the Main Idea and Details Chart.

Whale Sharks Use Geometry to Avoid Sinking

Science Writing from *ScienceDaily*

Why This Text

Students may have difficulty with technical words and phrases when they read science articles. Many science articles, such as this one about whale sharks, discuss complex ideas that call upon the reader's ability to reason abstractly. With the help of the close-reading questions, students will determine the meaning of technical words and phrases in the article. This close reading will lead students to understand how the author develops key ideas in different parts of the article.

Background Have students read the background and information about whale sharks. Introduce the article by explaining that all animals, including humans, must pay attention to their expenditure of energy. If an animal uses more energy than it consumes (as food), it will be forced to burn stored energy, normally fat. If the animal does not correct its "energy equation," it will eventually die. Whale sharks, like other fish, move in three dimensions, adding complexity to their energy calculations.

AS YOU READ Ask students to pay attention to the main ideas in the article. What technical words must they understand in order to analyze the article's central idea?

 Common Core Support

- cite strong and thorough textual evidence
- determine a central idea of a text
- determine the meaning of words and phrases
- analyze how ideas are developed in sections of a text

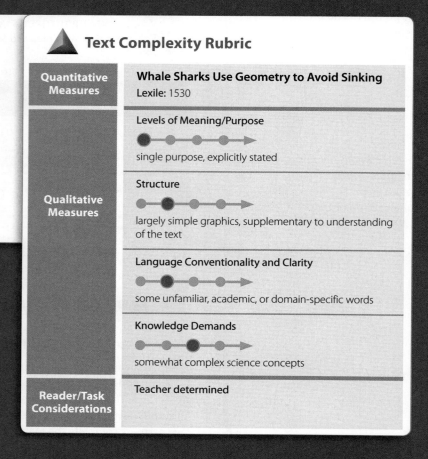

Text Complexity Rubric

Quantitative Measures	**Whale Sharks Use Geometry to Avoid Sinking** Lexile: 1530
Qualitative Measures	**Levels of Meaning/Purpose** — single purpose, explicitly stated
	Structure — largely simple graphics, supplementary to understanding of the text
	Language Conventionality and Clarity — some unfamiliar, academic, or domain-specific words
	Knowledge Demands — somewhat complex science concepts
Reader/Task Considerations	Teacher determined

Strategies for CLOSE READING

Determine Meanings and Analyze Ideas

Students should read this article carefully all the way through. Close-reading questions at the bottom of the page will help them focus on a thorough analysis of the article's ideas. As they read, students should jot down comments or questions about the text in the margins.

WHEN STUDENTS STRUGGLE . . .

To help students analyze ideas in "Whale Sharks Use Geometry to Avoid Sinking," have them work in small groups to fill out a chart like the one shown below.

CITE TEXT EVIDENCE For practice in determining meanings, ask students to cite text evidence for the definition of each term in the chart.

whale shark	"the largest fish species in the ocean" (line 1)
negative buoyancy	"the property of an animal . . . that causes it to sink, rather than float, in water" (footnote, page 67)
energy expenditure	"travel speed, which governs how much energy an animal uses" (lines 13–14)
	"to quantify the energetic cost of vertical movement" (line 25)
accelerometer	"a device that measures acceleration forces, allowing a scientist to determine the vertical angle at which it is moving" (footnote, page 68)

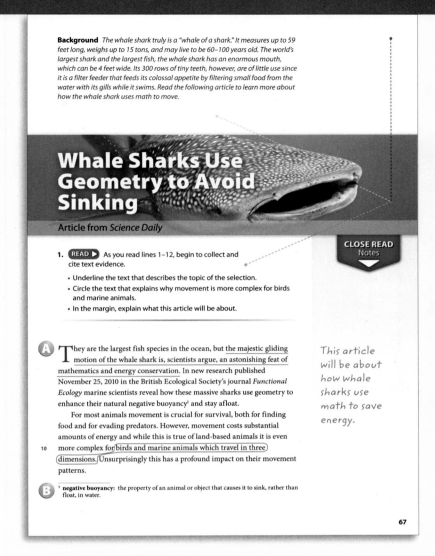

Background *The whale shark truly is a "whale of a shark." It measures up to 59 feet long, weighs up to 15 tons, and may live to be 60–100 years old. The world's largest shark and the largest fish, the whale shark has an enormous mouth, which can be 4 feet wide. Its 300 rows of tiny teeth, however, are of little use since it is a filter feeder that feeds its colossal appetite by filtering small food from the water with its gills while it swims. Read the following article to learn more about how the whale shark uses math to move.*

Whale Sharks Use Geometry to Avoid Sinking

Article from *Science Daily*

CLOSE READ
Notes

1. **READ ▶** As you read lines 1–12, begin to collect and cite text evidence.

- Underline the text that describes the topic of the selection.
- Circle the text that explains why movement is more complex for birds and marine animals.
- In the margin, explain what this article will be about.

A They are the largest fish species in the ocean, but the majestic gliding motion of the whale shark is, scientists argue, an astonishing feat of mathematics and energy conservation. In new research published November 25, 2010 in the British Ecological Society's journal *Functional Ecology* marine scientists reveal how these massive sharks use geometry to enhance their natural negative buoyancy[1] and stay afloat.

For most animals movement is crucial for survival, both for finding food and for evading predators. However, movement costs substantial amounts of energy and while this is true of land-based animals it is even
10　more complex for birds and marine animals which travel in three dimensions. Unsurprisingly this has a profound impact on their movement patterns.

B [1] **negative buoyancy:** the property of an animal or object that causes it to sink, rather than float, in water.

This article will be about how whale sharks use math to save energy.

67

---

1. **READ AND CITE TEXT EVIDENCE** Tell students that scientists publish their discoveries in specialized journals that recruit other scientists in the same field, "peers," to review the methods and findings of the discovery. Later, journalists may report on these discoveries for a wider, nonscientific audience.

A **ASK STUDENTS** to discuss how they determined which text to underline as the topic of the article. What clue(s) indicate that the text in lines 1–3 constitutes the topic? *The text is in the first sentence, where topics often appear. The text talks about sharks' "feat of mathematics," which echoes the title of the article. The author calls the sharks' feat of mathematics "astonishing," which makes the reader want to continue and find out more about this feat. The next sentence (lines 3–6) supports this text, explaining where the original research was published.*

Animals that live in the ocean also have to move vertically. This additional movement uses more energy.

C "The key factor for animal movement is travel speed, which governs how much energy an animal uses, the distance it will travel and how often resources are encountered," said lead author Adrian Gleiss from Swansea University. "However, oceanic animals not only have to consider their travel speed, but also how vertical movement will affect their energy expenditure, which changes the whole perspective."

20 For the past four years, Adrian Gleiss and Rory Wilson, from Swansea University, worked with Brad Norman from ECOcean Inc. to lead an international team to investigate the movements of whale sharks, Rhincodon typus, at Ningaloo Reef in Western Australia. They attached animal-borne motion sensors, accelerometers,[2] to the free-swimming whale sharks to measure their swimming activity and vertical movement, which
D allowed them to quantify the energetic cost of vertical movement.

[2] **accelerometer:** a device that measures acceleration forces, allowing a scientist to determine the vertical angle at which it is moving.

2. ◀ REREAD Reread lines 7–12. Why would having negative buoyancy require a whale shark to use more energy to move through the ocean?

The whale shark has to expend energy to counter its negative buoyancy, which would otherwise cause it to sink. Also, a shark moves in three directions at once.

3. READ ▶ Read lines 13–25 and continue to cite text evidence.
• Underline the key ideas in these lines.
• In the margin, explain the meaning of lines 13–18 in your own words.

E The team's data revealed that whale sharks are able to glide without investing energy into movement when descending, but they had to beat their tails when they ascended. This occurs because sharks, unlike many fish, have negative buoyancy.

30 Also, the steeper the sharks ascended, the harder they had to beat their tail and the more energy they had to invest. The whale sharks displayed two
F broad movement modes, one consisting of shallow ascent angles, which minimize the energetic cost of moving in the horizontal while a second characteristic of steeper ascent angles, optimized the energetic cost of vertical movement.

When moving down, whale sharks glide, without using energy. To go up, they beat their tails.

4. ◀ REREAD Reread lines 19–25. What does the "quantify the energetic cost of vertical movement" mean?

This means to find out the amounts of energy used to move up or down in the ocean.

5. READ ▶ As you read lines 26–40, continue to cite textual evidence.
• Underline the key points in each paragraph.
• In the margin of lines 26–29, explain the claim in your own words.

2. **REREAD AND CITE TEXT EVIDENCE**

B **ASK STUDENTS** to compare buoyancy with negative buoyancy. *Things like sticks, ducks, and otters have buoyancy, so they naturally float. Things like rocks, fishing lures, and whale sharks have negative buoyancy, so they naturally sink.* For animals with buoyancy, will diving or rising in water take energy? *They expend energy diving.* For animals with negative buoyancy, will diving or rising take energy? *They expend energy rising.*

3. **READ AND CITE TEXT EVIDENCE**

C **ASK STUDENTS** to explain the key ideas of lines 13–18. *Animals' travel speed determines how much energy they use. Oceanic animals also expend energy when they move vertically.*

FOR ELL STUDENTS Challenge students to identify the infinitive of the verb from which the second part of *animal-borne* comes. *to bear* Explain that *borne* is the past participle of *bear*, which means "to move while holding or supporting something."

4. **REREAD AND CITE TEXT EVIDENCE**

D **ASK STUDENTS** to take apart the phrase and then look for clues about the meaning of each term. What does the verb *quantify* mean? *Students should note that the accelerometers were used to measure two quantities—swimming activity and vertical movement.* What does the term *energetic cost* mean? *Students should reason that a cost is something that must be paid, so* energetic cost *must be the amount of energy "paid" by the sharks.* What does the term *vertical movement* mean? *Students should understand that* vertical movement *is "movement up or down".*

5. **READ AND CITE TEXT EVIDENCE**

E **ASK STUDENTS** to describe the three kinds of energy expenditure revealed by the accelerometer data. *Whale sharks don't expend energy when they descend. They expend energy when they ascend. They expend more energy when they ascend more steeply.*

"These results demonstrate how geometry plays a crucial role in movement strategies for animals moving in 3-dimensions," concluded Gleiss. "This use of negative buoyancy may play a large part in oceanic sharks being able to locate and travel between scarce and unpredictable food sources efficiently."

40

6. **◀ REREAD** Reread lines 30–40. In your own words, explain the two kinds of movements the whale sharks displayed.

When going up vertically, whale sharks either move with shallow angles or with steep angles.

SHORT RESPONSE

Cite Text Evidence   What claim does this article make about whale sharks? How is this claim supported? **Cite evidence from the text** in your explanation.

The article claims that whale sharks use geography in order to prevent sinking. The article goes on to explain that oceanic mammals move in three dimensions, so conserving energy is very important to them. They need to know how much energy they will use and also how much energy it will take for them to get to the next place. A study of whale sharks showed that these mammals used one of two broad movements: one which minimized the "energetic cost of moving in the horizontal" and another which "optimized the energetic cost of vertical movement."

70

6. REREAD AND CITE TEXT EVIDENCE

F **ASK STUDENTS** to describe the two kinds of movements from a whale shark's perspective. *Students should start by describing a shark that is swimming in a flat horizontal plane. To ascend in "a shallow" angle, the shark will move upward gently. To ascend at "a steeper" angle, the shark will move upward more sharply.*

SHORT RESPONSE

Cite Text Evidence   Students' responses should include text evidence that supports their positions. They should:

- state the article's claim about whale sharks.
- explain how a scientific team tested the claim.
- describe the results of the scientific study.

TO CHALLENGE STUDENTS . . .

For more context and deeper understanding, students can research whale sharks online.

ASK STUDENTS to summarize what they learned about whale sharks' diet and feeding strategy. *Students should point out that whale sharks are filter feeders. They open their large jaws and scoop up huge amounts of water, filtering out the phytoplankton and zooplankton, microscopic plants and animals. Whale sharks feed primarily near the ocean's surface, so their negative buoyancy—and its effect on their energy expenditure—is a critical factor in their feeding success.*

DIG DEEPER

With the class, return to Question 6, Reread. Have students share their responses to the question.

ASK STUDENTS to discuss what the scientists discovered about the two kinds of movements.

- What advantage does a whale shark get from the first "movement mode"? *When a shark swims at a shallow ascent angle, it minimizes the energy it expends to move horizontally.*

- What advantage does a whale shark get from the second "movement mode"? *When a shark swims at a steeper ascent angle, it "optimizes" the "energetic cost" of moving vertically. This implies that here, too, the shark is minimizing the amount of energy it uses, given its vertical movement.*

- Summarize how the whale shark "uses geometry" to its advantage. *When a whale shark wants to ascend, it swims at one of two kinds of angles—shallow or steep—which allows it to conserve as much energy as possible.*

ASK STUDENTS to return to their Short Response answer and revise it based on the class discussion.

COMPARE TEXT AND MEDIA
Musée des Beaux Arts

Landscape with the Fall of Icarus

Poem by W. H. Auden

Painting by Pieter Breughel the Elder

Why This Text and This Painting?

Students living in a world dominated by technology are regularly exposed to the interplay between words and images. This lesson explores how both mediums emphasize and negate content.

Key Learning Objective: The student will be able to analyze representations of a subject in different mediums.

 COMMON CORE

Common Core Standards

RL 1 Cite textual evidence.

RL 2 Determine a theme and analyze its development.

RL 5 Analyze an author's choices concerning how to structure a text

RL 6 Analyze a particular point of view.

RL 7 Analyze a subject or key scene in two different artistic mediums.

W 9 Draw evidence from texts to support analysis, reflection, and research.

SL 3 Evaluate a speaker's point of view, reasoning, and use of evidence.

SL 4 Present information clearly so that the development and style are appropriate to purpose, audience, and task.

Text Complexity Rubric

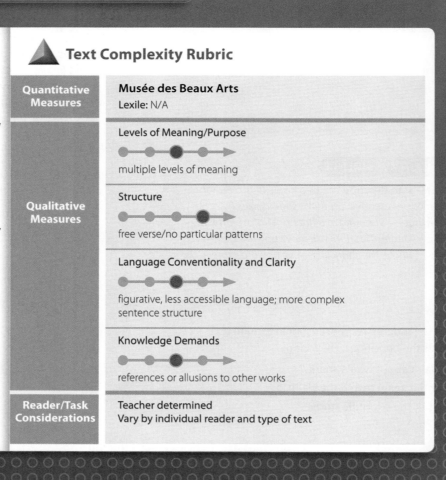

Quantitative Measures	**Musée des Beaux Arts** Lexile: N/A
Qualitative Measures	**Levels of Meaning/Purpose** multiple levels of meaning
	Structure free verse/no particular patterns
	Language Conventionality and Clarity figurative, less accessible language; more complex sentence structure
	Knowledge Demands references or allusions to other works
Reader/Task Considerations	Teacher determined Vary by individual reader and type of text

TEACH

CLOSE READ

Background Explain that myths serve several purposes within their cultures of origin. They may explain natural events, or they may provide people with cultural rules and values. Today, by studying the myths of any culture, modern scholars can learn about the points of view and cultural experiences of the original storytellers.

Share Ovid's description of the ploughman: "He [Daedalus] urged the boy [Icarus] to follow, and showed him the dangerous art of flying, moving his own wings, and then looking back at his son. Some angler catching fish with a quivering rod, or a shepherd leaning on his crook, or a ploughman resting on the handles of his plough, saw them, perhaps, and stood there amazed, believing them to be gods able to travel the sky." Explain that the ploughman is a feature of the myth that appears in the painting by Breughel, and therefore the poem by Auden.

Point out that the author states the point of view of the original storyteller of the legend of Icarus. The story focuses on two characters that upset the natural order: Daedalus, who builds the wings, and Icarus, who wants to fly higher and higher. According to the natural order, humans are not able to fly. The storyteller underscores this point of view by punishing the characters for their crimes; Icarus dies and Daedalus loses his son.

Musée des Beaux Arts

Landscape with the Fall of Icarus

Poem by W. H. Auden   Painting by Pieter Breughel the Elder

Background *According to a Greek myth, King Minos imprisoned the architect and inventor Daedalus and his son Icarus on the isle of Crete. In order to escape, Daedalus built two pairs of wings with feathers and wax. Before fleeing the island, he warned his son to not fly too high, lest the warm sunlight melt the wax and destroy the wings. Once airborne, however, Icarus became exhilarated with the joy and freedom of flight. Higher and higher he flew, until the wax on his wings did indeed begin to soften. The feathers separated, and the young man fell and drowned in a part of the Aegean called the Icarian Sea.*

The story of Icarus shows the danger of upsetting the natural order, either through artifice or ambition. It has fascinated visual artists from ancient sculptors through Rubens and Matisse. Writers and poets, too, have expanded on the legend; the Roman poet Ovid published a particularly influential version in AD 8. Over the centuries, painters and poets have consistently informed and alluded to each others' work on the subject.

Ovid's tale inspired perhaps the best known Icarus painting, a work once attributed to Pieter Breughel the Elder *(1525–1569). We know little about the life of the great Flemish painter, who became famous for his finely detailed, allegorical landscapes. Breughel began and ended his career in what is now Belgium, but he was greatly influenced by Italian art and spent several years painting in Italy.*

Breughel's Landscape with the Fall of Icarus *inspired a major 20th-century poet,* W. H. Auden. Auden *(1907–1973) first viewed the painting in a Brussels museum in 1938, shortly before war broke out in Europe. In 1939 he moved from his native England to New York City. "Musée des Beaux Arts" appeared in 1940. Auden taught at universities and wrote plays, prose, music lyrics, and over a dozen books of poems. His poetry, which features keen observation and direct, accessible language, had a profound influence on a generation of modern poets.*

APPLYING ACADEMIC VOCABULARY

perspective	incorporate

As you discuss the poem and the painting, incorporate the following Collection 4 academic vocabulary words: *perspective* and *incorporate*. To help students compare and contrast the poem and the painting, ask them to identify the details in the painting on which Auden bases his **perspective** that the painting is about the human response to suffering. Ask: Which details in the painting does Auden **incorporate** into his poem and why?

AS YOU READ Direct students to use the As You Read statement to focus their reading.

Analyze a Particular Point of View (LINES 14–17)

 COMMON CORE **RL 6**

Remind students of Ovid's lines regarding the ploughman you shared with them (page 189).

 ASK STUDENTS how Ovid and Auden differ in their idea of how the ploughman will react to Daedalus and Icarus. *(Ovid envisions that the ploughman will stop his work and stand and stare in amazement. Auden's poem says that the ploughman may find Icarus's fall and death unimportant.)* What does this show us about Auden's perspective on the human reaction to suffering? *(that humans are ignorant or uncaring about the suffering of others)*

Analyzing Representations in Different Mediums
(LINES 14–21)

 COMMON CORE **RL 1, RL 7**

Explain that when artists create works in response to an existing story, they make choices about which details to include and which to exclude. They may also choose to reinterpret the meaning of the story.

B **CITE TEXT EVIDENCE** Ask students to reread lines 14–21. Which items appear in the painting on p. 191? *(the ploughman, sun, white legs, green water, ship)* Are there elements of the painting that do not appear in the poem? What are they? *(shepherd, fisherman, natural elements such as trees, mountains, and birds)* Ask partners to discuss why Auden includes particular elements from the painting and excludes others. *(He focuses on the human reaction to suffering rather than the natural surroundings.)*

COLLABORATIVE DISCUSSION Have students summarize what the Old Masters understood about suffering. Does Auden agree or disagree? Make sure students support their responses with text evidence.

ASK STUDENTS to share questions they generate while reading and discussing the selection.

AS YOU READ Think about how the historical context in which Auden wrote the poem, just before World War II, might influence its theme. Write down any questions you generate during reading.

Musée des Beaux Arts
Poem by W. H. Auden

About suffering they were never wrong,
The Old Masters:[1] how well they understood
Its human position; how it takes place
While someone else is eating or opening a window or just
    walking dully along;
5 How, when the aged are reverently, passionately waiting
For the miraculous birth, there always must be
Children who did not specially want it to happen, skating
On a pond at the edge of the wood:
They never forgot
10 That even the dreadful martyrdom must run its course
Anyhow in a corner, some untidy spot
Where the dogs go on with their doggy life and the
    torturer's horse
Scratches its innocent behind on a tree.

In Breughel's *Icarus*, for instance: how everything turns away
15 Quite leisurely from the disaster; the ploughman may
Have heard the splash, the forsaken cry,
But for him it was not an important failure; the sun shone
As it had to on the white legs disappearing into the green
Water; and the expensive delicate ship that must have seen
20 Something amazing, a boy falling out of the sky,
Had somewhere to get to and sailed calmly on.

COLLABORATIVE DISCUSSION What did the "Old Masters" understand about suffering? With a partner, discuss Auden's own attitude toward their perspective. Cite specific evidence from the poems to support your ideas.

---

[1] **Old Masters:** Famous European painters of the Renaissance period.

SCAFFOLDING FOR ELL STUDENTS

Students may struggle with determining where one complete idea begins and ends in a poem like this one, since one sentence can span many lines and punctuation does not always follow line breaks. Have students reread the poem, this time focusing on punctuation and stopping at the appropriate times. At the end of each sentence, ask students to restate the idea in their own words.

AS YOU VIEW Consider the relationship between painting's title and its composition. Write down any questions you generate while viewing it.

Landscape with the Fall of Icarus
Painting by Pieter Breughel the Elder

Landscape with the Fall of Icarus, c. 1558, by Pieter Breughel the Elder (1525–1569), oil on panel transferred onto canvas, 73 x 112 cm.

COLLABORATIVE DISCUSSION Which image in the painting do you think is most important? Discuss how and why the artist emphasized this part of the scene. Point out details from the painting that support your ideas.

Image Credits: ©De Agostini/Getty Images

WHEN STUDENTS STRUGGLE...

To guide students with the analysis of the painting, provide these questions:

How has the artist arranged the elements of the painting?
- What is near? What is far away?
- What is high? What is low?
- What is big? What is small?

From what perspective is the viewer seeing the event of Icarus's drowning?

Have students answer these questions in pairs. Then lead students to discuss how the artist uses composition and perspective to convey meaning.

TEACH

CLOSE READ

AS YOU VIEW Direct students to use the As You View statement to focus their viewing.

Analyze a Particular Point of View
 COMMON CORE RL 6

Remind students that Ovid suggests that the ploughman might have stared at Icarus in amazement.

C **ASK STUDENTS** to study Breughel's ploughman. Is he staring at Icarus in amazement? If not, what is he doing? *(No, he continues with his work without noticing Icarus.)*

Analyzing Representations in Different Mediums
COMMON CORE RL 1, RL 7

Remind students of the chronological sequence of the artistic works: the original myth, Breughel's painting, and Auden's poem.

D **CITE TEXT EVIDENCE** Have students identify elements of Auden's poem that are not part of the two pieces that came before his poem. *(The first thirteen lines of Auden's poem are about the Old Masters and their attitude toward suffering.)* Have students identify the parts of the original story that Breughel leaves out. *(He includes only the death of Icarus, not the imprisonment of Daedalus, the building of the wings, or even why Icarus fell.)*

COLLABORATIVE DISCUSSION Explain that the foreground of a painting is the part that appears to be nearest to the viewer. The foreground often draws the viewer's eye first and therefore conveys importance. Ask: Is it easy or difficult for the viewer to find the drowning Icarus in the painting? What do the size and placement of the ploughman and Icarus tell viewers about the artist's message?

ASK STUDENTS to share questions they generate while viewing and discussing the painting.

Analyzing Representations in Different Mediums

COMMON CORE **RL 7**

Lead small student groups to prepare three-column charts. In the first column, have students write the three bulleted questions. In the second column, have students write responses based on Auden's poem. In the third column, have students write responses based on Breughel's painting. Remind students to cite text evidence where applicable. Have each group present its chart and analysis to the class.

Analyzing the Text and Image

COMMON CORE **RL 1, RL 2, RL 7**

Possible answers:

1. *Both works focus on the death of Icarus and withhold the events that lead to his death.*

2. *In the painting, Icarus appears as a tiny pair of legs because his death is of no consequence in the surrounding landscape. Icarus receives slightly greater prominence in the poem. He is mentioned by name in line 14; his legs are mentioned in line 18; and his fall is mentioned in line 20.*

3. *Sample answer: I agree with Auden's interpretation because Icarus appears in the painting only as a tiny, hard-to-find pair of legs. Without the title, viewers might not notice Icarus at all in the painting.*

> ✓ **Assess It!**
>
> **Online Selection Test**
> - Download an editable ExamView bank.
> - Assign and manage this test online.

Analyzing Representations in Different Mediums

COMMON CORE **RL 7**

A **medium** is a vehicle for artistic expression, or a mode of communication. Examples include drama, music, text, and the visual arts. Artists working in different media often depict the same subject. Since each medium offers its own particular strengths and limitations, however, these artists often emphasize different aspects of the subject or scene. As a result, they may develop and address different themes within the same topic. For example, the visual art medium (painting) does not allow Breughel to represent the entire moral of the myth in his work.

Auden, for his part, emphasizes another aspect of the theme after viewing two paintings in the Musées Royaux des Beaux-Arts, a Brussels museum. (Auden's first stanza refers to Breughel's painting *The Census at Bethlehem*.) When considered together, the Icarus myth, the painting, and the poem provide a much broader range of meaning than each delivers on its own. When comparing representations of a subject in different mediums, you might ask yourself the following questions:

- What details are emphasized in each treatment?
- What details are present in one treatment but absent in the other?
- What is each artist's attitude toward the subject?

Analyzing the Text and Image

COMMON CORE **RL 2, RL 7, SL 4**

Cite Text Evidence   Support your responses with evidence from the selections.

1. **Analyze** Describe how the two works incorporate the Icarus myth. Which parts of the story do they withhold, and which parts do they emphasize?

2. **Evaluate** Why does Icarus appear as a tiny pair of legs in a corner of the painting? Does he receive greater prominence in the poem? Explain.

3. **Synthesize** Auden interprets the scene as a human response to suffering. Do you agree or disagree with the poet's interpretation of the painting? Why?

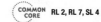

PERFORMANCE TASK

Speaking Activity: Comparison Plan and deliver a short speech in which you compare Auden's poem with *Landscape with the Fall of Icarus*.

- Begin planning your comparison by making a Venn diagram in which you list key details from the painting and the poem.
- Draft a short speech in which you point out the details and ideas that appear in both works.
- Draft a conclusion in which you analyze the significance of these shared details.
- Deliver your speech. Be sure to quote from Auden's poem and point out details in the painting.

Assign this performance task.

PERFORMANCE TASK

COMMON CORE **W 9, SL 4**

Speaking Activity Provide students with frames for their speeches.

1. The story of Icarus is popular among artists because _____.
2. In Auden's poem, the speaker describes _____. [include quotations]
3. In Breughel's painting, he emphasizes_____. [include descriptions]
4. These similarities suggest that both artists _____.

Evaluate a Speaker

TEACH

Before students complete the Performance Task, explain that when students evaluate speakers, they should consider the following elements:

- **Point of View** What is the speaker's opinion or perspective regarding the subject?
- **Reasoning** Does the speaker present clear and logical reasons that support his or her point of view?
- **Evidence** Does the speaker offer credible evidence to explain or clarify each reason?
- **Rhetoric** What methods of persuasion does the speaker employ?

Students may complete the Interactive Speaking and Listening Lesson, Analyzing and Evaluating Presentations, to learn more about providing feedback to speakers on their presentations.

PRACTICE AND APPLY

When students deliver their comparison speeches regarding Auden's poem and Breughel's painting, have the audience members use a rubric such as this one to evaluate the speakers.

Point of View	5 4 3 2 1
	(Circle one)
	The speaker's conclusion regarding the significance of the shared details is clearly stated and insightful.
Reasoning	5 4 3 2 1
	The speaker identifies and clearly states shared key details or ideas between the works.
Evidence	5 4 3 2 1
	The speaker presents clear examples from each work to support key details or ideas.
Rhetoric	5 4 3 2 1
	I find myself agreeing with the speaker's point of view.

Determine Theme

TEACH

Remind students that a theme is the life lesson contained within an artistic or literary work. Often, readers can determine theme by examining the details an artist or author includes.

For example, in Breughel's painting, Icarus's legs are very small and hard to locate at first glance.

What does this detail suggest about Icarus's suffering? It may suggest that Icarus's suffering is inconsequential or unimportant.

This idea may be one theme of the work: the suffering that seems very important to one person may not even be noticeable to others as they carry out their everday lives.

PRACTICE AND APPLY

Using a two-column chart such as this one, have student pairs gather details from Auden's poem about the actions of people in their everday lives, compared to the suffering of others:

Everyday Life	Suffering
• Someone is eating	• Torture
• Someone is opening a window	• Dreadful martyrdom
• _____	• _____

Lead students to discuss the relationship between the details in the first column and the details in the second column.

- How do those represented in the first column correspond to the examples of suffering detailed in the second column? *(They represent someone ignoring the suffering in the second column and carrying on with their own lives.)*
- Based on these details, what is one possible theme of the poem? *(In life, suffering is as commonplace as eating, opening a window, or walking. It is not worthy of special note.)*

Analyze Text Structure: Form in Poetry

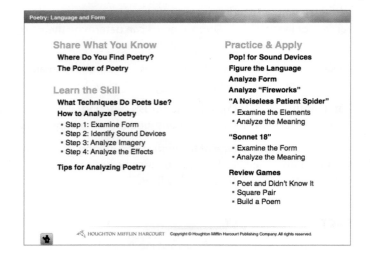

Poetry: Language and Form

Share What You Know
Where Do You Find Poetry?
The Power of Poetry

Learn the Skill
What Techniques Do Poets Use?
How to Analyze Poetry
- Step 1: Examine Form
- Step 2: Identify Sound Devices
- Step 3: Analyze Imagery
- Step 4: Analyze the Effects

Tips for Analyzing Poetry

Practice & Apply
Pop! for Sound Devices
Figure the Language
Analyze Form
Analyze "Fireworks"
"A Noiseless Patient Spider"
- Examine the Elements
- Analyze the Meaning

"Sonnet 18"
- Examine the Form
- Analyze the Meaning

Review Games
- Poet and Didn't Know It
- Square Pair
- Build a Poem

TEACH

Review the following elements of poetic form with students:

- **Free verse:** poetry in which there are no regular rhymes, stanzaic forms, or metrical patterns
- **Enjambment:** the continuation of meaning, without pause or break, from one line of poetry to the next

Explain to students that while the first three lines of the poem each have ten syllables, suggesting a metrical pattern, this regularity ends at line 4. Lead students in counting and marking the syllables in the first four lines.

Then have students circle the punctuation in the poem. Ask: Where does most of the punctuation occur—in the middle of lines or at the ends of lines? *(in the middle of lines)*

COLLABORATIVE DISCUSSION

Direct students to work in small groups to discuss the relationship between the form of the poem and its meaning. Ask: Why does Auden begin and then reject traditional patterned verse? Why does Auden's speaker repeatedly run one line into the next? *(It's as if the details of real life—eating, opening a window, walking along, and suffering—cannot be contained within the standard constraints of poetry. The Old Masters—and Auden—may capture glimpses of life, but they cannot capture life itself; it moves too quickly and fleetingly, as Icarus well knows.)*

Analyzing Representations in Different Mediums

RETEACH

Review the term *medium* and provide examples.

- Ask students to identify the artistic mediums of Auden and Breughel.
- Lead students to discuss the relationship between the medium and the content of an artistic representation. For example, how does the fact that Breughel paints influence his decisions about which part of the story to emphasize and which to leave absent? *(With painting, Breughel must focus on one moment in time.)* How does the fact that Auden writes influence his decisions regarding the content of his poem? *(With writing, Auden is able to include references to the painter and other works.)*

LEVEL UP TUTORIALS Assign the following *Level Up* tutorial: **Universal and Recurring Themes**

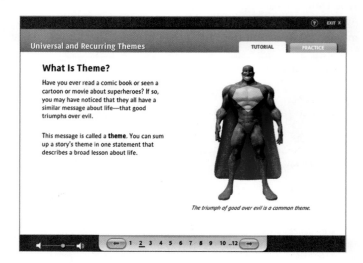

What Is Theme?

Have you ever read a comic book or seen a cartoon or movie about superheroes? If so, you may have noticed that they all have a similar message about life—that good triumphs over evil.

This message is called a **theme.** You can sum up a story's theme in one statement that describes a broad lesson about life.

The triumph of good over evil is a common theme.

CLOSE READING APPLICATION

Students can apply the skill to other works cited in the Background on p. 189, including Ovid's full text and the works of Matisse or Rubens. Have students work with a partner to identify which parts of the story are emphasized and absent in each representation. Ask: What is the artist's attitude toward the subject? What theme is present in each work?

COLLECTION 4
PERFORMANCE TASK A

PERFORMANCE TASK A

Present a Speech

This collection focuses on how we perceive the world around us, from the use of our senses and instincts to the help of scientific instruments. Look back at the anchor texts "We grow accustomed to the Dark" and "Before I got my eye put out" and at the other texts you have read in this collection. Synthesize your ideas about them by preparing and presenting a speech.

An effective speech

- focuses the audience's attention on a controlling idea
- has a logically structured body including transitions
- provides evidence from the texts that illustrate the controlling idea
- includes a satisfying conclusion that follows logically from the body of the speech
- demonstrates appropriate and clear use of language
- engages the reader with appropriate emphasis, volume, and gestures
- maintains a formal tone through the standard use of English

COMMON CORE

SL 4 Present information, findings, and evidence.
W 9a–b Draw evidence from literary or informational texts.

PLAN

Analyze the Text Think about the quotation from Henry David Thoreau that begins this collection: "The question is not what you look at, but what you see."

- Choose three texts from this collection, including at least one poem by Emily Dickinson. Identify how Thoreau's idea is illustrated in the texts you chose.
- Take notes on details from your three chosen texts that have to do with how people see or perceive things.
- Pay attention to specific examples and quotations from the texts that provide strong evidence of each author's ideas.

State Your Controlling Idea Based on these texts, write a statement of your controlling idea about how we perceive the world around us. This statement will be the central idea of your speech. Remember that you will need to provide sufficient evidence from the texts to support your controlling idea.

my Notebook

Use the annotation tools in your eBook to find evidence that supports your ideas. Save each piece of evidence to your notebook.

ACADEMIC VOCABULARY

As you share your ideas about how we see things, be sure to incorporate these words.

differentiate
incorporate
mode
orient
perspective

Collection Performance Task A **193**

PRESENT A SPEECH

COMMON CORE **SL 4, W 9a-b**

Introduce students to the Performance Task by reading the introductory paragraph with them and reviewing the criteria for what makes a good informative speech. Remind students that while their speeches should use correct grammar and a proper tone, the speeches should also be written to be delivered aloud, using language that flows naturally the way people really speak.

PLAN

ANALYZE THE TEXT

View It!

Professional Development Podcast:
Performance Task

Students should think of their controlling idea as the main message of their speech. If their audience comes away from the speech remembering only one thing, it should be a sentence that can summarize this idea. To help students stay focused while collecting evidence, suggest that students write down and keep in mind two or three specific questions so as not to get sidetracked in analysis that does not support their main point. For example: How would this author define the act of looking versus the act of seeing? What are some examples of ways people perceive the world in this text? What are some quotes from this poem that refer to looking or seeing?

PRODUCE

WRITE YOUR SPEECH

Instead of jumping right into the act of writing their speech down, students may find it more helpful to begin by recording themselves speaking aloud as if they were explaining their ideas to an engaged listener. Students should keep their outline in mind while they speak, but they may discover as they talk that their ideas might be more effective if presented in a different sequence. Students can then use this recording as a guide for writing their speech, making sure that each point builds on the one before it and that they are not trying to cover too much information. Remind students that it is better to make two or three points well than to drown the audience in a sea of unrelated or confusing observations. Add that because the audience will only hear this speech once, and will be unable to go back and reread a point again the way they would with a written essay, it is essential that students make it clear from the start what they will be telling the audience so that their audience can be listening with that in mind.

Get Organized Organize your notes in an outline. You will need to present your ideas clearly so that your audience—your classmates—can easily follow the evidence for your claim.

- Write your controlling idea in the introductory section of your outline. Be sure to refer to the quotation by Thoreau in this section. You may want to include an additional quotation or detail from one of your chosen texts to engage your readers.
- In the body of your outline, list the central ideas that support your controlling idea. Include each writer's perspective on how we see things.
- For each central idea, cite evidence from the three texts that supports the idea.
- Reiterate and support your controlling idea in the concluding section. End with a final, thought-provoking statement.

PRODUCE

Write Your Speech Use your notes and outline to write a clearly organized speech that presents your ideas about perception. Remember to include

- an engaging introduction, a logically ordered body, and an interesting conclusion
- transitions between the main sections of your speech
- details, quotations, and examples from the texts to support your controlling idea
- language that creates an appropriately formal tone for a speech
- a variety of grammatical structures that will keep your audience engaged and interested in your speech

Plan Your Presentation When you deliver your speech to your classmates, you will need to make it come alive with appropriate expression, volume, and gestures. Read over your draft, and mark places in the text where you might want to

- emphasize a word or detail
- pause to give the audience time to consider an important idea
- use gestures to convey meaning or emotion

my WriteSmart

Write your rough draft in myWriteSmart. Focus on getting your ideas down, rather than perfecting your choice of language.

Practice and Improve Practice your speech with a partner. Use the chart on the next page to review the characteristics of an effective speech. As you speak, remember to incorporate the presentation techniques you marked on your draft. As you listen to your partner's speech, ask yourself these questions:

my **WriteSmart**
Have your partner or a group of peers review your draft in myWriteSmart.

- Does the beginning of the speech draw me in?
- Is the controlling idea presented clearly and concisely, followed by ideas and evidence that support it?
- Can I follow the reasoning, organization, and development of the speech?
- Does the conclusion reinforce the central ideas of the speech?
- Does my partner use appropriate emphasis and gestures?
- Can I hear my partner clearly? Does he or she need to speak more loudly or softly?
- How is my partner's pace? Does he or she need to slow down or speed up?

After you and your partner have presented your speeches, give each other feedback, paying attention to the questions above. Mention what your partner did particularly well and what he or she could have done better. Then revise your draft based on your partner's feedback and your own observations of your speech. Make sure that your audience will both understand and enjoy it.

PRESENT

Make Your Speech Present your speech to the whole class. The audience should listen, take notes, and be prepared to ask questions.

- Introduce yourself and briefly state the topic of your speech.
- At the end of your speech, ask your audience if they have any questions or comments.
- Find out which aspects of your speech were particularly strong.
- Ask how your speech could be improved.
- Thank your audience for their time and attention.

REVISE

PRACTICE AND IMPROVE

Presenting a speech to a partner is a good time to gauge the effectiveness of various composition and presentation techniques. Point out that it will save time to fix large issues before smaller ones, so students should 1) check the effectiveness of their introduction, order of body points, and conclusion, 2) evaluate the transitions between each point, and 3) check sentence-level mechanical issues such as grammar and word choice. Some ways students might tweak their speeches to make them more effective when heard aloud include:

- using sentences of varying lengths to keep the sound of the speech from becoming boring or monotone.
- using balanced sentence structures that present ideas in a clear sequence or in parallel form.
- not using a complicated word when a simpler one would do.
- defining any difficult vocabulary or special terms that must be used.
- briefly summing up each point before using time-order words to transition to the next section of the speech.

PRESENT

MAKE YOUR SPEECH

Remind students to monitor the pace of their speech as they read it. A nervous student may find him or herself reading faster and faster until the words blur together. Students can use carefully planned pauses to emphasize a point and let its meaning sink into the audience's minds. Students can also raise their voice to accentuate an idea, but speakers should never shout. Although students can glance down at their papers, they should remember to maintain good eye contact with their listeners. Note that students should especially be aware of their hands. Good speakers do not jam their hands in their pockets or distract the attention of their audience by fidgeting with their fingers. Instead, good speakers use a few well-chosen gestures to punctuate their words.

PERFORMANCE TASK A

LANGUAGE

Have students look at the chart and identify how they did on the Performance Task in the Language category. Ask students to think about the tone and use of transitions in their speech. Ask them to use these criteria to make a list of suggestions they could follow when writing their next speech to make it more effective and engaging.

COLLECTION 4 **TASK A**
SPEECH

	Ideas and Evidence	Organization	Language
ADVANCED	• The speech begins memorably and engages the audience's attention. • A strong and interesting controlling idea is introduced at the start of the speech. • Information and supporting evidence are presented clearly, concisely, and logically so that the audience can follow the development of ideas.	• Central ideas and supporting evidence are presented in a logical and powerful way. • The speech maintains a consistent focus on the topic. • The speech ends with a satisfying and thought-provoking conclusion.	• The speech maintains a consistent and appropriately formal tone through the use of standard English. • The speech flows smoothly with the use of transitions and varied sentence structures. • The speaker is easy to understand and uses volume, pacing, and gestures appropriately.
COMPETENT	• The speech starts in a way that engages the audience. • A controlling idea is introduced at the start of the speech. • Information and supporting evidence are presented clearly and logically, although some unnecessary information is included.	• Central ideas and supporting evidence are presented in a mostly logical way. • The speech stays focused on the topic, with a few minor lapses. • The speech ends with an appropriate conclusion.	• The speech mostly maintains a formal tone through the use of standard English. • The speech mostly flows smoothly with the use of transitions and varied sentence structures. • The speaker is generally easy to understand.
LIMITED	• The speech has a somewhat bland opening that may not engage the audience. • A controlling idea is hinted at but not made clear at the start of the speech. • Most information and supporting evidence are presented clearly, but there is some unnecessary information and some gaps in logic.	• Central ideas and some supporting evidence are presented, but the reasoning is often unclear. • The speech strays from the topic in several places. • The speech ends with a brief concluding statement but leaves some ideas unresolved.	• The speech has an inconsistent tone, sometimes using nonstandard or very informal English. • The speech needs more transitions to clarify links between ideas and uses monotonous sentence structures. • The speaker is sometimes difficult to understand and may rush or speak in a monotone.
EMERGING	• The speech opens in a way that does not engage the audience. • There is no controlling idea. • Information is not presented clearly and logically, and supporting evidence is lacking.	• Central ideas and supporting evidence are difficult for the audience to identify and understand. • The speech lacks focus throughout. • The speech ends abruptly.	• The speech has an overly informal tone, using nonstandard English and/or slang. • The speech lacks transitions to clarify links between ideas and uses choppy simple sentences. • The speaker is often difficult to understand.

Write a Short Story

COMMON CORE

W 3a–e Write narratives.
W 4 Produce clear and coherent writing.

The texts in this collection focus on how individuals see things, both from a scientific viewpoint and from a more subjective, emotional perspective. Look back at the anchor text "Coming to Our Senses" and the other texts you have read in this collection. Synthesize your ideas about them by writing a suspenseful or surprising short story.

An effective short story

- begins by introducing a setting, a narrator, and a main character
- has an engaging plot with a central conflict that the characters try to resolve
- provides a clear sequence of events
- uses a variety of narrative techniques to develop characters, plot, theme, and suspense or surprise
- sets a pace that keeps the reader curious about the next plot event
- includes sensory language and descriptive details
- ends with a logical and satisfying resolution to the conflict

PLAN

Identify Narrative Techniques Choose three texts from this collection, including "Coming to Our Senses." What surprise or sudden insight is revealed in each text? How does the author keep you guessing or reveal the insight? Reread your chosen texts, taking notes on techniques the writers use to create suspense or surprise. Ask yourself these questions:

- What point of view does each writer use? Identify the narrator as first-person or third-person. How does the point of view affect how or when information is revealed?
- How does the writer use dialogue and descriptive details to create suspense or reveal insights?
- How does the writer control pacing? Look for passages with descriptive detail that makes readers slow down. Contrast them with passages in which events take place very quickly. How does the pacing allow for suspense or surprise?

myNotebook

Use the annotation tools in your eBook to identify vivid details and suspenseful techniques. Save to your notebook any details or techniques you might incorporate into your narrative.

ACADEMIC VOCABULARY

As you discuss narrative techniques with your group, try to use these words.

differentiate
incorporate
mode
orient
perspective

WRITE A SHORT STORY

COMMON CORE W 3a-e, W 4

Review with students the characteristics of a well-written short story. Note that the way a writer organizes and develops these basic elements will determine the tone and effect of the final story and whether it is suspenseful, funny, sad, romantic, or scary.

PLAN

IDENTIFY NARRATIVE TECHNIQUES

View It!

Professional Development Podcast:

Writing Narratives at the Secondary Level

Explain that although students would never want to plagiarize from published writers, or copy word for word their descriptions and turns of phrase, developing writers can learn a lot by studying the works of established writers and figuring out how they create their effects. Note that when analyzing texts, students can gather everything from broad strategies for how to structure a scene or reveal information about a character to specific lists of exciting action verbs or interesting dialogue tags to use.

PERFORMANCE TASK B

Have a Group Discussion Discuss your analysis of narrative
techniques in a group with two other classmates. Each classmate will
present his or her reflections on one text.

PLAN

HAVE A GROUP DISCUSSION

While evaluating the effectiveness of the techniques
being presented, students should look at the mechanics
of how different effects are created. Does the author
vary sentence length or use sentence fragments? Does
the author use many descriptive words or just a few?
What is the ratio of dialogue to description in a passage?
Does the author stay with the same point of view or
narrate the action from several vantage points? Then
have students consider how they could replicate each
technique in their own writing.

PLAN

GET ORGANIZED

Make sure that students understand that they can play
with the order of events in their story and do not have
to tell the events in chronological order. They might find
it more effective to open with an event from the middle
of a tale and then fill in background information using a
flashback scene or a character's thoughts or memories.

Add that although students should also feel free to play
with point of view, they might find it more effective to
limit themselves to one or two points of view instead of
leaping among the minds of different characters with no
ultimate plan or goal in mind. Have students consider
the benefits of different points of view. First person ("I
love to ski") and limited third person ("Julia loved to
ski") provide the reader with a deeper connection to
the character. Omniscient and unlimited third person
("Everyone in the family had their own feelings about
the trip.") offer a reader more information.

Have a Group Discussion Discuss your analysis of narrative
techniques in a group with two other classmates. Each classmate will
present his or her reflections on one text.

- Take turns presenting your analyses. Be sure to differentiate
  between the various techniques used to reveal sudden insights.

- After all three texts have been presented, evaluate the narrative
  techniques used in each text. Were any techniques more effective
  than others in creating suspense or surprise? Why?

- Decide which narrative techniques will be most useful when it is
  time to draft your own story.

Brainstorm Use a web diagram or other graphic organizer to
generate ideas for your narrative.

- Think about an experience, event, or conflict you know about
  that involved an element of suspense or surprise.

- Use your imagination to create characters, setting, plot, conflict,
  and theme related to this experience or event.

- Remember that this is a fictional account and that you are using
  ideas from real life to help you get started.

Get Organized Organize your notes. Combine the techniques
you identified in the texts with your own ideas in an outline or a
graphic organizer.

- Create an outline or use a story map to clarify the structure
  of your short story. Look back at the chosen texts from this
  collection to help you. Ask yourself:
  - *How does the story begin? What can I do to engage readers and
    make them want to keep reading?*
  - *What is the story's plot? What is the central conflict? Are there any
    other conflicts related to the central one?*
  - *What is the sequence of events? How do they lead to a
    climax—a turning point or moment of greatest intensity? When is
    the moment of sudden insight?*
  - *How does the story end? Is the conflict resolved? How?*
- Select which point of view you will use in your narrative. Take
  notes on other narrative techniques you plan to incorporate into
  the story.
- Flesh out your setting and characters. What will your readers want
  to know? Give details about the setting. Describe your characters'
  appearance, personality, and anything else that makes them
  stand out.
- Think about the details you will use to create suspense or surprise.

PRODUCE

DRAFT YOUR SHORT STORY

Rather than worrying about getting every word exactly right during the first draft, students should first focus on just putting words down on the page. Their outlines and graphic organizers should provide them with some guidance as they write, but if they hit a creative dead end, discover they need to add a new character or situation, or think their plot events would work better if they were to be narrated in a different order, students should always feel free to deviate from their original writing plan.

REVISE

IMPROVE YOUR DRAFT

When providing story feedback for their partners, students should remember the work they did analyzing the narrative techniques published writers use. Encourage them to provide concrete suggestions, such as specific ideas for a more effective way to open the story or places where more information about a character could be subtly added to the story.

PRESENT

GATHER ROUND

Before reading their finished story to an audience, students should listen to themselves reading the story aloud, perhaps even recording their reading so they can really study how it sounds and tweak any dull, repetitious, or monotonous parts. Although student readers should use pauses and emphasis to make their stories exciting, their work should be written well enough to be able to stand on its own and create a suspenseful atmosphere without relying on a person's voice to bring it to life.

PRODUCE

Draft Your Short Story Write a draft of your short story, following your notes, outline, and graphic organizers.

my WriteSmart

Write your rough draft in myWriteSmart. Focus on getting your ideas down rather than perfecting your choice of language.

- Begin by introducing the setting, the main character(s), and an experience or conflict that will be central to the plot.
- Describe a sequence of events surrounding the conflict. Pay attention to how you develop the element of surprise or suspense and the best moment to reveal a sudden insight.
- Use descriptive details, sensory language, and narrative techniques such as dialogue.
- Provide a satisfying ending that resolves the central conflict.

REVISE

my WriteSmart

Have your partner or a group of peers review your draft in myWriteSmart.

Improve Your Draft Exchange drafts with a partner. Use the chart on the next page to review the characteristics of an effective short story. When reading your partner's draft, ask yourself the following questions. Then use feedback from your partner to revise your draft.

- Does the story begin in an engaging way? What could the writer do to make the beginning more interesting or exciting?
- Is there anything confusing about the sequence of events? Did you see the surprise coming? Did you feel the suspense throughout the story?
- Are the characters fully developed—that is, are there enough details to make them seem real?
- Does the dialogue sound natural?
- Is the conflict resolved in a logical way?

PRESENT

Gather Round When your final draft is completed, read your narrative to a small group. Use your voice and gestures to present a lively reading. Be prepared to answer questions or respond to comments from your group members.

PERFORMANCE TASK B

ORGANIZATION

Have students look at the chart and identify how they did on the Performance Task in the Organization category. Ask them to think about the sequence of events and pacing in their story. Ask them to identify the aspect of their story that could be improved the most and come up with a strategy to help them develop this aspect better in their next piece of short fictional writing.

	Ideas and Evidence	Organization	Language
ADVANCED	• The short story begins memorably; the exposition clearly introduces the setting and a main character and establishes the conflict in a unique way. • The writer regularly uses precise description and realistic dialogue to develop characters and events. • The plot is thoroughly developed; the story reveals a significant theme. • The story ends by resolving the conflict and tying up loose ends.	• The sequence of events is effective, clear, and logical. • The pace and organization keep the reader curious about the next plot event.	• The point of view is effective and consistent throughout the story. • Vivid sensory details reveal the setting and characters. • Sentence beginnings, lengths, and structures vary and have a rhythmic flow. • Spelling, capitalization, and punctuation are correct. • Grammar and usage are correct.
COMPETENT	• The story introduces the setting, a main character, and a conflict, but it could be more engaging. • The writer often uses description and dialogue to develop characters and events. • The plot is adequately developed; the story suggests a theme. • The story resolves the conflict, but more details are needed to bring the plot to a satisfying conclusion.	• The sequence of events is mostly clear and logical. • The pace is usually effective.	• The point of view is mostly consistent. • A few more sensory details would help to describe the setting and characters. • Sentence beginnings, lengths, and structures mostly vary. • Some spelling, capitalization, and punctuation mistakes occur but are not distracting. • Some minor grammatical and usage errors appear in the story.
LIMITED	• The story opening is uneventful; the exposition identifies a setting and a main character but only hints at a conflict. • The writer occasionally uses description and dialogue to develop characters and events. • The plot development is uneven in a few places; a theme is only hinted at. • The story resolves some parts of the conflict.	• The sequence of events is confusing in a few places. • The pace often lags.	• The point of view shifts in a few places. • The sensory details are ordinary or not used regularly enough. • Sentence structures vary somewhat. • Spelling, capitalization, and punctuation are often incorrect • Grammar and usage are incorrect in many places.
EMERGING	• The short story is missing critical information about the setting and main character and doesn't set up a conflict. • The writer does not use description and dialogue to develop characters and events. • The plot is barely developed, and there is no recognizable theme. • The story lacks a clear resolution.	• There is no clear sequence of events, making it easy for the reader to lose interest in the plot. • The pace is ineffective.	• The story lacks a clear point of view. • Sensory details are rarely or never used to describe the setting and characters. • A repetitive sentence structure makes the writing monotonous. • Spelling, capitalization, and punctuation are incorrect throughout. • Many grammatical and usage errors change the meaning of the writer's ideas.

Image Credits: ©Ruthven Carstairs/Alamy Images

Absolute Power

"Be bloody, bold, and resolute; laugh to scorn
The power of man."

—*Macbeth*, Act IV, Scene 1

CONNECTING WORD AND IMAGE

ASK STUDENTS to discuss how the collection opener image and the collection quotation work together to create a connection.

PERFORMANCE TASK PREVIEW

Point out to students that they will complete one performance task at the end of the collection. The performance task will require them to further analyze the selections in the collection and to synthesize ideas about these analyses. They will present their findings in a variety of products.

ACADEMIC VOCABULARY

View It!

Professional Development Podcast:

Academic Vocabulary

Students can acquire facility with the academic vocabulary words through frequent, repeated exposure as they analyze and discuss the selections in the collection. Academic vocabulary can be used in the following instructional contexts. This will enable students to incorporate the academic vocabulary words into their working vocabulary.

- Collaborative Discussion at the end of each selection
- Analyzing the Text questions for each selection
- Selection-level Performance Task
- Vocabulary instruction (for Critical Vocabulary and/or for Vocabulary Strategy)
- Language and Style
- End-of-collection Performance Task for all selections in the collection

ASK STUDENTS to review the academic vocabulary word list for this collection. You may wish to pronounce each word aloud, so students hear the correct pronunciation. Then, discuss the definitions and the related forms for each word. Remind students that they will encounter these five academic vocabulary words throughout the collection.

Absolute Power

Human ambition is timeless, and its fruits are fleeting.

hmhfyi.com

COLLECTION

PERFORMANCE TASK Preview

At the end of this collection, you will have an opportunity to complete this task:

- Write an analysis explaining how Macbeth's character contains traits that all of us share.

ACADEMIC VOCABULARY

Study the words and their definitions in the chart below. You will use these words as you discuss and write about the texts in this collection.

Word	Definition	Related Forms
comprise (kəm-prīz´) *v.*	to consist or be made up of	comprising
incidence (ĭn´sĭ-dəns) *n.*	the occurrence or frequency of something	incident, coincidence
priority (prī-ôr´ĭ-tē) *n.*	something that is more important or considered more important than another thing	prioritize
thesis (thē´sĭs) *n.*	a statement or premise that is defended by an argument	hypothesis
ultimate (ŭl´tə-mĭt) *adj.*	concluding a process or progression; final	ultimately, ultimatum

USING COLLECTIONS YOUR WAY

Use the following information, along with the charts on the following pages, to help you decide how you want to introduce the collection. Based on your teaching style, your students' interests, or your instructional goals, you may want to structure the collection in various ways. You may choose different entry points each time you teach the collection.

"I love teaching traditional literature."

In this play, **William Shakespeare** presents a tragic hero as a means of exploring themes such as ambition, fate, greed, corruption, and the consequences of sacrificing morals to gain power.

The Tragedy of
Macbeth

Drama by William Shakespeare

William Shakespeare (1564–1616) was born in Stratford-upon-Avon to a fairly prosperous family. He attended the local grammar school, where he received a solid grounding in Latin and classical literature. When he was eighteen, he married Anne Hathaway. They had a daughter and then twins, a boy and a girl.

Sometime around 1590, Shakespeare left Stratford for London. He found work as an actor and began what was to be a highly successful career as a playwright. He belonged to a theater company known as the Lord Chamberlain's Men, which performed for Queen Elizabeth I; this company also renovated a theater known as the Globe for their own performances. Shakespeare's success enabled him to buy a house for his family in Stratford. He lived in that house after his retirement in 1612 but continued to write until his death four years later at the age of fifty-two.

Shakespeare is recognized as the most influential writer in the English language. He mastered the sonnet form, making it his own with his highly original approach; he composed long narrative poems; and he left a dramatic legacy unsurpassed by any playwright before or since. Four centuries later, his plays continue to be performed on stage and made into films.

Shakespeare's plays are often grouped based on when they were written. In the early 1590s, he wrote history plays and comedies with plots derived from earlier stories. In the late 1590s, he wrote comedies, including A Midsummer Night's Dream, in which he skillfully interwove complex plots to convey his themes. As the century ended, Shakespeare began exploring darker views of human nature in his work. Between 1600 and 1607, he wrote his greatest tragedies, including Macbeth, Hamlet, and King Lear. His later comedies, such as The Tempest, are often called tragicomedies, as they are tinged with sadness.

After Shakespeare died, his plays were published in an edition known as the First Folio. In the introduction, playwright Ben Jonson wrote that Shakespeare "was not of an age, but for all time."

The Tragedy of Macbeth **213**

Background In 1997, the BBC (British Broadcasting Corporation) produced a new version of Shakespeare's Scottish play—Macbeth on the Estate. Award-winning director Penny Woolcock reset the play as a modern crime drama and filmed it in the Ladywood Estate, a low-income housing development in Birmingham, England. Action was set in the estate's apartments, courtyards, and roofs, but the production retained Shakespeare's powerful language. Residents from the estate worked on the film and participated as actors. Reviews were polarized, with some critics preferring a more traditional approach and others embracing this affirmation of Shakespeare's universality.

MEDIA ANALYSIS

from
Macbeth on the Estate

Film directed by Penny Woolcock

AS YOU VIEW Consider how the modern setting creates a certain mood or tone. Write down any questions you have during viewing.

COLLABORATIVE DISCUSSION In a small group, discuss how the modern setting adds to the mood of the production. What atmosphere, or feeling, is conveyed? Cite specific images to support your ideas.

Macbeth on the Estate **293**

"I like to use a digital product as a starting point."

This version of *Macbeth* uses Shakespeare's words but depicts the setting as a crime scene set in modern times, showing the universal and timeless nature of Shakespeare's themes.

Background For many of his historical plays such as Macbeth, Shakespeare relied on the Chronicles, first published in 1577, as his main source. Raphael Holinshed is credited as the Chronicles' sole author, but many other writers contributed to this work. Although Shakespeare's Macbeth resembles the "historical" Macbeth in the Chronicles, most scholars do not consider the Chronicles to be a reliable document. In fact, the "real" Macbeth (c. 1005–1057) was a Scottish king whom those same scholars consider a just ruler, not a tragic hero.

from
Holinshed's
Chronicles

History by Raphael Holinshed

AS YOU READ Pay attention to the details on which Shakespeare drew to create his tragic hero. Write down any questions you generate during reading.

Duncan's Murder

It fortuned, as Macbeth and Banquo journeyed toward Forres, where the King then lay, they went sporting by the way together without other company save only themselves, passing through the woods and fields, when suddenly, in midst of a laund,[1] there met them three women in strange and wild apparel, resembling creatures of elder world; whom when they attentively beheld, wondering much at the sight, the first of them spoke and said, "All hail, Macbeth, Thane of Glamis!" (for he had lately entered into that dignity and office by the death of his father Sinel). The second of them said, "Hail, Macbeth, Thane of Cawdor!" But the third said, "All hail, Macbeth, that hereafter shalt be King of Scotland!"

Then Banquo. "What manner of women," saith he, "are you, that seem so little favorable unto me, whereas to my fellow here, besides high offices, ye assign also the kingdom, appointing forth

[1] **laund:** a clearing in the forest.

Holinshed's Chronicles **295**

"I like to connect literature to history."

This excerpt from **Raphael Holinshed's** historical text describes events in the life of the historical figure of Macbeth, and the text is thought to have been used by Shakespeare as source material for his tragedy *Macbeth*.

mySmartPlanner | **eBook** | **myNotebook** | **myWriteSmart** | **fyi** hmhfyi.com

Collection 5 Lessons	Media	Teach and Practice
Student Edition | **eBook**	▶ Video Links HISTORY A&E	**Close Reading and Evidence Tracking**
Argument by Michael Mack from "Why Read Shakespeare?"	🔊 **Audio** from "Why Read Shakespeare?"	
ANCHOR TEXT **Drama by William Shakespeare** *The Tragedy of Macbeth*	▶ **Video BIOGRAPHY** *William Shakespeare* 🔊 **Audio** *The Tragedy of Macbeth*	**Close Read Screencasts** • Modeled Discussion 1 (Act I, Scene 5, lines 35–44) • Modeled Discussion 2 (Act II, Scene 3, lines 112–126) • Modeled Discussion 3 (Act III, Scene 5, lines 23–33) • Modeled Discussion 4 (Act IV, Scene 2, lines 30–41) • Modeled Discussion 5 (Act V, Scene 5, lines 9–18) **Strategies for Annotation** • Analyze Structure • Analyze Shakespearean Drama • Analyze Character and Theme
CLOSE READER **Drama by William Shakespeare** from *The Tragedy of Macbeth*	🔊 **Audio** from *The Tragedy of Macbeth*	
Film by Penny Woolcock from *Macbeth on the Estate*	🔊 **Audio** from *Macbeth on the Estate*	
History by Raphael Holinshed from *Holinshed's Chronicles*	🔊 **Audio** from *Holinshed's Chronicles*	**Strategies for Annotation** • Archaic Language
Short Story by James Thurber "The Macbeth Murder Mystery"	🔊 **Audio** "The Macbeth Murder Mystery"	**Strategies for Annotation** • Analyze How an Author Draws On Shakespeare
Poem by Patricia Smith "5:00 P.M., Tuesday, August 23, 2005"	▶ **Video HISTORY** *Science of a Hurricane* 🔊 **Audio** "5:00 P.M., Tuesday, August 23, 2005"	**Strategies for Annotation** • Support Inferences About Word Choice
Collection 5 Performance Task: Write an Analytical Essay	**fyi** hmhfyi.com	**Interactive Lessons** Writing an Informative Text Writing as a Process Using Textual Evidence

	For Systematic Coverage of Writing and Speaking & Listening Standards	Interactive Lessons Writing a Narrative Producing and Publishing with Technology	Lesson Assessments Writing a Narrative Producing and Publishing with Technology

Assess		Extend	Reteach
Performance Task	**Online Assessment**	**Teacher eBook**	**Teacher eBook**
Speaking Activity: Argument	Selection Test	**Interactive Whiteboard Lesson >** Identify Fallacious Reasoning	**Analyze Argument and Rhetoric > Level Up Tutorial >** Analyzing Arguments
Writing Activity: Analysis Speaking Activity: Discussion Writing Activity: Analysis Speaking Activity: Debate Writing Activity: Argument	Selection Test	**Understand Use of Language: Archaic Words and Sentence Structures**	**Analyze Character and Theme > Level Up Tutorial >** Theme
Speaking Activity: Argument	Selection Test	**Use Media in Presentations**	**Analyze Representations > Level Up Tutorial >** Methods of Characterization
Speaking Activity: Discussion	Selection Test	**Analyzing Cultural Experience**	**Analyze Historical Text**
Writing Activity: Narrative	Selection Test	**Orient Readers of Narratives**	**Analyze How an Author Draws on Shakespeare > Level Up Tutorial >** Elements of Drama
Speaking Activity: Poetry Reading	Selection Test	**Analyze Complex Characters** **Integrate Various Sources of Information** **Interactive Whiteboard Lesson >** Analyze Poetic Form	**Support Inferences About Word Choice > Level Up Tutorial >** Figurative Language
Write an Analytical Essay	Collection Test		

Collection 5 Lessons	COMMON CORE Key Learning Objective	Performance Task
Argument by Michael Mack **Lexile 980** from "Why Read Shakespeare?" p. 203A	**The student will be able to...** analyze the use of rhetoric in an argument	Speaking Activity: Argument
ANCHOR TEXT **Drama by William Shakespeare** *The Tragedy of Macbeth,* p. 213A	**The student will be able to...** analyze interactions between characters and theme	Writing Activity: Analysis Speaking Activity: Discussion Writing Activity: Analysis Speaking Activity: Debate Writing Activity: Argument
Film by Penny Woolcock from *Macbeth on the Estate,* p. 293A	**The student will be able to...** analyze representations of a scene	Speaking Activity: Argument
History by Raphael Holinshed **Lexile 1630** from *Holinshed's Chronicles,* p. 295A	**The student will be able to...** analyze historical text	Speaking Activity: Discussion
Short Story by James Thurber **Lexile 580** "The Macbeth Murder Mystery," p. 301A	**The student will be able to...** analyze how an author draws on Shakespeare	Writing Activity: Narrative
Poem by Patricia Smith "5:00 P.M., Tuesday, August 23, 2005," p. 309A	**The student will be able to...** make and support inferences about word choice	Speaking Activity: Poetry Reading

Collection 5 Performance Tasks:
Write an Analytical Essay

Vocabulary Strategy	Language and Style	Student Instructional Support	CLOSE READER Selection
	Rhetorical Questions	**Scaffolding for ELL Students:** Analyze Argument and Rhetoric **When Students Struggle:** Understanding Unfamiliar Allusions **To Challenge Students:** Respond to Theme	
	Inverted Sentence Structure	**Scaffolding for ELL Students:** 214, 216, 217, 218, 222, 226, 228, 233, 236, 240, 243, 248, 254, 256, 262, 266, 270, 274, 286 **When Students Struggle:** 215, 219, 220, 223, 227, 229, 234, 238, 249, 252, 257, 258, 263, 265, 267, 269, 271, 275, 280, 283, 288 **To Challenge Students:** 224, 230, 239, 241, 246, 251, 264, 268, 273, 276	Drama by William Shakespeare from *The Tragedy of Macbeth*, p. 292b
		Scaffolding for ELL Students: Analyze Representations	
Archaic Language	Absolute Phrases	**Scaffolding for ELL Students:** Language **When Students Struggle:** • Use Images to Understand Text • Analyze Source Material • Absolute Phrases	
Words from Latin		**Scaffolding for ELL Students:** Language: Idioms **When Students Struggle:** How an Author Draws on Shakespeare **To Challenge Students:** Understanding Characters	
		Scaffolding for ELL Students: Vocabulary **When Students Struggle:** Extended Metaphor	

from Why Read Shakespeare?

Argument by Michael Mack

Why This Text?

Students will encounter different types of arguments and literature throughout their lives. This text addresses some of the reasons that people read literature in general and Shakespeare in particular.

View It!

Professional Development Podcast:

Teaching Argument

Key Learning Objective: The student will analyze the use of rhetoric in an argument.

Common Core Standards

RI 1 Cite textual evidence.

RI 4 Determine the meaning of words and phrases.

RI 5 Analyze how an author's ideas are developed by particular sentences or paragraphs.

RI 6 Determine an author's point of view and analyze how an author uses rhetoric.

RI 8 Delineate and evaluate the argument and specific claims in a text; identify false statements.

W 1 Write arguments using valid reasoning and relevant evidence.

SL 4 Present information clearly so that the development and style are appropriate to purpose, audience, and task.

L 3 Apply language in different contexts to make choices for style, and to comprehend more fully.

L 5 Demonstrate understanding of figurative language.

▲ Text Complexity Rubric

Quantitative Measures	*from* **Why Read Shakespeare?** **Lexile:** 980L
Qualitative Measures	**Levels of Meaning/Purpose** single purpose, explicitly stated
	Structure organization of main ideas and details complex, but clearly stated and generally sequential
	Language Conventionality and Clarity some unfamiliar, academic, or domain-specific words
	Knowledge Demands some references to other texts
Reader/Task Considerations	Teacher determined Vary by individual reader and type of text

Background Have students read the background information about the speech. Explain that a convocation is a general assembly that colleges typically have for freshmen students. Michael Mack, at the time of the 2008 speech, was the director of the University Honors Program and associate professor of English. In his speech, Mack presents his opinion on the value of reading Shakespeare in an effort to leave students eager to ask questions and seek meaningful answers about their educational experience.

AS YOU READ Direct students to use the As You Read statement to focus their reading.

Analyze Argument and Rhetoric (LINES 1–13)

COMMON CORE RI 6, RI 8

Sometimes the beginning of a speech includes an anecdote to warm up the audience. Other times, a speaker will begin by immediately making a claim and laying the groundwork for an argument.

Ⓐ CITE TEXT EVIDENCE Have students read the first five lines of the speech and identify the claim that Mack makes. *(Mack states that college should be a time for students to broaden their interests.)*

Explain that the goal of using a rhetorical technique is to engage the audience. Tell students that there are many different rhetorical techniques, including asking questions, using repetition, or adjusting the volume of one's voice.

Ⓑ ASK STUDENTS how the rhetorical questions in this section set the stage for Mack's argument and engage his audience. *(The first question [lines 2–3] introduces the topic; the second question [lines 7–8] appeals to the audience by showing the speaker's understanding of students' reluctance to read Shakespeare.)*

Background *In September 2008, a large freshman class gathered on the campus of the Catholic University of America (CUA) in Washington, D.C., to begin their college careers. As happens every September, the university faculty greeted them in a convocation. That year, the highlight of the gathering was a speech delivered by English professor* **Michael Mack.** *Mack began "Why Read Shakespeare?" with a disclosure: as a Shakespeare scholar, he was hardly objective. Still, he noted, the value of reading Shakespeare must, from time to time, be articulated.*

from Why Read Shakespeare?

Argument by Michael Mack

AS YOU READ Note each reason Mack provides to support his central argument that people should read Shakespeare. Write down any questions you generate during reading.

Ⓐ   If college is a time for asking questions, it also is a time for broadening your interests. Why should Shakespeare be one of those interests that you seek to develop at CUA? The obvious argument to the contrary is that reading Shakespeare is hard work—and not particularly rewarding, at least the first time round. I would like to begin by addressing what I take to be a perfectly honest response to a first reading of Shakespeare, namely "I don't get it; is it really worth the effort?"

Let me try to explain by comparing Shakespeare to music. We
10 all know that some kinds of music are easy on the ears. This is the ear candy that you like the very first time you hear it. And after you've heard it ten thousand times in twenty four hours, it turns into an ear worm that drives you crazy.

There also is music that you don't particularly like the first time you hear it. But, if you give it a chance, it grows on you. And you discover something new about it every time you listen. At a certain point, if you listen enough, you realize that what seemed random is   Ⓒ

SCAFFOLDING FOR ELL STUDENTS

Analyze Argument and Rhetoric Mack uses comparisons that his audience will relate to. In his comparing music to Shakespeare, Mack uses figurative language, or phrases that create sensory images. Ask students to explain the terms *ear candy (something that sounds sweet and easy to listen to but has no substance)* and *ear worm (a sound that wiggles its way into a person's mind).* Have students discuss how the use of the words *candy* and *worm* suggest images that are pleasant or disturbing.

TEACH

CLOSE READ

Analyze Argument and Rhetoric (LINES 16–20)

 COMMON CORE RI 6

Explain that comparison can be used as a rhetorical device. Sometimes the comparison is clear and direct, such as the speaker's comparison of listening to music and reading Shakespeare. Other times, the comparison uses language that requires further exploration.

C ASK STUDENTS to create a chart that lists terms that describe early and late reactions to listening to a piece of music.

First it seems:	Later it seems:
(random)	(complex)
(annoying)	(appealing, edgy)
(weird)	(strange, wonderful)

CRITICAL VOCABULARY

truncate: Mack refers to the short attention span of people today.

ASK STUDENTS to explain why having a truncated attention span might make reading Shakespeare's works difficult. (*Possible answer: Reading plays requires concentration and focused attention.*)

Analyze Argument

COMMON CORE RI 6

(LINES 50–59)

Explain that a good speaker often uses phrases that directly address an audience's potential concerns.

D ASK STUDENTS to analyze how Mack uses the rhetorical device of addressing a potential concern of his audience. (*Mack expresses his understanding about how his audience may feel about reading Shakespeare. He makes statements his audience will identify with ["I'm just a normal guy" and "I prefer something more scientific"] based on his assumption that his audience doesn't believe reading Shakespeare's works is for them.*)

204 Collection 5

---

really better described as "complex." What had been annoying now instead strikes you as appealingly edgy. And what initially seemed
20 weird now looks strangely wonderful. This is the way Shakespeare works. He gives you a serious headache the first time you try to understand him—and the second. But if you stick with him, you can expect a breakthrough, and the excitement and satisfaction of being able to say, "I get it."

The first time you listen to a piece of complex music, you hear but don't hear. Why should it be any surprise, then, that the first time people read Shakespeare they don't get it? What would be surprising—and a genuine cause for concern—would be if someone read Shakespeare and thought they'd understood him.
30 This phenomenon of people having difficulty understanding Shakespeare is hardly new. It predates by centuries our **truncated** attention spans and our preference for the fast cuts of modern video. It is a problem that the editors of the First Folio[1] addressed in 1623, just seven years after the death of Shakespeare. The editors, John Heminge and Henry Condell, were two of Shakespeare's fellow players and shareholders in the Globe.[2] Addressing the "great variety of readers" of the volume, they wrote:

> Read him, therefore; and again and again.
> And if then you do not like him, surely
40 you are in some manifest danger, not to
> understand him.

They did not expect readers to understand Shakespeare's works the first time they read them—and that's why they recommend rereading—"again and again." They recognize that Shakespeare is difficult, but they insist that he is worth the effort—and that if someone doesn't like Shakespeare, it's their fault, not his.

A Time for Exploring

The question Heminge and Condell don't answer—and the one I still haven't answered—is what you've understood when you've understood Shakespeare. When you get "it," what did you get?
50 I'd like to answer this by addressing in particular those who just don't see themselves as, well, the literary type. Some of you out there are thinking, "Reading Shakespeare—that's just not me: I'm just a normal guy, and the simple pleasures are good enough for me. Besides, what would my bowling buddies say?" I can hear others out there thinking, "I'm in a professional school, and I just want to get into my professional studies as quickly as

truncate
(trŭng′kāt) v. make shorter.

---

[1] **First Folio:** the first published collection of Shakespeare's plays.
[2] **the Globe:** the London theater at which Shakespeare was based.

204 Collection 5

APPLYING ACADEMIC VOCABULARY

comprise	thesis

As you discuss the speech, incorporate the following Collection 5 academic vocabulary words: *comprise* and *thesis*. As students discuss the speech, have them identify the arguments that **comprise** the speech. Then have students state the speech's **thesis** and identify the different arguments that support it.

E

possible." Still others are thinking, "I much prefer something more scientific—I believe in studying "real" things: fiction is fun to read on summer break, but . . ."

60   In response to these serious-minded objections to reading Shakespeare, I would like to suggest that what you find in Shakespeare is as serious as the subject matter of your other courses. We think of biology and chemistry, history and politics, psychology and sociology as subjects that are focused on the real world. Well, as with these subjects, Shakespeare offers us a lens on the real world in which we live.

In Shakespeare's time, great books were thought of as mirrors. When you read a great book, the idea is, you are looking into a mirror—a pretty special mirror, one that reflects the world in a way
70   that allows us to see its true nature. What is more, as we hold the volume of Shakespeare in front of us, we see that it reflects not only the world around us, but also ourselves. What is it that we find in Shakespeare? Nothing less than ourselves and the world—certainly worthy subjects to study in college.

Indeed, some of Shakespeare's **contemporaries** justified the seriousness of literary fictions by pointing out that Christ Himself used them. Take the parable of the prodigal son:[3] in this fiction you learn about sin and forgiveness. And you also learn about yourself. You realize that the story is about you—you are the prodigal son.
80   The problem is that you are not only the prodigal son but also the resentful, self-righteous older brother. As you interpret the

contemporary
(kən-těm′pə-rěr′ē) *n.*
one living at the
same time as.

---

[3] **parable of the prodigal son:** a New Testament story about a father who celebrates the return of a son who has squandered his birthright.

CLOSE READ

Analyze Word Choice   COMMON CORE RI 4, L 5
(LINES 55–66)

Remind students that words have **connotations,** which are the feelings or ideas associated with them, as well as **denotations,** which are their dictionary definitions. The words a writer chooses express the **tone,** or attitude, the writer has toward the subject.

Ⓔ **ASK STUDENTS** to discuss the denotation and connotation of *professional* and *scientific*. Then ask students to describe how Mack uses the meanings of the words and resulting tone to further develop his argument. *(Mack's use of "professional" and "scientific" in this context suggests that many people consider reading Shakespeare as entertainment and don't take it seriously as something that can be applied to life beyond college. Mack argues that Shakespeare is as relatable to the real world as any other subject is.)*

CRITICAL VOCABULARY

contemporary: The writer points out that Shakespeare's contemporaries also made arguments that people needed to take his work seriously.

ASK STUDENTS how the viewpoint(s) of Shakespeare's contemporaries supports Mack's thesis. *(Shakespeare's contemporaries argued that fiction should be taken seriously because Christ Himself used fiction in his teachings.)*

WHEN STUDENTS STRUGGLE . . .

One literary technique is to make allusions to literary works, historical events, or commonly held beliefs. Students may be unfamiliar with the story of the prodigal son. Provide these strategies to help students with unfamiliar allusions:

- Look for footnotes within the text that might explain the allusion.
- Conduct research to find a summary of the passage or an in-depth explanation.

ASK STUDENTS to explain how Mack's allusion to the prodigal son story helps develop his argument that literary fiction should be taken seriously. *(Mack suggests that interpreting fiction can help readers discover truths about themselves.)*

CLOSE READ

Analyze Argument

COMMON CORE **RI 4**

(LINES 88–106)

Inform students that one way to analyze an argument is to consider the reasons and examples a writer uses to strengthen an argument.

F CITE TEXT EVIDENCE Ask students to cite reasons that Mack uses to explain how learning about literature relates to learning about life. (*Learning about Macbeth's ambition helps readers see ambition in themselves [lines 88–91]; if one can better understand literature, one can better understand life [lines 93–94]; if one understands life, one can better understand literature [lines 95–96]; finding meaning in Shakespeare means one can find meaning in life [lines 98–100].*)

CRITICAL VOCABULARY

phantasmagoric: Mack characterizes Macbeth's behavior as being phantasmagoric.

ASK STUDENTS to describe a phantasmagoric state. (*having visions or hallucinations, sleepwalking, having difficulty understanding what is going on*)

vicarious: Mack says that readers can enjoy vicarious experiences by reading Shakespeare.

ASK STUDENTS to explain why Mack uses a flight simulator as an example of a vicarious experience and how that relates to reading Shakespeare. (*A flight simulator provides practice for real-world flying; reading Shakespeare provides practice for real-world experiences.*)

"What is it that we find in Shakespeare? Nothing less than ourselves and the world."

parable, you find that it interprets you—and in multiple ways. As you discover the true meaning of the parable you discover the truth about yourself.

In the case of *Macbeth*, we have a supreme reflection of ambition. But what makes the play terrifying is not that Macbeth looks like a fascist dictator[4]—a popular staging these days—but because he looks like us. If you don't see your own overreaching in the **phantasmagoric** restless ecstasy of Macbeth, you need to read

90   again. Either you don't understand the true nature of Macbeth's ambition or you don't know yourself. Or, quite possibly, both.

What we see in these examples is a fairly complex interplay of life and literature. Literature teaches you about life, and the better you understand literature, the better you understand life. It also is true, though, that the more you know about life, the better equipped you are to understand what you find in literature. This two-way mirroring means that learning about literature and learning about life go hand in hand. And it means that finding beauty and meaning in Shakespeare is a sort of proving ground for

100 finding beauty and meaning in life.

Indeed, as you learn to read Shakespeare, you are learning to read the world. As you interpret Shakespeare's characters, you are practicing figuring out life's characters. Struggling with the complexities involved in interpreting Shakespeare is a superb preparation for struggling with the complexities of life. Shakespeare offers a world of **vicarious** experience—a virtual reality, a sort of

phantasmagoric
(făn-tăzˊmə-gôrˊĭk)
adj. dreamlike or surreal.

vicarious
(vī-kârˊē-əs) *adj.*
seen through
the imagined
interpretations of
another.

---

[4] **fascist dictator:** authoritarian ruler of an oppressive, nationalistic government.

206 Collection 5

TO CHALLENGE STUDENTS . . .

Respond to Theme Have students respond to Mack's idea about the "interplay of life and literature" in lines 92–100.

- Have groups discuss what it means to say that finding meaning in Shakespeare "is a sort of proving ground for finding beauty and meaning in life." Ask students to provide reasons that support their claim.

- Invite students to debate which is more important—that literature teaches readers about life or that understanding life helps readers understand literature. Have students identify examples from literature they have read.

- Ask students to summarize their view of the interplay between literature and their own lives, explaining whether they see a connection and why.

flight simulator—that gives you a great advantage when it comes time to venture out into the real world.

So Shakespeare isn't just for literary types, he is for anyone who
110 is interested in navigating the real world. . . .

There is Knowledge and there is Knowledge

As I conclude, I would like to remind you that college isn't just about your head, it's also about the heart. And, returning to Shakespeare, I can say that he can be particularly helpful in understanding the heart. Read Shakespeare and spare yourself a world of bad dates.

Shakespeare shows how the head and the heart need each other. One of the most important things for you to come to understand is your own emotional life. Why do you feel the way you do? Have other people felt this way before? What have they done about it, and
120 how has it turned out?

By reading about the heart, your head and heart become more fully integrated. This integrity, when you understand what you feel and you hear with an understanding heart, is the mark of an educated person. . . .

So, again, "Why read Shakespeare?" I've proposed a link between getting to know Shakespeare and getting to know the world and ourselves. I encourage you to test out this hypothesis and to see if in becoming better at the art of reading Shakespeare, you become better at the art of living—to see if through reading
130 Shakespeare you become someone better equipped to find happiness in life, someone who more highly values what is truly valuable in life.

COLLABORATIVE DISCUSSION With a partner, discuss the reasons that Mack gives for why people should read Shakespeare. Cite specific evidence from the text to support your ideas.

CLOSE READ

Analyze Argument and Rhetoric (LINES 111–132)

COMMON CORE RI 8

Tell students that speakers and writers often conclude an argument by presenting ideas that both appeal to the audience's self-interest and support the author's claim.

G **ASK STUDENTS** to read the last few paragraphs of the speech and identify how Mack connects reading Shakespeare to the audience's self-interest. *(In lines 113–115, Mack states that reading Shakespeare can help students understand the heart and thus avoid bad dates.)* Then ask students to identify rhetorical questions Mack uses to connect with his audience. *(Why do you feel the way you do? Have other people felt this way before? What have they done about it, and how has it turned out? [lines 118–120])*

COLLABORATIVE DISCUSSION Have students pair up and discuss whether they agree with the reasons Mack gives for why people should read Shakespeare. Then have partners share their thoughts with the class as a whole.

ASK STUDENTS to share any questions they generated in the course of reading and discussing the selection.

APPLYING ACADEMIC VOCABULARY

priority	ultimate

As you discuss the speech, incorporate the following Collection 5 academic vocabulary words: *priority* and *ultimate*. Have students respond to the ideas within the argument as if they were giving Mack a critique. Students should identify the **ultimate** argument and then list additional arguments in order of decreasing **priority.** Students may even suggest arguments or examples that should be left out of the speech.

PRACTICE & APPLY

Analyze Argument and Rhetoric

COMMON CORE RI 6, RI 8

Help students understand the terms. Once students have examined the speech, have them summarize the claims. *(Shakespeare is difficult to understand, but his works can teach us about the world and ourselves. We can learn about life through literature. Reading Shakespeare prepares us to handle life's challenges.)*

Help students understand the different techniques a speaker can use to appeal to a specific audience. Ask students to consider ways the writer uniquely addresses the audience of college freshmen.

Analyze Argument and Rhetoric

COMMON CORE RI 6, RI 8

"Why Read Shakespeare?" is an **argument** in which the author attempts to persuade an audience to agree with his point of view. Michael Mack states a **claim,** or thesis, and supports it with valid reasoning and relevant evidence. He also makes these rhetorical choices, which appeal directly to his audience of college freshmen.

- The author directly addresses his audience's **potential concerns.** "Some of you out there are thinking, 'Reading Shakespeare—that's just not me: I'm just a normal guy, and the simple pleasures are good enough for me. Besides, what would my bowling buddies say?'" How might this question appeal to his audience?
- The author uses **comparisons** that his audience will relate to. He begins the speech by comparing Shakespeare to music. What assumption is the author making about his audience by using this comparison?
- The author appeals directly to the audience's **self-interest.** He explains that reading Shakespeare can ultimately help students understand matters of the heart: "Read Shakespeare and spare yourself a world of bad dates."

Analyzing the Text

COMMON CORE RI 1, RI 4, RI 5, RI 6, RI 8

Possible answers:

1. *Lines 35–46 refer to Heminge's and Condell's notion that people should read Shakespeare's works more than once in order to understand them. This suggests to current readers that they too will find reading Shakespeare difficult but worth the effort.*

2. *"Ear candy" is something that is easy to listen to. Mack uses this contemporary expression to connect to the audience of college students.*

3. *Mack operates on the assumption that literature teaches the reader about life. In lines 88–91, Mack states that readers should see their "own overreaching" in Macbeth's ambition. In addition, interpreting Shakespeare's characters gives the reader practice "figuring out life's characters" (lines 102–103).*

4. *Mack wanted to challenge the audience to test the hypothesis that becoming better at reading Shakespeare will result in becoming better at living.*

Analyzing the Text

COMMON CORE RI 1, RI 4, RI 5, RI 6, RI 8, W 1, SL 4

Cite Text Evidence Support your responses with evidence from the selection.

1. **Identify** Why did Shakespeare's contemporaries recommend rereading his works, and what might this information suggest to current readers?

2. **Infer** Mack uses the term "ear candy" in line 11. What does he mean by this term? How might the term appeal to his audience?

3. **Cite Evidence** What evidence does the author provide to support the claim that Shakespeare's works reflect the world and ourselves?

4. **Analyze** The author concludes the speech with a kind of challenge to his audience. Review lines 125–132, and then explain why he included this content.

PERFORMANCE TASK

Speaking Activity: Argument In his speech to college freshmen, Mack presents his opinion on the value of reading Shakespeare. Evaluate how successfully he appeals to his audience by writing and delivering a brief speech of your own.

- Present an argument about whether Mack succeeds in achieving the ultimate purpose of persuading his audience to read Shakespeare.
- Cite text evidence to discuss whether Mack's style and tone appeal to you as a student and whether you find the comparisons he makes relevant.

Assign this performance task.

PERFORMANCE TASK

COMMON CORE W 1, SL 4

Speaking Activity: Argument Have students work individually to write their speeches. Then have students practice giving their speeches in small groups and providing feedback to one another before presenting their speeches to the entire class.

Critical Vocabulary

truncate   contemporary   phantasmagoric   vicarious

Practice and Apply Complete the sentences to demonstrate your understanding of each Critical Vocabulary word.

1. When it comes to Shakespeare, our **truncated** attention spans might make it difficult to . . .

2. A **contemporary** of Shakespeare's may have understood the language in his works because . . .

3. Many readers like the **phantasmagoric** scenes in Shakespeare's plays because . . .

4. We get a **vicarious** thrill out of reading fiction because . . .

Language and Style: Rhetorical Questions

Rhetorical questions are questions that do not require a reply. Writers use them to suggest that their arguments make the answers to the questions obvious or self-evident. In "Why Read Shakespeare?" Michael Mack uses rhetorical questions for three distinct purposes: to engage the audience, to introduce a topic, and to make a point. For example, note Mack's use of a rhetorical question in lines 26–27:

> **Why should it be any surprise, then, that the first time people read Shakespeare they don't get it?**

The author asks this question to appeal to the audience, to let them know that he understands their reluctance to read Shakespeare. He doesn't really expect an answer. Now look at this example from line 49:

> **When you get "it," what did you get?**

This question also does not require an answer. Instead, it introduces a topic in a way that allows the listener to follow the argument.

In this example (lines 72–74), Mack asks a rhetorical question and then immediately answers it:

> **What is it that we find in Shakespeare? Nothing less than ourselves and the world—certainly worthy subjects to study in college.**

Here, the author reasons aloud to state one of the points of his argument.

Practice and Apply Look back at the speech you wrote for this selection's Performance Task. Revise your speech to add at least two rhetorical questions. Present your revised speech to a partner and discuss the effectiveness of the rhetorical questions.

PRACTICE & APPLY

Critical Vocabulary

Possible answers:

1. *When it comes to Shakespeare, our **truncated** attention spans might make it difficult to stay focused and put in the effort required to understand Shakespeare.*

2. *A **contemporary** of Shakespeare's may have understood the language in his works because he or she would have used similar language in everyday speech.*

3. *Many readers like the **phantasmagoric** scenes in Shakespeare's plays because they portray characters existing in a dreamlike state.*

4. *We get a **vicarious** thrill out of reading fiction because it is fun to imagine living a life as a different person.*

Language and Style: Rhetorical Questions

Be sure students understand the purposes of Mack's rhetorical questions in his speech. Then have students review their own speeches to find sections of text that specifically engage the audience, introduce the topic, and make a point. Have students rework the text to incorporate rhetorical questions in at least two parts of their speech. Challenge students to use rhetorical questions for two different purposes.

Answer:

Revisions will vary. Students' speeches should include the addition of at least two rhetorical questions.

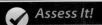 **Assess It!**

Online Selection Test
- Download an editable ExamView bank.
- Assign and manage this test online.

INTERACTIVE WHITEBOARD LESSON
Identify Fallacious Reasoning

 COMMON CORE

RI 8

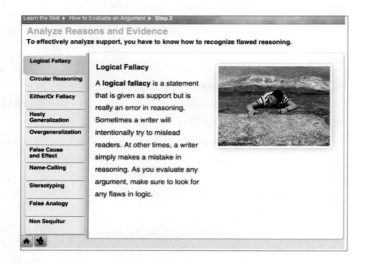

TEACH

Before having students write their arguments for the Performance Task, review the different types of logical fallacies, including the following:

- **False Cause and Effect:** This suggests that one event causes another. Although the two events are presented as being related, they do not have a cause-and-effect relationship.
- **Overgeneralization:** This kind of statement oversimplifies and does not take into consideration all the variables. Or it bases a conclusion on just a few variables. Words such as *all* or *never* are often used in overgeneralizations.
- **Either/Or Fallacy:** In this type of argument, the writer presents only two possible outcomes or viewpoints when more actually exist.

COLLABORATIVE DISCUSSION

Have pairs of students discuss Mack's comment from lines 114–115: "Read Shakespeare and save yourself a world of bad dates." Have students identify the logical fallacy used and revise the statement without using logical fallacies.

Analyze Argument and Rhetoric

 COMMON CORE

RI 6, RI 8

RETEACH

Review the terms *argument, claim, potential concerns, comparisons,* and *self-interest.* Then give an example from the text that raises a potential concern, such as the statement in lines 3–4 that "reading Shakespeare is hard work—and not particularly rewarding."

- Have students describe how Mack addresses this potential concern. *(He agrees with the concern and then says that eventually it will be worth the effort.)*
- Ask students to explain how this potential concern appeals to the self-interest of this audience. *(This is a concern that college students are likely to have. When Mack responds to this concern, he shows why reading Shakespeare would matter to this particular audience.)*

LEVEL UP TUTORIALS Assign the following *Level Up* tutorial: **Analyzing Arguments**

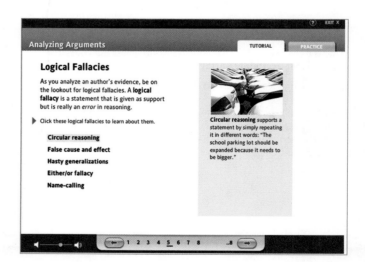

CLOSE READING APPLICATION

Have students apply the skill as they analyze the arguments that Mack makes. Direct students to work independently to identify rhetorical devices Mack uses to appeal directly to his audience. Ask students which of the three rhetorical choices (potential concerns, comparisons, and self-interest) Mack uses most effectively and which rhetorical choice Mack could have used more (or less) of in order to strengthen his argument.

*my*SmartPlanner   Create lesson plans and access resources online.

ANCHOR TEXT The Tragedy of Macbeth

Play by William Shakespeare

Why This Text?

Students regularly see dramatic presentations, whether in the movies, on television, or onstage. *The Tragedy of Macbeth* features many elements students may be familiar with, such as complex characters, a compelling plot, and themes that relate to real life. Students can experience the power and beauty of Shakespeare's language.

▶ **View It!**

Professional Development Podcast:

Text Complexity

Key Learning Objective: The student will be able to analyze interactions between characters and theme.

For additional practice:

Close Reader selection:
from The Tragedy of Macbeth

COMMON CORE Common Core Standards

RL 1 Cite textual evidence.

RL 2 Determine a theme and analyze its development; provide a summary of the text.

RL 3 Analyze how complex characters develop, interact, and develop a theme.

RL 4 Determine the meaning of words and phrases, including figurative language.

RL 5 Analyze an author's choices concerning structure.

RI 7 Analyze various accounts told in different mediums.

W 1 Write argument in an analysis.

W 2 Write informative essays to examine complex ideas.

SL 1 Participate in collaborative discussions and refer to evidence from texts to stimulate ideas.

L 3 Apply knowledge of language to understand its functions, make effective choices, and comprehend more fully.

L 5 Demonstrate understanding of figurative language.

L 5a Interpret figures of speech and analyze their role.

▲ Text Complexity Rubric

Quantitative Measures	**The Tragedy of Macbeth** Lexile: N/A
Qualitative Measures	**Levels of Meaning/Purpose** ●—●—●—●—▶ multiple levels of meaning
	Structure ●—●—●—●—▶ somewhat complex story concepts
	Language Conventionality and Clarity ●—●—●—●—▶ archaic, unfamiliar language
	Knowledge Demands ●—●—●—●—▶ somewhat unfamiliar experience and situation, fairly complex theme
Reader/Task Considerations	Teacher determined Vary by individual reader and type of text

Characteristics of Shakespearean Tragedy

Tragic Heroes

Explain that a tragic hero usually exhibits extraordinary abilities, such as bravery, but also has a tragic flaw, or a fatal error in judgment or weakness of character, that leads directly to his or her downfall. Not all tragedies end with a tragic hero's death; however, the tragic hero's unhappy end usually involves a loss of some kind. Although the tragic hero is an important person in society, the tragic flaw he or she has is not unique to the right and powerful. On some level, every reader or audience member identifies with the hero's tragic flaw. Encourage students to pay particular attention to how the choices Macbeth makes and the motivations for those choices set up his ultimate fate.

Dramatic Conventions

To help students understand the dramatic conventions, review the following:

- Both soliloquies and asides often hint at future plot events. While the stage directions indicate an aside, they do not indicate a soliloquy. Stage directions can show whether a character is on stage alone. A soliloquy will often occur after a stage direction indicates for the other characters to exit. Often, the tension between the character's words and the audience's responses reflects or heightens an internal conflict.

- Project on the whiteboard the beginning of Act I Scene 5. Point to the stage directions that indicate Lady Macbeth is alone on the stage. After she reads the letter, which is set off by quotation marks, she expresses her thoughts about the prophecies.

- Tell students that irony is a contrast between appearance or expectations and reality. In dramatic irony what appears to be true to one or more characters is known to be false by the audience because the audience has a more complete picture of the plot and characters.

- Give students an example of a real-life situation in which one group is aware of something another is not, such as a surprise party.

Shakespearean Drama

One reason Shakespeare's works have endured for over 400 years may be that his characters—figures from history and his imagination—transcend any particular time or place. Many of these characters are **archetypes**—familiar character types that appear over and over again in literature. The scheming characters and conspiracies at the heart of *The Tragedy of Macbeth* are as relevant today as they were in Shakespeare's time.

Characteristics of Shakespearean Tragedy

A **tragedy** is a drama in which a series of actions leads to the downfall of the main character, called the **tragic hero**. The plot builds to a **catastrophe,** or a disastrous final outcome, that usually involves the death of the hero and many others. To create suspense before this inevitable outcome and to help the audience understand the characters, Shakespeare used certain dramatic conventions, including dramatic irony, the soliloquy, and the aside.

Main Character	Dramatic Conventions
Tragic Hero • is of high social rank—a king, a prince, or a general • has a **tragic flaw**—an error in judgment or a character defect—that ultimately leads to his or her downfall • suffers complete ruin or death • faces his or her downfall with courage and dignity	**Dramatic Irony** • results when the audience knows more than one or more of the characters—for example, Duncan does not know that Macbeth is plotting against him, but the audience does • helps build suspense **Soliloquy** • is a speech given by a character alone on stage, used to reveal his or her private thoughts and feelings • may help the audience understand a character's motivation **Aside** • is a character's remark, either to the audience or to another character, that no one else on stage is supposed to hear • lets the audience in on a character's thoughts or secrets

WHEN STUDENTS STRUGGLE . . .

Language Review these literary terms with students.

plot: the series of related events that happen in a play or other narrative

conflict: a clash or struggle that drives the plot and must be resolved

antagonist: a character who opposes the hero (protagonist)

resolution: the part of the play in which the conflict or problems are settled

ASK STUDENTS to create a three-column chart. In the first two columns, have them list the terms and definitions. As they read the play, have them complete the third column with an example of each.

The Language of Shakespeare

Shakespearean language can be challenging because of its unfamiliar vocabulary and sentence structure, but it shouldn't stop you from getting caught up in the intriguing plot that drives *Macbeth*. Here are some keys to reading Shakespeare's language:

Blank Verse Shakespeare's plays are **verse dramas,** in which most of the dialogue is written in the metrical patterns of poetry. Shakespeare wrote primarily in **blank verse,** or unrhymed lines of iambic pentameter. **Iambic pentameter** is a pattern of rhythm that has five unstressed syllables (˘), each followed by a stressed syllable (′). Read these lines aloud, noticing how the rhythm mimics that of everyday speech:

> ˘ ′ ˘ ′ ˘ ′ ˘ ′ ˘ ′
> *God's benison go with you and with those*
> ˘ ′ ˘ ′ ˘ ′ ˘ ′ ˘ ′
> *That would make good of bad and friends of foes.*

Most of *Macbeth* is written in blank verse. In some places, however, Shakespeare broke the pattern to vary the rhythm, create dramatic tension, or distinguish low-ranking characters from those of higher rank.

Rhetorical Devices *Macbeth* is about power, ambition, and betrayal. The characters are constantly trying to persuade themselves, each other, and the audience of the rightness of their cause. As a result, the play is full of speeches that make masterful use of rhetorical devices, such as repetition, parallelism, and rhetorical questions.

Rhetorical Device	Example
REPETITION the use of words and phrases more than once to emphasize ideas	Thrice to thine, and thrice to mine And thrice again, to make up nine. —Act I, Scene 3, lines 35–36
PARALLELISM the repetition of grammatical structures to express ideas that are related or of equal importance	When the hurly-burly's done, When the battle's lost and won. —Act I, Scene 1, lines 3–4
RHETORICAL QUESTIONS the use of questions that require no answer to make the speaker's rightness seem self-evident	Do you not hope your children shall be kings When those that gave the Thane of Cawdor to me Promised no less to them? —Act I, Scene 3, lines 118–120

TO CHALLENGE STUDENTS . . .

Create Blank Verse Have students work in pairs to write several lines of blank verse. Give them a topic or allow them to choose their own. Remind students that although the meter should be a consistent iambic pentameter, there is no rhyme scheme. Have students mark their verses as in the example. Then invite pairs to share their lines with the class. Discuss the process of writing blank verse and the challenges that a writer might face.

The Language of Shakespeare

Blank Verse

To help students hear the stressed and unstressed syllables and to hear that blank verse is very close to the natural rhythms of English, read the two lines of iambic pentameter aloud. Explain that thoughts expressed in blank verse do not always appear as in this example—a sentence presented in one end-stopped line. Some sentences can stretch across several lines and can begin or end in the middle of a line, which is called an enjambment. Shakespeare usually uses blank verse, but sometimes he departs from it into either rhymed verse or prose. Tell students that when they read a passage in rhymed verse or prose, they should pause to figure out what point he is making or what he is trying to emphasize.

Rhetorical Devices

Explain that writers use rhetorical devices for emphasis and persuasion. Review the definitions and examples. Ask students to explain the effect of each example.

Then ask students to provide their own examples of each device. Write their examples on the board and ask them to describe the effect. Begin by illustrating repetition using the following sentence:

We are born to sorrow, pass our time in sorrow, end our days in sorrow.

Have students identify the repeated word and explain what the repetition accomplishes. *(sorrow; There is no avoiding sorrow—it is very much part of life.)*

Reading Shakespearean Drama

Reading Drama

Project page 214 or have students turn to that page. Point out the cast of characters, and explain that returning to the cast of characters as they read can help them remember who each character is and how they are related to each other.

Tell students to pay close attention to the stage directions as they provide important information about the setting, the action, and the characters. Stage directions will also point out asides and help them determine when dialogue is a soliloquy.

Project page 218 or have students turn to that page. Then have them identify examples of stage directions and dialogue. Ask students what sounds and movements are described. *(drums are beating; the witches are dancing in a circle)* Ask them how they know which events and dialogue occur before and after Macbeth and Banquo arrive. *(The stage directions note when the two men enter the scene.)*

Remind students to pay attention to the elements of tragedy as they read. Tell them to look for examples of foreshadowing, or clues that help readers predict the tragic outcome of the play. Have students share examples of foreshadowing from movies they've seen or books they've read.

Elizabethan Words to Know

Read each word aloud for students. Have them repeat the words. Then write this sentence on the board:

The king's issue never ere durst fly. So wherefore would he fly to thine home anon?

Have students identify which words can be replaced with entries from the glossary. Rewrite the sentence with their suggestions. *(The king's child never before dared to run away. So why would he flee to your home soon?)*

Remind students that Shakespeare also uses outdated grammatical forms, unusual word order, and unfamiliar vocabulary. Tell them to read carefully and stop periodically to summarize text in their own words to ensure understanding.

Reading Shakespearean Drama

Understanding Shakespearean drama can be challenging for modern readers. Use these strategies to help you appreciate and analyze *Macbeth*.

- Study the opening **cast of characters,** which in *Macbeth* will tell you the characters' ranks and how they are related to one another.

- Try to visualize the setting and action by using information in the **stage directions** and **dialogue.**

- Keep track of the characters, and think about what the words and actions reveal about their traits. Pay attention in particular to the actions and motivations of Macbeth and Lady Macbeth. At the end, consider how closely each fits the model of a **tragic hero**.

- Note examples of **foreshadowing,** and use each to predict events and better understand the characters' personalities.

- Use the **side notes** to understand unfamiliar words and expressions.

- Remember that the end of a line does not necessarily mean the end of a thought. Look closely at each line's punctuation, and try to figure out the meaning of the complete sentence or phrase.

- Paraphrase passages to help you understand characters' public personas as well as their private schemes. When you **paraphrase** a passage, you restate its key points in your own words.

Elizabethan Words to Know

Here are words that you will encounter often while reading *Macbeth*:

anon: soon	**naught:** nothing	**thither:** there
durst: dared	**nigh:** near	**'twixt:** between
ere: before	**perchance:** maybe	**whence:** where
fly: flee, run away	**prithee:** please	**wherefore:** why
hark: listen	**thence:** there	**whither:** where
hie: hurry	**thine:** your, yours	**withal:** also
issue: child, offspring		

WHEN STUDENTS STRUGGLE . . .

Encourage students to read slowly and paraphrase frequently to ensure their understanding of the plot and characters. Project lines 16–23 from Act I Scene 1 on the whiteboard. Paraphrase the first two lines, modeling for students how to use the marginal notes and the context. *(Macbeth used his bloody sword to bravely fight his way to face the rebel lord.)* Have students work with partners to paraphrase the remaining lines. Ask volunteers to share their paraphrases with the class. If students struggle, paraphrase the lines as a class.

Encourage students to take notes about Macbeth and Lady Macbeth as they read. Have them create a three-column chart for each character. Label each column "Act/Scene," "Actions," and "What Actions Reveal."

Biography Have students read the biography of Shakespeare. Explain that although Shakespeare wrote his tragedies, comedies, and histories centuries ago, they explore characters and universal themes that speak to people across the ages and around the world—not just Elizabethan England. His works continue to be widely read in classrooms and by casual readers and scholars, and his plays are frequently staged and regularly adapted to film. His popularity is not limited to the English-speaking world—his works have been adapted across a wide range of languages and cultures. Because of his timeless characters and themes, as well as the beauty of his language and style, Shakespeare is considered one of the most influential and famous English authors. As 16th century fellow playwright and friend Ben Jonson so aptly wrote in the preface to the First Folio, Shakespeare was the "Soule of the Age! The applause! delight! The wonder of our stage!"

Analyze Accounts in Different Mediums

 COMMON CORE **RI 7**

After students have read the biography of Shakespeare on this page, have them view the A&E video biography accessible through their eBooks. Ask students to discuss which details and ideas about Shakespeare's life are emphasized in each biography. Follow up by asking students how the nature of each medium might emphasize different aspects of Shakespeare's life.

The Tragedy of Macbeth

Drama by William Shakespeare

William Shakespeare *(1564–1616) was born in Stratford-upon-Avon to a fairly prosperous family. He attended the local grammar school, where he received a solid grounding in Latin and classical literature. When he was eighteen, he married Anne Hathaway. They had a daughter and then twins, a boy and a girl.*

Sometime around 1590, Shakespeare left Stratford for London. He found work as an actor and began what was to be a highly successful career as a playwright. He belonged to a theater company known as the Lord Chamberlain's Men, which performed for Queen Elizabeth I; this company also renovated a theater known as the Globe for their own performances. Shakespeare's success enabled him to buy a house for his family in Stratford. He lived in that house after his retirement in 1612 but continued to write until his death four years later at the age of fifty-two.

Shakespeare is recognized as the most influential writer in the English language. He mastered the sonnet form, making it his own with his highly original approach; he composed long narrative poems; and he left a dramatic legacy unsurpassed by any playwright before or since. Four centuries later, his plays continue to be performed on stage and made into films.

Shakespeare's plays are often grouped based on when they were written. In the early 1590s, he wrote history plays and comedies with plots derived from earlier stories. In the late 1590s, he wrote comedies, including A Midsummer Night's Dream, *in which he skillfully interwove complex plots to convey his themes. As the century ended, Shakespeare began exploring darker views of human nature in his work. Between 1600 and 1607, he wrote his greatest tragedies, including* Macbeth, Hamlet, *and* King Lear. *His later comedies, such as* The Tempest, *are often called tragicomedies, as they are tinged with sadness.*

After Shakespeare died, his plays were published in an edition known as the First Folio. *In the introduction, playwright Ben Jonson wrote that Shakespeare "was not of an age, but for all time."*

Image Credits: (r) ©Alfredo Dagli Orti/The Art Archive/Corbis; (c) ©Henry Steadman/Photolibrary/Getty Images; (l) ©Stockbyte/Getty Images

---

Close Read Screencasts   ▶ *View It!*

Modeled Discussion

Have students click the *Close Read* icons in their eBooks to access a screencast in which readers discuss and annotate the following key passage:

- Lady Macbeth discussing the impending death of Duncan (Scene 5, lines 35–44)

As a class, view and discuss this video.

TEACH

CLOSE READ

Background Shakespeare's *The Tragedy of Macbeth* has been performed on stage and in film countless times. The play has even been adapted to settings other than 11th century Scotland. In a 2010 adaptation, the play was set in a mid 20th century military society. In a 2006 adaptation of the play, all the main characters are gangsters in modern-day Austria.

Analyze Structure

Remind students that Shakespeare's plays, like most dramas, include a cast list, as well as brief descriptions noting societal roles or relationships between the major characters. Explain that some playwrights also include brief descriptions of the characters to help readers visualize them.

Ⓐ ASK STUDENTS to identify who Duncan is. *(The King of Scotland)* Tell them to explain who Macbeth is in relation to Duncan. *(Macbeth is one of the noblemen serving under Duncan.)* Ask them how understanding this relationship will help them as they read. What might they predict based on the character descriptions? (Macbeth might come into conflict with his king or one of his own peers.)

Explain that, along with the cast of characters, playwrights usually provide information about the setting at the beginning of the text.

Ⓑ ASK STUDENTS to identify what additional information is provided on this page. *(The time and place; Macbeth takes place in 11th century Scotland and England.)*

Background *It is believed that Shakespeare wrote* Macbeth *largely to please King James I. The Scottish-born king claimed to be descended from an 11th-century historical figure named Banquo. In* Macbeth, *the witches predict that Banquo will sire a long line of kings. James's interest in witchcraft—he wrote a book on the subject in 1597—may explain the prominence of the witches in the play. The play also addressed James's fears of assassination; he had survived several attempts on his life.*

THE TIME: The 11th century   **THE PLACE:** Scotland and England Ⓑ

CHARACTERS

Ⓐ **Duncan,** King of Scotland

His Sons
 Malcolm
 Donalbain

Ⓐ *Noblemen of Scotland*
 Macbeth
 Banquo
 Macduff
 Lennox
 Ross
 Menteith (měn-tēth´)
 Angus
 Caithness (kāth´nĭs)
Fleance (flā´əns), son to Banquo
Siward (syōō´ərd), earl of Northumberland, general of the English forces
Young Siward, his son

Seyton (sā´tən), an officer attending on Macbeth
Son, to Macduff
An English Doctor
A Scottish Doctor
A Porter
An Old Man
Three Murderers
Lady Macbeth
Lady Macduff
A Gentlewoman attending on Lady Macbeth
Hecate (hěk´ĭt), goddess of witchcraft
Three Witches
Apparitions
Lords, Officers, Soldiers, Messengers, and Attendants

Image Credits: ©AKG Images

SCAFFOLDING FOR ELL STUDENTS

Comprehension: Character Relationships Help students understand relationships between characters. Have students work in pairs to make a graphic representation of the cast of characters. For example, they can represent the relationship between Duncan and his noblemen as a family tree, using purple lines to denote royalty; within this large family tree they can show blood relations with red lines. Point out that not everyone will be connected to this large tree. Characters whose relationships are unknown, such as the Witches, Apparitions, and Murderers, can be included in the periphery with question marks.

ASK STUDENTS to make predictions about what will happen in the play, based on the cast of characters and their relationships.

AS YOU READ Notice the reactions of Macbeth and Banquo to the witches' words. Write down any questions you generate during reading.

ACT I

Scene 1 *An open place in Scotland.*

[*Thunder and lightning. Enter three* Witches.]

First Witch. When shall we three meet again?
In thunder, lightning, or in rain?

Second Witch. When the hurly-burly's done,
When the battle's lost and won.

5 **Third Witch.** That will be ere the set of sun.

First Witch. Where the place?

Second Witch.   Upon the heath.

Third Witch. There to meet with Macbeth.

First Witch. I come, Graymalkin.

Second Witch. Paddock calls.

Third Witch.   Anon.

10 **All.** Fair is foul, and foul is fair,
Hover through the fog and filthy air.

[*They exit.*]

Scene 2 *King Duncan's camp near the battlefield.*

[*Alarum within. Enter* King Duncan, Malcolm, Donalbain,
Lennox, *with* Attendants, *meeting a bleeding* Captain.]

Duncan. What bloody man is that? He can report,
As seemeth by his plight, of the revolt
The newest state.

Malcolm.   This is the sergeant
Who, like a good and hardy soldier, fought
5 'Gainst my captivity.—Hail, brave friend!
Say to the King the knowledge of the broil
As thou didst leave it.

Captain.   Doubtful it stood,
As two spent swimmers that do cling together
And choke their art. The merciless Macdonwald
10 (Worthy to be a rebel, for to that
The multiplying villainies of nature
Do swarm upon him) from the Western Isles
Of kerns and gallowglasses is supplied;

3 hurly-burly: turmoil; uproar.

8–9 Graymalkin . . . Paddock: two demon helpers in the form of a cat and a toad; **Anon:** at once.

[Stage Direction] Alarum within: the sound of a trumpet offstage, a signal that soldiers should arm themselves.

5 'Gainst my captivity: to save me from capture.

6 broil: battle.

9–13 Macdonwald's evils (**multiplying villainies**) swarm like insects around him. His army consists of soldiers (**kerns and gallowglasses**) from the Hebrides (**Western Isles**).

The Tragedy of Macbeth: Act I, Scene 2   **215**

WHEN STUDENTS STRUGGLE...

Point out that in lines 1–44 of Scene 2, Malcolm and Duncan learn about a bloody battle. Have students complete a chart like the one below.

Who led the battle?	Macbeth and Banquo on one side; Macdonwald, the King of Norway on the other
What does Duncan learn about Macbeth?	Macbeth fought bravely (and brutally) to defeat the opposing armies.
Where does Duncan learn this information?	at a camp near the battlefield
Why does Duncan order Cawdor's execution?	he is a traitor; he helped the King of Norway
How does Duncan plan to reward Macbeth?	He will make Macbeth the new Thane of Cawdor.

TEACH

CLOSE READ

AS YOU READ Have students notice the reactions of Macbeth and Banquo to the witches' words. Have them write down any questions they generate during reading.

Analyze Theme (Scene 1, line 10)   RL 2

Remind students the theme is the message about life or humanity the author wants to share with the reader. A work of literature, especially one as complex and intense as *Macbeth,* can have multiple themes. Direct students' attention to line 10, and have them read it aloud.

C ASK STUDENTS what the three witches mean. *(They are saying that things are not as they appear: what seems fair is actually foul and what seems foul is actually fair.)* Then ask students to make a prediction about the significance of this statement to the drama as a whole. *(Answers will vary. Students may predict that it could become a theme.)*

Determine Figurative Meanings (Scene 2, lines 8–9)   RL 4

Remind students that figurative language is not to be read literally. An author uses figurative language, such as metaphors and similes, in order to compare two things to help a reader better understand difficult or unfamiliar ideas. Have students read the lines that compare the battle to two exhausted swimmers clinging to each other.

D ASK STUDENTS to identify the figurative language in these lines and to explain what comparison Shakespeare is making. *(He is using a simile to compare the two warring armies to two exhausted swimmers who are clinging to each other.)* Ask students to explain what idea Shakespeare is trying to communicate through this simile. *(He is showing how each army is so exhausted that it is barely able to carry on the fight. Each army also feels it is near defeat.)*

Analyze Character

COMMON CORE RL 3

(LINES 16–23)

Remind students that authors don't always explicitly say what they mean. Readers must use details from the text to make inferences, or logical assumptions, about the characters or actions. Have students reread lines 16–23.

 CITE TEXT EVIDENCE Tell students to explain what the Captain says Macbeth has done to Macdonwald. *(He has slain the rebel lord Macdonwald.)* Have students use details in the Captain's description of the act to make inferences about Macbeth, citing evidence in the text to support their inference. *(Macbeth is brave, but the description "with his brandished steel, which smoked with bloody execution" shows that he is a ruthless and violent person. Without addressing his foe, Macbeth "unseam(s) him," or slices him open from his stomach to his jaw, and then puts his head on the castle walls.)* Then have students compare their inferences to the description of a tragic hero in the introduction to Shakespearean tragedy. *(Macbeth is an important person with "extraordinary abilities.")*

And Fortune, on his damnèd quarrel smiling,
15 Showed like a rebel's whore. But all's too weak;
For brave Macbeth (well he deserves that name),
Disdaining Fortune, with his brandished steel,
Which smoked with bloody execution,
Like valor's minion, carved out his passage
20 Till he faced the slave;
Which ne'er shook hands, nor bade farewell to him,
Till he unseamed him from the nave to th' chops,
And fixed his head upon our battlements.

Duncan. O valiant cousin, worthy gentleman!

25 **Captain.** As whence the sun 'gins his reflection
Shipwracking storms and direful thunders break,
So from that spring whence comfort seemed to come
Discomfort swells. Mark, King of Scotland, mark:
No sooner justice had, with valor armed,
30 Compelled these skipping kerns to trust their heels,
But the Norweyan lord, surveying vantage,
With furbished arms and new supplies of men,
Began a fresh assault.

Duncan. Dismayed not this our captains, Macbeth and Banquo?

35 **Captain.** Yes, as sparrows eagles, or the hare the lion.
If I say sooth, I must report they were
As cannons overcharged with double cracks,
So they doubly redoubled strokes upon the foe.
Except they meant to bathe in reeking wounds
40 Or memorize another Golgotha,
I cannot tell—
But I am faint. My gashes cry for help.

Duncan. So well thy words become thee as thy wounds:
They smack of honor both.—Go, get him surgeons.

[*The* Captain *is led off by* Attendants.]
[*Enter* Ross *and* Angus.]
45 Who comes here?

Malcolm.   The worthy Thane of Ross.

Lennox. What a haste looks through his eyes!
So should he look that seems to speak things strange.

Ross. God save the King.

Duncan. Whence cam'st thou, worthy thane?

50 **Ross.** From Fife, great king,
Where the Norweyan banners flout the sky

19 valor's minion: the favorite of valor, meaning the bravest of all.

22 unseamed him . . . chops: split him open from the navel to the jaw.

25–28 As the rising sun is sometimes followed by storms, a new assault on Macbeth began.

36 sooth: the truth.

37 double cracks: a double load of ammunition.

39–40 The officer claims he cannot decide whether (**except**) Macbeth and Banquo wanted to bathe in blood or make the battlefield as famous as Golgotha, the site of Christ's crucifixion.

45 Thane: a Scottish noble.

49–59 Ross has arrived from Fife, where Norway's troops had invaded. There the king of Norway, with the Thane of Cawdor, met Macbeth (described as the husband of **Bellona**, the goddess of war). Macbeth, in heavy armor (**proof**), challenged the enemy.

SCAFFOLDING FOR ELL STUDENTS

Vocabulary: Connotations English Language Learners may need guidance in understanding how a word's connotation, or associated feelings, can help readers understand or visualize a character. Using a whiteboard, project lines 16–23. Have volunteers read the lines aloud. If necessary, help them define the words or understand the scene. Then Invite volunteers to do the following:

- Highlight words that have a positive connotation regarding Macbeth.
- Underline words that have violent or brutal connotations.

ASK STUDENTS how these words help them understand the character of Macbeth and to explain whether or not Macbeth has any of the characteristics of a tragic hero described in the introduction to Shakespearean tragedy.

And fan our people cold.
Norway himself, with terrible numbers,
Assisted by that most disloyal traitor,
55   The Thane of Cawdor, began a dismal conflict,
Till that Bellona's bridegroom, lapped in proof,
Confronted him with self-comparisons,
Point against point, rebellious arm 'gainst arm,
Curbing his lavish spirit. And to conclude,
60   The victory fell on us.

Duncan.   Great happiness!

Ross. That now Sweno,
The Norways' king, craves composition.
Nor would we deign him burial of his men
Till he disbursèd at Saint Colme's Inch
65   Ten thousand dollars to our general use.

Duncan. No more that Thane of Cawdor shall deceive
Our bosom interest. Go, pronounce his present death,
And with his former title greet Macbeth.

Ross. I'll see it done.

70   **Duncan.** What he hath lost, noble Macbeth hath won.

[*They exit.*]

Scene 3   *A bleak place near the battlefield.*

[*Thunder. Enter the three* Witches.]

First Witch. Where hast thou been, sister?

Second Witch. Killing swine.

Third Witch. Sister, where thou?

First Witch. A sailor's wife had chestnuts in her lap
5   And munched and munched and munched. "Give me," quoth I.
"Aroint thee, witch," the rump-fed runnion cries.
Her husband's to Aleppo gone, master o' th' *Tiger*;
But in a sieve I'll thither sail
And, like a rat without a tail,
10   I'll do, I'll do, and I'll do.

Second Witch. I'll give thee a wind.

First Witch. Th' art kind.

Third Witch. And I another.

First Witch. I myself have all the other,
15   And the very ports they blow,
All the quarters that they know

62 craves composition: wants a treaty.

63 deign: allow.

64 disbursèd at Saint Colme's Inch: paid at Saint Colme's Inch, an island in the North Sea.

66–67 deceive our bosom interest: betray our friendship; **present death:** immediate execution.

6 "Aroint thee, witch," . . . **runnion cries:** "Go away, witch!" the fatbottomed (**rump-fed**), ugly creature (**runnion**) cries.

7–8 The woman's husband, the master of a merchant ship (**th'** *Tiger*), has sailed to Aleppo. The witch will pursue him. Witches were thought to sail on strainers (**sieve**).

14–23 The witch controls the winds, covering all points of a compass (**shipman's card**). She will make the sailor sleepless, keeping his eyelids (**penthouse lid**) from closing. Thus, he will lead an accursed (**forbid**) life for weeks (**sev'nnights**), wasting away with fatigue.

The Tragedy of Macbeth: Act I, Scene 3   **217**

CLOSE READ

Summarize the Text

(LINES 66–70)

Explain to students that when reading difficult or complicated text, it is helpful to stop periodically and paraphrase or summarize what they are reading. Have students reread lines 66–70.

F **ASK STUDENTS** to summarize the exchange between Duncan and Ross. (*Duncan condemns the current Thane of Cawdor to death and tells Ross that Macbeth will be the new Thane of Cawdor.*) Ask them why Macbeth is given this reward. (*He played a key role in defeating the rebel lord and the Norwegian army.*)

Analyze Character

(LINES 4–25)

Explain that a character's actions and how he or she interacts with other characters can provide a reader with insight into the character's motivations.

G **ASK STUDENTS** what the witches are discussing. (*A sailor's wife refused to share chestnuts with the First Witch, so she is placing a curse on the woman's husband; the other witches offer to help her get her revenge.*) Ask students what this act suggests about the witches. (*The witches are evil, vindictive, and likely untrustworthy.*)

SCAFFOLDING FOR ELL STUDENTS

Vocabulary: Archaic Language Explain that many words and phrases in the play are no longer used in modern English. Encourage students to keep a vocabulary journal, one for high-utility terms and one for archaic terms. As you read, point out some of the archaic terms and define them. On this page, you may point out the words *quoth* ("said"), *thither* ("there"), *shalt* ("shall"), and *thine* ("yours").

ASK STUDENTS to point out other archaic words and help them use the context to determine the meaning. An example is *thrice* on page 218. The witches say the word three times and then say "to make up nine." Explain that three times three is nine, so *thrice* must mean "three times."

Analyze Theme

COMMON CORE **RL 2**

(LINE 38)

Tell students that authors develop their themes
over the course of a text. Readers must use details
throughout the story to recognize how the author
continues to refine it. Have students recall their
discussion on page 215 about the witches' line "Fair
is foul, and foul is fair" and how this line hints at one
theme. Have them relate this line and discussion to
what Macbeth says in line 38.

 ASK STUDENTS why Macbeth calls the day both
foul and fair. *(It is foul because the day was filled with
violence and death; it is fair because they ultimately
won.)* Have them explain how the line relates to the
theme and why it is relevant that Macbeth is saying
this line. *(The theme is that things may not always truly
be as they appear. It's relevant that Macbeth is saying
it because it may mean that he is going to embody the
witches' "mixing up" of the foul and the fair.)*

> I' th' shipman's card.
> I'll drain him dry as hay.
> Sleep shall neither night nor day
> 20 Hang upon his penthouse lid.
> He shall live a man forbid.
> Weary sev'nnights, nine times nine,
> Shall he dwindle, peak, and pine.
> Though his bark cannot be lost,
> 25 Yet it shall be tempest-tossed.
> Look what I have.
>
> **Second Witch.** Show me, show me.
>
> **First Witch.** Here I have a pilot's thumb,
> Wracked as homeward he did come.
>
> [*Drum within*]
>
> 30 **Third Witch.** A drum, a drum!
> Macbeth doth come.
>
> **All.** [*Dancing in a circle*] The Weïrd Sisters, hand in hand,
> Posters of the sea and land,
> Thus do go about, about,
> 35 Thrice to thine, and thrice to mine
> And thrice again, to make up nine.
> Peace, the charm's wound up.
>
> [*Enter* Macbeth *and* Banquo.]
>
> **Macbeth.** So foul and fair a day I have not seen.

33 posters: quick
riders.

36 Nine was
considered a
magical number by
superstitious people.

Image Credits: ©Michael Shay/Taxi/Getty Images

SCAFFOLDING FOR ELL STUDENTS

Vocabulary: Multiple-Meaning Words To recognize the theme, students need
to understand the meanings of *foul* and *fair* as used in the play. They may be familiar
with the term "foul ball" or a "fair" as a carnival-like event. Explain that Shakespeare
is using different meanings of the words and with strong connotations, or feelings.
In this instance, *foul* means "wicked or immoral"; *fair* means "just or appropriate" or
"beautiful."

ASK STUDENTS to work with partners to figure out the meaning of these multiple-
meaning words based on context clues: *state* (Scene 2, line 3); *Fortune* (Scene 2, line
14); *steel* (Scene 2, line 17); *slave* (Scene 2, line 20) ; *strokes* (Scene 2, line 38); *pine*
(Scene 3, line 23); *hail* (Scene 3, line 48); *start* (Scene 3, line 51); *get* (Scene 3, line 67).

Banquo. How far is 't called to Forres?—What are these,
40 So withered, and so wild in their attire,
That look not like th' inhabitants o' th' earth
And yet are on 't?—Live you? Or are you aught
That man may question? You seem to understand me
By each at once her choppy finger laying
45 Upon her skinny lips. You should be women,
And yet your beards forbid me to interpret
That you are so.

Macbeth. Speak, if you can. What are you?

First Witch. All hail, Macbeth! Hail to thee, Thane of Glamis!

Second Witch. All hail, Macbeth! Hail to thee, Thane of Cawdor!

50 **Third Witch.** All hail, Macbeth, that shalt be king hereafter!

Banquo. Good sir, why do you start and seem to fear
Things that do sound so fair? I' th' name of truth,
Are you fantastical, or that indeed
Which outwardly you show? My noble partner
55 You greet with present grace and great prediction
Of noble having and of royal hope,
That he seems rapt withal. To me you speak not.
If you can look into the seeds of time
And say which grain will grow and which will not,
60 Speak, then, to me, who neither beg nor fear
Your favors nor your hate.

First Witch. Hail!

Second Witch. Hail!

Third Witch. Hail!

65 **First Witch.** Lesser than Macbeth and greater.

Second Witch. Not so happy, yet much happier.

Third Witch. Thou shalt get kings, though thou be none.
So all hail, Macbeth and Banquo!

First Witch. Banquo and Macbeth, all hail!

70 **Macbeth.** Stay, you imperfect speakers. Tell me more.
By Sinel's death I know I am Thane of Glamis.
But how of Cawdor? The Thane of Cawdor lives
A prosperous gentleman, and to be king
Stands not within the prospect of belief,
75 No more than to be Cawdor. Say from whence
You owe this strange intelligence or why

42–46 aught: anything; **choppy:** chapped; **your beards:** Beards on women identified them as witches.

53 are you fantastical: Are you (the witches) imaginary?

54–57 The witches' prophecies of noble possessions (**having**)—the lands and wealth of Cawdor—and kingship (**royal hope**) have left Macbeth dazed (**rapt withal**).

CLOSE READ

Analyze Character
COMMON CORE RL 3

(LINES 48–60; 60–76)

Remind students that what characters say and do and how others react to them reveals a great deal about their personalities and motivations. Have students reread lines 48–61 and lines 65–76.

 ASK STUDENTS what the witches say to Macbeth. *(In lines 48–50, the witches greet him using three titles, predicting he will be king. In lines 65–76, they predict that he will not be happy and suggest that not his, but Banquo's heirs, will inherit the throne.)* How does Macbeth respond? *(In lines 51–52, Banquo indicates that Macbeth seems fearful of the witches' prophecy. Later, Macbeth wants to know more about their prophecy and where the witches' information comes from.)* Have them explain what Macbeth's response reveals about his character. *(His reaction suggests that he is both avidly interested in and afraid of the prophecy. Perhaps Macbeth has already thought through the violence that would be involved in making the prophecy a reality.)*

Analyze Shakespearean Drama
COMMON CORE RL 5

(LINES 48–50; 70–76)

Remind students that a tragic hero comes to ruin because of a tragic flaw, which can be an error in judgment or a weakness in character.

J ASK STUDENTS how the witches' greeting and Macbeth's reaction to it could foreshadow his tragic flaw. *(Their greeting foreshadows events to come—somehow Macbeth will become first Thane of Cawdor, then king. Macbeth seems electrified by the prophecy; his tragic flaw may be a secret desire to achieve these goals.)*

WHEN STUDENTS STRUGGLE . . .

Ask students to reread lines 48–52 and discuss why Macbeth seems both surprised and frightened by what the witches say. Remind students that Duncan ordered the Thane of Cawdor's death and the awarding of his title to Macbeth, but Macbeth wasn't present to hear about these developments. *(The witches call Macbeth the Thane of Glamis, the Thane of Cawdor, and king. These titles surprise Macbeth because as far as he knows, the only title that he possesses is Thane of Glamis. He is frightened because the witches themselves present an eerie spectacle, and the titles with which they greet him would suggest that something bad might happen, or has already happened, to the Thane of Cawdor and the king.)*

Summarize the Text

COMMON CORE **RL 2**

(LINES 79–85)

Remind students that paraphrasing and summarizing are important reading strategies that they should employ throughout a text to ensure their understanding of the plot and characters. Have students reread lines 79–85.

K **ASK STUDENTS** to summarize the exchange between Banquo and Macbeth. *(After the witches have given their prophecy, they vanish. Banquo wonders whether they are insane, while Macbeth seems to believe they were really there and wishes they would have stayed longer to explain their prophecy.)* What do these different reactions suggest about their characters? *(Macbeth's willingness to believe*

Analy...

(LINES 8...

Tell st... ...s a char... ...personality and motives is through what others say about him or her. However, since characters are not always reliable, readers must consider what they know about all the characters to understand which characters are reliable, which ones are naïve, and which ones may have hidden motives.

L **ASK STUDENTS** what Ross says in lines 89–100. *(Ross says the King and his subjects all praise Macbeth for his bravery in defense of the kingdom; they all see Macbeth as a noble hero.)* Ask students if they think this is a fair and accurate assessment of Macbeth. Why or why not? *(Students may say that it is fair in that Macbeth was very brave, but they may suggest he is not as noble as the king and others seem to think.)*

Upon this blasted heath you stop our way
With such prophetic greeting. Speak, I charge you.

[Witches *vanish.*]

Banquo. The earth hath bubbles, as the water has,
80 And these are of them. Whither are they vanished?

     80 whither: where.

Macbeth. Into the air, and what seemed corporal melted,
As breath into the wind. Would they had stayed!

     81 corporal: physical; real.

Banquo. Were such things here as we do speak about?
Or have we eaten on the insane root
85 That takes the reason prisoner?

     84 insane root: A number of plants were believed to cause insanity when eaten.

Macbeth. Your children shall be kings.

Banquo.   You shall be king.

Macbeth. And Thane of Cawdor too. Went it not so?

Banquo. To th' selfsame tune and words.—Who's here?

[Enter Ross *and* Angus.]

Ross. The King hath happily received, Macbeth,
90 The news of thy success, and, when he reads
Thy personal venture in the rebels' fight,
His wonders and his praises do contend
Which should be thine or his. Silenced with that,
In viewing o'er the rest o' th' selfsame day
95 He finds thee in the stout Norweyan ranks,
Nothing afeard of what thyself didst make,
Strange images of death. As thick as hail
Came post with post, and every one did bear
Thy praises in his kingdom's great defense,
100 And poured them down before him.

     92–93 King Duncan hesitates between awe (**wonders**) and gratitude (**praises**) and is, as a result, speechless.

     96–97 Although Macbeth left many dead (**strange images of death**), he obviously did not fear death himself.

Angus.   We are sent
To give thee from our royal master thanks,
Only to herald thee into his sight,
Not pay thee.

Ross. And for an earnest of a greater honor,
105 He bade me, from him, call thee Thane of Cawdor,
In which addition, hail, most worthy thane,
For it is thine.

     104 earnest: partial payment.

     106 addition: title.

Banquo.   What, can the devil speak true?

Macbeth. The Thane of Cawdor lives. Why do you dress me
In borrowed robes?

Angus.   Who was the Thane lives yet,
110 But under heavy judgment bears that life

WHEN STUDENTS STRUGGLE...

Frequent asides can be an added challenge for students reading Shakespeare. Remind students that an aside is a brief speech that other characters cannot hear. Authors use asides to reveal a character's private thoughts and feelings. In order to better understand Macbeth, students need to be able to distinguish between what Macbeth says to other characters and what he says to himself. Project lines 117–146 on a whiteboard. Have students closely study Macbeth's lines to determine when he is speaking to others and when he is speaking to himself.

Which he deserves to lose. Whether he was combined
With those of Norway, or did line the rebel
With hidden help and vantage, or that with both
He labored in his country's wrack, I know not;
115 But treasons capital, confessed and proved,
Have overthrown him.

    Macbeth [*aside*].   Glamis and Thane of Cawdor!
The greatest is behind. [*To Ross and* Angus] Thanks for your pains.
[*Aside to* Banquo] Do you not hope your children shall be kings
When those that gave the Thane of Cawdor to me
120 Promised no less to them?

    Banquo.   That, trusted home,
Might yet enkindle you unto the crown,
Besides the Thane of Cawdor. But 'tis strange.
And oftentimes, to win us to our harm,
The instruments of darkness tell us truths,
125 Win us with honest trifles, to betray 's
In deepest consequence.—
Cousins, a word, I pray you.   [*They step aside.*]

    Macbeth [*aside*].   Two truths are told
As happy prologues to the swelling act
Of the imperial theme.—I thank you, gentlemen.
130 [*Aside*] This supernatural soliciting
Cannot be ill, cannot be good. If ill,
Why hath it given me earnest of success
Commencing in a truth? I am Thane of Cawdor.
If good, why do I yield to that suggestion
135 Whose horrid image doth unfix my hair
And make my seated heart knock at my ribs
Against the use of nature? Present fears
Are less than horrible imaginings.
My thought, whose murder yet is but fantastical,
140 Shakes so my single state of man
That function is smothered in surmise,
And nothing is but what is not.

    Banquo.   Look how our partner's rapt.

    Macbeth [*aside*]. If chance will have me king, why, chance may
       crown me
Without my stir.

    Banquo.   New honors come upon him,
145 Like our strange garments, cleave not to their mold
But with the aid of use.

111–116 Whether the former thane of Cawdor allied (**combined**) with the king of Norway or supported the traitor Macdonwald (**did line the rebel**), he is guilty of treasons that deserve the death penalty (**treasons capital**), having aimed at the country's ruin (**wrack**).

120 home: fully; completely.

121 enkindle you unto: inflame your ambitions.

123–126 Banquo warns that evil powers often offer little truths to tempt people. The witches may be lying about what matters most (**in deepest consequence**).

144 my stir: my doing anything.

The Tragedy of Macbeth: Act I, Scene 3   **221**

Have volunteers do the following:
- Highlight text in which Macbeth addresses other characters.
- Draw a box around text in which Macbeth is speaking to himself.

Then draw a two-column chart with the headings *What He Says* and *What He Thinks*. As a class, complete the chart. Encourage students to use a similar method of marking asides from dialogue as they read the play to help them better understand the motivations of characters.

ASK STUDENTS to explain how differentiating between asides and dialogue helps them understand Macbeth as a character. (*Macbeth is concerned with keeping up appearances, but in his asides he reveals his desires and his true nature to readers.*)

CLOSE READ

Analyze Character

COMMON CORE **RL 3**

(LINES 118–126)

Tell students that when analyzing a character, readers must consider the character's words and their reactions to situations. Readers need to continually analyze these character details because a character's motivations may change or conflict.

Ⓜ **ASK STUDENTS** to contrast Banquo's and Macbeth's reactions now that the first part of the witches' prophecy has come true. (*Macbeth seems to think the prophecy is a good thing. Banquo is not as convinced because the source of the prophecy—the witches—appears to be evil. Banquo is worried that there may be consequences and warns Macbeth about possible results of his ambitions.*) Ask them what these reactions tell them about Macbeth's ambition. (*Now that he has been given a reward, and it's been hinted that he'll receive more, he wants it all. He doesn't seem to care that there may be dreadful consequences if he is to achieve his goal.*)

Analyze Theme

COMMON CORE **RL 2**

(LINES 143–144)

Tell students that a literary work may have multiple themes that are intertwined or that build on each other. Remind students that one theme that has emerged involves appearances vs. reality.

Ⓝ **ASK STUDENTS** to identify another theme that has emerged involving Macbeth specifically. (*Unbridled ambition may have tragic consequences.*) Explain that lines 143–144 suggest another theme. Ask what Macbeth means in these lines. (*He believes the witches' prophecy will come true without his needing to do anything to make that happen.*) Have students explain what theme this helps establish. (*Once a person's fate has been decided, there is nothing he or she can do to change it.*)

Analyze Character
COMMON CORE RL 3

(LINES 146–147)

Tell students that a character's beliefs may direct his or her actions. Then have them read Macbeth's aside in lines 146–147.

 ASK STUDENTS what these lines reveal about Macbeth's beliefs. *(Answers will vary. The lines seem to suggest that time is like water; it will run through the "roughest day"—just as water runs through the roughest terrain, often erasing whatever was in its path. Therefore, people's plans and actions amount to little.)*

Analyze Theme
COMMON CORE RL 1, RL 2

(LINES 11–14)

Remind students that authors develop their themes throughout the text. Have students recall the theme related to the witches' "fair is foul, foul is fair" statement. Tell them to consider how the king's statement about the rebellious former Thane of Cawdor relates to this theme.

P CITE TEXT EVIDENCE What does Duncan say about the former Thane of Cawdor? *(He says that he had total trust for the former Thane, believing him to be a gentleman.)* Have students use text evidence to explain how Duncan's first line supports the theme about appearances vs. reality. *(The line supports the theme that things are not always as they appear. In line 12, Duncan says a person cannot judge someone's character by his face. It is impossible to tell what someone is thinking based on expressions or looks, which may conceal a hidden agenda or nature.)*

O **Macbeth** [*aside*].   Come what come may,
Time and the hour runs through the roughest day.

Banquo. Worthy Macbeth, we stay upon your leisure.

Macbeth. Give me your favor. My dull brain was wrought
150 With things forgotten. Kind gentlemen, your pains
Are registered where every day I turn
The leaf to read them. Let us toward the King.
[*Aside to* Banquo] Think upon what hath chanced, and
        at more time,
The interim having weighed it, let us speak
155 Our free hearts each to other.

Banquo.   Very gladly.

Macbeth. Till then, enough.—Come, friends.

[*They exit.*]

Scene 4 *A room in the king's palace at Forres.*

[*Flourish. Enter* King Duncan, Lennox, Malcolm, Donalbain, *and* Attendants.]

Duncan. Is execution done on Cawdor? Are not
Those in commission yet returned?

Malcolm.   My liege,
They are not yet come back. But I have spoke
With one that saw him die, who did report
5 That very frankly he confessed his treasons,
Implored your Highness' pardon, and set forth
A deep repentance. Nothing in his life
Became him like the leaving it. He died
As one that had been studied in his death
10 To throw away the dearest thing he owed
As 'twere a careless trifle.

Duncan.   There's no art
P To find the mind's construction in the face.
He was a gentleman on whom I built
An absolute trust.

[*Enter* Macbeth, Banquo, Ross, *and* Angus.]
                O worthiest cousin,
15 The sin of my ingratitude even now
Was heavy on me. Thou art so far before
That swiftest wing of recompense is slow
To overtake thee. Would thou hadst less deserved,
That the proportion both of thanks and payment
20 Might have been mine! Only I have left to say,
More is thy due than more than all can pay.

222 Collection 5

146–147 Come what ... roughest day: The future will arrive no matter what.

148 stay: wait.

150–152 your pains ... read them: I will always remember your efforts. The metaphor refers to keeping a diary and reading it regularly.

153–155 Macbeth wants to discuss the prophecies later, after he and Banquo have had time to think about them.

2 those in commission: those who have the responsibility for Cawdor's execution.

6 set forth: showed.

8–11 He died as ... trifle: He died as if he had rehearsed (**studied**) the moment. Though losing his life (**the dearest thing he owed**), he behaved with calm dignity.

14–21 The king feels that he cannot repay (**recompense**) Macbeth enough. Macbeth's qualities and accomplishments are of greater value than any thanks or payment Duncan can give.

SCAFFOLDING FOR ELL STUDENTS

Vocabulary: Transitive and Intransitive Verbs Write or project lines 7–8 on the board. Ask students what the line means. *(Nothing in his life made him look better than his dying.)* Ask what *became* means in this sentence. *(to show in a positive light)* Point out that *became* takes this definition only when it is **transitive**—when it carries an object (a noun or pronoun—in this case, *him.*) Explain that transitive verbs and **intransitive verbs** (those that do not carry an object) often have related meanings; but some, like *become*, have very different meanings.

ASK STUDENTS to look at the transitive verbs *invest* (line 40) and *bid* (line 57), explain their meanings in the text, and explain their more familiar meanings as intransitive verbs.

Macbeth. The service and the loyalty I owe
In doing it pays itself. Your Highness' part
Is to receive our duties, and our duties

25 Are to your throne and state children and servants,
Which do but what they should by doing everything
Safe toward your love and honor.

Duncan.   Welcome hither.
I have begun to plant thee and will labor
To make thee full of growing.—Noble Banquo,

30 That hast no less deserved nor must be known
No less to have done so, let me enfold thee
And hold thee to my heart.

Banquo.   There, if I grow,
The harvest is your own.

Duncan.   My plenteous joys,
Wanton in fullness, seek to hide themselves

35 In drops of sorrow.—Sons, kinsmen, thanes,
And you whose places are the nearest, know
We will establish our estate upon
Our eldest, Malcolm, whom we name hereafter
The Prince of Cumberland; which honor must

40 Not unaccompanied invest him only,
But signs of nobleness, like stars, shall shine
On all deservers.—From hence to Inverness,
And bind us further to you.

Macbeth. The rest is labor which is not used for you.

45 I'll be myself the harbinger and make joyful
The hearing of my wife with your approach.
So humbly take my leave.

Duncan.   My worthy Cawdor.

Macbeth [*aside*]. The Prince of Cumberland! That is a step
On which I must fall down or else o'erleap,

50 For in my way it lies. Stars, hide your fires;
Let not light see my black and deep desires.
The eye wink at the hand, yet let that be
Which the eye fears, when it is done, to see.

[*He exits.*]

Duncan. True, worthy Banquo. He is full so valiant,

55 And in his commendations I am fed:
It is a banquet to me.—Let's after him,
Whose care is gone before to bid us welcome.
It is a peerless kinsman.

[*Flourish. They exit.*]

28–29 The king plans to give more honors to Macbeth.

33–35 My plenteous . . . sorrow: The king is crying tears of joy.

39 Prince of Cumberland: the title given to the heir to the Scottish throne.

42 Inverness: site of Macbeth's castle, where the king has just invited himself, giving another honor to Macbeth.

45 harbinger: a representative sent before a royal party to make proper arrangements for its arrival.

CLOSE READ

Analyze Character
COMMON CORE **RL 2, RL 3**
(LINES 27–30)

Remind students that a character's words can reveal personality and motivations. A writer can also use a character's words to foreshadow events or develop the theme. Recall with students Duncan's statement on the previous page about how he had placed his absolute trust in the former Thane of Cawdor.

Q **ASK STUDENTS** what Duncan plans to do. (*He is going to reward Macbeth even more.*) Have them explain why he is doing this. (*He's rewarding Macbeth for defeating the rebels and the Norwegians.*) Given Duncan's earlier statement, ask what this reveals about Duncan's nature. How do his words help develop the plot or hint at future events? (*Duncan earlier stated that he misplaced his trust, and it nearly cost him. Now he is putting total trust in Macbeth, who has ambitions to be king. This suggests that Duncan is naïve and cannot see what Macbeth truly desires. Trusting Macbeth and giving him more power hints at Duncan's undoing.*)

Analyze Theme
COMMON CORE **RL 2**
(LINES 48–53)

Remind students that a story's theme is its message about life or human nature. Recall with students one of the play's themes suggested by Macbeth's earlier statement "If chance will have me king, why chance/ may crown me / Without my stir."

R **ASK STUDENTS** to paraphrase lines 48–53. (*Macbeth realizes that Malcolm now stands between him and the throne. He says he must hide his desire to kill Malcolm, yet still do it.*) How do these lines contrast with his earlier thoughts about his destiny? (*Earlier he suggested that his fate was to be king, therefore he didn't need to take action. Now he's suggesting he will need to act in order to ensure his desires and destiny.*) How do Macbeth's thoughts help develop the theme? (*He realizes that one's fate cannot be left to chance.*)

WHEN STUDENTS STRUGGLE . . .

Students need to understand why Macbeth now sees Malcom as a threat. Have them reread lines 33–43. Ask them to explain what Duncan is saying and why this information propels the plot. (*Duncan tells Macbeth and Banquo that Malcolm is next in line for the throne of Scotland. This information is important because now that Macbeth has been told Malcolm is to be the next king, he likely sees Malcolm as a threat to his goals and may plan to remove him.*) Have students work together to create a plot diagram with the main events in Scenes 1–4. As they read the rest of the play, encourage them to continue plotting the main events to help them understand how the characters' actions build to the climax and then the resolution.

Analyze Character

COMMON CORE RL 1, RL 3

(LINES 12–27)

Remind students that a soliloquy is a speech made when a character is alone on the stage. Playwrights use soliloquies to reveal a character's inner thoughts and emotions. In lines 12–27, Lady Macbeth reveals her thoughts about the prophecies, herself, and her husband.

S **ASK STUDENTS** what they can infer about Lady Macbeth based on her soliloquy. (*She believes in the prophecy, but believes that Macbeth must act in order to make it a reality. She considers herself more ruthless and hopes she can use her cunning ways to convince Macbeth of what he must do in order to become king.*)

Tell students that another way readers can learn about a character is through the way others perceive him or her. Point out Lady Macbeth's line regarding her husband, "Yet do I fear thy nature."

T **CITE TEXT EVIDENCE** Ask students to explain what "nature" of Macbeth the Lady Macbeth fears. Remind them to use text evidence to support their response. (*She acknowledges that he has ambition, but in lines 13–18 she worries that he may lack the necessary strength or ruthlessness to become king.*) Based on Macbeth's words and actions so far, ask students if they believe Lady Macbeth has reason to be concerned. (*While Macbeth has shown some noble traits, he has begun to show that he's willing to do whatever is necessary to gain the throne.*)

Scene 5 *Macbeth's castle at Inverness.*

[*Enter* Lady Macbeth, *alone, with a letter.*]

Lady Macbeth. [*Reading the letter*] "They met me in the day of success, and I have learned by the perfect'st report they have more in them than mortal knowledge. When I burned in desire to question them further, they made themselves air, into which they

5   vanished. Whiles I stood rapt in the wonder of it came missives from the King, who all-hailed me 'Thane of Cawdor,' by which title, before, these Weïrd Sisters saluted me and referred me to the coming on of time with 'Hail, king that shalt be.' This have I thought good to deliver thee, my dearest partner of greatness, that

10 thou might'st not lose the dues of rejoicing by being ignorant of what greatness is promised thee. Lay it to thy heart, and farewell."
        Glamis thou art, and Cawdor, and shalt be
    What thou art promised. Yet do I fear thy nature;
    It is too full o' th' milk of human kindness

15 To catch the nearest way. Thou wouldst be great,
    Art not without ambition, but without
    The illness should attend it. What thou wouldst highly,
    That wouldst thou holily; wouldst not play false
    And yet wouldst wrongly win. Thou'd'st have, great Glamis,

20 That which cries "Thus thou must do," if thou have it,
    And that which rather thou dost fear to do,
    Than wishest should be undone. Hie thee hither,
    That I may pour my spirits in thine ear
    And chastise with the valor of my tongue

25 All that impedes thee from the golden round

13–18 Lady Macbeth fears her husband is too good (**too full o' th' milk of human kindness**) to seize the throne by murder (**the nearest way**). Lacking the necessary wickedness (**illness**), he wants to gain power virtuously (**holily**).

TO CHALLENGE STUDENTS . . .

Portray Complex Characters Remind students that dramas are meant to be seen. When watching a play, viewers can see how a character acts or feels. When reading a play, they can often rely on stage directions to better understand the action and characters. Point out that Shakespeare does not provide detailed stage directions. Instead, readers must pay close attention to details and clues about the characters to determine their feelings, movements, and reactions.

ASK STUDENTS to reread Act 1, Scene 5, focusing on details that help them visualize how the characters look, feel, and act. Then have them add their own detailed stage directions throughout the scene to help readers visualize the characters and actions.

Explain that when staging a play, directors refer to stage directions but also interpret

Which fate and metaphysical aid doth seem
To have thee crowned withal.

[*Enter* Messenger.]

                What is your tidings?

Messenger. The King comes here tonight.

Lady Macbeth.   Thou'rt mad to say it!
Is not thy master with him? who, were't so,
30 Would have informed for preparation.

Messenger. So please you, it is true. Our Thane is coming.
One of my fellows had the speed of him,
Who, almost dead for breath, had scarcely more
Than would make up his message.

32 had the speed of him: rode faster than he.

Lady Macbeth.   Give him tending.
35 He brings great news.

[Messenger *exits.*]

             The raven himself is hoarse
That croaks the fatal entrance of Duncan
Under my battlements. Come, you spirits
That tend on mortal thoughts, unsex me here,
And fill me from the crown to the toe top-full
40 Of direst cruelty. Make thick my blood.
Stop up th' access and passage to remorse,
That no compunctious visitings of nature
Shake my fell purpose, nor keep peace between
Th' effect and it. Come to my woman's breasts
45 And take my milk for gall, you murd'ring ministers,
Wherever in your sightless substances
You wait on nature's mischief. Come, thick night,
And pall thee in the dunnest smoke of hell,
That my keen knife see not the wound it makes,
50 Nor heaven peep through the blanket of the dark
To cry "Hold, hold!"

[*Enter* Macbeth.]

            Great Glamis, worthy Cawdor,
Greater than both by the all-hail hereafter!
Thy letters have transported me beyond
This ignorant present, and I feel now
55 The future in the instant.

Macbeth.   My dearest love,
Duncan comes here tonight.

Lady Macbeth.   And when goes hence?

35 raven: The harsh cry of the raven, a bird symbolizing evil and misfortune, was supposed to indicate an approaching death.

37–51 Lady Macbeth calls on the spirits of evil to rid her of feminine weakness (**unsex me**) and to block out guilt. She wants no normal pangs of conscience (**compunctious visitings of nature**) to get in the way of her murderous plan. She asks that her mother's milk be turned to bile (**gall**) by the unseen evil forces (**murd'ring ministers, sightless substances**) that exist in nature. Furthermore, she asks that the night wrap (**pall**) itself in darkness as black as hell so that no one may see or stop the crime.

CLOSE READ

Analyze Language

 COMMON CORE RL 3, RL 4

(LINES 35–50)

Remind students that authors choose words carefully to reveal information about characters and set the mood, or atmosphere. Point out that Shakespeare uses descriptive details and words with powerful connotations in Lady Macbeth's soliloquy.

Ⓤ ASK STUDENTS to identify words or phrases with strong connotations in Lady Macbeth's soliloquy. *(fatal, battlements, mortal, direst cruelty, remorse, compunctions, murd'ring, mischief, thick night, dunnest smoke of hell, blanket of the dark)* Ask students what mood these words create and what they reveal about Lady Macbeth. *(The words create a dark and terrifying mood and indicate that she is calling upon evil spirits to help her achieve her goals. It shows she has incredible will and courage to address these evil spirits and is not afraid to be ruthless or wicked if it serves her purpose.)*

scenes and characters in their own unique way.

Ask students to pair up to perform Lady Macbeth's soliloquy either in lines 1–27 or lines 35–51, using the stage directions they wrote for Scene 5. One student will direct and the other will perform. They should consider details such as:

- how the character moves during the scene
- whether or not the character is addressing the audience
- what kind of facial expressions and gestures the character makes when delivering the lines

Encourage them to experiment with different direction to see what works best. Then have them perform the soliloquy for the class.

Analyze Theme
COMMON CORE RL 2

(Scene 5, lines 60–63)

Remind students that longer literary works often have multiple themes that may relate to each other. Authors refine their themes as the plot unfolds. Have students reread lines 60–63 and recall some of the themes that have been discussed.

 ASK STUDENTS how these lines reflect one or more of the themes. How do these themes relate to each other? *(Lady Macbeth is telling Macbeth to appear innocent and non-threatening in order to hide his brutal plans. Her words develop the themes of appearance vs. reality and the dangers of ambition. At this point in the play, the themes come together, as Lady Macbeth advises her husband to conceal his ambition and wicked plan in order to achieve their goal.)*

Analyze Language
COMMON CORE RL 4

(Scene 5, lines 62–63)

Remind students that figurative language, such as similes, metaphors, and allusions, helps readers understand or visualize complex ideas or emotions.

W **ASK STUDENTS** what Lady Macbeth tells her husband to act like. *(a serpent)* Why is a serpent an appropriate comparison? *(Snakes are cold-blooded animals; they are ruthless hunters. As a biblical allusion, snakes also symbolize evil.)* Tell them to share who they think is more like a serpent—Macbeth or Lady Macbeth—and to support their answer. *(Students may say Lady Macbeth is more cold-blooded than Macbeth because she does not have merely the desire for power; she has made detailed, grisly plans for achieving it.)*

Macbeth. Tomorrow, as he purposes.

Lady Macbeth.   O, never
Shall sun that morrow see!
Your face, my thane, is as a book where men
60 May read strange matters. To beguile the time,
Look like the time. Bear welcome in your eye,
Your hand, your tongue. Look like th' innocent flower,
But be the serpent under 't. He that's coming
Must be provided for; and you shall put
65 This night's great business into my dispatch,
Which shall to all our nights and days to come
Give solely sovereign sway and masterdom.

Macbeth. We will speak further.

Lady Macbeth.   Only look up clear.
To alter favor ever is to fear.
70 Leave all the rest to me.

[They exit.]

Scene 6 *In front of Macbeth's castle.*

[Hautboys and Torches. Enter King Duncan, Malcolm, Donalbain, Banquo, Lennox, Macduff, Ross, Angus, and Attendants.]

Duncan. This castle hath a pleasant seat. The air
Nimbly and sweetly recommends itself
Unto our gentle senses.

Banquo.   This guest of summer,
The temple-haunting martlet, does approve,
5 By his loved mansionry, that the heaven's breath
Smells wooingly here. No jutty, frieze,
Buttress, nor coign of vantage, but this bird
Hath made his pendant bed and procreant cradle.
Where they most breed and haunt, I have observed,
10 The air is delicate.

[Enter Lady Macbeth.]

Duncan.   See, see, our honored hostess!—
The love that follows us sometime is our trouble,
Which still we thank as love. Herein I teach you
How you shall bid God 'ild us for your pains
And thank us for your trouble.

Lady Macbeth.   All our service,
15 In every point twice done and then done double,
Were poor and single business to contend

60–63 To beguile . . . under 't: To fool (**beguile**) everyone, act as expected at such a time.

65 my dispatch: my management.

67 give solely sovereign sway: bring absolute royal power.

69 To alter . . . fear: To change your expression (**favor**) is a sign of fear.

[Stage Direction] **hautboys:** oboes.

1 seat: location.

3–10 The martin (**martlet**) usually built its nest on a church (**temple**), where every projection (**jutty**), sculptured decoration (**frieze**), support (**buttress**), and convenient corner (**coign of vantage**) offered a good nesting site. Banquo sees the presence of the martin's hanging (**pendant**) nest, a breeding (**procreant**) place, as a sign of healthy air.

16 single business: weak service.

SCAFFOLDING FOR ELL STUDENTS

Vocabulary and Comprehension As a class, listen to the audio recording of Scene 5, while students read along. Then ask students to look at the word *fell* (line 43). Help students use context clues to define it. *(The side gloss explanation matching "fell purpose" would be "murderous plan," so* fell *must mean "murderous" or just "evil.")* Break students into small groups to define these terms:

- damnest (Scene 5, line 48) *("darkest")*
- approve (Scene 6, line 4) *("prove")*
- late dignities (Scene 6, line 19) *("recent honors")*

Have groups summarize the scene and discuss points of confusion with the class.

Against those honors deep and broad wherewith
Your Majesty loads our house. For those of old,
And the late dignities heaped up to them,
20 We rest your hermits.

Duncan.   Where's the Thane of Cawdor?
We coursed him at the heels and had a purpose
To be his purveyor; but he rides well,
And his great love (sharp as his spur) hath helped him
To his home before us. Fair and noble hostess,
25 We are your guest tonight.

Lady Macbeth.   Your servants ever
Have theirs, themselves, and what is theirs in compt
To make their audit at your Highness' pleasure,
Still to return your own.

Duncan.   Give me your hand.

[*Taking her hand*]

Conduct me to mine host. We love him highly
30 And shall continue our graces towards him.
By your leave, hostess.

[*They exit.*]

Scene 7 *A room in Macbeth's castle.*

P5   P7

[*Hautboys. Torches. Enter a* Sewer, *and divers* Servants *with
dishes and service over the stage. Then enter* Macbeth.]

Macbeth. If it were done when 'tis done, then 'twere well
It were done quickly. If th' assassination
Could trammel up the consequence and catch
With his surcease success, that but this blow
5 Might be the be-all and the end-all here,
But here, upon this bank and shoal of time,
We'd jump the life to come. But in these cases
We still have judgment here, that we but teach
Bloody instructions, which, being taught, return
10 To plague th' inventor. This even-handed justice
Commends th' ingredient of our poisoned chalice
To our own lips. He's here in double trust:
First, as I am his kinsman and his subject,
Strong both against the deed; then, as his host,
15 Who should against his murderer shut the door,
Not bear the knife myself. Besides, this Duncan
Hath borne his faculties so meek, hath been
So clear in his great office, that his virtues
Will plead like angels, trumpet-tongued, against

20 we rest your hermits: we can only repay you with prayers. The rich hired hermits to pray for the dead.

21 coursed him at the heels: followed closely.

22 purveyor: one who makes advance arrangements for a royal visit.

25–28 Legally, Duncan owned everything in his kingdom. Lady Macbeth politely says that they hold his property in trust (**compt**), ready to return it (**make their audit**) whenever he wants.

[Stage Direction] **Sewer:** the steward, the servant in charge of arranging the banquet and tasting the king's food; **divers:** various.

1–10 If Duncan's murder would have no negative consequences and be successfully completed with his death (**surcease**), then Macbeth would risk eternal damnation. He knows, however, that terrible deeds (**bloody instructions**) often backfire.

The Tragedy of Macbeth: Act I, Scene 7 **227**

CLOSE READ

Analyze Shakespearean Drama (Scene 6, lines 24–31)

Remind students that in dramatic irony, the audience is privy to information of which a character is unaware. Have students reread the dialogue between Duncan and Lady Macbeth.

X ASK STUDENTS how the way the king addresses Lady Macbeth shows dramatic irony. *(He calls her "Fair and noble hostess" and makes a point of saying that he and his men are her guests. He also says how highly he loves Macbeth and will continue to show graces to him. Lady Macbeth claims that they will return his property whenever he wants. The dramatic irony comes from Duncan thinking he is in a safe place in the hands of noble people, when in fact they are planning on murdering him under their roof. Duncan also does not know that Lady Macbeth has no plans of returning his lands and plans to usurp his kingdom.)*

Analyze Character

(Scene 7, lines 1–28)

Scene 7 begins with a famous soliloquy in which Macbeth acknowledges that ambition alone drives him to kill Duncan.

Y CITE TEXT EVIDENCE Ask students what change has occurred in Macbeth's character. *(Macbeth acknowledges that "vaulting ambition" is the only reason for him to kill Duncan [lines 26–27]. This acknowledgment shows that he is thinking clearly at this point, for he knows that he has no justification for killing Duncan. In fact, he recognizes several reasons for not murdering the king [line 13–20].)*

WHEN STUDENTS STRUGGLE...

Have students reread lines 7–12. Explain that Macbeth is saying there is punishment ("judgment") for evil in this life. If he does something evil ("teach / Bloody instructions"), then something evil will happen to him ("return / To plague th'inventor") Help students understand other passages of this soliloquy that confuse them.

ASK STUDENTS to practice fluency through echo reading. Read the soliloquy with expression, pausing after each sentence so that the class can read the same line, with the same expression.

Analyze Character

 COMMON CORE RL 3

(LINES 25–28, 30–35)

Explain that in dramas, another character may act as a **catalyst,** someone who drives the hero into action. Lady Macbeth plays this role, as the "spur" who will "prick the sides of [Macbeth's] intent."

Z ASK STUDENTS to predict what lines 25–28 foreshadow. *(that Lady Macbeth will spur Macbeth on to murder Duncan.)*

Remind students that a well-developed character is complex and often has multiple or contradictory motivations. In tragedies, the hero, while in some ways noble, is also flawed. This contradiction leads to internal conflict as the hero struggles to decide which motivation is more important.

A2 CITE TEXT EVIDENCE Ask students what Macbeth's thoughts and his declaration to Lady Macbeth reveal about his motivations and internal conflict. Remind students to use evidence from the text to support their answers. *(Up to this point, Macbeth has progressively revealed more and more of his ambition and the great and violent lengths he is willing to go in order to achieve his goals. In this scene, however, he shows doubt that evil deeds may justify the ends and wants to call off the plans [line 31]. He struggles because he wants to be king, yet he doesn't want to kill a good king.)*

20 The deep damnation of his taking-off;
And pity, like a naked newborn babe
Striding the blast, or heaven's cherubin horsed
Upon the sightless couriers of the air,
Shall blow the horrid deed in every eye,
25 That tears shall drown the wind. I have no spur
To prick the sides of my intent, but only
Vaulting ambition, which o'erleaps itself
And falls on th' other—

[*Enter* Lady Macbeth.]

               How now? What news?

Lady Macbeth. He has almost supped. Why have you left the
    chamber?

30 **Macbeth.** Hath he asked for me?

Lady Macbeth.   Know you not he has?

Macbeth. We will proceed no further in this business.
He hath honored me of late, and I have bought
Golden opinions from all sorts of people,
Which would be worn now in their newest gloss,
35 Not cast aside so soon.

Lady Macbeth.   Was the hope drunk
Wherein you dressed yourself? Hath it slept since?

32–35 I have . . . so soon: The praises that Macbeth has received are, like new clothes, to be worn, not quickly thrown away.

35–38 Lady Macbeth sarcastically suggests that Macbeth's ambition must have been drunk, because it now seems to have a hangover (**to look so green and pale**).

SCAFFOLDING FOR ELL STUDENTS

Analyze Language: Sarcasm Students may struggle with the concept of sarcasm. Tell students it's a form of verbal irony. Sarcasm is a critical remark stated in a way that is the opposite of what it means. It's meant to hurt or mock someone. In line 30, Lady Macbeth is mocking Macbeth because he knows the answer to his own question and didn't need to ask it. Her other questions are also sarcastic, suggesting that he must have been drunk. Demonstrate sarcasm in situations that are familiar to students.

Work with students to analyze examples of sarcasm in lines 37–45. *(Lady Macbeth asks if her husband's ambition was drunk, knowing this is not the case. She asks if he is as pathetic as a "poor cat," knowing full well he has just conducted himself bravely in battle.)*

Image Credits: ©Andrew Lockie/Flickr/Getty Images

And wakes it now, to look so green and pale
At what it did so freely? From this time
Such I account thy love. Art thou afeard
40 To be the same in thine own act and valor
As thou art in desire? Wouldst thou have that
Which thou esteem'st the ornament of life
And live a coward in thine own esteem,
Letting "I dare not" wait upon "I would,"
45 Like the poor cat i' th' adage?

Macbeth.   Prithee, peace.
I dare do all that may become a man.
Who dares do more is none.

Lady Macbeth.   What beast was't, then,
That made you break this enterprise to me?
When you durst do it, then you were a man;
50 And to be more than what you were, you would
Be so much more the man. Nor time nor place
Did then adhere, and yet you would make both.
They have made themselves, and that their fitness now
Does unmake you. I have given suck, and know
55 How tender 'tis to love the babe that milks me.
I would, while it was smiling in my face,
Have plucked my nipple from his boneless gums
And dashed the brains out, had I so sworn as you
Have done to this.

Macbeth.   If we should fail—

Lady Macbeth.   We fail?
60 But screw your courage to the sticking place
And we'll not fail. When Duncan is asleep
(Whereto the rather shall his day's hard journey
Soundly invite him), his two chamberlains
Will I with wine and wassail so convince
65 That memory, the warder of the brain,
Shall be a fume, and the receipt of reason
A limbeck only. When in swinish sleep
Their drenchèd natures lie as in a death,
What cannot you and I perform upon
70 Th' unguarded Duncan? What not put upon
His spongy officers, who shall bear the guilt
Of our great quell?

Macbeth.   Bring forth men-children only,
For thy undaunted mettle should compose
Nothing but males. Will it not be received,

39–45 Lady Macbeth criticizes Macbeth's weakened resolve and compares him to a cat in a proverb (**adage**) who wouldn't catch fish because it feared wet feet.

54 I have given suck: I have nursed a baby.

60 When each string of a guitar or lute is tightened to the peg (**sticking place**), the instrument is ready to be played.

65–67 Lady Macbeth will get the guards so drunk that their reason will become like a still (**limbeck**), producing confused thoughts.

72 quell: murder.

72–74 Bring forth . . . males: Your bold spirit (**undaunted mettle**) is better suited to raising males than females.

CLOSE READ

Analyze Language

COMMON CORE RL 4

(LINES 36–45)

Explain that sarcasm is a type of verbal irony. Sarcasm is a critical remark in the form of a statement in which literal meaning is opposite actual meaning. Sarcasm is mocking and intended to hurt someone.

 ASK STUDENTS about the effect of the sarcasm in Lady Macbeth's lines. (*Her sarcasm emphasizes how cruel she has become. Not only does she want to kill Duncan, but she mocks her husband for doubting whether or not it is right. Her mockery is an attempt to bully him into killing Duncan.*)

Summarize the Text

COMMON CORE RL 2

(LINES 72–74)

Remind students that pausing to paraphrase or summarize text will help them ensure they understand complex plots and characters.

 ASK STUDENTS to paraphrase what Macbeth says to Lady Macbeth. (*He says she should only give birth to sons because her manner is better suited to raising sons than daughters.*) Have them explain how this line reflects Lady Macbeth's earlier request (Scene 5, line 38) that the dark spirits "unsex her." (*Earlier she asked to have her "feminine" qualities, such as compassion or tenderness, eliminated so she could accomplish her task. Here Macbeth is admitting that he sees very little of the compassion or tenderness one associates with a mother raising daughters.*)

WHEN STUDENTS STRUGGLE . . .

To make sure students understand the kind of pressure Lady Macbeth is putting on her husband, make sure they understand her speech in lines 47–59. Ask volunteers how Lady Macbeth uses shame to pressure her husband into carrying out their plan. (*First she says that Macbeth isn't a man if he doesn't kill Duncan. Then she says that if she had made a promise to Macbeth, even if it were to kill her own infant, she would do it.*)

ASK STUDENTS to discuss whether Macbeth admires or fears his wife when he says, in lines 72–74, "bring forth men-child only. . . ."

Analyze Theme

COMMON CORE RL 1, RL 2

(LINES 77–82)

Remind students that a story's theme, or its message about life, can be revealed through characters' words, thoughts, and actions. Have them consider the themes they have been discussing so far.

D2 **CITE TEXT EVIDENCE** Ask students how the dialogue between Lady Macbeth and Macbeth reflects one of the themes of the play. Have them use text evidence to support their response. *(Lady Macbeth says they will "make our griefs and clamor roar" upon Duncan's death, and Macbeth says "False face must hide what the false heart doth know." They are already preparing to hide their violent crime against their king by pretending to grieve, reflecting the theme that appearances can be deceiving.)*

COLLABORATIVE DISCUSSION Have partners note specific evidence for each character to support their assessment. Tell them to consider what they know about each character and how that contributes to their answer.

ASK STUDENTS to share any questions they generated in the course of reading and discussing the selection.

---

75 When we have marked with blood those sleepy two
Of his own chamber and used their very daggers,
That they have done 't?

Lady Macbeth.   Who dares receive it other,
As we shall make our griefs and clamor roar
Upon his death?

Macbeth.   I am settled and bend up
80 Each corporal agent to this terrible feat.
Away, and mock the time with fairest show.
False face must hide what the false heart doth know.

[*They exit.*]

79–82 Now that Macbeth has made up his mind, every part of his body (**each corporal agent**) is tightened like a bow. He and Lady Macbeth will deceive everyone (**mock the time**), hiding their evil plan with gracious faces.

COLLABORATIVE DISCUSSION With a partner, compare how Banquo and Macbeth each react to the witches' words. What might be the reason for Macbeth's reaction? Cite specific textual evidence from the play to support your ideas.

TO CHALLENGE STUDENTS . . .

Analyze Argument and Character Have students reread Scene 7, comparing Lady Macbeth's way of arguing to Macbeth's and noting whether their different ways of arguing conform to typical gender stereotypes of the time. *(Possible answer: Lady Macbeth argues emotionally. She calls on her relationship with Macbeth, questions his manhood, and makes the wild claim that she would murder her baby if she'd promised to. Macbeth's argument is much more rational: He weighs the consequences of murdering Duncan. Their argument styles seem to fall into typical gender stereotypes of the time.)*

Analyzing the Text

COMMON CORE · RL 3, RL 4, RL 5, W 2, L 5a

Cite Text Evidence   Support your responses with evidence from the selection.

1. **Analyze** What is the purpose of the first scene? Explain.

2. **Infer** Reread lines 16–23 of Scene 2. What impression of Macbeth is created by these details?

3. **Draw Conclusions** A **paradox** is an apparent contradiction that reveals a truth. The witches end the first scene with a paradox: "Fair is foul, and foul is fair." Explain the ways in which this contradiction is shown to be true in Act I.

4. **Predict** Review lines 2–14 in Scene 4. What does this description of the previous Thane of Cawdor's actions and ultimate fate **foreshadow**, or hint at, for Macbeth?

5. **Analyze** How is Macbeth's conflict intensified by the events in Scene 4? What lines from his aside in Scene 4 (lines 48–53) develop the audience's understanding of this conflict?

6. **Interpret** Reread Lady Macbeth's soliloquy, lines 35–51, in Scene 5. Why does she ask for the spirits to fill her with "direst cruelty" and "make thick my blood"? What does this speech reveal about her character?

7. **Analyze** Explain the dramatic irony of Duncan's reaction when he arrives at Macbeth's castle.

8. **Draw Conclusions** Review lines 28–32 in Scene 4 and Duncan's lines in Scene 6. How does Duncan's language in these passages convey his character? Explain.

PERFORMANCE TASK

Writing Activity: Analysis How are Macbeth and Lady Macbeth different? Use their major speeches in Scene 7 to contrast their characters.

- First, identify what lines 1–28 reveal about Macbeth as he lists the reasons they should not go ahead with the plan. What does he decide?

- Next, consider what is revealed about Lady Macbeth's character through her reaction to Macbeth's decision and her response in lines 47–59.
- Summarize their key differences in a paragraph.

Assign this performance task.

PERFORMANCE TASK

COMMON CORE · W 2, RL 3

Writing Activity: Analysis Tell students to consider using a Venn diagram to compare and contrast Macbeth and Lady Macbeth. In addition to focusing on the lines in Scene 7, encourage them to consider what they've already learned about these two characters, citing scene and line references to support those conclusions as well.

PRACTICE & APPLY

Analyzing the Text

COMMON CORE · RL 1, RL 2, RL 3, RL 4, RL 5, L 5a

Possible answers:

1. *The first scene not only foreshadows the violence of the play with thunder and lightning, but it also sets up the theme of "fair is foul, and foul is fair" that runs through the play.*

2. *The Captain's description of Macbeth on the battlefield creates an impression of a man who is courageous ("brave Macbeth"; "valor's minion") yet vicious and violent ("carved out his passage"; "unseamed him"; "fixes his head upon our battlements").*

3. *The characters of Macbeth and Lady Macbeth both reflect the paradox of "fair is foul, and foul is fair." Both characters outwardly show loyalty, respect, and obedience to the king, while inwardly and with each other, they plot his death. This shows that while they appear to be one thing, they are in fact something else entirely.*

4. *Duncan had placed complete trust in the former Thane of Cawdor, and he was betrayed. So, the Thane of Cawdor died for his crimes. Duncan then places trust in Macbeth as his new Thane of Cawdor. However, like the previous thane, Macbeth has a treacherous heart, which foreshadows that Macbeth will end up dying for the crimes he will soon commit.*

5. *Before Scene 4, Macbeth thought that to gain the crown, he only needed to rely on the prophecy and would not need to act himself ("Without my stir"). In Scene 4, Duncan says Malcolm is next in line for the throne, so the conflict is intensified once there is a new obstacle between Macbeth and the throne.*

6. *Lady Macbeth knows that what she and Macbeth are planning will require her to harden her heart against emotions, such as compassion or guilt. This shows that her ambition drives her every action.*

7. *Duncan talks about what a pleasant and welcoming place Macbeth's castle is, but the audience knows it's a dangerous place since the Macbeths are planning to kill him in their home.*

8. *Duncan praises Banquo and Macbeth for their loyalty and looks to reward them and keep them close ("hold thee to my heart"), and he praises how warm and welcoming the site of his future murder is. These lines reveal Duncan to be naïve and overly trusting.*

Make Inferences

COMMON CORE **RL 1**

(LINES 6–20)

In lines 6–8, Banquo asks that "cursèd thoughts" leave him so that he can sleep.

(A) CITE TEXT EVIDENCE Ask students to read ahead to find the probable cause of Banquo's insomnia. (*In lines 19–20, Banquo confides to Macbeth that he dreamt of the witches' prophecy. This troubling prophecy is probably the cause of his sleeplessness.*)

Analyze Author's Choices: Tension and Surprise

COMMON CORE **RL 1, RL 5**

(LINES 16–18)

Tell students that playwrights use various techniques to build **suspense,** or tension. Explain that **dramatic irony**—when the audience knows something that one or more characters do not know—is one such technique.

(B) CITE TEXT EVIDENCE Ask students to paraphrase lines 16–18. (*In lines 16–18, Macbeth tells Banquo that he and his wife could not entertain King Duncan as they would have liked because they were unprepared.*) What makes these remarks ironic? (*In Act I, Macbeth and his wife made plans to kill the king.*) How does this help build suspense? (*Because the audience knows Macbeth's plans, they wait for the moment when his actions will be carried out.*)

AS YOU READ Look for details about how Macbeth conceals his plot. Write down any questions you generate during reading.

ACT II

Scene 1 *The court of Macbeth's castle.*

[*Enter* Banquo, *and* Fleance *with a torch before him.*]

Banquo. How goes the night, boy?

Fleance. The moon is down. I have not heard the clock.

Banquo. And she goes down at twelve.

Fleance.   I take 't, 'tis later, sir.

Banquo. Hold, take my sword. [*Giving his sword to* Fleance]

> There's husbandry in heaven;
5 Their candles are all out. Take thee that too.
   A heavy summons lies like lead upon me,
   And yet I would not sleep. Merciful powers,
   Restrain in me the cursèd thoughts that nature
   Gives way to in repose.

[*Enter* Macbeth, *and a* Servant *with a torch.*]

> Give me my sword.—Who's there?

10 **Macbeth.** A friend.

Banquo. What, sir, not yet at rest? The King's abed.
He hath been in unusual pleasure, and
Sent forth great largess to your offices.
This diamond he greets your wife withal,
15 By the name of most kind hostess, and shut up
In measureless content. [*He gives* Macbeth *a diamond.*]

Macbeth.   Being unprepared,
Our will became the servant to defect,
Which else should free have wrought.

Banquo.   All's well.
I dreamt last night of the three Weïrd Sisters.
20 To you they have showed some truth.

Macbeth.   I think not of them.
Yet, when we can entreat an hour to serve,
We would spend it in some words upon that business,
If you would grant the time.

Banquo.   At your kind'st leisure.

Macbeth. If you shall cleave to my consent, when 'tis,
25 It shall make honor for you.

Banquo.   So I lose none
In seeking to augment it, but still keep

4–5 The heavens show economy (**husbandry**) by keeping the lights (**candles**) out—it is a starless night.

6 heavy summons: desire for sleep.

13 largess to your offices: gifts to the servants' quarters.

15 shut up: went to bed.

21 can entreat an hour: both have the time.

24–28 Macbeth asks Banquo for his support (**cleave to my consent**), promising honors in return. Banquo is willing to increase (**augment**) his honor provided he can keep a clear conscience and remain loyal to the king (**keep my bosom . . . clear**).

Close Read Screencasts   View It!

Modeled Discussions

Have students click the *Close Read* icons in their eBooks to access a screencast in which readers discuss and annotate the following key passage:

- Lady Macbeth, Banquo, Malcolm, and Donalbain react to Duncan's murder (Scene 3, lines 112–126)

As a class, view and discuss this video.

C My bosom franchised and allegiance clear,
I shall be counseled.

Macbeth.   Good repose the while.

Banquo. Thanks, sir. The like to you.

[Banquo *and* Fleance *exit.*]

30 **Macbeth.** Go bid thy mistress, when my drink is ready,
She strike upon the bell. Get thee to bed.

[Servant *exits.*]

D Is this a dagger which I see before me,
The handle toward my hand? Come, let me clutch thee.
I have thee not, and yet I see thee still.
35 Art thou not, fatal vision, sensible
To feeling as to sight? or art thou but
A dagger of the mind, a false creation
Proceeding from the heat-oppressèd brain?
I see thee yet, in form as palpable
40 As this which now I draw. [*He draws his dagger.*]
Thou marshal'st me the way that I was going,
And such an instrument I was to use.
Mine eyes are made the fools o' th' other senses
Or else worth all the rest. I see thee still,
45 And, on thy blade and dudgeon, gouts of blood,
Which was not so before. There's no such thing.
It is the bloody business which informs
Thus to mine eyes. Now o'er the one-half world
Nature seems dead, and wicked dreams abuse
50 The curtained sleep. Witchcraft celebrates
Pale Hecate's off'rings, and withered murder,
Alarumed by his sentinel, the wolf,
Whose howl's his watch, thus with his stealthy pace,
With Tarquin's ravishing strides, towards his design
55 Moves like a ghost. Thou sure and firm-set earth,
Hear not my steps, which way they walk, for fear
Thy very stones prate of my whereabouts
And take the present horror from the time,
Which now suits with it. Whiles I threat, he lives.
60 Words to the heat of deeds too cold breath gives.

[*A bell rings.*]

I go, and it is done. The bell invites me.
Hear it not, Duncan, for it is a knell
That summons thee to heaven or to hell.

[*He exits.*]

32–42 Macbeth sees a dagger hanging in midair before him and questions whether it is real (**palpable**) or the illusion of a disturbed (**heat-oppressèd**) mind. The floating, imaginary dagger, which leads (**marshal'st**) him to Duncan's room, prompts him to draw his own dagger.

43–44 Either his eyes are mistaken (**fools**) or his other senses are.

45 He sees drops of blood on the blade and handle.

62 knell: funeral bell.

TEACH

CLOSE READ

Support Inferences
(LINES 25–28)

COMMON CORE **RL 1**

Explain that readers use information explicitly stated in a text to make **inferences,** or logical conclusions, about the implied meaning. Remind them to use the side margin notes to help understand Shakespeare's language.

C CITE TEXT EVIDENCE Ask students what inference they can make after reading lines 25–28. *(Banquo is worried that Macbeth may ask him to do something that opposes the king.)* Then have them identify specific information that supports their inference. *("…keep/My bosom franchised and allegiance clear")*

Analyze Character and Theme (LINES 32–42)

COMMON CORE **RL 2, RL 3**

Have a student volunteer summarize Macbeth's encounter with the three witches in Act I. Point out that this meeting set up the **theme** about the roles of fate vs. free will in determining one's actions.

D ASK STUDENTS how Shakespeare uses Macbeth's dialogue to develop the theme of fate vs. free will. *(Macbeth seems to take the vision of the dagger pointing toward the king's room in lines 32–42 as evidence that he is merely working toward his fate.)*

SCAFFOLDING FOR ELL STUDENTS

Summarize Shakespearean Language Work with students to translate Macbeth's soliloquy (Scene 1, lines 32–63) into plain language. Read a few lines at a time, pausing as volunteers summarize them:

- Lines 32–48: Macbeth sees a dagger in front of him. He is aware that the dagger exists in his imagination only, and he draws his own dagger. He sees blood, but knows it is only evil thoughts plaguing him.

- Lines 48–55: Macbeth knows that this is a time of wicked dreams that are moving toward their fulfillment.

- Lines 59–60: Simply thinking and talking about his plan is not enough. Words cannot replace actions.

Analyze Author's Choices: Tension and Surprise

COMMON CORE RL 1, RL 4, RL 5

(LINES 15–19)

Tell students that the way a playwright uses words and punctuation can create tension or emotion in a scene.

E **CITE TEXT EVIDENCE** Ask students to explain how Shakespeare creates tension in lines 15–19. Then have them identify specific examples to support their answer. *(Shakespeare uses short, choppy dialogue between Macbeth and his wife—"When?" "Now," "Ay," "Hark!"—to create tension. The questions and exclamations also add a stressful feeling to the scene.)*

Scene 2 *Macbeth's castle.*

[*Enter* Lady Macbeth.]

Lady Macbeth. That which hath made them drunk hath made
    me bold.
What hath quenched them hath given me fire. Hark!—Peace.
It was the owl that shrieked, the fatal bellman,
Which gives the stern'st good-night. He is about it.
5 The doors are open, and the surfeited grooms
Do mock their charge with snores. I have drugged their possets,
That death and nature do contend about them
Whether they live or die.

    Macbeth [*within*].   Who's there? what, ho!

    Lady Macbeth. Alack, I am afraid they have awaked,
10 And 'tis not done. Th' attempt and not the deed
Confounds us. Hark!—I laid their daggers ready;
He could not miss 'em. Had he not resembled
My father as he slept, I had done 't.

[*Enter* Macbeth *with bloody daggers.*]

                    My husband?

    Macbeth. I have done the deed. Didst thou not hear a noise?

15 **Lady Macbeth.** I heard the owl scream and the crickets cry.
Did not you speak?

    Macbeth.   When?

    Lady Macbeth.   Now.

    Macbeth.   As I descended?

    Lady Macbeth. Ay.

    Macbeth.   Hark!—Who lies i' th' second chamber?

    Lady Macbeth. Donalbain.

    Macbeth.   This is a sorry sight.

    Lady Macbeth. A foolish thought, to say a sorry sight.

20 **Macbeth.** There's one did laugh in 's sleep, and one cried
    "Murder!"
That they did wake each other. I stood and heard them.
But they did say their prayers and addressed them
Again to sleep.

    Lady Macbeth. There are two lodged together.

    Macbeth. One cried "God bless us" and "Amen" the other,
25 As they had seen me with these hangman's hands,

3 fatal bellman: town crier.

5 surfeited grooms: drunken servants.

6 possets: drinks.

11 confounds: destroys. If Duncan survives, they will be killed (as his attempted murderers).

25 As: as if. He imagines that the sleepers could see him.

WHEN STUDENTS STRUGGLE . . .

This important scene describes the murder of Duncan. Have students use a chart like the one below to piece together the events leading up to and after the murder.

| Lady Macbeth drugs the servants and leaves their daggers ready for Macbeth. | → | Macbeth kills Duncan while his wife waits in another room. | → | Macbeth hears voices; he's afraid he's been discovered. | → | Macbeth returns to his wife. She scolds him for bringing the daggers and returns to Duncan's room to plant the bloody evidence on his servants. |

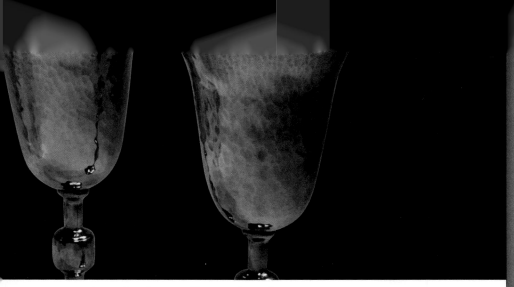

Image Credits: ©Getty Images

F

List'ning their fear. I could not say "Amen"
When they did say "God bless us."

Lady Macbeth. Consider it not so deeply.

Macbeth. But wherefore could not I pronounce "Amen"?
30   I had most need of blessing, and "Amen"
Stuck in my throat.

Lady Macbeth.   These deeds must not be thought
After these ways; so, it will make us mad.

Macbeth. Methought I heard a voice cry "Sleep no more!
Macbeth does murder sleep"—the innocent sleep,
35   Sleep that knits up the raveled sleave of care,
The death of each day's life, sore labor's bath,
Balm of hurt minds, great nature's second course,
Chief nourisher in life's feast.

Lady Macbeth.   What do you mean?

Macbeth. Still it cried "Sleep no more!" to all the house.
40   "Glamis hath murdered sleep, and therefore Cawdor
Shall sleep no more. Macbeth shall sleep no more."

Lady Macbeth. Who was it that thus cried? Why, worthy thane,
You do unbend your noble strength to think
So brainsickly of things. Go get some water
45   And wash this filthy witness from your hand.—
Why did you bring these daggers from the place?

34–38 Sleep eases worries (**knits up the raveled sleave of care**), relieves the aches of physical work (**sore labor's bath**), soothes the anxious (**hurt minds**), and nourishes like food.

The Tragedy of Macbeth: Act II, Scene 2   **235**

Analyze Character and Theme (LINES 56–72)

COMMON CORE RL 1, RL 2, RL 3

As they read, remind students to continue looking for evidence that develops the theme through characters' interactions.

H CITE TEXT EVIDENCE Have students reread the dialogue between Macbeth and his wife in lines 56–72. Then have them cite details that shape and refine the theme of guilt. *(Lines 58–61, where Macbeth says all of the oceans could not wash the blood from his hands, and would instead turn the ocean red; line 72, where he says he wishes the knocking would wake the king, who is now dead.)* Ask students whether Lady Macbeth feels the same guilt, and explain how they know. *(Lady Macbeth does not feel any guilt. In line 65, she says "A little water clears us of this deed.")* Ask students to form a preliminary statement of a theme about guilt based on their responses. *(Responses will vary. Students may say that guilt is proportionate to the virtue of the person who commits the crime, since Macbeth is nearly mad with guilt, but Lady Macbeth feels none. Accept reasonable responses supported by the text.)*

Analyze Author's Choices (LINES 1–2)

COMMON CORE RL 4, RL 5

Remind students that Shakespeare often employs dramatic irony, keeping his characters in the dark about things the audience knows.

I ASK STUDENTS to identify the ironic statement the porter makes. *(In lines 1–2, he compares himself to the porter for the gates to hell.)* What makes this statement ironic? *(The audience knows the king has been murdered, but the porter does not.)*

They must lie there. Go carry them and smear
The sleepy grooms with blood.

  Macbeth.   I'll go no more.
I am afraid to think what I have done.
50 Look on 't again I dare not.

  Lady Macbeth.   Infirm of purpose!
Give me the daggers. The sleeping and the dead
Are but as pictures. 'Tis the eye of childhood
That fears a painted devil. If he do bleed,
I'll gild the faces of the grooms withal,
55 For it must seem their guilt.

  [*She exits with the daggers. Knock within.*]

  Macbeth.   Whence is that knocking?
How is 't with me when every noise appalls me?
What hands are here? Ha, they pluck out mine eyes.
Will all great Neptune's ocean wash this blood
Clean from my hand? No, this my hand will rather
60 The multitudinous seas incarnadine,
Making the green one red.

  [*Enter* Lady Macbeth.]

  Lady Macbeth. My hands are of your color, but I shame
To wear a heart so white.   [*Knock*]

        I hear a knocking
At the south entry. Retire we to our chamber.
65 A little water clears us of this deed.
How easy is it, then! Your constancy
Hath left you unattended.   [*Knock*]

        Hark, more knocking.
Get on your nightgown, lest occasion call us
And show us to be watchers. Be not lost
70 So poorly in your thoughts.

  Macbeth. To know my deed 'twere best not know myself.
             [*Knock*]
Wake Duncan with thy knocking. I would thou couldst.

  [*They exit.*]

Scene 3 *Within Macbeth's castle, near the gate.*

[*Knocking within. Enter a* Porter.]

  Porter. Here's a knocking indeed! If a man were porter of hell gate, he should have old turning the key. [*Knock*] Knock, knock, knock! Who's there, i' th' name of Beelzebub? Here's a farmer that hanged himself on th' expectation of plenty. Come in time!

54–55 She'll cover (**gild**) the servants with blood, blaming them for the murder.

59–61 this my hand . . . one red: The blood on my hand will redden (**incarnadine**) the seas.

66–67 Your constancy . . . unattended: Your courage has left you.

68–69 lest . . . watchers: in case we are called for and found awake (**watchers**), which would look suspicious.

71 To know . . . myself: To come to terms with what I have done, I must lose my conscience.

2 old turning the key: plenty of key turning. Hell's porter would be busy in such evil times.

3 Beelzebub: a devil.

SCAFFOLDING FOR ELL STUDENTS

Analyze Character and Theme Work with students to translate Macbeth's dialogue in lines 56–61 into plain language. Then have students summarize Macbeth's words. When they have finished, use the following questions to scaffold students' understanding.

ASK STUDENTS why Macbeth has blood on his hands. *(He just returned from killing the king.)* The blood is evidence of what crime? *(murder)* What does the blood symbolize? *(Guilt over what he's done.)* Have partners use a chart like the one shown to cite evidence of how the theme of guilt is developed and refined throughout the play. They can return to the chart later in the play to add more details.

5 Have napkins enough about you; here you'll sweat for 't. [*Knock*]
Knock, knock! Who's there, in th' other devil's name? Faith,
here's an equivocator that could swear in both the scales against
either scale, who committed treason enough for God's sake
yet could not equivocate to heaven. O, come in, equivocator.
10 [*Knock*] Knock, knock, knock! Who's there? Faith, here's an
English tailor come hither for stealing out of a French hose.
Come in, tailor. Here you may roast your goose. [*Knock*] Knock,
knock! Never at quiet. —What are you? —But this place is too
cold for hell. I'll devilporter it no further. I had thought to have
15 let in some of all professions that go the primrose way to th'
everlasting bonfire. [*Knock*] Anon, anon! [*The* Porter *opens the
door to* Macduff *and* Lennox.] I pray you, remember the porter.

Macduff. Was it so late, friend, ere you went to bed
That you do lie so late?

20 **Porter.** Faith, sir, we were carousing till the second cock, and
drink, sir, is a great provoker of three things.

Macduff. What three things does drink especially provoke?

Porter. Marry, sir, nose-painting, sleep, and urine. Lechery, sir, it
provokes and unprovokes. It provokes the desire, but it takes
25 away the performance. Therefore much drink may be said
to be an equivocator with lechery. It makes him, and it mars
him; it sets him on, and it takes him off; it persuades him and
disheartens him; makes him stand to and not stand to; in
conclusion, equivocates him in a sleep and, giving him the lie,
30 leaves him.

Macduff. I believe drink gave thee the lie last night.

Porter. That it did, sir, i' th' very throat on me; but I requited
him for his lie, and, I think, being too strong for him, though he
took up my legs sometime, yet I made a shift to cast him.

35 **Macduff.** Is thy master stirring?

[*Enter* Macbeth.]

Our knocking has awaked him. Here he comes.

[Porter *exits*.]

Lennox. Good morrow, noble sir.

Macbeth.   Good morrow, both.

Macduff. Is the King stirring, worthy thane?

Macbeth.   Not yet.

Macduff. He did command me to call timely on him.
40 I have almost slipped the hour.

3–11 The porter pretends he is welcoming a farmer who killed himself after his schemes to get rich (**expectation of plenty**) failed, a double talker (**equivocator**) who perjured himself yet couldn't talk his way into heaven, and a tailor who cheated his customers by skimping on material (**stealing out of a French hose**).

31–34 Alcohol is described as a wrestler thrown off (**cast**) by the porter, who thus paid him back (**requited him**) for disappointment in love. *Cast* also means "to vomit" and "to urinate."

39 timely: early.

40 slipped the hour: missed the time.

The Tragedy of Macbeth: Act II, Scene 3   **237**

CLOSE READ

Analyze Author's Choices RL 4, RL 5

(LINES 1–16)

Explain that **comic relief** is a technique playwrights use to provide relief from emotional tension.

J ASK STUDENTS to reread lines 1–16. How does Shakespeare use the porter as comic relief? (*By having the porter joke about how busy hell is—with the farmer, equivocator, and tailor entering it—the tension from the previous scene is lessened some.*) Ask students what they notice about the printed lines and how they differ from the lines in the rest of the drama. (*The porter's lines are in prose rather than blank verse.*) Ask students what the effect of this choice is. (*It underscores that the porter's speech is less formal than the other characters', highlighting the fact that he is of a lower social status and that his comic lines are not as important as the other characters'.*)

Theme: Guilt		
Macbeth thinks he heard someone say "Macbeth does murder sleep."	Macbeth thinks all the water in the ocean could not wipe his hands clean of the blood.	Lady Macbeth says a little water will wash away their guilt.

Analyze Author's Choices (LINES 48–55)

 COMMON CORE RL 1, RL 4, RL 5

Explain that playwrights use specific word choice to create a particular **mood** in a literary work. The mood, or the general feeling and emotions that the writing creates for the reader, can be established with language, setting, and characters' actions.

K **CITE TEXT EVIDENCE** Have students identify the words that set a foreboding mood in lines 48–55. *(unruly, lamenting, screams of death, prophesying, dire, clamored, feverous)*

Determine Figurative Meanings (LINES 65–67)

COMMON CORE RL 5

Ask for a student volunteer to define the term **figurative meaning**. *(language such as metaphors, similes, and hyperbole that does not use words or terms literally)* Explain that playwrights use figurative meanings of words to create a vivid imagery and depth of meaning and to convey a mood.

L **ASK STUDENTS** what metaphor Macduff makes in lines 65–67. *(He compares his shock of learning the king is dead to being turned to stone by a Gorgon.)* Why is this metaphor effective? *(It conveys Macduff's despair at the situation.)*

Macbeth.   I'll bring you to him.

Macduff. I know this is a joyful trouble to you,
But yet 'tis one.

Macbeth. The labor we delight in physics pain.
This is the door.

43 physics: cures.

Macduff.   I'll make so bold to call,
45 For 'tis my limited service. [Macduff *exits.*]

45 limited service: appointed duty.

Lennox. Goes the King hence today?

Macbeth. He does. He did appoint so.

Lennox. The night has been unruly. Where we lay,
Our chimneys were blown down and, as they say,

50 Lamentings heard i' th' air, strange screams of death,
And prophesying, with accents terrible,
Of dire combustion and confused events
New hatched to th' woeful time. The obscure bird
Clamored the livelong night. Some say the earth
55 Was feverous and did shake.

Macbeth.   'Twas a rough night.

Lennox. My young remembrance cannot parallel
A fellow to it.

[*Enter* Macduff.]

Macduff.   O horror, horror, horror!
Tongue nor heart cannot conceive nor name thee!

Macbeth and Lennox. What's the matter?

60 **Macduff.** Confusion now hath made his masterpiece.
Most sacrilegious murder hath broke ope
The Lord's anointed temple and stole thence
The life o' th' building.

60–63 Macduff mourns Duncan's death as the destruction (**confusion**) of order and as sacrilegious, violating all that is holy. In Shakespeare's time the king was believed to be God's sacred representative on earth.

Macbeth.   What is 't you say? The life?

Lennox. Mean you his majesty?

65 **Macduff.** Approach the chamber and destroy your sight
With a new Gorgon. Do not bid me speak.
See and then speak yourselves.

L

66 new Gorgon: Macduff compares the shocking sight of the corpse to a Gorgon. In Greek mythology, anyone who saw a Gorgon turned to stone.

[Macbeth *and* Lennox *exit.*]

                    Awake, awake!
Ring the alarum bell.—Murder and treason!
Banquo and Donalbain, Malcolm, awake!
70 Shake off this downy sleep, death's counterfeit,
And look on death itself. Up, up, and see

70 counterfeit: imitation.

WHEN STUDENTS STRUGGLE . . .

Line 35 marks Macbeth's first entrance since murdering Duncan. Ask students how Macbeth reacted to his crime at the end of the last scene. Have students read to line 74 and then describe Macbeth's behavior, both before and after the discovery of Duncan's murder. Have students pay attention to how both Macbeth and his wife behave once they are together on the stage. Remind students that, as readers of a play, but not viewers, we have only the actor's words to suggest their behavior. We have to infer how well their words mask their inner thoughts and feelings.

ASK STUDENTS to debate whether Macbeth or his wife would have a more difficult time pretending shock and horror at the discovery of Duncan's murder. Have them defend their responses with evidence from this and earlier scenes.

The great doom's image. Malcolm. Banquo.
As from your graves rise up and walk like sprites
To countenance this horror.—Ring the bell.

[*Bell rings.*]
[*Enter* Lady Macbeth.]

75 **Lady Macbeth.** What's the business,
That such a hideous trumpet calls to parley
The sleepers of the house? Speak, speak!

Macduff.   O gentle lady,
'Tis not for you to hear what I can speak.
The repetition in a woman's ear
80 Would murder as it fell.

[*Enter* Banquo.]

                              O Banquo, Banquo,
Our royal master's murdered.

Lady Macbeth.   Woe, alas!
What, in our house?

Banquo.   Too cruel anywhere. —
Dear Duff, I prithee, contradict thyself
And say it is not so.

[*Enter* Macbeth, Lennox, *and* Ross.]

85 **Macbeth.** Had I but died an hour before this chance,
I had lived a blessèd time; for from this instant
There's nothing serious in mortality.
All is but toys. Renown and grace is dead.
The wine of life is drawn, and the mere lees
90 Is left this vault to brag of.

[*Enter* Malcolm *and* Donalbain.]

Donalbain. What is amiss?

Macbeth.   You are, and do not know 't.
The spring, the head, the fountain of your blood
Is stopped; the very source of it is stopped.

Macduff. Your royal father's murdered.

Malcolm.   O, by whom?

95 **Lennox.** Those of his chamber, as it seemed, had done 't.
Their hands and faces were all badged with blood.
So were their daggers, which unwiped we found
Upon their pillows. They stared and were distracted.
No man's life was to be trusted with them.

72 great doom's image: a picture like the Last Judgment, the end of the world.

73 sprites: spirits. The spirits of the dead were supposed to rise on Judgment Day.

76 trumpet calls to parley: She compares the clanging bell to a trumpet used to call two sides of a battle to negotiation.

86–90 for from . . . brag of: From now on, nothing matters (**there's nothing serious**) in human life (**mortality**); even fame and grace have been made meaningless. The good wine of life has been removed (**drawn**), leaving only the dregs (**lees**).

96 badged: marked.

CLOSE READ

Analyze Author's Choices: Tension and Surprise

COMMON CORE RL 4, RL 5

(LINES 75–80)

Remind students that dramatic irony helps build suspense.

 ASK STUDENTS to reread lines 75–80. Why are Lady Macbeth's words ironic? *(She asks what the commotion is about, but she already knows.)* How does this create suspense? *(The audience wonders if Macbeth's crime—and her part in it—will be discovered.)* How do Macduff's words in lines 75–78 ironically echo Lady Macbeth's speech in Act I, in which she calls on the spirits of evil to "unsex her"? (Macduff thinks Lady Macbeth is too gentle and womanly to hear about Duncan's murder. In Act I, Lady Macbeth wanted to rid herself of womanly weakness in order to carry out a grisly plot.)*

Analyze Character and Theme (LINES 85–90)

COMMON CORE RL 1, RL 2, RL 3

Remind students to continue looking for evidence that develops the theme through the characters' interactions.

N **CITE TEXT EVIDENCE** Ask students how the theme of guilt is refined in lines 85–90. *(Macbeth reveals the depth of his guilt by telling Lennox and Ross that, with the king now dead, everything good is gone.)*

TO CHALLENGE STUDENTS . . .

Analyze Theme Act Two, Scene 3 would have shocked audiences in Shakespeare's day; have students discuss why. Provide the following prompts for guidance:

- Briefly research the concept of the divine right of kings and of regicide in Elizabethan times.
- Consider how Macduff's statement about "Confusion" (line 58) fits into the drama's themes.
- Think about the effect of Duncan's murder taking place offstage.

Have students write a summary of their discussion afterwards.

Analyze Character and Theme (LINES 102–112)

COMMON CORE RL 2, RL 3

Remind students that the theme is often implied by characters' actions.

O ASK STUDENTS to reread lines 102–112. How does Shakespeare invoke the theme of guilt here? *(After Macbeth details the gruesome scene of the king's murder, Lady Macbeth faints. Her fainting suggests her feelings of guilt as the realization of what has happened hits her. On the other hand, her fainting may be an act—an appearance devised to distract Macduff from questioning Macbeth further and uncovering the reality of the murder.)*

Tell students that a theme can also be explicitly addressed. Recall that fate is another theme in *Macbeth*.

P ASK STUDENTS to reread lines 115–117. What is Donalbain's fear? *(That he and his brother will suffer the same fate as his father while at Macbeth's castle.)*

---

100 **Macbeth.** O, yet I do repent me of my fury,
That I did kill them.

Macduff.   Wherefore did you so?

Macbeth. Who can be wise, amazed, temp'rate, and furious,
Loyal, and neutral, in a moment? No man.
Th' expedition of my violent love
105 Outrun the pauser, reason. Here lay Duncan,
His silver skin laced with his golden blood,
And his gashed stabs looked like a breach in nature
For ruin's wasteful entrance; there the murderers,
Steeped in the colors of their trade, their daggers
110 Unmannerly breeched with gore. Who could refrain
That had a heart to love, and in that heart
Courage to make 's love known?

Lady Macbeth.   Help me hence, ho!

Macduff. Look to the lady.

Malcolm [*aside to* Donalbain]. Why do we hold our tongues,
That most may claim this argument for ours?

Donalbain [*aside to* Malcolm].
115 What should be spoken here, where our fate,
Hid in an auger hole, may rush and seize us?
Let's away. Our tears are not yet brewed.

Malcolm [*aside to* Donalbain].
Nor our strong sorrow upon the foot of motion.

Banquo. Look to the lady.

[Lady Macbeth *is assisted to leave.*]

120 And when we have our naked frailties hid,
That suffer in exposure, let us meet
And question this most bloody piece of work
To know it further. Fears and scruples shake us.
In the great hand of God I stand, and thence
125 Against the undivulged pretense I fight
Of treasonous malice.

Macduff.   And so do I.

All.   So all.

Macbeth. Let's briefly put on manly readiness
And meet i' th' hall together.

All.   Well contented.

[*All but* Malcolm *and* Donalbain *exit.*]

104–105 He claims his emotions overpowered his reason, which would have made him pause to think before he killed Duncan's servants.

107 breach: a military term to describe a break in defenses, such as a hole in a castle wall.

112 Lady Macbeth faints.

120–121 Banquo suggests that they all meet to discuss the murder after they have dressed (**our naked frailties hid**), since people are shivering in their nightclothes (**suffer in exposure**).

123–126 Though shaken by fears and doubts (**scruples**), he will fight against the secret plans (**undivulged pretense**) of the traitor.

* 2015 PY

SCAFFOLDING FOR ELL STUDENTS

Language: Shakespeare's English Explain that Shakespeare used apostrophes where he dropped a letter, left words out entirely, and varied the word order from conventional patterns of modern English. Provide the following example.

Who could refrain/That had a heart to love, and in that heart/

[had] Courage to make 's [his] love known? (lines 110–112)

Have mixed-language ability groups study different passages from this scene, filling in missing words and letters and experimenting with word order when necessary. Then have the groups work together to paraphrase each passage. Each group should present their paraphrases to the class.

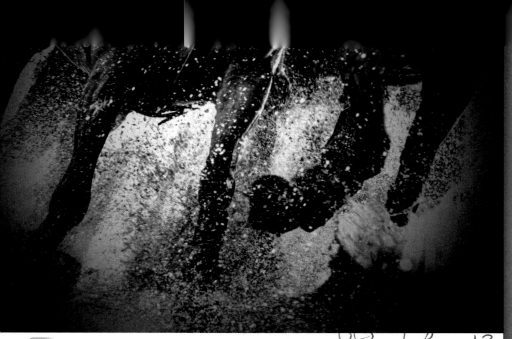

Malcolm. What will you do? Let's not consort with them.
130 To show an unfelt sorrow is an office
Which the false man does easy. I'll to England.

Donalbain. To Ireland I. Our separated fortune
Shall keep us both the safer. Where we are,
There's daggers in men's smiles. The near in blood,
135 The nearer bloody.

Malcolm.   This murderous shaft that's shot
Hath not yet lighted, and our safest way
Is to avoid the aim. Therefore to horse,
And let us not be dainty of leave-taking
But shift away. There's warrant in that theft
140 Which steals itself when there's no mercy left.

[*They exit.*]

Scene 4 *Outside Macbeth's castle.*

[*Enter* Ross *with an* Old Man.]

Old Man. Threescore and ten I can remember well,
Within the volume of which time I have seen
Hours dreadful and things strange, but this sore night
Hath trifled former knowings.

129–131 Malcolm does not want to join (**consort with**) the others because one of them may have plotted the murder.

139–140 There's . . . **left:** There's good reason (**warrant**) to steal away from a situation that promises no mercy.

1–4 Nothing the old man has seen in 70 years (**threescore and ten**) has been as strange and terrible (**sore**) as this night. It has made other times seem trivial (**hath trifled**) by comparison.

Image Credits: ©Cristina Corduneanu/Flickr/Getty Images

CLOSE READ

Support Inferences
(LINES 129–140)

COMMON CORE RL 1, RL 3

Remind students that an inference is a logical conclusion based on text evidence. Then recall that Malcolm is next in line to be king.

Q CITE TEXT EVIDENCE Ask students what inference they can make about the kind of king Malcolm will be. *(Malcolm will be a weak, cowardly king; Malcolm will be a shrewd king.)* Then have them identify specific information that supports their inference. *(In lines 120–121, Banquo suggests everyone should meet to discuss the murder because he suspects a traitor. But in lines 129–131, Malcolm tells his brother they should not stay and that he is going to England. This could suggest either cowardice or a recognition that he might well be the next victim and should escape to protect his eventual succession to the throne.)*

TO CHALLENGE STUDENTS . . .

Analyze Language Tell students that many directors have interpreted Shakespeare's original work, but set them in different times or cultures. Have students work in small groups. Tell them to choose a scene from *Macbeth* and rewrite it, applying the following principles:

• Choose a modern-day setting.

• Use contemporary language to paraphrase the scene line by line.

• Create roles based on an organizational hierarchy that makes sense in the modern context.

Have students present their staging to the class.

Analyze Character and Theme (LINES 20–30)

COMMON CORE RL 2, RL 3

Remind students that a major theme in *Macbeth* involves ambition, particularly Macbeth's ambition to gain the crown once he hears the three witches' prophecy. Guide the class to understand that playwrights may use characters to develop a theme indirectly.

(R) **ASK STUDENTS** to reread lines 20–30. How does the exchange between Macduff and Ross support the theme of ambition? *(In lines 27–29, Ross wonders at the princes' ambition, that they would pay someone to have their own father killed so they could take the crown. Though Ross is wrong about the guilty party, he is correct in that it is "thriftless ambition" that led to the king's murder.)*

Ross.   Ha, good father,
5 Thou seest the heavens, as troubled with man's act,
    Threaten his bloody stage. By th' clock 'tis day,
    And yet dark night strangles the traveling lamp.
    Is 't night's predominance or the day's shame
    That darkness does the face of earth entomb
10 When living light should kiss it?

Old Man.   'Tis unnatural,
    Even like the deed that's done. On Tuesday last
    A falcon, tow'ring in her pride of place,
    Was by a mousing owl hawked at and killed.

Ross. And Duncan's horses (a thing most strange and certain),
15 Beauteous and swift, the minions of their race,
    Turned wild in nature, broke their stalls, flung out,
    Contending 'gainst obedience, as they would
    Make war with mankind.

Old Man.   'Tis said they eat each other.

Ross. They did so, to th' amazement of mine eyes
20 That looked upon 't.
    [*Enter* Macduff.]
                        Here comes the good Macduff.—
    How goes the world, sir, now?

Macduff.   Why, see you not?

Ross. Is 't known who did this more than bloody deed?

Macduff. Those that Macbeth hath slain.

Ross.   Alas, the day,
    What good could they pretend?

Macduff.   They were suborned.
25 Malcolm and Donalbain, the King's two sons,
    Are stol'n away and fled, which puts upon them
    Suspicion of the deed.

Ross.   'Gainst nature still!
    Thriftless ambition, that will ravin up
    Thine own lives' means. Then 'tis most like
30 The sovereignty will fall upon Macbeth.

Macduff. He is already named and gone to Scone
    To be invested.

Ross.   Where is Duncan's body?

6–10 By th' clock . . . kiss it: Though daytime, an unnatural darkness blots out the sun (**strangles the traveling lamp**).

12–13 The owl would never be expected to attack a high-flying (**tow'ring**) falcon, much less defeat one.

15 minions: best or favorites.

17 Contending 'gainst obedience: The well-trained horses rebelliously fought against all constraints.

24 What . . . pretend: Ross wonders what the servants could have hoped to achieve (**pretend**) by killing; **suborned:** hired or bribed.

27–29 He is horrified by the thought that the sons could act contrary to nature (**'gainst nature still**) because of wasteful (**thriftless**) ambition and greedily destroy (**ravin up**) their father, the source of their own life (**thine own lives' means**).

31–32 Macbeth went to the traditional site (**Scone**) where Scotland's kings were crowned.

APPLYING ACADEMIC VOCABULARY

comprise	ultimate

As you discuss Shakespeare's play, incorporate the Collection 5 academic vocabulary words *comprise* and *ultimate*. Ask students to explain what events in this act **comprised** the unnatural happenings of the night, and what Ross seems to consider the **ultimate** betrayal.

Macduff. Carried to Colmekill,
The sacred storehouse of his predecessors

35 And guardian of their bones.

Ross.   Will you to Scone?

Macduff. No, cousin, I'll to Fife.

Ross.   Well, I will thither.

Macduff. Well, may you see things well done there. Adieu,
Lest our old robes sit easier than our new.

Ross. Farewell, father.

40 **Old Man.** God's benison go with you and with those
That would make good of bad and friends of foes.

[*All exit.*]

40–41 The old man gives his blessing (**benison**) to Macduff and all those who would bring peace to the troubled land.

COLLABORATIVE DISCUSSION How do Macbeth and Lady Macbeth conceal and carry out their plot? With a partner, discuss which parts of the plan go smoothly and which do not. Cite specific textual evidence from the play to support your ideas.

CLOSE READ

Determine Figurative Meaning (LINES 38–39)

COMMON CORE RL 4

Tell students that *adieu*, like *adios*, literally means "to God" (*Goodbye*, for that matter, is a contraction of the expression "God be with you.") Sometimes writers intend the word to be taken not just as a farewell but as a blessing.

S **ASK STUDENTS** what warning McDuff conveys in lines 38–39 through the clothing metaphor? (*McDuff is telling Ross to go with God, because he fears that with Macbeth as king instead of Duncan, their new situation ("new robes") may not suit them as well as their old one did.*)

COLLABORATIVE DISCUSSION Have partners review the text for examples of Macbeth and Lady Macbeth carrying out their plot. Tell students to create a two-column chart to take notes on each example. One column is for examples that show the plan going smoothly. The other column is for examples that show the plan not going well. Have partners share their conclusions with the class as a whole. Accept all reasonable responses.

ASK STUDENTS to share any questions they generated in the course of reading and discussing the selection.

SCAFFOLDING FOR ELL STUDENTS

Vocabulary: Antonyms Remind students that a paradox is a statement that seems contradictory but actually reveals a truth. One critical theme in Macbeth is based on the paradoxical statement "Fair is foul, and foul is fair" (Act I, Scene 1, line 10). Point out that *foul* and *fair* are antonyms, words with opposite meaning. Ask students how this paradoxical statement reveals a theme. (*Things that seem good may be bad, and things that seem bad may be good.*) Project or write lines 40–41 on a whiteboard. Ask a volunteer to underline or highlight words that echo this theme.

Old Man.   God's benison go with you and with those
That would make good of bad and friends of foes.

ASK STUDENTS how these lines develop the theme. (*They express a desire to have justice restored.*) Have students look for antonyms used in a similar way throughout the remainder of the drama.

PRACTICE & APPLY

Analyzing the Text 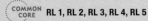 RL 1, RL 2, RL 3, RL 4, RL 5

Possible answers:

1. *All of those passages demonstrate Macbeth's guilt over murdering King Duncan.*

2. *Though the porter scene provides humor, it also increases the tension because the audience knows about the murder and waits in suspense to see when it will be revealed.*

3. *Macbeth says he killed Duncan's servants because he was overcome with emotion after learning they murdered the king, but the audience knows he's the guilty party. This second act of murder further pushed Macbeth toward his tragic fall.*

4. *The use of blood symbolizes guilt and family; sleep symbolizes innocence; and darkness symbolizes evil.*

5. *Donalbain is referring to how welcoming everyone was when the king arrived to Macbeth's castle, yet someone there was a traitor and murderer; they may have been smiling, but someone there was planning murder. Since he does not know who is guilty, he and his brother think it best to leave. The nobles take this as a sign that the princes are guilty in plotting their father's murder.*

6. *All of the actions described in these lines—the night swallowing the day, an owl killing a falcon, the horses behaving wildly—are unnatural, reflecting the unnatural act of killing the king. This description foreshadows Macbeth's violent reign and eventual downfall.*

7. *Macduff is a loyal nobleman. By saying he will not attend the coronation (line 36), the suggestion is that he does not accept Macbeth as his king.*

8. *The mood in Act II is menacing, ominous, and foreboding. In Scene 1, Macbeth has a vision of a bloody dagger and talks about Hecate, the Greek goddess of the underworld (lines 32–42, 50–55); in Scene 2, after killing the king, Macbeth worries about how he could not say a prayer when he needed it most (lines 24–31) and how he'll never get the blood off his hands (lines 58–61); at the beginning of Scene 3, the porter likens himself to the porter at hell's gate; in Scene 4, Ross and the Old Man discuss the unnatural events following the king's death. (lines 6–19)*

 eBook *Annotate It!*

Analyzing the Text

COMMON CORE RL 1, RL 2, RL 3, RL 4, RL 5, SL 1a

Cite Text Evidence   Support your responses with evidence from the selection.

1. **Analyze** Macbeth's active imagination contributes to his internal conflict. Explain what these passages reveal about this conflict.

   - the appearance of the dagger (Scene 1, lines 32–48)
   - the voice after the murder (Scene 2, lines 33–41)
   - his refusal to return to the room (Scene 2, lines 48–50)
   - his words after the discovery of Duncan's death (Scene 3, lines 85–90)

2. **Draw Conclusions** How does the porter's scene increase tension and suspense?

3. **Analyze** Explain the dramatic irony of lines 100–112 in Scene 3. Why is Macbeth's action significant?

4. **Identify Patterns** Throughout the play **symbols**, or objects or ideas that stand for something other than themselves, are used to represent major ideas and themes. What is symbolized by the repeated incidences of images of blood, sleep, and darkness?

5. **Interpret** Explain how Donalbain's statement that "There's daggers in men's smiles" relates to the sons' decision to flee. How is their action interpreted by Duncan's nobles?

6. **Draw Conclusions** What do the images in lines 6–19 of Scene 4 suggest about the act of killing the king? What is foreshadowed about Macbeth's reign by the description in these lines?

7. **Infer** Explain Macduff's attitude toward Macbeth and his coronation. Use specific details from the text to support this inference.

8. **Cite Evidence** What is the mood or atmosphere of Act II? What images or details in characters' speeches help to create this mood?

PERFORMANCE TASK

Speaking Activity: Discussion Why does Lady Macbeth faint? Is it a distraction or is it real? Support your conclusion with evidence from the text.

- Jot down ideas about what Lady Macbeth does and says in Act II that might explain why she faints.

- In a small group, discuss these ideas and your interpretation of her action. Together, draw one or more conclusions about her motives.
- Summarize the group discussion and present your ideas to the class.

Assign this performance task.

PERFORMANCE TASK

COMMON CORE SL 1, W 4

Speaking Activity: Discussion Explain to students that to prepare for their discussion they should reread Scene 2 and lines 102–112 of Scene 4. Tell them to look for and write down any evidence supporting their conclusions about Lady Macbeth's sincerity in fainting.

AS YOU READ Direct students to use the As You Read statement to focus their reading.

Analyze Character: Dialogue (LINES 1–10)

COMMON CORE RL 3

Explain to students that in drama, the dialogue provides most of the information about the characters. Authors reveal characters through what they say, what is said about them, and how they act.

(A) CITE TEXT EVIDENCE Have students read lines 1–10 and cite specific dialogue supporting the idea that Banquo is hopeful about the prediction of the Weird Women. *("But that myself should be the root and father / Of many kings." [lines 5–6] and "May they not be my oracles as well, / And set me up in hope?" [lines 9–10].)*

Analyze Word Choice

COMMON CORE RL 4

(LINES 3, 15–18)

Point out that in dialogue, the tone refers to the mood or feelings that characters project or the way characters sound to others.

(B) ASK STUDENTS to consider what they have learned about Banquo's suspicions about Macbeth. Then ask them to identify and explain Banquo's tone as he addresses Macbeth. *(Banquo is careful to mask his suspicion that Macbeth has acted "most foully" and speaks in a respectful tone as he voices his allegiance to his king.)*

Tell students that Shakespeare often uses double meanings for words and phrases as a way of adding layers to meaning.

(C) ASK STUDENTS to explain what double meaning might be intended by Banquo's statement that his "duties / Are with a most indissoluble tie / Forever knit." *(Banquo says explicitly that he will follow the king's commands, but this could also mean that the two men's fates are connected.)*

AS YOU READ Pay attention to the details that describe the condition of Scotland under Macbeth's rule. Write down any questions you generate during reading.

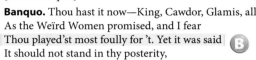

ACT III

Scene 1 *Macbeth's palace at Forres.*

[*Enter* Banquo.]

Banquo. Thou hast it now—King, Cawdor, Glamis, all
As the Weïrd Women promised, and I fear
Thou played'st most foully for 't. Yet it was said
It should not stand in thy posterity,
5 But that myself should be the root and father
Of many kings. If there come truth from them
(As upon thee, Macbeth, their speeches shine),
Why, by the verities on thee made good,
May they not be my oracles as well,
10 And set me up in hope? But hush, no more.

[*Sennet sounded. Enter* Macbeth *as King*, Lady Macbeth, Lennox,
Ross, Lords, *and* Attendants.]

Macbeth. Here's our chief guest.

Lady Macbeth.   If he had been forgotten,
It had been as a gap in our great feast
And all-thing unbecoming.

Macbeth. Tonight we hold a solemn supper, sir,
15 And I'll request your presence.

Banquo.   Let your Highness
Command upon me, to the which my duties
Are with a most indissoluble tie
Forever knit.

Macbeth.   Ride you this afternoon?

Banquo. Ay, my good lord.

20 **Macbeth.** We should have else desired your good advice
(Which still hath been both grave and prosperous)
In this day's council, but we'll take tomorrow.
Is 't far you ride?

Banquo. As far, my lord, as will fill up the time
25 'Twixt this and supper. Go not my horse the better,
I must become a borrower of the night
For a dark hour or twain.

Macbeth.   Fail not our feast.

Banquo. My lord, I will not.

[Stage Direction] Sennet sounded: A trumpet is sounded.

14–15 A king usually uses the royal pronoun *we*. Macbeth switches to *I* with Banquo.

15–18 Banquo says he is duty bound to serve the king.

21 grave and prosperous: thoughtful and profitable.

25–27 If his horse goes no faster than usual, he'll be back an hour or two (**twain**) after dark.

Close Read Screencasts   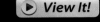 ▶ View It!

Modeled Discussion

Have students click the *Close Read* icons in their eBooks to access a screencast in which readers discuss and annotate the following key passage:

- Hecate's meeting with the witches (Scene 5, lines 23-33)

As a class, view and discuss this video.

Analyze Character   COMMON CORE RL 1, RL 3

(LINES 29–71)

Explain that **irony** in dialogue can reveal to the audience aspects about a character that other characters fail to recognize.

D CITE TEXT EVIDENCE Have students read Macbeth's dialogue in lines 29–35. Ask them to cite an example of irony. (*Macbeth states that Malcolm and Donalbain are "not confessing / Their cruel parricide, filling their hearers / With strange invention." He's saying that Malcolm and Donalbain are telling lies, when in fact Macbeth himself is telling lies.*)

Explain that a **soliloquy** is a monologue in which a character reveals information, thoughts, and feelings to the audience but not to other characters.

E CITE TEXT EVIDENCE Have students cite text evidence in Macbeth's soliloquy (lines 47–71) that explains Macbeth's assessment of Banquo. Then ask students to explain what is revealed about Macbeth's character. (*Believing in the prophecy made by the sisters, Macbeth feels that murdering Duncan will eventually benefit Banquo and his line, not Macbeth's. Therefore, Banquo is the one threat to him ["There is none but he / Whose being I do fear"]. Macbeth considers Banquo's cautiousness, his "wisdom that doth guide his valor / To act in safety." This suggests Macbeth is thinking of doing harm to him. We know that Macbeth killed Duncan, and now Macbeth sees Banquo as a threat. This soliloquy reveals Macbeth's bitterness about the prophecy and Banquo's apparent nobility and fitness to be king. It also reveals Macbeth's ambition and the ruthlessness with which he will pursue it.*)

Analyze Theme (LINES 65–71) COMMON CORE RL 2

Soliloquies often reveal major themes.

F ASK STUDENTS what theme is developed in these lines. (*The theme of fate vs. free will comes back into play; the last two lines of the soliloquy reveal that Macbeth is willing to fight to the end ["to th' utterance"] against what he now sees as his fate.*)

Macbeth. We hear our bloody cousins are bestowed
In England and in Ireland, not confessing
Their cruel parricide, filling their hearers
With strange invention. But of that tomorrow,
When therewithal we shall have cause of state
Craving us jointly. Hie you to horse. Adieu,
35 Till you return at night. Goes Fleance with you?

Banquo. Ay, my good lord. Our time does call upon 's.

Macbeth. I wish your horses swift and sure of foot,
And so I do commend you to their backs.
Farewell.

[Banquo *exits.*]

40 Let every man be master of his time
Till seven at night. To make society
The sweeter welcome, we will keep ourself
Till suppertime alone. While then, God be with you.

[Lords *and all but* Macbeth *and a* Servant *exit.*]

Sirrah, a word with you. Attend those men
45 Our pleasure?

Servant. They are, my lord, without the palace gate.

Macbeth. Bring them before us.

[Servant *exits.*]

To be thus is nothing,
But to be safely thus. Our fears in Banquo
Stick deep, and in his royalty of nature
50 Reigns that which would be feared. 'Tis much he dares,
And to that dauntless temper of his mind
He hath a wisdom that doth guide his valor
To act in safety. There is none but he
Whose being I do fear; and under him
55 My genius is rebuked, as it is said
Mark Antony's was by Caesar. He chid the sisters
When first they put the name of king upon me
And bade them speak to him. Then, prophet-like,
They hailed him father to a line of kings.
60 Upon my head they placed a fruitless crown
And put a barren scepter in my grip,
Thence to be wrenched with an unlineal hand,
No son of mine succeeding. If 't be so,
For Banquo's issue have I filed my mind;
65 For them the gracious Duncan have I murdered,
Put rancors in the vessel of my peace   **F**

---

29 bloody cousins: murderous relatives (Malcolm and Donalbain); **bestowed:** settled.

32 strange invention: lies; stories they have invented.

33–34 when . . . jointly: when matters of state will require the attention of us both.

40 be master of his time: do what he wants.

43 while: until.

44–45 sirrah: a term of address to an inferior; **Attend . . . pleasure:** Are they waiting for me?

47–48 To be thus . . . safely thus: To be king is worthless unless my position as king is safe.

51 dauntless temper: fearless temperament.

55–56 Banquo's mere presence forces back (**rebukes**) Macbeth's ruling spirit (**genius**). In ancient Rome, Caesar, who became emperor, had the same effect on his rival, Mark Antony.

60–69 They gave me a childless (**fruitless, barren**) rule, which will be taken away by someone outside my family (**unlineal**). I have committed murder, poisoned (**filed**) my mind, and destroyed my soul (**eternal jewel**) only to benefit Banquo's heirs.

TO CHALLENGE STUDENTS . . .

Analyze Character Interactions After students read the interaction between Macbeth and the murderers, have them work in small groups to complete one of the following activities:

- Debate whether Macbeth manipulates the murderers into agreeing with him. Have students use evidence from the dialogue, other literary works, or knowledge of others who have exhibited qualities similar to Macbeth.

- Discuss whether Shakespeare intended to show Macbeth as a manipulator in this scene. Ask students to cite specific language or tone for support.

- Have groups summarize their discussions to the class. Challenge students to take the minority view and support it with evidence and experience.

Only for them, and mine eternal jewel
Given to the common enemy of man
To make them kings, the seeds of Banquo kings.

E

F

70 Rather than so, come fate into the list,
And champion me to th' utterance.—Who's there?

[*Enter* Servant *and two* Murderers.]

G

[*To the* Servant] Now go to the door, and stay there till we call.

[Servant *exits*.]

Was it not yesterday we spoke together?

Murderers. It was, so please your Highness.

Macbeth. Well then, now

75 Have you considered of my speeches? Know
That it was he, in the times past, which held you
So under fortune, which you thought had been
Our innocent self. This I made good to you
In our last conference, passed in probation with you

80 How you were borne in hand, how crossed, the instruments,
Who wrought with them, and all things else that might
To half a soul and to a notion crazed
Say "Thus did Banquo."

First Murderer. You made it known to us.

Macbeth. I did so, and went further, which is now

85 Our point of second meeting. Do you find
Your patience so predominant in your nature
That you can let this go? Are you so gospeled
To pray for this good man and for his issue,
Whose heavy hand hath bowed you to the grave

90 And beggared yours forever?

First Murderer. We are men, my liege.

Macbeth. Ay, in the catalogue you go for men,
As hounds and greyhounds, mongrels, spaniels, curs,
Shoughs, water-rugs, and demi-wolves are clept
All by the name of dogs. The valued file

95 Distinguishes the swift, the slow, the subtle,
The housekeeper, the hunter, every one
According to the gift which bounteous nature
Hath in him closed; whereby he does receive
Particular addition, from the bill

100 That writes them all alike. And so of men.
Now, if you have a station in the file,
Not i' th' worst rank of manhood, say 't,
And I will put that business in your bosoms

75–83 Macbeth supposedly proved (**passed in probation**) Banquo's deception (**how you were borne in hand**), methods, and allies. Even a half-wit (**half a soul**) or a crazed person would agree that Banquo caused their trouble.

87–90 He asks whether they are so influenced by the gospel's message of forgiveness (**so gospeled**) that they will pray for Banquo and his children despite his harshness, which will leave their own families beggars.

91–100 The true worth of a dog can be measured only by examining the record (**valued file**) of its special qualities (**particular addition**).

103–107 Macbeth will give them a secret job (**business in your bosoms**) that will earn them his loyalty (**grapples you to the heart**) and love. Banquo's death will make this sick king healthy.

The Tragedy of Macbeth: Act III, Scene 1 **247**

CLOSE READ

Analyze Structure

COMMON CORE **RL 5**

(LINES 71–104)

Explain that the structure of a play includes stage directions and dialogue. These elements can include information that furthers the action of the plot.

G **ASK STUDENTS** to explain how the stage directions and dialogue further the action of the plot. Then ask students to compare the nature of the First Murderer's dialogue to Macbeth's. (*The stage direction states that a Servant and "two Murderers" enter the scene. This lets the reader know that the action that will follow has something to do with plotting or committing a murder. The dialogue that follows between Macbeth and the Murderers reveals that they had spoken earlier ["Have you considered of my speeches" and "Our point of second meeting"]. The dialogue of the First Murderer differs from Mabcbeth's in its brevity and directness. When Macbeth appeals to the Murderers' pride to persuade them to take revenge against Banquo for his alleged misdeeds against them, the First Murderer agrees simply and directly, "We are men, my liege." Macbeth then replies with a lengthy and elaborate simile, comparing the cataloguing of dog breeds to the ranking of men. Macbeth is pointing out that the Murderers would be men of standing under his protection if they carry out the plot to murder Banquo.*)

Strategies for Annotation

🖉 🗐 **Annotate it!**

Analyze Structure

COMMON CORE **RL 5**

Have students use their eBook annotation tools to analyze the text. Ask them to do the following.

- Highlight in yellow lines 67–71.
- Underline dialogue Macbeth says to himself.
- On a note, explain how the dialogue furthers the action of the plot.

Only for them, and mine eternal jewel

Given to the common enemy of man

To make them kings, the seeds of Banquo kings.

Rather than so, come fate into the list,

And champion me to th' utterance.—Who's there?

Macbeth's dialogue indicates his intention to fight fate and prevent Banquo's line from becoming kings.

Analyze Language

COMMON CORE RL 4, L 5

(LINES 104–123)

Remind students of the characteristics of iambic pentameter and that this meter is used throughout Shakespeare's plays. Then point out that Shakespeare often uses an inverted sentence structure in which subjects, predicates, objects, and prepositional phrases don't follow the pattern of usual speech.

H ASK STUDENTS to scan the meter in lines 115–122 and identify the meter. *(The lines scan as iambic pentameter.)* Then ask students to change the sentence structure of the following line: "And though I could / With barefaced power sweep him from my sight." Ask them to restructure the sentence so that it would sound more like usual speech. *(And though I could sweep him from my sight with barefaced power.)* Then have students scan the restructured lines. Ask students how Shakespeare's use of inverted sentence structure affects iambic pentameter. *(Iambic pentameter consists of five metrical feet, each consisting of an unaccented syllable followed by an accented syllable. Prepositional phrases begin with an unaccented preposition, so placing them where an unaccented syllable is needed preserves the meter. Usual speech would interrupt the meter.)*

Whose execution takes your enemy off,
105   Grapples you to the heart and love of us,
Who wear our health but sickly in his life,
Which in his death were perfect.

Second Murderer.   I am one, my liege,
Whom the vile blows and buffets of the world
Hath so incensed that I am reckless what
110   I do to spite the world.

First Murderer.   And I another
So weary with disasters, tugged with fortune,
That I would set my life on any chance,
To mend it or be rid on 't.

Macbeth.   Both of you
Know Banquo was your enemy.

Murderers.   True, my lord.

115   **Macbeth.** So is he mine, and in such bloody distance
That every minute of his being thrusts
H Against my near'st of life. And though I could
With barefaced power sweep him from my sight
And bid my will avouch it, yet I must not,
120   For certain friends that are both his and mine,
Whose loves I may not drop, but wail his fall
Who I myself struck down. And thence it is
That I to your assistance do make love,

I

111 tugged with: knocked about by.

115–117 Banquo is near enough to draw blood, and like a menacing swordsman, his mere presence threatens (**thrusts against**) Macbeth's existence.

119 bid my will avouch it: justify it as my will.

SCAFFOLDING FOR ELL STUDENTS

Analyze Poetic Language Students may have difficulty understanding the inverted or other nonstandard sentence structures in *Macbeth*. Have students make a chart like the one shown and work in pairs to rewrite the lines to help determine their meanings.

Original Line	Standard English Order
Line 35: . . . Goes Fleance with you?	*(Is Fleance going with you?)*
Line 36: . . . Our time does call upon's.	*(It's time to)*
Lines 42–43: . . . we will keep ourself / Till suppertime alone. . . .	*(We'll keep to ourselves until suppertime)*

Masking the business from the common eye
125 For sundry weighty reasons.

Second Murderer.   We shall, my lord,
Perform what you command us.

First Murderer.   Though our lives—

Macbeth. Your spirits shine through you. Within this hour at most
I will advise you where to plant yourselves,
Acquaint you with the perfect spy o' th' time,
130 The moment on 't, for 't must be done tonight
And something from the palace; always thought
That I require a clearness. And with him
(To leave no rubs nor botches in the work)
Fleance, his son, that keeps him company,
135 Whose absence is no less material to me
Than is his father's, must embrace the fate
Of that dark hour. Resolve yourselves apart.
I'll come to you anon.

Murderers.   We are resolved, my lord.

Macbeth. I'll call upon you straight. Abide within.

[*Murderers exit.*]

140 It is concluded. Banquo, thy soul's flight,
If it find heaven, must find it out tonight.

[*He exits.*]

Scene 2 *Macbeth's palace at Forres.*

[*Enter* Lady Macbeth *and a* Servant.]

Lady Macbeth. Is Banquo gone from court?

Servant. Ay, madam, but returns again tonight.

Lady Macbeth. Say to the King I would attend his leisure
For a few words.

Servant.   Madam, I will.

[*He exits.*]

Lady Macbeth.   Naught's had, all's spent,
5 Where our desire is got without content.
'Tis safer to be that which we destroy
Than by destruction dwell in doubtful joy.

[*Enter* Macbeth.]

How now, my lord? Why do you keep alone,
Of sorriest fancies your companions making,
10 Using those thoughts which should indeed have died

127 Your spirits shine through you: Your courage is evident.

131–132 something from . . . clearness: The murder must be done away from the palace so that I remain blameless (**I require a clearness**).

135 absence: death.

137 Resolve yourselves apart: Decide in private.

139 straight: soon.

4–7 Nothing (naught) has been gained; everything has been wasted (**spent**). It would be better to be dead like Duncan than to live in uncertain joy.

CLOSE READ

Analyze Characters   COMMON CORE RL 1, L 3

(LINES 114–139)

Tell students that a well-rounded character changes in the course of a drama. In tragedy, the hero's tragic flaw becomes more pronounced as the drama progresses.

I **ASK STUDENTS** how the planning of this murder differs from the planning of Duncan's murder. (*Macbeth seems much more resolved and devious than he did during the planning of Duncan's murder, when Lady Macbeth had to spur him on. There is no evidence that Lady Macbeth helped him plan this murder.*) How does the change signal a change in Macbeth's character, a deepening of his tragic flaw? (*Macbeth's ambition seems to be winning the battle with his conscience.*)

Tell students that since drama does not generally have a narrator, most of what the audience learns about characters is through their actions and dialogue.

J **CITE TEXT EVIDENCE** Have students examine Macbeth's dialogue and ask them to explain the reason Macbeth gives for ordering Fleance killed in lines 133–136. (*Macbeth tells the murderers that they should kill Fleance in order to make sure there are no witnesses or evidence ["no rubs nor botches in the work"].*) Ask students to explain the real reason Macbeth wants Fleance dead. (*Macbeth wants to protect his place as king, and Fleance is as much a threat to Macbeth as Banquo, since the witches prophesied that Banquo's heir would be king.*)

WHEN STUDENTS STRUGGLE . . .

Provide the following strategy to help students determine the meaning of figurative language and other expressions they encounter as they read *Macbeth*. Model the strategy with the expression, "the common eye" (line 124):

- Read the expression and consider its literal meaning. (*The common eye could refer to something that most people would see—something public.*)
- Decide if the literal meaning makes sense. If not, consider how it may help to determine the intended meaning. (*It refers to how most people view something—not physically, but what they would think about it.*)
- Think about any similar expressions (e.g., the public eye) in modern speech and writing that have similar meaning.

Interpret Figurative Language (LINES 11–27)

 COMMON CORE L 5

Explain to students that a writer can use imagery to create a picture for the audience. Sometimes the imagery in dialogue contains symbolism, or words or ideas that represent other words or ideas.

K **ASK STUDENTS** to identify the animal imagery Macbeth uses. *(the snake)* Then ask them what he means by "scorched the snake, not killed it." *(The snake is a symbol for the obstacles to their ambition. A merely wounded snake can still harm Macbeth and Lady Macbeth.)* Ask students in what way the image of the snake is ironic, coming from Macbeth. *(Macbeth uses the image of the snake to characterize himself as a victim, when in fact he is the predator.)*

Analyze Character

(LINES 29–34)

 COMMON CORE RL 3

Remind students to continue to examine dialogue to learn about how a character feels, what the character is thinking, or how others view the character.

L **ASK STUDENTS** to explain what instruction Macbeth gives to Lady Macbeth with regard to speaking about Banquo. *(He tells her to use flattery and honor when talking about Banquo ["present him eminence / Both with eye and tongue"].)* Then ask which phrase suggests they should hide their true feelings. *("make our faces vizards to our hearts")* Finally, ask students what Lady Macbeth's comment in line 34 tells the reader about the difference between Macbeth's words and the way he might be acting. *(After Macbeth gives his wife instructions, she says "You must leave this," implying that he seems upset. Though his instructions sound cool-headed, he is apparently quite distressed.)*

With them they think on? Things without all remedy
Should be without regard. What's done is done.

Macbeth. We have scorched the snake, not killed it.
She'll close and be herself whilst our poor malice
15   Remains in danger of her former tooth.
But let the frame of things disjoint, both the worlds suffer,
Ere we will eat our meal in fear, and sleep
In the affliction of these terrible dreams
That shake us nightly. Better be with the dead,
20   Whom we, to gain our peace, have sent to peace,
Than on the torture of the mind to lie
In restless ecstasy. Duncan is in his grave.
After life's fitful fever he sleeps well.
Treason has done his worst; nor steel nor poison,
25   Malice domestic, foreign levy, nothing
Can touch him further.

Lady Macbeth.   Come on, gentle my lord,
Sleek o'er your rugged looks. Be bright and jovial
Among your guests tonight.

Macbeth.   So shall I, love,
And so I pray be you. Let your remembrance
30   Apply to Banquo; present him eminence
Both with eye and tongue: unsafe the while that we
Must lave our honors in these flattering streams
And make our faces vizards to our hearts,
Disguising what they are.

Lady Macbeth.   You must leave this.

35 **Macbeth.** O, full of scorpions is my mind, dear wife!
Thou know'st that Banquo and his Fleance lives.

Lady Macbeth. But in them Nature's copy's not eterne.

Macbeth. There's comfort yet; they are assailable.
Then be thou jocund. Ere the bat hath flown
40   His cloistered flight, ere to black Hecate's summons
The shard-borne beetle with his drowsy hums
Hath rung night's yawning peal, there shall be done
A deed of dreadful note.

Lady Macbeth.   What's to be done?

Macbeth. Be innocent of the knowledge, dearest chuck,
45   Till thou applaud the deed.—Come, seeling night,
Scarf up the tender eye of pitiful day,
And with thy bloody and invisible hand
Cancel and tear to pieces that great bond

16–22 He would rather have the world fall apart (**the frame of things disjoint**) than be afflicted with such fears and nightmares. Death is preferable to life on the torture rack of mental anguish (**restless ecstasy**).

27 sleek: smooth.

30 present him eminence: pay special attention to him.

32 lave . . . streams: wash (**lave**) our honor in streams of flattery—that is, falsify our feelings.

33 vizards: masks.

37 in them . . . not eterne: Nature did not give them immortality.

39–43 jocund: cheerful; merry; **Ere the bat . . . note:** Before nightfall, when the bats and beetles fly, something dreadful will happen.

44 chuck: chick (a term of affection).

45 seeling: blinding.

48 great bond: Banquo's life.

APPLYING ACADEMIC VOCABULARY

| comprise | incidence |

Use these academic vocabulary words as students continue discussing *Macbeth*: *comprise* and *incidence*. Have students identify specific events and details that **comprised** Banquo and Macbeth's meeting with the Weird Sisters. Have students consider Banquo's reflections on this meeting at the beginning of Act III, and then challenge students to make generalizations about other **incidences** of a character reflecting on a revelation or suggestion about his or her fate.

Which keeps me pale. Light thickens, and the crow
50　Makes wing to th' rooky wood.
Good things of day begin to droop and drowse,
Whiles night's black agents to their preys do rouse.—
Thou marvel'st at my words, but hold thee still.
Things bad begun make strong themselves by ill.
55　So prithee go with me.

[*They exit.*]

Scene 3　*A park near the palace.*

[*Enter three* Murderers.]

First Murderer. But who did bid thee join with us?

Third Murderer.　　　　　　　　　　　Macbeth.

Second Murderer [*to the* First Murderer].
He needs not our mistrust, since he delivers
Our offices and what we have to do
To the direction just.

First Murderer.　　　Then stand with us.—
5　The west yet glimmers with some streaks of day.
Now spurs the lated traveler apace
To gain the timely inn, and near approaches
The subject of our watch.

Third Murderer.　　　Hark, I hear horses.

Banquo [*within*]. Give us a light there, ho!

Second Murderer.　　　　　　　Then 'tis he. The rest
10　That are within the note of expectation
Already are i' th' court.

First Murderer.　　　His horses go about.

Third Murderer. Almost a mile; but he does usually
(So all men do) from hence to th' palace gate
Make it their walk.

[*Enter* Banquo *and* Fleance, *with a torch*.]

Second Murderer. A light, a light!

Third Murderer.　　　　　　　'Tis he.

15　**First Murderer.** Stand to 't.

Banquo. It will be rain tonight.

First Murderer.　　　　Let it come down!

[*The three* Murderers *attack*.]

Banquo. O, treachery! Fly, good Fleance, fly, fly, fly!
Thou mayst revenge—O slave!

---

50 rooky: gloomy; also, filled with rooks, or crows.

54 Things brought about through evil need additional evil to make them strong.

2–5 He needs . . . just: Macbeth should not be distrustful, since he gave us the orders (**offices**) and we plan to follow his directions exactly.

6 lated: tardy; late.

9 Give us a light: Banquo, nearing the palace, calls for servants to bring a light.

9–11 Then 'tis . . . court: It must be Banquo, since all the other expected guests are already in the palace.

15 Stand to 't: Be prepared.

18 Thou mayst revenge: You might live to avenge my death.

CLOSE READ

Analyze Imagery
(LINES 51–52)

COMMON CORE　RL 4, L 5

Point out that imagery in dialogue can create vivid pictures for the reader and is often symbolic.

Ⓜ **ASK STUDENTS** to explain how Macbeth describes the ending of day. (*Good things about the day begin to fade.*) Then ask students to cite which words describe the images of predators and prey. (*"night's black agents to their preys do rouse"*) Ask students what "black agents" might refer to. (*the murderers or the unfolding of Macbeth's plan to kill Banquo*) Ask students how this imagery contributes to the overall mood of Scene 2. (*The imagery is in keeping with the overall dark mood of the scene.*)

TO CHALLENGE STUDENTS . . .

Drama and the Stage Director As students read *Macbeth*, have them consider the importance of the director and the director's view in how the drama is portrayed.

ASK STUDENTS to discuss different ways that a particular scene could be portrayed. Then have students explain the reasons a director might choose to portray it one way or the other. (*Possible answer: In Act III Scene 3, the director might show the murderers as inept to create comic relief in the middle of a very serious act. Or the director might draw out the fight between the murderers and Banquo and Fleance, having Fleance fight bravely before fleeing. This would plant an idea about Fleance's character in the audience's mind.*)

Analyze Language

COMMON CORE RL 4, L 5

(LINES 9–23)

Explain to students that words or phrases in dialogue that shift in tone can convey a change in a character's emotion, may reveal a significant point in the plot, or point to an underlying theme.

(N) CITE TEXT EVIDENCE Have students cite text evidence in Macbeth's conversation with the Murderer (lines 9–23) that reveals Macbeth's abrupt change in tone and attitude regarding the events surrounding Banquo's murder. *(When the Murderer enters the banquet hall, Macbeth's words express a feeling of victory and satisfaction ["Thou art the best o' th' cutthroats" and "thou art the nonpareil."]. Upon learning of Fleance's escape, Macbeth's tone abruptly changes ["Then comes my fit again"], and he reveals that until this moment, he had felt invincible ["I had else been perfect, / Whole as the marble, founded as the rock, / As broad and general as the casing air."]. This event has caused Macbeth to lose his confidence.)*

Analyze Shakespearean Drama

COMMON CORE RL 5

(LINES 21–25)

Remind students that an aside is a conversation between characters that is not meant to be heard by the other characters on stage.

(O) ASK STUDENTS to explain which sentences in lines 21–25 are spoken by Macbeth as an aside and how they can tell where the aside begins and ends. *(The stage direction "[aside]" indicates that Macbeth is speaking lines that only the audience can hear. He wouldn't reveal his true thoughts and feelings about Fleance's escape to the murderer. The dash in line 25 indicates that Macbeth is now addressing the Murderer.)*

[*He dies.* Fleance *exits.*]

Third Murderer. Who did strike out the light?

First Murderer.   Was 't not the way?   **19 Was 't not the way:** Isn't that what we were supposed to do?

20 **Third Murderer.** There's but one down. The son is fled.

Second Murderer. We have lost best half of our affair.

First Murderer. Well, let's away and say how much is done.

[*They exit.*]

Scene 4 *The hall in the palace.*

[*Banquet prepared. Enter* Macbeth, Lady Macbeth, Ross, Lennox, Lords, *and* Attendants.]

Macbeth. You know your own degrees; sit down. At first   **1 your own degrees:** where your rank entitles you to sit.
And last, the hearty welcome.

[*They sit.*]

Lords.   Thanks to your Majesty.

Macbeth. Ourself will mingle with society
And play the humble host.

5 Our hostess keeps her state, but in best time   **5 keeps her state:** sits on her throne rather than at the banquet table.
We will require her welcome.

Lady Macbeth. Pronounce it for me, sir, to all our friends,
For my heart speaks they are welcome.

[*Enter* First Murderer *to the door.*]

(N)

Macbeth. See, they encounter thee with their hearts' thanks.
10 Both sides are even. Here I'll sit i' th' midst.
Be large in mirth. Anon we'll drink a measure   **11 measure:** toast. Macbeth keeps talking to his wife and guests as he casually edges toward the door to speak privately with the murderer.
The table round. [*Approaching the* Murderer] There's blood upon thy face.

Murderer. 'Tis Banquo's then.

Macbeth. 'Tis better thee without than he within.
15 Is he dispatched?   **15 dispatched:** killed.

Murderer. My lord, his throat is cut. That I did for him.

Macbeth. Thou art the best o' th' cutthroats,
Yet he's good that did the like for Fleance.
If thou didst it, thou art the nonpareil.   **19 nonpareil:** best.

20 **Murderer.** Most royal sir, Fleance is 'scaped.

Macbeth [*aside*]. Then comes my fit again. I had else been   **(O)**
    perfect,
Whole as the marble, founded as the rock,
As broad and general as the casing air.   **23 casing:** surrounding.

WHEN STUDENTS STRUGGLE . . .

One way to help students more fully understand the language of Shakespeare is to have them read the dialogue aloud using proper vocal inflection. Use the dialogue between Macbeth and the First Murderer to model this strategy.

- Read lines 12–32 aloud and have students echo-read after you.
- Discuss with students the meanings of the lines. Ask them to rephrase the language using modern phrases or words; provide corrective feedback.
- Have a pair of students read the dialogue aloud for the class. Select different pairs of students to read it again.

ASK STUDENTS to describe how reading the lines aloud helped them to better understand the language.

But now I am cabined, cribbed, confined, bound in **(P)**
25 To saucy doubts and fears.—But Banquo's safe?

Murderer. Ay, my good lord. Safe in a ditch he bides, **(Q)**
With twenty trenchèd gashes on his head,
The least a death to nature.

Macbeth.   Thanks for that.
There the grown serpent lies. The worm that's fled
30 Hath nature that in time will venom breed,
No teeth for th' present. Get thee gone. Tomorrow
We'll hear ourselves again.

[*Murderer exits.*]

Lady Macbeth.   My royal lord,
You do not give the cheer. The feast is sold
That is not often vouched, while 'tis a-making,
35 'Tis given with welcome. To feed were best at home;
From thence, the sauce to meat is ceremony;
Meeting were bare without it.

[*Enter the Ghost of* Banquo, *and sits in* Macbeth's *place.*]

Macbeth [*to* Lady Macbeth]. Sweet remembrancer!—
Now, good digestion wait on appetite
And health on both!

Lennox.   May't please your Highness sit.

40 **Macbeth.** Here had we now our country's honor roofed,
Were the graced person of our Banquo present,
Who may I rather challenge for unkindness
Than pity for mischance.

Ross.   His absence, sir,
Lays blame upon his promise. Please 't your Highness
45 To grace us with your royal company?

Macbeth. The table's full.

Lennox.   Here is a place reserved, sir.

Macbeth. Where?

Lennox. Here, my good lord. What is 't that moves your Highness?

Macbeth. Which of you have done this?

Lords.   What, my good lord?

50 **Macbeth** [*to the* Ghost]. Thou canst not say I did it. Never shake
Thy gory locks at me.

Ross. Gentlemen, rise. His Highness is not well.

29 worm: little serpent, that is, Fleance.

31 no teeth for th' present: too young to cause harm right now.

32 hear ourselves: talk together.

32–37 Macbeth must not forget his duties as host. A feast will be no different from a meal that one pays for unless the host gives his guests courteous attention (**ceremony**), the best part of any meal.

37 sweet remembrancer: a term of affection for his wife, who has reminded him of his duty.

40–43 The best people of Scotland would all be under Macbeth's roof if Banquo were present too. He hopes Banquo's absence is due to rudeness rather than to some accident (**mischance**).

46 Macbeth finally notices that Banquo's ghost is present and sitting in the king's chair.

TEACH

CLOSE READ

Analyze Word Choice

COMMON CORE RL 4, L 5b

(LINES 21–25)

Remind students that an **aside** consists of lines between characters (or that a character says to himself) that are not meant to be heard by the other characters on stage.

(P) **ASK STUDENTS** to point out and analyze the words Macbeth uses to indicate his feelings about the news of Fleance. (*"Whole as the marble, founded as the rock," indicates he was confident in the plan and that it was solid. As a result of Fleance not being killed, he feels "cabined, cribbed, confined," indicating he is trapped by his "saucy doubts and fears." He is overwhelmed by fear and worry about the future.*)

Tell students that readers analyze the words a writer chooses by considering the overall context. Sometimes a writer uses a word that has a meaning that is quite different from the connotation or denotation.

(Q) **ASK STUDENTS** what Macbeth means when he uses the word *safe* to describe the plan. (*Macbeth wants to be sure that the plan went smoothly. He is not asking about Banquo's well-being.*)

APPLYING ACADEMIC VOCABULARY

ultimate	priority

Use the academic vocabulary words *ultimate* and *priority* to discuss Lady Macbeth's response (lines 32–37) to her husband's actions at the feast. Have students explain what Lady Macbeth feels her husband's **priority** should be to his guests at the feast. Then have students contrast Lady Macbeth's view of the **ultimate** goal of the dinner with the way that Macbeth behaves.

Analyze Author's Choices: Tension and Surprise

COMMON CORE RL 5

(LINES 53–68)

Remind students that dramatic irony is created when the characters know less about what is happening than the audience does.

(R) CITE TEXT EVIDENCE Ask students to describe what Lady Macbeth tells her guests about Macbeth's outburst. *(In lines 53–54, Lady Macbeth makes an excuse for her husband, saying that he has been prone to fits since he was a child. In lines 55–58, she tells them to go ahead and eat and not to fuss over him because it will embarrass him.)* Then ask students to cite evidence that supports the dramatic irony that Lady Macbeth believes Macbeth's fears are still about Duncan. *(In lines 62–64, Lady Macbeth is angry with Macbeth about what she perceives as his imaginary fears about killing Duncan. Lady Macbeth does not know Banquo is dead or that Macbeth had him killed.)*

Lady Macbeth. Sit, worthy friends. My lord is often thus
And hath been from his youth. Pray you, keep seat.
55 The fit is momentary; upon a thought
He will again be well. If much you note him
You shall offend him and extend his passion.
Feed and regard him not. [*Drawing* Macbeth *aside*] Are you a man?

Macbeth. Ay, and a bold one, that dare look on that
60 Which might appall the devil.

Lady Macbeth.   O, proper stuff !
This is the very painting of your fear.
This is the air-drawn dagger which you said
Led you to Duncan. O, these flaws and starts,
Impostors to true fear, would well become
65 A woman's story at a winter's fire,
Authorized by her grandam. Shame itself!
Why do you make such faces? When all's done,
You look but on a stool.

Macbeth. Prithee see there. Behold, look! [*To the* Ghost] Lo, how
    say you?
70 Why, what care I? If thou canst nod, speak too.—
If charnel houses and our graves must send
Those that we bury back, our monuments
Shall be the maws of kites.

[Ghost *exits.*]

Lady Macbeth.   What, quite unmanned in folly?

60–68 She dismisses his hallucination as utter nonsense (**proper stuff**). His outbursts (**flaws and starts**) are the product of imaginary fears (**impostors to true fear**) and are unmanly, the kind of behavior described in a woman's story.

71–73 If burial vaults (**charnel houses**) give back the dead, then we may as well throw our bodies to the birds (**kites**), whose stomachs (**maws**) will become our tombs (**monuments**).

SCAFFOLDING FOR ELL STUDENTS

Analyze Author's Choices: Tension and Surprise Students may have trouble identifying irony when they are unsure of word meaning. Explain that denotation of a word is its literal meaning. The connotation of a word refers to the associations or emotions related to that word. For example, in line 58, Lady Macbeth asks Macbeth "Are you a man?" Ask students what the denotation of *man* is. Then ask what connotation Lady Macbeth may be using for *man*. *(She is asking Macbeth if he is a strong person. The connotation of a man is someone who is a leader and can be in charge.)*

Macbeth. If I stand here, I saw him.

Lady Macbeth.   Fie, for shame!

75 **Macbeth.** Blood hath been shed ere now, i' th' olden time,
Ere humane statute purged the gentle weal;
Ay, and since too, murders have been performed
Too terrible for the ear. The time has been
That, when the brains were out, the man would die,
80 And there an end. But now they rise again
With twenty mortal murders on their crowns
And push us from our stools. This is more strange
Than such a murder is.

Lady Macbeth.   My worthy lord,
Your noble friends do lack you.

Macbeth.   I do forget.—
85 Do not muse at me, my most worthy friends.
I have a strange infirmity, which is nothing
To those that know me. Come, love and health to all.
Then I'll sit down.—Give me some wine. Fill full.

[*Enter* Ghost.]

I drink to the general joy o' th' whole table
90 And to our dear friend Banquo, whom we miss.
Would he were here! To all and him we thirst,
And all to all.

Lords.   Our duties, and the pledge.

[*They raise their drinking cups.*]

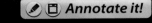

Macbeth [*to the* Ghost]. Avaunt, and quit my sight! Let the earth
hide thee.
Thy bones are marrowless; thy blood is cold;
95 Thou hast no speculation in those eyes
Which thou dost glare with.

Lady Macbeth.   Think of this, good peers,
But as a thing of custom. 'Tis no other;
Only it spoils the pleasure of the time.

Macbeth [*to the* Ghost]. What man dare, I dare.
100 Approach thou like the rugged Russian bear,
The armed rhinoceros, or th' Hyrcan tiger;
Take any shape but that, and my firm nerves
Shall never tremble. Or be alive again
And dare me to the desert with thy sword.
105 If trembling I inhabit then, protest me

75–78 Macbeth desperately tries to justify his murder of Banquo. Murder has been common from ancient times to the present, though laws (**humane statute**) have tried to rid civilized society (**gentle weal**) of violence.

85 muse: wonder.

93–96 avaunt: go away. Macbeth tells Banquo that he is only a ghost, with unreal bones, cold blood, and no consciousness (**speculation**).

99–104 Macbeth would be willing to face Banquo in any other form, even his living self.

105–106 If trembling . . . girl: If I still tremble, call me a girl's doll.

The Tragedy of Macbeth: Act III, Scene 4   **255**

CLOSE READ

Analyze Shakespearean Drama

COMMON CORE RL 5

(LINES 74–96)

Point out that when the characters do not share the same knowledge of plot events, they will react differently from one another. This dramatic irony creates tension.

S ASK STUDENTS to contrast the way the guests at the table would interpret Macbeth's lines to the way the audience would interpret them. (*The guests do not know when the toast ends and the outburst begins. Macbeth's words indicate his honor to Banquo, but the audience knows that Macbeth's toast is a lie meant to aid in the cover up of Macbeth's part in Banquo's murder.*)

Strategies for Annotation ✎ 🗐 Annotate it!

Analyze Shakespearean Drama   COMMON CORE RL 5

Share these strategies for guided or independent analysis of complex dramatic irony.

- Underline words Macbeth speaks that would confuse his dinner guests.
- Highlight in blue words that indicate Lady Macbeth is making excuses for Macbeth.

Write a note that describes how the guests might view Macbeth's speech.

Macbeth [*to the* Ghost] . . . Thou hast no speculation in those eyes

Which thou dost glare with.

Lady Macbeth Think of this, good peers,

But as a thing of custom. 'Tis no other;

Only it spoils the pleasure of the time.

The guests might wonder who Macbeth thinks is glaring at him.

Analyze Theme

COMMON CORE **RL 2**

(LINES 136–138)

Remind students that a playwright develops a theme throughout the course of a drama. Readers make inferences about the developments of a theme based on details found in the text.

T **CITE TEXT EVIDENCE** Have students reread these lines and cite words that indicate that Macbeth has gone too far in his quest for power. (*"Stepped in so far that, should I wade no more"*) Ask students which theme is being developed in this scene. (*The theme involves ambition; ambition has driven Macbeth to the point of no return.*)

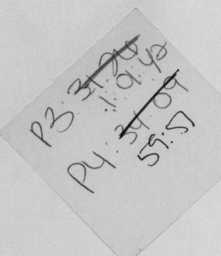

The baby of a girl. Hence, horrible shadow!
Unreal mock'ry, hence!

[Ghost *exits.*]

                  Why, so, being gone,
I am a man again.—Pray you sit still.

Lady Macbeth. You have displaced the mirth, broke the good
    meeting
110 With most admired disorder.

Macbeth.   Can such things be
And overcome us like a summer's cloud,
Without our special wonder? You make me strange
Even to the disposition that I owe,
When now I think you can behold such sights
115 And keep the natural ruby of your cheeks
When mine is blanched with fear.

Ross.   What sights, my lord?

Lady Macbeth. I pray you speak not. He grows worse and worse.
Question enrages him. At once, good night.
Stand not upon the order of your going,
120 But go at once.

Lennox.   Good night, and better health
Attend his Majesty.

Lady Macbeth.   A kind good night to all.

[Lords *and all but* Macbeth *and* Lady Macbeth *exit.*]

Macbeth. It will have blood, they say; blood will have blood.
Stones have been known to move, and trees to speak;
Augurs and understood relations have
125 By maggot pies and choughs and rooks brought forth
The secret'st man of blood.—What is the night?

Lady Macbeth. Almost at odds with morning, which is which.

Macbeth. How say'st thou that Macduff denies his person
At our great bidding?

Lady Macbeth.   Did you send to him, sir?

130 **Macbeth.** I hear it by the way; but I will send.
There's not a one of them but in his house
I keep a servant fee'd. I will tomorrow
(And betimes I will) to the Weïrd Sisters.
More shall they speak, for now I am bent to know
135 By the worst means the worst. For mine own good,
T   All causes shall give way. I am in blood

110 admired: astonishing.

110–116 Macbeth is bewildered by his wife's calm, which makes him seem a stranger to himself (**strange even to the disposition that I owe**): she has all the courage, while he is white (**blanched**) with fear.

119 Stand . . . going: Don't worry about the proper formalities of leaving.

122–126 Macbeth fears that Banquo's murder (**it**) will be revenged by his own murder. Stones, trees, or talking birds (**maggot pies and choughs and rooks**) may reveal the hidden knowledge (**augurs**) of his guilt.

128–129 How say'st . . . bidding: What do you think of Macduff's refusal to come?

131–132 Macbeth has paid (**fee'd**) household servants to spy on every noble, including Macduff.

133 betimes: early.

134 bent: determined.

135–140 Macbeth will do anything to protect himself. He will act on his unnatural (**strange**) thoughts without having examined (**scanned**) them.

SCAFFOLDING FOR ELL STUDENTS

Language: Print Clues Students may struggle with heavily glossed passages, such as lines 121–144. Review the glosses as a class. Then, read short sections of the text aloud. Have students listen carefully and then summarize to a partner what they have heard. As students explain what they think is taking place, discuss their responses and help them correct any misunderstandings.

ASK STUDENTS how they would describe Macbeth's character at this point. (*He seems paranoid: He is worried that Macduff is plotting against him, and he has paid spies in Macduff's house. He has become completely amoral: He plans to consult with the witches.*)

Stepped in so far that, should I wade no more,
Returning were as tedious as go o'er.
Strange things I have in head, that will to hand,
140 Which must be acted ere they may be scanned.

Lady Macbeth. You lack the season of all natures, sleep.

Macbeth. Come, we'll to sleep. My strange and self-abuse
Is the initiate fear that wants hard use
We are yet but young in deed.

[*They exit.*]

Scene 5 *A heath.*

[*Thunder. Enter the three* Witches, *meeting* Hecate.]

First Witch. Why, how now, Hecate? You look angerly.

Hecate. Have I not reason, beldams as you are,
Saucy and overbold, how did you dare
To trade and traffic with Macbeth
5   In riddles and affairs of death,
And I, the mistress of your charms,
The close contriver of all harms,
Was never called to bear my part
Or show the glory of our art?
10   And which is worse, all you have done
Hath been but for a wayward son,
Spiteful and wrathful, who, as others do,
Loves for his own ends, not for you.
But make amends now. Get you gone,
15   And at the pit of Acheron
Meet me i' th' morning. Thither he
Will come to know his destiny.
Your vessels and your spells provide,
Your charms and everything beside.
20   I am for th' air. This night I'll spend
Unto a dismal and a fatal end.
Great business must be wrought ere noon.
Upon the corner of the moon
There hangs a vap'rous drop profound.
25   I'll catch it ere it come to ground,
And that, distilled by magic sleights,
Shall raise such artificial sprites
As by the strength of their illusion
Shall draw him on to his confusion.
30   He shall spurn fate, scorn death, and bear
His hopes 'bove wisdom, grace, and fear.

141 season: preservative.

142–144 His vision of the ghost (**strange and self-abuse**) is only the result of a beginner's fear (**initiate fear**), to be cured with practice (**hard use**).

2 beldams: hags.

13 loves . . . you: cares only about his own goals, not about you.

15 Acheron: a river in hell, according to Greek mythology.

20–21 This . . . end: Tonight I'm working for a disastrous (**dismal**) and fatal end for Macbeth.

23–29 Hecate will obtain a magical drop from the moon, treat it with secret art, and so create spirits (**artificial sprites**) that will lead Macbeth to his destruction (**confusion**).

The Tragedy of Macbeth: Act III, Scene 5 **257**

CLOSE READ

Analyze the Impact of Word Choice (LINES 1-33)

COMMON CORE RL 4

Point out that the specific words and phrases a writer chooses, as well as rhyme and rhythm, help evoke a sense of time and place and establish a mood, or atmosphere.

CITE TEXT EVIDENCE Have students identify the setting and the words Hecate uses that establish a particular mood. (*This portion of the scene appears to be an otherworldly place where the gods/fates live. She speaks about beldams, charms, the pit of Acheron, destiny, and spells. She talks of magic when she describes catching a drop of a "vapor" from the moon. The language and setting combine to create an eerie mood.*) Have students cite examples of Hecate's use of rhyme and identify the rhyme scheme. (*are/dare; Macbeth/death; charms/harms; part/art; couplet – aa, bb, cc, etc.*) Ask students how this rhyme scheme, a departure from the usual iambic pentameter, affects the mood of the passage. (*The sing-song rhyme and rhythm are at odds with Hecate's menacing language, creating a disturbing atmosphere.*)

WHEN STUDENTS STRUGGLE . . .

Use Hecate's monologue to help build students' fluency. In mixed-ability pairs, have students conduct paired oral reading.

- In each pair, student A will read the first line, and student B will read the second, rhyming line.
- Have students pause to work out the meaning of unfamiliar words, such as "saucy," "wayward," "spiteful," "wrathful," and "sleights," and to consult the side-glosses.
- After finishing the monologue, ask students to summarize Hecate's main point. (*Hecate tells the witches they should not have dealt with Macbeth independently. She will cause Macbeth to fall by making him overconfident.*)

Analyze Impact of Word Choice: Tone

COMMON CORE RL 2, RL 3

(LINES 1–39)

Tell students that summarizing and paraphrasing dialogue can help them understand the development of the plot. However, students must be aware of the nuances in a speech that reveal a character's true meaning; an objective summary of Lennox's speech would not capture his ironic tone.

V **ASK STUDENTS** to paraphrase Lennox's speech. Then have students describe Lennox's attitude toward Macbeth. *(Lennox sums up the crimes that have taken place. However, Lennox's tone seems to be ironic: He emphasizes that all of the alleged murderers are dead or have fled—a fact which observers may find too convenient. He also says Macbeth was "wise" to kill the servants who allegedly killed Duncan, suggesting that Macbeth did so not out of rage but out of cunning. Finally, he refers to his recent dinner with Macbeth as "The tyrant's feast"—his most direct criticism of Macbeth in the entire speech. The dialogue shows that some are suspicious of Macbeth and will act on their suspicions.)*

Determine Figurative Meanings (LINES 5–7)

COMMON CORE RL 4, L 3

Tell students that writers can use figurative language to create irony because it allows the writer to convey two meanings at once.

W **CITE TEXT EVIDENCE** Have students explain the specific, literal meaning of the lines "Banquo walked too late" and "men must not walk too late." Have them explain the figurative meaning as well. *(Scene 3, line 14 indicates that Banquo was attacked by murderers while walking by night. However, Lennox also means that they are all living in dangerous times, when nobody is safe from treachery; "to walk late" is to risk death, which is what happened to Banquo.)*

And you all know, security
Is mortals' chiefest enemy.

[*Music and a song*]

Hark! I am called. My little spirit, see,
35   Sits in a foggy cloud and stays for me.

[*Hecate exits.*]

[*Sing within "Come away, come away," etc.*]

First Witch. Come, let's make haste. She'll soon be back again.

[*They exit.*]

Scene 6 *The palace at Forres.*

[*Enter* Lennox *and another* Lord.]

Lennox. My former speeches have but hit your thoughts,
Which can interpret farther. Only I say
Things have been strangely borne. The gracious Duncan
Was pitied of Macbeth; marry, he was dead.
5   And the right valiant Banquo walked too late,
Whom you may say, if 't please you, Fleance killed,
For Fleance fled. Men must not walk too late.
Who cannot want the thought how monstrous
It was for Malcolm and for Donalbain
10   To kill their gracious father? Damnèd fact,
How it did grieve Macbeth! Did he not straight
In pious rage the two delinquents tear
That were the slaves of drink and thralls of sleep?
Was not that nobly done? Ay, and wisely, too,
15   For 'twould have angered any heart alive
To hear the men deny 't. So that I say
He has borne all things well. And I do think
That had he Duncan's sons under his key
(As, an 't please heaven, he shall not) they should find
20   What 'twere to kill a father. So should Fleance.
But peace. For from broad words, and 'cause he failed
His presence at the tyrant's feast, I hear
Macduff lives in disgrace. Sir, can you tell
Where he bestows himself?

Lord.   The son of Duncan
25   (From whom this tyrant holds the due of birth)
Lives in the English court and is received
Of the most pious Edward with such grace
That the malevolence of fortune nothing
Takes from his high respect. Thither Macduff
30   Is gone to pray the holy king upon his aid

34–35 Hecate has a demon helper (**my little spirit**), to which she is raised by pulley to "the heavens" of the stage.

1–3 Lennox and the other lord have shared suspicions of Macbeth.

6–7 Fleeing the scene of the crime must make Fleance guilty of his father's murder.

8–10 Everyone agrees on the horror of Duncan's murder by his sons.

12 pious: holy.

21 from broad words: because of his frank talk.

24 bestows himself: is staying.

25 Macbeth keeps Malcolm from his rightful throne.

27 Edward: Edward the Confessor, king of England from 1042 to 1066, a man known for his virtue and religion.

28–29 that . . . respect: Despite his bad fortune, Malcolm is treated respectfully by Edward.

29–37 Macduff wants the king to persuade the people of Northumberland and their earl, Siward, to join Malcolm's cause.

WHEN STUDENTS STRUGGLE . . .

Summarizing events can help students keep track of a long text with a complex plot. Summarizing can also help students get a better sense of what to expect as the story unfolds. Guide students in using a graphic organizer to summarize events so far:

- Use the dialogue in Scene 6 to help students recall the main events.
- Demonstrate how students can use a time line or sequence chart to show the order of the events.
- Demonstrate how students can use a web diagram to cluster important events around specific characters.

ASK STUDENTS to choose a graphic organizer and use it to help them summarize the events of Act III.

To wake Northumberland and warlike Siward
That, by the help of these (with Him above
To ratify the work), we may again
Give to our tables meat, sleep to our nights,
35 Free from our feasts and banquets bloody knives,
Do faithful homage, and receive free honors,
All which we pine for now. And this report
Hath so exasperate the King that he
Prepares for some attempt of war.

Lennox.   Sent he to Macduff?

40 **Lord.** He did, and with an absolute "Sir, not I,"
The cloudy messenger turns me his back
And hums, as who should say, "You'll rue the time
That clogs me with this answer."

Lennox.   And that well might
Advise him to a caution t' hold what distance
45 His wisdom can provide. Some holy angel
Fly to the court of England and unfold
His message ere he come, that a swift blessing
May soon return to this our suffering country
Under a hand accursed.

Lord.   I'll send my prayers with him.

[*They exit.*]

40–43 The messenger, fearing Macbeth's anger, was unhappy (**cloudy**) with Macduff's refusal to cooperate. Because Macduff burdens (**clogs**) him with bad news, he will not hurry back.

COLLABORATIVE DISCUSSION Are the people happy about Macbeth's rule? Why or why not? With a partner, discuss what is revealed about the way in which Macbeth governs. Cite specific textual evidence from the play to support your ideas.

CLOSE READ

Analyze Shakespearean Drama

COMMON CORE RL 2

(LINES 29–34)

Explain that in Shakespeare's play, some scenes serve to advance the plot through exposition. (For example, students may recall Scene 2 in Act I, where Duncan learns how Macbeth defeated the Thane of Cawdor.) These scenes explain actions that have happened offstage, rather than show them directly.

Ⓧ CITE TEXT EVIDENCE Ask students to explain what life in Scotland under Macbeth has been like, and how some noblemen plan to put an end to Macbeth's rule. *(The Lord mentions that the people have been hungry and worried [lines 32–34], and that bloody intrigues have replaced honorable service and its rewards [lines 35–37]. Macduff wants the King of England to persuade the people of Northumberland and their aggressive earl Siward to join Malcolm's cause in defeating Macbeth [lines 29–37].)*

COLLABORATIVE DISCUSSION Have students pair up and discuss the different views that characters have of Macbeth and his rule. Then have partners share their thoughts with the class as a whole.

ASK STUDENTS to share any questions they generated in the course of reading and discussing this portion of *Macbeth*.

APPLYING ACADEMIC VOCABULARY

> thesis

Use the academic vocabulary word *thesis* as students discuss Act III of *Macbeth*. Tell students to think about what they would write about if they were to use Act III of *Macbeth* to support a thesis about fate, power and ambition, guilt, appearance vs. reality, or some other important theme. Have students give a brief explanation of what their paper might say, explaining what the **thesis** would be and how Act III would help support that thesis.

PRACTICE & APPLY

Analyzing the Text COMMON CORE RL 1, RL 3, RL 4, RL 5

Possible answers:

1. Macbeth feels threatened because the prophecy states that Banquo's sons will be kings. His discussion with the murderers reveals that he can be just as conniving as his wife. The fact that he hired assassins may reflect his aversion to murdering his allies (murdering Duncan distressed him); on the other hand, it may simply reflect his heightened status.

2. Both characters are uneasy about the murder; they share fewer of their concerns with each other.

3. Fleance's escape suggests that the prophecy is going to come true. Macbeth is not lucky, but is rather creating the very situation he is trying to avoid.

4. Banquo's ghost represents Macbeth's fear and his guilt. Lady Macbeth remains calm but is becoming angry with Macbeth; she publicly supports her husband while privately bullying and cajoling him to be strong.

5. Macbeth realizes he has done horrible things. He feels trapped because he is in too deep.

6. Scene 5 shows that while they believe he is at fault for his own downfall, the goddesses actively work to ensure that Macbeth will fall.

7. "How it did grieve Macbeth" and "Was that not nobly done" are words Lennox uses to describe Macbeth's outrage at Banquo's death, when in fact, Macbeth had Banquo murdered.

8. There will be a war (lines 30–34 and 38–39).

 **eBook** *Annotate It!*

Analyzing the Text COMMON CORE RL 1, RL 3, RL 4, RL 5, W 2

Cite Text Evidence   Support your responses with evidence from the selection.

1. **Infer**   Reread lines 47–56 in Scene 1. Why does Macbeth fear Banquo and feel threatened by his "being"? What is suggested about Macbeth's character through his action of hiring murderers to carry out his plan?

2. **Analyze**   What do these passages in Scene 2 suggest about the effect of Duncan's death on Macbeth, Lady Macbeth, and their relationship?
   - lines 4–7 ("Nought's had, all's spent . . . doubtful joy.")
   - lines 16–26 ("But let the frame of things disjoint . . . him further.")
   - lines 44–55 ("Be innocent of the knowledge . . . go with me.")

3. **Draw Conclusions**   What does Fleance's escape suggest about Macbeth's luck?

4. **Analyze**   What does Banquo's ghost in Scene 4 represent? Explain how the presence of the ghost affects Lady Macbeth's behavior, even though she cannot see it.

5. **Compare**   Review lines 135–140 in Scene 4. In what way does this speech reveal a change in Macbeth's attitude from how he has felt in the past about his deeds?

6. **Draw Conclusions**   Some critics believe that Scene 5 was not part of the original text but was added to the play later. What is the purpose of Scene 5?

7. **Analyze**   Review Lennox's speech in lines 1–20 of Scene 6. What words and phrases in this speech convey an ironic tone?

8. **Predict**   What possible plot developments are foreshadowed in Scene 6? Cite text evidence to support your prediction.

PERFORMANCE TASK

Writing Activity: Analysis   How does dramatic irony intensify the impact of Act III?

- Create a three-column chart with these headings: *Lines; What characters do or say; What the audience knows.*
- With a partner, identify the two strongest instances of dramatic irony in Act III, and complete the chart with details from those instances.

- Using details from your chart, discuss in a paragraph or two the impact of dramatic irony on the audience's understanding of Macbeth's character.

PERFORMANCE TASK   COMMON CORE RL 5, W 2

Assign this performance task.

Writing Activity: Analysis   Have students work in pairs to complete their charts and then write their paragraphs on their own. Some prominent examples of dramatic irony from Act III include the following:

- **Scene 1.** Lines 15–18: Banquo pledges his duty to Macbeth, but we know he is suspicious of Macbeth. Lines 29–32: Macbeth talks of the "cruel parricide" committed by Duncan's sons; we know they are innocent.

- **Scene 2.** Lines 29–34: Macbeth tells Lady Macbeth to look after Banquo at the banquet; Banquo will be murdered before the banquet.

Have students exchange papers with their partners. Partners should read each other's papers to be sure they include details from the chart. Partners should then make suggestions for revisions in grammar, usage, and clarity. Finally, have students revise their paragraphs.

TEACH

CLOSE READ

AS YOU READ Direct students to the As You Read note to focus their reading.

Analyze Character and Theme (LINES 1–21)

COMMON CORE RL 1, RL 2, RL 3

Explain to students that playwrights often use scene descriptions and stage directions to set the mood and establish the tone for dialogue that follows.

(A) **CITE TEXT EVIDENCE** Have students describe the mood that is established in the scene description and stage direction at the beginning of Scene 1. What elements help to create that mood? What tone might readers expect in the dialogue that follows? How does the stage direction further readers' understanding of the witches? Have students support their responses with text evidence. *(A "boiling cauldron," often symbolic of witchcraft, in the middle of a "cave" sets a dark and gloomy mood. The sound of "thunder" as the witches enter establishes a threatening tone for the dialogue and characterizes the witches as being powerful and evil.)*

Explain that a **couplet** is created by two consecutive, often rhymed, lines of poetry that work together to make a point or to express an idea.

(B) **ASK STUDENTS** to identify the repeated couplet in the witches' dialogue. *(The repeated couplet appears in lines 10–11 and 20–21: "Double, double . . . cauldron bubble.")* What point or idea does the couplet express? *(These are magic words for the potion the witches are concocting and may be a further sign of the witches' power to concoct or foresee future struggles and trouble.)*

AS YOU READ Pay attention to details that reveal Macbeth's willingness to embrace evil. Write down any questions you generate during reading.

ACT IV

(A) **Scene 1** *A cave. In the middle, a boiling cauldron.*

[Thunder. Enter the three Witches.]

First Witch. Thrice the brinded cat hath mewed.

Second Witch. Thrice, and once the hedge-pig whined.

Third Witch. Harpier cries "'Tis time, 'tis time!"

First Witch. Round about the cauldron go;
5   In the poisoned entrails throw.
  Toad, that under cold stone
  Days and nights has thirty-one
  Sweltered venom sleeping got,
  Boil thou first i' th' charmed pot.

[The Witches circle the cauldron.]

(B) 10 **All.** Double, double toil and trouble;
  Fire burn, and cauldron bubble.

Second Witch. Fillet of a fenny snake
  In the cauldron boil and bake.
  Eye of newt and toe of frog,
15   Wool of bat and tongue of dog,
  Adder's fork and blindworm's sting,
  Lizard's leg and howlet's wing,
  For a charm of powerful trouble,
  Like a hell-broth boil and bubble.

20 **All.** Double, double toil and trouble;
  Fire burn, and cauldron bubble.

Third Witch. Scale of dragon, tooth of wolf,
  Witch's mummy, maw and gulf
  Of the ravined salt-sea shark,
25   Root of hemlock digged i' th' dark,
  Liver of blaspheming Jew,
  Gall of goat and slips of yew
  Slivered in the moon's eclipse,
  Nose of Turk and Tartar's lips,
30   Finger of birth-strangled babe
  Ditch-delivered by a drab,
  Make the gruel thick and slab.
  Add thereto a tiger's chaudron
  For th' ingredience of our cauldron.

1–3 Magical signals and the call of the third witch's attending demon (**harpier**) tell the witches to begin.

4–34 The witches are stirring up a magical stew to bring trouble to humanity. Their recipe includes intestines (**entrails, chaudron**), a slice (**fillet**) of snake, eye of salamander (**newt**), snake tongue (**adder's fork**), a lizard (**blindworm**), a baby owl's (**howlet's**) wing, a shark's stomach and gullet (**maw and gulf**), the finger of a baby strangled by a prostitute (**drab**), and other gruesome ingredients. They stir their brew until it is thick and slimy (**slab**).

Close Read Screencasts   **View It!**

Modeled Discussion

Have students click the *Close Read* icons in their eBooks to access a screencast in which readers discuss and annotate the following key passage:

- Lady Macduff reacting to a message about her husband's death (Scene 2, lines 30– 41)

As a class, view and discuss this video.

Analyze Character and Theme (LINES 50–61)

COMMON CORE RL 1, RL 2, RL 3

Remind students that Shakespeare uses powerful imagery to support theme and character.

C CITE TEXT EVIDENCE Have students identify the images Macbeth uses in his speech. *(violent wind storms that pound churches [lines 52–53], flatten crops and trees [line 55], topple castles [line 56], and crumble palaces and pyramids [line 57]; storm waves that sink ships [lines 53–54])*

D ASK STUDENTS who Macbeth says can set loose these storms. *(Macbeth is speaking to the witches when he says in line 52 "you untie the winds and let them fight.")*

E ASK STUDENTS what this speech suggests about Macbeth and how the speech supports theme. *(Macbeth acknowledges the witches' power to control nature and create chaos in the world, but he doesn't care what happens as long as he gets the answers to his questions. The speech suggests that Macbeth will be ruthless in his quest for power.)*

---

35   **All.** Double, double toil and trouble;
    Fire burn, and cauldron bubble.

    Second Witch. Cool it with a baboon's blood.
    Then the charm is firm and good.

    [*Enter* Hecate *and the other three* Witches.]

    Hecate. O, well done! I commend your pains,
40   And everyone shall share i' th' gains.
    And now about the cauldron sing
    Like elves and fairies in a ring,
    Enchanting all that you put in.

    [*Music and a song: "Black Spirits," etc.* Hecate *exits.*]

    Second Witch. By the pricking of my thumbs,
45   Something wicked this way comes.
    Open, locks,
    Whoever knocks.

    [*Enter* Macbeth.]

    Macbeth. How now, you secret, black, and midnight hags?
    What is 't you do?

    All.   A deed without a name.

50   **Macbeth.** I conjure you by that which you profess
    (Howe'er you come to know it), answer me.
    Though you untie the winds and let them fight   **D**
    Against the churches, though the yeasty waves
    Confound and swallow navigation up,
55   Though bladed corn be lodged and trees blown down,
    Though castles topple on their warders' heads,
    Though palaces and pyramids do slope
    Their heads to their foundations, though the treasure
    Of nature's germens tumble all together
60   Even till destruction sicken, answer me   **E**
    To what I ask you.

    First Witch.   Speak.

    Second Witch.   Demand.

    Third Witch.   We'll answer.

    First Witch. Say if th' hadst rather hear it from our mouths
    Or from our masters'.

    Macbeth.   Call 'em. Let me see 'em.

    First Witch. Pour in sow's blood that hath eaten
65   Her nine farrow; grease that's sweaten
    From the murderers' gibbet throw
    Into the flame.

50–61 Macbeth calls upon (**conjure**) the witches in the name of their dark magic (**that which you profess**). Though they unleash winds to topple churches and make foaming (**yeasty**) waves to destroy (**confound**) ships, though they flatten wheat (**corn**) fields, destroy buildings, and reduce nature's order to chaos by mixing all seeds (**germens**) together, he demands an answer to his question.

63 masters: the demons whom the witches serve.

65–66 farrow: newborn pigs; **grease . . . gibbet:** grease from a gallows where murderers were hung.

SCAFFOLDING FOR ELL STUDENTS

Vocabulary: Word Associations English learners can get a general idea of what is happening without understanding each word. Using a whiteboard, project lines 4–9 of Scene 1 and ask volunteers to highlight key words that describe what the witches are doing.

ASK STUDENTS what associations they make with the words *poisoned*, *toad*, *venom*, and *charmed*. *(Together these words evoke a sinister, disturbing mood.)* Ask: What are the witches doing? *(circling the cauldron, adding the first ingredients of a powerful potion)*

First Witch. Round about the cauldron go;

In the poisoned entrails throw.

Toad, that under cold stone . . .

Sweltered venom sleeping got,

Boil thou first i' th' charmed pot.

All.   Come high or low;
Thyself and office deftly show.

[*Thunder. First Apparition, an Armed Head.*]

F

Macbeth. Tell me, thou unknown power—

First Witch.   He knows thy thought.
70 Hear his speech but say thou naught.

First Apparition. Macbeth! Macbeth! Macbeth! Beware Macduff!
Beware the Thane of Fife! Dismiss me. Enough.

[*He descends.*]

Macbeth. Whate'er thou art, for thy good caution, thanks.
Thou hast harped my fear aright. But one word more—

75 **First Witch.** He will not be commanded. Here's another
More potent than the first.

[*Thunder. Second Apparition, a Bloody Child.*]

Second Apparition. Macbeth! Macbeth! Macbeth!—

Macbeth. Had I three ears, I'd hear thee.

Second Apparition. Be bloody, bold, and resolute. Laugh to scorn

G
80 The power of man, for none of woman born
Shall harm Macbeth.

[*He descends.*]

Macbeth. Then live, Macduff; what need I fear of thee?
But yet I'll make assurance double sure
And take a bond of fate. Thou shalt not live,
85 That I may tell pale-hearted fear it lies,
And sleep in spite of thunder.

[*Thunder. Third Apparition, a Child Crowned, with a tree in his hand.*]

H

                    What is this
That rises like the issue of a king
And wears upon his baby brow the round
And top of sovereignty?

All.   Listen, but speak not to 't.

90 **Third Apparition.** Be lion-mettled, proud, and take no care
Who chafes, who frets, or where conspirers are.
Macbeth shall never vanquished be until
Great Birnam Wood to high Dunsinane Hill
Shall come against him.   [*He descends.*]

Macbeth.   That will never be.
95 Who can impress the forest, bid the tree

Sidenotes:

[Stage Direction] Each of the three apparitions holds a clue to Macbeth's future.

74 harped: guessed.

84 The murder of Macduff will give Macbeth a guarantee (**bond**) of his fate and put his fears to rest.

87 issue: child.

88–89 the round and top: the crown.

90–94 The third apparition tells Macbeth to take courage. He cannot be defeated unless Birnam Wood travels the 12-mile distance to Dunsinane Hill, where his castle is located.

95 impress: force into service.

The Tragedy of Macbeth: Act IV, Scene 1   **263**

CLOSE READ

Analyze Character and Theme (LINES 69–94)

COMMON CORE RL 1, RL 2, RL 3

Explain to students that a **symbol** is a person, place, or object that has a concrete meaning for itself and also stands for something beyond itself, such as an idea or feeling.

F **ASK STUDENTS** what the armed head, or head wearing armor, may symbolize. (*Armor is used in battle, so the armed head suggests that Macbeth will be involved in battle. Lines 71–72 suggest that the battle will be against Macduff.*)

G **CITE TEXT EVIDENCE** Have students identify the text related to the second apparition that may give Macbeth a false sense of security. (*"None of woman born shall harm Macbeth" in lines 80–81 may make Macbeth think he is safe from everyone since all people are born of women.*)

H **ASK STUDENTS** to reread the stage direction and text related to the third apparition. Have them explain what this apparition represents and how the apparition's words to Macbeth may affect him. (*The crowned child represents a future king and the tree stands for Great Birnam Wood. The apparition's words may make Macbeth feel safe since a wooded forest cannot move.*) Finally, ask students how the symbolism of the three apparitions might foreshadow future events related to a theme. (*The first two apparitions are bloody ones, suggesting future violence in Macbeth's relentless pursuit of power. The third apparition might foreshadow that someone's child will supplant Macbeth as king.*)

WHEN STUDENTS STRUGGLE . . .

Students might miss the reversal that occurs in lines 82–86. Read the lines aloud, emphasizing the shift that occurs between lines 82 and 83. Then discuss how the speech relates to theme and character in this scene.

ASK STUDENTS to explain Macbeth's contradictory comments. (*In line 82, Macbeth says he has nothing to fear from Macduff, so Macduff shall live. Macbeth changes his mind in lines 83–86, saying that he wants to be double sure he has nothing to fear. He has decided to kill Macduff to calm his fears.*)

Discuss the theme Macbeth's comments reflect and what his comments reveal about his character. (*Macbeth's comments relate to the theme of ambition and show that Macbeth will do anything to secure his throne.*)

Analyze Character and Theme (LINES 97–105)

COMMON CORE RL 1, RL 2, RL 3

Explain that Macbeth's speech after the third apparition descends (lines 97–105) reveals much about theme and character.

Ⓘ CITE TEXT EVIDENCE Have students cite text that reflects Macbeth's ego and ambition. *(In line 98, Macbeth's ego is evident when he refers to himself as "our high-placed Macbeth," and in lines 104–105, his ego and ambition combine to make him so bold as to demand that the ghost reveal whether Banquo's descendants will become kings and to curse the ghost when he doesn't receive a response.)*

Have students recall the witches' prophecy to Banquo in Act I, Scene 3 that Banquo shall father kings, but Banquo himself will not be king.

Ⓙ ASK STUDENTS to make an inference about what is going through Macbeth's mind after seeing the apparitions of eight kings that look like Banquo (lines 112–122). *(Macbeth is obviously upset by the apparition [lines 115–116, 118, and 122]; he is probably worried that the reassurance he received from the three earlier apparitions was false.)*

Ⓘ
Unfix his earthbound root? Sweet bodements, good!
Rebellious dead, rise never till the wood
Of Birnam rise, and our high-placed Macbeth
Shall live the lease of nature, pay his breath
100 To time and mortal custom. Yet my heart
Throbs to know one thing. Tell me, if your art
Can tell so much: shall Banquo's issue ever
Reign in this kingdom?

    All.   Seek to know no more.

    Macbeth. I will be satisfied. Deny me this,
105 And an eternal curse fall on you! Let me know!

                [*Cauldron sinks. Hautboys.*]

    Why sinks that cauldron? And what noise is this?

    First Witch. Show.

    Second Witch. Show.

    Third Witch. Show.

110   **All.** Show his eyes, and grieve his heart.
    Come like shadows; so depart.

    [*A show of eight kings, the eighth king with a glass in his hand, and* Banquo *last.*]

Ⓙ
    Macbeth. Thou art too like the spirit of Banquo. Down!
    Thy crown does sear mine eyeballs. And thy hair,
    Thou other gold-bound brow, is like the first.
115   A third is like the former.—Filthy hags,
    Why do you show me this?—A fourth? Start, eyes!
    What, will the line stretch out to th' crack of doom?
    Another yet? A seventh? I'll see no more.
    And yet the eighth appears who bears a glass
120   Which shows me many more, and some I see
    That twofold balls and treble scepters carry.
    Horrible sight! Now I see 'tis true,

96 bodements: prophecies.

97–100 Macbeth boasts that he will never again be troubled by ghosts (**rebellious dead**) and that he will live out his expected life span (**lease of nature**). He believes he will die (**pay his breath**) by natural causes (**mortal custom**).

[Stage Direction] **A show . . . :** Macbeth next sees eight kings, the last carrying a mirror (**glass**). According to legend, Fleance escaped to England, where he founded the Stuart family, to which King James belonged.

112–124 All eight kings look like Banquo. The mirror shows a future with many more Banquo look-alikes as kings. The twofold balls and treble scepters foretell the union of Scotland and England in 1603, the year that James became king of both realms. Banquo, his hair matted (**boltered**) with blood, claims all the kings as his descendants.

Image Credits: ©James Steidl/Shutterstock

TO CHALLENGE STUDENTS . . .

Analyze Character and Theme Remind students that Shakespeare wrote *Macbeth* during the reign of James I, who claimed to be a direct descendant of Banquo.

ASK STUDENTS to examine how the historical time and place may have influenced Shakespeare's development of Banquo and the theme in *Macbeth*. *(Shakespeare may have wanted to flatter James I and thus portrayed Banquo and his descendants as being honorable monarchs who exhibit the qualities of a good king as opposed to those of a tyrant like Macbeth.)*

For the blood-boltered Banquo smiles upon me
And points at them for his.

[*The* Apparitions *disappear.*]

What, is this so?

125 **First Witch.** Ay, sir, all this is so. But why
Stands Macbeth thus amazedly?
Come, sisters, cheer we up his sprites
And show the best of our delights.
I'll charm the air to give a sound
130 While you perform your antic round,
That this great king may kindly say
Our duties did his welcome pay.

[*Music. The* Witches *dance and vanish.*]

Macbeth. Where are they? Gone? Let this pernicious hour
Stand aye accursèd in the calendar!—
135 Come in, without there.

[*Enter* Lennox.]

Lennox.   What's your Grace's will?

Macbeth. Saw you the Weïrd Sisters?

Lennox.   No, my lord.

Macbeth. Came they not by you?

Lennox.   No, indeed, my lord.

Macbeth. Infected be the air whereon they ride,
And damned all those that trust them! I did hear
140 The galloping of horse. Who was 't came by?

Lennox. 'Tis two or three, my lord, that bring you word
Macduff is fled to England.

Macbeth.   Fled to England?

Lennox. Ay, my good lord.

Macbeth [*aside*]. Time, thou anticipat'st my dread exploits.
145 The flighty purpose never is o'ertook
Unless the deed go with it. From this moment
The very firstlings of my heart shall be
The firstlings of my hand. And even now,
To crown my thoughts with acts, be it thought and done:
150 The castle of Macduff I will surprise,
Seize upon Fife, give to th' edge o' th' sword
His wife, his babes, and all unfortunate souls
That trace him in his line. No boasting like a fool;
This deed I'll do before this purpose cool.

133 pernicious: evil.

134 aye: always.

135 After the witches vanish, Macbeth hears noises outside the cave and calls out.

144–156 Frustrated in his desire to kill Macduff, Macbeth blames his own hesitation, which gave his enemy time to flee. He concludes that one's plans (**flighty purpose**) are never achieved (**o'ertook**) unless carried out at once. From now on, Macbeth promises, he will act immediately on his impulses (**firstlings of my heart**) and complete (**crown**) his thoughts with acts. He will surprise Macduff's castle at Fife and kill his wife and children.

CLOSE READ

Analyze Character and Theme (LINES 141–154)

COMMON CORE   RL 1, RL 2, RL 3

Lennox tells Macbeth that Macduff has fled Scotland and gone to England. Point out that Shakespeare reveals much about Macbeth's character at the end of this scene.

K   **CITE TEXT EVIDENCE** Have students examine Macbeth's reaction to the news that Macduff has fled to England. Ask students to describe the reaction and cite the evidence. (*Macbeth's question in line 142 suggests that he is frustrated that Macduff has escaped, and lines 144–146 show that Macbeth blames himself for not acting quickly enough to stop Macduff.*) What does Macbeth say he will do from now on, and what action is he planning to take? (*He says in lines 146–153 that from now on he will act immediately upon his thoughts instead of hesitating. He plans to capture Macduff's castle and kill his wife and children.*)

L   **ASK STUDENTS** why Macbeth decides to kill Macduff's family (lines 150–153). (*Macbeth may think the prophecy that Banquo's descendants will rule Scotland may come true if Macduff joins forces with others against him, and Fleance, Banquo's son who escaped in Act III, becomes king. Macbeth also may think that killing Macduff's family is the only way to ensure that Macduff's immediate relatives and future descendants cannot hurt him.*)

M   **ASK STUDENTS** what Macbeth's speech, culminating in line 154, reveals about his changing character. (*Macbeth is becoming increasingly irrational, impulsive, and violent.*) How does his speech develop a theme of the drama? (*His increasingly irrational, impulsive, and violent nature supports a theme about the perils of power and ambition.*)

WHEN STUDENTS STRUGGLE . . .

Elicit from students a definition of **verbal irony.** (*a contrast between what is said and what is meant*) Then direct students to lines 138–139.

ASK STUDENTS what is ironic about Macbeth's statement damning all those who trust the witches. (*It is ironic because Macbeth earlier had entrusted himself to the witches' prophecies, so he therefore is damning himself.*) Ask students to consider what this irony reveals about Macbeth's character by answering this question: Is Macbeth aware enough to recognize the irony in his statement? (*Some students may believe Macbeth is completely unhinged, and can't see the contradiction in what he's saying. Others mays believe he is aware of the irony—aware that he is damned.*)

Analyze Character

COMMON CORE RL 1, RL 2, RL 3

(LINES 3–17)

Lady Macduff believes that her husband is a traitor who fled the country to save himself while abandoning her and her children, leaving them to fend for themselves against Macbeth. Point out that Shakespeare again uses irony to reveal character.

(N) **CITE TEXT EVIDENCE** Have students identify and explain the irony. *(In lines 3–4, Lady Macduff says that her husband's fears led him to become a traitor by fleeing the country. Lady Macduff's statements are ironic because Ross knows that Macduff has bravely set off on a mission to defeat Macbeth, saying in lines 16–17 that Macduff "is noble, wise, judicious, and best knows / The fits o' th' season.")*

ASK STUDENTS why Lady Macduff tells her son that his father is dead, even though the boy heard her discussion with Ross. *(Possible answer: Lady Macduff is upset her husband has left his family undefended. In her opinion, Macduff's absence is like death because it has left the family without its chief protector.)*

---

155 But no more sights!—Where are these gentlemen?
　　　Come bring me where they are.

　　　[*They exit.*]

　　　Scene 2 *Macduff's castle at Fife.*

　　　[*Enter* Lady Macduff, *her* Son, *and* Ross.]

　　　Lady Macduff. What had he done to make him fly the land?

　　　Ross. You must have patience, madam.

　　　Lady Macduff. 　　　　　　　　　He had none.
　　　His flight was madness. When our actions do not,
　　　Our fears do make us traitors.

　　　Ross. 　　　　　　　　You know not
　5　Whether it was his wisdom or his fear.

　　　Lady Macduff. Wisdom? To leave his wife, to leave his babes,
　　　His mansion and his titles in a place
　　　From whence himself does fly? He loves us not;
　　　He wants the natural touch; for the poor wren
　10　(The most diminutive of birds) will fight,
　　　Her young ones in her nest, against the owl.
　　　All is the fear, and nothing is the love,
　　　As little is the wisdom, where the flight
　　　So runs against all reason.

　　　Ross. 　　　　　　　　My dearest coz,
　15　I pray you school yourself. But for your husband,
　　　He is noble, wise, judicious, and best knows
　　　The fits o' th' season. I dare not speak much further;
　　　But cruel are the times when we are traitors
　　　And do not know ourselves; when we hold rumor
　20　From what we fear, yet know not what we fear,
　　　But float upon a wild and violent sea
　　　Each way and move—I take my leave of you.
　　　Shall not be long but I'll be here again.
　　　Things at the worst will cease or else climb upward
　25　To what they were before.—My pretty cousin,
　　　Blessing upon you.

　　　Lady Macduff. Fathered he is, and yet he's fatherless.

　　　Ross. I am so much a fool, should I stay longer
　　　It would be my disgrace and your discomfort.
　30　I take my leave at once. 　　　　　　[*Ross exits.*]

　　　Lady Macduff. 　　　　　Sirrah, your father's dead.
　　　And what will you do now? How will you live?

3–4 Macduff's wife is worried that others will think her husband a traitor because his fears made him flee the country (**our fears do make us traitors**), though he was guilty of no wrongdoing

9 wants the natural touch: lacks the instinct to protect his family.

14 coz: cousin (a term used for any close relation).

15 school: control; **for:** as for.

17 fits o' th' season: disorders of the present time.

18–22 Ross laments the cruelty of the times that made Macduff flee. Fears make people believe (**hold**) rumors, though they do not know what to fear and drift aimlessly like ships tossed by a tempest.

28–30 Moved by pity for Macduff's family, Ross is near tears (**my disgrace**). He will leave before he embarrasses himself.

SCAFFOLDING FOR ELL STUDENTS

Analyze Character English learners may better understand Shakespeare's development of characters in Scene 2 by reading aloud. Have students read one character's speech at a time. After each speech, have students explain in their own words the main idea(s) expressed by the character.

ASK STUDENTS what they learn about the key characters in this scene.

- Lady Macduff *(She is angry with her husband, thinks he is a coward for deserting his family, and is afraid for the safety of her children and herself.)*

- Ross *(He defends Macduff's courage and honor, and although he likely knows why Macduff fled the country, he tries to protect Lady Macduff by not revealing anything for which she could be implicated.)*

Son. As birds do, mother.

Lady Macduff.   What, with worms and flies?

Son. With what I get, I mean; and so do they.

Lady Macduff. Poor bird, thou'dst never fear the net nor lime,
35 The pitfall nor the gin.

Son. Why should I, mother? Poor birds they are not set for.
My father is not dead, for all your saying.

Lady Macduff. Yes, he is dead. How wilt thou do for a father?

Son. Nay, how will you do for a husband?

40 Lady Macduff. Why, I can buy me twenty at any market.

Son. Then you'll buy 'em to sell again.

Lady Macduff. Thou speak'st with all thy wit,
And yet, i' faith, with wit enough for thee.

Son. Was my father a traitor, mother?

45 Lady Macduff. Ay, that he was.

Son. What is a traitor?

Lady Macduff. Why, one that swears and lies.

Son. And be all traitors that do so?

Lady Macduff. Every one that does so is a traitor and must be
hanged.

50 Son. And must they all be hanged that swear and lie?

32–35 The spirited son refuses to be defeated by their bleak situation. He will live as birds do, taking whatever comes his way. His mother responds in kind, calling attention to devices used to catch birds: nets, sticky birdlime (**lime**), snares (**pitfall**), and traps (**gin**).

40–43 Lady Macduff and her son affectionately joke about her ability to find a new husband. She expresses admiration for his intelligence (**with wit enough**).

The Tragedy of Macbeth: Act IV, Scene 2   **267**

Image Credits: ©Philip Dunn/Alamy Images

CLOSE READ

Analyze Character

COMMON CORE   RL 1, RL 3, RL 4

(LINES 32–50)

Shakespeare develops the son's character through dialogue between Lady Macduff and her son. Explain to students that in Elizabethan times children were often given adult responsibilities and were expected to behave, think, and speak maturely. Lady Macduff has bluntly told her son that his father is dead and asked what the son will do now—how he will live.

CITE TEXT EVIDENCE Have students cite evidence of the son's maturity. *(In lines 32–33, the son responds to his mother's question by saying he will survive as birds do, taking what comes his way. The son further shows maturity by telling his mother in line 37 that he knows his father is not dead despite what she has told him. The son's questions about his father being a traitor and about the meaning of the word "traitor" in lines 46, 48, and 50 reveal critical thinking skills and logic that one might expect only in adults.)* Ask students to describe the son's character in one or two words. *(Accept reasonable responses that are supported by text evidence, such as "loyal", "courageous," "witty," and "wise.")*

WHEN STUDENTS STRUGGLE . . .

Remind students that Shakespeare often leaves words out and uses an inverted word order, putting verbs before subjects and objects before verbs.

ASK STUDENTS these questions to show them how to restate the son's question in line 48:

- What does "all" refer to in the son's question? *(all people)*
- What words does "do so" refer to? *(swear and lie)*
- Where would you place "do so" in the question in contemporary English? *(after "all")*
- How would you restate the question in contemporary English?
  (And are all people who swear and lie traitors?)

Analyze Character and Theme (LINES 69–79)

COMMON CORE   RL 1, RL 2, RL 3, RL 5

Remind students that Shakespeare often uses a **soliloquy,** a speech spoken by a character to him- or herself while alone, to reveal the character's inner thoughts, feelings, and plans to the audience. Point out that Lady Macduff's speech in lines 69–75 is a soliloquy.

(P) ASK STUDENTS to paraphrase Lady Macduff's thoughts about "this earthly world." *(Why should I flee when I have done nothing wrong? But I must remember that here on Earth doing evil is often applauded, whereas doing good is sometimes dangerous and foolish. So why do I present the womanly defense that I am innocent?)* What theme developing since Act I do the ideas in this soliloquy support? *(Lady Macduff's observation about the outcomes of doing harm versus doing good echo the theme of "fair is foul, and foul is fair.")*

(Q) CITE TEXT EVIDENCE Ask students to describe how the son feels about his father. Be sure they support their answers with text evidence. *(In line 79, Macduff's son reacts quickly, vehemently accusing the murderer of being a liar and a villain. The son clearly admires and loves his father and is willing to defend him, even in a situation that looks deadly for himself.)*

Lady Macduff. Every one.

Son. Who must hang them?

Lady Macduff. Why, the honest men.

Son. Then the liars and swearers are fools, for there are liars and
55   swearers enough to beat the honest men and hang up them.

Lady Macduff. Now God help thee, poor monkey! But how wilt thou do for a father?

Son. If he were dead, you'd weep for him. If you would not, it were a good sign that I should quickly have a new father.

60   **Lady Macduff.** Poor prattler, how thou talk'st!

[*Enter a* Messenger.]

Messenger. Bless you, fair dame. I am not to you known,
Though in your state of honor I am perfect.
I doubt some danger does approach you nearly.
If you will take a homely man's advice,
65   Be not found here. Hence with your little ones!
To fright you thus methinks I am too savage;
To do worse to you were fell cruelty,
Which is too nigh your person. Heaven preserve you!
I dare abide no longer.   [Messenger *exits.*]

Lady Macduff.   Whither should I fly?
70   I have done no harm. But I remember now
I am in this earthly world, where to do harm
Is often laudable, to do good sometime
Accounted dangerous folly. Why then, alas,
Do I put up that womanly defense
75   To say I have done no harm?

[*Enter* Murderers.]

                    What are these faces?

Murderer. Where is your husband?

Lady Macduff. I hope in no place so unsanctified
Where such as thou mayst find him.

Murderer.   He's a traitor.

Son. Thou liest, thou shag-eared villain!

Murderer.   What, you egg!

[*Stabbing him*]
80   Young fry of treachery!

Son.   He has killed me, mother.
Run away, I pray you,

54–60 Her son points out that traitors outnumber honest men in this troubled time. The mother's terms of affection, **monkey** and **prattler** (childish talker), suggest that his playfulness has won her over.

61–69 The messenger, who knows Lady Macduff is an honorable person (**in your state of honor I am perfect**), delivers a polite but desperate warning, urging her to flee immediately. While he apologizes for scaring her, he warns that she faces a deadly (**fell**) cruelty, one dangerously close (**too nigh**).

77 unsanctified: unholy.

79 shag-eared: long-haired.

80 young fry: small fish.

TO CHALLENGE STUDENTS . . .

Analyze Character and Theme Explain that dramatists often use a written letter as a device to provide the audience with information related to character, theme, or plot.

ASK STUDENTS to imagine that, when Macduff arrived in England, he sent a letter to Lady Macduff that she never received. Have students write Macduff's letter, including

- an explanation of his sudden departure,
- reasons for leaving his family behind, and
- instructions or a personal message to his wife and son.

Remind students to base the contents of the letter on details of plot, theme, and character from the text. Encourage students to share their letters in small groups.

[Lady Macduff *exits, crying "Murder!" followed by the* Murderers *bearing the* Son's *body.*]

Scene 3 *England. Before King Edward's palace.*

[*Enter* Malcolm *and* Macduff.]

Malcolm. Let us seek out some desolate shade and there
Weep our sad bosoms empty.

Macduff.   Let us rather
Hold fast the mortal sword and, like good men,
Bestride our downfall'n birthdom. Each new morn
5   New widows howl, new orphans cry, new sorrows
Strike heaven on the face, that it resounds
As if it felt with Scotland, and yelled out
Like syllable of dolor.

Malcolm.   What I believe, I'll wail;
What know, believe; and what I can redress,
10   As I shall find the time to friend, I will.
What you have spoke, it may be so, perchance.
This tyrant, whose sole name blisters our tongues,
Was once thought honest. You have loved him well.
He hath not touched you yet. I am young, but something
15   You may deserve of him through me, and wisdom
To offer up a weak, poor, innocent lamb
T' appease an angry god.

Macduff. I am not treacherous.

Malcolm.   But Macbeth is.
A good and virtuous nature may recoil
20   In an imperial charge. But I shall crave your pardon.
That which you are, my thoughts cannot transpose.
Angels are bright still, though the brightest fell.
Though all things foul would wear the brows of grace,
Yet grace must still look so.

Macduff.   I have lost my hopes.

25   **Malcolm.** Perchance even there where I did find my doubts.
Why in that rawness left you wife and child,
Those precious motives, those strong knots of love,
Without leave-taking? I pray you,
Let not my jealousies be your dishonors,
30   But mine own safeties. You may be rightly just,
Whatever I shall think.

Macduff.   Bleed, bleed, poor country!
Great tyranny, lay thou thy basis sure,
For goodness dare not check thee. Wear thou thy wrongs;

1–8 Macduff advises that they grab a deadly (**mortal**) sword and defend their homeland (**birthdom**). The anguished cries of Macbeth's victims strike heaven and make the skies echo with cries of sorrow (**syllable of dolor**).

8–15 Malcolm will strike back only if the time is right (**as I shall find the time to friend**). Macduff may be sincere, but he may be deceiving Malcolm to gain a reward from Macbeth (**something you may deserve of him through me**).

18–24 Even a good person may fall (**recoil**) into wickedness because of a king's command (**imperial charge**). Suspicions cannot change (**transpose**) the nature (**that which you are**) of an innocent person. Virtue cannot be damaged even by those like Lucifer (**the brightest angel**), who can disguise themselves as virtuous (**wear the brows of grace**).

26 rawness: vulnerability.

29 jealousies: suspicions.

CLOSE READ

Analyze Character and Theme (LINES 2–17)

COMMON CORE RL 1, RL 2, RL 3, RL 4

Remind students that **dramatic irony** occurs when the reader or viewer knows something that a character does not know. Shakespeare uses dramatic irony at the beginning of Scene 3 to create intense sympathy for Macduff.

R CITE TEXT EVIDENCE Have students explain what is ironic about Macduff's speech in lines 2–8. (*Macduff's speech is ironic because he does not yet know that the "new sorrows" he speaks of in line 5 have already befallen him. Instead of the "new widows" and "new orphans" in Scotland that Macduff describes in line 5, it is Macduff himself who has lost his loved ones.*)

S ASK STUDENTS to explain the irony in Malcolm's speech in lines 8–17. (*In line 14, Malcolm tells Macduff that Macbeth "hath not touched you yet," but the audience knows Macbeth has had Macduff's wife and children killed.*)

WHEN STUDENTS STRUGGLE . . .

Remind students that they last saw Malcolm when he left Scotland in Act II, Scene 3. To better understand Malcolm's character, have students track details about him in Act IV, Scene 3.

ASK STUDENTS to create a web diagram. In the center circle, have students write "Malcolm after leaving Scotland." In the surrounding circles, have students list details from Act IV, Scene 3 about Malcolm's character traits and the evidence that supports these traits.

shrewd and cautious, as he pretends to be what he is not to test Macduff's loyalty

self-assured, as he has won the support of King Edward who is giving him Siward's help and troops to fight Macbeth

loyal to Scotland, as he plans to fight against Macbeth's tyranny

MALCOLM *after leaving Scotland*

Analyze Character

COMMON CORE RL 1, RL 2, RL 3

(LINES 44–102)

Malcolm tests Macduff's loyalty to Scotland by pretending that he would be a worse tyrant than Macbeth. Audiences in Shakespeare's day knew the legend of Macbeth and understood Malcolm's ruse. Students reading for the first time, however, do not become aware of the dramatic irony until Macduff does, when Malcolm reveals his true purpose in lines 114–137. Therefore, as students read lines 44–102, focus on comprehension and on looking for clues to Malcolm's motivation.

(T) CITE TEXT EVIDENCE Ask students what kind of king Malcolm claims he would be. *(In lines 50–55, Malcolm says that people would think that Macbeth was innocent if they knew how evil he himself was. In lines 60–65, he says that no woman would be safe from his boundless lust.)* Ask students why Malcolm would admit to this huge character flaw. *(Accept reasonable responses.)*

The title is affeered.—Fare thee well, lord.

35 I would not be the villain that thou think'st
For the whole space that's in the tyrant's grasp,
And the rich East to boot.

Malcolm. Be not offended.
I speak not as in absolute fear of you.
I think our country sinks beneath the yoke.
40 It weeps, it bleeds, and each new day a gash
Is added to her wounds. I think withal
There would be hands uplifted in my right;
And here from gracious England have I offer
Of goodly thousands. But, for all this,
45 When I shall tread upon the tyrant's head
Or wear it on my sword, yet my poor country
Shall have more vices than it had before,
More suffer, and more sundry ways than ever,
By him that shall succeed.

Macduff. What should he be?

50 **Malcolm.** It is myself I mean, in whom I know
All the particulars of vice so grafted
That, when they shall be opened, black Macbeth
Will seem as pure as snow, and the poor state
Esteem him as a lamb, being compared
55 With my confineless harms.

Macduff. Not in the legions
Of horrid hell can come a devil more damned
In evils to top Macbeth.

Malcolm. I grant him bloody,
Luxurious, avaricious, false, deceitful,
Sudden, malicious, smacking of every sin
60 That has a name. But there's no bottom, none,
In my voluptuousness. Your wives, your daughters,
Your matrons, and your maids could not fill up
The cistern of my lust, and my desire
All continent impediments would o'erbear
65 That did oppose my will. Better Macbeth
Than such an one to reign.

Macduff. Boundless intemperance
In nature is a tyranny. It hath been
Th' untimely emptying of the happy throne
And fall of many kings. But fear not yet
70 To take upon you what is yours. You may
Convey your pleasures in a spacious plenty

34 affeered: confirmed.

46–49 yet my . . . succeed: To test Macduff's honor and loyalty, Malcolm begins a lengthy description of his own fictitious vices.

50–55 Malcolm says that his own vices are so plentiful and deeply planted (**grafted**) that Macbeth will seem innocent by comparison.

58 luxurious: lustful.

61 voluptuousness: lust.

63 cistern: large storage tank.

63–65 His lust is so great that it would overpower (**o'erbear**) all restraining obstacles (**continent impediments**).

66–76 Macduff describes uncontrolled desire (**boundless intemperance**) as a tyrant of human nature that has caused the early (**untimely**) downfall of many kings.

SCAFFOLDING FOR ELL STUDENTS

Vocabulary: Suffixes Direct students to line 58. Point out the words *luxurious* and *avaricious*. Tell students that words ending in *–ous* or *–ious* act as adjectives. Ask them who is being described as avaricious. *(Macbeth)* Have students work with a partner to look for other words that end in or contain *–ious* or *–ous*: *("gracious," line 43; "malicious," line 59; "voluptuousness," line 61; "spacious," line 71; "pernicious," line 85)* Have them determine the meaning of each.

ASK STUDENTS to summarize what Malcolm says he would be like as king, using five of the words in the paragraph above.

And yet seem cold—the time you may so hoodwink.
We have willing dames enough. There cannot be
That vulture in you to devour so many
75 As will to greatness dedicate themselves,
Finding it so inclined.

Malcolm.   With this there grows
In my most ill-composed affection such
A stanchless avarice that, were I king,
I should cut off the nobles for their lands,
80 Desire his jewels, and this other's house;
And my more-having would be as a sauce
To make me hunger more, that I should forge
Quarrels unjust against the good and loyal,
Destroying them for wealth.

Macduff.   This avarice
85 Sticks deeper, grows with more pernicious root
Than summer-seeming lust, and it hath been
The sword of our slain kings. Yet do not fear.
Scotland hath foisons to fill up your will
Of your mere own. All these are portable,
90 With other graces weighed.

Malcolm. But I have none. The king-becoming graces,
As justice, verity, temp'rance, stableness,
Bounty, perseverance, mercy, lowliness,
Devotion, patience, courage, fortitude,
95 I have no relish of them but abound
In the division of each several crime,
Acting it many ways. Nay, had I power, I should
Pour the sweet milk of concord into hell,
Uproar the universal peace, confound
100 All unity on earth.

Macduff.   O Scotland, Scotland!

Malcolm. If such a one be fit to govern, speak.
I am as I have spoken.

Macduff.   Fit to govern?
No, not to live.—O nation miserable,
With an untitled tyrant bloody-sceptered,
105 When shalt thou see thy wholesome days again,
Since that the truest issue of thy throne
By his own interdiction stands accursed
And does blaspheme his breed?—Thy royal father
Was a most sainted king. The queen that bore thee,
110 Oft'ner upon her knees than on her feet,

76–78 Malcolm adds insatiable greed (**stanchless avarice**) to the list of evils in his disposition (**affection**).

84–90 Macduff recognizes that greed is a deeper-rooted problem than lust, which passes as quickly as the summer (**summer-seeming**). But the king's property alone (**of your mere own**) offers plenty (**foisons**) to satisfy his desire. Malcolm's vices can be tolerated (**are portable**).

91–95 Malcolm lists the kingly virtues he lacks: truthfulness (**verity**), consistency (**stableness**), generosity (**bounty**), humility (**lowliness**), and religious devotion.

102–114 Macduff can see no relief for Scotland's suffering under a tyrant who has no right to the throne (**untitled**). The rightful heir (**truest issue**), Malcolm, bans himself from the throne (**by his own interdiction**) because of his evil. Malcolm's vices slander his parents (**blaspheme his breed**)—his saintly father and his mother who renounced the world (**died every day**) for her religion.

The Tragedy of Macbeth: Act IV, Scene 3   **271**

CLOSE READ

Analyze Character and Theme (LINES 73–110)

COMMON CORE RL 1, RL 2, RL 3, RL 4

Explain to students that Malcolm continues to try to dissuade Macduff from enlisting his aid.

CITE TEXT EVIDENCE Ask students to summarize the conversation between Macduff and Malcolm. *(In lines 73–76, Macduff responds to Malcolm's admission of lust by saying there are plenty of admiring women in Scotland to meet his needs. Malcolm then claims his unquenchable greed would cause him to destroy the nobility to gain their wealth [lines 84–90]. Macduff responds to Malcolm's admission of unquenchable greed by saying there is plenty of wealth in Scotland to satisfy Malcolm's greed. Finally, Malcolm claims he has not a single kingly virtue, and if he could, he would destroy peace throughout the world. At last, Macduff agrees that Malcolm is not fit to rule or even live [lines 102–114].)*

ASK STUDENTS whether Macduff seems honorable. *(Possible answer: At first, Macduff seems to have questionable honor, because he is willing to support immoral qualities, such as unrestrained lust and greed, in order to eliminate Macbeth. His final outburst, however, reveals a loathing for Malcolm and the immorality he claims. It seems as if he had been trying to convince himself against his better nature that Malcolm could replace Macbeth.)*

WHEN STUDENTS STRUGGLE . . .

Students can help each other to understand characters' complex speeches. Have students work with a partner or in small groups.

ASK STUDENTS to each select a speech that they are having trouble understanding and read it aloud. Remind students to use the following reading tips:

- Read difficult passages slowly and clearly.
- Use the punctuation as guides for pausing (commas) and stopping (periods).
- Read with meaning to communicate your understanding to listeners.
- After reading, ask and answer questions to clarify ideas.

Analyze Character and Theme (LINES 114–132)

COMMON CORE RL 1, RL 3, RL 4

In this passage, Malcolm reveals his true character and his plans for Macbeth, and the **dramatic irony** of the preceding passages is revealed.

V CITE TEXT EVIDENCE Have students identify the point at which the audience knows Malcolm has been testing Macduff all along. *(In lines 114–117, Malcolm tells Macduff that his passionate outburst has convinced Malcolm of his "good truth and honor." Then, in lines 121–131, Malcolm explains that his previous claims to evil were only a pretense.)*

ASK STUDENTS to review lines 125–132 to identify the qualities that Malcolm says he truly has. *(He says he is a virgin, not greedy, faithful, trustworthy, loyal, truthful, and humble.)*

Died every day she lived. Fare thee well.
These evils thou repeat'st upon thyself
Have banished me from Scotland.—O my breast,
Thy hope ends here!

    Malcolm.   Macduff, this noble passion,
115 Child of integrity, hath from my soul
     Wiped the black scruples, reconciled my thoughts
     To thy good truth and honor. Devilish Macbeth
     By many of these trains hath sought to win me
     Into his power, and modest wisdom plucks me
120 From overcredulous haste. But God above
     Deal between thee and me, for even now
     I put myself to thy direction and
     Unspeak mine own detraction, here abjure
     The taints and blames I laid upon myself
125 For strangers to my nature. I am yet
     Unknown to woman, never was forsworn,
     Scarcely have coveted what was mine own,
     At no time broke my faith, would not betray
     The devil to his fellow, and delight
130 No less in truth than life. My first false speaking
     Was this upon myself. What I am truly
     Is thine and my poor country's to command—
     Whither indeed, before thy here-approach,
     Old Siward with ten thousand warlike men,
135 Already at a point, was setting forth.

114–125 Macduff has finally convinced Malcolm of his honesty. Malcolm explains that his caution (**modest wisdom**) resulted from his fear of Macbeth's tricks. He takes back his accusations against himself (**unspeak mine own detraction**) and renounces (**abjure**) the evils he previously claimed.

133–137 Malcolm already has an army, 10,000 troops belonging to old Siward, the earl of Northumberland. Now that Macduff is an ally, he hopes the battle's result will match the justice of their cause (**warranted quarrel**).

Image Credits: ©AKG Images

272 Collection 5

APPLYING ACADEMIC VOCABULARY

comprise	ultimate

As you discuss Malcolm's speech, incorporate the following Collection 5 academic vocabulary words: *comprise* and *ultimate*. Ask students what Malcolm's **ultimate** goal was in pretending to be more tyrannical than Macbeth. *(to find out whether Macduff's motivation in asking Malcolm to return to Scotland is pure)* Then ask whether Malcolm's descriptions of his true self **comprise** the qualities of a true king or of a tyrant. *(These are the qualities of a true king.)*

Now we'll together, and the chance of goodness
Be like our warranted quarrel. Why are you silent?

Macduff. Such welcome and unwelcome things at once
'Tis hard to reconcile.

[*Enter a* Doctor.]

140 **Malcolm.** Well, more anon.—Comes the King forth, I pray you?

Doctor. Ay, sir. There are a crew of wretched souls
That stay his cure. Their malady convinces
The great assay of art, but at his touch
(Such sanctity hath heaven given his hand)
145 They presently amend.

Malcolm.   I thank you, doctor.

[Doctor *exits.*]

Macduff. What's the disease he means?

Malcolm.   'Tis called the evil:
A most miraculous work in this good king,
Which often since my here-remain in England
I have seen him do. How he solicits heaven
150 Himself best knows, but strangely visited people
All swoll'n and ulcerous, pitiful to the eye,
The mere despair of surgery, he cures,
Hanging a golden stamp about their necks
Put on with holy prayers; and, 'tis spoken,
155 To the succeeding royalty he leaves
The healing benediction. With this strange virtue,
He hath a heavenly gift of prophecy,
And sundry blessings hang about his throne
That speak him full of grace.

[*Enter* Ross.]

Macduff.   See who comes here.

160 **Malcolm.** My countryman, but yet I know him not.

Macduff. My ever-gentle cousin, welcome hither.

Malcolm. I know him now.—Good God betimes remove
The means that makes us strangers!

Ross.   Sir, amen.

Macduff. Stands Scotland where it did?

Ross.   Alas, poor country,
165 Almost afraid to know itself. It cannot
Be called our mother, but our grave, where nothing
But who knows nothing is once seen to smile;
Where sighs and groans and shrieks that rent the air

141–159 Edward the Confessor, king of England, could reportedly heal the disease of scrofula (**the evil**) by his saintly touch. The doctor describes people who cannot be helped by medicine's best efforts (**the great assay of art**) waiting for the touch of the king's hand. Edward has cured many victims of this disease. Each time, he hangs a gold coin around their neck and offers prayers, a healing ritual that he will teach to his royal descendants (**succeeding royalty**).

162–163 Good God ... strangers: May God remove Macbeth, who is the cause (**means**) of our being strangers.

The Tragedy of Macbeth: Act IV, Scene 3   **273**

CLOSE READ

Analyze Language

COMMON CORE   RL 1, RL 4

(LINES 141–159)

Point out to students that the entrance of a doctor at this point may seem out of place, but the information revealed is related to a key theme.

 CITE TEXT EVIDENCE Have students explain what the reader learns about King Edward from the doctor's and Malcolm's speeches. *(In lines 141–144, the doctor says that the king's "touch" heals sick "souls" through the power given him by "heaven." In line 147, Malcolm calls Edward "this good king" and says in lines 152–154 that the king "cures" the sick by saying "prayers" as he hangs "a golden stamp about their necks." Then in lines 155–156, he says he's heard that the king's "succeeding royalty" will have the power to perform the same "healing benediction.")*

Explain to students that Shakespeare is making an **analogy,** a comparison between two things for the purpose of clarifying the less familiar of the two.

ASK STUDENTS to think about how Scotland under Macbeth's rule can be used in an analogy to a sick patient. *(Under Macbeth's rule, Scotland is like a patient sick with disease.)* Ask students to carry the analogy further to explain how King Edward's healing powers may be related to conditions in Scotland. *(Scotland needs to be healed by the "touch" of a good king.)*

TO CHALLENGE STUDENTS . . .

Analyze Character and Theme Act IV contains references to King Edward that contrast sharply with references to Macbeth.

ASK STUDENTS to find and contrast these references. For example, in Scene 3, lines 147–159, we learn that King Edward has the power to heal, and that he also has the gift of prophecy. Ask students to compare this characterization of King Edward with Macbeth's consultation with the witches earlier in Act IV. Students may want to record their findings in a two-column comparison-contrast chart. Remind them to write down the line numbers for each reference. Have students share their findings in groups.

Analyze Character and Theme (LINES 164–180)

COMMON CORE RL 1, RL 2, RL 3, RL 5

Remind students that the events in a tragedy are set in motion by a decision that is often an error in judgment caused by a **tragic flaw,** or quality that leads to the tragic hero's downfall. Succeeding events are linked in a cause-and-effect relationship and lead to a disastrous conclusion.

X CITE TEXT EVIDENCE Have students identify the series of events described by Ross that will likely lead to a disastrous conclusion for Macbeth. (*Ross says that in Scotland, no one smiles anymore [line 167]; sighs, groans, and shrieks are made, but no one notices [lines 168–169]; violent sorrow is commonplace [lines 169–170]; people don't want to know who died when they hear the funeral bells [lines 170–171]; and good men die before they're even sick [line 173].*) Have students identify the cascade of character flaws in Macbeth that has likely caused these events to unfold. (*Macbeth's unbridled ambition has led him to become more and more ruthless, impulsive, and paranoid, leading to misery for his subjects.*)

Tell students that in the exchange between Ross and Macduff, Shakespeare uses **ambiguity,** a technique in which a word, phrase, or event has more than one meaning or can be interpreted in more than one way.

Y ASK STUDENTS to explain the ambiguity of Macduff's use of "at their peace" in line 179 and Ross's response of "at peace" in line 180. (*Macduff is asking if Macbeth disturbed his family's peaceful life in the castle, but Ross responds vaguely that the family was at peace, a play on the expression "rest in peace" that is used to wish someone who has died eternal rest and peace.*)

Are made, not marked; where violent sorrow seems
170 A modern ecstasy. The dead man's knell
Is there scarce asked for who, and good men's lives
Expire before the flowers in their caps,
Dying or ere they sicken.

Macduff. O relation too nice and yet too true!

175 **Malcolm.** What's the newest grief?

Ross. That of an hour's age doth hiss the speaker.
Each minute teems a new one.

Macduff.   How does my wife?

Ross. Why, well.

Macduff.   And all my children?

Ross.   Well too.

Macduff. The tyrant has not battered at their peace?

180 **Ross.** No, they were well at peace when I did leave 'em.

Macduff. Be not a niggard of your speech. How goes 't?

Ross. When I came hither to transport the tidings
Which I have heavily borne, there ran a rumor
Of many worthy fellows that were out;
185 Which was to my belief witnessed the rather
For that I saw the tyrant's power afoot.
Now is the time of help. Your eye in Scotland
Would create soldiers, make our women fight
To doff their dire distresses.

Malcolm.   Be 't their comfort
190 We are coming thither. Gracious England hath
Lent us good Siward and ten thousand men;
An older and a better soldier none
That Christendom gives out.

Ross.   Would I could answer
This comfort with the like. But I have words
195 That would be howled out in the desert air,
Where hearing should not latch them.

Macduff.   What concern they—
The general cause, or is it a fee-grief
Due to some single breast?

Ross.   No mind that's honest
But in it shares some woe, though the main part
200 Pertains to you alone.

174 relation too nice: news that is too accurate.

176–177 If the news is more than an hour old, listeners hiss at the speaker for being outdated; every minute gives birth to a new grief.

180 well at peace: Ross knows about the murder of Macduff's wife and children, but the news is too terrible to report.

182–189 Ross mentions the rumors of nobles who are rebelling (**out**) against Macbeth. Ross believes the rumors because he saw Macbeth's troops on the march (**tyrant's power afoot**). The presence (**eye**) of Malcolm and Macduff in Scotland would help raise soldiers and remove (**doff**) Macbeth's evil (**dire distresses**).

195 would: should.

196 latch: catch.

197 fee-grief: private sorrow.

198–199 No mind . . . woe: Every honorable (**honest**) person shares in this sorrow.

SCAFFOLDING FOR ELL STUDENTS

Language and Vocabulary: Sentence Patterns, Contractions, Context Clues English learners will better understand Shakespeare's dialogue, as well as characters and theme, by using strategies to clarify confusing sentences.

- When the verb precedes the subject, or the object precedes both the subject and verb, rearrange the words in Standard English word order. Add a helping verb and other words as needed.

- An apostrophe frequently indicates a **contraction,** meaning that one or more letters are missing. Use context clues to figure out the intended word.

ASK STUDENTS to work with a partner to restate confusing sentence constructions in Scene 3.

Macduff.   If it be mine,
Keep it not from me. Quickly let me have it.

Ross. Let not your ears despise my tongue forever,
Which shall possess them with the heaviest sound
That ever yet they heard.

Macduff.   Hum! I guess at it.

205 **Ross.** Your castle is surprised, your wife and babes
Savagely slaughtered. To relate the manner
Were on the quarry of these murdered deer
To add the death of you.

Malcolm.   Merciful heaven!
What, man, ne'er pull your hat upon your brows.
210 Give sorrow words. The grief that does not speak
Whispers the o'erfraught heart and bids it break.

Macduff. My children too?

Ross. Wife, children, servants, all that could be found.

Macduff. And I must be from thence? My wife killed too?

215 **Ross.** I have said.

Malcolm. Be comforted.
Let's make us med'cines of our great revenge
To cure this deadly grief.

Macduff. He has no children. All my pretty ones?
220 Did you say "all"? O hell-kite! All?
What, all my pretty chickens and their dam
At one fell swoop?

Malcolm. Dispute it like a man.

Macduff.   I shall do so,
But I must also feel it as a man.
225 I cannot but remember such things were
That were most precious to me. Did heaven look on
And would not take their part? Sinful Macduff,
They were all struck for thee! Naught that I am,
Not for their own demerits, but for mine,
230 Fell slaughter on their souls. Heaven rest them now.

Malcolm. Be this the whetstone of your sword. Let grief
Convert to anger. Blunt not the heart; enrage it.

Macduff. O, I could play the woman with mine eyes
And braggart with my tongue! But, gentle heavens,
235 Cut short all intermission! Front to front
Bring thou this fiend of Scotland and myself.

206–208 Ross won't add to Macduff's sorrow by telling him how his family was killed. He compares Macduff's dear ones to the piled bodies of killed deer (**quarry**).

210–211 The grief . . . break: Silence will only push an overburdened heart to the breaking point.

219–222 He has no children: possibly a reference to Macbeth, who has no children to be killed for revenge. Macduff compares Macbeth to a bird of prey (**hell-kite**) who kills defenseless chickens and their mother.

228 naught: nothing.

231 whetstone: grindstone used for sharpening.

CLOSE READ

Analyze Character and Theme (LINES 200–224)

 COMMON CORE   RL 1, RL 2, RL 3

Remind students that playwrights use dialogue, gestures, and body movement to convey the characters' thoughts and feelings.

Z CITE TEXT EVIDENCE Have students use the dialogue between Ross and Macduff to make inferences about these characters' feelings. How does Ross feel about having to tell Macduff about the murders of his wife and children? *(Ross dreads having to give Macduff the news. In line 202, Ross hopes that Macduff will not hate him forever.)* How does Macduff feel about his family's death? *(Macduff has trouble taking in the information or accepting what he has heard. After Ross tells him "your wife and babes" have been slaughtered in lines 205–206, Macduff asks questions that have already been answered—"My children too?" in line 212 and "My wife killed too?" in line 214.)*

Remind students that one of the themes in the play is the exploration of gender. (Have students recall Lady Macbeth's wish to "unsex" herself in order to have the boldness to kill Duncan.) Point out that in line 223 Malcolm urges Macduff to deal with his grief "like a man." In lines 223–224, Macduff says he will do so, but he must also feel his grief "as a man."

A2 ASK STUDENTS how Malcolm's and Macduff's ideas of manhood differ. *(Malcolm relates manhood to aggression and revenge, whereas Macduff knows that manhood also involves honoring the dead by being sensitive and feeling grief.)*

WHEN STUDENTS STRUGGLE . . .

Some students may have difficulty inferring the feelings of Ross, Macduff, and Malcolm from the dialogue. Have students work in groups of three, each taking the role of one of the characters to read aloud lines 204–235.

1. Direct students to read through the dialogue for understanding, stopping to discuss the best way to read each character's lines using vocal tone, emphasis, and pacing.

2. Have groups read through the dialogue again, incorporating the tone, emphasis, and pacing agreed on earlier.

3. Ask groups to discuss the feelings each character's dialogue conveys.

Analyze Character and Theme (LINE 238)

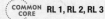 COMMON CORE RL 1, RL 2, RL 3

Shakespeare continues to make references to gender when Malcolm says in line 238, "This tune goes manly."

B2 ASK STUDENTS to explain Malcolm's meaning. *(Malcolm is saying that Macduff sounds like a man now that he is angry and wants to confront Macbeth.)*

COLLABORATIVE DISCUSSION Have partners support their ideas with specific cause-and-effect relationships. Then have them share their ideas with the class. Accept all reasonable responses.

ASK STUDENTS to share any questions they generated in the course of reading and discussing the selection.

Within my sword's length set him. If he scape,
Heaven forgive him too.

B2 **Malcolm.**   This tune goes manly.
Come, go we to the King. Our power is ready;
240 Our lack is nothing but our leave. Macbeth
Is ripe for shaking, and the powers above
Put on their instruments. Receive what cheer you may.
The night is long that never finds the day.

[*They exit.*]

239–243 Our troops are ready to attack, needing only the king's permission (**our lack is nothing but our leave**). Like a ripe fruit, Macbeth is ready to fall, and heavenly powers are preparing to assist us.

COLLABORATIVE DISCUSSION With a partner, discuss how Macbeth descends further into evil. Cite specific textual evidence from the play to support your ideas.

TO CHALLENGE STUDENTS . . .

Discuss an Issue At the end of Act IV, Macduff's speech foreshadows a final confrontation between Macbeth and Macduff. Present this issue: Should Macduff confront Macbeth but spare his life, or should Macduff confront and kill Macbeth? Have students discuss the issue in a small group. Each student should begin by taking a side and stating a position. Students' opinions should:

- focus on the issue,
- present a clear position supported by text evidence,
- demonstrate understanding of theme and character,
- reflect effective organization of ideas, and
- include effective logical, emotional, and ethical appeals.

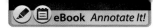
Analyzing the Text

COMMON CORE · RL 1, RL 3, RL 5, SL 1a–d

Cite Text Evidence   Support your responses with evidence from the selection.

1. **Analyze** How does Macbeth interpret the prophecies pronounced by the first three apparitions? Explain how knowledge of the witches' intent affects the audience's perception of these prophecies. ✓

2. **Infer** What is the purpose of the appearance and speech of the messenger in Scene 2? Who might have sent this messenger?

3. **Draw Conclusions** Lady Macduff and Malcolm both question Macduff's motives for fleeing Scotland. Think about the crimes Macbeth has already committed. Why might the nature of these crimes have led Macduff to believe his family would be safe at his castle? ✓

4. **Infer** Why might Shakespeare have decided to show the murder of Lady Macduff and her children on stage? Explain how watching this scene rather than hearing about the event occurring offstage might affect the audience's view of Macbeth. ✓

5. **Cite Evidence** What is Malcolm's initial attitude toward Macduff? What is shown about Malcolm through the way he assesses Macduff's sincerity?

6. **Interpret** Explain the dramatic irony of these lines in Scene 3:
   - lines 4–8 ("Each new morn . . .")
   - line 14 ("He hath not touched you yet.")
   - line 180 ("No, they were well at peace when I did leave 'em.")

7. **Analyze** Consider the description of Edward, the English king, in lines 146–159 of Scene 3. Why is this passage included in the play?

PERFORMANCE TASK

 **my WriteSmart**

Speaking Activity: Debate Some directors omit much of the scene in which Malcolm tests Macduff. What would be lost or gained by omitting this part of the play?

- With a group, come to a consensus on the significance of that part of Scene 3. Identify reasons and evidence to support your opinion.

- Present your argument in the form of a panel discussion or debate. Have other groups present their opposing arguments.
- Ask listening classmates to evaluate which argument is most compelling and why.

Assign this performance task.   **my WriteSmart**

PERFORMANCE TASK

COMMON CORE · SL 1a–d

Speaking Activity: Debate Have groups plan for the debate or panel discussion by preparing an outline for the arguments they will make and the evidence they will present to support the arguments.

PRACTICE & APPLY

Analyzing the Text   COMMON CORE · RL 1, RL 3, RL 5

Possible answers:

1. *Macbeth manages to convince himself from the prophecies that he is safe, but despite the second apparition's assurance (or warning) that "none of woman born" will hurt Macbeth, he decides to kill Macduff just for peace of mind. The audience knows that the witches intend to increase trouble from the line "Double, double, toil and trouble," so the audience sees the prophecies as trickery.*

2. *The messenger has come to warn Lady Macduff to give her a chance of escape. Lady Macbeth, who is plagued with guilt over her role in the murder of Duncan and possibly having knowledge of her husband's plan, may have sent the messenger.*

3. *Previously, Macbeth killed grown men who were his enemies, not defenseless women and children who pose no threat to him.*

4. *Shakespeare has built up interest and sympathy for Macduff's son earlier in the scene, so by showing the son defending his father's honor and being murdered onstage, Shakespeare increases the audience's emotions and awareness that Macbeth is now murdering innocent people for no purpose. Seeing the murder onstage is much more effective than hearing it from offstage.*

5. *In Scene 3, Malcolm is suspicious of Macduff at first (lines 11, 14–17). Through his test of Macduff's character, Malcolm shows that he is extremely cautious (lines 25–31) and clever (lines 123–125).*

6. *Lines 4–8: Macduff's reference to "new widows" and "new orphans" is ironic because the audience knows that Macduff's wife and children have been murdered. Line 14: Malcolm's words that Macbeth "has not touched you [Macduff] yet" are ironic because the audience knows that Macbeth has indirectly "touched" Macduff by having his family murdered. Line 180: Ross's reference to "at peace" is ironic because the audience knows that Macduff's family is now "resting at peace" in death.*

7. *Shakespeare may have included the passage to contrast the healing powers of the good King Edward with the destructive powers of the evil King Macbeth.*

AS YOU READ Direct students to use the As You Read note to focus their reading.

Analyze Plot and Character (LINES 1–17)

COMMON CORE RL 2, RL 3

Explain to students that instead of telling the audience everything about a scene by using stage directions, a playwright can develop the plot by using characters' dialogue.

 CITE TEXT EVIDENCE Ask students to explain what the gentlewoman wants the doctor to do and why. Be sure students cite evidence from the text. *(She wants him to see the strange behavior of Lady Macbeth so that someone else will be a witness to it besides her. She tells the doctor in lines 14–15 that she will not describe the behavior until she has another witness to confirm what she is seeing, and in line 17 she commands the doctor to stand close and observe Lady Macbeth. In this way we will learn about a change in Lady Macbeth as the doctor witnesses it.)*

Analyze Language: Archaic Words (LINES 27–31)

COMMON CORE RL 4

Remind students that contractions are formed by replacing a letter or letters in a word with an apostrophe. Over time, some once-common contractions fell out of fashion and are now rarely used.

B **ASK STUDENTS** to identify an example of a contraction that would sound unfamiliar to modern ears and one that would sound familiar, and to explain the meaning of each. *(In line 27, Lady Macbeth uses the familiar contraction "here's" to tell the location of a spot. In line 31, she uses the unfamiliar contraction "do 't" (do it) to say that it is time to take action.)*

AS YOU READ Pay attention to whether the prophecies pronounced by the apparitions are fulfilled. Write down any questions you generate during reading.

ACT V

Scene 1 *Macbeth's castle at Dunsinane.*

[*Enter a* Doctor of Physic *and a* Waiting Gentlewoman.]

 Doctor. I have two nights watched with you but can perceive no truth in your report. When was it she last walked?

Gentlewoman. Since his Majesty went into the field, I have seen her rise from her bed, throw her nightgown upon her,
5 unlock her closet, take forth paper, fold it, write upon' t, read it, afterwards seal it, and again return to bed; yet all this while in a most fast sleep.

    3 went into the field: went to battle.

Doctor. A great perturbation in nature, to receive at once the benefit of sleep and do the effects of watching. In this slumb'ry
10 agitation, besides her walking and other actual performances, what at any time have you heard her say?

    8–9 A great . . . of watching: To behave as though awake (**watching**) while sleeping is a sign of a greatly troubled nature.

Gentlewoman. That, sir, which I will not report after her.

Doctor. You may to me, and 'tis most meet you should.

    13 meet: appropriate.

Gentlewoman. Neither to you nor anyone, having no witness to
15 confirm my speech.

[*Enter* Lady Macbeth *with a taper.*]

Lo you, here she comes. This is her very guise and, upon my life, fast asleep. Observe her; stand close.

    16 guise: usual manner.

    17 stand close: hide yourself.

Doctor. How came she by that light?

    18 that light: her candle.

Gentlewoman. Why, it stood by her. She has light by her
20 continually. 'Tis her command.

Doctor. You see her eyes are open.

Gentlewoman. Ay, but their sense are shut.

Doctor. What is it she does now? Look how she rubs her hands.

Gentlewoman. It is an accustomed action with her to seem thus
25 washing her hands. I have known her continue in this a quarter of an hour.

Lady Macbeth. Yet here's a spot.

B **Doctor.** Hark, she speaks. I will set down what comes from her, to satisfy my remembrance the more strongly.

30 **Lady Macbeth.** Out, damned spot, out, I say! One. Two. Why then, 'tis time to do 't. Hell is murky. Fie, my lord, fie, a soldier and afeard? What need we fear who knows it, when none can **C**

278 Collection 5

Close Read Screencasts   View It!

Modeled Discussions

Have students pair up and do an independent close read of the following passage—Macbeth learning of his wife's death (Scene 5, lines 9–18).

As a class, discuss the passage.

call our power to account? Yet who would have thought the old
man to have had so much blood in him?

35 **Doctor.** Do you mark that?

Lady Macbeth. The Thane of Fife had a wife. Where is she now?
What, will these hands ne'er be clean? No more o' that, my lord,
no more o' that. You mar all with this starting.

Doctor. Go to, go to. You have known what you should not.

40 **Gentlewoman.** She has spoke what she should not, I am sure of
that. Heaven knows what she has known.

Lady Macbeth. Here's the smell of the blood still. All the
perfumes of Arabia will not sweeten this little hand. O, O, O!

Doctor. What a sigh is there! The heart is sorely charged.

45 **Gentlewoman.** I would not have such a heart in my bosom for
the dignity of the whole body.

Doctor. Well, well, well.

Gentlewoman. Pray God it be, sir.

Doctor. This disease is beyond my practice. Yet I have known
50 those which have walked in their sleep, who have died holily in
their beds.

Lady Macbeth. Wash your hands. Put on your nightgown. Look
not so pale. I tell you yet again, Banquo's buried; he cannot come
out on 's grave.

55 **Doctor.** Even so?

Lady Macbeth. To bed, to bed. There's knocking at the gate.
Come, come, come, come. Give me your hand. What's done
cannot be undone. To bed, to bed, to bed.

[Lady Macbeth *exits.*]

Doctor. Will she go now to bed?

60 **Gentlewoman.** Directly.

Doctor. Foul whisp'rings are abroad. Unnatural deeds
Do breed unnatural troubles. Infected minds
To their deaf pillows will discharge their secrets.
More needs she the divine than the physician.
65 God, God forgive us all. Look after her.
Remove from her the means of all annoyance
And still keep eyes upon her. So good night.
My mind she has mated, and amazed my sight.
I think but dare not speak.

Gentlewoman.   Good night, good doctor.

[*They exit.*]

36–38 Lady Macbeth
shows guilt about
Macduff's wife. Then she
addresses her husband,
as if he were having
another ghostly fit
(**starting**).

44 sorely charged:
heavily burdened.

45–46 The
gentlewoman says that
she would not want
Lady Macbeth's heavy
heart in exchange for
being queen.

49 practice: skill.

54 on 's: of his.

**61 Foul whisp'rings are
abroad:** Rumors of evil
deeds are circulating.

64 She needs a priest
more than a doctor.

66 annoyance: injury.
The doctor may be
worried about the
possibility of Lady
Macbeth's committing
suicide.

68 mated: astonished.

The Tragedy of Macbeth: Act V, Scene 1   **279**

Analyze Character and Theme (LINES 30–38)

COMMON CORE   RL 2, RL 3

Remind students that one way to determine theme is
to examine how events that happen over the course
of a play change the characters. Tell students to keep
in mind earlier events and compare a character's
present actions to those earlier in the play to observe
how the character may or may not have changed.

C CITE TEXT EVIDENCE Ask students to examine
Lady Macbeth's behavior and describe what appears
to have happened to her and how they can tell,
using what they know about Lady Macbeth's words
and actions earlier in the play. *(Earlier, in Act II, Scene
2, lines 51–66, Macbeth was the one who shrank from
blood and worried about washing his hands clean after
murdering Duncan. Lady Macbeth seemed unbothered
by their actions and was sure a little water would wash
their crime away. Now Lady Macbeth is sleepwalking;
recalling the people she and Macbeth have caused
to be murdered, such as Duncan and Lady Macduff;
and fruitlessly trying to wash her hands clean of guilt.
Earlier, she did not care, but now she seems haunted by
their actions.)*

Strategies for Annotation   🖊 📑 Annotate it!

Analyze Character and Theme

COMMON CORE   RL 2, RL 3

Have students locate passages that parallel lines from earlier in the play to help
them analyze the development of Lady Macbeth's character. Ask them to use
their eBook annotation tools to do the following:

- Highlight in yellow a sentence to compare with Lady Macbeth's words in
  Act II, Scene 2, lines 53–55: "If he do bleed, I'll gild the faces of the grooms
  withal, for it must seem their guilt."

- Highlight in blue a sentence to compare with Macbeth's words in Act II,
  Scene 2, lines 58–61: "Will all great Neptune's ocean wash this blood clean
  from my hand?"

call our power to account? Yet who would have thought the old
man to have had so much blood in him?

Doctor. Do you mark that?

Lady Macbeth. The Thane of Fife had a wife. Where is she now?
What, will these hands ne'er be clean? No more o' that, my lord,

The Tragedy of Macbeth: Act V, Scene 1   **279**

Analyze Character and Theme (LINES 6–13)

COMMON CORE RL 2, RL 3

Explain that students can recall important dialogue from earlier in a play to help them trace the development of the play's themes.

D ASK STUDENTS to identify where Menteith and the other noblemen in this scene are going to meet up with the English soldiers to march against Macbeth. *(near Birnam Wood)* Why is this setting important? *(In Act IV, Scene 1, lines 92–94, an apparition told Macbeth that he would never be conquered until Great Birnam Wood comes to Dunsinane Hill. Macbeth has now fortified himself inside Dunsinane and Malcolm and his allies are preparing for attack inside Birnam Wood. Whatever happens next will prove how true the prophecy is.)*

Interpret Figurative Language (LINES 16–22)

COMMON CORE RL 4, L 5

Tell students that writers sometimes use **similes,** figures of speech that compare two things using the word *like* or *as.* A simile can lend emotional depth to a character's words.

E ASK STUDENTS to reread Angus's dialogue in lines 16–22. What does Angus mean when he says "Those he commands move only in command/ Nothing in love"? *(Macbeth's subjects follow his commands only because he is their king, not because they have any affection or respect for him.)* What simile does Angus use in these lines? What does it mean? How is it an effective use of language? *(Angus compares Macbeth's title to a robe that is too big for him. The simile means that Macbeth is not worthy to be king. It's an effective use of language because the comparison of a giant to a dwarfish thief makes it clear that Macbeth doesn't deserve to wear the robe of a king.)*

Scene 2 *The country near Dunsinane.*

[Drum and Colors. Enter Menteith, Caithness, Angus, Lennox, *and* Soldiers.]

Menteith. The English power is near, led on by Malcolm,
His uncle Siward, and the good Macduff.
Revenges burn in them, for their dear causes
Would to the bleeding and the grim alarm
5   Excite the mortified man.

Angus.   Near Birnam Wood
Shall we well meet them. That way are they coming.

D

Caithness. Who knows if Donalbain be with his brother?

Lennox. For certain, sir, he is not. I have a file
Of all the gentry. There is Siward's son
10 And many unrough youths that even now
Protest their first of manhood.

Menteith.   What does the tyrant?

Caithness. Great Dunsinane he strongly fortifies.
Some say he's mad; others that lesser hate him
Do call it valiant fury. But for certain
15 He cannot buckle his distempered cause
Within the belt of rule.

Angus.   Now does he feel
His secret murders sticking on his hands.
Now minutely revolts upbraid his faith-breach.
Those he commands move only in command,
E 20 Nothing in love. Now does he feel his title
Hang loose about him, like a giant's robe
Upon a dwarfish thief.

Menteith.   Who, then, shall blame
His pestered senses to recoil and start
When all that is within him does condemn
25 Itself for being there?

Caithness.   Well, march we on
To give obedience where 'tis truly owed.
Meet we the med'cine of the sickly weal,
And with him pour we in our country's purge
Each drop of us.

Lennox.   Or so much as it needs
30 To dew the sovereign flower and drown the weeds.
Make we our march towards Birnam.

[They exit marching.]

3–5 for their dear . . . man: The cause of Malcolm and Macduff is so deeply felt that a dead (**mortified**) man would respond to their call to arms (**alarm**).

10–11 many . . . manhood: many soldiers who are too young to grow beards (**unrough**).

15–16 Like a man so swollen with disease (**distempered**) that he cannot buckle his belt, Macbeth cannot control his evil actions.

18 Every minute, revolts against Macbeth shame him for his treachery (**faith-breach**).

22–25 Macbeth's nerves, troubled by guilt, (**pestered senses**) have made him jumpy.

25–29 They give their loyalty to the only help (**med'cine**) for the sick country (**weal**). They are willing to sacrifice their last drop of blood to cleanse (**purge**) Scotland.

29–31 Lennox compares Malcolm to a flower that needs the blood of patriots to water (**dew**) it and drown out weeds like Macbeth.

WHEN STUDENTS STRUGGLE . . .

After students read lines 1–18 of Scene 3, discuss how Macbeth acts in this scene and how different he is from the way he was in earlier acts. Suggest that they compare his previous interactions with Lady Macbeth and his level of self-confidence with how he feels now and how he treats the servant.

ASK STUDENTS to use a chart like the one to the right to record information about what Macbeth thinks, says, and does. Students can use a similar chart to collect information from other parts of the play and then compare the details to trace how Macbeth changes from scene to scene.

Scene 3 *Dunsinane. A room in the castle.*

[*Enter* Macbeth, *the* Doctor, *and* Attendants.]

Macbeth. Bring me no more reports. Let them fly all.
Till Birnam Wood remove to Dunsinane
I cannot taint with fear. What's the boy Malcolm?
Was he not born of woman? The spirits that know
5 All mortal consequences have pronounced me thus:
"Fear not, Macbeth. No man that's born of woman
Shall e'er have power upon thee." Then fly, false thanes,
And mingle with the English epicures.
The mind I sway by and the heart I bear
10 Shall never sag with doubt nor shake with fear.

[*Enter* Servant.]

The devil damn thee black, thou cream-faced loon!
Where got'st thou that goose-look?

Servant. There is ten thousand—

Macbeth.   Geese, villain?

Servant.   Soldiers, sir.

Macbeth. Go prick thy face and over-red thy fear,
15 Thou lily-livered boy. What soldiers, patch?
Death of thy soul! Those linen cheeks of thine
Are counselors to fear. What soldiers, whey-face?

Servant. The English force, so please you.

Macbeth. Take thy face hence.

[Servant *exits.*]

                                        Seyton!—I am sick at heart
20 When I behold—Seyton, I say!—This push
Will cheer me ever or disseat me now.
I have lived long enough. My way of life
Is fall'n into the sere, the yellow leaf,
And that which should accompany old age,
25 As honor, love, obedience, troops of friends,
I must not look to have, but in their stead
Curses, not loud but deep, mouth-honor, breath
Which the poor heart would fain deny and dare not.—
Seyton!

[*Enter* Seyton.]

30 **Seyton.** What's your gracious pleasure?

Macbeth.   What news more?

Seyton. All is confirmed, my lord, which was reported.

---

1 Macbeth wants no more news of thanes who have gone to Malcolm's side.

2–10 Macbeth will not be infected (**taint**) with fear, because the witches (**spirits**), who know all human events (**mortal consequences**), have convinced him that he is invincible. He mocks the self-indulgent English (**English epicures**), then swears that he will never lack confidence.

11 **loon:** stupid rascal.

12 **goose-look:** look of fear.

14–17 Macbeth suggests that the servant cut his face so that blood will hide his cowardice. He repeatedly insults the servant, calling him a coward (**lily-livered**) and a clown (**patch**) and making fun of his white complexion (**linen cheeks, whey-face**).

20–28 **This push . . . dare not:** The upcoming battle will either make Macbeth secure (**cheer me ever**) or dethrone (**disseat**) him. He bitterly compares his life to a withered (**sere**) leaf. He cannot look forward to old age with friends and honor, but only to curses and empty flattery (**mouthhonor, breath**) from those too timid (**the poor heart**) to tell the truth.

TEACH

CLOSE READ

Analyze Character and Theme (LINES 1–18)

COMMON CORE RL 2, RL 3

Explain to students that observing the way a character treats other characters in a play is another way to trace changes in the character's personality over time.

F **ASK STUDENTS** how Macbeth's attitude here is different from his previous attitude in the play, particularly in the way he treats the servant. *(Earlier, Macbeth was jumpy and jittery because of his actions. Now, because he believes that the witches prophesized that he will never be conquered, he is so confident that he says he will never doubt or shake with fear [line 10]. He even mocks the servant for being a pale-faced coward [line 11], when earlier in the play it was Lady Macbeth urging Macbeth not to be afraid.)*

Macbeth Thinks	Macbeth Says	Macbeth Does
Because a forest should not literally be able to travel to a castle and because Malcolm was "born of woman," Macbeth does not think he can be defeated.	His mind and heart will never have doubt or fear.	He insults the servant, calling him a "cream-faced loon" and a "lily-livered boy."

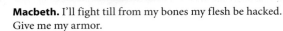

Analyze Language

COMMON CORE RL 1, RL 4

(LINES 38–46)

Review the dialogue between Macbeth and the doctor.

G **CITE TEXT EVIDENCE** Ask students to identify what ails Lady Macbeth. Have students cite the evidence for their answers. *(Lady Macbeth cannot sleep because she is plagued by what the doctor calls "thick-coming fancies" [line 38]. These are visions of the past actions that she and Macbeth took to murder Duncan, and manifestations of the guilt she feels, such as trying to wash her hands clean of blood.)* What does Macbeth wish the doctor could do? *(Macbeth wishes in lines 39–45 that the doctor could remove all of the sad memories that are inside Lady Macbeth's head.)*

Analyze Character and Theme (LINES 49–56)

COMMON CORE RL 5

Remind students that the words spoken by a character as a play progresses give the audience a deeper understanding of him or her. Also remind students that various plots begin to come together during the last act of a drama. Have students pay attention to how Shakespeare interweaves an exchange about Lady Macbeth with comments about Scotland.

H **ASK STUDENTS** to explain what Macbeth's dialogue to the doctor in lines 49–56 says about Macbeth. *(Possible answer: He still cares for Scotland, just as he grieves for his wife. He is not so evil and self-centered as to care only about his own wants.)* Remind students that Shakespeare uses irony throughout this play. Ask: What is ironic about Macbeth asking the doctor to cure Scotland's "disease?" *(Macbeth himself is the source of that "disease.")*

Macbeth. I'll fight till from my bones my flesh be hacked.
Give me my armor.

Seyton. 'Tis not needed yet.

Macbeth. I'll put it on.
35 Send out more horses. Skirr the country round.
Hang those that talk of fear. Give me mine armor.—
How does your patient, doctor?

Doctor. Not so sick, my lord,
As she is troubled with thick-coming fancies
That keep her from her rest.

Macbeth. Cure her of that.
40 Canst thou not minister to a mind diseased,
Pluck from the memory a rooted sorrow,
Raze out the written troubles of the brain,
And with some sweet oblivious antidote
Cleanse the stuffed bosom of that perilous stuff
45 Which weighs upon the heart?

Doctor. Therein the patient
Must minister to himself.

Macbeth. Throw physic to the dogs, I'll none of it.—
Come, put mine armor on. Give me my staff.

[Attendants *begin to arm him.*]

Seyton, send out.—Doctor, the thanes fly from me.—
50 Come, sir, dispatch.—If thou couldst, doctor, cast
The water of my land, find her disease,
And purge it to a sound and pristine health,
I would applaud thee to the very echo
That should applaud again.—Pull 't off, I say.—
55 What rhubarb, senna, or what purgative drug
Would scour these English hence? Hear'st thou of them?

35 skirr: scour.

47–54 Macbeth has lost his faith in the ability of medicine (**physic**) to help his wife. He says that if the doctor could diagnose Scotland's disease (**cast . . . land**) and cure it, Macbeth would never stop praising him.

54 Pull 't off: Macbeth is referring to a piece of armor.

56 scour: purge; **them:** the English.

Doctor. Ay, my good lord. Your royal preparation
Makes us hear something.

Macbeth. Bring it after me.—
I will not be afraid of death and bane
60 Till Birnam Forest come to Dunsinane.

58–60 Macbeth leaves for battle, telling Seyton to bring the armor.

Doctor [aside]. Were I from Dunsinane away and clear,
Profit again should hardly draw me here.

[*They exit.*]

Scene 4 *The country near Birnam Wood.*

[*Drum and Colors. Enter* Malcolm, Siward, Macduff, Siward's son, Menteith, Caithness, Angus, *and* Soldiers, *marching.*]

Malcolm. Cousins, I hope the days are near at hand
That chambers will be safe.

Menteith. We doubt it nothing.

Siward. What wood is this before us?

Menteith. The wood of Birnam.

Malcolm. Let every soldier hew him down a bough
5 And bear 't before him. Thereby shall we shadow
The numbers of our host and make discovery
Err in report of us.

Soldiers. It shall be done.

Siward. We learn no other but the confident tyrant
Keeps still in Dunsinane and will endure
10 Our setting down before 't.

10 setting down: siege.

Malcolm. 'Tis his main hope;
For, where there is advantage to be given,
Both more and less have given him the revolt,
And none serve with him but constrainèd things
Whose hearts are absent too.

10–14 Malcolm says that men of all ranks (**both more and less**) have abandoned Macbeth. Only weak men forced into service remain with him.

Macduff. Let our just censures
15 Attend the true event, and put we on
Industrious soldiership.

14–16 Macduff warns against overconfidence and advises that they focus on fighting.

Siward. The time approaches
That will with due decision make us know
What we shall say we have and what we owe.
Thoughts speculative their unsure hopes relate,
20 But certain issue strokes must arbitrate;
Towards which, advance the war.

16–21 Siward says that the approaching battle will decide whether their claims will match what they actually possess (**owe**). Now, their hopes and expectations are guesswork (**thoughts speculative**); only fighting (**strokes**) can settle (**arbitrate**) the issue.

[*They exit marching.*]

WHEN STUDENTS STRUGGLE...

Remind students to use the stage directions to help them visualize the actions in the play. This will help them understand the dialogue and infer other actions that aren't explicitly stated.

ASK STUDENTS to read the stage directions at the beginning of Scene 4. Have them visualize the characters marching through the countryside near a forest. The characters are talking as they march along. They look at one another as they speak. Perhaps they stop briefly and Siward gestures toward Birnam Wood as he asks about it. Have volunteers act out this scene, using gestures that seem reasonable in the context of the play.

CLOSE READ

Analyze Character and Theme (LINES 4–7)

COMMON CORE RL 2, RL 3

Remind students that plot events can help develop a theme.

CITE TEXT EVIDENCE Ask students to identify what event on this page relates to prophecies. (*In lines 4–7, Malcolm commands that his troops cut tree boughs from the forest of Birnam and hold them in front of them as they advance. This will make it look like the forest is coming to Dunsinane, which is one of the events the apparation's prophecy said must happen before Macbeth can be defeated.*)

Analyze Character and Theme (LINES 14–16)

COMMON CORE RL 2, RL 3

Explain that sometimes the development of a drama's theme can be better understood by comparing the hero to another character.

ASK STUDENTS to reread Macduff's dialogue and compare his attitude toward warfare with Macbeth's. (*In the previous scene, Macbeth was boastful about not being afraid and sure he could not be beaten. In contrast, in lines 14–16, Macduff is more cautious and says his side will be best served by focusing on fighting industriously.*)

TEACH

CLOSE READ

Analyze Character and Theme (LINES 17–28)

COMMON CORE RL 3, RL 5

Remind students that a soliloquy is a speech that a character makes alone on the stage, to reveal his or her thoughts to the audience.

(K) ASK STUDENTS to reread lines 17–28 and explain how they reflect Macbeth's state of mind in the latter part of the play. Suggest students recall previous details from this act that relate to how he is feeling now. *(In Scene 3, Macbeth said in lines 22–26 that he had already lived long enough, that his way of life was passing, and that he would not be able to enjoy an old age with friends. Now that Lady Macbeth has died, he is truly alone and has even less to look forward to. The repetition of the word "tomorrow" in line 19 and the word "day" in line 20 and the description of the way time moves as creeping at a "petty pace" emphasizes how dreadful Macbeth finds life now. He will still fight, but he compares life in lines 26–28 to "a tale told by an idiot" that ultimately means nothing.)*

Scene 5 *Dunsinane. Within the castle.*

[*Enter* Macbeth, Seyton, *and* Soldiers, *with Drum and Colors.*]

Macbeth. Hang out our banners on the outward walls.
The cry is still "They come!" Our castle's strength
Will laugh a siege to scorn. Here let them lie
Till famine and the ague eat them up.
5 Were they not forced with those that should be ours,
We might have met them dareful, beard to beard,
And beat them backward home.

[*A cry within of women.*]

　　　　　　　　　　　What is that noise?

Seyton. It is the cry of women, my good lord. [*He exits.*]

Macbeth. I have almost forgot the taste of fears.
10 The time has been my senses would have cooled
To hear a night-shriek, and my fell of hair
Would at a dismal treatise rouse and stir
As life were in 't. I have supped full with horrors.
Direness, familiar to my slaughterous thoughts,
15 Cannot once start me.

[*Enter* Seyton.]

　　　　　　　　　Wherefore was that cry?

Seyton. The Queen, my lord, is dead.

Macbeth. She should have died hereafter.
There would have been a time for such a word.
Tomorrow and tomorrow and tomorrow
20 Creeps in this petty pace from day to day
To the last syllable of recorded time,
And all our yesterdays have lighted fools
The way to dusty death. Out, out, brief candle!
Life's but a walking shadow, a poor player
25 That struts and frets his hour upon the stage
And then is heard no more. It is a tale
Told by an idiot, full of sound and fury,
Signifying nothing.

[*Enter a* Messenger.]

Thou com'st to use thy tongue: thy story quickly.

30 **Messenger.** Gracious my lord,
I should report that which I say I saw,
But know not how to do 't.

Macbeth.　　　　　Well, say, sir.

4 ague: fever.

5–7 Macbeth complains that the attackers have been reinforced (**forced**) by deserters (**those that should be ours**), which has forced him to wait at Dunsinane instead of seeking victory on the battlefield.

9–15 There was a time when a scream in the night would have frozen Macbeth in fear and a terrifying tale (**dismal treatise**) would have made the hair on his skin (**fell of hair**) stand on end. But since he has fed on horror (**direness**), it cannot stir (**start**) him anymore.

17–18 Macbeth wishes that his wife had died later (**hereafter**), when he would have had time to mourn her.

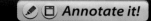

Strategies for Annotation　🖉 🗐 **Annotate it!**

Analyze Character and Theme

COMMON CORE RL 3, RL 5

Students can use their eBook annotation tools to help them analyze a soliloquy and gain insight into a character. Point out that the rhythm of certain lines in this soliloquy emphasizes Macbeth's attitude. Have students tap their foot and notice the rhythm as they do the following:

- Highlight in yellow the repeated words that correspond to the rhythm established by the foot tapping.
- Highlight in pink repeated words that do not follow the rhythm.
- Discuss with a partner the effect of the repetition in each case and explain why the author may have used the repetition.

There would have been a time for such a word.

Tomorrow and tomorrow and tomorrow

Creeps in this petty pace from day to day

To the last syllable of recorded time,

And all our yesterdays have lighted fools

The way to dusty death. Out, out, brief candle!

Messenger. As I did stand my watch upon the hill,
I looked toward Birnam, and anon methought

35 The wood began to move.

Macbeth.   Liar and slave!

Messenger. Let me endure your wrath, if 't be not so.
Within this three mile may you see it coming.
I say, a moving grove.

Macbeth.   If thou speak'st false,
Upon the next tree shall thou hang alive

40 Till famine cling thee. If thy speech be sooth,
I care not if thou dost for me as much.—
I pull in resolution and begin
To doubt th' equivocation of the fiend,
That lies like truth. "Fear not till Birnam Wood

45 Do come to Dunsinane," and now a wood
Comes toward Dunsinane. —Arm, arm, and out!—
If this which he avouches does appear,
There is nor flying hence nor tarrying here.
I 'gin to be aweary of the sun

50 And wish th' estate o' th' world were now undone.—
Ring the alarum bell! —Blow wind, come wrack,
At least we'll die with harness on our back.

[*They exit.*]

Scene 6 *Dunsinane. Before the castle.*

[*Drum and Colors. Enter* Malcolm, Siward, Macduff, *and their
army, with boughs.*]

Malcolm. Now near enough. Your leafy screens throw down
And show like those you are. —You, worthy uncle,
Shall with my cousin, your right noble son,
Lead our first battle. Worthy Macduff and we

5 Shall take upon 's what else remains to do,
According to our order.

Siward.   Fare you well.
Do we but find the tyrant's power tonight,
Let us be beaten if we cannot fight.

Macduff. Make all our trumpets speak; give them all breath,
10 Those clamorous harbingers of blood and death.

[*They exit. Alarums continued.*]

38–52 The messenger's news has dampened Macbeth's determination (**resolution**); Macbeth begins to fear that the witches have tricked him (**to doubt th' equivocation of the fiend**). His fear that the messenger tells the truth (**avouches**) makes him decide to confront the enemy instead of staying in his castle. Weary of life, he nevertheless decides to face death and ruin (**wrack**) with his armor (**harness**) on.

1–6 Malcolm commands the troops to put down their branches (**leafy screens**) and gives the battle instructions.

7 power: forces.

10 harbingers: announcers.

CLOSE READ

Analyze Character and Theme (LINES 33–52)

COMMON CORE RL 2, RL 3

Point out to students that examining how a character responds in a crisis can reveal insights into his or her personality and state of mind.

CITE TEXT EVIDENCE Ask students to describe Macbeth's attitude toward the upcoming fight and to use details from the text to explain why he feels this way. (*In lines 33–35, Macbeth hears that it looks like the wood of Birnam is moving toward his castle. At first he grows angry and calls the messenger a liar, but then he returns to his earlier hopeless state of mind in which he said that life is meaningless. Macbeth says in line 49 that he has grown weary of the sun, or of life. Growing weary of life and thinking it means nothing shows that Macbeth is becoming aware of the fact that his evil actions have ruined his life. There is nothing left for him to do but die, as he states in line 52.*)

Analyze Character and Theme (LINES 1–13)

COMMON CORE RL 2, RL 3

Explain to students that a character's dialogue in a play may remind the audience of important things that happened earlier in the play. The audience must keep these things in mind to help them understand the significance of the actions taking place in the current scene.

M ASK STUDENTS to explain how Macbeth's attitude toward fighting changes over the course of this scene with Young Siward, and why. *(Before fighting, in lines 2–4, Macbeth recalls the third prophecy about him being unable to be killed by anyone except one not born of woman. After killing Young Siward, Macbeth grows in confidence and laughs at weapons carried by anyone born from a woman because he thinks this prophecy protects him from harm.)*

Analyze Language: Archaic Words (LINES 14–23)

COMMON CORE RL 4

Point out that the play uses many archaic English verb tenses. For example, when the subject of a sentence is *thou*, the verb following this subject uses the ending -*est* or -*st*.

N ASK STUDENTS to identify two examples of verbs ending in -*est* (or -*st*) and to explain the way each is used. *(In line 15, Macduff uses the verb "beest" in place of "are." In line 20, he uses the verb "shouldst" in place of "should.")*

Scene 7 *Another part of the battlefield.*

[*Enter* Macbeth.]

Macbeth. They have tied me to a stake. I cannot fly,
But, bear-like, I must fight the course. What's he
That was not born of woman? Such a one
Am I to fear, or none.

[*Enter* Young Siward.]

5 **Young Siward.** What is thy name?

Macbeth.   Thou'lt be afraid to hear it.

Young Siward. No, though thou call'st thyself a hotter name
Than any is in hell.

Macbeth.   My name's Macbeth.

Young Siward. The devil himself could not pronounce a title
More hateful to mine ear.

Macbeth.   No, nor more fearful.

10 **Young Siward.** Thou liest, abhorrèd tyrant. With my sword
I'll prove the lie thou speak'st.

[*They fight, and* Young Siward *is slain.*]

Macbeth.   Thou wast born of woman.
But swords I smile at, weapons laugh to scorn,
Brandished by man that's of a woman born. [*He exits.*]

[*Alarums. Enter* Macduff.]

Macduff. That way the noise is. Tyrant, show thy face!
15 If thou beest slain, and with no stroke of mine,
My wife and children's ghosts will haunt me still.
I cannot strike at wretched kerns, whose arms
Are hired to bear their staves. Either thou, Macbeth,
Or else my sword with an unbattered edge
20 I sheathe again undeeded. There thou shouldst be;
By this great clatter, one of greatest note
Seems bruited. Let me find him, Fortune,
And more I beg not.

[*He exits. Alarums.*]
[*Enter* Malcolm *and* Siward.]

Siward. This way, my lord. The castle's gently rendered.
25 The tyrant's people on both sides do fight,
The noble thanes do bravely in the war,
The day almost itself professes yours,
And little is to do.

1–4 Macbeth compares himself to a bear tied to a post (a reference to the sport of bearbaiting, in which a bear was tied to a stake and attacked by dogs).

14–20 Macduff hopes to find Macbeth before someone else has the chance to kill him. Macduff does not want to fight the miserable hired soldiers (**kerns**), who are armed only with spears (**staves**). If he can't fight Macbeth, Macduff will leave his sword unused (**undeeded**).

22 bruited: rumored or heard.

24 gently rendered: surrendered without a fight.

27 You have almost won the day.

28–29 During the battle many of Macbeth's men deserted to Malcolm's army.

SCAFFOLDING FOR ELL STUDENTS

Language: Archaic Verb Endings Have mixed language-ability jigsaw groups work together to make a list of verbs in lines 1–28 that end in -*est* or -*st* and follow the subject word *thou*. For example, *call'st* (line 6), *liest* (line 10), *speak'st* (line 11), and *wast* (line 12). Then have the groups work together to use context clues and their knowledge of modern verb tenses to figure out the modern way to say the same verb. Finally, have students reread each line from the play using *you* and the modern form of the verb to make sure they understand the meaning of each sentence.

Malcolm.　　　We have met with foes
That strike beside us.

Siward.　　　　　Enter, sir, the castle.

[*They exit. Alarum.*]

Scene 8 *Another part of the battlefield.*

[*Enter* Macbeth.]

Macbeth. Why should I play the Roman fool and die
On mine own sword? Whiles I see lives, the gashes
Do better upon them.

[*Enter* Macduff.]

Macduff.　　　　　Turn, hellhound, turn!

Macbeth. Of all men else I have avoided thee.
5　But get thee back. My soul is too much charged
With blood of thine already.

Macduff.　　　　　I have no words;
My voice is in my sword, thou bloodier villain
Than terms can give thee out.

[*Fight. Alarum.*]

Macbeth.　　　　　Thou losest labor.
As easy mayst thou the intrenchant air
10　With thy keen sword impress as make me bleed.
Let fall thy blade on vulnerable crests;
I bear a charmèd life, which must not yield
To one of woman born.

Macduff.　　　　　Despair thy charm,
And let the angel whom thou still hast served
15　Tell thee Macduff was from his mother's womb
Untimely ripped.

Macbeth. Accursèd be that tongue that tells me so,
For it hath cowed my better part of man!
And be these juggling fiends no more believed
20　That palter with us in a double sense,
That keep the word of promise to our ear
And break it to our hope. I'll not fight with thee.

Macduff. Then yield thee, coward,
And live to be the show and gaze o' th' time.
25　We'll have thee, as our rarer monsters are,
Painted upon a pole, and underwrit
"Here may you see the tyrant."

1–3 Macbeth refuses to commit suicide in the style of a defeated Roman general.

4–6 Macbeth does not want to fight Macduff, having already killed so many members of Macduff's family.

8–13 Macbeth says that Macduff is wasting his effort. Trying to wound Macbeth is as useless as trying to wound the invulnerable (**intrenchant**) air. Macduff should strike at the helmets (**crests**) of more vulnerable foes.

15–16 Macduff . . . **untimely ripped:** Macduff was a premature baby delivered by cesarean section, an operation that removes the child directly from the mother's womb.

18　cowed: made fearful.

19–22 The cheating witches (**juggling fiends**) have tricked him (**palter with us**) with words that have double meanings.

23–27 Macduff tells Macbeth to surrender and become a public spectacle (**the show and gaze o' th' time**), with his picture displayed (**painted upon a pole**) as if he were in a circus sideshow.

Analyze Character and Theme (LINES 1–14)

COMMON CORE　RL 2, RL 3

Explain to students that the audience can take final stock of Macbeth's character by examining how he interacts with Macduff in lines 1–14 and why Macbeth makes the decisions he does before his death.

Ⓞ CITE TEXT EVIDENCE Ask students to identify some character traits that Macbeth shows in this final scene. Remind them to cite evidence from the text to support their ideas. *(Even after all of the evil deeds he has done, and even though he wants to fight instead of commit suicide [lines 1–2], Macbeth shows some remorse and goodness by refusing to fight Macduff at first. His reason, given in lines 4–6, is that his conscience is already stained with enough blood from Macduff's family for having murdered his wife and children, so he does not want more Macduff blood on his hands. At the same time, Macbeth shows arrogance as he tells Macduff in lines 12–13 that he believes he possesses a charmed life and cannot be killed by anyone born of a woman, so he is sure that he will win if he and Macduff fight.)*

Analyze Character and Theme (LINES 27–34)

COMMON CORE RL 2, RL 3

Remind students that in the course of a drama, characters change, but some character traits remain constant. Also point out that the final impression a character leaves on the audience can affect the way the audience ultimately views this character and his or her actions.

P **ASK STUDENTS** to examine how Macbeth faces death and compare his character here to characterizations earlier in the play, such as the Captain's description of him in Act I, Scene 2. Have them consider what traits have stayed the same throughout the entire play. *(Macbeth has always been a brave fighter—the Captain in Act I, Scene 2, describes him in line 16 as brave—and it was his prowess on the battlefield that first won him a title from Duncan. Therefore, it is no surprise that he chooses to die fighting Macduff. At the same time, he has always been proud and has grown increasingly arrogant, so it is not a surprise that he refuses to bow to Malcolm. Furthermore, in Act I, Macbeth disdains Fortune [line 17] and makes his own luck through the strength of his fighting. Over the course of the play, however, he comes to listen closely to the prophecies of the witches and rely on them to direct his future instead of relying on his own values and beliefs.)*

Macbeth.   I will not yield
To kiss the ground before young Malcolm's feet
And to be baited with the rabble's curse.
30 Though Birnam Wood be come to Dunsinane
And thou opposed, being of no woman born,
Yet I will try the last. Before my body
I throw my warlike shield. Lay on, Macduff,
And damned be him that first cries "Hold! Enough!"

[*They exit fighting. Alarums.*]
[*They enter fighting, and* Macbeth *is slain.* Macduff *exits carrying off* Macbeth's *body. Retreat and flourish. Enter, with Drum and Colors,* Malcolm, Siward, Ross, Thanes, *and* Soldiers.]

35 **Malcolm.** I would the friends we miss were safe arrived.

Siward. Some must go off; and yet by these I see
So great a day as this is cheaply bought.

Malcolm. Macduff is missing, and your noble son.

Ross. Your son, my lord, has paid a soldier's debt.
40 He only lived but till he was a man,
The which no sooner had his prowess confirmed
In the unshrinking station where he fought,
But like a man he died.

Siward.   Then he is dead?

Ross. Ay, and brought off the field. Your cause of sorrow
45 Must not be measured by his worth, for then
It hath no end.

[Stage Direction] **Retreat . . . :** The first trumpet call (**retreat**) signals the battle's end. The next one (**flourish**) announces Malcolm's entrance.

36–37 Though some must die (**go off**) in battle, Siward can see that their side does not have many casualties.

Image Credits: ©David Muscroft/Superstock/Glow Images

WHEN STUDENTS STRUGGLE . . .

Tell students to take time to clarify what subject a pronoun refers to in order to help them understand the meaning of a passage.

ASK STUDENTS to reread Ross's dialogue in lines 44–46. Ask: What is the cause of sorrow that Ross refers to? *(the death of Siward's son)* What does the pronoun "It" refer to? *(the sorrow felt by his son's death)* What does Ross mean by these words of comfort? *(Ross knows that Siward loved his son dearly and that his son's worth had no end. So if Siward's sorrow matches his son's worth, Siward's sorrow will never end.)*

Siward.   Had he his hurts before?

Ross. Ay, on the front.

Siward.   Why then, God's soldier be he!
Had I as many sons as I have hairs,
I would not wish them to a fairer death;
50   And so his knell is knolled.

Malcolm. He's worth more sorrow, and that I'll spend for him.

Siward. He's worth no more.
They say he parted well and paid his score,
And so, God be with him. Here comes newer comfort.

[*Enter Macduff with Macbeth's head.*]

55   **Macduff.** Hail, King! for so thou art. Behold where stands
Th' usurper's cursèd head. The time is free.
I see thee compassed with thy kingdom's pearl,
That speak my salutation in their minds,
Whose voices I desire aloud with mine.
60   Hail, King of Scotland!

All.   Hail, King of Scotland!

[*Flourish*]

Malcolm. We shall not spend a large expense of time
Before we reckon with your several loves
And make us even with you. My thanes and kinsmen,
Henceforth be earls, the first that ever Scotland
65   In such an honor named. What's more to do,
Which would be planted newly with the time,
As calling home our exiled friends abroad
That fled the snares of watchful tyranny,
Producing forth the cruel ministers
70   Of this dead butcher and his fiend-like queen
(Who, as 'tis thought, by self and violent hands,
Took off her life)—this, and what needful else
That calls upon us, by the grace of grace,
We will perform in measure, time, and place.
75   So thanks to all at once and to each one,
Whom we invite to see us crowned at Scone.

[*Flourish. All exit.*]

COLLABORATIVE DISCUSSION With a partner, discuss how each
prophecy is fulfilled in spite of its seeming impossibility. Cite specific
textual evidence from the play to support your ideas.

46 hurts before: wounds in the front of his body, which indicate he died facing his enemy.

50 knell is knolled: Young Siward's death bell has already rung.

[Stage Direction] Macduff is probably carrying Macbeth's head on a pole.

56–57 The time ... pearl: Macduff declares that the age (**time**) is now freed from tyranny. He sees Malcolm surrounded by Scotland's noblest men (**thy kingdom's pearl**).

61–76 Malcolm promises that he will quickly reward his nobles according to the devotion (**several loves**) they have shown. He gives the thanes new titles (**henceforth be earls**) and declares his intention, as a sign of the new age (**planted newly with the time**), to welcome back the exiles who fled Macbeth's tyranny and his cruel agents (**ministers**).

CLOSE READ

Analyze Character and Theme (LINES 46–50)

COMMON CORE   RL 2, RL 3

Explain to students that when audience members reach the end of a play, they can put together clues they have gathered from the actions of the characters to fully formulate the important themes of the play.

Q ASK STUDENTS to identify what Siward wishes to find out about the way his son died and why this is important to him. (*In lines 46–49, Siward confirms that his son's wounds are on the front of his body. This reassures him that his son fought bravely, facing his enemy head-on instead of running away like a coward.*) How might this relate to Macbeth's behavior throughout the play? (*Although Macbeth was a brave fighter on the battlefield and faced his death head-on, he ruined his life and reputation by taking secretive, cowardly actions, such as killing people under the cover of darkness while they were sleeping.*) What theme might you formulate based on these observations? (*Bold action and courageous action are not necessarily the same thing.*)

COLLABORATIVE DISCUSSION Have partners first identify each prophecy in Act V and explain why each would seem impossible to fulfill. Then have partners pinpoint where in the play each prophecy comes to fruition. Finally, invite pairs to present to the class their detailed, well-supported explanations of how each came true.

ASK STUDENTS to share any questions they generated in the course of reading and discussing the selection.

TEACH

CLOSE READ

Analyze Character and Theme

Help students understand that the theme of a work of literature is more than just one main idea. It is the message of the text that the author wishes to share with an audience. Emphasize that one literary text may have more than one theme and that different people might identify different themes. Remind students, however, that they should be able to cite details from the text to support any ideas they have about theme. Also, make sure students understand that although a theme is usually related to a concept like fate, amibition, love, and so on, a theme is stated in the form of a sentence. *(One theme in "The Tragedy of Macbeth" is that making a bad decision and staying committed to it can lead to other bad choices and create a chain of destructive events.)*

To help students determine the themes, they can use these strategies:

- Frequently ask yourself why Macbeth is acting as he does and think about the cause and effect relationships that link each action to the next.
- Make a list of Macbeth's character traits and trace which ones remain the same for the entire play and which ones change.

Analyze Character and Theme

The **theme** of a work of literature is the insight about life and human nature that the writer wants to communicate. Theme is conveyed through the writer's development of elements such as character and plot.

In his play, Shakespeare presents several themes. These ideas are brought out by the actions, thoughts, and feelings of the characters, particularly those of Macbeth.

Macbeth is a multi-dimensional, complex character who changes as a result of the decisions he makes and the way he reacts to conflict. Consider these key aspects of the interplay between character and theme together with examples from the play:

How the character changes over time	Early in Act I: Macbeth, loyal to Duncan, wins a great victory for the king.
	Later in Act I: Macbeth considers murdering the king based on the words of the witches and Lady Macbeth.
	Act II: Hoping the violence will end there, Macbeth murders the king and his guards.
	Act III: Macbeth has Banquo killed on the basis of mere suspicions, but he also begins to show signs of a guilty conscience.
How the character interacts with others	Once the first prophecy is fulfilled, Macbeth unquestioningly believes all the witches say, and seeks their advice.
	Macbeth solves conflicts, both real and imagined, by murdering anyone who might oppose him.
How the character advances the plot	Macbeth's decision to have Macduff's family murdered leads to his own death at Macduff's hands.

Through Macbeth's conflict, his subsequent actions, his thoughts, and his feelings, Shakespeare conveys profound lessons about the consequences of a person's decisions. Each poor decision Macbeth makes paves the way for the next, until by Act III he says "I am in blood / Stepped in so far that, should I wade no more, / Returning were as tedious as go o'er." Consider what theme is expressed through Macbeth's character and fate.

Strategies for Annotation 🖊 🗐 *Annotate it!*

Analyze Character and Theme

Students can review the whole play and collect clues about Macbeth's character and how he changes over the course of the play. Share these strategies for guided or independent analysis:

- Highlight in blue the words a character uses to describe Macbeth's character.
- Highlight in yellow the words a character uses to describe Macbeth's actions.

For brave Macbeth (well he deserves that name),

Disdaining Fortune, with his brandished steel,

Which smoked with bloody execution,

Like valor's minion, carved out his passage

Till he faced the slave;

@ end of play, analyze how Macbeth can be viewed in a tragic light (you empathize w/ him despite a great character flaw)

utilizing ~~TIQA~~ TIQA — who is most at fault for Duncan's murder? for Macbeth's downfall?

~~Compare Macbeth~~

→

talk to Brian

↳ he wanted to do Macbeth rap,

maybe we can make time, & instead cl can do the Macbeth kids book project

use sounds effects

Alyssa?
possibly

Cooper Dees?
Shakespearean actor award

8:02

8:45

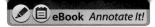

Analyzing the Text

COMMON CORE RL 1, RL 2, RL 3, RL 5, W 1

Cite Text Evidence Support your responses with evidence from the selection.

1. **Analyze** Using these passages as a guide, explain how Macbeth's attempt to resolve his conflict changes him. What message does Shakespeare convey through his change?

   - Act I, Scene 3, lines 130–142; Scene 7, lines 31–35
   - Act II, Scene 2, lines 56–61
   - Act III, Scene 4, lines 93–96; lines 122–126
   - Act V, Scene 3, lines 19–28; scene 5, lines 9–15

2. **Evaluate** Explain how Lady Macbeth's actions in Act V, Scene 1, draw meaning from the images of blood, darkness, and sleep that have run through the play. Does her deterioration redeem her character in the eyes of the audience? Why or why not?

3. **Analyze** In what ways do Macbeth's strengths contribute to his downfall? Cite examples from the entire play to support your ideas.

4. **Cite Evidence** What moment might be called the climax, or highest point of tension, in Act V? What is clear to the audience and to Macbeth at this point?

5. **Identify Patterns** The witches are sometimes seen as representing fate, or destiny. Do they merely reveal what will happen, or do they manipulate events?

6. **Analyze** In Shakespeare's tragedies, often the main character is given a chance to say something significant about his life just before he dies. What speech might function as Macbeth's farewell, even though it doesn't occur in Act V, Scene 8? Defend your choice with evidence from the text.

7. **Compare** Review Malcolm's last speech in Act V, Scene 8. How are his words an echo of Duncan's language earlier in the play? How does this speech thematically and structurally unify the play?

PERFORMANCE TASK

Writing Activity: Argument Is Macbeth a tragic hero? Refer to the introductory essay on Shakespearean Drama, and explore your ideas in an essay.

- Review the definition of a tragic hero. Decide which of the characteristics Macbeth embodies. Find details in the text to support your thesis.

- Organize your ideas logically. Write an essay in which you defend your view of Macbeth.
- Use the conventions of standard written English in your essay.

The Tragedy of Macbeth, Act V **291**

Assign this performance task.

PERFORMANCE TASK

COMMON CORE W 1

Writing Activity: Argument Suggest that students use a two-column chart to help them organize evidence they collect, writing each characteristic of a tragic hero in the left column and recording evidence for that characteristic in the text in the right column. Remind students to begin their essays with a strong thesis statement that clearly describes the position they will be defending.

PRACTICE & APPLY

Analyzing the Text
COMMON CORE RL 1, RL 2, RL 3, RL 5

Possible answers:

1. *In Act I, Macbeth is horrified by the idea of murder (Scene 3) and decides not to act because the king has honored him (Scene 7). By Act II, he has committed murder but is haunted and apalled by it (Scene 2). In Act III, he rails against the spectre that haunts him, but seems to blame it, not himself, for his troubles (Scene 4). By Act V, he recognizes both that he has ruined any chance his soul had for peace (Scene 3) and that he is no longer moved by violence (Scene 5). Shakespeare conveys a message that acting immorally to feed ambition destroys the soul.*

2. *In Act II, Scene 2, lines 44–48, the image of blood was related to guilt. Darkness was associated with evil actions, such as the murders of Duncan and Banquo. Sleep is a peaceful time interrupted by nightmares and terrible acts. In Act II, Scene 2, lines 33–41, Macbeth imagines that he hears a voice cry out that Macbeth murders peaceful sleep. In Act V, as she sleepwalks and relives her guilt, Lady Macbeth has commanded that there be a light by her at all times (Scene 1, lines 18–19), as if to keep darkness at bay. Her deterioration redeems her somewhat in the eyes of the audience because, unlike her husband, she seems to recognize that they have done so terrible a thing that nothing could wash away their guilt.*

3. *Macbeth has confidence in his worth and ability, which helps him be a great general. He is also devoted to his wife. Once he hears prophecies about becoming king, however, his courage and his marital devotion both contribute to his downfall. (Students should cite representative passages from throughout the drama to support their responses.)*

4. *In lines 27–34 of Scene 8, Macbeth faces the realization that the prophecies have come true. Both the audience and Macbeth now know he is doomed.*

5. *The witches manipulate events. Hecate calls them to task in Act III, Scene 5, for giving Macbeth information without her involvement, and she herself plans in lines 20–33 to confuse him with spirits and destroy him.*

6. *In Act V, Scene 5, lines 23–28, Macbeth compares life to an actor with a small part to play and says that the play itself ultimately has no meaning. This highlights how his own actions do not really amount to anything of worth.*

7. *Just as Malcolm's father rewarded his loyal followers in Act I, Scene 4, lines 39–43, Malcolm rewards his nobles by making them earls. Macbeth's anger at Malcolm being named heir earlier in the play sets the tragedy in motion. Now Malcolm establishes a new order.*

The Tragedy of Macbeth, Act V **291**

PRACTICE & APPLY

Language and Style: Inverted Sentence Structure

 COMMON CORE **L 3**

If students have trouble untangling the syntax and meaning of sentences with an inverted sentence structure, suggest that they label the parts of the sentence (*S* for subject, *V* for verb, *O* for object) before trying to reorder them in a more conventional way. Also, students can read the sentences aloud to listen to the way they sound and see how they might be reorganized to sound clearer.

Answers:

1. *Oh, dear wife, my mind is full of scorpions!*

2. *I'll fight until my flesh is hacked from my bones.*

3. *We retire to our chamber.*

4. *I have murdered the gracious Duncan for them.*

5. *Then my fit comes again.*

Students' original sentences will vary but should use inverted structures similar to those shown in Shakespeare's sentences.

> ### ✔ Assess It!
>
> **Online Selection Test**
> • Download an editable ExamView bank.
> • Assign and manage this test online.

Language and Style: Inverted Sentence Structure

 COMMON CORE **L 3**

A key aspect of Shakespeare's style is his use of inverted sentence structure. In an **inverted sentence**, the normal word order is reversed. Some examples of inverted structure include: all or part of the predicate comes before the subject; a subject comes between a helping verb and a main verb; a direct object precedes a verb, and a prepositional phrase comes before the noun or verb it modifies. Shakespeare includes many of these inverted sentence structures in his play.

> Read these lines from *The Tragedy of Macbeth*:

> **Come, go we to the King. (Act IV, Scene 3, line 239)**

> **The castle of Macduff I will surprise. (Act IV, Scene 1, line 150)**

Notice that in the first example the verb *go* precedes the subject *we*. In the second example, the direct object *the castle* and its modifier *of Macduff* appear before both the subject *I* and the verb phrase *will surprise*. Shakespeare could have written the lines this way:

> **Come, we go to the King.**

> **I will surprise the castle of Macduff.**

Instead, Shakespeare chose to use inverted structures for poetic effect.

Writers also use inverted sentence structures to add variety to their writing or to emphasize a word or an idea.

Practice and Apply Working independently, identify the part that is inverted in each of Shakespeare's sentences below. Rewrite each sentence without the inversion. Then, working with a partner, write five original sentences on topics of your choice that use the same inverted structures found in Shakespeare's sentences.

1. O, full of scorpions is my mind, dear wife! (Act III, Scene 2, line 35)

2. I'll fight till from my bones my flesh be hacked. (Act V, Scene 3, line 32)

3. Retire we to our chamber. (Act II, Scene 2, line 64)

4. For them the gracious Duncan have I murdered. (Act III, Scene 1, line 65)

5. Then comes my fit again. (Act III, Scene 4, line 21)

Understand Use of Language: Archaic Words and Sentence Structures

COMMON CORE

L 3

TEACH

Although Shakespeare's works brought to the English language a multitude of new words that people use even today, students may struggle to decipher his poetic sentence structures and understand the meaning of the archaic words that have fallen out of fashion.

To untangle a sentence, students can diagram its parts. Suggest that they find the subject (who or what the sentence is about) and the predicate (what the subject is or does). Then they can separate out any other clauses and consider the function of each one.

Suggest that students use the following strategies when they come across an unfamiliar word:

- Search the surrounding dialogue for context clues that might help them figure out the meaning.
- Try to break the word down into base or root words, suffixes, and prefixes and figure out the meaning from these parts.
- Use a dictionary to look up the definition of any unfamiliar words as necessary.
- Use the word in a sentence of their own to solidify their understanding of its meaning.

PRACTICE AND APPLY

Display several sentences from the play that use archaic sentence structures and have students figure out the meaning of each one. For example, display Act V, Scene 7, lines 12–13 and have students rearrange the words to reflect modern English structure. *(The subject is "I" and the predicate is "smile at [swords]." Modern structure might be, "I smile at swords and laugh to scorn at weapons brandished by man that's born of a woman.")*

Pick out various sections of the play that contain archaic words and have students practice figuring out the meaning of each one. For example, display Act V, Scene 1, lines 22–24, and have students work to figure out the meaning of the word *accustomed*. *(The context tells the audience that Lady Macbeth performs this action over and over. The word "custom" means "habit." Therefore, "accustomed" probably means "usual or regular.")*

Analyze Character and Theme

COMMON CORE

RL 2,
RL 3

 LEVEL UP TUTORIALS Assign the following *Level Up* tutorial: **Theme**

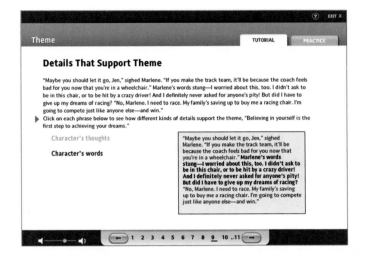

RETEACH

Explain that theme is an author's message about life or humanity. Unlike a topic or a key concept in a literary work, which can be stated in a word or two (for example, freedom), the theme is stated in the form of a sentence (for instance, Freedom comes with responsibilities). Usually a work's themes must be inferred, and complex works like Macbeth have many themes. To identify theme in a complex work, students should pick one of the work's topics or key concepts (for example, false appearances) and then examine the following elements related to that topic: setting, character, symbolism, conflict, and resolution. Work with students to create a cluster diagram with the topic in the middle surrounded by the elements and a brief description (for example, Character: The Macbeths play gracious hosts but hide a fiendish plot).

Ask students to reflect on what they have discovered and what comment about the human experience Shakespeare is making (for example, a fair appearance can hide a foul reality).

CLOSE READING APPLICATION

Students can analyze the theme of another literary work—such as a novel, short story , or film—by creating another cluster diagram. Make sure students cite text examples. Then have students reflect on and write down the author's message about the human experience.

from The Tragedy of Macbeth

Drama by William Shakespeare

Why This Text

In *Macbeth*, Shakespeare uses a rousing narrative about kings, battles, and witches to examine several themes, including the corrupting effect of uncontrolled ambition, the qualities of a good ruler, and whether a person's destiny is determined by his or her own fate. With the help of the close-reading questions, students will analyze how the main characters develop and interact with one another. This close reading will lead students to an understanding of how the characters' actions advance the plot and develop the theme.

Background Have students read the background about the play *Macbeth* and its author, William Shakespeare. Macbeth and Duncan are mentioned in early Scottish historical accounts. However, Shakespeare probably relied more on a later work, *The Chronicles of England, Scotland, and Ireland*, by Raphael Holinshed. This publication, first put out in 1577, depicted a more ruthless Macbeth than the original records did, and Shakespeare followed Holinshed's version in this regard.

AS YOU READ Remind students that a drama depends on dialogue to reveal how a character changes over time. When and how does Macbeth show that he is beginning to crave and feel entitled to the crown of Scotland?

Common Core Support

- cite strong and thorough textual evidence
- determine a theme or central idea and analyze its development
- analyze how complex characters develop
- analyze the impact of specific word choices

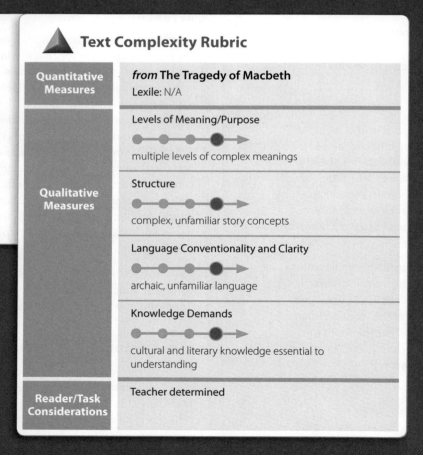

Text Complexity Rubric

Quantitative Measures	*from* The Tragedy of Macbeth Lexile: N/A
Qualitative Measures	**Levels of Meaning/Purpose** multiple levels of complex meanings
	Structure complex, unfamiliar story concepts
	Language Conventionality and Clarity archaic, unfamiliar language
	Knowledge Demands cultural and literary knowledge essential to understanding
Reader/Task Considerations	Teacher determined

Strategies for CLOSE READING

Analyze Character and Theme

Students should read Act I carefully all the way through. Close-reading questions at the bottom of the pages will help them understand how the characters develop and change. As they read, students should jot down comments or questions about the text in the margins.

WHEN STUDENTS STRUGGLE . . .

To help students understand how characters' dialogue reveals their inner nature, have them work in small groups to fill out a chart like the one shown below.

CITE TEXT EVIDENCE For practice in analyzing character development, ask students to give text examples showing what Macbeth's intentions are and how they change over the course of Act I.

Macbeth's Words	Macbeth's Development
". . . to be king Stands not within the prospect of belief . . ." (Act I, Scene 3, lines 73–74)	At this point, Macbeth has not thought of becoming king and finds the idea unbelievable.
"Glamis and Thane of Cawdor! The greatest is behind." (Act 1, Scene 3, lines 117–118)	Macbeth has realized that the prophecy could come true, and he feels the first urge for the throne.
". . . why do I yield to that suggestion Whose horrid image doth unfix my hair And make my seated heart knock at my ribs Against the use of nature?" (Act I, Scene 3, lines 134–137)	Macbeth wants the throne so much that he's thinking of a horrible way of reaching his goal—murder.

Background *Macbeth is a tragedy: a kind of play in which human actions have their own inevitable consequences, in which the characters' bad deeds, errors, and crimes are never forgiven or rectified. In* **William Shakespeare's** *tragedies the main character, or tragic hero, is usually a high-ranking person distinguished by bravery and intelligence. The hero's character also includes a fatal weakness or tragic flaw that permits an ill-judged action to lead remorselessly to catastrophe.*

from
The Tragedy of
Macbeth
Drama by William Shakespeare

CLOSE READ
Notes

THE TIME: The 11th century   **THE PLACE:** Scotland and England

CHARACTERS

Duncan, King of Scotland

His Sons
  Malcolm
  Donalbain

Noblemen of Scotland
  Macbeth
  Banquo
  Lennox
  Ross
  Angus

Lady Macbeth
Three Witches
Captain
Messenger
Attendants

73

1. **READ ▶** As you read Scene 1, and Scene 2 lines 1–24, begin to collect and cite text evidence.

- In the margin, explain where the witches plan to meet again, and why.
- Underline the witches' references to threatening aspects of nature.
- In the margin, explain the characteristics Macbeth shows in battle.

The play opens in a wild and lonely place in medieval Scotland. The king of Scotland, Duncan, along with his sons Malcolm and Donalbain, is engaged in a war against Scottish rebels and then faces an attack by the king of Norway. However, the first characters Shakespeare introduces are supernatural beings—witches who seem able to foretell the future.

ACT I

Scene 1 • *An open place in Scotland.*

[*Thunder and lightning. Enter three* Witches.]
Ⓐ Ⓑ **First Witch.** When shall we three meet again?
In thunder, lightning, or in rain?
Second Witch. When the hurly-burly's done,
When the battle's lost and won.
5 **Third Witch.** That will be ere the set of sun.
First Witch. Where the place?
Second Witch.   Upon the heath.
Third Witch. There to meet with Macbeth.
First Witch. I come, Graymalkin.
Second Witch. Paddock[1] calls.
Third Witch.   Anon.[2]
10 **All.** Fair is foul, and foul is fair,
Hover through the fog and filthy air.
[*They exit.*]

[1] **Graymalkin . . . Paddock:** two demons in the form of a cat and a toad.
[2] **anon:** soon.

The witches plan to meet after the battle is over to talk to Macbeth.

2. **◀ REREAD** Reread Scene 1. Describe the mood or atmosphere created by the witches and the weather.

The witches create an atmosphere of mystery and potential danger. The thunder, lightning, and "fog and filthy air" are unsettling.

74

Scene 2 • *King Duncan's camp near the battlefield.*

[*Alarum within.[3] Enter* King Duncan, Malcolm, Donalbain, Lennox, *with* Attendants, *meeting a bleeding* Captain.]
Duncan. What bloody man is that? He can report,
As seemeth by his plight, of the revolt
The newest state.
Malcolm.   This is the sergeant
Who, like a good and hardy soldier, fought
5 'Gainst my captivity.[4]—Hail, brave friend!
Say to the King the knowledge of the broil[5]
As thou didst leave it.
Captain.   Doubtful it stood,
As two spent swimmers that do cling together
And choke their art.[6] The merciless Macdonwald
10 (Worthy to be a rebel, for to that
The multiplying villainies of nature
Do swarm upon him) from the Western Isles
Of kerns and gallowglasses[7] is supplied;
And Fortune, on his damnèd quarrel smiling,
15 Showed like a rebel's whore. But all's too weak;
For brave Macbeth (well he deserves that name),
Disdaining Fortune, with his brandished steel,
Which smoked with bloody execution,
Like valor's **minion**, carved out his passage
20 Till he faced the slave;

minion:
*follower;
favorite*

[3] **Alarum within:** the sound of a trumpet offstage, signaling soldiers to arm themselves.
[4] **'Gainst my captivity:** to save me from capture.
[5] **broil:** battle.
[6] **choke their art:** drown each other.
[7] **kerns and gallowglasses:** foot soldiers and armed horsemen.

3. **READ ▶** As you read Scene 2, lines 25–70, continue to cite textual evidence.

- Circle the name of the captain who fights alongside Macbeth. Then, circle the lines that describe the two men in battle.
- In the margin, explain the animal analogies (line 35).
- In the margin, summarize Ross's report to Duncan (lines 50–60).

75

---

1. **READ AND CITE TEXT EVIDENCE** Note to students that it's important to understand the kind of person Macbeth is at the start of the play.

Ⓐ **ASK STUDENTS** to read lines 1–24 of Scene 2. What do we learn about Macbeth? Who speaks about him, and why is that person's evidence trustworthy? *We learn that Macbeth was brave in battle. We do not witness Macbeth's actions in battle directly. We hear about what he did from the wounded Captain, who is trustworthy because he fought alongside Macbeth and watched what he did.*

2. **REREAD AND CITE TEXT EVIDENCE**

Ⓑ **ASK STUDENTS** to reread Scene 1. In what way does opening the play with witches affect the mood of the play? *Students might say that the witches give the play a creepier, foreboding air. Knowing that they mention Macbeth's name piques our interest.*

3. **READ AND CITE TEXT EVIDENCE** Shakespeare often refers to noblemen in a traditional shortened style. Here, the thane of a place is called by the place name: the Thane of Ross (a Scottish region) is called *Ross*. The king of Norway is called *Norway*.

Ⓒ **ASK STUDENTS** to look at lines 45–60 of Scene 2. What enemies does the Thane of Ross tell Duncan about? Who is "Bellona's bridegroom," and what are his actions? *Ross tells about the rebel Scottish noble, the Thane of Cawdor, and his ally the King of Norway. Macbeth is Bellona's bridegroom. He fights these two enemies effectively, and "the victory fell on us" (line 60).*

Critical Vocabulary: minion (line 19) Ask students to share their definitions of *minion*. Ask them how the word helps Shakespeare to create a personification of valor.

> " Go, pronounce his present death, And with his former title greet Macbeth. "

He is brave and very fierce and ruthless.

Which ne'er shook hands, nor bade farewell to him,
Till he unseamed him from the nave to th' chops,[8]
And fixed his head upon our battlements.
Duncan. O valiant cousin, worthy gentleman!

25 **Captain.** As whence the sun 'gins his reflection
Shipwracking storms and direful thunders break,
So from that spring whence comfort seemed to come
Discomfort swells. Mark, King of Scotland, mark:
No sooner justice had, with valor armed,
30 Compelled these skipping kerns to trust their heels,
But the Norweyan lord, surveying vantage,
With furbished arms and new supplies of men,
Began a fresh assault.
Duncan. Dismayed not this our captains, Macbeth and Banquo?

35 **Captain.** Yes, as sparrows eagles, or the hare the lion.
If I say sooth, I must report they were
As cannons overcharged with double cracks,
So they doubly redoubled strokes upon the foe.
Except they meant to bathe in reeking wounds
40 Or memorize another Golgotha,[9]
I cannot tell—
But I am faint. My gashes cry for help.
Duncan. So well thy words become thee as thy wounds:
They smack of honor both.—Go, get him surgeons.
[*The Captain is led off by Attendants.*]
[*Enter Ross and Angus.*]
45 Who comes here?
Malcolm.   The worthy Thane[10] of Ross.
Lennox. What a haste looks through his eyes!
So should he look that seems to speak things strange.
Ross. God save the King.

The captains don't fear the Norwegian attackers any more than a powerful animal fears a weak one.

[8] **unseamed him from the nave to th' chops:** split him open from navel to jaw.
[9] **memorize another Golgotha:** make the battlefield as famous as Golgotha, the site of Christ's crucifixion.
[10] **Thane:** a rank of Scottish nobleman.

76

Duncan. Whence cam'st thou, worthy thane?
50 **Ross.** From Fife, great king,
Where the Norweyan banners flout the sky
And fan our people cold.
Norway himself, with terrible numbers,
Assisted by that most disloyal traitor,
55 The Thane of Cawdor, began a dismal conflict,
Till that Bellona's bridegroom,[11] lapped in proof,
Confronted him with self-comparisons,[12]
Point against point, rebellious arm 'gainst arm,
Curbing his lavish spirit. And to conclude,
60 The victory fell on us.
Duncan.   Great happiness!
Ross. That now Sweno,
The Norways' king, craves composition.[13]
Nor would we deign him burial of his men
Till he disbursèd at Saint Colme's Inch
65 Ten thousand dollars to our general use.
Duncan. No more that Thane of Cawdor shall deceive
Our bosom interest. Go, pronounce his present death,
And with his former title greet Macbeth.
Ross. I'll see it done.
70 **Duncan.** What he hath lost, noble Macbeth hath won.
[*They exit.*]

[11] **Bellona's bridegroom:** Macbeth is referred to as the groom of Bellona, the Roman goddess of war.
[12] **self-comparisons:** equal deeds.
[13] **craves composition:** wants a treaty.

Ross reports that the invading king of Norway and the Thane of Cawdor were challenged and defeated by Macbeth.

4. ◀ **REREAD**   Reread Scene 2, lines 66–70. Who is punished, and who is rewarded? What is the punishment, and what is the reward? Support your answer with explicit textual evidence.

The Thane of Cawdor is stripped of his title and condemned to death, and Macbeth is made Thane of Cawdor in his place. According to Duncan, what the traitorous Thane of Cawdor "hath lost, noble Macbeth hath won."

77

FOR ELL STUDENTS Clarify that gashes (line 42) are long cuts or wounds in the flesh.

4. **REREAD AND CITE TEXT EVIDENCE**   One of Shakespeare's themes in *Macbeth* is the qualities of a good king. It's important to notice the powers that a king has in this time so as to evaluate whether or not they act justly.

D ASK STUDENTS to reread lines 50–70. How did the battle end for the Thane of Cawdor? What gives Duncan the right to decide on what happens to the thane now? *The Thane of Cawdor was defeated in battle against the forces of King Duncan of Scotland. As king, Duncan has the right to decide on a punishment for a rebel. He also has the right to take away someone's noble rank and title.*

CLOSE READ
Notes

CLOSE READ
Notes

Scene 3 • *A bleak place near the battlefield.*

[*Thunder. Enter the three* Witches.]
First Witch. Where hast thou been, sister?
Second Witch. Killing swine.
Third Witch. Sister, where thou?
First Witch. A sailor's wife had chestnuts in her lap
5   And munched and munched and munched. "Give me," quoth I.
"Aroint thee,¹⁴ witch," the rump-fed runnion¹⁵ cries.
Her husband's to Aleppo gone, master o' th' *Tiger*;
But in a sieve I'll thither sail
And, like a rat without a tail,
10   I'll do, I'll do, and I'll do.
Second Witch. I'll give thee a wind.
First Witch. Th' art kind.
Third Witch. And I another.
First Witch. I myself have all the other,
15   And the very ports they blow,
All the quarters that they know
I' th' shipman's card.¹⁶
I'll drain him dry as hay.
Sleep shall neither night nor day
20   Hang upon his penthouse lid.
He shall live a man forbid.
Weary sev'nnights,¹⁷ nine times nine,
Shall he dwindle, peak, and pine.
Though his bark cannot be lost,
25   Yet it shall be tempest-tossed.

¹⁴**Aroint thee:** Go away.
¹⁵**rump-fed runion:** fat-bottomed, ugly creature.
¹⁶**card:** compass.
¹⁷**sev'nnights:** weeks.

They are very powerful and will travel great distances to harm people. They do things for revenge, to get even with people, or just for fun.

5. **READ ▶** As you read Scene 3, lines 1–37, continue to cite textual evidence.

• Underline examples of the witches' malicious behavior or plans for such behavior.
• In the margin, explain the extent of the witches' power and the way in which they use it (lines 8–25).

78

Look what I have.
Second Witch. Show me, show me.
First Witch. Here I have a pilot's thumb,
Wracked as homeward he did come.
[*Drum within*]
30   **Third Witch.** A drum, a drum!
Macbeth doth come.
All. [*Dancing in a circle*] The Weïrd¹⁸ Sisters, hand in hand,
Posters¹⁹ of the sea and land,
Thus do go about, about,
35   Thrice to thine, and thrice to mine
And thrice again, to make up nine.
Peace, the charm's wound up.
[*Enter* Macbeth *and* Banquo.]
Macbeth. So foul and fair a day I have not seen.
Banquo. How far is 't called to Forres?—What are these,
40   So withered, and so wild in their attire,
That look not like th' inhabitants o' th' earth
And yet are on 't?—Live you? Or are you aught
That man may question? You seem to understand me
By each at once her choppy finger laying

¹⁸**Weïrd:** related to the Old English word *wyrd* (fate or personal destiny); these "weïrd sisters" manipulate fate.
¹⁹**posters:** quick riders.

6. **◀ REREAD** Reread Scene 3, lines 8–25. *Fate* is a theme in *Macbeth*. If the witches can foresee the fate of others, what effect or influence do you think they will have on the outcome of the play?

They will probably influence a bad outcome for people, not a good one.

7. **READ ▶** As you read Scene 3, lines 38–88, continue to cite textual evidence.

• Underline the witches' predictions for Macbeth and Banquo, and restate them in the margin.
• In the margin, explain why Macbeth disbelieves the witches at first (lines 71–75).

79

---

5. **READ AND CITE TEXT EVIDENCE**

E ASK STUDENTS to look at lines 1–37 of Scene 3. What do the witches reveal about their character and actions through their dialogue? *The witches are spiteful and mean. They tell one another about casual acts of malice and vandalism, such as killing swine (pigs) and planning to harm the husband of a woman who offended one witch.*

FOR ELL STUDENTS The use of old forms of English can be challenging for any student, but even more so for your ELL students. Guide them through the text by pointing out that they may recognize many words if they read them aloud—the spelling may be different but the context and the sound of the spoken words will give them clues to their meaning.

6. **REREAD AND CITE TEXT EVIDENCE** Shakespeare gets the witches' prophecies about Macbeth and Banquo almost word for word from Holinshed, where the men encounter three women described as perhaps "goddesses of destiny,… or fairies." However, in Holinshed the women are not portrayed as sinister.

F ASK STUDENTS to reread lines 8–25 of Scene 3. How does Shakespeare foreshadow the kind of influence his witches might have? *By showing us to what lengths the witches will go to to punish their enemies, Shakespeare shows their capacity for evil.*

7. **READ AND CITE TEXT EVIDENCE** Macbeth is already the Thane of Glamis. He inherited the title on his father's death.

G ASK STUDENTS to explain the witches' predictions. *One witch calls Macbeth "king hereafter," but audiences have seen the current king of Scotland, Duncan.*

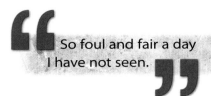

> So foul and fair a day
> I have not seen.

He thinks that the Thane of Cawdor is alive and that it's unlikely that he (Macbeth) could become king.

I By Sinel's[22] death I know I am Thane of Glamis.
But how of Cawdor? The Thane of Cawdor lives
A prosperous gentleman, and to be king
Stands not within the prospect of belief,
75 No more than to be Cawdor. Say from whence
You owe this strange intelligence or why
Upon this blasted heath you stop our way
With such prophetic greeting. Speak, I charge you.
[Witches *vanish*.]
Banquo. The earth hath bubbles, as the water has,
80 And these are of them. Whither are they vanished?
Macbeth. Into the air, and what seemed **corporal** melted,
As breath into the wind. Would they had stayed!
Banquo. Were such things here as we do speak about?
Or have we eaten on the insane root
85 That takes the reason prisoner?
Macbeth. Your children shall be kings.
Banquo.   You shall be king.
Macbeth. And Thane of Cawdor too. Went it not so?
Banquo. To th' selfsame tune and words.—Who's here?

corporal:
physical, real

²²**Sinel:** Macbeth's father.

45 Upon her skinny lips. You should be women,
And yet your beards forbid me to interpret
That you are so.
Macbeth.   Speak, if you can. What are you?
First Witch. All hail, Macbeth! Hail to thee, Thane of Glamis!
Second Witch. All hail, Macbeth! Hail to thee, Thane of Cawdor!
G 50 **Third Witch.** All hail, Macbeth, that shalt be king hereafter!
Banquo. Good sir, why do you start and seem to fear
Things that do sound so fair? I' th' name of truth,
Are you **fantastical**, or that indeed
Which outwardly you show? My noble partner
H 55 You greet with present grace and great prediction
Of noble having and of royal hope,
That he seems **rapt** withal. To me you speak not.
If you can look into the seeds of time
And say which grain will grow and which will not,
60 Speak, then, to me, who neither beg nor fear
Your favors nor your hate.
First Witch. Hail!
Second Witch. Hail!
Third Witch. Hail!
65 **First Witch.** Lesser than Macbeth and greater.
Second Witch. Not so happy,²⁰ yet much happier.
Third Witch. Thou shalt get²¹ kings, though thou be none.
So all hail, Macbeth and Banquo!
First Witch. Banquo and Macbeth, all hail!
70 **Macbeth.** Stay, you imperfect speakers. Tell me more.

fantastical:
imaginary

rapt:
mesmerized

Banquo will father kings, but he will not be a king.

²⁰**happy:** fortunate (related to *happenstance* and *perhaps*).
²¹**get:** beget; be the ancestor of.

8. **◀ REREAD** Reread lines 39–47 and 70–78. How do Banquo's reactions to the witches differ from Macbeth's? What does Macbeth's reaction suggest about his character? Support your response with explicit textual evidence.

Banquo is repulsed by the witches and says that they do not resemble "inhabitants of the earth." Macbeth refers to the witches in milder terms, calling them "imperfect speakers." Macbeth wants to hear more about where they received their "strange intelligence."

9. **READ ▶** As you read lines 89–127, continue to cite textual evidence.

- Circle what Macbeth and Banquo learn that confirms the witches' statements.
- Underline the moment Macbeth's feelings seem to change and intensify.
- In the margin, describe Macbeth's new feelings.

Critical Vocabulary: fantastical (line 53) Ask students to share their definitions of *fantastical*. Ask them what the word conveys about Banquo's reaction to encountering these creatures. *He thinks they may be an illusion.*

Critical Vocabulary: rapt (line 57) Ask students to share their definitions of *rapt*. Ask them what the word shows about how Macbeth reacts to the witches' prophecies. *Macbeth is paying very close attention to their words.*

FOR ELL STUDENTS Clarify that the adverb *withal* is an archaic form of the adverbial phrase *with that*.

8. **REREAD AND CITE TEXT EVIDENCE**

H **ASK STUDENTS** to reread lines 51–61. What clue does Banquo's view of Macbeth's reaction in lines 55–57 offer? *Banquo sees that Macbeth is "rapt" after hearing the witches.*

9. **READ AND CITE TEXT EVIDENCE**

I **ASK STUDENTS** how the fact that the audience has seen Macbeth named Thane of Cawdor creates foreboding. *The witches are telling the truth about Cawdor. They might also be right about Macbeth's becoming king. For that to happen, Duncan would have to die.*

Critical Vocabulary: corporal (line 81) Ask students to share their definitions of *corporal*. Ask what the word shows about how solid the witches seemed when the men encountered them. *At first they seemed solid, but then vanished "as breath into the wind."*

[*Enter Ross and* Angus.]

Ross. The King hath happily received, Macbeth,
90 The news of thy success, and, when he reads
Thy personal venture in the rebels' fight,
His wonders and his praises do contend
Which should be thine or his. Silenced with that,
In viewing o'er the rest o' th' selfsame day
95 He finds thee in the stout Norweyan ranks,
Nothing afeard of what thyself didst make,
Strange images of death. As thick as hail
Came post with post, and every one did bear
Thy praises in his kingdom's great defense,
100 And poured them down before him.

Angus.   We are sent
To give thee from our royal master thanks,
Only to herald thee into his sight,
Not pay thee.

Ross. And for an earnest²³ of a greater honor,
105 He bade me, from him, call thee Thane of Cawdor,
In which addition, hail, most worthy thane,
For it is thine.

Banquo.   What, can the devil speak true?

Macbeth. The Thane of Cawdor lives. Why do you dress me
In borrowed robes?

Angus.   Who was the Thane lives yet,
110 But under heavy judgment bears that life
Which he deserves to lose. Whether he was combined²⁴
With those of Norway, or did line²⁵ the rebel
With hidden help and vantage, or that with both
He labored in his country's wrack, I know not;
115 But treasons capital, confessed and proved,
Have overthrown him.

Macbeth. [*Aside*]   Glamis and Thane of Cawdor!
The greatest is behind.²⁶ [*To Ross and* Angus] Thanks for your pains.
[*Aside to* Banquo] Do you not hope your children shall be kings
When those that gave the Thane of Cawdor to me
120 Promised no less to them?

Macbeth is excited and begins to consider becoming king.

———
²³**earnest:** partial payment.
²⁴**combined:** allied.
²⁵**line:** support.
²⁶**behind:** yet to come.

82

Banquo.   That, trusted home,²⁷
Might yet enkindle you²⁸ unto the crown,
Besides the Thane of Cawdor. But 'tis strange.
And oftentimes, to win us to our harm,
The instruments of darkness tell us truths,
125 Win us with honest trifles, to betray 's
In deepest consequence.—
Cousins, a word, I pray you.   [*They step aside.*]

Macbeth. [*Aside*]   Two truths are told
As happy prologues to the swelling act
Of the imperial theme.—I thank you, gentlemen.
130 [*Aside*] This supernatural soliciting
Cannot be ill, cannot be good. If ill,
Why hath it given me earnest of success
Commencing in a truth? I am Thane of Cawdor.
If good, why do I yield to that suggestion
135 Whose horrid image doth unfix my hair
And make my seated heart knock at my ribs

———
²⁷**home:** fully.
²⁸**enkindle you:** inflame your ambitions.

He wonders whether the witches' prophecy is good or bad and admits that he's already considered killing Duncan to complete the prophecy.

10. ◀ **REREAD** Reread Scene 3, lines 116–127. Contrast Macbeth's and Banquo's reactions to the realization that the first of the witches prophecies has come true. Support your answer with explicit textual evidence.

Banquo warns that evil powers often offer little, or inconsequential, truths to tempt people. These "instruments of darkness" may be lying about what matters most, the "deepest consequence."

11. **READ** ▶ As you read Scene 3, lines 128–156, continue to cite textual evidence.
   • Circle the text that shows Macbeth's conflicting feelings about the witches' prophecy. In the margin, explain what Macbeth is thinking.
   • In the margin, tell what Macbeth's comment about chance shows about the kind of action he thinks about taking at this moment (lines 143–144).

83

FOR ELL STUDENTS Explain that the compound word *overthrow* does not mean "to throw something over something else" but "to overcome, or bring about downfall."

---

10. **REREAD AND CITE TEXT EVIDENCE**

J **ASK STUDENTS** to reread lines 118–127. What does Banquo think about what the witches have foretold? *Banquo assumes that the witches are "instruments of darkness," so even a truth from them could be dangerous. Macbeth decides that if two of the prophecies are true, the third one might be also.*

11. **READ AND CITE TEXT EVIDENCE**

K **ASK STUDENTS** to read lines 130–136. What contradictory words or phrases does Macbeth use? How do these words show conflict? *He uses the opposites "good" and "ill" (evil). He uses the positive idea of "truth" and the negative idea of a "horrid image." He is eager for the prize, but repelled by what he might have to do to get it.*

He is horrified
at the thought
of killing the
king and hopes
that maybe he
will become
king by
chance,
without
committing
murder.

Against the use of nature? Present fears
Are less than horrible imaginings.
My thought, whose murder yet is but fantastical,
140   Shakes so my single state of man
That function is smothered in surmise,
And nothing is but what is not.
Banquo.   Look how our partner's rapt.
Macbeth. [*Aside*] If chance will have me king, why, chance may crown me
Without my stir.²⁹
Banquo.   New honors come upon him,
145   Like our strange garments, cleave not to their mold
But with the aid of use.
Macbeth. [*Aside*]   Come what come may,
Time and the hour runs through the roughest day.
Banquo. Worthy Macbeth, we stay upon your leisure.
Macbeth. Give me your favor. My dull brain was wrought
150   With things forgotten. Kind gentlemen, your pains
Are registered where every day I turn
The leaf to read them. Let us toward the King.
[*Aside to* Banquo] Think upon what hath chanced, and at more time,
The interim having weighed it, let us speak
155   Our free hearts each to other.
Banquo.   Very gladly.
Macbeth. Till then, enough.—Come, friends.
[*They exit.*]

²⁹**my stir:** my doing anything.

12. **◀ REREAD AND DISCUSS** Reread Scene 3, lines 128–156. In a small
group, discuss the influences of fate and ambition on Macbeth. Cite
evidence from the text in your discussion.

13. **READ ▶** As you read Scene 4, lines 1–58, cite textual evidence.

• In the margin, explain why Malcolm's speech reminds the audience of the
theme of betrayal (lines 2–11).
• Underline the passage that throws doubt on Duncan's judge of character.
• Underline Duncan's announcement in lines 35–39 and circle Macbeth's
reaction in lines 48–53.

84

Scene 4 • *A room in the king's palace at Forres.*

[*Flourish. Enter* King Duncan, Lennox, Malcolm, Donalbain, *and*
Attendants.]
Duncan. Is execution done on Cawdor? Are not
Those in commission yet returned?
Malcolm.   My liege,
They are not yet come back. But I have spoke
With one that saw him die, who did report
5   That very frankly he confessed his treasons,
Implored your Highness' pardon, and set forth
A deep repentance. Nothing in his life
Became him like the leaving it. He died
As one that had been studied in his death
10   To throw away the dearest thing he owed³⁰
As 'twere a careless trifle.
Duncan.   There's no art
To find the mind's construction in the face.
He was a gentleman on whom I built
An absolute trust.
[*Enter* Macbeth, Banquo, Ross, *and* Angus.]
              O worthiest cousin,
15   The sin of my ingratitude even now
Was heavy on me. Thou art so far before
That swiftest wing of recompense is slow
To overtake thee. Would thou hadst less deserved,
That the proportion both of thanks and payment
20   Might have been mine! Only I have left to say,
More is thy due than more than all can pay.
Macbeth. The service and the loyalty I owe
In doing it pays itself. Your Highness' part
Is to receive our duties, and our duties
25   Are to your throne and state children and servants,
Which do but what they should by doing everything
Safe toward your love and honor.

³⁰**owed:** owned.

Malcolm talks
about
Cawdor's
death as
punishment for
the betrayal
of Duncan and
Scotland.

85

---

12. REREAD AND DISCUSS USING TEXT EVIDENCE

Ⓛ ASK STUDENTS to cite evidence of Macbeth being guided
by fate and of Macbeth being guided by his own ambition.
*Macbeth has been pushed by fate: "I am Thane of Cawdor" (line 133).
His willingness to further his position is shown: "why do I yield to that
suggestion . . ." (line 134). He hopes, however, that his ambition might
be fulfilled without his actions (lines 143–144).*

13. READ AND CITE TEXT EVIDENCE

Ⓜ ASK STUDENTS to read Scene 4, lines 1–12, and reread
Scene 2, lines 65–70, where Duncan punishes the former Thane of
Cawdor. What was Cawdor's crime? *He rebelled against his king
and his country, which is treason.*

FOR ELL STUDENTS Explain that the phrase *my liege* is a form of
address to a lord. It is equivalent to "my lord."

Duncan. Welcome hither.
I have begun to plant thee and will labor
To make thee full of growing.—Noble Banquo,
30 That hast no less deserved nor must be known
No less to have done so, let me enfold thee
And hold thee to my heart.
Banquo. There, if I grow,
The harvest is your own.
Duncan. My plenteous joys,
Wanton in fullness, seek to hide themselves
35 In drops of sorrow.—Sons, kinsmen, thanes,
And you whose places are the nearest, know
We will establish our estate[31] upon
Our eldest, Malcolm, whom we name hereafter
The Prince of Cumberland;[32] which honor must
40 Not unaccompanied invest him only,
But signs of nobleness, like stars, shall shine
On all deservers.—From hence to Inverness,[33]
And bind us further to you.
Macbeth. The rest is labor which is not used for you.
45 I'll be myself the **harbinger** and make joyful
The hearing of my wife with your approach.
So humbly take my leave.
Duncan. My worthy Cawdor.
Macbeth. [*Aside*] The Prince of Cumberland! That is a step
On which I must fall down or else o'erleap,
50 For in my way it lies. Stars, hide your fires;
Let not light see my black and deep desires.
The eye wink at the hand, yet let that be
Which the eye fears, when it is done, to see.
[*He exits.*]
Duncan. True, worthy Banquo. He is full so valiant,
55 And in his commendations I am fed:
It is a banquet to me.—Let's after him,
Whose care is gone before to bid us welcome.
It is a peerless kinsman.
[*Flourish. They exit.*]

wanton:
unrestrained

harbinger:
a messenger
sent ahead to
announce
an arrival

[31] **estate:** succession of heirs.
[32] **The Prince of Cumberland:** the title given to the heir of the Scottish throne.
[33] **Inverness:** Macbeth's castle; it was an honor to have the king visit one's home.

86

Scene 5 • *Macbeth's castle at Inverness.*

(O) [*Enter Lady Macbeth, alone, with a letter.*]
Lady Macbeth. [*Reading the letter*] "They met me in the day of success,
and I have learned by the perfect'st report they have more in them than
mortal knowledge. When I burned in desire to question them further,
they made themselves air, into which they vanished. Whiles I stood rapt
5 in the wonder of it came missives from the King, who all-hailed me
'Thane of Cawdor,' by which title, before, these Weïrd Sisters saluted
me and referred me to the coming on of time with 'Hail, king that shalt
be.' This have I thought good to deliver thee, my dearest partner of
greatness, that thou might'st not lose the dues of rejoicing by being
10 ignorant of what greatness is promised thee. Lay it to thy heart, and
(P) farewell."
Glamis thou art, and Cawdor, and shalt be
What thou art promised. Yet do I fear thy nature;
It is too full o' th' milk of human kindness
15 To catch the nearest way. Thou wouldst be great,
Art not without ambition, but without
The illness[34] should attend it. What thou wouldst highly,
That wouldst thou holily;[35] wouldst not play false
And yet wouldst wrongly win. Thou'd'st have, great Glamis,

[34] **illness:** wickedness, ruthlessness.
[35] **holily:** virtuously.

She worries
that he is too
weak to kill
Duncan. She
sees his
ambition, but
says that he
lacks the
ruthlessness
to seize his
"promised"
destiny.

14. ◀ REREAD Reread Scene 4, lines 48–53. What does Macbeth admit in
this aside? Based on these lines, what do you think is Macbeth's tragic
flaw? Cite text evidence in your response.

Macbeth admits that he hopes the king will be murdered. Ruthless
ambition is his tragic flaw. He recognizes his "black and deep
desires" but still hopes Duncan will die so that he can become king.

15. READ ▶ As you read Scene 5, lines 1–51, continue to cite textual
evidence.

- In the margin, sum up Lady Macbeth's misgivings about her husband
  (lines 13–15).
- In the margin, list some adjectives that describe Lady Macbeth's character
  (lines 35–51). Explain what she is asking for in this soliloquy.

87

Critical Vocabulary: wanton (line 34) Ask students to share
their definitions of *wanton*. Ask them what the word conveys
about Duncan's character and approach to people. *He is very
open and trusting.*

Critical Vocabulary: harbinger (line 45) Ask students to share
their definitions of *harbinger*. Ask them why Macbeth might
want to travel home ahead of the king. *He is starting to hatch
plans and wants to prepare.*

14. REREAD AND CITE TEXT EVIDENCE Explain to students that
an aside is spoken aloud by a character but heard only by the
audience.

(N) **ASK STUDENTS** to reread lines 48–53 of Scene 4. In what
way is the naming of the Prince of Cumberland an obstacle? *The
naming of an heir to the throne means that there is one more person
between Macbeth and his goal.*

15. READ AND CITE TEXT EVIDENCE

(O) **ASK STUDENTS** what traits Lady Macbeth seems to value in
a person. What does that outlook say about her? *She values
ambition, and she seems to value ruthlessness to achieve a goal. She
faults Macbeth for not being ruthless enough. This means that she
would probably stop at nothing to get what she wants.*

20   That which cries "Thus thou must do," if thou have it,
      And that which rather thou dost fear to do,
      Than wishest should be undone. Hie thee hither,
      That I may pour my spirits in thine ear
      And chastise with the valor of my tongue
25   All that impedes thee from the golden round
      Which fate and metaphysical aid doth seem
      To have thee crowned withal.
      [*Enter* Messenger.]
                              What is your tidings?
      Messenger. The King comes here tonight.
      Lady Macbeth.   Thou'rt mad to say it!
      Is not thy master with him? who, were't so,
30   Would have informed for preparation.
      Messenger. So please you, it is true. Our Thane is coming.
      One of my fellows had the speed of him,
      Who, almost dead for breath, had scarcely more
      Than would make up his message.
      Lady Macbeth.   Give him tending.
35   He brings great news.
      [Messenger *exits.*]
                              The raven³⁶ himself is hoarse
      That croaks the fatal entrance of Duncan
      Under my battlements. Come, you spirits
      That tend on mortal thoughts, unsex me here,
      And fill me from the crown to the toe top-full
40   Of direst cruelty. Make thick my blood.
      Stop up th' access and passage to remorse,
      That no compunctious visitings of nature³⁷
      Shake my fell purpose, nor keep peace between
      Th' effect and it. Come to my woman's breasts
45   And take my milk for gall,³⁸ you murd'ring ministers,³⁹
      Wherever in your sightless⁴⁰ substances
      You wait on nature's mischief. Come, thick night,
      And pall⁴¹ thee in the dunnest smoke of hell,

      ─────────────────────
      ³⁶**raven:** a bird that often symbolizes evil or misfortune.
      ³⁷**compunctious visitings of nature:** the natural pangs of a guilty conscience.
      ³⁸**gall:** bile, a bitter substance produced by the liver.
      ³⁹**ministers:** agents.
      ⁴⁰**sightless:** invisible.
      ⁴¹**pall:** wrap, cover.

ruthless
ambitious
treacherous
manipulative
deadly

She wants to replace her femininity with the ability to commit murder.

88

That my keen knife see not the wound it makes,
50   Nor heaven peep through the blanket of the dark
      To cry "Hold, hold!"
      [*Enter* Macbeth.]
                        Great Glamis, worthy Cawdor,
   Q Greater than both by the all-hail hereafter!
      Thy letters have transported me beyond
      This ignorant present, and I feel now
55   The future in the instant.
      Macbeth.   My dearest love,
   R Duncan comes here tonight.
      Lady Macbeth.   And when goes hence?
      Macbeth. Tomorrow, as he purposes.
      Lady Macbeth.   O, never
      Shall sun that morrow see!
      Your face, my thane, is as a book where men
60   May read strange matters. To beguile the time,
      Look like the time. Bear welcome in your eye,
      Your hand, your tongue. Look like th' innocent flower,
      But be the serpent under 't. He that's coming
      Must be provided for; and you shall put
65   This night's great business into my dispatch,⁴²
      Which shall to all our nights and days to come
      Give solely sovereign sway and masterdom.
      Macbeth. We will speak further.
      Lady Macbeth.   Only look up clear.
      To alter favor ever is to fear.⁴³
70   Leave all the rest to me.
      [*They exit.*]

      ─────────────────────
      ⁴²**dispatch:** management.
      ⁴³**to alter favor ever is to fear:** to change expression (**favor**) is a sign of fear.

16. ◀ **REREAD AND DISCUSS** Reread Scene 5, lines 11–27, and 35–51. With a small group, discuss the kind of woman revealed in these speeches. How does she feel about her husband? What motivates her plans for the future?

17. **READ** ▶ As you read Scene 5, lines 52–70, continue to cite textual evidence.
    • Underline the words that Lady Macbeth uses to greet her husband. Then, circle the way Macbeth addresses Lady Macbeth when he first sees her.
    • In the margin, explain what their greetings say about their relationship.

She addresses him by his rank, while he uses a term of endearment. She is more ruthless than he is, and maybe he loves her more than she loves him.

89

FOR ELL STUDENTS Encourage students to guess the meaning of the adverb *hither* by looking at context clues around the word.

16. **REREAD AND DISCUSS USING TEXT EVIDENCE**

P **ASK STUDENTS** how long it takes for Lady Macbeth to believe the prophecy about Macbeth's kingship. What is the first thing she says after reading the letter? *She believes the prophecy at once. She says that he "shalt be what thou art promised." She is ready to work toward the goal of kingship.*

17. **READ AND CITE TEXT EVIDENCE**

Q **ASK STUDENTS** to read lines 52–70 of Scene 5. What does Lady Macbeth want her husband to do? *She wants Macbeth to "Look like th' innocent flower, But be the serpent under 't" (lines 62–63) and tells him to "Leave all the rest to me (line 70)." She has already planned the murder of Duncan.*

Scene 6 • In front of Macbeth's castle.

[*Hautboys and Torches. Enter* King Duncan, Malcolm, Donalbain, Banquo, Lennox, Macduff, Ross, Angus, *and Attendants.*]

Duncan. This castle hath a pleasant seat. The air
Nimbly and sweetly recommends itself
Unto our gentle senses.

Banquo.   This guest of summer,
The temple-haunting martlet,[44] does approve,
5   By his loved mansionry, that the heaven's breath
Smells wooingly here. No jutty, frieze,
Buttress, nor coign of vantage, but this bird
Hath made his pendant bed and procreant cradle.
Where they most breed and haunt, I have observed,
10   The air is delicate.
[*Enter* Lady Macbeth.]

Duncan.   See, see, our honored hostess!—
The love that follows us sometime is our trouble,
Which still we thank as love. Herein I teach you
How you shall bid God 'ield[45] us for your pains

It is ironic because it contrasts with the brutal plot being hatched in the castle.

Ⓢ Ⓣ

[44]**martlet:** a house martin—a small bird that often nests on buildings such as churches.
[45]**'ield:** yield (i.e., thank you).

---

18. ◀ **REREAD** Reread Scene 5, lines 56–70. Compare the intensity of ambition displayed by Macbeth and Lady Macbeth. Which one seems more likely to commit to a murderous plan? Support your response with explicit text evidence.

Her ambition seems even greater than his. She seems ready to kill Duncan this very night. He doesn't seem ready to kill the king, because he talks about how Duncan will leave the castle tomorrow.

19. **READ** ▶ As you read Scene 6, lines 1–31, continue to cite textual evidence.

• Underline the positive, benevolent images of nature that Duncan and Banquo use.
• In the margin, explain why this imagery is an example of dramatic irony (lines 1–10).

90

> "The love that follows us sometime is our trouble, Which still we thank as love."

And thank us for your trouble.

Lady Macbeth.   All our service,
15   In every point twice done and then done double,
Were poor and single business to contend
Against those honors deep and broad wherewith
Your Majesty loads our house. For those of old,
And the late dignities heaped up to them,
20   We rest your hermits.[46]

Duncan.   Where's the Thane of Cawdor?
We coursed him at the heels and had a purpose
To be his purveyor; but he rides well,
And his great love (sharp as his spur) hath helped him
To his home before us. Fair and noble hostess,
25   We are your guest tonight.

Lady Macbeth.   Your servants ever
Have theirs, themselves, and what is theirs in compt
To make their audit at your Highness' pleasure,
Still to return your own.

Duncan.   Give me your hand.
[*Taking her hand*]
Conduct me to mine host. We love him highly
30   And shall continue our graces towards him.
By your leave, hostess.
[*They exit.*]

[46]**hermits:** we (as hermits) will pray for you. Hermits were often paid to pray for another's soul.

---

20. ◀ **REREAD** Reread Scene 6, lines 10–31. Compare and contrast the words of King Duncan and those of Lady Macbeth. Support your answer with explicit textual evidence.

While both Duncan and Lady Macbeth sound warm and gracious, only Duncan is sincere. Lady Macbeth may seem polite and humble, but she is really plotting to murder the king.

91

---

18. REREAD AND CITE TEXT EVIDENCE

Ⓡ **ASK STUDENTS** to look back at lines 56–58 of Scene 5. What do these lines show about Macbeth's and Lady Macbeth's intentions at this point? *Macbeth says that Duncan will safely leave Inverness Castle "Tomorrow, as he purposes." Lady Macbeth says "O, never Shall sun that morrow see!" She's ready to end Duncan's life that very night.*

19. READ AND CITE TEXT EVIDENCE
In dramatic irony, the audience knows more than the characters.

Ⓢ **ASK STUDENTS** to explain the irony of Duncan's speech to Lady Macbeth in lines 10–14. *The identity of the speakers adds irony. Duncan is likely walking into a death trap in this castle, yet he is graciously thanking Lady Macbeth for her hospitality.*

20. REREAD AND CITE TEXT EVIDENCE

Ⓣ **ASK STUDENTS** to reread lines 10–31 of Scene 6. What does the audience already know of Duncan? What has Shakespeare already shown us about Lady Macbeth? *In every appearance so far, Duncan has been straightforward and fair. He has punished a wrongdoer, the traitor, and has rewarded those who have helped him, including Macbeth himself. Lady Macbeth has shown herself to be ambitious and ruthless.*

Scene 7 • *A room in Macbeth's castle.*

[*Hautboys. Torches. Enter a Sewer, and divers Servants*[47] *with dishes and service over the stage. Then enter Macbeth.*]

Macbeth. If it were done when 'tis done, then 'twere well
It were done quickly. If th' assassination
Could trammel up the consequence and catch
With his surcease[48] success, that but this blow
5 Might be the be-all and the end-all here,
But here, upon this bank and shoal of time,
We'd jump the life to come. But in these cases
We still have judgment here, that we but teach
Bloody instructions, which, being taught, return
10 To plague th' inventor. This even-handed justice
Commends th' ingredience of our poisoned chalice
To our own lips. He's here in double trust:
First, as I am his kinsman and his subject,
Strong both against the deed; then, as his host,
15 Who should against his murderer shut the door,
Not bear the knife myself. Besides, this Duncan
Hath borne his faculties so meek, hath been
So clear in his great office, that his virtues
Will plead like angels, trumpet-tongued, against
20 The deep damnation of his taking-off;
And pity, like a naked newborn babe,
Striding the blast, or heaven's cherubin horsed
Upon the sightless couriers of the air,
Shall blow the horrid deed in every eye,

---

[47] **Hautboys . . . a Sewar, and divers Servants:** oboes (**hautboys**) . . . a steward, or servant responsible for arranging the banquet (**sewer**), and various (**divers**) servants.
[48] **surcease:** completion.

21. **READ ▶** As you read Scene 7, lines 1–45, continue to cite textual evidence.
• Underline Macbeth's reasons for not harming Duncan.
• In the margin, sum up the conversation between Macbeth and Lady Macbeth (lines 31–45).

92

> " If it were done
> when 'tis done,
> then 'twere well
> It were done quickly. "

25 That tears shall drown the wind. I have no spur
To prick the sides of my intent, but only
Vaulting ambition, which o'erleaps itself
And falls on th' other—
[*Enter Lady Macbeth.*]
                                    How now? What news?
Lady Macbeth. He has almost supped.
Why have you left the chamber?
30 **Macbeth.** Hath he asked for me?
Lady Macbeth.   Know you not he has?
Macbeth. We will proceed no further in this business.
He hath honored me of late, and I have bought
Golden opinions from all sorts of people,
Which would be worn now in their newest gloss,
35 Not cast aside so soon.
Lady Macbeth.   Was the hope[49] drunk
Wherein you dressed yourself? Hath it slept since?
And wakes it now, to look so green and pale
At what it did so freely? From this time
Such I account thy love. Art thou afeard
40 To be the same in thine own act and valor
As thou art in desire? Wouldst thou have that
Which thou esteem'st the ornament of life

---

[49] **hope:** ambition.

Macbeth wants to stop all plans of murder. He cites the honor Duncan and others have shown him. Lady Macbeth is sarcastic, mocking, and critical and calls him a coward.

22. **◀ REREAD** Reread Scene 7, lines 12–28 and lines 31–35. What does Macbeth's reasoning show about his state of mind? Cite explicit text evidence in your response.

He is thinking clearly at this point because he knows that there is no justification for killing Duncan. He cannot kill the king simply to satisfy his own "vaulting ambition."

93

---

21. **READ AND CITE TEXT EVIDENCE**

Ⓤ ASK STUDENTS to recall what they already know about Macbeth in battle. Then, ask them how Lady Macbeth contradicts what they read about Macbeth in lines 36–45. *Lady Macbeth tries to goad him by calling him a coward. This statement is disproved by the fact that he was extremely brave in battle.*

22. **REREAD AND CITE TEXT EVIDENCE** In many societies, hospitality—the obligation of a host to a guest, and vice versa—is a duty and sometimes even a law of the culture. The host is obligated not just to feed a guest generously but also to protect the guest. To violate hospitality is to dishonor oneself and is an especially shameful act of betrayal.

Ⓥ ASK STUDENTS to reread Scene 7, lines 1–28. What does Macbeth realize at this moment about his motive for killing Duncan? What does he realize about his obligations to Duncan? *Macbeth sees that all he has to spur himself on is "vaulting ambition." He knows that Duncan is at Inverness on "double trust," meaning (1) that Macbeth is Duncan's "kinsman and his subject" and (2) that Macbeth, as Duncan's host, "should against his murderer shut the door, not bear the knife myself."*

And live a coward in thine own esteem,
Letting "I dare not" wait upon "I would,"
45 Like the poor cat i' th' adage?[50]

Macbeth.   Prithee, peace.
I dare do all that may become a man.
Who dares do more is none.

Lady Macbeth.   What beast was't, then,
That made you break this enterprise to me?
When you durst[51] do it, then you were a man;
50 And to be more than what you were, you would
Be so much more the man. Nor time nor place
Did then adhere,[52] and yet you would make both.
They have made themselves, and that their fitness now
Does unmake you. I have given suck, and know
55 How tender 'tis to love the babe that milks me.
I would, while it was smiling in my face,
Have plucked my nipple from his boneless gums
And dashed the brains out, had I so sworn as you
Have done to this.

Macbeth.   If we should fail—

Lady Macbeth.   We fail?
60 But screw your courage to the sticking place
Ⓦ And we'll not fail. When Duncan is asleep
(Whereto the rather shall his day's hard journey
Soundly invite him), his two chamberlains
Will I with wine and wassail so convince
65 That memory, the warder of the brain,

---

[50] **poor cat i' th' adage:** a cat in a proverb (**adage**) that wouldn't catch fish because it feared wet feet.
[51] **durst:** dared.
[52] **adhere:** agree.

---

23. **READ** ▶ As you read lines 46–82, continue to cite text evidence.

• In the margin, summarize what Lady Macbeth says to urge Macbeth to act (lines 47–59).

• In the margin, explain how Lady Macbeth plans to accomplish the deed and avoid suspicion (lines 59–73).

• In the margin, make an inference about the way Macbeth feels about his wife (lines 72–77).

94

Shall be a fume, and the receipt of reason
A limbeck[53] only. When in swinish sleep
Their drenchèd natures lie as in a death,
What cannot you and I perform upon
70 Th' unguarded Duncan? What not put upon
His spongy officers, who shall bear the guilt
Of our great quell?

Macbeth.   Bring forth men-children only,
For thy undaunted mettle[54] should compose
Nothing but males. Will it not be received,
75 When we have marked with blood those sleepy two
Of his own chamber and used their very daggers,
That they have done 't?

Lady Macbeth.   Who dares receive it other,
As we shall make our griefs and clamor roar
Upon his death?

Macbeth.   I am settled and bend up
80 Each corporal agent to this terrible feat.
Away, and mock the time with fairest show.
False face must hide what the false heart doth know.
[*They exit.*]

---

[53] **limbeck:** a still for making liquor.
[54] **mettle:** spirit.

95

She attacks Macbeth's manliness, and says that she herself would kill her own child if she broke her promise to Macbeth.

Lady Macbeth wants to get the king's attendants drunk so they can't defend the king. She will make sure the attendants are blamed.

He seems to admire her. He says that her bold spirit is best suited for raising males.

---

23. **READ AND CITE TEXT EVIDENCE**

Ⓦ **ASK STUDENTS** to read lines 61–72 of Scene 7. What does Lady Macbeth's plan show about her character? *Students should understand that by being ready to kill the king after Macbeth's hesitation, she shows her boldness. Her plan to get the chamberlains drunk shows that she is crafty. Her willingness to frame Duncan's servants for the murder shows that she doesn't care how many people are hurt as long as she can reach her goals. The fact that she will violate the tradition of hospitality (as outlined by Macbeth in lines 14–16) shows that she is capable of betraying any moral standard and probably has no boundaries.*

FOR ELL STUDENTS Explain that the accent on the second *e* in *drenchéd* makes the second syllable voiced, so it is a two-syllable word and fits the meter. In modern English, the word has one syllable.

24. **◀ REREAD** Reread lines 46–82. How would you characterize Lady
Macbeth's way of arguing? How effective is she in getting what she
wants? Cite explicit text evidence in your response.

Lady Macbeth argues emotionally, practically bullying Macbeth into
complying with her plan to murder Duncan. She accuses Macbeth of
being a coward and makes a wild claim that she would murder her
own baby. In the end, Macbeth agrees with her plan and says, "I am
settled."

SHORT RESPONSE

Cite Text Evidence What forces and influences, external and internal, drive
Macbeth toward his final decision at the end of Scene 7? In what ways does he try
to withstand the urge to act against Duncan? **Cite text evidence** in your response.

Macbeth responds to both external and internal influences. The first
external influence is the prophecy of the witches. When Macbeth
learns that the witches were right about his becoming Thane of
Cawdor, he realizes that their prophecy about his kingship might also
come true. The other main external influence on his actions is the
ruthless ambition of his wife. Lady Macbeth doesn't hesitate at all to
plan for Duncan's immediate murder. She intimidates Macbeth into
taking action. Macbeth's internal force is his own powerful ambition.
He tries to resist the urge to act on his ambition by considering his
obligations to Duncan as his host, his kinsman, and his subject, and
also because of Duncan's virtue as a king and a man who shows
generosity toward him, but in the end Macbeth submits to his
overwhelming ambition, his tragic flaw.

96

---

24. REREAD AND CITE TEXT EVIDENCE

Ⓧ ASK STUDENTS to reread lines 30–45—in which the basis
of the argument is established—in order to more completely
understand how Lady Macbeth turns the argument. What
argument does each of the two people make? *Macbeth argues*
that the king "hath honored me of late," and he'd rather not cast
aside this praise just yet. Lady Macbeth tries to shame Macbeth. She
asks if he's afraid to act in a way that reflects his ambition to be king.

SHORT RESPONSE

Cite Text Evidence Students' responses should include text
evidence that supports their positions. They should:

- identify the influences that propel Macbeth to action.
- analyze Macbeth's efforts to reason why he should spare
  Duncan's life.
- name the action Macbeth decides to take at the end of Scene 7.

TO CHALLENGE STUDENTS . . .

Shakespeare wrote many plays about rulers and power. *Macbeth,*
Hamlet, and *King Lear* are classified among his tragedies, along
with *Julius Caesar,* about the ruler of Rome. He also wrote many
plays about English kings, which are traditionally grouped
together as his histories. Some examples of his history plays are
Richard II, Richard III, and *Henry V.*

ASK STUDENTS to research one play mentioned above (except
Macbeth) by reading a synopsis of the play to see what happens
to the title character. Have students write one or two paragraphs
from their research telling about what changes the most
important characters go through and how those changes affect
the country over which the title character rules. Have students
compare their findings with those of other students.

DIG DEEPER

With the class, return to Question 12, the Reread and Discuss
question on page 84. Have students share their responses.

ASK STUDENTS to cite text evidence leading to their
conclusions about the role played by fate versus that played by
Macbeth's own ambition on his behavior and actions.

- Have students reread all of Scene 1 and Scene 3, lines
  1–78. Ask why Shakespeare chose to feature the witches
  so extensively instead of just having them announce
  the prophecy. *He might want to show that they and their*
  prophecy—and therefore, the importance of fate—are
  important to the story.

- Have students reread lines 116–144. How does Macbeth react
  to the news that one of the witches' prophecies has already
  come true? *He immediately thinks about himself on the throne*
  ("The greatest is behind"). He starts imagining what it might take
  to bring about his becoming king (lines 134–142).

ASK STUDENTS to continue their discussion and re-examine
their views now that they have read later scenes.

MEDIA *from* **Macbeth on the Estate**

Film directed by Penny Woolcock

Why This Text?

Students regularly view different interpretations of classics through films, videos on the Internet, and television. This lesson explores the choices a director made when interpreting Shakespeare's *Macbeth*.

Key Learning Objective: The student will be able to analyze representations of a scene.

COMMON CORE Common Core Standards

RL 2 Determine a theme and analyze its development.

RL 7 Analyze a subject or a key scene in two different artistic mediums.

SL 4 Present information clearly so that the development and style are appropriate to purpose, audience, and task.

SL 5 Make strategic use of digital media to enhance understanding of findings, reasoning, and evidence in presentations.

▲ Text Complexity Rubric

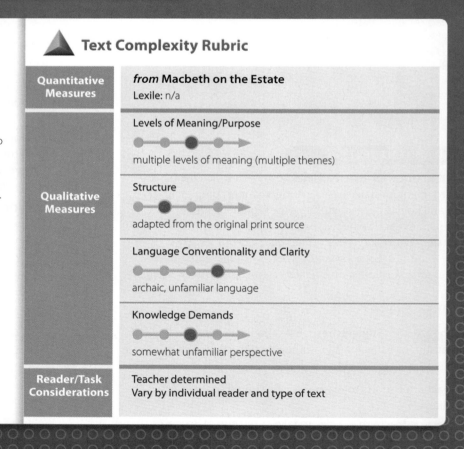

Quantitative Measures	*from* **Macbeth on the Estate** Lexile: n/a
Qualitative Measures	**Levels of Meaning/Purpose** multiple levels of meaning (multiple themes)
	Structure adapted from the original print source
	Language Conventionality and Clarity archaic, unfamiliar language
	Knowledge Demands somewhat unfamiliar perspective
Reader/Task Considerations	Teacher determined Vary by individual reader and type of text

CLOSE READ

Background Have students read the background and information about the director. Tell students that Penny Woolcock is an award-winning filmmaker, director, and screenwriter. Her interpretation of *Macbeth* includes portraying Macbeth and the other lords as rivals whose battles take place in an inner-city setting. Woolcock knew many would criticize and be shocked by her representation, but she wanted to create a version of *Macbeth* that was accessible to modern audiences.

AS YOU VIEW Direct students to use the As You View activity to focus their viewing. Have them write down any questions they have during viewing.

Analyze Representations

 RL 7, SL 5

Explain that when adapting a literary work to film, directors make choices about what to include and what to emphasize. Tell students that this clip is from Act V, Scene 5. Point out which actor is Macbeth and which is Seyton.

ASK STUDENTS to view the first 50 seconds of the film clip several times and compare it with the original play. Ask what part of Seyton's dialogue is not included in the video and why Woolcock made this decision. *(Woolcock left out "is dead." This creates suspense while Macbeth runs to find out what has happened.)*

ASK STUDENTS what is emphasized in the scene and to explain the effect this has on the audience. *(Lady Macbeth's death is emphasized by showing her body, creating sympathy for her. It also creates sympathy for Macbeth because we see his reaction to her death.)*

COLLABORATIVE DISCUSSION Have students work in small groups to discuss how the modern setting and specific images affect the mood of the production.

ASK STUDENTS to share any questions they generated while viewing and discussing the clip.

Background *In 1997, the BBC (British Broadcasting Corporation) produced a new version of Shakespeare's Scottish play—Macbeth on the Estate. Award-winning director Penny Woolcock reset the play as a modern crime drama and filmed it in the Ladywood Estate, a low-income housing development in Birmingham, England. Action was set in the estate's apartments, courtyards, and roofs, but the production retained Shakespeare's powerful language. Residents from the estate worked on the film and participated as actors. Reviews were polarized, with some critics preferring a more traditional approach and others embracing this affirmation of Shakespeare's universality.*

MEDIA ANALYSIS

from
Macbeth on the Estate

Film directed by Penny Woolcock

AS YOU VIEW Consider how the modern setting creates a certain mood or tone. Write down any questions you have during viewing.

Image Credits: (t) ©MJ Kim/Getty Images; (c) (b) ©BBC Motion Gallery

COLLABORATIVE DISCUSSION In a small group, discuss how the modern setting adds to the mood of the production. What atmosphere, or feeling, is conveyed? Cite specific images to support your ideas.

SCAFFOLDING FOR ELL STUDENTS

Analyze Representations Have partners or small groups of mixed proficiencies reread the beginning of Act V and discuss or draw the way they visualized the setting and characters of Macbeth. Then have partners view the film clip several times, making notes about how the setting and characters are different from what they imagined.

ASK STUDENTS which representation they feel is more effective and why.

Analyze Representations COMMON CORE RL 7

Help students understand the meaning of the terms. Point out that the choices a director makes about setting and sets, film shots and angles, and actors can drastically change a production. Have students cite examples of how each of these aspects affected how the scene from Shakespeare's *Macbeth* was represented in this particular film.

Analyzing the Media COMMON CORE RL 2, RL 7

Possible answers:

1. *The scene is staged on the sidewalk at a public housing building that is grim and cold and shabby. The people are unemotional, even as they stare at Lady Macbeth's body. These aspects set a bleak tone of the scene.*

2. *Omitted from the scene are: lines 1–6 and half of line 7; through half of line 8 through half of line 12; "is dead" from line 16; lines 29 through half of line 44; and half of line 45 through line 48. The omission of these lines speeds the pace, which increases tension. By leaving out lines 29–43, we don't see Macbeth threatening the messenger who comes to tell him about the moving grove. These lines would not make sense based on the city scene. The omission also makes him seem less angry and more regretful.*

3. *The actor's pauses in the speech from lines 18–28 emphasize Macbeth's sorrow and regret for what has happened to his wife. The actor's expression when saying lines 51–52 make it easier to see how, while he is saddened by what has happened, he is determined to meet what comes next as best he can.*

Analyze Representations COMMON CORE RL 7

The "Tomorrow and tomorrow and tomorrow" speech—Macbeth's reaction to Lady Macbeth's death amid his preparations for war—is one of Shakespeare's most famous scenes. Every actor or director attempting this scene brings a unique approach to it, comprising a personal reading of Shakespeare's words and a particular message or feeling he or she wants to communicate through the speech. Consider what this production emphasizes in the scene as well as what it omits from the original play. In addition, think about how the director uses the medium of film in concert with Shakespeare's words.

- **Setting/Sets:** How do background noise, buildings, and other features of the location affect the tone and theme of the scene?
- **Film shots and angles:** What is the effect of multiple shots of the bystanders from various angles?
- **Actors:** Why might the director have chosen to surround Lady Macbeth's body with bystanders when the play did not?

Analyzing the Media COMMON CORE RL 7, RL 2, SL 4

Cite Text Evidence   Support your responses with evidence from the selection.

1. **Analyze** How do the choices made by the director of *Macbeth on the Estate* help convey tone? Cite specific images and staging to support your answer.

2. **Compare** Which passages of Shakespeare's original text are omitted from this production of the scene? Explain how leaving out these lines affects the pacing and theme of the scene.

3. **Evaluate** How do the actors' use of emphasis and expression add meaning to this scene and help clarify your understanding? Cite specific lines.

PERFORMANCE TASK

Speaking Activity: Argument How effective was this modern resetting of *Macbeth* in expressing key theme of Shakespeare's play? Discuss your thesis in a short speech.

- Review the clip, making notes of themes that emerge through the modern setting. Cite specific details from the film in your notes.
- Compare those themes to major themes of the play.

- Draft a statement expressing your overall evaluation of the modern production's effectiveness.
- Present your evaluation in a short speech in which you support your claim with specific, relevant evidence from both the film and the play.

Assign this performance task.

PERFORMANCE TASK COMMON CORE SL 4

Speaking Activity: Argument Explain to students that their speeches should include a precise claim about whether the theme in the film clip is different from the themes of the play. Remind them to include specific, relevant examples from both the clip and the play to support their claims.

Use Media in Presentations

TEACH

Tell students they can make use of digital media to enhance their presentations. Explain that when using digital media, they need to think about the purpose of their presentation and which element—or elements—would be most effective toward that purpose. Deciding when and how to include digital media in a presentation is an important part of the planning process. Students can use media they create—for example, digital photographs, posters or pictures they make and then digitize, recordings of sounds or music, or videos—or they can search online for existing material. Explain that if they use material created by someone else they must credit the original source.

Before having students make their presentations for the Performance Task, discuss different types of digital media and how they could be incorporated into their presentations. Then have them consider the following questions:

- **Textual** (for a slide presentation or PowerPoint presentation) Which font might best convey the mood or theme of *Macbeth* or the film? How large should the font be so the audience can read the slides?

- **Audio** Would a short clip of the audio from the film help prove a point?

- **Visual** Could a photograph or still from the film clip enhance your evaluation?

PRACTICE AND APPLY

Have students work in groups to discuss which types of media they could use to enhance their speeches for the Performance Task, and what the final product might look like. Then have them develop a basic plan for their projects. Allow students time to find or create the media they will incorporate.

Analyze Representations

RETEACH

Review the choices a director makes when staging a production of an original work. Point out that how closely a director stays to the original source can make subtle or drastic changes to the mood and tone of a presentation.

Have students examine Scene 5 for stage directions. Ask them to explain how Shakespeare's stage directions determine the choices that directors might make. *(Possible answer: The lack of detailed stage direction allows directors to set their adaptations in a different time period, country, or culture.)* Ask students to explain why a director might want to make drastic changes to an original source. *(Possible answer: Changing certain aspects of the original allows the director to get across a particular point.)*

 LEVEL UP TUTORIALS Assign the following *Level Up* tutorial: **Methods of Characterization**

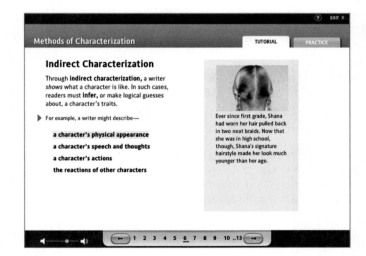

CLOSE READING APPLICATION

Students can apply the skill to media representation of a familiar piece of literature. Ask them to select a scene in the video adaptation and note in detail how it differs from the original in choices made by the director in setting and staging and choices made by an actor in characterization.

from Holinshed's Chronicles

History by Raphael Holinshed

Why This Text?

Students regularly read both literature and informational texts, but they don't often have the opportunity to see how an author draws from informational text to create the plot, theme, and characters of a fictional work. This lesson explores Shakespeare's likely source of many elements in *Macbeth*.

View It!

Professional Development Podcast:

Text-Dependent Analysis

Key Learning Objective: The student will analyze historical text.

Common Core Standards

RL 6 Analyze a particular cultural experience.

RL 9 Analyze how an author draws on source material.

RI 1 Cite textual evidence.

RI 2 Determine a central idea and analyze its development.

RI 3 Analyze how the author unfolds ideas or events.

RI 4 Determine the meaning of words and phrases.

RI 5 Analyze how an author's ideas are developed by particular sentences or paragraphs.

RI 6 Determine an author's point of view and analyze how an author uses rhetoric.

RI 9 Analyze seminal documents of historical and literary significance.

SL 1 Participate in collaborative discussions.

SL 4 Present information clearly.

L 1b Use various types of phrases.

L 3 Apply language to make choices for style, and to comprehend more fully.

L 4 Determine the meaning of unknown and multiple-meaning words.

Text Complexity Rubric

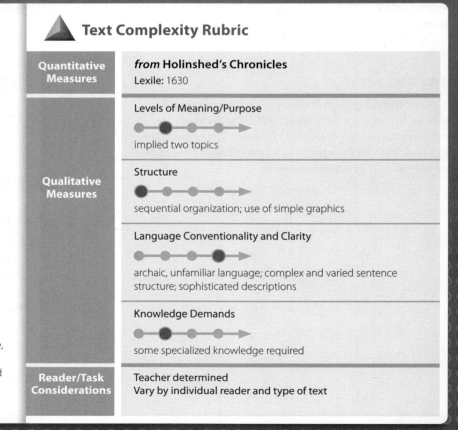

Quantitative Measures

Qualitative Measures

Reader/Task Considerations

	from Holinshed's Chronicles
	Lexile: 1630

Levels of Meaning/Purpose

implied two topics

Structure

sequential organization; use of simple graphics

Language Conventionality and Clarity

archaic, unfamiliar language; complex and varied sentence structure; sophisticated descriptions

Knowledge Demands

some specialized knowledge required

Reader/Task Considerations

Teacher determined
Vary by individual reader and type of text

Background *Holinshed's Chronicles* is an extensive compilation of historical writings about England, Scotland, and Ireland. The main contributors were men of varying origins and upbringings that influenced their political and religious views. Thus, their interpretations of British history may not be the most accurate or the most reliable. Regardless of the trustworthiness of the writings, the *Chronicles* became a valuable source of historical and political details—as well as inspiration—for authors of Elizabethan literature such as William Shakespeare, Edmund Spenser, Samuel Daniel, and Michael Drayton.

AS YOU READ Direct students to the As You Read note to focus their reading. Encourage them to generate questions about unfamiliar words or text content as they read.

Archaic Language (LINES 1–9)   COMMON CORE RI 1, L 1b, L 3

Point out that the first sentence is long and contains archaic language, which makes it difficult to understand. Explain that identifying the three participial phrases and their purposes in the sentence may help improve comprehension.

A **ASK STUDENTS** to identify the three participial phrases and explain their purpose in the sentence. *(In lines 3–4, "passing through the woods and fields" describes the land where Macbeth and Banquo were traveling; in lines 5–6, "resembling creatures of elder world" describes the three women's appearance; and in line 7, "wondering much at the sight" describes the men's reaction to what they were seeing. Each of the phrases adds descriptive details.)*

Analyze Source Material   COMMON CORE RL 9, RI 1
(LINES 1–11)

Explain to students that this excerpt from the *Chronicles* was likely the major source that Shakespeare referred to when he was writing *Macbeth*.

B **CITE TEXT EVIDENCE** Have students identify historical details in the first paragraph that Shakespeare probably drew on when developing the plot and characters in Macbeth. *("Macbeth and Banquo journeyed toward Forres" [line 1]; "in midst of a laund" [line 4]; "three women in strange and wild apparel" [line 5]; "All hail, Macbeth, Thane of Glamis!" [lines 7–8]; Macbeth's father, "Sinel" [line 9]; "Hail, Macbeth, Thane of Cawdor!" [line 10]; "All hail, Macbeth, that hereafter shalt be King of Scotland!" [line 11])*

Background *For many of his historical plays such as Macbeth, Shakespeare relied on the* Chronicles, *first published in 1577, as his main source. Raphael Holinshed is credited as the* Chronicles' *sole author, but many other writers contributed to this work. Although Shakespeare's Macbeth resembles the "historical" Macbeth in the* Chronicles, *most scholars do not consider the* Chronicles *to be a reliable document. In fact, the "real" Macbeth (c. 1005–1057) was a Scottish king whom those same scholars consider a just ruler, not a tragic hero.*

from
Holinshed's Chronicles

History by Raphael Holinshed

AS YOU READ Pay attention to the details on which Shakespeare drew to create his tragic hero. Write down any questions you generate during reading.

Duncan's Murder

 It fortuned, as Macbeth and Banquo journeyed toward Forres, where the King then lay, they went sporting by the way together without other company save only themselves, passing through the woods and fields, when suddenly, in midst of a laund,[1] there met them three women in strange and wild apparel, resembling creatures of elder world; whom when they attentively beheld, wondering much at the sight, the first of them spoke and said, "All hail, Macbeth, Thane of Glamis!" (for he had lately entered into that dignity and office by the death of his father Sinel). The second of
10 them said, "Hail, Macbeth, Thane of Cawdor!" But the third said, "All hail, Macbeth, that hereafter shalt be King of Scotland!"

    Then Banquo. "What manner of women," saith he, "are you, that seem so little favorable unto me, whereas to my fellow here, besides high offices, ye assign also the kingdom, appointing forth

Image Credits: Richard Phipps/Illustration Ltd.

---

[1] **laund:** a clearing in the forest.

SCAFFOLDING FOR ELL STUDENTS

Language Project lines 1–11. Invite students to draw vertical lines to separate a lengthy sentence into parts and highlight in green words they don't understand. Then students can use context clues, footnotes, and a dictionary to determine the meanings.

It fortuned, as Macbeth and Banquo journeyed toward Forres, where the King then lay,|they went sporting by the way together without other company save only themselves, passing through the woods and fields,|when suddenly, in the midst of a laund,

Analyze Source Material (LINES 15–20)

COMMON CORE RL 9, RI 1, RI 2, RI 5

Shakespeare drew many details from the Chronicles, but he changed some of them slightly, omitted others, and introduced some at different points in the play rather than all at once.

Ⓒ **CITE TEXT EVIDENCE** Have students identify three details in lines 15–20 of the Chronicles that Shakespeare changed, omitted, or moved to a later scene in the play. *(In line 17, "but with an unlucky end" is worded in a riddle and appears later in Act IV, Scene 1 of the play; in line 17, "neither shall he leave any issue behind" does not appear in the play; in lines 19–20, "of thee those shall be born which shall govern the Scottish kingdom by long order of continual descent" is enhanced with new details of "eight" kings that resemble Banquo that appear later in Act IV, Scene 1 of the play.)*

Lines 30–33 contain a major fact that differs greatly from Shakespeare's version of events.

Ⓓ **ASK STUDENTS** to identify the difference between Shakespeare's version of events and the Chronicles in the second paragraph. *(In the Chronicles, Macbeth talked with friends about how he might lay claim to the throne upon Duncan's death. [lines 30–33] In Shakespeare's play, the only person Macbeth confides in is his wife.)*

CRITICAL VOCABULARY

usurp: According to the Chronicles, Macbeth was worried that his ascension to the throne would be blocked.

ASK STUDENTS why Macbeth thought he might have to usurp the kingdom by force. *(Lines 25–29 reveal that King Duncan had named his son Malcolm to succeed him to the throne upon his death.)*

Ⓒ nothing for me at all?" "Yes," saith the first of them, "we promise greater benefits unto thee than unto him, for he shall reign indeed, but with an unlucky end; neither shall he leave any issue behind him to succeed in his place, where contrarily thou indeed shalt not reign at all, but of thee those shall be born which shall govern the
20 Scottish kingdom by long order of continual descent." Herewith the foresaid women vanished immediately out of their sight. . . . Shortly after, the Thane of Cawdor being condemned at Forres of treason against the King committed, his lands, livings, and offices were given of the King's liberality to Macbeth. . . .

Ⓓ Shortly after it chanced that King Duncan, having two sons by his wife (which was the daughter of Siward Earl of Northumberland), he made the elder of them (called Malcolm) Prince of Cumberland, as it were thereby to appoint him his successor in the kingdom immediately after his decease. Macbeth,
30 sore troubled herewith, for that he saw by this means his hope sore hindered . . . he began to take counsel how he might **usurp** the kingdom by force, having a just quarrel[2] so to do (as he took the matter), for that Duncan did what in him lay to defraud him of all manner of title and claim which he might, in time to come, pretend[3] unto the crown.

The words of the three Weird Sisters also (of whom before ye have heard) greatly encouraged him hereunto; but specially his wife lay sore upon him to attempt the thing, as she that was very ambitious, burning in unquenchable desire to bear the name of a

usurp
(yo͞o-sûrp´) *v.* to take control of illegally.

---

[2] **quarrel:** reason or cause.
[3] **pretend:** lay claim.

WHEN STUDENTS STRUGGLE . . .

Explain that the image is a woodcut illustration that appears in *Holinshed's Chronicles.*

ASK STUDENTS to compare details in the image with details in lines 1–11 of the Chronicles. In what ways does the image clarify the text? *(Showing the men riding horses clarifies the meaning of "sporting" in line 2.)* Which details in the image are not what you envisioned after reading the text? *(Answers will vary.)* How does Shakespeare's play differ from the details in the image or text lines 1–11? *(Shakespeare adds description and slightly more dialogue. He does not describe the men's clothing or mode of transportation; in addition, Banquo provides more details about the witches, saying they are "withered," "wild in their attire," have "choppy finger," "skinny lips," and "beards." The witches' dialogue has the same meaning but added phrases for dramatic effect.)*

40 queen. At length, therefore, communicating his purposed intent
with his trusty friends, amongst whom Banquo was the chiefest,
upon confidence of their promised aid he slew the King at Inverness
or (as some say) at Bothgowanan, in the sixth year of his reign.

Banquo's Murder

This was but a counterfeit zeal of equity[4] showed by him, partly
against his natural inclination, to purchase thereby the favor of
the people. Shortly after, he began to show what he was, instead of
equity practicing cruelty. For the prick of conscience (as it chanceth
ever in tyrants and such as attain to any estate by unrighteous
means) caused him ever to fear lest he should be served of the same
50 cup as he had ministered to his **predecessor**. The words also of
the three Weird Sisters would not out of his mind, which as they
promised him the kingdom, so likewise did they promise it at the
same time unto the posterity of Banquo. He willed therefore the
same Banquo, with his son named Fleance, to come to a supper that
he had prepared for them; which was indeed, as he had devised,
present death at the hands of certain murderers whom he hired
to execute that deed, appointing them to meet with the same
Banquo and his son without the palace, as they returned to their
lodgings, and there to slay them, so that he would not have his
60 house slandered but that in time to come he might clear himself
if anything were laid to his charge upon any suspicion that might
arise.
    It chanced by the benefit of the dark night that, though the
father were slain, yet the son, by the help of almighty God reserving
him to better fortune, escaped that danger; and afterward, having
some inkling (by the **admonition** of some friends which he had
in the court) how his life was sought no less than his father's, who
was slain not by chance-medley[5] (as by the handling of the matter
Macbeth would have had it to appear) but even upon a prepensed[6]
70 device, whereupon to avoid further peril he fled into Wales.

predecessor
(prĕd´ĭ-sĕs´ər) *n.* the
person who held a
position prior to the
current holder.

admonition
(ăd´mə-nĭsh´ən) *n.* a
warning.

COLLABORATIVE DISCUSSION In a small group, discuss similarities and
differences between this excerpt from the *Chronicles* and Shakespeare's
Macbeth. Support your ideas with evidence from both texts.

---

[4] **counterfeit zeal of equity:** a false show of fairness.
[5] **chance-medley:** accident.
[6] **prepensed:** intentional.

TO CHALLENGE STUDENTS . . .

Analyze Source Material Students may be interested in learning how the
historical Macbeth actually had a claim to the throne.

ASK STUDENTS to search the Internet or the FYI Website to gather details
about the system of succession in Scotland in the eleventh century and to
find out how Macbeth had a legitimate claim to the throne. Suggest that
students investigate details about Duncan I, Macbeth, and Malcolm III. Have
students share their findings in small groups. *(According to the Celtic system
of succession, any male could be a successor if his father, grandfather, or great-
grandfather had been king. Macbeth was probably a grandson of King Kenneth
II. Macbeth's wife was a Gruoch, a descendant of King Kenneth III.)*

CLOSE READ

Analyze Source Material
COMMON CORE   RL 9, RI 1, RI 2, RI 4, RI 5
(LINES 40–44)

Draw students' attention to the top of the page.
Explain that one major difference between
Holinshed's details and Shakespeare's details appears
in lines 40–44.

E **CITE TEXT EVIDENCE** According to the
Chronicles, what action did Macbeth take? *(Macbeth
shared his plan to murder Duncan with several close
friends, including Banquo, who promised to help him.
Macbeth then murdered the king.)* Where was the king
killed? *(Lines 43–44 reveal that he was killed either at
Inverness or Bothgowanan.)* How do these details
differ in Shakespeare's play? *(Macbeth confides only in
his wife; Bothgowanan is never mentioned as the place
where Duncan was killed.)*

> **CRITICAL VOCABULARY**
>
> **predecessor**: Lines 47–50 of the Chronicles gives
> a reason why Macbeth decided to kill Banquo.
> **ASK STUDENTS** who Macbeth's predecessor was
> and why this detail was a factor in his decision.
> *(Macbeth's predecessor was King Duncan. Macbeth
> was afraid that Banquo would try to kill him because
> he himself had killed King Duncan.)*
>
> **admonition**: The text says that Banquo's
> son Fleance escaped by fleeing to Wales.
> **ASK STUDENTS** what admonition caused Fleance's
> action. *(Lines 66–68 state that Fleance's friends
> warned him his life was in jeopardy because his
> father's death was not an accident, despite what
> Macbeth wanted people to believe.)*

COLLABORATIVE DISCUSSION Have students
prepare for the group discussion by organizing the
similarities and differences in the two selections in the
Interactive Graphic Organizer: Comparison-Contrast
Chart. Then have students discuss their findings in small
groups.

ASK STUDENTS to share any questions they
generated in the course of reading and discussing the
selection.

PRACTICE & APPLY

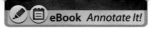
Analyze Source Material

 RL 9, RI 1

After students have read the first paragraph, ask them to identify the steps to take when reading a historical text. ([1] *Read slowly to be sure you understand. [2] Read the footnote definitions. [3] Paraphrase sentences. [4] Evaluate the historical significance of the text.*)

Analyzing the Text

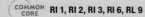 **RI 1, RI 2, RI 3, RI 6, RL 9**

Possible answers:

1. *Yes, the direct quotations of the women and Banquo support the author's purpose of providing details of the event and make the history interesting to read. OR No, the source of the direct quotations is not cited, so it is possible the quotations were fabricated to make the event more interesting to read.*

2. *King Duncan: In both texts, Macbeth's motivations came from his feeling that Duncan had wronged him by appointing his son Malcolm Prince of Cumberland and successor to the throne and the Weird Sisters' predictions. In the Chronicles, Macbeth's wife wanted to be queen, but she was not her husband's accomplice. In Shakespeare's play, Macbeth's wife was his accomplice in Duncan's murder, and Macbeth also was motivated by his unchecked ambition for power. Banquo: In both texts, Macbeth's motivation was to eliminate Banquo and his son Fleance so they would be unable to father future generations of kings of Scotland (lines 39–41). Students may say Shakespeare is more successful in conveying Macbeth's motivations because his characterization of Macbeth is more complex and interesting than in Holinshed's account. Additionally, Shakespeare presents usurping the throne as a despicable crime, whereas Holinshed's narrative is more neutral.*

3. *Shakespeare transformed Macbeth to be a much more dramatic character for the stage through dialogue that creates emotional relationships between characters. He portrayed Macbeth as a negative character to please King James.*

Analyze Source Material

 RI 1, RL 9

When reading historical text, you will encounter unfamiliar words and sentence structures that require you to slow down and make sure you understand the author's explicit meaning. Use footnote definitions of challenging words, and try to paraphrase, or restate in your own words, any sentences that don't at first make sense to you. Once you understand the basic information being conveyed, then you can evaluate the historical significance of the text.

As you read the excerpt from the *Chronicles*, you should have noticed ways in which Shakespeare drew upon and transformed this source material to create his character of Macbeth. For example, lines 1–10 from the Holinshed text describes how Macbeth and Banquo came upon "three women in strange and wild apparel, resembling creatures of elder world." In Act I, Scene 3 of *Macbeth*, Shakespeare expands on Holinshed's description of this encounter, bringing it to life.

Analyzing the Text

RI 1, RI 2, RI 3, RI 6, RL 9, SL 1

Cite Text Evidence   Support your responses with evidence from the selection.

1. **Interpret** Direct quotations comprise much of the content of lines 1–20. Is the use of direct quotations effective in supporting the author's purpose in this text? Explain.

2. **Compare** In both the play and the history, Macbeth can be viewed as a flawed, tragic hero. What are the similarities and differences in how each text conveys Macbeth's motivations for killing Duncan and Banquo? Which author is more successful in conveying Macbeth's motivations, and why? Cite textual evidence to support your answer.

3. **Evaluate** Based on your understanding of Shakespeare's context for writing *Macbeth*, how and why did he transform the character from the *Chronicles* to suit his purpose? Consider his priority, and cite evidence from both works.

PERFORMANCE TASK

Speaking Activity: Discussion In a small group, discuss *Macbeth* and *Chronicles*:

- What events and characters are similar? What differences did you notice?
- What does each work reveal about that author's point of view toward Macbeth?

- What might account for differences between the two views of Macbeth?
- Take notes and cite evidence from each text to support your ideas. Then, write a paragraph summarizing your discussion.

Assign this performance task.

PERFORMANCE TASK **RI 1, RI 3, RL 9, SL 1**

Speaking Activity: Discussion Before students meet in their groups, have them organize their notes of comparisons and contrasts between the two texts. Suggest that students use the Interactive Graphic Organizer: Comparison-Contrast Chart. Encourage students to take notes during their group discussion to aid them later when they write the summary of the discussion. Have each group present its summary to the class.

Critical Vocabulary

usurp   predecessor   admonition

Practice and Apply For each Critical Vocabulary word, choose which of the two situations best fits the word's meaning, and explain why your choice is correct.

1. usurp
   a. a player taking over as team captain when the captain is sick
   b. a coach appointing a temporary team captain

2. predecessor
   a. an earlier president
   b. the newly-elected president

3. admonition
   a. a gentle reminder
   b. a stern warning

Vocabulary Strategy: Archaic Language

Many words and phrases in the *Chronicles* are **archaic**, rarely used because they belong to an earlier period of history. Determining their meanings is essential to understanding ideas and events in the text. Here are three strategies you can use:

- Use general and specialized **reference material**, both print and digital. These may include dictionaries for defining specific words; encyclopedias for providing an explanation of places, events, and people; and a search engine for finding specialized online resources to define more obscure references.
- Consult the **footnotes**. For example, in the *Chronicles*, you can use the footnote for *laund* to learn that it means "an open space or clearing in a forest."
- **Recast** sentences containing an archaic word or phrase. First, use context clues to determine the general meaning of the sentence. Then, rewrite the sentence in your own words while retaining the archaic word or phrase. Try changing the position of the archaic word or phrase in your sentence to test how this affects the general meaning of the sentence.

Practice and Apply Use print or digital resource materials to define or explain each archaic word or phrase from the *Chronicles*.

creatures of elder world (line 6)	livings (line 23)
beheld (line 6)	hereunto (line 37)
Thane (line 8)	chanceth (line 47)
saith (line 12)	laid to his charge (line 61)

TEACH

CLOSE READ

Critical Vocabulary

Answers:

1. *a, The player is taking control without permission.*

2. *a, The predecessor is the president who held the position prior to the current president.*

3. *b, An admonition is a warning, not a reminder.*

Vocabulary Strategy: Archaic Language

Possible answers:

- **creatures of elder world (line 6):** fairies
- **beheld (line 6):** *held in view; looked upon*
- **Thane (line 8):** *a person who held rank with an earl's son and held lands of the king*
- **saith (line 12):** *said*
- **livings (line 23):** *residences*
- **hereunto (line 37):** *regarding this point*
- **chanceth (line 47):** *third-person singular of "chance"*
- **laid to his charge (line 61):** *if charges were brought against him*

Strategies for Annotation   **Annotate it!**

Archaic Language

Have students locate the sentences containing *creatures of elder world, beheld, Thane, saith, livings, hereunto, chanceth,* and *laid to his charge* in *Holinshed's Chronicles,* then use their eBook annotation tools to:

- Highlight each archaic word or phrase.
- Underline clues to its meaning.
- Search for a meaning in other resources.
- Attach a note about the meaning.
- Rephrase the sentence containing archaic language.

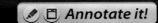

the kingdom by force, **having a just quarrel**[2] so to do (as he took the matter), for that Duncan did what in him lay to **defraud him of all manner of title and claim** which he might, in time to come, pretend[3] unto the crown.

Language and Style: Absolute Phrases

 L 1b

Explain that authors use **absolute phrases** to add details to their sentences. An absolute phrase describes the entire main clause of the sentence and is always set off by commas. Write one of the practice phrases on the board and work together as a class to identify the absolute phrase and its purpose in the sentence.

PRACTICE AND APPLY

Divide students into pairs and have them work together to write three sentences with absolute clauses. When they are finished, have them share their work with the class.

Answers: *Students' sentences should compare Holinshed's* Chronicles *with Shakespeare's* Macbeth *and should contain an absolute phrase set off with commas. For example: Shakespeare embellished the historical information in* Holinshed's Chronicles, *drama requiring more details about characters.*

Assess It!

Online Selection Test
- Download an editable ExamView bank.
- Assign and manage this test online.

Language and Style: Absolute Phrases

 L 1b

To add information and variety to sentences, writers often use absolute phrases. An **absolute phrase** consists of a noun and a participle (a verb form ending in *–ed* or *–ing* that acts as an adjective), and is always set off with commas. Absolute phrases may also contain the participle's object and any modifiers. Because absolute phrases describe the entire main clause of the sentence, they function as modifiers.

Look at this example of an absolute phrase from Holinshed's *Chronicles*:

> Shortly after, the Thane of Cawdor being condemned at Forres of treason against the King committed, his lands, livings, and offices were given of the King's liberality to Macbeth. . . .

Because this sentence contains archaic language, it may be challenging to understand. However, by identifying the absolute phrase and determining its meaning, readers can comprehend the entire sentence and its significance. In this sentence, the absolute phrase explains why Macbeth gained the "lands, livings, and offices" of the Thane of Cawdor—because the Thane, or lord, was convicted of being disloyal to the King. This incidence of treason thus allowed the second witch's prophecy for Macbeth to be fulfilled.

This chart shows two other examples of absolute phrases.

Absolute Phrase	What It Modifies
Its wheels squealing, the horse-drawn carriage took the corner too fast.	The noun *wheels* is modified by the participle *squealing* and the modifier *Its*. This absolute phrase modifies, or describes, the rest of the sentence, *the horse-drawn carriage took the corner too fast*.
Macbeth thought only about the witches' prophecies, his mind captured by these wild creatures.	The noun *mind* is modified by the participle *captured* and the additional modifiers *his* and *by these wild creatures*. This absolute phrase modifies the rest of the sentence, *Macbeth thought only about the witches' prophecies*.

Practice and Apply Work with a partner to write three sentences that include absolute phrases comparing Holinshed's *Chronicles* with Shakespeare's *Macbeth*. Choose your most effective sentence to share with the class.

WHEN STUDENTS STRUGGLE . . .

Demonstrate how the example sentence above was constructed, using the steps below:

- **Write two separate sentences:** Drama requires more details about characters. Shakespeare embellished the historical information in *Holinshed's Chronicles*.

- **Turn the first into an absolute phrase with a verb in its participle form:** Drama requiring more details about characters

- **Place the absolute phrase at the beginning, middle, or end of the second sentence:** Shakespeare embellished the historical information in *Holinshed's Chronicles,* drama requiring more details about characters.

ASK STUDENTS to use the steps to complete the Practice and Apply activity.

Analyzing Cultural Experience

RL 6, RI 1, SL 1

TEACH

Tell students that analyzing the **cultural experience** of details in historical documents, such as *Holinshed's Chronicles,* can help readers to get a better understanding of the historical events as well as the customs, values, and beliefs of the time.

Suggest that students answer the following questions about the historical text as they read:

1. What do you learn about the people during this time period and their way of life—their laws, traditions, beliefs, attitudes, behaviors, language?

2. What details about the people and events are the most interesting or engaging? Are these the same details that Shakespeare incorporated into or altered in *Macbeth?*

PRACTICE AND APPLY

Display the first paragraph (lines 1–11) of the *Chronicles* on the board or on a device. Ask volunteers to answer questions 1 and 2 by pointing out details about the people (*Macbeth is Thane of Glamis, Thane of Cawdor, future king of Scotland, son of Sinel; Banquo, the three women seem to be "creatures of elder world," wearing "strange and wild apparel"*) and their way of life (*ride horses; region of woods and fields; system whereby noble titles and offices are passed to descendants; formal, outdated language*). Students may want to record their notes in the Interactive Graphic Organizer: Cluster Diagram.

When students have finished analyzing the first paragraph, have them work with a partner or in small groups to continue analyzing details of the cultural experience in each paragraph of *Holinshed's Chronicles,* using a different Cluster Diagram for each one. When all groups are finished, ask them to share a summary of cultural context revealed by Holinshed and used by Shakespeare.

Analyze Historical Text

RI 1, RI 2, RI 3, RI 5, RI 6, RI 9, SL 1, SL 1a, SL 4

RETEACH

Explain to students that a historical text is anything from the past that helps us learn what happened and why. Ask students to identify types of historical texts. *(Possible answers: a written document, photograph or painting, monument, map, video or film)*

Provide students with the following steps for analyzing a historical text:

-   **Identify the author and the author's purpose.** Did the author observe the events, or did the author obtain information from other sources? Was the author personally involved in the events? Does he or she show any biases?

-   **Examine the production of the document.** Was the document created at the time of the event or years later? Is the language contemporary, or is it archaic with unfamiliar sentence structures and words whose meanings may have changed over time? Was the document meant to be public or private? Is the text in its original language, or is it an authoritative translation?

-   **Analyze the content.** What important details are provided? What does the document reveal about the culture at the time? Does it present a consistent story? If there are contradictions, why? If there are factual errors, why? Is the information reliable? Do other credible sources confirm the details?

-   **Evaluate the evidence.** How does the historical text affect your understanding of the topic?

CLOSE READING APPLICATION

Have partners or small groups of students apply the skill to a historical text of their choosing and present a summary of their assessment of the value of the text as a historical source. Remind students to cite evidence to support their analysis.

The Macbeth Murder Mystery

Short Story by James Thurber

Why This Text?

To become truly proficient readers, students must know the conventions of different genres and be able to recognize new levels of meaning that are created when a writer manipulates these conventions. This lesson explores two characters' readings of the tragic drama *Macbeth* through their conception of it as a classic English murder mystery.

▶ View It!

Professional Development Podcast:

Text-Dependent Analysis

Key Learning Objective: The student will be able to analyze how an author draws on Shakespeare.

COMMON CORE — Common Core Standards

RL 1 Cite textual evidence.

RL 4 Determine the meaning of words and phrases.

RL 9 Analyze how an author draws on source material.

W 3 Write narratives to develop events using effective technique, details, and event sequences.

W 3a Engage the reader by setting out a situation, establishing point(s) of view, and introducing characters.

L 4b Identify and use patterns of word changes that indicate different meanings.

L 4c Consult reference materials to find pronunciation or clarify meaning.

▲ Text Complexity Rubric

Quantitative Measures	**The Macbeth Murder Mystery** Lexile: 580L
Qualitative Measures	**Levels of Meaning/Purpose**  multiple levels of meaning
	Structure simple, linear chronology; one consistent point of view
	Language Conventionality and Clarity some unfamiliar language and less straightforward sentence structure
	Knowledge Demands increased amount of literary knowledge useful
Reader/Task Considerations	Teacher determined Vary by individual reader and type of text

Background Have students read the background and information about the author. Then explain how Thurber's idea to have a character uniquely interpret some key events in *Macbeth* allows the author to examine the tragedy as if it were an English murder mystery. Point out to students that Shakespearean dramatic tragedies and murder mysteries do have some things in common. In a classic English murder mystery, everyday life is interrupted by a death in a community and order is restored once the detective solves the case and catches the murderer. In Shakespearean tragedies such as *Macbeth* and *Hamlet*, a hero's downfall causes chaos in a setting and the truth about his or her actions must be revealed before order can be restored.

AS YOU READ Direct students to use the As You Read statement to focus their reading.

Analyze How an Author Draws on Shakespeare

COMMON CORE RL 1, RL 9

(LINES 5–12)

Explain to students that to help the reader understand why the characters interpret Shakespeare in the way that they do, Thurber provides clues about their personalities at the beginning of the story.

Ⓐ CITE TEXT EVIDENCE Ask students to identify clues Thurber supplies in the first paragraph about what kind of a reader the American lady is. (*The American lady's powers of observation are narrow. She bought the book because it resembled the Penguin murder mysteries and was on the counter with them. In lines 6–7, she admits that she bought the book without "looking at it carefully," and in line 12 she admits that she didn't notice that its jacket was a different color than the covers of detective stories. She wants and is prepared to read a mystery story. However, the book she actually reads is* The Tragedy of Macbeth *[line 14].*) Ask students to cite evidence about the personality of the narrator. (*The narrator murmers "sympathetically" to the American lady [line 8] about her being mad at discovering that the book she selected "was Shakespeare." The narrator is kind and doesn't wish to upset the lady.*)

Background *English murder mysteries follow a predictable framework and typically contain these elements that help readers predict the conclusion: a dead body; an intelligent detective; an isolated setting; a group of suspects; clues, some of which are misleading; a surprise twist; a capture; and an explanation of how the crime was committed.*

James Thurber (1894–1961) *was an American humor writer and cartoonist. He began his career as a journalist and went on to write essays, short stories, fables, fairy tales, picture books, and plays. In 1997, the Thurber Prize for American Humor was created in his honor.*

The Macbeth Murder Mystery

Short Story by James Thurber

AS YOU READ Look for evidence of how James Thurber uses humor to transform Shakespeare's dramatic tragedy *Macbeth* into a murder mystery. Write down any questions you generate during reading.

"It was a stupid mistake to make," said the American woman I had met at my hotel in the English lake country, "but it was on the counter with the other Penguin books—the little sixpenny[1] ones, you know, with the paper covers—and I supposed of course it was a detective story. All the others were detective stories. I'd read all the others, so I bought this one without really looking at it carefully. You can imagine how mad I was when I found out it was Shakespeare." I murmured something sympathetically. "I don't see why the Penguin-books people had to get out Shakespeare's plays
10 in the same size and everything as the detective stories," went on my companion. "I think they have different-colored jackets," I said. "Well, I didn't notice that," she said. "Anyway, I got real comfy in bed that night and all ready to read a good mystery story and here I had 'The Tragedy of Macbeth'—a book for high-school students.

---

[1] **sixpenny:** a former British monetary unit that is equal to six pennies.

The Macbeth Murder Mystery **301**

Image Credits: (t) ©MLM/AP Images; (bg) ©Powered by Light RF/Alamy Images; (r) ©CSA Images/Archive/Getty Images

SCAFFOLDING FOR ELL STUDENTS

Language: Idioms The characters' informal way of speaking and the use of idioms contrast with the archaic lines from Shakespeare that are featured in the story. This could potentially confuse English language learners. Remind students that idioms are expressions whose meanings differ from the literal meanings of the words that make them up. Pair students of mixed-language ability and have partners work together to identify confusing phrases, such as "just crazy" (line 16), "cut in" (line 23), "on and on like that" (line 60), and "All that stuff" (line 61). Then have students use context clues to figure out the meaning of each phrase. Students can check their answers by rereading the sentence in which the idiom originally appeared while substituting their definition in the idiom's place.

Analyze How an Author Draws on Shakespeare

COMMON CORE RL 9

(LINES 25–29)

For this story to make the most sense, the reader must have a previous knowledge of what kind of literary work *Macbeth* is. The reader should keep in mind what he or she already knows about the plot and characters of *Macbeth* when interpreting the actions of the narrator and the lady.

B **ASK STUDENTS** to describe how the American lady feels about *Macbeth* and why. *(She says she doesn't like the play, and the reason she gives is that she doesn't think Macbeth actually killed the King [line 27].)* Evaluate how well the lady read *Macbeth*, judging from the evidence given in the story at this point. *(She interpreted the play as if Shakespeare is a mystery writer trying to trick the reader and keep him or her in suspense. She is focusing on a problem that is not presented in* Macbeth—*who really killed King Duncan—and judging all the characters by how likely they are to have committed this murder.)*

CRITICAL VOCABULARY

decisively: The American lady asserts strongly that she did not like *Macbeth*.

ASK STUDENTS to discuss how this word choice fits in with the rest of what they know about the lady's character. *(Once she makes a judgment or decision, she is very sure that she is right. She is equally decisive about all of her other ideas about how to figure out what "really happened" in* Macbeth.)*

Like 'Ivanhoe.'" "Or 'Lorna Doone,'"[2] I said. "Exactly," said the American lady. "And I was just crazy for a good Agatha Christie, or something. Hercule Poirot[3] is my favorite detective." "Is he the rabbity one?" I asked. "Oh, no," said my crime-fiction expert. "He's the Belgian one. You're thinking of Mr. Pinkerton, the one that
20 helps Inspector Bull.[4] He's good, too."

Over her second cup of tea my companion began to tell the plot of a detective story that had fooled her completely—it seems it was the old family doctor all the time. But I cut in on her. "Tell me," I said. "Did you read 'Macbeth'?" "I had to read it," she said. "There wasn't a scrap of anything else to read in the whole room." "Did you like it?" I asked. "No, I did not," she said, **decisively**. "In the first place, I don't think for a moment that Macbeth did it." I looked at her blankly. "Did what?" I asked. "I don't think for a moment that he killed the King," she said. "I don't think the Macbeth woman
30 was mixed up in it, either. You suspect them the most, of course, but those are the ones that are never guilty—or shouldn't be, anyway." "I'm afraid," I began, "that I—" "But don't you see?" said the American lady. "It would spoil everything if you could figure out right away who did it. Shakespeare was too smart for that. I've read that people never have figured out 'Hamlet,' so it isn't likely Shakespeare would have made 'Macbeth' as simple as it seems." I thought this over while I filled my pipe. "Who do you suspect?" I asked, suddenly. "Macduff," she said, promptly. "Good God!" I whispered, softly.
40 "Oh, Macduff did it, all right," said the murder specialist. "Hercule Poirot would have got him easily." "How did you figure it out?" I demanded. "Well," she said, "I didn't right away. At first I suspected Banquo. And then, of course, he was the second person killed. That was good right in there, that part. The person you suspect of the first murder should always be the second victim." "Is that so?" I murmured. "Oh, yes," said my informant. "They have to keep surprising you. Well after the second murder I didn't know who the killer was for a while." "How about Malcolm and Donalbain, the King's sons?" I asked. "As I remember it,
50 they fled right after the first murder. That looks suspicious." "Too suspicious," said the American lady. "Much too suspicious. When they flee, they're never guilty. You can count on that." "I

decisively
(dĭ-sī′sĭv-lē) *adv.* in a firm and resolute manner.

---

[2] **Ivanhoe . . . Lorna Doone:** historical romance novels set in England and written in the 1800s by Sir Walter Scott and Richard Doddridge Blackmore, respectively.

[3] **Agatha Christie . . . Hercule Poirot:** Agatha Christie is a British author of crime novels, short stories, and plays; Hercule Poirot is a Belgian detective character who appears in many of her works.

[4] **Mr. Pinkerton . . . Inspector Bull:** series characters in American David Frome's (pseudonym for Zenith Jones Brown) mystery novels.

302 Collection 5

Strategies for Annotation ✐ 🗐 *Annotate it!*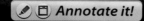

Analyze How an Author Draws on Shakespeare

COMMON CORE RL 9

Have students use their eBook annotation tools to analyze the text. Ask them to do the following:

- Highlight in blue statements that provide clues about the conventions of murder mysteries as the American lady understands them.
- Write a note that explains why each convention provides an inappropriate method to use to interpret a Shakespearean tragedy.

You suspect them the most, of course, but those are the ones that are never guilty—or shouldn't be, anyway." "I'm afraid," I began, "that I—" "But don't you see?" said the American lady. "It would spoil everything if you could figure out right away who did it. Shakespeare was too smart for that.

Macbeth and Lady Macbeth are not suspects in a murder mystery. They are a tragic hero and a heroine.

think for a moment that Macbeth did it."

believe," I said, "I'll have a brandy," and I summoned the waiter. My companion leaned toward me, her eyes bright, her teacup quivering. "Do you know who discovered Duncan's body?" she demanded. I said I was sorry, but I had forgotten. "Macduff discovers it," she said, slipping into the historical present. "Then he comes running downstairs and shouts, 'Confusion has broke open the Lord's anointed temple' and '**Sacrilegious** murder has made his
60 masterpiece' and on and on like that." The good lady tapped me on the knee. "All that stuff was rehearsed," she said. "You wouldn't say a lot of stuff like that, off-hand, would you—if you had found a body?" She fixed me with a glittering eye. "I—" I began. "You're right!" she said. "You wouldn't! Unless you had practiced it in advance. 'My God, there's a body in here!' is what an innocent man would say." She sat back with a confident glare.

I thought for a while. "But what do you make of the Third Murderer?" I asked. "You know, the Third Murderer has puzzled 'Macbeth' scholars for three hundred years." "That's because
70 they never thought of Macduff," said the American lady. "It was Macduff, I'm certain. You couldn't have one of the victims murdered by two ordinary thugs—the murderer always has to be somebody important." "But what about the banquet scene?" I asked, after a moment. "How do you account for Macbeth's guilty actions there, when Banquo's ghost came in and sat in his chair?" The lady leaned forward and tapped me on the knee again. "There wasn't any ghost," she said. "A big, strong man like that doesn't go around seeing ghosts—especially in a brightly lighted banquet hall with dozens of people around. Macbeth was shielding somebody!" "Who
80 was he shielding?" I asked. "Mrs. Macbeth, of course," she said. "He

sacrilegious
(săk´rə-lĭj´əs) *adj.*
grossly irreverent toward what is sacred.

Image Credit: ©Houghton Mifflin Harcourt

WHEN STUDENTS STRUGGLE . . .

How an Author Draws on Shakespeare Students must remember and understand the original text of *Macbeth* in order to recognize how incorrectly the American lady is interpreting the play. As needed, have students return to the play and reread the portions referenced by the American lady to refresh their memories of the dialogue and actions of the characters. Then have them take notes comparing what actually happens in the play (and the significance of each event) with the way the American lady is interpreting each event.

Analyze How an Author Draws on Shakespeare
COMMON CORE RL 4, RL 9

(LINES 55–66)

Explain that because Shakespeare wrote his works during a different era than the time period in which many English mystery novel writers lived, he used language in different ways than they did.

C **ASK STUDENTS** to summarize the American lady's case for why the character Macduff is the murderer and explain how knowledge of the original Shakespearean text can help the reader evaluate her theory better. *(She thinks Macduff killed the king because when he discovered the body, he shouted, using poetic language [lines 58–60]. She thinks his words were rehearsed [line 61] because an innocent man would speak more plainly and shockingly state that he found a body [line 65]. She is misinterpreting the play because poetic language is exactly the kind of language that a character in a Shakespearean tragedy would use. The point of Macduff's speech is not just to announce that someone is dead but to emphasize that to have murdered the king in this manner is a complete violation of morality.)*

CRITICAL VOCABULARY

sacrilegious: Macduff describes the murder of King Duncan as a violation against something sacred or holy.

ASK STUDENTS to explain why Macduff might use this word to describe the King's murder. *(Macduff refers to King Duncan as the Lord's anointed temple, which means that God chose this man to be king. Therefore, killing God's chosen ruler would mean violating something sacred.)*

Analyze How an Author Draws on Shakespeare

COMMON CORE **RL 9**

(LINES 81–90)

Explain to students that authors of murder mystery novels include some details in their descriptions that turn out to be important clues. Readers of murder mysteries are supposed to put the clues together and make logical deductions to interpret plot events and the behavior of the characters. Dramatists, however, often use descriptive details to convey meaning through a pattern of repeated images and symbols.

D **ASK STUDENTS** to summarize the American lady's explanation for Macbeth and Lady Macbeth's suspicious behavior in the play. (*She thinks that they were acting guilty to protect each other [line 90].*) Have students recall the sleepwalking scene in *Macbeth* and evaluate the way that the American lady interprets it. (*She says that the proof that Lady Macbeth was acting guilty on purpose by sleepwalking is that Lady Macbeth was carrying a light, and real sleepwalkers do not need to bring a light because they have "second sight" [line 88]. If the lady were actually reading a murder mystery novel, this would be a good deduction. However, because* Macbeth *is a dramatic tragedy, the taper that Lady Macbeth carries is part of a pattern of imagery dealing with light and darkness.*)

CRITICAL VOCABULARY

secluded: The narrator escorts the American lady to a private spot where he can tell her his theory.

ASK STUDENTS to explain why the narrator wants to hold their conversation in a secluded spot. (*He doesn't want other people to overhear their conversation, which goes along with the air of secrecy that usually accompanies the solving of a mystery.*)

contention: The narrator makes a strong assertion that the "old Man" who enters in Act II, Scene 4, is "old Mr. Macbeth."

ASK STUDENTS to describe how the narrator supports his contention. (*The narrator offers what seems to be sound evidence on which to base his idea: Lady Macbeth's father's motive for murdering Duncan was to make his daughter queen.*)

D thought she did it and he was going to take the rap himself. The husband always does that when the wife is suspected." "But what," I demanded, "about the sleepwalking scene, then?" "The same thing, only the other way around," said my companion. "That time she was shielding him. She wasn't asleep at all. Do you remember where it says, 'Enter Lady Macbeth with a taper'?" "Yes," I said. "Well, people who walk in their sleep never carry lights!" said my fellow-traveler. "They have second sight. Did you ever hear of a sleepwalker carrying a light?" "No," I said, "I never did." "Well,
90 then, she wasn't asleep. She was acting guilty to shield Macbeth." "I think," I said, "I'll have another brandy," and I called the waiter. When he brought it, I drank it rapidly and rose to go. "I believe," I said, "that you have got hold of something. Would you lend me that 'Macbeth'? I'd like to look it over tonight. I don't feel, somehow, as if I'd ever really read it." "I'll get it for you," she said. "But you'll find that I am right."

I read the play over carefully that night, and the next morning, after breakfast, I sought out the American woman. She was on the putting green, and I came up behind her silently and took her arm.
100 She gave an exclamation. "Could I see you alone?" I asked, in a low voice. She nodded cautiously and followed me to a **secluded** spot. "You've found out something?" she breathed. "I've found out," I said triumphantly, "the name of the murderer!" "You mean it wasn't Macduff?" she said. "Macduff is as innocent of those murders," I said, "as Macbeth and the Macbeth woman." I opened the copy of the play, which I had with me, and turned to Act II, Scene 2. "Here," I said, "you will see where Lady Macbeth says, 'I laid their daggers ready. He could not miss 'em. Had he not resembled my father as he slept, I had done it.' Do you see?" "No," said the American woman,
110 bluntly, "I don't." "But it's simple!" I exclaimed. "I wonder I didn't see it years ago. The reason Duncan resembled Lady Macbeth's father as he slept is that it actually was her father!" "Good God!" breathed my companion, softly. "Lady Macbeth's father killed the King," I said, "and hearing someone coming, thrust the body under the bed and crawled into the bed himself." "But," said the lady, "you can't have a murderer who only appears in the story once. You can't have that." "I know that," I said, and I turned to Act II, Scene 4. "It says here, 'Enter Ross with an old Man.' Now, that old man is never identified and it is my **contention** that he was old Mr. Macbeth,
120 whose ambition it was to make his daughter Queen. There you have your motive." "But even then," cried the American lady, "he's still a minor character!" "Not," I said, gleefully, "when you realize that he was also one of the weird sisters in disguise!" "You mean one of the three witches?" "Precisely," I said. "Listen to this speech of

secluded
(sĭ-klōō′dĭd) *adj.* hidden from view.

contention
(kən-tĕn′shən) *n.* an assertion put forward in argument.

APPLYING ACADEMIC VOCABULARY

comprise	thesis

As you discuss this short story, incorporate the following Collection 5 academic vocabulary words: *comprise* and *thesis*. To explore the American lady's reading of *Macbeth* and the case she makes for who the real murderer is in the play, ask students to identify her **thesis** and the various points that **comprise** it.

the old man's. 'On Tuesday last, a falcon towering in her pride of place, was by a mousing owl hawk'd at and kill'd.' Who does that sound like?" "It sounds like the way the three witches talk," said my companion, reluctantly. "Precisely!" I said again. "Well, said the American woman, "maybe you're right, but—" "I'm sure I am,"
130 I said. "And do you know what I'm going to do now?" "No," she said. "What?" "Buy a copy of 'Hamlet,'" I said, "and solve that!" My companion's eyes brightened. "Then," she said, "you don't think Hamlet did it?" "I am," I said, "absolutely positive he didn't." "But who," she demanded, "do you suspect?" I looked at her **cryptically**. "Everybody," I said, and disappeared into a small grove of trees as silently as I had come.

cryptically
(krĭp′tĭk-lē) *adv.*
in a secretive or mysterious manner.

COLLABORATIVE DISCUSSION With a partner, discuss the characteristics of murder mysteries you've read or seen. Which characteristics does Thurber use to classify *Macbeth* as a murder mystery? In your discussion, cite evidence from the text.

TO CHALLENGE STUDENTS . . .

To guide and deepen students' understanding of the characters in this short story, have them discuss and compare how the American lady and the narrator each think about and interpret the works of Shakespeare. Ask them to consider questions such as how much background knowledge each character has about Shakespeare's works, how people have historically read and studied them, how each character feels about Shakespeare's works at the beginning of the story, and how each feels about his works at the end. In particular, have students focus on the sections in which each character presents his or her "solution" of *Macbeth*.

CLOSE READ

Analyze How an Author Draws on Shakespeare

COMMON CORE **RL 9**

(LINES 131–135)

Point out that the plot of Thurber's story revolves around two characters who discuss *Macbeth* in terms of a murder mystery novel rather than a Shakespearean tragedy. Then explain that when literary critics try to "solve" *Hamlet*, what they are usually trying to do is to figure out why Hamlet takes so long to kill the king.

E **CITE TEXT EVIDENCE** Ask students to explain what the narrator means when he says he will "solve" *Hamlet*. *(He is planning to reread* Hamlet *as if it were written as a murder mystery. He says in line 133 that he is sure Hamlet didn't do it, and he adds in line 135 that he suspects "everybody." Discounting the obvious suspect and suspecting all other characters are two conventions of murder mystery novels that he learned from the American lady.)*

> **CRITICAL VOCABULARY**
>
> **cryptically**: The narrator doesn't want to reveal outright who he suspects "did it" in *Hamlet*.
>
> **ASK STUDENTS** to explain why looking cryptically at the American lady at this point is a good choice of words on Thurber's part. *(The narrator is aware of the plot points of* Hamlet, *so for him to give a cryptic look when stating that he suspects that everybody "did it" is ironic and humorous. It shows that he will enjoy reading* Hamlet *as if it were a murder mystery.)*

COLLABORATIVE DISCUSSION Have student pairs use the Background note to start brainstorming a list of the conventions of murder mysteries. Suggest that they consider how each kind of story element is typically used in mystery stories, examining the use of characters, settings, plot events, and types of language. Then have students compare how mystery stories use these elements with the way the American lady claims that Shakespeare uses them in *Macbeth*. Invite pairs to share their findings with the class.

ASK STUDENTS to share any questions they generated in the course of reading and discussing the selection.

Analyze How an Author Draws on Shakespeare RL 9

Make sure students understand what a satire is. Then brainstorm some characteristics of dramatic tragedies. *(For example, the plot centers on the downfall of a tragic hero or heroine who is often in possession of a fatal flaw that causes his or her doom. The hero's actions introduce chaos into the setting, and order must be restored at the end. The characters speak using soliloquies and asides.)*

Once students understand the conventions of both genres, have them answer the questions.

Possible answers:

- *Thurber refers to the plot events, characters, and dialogue in Macbeth.*
- *The plot events and dialogue are read as if they were written in a murder mystery.*
- *If a reader is reading for the purpose of solving a mystery, then normal character actions take on different meanings. Characters' motivations are interpreted with suspicion and with the expectation that there will be a plot twist.*
- *Thurber could be ridiculing rigid thinking; that is, the insistence of some people on interpreting events through a narrow viewpoint.*

Analyze How an Author Draws on Shakespeare RL 9

The works of William Shakespeare have influenced many authors over the centuries. Shakespeare's plays contain insights on human nature that are timeless. For example, his tragedy *Macbeth* is known for themes of uncontrolled ambition, betrayal, and corrupting power, themes shared by many literary works. Not only are Shakespeare's themes familiar, but his characters and conflicts are as well. When an author refers to a Shakespearean character, such as Lady Macbeth, or to a situation, such as King Duncan's murder, that reference makes a connection with the audience and deepens our understanding of the author's work.

In "The Macbeth Murder Mystery," James Thurber draws upon Shakespeare's *Macbeth* to create a **satire**, a literary work that ridicules a vice or folly found in society. Satirists use humor in their works to cause people to change how they think or what their priorities are. Readers of Thurber's short story will be familiar with the references to *Macbeth*, but the unexpected way Thurber's characters transform the tragedy into a formulaic British murder mystery allows him to comment on how people approach literature. As you analyze "The Macbeth Murder Mystery," consider these questions:

> **To which elements of Shakespeare's play does Thurber refer in his story?**
>
> **How are the play's elements transformed in the short story?**
>
> **What effect do these changes have on the characters? on the reader?**
>
> **What issue does Thurber ridicule in his story?**

306 Collection 5

Strategies for Annotation  Annotate it!

Analyze How an Author Draws on Shakespeare RL 9

Share this strategy for guided or independent analysis:

- Highlight in yellow information about the way the narrator interprets his evidence.
- Write a note to explain how the narrator is misinterpreting Shakespeare.

slept, I had done it.' Do you see?" "No," said the American woman, bluntly, "I don't." "But it's simple!" I exclaimed. "I wonder I didn't see it years ago. The reason Duncan resembled Lady Macbeth's father as he slept is that it actually was her father!"

> The narrator is imposing a plot twist that might have been used by a mystery writer but not by Shakespeare.

Analyzing the Text

COMMON CORE RL 1, RL 4, RL 9, W 3

Cite Text Evidence Support your responses with evidence from the selection.

1. **Connect** Writers use **satire** to ridicule follies or foolish ideas commonly held in a society. What does Thurber ridicule in his satire? What point does he make regarding the expectations of reading different types of literature?

2. **Draw Conclusions** The American woman explains why some characters in the play are not guilty of Macbeth's murder. What reasons does she provide to prove that Malcolm, Donalbain, Macbeth, and Lady Macbeth are innocent? Does she have an understanding of Shakespeare's play? Explain your answer.

3. **Interpret** In lines 94–95, the narrator says of Shakespeare's play, "I don't feel, somehow, as if I'd ever really read it." In what way is this statement ironic? How does this incidence of irony add to Thurber's satire?

4. **Compare** In the last paragraph, the narrator presents his solution to *Macbeth*'s murder mystery. How does his version of Duncan's murder differ from Shakespeare's? Explain how the characters are recast and the events of the play are changed.

5. **Analyze** Thurber is known for his humor and wit. How does he convey humor in this story? Cite details from the text to support your response.

PERFORMANCE TASK

Writing Activity: Narrative In this story, characters misinterpret a dramatic tragedy as a murder mystery. How does the understanding of literary genres shape the interpretation of a story? Can characteristics of one genre be applied to another for a different interpretation? Explore these ideas by transforming one type of story into another.

1. With a partner, choose a familiar fable or fairy tale. Note the elements that make the story you chose a fable or fairy tale.

2. Think about the conflict or characters in the story. In what different genre might the conflict or characters appear? List the elements of the new genre. Genres you might consider include romance, science fiction, mystery, and comedy.

3. Rewrite your story so that it maintains the same events but contains the characteristics of the new genre. For example, a fairy tale can be rewritten as a science fiction story by eliminating the magical elements and by changing the setting.

4. Exchange your story with another pair and try to identify the fairy tale or fable your classmates used as their source.

Assign this performance task.

PERFORMANCE TASK

COMMON CORE W 3

Writing Activity: Narrative Before pairing students, discuss the conventions of different genres. Have students name stories from specific genres and chart elements found in each. (In fairy tales, events repeat three times, a female character is in distress, and a moral is taught.) Have partners choose a familiar story to reinterpret. Have them identify the genre and chart the conventions of the story they will rewrite. Remind them to refer to their charts while rewriting.

Analyzing the Text

COMMON CORE RL 1, RL 4, RL 9

Possible answers:

1. *Thurber could be ridiculing people who can only view life through a narrow viewpoint. Thurber makes the point that knowing the conventions of different genres of literature will allow readers to understand different levels of meaning as the writers intended.*

2. *She thinks Malcolm and Donalbain are innocent because they fled (line 50), and guilty people never flee in murder mysteries. She thinks Macbeth and Lady Macbeth are innocent because people suspect them the most (line 30), and the characters the reader suspects the most are never guilty. She understands the text according to the conventions of a mystery novel but not as a Shakespearean tragedy, so she doesn't have an understanding of Macbeth.*

3. *It's ironic because he has read it before and understood it because he understood the conventions of a dramatic tragedy. It adds to the satire because the lady's belief that her interpretation is the right one is leading the narrator to doubt his own interpretation. There is irony in that as well. The informed person, who knows a truth about something, is led down the path of disbelief by the incorrect assertions of the uninformed person.*

4. *The narrator speculates that Lady Macbeth's father is actually a character in the play (he appears as the Old Man [line 118] with Ross and disguised as one of the three witches). He suggests that it was actually Lady Macbeth's father who killed Duncan. The father then hid Duncan's body under the bed and crawled into the bed himself so that it really was her father whom Lady Macbeth saw. The narrator adds that the father's motive was to make Lady Macbeth queen.*

5. *The American lady's misreading of the play is funny because she keeps interpreting the text differently from the way the narrator and the reader expect her to. Initially, the narrator is so shocked by her claims that he stares at her (line 28), whispers "Good God!" (lines 38–39), and orders brandy to cope with her assertions (lines 53 and 91–92). Another layer of humor is brought in when the narrator gets drawn into "solving" the play. The reader can laugh at his actions and the images of him giving cryptic looks and hiding in a grove of trees (lines 134–135).*

PRACTICE & APPLY

Critical Vocabulary

COMMON CORE   L 4b, L 4c

Possible answers:

1. *"Contention" goes with a disagreement because when two people disagree with one another, each person is asserting something he or she believes.*

2. *"Cryptically" goes with a mysterious note because someone communicating secretly is conveying information in a mysterious way.*

3. *"Decisively" goes with a judge's ruling because a judge makes a firm decision about a court case.*

4. *"Sacrilegious" goes with swearing in anger because often people who swear use sacred words in an improper way.*

5. *"Secluded" goes with a secret hideout because people searching for a place in which to hide often pick a place that is hard for others to see or find.*

Vocabulary Strategy: Words from Latin

Possible answers:

Provide students with a chart such as the one shown below to organize their answers.

 Assess It!

Online Selection Test
- Download an editable ExamView bank.
- Assign and manage this test online.

Critical Vocabulary

COMMON CORE   L 4b, L 4c

decisively   sacrilegious   secluded   contention   cryptically

Practice and Apply   Explain which Critical Vocabulary word is most closely associated with each idea or situation.

1. Which Critical Vocabulary word goes with a disagreement? Why?

2. Which Critical Vocabulary word goes with a mysterious note? Why?

3. Which Critical Vocabulary word goes with a judge's ruling? Why?

4. Which Critical Vocabulary word goes with swearing in anger? Why?

5. Which Critical Vocabulary word goes with a secret hideout? Why?

Vocabulary Strategy: Words from Latin

A word's **etymology** shows the ultimate origin and historical development of that word. Many English words are derived from Latin ones. For example, the Critical Vocabulary word *sacrilegious* comes from the Latin word *sacer*, which means "holy." *Sacrilegious* contains the root or basic word part *sacr–*. Understanding a word's etymology will help you grasp the word's meaning. In addition, knowing the meaning of roots will help you define other words with similar roots.

Practice and Apply   Follow these steps to complete the activity:

1. Use a dictionary to look up the etymology of each word in the chart, and write the meaning of its Latin root.

2. Identify two additional words that contain the same Latin root.

3. Write three sentences for each root, one using the word from the selection and two others using the additional related words you identified.

Word	Root
suspected (line 43)	*spec–*
certain (line 71)	*cert–*
exclamation (line 100)	*clam–*
motive (line 121)	*mot–*

Word/Root	Meaning of Root	Additional Words	Sentences
suspected/spec–	*to look, watch, see, or observe*	*spectacle, inspect*	*She suspected he was a criminal.* *The circus put on a spectacle.* *Inspect the plant for bugs.*
certain/cert–	*to be sure*	*certificate, ascertain*	*She was certain he did it.* *This certificate proves I graduated.* *Can we ever ascertain the truth?*
exclamation/clam–	*to cry out*	*clamor, acclaim*	*She yelled with a loud exclamation.* *I could not hear him over the clamor.* *Her book was met with great acclaim.*
motive/mot–	*to move*	*emotion, motion*	*What is your motive for helping me?* *She felt many emotions when singing.* *Kick the ball to set it in motion.*

Orient Readers of Narratives

W 3a

TEACH

Explain to students that a proficient reader uses clues to orient himself or herself in order to understand and interpret what is going on in a short story. Examining the methods Thurber uses to provide his reader with such information can prepare students for establishing these elements in the fables or fairy tales they write for their Performance Task.

Point out some essential parts of a narrative:

- the introduction of a narrator or point of view from which the events will be experienced
- the description of a setting
- the presentation of an interesting situation
- the development of characters

Note that these parts can be presented to the reader through straight description or lines of dialogue.

PRACTICE AND APPLY

Have students describe the narrator or the point of view from which this story is told, including details Thurber provides to help the reader understand the narrator. *(The narrator tells the story from a first-person point of view. The details included, such as the narrator smoking a pipe and drinking brandies, could indicate that the narrator is a man.)*

Have students identify the setting of this story, citing details that help them orient themselves. *(The setting is a hotel in the English lake country [line 2] that includes a restaurant [line 53] and a golf course [line 99].)*

Have students identify the situation of the story. *(The narrator meets an American lady who makes a case for how one could interpret* Macbeth *as a murder mystery. The narrative traces the development of the narrator's reaction to this method of reading Shakespeare.)*

Have students point out some techniques Thurber uses to help readers follow the development of the characters. *(Thurber uses dialogue and short descriptions of actions to reveal things about the characters' personalities. For example, at first the narrator stares at the lady blankly [line 28] and tries to interrupt her to correct her [line 32]. He eventually changes his attitude and enthusiasm for reading* Macbeth *in her way. This is conveyed by his assuming the role of a mysterious detective coming up behind her silently to share his theory [line 99] and how "gleefully" [line 122] he does so.)*

Analyze How an Author Draws on Shakespeare

RL 9

RETEACH

Review the term *satire* and have students consider what Thurber is satirizing in his short story. Have students think about how the American lady interprets *Macbeth* and how well she understands the point of view from which it was written and the culture from which it comes.

- Have students describe what kind of a reader the American lady is and how she decides what to read next. *(The American lady likes to read only mystery novels, and she wants to read another one. When* Macbeth *turns out to be a tragedy, she reads it as a mystery novel anyway.)*
- Have students identify the satirical point they think Thurber is making through having a character misinterpret *Macbeth*. *(By reading the play as a murder mystery, the American lady misses out on the play's real meaning. Thurber may also be making a point about American readers of Shakespeare since he deliberately chose to portray an American.)*

 LEVEL UP TUTORIALS Assign the following *Level Up* tutorial: **Elements of Drama**

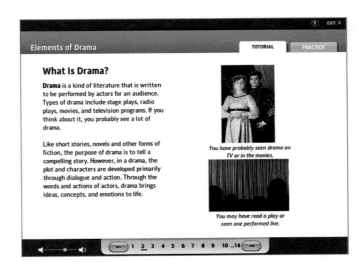

CLOSE READING APPLICATION

Students can apply this skill to reading another satirical work. Remind students to ask themselves if they think the author agrees with the actions of the characters or if he or she is using humor to make a point.

5 P.M., Tuesday, August 23, 2005

Poem by Patricia Smith

Why This Text?

Students regularly see important events reported in the news or dramatized on television and in film. They may not be as familiar with how such events can be depicted in poetry. This lesson explores how Patricia Smith dramatizes a developing hurricane, Hurricane Katrina, by personifying the storm.

Key Learning Objective: The student will be able to make and support inferences about word choice.

 ### Common Core Standards

RL 1 Cite textual evidence to support inferences.

RL 2 Determine a theme and analyze its development.

RL 3 Analyze how complex characters develop, interact, and advance the plot

RL 4 Determine the meaning of words and phrases, including figurative and connotative meanings; analyze the impact of word choices on tone.

RL 5 Analyze an author's choices concerning how to structure a text.

W 2 Write informative texts to examine complex ideas.

W 9a Draw evidence from literary texts to support analysis.

SL 2 Integrate multiple sources of information presented in diverse media or formats.

SL 6 Adapt speech to a variety of contexts and tasks.

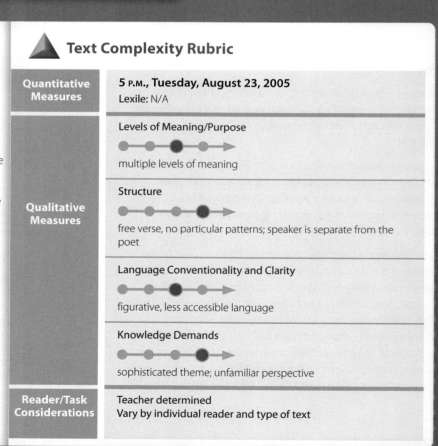

Text Complexity Rubric

Quantitative Measures	**5 P.M., Tuesday, August 23, 2005** Lexile: N/A
Qualitative Measures	**Levels of Meaning/Purpose** multiple levels of meaning
	Structure free verse, no particular patterns; speaker is separate from the poet
	Language Conventionality and Clarity figurative, less accessible language
	Knowledge Demands sophisticated theme; unfamiliar perspective
Reader/Task Considerations	Teacher determined Vary by individual reader and type of text

CLOSE READ

5 P.M., Tuesday, August 23, 2005

Poem by Patricia Smith

For more context and historical background, students can view the video "Science of a Hurricane" in their eBooks.

Background Have students read the background information about hurricanes and Hurricane Katrina. To help students appreciate the ferocity of the storm, explain that by the time Katrina hit the Gulf Coast, the winds measured 100–140 miles per hour, and rain fell at the rate of about one inch per hour. While the hurricane caused massive destruction across 400 miles of the coast (as well as inland), it is the damage caused in New Orleans that has become one of the most lasting images of the storm's devastating power. When the storm was finished, 80 percent of New Orleans was under water. Most of this flooding was the result of breaks in the levee that holds back the water from Lake Pontchartrain. In some flooded areas, the water was so deep, people had to climb on the roofs of their homes to avoid it, and there they waited to be rescued. While the city and other coastal areas have made progress toward recovery in the years since, the process of rebuilding continues.

Patricia Smith Have students read the background information about the author. Explain that just as Shakespeare's plays were meant to be performed, so too are Smith's poems. Her persona poetry lends itself to performance. In a persona poem, the writer becomes another person, an animal, or an object—even a hurricane!

Background *A hurricane develops in stages. At any point, the storm may either fall apart or become more organized and intense, progressing to the next stage. In the first stage, a tropical disturbance occurs, in which loosely-organized, heavy rain clouds develop. The storm system draws moisture from the warm, humid air on the ocean's surface. This warm air rises and cooler air moves down to replace it, creating a swirling pattern of winds, a tropical depression. If the winds reach 39 to 73 miles per hour, the depression becomes a tropical storm. At 74 miles per hour, the storm becomes a hurricane.*

On August 23, 2005, a tropical depression formed off the southern coast of the United States. It would develop over the next few days into Hurricane Katrina, first sweeping over the east coast of Florida and then homing in on Mississippi and Louisiana, where it made a second landfall on August 29. One of the most powerful and devastating hurricanes to ever hit U.S. soil, Katrina's massive winds and torrential rainfall created a storm surge of more than 25 feet, breaching a crucial levee and plunging most of the city of New Orleans under water. The hurricane was responsible for at least 1,800 deaths, and it forever changed the Gulf Coast and its inhabitants.

Patricia Smith (b. 1955) *is an award-winning poet, performance artist, and four-time National Poetry Slam champion. She is known for using personas—first-person voices that range from gang members to monsters of Greek mythology—to expose uncomfortable truths about situations that most people don't want to face. Her work evokes such themes as self-destruction, betrayal, and vindictiveness, highlighting the spiritual and political impact of the subjects she explores. This poem appears in her book* Blood Dazzler, *a collection that traces the environmental and human costs of Hurricane Katrina. The book earned Smith a National Book Award nomination in 2008.*

SCAFFOLDING FOR ELL STUDENTS

Vocabulary The concept of connotative meaning might be difficult. Point out the word *belittle* in line 10 of the poem. Explain that other words or phrases, such as *make light of* or *dismiss*, mean roughly the same thing, but they don't carry the harsher tone that *belittle* implies.

ASK STUDENTS to consider the word *harbors* in line 22. Tell them that it has a similar meaning to *contains* and *shelters*. Ask what connotation *harbors* has that would explain why the poet chose this word as opposed to a similar word. *("Shelters" and "contains" do not have the emotional impact of "harbors." "Harbors" implies a larger and grander gesture, as well as protection.)*

AS YOU READ Direct students to use the As You Read note to focus their reading.

Support Inferences About Word Choice (LINES 6–23) COMMON CORE RL 4

Remind students that a poet often chooses a specific word for its connotative meaning—a meaning that goes beyond the literal and evokes the feelings associated with the word. Connotative meanings can help establish tone, or attitude toward the subject.

A **ASK STUDENTS** to find the words and phrases *thrashing, how dare, I will require,* and *unbridled.* Have them discuss the connotations of these words and phrases, and share what tone they create. *("Thrashing" and "unbridled" suggest dangerous and uncontrollable. "How dare" and "I will require" suggest a powerful person who expects obedience. The tone created is both demanding and threatening.)* Have students find words and phrases that also develop a tone of ominous patience. *("can wait for it," "console myself," and "bored breath")*

Remind students that a metaphor is a comparison of two unlike things that may share certain characteristics, and that an extended metaphor is a metaphor that is developed at length in a work.

B **CITE TEXT EVIDENCE** Have students identify the poem's extended metaphor, and explain how it is also an example of personification. Remind students to cite text evidence to support their answer. *(The extended metaphor is of the developing hurricane as a powerful, dangerous woman. There are numerous references to parts of the body [for example, lines 7, 9, and 18], and in the fourth stanza it becomes clear that the speaker is a woman.)*

COLLABORATIVE DISCUSSION Have students pair up and discuss specific evidence that the poet uses to develop the voice of the speaker. Have them consider whether, when reading the poem, they tended to view the speaker as more human or more natural force.

ASK STUDENTS to share any questions they generated in the course of reading and discussing the selection.

AS YOU READ Note words and phrases that reveal the speaker's character. Write down any questions you generate during reading.

5 P.M., Tuesday, August 23, 2005

"Data from an Air Force reserve unit reconnaissance aircraft . . . along with observations from the Bahamas and nearby ships . . . indicate the broad low pressure area over the southeastern Bahamas has become organized enough to be classified as tropical depression twelve."

5   —NATIONAL HURRICANE CENTER

A muted thread of gray light, hovering ocean,
becomes throat, pulls in wriggle, anemone, kelp,[1]
widens with the want of it. I become

A   a mouth, thrashing hair, an overdone eye. How dare
10 the water belittle my thirst, treat me as just
another
small
disturbance,

try to feed me
15 from the bottom of its hand?

I will require praise,
unbridled winds to define my body,
a crime behind my teeth
because

B 20 every woman begins as weather,
sips slow thunder, knows her hips. Every woman
harbors a chaos, can
wait for it, straddling a fever.

For now,
25 I console myself with small furies,
those dips in my dawning system. I pull in
a bored breath. The brine[2] shivers.

COLLABORATIVE DISCUSSION How would you describe the poem's speaker? With a partner, discuss how the poet creates a vivid character as the voice of the poem. Cite specific lines to support your ideas.

---

[1] **anemone, kelp:** sea anemones are brightly colored, tentacled sea creatures; kelp is a kind of seaweed.
[2] **brine:** salt water or sea water.

WHEN STUDENTS STRUGGLE . . .

To help students identify and understand the extended metaphor, have pairs work together to identify the words that create the metaphor. Display the poem on a whiteboard. Have one student in the pair highlight words that suggest the human body. *(throat, mouth, hair, eye, body, teeth, hips)* Have the other student underline pronouns and other words that suggest the speaker is a living being. *(my thirst, me, I, feed me, myself, breath)*

Have each pair work together to write a few sentences explaining how the extended metaphor in the poem develops. Remind them to use text evidence to support their answer.

Support Inferences About Word Choice

Poetry packs a lot of meaning into a small space, so poets must choose and arrange their words carefully. Using **figurative language**, or words that communicate meaning beyond the literal interpretation, is one way a poet can add an extra dimension to the text. One example is a **metaphor**, a figure of speech that implies a comparison between two unlike things that share a key characteristic. An **extended metaphor** is developed at length, often continuing across several stanzas or throughout the poem.

Another figure of speech often used by poets is **personification**, in which human qualities are given to a nonhuman subject. Like a metaphor, personification makes a comparison between two things that are dissimilar in order to shed new light on one or both of them.

Poets also choose words for their **connotative** meanings, or the feelings associated with them. By interpreting the figurative and connotative language in a poem, readers can infer the speaker's **tone**, or attitude toward the subject, which often reveals the poet's meaning.

Consider the questions in the chart to help you analyze the poem.

Words from Text	Analysis
A muted thread of gray light, hovering ocean, becomes throat . . .	**This image sets the scene for what is to come.** • What is the "thread of gray light"? • In what way is a developing hurricane like a throat?
. . . How dare the water belittle my thirst, treat me as just another small disturbance . . .	**These lines develop the character of the poem's speaker.** • From whose point of view is this poem presented? • What effect does the use of single words on each line create?
every woman begins as weather, . . . Every woman harbors a chaos . . .	**These lines develop a comparison.** • Is it literally true that "every woman begins as weather"? • What is being compared in these lines?
For now, I console myself with small furies, . . . I pull in a bored breath. The brine shivers.	**The poem ends on a suspenseful note.** • What is the speaker's tone in these lines? • Why does the brine shiver?

CLOSE READ

Support Inferences About Word Choice

To make sure students understand each boldfaced term, have them work together in pairs to paraphrase the meaning of each term. Students can take turns explaining a term while the partner provides an example from the poem. Then ask pairs to discuss the text examples and questions in the chart.

Possible answers:

- *The "thread of gray light" is the storm clouds or the horizon.*
- *A developing hurricane is like a throat because it is widening to swallow everything in its path.*
- *The poem is presented from the point of view of the hurricane.*
- *The use of single-word lines emphasizes the idea that the water seems to view the hurricane as a minor nuisance, not befitting its importance.*
- *It is not literally true that "every woman begins as weather." This line is a metaphor.*
- *A woman is compared to a developing storm: "begins as weather" is the power of birth, and "harbors a chaos" is a woman's and a storm's ability to create or increase something.*
- *The tone is both patient and condescending. The storm knows it will grow, so it is patient, and it knows that respect for it will grow in time.*
- *The brine shivers because the sea begins to realize just how powerful this storm is going to be.*

Strategies for Annotation ✏️ 📄 *Annotate it!*

Support Inferences About Word Choice

Have students use their eBook annotation tools to analyze the poet's word choice, focusing on how the storm and the ocean are personified, or given human qualities. Then students will analyze the interaction of the two.

- Highlight in yellow details that personify the hurricane.
- Highlight in blue details that personify the ocean.
- How does the personified interaction between the storm and the ocean reflect how an actual hurricane interacts with the ocean?

a mouth, thrashing hair, an overdone eye. How dare
the water belittle my thirst, treat me as just

another

small

disturbance,

Analyzing the Text COMMON CORE RL 1, RL 2, RL 4, RL 5

Possible answers:

1. *The quotation establishes that the poem is about a hurricane. It provides a stark contrast to the poem: the language in the quotation is very clinical; there is no drama to it; and it speaks of the storm as an inanimate object. The poem, on the other hand, uses vibrant language; establishes a dramatic and ominous tone; and speaks of the hurricane as a powerful, determined living being.*

2. *The hurricane is personified. The use of the first-person pronouns ("I," "me," "my"); the references to a body ("mouth," "thrashing hair," "my body," "my teeth," "hips," "breath"); and the comparison to a woman all give it human qualities.*

3. *The speaker's tone is patient, confident, and threatening. The patience and confidence are evident in the way the speaker recognizes that she is just a growing storm now, but she will soon be a full-blown hurricane ("I will"; "For now"). The threatening tone is evident in the way the speaker reacts to being challenged ("How dare the water belittle my thirst") and what she will soon unleash ("Every woman harbors a chaos"; "The brine shivers").*

4. *Words with strong connotations include "thrashing," "unbridled," "chaos," and "furies." These words create a feeling of dread in the anticipation of a powerful, uncontrollable force.*

5. *The speaker seems offended that she is being dismissed so carelessly. The short, clipped lines are meant to reflect the abrupt, dismissive attitude being shown to the speaker. They create both an offended tone and a menacing one. The speaker does not appreciate being treated so lightly and dismissively.*

6. *One theme the poet conveys is that natural forces need to be respected—they cannot be treated lightly. Other possible themes are that the powerful gain their power from things other than themselves, that power can be destructive, and that the powerful are doomed to self-destruction—though not stated, a hurricane weakens and falls apart once the source of its power, the warm waters, is removed.*

✔ Assess It!

Online Selection Test
- Download an editable ExamView bank.
- Assign and manage this test online.

✎ 📖 **eBook** *Annotate It!*

Analyzing the Text COMMON CORE RL 1, RL 2, RL 4, RL 5, SL 6

Cite Text Evidence   Support your responses with evidence from the selection.

1. **Draw Conclusions** Why does the poet begin this poem with a quotation from the National Hurricane Center? What does this information convey to the reader?

2. **Cite Evidence** What nonhuman subject is personified in the poem? Identify specific words and phrases that give the subject human qualities.

3. **Analyze** Describe the speaker's tone in this poem. What words and phrases does the poet use to establish this tone?

4. **Interpret** What words and phrases from the poem have especially strong connotative meanings? What feelings do they convey?

5. **Analyze** Read the first two stanzas aloud, keeping in mind the voice and personality of the speaker. How do the short lines at the end of this passage affect tone and meaning?

6. **Infer** What ultimate **theme**, or deeper message about life, does the poet convey through the personification and imagery in the poem?

PERFORMANCE TASK

Speaking Activity: Poetry Reading Patricia Smith is a National Poetry Slam Champion, and this poem is meant to be spoken. Work with a small group to adapt the poem for a male voice and practice reading it aloud.

1. Discuss what words and phrases in the poem stand out and what figurative and connotative meanings they have. How should those words be spoken? Ominously? Angrily?

2. Think about how the poem could have instead personified the hurricane as male. Discuss what words and phrases could be substituted to adapt this poem for a male voice.

3. Take turns reading the poem aloud, emphasizing key words and phrases. Read both versions, demonstrating both female and male voices.

4. Write a brief summary of what you learned by reading the poem aloud and by adapting the language to suit a male speaker.

Assign this performance task.

PERFORMANCE TASK COMMON CORE RL 4, SL 6

Speaking Activity: Poetry Reading Have small groups use unique markings to separately identify words and phrases with figurative and connotative meanings, and words and phrases that indicate a female speaker (note that there may be overlap). Encourage students to be prepared to explain and support any substitutions they make. The readings should demonstrate an understanding of pace and tone, and the summaries should reflect an understanding of the speaker's role in the poem.

Analyze Complex Characters

RL 3, W 2, W 9a

TEACH

Explain that engaging literature has complex characters, or characters with depth, who are not just one-dimensional. When analyzing a complex character, readers should consider:

- **What the character says and does:** Just as with real people, you can tell a lot about what kind of person a character is by the things he or she says and does, especially how he or she treats others.
- **How other characters react to the character:** A reader can learn about a character by the way other characters react to him or her. Do they act like they don't trust the character? Do they say things that suggest they're afraid of the character? Readers should ask themselves questions like, "What makes this character untrustworthy?" "Why should this character be feared?"
- **What the character thinks:** A character's thoughts may be as revealing as his or her actions. Also, be aware of contradictions between a character's actions and thoughts. By evaluating such contrasts, the reader gains deeper insight into what truly motivates the character.

PRACTICE AND APPLY

Have students compare the speaker of this poem with either Macbeth or Lady Macbeth. They should start by listing key traits of both characters, focusing on traits shared by Smith's and Shakespeare's characters. Then to elaborate on ideas, they should ask themselves:

- What traits are revealed by the characters' words and actions?
- How do other "characters" in both works (such as the water in the poem) react to the chosen characters?
- What inner thoughts reveal key traits?
- What motivations and desires are shared by the poem's speaker and either Macbeth or Lady Macbeth?

Encourage students to note any contrasts as well as comparisons, and discuss their conclusions in a one-page character analysis.

Integrate Various Sources of Information

SL 2

TEACH

Explain that reading a text along with information from other sources can enhance the reader's experience of the text, and provide supporting or contrasting information that helps readers form a deeper understanding and appreciation of the text. When integrating information from various sources, readers should look for these characteristics:

- **Similarities:** Identifying similarities between a text that you are reading and other sources can lend credibility to information provided in the text. For example, if you're reading a historical novel in which the characters fight in a famous battle, and a reliable history source supports the details of the battle, you can have more confidence that the novel's author is providing accurate information.
- **Differences:** What does it mean if conflicts of information are revealed when reading multiple texts? Using the example above, what if the novel's author provided information that contradicted the historical source? A critical reader would note these differences, and consider why these differences occurred. What purpose might a fiction author have for deviating from the facts?
- **Multimedia:** While words are powerful, they do have their limits. Different types of media—video, audio recordings, online interactive experiences—can offer additional information for readers to integrate with the original text. Imagine if readers of that historical novel watched a video of archival war footage. The sights and sounds could contribute to what they imagined, and lend credibility to the author's portrayal.

PRACTICE AND APPLY

Have students create a three-circle Venn diagram, with one circle each for the poem, the History Channel video, and the National Hurricane Center statement at the beginning of the poem. Tell students to determine where the representations differ, and to use these differences to discuss the following:

- Are there any factual differences? How can these differences be accounted for? Which source seems most credible?
- How do these differences (as well as the similarities) contribute to an understanding and appreciation of the poem?

Analyze Poetic Form

COMMON CORE
RL 5

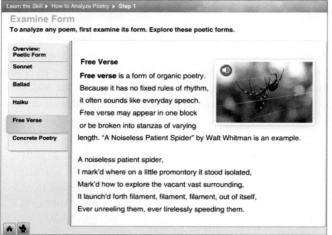

TEACH

Before having students do the Performance Task, review with them how a poem's form contributes to the voice of the speaker and the sound of the poem as it's read.

Discuss with students whether Smith's poem is considered a traditional form or an organic form, and have them support their answers. *(Its lack of regular rhythm and rhyme make it an organic form.)* Ask them why they think "organic" is a fitting label for the content. *(One connotation of organic is "natural," and the poem is about a force of nature.)*

Have students identify which of the tabs reflects the specific form used in Smith's poem, and explain their choice. *(The poem is identifiable as free verse due to its loose structure, varying stanza length, and everyday speech.)* Ask them why this form is appropriate, and how it contributes to meaning and building tension in the poem. *(The loose form reflects the chaos of a hurricane; the shorter, later stanzas give the feeling that things are beginning to happen faster; the everyday language and images are fitting for the personification of the hurricane as speaker.)*

COLLABORATIVE DISCUSSION

Direct students to consider how the free verse form of "5 P.M., Tuesday, August 23, 2005" affects how it sounds as they read the poem aloud in the Performance Task. Encourage students to also consider what effect, if any, changing the gender of the speaker has had on the form.

Support Inferences About Word Choice

COMMON CORE
RL 1, RL 4

RETEACH

Review the terms *figurative language, metaphor, extended metaphor, personification, connotative,* and *tone.* Remind students that poets choose words to create specific meanings and feelings. Often no other word would do. Changing them can alter a poem's meaning or message.

- Ask students to consider the phrase *thrashing hair* in line 9 and what it contributes to the extended metaphor. *(The metaphor evokes tendrils of cloud whirling in a hurricane and makes the storm seem distinctly feminine.)*
- Have students consider the word *dawning* in line 26 and what it contributes to the tone. Ask: Why does the poet choose the word *dawning* instead of a comparable word, such as *beginning* or *brewing*? *("Dawning" suggests the horizon, or as far as the eye can see. Use of this word suggests not just a beginning, but how immense and overwhelming the storm will be.)*

 LEVEL UP TUTORIALS Assign the following *Level Up* tutorial: **Figurative Language**

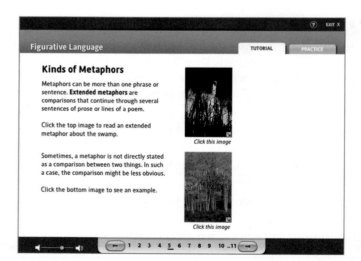

CLOSE READING APPLICATION

Students can apply the skill to the revised poems they did in the Performance Task. Have each student take one of the revised poems and evaluate the newly introduced words or phrases. Ask: Why do you think the writer used this particular word or phrase? How does it affect meaning? Does it add to, take away from, or change in some other way the meaning of Smith's poem?

Write an Analytical Essay

COMMON CORE

W 2a–f Write informative/ explanatory texts.

W 9a–b Draw evidence from literary or informational texts to support analysis.

This collection focuses on human ambition and our eternal quest for power. In his speech "Why Read Shakespeare?" Michael Mack argues that if you don't see yourself in Macbeth's ambition, you're either misreading the play or misreading yourself. Review the texts in this collection, including the anchor, Shakespeare's *Macbeth*. Then synthesize your ideas by writing an analysis that explains how one aspect of Macbeth's character represents a universal human trait.

An effective analytical essay

- includes a clear controlling idea about the universality of one of Macbeth's key personality traits
- begins by engaging the reader with an interesting observation, quotation, or detail from one of the selections
- organizes central ideas in a logically structured body that clearly develops the controlling idea
- uses transitions to show how ideas are related
- includes quotations or examples from the texts to illustrate central ideas
- has a concluding section that follows logically from the body of the essay and sums up the central ideas of the analysis

PLAN

Analyze the Texts Review *Macbeth* and two other texts in the collection.

- Take notes on Macbeth's character traits. Which of his traits are revealed in other texts in this collection and in people today? Which one of these traits will be your focus?
- Choose the two other texts in the collection that provide the strongest support for your conclusion about the universality of the character trait you have chosen.
- Write down important details, examples, and relevant quotations from all three texts that support your central idea.

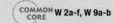

my Notebook

Use the annotation tools in your eBook to find evidence that supports your ideas about ambition. Save each piece of evidence to your notebook.

ACADEMIC VOCABULARY

As you share your ideas about ambition, be sure to use these words.

comprise
incidence
priority
thesis
ultimate

WRITE AN ANALYTICAL ESSAY

COMMON CORE **W 2a-f, W 9a-b**

Introduce students to the Performance Task by reading the introductory paragraph with them and reviewing the criteria for an effective analytical essay. Point out that their finished essays should contain a clearly communicated central idea that is well supported by accurate analysis of several texts and written using correct grammar and language conventions.

PLAN

ANALYZE THE TEXTS

View It!

Professional Development Podcast:

Performance Task

Remind students that they can identify a character's traits by examining what he or she thinks, says, and does; what other characters in the text say and think about the character; and how other characters react to him or her. A trait is not a passing emotion or a single reaction, so students should identify a pattern of behavior in the text. Explain to students that some traits may be more dominant than others and that students should consider which traits best describe the character, even if several different traits are present in his or her personality. When evaluating a complex character, students can examine how various traits come to the forefront or subside over the course of the narrative.

PERFORMANCE TASK

PLAN

GET ORGANIZED

Students have several choices for how to organize their essays in a logical manner. They might devote a paragraph or a section to analyzing each text in turn. They might also analyze a different aspect about their chosen trait in each section, incorporating examples from all three texts each time.

PRODUCE

DRAFT YOUR ESSAY

Remind students that their analyses must be supported by specific evidence from each text. Review some types of evidence that they might include:

- Summaries: relevant events from the text summed up in the student's own words.
- Paraphrases: important dialogue or narration from the text restated by the student.
- Quotations: specific words, phrases, and sentences presented word for word with a citation explaining exactly where they come from.
- Details: bits of information from the text, including descriptions of the appearance or actions of a character.

Get Organized Prioritize your ideas in a graphic organizer.

- Write a controlling idea, or thesis statement, about how your chosen trait is a human quality that all people exhibit to some extent or at certain times.

- Decide which organizational pattern you will use to develop your essay. In what order will you present your supporting examples and ideas? Be sure your ideas are presented in a logical order that flows from one to the next.

- Use your organizational pattern to sort the evidence you have gathered from the selections. Match each piece of evidence to the idea it best supports. A hierarchy diagram can help you organize your reasons and evidence for the body of your essay.

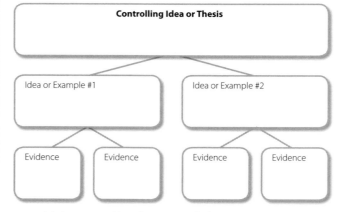

- Jot down some ideas for your conclusion.

PRODUCE

Draft Your Essay Write a draft of your essay, following your graphic organizer. As you work on your draft, consider your purpose and audience. Remember that essay writing requires formal language and a respectful tone. Essays that analyze literary texts should be appropriate for an academic context.

*my*WriteSmart

Write your rough draft in *my*WriteSmart. Focus on getting your ideas down, rather than perfecting your choice of language.

- Introduce a clear and concise controlling idea. Include an interesting quotation or detail in the introductory paragraph to draw in your audience.

- Present your details, quotations, and examples from the selections in logically ordered paragraphs. Each paragraph should have a central idea related to your thesis with evidence to support it. Explain how each piece of evidence supports the central idea.

- Use transitions to connect the main sections of your essay and to clarify the relationships among your ideas.
- Write a conclusion that summarizes your analysis and presents a final synthesis of your central ideas.

REVISE

Exchange Essays Share your essay with a partner. Use the chart on the next page to review the characteristics of an effective analytical essay. As you read your partner's essay, consider these questions:

my **WriteSmart**

Have your partner or a group of peers review your draft in *my*WriteSmart. Ask your reviewers to note any evidence that does not support the controlling idea.

- Does the introduction correctly identify all three titles and authors?
- Does your partner's controlling idea include a perspective from all three texts on how Macbeth exhibits a universal human trait?
- Are the ideas in the essay developed in a logical order, using appropriate transitions to connect them?
- Has the writer provided sufficient and relevant textual evidence in a logically organized way?
- Are any sections of the essay confusing? What additional information or explanation could help clarify the writer's ideas?
- Does the writer maintain a formal style and objective tone?
- Is the conclusion an accurate summary of the analysis? Does it eloquently synthesize the central ideas of the essay?

Tell your partner which aspects of the essay are particularly strong, and point out any areas that need clarification. Allow your partner to give you feedback on your essay. Then use the information from your feedback session to improve your draft. Make sure it is clear, coherent, and engaging.

PRESENT

Share Your Essay When your final draft is completed, read your essay aloud to a small group. The audience should listen, take notes, and be prepared to comment or ask questions.

REVISE

EXCHANGE ESSAYS

Note that a point can be well supported with several examples from the text yet not actually relate to the main idea that a student is trying to make. Partners should help each other evaluate not only whether there are holes in the logic of each other's papers but also if there are extraneous points being made that could be cut to ensure a tighter focus on the main thesis being defended.

PRESENT

SHARE YOUR ESSAY

Pair or group students who chose to write about similar or identical traits and have them share their essays with the same audience. As part of the post-presentation discussion, suggest that the audience compare the texts each writer chose to analyze and the examples he or she selected as support, evaluating how effectively each writer structured his or her analysis.

PERFORMANCE TASK

ORGANIZATION

Have students look at the chart and identify how they did on the Performance Task in the Organization category. Ask them to evaluate how well they organized central ideas and supporting evidence and used transitions to effectively show connections between ideas. Have students choose one area that needs improvement and outline a strategy to do so.

COLLECTION 5 TASK
ANALYTICAL ESSAY

	Ideas and Evidence	Organization	Language
ADVANCED	• An eloquent introduction includes titles and authors of selections; a clear controlling idea describes the view of the chosen trait presented in the texts. • Specific, relevant details support the central ideas. • A satisfying conclusion synthesizes the ideas and summarizes the analysis.	• Central ideas and supporting evidence are organized effectively and logically throughout the essay. • Varied transitions successfully show the relationships between ideas.	• The analysis uses an appropriately formal style and a knowledgeable, objective tone. • Language is precise and captures the writer's thoughts with originality. • Sentence beginnings, lengths, and structures vary and flow well. • Spelling, capitalization, and punctuation are correct. • Grammar and usage are correct.
COMPETENT	• The introduction identifies selection titles and authors but could be more engaging; the controlling idea identifies the chosen trait but may be cursory. • Most central ideas are adequately supported. • The concluding section synthesizes most of the ideas and summarizes most of the analysis.	• The organization of central ideas and supporting evidence is usually easy to follow. • Transitions generally clarify the relationships between ideas.	• The style is generally formal, and the tone usually communicates confidence. • Most language is precise. • Sentence beginnings, lengths, and structures vary somewhat. • A few spelling, capitalization, and punctuation mistakes occur. • Some grammatical and usage errors occur but do not interfere with understanding.
LIMITED	• The introduction identifies the selections; the controlling idea only hints at the main idea of the analysis. • Details support some central ideas but are often too general. • The concluding section gives an incomplete summary of the analysis and merely restates the thesis.	• Most central ideas are organized logically, but supporting details may be out of place. • More transitions are needed throughout the essay to connect ideas.	• The style is often informal, and the tone reflects a superficial understanding of the texts. • Language is repetitive or vague at times. • Sentence structures barely vary, and some fragments or run-on sentences are present. • Spelling, capitalization, and punctuation are often incorrect. • Grammar and usage are incorrect in many places, sometimes making the writer's ideas unclear.
EMERGING	• The appropriate elements of an introduction are missing. • Details and evidence are irrelevant or missing. • The analysis lacks a concluding section.	• A logical organization is not used; ideas are presented randomly. • Transitions are not used, making the essay difficult to understand.	• Style and tone are inappropriate. • Language is inaccurate, repetitive, and vague. • Repetitive sentence structure, fragments, and run-on sentences make the writing difficult to follow. • Numerous errors in spelling, capitalization, or punctuation occur. • Many grammar and usage errors interfere with the writer's ideas.

Image Credits: *Calle II, 2008* (oil on canvas) ©Bill Jacklin/Private Collection/The Bridgeman Art Library

Hard-Won Liberty

❝There is no easy walk to freedom anywhere.❞

—Nelson Mandela

CONNECTING WORD AND IMAGE

ASK STUDENTS to discuss how the collection opener image and the collection quotation work together to create a connection.

PERFORMANCE TASK PREVIEW

Point out to students that they will complete one performance task at the end of the collection. The performance task will require them to further analyze the selections in the collection and to synthesize ideas about these analyses. They will present their findings in a written argument.

ACADEMIC VOCABULARY

View It!

Professional Development Podcast:

Academic Vocabulary

Students can acquire facility with the academic vocabulary words through frequent, repeated exposure as they analyze and discuss the selections in the collection. Academic vocabulary can be used in the following instructional contexts. This will enable students to incorporate the academic vocabulary words into their working vocabulary.

- Collaborative Discussion at the end of each selection
- Analyzing the Text questions for each selection
- Selection-level Performance Task
- Vocabulary instruction (for Critical Vocabulary and/or for Vocabulary Strategy)
- Language and Style
- End-of-collection Performance Task for all selections in the collection

ASK STUDENTS to review the academic vocabulary word list for this collection. You may wish to pronounce each word aloud, so students hear the correct pronunciation. Then discuss the definitions and the related forms for each word. Remind students that they will encounter these five academic vocabulary words throughout the collection.

Hard Won Liberty

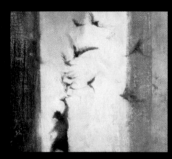

This collection travels around the world to explore how people win their freedom from oppression.

hmhfyi.com

COLLECTION

PERFORMANCE TASK Preview

At the end of this collection, you will have the opportunity to complete this task:

- Write an argument that answers this question: What constitutes true freedom?

ACADEMIC VOCABULARY

Study the words and their definitions in the chart below. You will use these words as you discuss and write about the texts in this collection.

Word	Definition	Related Forms
comprehensive (kŏm´prĭ-hĕn´sĭv) *adj.*	complete or of sufficient scope to include all aspects	comprehensively, comprehension
equivalent (ĭ-kwĭv´ə-lənt´) *adj.*	equal to or similar	equivalence, equivalently
incentive (ĭn-sĕn´tĭv) *n.*	an inducement or motivation to do something	disincentive, incentivize
innovate (ĭn´ə-vāt) *v.*	to change or develop through new or original methods, processes, or ideas	innovation, innovator, innovative
media (mē´dē-ə) *n.*	a means or vehicle for communication	medium

USING COLLECTIONS YOUR WAY

Use the following information, along with the charts on the following pages, to help you decide how you want to introduce the collection. Based on your teaching style, your students' interests, or your instructional goals, you may want to structure the collection in various ways. You may choose different entry points each time you teach the collection.

"I like to connect literature to history."

This letter written by **Martin Luther King Jr.** includes universal themes and historical references that supported his call for justice and helped achieve a strong impact on the civil rights cause.

Martin Luther King Jr. (1929–1968) led a nonviolent protest in 1963 against lunch counter segregation in Birmingham, Alabama. He was jailed along with many of his supporters. While in jail, King wrote this letter in response to the local clergy. As a Baptist minister and a leader of the civil rights movement, King helped to organize the 1963 March on Washington, where he delivered his "I Have a Dream" speech. His leadership was crucial in passing the Civil Rights Act of 1964. In the same year, he received the Nobel Peace Prize. King was assassinated in 1968.

Letter from Birmingham Jail

Argument by Martin Luther King Jr.

AS YOU READ Pay attention to what King hoped to achieve in Birmingham. Write down any questions you generate during reading.

April 16, 1963
My Dear Fellow Clergymen:

While confined here in the Birmingham city jail, I came across your recent statement calling my present activities "unwise and untimely." Seldom do I pause to answer criticism of my work and ideas. If I sought to answer all the criticisms that cross my desk, my secretaries would have little time for anything other than such correspondence in the course of the day, and I would have no time for constructive work. But since I feel that you are men of genuine good will and that your criticisms are sincerely set forth, I want to try to answer your statement in what I hope will be patient and reasonable terms.

I think I should indicate why I am here in Birmingham, since you have been influenced by the view which argues against "outsiders coming in." I have the honor of serving as president of the Southern Christian Leadership Conference, an organization

Letter from Birmingham Jail **319**

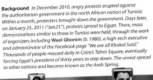

Background In December 2010, angry protests erupted against the authoritarian government in the north African nation of Tunisia. Within a month, protesters brought down the government. Days later, on January 25, 2011 ("Jan25"), protests spread to Egypt. There, mass demonstrations similar to those in Tunisia were held, through the work of organizers including **Wael Ghonim** (b. 1980), a high-tech executive and administrator of the Facebook page "We are all Khaled Said." Thousands of people massed daily in Cairo's Tahrir Square, eventually forcing Egypt's president of thirty years to step down. The unrest spread to other nations and became known as the Arab Spring.

"I emphasize informational texts."

This informational text excerpt compiles and summarizes information about the 2011 demonstrations in Egypt that were organized to protest the country's government and demand rights.

from

Revolution 2.0

Memoir by Wael Ghonim

AS YOU READ Identify how the author organizes information and think about the kinds of information the author includes in the document. Write down any questions you generate during reading.

I continued to rally supporters on the page. I shared writings, images, and designs made by the page members that promised a victorious Jan25. I tried to induce confidence and belief that youth would be capable of leading change. I also highlighted the government's frightened reactions.

I decided to compile all the information relevant to Jan25 in a document that was easy to print and to distribute online. It summarized the reasons for protesting and for choosing this day and these locations. It also described the unified chants that had been chosen and provided phone numbers for activists responsible for supporting arrested protesters and for redirecting demonstrators to other locations if the protests at any one place were obstructed. I uploaded the file to Google Docs, where more than 50,000 people accessed it. Its content was also **disseminated** through various online forums, political websites, Facebook pages, and Twitter accounts.

disseminate (dĭ-sĕm′ə-nāt′) v. to spread or circulate widely.

Revolution 2.0 **341**

"I love to concentrate on contemporary literature."

This modern story focuses on universal themes, such as political imprisonment, injustice, and power—building suspense by relating the events in the life of an escaped prisoner who is trying to avoid being discovered.

Background The protagonist of "The Briefcase" is a political prisoner in an unnamed country, a man who has been arrested for associating with the wrong people. Political prisoners are detained, imprisoned, and sometimes executed, without benefit of trial or jury, due to political associations or beliefs that conflict with those of the people in power. Such detentions happen all over the world under regimes that hold absolute power over the people and the press. In this story, author **Rebecca Makkai** (b. 1978) innovates the universality of political imprisonment through the use of basic astronomy.

The Briefcase

Short Story by Rebecca Makkai

AS YOU READ Pay attention to details that reveal something about the chef's character. Write down any questions you generate during reading.

He thought how strange that a political prisoner, marched through town in a line, chained to the man behind and chained to the man ahead, should take comfort in the fact that all this had happened before. He thought of other chains of men on other islands of the Earth, and he thought how since there have been men there have been prisoners. He thought of mankind as a line of miserable monkeys chained at the wrist, dragging each other back into the ground.

In the early morning of December first the sun was finally warming them all, enough that they could walk faster. With his left hand, he adjusted the loop of steel that cuffed his right hand to the line of doomed men. His hand was starved, his wrist was thin, his body was cold: the cuff slipped off. In one beat of the heart he looked back to the man behind him and forward to the man limping ahead, and knew that neither saw his naked, red wrist; each saw

The Briefcase **361**

COLLECTION 6 DIGITAL OVERVIEW

mySmartPlanner | **eBook** | **my**Notebook | ✓**my**WriteSmart | **fyi** hmhfyi.com

Collection 6 Lessons	Media	Teach and Practice
Student Edition | eBook	▶ Video Links	**Close Reading and Evidence Tracking**
ANCHOR TEXT — **Argument by Martin Luther King Jr.** "Letter from Birmingham Jail"	▶ **Video BIOGRAPHY** *Class of the 20th Century: 1963–1968* 🔊 **Audio** " Letter from Birmingham Jail"	**Close Read Screencasts** • Modeled Discussion 1 (lines 1–12) • Modeled Discussion 2 (lines 183–194) • Close Read application (lines 461–474) **Strategies for Annotation** • Analyze Argument in a Seminal Document • Context Clues • Repetition and Parallelism
CLOSE READER — **Speech by Josephine Baker** Speech at the March on Washington	🔊 **Audio** Speech at the March on Washington	
Memoir by Wael Ghonim from *Revolution 2.0*	🔊 **Audio** from *Revolution 2.0*	**Strategies for Annotation** • Domain-specific Words
Argument by Mohandas K. Gandhi from "Letter to Viceroy, Lord Irwin"	🔊 **Audio** from "Letter to Viceroy, Lord Irwin"	**Strategies for Annotation** • Analyze Argument and Rhetoric • Denotations and Connotations
Documentary Film by BBC from *Gandhi: The Rise to Fame*	🔊 **Audio** from *Gandhi: The Rise to Fame*	**Strategies for Annotation** • Analyze Accounts in Different Mediums
Short Story by Rebecca Makkai "The Briefcase"	🔊 **Audio** "The Briefcase"	**Strategies for Annotation** • Analyze Character and Theme
CLOSE READER — **Short Story by Christine Lee Zilka** "Bile"	🔊 **Audio** "Bile"	
Poem by Jimmy Santiago Baca "Cloudy Day"	🔊 **Audio** "Cloudy Day"	
Collection 6 Performance Task: Write an Argument	**fyi** hmhfyi.com	**Interactive Lessons** Writing an Argument Using Textual Evidence

		For Systematic Coverage of Writing and Speaking & Listening Standards	**Interactive Lessons** Writing Informative Texts Giving a Presentation	**Lesson Assessments** Writing Informative Texts Giving a Presentation

Assess		Extend	Reteach
Performance Task	**Online Assessment**	**Teacher eBook**	**Teacher eBook**
Writing Activity: Comparison	Selection Test	**Analyzing Themes in Seminal Documents**	**Analyze Argument in a Seminal Document > Level Up Tutorial >** Analyzing Arguments
Speaking Activity: Research	Selection Test	**Integrate Information Sources**	**Analyze Evidence and Author's Ideas > Level Up Tutorial >** Informational Text
Writing Activity: Analysis	Selection Test		
Speaking Activity: Debate		**Synthesize Sources**	**Analyze Accounts in Different Mediums > Level Up Tutorial >** Primary and Secondary Sources
Writing Activity: Personal Letter	Selection Test	**Analyze Tone > Interactive Whiteboard Lesson >** Word Choice and Tone	**Analyze Character and Theme > Level Up Tutorial >** Theme
Speaking Activity: Discussion	Selection Test	**Analyze Author's Choices: Text Structure** **Vocabulary Strategy: Denotations and Connotations > WordSharp Interactive Tutorial >** Denotative and Connotative Meanings **Respond in Discussions > Interactive Lesson >** Participating in Collaborative Discussions	**Analyze Theme and Tone > Level Up Tutorial >** Tone
Write an Argument	Collection Test		

Collection 6 Lessons	Key Learning Objective	Performance Task
ANCHOR TEXT **Argument by Martin Luther King, Jr.** *Letter from Birmingham Jail,* **p. 319A** **Lexile 1190**	**The student will be able to...** analyze argument in a seminal document	Writing Activity: Comparison
Memoir by Wael Ghonim from *Revolution 2.0,* **p. 341A** **Lexile 1100**	**The student will be able to...** analyze evidence and ideas in a functional document	Speaking Activity: Research
Argument by Mohandas K. Gandhi from *Letter to Viceroy, Lord Irwin,* **p. 351A** **Lexile 1210**	**The student will be able to...** analyze an argument and rhetoric and compare accounts in different mediums	Writing Activity: Analysis
Documentary Film by BBC from *Gandhi: The Rise to Fame,* **p. 359A**	**The student will be able to...** analyze an argument and rhetoric and compare accounts in different mediums	Speaking Activity: Debate
Short Story by Rebecca Makkaii *The Briefcase,* **p. 361A** **Lexile 860**	**The student will be able to...** analyze interactions between character and theme in a short story	Writing Activity: Personal Letter
Poem by Jimmy Santiago Baca *Cloudy Day,* **p. 373A**	**The student will be able to...** analyze how a poem's shift in tone contributes to its theme	Speaking Activity: Discussion

Collection 6 Performance Tasks:
Write an Argument

Vocabulary Strategy	Language and Style	Student Instructional Support	CLOSE READER Selection
Context Clues	Repetition and Parallelism	**Scaffolding for ELL Students:** • Understand Purpose • Analyze Conclusions • Rhetorical Questions • Understand Comparisons • Vocabulary: Prefixes **When Students Struggle:** • Understand Point of View • Understand Allusions • Understand Development of a Claim **To Challenge Students:** • Personal Views • Conduct Research • Summarize • Different Perspective	Speech by Josephine Baker Speech at the March on Washington, p. 340b **Lexile 860**
Domain-specific Words	Colons	**Scaffolding for ELL Students:** • Analyze Language: Infinitives • Analyze Author's Ideas **When Students Struggle:** • Development of Ideas • Text Formatting Strategies **To Challenge Students:** Analyze Author's Ideas	
Denotations and Connotations		**Scaffolding for ELL Students:** • Focus on Facts in Informational Text • Analyze Argument **When Students Struggle:** Comprehend Word Choice in Rhetoric **To Challenge Students:** Respond to an Argument	
		Scaffolding for ELL Students: Analyze Accounts in Different Mediums	
	Semicolons	**Scaffolding for ELL Students:** • Understand Time Sequence • Understand Dialogue **When Students Struggle:** • Understand Complicated Sentence Structure: Colons and Semicolons • Understand Character: Inner Dialogue **To Challenge Students:** • Exploring Themes • Explore Theme: Identity	Short Story by Christine Lee Zilka "Bile," p. 372b **Lexile 670**
	Prepositional Phrases	**Scaffolding for ELL Students:** Reading Comprehension: Imagery **When Students Struggle:** Similes and Metaphors	

ANCHOR TEXT EXEMPLAR

Letter from Birmingham Jail

Argument by Martin Luther King Jr.

Why This Text?

Students encounter arguments every day. As they become more aware of history and culture, they will also encounter arguments in seminal documents of historical significance. This lesson analyzes the argument developed by Martin Luther King Jr. in defense of his direct action against segregation in Birmingham, Alabama.

▶ **View It!**

Professional Development Podcast:

Teaching Argument

Key Learning Objective: The student will be able to analyze argument in a seminal document.

For practice and application:

Close Reader selection
"Speech at the March on Washington"
speech by Josephine Baker

Common Core Standards

COMMON CORE

RI 1 Cite textual evidence.

RI 2 Determine a central idea of a text.

RI 4 Analyze the cumulative impact of specific word choices.

RI 5 Analyze how an author's ideas are developed by particular sentences or paragraphs.

RI 6 Determine author's point of view/purpose; analyze how an author uses rhetoric to advance that point of view or purpose.

RI 8 Delineate and evaluate the argument and specific claims in a text.

RI 9 Analyze seminal U.S. documents of historical and literary significance.

W 5 Strengthen writing by planning, revising, editing, rewriting, or trying a new approach.

W 9b Apply grades 9–10 Reading standards to literary nonfiction.

W 10 Write over extended and shorter time frames for a range of tasks, purposes, and audiences.

L 1a Use parallel structure.

L 4a Use context as a clue to the meaning of a word.

L 4d Verify the preliminary determination of the meaning of a word.

L 5b Analyze nuances in words with similar denotations.

▲ Text Complexity Rubric

Quantitative Measures	**Letter from Birmingham Jail** Lexile: 1190L
Qualitative Measures	**Levels of Meaning/Purpose** multiple purposes; implied, subtle
	Structure organization of main ideas and details complex but mostly explicit
	Language Conventionality and Clarity increased unfamiliar, academic, or domain-specific words; more complex sentence structure
	Knowledge Demands specialized knowledge required; somewhat complex civics concepts
Reader/Task Considerations	Teacher determined Vary by individual reader and type of text

For more context and historical background, students can view the video "Class of the 20th Century: 1963–1968" in their eBooks.

Background Have students read the background and information about the author. Martin Luther King Jr.'s position on nonviolent direct action was influenced by the views of India's Mohandas Gandhi. A federal U.S. holiday, celebrated annually in January, was established in 1986 to honor King's accomplishments and legacy.

AS YOU READ Direct students to use the As You Read note to focus their reading.

Analyze Accounts in Different Mediums

COMMON CORE **RI 7**

After students have read the biography of Martin Luther King Jr. on this page, have them view the History video discussing King and the civil rights movement accessible through their eBooks. Ask students to discuss which aspects of King's life are emphasized in each source. Follow up by asking students how the nature of each medium might spotlight different details about King and the civil rights movement.

Analyze Argument in a Seminal Document (LINES 2–12)

COMMON CORE **RI 8, RI 9**

Tell students that arguments address specific claims and a specific audience.

 ASK STUDENTS to identify one claim opposing King's work to which he is responding in the first paragraph of the letter. To whom is he responding, and why is this audience significant? *(King is responding to the claim that his work is "unwise and untimely" [lines 4–5]. He is responding to a group of fellow religious leaders, which is significant because he can address them seriously as equals; he can expect them to be thoughtful people, not angry rabble-rousers.)*

counter segregation in Birmingham, Alabama. He was jailed along with many of his supporters. While in jail, King wrote this letter in response to the local clergy. As a Baptist minister and a leader of the civil rights movement, King helped to organize the 1963 March on Washington, where he delivered his "I Have a Dream" speech. His leadership was crucial in passing the Civil Rights Act of 1964. In the same year, he received the Nobel Peace Prize. King was assassinated in 1968.

Letter from Birmingham Jail

Argument by Martin Luther King Jr.

Image Credits: (l) ©CSU Archives/Everett Collection Inc./Alamy Images; (r) ©Bill Hudson/AP Images

AS YOU READ Pay attention to what King hoped to achieve in Birmingham. Write down any questions you generate during reading.

April 16, 1963
My Dear Fellow Clergymen:

While confined here in the Birmingham city jail, I came across your recent statement calling my present activities "unwise and untimely." Seldom do I pause to answer criticism of my work and ideas. If I sought to answer all the criticisms that cross my desk, my secretaries would have little time for anything other than such correspondence in the course of the day, and I would have no time for constructive work. But since I feel that you are men of genuine
10   good will and that your criticisms are sincerely set forth, I want to try to answer your statement in what I hope will be patient and reasonable terms.

   I think I should indicate why I am here in Birmingham, since you have been influenced by the view which argues against "outsiders coming in." I have the honor of serving as president of the Southern Christian Leadership Conference, an organization

Letter from Birmingham Jail   **319**

Modeled Discussions

Have students click the *Close Read* icons in their eBooks to access two screencasts in which readers discuss and annotate the following key passages:

- the date, salutation, and introductory paragraph (lines 1–12)
- King's discussion of just and unjust laws (lines 183–194)

As a class, view and discuss at least one of these videos. Then have students pair up to do an independent close read of an additional passage—King's request for southern white ministers to support integration because it is morally right to do so (lines 461–474).

Analyze Argument in a Seminal Document

COMMON CORE RI 8, RI 9

(LINES 17–43)

Explain to students the three different types of reasons that King provides in his letter to justify his presence in Birmingham.

Organizational reasons relate to any associations with organizations or groups of people.

Religious or **historical reasons** relate to religious or historical people, places, things, or events.

Moral reasons relate to morality, or what is considered right or wrong.

Ⓑ **CITE TEXT EVIDENCE** Have students choose one type of reason and work in pairs to cite an example from lines 17–43. Then have them explain why the example fits their chosen reason. Invite volunteers to share their explanations with the class. Accept all reasonable responses. *(Possible answer: King states a moral reason that he is in Birmingham: because "injustice is here" [lines 27–28]. This is a moral reason because injustice relates to what is considered right or wrong.)*

Explain that an **allusion** is an indirect reference to a famous person, place, event, or literary work.

Ⓒ **ASK STUDENTS** to identify a religious allusion on the page. *(King alludes to prophets in the eighth century B.C. and the Apostle Paul, who carried the word of the gospel beyond their home towns.)* Ask students to explain why King included religious allusions in his letter. *(King was writing to clergymen, so he could expect references to Biblical events to resonate with them.)*

CRITICAL VOCABULARY

cognizant: King is aware that communities and states are connected.

ASK STUDENTS how King was cognizant of injustices in Birmingham if he did not live there. *(King was informed by an affiliate organization that is present in Birmingham.)*

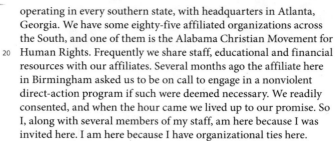

Ⓑ operating in every southern state, with headquarters in Atlanta, Georgia. We have some eighty-five affiliated organizations across the South, and one of them is the Alabama Christian Movement for
20 Human Rights. Frequently we share staff, educational and financial resources with our affiliates. Several months ago the affiliate here in Birmingham asked us to be on call to engage in a nonviolent direct-action program if such were deemed necessary. We readily consented, and when the hour came we lived up to our promise. So I, along with several members of my staff, am here because I was invited here. I am here because I have organizational ties here.

But more basically, I am in Birmingham because injustice is here. Just as the prophets of the eighth century B.C. left their villages and carried their "thus saith the Lord" far beyond the
30 boundaries of their home towns, and just as the Apostle Paul left his village of Tarsus and carried the gospel of Jesus Christ to the far corners of the Greco-Roman world, so am I compelled to carry the gospel of freedom beyond my own home town. Like Paul, I must constantly respond to the Macedonian call for aid.[1]   Ⓒ

Moreover, I am **cognizant** of the interrelatedness of all communities and states. I cannot sit idly by in Atlanta and not be concerned about what happens in Birmingham. Injustice anywhere is a threat to justice everywhere. We are caught in an inescapable network of mutuality, tied in a single garment of destiny. Whatever
40 affects one directly, affects all indirectly. Never again can we afford to live with the narrow, provincial "outside agitator" idea. Anyone who lives inside the United States can never be considered an outsider anywhere within its bounds.

You deplore the demonstrations taking place in Birmingham. But your statement, I am sorry to say, fails to express a similar concern for the conditions that brought about the demonstrations. I am sure that none of you would want to rest content with the superficial kind of social analysis that deals merely with effects and does not grapple with underlying causes. It is unfortunate that
50 demonstrations are taking place in Birmingham, but it is even more unfortunate that the city's white power structure left the Negro community with no alternative.

In any nonviolent campaign there are four basic steps: collection of the facts to determine whether injustices exist; negotiation; self-purification; and direct action. We have gone through all these steps in Birmingham. There can be no gainsaying the fact that racial injustice engulfs this community. Birmingham is probably the most thoroughly segregated city in the United States. Its ugly record of brutality is widely known. Negroes have

cognizant
(kŏg′nĭ-zənt) *adj.*
aware or conscious of.

---

[1] **Macedonian call for aid:** according to the Bible (Acts 16), the apostle Paul received a vision calling him to preach in Macedonia, an area north of Greece.

320   Collection 6

SCAFFOLDING FOR ELL STUDENTS

Understand Purpose To help students understand King's purpose in writing the letter and to practice citing text evidence, read aloud the first paragraph and ask students to identify to whom King is writing. *(other clergymen)* Then ask how these people described King's protest activities. *("unwise and untimely")* Direct students to the final sentence in this paragraph and ask them to explain why King is writing this letter to the clergymen. *("to answer your statement")* Have students read lines 13–28 independently.

ASK STUDENTS who invited King to Birmingham. *("affiliate in Birmingham")* Then ask why King decided to go. *("because injustice is here")*

experienced grossly unjust treatment in the courts. There have
been more unsolved bombings of Negro homes and churches in
Birmingham than in any other city in the nation. These are the
hard, brutal facts of the case. On the basis of these conditions,
Negro leaders sought to negotiate with the city fathers. But the
latter consistently refused to engage in good-faith negotiation.

Then, last September, came the opportunity to talk with
leaders of Birmingham's economic community. In the course of the
negotiations, certain promises were made by the merchants—for
example, to remove the stores' humiliating racial signs.[2] On the
basis of these promises, the Reverend Fred Shuttlesworth and the
leaders of the Alabama Christian Movement for Human Rights
agreed to a **moratorium** on all demonstrations. As the weeks
and months went by, we realized that we were the victims of a
broken promise. A few signs, briefly removed, returned; the others
remained.

As in so many past experiences, our hopes had been blasted,
and the shadow of deep disappointment settled upon us. We had
no alternative except to prepare for direct action, whereby we
would present our very bodies as a means of laying our case before
the conscience of the local and the national community. Mindful
of the difficulties involved, we decided to undertake a process of
self-purification. We began a series of workshops on nonviolence,
and we repeatedly asked ourselves: "Are you able to accept blows
without **retaliating**?" "Are you able to endure the ordeal of jail?"
We decided to schedule our direct-action program for the Easter
season, realizing that except for Christmas, this is the main
shopping period of the year. Knowing that a strong economic-
withdrawal program[3] would be the by-product of direct action, we
felt that this would be the best time to bring pressure to bear on the
merchants for the needed change.

Then it occurred to us that Birmingham's mayoralty election
was coming up in March, and we speedily decided to postpone
action until after election day. When we discovered that the
Commissioner of Public Safety, Eugene "Bull" Connor, had
piled up enough votes to be in the run-off, we decided again
to postpone action until the day after the run-off so that the
demonstrations could not be used to cloud the issues. Like many
others, we waited to see Mr. Connor defeated, and to this end we
endured postponement after postponement. Having aided in this
community need, we felt that our direct-action program could be
delayed no longer.

moratorium
(môr′ə-tôr′ē-əm) *n.*
a temporary
suspension or
agreed-upon delay.

retaliate
(rĭ-tăl′ē-āt′) *v.* to
respond in kind to
having been acted
upon, often with
harmful intent.

---

[2] **racial signs:** signs that marked segregated areas of buildings and other
facilities.
[3] **economic withdrawal program:** boycott.

CLOSE READ

Analyze Argument
COMMON CORE RI 5, RI 8
(LINES 66–101)

Point out to students that this entire page of the
letter discusses recent events in Birmingham in detail.

D **ASK STUDENTS** why King might have taken
the time so early in the letter to delve into such
minute detail about steps taken and recent events in
Birmingham. (*King is responding to the claim that his
work is "untimely" by carefully detailing the evidence
that shows, on the contrary, that his work is long
overdue. The many thoughtfully considered delays he
cites illustrate that King and those working with him are
far from hasty in their actions.*)

CRITICAL VOCABULARY

moratorium: Because of promises made by local
merchants, leaders of the Alabama Christian
Movement for Civil Rights agreed to suspend their
demonstrations in Birmingham.

ASK STUDENTS to discuss why the leaders of the
Alabama Christian Movement for Human Rights
agreed to a moratorium on all direct actions. (*They
wanted to show they would honor negotiated terms.*)

retaliate: The workshops on nonviolence were
designed to ensure that participants in direct
actions would not react in a harmful way even if
harm came to them.

ASK STUDENTS what might happen if participants
retaliated against police who struck blows.
(*Participants and police officers would both be
injured.*)

APPLYING ACADEMIC VOCABULARY

media	incentive

As you discuss King's letter, incorporate the following Collection 6 academic
vocabulary words: *media* and *incentive*. Tell students that this letter was
disseminated, or released, by the **media** to the public. King used old
newspapers as his stationery. His lawyers had to smuggle portions of the
letter out of the Birmingham jail in order for it to be published in magazines.
As students explore the specific details that relate to the four steps taken
by King and others, have them identify the **incentive** that led to the
implementation of step four, direct action.

Analyze Rhetoric

COMMON CORE RI 4, RI 6

(LINES 104–119)

Explain that writers of arguments can use repetition sparingly to make their ideas more memorable for readers.

E **CITE TEXT EVIDENCE** Ask students to identify all of the instances of the word *tension* in these lines. *(King uses the word* tension *seven times [lines 106, 109, 111, 112, 114, and 117].)* Have students identify the ways in which the meaning and tone of the word *tension* change over the course of the paragraph. *(At first,* tension *seems to hold a negative connotation, but as King refines its meaning, the tone surrounding* tension *becomes clearly positive.)*

You may well ask: "Why direct action? Why sit-ins, marches and so forth? Isn't negotiation a better path?" You are quite right in calling for negotiation. Indeed, this is the very purpose of direct action. Nonviolent direct action seeks to create such a crisis and foster such a tension that a community which has constantly refused to negotiate is forced to confront the issue. It seeks so to dramatize the issue that it can no longer be ignored. My citing the creation of tension as part of the work of the nonviolent-resister 110 may sound rather shocking. But I must confess that I am not afraid of the word "tension." I have earnestly opposed violent tension, but there is a type of constructive, nonviolent tension which is necessary for growth. Just as Socrates[4] felt that it was necessary to create a tension in the mind so that individuals could rise from the bondage of myths and half-truths to the unfettered realm of creative analysis and objective appraisal, so must we see the need for nonviolent gadflies to create the kind of tension in society that will help men rise from the dark depths of prejudice and racism to the majestic heights of understanding and brotherhood.

120 The purpose of our direct-action program is to create a situation so crisis-packed that it will inevitably open the door to negotiation. I therefore concur with you in your call for negotiation. Too long has our beloved Southland been bogged down in a tragic effort to live in monologue rather than dialogue.

One of the basic points in your statement is that the action that I and my associates have taken in Birmingham is untimely. Some have asked: "Why didn't you give the new city administration time to act?" The only answer that I can give to this query is that the new Birmingham administration must be prodded about as much 130 as the outgoing one, before it will act. . . . My friends, I must say to you that we have not made a single gain in civil rights without determined legal and nonviolent pressure. Lamentably, it is an historical fact that privileged groups seldom give up their privileges voluntarily. Individuals may see the moral light and voluntarily give up their unjust posture; but, as Reinhold Niebuhr[5] has reminded us, groups tend to be more immoral than individuals.

We know through painful experience that freedom is never voluntarily given by the oppressor; it must be demanded by the oppressed. Frankly, I have yet to engage in a direct-action campaign 140 that was "well timed" in the view of those who have not suffered unduly from the disease of segregation. For years now I have heard the word "Wait!" It rings in the ear of every Negro with piercing

---

[4] **Socrates:** (c. 470–399 B.C.) Greek philosopher and major influence in the development of Western thought.

[5] **Reinhold Niebuhr:** (1892–1971) American theologian whose writings address moral and social problems.

WHEN STUDENTS STRUGGLE . . .

Tell students that arguments present different points of view. Help students visualize the two sides of an argument by flipping a coin and discussing the idiom, "the other side of the coin." Remind students that King and others favored direct action and that the clergymen favored negotiation. Have students work in pairs. Using a timer, direct one student to argue in favor of the use of direct action (sit-ins and marches) for one minute. After a minute, have the other student argue for one minute in favor of negotiation. Explain that knowing and addressing an opposing view can help a writer be more convincing.

Martin Luther King Jr. (seated at left of table) speaks at a news conference in Birmingham, AL, in May of 1963.

familiarity. This "Wait" has almost always meant "Never." We must come to see, with one of our distinguished jurists, that "justice too long delayed is justice denied."

We have waited for more than 340 years for our constitutional and God-given rights. The nations of Asia and Africa are moving with jetlike speed toward gaining political independence, but we still creep at horse-and-buggy pace toward gaining a cup of coffee
150 at a lunch counter. Perhaps it is easy for those who have never felt the stinging darts of segregation to say, "Wait." But when you have seen vicious mobs lynch your mothers and fathers at will and drown your sisters and brothers at whim; when you have seen hate-filled policemen curse, kick and even kill your black brothers and sisters; when you see the vast majority of your twenty million Negro brothers smothering in an airtight cage of poverty in the midst of an affluent society; when you suddenly find your tongue twisted and your speech stammering as you seek to explain to your six-year-old daughter why she can't go to the public amusement
160 park that has just been advertised on television, and see tears

Analyze Rhetoric   COMMON CORE RI 6, L 1a

(LINES 151–179)

Explain that **parallelism** is the use of similar grammatical forms to express ideas that are related or equal in importance.

F **CITE TEXT EVIDENCE** Ask students to identify the parallel structure used in this passage. *(King repeats "when you" at the beginning of each subordinate clause in the sentence that begins on line 151. Each clause states a response to the preceding sentence, "Perhaps it is easy for those who have never felt the stinging darts of segregation to say, "Wait.")* Ask students what effect this use of parallel structure has on King's argument. *(By using parallel structure to link examples of the injustices faced on a daily basis by African Americans, King makes clear to readers the pervasiveness of this pattern of discrimination.)*

Analyze Argument in a Seminal Document

(LINES 183–194)

Tell students that seminal documents may refer to other seminal documents to support ideas.

G **ASK STUDENTS** to what other seminal document King refers in this paragraph. *(King refers to the 1954 Supreme Court decision that ended racial segregation in public schools.)* Ask students which of King's three reasons for being in Birmingham is supported by this distinction between just and unjust laws. *(This discussion supports the idea that King is in Birmingham for moral reasons.)*

welling up in her eyes when she is told that Funtown is closed to colored children, and see ominous clouds of inferiority beginning to form in her little mental sky, and see her beginning to distort her personality by developing an unconscious bitterness toward white people; when you have to concoct an answer for a five-year-old son who is asking: "Daddy, why do white people treat colored people so mean?"; when you take a cross-country drive and find it necessary to sleep night after night in the uncomfortable corners of your automobile because no motel will accept you; when you are
170 humiliated day in and day out by nagging signs reading "white" and "colored"; when your first name becomes "nigger," your middle name becomes "boy" (however old you are) and your last name becomes "John," and your wife and mother are never given the respected title "Mrs."; when you are harried by day and haunted by night by the fact that you are a Negro, living constantly at tiptoe stance, never quite knowing what to expect next, and are plagued with inner fears and outer resentments; when you are forever fighting a degenerating sense of "nobodiness"—then you will understand why we find it difficult to wait. There comes a
180 time when the cup of endurance runs over, and men are no longer willing to be plunged into the abyss of despair. I hope, sirs, you can understand our legitimate and unavoidable impatience.

You express a great deal of anxiety over our willingness to break laws. This is certainly a legitimate concern. Since we so diligently urge people to obey the Supreme Court's decision of 1954 outlawing segregation in the public schools,[6] at first glance it may seem rather paradoxical for us consciously to break laws. One may well ask: "How can you advocate breaking some laws and obeying others?" The answer lies in the fact that there are two types of laws:
190 just and unjust. I would be the first to advocate obeying just laws. One has not only a legal but a moral responsibility to obey just laws. Conversely, one has a moral responsibility to disobey unjust laws. I would agree with St. Augustine[7] that "an unjust law is no law at all."

Now, what is the difference between the two? How does one determine whether a law is just or unjust? A just law is a man-made code that squares with the moral law or the law of God. An unjust law is a code that is out of harmony with the moral law. To put it in the terms of St. Thomas Aquinas:[8] An unjust law is a
200 human law that is not rooted in eternal law and natural law. Any

G

---

[6] **Supreme Court . . . public schools:** The U.S. Supreme Court's decision in the case *Brown* v. *Board of Education of Topeka, Kansas.*

[7] **St. Augustine:** North African bishop (A.D. 354–430) regarded as a founder of Christianity.

[8] **St. Thomas Aquinas:** noted philosopher and theologian (1225–1274).

WHEN STUDENTS STRUGGLE . . .

To help students understand the importance of effective evidence and the effects of **allusions,** indirect references to famous people, places, events, or literary works, direct them to the allusion that appears in lines 193–194. Have students consider King's audience and the information in the footnote about St. Augustine.

ASK STUDENTS why St. Augustine's quote would appeal to King's audience. *(King is speaking to religious leaders in Birmingham. St. Augustine was an important religious leader. The clergymen in Birmingham may be convinced by St. Augustine's words.)*

law that uplifts human personality is just. Any law that degrades human personality is unjust. All segregation statutes are unjust because segregation distorts the soul and damages the personality. It gives the segregator a false sense of superiority and the segregated a false sense of inferiority. Segregation, to use the terminology of the Jewish philosopher Martin Buber,[9] substitutes an "I-it" relationship for an "I-thou" relationship and ends up relegating persons to the status of things. Hence segregation is not only politically, economically and sociologically unsound, it is morally

210 wrong and sinful. Paul Tillich[10] has said that sin is separation. Is not segregation an existential expression of man's tragic separation, his awful estrangement, his terrible sinfulness? Thus it is that I can urge men to obey the 1954 decision of the Supreme Court, for it is morally right; and I can urge them to disobey segregation ordinances, for they are morally wrong.

Let us consider a more concrete example of just and unjust laws. An unjust law is a code that a numerical or power majority group compels a minority group to obey but does not make binding on itself. This is *difference* made legal. By the same token, a just law

220 is a code that a majority compels a minority to follow and that it is willing to follow itself. This is *sameness* made legal.

Let me give another explanation. A law is unjust if it is inflicted on a minority that, as a result of being denied the right to vote, had no part in enacting or devising the law. Who can say that the legislature of Alabama which set up that state's segregation laws was democratically elected? Throughout Alabama all sorts of devious methods are used to prevent Negroes from becoming registered voters, and there are some counties in which, even though Negroes constitute a majority of the population, not a single Negro is

230 registered. Can any law enacted under such circumstances be considered democratically structured?

Sometimes a law is just on its face and unjust in its application. For instance, I have been arrested on a charge of parading without a permit. Now, there is nothing wrong in having an ordinance which requires a permit for a parade. But such an ordinance becomes unjust when it is used to maintain segregation and to deny citizens the First-Amendment privilege of peaceful assembly and protest.

I hope you are able to see the distinction I am trying to point out. In no sense do I advocate evading or defying the law, as

240 would the rabid segregationist. That would lead to anarchy. One who breaks an unjust law must do so openly, lovingly, and with

---

[9] **Martin Buber:** influential philosopher (1878–1965) with a great impact on Jewish and Christian theology.
[10] **Paul Tillich:** (1886–1965) influential German-American philosopher and Christian theologian.

APPLYING ACADEMIC VOCABULARY

comprehensive	equivalent

As you discuss King's letter, incorporate the following Collection 6 academic vocabulary words: *comprehensive* and *equivalent*. Point out to students that King has written a **comprehensive** argument using reasons and evidence to support his claim that the direct action was a violation of an unjust law, and therefore did not truly constitute a violation. As you further evaluate King's explanation of just and unjust laws, ask students to explain how the Supreme Court ruling of 1954, which gave African American and white school children **equivalent** rights, is a just law.

CLOSE READ

Analyze Argument in a Seminal Document

COMMON CORE **RI 8**

(LINES 205–210)

Remind students that strong arguments show a consistent awareness of audience.

H **CITE TEXT EVIDENCE** Ask students to cite two references or allusions in this passage chosen to appeal to King's audience of fellow clergymen. *(King cites two influential theologians to support his point about the immorality of segregation [lines 206 and 210].)* Ask students why these references are well suited to King's audience. *(By making these references, King reminds his readers that he is one of them—a well-educated religious authority. While these references might not be suited to a more general audience, using them in this context allows King to communicate to his specific audience that they are, in effect, members of the same exclusive club.)*

Analyze Argument in a Seminal Document

COMMON CORE **RI 8, RI 9**

(LINES 216–237)

Tell students that a well crafted argument moves from general ideas to specific examples.

I **CITE TEXT EVIDENCE** Have students identify the specific examples King provides of either unjust laws or the unjust application of just laws. *(King notes segregation laws on which those who suffered the effects were not allowed to vote [lines 224–231] and the use of a parade permit ordinance to stop protests [lines 233–237].)* Ask students why concrete examples such as those King provides are important here. *(Without specific examples, readers may consider the claim too vague, or they may identify their own examples, which might not fit King's definition of just and unjust laws.)*

Analyze Argument in a Seminal Document

COMMON CORE RI 8, RI 9

(LINES 247–264)

If necessary, remind students that an **allusion** is an indirect reference to a famous person, place, event, or literary work.

J **ASK STUDENTS** to identify the allusions in these two paragraphs. *(King alludes to events in the Bible, in ancient Greece and Rome, in American history, in World War II, and in the Cold War.)* Ask students how King uses these allusions to support his argument in favor of civil disobedience. *(King carefully chooses these allusions, spanning nearly all of recorded history, to show that those who practiced civil disobedience were in the right, opposing tyrannical powers. His readers may begin to see civil rights protesters as part of this long tradition.)*

Analyze Rhetoric

COMMON CORE RI 4, RI 6

(LINES 265–267)

Remind students that authors of arguments choose words carefully for their connotations.

K **ASK STUDENTS** what tone King creates through his word choices in these lines. *(When King says "I must make two honest confessions"; "I must confess"; and "I have been gravely disappointed," he creates a humble, almost apologetic, tone.)* Ask students what effect this shift in tone might have on King's audience. *(Up to this point, King has been direct and forceful in his argument. His shift in tone will grab his readers' attention and may make a connection with those clergy members who are accustomed to hearing confessions from their congregants.)*

---

a willingness to accept the penalty. I submit that an individual who breaks a law that conscience tells him is unjust, and who willingly accepts the penalty of imprisonment in order to arouse the conscience of the community over its injustice, is in reality expressing the highest respect for law.

J   Of course, there is nothing new about this kind of civil disobedience. It was evidenced sublimely in the refusal of Shadrach, Meshach and Abednego to obey the laws of Nebuchadnezzar,[11] on
250 the ground that a higher moral law was at stake. It was practiced superbly by the early Christians, who were willing to face hungry lions and the excruciating pain of chopping blocks rather than submit to certain unjust laws of the Roman Empire. To a degree, academic freedom is a reality today because Socrates practiced civil disobedience. In our own nation, the Boston Tea Party[12] represented a massive act of civil disobedience.

     We should never forget that everything Adolf Hitler did in Germany was "legal" and everything the Hungarian freedom fighters[13] did in Hungary was "illegal." It was "illegal" to aid and
260 comfort a Jew in Hitler's Germany. Even so, I am sure that, had I lived in Germany at the time, I would have aided and comforted my Jewish brothers. If today I lived in a Communist country where certain principles dear to the Christian faith are suppressed, I would openly advocate disobeying that country's antireligious laws.

     I must make two honest confessions to you, my Christian and Jewish brothers. First, I must confess that over the past few years I have been gravely disappointed with the white moderate. **K** I have almost reached the regrettable conclusion that the Negro's great stumbling block in his stride toward freedom is not the
270 White Citizen's Counciler or the Ku Klux Klanner,[14] but the white moderate, who is more devoted to "order" than to justice; who prefers a negative peace which is the absence of tension to a positive peace which is the presence of justice; who constantly says: "I agree with you in the goal you seek, but I cannot agree with your methods of direct action"; who paternalistically believes he can set the timetable for another man's freedom; who lives by a mythical concept of time and who constantly advises the Negro to wait for a "more convenient season." Shallow understanding from people of good will is more frustrating than absolute misunderstanding from

---

[11] **refusal . . . Nebuchadnezzar:** Biblical account of three Hebrews condemned for refusing to worship an idol as required by the King of Babylon. The three were miraculously protected from the flames into which they were thrown.

[12] **Boston Tea Party:** a 1773 protest against the British Tea Act in which American colonists dumped 342 chests of tea into Boston Harbor.

[13] **Hungarian freedom fighters:** participants in the 1956 revolt against Hungary's Soviet-backed government.

[14] **White . . . Klanner:** members of white-supremacist groups.

SCAFFOLDING FOR ELL STUDENTS

Analyze Conclusions Explain that a **conclusion** is a judgment based on related details or events. Help students trace the development of a conclusion. Direct students to King's conclusion about white moderates that appears in lines 278–280. Read the sentence aloud and define words and phrases students may not understand (*Shallow, good will, frustrating, absolute, ill will*). Then explain that King based his conclusions on specific reasons. Read lines 270–278 aloud, pausing after each relative clause that provides a reason for King's disappointment and making sure students understand the words. Encourage students to paraphrase each reason.

ASK STUDENTS to explain how one specific reason shows King's frustration.

CLOSE READ

Analyze Argument in a Seminal Document

COMMON CORE   RI 5, RI 8

(LINES 282–290)

Remind students that every section of an argument contributes to its central claim and purpose.

Ⓛ ASK STUDENTS why King discusses white moderates, who were generally sympathetic to the cause of civil rights, in his letter. *(King's audience may include some white moderates, and these readers might otherwise think King does not refer to them when discussing roadblocks in progress toward equal rights for all.)* Ask students what implied counterclaim King addresses here. *(The implied counterclaim is that civil rights advances should only proceed in peaceful, law-abiding ways that do not disturb the established order.)*

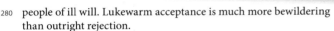

280 people of ill will. Lukewarm acceptance is much more bewildering than outright rejection.

I had hoped that the white moderate would understand that law and order exist for the purpose of establishing justice and that when they fail in this purpose they become the dangerously structured dams that block the flow of social progress. I had hoped that the white moderate would understand that the present tension in the South is a necessary phase of the transition from an obnoxious negative peace, in which the Negro passively accepted his unjust plight, to a substantive and positive peace, in which all men will
290 respect the dignity and worth of human personality. Actually, we who engage in nonviolent direct action are not the creators of tension. We merely bring to the surface the hidden tension that is already alive. We bring it out in the open, where it can be seen and dealt with. Like a boil that can never be cured so long as it is covered up but must be opened with all its ugliness to the natural medicines of air and light, injustice must be exposed, with all the

Letter from Birmingham Jail   **327**

Analyze Argument in a Seminal Document

COMMON CORE · RI 1, RI 8, RI 9

(LINES 299–336)

Remind students that a **counterargument** is an argument a writer includes to address a reader's potential opposing view, or counterclaim.

Ⓜ CITE TEXT EVIDENCE Ask students to use text evidence in lines 299–312 to state King's counterargument to the assertion that the actions of Birmingham's African American community precipitated violence and must be condemned. Ask students to explain one example King uses to address the clergymen's statement. *(King questions the logic of this assertion. He writes that it is like suggesting a robbed man be condemned for possessing the money that precipitated the evil act of robbery [line 303]. King states that it is wrong to urge an individual to cease efforts to gain his basic constitutional rights because the quest may precipitate violence [line 311].)*

Ⓝ CITE TEXT EVIDENCE Ask students why it is important in lines 313–336 for King to address the counterclaim that African Americans will eventually receive equal rights. *(If his readers believe that achieving equal rights is simply a matter of time, they will not support King's use of disruptive tactics that will speed the process along.)* Then have students identify King's counterargument and cite his reasons. *(King's counterargument is that "time itself is neutral." King calls the myth a "tragic misconception." His reasons include that it is a "strangely irrational notion" that time "will inevitably cure all ills." King states that human progress is not inevitable; rather, "it comes through the tireless efforts of men" [lines 320–328].)*

CRITICAL VOCABULARY

precipitate: King does not agree with the clergymen's assertion that the peaceful direct action caused the police to act violently toward participants.

ASK STUDENTS to identify what precipitated, or caused, a man to be robbed. *("possession of money")*

---

tension its exposure creates, to the light of human conscience and the air of national opinion before it can be cured.

300   In your statement you assert that our actions, even though peaceful, must be condemned because they **precipitate** violence. But is this a logical assertion? Isn't this like condemning a robbed man because his possession of money precipitated the evil act of robbery? Isn't this like condemning Socrates because his unswerving commitment to truth and his philosophical inquiries precipitated the act by the misguided populace in which they made him drink hemlock? Isn't this like condemning Jesus because his unique God-consciousness and never-ceasing devotion to God's will precipitated the evil act of crucifixion? We must come to see that, as the federal courts have consistently affirmed, it is

310 wrong to urge an individual to cease his efforts to gain his basic constitutional rights because the quest may precipitate violence. Society must protect the robbed and punish the robber.

    I had also hoped that the white moderate would reject the myth concerning time in relation to the struggle for freedom. I have just received a letter from a white brother in Texas. He writes: "All Christians know that the colored people will receive equal rights eventually, but it is possible that you are in too great a religious hurry. It has taken Christianity almost two thousand years to accomplish what it has. The teachings of Christ take time to come

320 to earth." Such an attitude stems from a tragic misconception of time, from the strangely irrational notion that there is something in the very flow of time that will inevitably cure all ills. Actually, time itself is neutral; it can be used either destructively or constructively. More and more I feel that the people of ill will have used time much more effectively than have the people of good will. We will have to repent in this generation not merely for the hateful words and actions of the bad people but for the appalling silence of the good people. Human progress never rolls in on wheels of inevitability; it comes through the tireless efforts of men willing to be coworkers

330 with God, and without this hard work, time itself becomes an ally of the forces of social stagnation. We must use time creatively, in the knowledge that the time is always ripe to do right. Now is the time to make real the promise of democracy and transform our pending national elegy into a creative psalm[15] of brotherhood. Now is the time to lift our national policy from the quicksand of racial injustice to the solid rock of human dignity.

    You speak of our activity in Birmingham as extreme. At first I was rather disappointed that fellow clergymen would see my nonviolent efforts as those of an extremist. I began thinking

precipitate
(prĭ-sĭp´ĭ-tāt´) v. to cause something to happen rapidly or unexpectedly.

---

[15] **elegy . . . psalm:** an elegy is a lament for the dead; a psalm is a song of praise.

328 Collection 6

TO CHALLENGE STUDENTS . . .

Personal Views King said, "More and more I feel that the people of ill will have used time much more effectively than have the people of good will." Ask students to identify ways in which "the people of ill will" used time effectively. Then ask whether students agree with King that those opposing civil rights were more effective than those working for change. Be sure they support their views with evidence from the text.

Finally, challenge students to work in groups to discuss King's statement as it relates to the present day. Whom would they define as current people of good will and ill will, and why? Who has used time more effectively in advancing a cause?

340 about the fact that I stand in the middle of two opposing forces
in the Negro community. One is a force of **complacency**, made
up in part of Negroes who, as a result of long years of oppression,
are so drained of self-respect and a sense of "somebodiness" that
they have adjusted to segregation; and in part of a few middle-
class Negroes who, because of a degree of academic and economic
security and because in some ways they profit by segregation, have
become insensitive to the problems of the masses. The other force
is one of bitterness and hatred, and it comes perilously close to
advocating violence. It is expressed in the various black nationalist
350 groups that are springing up across the nation, the largest and best
known being Elijah Muhammad's Muslim movement.[16] Nourished
by the Negro's frustration over the continued existence of racial
discrimination, this movement is made up of people who have lost
faith in America, who have absolutely repudiated Christianity, and
who have concluded that the white man is an incorrigible "devil."

I have tried to stand between these two forces, saying that we
need emulate neither the "do-nothingism" of the complacent nor
the hatred and despair of the black nationalist. For there is the
more excellent way of love and nonviolent protest. I am grateful to
360 God that, through the influence of the Negro church, the way of
nonviolence became an integral part of our struggle.

If this philosophy had not emerged, by now many streets of the
South would, I am convinced, be flowing with blood. . . .

Oppressed people cannot remain oppressed forever. The
yearning for freedom eventually **manifests** itself, and that is
what has happened to the American Negro. Something within
has reminded him of his birthright of freedom, and something
without has reminded him that it can be gained. Consciously or
unconsciously, he has been caught up by the *Zeitgeist*,[17] and with
370 his black brothers of Africa and his brown and yellow brothers of
Asia, South America and the Caribbean, the United States Negro
is moving with a sense of great urgency toward the promised land
of racial justice. If one recognizes this vital urge that has engulfed
the Negro community, one should readily understand why public
demonstrations are taking place. The Negro has many pent-up
resentments and latent frustrations, and he must release them. So
let him march; let him make prayer pilgrimages to the city hall; let
him go on freedom rides—and try to understand why he must do
so. If his repressed emotions are not released in nonviolent ways,

complacency
(kəm-plā´sən-sē) *n.*
contented self-
satisfaction.

manifest
(măn´ə-fĕst´) *v.* to
show or reveal.

---

[16] **black nationalist . . . Elijah Muhammad's Muslim movement:** groups
that proposed economic and social independence for African American
communities, including the Nation of Islam, founded in 1930 and led by Elijah
Muhammad (1897–1975) from 1934 until his death.

[17] ***Zeitgeist* (tsīt´gīst´):** German for "the spirit of the time," referring to the
attitudes and beliefs of most people living during a period.

Letter from Birmingham Jail **329**

CLOSE READ

Analyze Argument in a Seminal Document

COMMON CORE RI 8, RI 9

(LINES 340–363)

Remind students that writers of arguments must
clearly delineate claims.

CITE TEXT EVIDENCE Ask students to identify the
"two opposing forces" King discusses in this section.
*(King distinguishes between a force of "complacency"
that allows some African Americans to accept things
as they are and an angry force exemplified by Elijah
Muhammad's Muslim movement.)* Ask students
how King's discussion of these two forces serves
his purpose. *(King is able to position himself as a
reasonable force for positive change by contrasting his
nonviolent action with the other forces' inaction on the
one hand and tendency toward violence on the other.)*

CRITICAL VOCABULARY

complacency: King expresses the idea that some
African Americans are content with the way
society is structured.

ASK STUDENTS to explain the two reasons why
some African Americans are complacent. *(They
are "so drained of self-respect " from "long years
of oppression," or they "profit" in some way from
segregation.)*

manifest: King explains why the long-suppressed
desire for civil rights is finally becoming apparent.

ASK STUDENTS to identify the two reminders that
have manifested within and without the African
American man. *("his birthright of freedom" and "that
it can be gained")*

WHEN STUDENTS STRUGGLE . . .

Help student pairs trace the development of a claim by completing a graphic
organizer. Direct students to read lines 364–384. Tell students that as they read they
should consider King's opinion regarding "oppressed people," his reasons for his
opinion, and the specific actions he thinks "oppressed people" should take.

Opinion	"Oppressed people cannot remain oppressed forever."
Reasons	"They have a "yearning for freedom."
Action	"march," "prayer pilgrimages to city hall," "freedom rides," "nonviolent direct action"

Analyze Rhetoric

RI 4, RI 6

(LINES 384–410)

Remind students that controlled use of repetition is a powerful rhetorical tool used by writers of arguments.

P ASK STUDENTS how King shifts the idea of being "extremist" from something negative to something positive. *(King initially objects to being called an extremist but gradually shifts the word's tone by alluding to great historical figures who could be categorized as extremists.)* Then ask students how the concluding sentence of this passage (lines 408–410) directly addresses his audience. *(King concludes the passage by saying that "creative extremists," may be exactly what are needed, which addresses the claim that his actions are "unwise.")*

---

380 they will seek expression through violence; this is not a threat but a fact of history. So I have not said to my people: "Get rid of your discontent." Rather, I have tried to say that this normal and healthy discontent can be channeled into the creative outlet of nonviolent direct action. And now this approach is being termed extremist.

But though I was initially disappointed at being categorized as an extremist, as I continued to think about the matter I gradually gained a measure of satisfaction from the label. Was not Jesus an extremist for love: "Love your enemies, bless them that curse you, do good to them that hate you, and pray for them 390 which despitefully use you, and persecute you." Was not Amos[18] an extremist for justice: "Let justice roll down like waters and righteousness like an ever-flowing stream." Was not Paul an extremist for the Christian gospel: "I bear in my body the marks of the Lord Jesus." Was not Martin Luther[19] an extremist: "Here I stand; I cannot do otherwise, so help me God." And John Bunyan:[20] "I will stay in jail to the end of my days before I make a butchery of my conscience." And Abraham Lincoln: "This nation cannot survive half slave and half free." And Thomas Jefferson: "We hold these truths to be self-evident, that all men are created equal . . ." 400 So the question is not whether we will be extremists, but what kind of extremists we will be. Will we be extremists for hate or for love? Will we be extremists for the preservation of injustice or for the extension of justice? In that dramatic scene on Calvary's hill[21] three men were crucified. We must never forget that all three were crucified for the same crime—the crime of extremism. Two were extremists for immorality, and thus fell below their environment. The other, Jesus Christ, was an extremist for love, truth and goodness, and thereby rose above his environment. Perhaps the South, the nation and the world are in dire need of creative 410 extremists.

I had hoped that the white moderate would see this need. Perhaps I was too optimistic; perhaps I expected too much. I suppose I should have realized that few members of the oppressor race can understand the deep groans and passionate yearnings of the oppressed race, and still fewer have the vision to see that injustice must be rooted out by strong, persistent and determined action. I am thankful, however, that some of our white brothers in the South have grasped the meaning of this social revolution and

---

[18] **Amos:** Hebrew prophet whose words are recorded in the Old Testament book bearing his name.

[19] **Martin Luther:** (1483-1546) German monk who launched the Protestant Reformation.

[20] **John Bunyan:** (1628-1688) English preacher and writer, author of *The Pilgrim's Progress.*

[21] **Calvary's hill:** the site of Jesus' crucifixion.

SCAFFOLDING FOR ELL STUDENTS

Rhetorical Questions Tell students that a **rhetorical question** is a question that does not require an answer. Writers use rhetorical questions in order to grab a reader's interest and to emphasize an idea. Direct students to the rhetorical questions that appear in lines 401–403. Make sure students understand "preservation of injustice" and "extension of justice."

ASK STUDENTS to identify the two ideas that King wants to emphasize. *(love and justice)*

" WILL WE BE EXTREMISTS FOR HATE OR FOR LOVE? "

committed themselves to it. They are still all too few in quantity,
420 but they are big in quality. Some—such as Ralph McGill, Lillian
Smith, Harry Golden, James McBride Dabbs, Ann Braden and
Sarah Patton Boyle—have written about our struggle in eloquent
and prophetic terms. Others have marched with us down nameless
streets of the South. They have languished in filthy, roach-infested
jails, suffering the abuse and brutality of policemen who view them
as "dirty nigger-lovers." Unlike so many of their moderate brothers
and sisters, they have recognized the urgency of the moment and
sensed the need for powerful "action" antidotes to combat the
disease of segregation.

430 Let me take note of my other major disappointment. I have
been so greatly disappointed with the white church and its
leadership. Of course, there are some notable exceptions. I am not
unmindful of the fact that each of you has taken some significant
stands on this issue. I commend you, Reverend Stallings, for your
Christian stand on this past Sunday, in welcoming Negroes to your
worship service on a nonsegregated basis. I commend the Catholic
leaders of this state for integrating Spring Hill College several years
ago.

But despite these notable exceptions, I must honestly reiterate
440 that I have been disappointed with the church. I do not say this as
one of those negative critics who can always find something wrong
with the church. I say this as a minister of the gospel, who loves the
church; who was nurtured in its bosom; who has been sustained by
its spiritual blessings and who will remain true to it as long as the
cord of life shall lengthen.

CLOSE READ

Analyze Rhetoric

COMMON CORE RI 4, RI 6

(LINES 423–429)

Explain to students that writers often make specific word choices based on connotation to convey nuances of meaning.

Q **CITE TEXT EVIDENCE** Have students identify words with negative connotations in this passage. *(languished, filthy, roach-infested, jails, suffering, abuse, brutality, dirty; you may choose either to omit or to discuss the most negative word in the passage,* nigger, *depending on your assessment of your students.)* Ask students in what way King contrasts these negative words with the positive situation he is describing. *(King writes in glowing terms of white allies in the cause of civil rights for all, while graphically illustrating the difficulties they are enduring for the cause.)*

TO CHALLENGE STUDENTS . . .

Conduct Research Explain that many media personalities present on television or on the radio are powerful forces for change. Point out that the same can be said of the media personalities during the civil rights movement, such as those King mentions: Ralph McGill, Lillian Smith, Harry Golden, James McBride Dabbs, Ann Braden, and Sarah Patton Boyle.

Have students work in groups of six. Each student in the group should select one of the six people. Challenge students to research that person, noting his or her contributions to the civil rights movement and any praise received or consequences suffered. Once students have completed their research, have the groups of six discuss their findings.

Analyze Argument in a Seminal Document

 COMMON CORE RI 8, RI 9

(LINES 446–485)

Explain that contrasts can provide powerful and memorable support for an argument.

R **CITE TEXT EVIDENCE** Have students identify at least one contrast between what King expected from religious leaders and what actually happened. *(King expected leaders in Montgomery to support the bus protest; instead, many either did nothing or openly opposed the movement [lines 446–454]. He also expected church leaders to support desegregation on moral, rather than merely legal, grounds [lines 461–465].)* Ask students how the contrast between what King expected and what actually happened supports his claim and addresses his audience. *(His audience of religious leaders may see that people expect positive action from organized religion. His readers may become concerned that many people will become disillusioned by the lack of action from religious institutions.)*

When I was suddenly catapulted into the leadership of the bus protest in Montgomery, Alabama,[22] a few years ago, I felt we would be supported by the white church. I felt that the white ministers, priests and rabbis of the South would be among our strongest 450 allies. Instead, some have been outright opponents, refusing to understand the freedom movement and misrepresenting its leaders; all too many others have been more cautious than courageous and have remained silent behind the anesthetizing security of stained glass windows.

In spite of my shattered dreams, I came to Birmingham with the hope that the white religious leadership of this community would see the justice of our cause and, with deep moral concern, would serve as the channel through which our just grievances could reach the power structure. I had hoped that each of you would 460 understand. But again I have been disappointed.

I have heard numerous southern religious leaders admonish their worshipers to comply with a desegregation decision because it is the law, but I have longed to hear white ministers declare: "Follow this decree because integration is morally right and because the Negro is your brother." In the midst of blatant injustices inflicted upon the Negro, I have watched white churchmen stand on the sideline and mouth pious irrelevancies and sanctimonious trivialities. In the midst of a mighty struggle to rid our nation of racial and economic injustice, I have heard many ministers 470 say: "Those are social issues, with which the gospel has no real concern." And I have watched many churches commit themselves to a completely otherworldly religion which makes a strange, un-Biblical distinction between body and soul, between the sacred and the secular.

I have traveled the length and breadth of Alabama, Mississippi and all the other southern states. On sweltering summer days and crisp autumn mornings I have looked at the South's beautiful churches with their lofty spires pointing heavenward. I have beheld the impressive outlines of her massive religious-education 480 buildings. Over and over I have found myself asking: "What kind of people worship here? Who is their God? Where were their voices when the lips of Governor Barnett dripped with words of interposition and nullification? Where were they when Governor Wallace[23] gave a clarion call for defiance and hatred? Where were their voices of support when bruised and weary Negro men and

---

[22]**bus protest in Montgomery, Alabama:** the 1955–1956 boycott that ended segregated seating in Montgomery's transportation system.
[23]**Gov. Barnett . . . Gov. Wallace:** Ross Barnett (1898–1987) and George Wallace (1919–1998), segregationist governors of Mississippi and Alabama, respectively, during the 1960s.

SCAFFOLDING FOR ELL STUDENTS

Understand Comparisons Explain that writers of arguments may make comparisons, discussing similarities or differences, in order to explain a claim. Help students understand the claim King makes about churches during his time by having them complete a chart that outlines how the contemporary churches, or churches during King's time, are different from those of the past.

Have students read lines 497–516. Encourage them to seek help for unfamiliar words and phrases (*agitators, God-intoxicated, astronomically intimidated, ineffectual, archdefender, status quo, sanction*). Then have pairs complete a chart like the one shown, listing words and phrases noting differences between the two churches. Depending on your students' needs, you may want to model a few examples for them.

women decided to rise from the dark dungeons of complacency to the bright hills of creative protest?"

Yes, these questions are still in my mind. In deep disappointment I have wept over the laxity of the church. But be
490 assured that my tears have been tears of love. There can be no deep disappointment where there is not deep love. Yes, I love the church. How could I do otherwise? I am in the rather unique position of being the son, the grandson and the great-grandson of preachers. Yes, I see the church as the body of Christ. But, oh! How we have blemished and scarred that body through social neglect and through fear of being nonconformists.

There was a time when the church was very powerful—in the time when the early Christians rejoiced at being deemed worthy to suffer for what they believed. In those days the church was not
500 merely a thermometer that recorded the ideas and principles of popular opinion; it was a thermostat that transformed the **mores** of society. Whenever the early Christians entered a town, the people in power became disturbed and immediately sought to convict the Christians for being "disturbers of the peace" and "outside agitators." But the Christians pressed on, in the conviction that they were "a colony of heaven," called to obey God rather than man. Small in number, they were big in commitment. They were too God-intoxicated to be "astronomically intimidated." By their effort and example they brought an end to such ancient evils as
510 infanticide and gladiatorial contests.[24]

Things are different now. So often the contemporary church is a weak, ineffectual voice with an uncertain sound. So often it is an archdefender of the status quo. Far from being disturbed by the presence of the church, the power structure of the average community is consoled by the church's silent—and often even vocal—sanction of things as they are.

But the judgment of God is upon the church as never before. If today's church does not recapture the sacrificial spirit of the early church, it will lose its authenticity, forfeit the loyalty of millions,
520 and be dismissed as an irrelevant social club with no meaning for the twentieth century. Every day I meet young people whose disappointment with the church has turned into outright disgust.

Perhaps I have once again been too optimistic. Is organized religion too inextricably bound to the status quo to save our nation and the world? Perhaps I must turn my faith to the inner spiritual church, the church within the church, as the true *ekklesia*[25] and

mores
(môr′āz) *n.*
established customs and conventions.

---

[24] **ancient evils . . . contests:** despicable past practices of killing unwanted babies and of forcing men to fight to the death for sport.

[25] *ekklesia* (ĭ-klē′zē-ə): a Greek term meaning "an assembly of people for worship," often translated into English as "church."

Letter from Birmingham Jail **333**

CLOSE READ

Analyze Argument in a Seminal Document

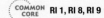

RI 1, RI 8, RI 9

(LINES 497–510)

Ask students to continue to look for claims and arguments and the reasons and evidence King uses to support them.

S **CITE TEXT EVIDENCE** Have students identify the central claim that King makes in this paragraph and the reasons and evidence he uses to support it. *(King claims that the early church was more powerful than the modern one. He offers the reason that the early Christians "rejoiced . . . to suffer for what they believed" [lines 498–499] and that the church "transformed the mores of society" [lines 501-502]. These reasons are supported by the evidence that early Christians entering a town were often arrested [lines 502–505] and that their efforts brought an end to "such ancient evils such as infanticide and gladiatorial contests" [lines 509–510].)*

CRITICAL VOCABULARY

mores: King states that the church determined the established customs and conventions of society.

ASK STUDENTS to compare the mores of a society that would allow infanticide and gladiatorial contests with our own. *(Accept all reasonable responses.)*

Churches of the past	Churches during King's time period
powerful	weak
transformed the mores of society	ineffectual
disturbed power	defender of status quo
committed	does not disturb community
ended evils	

Analyze Rhetoric

COMMON CORE RI 6

(LINES 540–557)

Ask students to watch for images with positive connotations that support King's argument.

T CITE TEXT EVIDENCE Ask students to identify references to American history in this paragraph. *(King refers to the landing of pilgrims at Plymouth Rock, Jefferson's writing the Declaration of Independence, slavery, and the growth of cotton production.)* Ask students how these references support the idea that African Americans deserve equal rights. *(African Americans have been present through all of American history and are crucial to the nation's economic development; it follows logically that they should have the same rights as all other Americans.)*

Analyze Argument in a Seminal Document

COMMON CORE RI 6, RI 8

(LINES 558–571)

Remind students that King's letter is a direct response to counterclaims made by a group of religious leaders.

U ASK STUDENTS what counterclaim in the clergymen's letter King is addressing here. *(King is responding to the clergymen's praise for the Birmingham police force, with which he strongly disagrees.)* Then ask students what evidence King's counterargument provides. *(King provides specific, unflinching details about the wrongs perpetrated by the Birmingham police against protesters, including physical violence, verbal abuse, and denial of food.)*

---

the hope of the world. But again I am thankful to God that some noble souls from the ranks of organized religion have broken loose from the paralyzing chains of conformity and joined us as active
530 partners in the struggle for freedom. They have left their secure congregations and walked the streets of Albany, Georgia, with us. They have gone down the highways of the South on tortuous rides for freedom. Yes, they have gone to jail with us. Some have been dismissed from their churches, have lost the support of their bishops and fellow ministers. But they have acted in the faith that right defeated is stronger than evil triumphant. Their witness has been the spiritual salt that has preserved the true meaning of the gospel in these troubled times. They have carved a tunnel of hope through the dark mountain of disappointment.
540 I hope the church as a whole will meet the challenge of this decisive hour. But even if the church does not come to the aid of justice, I have no despair about the future. I have no fear about the outcome of our struggle in Birmingham, even if our motives are at present misunderstood. We will reach the goal of freedom in Birmingham and all over the nation, because the goal of America is freedom. Abused and scorned though we may be, our destiny is tied up with America's destiny. Before the pilgrims landed at Plymouth, we were here. Before the pen of Jefferson etched the majestic words of the Declaration of Independence across the pages of history, we
550 were here. For more than two centuries our forebears labored in this country without wages; they made cotton king; they built the homes of their masters while suffering gross injustice and shameful humiliation—and yet out of a bottomless vitality they continued to thrive and develop. If the inexpressible cruelties of slavery could not stop us, the opposition we now face will surely fail. We will win our freedom because the sacred heritage of our nation and the eternal will of God are embodied in our echoing demands.

Before closing I feel impelled to mention one other point in your statement that has troubled me profoundly. You warmly
560 commended the Birmingham police force for keeping "order" and "preventing violence." I doubt that you would have so warmly commended the police force if you had seen its dogs sinking their teeth into unarmed, nonviolent Negroes. I doubt that you would so quickly commend the policemen if you were to observe their ugly and inhumane treatment of Negroes here in the city jail; if you were to watch them push and curse old Negro women and young Negro girls; if you were to see them slap and kick old Negro men and young boys; if you were to observe them, as they did on two occasions, refuse to give us food because we wanted to sing our
570 grace together. I cannot join you in your praise of the Birmingham police department.

334 Collection 6

TO CHALLENGE STUDENTS . . .

Have students reread lines 527–539 and summarize them by identifying who King is writing about and what they have done. *(King is writing about the "noble souls" [line 528] of organized religion who worked to advance civil rights for African Americans in the South by becoming "active partners" [lines 529–530] in direct actions, going on freedom rides, and even going to jail for standing up for what is morally right.)*

ASK STUDENTS to discuss how this passage gives them insight into King's assertions about organized religion being bound to the status quo. *(Some of the individuals who became active participants in the movement were "dismissed from their churches" or "have lost support of their bishops and fellow ministers [lines 534–535]. This illustrates the firm stance that organized religion had taken against challenging the status quo.)*

Image Credits: ©AP Images

It is true that the police have exercised a degree of discipline in handling the demonstrators. In this sense they have conducted themselves rather "nonviolently" in public. But for what purpose? To preserve the evil system of segregation. Over the past few years I have consistently preached that nonviolence demands that the means we use must be as pure as the ends we seek. I have tried to make clear that it is wrong to use immoral means to attain moral ends. But now I must affirm that it is just as wrong, or perhaps even
580 more so, to use moral means to preserve immoral ends. Perhaps Mr. Connor and his policemen have been rather nonviolent in public, as was Chief Pritchett in Albany, Georgia, but they have used the moral means of nonviolence to maintain the immoral end of racial injustice. As T. S. Eliot has said: "The last temptation is the greatest treason: To do the right deed for the wrong reason."

I wish you had commended the Negro sit-inners and demonstrators of Birmingham for their sublime courage, their willingness to suffer and their amazing discipline in the midst of great **provocation**. One day the South will recognize its real heroes.
590 They will be the James Merediths,[26] with the noble sense of purpose that enables them to face jeering and hostile mobs, and with the agonizing loneliness that characterizes the life of the pioneer.

provocation
(prŏv´ə-kā´shən) *n.* an action intended to elicit an angered response.

---
[26]**James Merediths:** people like James Meredith, who endured violent opposition from whites to become the first African American to attend the University of Mississippi.

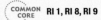

Analyze Argument in a Seminal Document

COMMON CORE RI 1, RI 8, RI 9

(LINES 572–585)

Remind students that a well-structured argument reiterates key ideas.

Ⓥ CITE TEXT EVIDENCE Ask students to cite words and ideas in this section of the text that echo earlier ideas in the letter, including King's stated reasons for being in Birmingham. *(The use of the words* moral, immoral, *and* wrong *in this section link back to King's stated moral reason for coming to Birmingham. The ideas in this section also link back to the earlier discussion of just and unjust laws.)*

> **CRITICAL VOCABULARY**
>
> **provocation:** King points out that the demonstrators received no praise for their refusal to respond with violence even when they were faced with actions intended to elicit anger.
>
> **ASK STUDENTS** to identify the type of provocation James Meredith endured. *(He faced "jeering and hostile mobs.")*

SCAFFOLDING FOR ELL STUDENTS

Vocabulary: Prefixes Remind students that English words can have multiple parts. A **prefix** is a word part added to the beginning of a word. Prefixes have their own unique meanings, and understanding those meanings will help students define unfamiliar words. Point out *immoral* (lines 578, 580, 583) and *nonviolent/nonviolence* (lines 581, 583). Explain: *im-* and *non-* mean "without" or "not." Therefore, *immoral* means "not moral" or "without good behavior." *Nonviolent* means "not violent" or "not harmful."

ASK STUDENTS to define *nonsegregated* (line 436), *nonconformists* (line 496) and *impatience* (line 616), using each word's context to form a preliminary definition and a dictionary to confirm the definition.

Analyze Argument in a Seminal Document

COMMON CORE RI 1, RI 8, RI 9

(LINES 607–608)

If necessary, remind students that **allusions** are references to a famous person, place, event, or literary work.

Ⓦ CITE TEXT EVIDENCE Ask students to identify the two seminal documents that King references as historical allusions on this page. *(King refers to the Constitution and the Declaration of Independence.)* Then ask what effect references to these particular seminal documents might have on King's audience. *(Throughout the letter, King has advocated liberty and responded to the clergymen's apparent preference for law and order over disruptive action. By citing the Declaration of Independence, he links the civil rights cause to the cause of American independence. And by citing the Constitution, he emphasizes the legal foundation for his actions.)*

COLLABORATIVE DISCUSSION Have students pair up and discuss the evidence that they found most compelling. Ask them to consider whether one of the specific types of reasons impacted their reactions in any particular way.

ASK STUDENTS to share any questions they generated in the course of reading and discussing the selection.

They will be old, oppressed, battered Negro women, symbolized in a seventy-two-year-old woman in Montgomery, Alabama, who rose up with a sense of dignity and with her people decided not to ride segregated buses, and who responded with ungrammatical profundity to one who inquired about her weariness: "My feets is tired, but my soul is at rest." They will be the young high school and college students, the young ministers of the gospel and a host 600 of their elders, courageously and nonviolently sitting in at lunch counters and willingly going to jail for conscience' sake. One day the South will know that when these disinherited children of God sat down at lunch counters, they were in reality standing up for what is best in the American dream and for the most sacred values in our Judaeo-Christian heritage, thereby bringing our nation back to those great wells of democracy which were dug deep by the founding fathers in their formulation of the Constitution and the Declaration of Independence. Ⓦ

Never before have I written so long a letter. I'm afraid it is much 610 too long to take your precious time. I can assure you that it would have been much shorter if I had been writing from a comfortable desk, but what else can one do when he is alone in a narrow jail cell other than write long letters, think long thoughts and pray long prayers?

If I have said anything in this letter that overstates the truth and indicates an unreasonable impatience, I beg you to forgive me. If I have said anything that understates the truth and indicates my having a patience that allows me to settle for anything less than brotherhood, I beg God to forgive me.

620 I hope this letter finds you strong in the faith. I also hope that circumstances will soon make it possible for me to meet each of you, not as an integrationist or a civil-rights leader but as a fellow clergyman and a Christian brother. Let us all hope that the dark clouds of racial prejudice will soon pass away and the deep fog of misunderstanding will be lifted from our fear-drenched communities, and in some not too distant tomorrow the radiant stars of love and brotherhood will shine over our great nation with all their scintillating beauty.

Yours for the cause of Peace and Brotherhood,
Martin Luther King, Jr.

COLLABORATIVE DISCUSSION What parts of King's argument do you find most compelling? Discuss your reaction to the letter with a partner. Cite specific evidence from the text to support your ideas.

TO CHALLENGE STUDENTS . . .

Different Perspective Ask students to make inferences about what the clergymen, the media, and the general public may have thought about King's letter.

Challenge students to think of these viewpoints and write a response to King's letter. Tell students to consider the social dynamics of the time to recognize that a response may be favorable or unfavorable. Regardless of the nature of the response, it should be respectful. Inform students their responses can take a variety of forms, such as:

- a reply letter to King written from the perspective of one of the local clergymen
- an article written from the perspective of a local newspaper reporter
- an editorial written from the perspective of either an African American or white person after he or she has read King's published letter

Analyze Argument in a Seminal Document

COMMON CORE RI 8, RI 9

When you analyze an argument, you must identify the **claims**, or the writer's positions on the issue or problem. You also need to examine and evaluate the reasons and evidence used to support the claims, while also looking at the counterarguments provided to address opposing views. For example, in "Letter from Birmingham Jail," note the different types of reasons King provides to justify his presence in Birmingham and consider questions that might help you assess the validity of his reasoning and the relevance and sufficiency of his evidence.

Organizational Reasons	Religious/Historical Reasons	Moral Reasons
"I am here because I have organizational ties here."	"Just as the prophets . . . so am I compelled to carry the gospel of freedom beyond my own home town."	"I cannot sit idly by in Atlanta and not be concerned about what happens in Birmingham."
• What facts does King provide to contest the idea that he is an outsider?	• How does this reasoning appeal to the shared beliefs of King's audience?	• Is this a valid statement? What evidence supports this reasoning?

Although King's letter was addressed to his "Fellow Clergymen," it was disseminated by the media to the public. To better comprehend why this letter, a seminal U.S. document, had such an impact on the civil rights cause, think about the **themes**, or the underlying messages, that King wants his audience to understand. As you explore the themes and consider the impact of King's letter, consider these questions:

- A **universal theme** is a message that can be found throughout the literature of all time periods. What universal themes does King explore in his letter? What makes these themes universal?
- An **allusion** is an indirect reference to a famous person, place, event, or literary work. King uses allusions to help connect the civil rights movement to other historical and religious figures and events. In what ways do allusions add power to King's letter? How might they help promote his cause? How might they influence other groups of people?

CLOSE READ

Analyze Argument in a Seminal Document

COMMON CORE RI 8, RI 9

Review with students the examples of the different types of reasons King presents in his letter. Remind students that evidence to support reasons may come in the form of facts, personal experiences, examples, or quotes. Explain that in order for a writer to convince an audience, the writer should provide sufficient evidence that is relevant, credible, and valid.

Help students understand the terms *theme, universal theme,* and *allusion.* Guide students in a discussion in which they offer responses to the questions that identify themes and the effects of allusions. Encourage students to return to the selection and cite text evidence to support their responses.

Strategies for Annotation  *Annotate it!*

Analyze Argument in a Seminal Document

COMMON CORE RI 8, RI 9

Share these strategies for guided or independent analysis:
- Highlight in green the reason King is protesting in Birmingham.
- Highlight in blue evidence that supports the reason.
- On a note, explain whether King's evidence is valid.

the fact that racial injustice engulfs this community. Birmingham is probably the most thoroughly segregated city in the United States. Its ugly record of brutality is widely known. Negroes have experienced grossly unjust treatment in the courts. There have been more unsolved bombings of Negro homes and churches in Birmingham than in any other city in the nation.

Analyzing the Text COMMON CORE RI 1, RI 2, RI 8, RI 9

Possible answers:

1. *King wrote in response to a statement from clergymen who criticized his "unwise and untimely" involvement in a nonviolent direct action against segregation. King is supporting his claim that breaking an unjust law and accepting the penalty to demonstrate injustice to society is actually expressing respect for law. He bases this on an earlier claim that "determined legal and nonviolent pressure" in the form of direct actions is the only successful means for bringing about gains in the civil rights movement (lines 130–132).*

2. *King defines just laws as "manmade code[s] that square with the moral law or the law of God" (lines 196–197). Unjust laws are "code[s] that are out of harmony with moral law" (lines 199–200). His counterargument responds to the opposing view that there is no justification for selectively breaking laws. King provides his rationale: King and the other participants in the direct action had a moral responsibility to disobey an unjust law.*

3. *Shadrach, Meshach and Abednego refused to obey Nebuchadnezzar's morally unjust laws. Early Christians faced death to protest unjust Roman laws. The Boston Tea Party was a direct action against an unjust law.*

4. *The four basic steps are: (1) "collection of the facts to determine whether injustices exist," (2) "negotiation," (3) "self-purification," (4) and "direct action." King's organization: (1) determined that racial injustice was widespread in the community; (2) negotiated with merchants; (3) held workshops to ensure that participants would be nonviolent and could endure the hardship of jail; (4) planned direct action (lines 53–90).*

5. *King means that he expects people of ill will to completely reject the plight of the oppressed. However, he finds it frustrating that those who have some amount of understanding that injustices exist do not want to immediately rectify those injustices.*

6. *King is referring to the resentment felt by African Americans who "Wait" for equal rights but are continually denied them. He provides descriptive examples and personal experiences to illustrate and explain the denied rights as well as the injustices African Americans endure that create a "sense of 'nobodiness'" (lines 151–179).*

7. *King writes that the communities and states of the United States are interrelated. He uses valid reasoning, saying that citizens are part of a mutual network that can be affected directly or indirectly, but that those effects will impact everyone (lines 37–43).*

eBook *Annotate It!*

Analyzing the Text COMMON CORE RI 1, RI 2, RI 8, RI 9, W 9b, W 10

Cite Text Evidence   Support your responses with evidence from the selection.

1. **Summarize** Based on details in the letter, what do you know about King's position and the events that prompted him to write this letter? What claim is he supporting in this argument?

2. **Analyze** How does King define just and unjust laws? To what opposing view is he providing a counterargument? Consider how defining certain laws as unjust provides an incentive for his readers to support his actions.

3. **Cite Evidence** Provide three examples of allusions that King uses to support his reasoning about his claim. How does this type of evidence strengthen his argument?

4. **Summarize** According to King, what are the four basic steps in a nonviolent campaign, and how did King's organization follow these steps in Birmingham?

5. **Interpret** What does King mean when he says "Shallow misunderstanding from people of good will is more frustrating than absolute misunderstanding from people of ill will"?

6. **Draw Conclusions** King says that "This 'Wait' has almost always meant 'Never.'" To what does he refer, and how does he defend his position?

7. **Analyze** Discuss whether King uses valid reasoning when he states that "Injustice anywhere is a threat to justice everywhere." What evidence does he provide to support this idea?

PERFORMANCE TASK

Writing Activity: Comparison Seminal U.S. texts often center on the themes of rights and freedom. Compare the ideas in King's letter with those in President Franklin Roosevelt's seminal "Four Freedoms" speech (See page R22).

1. As you read Roosevelt's speech and reread King's letter, make notes about how they both address related themes and equivalent concepts.

2. Write an essay in which you explain how the two documents explore people's fundamental human rights and what the two authors want done to end the injustice.

Assign this performance task.

PERFORMANCE TASK COMMON CORE RI 9, W 9b, W 10

Writing Activity: Comparison Provide students with context for Roosevelt's "Four Freedoms" speech. Explain that it was delivered to Congress on January 6, 1941, 11 months prior to the United States' declaration of war against Germany. Ask students to read the speech and to note similarities in ideas and themes to King's letter. Then have students reread King's letter to find key points of similarity. Ask students to cite text evidence from both pieces to support their comparisons.

Critical Vocabulary

COMMON CORE L 4a

cognizant	moratorium	retaliate	precipitate
complacency	manifest	mores	provocation

Practice and Apply Use your understanding of the Critical Vocabulary words to answer the following questions. Then, explain your answers to a partner.

1. Which might cause someone to **retaliate**: Losing a point in a game because of a foul or getting a well-deserved award?

2. Which might cause a brief **moratorium** on road building, a bad storm or potholes?

3. If I am **cognizant** of your plans, do I know about them or have I forgotten them?

4. If a movie reflected a society's **mores**, would it show traditional or unconventional practices?

5. If a motive for a crime begins to **manifest** itself, will it be easier or harder to prove the suspect's guilt?

6. What might be a **provocation** for war, breaking a treaty or signing one?

7. If you show **complacency** toward a bossy friend, how do you respond to his or her demands?

8. If my actions **precipitate** an accident, do I cause the accident or prevent it?

Vocabulary Strategy: Context Clues

A word's **context,** the words and sentences that surround it, often gives clues to its meaning. Context can also add shades of meaning to a word. Consider how context shapes the meaning of the word *tension* in King's letter:

Definition	Context Clues
tension: a strained relationship	"Nonviolent direct action seeks to . . . foster such a **tension** that a community . . . is forced to confront the issue."; "I have earnestly opposed violent **tension**, but there is a type of constructive, nonviolent **tension** which is necessary for growth"; "Just as Socrates felt that it was necessary to create a **tension** in the mind . . . so must we . . . create the kind of **tension** in society that will help men rise from the dark depths of prejudice."

As you can see from the context, King's use of the word *tension* describes a powerful force, one that can be positive rather than violent or hostile. Think about how replacing it with an equivalent word, such as *conflict*, might change King's intended meaning.

Practice and Apply Use context clues to define the words *moderate* (lines 266–280), *condemned/condemning* (lines 299–311), and *extremist* (lines 385–410). Verify your preliminary definition of each word in a dictionary. Then, in a small group, discuss how King adds nuances to each word's meaning in the context of his letter.

Letter from Birmingham Jail **339**

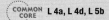

Critical Vocabulary

COMMON CORE L 4a, L 4d, L 5b

Possible answers:

1. *Losing a point in a game because of a foul: A person might want to retaliate, or get back at someone, after believing he or she had been wronged or harmed.*

2. *A bad storm: A moratorium, or suspension, in road building might be caused by a bad storm because winds and heavy rain make road building difficult.*

3. *I know about them: If I'm cognizant, I know they exist.*

4. *Traditional practices: Society's mores are the customs and ways people act.*

5. *Easier: When something manifests, it becomes apparent. So if a motive manifests itself, then it will be easier to connect the crime to someone.*

6. *Breaking a treaty: A treaty is an agreement of terms for peace, so keeping its terms would maintain peace. Doing something to elicit an angered response, such as breaking the treaty, would be a provocation for war.*

7. *I give in to his or her demands: Showing complacency means that I'm satisfied with how things are.*

8. *Your actions cause the accident: Preventing an accident is the opposite of precipitating one.*

Vocabulary Strategy: Context Clues

Possible answers:

1. *moderate: a person who prefers order to confrontation and whose views are not extreme.*

2. *condemned/condemning: to judge and punish harshly for an action considered a crime or harmful to others.*

3. *extremist: a person who acts in a bold, unconventional, and some times risky manner in order to support or defend a point of view.*

Strategies for Annotation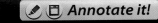

Context Clues

COMMON CORE L 4a

Have students locate the sentences containing *moderate, condemned/condemning,* and *extremist,* and use their eBook annotation tools to:

- Highlight in yellow each targeted word.
- Underline words and sentences that give clues to the word's meaning.
- On a note, record a definition of the word in your own words.

Was not Martin Luther an extremist: "Here I stand; I cannot do otherwise, so help me God." And John Bunyan: "I will stay in jail to the end of my days before I make a butchery of my conscience."

extremist: one who supports views with extreme actions

Letter from Birmingham Jail **339**

PRACTICE & APPLY

Repetition and Parallelism

COMMON CORE W 5, L 1a

Point out the word *resonate* and explain that it can mean to call forth or suggest images, feelings, and memories. It can also mean to echo or reverberate. To emphasize how King's use of **repetition** and **parallelism** sounds, read aloud, or have volunteers read aloud, the examples or original passages in the text. Ask students to discuss how listening to these examples makes them feel and any images or memories that are called forth.

Possible answers:

Answers will vary. When students have completed their revisions, they should be able to point to two examples of repetition and two examples of parallelism in their essays.

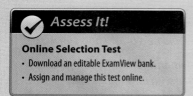

✔ *Assess It!*

Online Selection Test
- Download an editable ExamView bank.
- Assign and manage this test online.

Grammar in Context: Repetition and Parallelism

COMMON CORE W 5, L 1a

Repetition is a technique in which a sound, word, or phrase is repeated for emphasis or unity. **Parallelism** is the use of similar grammatical forms to express ideas that are related or equal in importance. King skillfully uses repetition and parallelism to make his message resonate with his audience. Consider the following examples and their effects:

Example	Effects
"**when you** have seen vicious mobs . . . **when you** have seen hate-filled policemen . . . **when you** see the vast majority of your twenty million Negro brothers smothering . . . **when you** suddenly find your tongue twisted . . . **when you** have to concoct an answer . . . **when you** take a cross-country drive . . . **when you** are humiliated . . . **when you** are harried by day and haunted by night . . . **when you** are forever fighting . . . —**then you** will understand why we find it difficult to wait."	Starting each subordinate clause with the words *when you* and then varying the parallel structure to *then you* emphasizes and dramatizes King's point that African Americans have waited long enough for their constitutional and God-given rights.
"the white moderate, **who** is more devoted to 'order' than to justice; **who** prefers a negative peace . . . **who** constantly says . . . **who** paternalistically believes . . . **who** lives by a mythical concept of time and **who** constantly advises the Negro to wait."	The relative pronoun *who* draws attention to the reasons King is frustrated with the white moderate.
"**Was not** Jesus an **extremist** for love . . . **Was not** Amos an **extremist** for justice . . . **Was not** Paul an **extremist** for the Christian gospel . . . **Was not** Martin Luther an **extremist** . . . **And** John Bunyan . . . **And** Abraham Lincoln . . . **And** Thomas Jefferson . . . So the question is not whether **we will be extremists**, but what kind of **extremists we will be**. **Will we be extremists** for hate or for love? **Will we be extremists** for the preservation of injustice or for the extension of justice?"	The repetition of the words *extremist* and *and* and the parallel structures created by the verbal phrase *was not* and the clause *we will be/will we be* link King's approach to that of other religious and historical figures.

Practice and Apply Locate other examples of repetition and parallel structure in King's letter and consider their effects. Then, look back at the essay you wrote for this selection's Performance Task. Revise your essay to include two examples each of repetition and parallelism. Discuss with a partner the effects of your revisions.

Strategies for Annotation ✐ 🗂 *Annotate it!*

Repetition and Parallelism

COMMON CORE L 1a

Have students use their eBook annotation tools to analyze the text. Ask them to do the following:

- Underline two additional examples of parallelism used to express ideas that are related or equal in importance.
- Highlight in yellow two additional examples of repetition used for emphasis or unity.

If I have said anything in this letter that overstates the truth and indicates an unreasonable impatience, I beg you to forgive me. If I have said anything that understates the truth and indicates my having a patience that allows me to settle for anything less than brotherhood, I beg God to forgive me.

Analyze Themes in Seminal Documents

TEACH

Remind students of the definition of **theme,** an underlying message. Also explain that themes of seminal documents often express messages about societal ideals or values. Before students complete the Performance Task, offer these steps for analyzing themes in a seminal text:

1. Identify the key values or ideas presented in the document. Consider such examples as freedom, bravery, equality, and justice.
2. Cite text evidence associated with each key value or idea. Look for specific examples, repeated words or ideas, symbols, and images.
3. Determine the outcome the writer wants to occur or the action the audience should take.

PRACTICE AND APPLY

Provide students with an analysis chart like the one below. Have students pair up to complete the chart in order to analyze the themes in King's letter and Roosevelt's speech. Remind students to refer to their completed charts as they write the essay for this selection's Performance Task.

Document	Key Ideas or Values	Text Evidence	Desired Outcome or Action
"Letter from Birmingham Jail"			
"Four Freedoms" speech			

Analyze Argument in a Seminal Document

RETEACH

Review that a **claim** is a writer's position on an issue or a problem and that **reasons** and **evidence** are used to support a claim; **counterarguments** address an opposing view. Help students understand the elements of an argument by analyzing an issue related to freedom. Present the claim: "Even though freedom of speech is a protected right, it should have limitations."

Ask students to offer a reason or evidence to support this claim. *(Sample reason: Words can sometimes incite anger and cause people to do harm to others.)*

Then ask students to offer a counterargument to the opposing view that speech should not have limitations. *(Sample counterargument: Limitations of speech limit debates on important issues. For example, if speaking out against segregationist laws were illegal, the civil rights movement may not have been successful.)*

 LEVEL UP TUTORIALS Assign the following *Level Up* tutorial to students: **Analyzing Arguments**

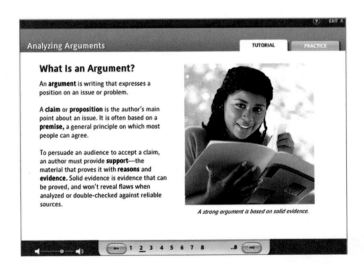

COLLABORATIVE DISCUSSION

Students can apply the skill to another seminal document that presents an argument. Have students work independently to identify the author's position on an issue or problem, reasons that support the claim, and counterarguments that address opposing views. Ask students whether they consider the reasons and evidence convincing.

Speech at the March on Washington

Speech by Josephine Baker

Background Have students read the background feature about Josephine Baker and the context for her speech. Tell students that over 250,000 people participated in the March on Washington on August 28, 1963. It was on this day, before the crowd that had gathered to call for civil and economic rights for African Americans, that Dr. Martin Luther King Jr. delivered his famous "I Have a Dream" speech.

AS YOU READ Ask students to note the various claims that the speaker makes throughout her speech. How soon into the speech does she make her purpose known?

Common Core Support

- cite strong and thorough textual evidence
- analyze in detail how an author's claims are developed
- analyze themes in historical texts

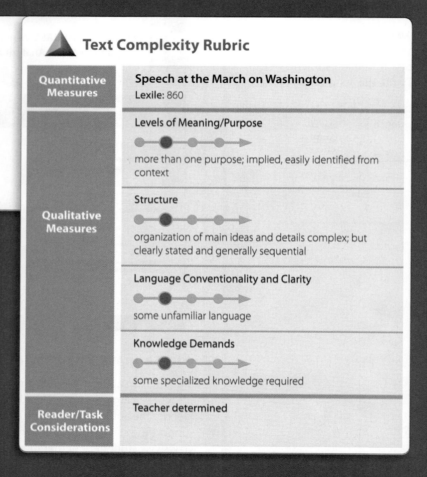

Text Complexity Rubric

Quantitative Measures	Speech at the March on Washington Lexile: 860
Qualitative Measures	**Levels of Meaning/Purpose** more than one purpose; implied, easily identified from context
	Structure organization of main ideas and details complex; but clearly stated and generally sequential
	Language Conventionality and Clarity some unfamiliar language
	Knowledge Demands some specialized knowledge required
Reader/Task Considerations	Teacher determined

Strategies for CLOSE READING

Analyze an Argument

Students should read the speech carefully, identifying Josephine Baker's claims, or positions on issues, and the reasons she gives to support her claims. Close-reading questions at the bottom of the page will help students collect and cite text evidence to identify claims made in the argument as well as supporting reasons and details. As they read, students should jot down the reasons Baker gives for speaking out about racism in the United States.

WHEN STUDENTS STRUGGLE . . .

To help students analyze the argument in Baker's historic speech, have them work in small groups to fill out a chart like the one shown below.

CITE TEXT EVIDENCE For practice analyzing an argument, ask students to cite text evidence that supports each of the claims Baker makes in her speech.

Claim	Supporting Details
As a child in the U.S., she encountered racism.	". . . they burned me out of my home . . . ." (line 10)
	". . . the conductor directed me to the last car." (line 16)
Life for African Americans was better in France than in the United States.	"I could go into any restaurant I wanted to . . ." (line 19)
	". . . I could drink water anyplace I wanted to . . ." (lines 19–20)
	". . . I didn't have to go to a colored toilet . . ." (line 20)
When she returned to the United States, she once again encountered racism.	". . . they would not let me check into the good hotels because I was colored, or eat in certain restaurants." (lines 38–39)
	". . . I was hounded by the government agencies in America . . ." (lines 53–54)

Background Josephine Baker *(1906–1975) was an African American dancer and singer who became an international musical and political icon. After dropping out of high school, Baker joined a vaudeville troupe as a dancer and headed to New York City. In the 1920s, she moved to France, where she became an overnight sensation, dancing and singing in cabarets. In the 1950s and 1960s, she joined the fight for civil rights, refusing to perform for segregated audiences and eventually adopting 12 multiethnic children. In 1963, Baker was asked to speak at the March on Washington, along with Martin Luther King, Jr. and other civil rights leaders.*

Speech at the March on Washington

Speech by Josephine Baker

CLOSE READ
Notes

1. **READD** As you read lines 1–13, begin to collect and cite text evidence.

   • Underline the statement Baker gives to introduce herself.
   • In the margin, explain Baker's reasons for speaking out.
   • Circle the difference between Josephine Baker and other African Americans.

Friends and family . . . you know I have lived a long time and I have come a long way. And you must know now that what I did, I did originally for myself. Then later, as these things began happening to me, I wondered if they were happening to you, and then I knew they must be. And I knew that you had no way to defend yourselves, as I had.

And as I continued to do the things I did, and to say the things I said, they began to beat me. Not beat me, mind you, with a club—but you know, I have seen that done too—but they beat me with their pens, with their writings. And friends, that is much worse.

10 When I was a child and they burned me out of my home, I was frightened and I ran away. Eventually I ran far away. It was to a place called France. Many of you have been there, and many have not. But I must tell you, ladies and gentlemen, in that country I never feared.

Baker has been the victim of racism, like other African Americans.

99

---

1. **READ AND CITE TEXT EVIDENCE** Discuss with students what Baker means when she says "And I knew that you had no way to defend yourselves, as I had" (line 5). *Being a successful celebrity probably gave Baker certain economic advantages that disadvantaged African Americans could not enjoy.*

A **ASK STUDENTS** to identify details in the text that support the idea that Josephine Baker had been the victim of racism. *"they beat me with their pens, with their writings" (lines 8–9) and "When I was a child and they burned me out of my home" (line 10).*

But I must tell you, when I was young in Paris, strange things happened to me. And these things had never happened to me before. When I left St. Louis a long time ago, the conductor directed me to the last car. And you all know what that means.

C
20 But when I ran away, yes, when I ran away to another country, I didn't have to do that. I could go into any restaurant I wanted to, and I could drink water anyplace I wanted to, and I didn't have to go to a colored toilet either, and I have to tell you it was nice, and I got used to it, and I liked it, and I wasn't afraid anymore that someone would shout at me and say, "Go to the end of the line."

So over there, far away, I was happy, and because I was happy I had some success, and you know that too.

Then, after a long time, I came to America to be in a great show for Mr. Ziegfeld,[1] and you know Josephine was happy. You know that. Because I wanted to tell everyone in my country about myself. I wanted to let everyone know that I made good, and you know too that that is only natural.

30 But on that great big beautiful ship, I had a bad experience. A very important star was to sit with me for dinner, and at the last moment I discovered she didn't want to eat with a colored woman. I can tell you it was some blow.

And I won't bother to mention her name, because it is not important, and anyway, now she is dead.

[1] **Mr. Ziegfeld:** Florenz Ziegfeld (1867–1932) was an American theater producer known for his series of theatrical revues called the Ziegfeld Follies.

Baker was happier in France because blacks were not segregated from whites. Baker was also able to achieve success in France.

2. ◀ **REREAD** Reread lines 6–13. What are the most important points Baker makes in these lines?

In America, Josephine Baker was burned out of her home and attacked by writers because of the color of her skin. Her experience was very different once she moved to France.

3. **READ** ▶ As you read lines 14–41, continue to cite textual evidence.
- Underline examples of segregation in America.
- In the margin, explain why Baker was happier in France (lines 18–30).

D
And when I got to New York way back then, I had other blows—when they would not let me check into the good hotels because I was colored, or eat in certain restaurants. And then I went to Atlanta, and it was a horror to
40 me. And I said to myself, I am Josephine, and if they do this to me, what do they do to the other people in America?

E F
You know, friends, that I do not lie to you when I tell you I have walked into the palaces of kings and queens and into the houses of presidents. And much more. But I could not walk into a hotel in America and get a cup of coffee, and that made me mad. And when I get mad, you know that I open my big mouth. And then look out, 'cause when Josephine opens her mouth, they hear it all over the world.

So I did open my mouth, and you know I did scream, and when I
50 demanded what I was supposed to have and what I was entitled to, they still would not give it to me.

So then they thought they could smear me, and the best way to do that was to call me a communist. And you know, too, what that meant. Those were dreaded words in those days, and I want to tell you also that I was hounded by the government agencies in America, and there was never one ounce of proof that I was a communist. But they were mad. They were mad because I told the truth. And the truth was that all I wanted was a cup of coffee. But I wanted that cup of coffee where *I* wanted to drink it, and I had the money to pay for it, so why shouldn't I have it where I wanted it?

Josephine Baker "opens her mouth" because she is denied what she feels she is entitled to.

4. ◀ **REREAD** Reread lines 37–41. Explain Josephine Baker's thinking in these lines. Why is she concerned with "the other people in America"?

Baker was shocked at the segregational policies in New York and Atlanta. She is concerned because she realizes that as badly as she is treated, other African Americans from everyday life are probably treated even worse.

5. **READ** ▶ As you read lines 42–58, continue to cite textual evidence.
- In the margin, explain why Josephine Baker "opens her mouth."
- Underline text that explains what happened as a result of Baker's protests.

2. **REREAD AND CITE TEXT EVIDENCE** Explain to students that Baker does not always state her claims directly.

B **ASK STUDENTS** to identify evidence in the text that supports the idea that life in France was better for Josephine Baker than life had been in the United States. *"When I was a child and they burned me out of my home, I was frightened and ran away. Eventually I ran far away. It was to a place called France.... But I must tell you ... in that country, I never feared" (lines 10–13).*

3. **READ AND CITE TEXT EVIDENCE**

C **ASK STUDENTS** to identify evidence in the text that helps them understand how Baker's life in France was free of racism. *"I could go into any restaurant I wanted to, and I could drink water anyplace I wanted to, and I didn't have to go to a colored toilet either ... and I wasn't afraid anymore that someone would shout at me and say, 'go to the end of the line'" (lines 19–23).*

4. **REREAD AND CITE TEXT EVIDENCE**

D **ASK STUDENTS** to find details that support the idea that segregationist policies were imposed in New York City and Atlanta. *Students should cite evidence in lines 38–40.*

5. **READ AND CITE TEXT EVIDENCE** Discuss with students what Baker means when she says, "So I did open my mouth, and you know I did scream ... " *Possible response: Baker probably spoke to the press about the racist treatment she had been subjected to.*

E **ASK STUDENTS** to identify the text evidence that Baker uses to refute that she was a communist. *" ... there was never one ounce of proof that I was a communist" (lines 54–55).*

FOR ELL STUDENTS Tell ELL students that *hounds* are "hunting dogs." Then ask students what *hounded* (line 54) might mean. *hunted down*

G H 60 Friends and brothers and sisters, that is how it went. And when I screamed loud enough, they started to open that door just a little bit, and we all started to be able to squeeze through it.

Now, I am not going to stand in front of all of you today and take credit for what is happening now. I cannot do that. But I want to take credit for telling you how to do the same thing, and when you scream, friends, I know you will be heard. And you will be heard now.

But you young people must do one thing, and I know you have heard this story a thousand times from your mothers and fathers, like I did from my mama. I didn't take her advice. But I accomplished the same in another fashion. You must get an education. You must go to school, and you must

70 learn to protect yourself. And you must learn to protect yourself with the pen, and not the gun. Then you can answer them, and I can tell you—and I don't want to sound corny—but friends, the pen really is mightier than the sword.

. . .

She wants young people to get an education so that they can protect themselves from racism.

> I want you to have a chance at what I had. But I do not want you to have to run away to get it.

I am not a young woman now, friends. My life is behind me. There is not too much fire burning inside me. And before it goes out, I want you to use what is left to light that fire in you. So that you can carry on, and so that you can do those things that I have done. Then, when my fires have burned out, and I go where we all go someday, I can be happy.

I You know, I have always taken the rocky path. I never took the easy

80 one, but as I grew older, and as I knew I had the power and the strength, I took that rocky path, and I tried to smooth it out a little. I wanted to make it easier for you. I want you to have a chance at what I had. But I do not want you to have to run away to get it. And mothers and fathers, if it is too late for you, think of your children. Make it safe here so they do not have to run away, for I want for you and your children what I had.

6. ◀ REREAD Reread lines 42–58. How does Baker's claim of the rights afforded to her in other countries strengthen her argument? Support your answer with explicit textual evidence.

Baker argues that because she has walked "into the palaces of kings and queens and into the houses of presidents" in other countries, she is certainly entitled to a "cup of coffee where I wanted to drink it," especially since she "had the money to pay for it." African Americans only wanted to be treated the same as other citizens.

7. READ ▶ As you read lines 59–78, continue to cite textual evidence.
• Underline text describing the results of Baker's "screaming."
• In the margin, explain Baker's advice for young people.
• Circle text describing the benefits of protecting oneself with a pen.

8. ◀ REREAD Reread lines 59–73. What does Josephine Baker give herself credit for in the civil rights movement? How does this reasoning appeal to the shared beliefs of her audience? Support your answer with explicit textual evidence.

Baker claims "credit for telling you how to do the same thing," meaning "screaming" or making a loud noise of dissent. By challenging her audience to follow her lead and scream as well, their strength in numbers will continue what she has started, for "when you scream, friends, I know you will be heard."

9. READ ▶ As you read lines 79–96, continue to cite textual evidence.
• Underline text describing what Baker has done for African Americans.
• Circle text explaining what Josephine Baker asks the audience to do for future generations.

6. REREAD AND CITE TEXT EVIDENCE

F **ASK STUDENTS** to identify details in the text that describe the rights Baker enjoyed in other countries. *Baker says, ". . . I have walked into the palaces of kings and queens and into the house of presidents. And much more" (lines 42–44).*

7. READ AND CITE TEXT EVIDENCE Help students understand that Baker was not literally screaming and that she is using a figure of speech.

G **ASK STUDENTS** to cite text evidence describing what Baker thinks young people must do to help themselves and to end racism. *Baker tells young people, "You must get an education. You must go to school, and you learn to protect yourself. And you must learn to protect yourself with the pen, and not the gun" (lines 69–71).*

8. REREAD AND CITE TEXT EVIDENCE

H **ASK STUDENTS** to cite text evidence in which Baker explains the results of the actions she took, and how they affected others. *When she "screamed loud enough, they started to open that door just a little bit" (line 60). Because the door was now open, "we all started to be able to squeeze through it" (line 61).*

9. READ AND CITE TEXT EVIDENCE Remind students that Josephine Baker went to France as a young woman and became a successful and famous entertainer.

I **ASK STUDENTS** to explain what Baker's claim in lines 80–82 means in the context of her having become a famous entertainer. *She broke down racist barriers and became an example of a successful African American woman.*

CLOSE READ
Notes

Ladies and gentlemen, my friends and family, I have just been handed a little note, as you probably saw. It is an invitation to visit the President of the United States in his home, the White House.

90   I am greatly honored. But I must tell you that a colored woman—or, as you say it here in America, a black woman—is not going there. It is a woman. It is Josephine Baker.

It is a great honor for me. Someday I want you children out there to have that great honor too. And we know that that time is not someday. We know that that time is *now.*

I thank you, and may God bless you. And may He continue to bless you long after I am gone.

10. ◀ REREAD AND DISCUSS Reread lines 86–91. In a small group, discuss what Baker means by saying "a black woman—is not going there."

SHORT RESPONSE

Cite Text Evidence What universal themes does Baker explore in her speech? What makes these themes universal? Review your reading notes, and be sure to **cite text evidence** in your response.

In her speech, Baker explores the universal themes of a desire for equality, the pursuit of freedom, and the strength of numbers. She compares her experiences in France to the way she was treated in America ("So over there, far away, I was happy, and because I was happy I had some success, and you know that too."). Baker challenges her audience to rise up when they are being treated unfairly, for "when you scream, friends, I know you will be heard. And you will be heard now." These themes are universal because they can be seen as basic inalienable rights for all people.

104

In 1927, Josephine Baker earned more money than any other entertainer in Europe. However, her legacy is based on much more than her celebrity as a performer.

ASK STUDENTS to research Josephine Baker's life—especially those areas in which she worked against oppression and racism.

- What did Baker do during World War II? How was she recognized for her work? *She worked with the French resistance as an underground courier, smuggling messages. She was a sub-lieutenant in the Free French forces, entertaining the troops. After the war, the French government awarded Baker the Legion of Honor and the Croix du Guerre.*

- How did Baker fight against racism in the United States? *She supported the civil rights movement, joining demonstrations and refusing to perform to segregated audiences. In 1951, the NAACP named her Most Outstanding Woman of the Year. The NAACP also named May 20 as Josephine Baker Day.*

---

10. **REREAD AND DISCUSS USING TEXT EVIDENCE** Explain to students that they are reading the text of a speech. In lines 86–88, Baker has been handed a note inviting her to visit President Kennedy at the White House as she was speaking.

ⓙ **ASK STUDENTS** to find details in lines 89–91 that clarify what Baker means by "a black woman—is not going there." *She means that she is not identified solely as a black woman. She is going as ". . . a woman. It is Josephine Baker" (lines 90–91).*

SHORT RESPONSE

Cite Text Evidence Students should:

- identify the universal themes that Baker talks about in her speech.
- explain why these themes are universal.
- cite text evidence to support their ideas.

DIG DEEPER

With the class, return to Question 5, Read. Have students share and discuss their responses.

ASK STUDENTS to identify specific text evidence in lines 42–58 that helps them respond to both bulleted items.

• Have students explain why they think Baker feels that she is entitled to certain basic civil rights and as a result "opens her mouth." *In lines 42–43, she says that she has walked into the palaces of kings and queens and into the houses of presidents. Her reasoning seems to be that in Europe she was not denied anything and in fact was treated as royalty, and that now back in the United States, she has not been allowed into certain hotels for something as insignificant as a cup of coffee. She is outraged by the denial of basic civil rights.*

• Have students discuss the evidence they underlined in response to the second bulleted item to ensure their understanding of concepts addressed in the text. Ask students to discuss what they know about communism. *Students should recall that communism is a political ideology that was adopted by the government of the former USSR (Union of Soviet Socialist Republics), which included Russia and fourteen other eastern European republics. You might explain that during the 1960s, the United States and the USSR were politically hostile to one another and that there were also several tense military confrontations. It was a period known as the Cold War. Because of these tensions, being referred to as a communist could have had seriously negative consequences on Josephine Baker's reputation and the public's impression of her.*

ASK STUDENTS to return to their Short Response answer and revise it based on the class discussion.

CLOSE READING NOTES

Revolution 2.0

Memoir by Wael Ghonim

Why This Text?

Today, students live in a global community. Nations are connected via economics and technology. This lesson explores how one writer uses technology to develop an idea and offer evidence to gather support for an international socio-political cause.

View It!

Professional Development Podcast:
Informational Text

Key Learning Objective: The students will be able to analyze evidence and ideas in a functional document.

Common Core Standards

RI 1 Cite textual evidence.

RI 3 Analyze how the author unfolds ideas or events.

RI 4 Determine the meaning of words and phrases.

RI 5 Analyze how an author's ideas are developed by particular sentences or paragraphs.

RI 6 Determine an author's point of view and analyze how an author uses rhetoric.

RI 8 Delineate specific claims in a text.

W 7 Conduct short research projects.

W 8 Gather relevant information from multiple authoritative sources.

SL 2 Integrate multiple sources of information presented in diverse media or formats.

SL 4 Present information clearly so that the development and style are appropriate to purpose, audience, and task.

L 2b Use a colon to introduce a list or quotation.

L 4d Verify the preliminary definition of the meaning of a word or phrase.

L 6 Acquire and use general academic words and phrases.

Text Complexity Rubric

Quantitative Measures	**Revolution 2.0** Lexile: 1100L
Qualitative Measures	**Levels of Meaning/Purpose** more than one purpose; easily identified from context
	Structure organization of main ideas and details complex, but mostly explicit; may exhibit disciplinary traits
	Language Conventionality and Clarity increased unfamiliar, academic, or domain-specific words
	Knowledge Demands somewhat complex social studies concepts
Reader/Task Considerations	Teacher determined Vary by individual reader and type of text

CLOSE READ

Background Explain that the author worked as part of a group of anonymous administrators for the Facebook page that helped spark the Egyptian revoluion. Elsewhere in *Revolution 2.0,* he notes two reason for this group approach: first, organizers wanted a wide range of viewpoints included in the protests; and second, if no one person was responsible for the page, all were less likely to be caught by authorities. However, Ghonim was arrested for his involvement and held for 11 days at the height of the protests.

AS YOU READ Direct students to use the As You Read prompt to focus their reading. Encourage them to keep a list of any questions they may have while they are reading this selection.

Analyze Ideas and Evidence (LINES 6–16)

COMMON CORE **RI 3, RI 5**

Explain that authors organize evidence to support their key ideas. Point out that this author clearly states how he worked toward his goals

(A) CITE TEXT EVIDENCE Ask students to reread lines 6–16 and explain what steps the author takes to achieve his stated goals. *(He compiles relevant information for protestors in an easy-to-print document and uploads the document online for easy access by supporters.)*

CRITICAL VOCABULARY

disseminated: By using technology, Ghonim was able to circulate his ideas to a wide audience.
ASK STUDENTS how Ghonim used technology to disseminate information. *(He organized information on a Facebook page, which was accessible to most everyone and able to reach beyond political boundaries.)*

Background *In December 2010, angry protests erupted against the authoritarian government in the north African nation of Tunisia. Within a month, protesters brought down the government. Days later, on January 25, 2011 ("Jan25"), protests spread to Egypt. There, mass demonstrations similar to those in Tunisia were held, through the work of organizers including* **Wael Ghonim** *(b. 1980), a high-tech executive and administrator of the Facebook page "We are all Khaled Said." Thousands of people massed daily in Cairo's Tahrir Square, eventually forcing Egypt's president of thirty years to step down. The unrest spread to other nations and became known as the Arab Spring.*

from
Revolution 2.0
Memoir by Wael Ghonim

AS YOU READ Identify how the author organizes information and think about the kinds of information the author includes in the document. Write down any questions you generate during reading.

I continued to rally supporters on the page. I shared writings, images, and designs made by the page members that promised a victorious Jan25. I tried to induce confidence and belief that youth would be capable of leading change. I also highlighted the government's frightened reactions.

I decided to compile all the information relevant to Jan25 in a document that was easy to print and to distribute online. It summarized the reasons for protesting and for choosing this day and these locations. It also described the unified chants
10 that had been chosen and provided phone numbers for activists responsible for supporting arrested protesters and for redirecting demonstrators to other locations if the protests at any one place were obstructed. I uploaded the file to Google Docs, where more than 50,000 people accessed it. Its content was also **disseminated** through various online forums, political websites, Facebook pages, and Twitter accounts.

(A)

disseminate (dĭ-sĕm′ə-nāt′) *v.* to spread or circulate widely.

Revolution 2.0 **341**

SCAFFOLDING FOR ELL STUDENTS

Analyze Language Using a whiteboard, project lines 1–5. Explain that an **infinitive** is made up of the word *to* followed by the simple form of a verb. Infinitives can be used as nouns, adjectives, or adverbs. Invite volunteers to mark up the lines:

- Highlight in green the infinitive in the first sentence.
- Highlight in yellow the infinitive in the third sentence.

ASK STUDENTS what two goals of the writer the infinitive expresses.

Analyze Evidence and Author's Ideas (LINES 17–29)

COMMON CORE RI 1, RI 5

Remind students that one of the author's goals for his writing is to present information in a way that makes understanding it easier for readers. Draw students' attention to the heading and subheading. Explain that such headings create points of focus for readers.

B CITE TEXT EVIDENCE Ask students to cite the text that shows the focus of the article. *(the first heading, "Everything You Need to Know about Jan25")* Have students explain how the focus of this section of the article is determined by citing evidence from the text. *(The focus is on who is involved in the movement, as determined by the subhead, "Who Are We?" This section explains that these people are Egyptians who wish to defend their rights, but who are not influenced by specific politics or ideologies, as explained by this text: "not influenced by any political party, group, movement, or organization" [lines 25–26], "does not support any person or specific ideology" [lines 26–27], and "belongs to all Egyptians who wish to defend their rights" [lines 27–28].)*

CRITICAL VOCABULARY

ideology: Ghonim is careful to explain that supporters of the page are not influenced by specific beliefs.

ASK STUDENTS to identify specific examples Ghonim mentions that would possibly further a particular ideology. *(political party, group, movement, organization, person)*

Everything You Need to Know about Jan25

Important note: Please visit the page regularly for frequent updates.

Who Are We?

The call for protests on Jan25 began from the Facebook page "*Kullena Khaled Said,*" a page created to support the case of
20 Khaled Said, who was beaten and tortured to death on the street in Alexandria in June of 2010. The call was spontaneous and not planned by any political or popular force. After the invitation spread, and because of events in Tunisia, many Egyptians were encouraged to participate and spread the word. The Facebook page is not influenced by any political party, group, movement, or organization. It is independent and does not support any person or specific **ideology**. It belongs to all Egyptians who wish to defend their rights. The page is managed through its member volunteers, and this is the secret to its success.

ideology
(ī´dē-ŏl´ə-jē) *n.* a system of doctrines or beliefs.

APPLYING ACADEMIC VOCABULARY

media	comprehensive

As you discuss the Facebook page, incorporate the following Collection 6 academic vocabulary words: *media* and *comprehensive*. To reiterate how Ghonim communicates with supporters, ask students how **media** plays a role in his plans. As they analyze the format and content of the page, ask students how Ghonim achieves his **comprehensive** goal of telling readers everything they need to know about Jan25.

Why Protest?

30 Egypt is going through one of the worst periods in its history on all fronts. Despite the reports propagated by the government that aim to polish its image, reality is unfortunately different. Our collective participation on Jan25 is the beginning of the end—the end of silence, acceptance, and submission to all that is happening in our country, and the beginning of a new page of coming forward and demanding our rights. Jan25 is not a revolution in the sense of a coup,[1] but rather a revolution against our government to let them know that we have taken interest in one another's problems and that we shall reclaim all our rights and will not be silent anymore.

40   There are 30 million Egyptians suffering from depression, including 1.5 million with severe depression. There were more than 100,000 suicide attempts in 2009, resulting in the deaths of 5,000 people. There are 48 million poor citizens in Egypt, including 2.5 million who live in extreme poverty. 12 million Egyptians have no shelter, including 1.5 million who live in cemeteries. Habitual corruption has led to graft[2] totaling more than 39 billion pounds[3] during one year alone. And Egypt ranks 115th out of 139 nations in the Corruption Perceptions Index. More than three million young Egyptians are unemployed; the unemployment rate among 50 youth has surpassed 30 percent. Egypt also came in last place among 139 countries in terms of hiring transparency. We have the highest rate of newborn deaths in the world: 50 of every 1,000 newborn Egyptians die. Half of Egypt's children are anemic, and eight million Egyptians are infected with hepatitis C. More than 100,000 citizens suffer from cancer every year because of water pollution. Our rate of ambulance cars to citizens is 1:35,000. Egypt's emergency law has caused the death of many Egyptians as the result of torture and also facilitated the arrests of thousands without official warrants. Security forces' involvement in monitoring 60 politicians and blocking their activism has led to shameless rigging of parliamentary elections, producing a people's assembly that was more than 90 percent controlled by the ruling party . . .

Why Jan25?

In 1952, using simple rifles, our forefathers in the police force fought the British army's tanks. Fifty became martyrs, and more than 100 were taken as prisoners. They were heroic and offered a model of sacrificing one's life for one's homeland. Now, more

---

[1] **coup:** a sudden, unlawful seizure of government power.
[2] **graft:** illegal or unethical exchanges of money.
[3] **pounds:** the main unit of Egyptian currency.

Revolution 2.0 **343**

WHEN STUDENTS STRUGGLE . . .

To guide students' understanding of how the author develops ideas, have students use a graphic organizer, such as the one below, to record specific evidence that supports key ideas.

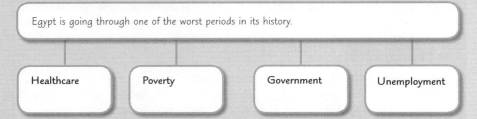

> Egypt is going through one of the worst periods in its history.

| Healthcare | Poverty | Government | Unemployment |

Analyze Author's Ideas
COMMON CORE RI 1, RI 5, RI 8

(LINES 30–39)

Note that this portion of the memoir functions as an argument. Remind students that persuasive arguments are often structured through the statement of reasons why readers should act or change their thinking. Generally, these reasons are followed by the presentation of supporting evidence.

C CITE TEXT EVIDENCE Ask students to reread lines 30–39 and explain how the author uses the subheading to focus readers. *(The subheading asks the same question readers may be asking.)* What reasons does the author give for joining the protest? *("Egypt is going through one of the worst periods in its history on all fronts" [lines 30–31]. The protest will end "silence, acceptance, and submission" [line 34] with regard to current events and allow Egyptians to reclaim their rights.)*

Analyze Evidence
COMMON CORE RI 8

(LINES 40–62)

Explain that in order to support his or her claim, an author may provide different types of evidence. This evidence may include **facts,** statements that may be proven true through reliable sources, or **statistics,** special types of facts based on numerical information.

D CITE TEXT EVIDENCE Have students reread lines 40–62. Ask them to cite one fact the author includes as evidence to support his claim. *("Egypt's emergency law has caused the death of many Egyptians as the result of torture and also facilitated the arrests of thousands without official warrants" [lines 56–59].)* What is one statistic the author includes as evidence? *("There are 48 million poor citizens in Egypt, including 2.5 million who live in extreme poverty" [lines 43–44].)* Ask student pairs to discuss how this evidence helps to clarify the reasons stated in lines 30–39. *(This evidence illustrates the author's reasons by showing that this is one of Egypt's worst periods, which includes poor health care, poverty, corruption, unemployment, pollution, torture, and lawlessness.)*

Analyze Development of Ideas (LINES 74–99)

COMMON CORE RI 1, RI 5

Explain that in this section, the text shifts from detailing an argument to providing information.

 CITE TEXT EVIDENCE Ask students how the author organizes the people's list of demands. *(Under the heading, "What Are Our Demands?" he clearly labels each demand: Demand One and so on.)* Then have students summarize the demands. *(Demand one: Work on the poverty problem by raising minimum wage and giving unemployment benefits to citizens. Demand two: Eliminate the state of emergency law. Demand three: Fire the Minister of Interior. Demand four: Limit presidents to two terms to prevent corruption and other abuses of power.)*

CRITICAL VOCABULARY

annul: Ghonim demands that an emergency law that violates the rights of citizens be declared invalid.

ASK STUDENTS why protestors might want to annul a law that empowers officials against citizens. *(Laws should protect citizens, not be used as weapons against them.)*

---

than 50 years later, we suffer from a police force that has become a machine for torturing and humiliating Egyptians. We chose this day specifically because it represents the fusion of the police and
70   the people. We hope that decent and honest officers will join our ranks on Jan25 because our cause is one with theirs. Jan25 is a national holiday, which should allow all Egyptians to participate without hurting their productivity on any level.

What Are Our Demands?

Demand One: Addressing the poverty problem before it explodes by respecting the judiciary's verdict to increase the minimum wage fairly, particularly in health care and education, in order to improve the services offered to the people. Also, to issue unemployment benefits that reach up to 500 Egyptian pounds, for a limited period, for every university graduate unable to find a job.
80   Demand Two: **Annulling** the emergency law, which has led to the control of Egypt by the security apparatus and has allowed the illegal arrest of political opposition members without cause. We demand that attorneys general take charge of police stations to stop the routine torture practices that take place there. We also demand implementation of the judiciary's verdicts by the government.

Demand Three: Firing Minister of Interior Habib el-Adly. His loose security measures have led to terrorist attacks as well as the spread of crime at the hands of police officers and other Ministry of Interior forces.
90   Demand Four: Placing a two-term limit on the presidency. Absolute power corrupts, and no advanced nation allows a president to stay in power for decades. It is our right to choose our president, and it is our right not to have a president monopolize power until his death.

Of course Egyptians have many further demands in areas such as health and education. We begin by moving together, pressuring the government, and achieving one demand at a time. This is our role as a people: to direct the government, hold it accountable, and determine its priorities.

annul
(ə-nŭl´) *v.* render or declare invalid.

Time and Place of Protests

100 It is very important to realize that the point of the protests is to mobilize all people to our side. Everyone is frustrated and dissatisfied with the nation's condition. We must encourage them to participate. This is why we must organize marches in all working-class neighborhoods. And people must move together in numbers of more than ten until they reach the protest destination. And by the way, the locations are not just the ones mentioned here. There are other locations that have not been announced where protests

---

TO CHALLENGE STUDENTS . . .

Analyze Author's Ideas Ask students to consider why posting these demands on Facebook and formatting them using headings is an effective choice.

ASK STUDENTS to work in pairs or small groups to extract information from the section titled "What Are Our Demands?" and format and phrase the information in ways that may make ideas clearer or be more appealing to the audience. Instruct students to focus on print text features as if the information will appear on a flyer, poster, or web page.

Display students' products. Then lead them to compare and contrast the effectiveness of the original text with their products. Ask students which version best communicates information and appeals to potential supporters.

will be organized in different governorates.[4] The important thing is for you to come out and express your anger in whatever way
110 you can.

Greater Cairo: Shubra Roundabout, Matariyya Square, Cairo University, the Arab League Street

Alexandria: Al-Manshiyya Square, Mahatet Masr Square

Important note: Other groups are organizing protests and marches in popular neighborhoods all over Cairo, Giza, Alexandria, and many other cities across Egypt. If you are in a working-class neighborhood, come out on Jan25 and join them . . .

F | **Protesting Guidelines**

1. The protests are peaceful. We are peace advocates and not advocates of violence. We are demanding our rights and
120 must uphold the rights of others. We will not respond to any provocation from security forces and lose control. This is what they want us to do. One of the security forces' main goals is to portray the protesters as thugs who want to destroy our country. We must discipline ourselves and refrain from foolishness or any violations of the law, and we must not endanger any person's life or cause harm to any public or private property. If you see someone behaving violently, please circle around this person and take him out of the protest.

130 2. Please be at the protest location promptly at the determined time. Delays will hinder our efforts and risk the failure of the protest. Being present at the same time makes it easy to start the protest and makes it hard for the security forces to prevent it.

3. When leaving your house, do not carry anything you don't need, such as membership cards or licenses or credit cards. Carry only your personal ID and a sum of money sufficient for an emergency. Please don't bring your watch or anything easily breakable. The ideal attire would be sportswear or
140 jeans along with a jacket to keep warm in case the protest runs long or develops into a sit-in. Please bring a large bottle of water, because there is always a shortage of water inside the protest.

4. Please carry the Egyptian flag and refrain from carrying any signs of a political party, movement, group, organization, or religious sect. Jan25 is for all Egyptians. We are all

G

---

[4] **governorates:** the 27 political districts of Egypt, each headed by a governor.

Revolution 2.0 **345**

CLOSE READ

Analyze Author's Ideas   COMMON CORE RI 5
(LINES 118–146)

Remind students that writers use subheads to organize their thoughts and put emphasis on particular points or ideas. Point out to students that the structure of the subheadings changes after line 99.

F **ASK STUDENTS** to look back at the first four subheadings and describe their structure. *(They are phrased as questions.)* Then ask them to examine the remaining three subheadings and describe their structure. *(They are phrased as noun phrases, not questions.)* Why does the author change the structure of the subheadings? *(He moves from persuading readers to join the protest to telling them how to participate.)* How does this relate to the author's purpose for writing? *(As the subhead structure changes, the author shifts from persuasive writing to functional writing.)*

Draw students' attention to the structure of the section titled "Protesting Guidelines." Point out that some of the guidelines in the list relate to philosophical issues and others relate to logistical or planning issues.

G **ASK STUDENTS** why the author is using a numbered list here. *(The numbered list organizes the steps and makes it easy for the readers to follow. This information provides them with steps to follow if they want to participate in a protest.)* How do items 1 and 4 help the cause succeed? *(By remaining peaceful, the protesters show their concerns are legitimate. By including all Egyptians, the protesters show that they are not like the government they are opposing.)* How will items 2 and 3 help the protests function smoothly? *(By arriving on time and bringing only necessities, the protesters help to ensure that the protests remain focused.)*

SCAFFOLDING FOR ELL STUDENTS

Analyze Author's Ideas Project lines 118–146. Explain that the author combines guidelines with explanation. Invite volunteers to mark up the lines by highlighting the guidelines in green and the explanations in yellow.

Please be at the protest location promptly at the determined time. Delays will hinder our efforts and risk the failure of the protest.

Analyze Evidence and Author's Ideas (LINES 152–158)

COMMON CORE   RI 5

Point out that the author continues to develop his thoughts by stating and explaining guidelines for the protest in a list.

H **ASK STUDENTS** to reread and paraphrase item 6. *(Do not fight with Central Security.)* Why does the author provide details about who the Central Security people are? *(To help protestors understand that they are not the enemy, the government is. Central Security is made up of citizens like those protesting.)*

Tell students that by organizing his points in a specific order, the author is able to emphasize key ideas. Draw students' attention to the "Unified Chants" subhead on this page. Point out that the author saves this explanation for the end of the document because it is memorable, and therefore powerful. In fact, Ghonim declares unified chants as one of the most powerful protest tools.

I **ASK STUDENTS** to examine the section of text titled "Unified Chants," and explain why the author uses bullets to separate the items in this list. *(The bullets separate the words to different chants. The bulleted list also makes it easy for the reader to scan the chants and focus on each as desired.)* Then have students cite text evidence to answer these questions: What two themes do all of the chants listed include? *("unemployment and poverty")* Why did organizers choose these two themes? *(They are "issues that concern all Egyptians.")* Why will protestors chant these words in unison? *(They want to show the government the Egyptian people are united over these issues and will "act as one.")*

CRITICAL VOCABULARY

divisive: Ghonim stresses that the protest is for all Egyptians; he does not want the protest to cause division or disagreement among the citizenry.
ASK STUDENTS why the author wants the protest to be unifying, not divisive. *(The people already feel divided from the government. He wants to create an opposite effect with the protest.)*

---

demanding equal rights and social justice and do not want to be **divisive.**

divisive
(dĭ-vī´sĭv) *adj.*
causing division or disagreement.

5. If you are not an experienced protester, leave the front lines
150 for experienced protesters to lead the march in order to avoid conflicting decisions.

6. The chants are unified and agreed upon. Please refrain from all profanity and do not enter into quarrels with security force members. Central Security is not your enemy. They are guards who have been forced to spend their compulsory military service in this capacity, and if they disobeyed the orders they would be punished badly. Try as much as possible to target your anger at the real enemy. **H**

7. Try as much as possible not to disturb traffic. We are not out
160 to punish the citizens but to demand our rights. Try not to interrupt traffic flow deliberately. It is understandable that when tens of thousands of people take to the streets, traffic flow will be affected. This is not what we are referring to.

8. Do not come out alone. It is very important not to come out alone, because friends come in handy in situations like these. Please be with someone and talk someone into coming out together, just like we take to the stadiums when there is a match to watch.

F **Unified Chants**

The unified chants are one of the most important protest ideas. We
170 are all out for the sake of Egypt, and we must unite and act as one. We will all stick to the chants together and will focus on the issues of unemployment and poverty. These are the issues that concern all Egyptians. These are the chants that have been agreed upon:

J
- Long live Egypt . . . Long live Egypt
- Bread . . . Freedom . . . Human dignity
- Dear freedom, where are you? . . . Emergency law is keeping us away from you
- We will not fear, we will not bow . . . Like we've done for so long
180 - Beloved people of Tunisia . . . The revolution sun will not set
- We shall sacrifice our blood and lives for you, dear Egypt
- Raise your voice up high . . . With injustice we will not comply
- Alert the people and rock the universe . . . We will not let our homeland go
- Minimum wage now . . . before all the Egyptians revolt

I

APPLYING ACADEMIC VOCABULARY

incentive	innovate

As you discuss the selection, incorporate the following Collection 6 academic vocabulary words: *incentive* and *innovate*. To reflect on the author's goals, have students identify the **incentives** Egyptians may have had to participate in the protest and to follow the stated guidelines. To analyze the protest strategies, discuss which strategies organizers borrowed from history and which strategies they **innovated.**

- It's my right to find work and live . . . The petty income is not enough
- Let's make it happen, Egyptians, wake your spirit . . . The gates of liberty are open
190
- Let's go, people, transcend the fear . . . Let the whole world know
- A people with the civilization and glory of years . . . Will not bow until Judgment Day

♡ *1,977 likes*   ◯ *1,527 comments*   *506,871 | views*

COLLABORATIVE DISCUSSION With a partner, discuss how the organization of the document makes it easy or difficult for someone participating in the protests to use. Cite specific textual evidence to support your ideas.

CLOSE READ

Determine Meaning   COMMON CORE RI 4

(LINES 174–194)

Remind students that authors choose their words carefully to convey a specific purpose or meaning. The words and phrases in the chants were chosen to evoke specific emotions and rally supporters.

🄹 **ASK STUDENTS** to reread the second chant, "Bread . . . Freedom . . . Human dignity." Ask students what the word *bread* stands for and why it's important to Egyptians. *(food; it's a basic human need that was not being met for these people.)* Have students reread the chant on lines 184–185 and explain what it means by "rock the universe." *(cause a change that makes a real difference to the world)* Have students read aloud the chant on lines 189–190 and discuss the meaning of the phrases "wake your spirit" *(get passionate about this)* and "The gates of liberty are open." *(This is the opportunity for them to gain their freedom.)* Ask students to discuss the effect this chant is meant to have. *(It's meant to get people passionate about change and fighting for their freedom. The author and his fellow organizers want to get people inspired and motivated to make a change.)*

COLLABORATIVE DISCUSSION Ask students to consider the information a protester would need to know, such as *Why should I participate? When and where is the protest? What should I bring? How do I participate?* Then have students check whether they can quickly find this information in the document.

ASK STUDENTS to share any questions they generate during the course of reading the selection.

WHEN STUDENTS STRUGGLE . . .

To guide students' understanding of formatting, have partners work together to create a three-column chart like the one below to identify a formatting strategy, describe the information that it includes, and explain how it helps the reader understand or use the information.

Formatting Strategy	Information	Understanding
bullets	chants for protest	separates each chant, quick reference for protesters

PRACTICE & APPLY

Analyze Evidence and Author's Ideas

COMMON CORE RI 1, RI 5

Make sure that students understand that part of this document is persuasive and part of it is functional. Tell the class that a functional document contains specific directions that readers can easily follow. Then review the characteristics of a functional document with the class. To illustrate these characteristics, explain that in *Revolution 2.0*, the author persuades readers to participate in the protest, and then he shifts to the functional task of telling them when, where, and how to participate. Have students work with partners to respond in writing to each of the bulleted questions.

Analyzing the Text

COMMON CORE RI 1, RI 3, RI 4, RI 5, RI 6

Possible answers:

1. *This strategy is effective because the author clarifies the intent of the organizers; they are not associated with any political party or ideology. Instead, they support the rights of all Egyptians.*

2. *These words and phrases support a tone of reason and control: peaceful; discipline; refrain; equal rights; social justice. This tone may convince readers to join the cause because it emphasizes that the protest is well thought-out and organized.*

3. *One statistic he cites is, "There were more than 100,000 suicide attempts in 2009, resulting in the deaths of 5,000 people." These statistics serve as evidence to convince readers to join the protest.*

4. *Key ideas are refined through labels, statements of demands, and short explanations of the reasons behind each demand. This section defines the tangible goals of the protest.*

5. *Social media may have been effective in inspiring young Egyptians to take action because many young people use social media; social media reaches large numbers of people; and social media crosses national boundaries, which creates a global audience for the writer's work.*

eBook *Annotate It!*

Analyze Evidence and Author's Ideas

 COMMON CORE RI 1, RI 5

The excerpt from *Revolution 2.0* is in part a **functional document**, a text that provides directions for performing a task. Functional documents can include schedules or directions for installing software. They are written with clear, concise language and organized to help readers quickly acquire information needed to achieve a goal. Effective functional documents have these characteristics:

- Clear **headings** that enable readers to locate information easily. How do the headings in the selection help direct readers' attention?
- A clear and logical **structure** or organization. For example, notice where the author places the unified chants in the document. Why is this location logical?
- Clear, concise **language.** Note that each demand the author provides begins with a verb, for example, "annulling the emergency law." Why might writing the demands in such a way be effective?

Analyzing the Text

 COMMON CORE RI 1, RI 3, RI 4, RI 5, RI 6, W 7, W 8, SL 2, SL 4

Cite Text Evidence   Support your responses with evidence from the selection.

1. **Analyze** The author begins by introducing the organizers of the demonstrations. Why is this an effective way to begin the document?

2. **Interpret** Note the wording of the Protesting Guidelines. What word choices create a tone of reason and control? How might this tone affect readers?

3. **Cite Evidence** The author cites several statistics in the section "Why Protest?" What are some of these statistics, and what is their function in the document?

4. **Interpret** How are key ideas refined with clear and concise language in the section "What Are Our Demands?" What purpose does this section serve?

5. **Evaluate** Based on this excerpt, why might the use of social media to innovate the idea of a national revolution have been effective in inspiring young Egyptians to take action?

PERFORMANCE TASK

Speaking Activity: Research Much has happened in Egypt since the events mentioned in this excerpt. Choose one section of the text, and give a short speech about current developments having to do with the section you chose.

1. Research current developments regarding one subtopic, for example difficulties Egyptians face. Note your sources and find photos or other media to support your ideas.

2. In a speech, compare ideas in your chosen section of the text with information from your research. Conclude with your view of whether or not progress has been achieved.

Assign this performance task.

PERFORMANCE TASK

COMMON CORE W 7, W 8, SL 2, SL 4

Speaking Activity: Research Provide students with charts such as the following to help them organize their research and their speeches.

What is the situation as it is described in the text?	
What is the current situation regarding this issue?	
Does the current situation show progress in this area?	

Critical Vocabulary

disseminate   ideology   annul   divisive

Practice and Apply Answer each question to demonstrate your understanding of the Critical Vocabulary words.

1. How might a discussion about pets become **divisive?**

2. What is a rule you would like to **annul?**

3. What is the most effective way to **disseminate** information about a class party?

4. How might a political candidate's **ideology** affect his or her actions once elected?

Vocabulary Strategy: Domain-specific Words

Reading and writing about a specific field, such as social studies or science, will require knowledge of **domain-specific words.** For example, if you were to read a science book about geology, you would need to be familiar with terms like *mantle*, *inner core*, and *magma*. Likewise, the author of *Revolution 2.0* uses words that are specific to politics. For example, the Critical Vocabulary word *ideology* is used to discuss how an Egyptian Facebook page is independent of influence from a specific group or set of ideas.

To help you determine the meaning of domain-specific words and phrases in a passage, use these strategies:

- Think about what you just read and **paraphrase** it.

- Think about the **context** of the passage. For example, in the section "What Are Our Demands?" Demand One uses the term *judiciary* in the context of fairness and verdicts. Those are clues to the word's meaning.

- Make an initial **guess** at the word's meaning. For example, you might guess that *judiciary* means "justice."

- Determine whether your guess makes sense in the context of the passage. If not, think of **alternatives.** What alternatives can you think of as meanings for the word *judiciary*?

- If you cannot determine the meaning of the word by its context, look up the word in a dictionary, glossary, or specialized **reference** book.

Practice and Apply Work with a partner to complete these activities.

1. Find these domain-specific words and phrases in the text: *hiring transparency* (line 51), *warrants* (line 59), *parliamentary* (line 61), and *security apparatus* (line 81). Reread the section in which each term appears, and write a definition of the word or phrase based on your understanding of its context.

2. Compare your definition to the definition found in a dictionary, digital reference source, or specialized reference book.

PRACTICE & APPLY

Critical Vocabulary

Possible answers:

1. *Two people might disagree if one person favors dogs and another favors cats.*

2. *I would like to make the no gum rule invalid because I know how to chew gum quietly and dispose of it properly.*

3. *The most effective way to let everyone know all the details of a class party is by texting or tweeting.*

4. *A political candidate's beliefs might cause him to work for or against certain laws.*

Vocabulary Strategy: Domain-specific Words

Term	My Definition	Dictionary Definition
hiring transparency	*clarity of rules for hiring someone for a job*	*obvious or easily detected hiring practices*
warrants	*legal documents for someone's arrest*	*judicial orders for an arrest*
parliamentary	*related to the government*	*of or concerning a lawmaking body*
security apparatus	*police or military force*	*political organization charged with making and enforcing laws*

Strategies for Annotation ✐ ▣ *Annotate it!*

Domain-specific Words

Encourage students to use their eBook annotation tools to identify context clues that will help them define domain-specific terms:

- Highlight in yellow context clues for *hiring transparency.*
- Highlight in green context clues for *warrants.*
- Highlight in blue context clues for *parliamentary.*
- Highlight in pink context clues for *security apparatus.*

pollution. Our rate of ambulance cars to citizens is 1:35,000. Egypt's emergency law has caused the death of many Egyptians as the result of torture and also facilitated the 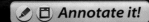 arrests of thousands without official warrants. Security forces' involvement in monitoring

Language and Style: Colons

Guide a class discussion about the effective use of punctuation in writing. Explain that in addition to signaling the end of a sentence or idea, punctuation can help create a specific mood and emphasize ideas. After reviewing the use of the colon, have student volunteers rewrite the three examples in the chart without the colons. For example, *In greater Cairo, protests will be held at Shubra Roundabout, Matariyya Square, Cairo University, and the Arab League Street.* Then lead students to compare and contrast each pair of items. Ask them what effect the colon has in each example.

Possible answers:

1. *Students may note that in addition to allowing for the spread of information within Egypt and the Middle East, social media allowed information to spread to democratic countries, which garnered additional support and focused international attention on the Egyptian government responses.*

2. *Students' paragraphs should include statements and clear explanations of ideas as well as supporting evidence.*

3. *Verify that students' paragraphs contain a minimum of four uses of the colon: one list, two key ideas, and one important point.*

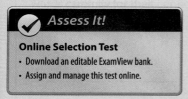

✔ Assess It!

Online Selection Test
- Download an editable ExamView bank.
- Assign and manage this test online.

Language and Style: Colons

Authors use punctuation not only to help them construct meaning in a text but also to help them organize ideas. In *Revolution 2.0*, the author uses colons for several purposes. A colon acts as a signal to readers to be alert because something important will follow. In a text that provides directions for action, the use of colons is particularly effective. Colons allow the writer to organize the information, to make it clear and concise, and to add emphasis where necessary.

Read this sentence from the selection:

This is our role as a people: to direct the government, hold it accountable, and determine its priorities.

The author could instead have written the sentence this way:

Our role as a people is to direct the government, to hold it accountable, and to determine its priorities.

While the revised example makes sense, it may not catch the reader's attention. By using a colon to prepare readers for something important, the author adds emphasis to his statement.

In addition to using colons for emphasis, Ghonim also uses colons in these ways:

Purpose	Example
to introduce lists	Greater Cairo: Shubra Roundabout, Matariyya Square, Cairo University, the Arab League Street
to concisely present key ideas	Demand One: Addressing the poverty problem . . .
to draw attention to the most important points for action	Important note: Please visit the page regularly for frequent updates.

Practice and Apply Work with a partner to complete the following steps.

1. First, discuss your response to the selection, considering the role of social media in Egypt's revolution.

2. Next, collaborate with your partner to draft a paragraph that conveys the ideas you discussed.

3. Finally, revise the paragraph to include a list introduced by a colon, two or more key ideas introduced by colons, and one important point introduced by a colon.

Integrate Information Sources

TEACH

Many speeches or presentations include multimedia elements such as photographs or short films, charts or diagrams, or audio clips. While such elements may make a speech more interesting to an audience, it is important for students to evaluate the credibility and accuracy of such sources before integrating them into a presentation.

- **Creator** Is the creator an identifiable, reputable person who is recognized as an expert in the field?
- **Producer** Is the producer affiliated with a respected organization?
- **Relevancy** Is the source current?
- **Point of View** Are multiple perspectives on the issue presented?
- **Polish** Is the source well documented and free from errors?

PRACTICE AND APPLY

As students create their speeches in response to the Performance Task for this selection, have them integrate multiple sources of information presented in diverse media formats into their speeches. For example, students may consider including the following multimedia elements:

- photographs of past or current conditions in Egypt
- a short film clip from an Arab Spring protest in Egypt
- charts or graphs of statistical information related to health care, unemployment, or government corruption in Egypt
- a short audio clip from an Egyptian who participated in an Arab Spring protest or who can comment on present conditions in Egypt

Remind students to use the questions above to evaluate the credibility and accuracy of each source before choosing to include it in their speeches.

For additional information, students can complete the relevant lessons found in the Interactive Speaking and Listening Lesson: Using Media in a Presentation.

Analyze Evidence and Author's Ideas

RETEACH

Review the terms *analyze, evidence,* and *idea,* and how an author develops an idea through supporting evidence and formatting. When a reader analyzes a text, he or she identifies these elements and assesses their effectiveness.

- Remind students that Ghonim states two purposes for the Facebook page: to rally supporters and induce confidence.
- Ask students what evidence the organizers provide to rally supporters. *(The page provides facts and statistics about the situation in Egypt.)* Ask if they would support the revolution based on the evidence provided. Why or why not?
- Ask students how formatting techniques make supporters confident they understand how to join the protests and cause change. *(Subheadings, labels, bullets, and numbering draw attention to the key pieces of information supporters need.)* Ask students whether they can think of anything else supporters would need to know to take action.

 LEVEL UP TUTORIALS Assign screens 7–9 and 11–13 of the following *Level Up* tutorial: **Informational Text**

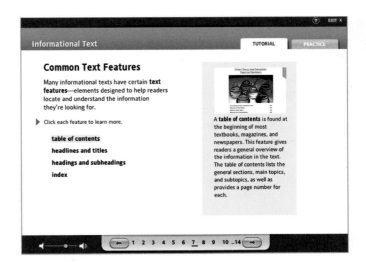

CLOSE READING APPLICATION

Students can apply the skill to another functional document such as directions for installing software or building a model. Have them work independently to analyze evidence and organization. Ask students how the author uses structure and evidence to develop a key idea.

from Letter to Viceroy, Lord Irwin

MEDIA *from* Gandhi: The Rise to Fame

Argument by Mohandas K. Gandhi

Documentary Film by BBC

Why These Texts?

Ideas that change the world do not materialize out of thin air. The nonviolent protests of the American civil rights movement and the Arab Spring stem largely from Gandhi's successful use of nonviolence. This lesson explores how Gandhi appeals to his audience and reinforces his argument to accomplish social change.

Key Learning Objective: The student will be able to analyze an argument and rhetoric and compare accounts in different mediums.

Common Core Standards

RI 1 Cite textual evidence.

RI 2 Determine a central idea and analyze its development.

RI 3 Analyze how author unfolds ideas or events.

RI 4 Analyze the impact of word choices on tone.

RI 5 Analyze how an author's ideas are developed by particular sentences or paragraphs.

RI 6 Determine an author's point of view and analyze how an author uses rhetoric.

RI 7 Analyze various accounts of a subject told in different mediums.

RI 8 Delineate and evaluate the argument and specific claims in a text; identify false statements.

W 2 Write informative texts to convey complex ideas, concepts, and information.

W 7 Conduct short research projects to answer a question.

W 9 Draw evidence from texts to support analysis, reflection, and research.

SL 1 Participate in collaborative discussions with diverse partners.

L 3a Write and edit work so that it conforms to the guidelines in a style manual.

L 5b Analyze nuances in words with similar denotations.

 Text Complexity Rubric

	Letter to Viceroy, Lord Irwin	Gandhi: The Rise to Fame
Quantitative Measures	Lexile: 1210L	Lexile: N/A
Qualitative Measures	**Levels of Meaning/Purpose** more than one purpose, easily identified	**Levels of Meaning/Purpose** multiple levels of meaning
	Structure organization of main idea and details complex but mostly explicit	**Structure** organization of main ideas and details complex, but mostly explicit
	Language Conventionality and Clarity complex and varied sentence structure	**Language Conventionality and Clarity** some unfamiliar, academic, or domain-specific words
	Knowledge Demands complex social studies concepts	**Knowledge Demands** somewhat complex social studies concepts
Reader/Task Considerations	Teacher determined Vary by individual reader and type of text	Teacher determined Vary by individual reader and type of text

TEACH

CLOSE READ

Background Have students read the background information. Explain that the term *satyagraha* is a Hindi word that means to insist on the truth. As a founder and practitioner of satyagraha, Gandhi believed in the power of nonviolence and the refusal to cooperate with injustice as means for combating evil and establishing truth. He also disapproved of secrecy. This philosophy demands that an opponent, such as Lord Irwin, be warned prior to any action.

Mohandas K. Gandhi Have students read the biographical information about Gandhi. Tell them that he began his career as a lawyer, training in England and practicing in South Africa. His first civil rights efforts took place there, as he led protests against the discrimination Indians faced in South Africa. He took the nonviolent methods he honed there back to India in 1915. Less than a year after helping India achieve independence, Gandhi was shot and killed by one of his own countrymen, a Hindu nationalist who opposed nonviolence.

from
Letter to Viceroy, Lord Irwin

MEDIA

from **Gandhi: The Rise to Fame**

Argument by Mohandas K. Gandhi   **Documentary Film by BBC**

Background *The Salt March, also known as the Salt Satyagraha, took place in India in 1930. The March protested the living conditions endured by the Indian people, including a high tax on salt and a prohibition against producing salt independently. Mohandas Gandhi, already a prominent leader in the Indian independence movement, wrote this letter on March 2, 1930. The British colonial government refused Gandhi's demands. Beginning on March 12, a group of Indians marched over 200 miles to the sea to protest the salt tax. On April 5, Gandhi arrived at the sea and then on April 6 broke the law by picking up handfuls of salt—essentially producing salt without paying the tax. This action sparked a national campaign of nonviolent protest that eventually led to Indian independence from Britain in 1947.*

Mohandas K. Gandhi (1869–1948), *often called by the title "Mahatma" ("Great Soul"), was one of the people who spearheaded the Indian drive for independence from British rule. His leadership helped the Indian people achieve independence through non-cooperation with unfair laws imposed by the British. His actions also inspired leaders of the American civil rights movement, such as Martin Luther King Jr., to follow his example on the path to achieving their goals.*

Image Credits: (b) ©Popperfoto/Getty Images; (t) ©Sam Panthaky/AFP/Getty Images

---

SCAFFOLDING FOR ELL STUDENTS

Help focus students' attention on the information about the Salt March and Gandhi with these questions:

- What country ruled India in the first half of the 20th century? *(Great Britain)*
- When and where did the Salt March take place? *(1930, India)*
- What was the purpose of the Salt March? *(to protest the salt tax and the poor living conditions of the Indian people under British rule)*
- How did Gandhi break the law when he reached the sea? *(He picked up handfuls of salt. Technically he was producing salt without paying the tax.)*
- What American civil rights leader did Gandhi inspire? *(Martin Luther King Jr.)*

AS YOU READ Direct students to use the As You Read note to focus their reading.

Analyze Rhetoric (LINES 1–15)   RI 1, RI 6

Remind students that Gandhi's audience is a British official. With his audience in mind, Gandhi makes two important points in the opening paragraphs of his letter.

(A) CITE TEXT EVIDENCE Have students reread the first two paragraphs. Ask them what Gandhi would prefer to an act of civil disobedience. *(to work with the Viceroy to find a solution)* Have students identify what evidence shows this. *("I would fain approach you and find a way out" [lines 2–3].)* Note that Gandhi finds the British laws to be a "curse" but does not extend this opinion to all things British. Ask students what examples he provides. *(He doesn't think Englishmen are worse than other people, many Englishmen are his friends, and many are courageous for speaking against British rule.)* Ask students how these points might affect Gandhi's audience. *(The Viceroy may appreciate the opportunity to fix the problem before the situation gets out of control. He may appreciate Gandhi's ability to separate the issues from the people involved.)*

Analyze Argument   RI 1, RI 8
(LINES 16–24)

Point out that Gandhi begins his argument by stating a cause and its effects.

(B) ASK STUDENTS to reread lines 16–24. Ask them what the cause of India's problems is, according to Gandhi. *(British rule)* Then ask students to identify the effects of British rule on India. *(poverty, serfdom, cultural ruin, spiritual degradation, helplessness)*

CRITICAL VOCABULARY

unpalatable: Gandhi acknowledges that some truths may be unpleasant to hear.

ASK STUDENTS to discuss why British officials may find the Indian point of view unpalatable. *(The Indian point of view may be unpleasant to British officials because it is a negative review of their involvement in India.)*

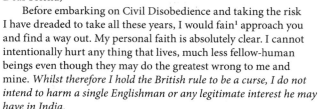

from Letter to Viceroy, Lord Irwin

Argument by Mohandas K. Gandhi

AS YOU READ Identify ways in which Gandhi appeals to his audience, an important British official. Write down any questions you generate during reading.

Dear Friend,

(A) Before embarking on Civil Disobedience and taking the risk I have dreaded to take all these years, I would fain[1] approach you and find a way out. My personal faith is absolutely clear. I cannot intentionally hurt any thing that lives, much less fellow-human beings even though they may do the greatest wrong to me and mine. *Whilst therefore I hold the British rule to be a curse, I do not intend to harm a single Englishman or any legitimate interest he may have in India.*

10 I must not be misunderstood. Though I hold the British rule in India to be a curse, I do not therefore consider Englishmen in general to be worse than any other people on earth. I have the privilege of claiming many Englishmen as dearest friends. Indeed much that I have learnt of the evil of British rule is due to the writings of frank and courageous Englishmen who have not hesitated to tell the **unpalatable** truth about that rule.

And why do I regard the British rule as a curse?

(B) It has impoverished the dumb millions by a system of progressive exploitation and by a ruinously expensive military and civil administration which the country can never afford.

20 It has reduced us politically to serfdom.[2] It has sapped the foundations of our culture, and, by the policy of disarmament,[3] it has degraded us spiritually. Lacking inward strength, we have been reduced by all but universal disarmament to a state bordering on cowardly helplessness.

. . . If India is to live as a nation, if the slow death by starvation of her people is to stop, some remedy must be found for immediate relief. The proposed conference is certainly not the remedy. It is not a matter of carrying conviction by argument. The matter resolves itself into one of matching forces. Conviction or no conviction

30 Great Britain would defend her Indian commerce and interest by all the forces at her command. India must consequently evolve

unpalatable
(ŭn-pălʹə-tə-bəl) *adj.*
unpleasant or unacceptable.

---

[1] **fain:** with pleasure.
[2] **serfdom:** the lowest class of a feudal system, which held people in bondage.
[3] **disarmament:** the reduction or elimination of weapons.

SCAFFOLDING FOR ELL STUDENTS

Analyze Argument Using a whiteboard, project lines 16–24. Invite volunteers to mark up the text:

- Highlight in green the cause of India's problems.
- Highlight in yellow the effects of this cause.

And why do I regard the British rule as a curse ?

It has impoverished the dumb millions by a system of…

It has reduced us politically to serfdom. It has sapped the

"My ambition is no less than to convert the British people through non-violence and thus make them see the wrong they have done to India."

©General Photographic Agency/Hulton Archive/Getty Images

force enough to free herself from that embrace of death. It is common cause that, however disorganized and for the time being insignificant it may be, the party of violence is gaining ground and making itself felt. Its end is the same as mine. But I am convinced that it cannot bring the desired relief to the dumb millions. And the conviction is growing deeper and deeper in me that nothing but **unadulterated** non-violence can check the organized violence of the British Government. Many think that non-violence is not an active
40 force. It is my purpose to set in motion that force as well against the organized violent force of the British rule as the unorganized violent force of the growing party of violence. To sit still would be to give rein to both the forces above mentioned. Having an unquestioning and immovable faith in the efficacy of non-violence as I know it, it would be sinful on my part to wait any longer. . . .

I know that in embarking on non-violence, I shall be running what might fairly be termed a mad risk, but the victories of truth have never been won without risks, often of the gravest character. Conversion of a nation that has consciously or unconsciously
50 preyed upon another far more numerous, far more ancient and no less cultured than itself is worth any amount of risk.

I have deliberately used the word conversion. For my ambition is no less than to convert the British people through non-violence and thus make them see the wrong they have done to India. I do not seek to harm your people. I want to serve them even as I

unadulterated
(ŭnˊə-dŭlˊtə-rāˊtĭd)
adj. pure and untainted.

Letter to Viceroy, Lord Irwin **353**

APPLYING ACADEMIC VOCABULARY

equivalent	incentive

As you discuss Gandhi's letter, incorporate the following Collection 6 academic vocabulary words: *equivalent* and *incentive*. To help students understand Gandhi's belief in the power of nonviolence, discuss why he believes nonviolence is **equivalent** to or even stronger than violence. When discussing the "mad risk" Gandhi is willing to take in service of his cause, have students identify the **incentives** for taking this risk.

CLOSE READ

Analyze Rhetoric
 COMMON CORE — RI 1, RI 6
(LINES 32–45)

Point out that Gandhi identifies three forces involved in the situation in India.

C **CITE TEXT EVIDENCE** Have students reread lines 32–45. Ask students what three forces Gandhi identifies. *(Indian party of violence; Gandhi's force of non-violence; British government)* Ask students which force Gandhi plans to combat with nonviolent force. *(both the British government and the Indian party of violence)* Have students identify the lines that indicate this plan. *(lines 40–42)* Finally, ask students why Gandhi's opposition to the Indian party of violence might appeal to his audience, the Viceroy. *(The Viceroy might consider Gandhi an ally against a violent opposition and therefore be inclined to work with him so as to avoid violence.)*

Analyze Argument and Rhetoric (LINES 52–54)
 COMMON CORE — RI 1, RI 6, RI 8

Draw students' attention to Gandhi's explicit statement of purpose, both in the text and in the quote pulled from the text.

D **ASK STUDENTS** to reread lines 52–54. Have them identify Gandhi's purpose. *(He wants to serve both the Indian people and the British by using nonviolence to reveal the wrongs British rule has perpetrated on India.)* Ask students how Gandhi uses this purpose to try to appeal to his audience. *(Gandhi claims that his actions are not against the British people, but in service to them.)*

> #### CRITICAL VOCABULARY
>
> **unadulterated**: Gandhi describes his vision of nonviolence as pure and having no exceptions.
>
> **ASK STUDENTS** to discuss why nonviolence must be unadulterated to be effective. *(If nonviolence is tainted by violence or corruption, it loses its impact and credibility and becomes like the forces it opposes.)*

Analyze Rhetoric

COMMON CORE   RI 1, RI 6

(LINES 57–63)

Draw students' attention to the comparison Gandhi makes between the British and his family.

E   **ASK STUDENTS** to reread lines 57–63. Ask students against what other group Gandhi has used the same "weapon" he plans to use against the British. *(his family)* Then ask how this comparison might affect Gandhi's audience. *(The Viceroy might understand that Gandhi's "weapon" is not intended to harm anyone because Gandhi loves his family and wouldn't hurt them. Also, this rhetoric underscores the point that Gandhi considers the British to be members of his larger family.)*

Explain to students that words have both denotations, or dictionary definitions, and connotations, or associated meanings and emotions.

F   **CITE TEXT EVIDENCE** Ask students to reread lines 69–77. Point out that Gandhi describes a future relationship between Great Britain and India after greed has been eliminated from the relationship. Ask students what words Gandhi uses to describe this future relationship. *(friendly, conference, equals, common good, voluntary fellowship, mutual help)* Finally, ask how these words might affect the Viceroy. *(The positive connotations might help persuade the Viceroy to think positively about Gandhi's argument.)*

CRITICAL VOCABULARY

humility: Gandhi expresses no superiority over others; he views himself as equal to others, including the Indian poor and the Viceroy.

ASK STUDENTS to discuss how the quality of humility may have contributed to Gandhi's success as a leader. *(People are willing to listen to and follow someone with whom they can identify and who does not exhibit arrogance or the abuse of social power.)*

Gandhi (fourth from left) walks with his followers during the 1930 Salt March.

want to serve my own. I believe that I have always served them. I served them up to 1919 blindly. But when my eyes were opened, and I conceived non-cooperation the object still was to serve them. I employed the same weapon that I have in all **humility**
60   successfully used against the dearest members of my family. If I have equal love for your people with mine, it will not long remain hidden. It will be acknowledged by them even as the members of my family acknowledged it after they had tried me for several years. If the people join me as I expect they will, the sufferings they will undergo, unless the British nation sooner retraces its steps, will be enough to melt the stoniest hearts.

The plan through civil disobedience will be to combat such evils as I have sampled out.

If we want to sever the British connection it is because of such
70   evils. When they are removed the path becomes easy. Then the way to friendly negotiation will be open. If the British commerce with India is purified of greed, you will have no difficulty in recognizing our independence. I respectfully invite you then to pave the way for an immediate removal of those evils and thus open a way for a real conference between equals, interested only in promoting the common good of mankind through voluntary fellowship and in arranging terms of mutual help and commerce suited to both. You have unnecessarily laid stress upon the communal problems that unhappily affect this land. Important though they undoubtedly
80   are for the consideration of any scheme of government, they have

humility
(hyōō-mĭl´ĭ-tē) *n.* modesty; lack of superiority over others.

Image Credits: ©Photo by Mansell/Time & Life Pictures/Getty Images;

354   Collection 6

WHEN STUDENTS STRUGGLE . . .

To guide students' comprehension of word choice as part of rhetoric, have them work in pairs to make word charts. Ask students to choose five words with positive connotations and five words with negative connotations from Gandhi's letter. Then have students explain their associations.

Word from Letter	Connotation	Explanation
weapon	negative	makes me think of anger and fighting
fellowship	positive	makes me think of love and friendship

little bearing on the greater problems which are above communities and which affect them all equally. *But if you cannot see your way to deal with these evils and my letter makes no appeal to your heart, on the 11th day of this month, I shall proceed with such co-workers of the Ashram[4] as I can take to disregard the provisions of the Salt laws.* I regard this tax to be the most **iniquitous** of all from the poor man's standpoint. As the Independence Movement is essentially for the poorest in the land, the beginning will be made with this evil. The wonder is, that we have submitted to the cruel monopoly[5] for so long. It is, I know, open to you to frustrate my design by arresting me. I hope that there will be tens of thousands ready in a disciplined manner to take up the work after me, and in the act of disobeying the Salt Act to lay themselves open to the penalties of a law that should never have disfigured the Statute-book.

I have no desire to cause you unnecessary embarrassment or any at all so far as I can help. If you think that there is any substance in my letter, and if you will care to discuss matters with me, and if to that end you would like me to postpone publication of this letter, I shall gladly refrain on receipt of a telegram to that effect soon after this reaches you. You will however do me the favor not to deflect me from my course unless you can see your way to conform to the substance of this letter.

This letter is not in any way intended as a threat, but is a simple and sacred duty **peremptory** on a civil resister. Therefore I am having it specially delivered by a young English friend, who believes in the Indian cause and is a full believer in non-violence and whom Providence[6] seems to have sent to me as it were for the very purpose.

iniquitous
(ĭ-nĭkʹwĭ-təs) *adj.*
wicked, evil.

peremptory
(pə-rĕmpʹtə-rē) *adj.*
imperative; required;
not able to be denied.

I remain,
Your Sincere friend,

M.K. Gandhi

COLLABORATIVE DISCUSSION How does Gandhi appeal to his audience? Cite specific words, phrases, and examples from the text.

---

[4] **Ashram:** a secluded residence of a Hindu religious leader and followers.
[5] **monopoly:** the complete and exclusive control of a product or service.
[6] **Providence:** God or a supernatural power.

CLOSE READ

Analyze Rhetoric

COMMON CORE RI 1, RI 6

(LINES 95–102)

Tell students that before closing, Gandhi makes an offer to the Viceroy.

G **CITE TEXT EVIDENCE** Ask students to reread lines 95–102. Ask students what Gandhi offers the Viceroy. *(Gandhi offers to meet with the Viceroy and withhold the publication of the letter.)* Ask how this offer might affect the Viceroy. *(If the Viceroy is worried about embarrassment among his colleagues for allowing the protest movement to grow, he may appreciate Gandhi's offer.)* Point out that, in return, Gandhi asks something of the Viceroy. Ask students to identify this request in the text. *("You will however do me the favor not to deflect me from my course . . ." [lines 100–101].)*

CRITICAL VOCABULARY

iniquitous: Gandhi thinks that the salt tax is the most immoral of the British demands on the Indian people.

ASK STUDENTS to identify why Gandhi finds the salt tax so iniquitous. *(The law is evil because it disproportionately affects India's poorest people.)*

peremptory: Gandhi says that he requires himself, by virtue of his commitment to civil disobedience, to send the letter to the Viceroy, announcing his intentions before acting.

ASK STUDENTS to discuss how Gandhi's reminder that this letter is peremptory may affect the Viceroy. *(The Viceroy may acknowledge the requirement and not interpret the letter as a threat. He may see that he is dealing with a person of good faith and character.)*

TO CHALLENGE STUDENTS . . .

To help students examine multiple perspectives on a topic, have them write one or two paragraphs in response to the following prompt:

Imagine you are Viceroy Lord Irwin, and you have received a letter from Mohandas K. Gandhi. The letter requests your help in dismantling British rule in India for the good of the Indian people, who are suffering from poverty, due in part to British rule. You disagree with Gandhi's point of view and support British rule in India. Write a one- or two-paragraph letter in response to Gandhi's letter.

COLLABORATIVE DISCUSSION Ask students to assume the role of the Viceroy, who supports British rule. Ask students which words, phrases, or examples in the letter might cause them to consider Gandhi's point of view and to explain why. Have student groups discuss this question and take notes. Have volunteers from each group present the ideas to the class.

ASK STUDENTS to share any questions they generate while reading and discussing the selection.

TEACH

CLOSE READ

Analyze Argument and Rhetoric

COMMON CORE RI 6, RI 8

Review the terms *claim, valid, relevant,* and *rhetoric* with students. Then have student pairs complete three-column charts like the sample below in response to the questions in the "Questions to Ask about the Text" column. First, ask students to find text evidence that will help them respond to each question. Then have them answer each question. Have a different pair of students present the information for each question. After each presentation, ask the listening audience to contribute additional ideas.

Question	Text Evidence	Response
How does Gandhi use the rhetorical question in line 16 to help define his claim?	"And why do I regard the British rule as a curse?"	Gandhi's answer to this question establishes the reasons for his claim that British rule should end.

Analyze Argument and Rhetoric

COMMON CORE RI 6, RI 8

A formal argument sets forth a specific claim and supports it with valid reasoning and relevant evidence. In his letter, Gandhi crafted his argument and rhetoric to appeal to his specific audience, the Viceroy of India. In doing this, Gandhi hoped that his argument would sway the Viceroy to improve the living conditions of the Indian people. As you analyze the argument and rhetoric of the letter, consider these elements and questions:

Elements to Consider	Questions to Ask about the Text
The **claim**—the central point of the argument—should be specific and reasonable.	How does Gandhi use the rhetorical question in line 16 to help define his claim?
Reasons that support a claim must be **valid**—both accurate and logical. No matter how appealing a reason may be, readers should ask themselves how it supports the writer's position and whether it is really true.	What is Gandhi's point of view about the English people? How does he use the distinction he makes between the English people and British rule to contribute to the power of his argument?
Evidence that is **relevant** must be used to elaborate on reasons. In other words, the evidence must be clearly linked to the reason and be sufficient, or comprehensive enough to provide solid support. Irrelevant or insufficient evidence weakens a writer's argument.	Why does Gandhi state in lines 64–66 that the suffering of the Indian people will be "enough to melt the stoniest hearts"?
Rhetoric is what writer uses to effectively communicate ideas to an audience. A writer can construct a strong argument by establishing credibility and using an appropriate tone. Rhetoric can include emotionally charged words and appeals as well as memorable phrasing. The use of rhetoric can determine whether readers accept or reject an argument.	How do Gandhi's use of language and the style of the letter give the Viceroy an incentive to consider the power and persuasiveness of Gandhi's argument?

Strategies for Annotation 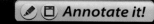 *Annotate it!*

Analyze Argument and Rhetoric

COMMON CORE RI 6, RI 8

Encourage students to use their eBook annotation tools to identify text evidence for their three-column charts.

- Highlight in yellow the rhetorical question in line 16.
- Highlight in green Gandhi's point of view regarding the English people and British rule.
- Highlight in blue examples of rhetoric that might help persuade the Viceroy to consider Gandhi's argument.

Indeed much that I have learnt of the evil of British rule is due to the writings of frank and courageous Englishmen who have not . . . real conference between equals, interested only in promoting the common good of mankind through voluntary fellowship and in arranging terms of mutual help and commerce suited to both. You

Analyzing the Text

COMMON CORE RI 1, RI 3, RI 4, RI 5, RI 6, RI 8, W 2, W 9

Cite Text Evidence   Support your responses with evidence from the selection.

1. **Cause/Effect** Identify positive statements Gandhi makes about the English (or British) people. What effect might these statements have on his reader? Why?

2. **Analyze** Identify Gandhi's central claim in this letter. What key reasons does he provide to support this claim?

3. **Evaluate** Notice how Gandhi structures this argument. Why is this order of ideas effective?

4. **Draw Conclusions** Identify the places where Gandhi uses the word *curse* and where he uses the word *conversion*. Why are these word choices significant, and how do they affect his tone?

5. **Analyze** What similarities and differences does Gandhi point out between his movement and the "party of violence"? Why is it important for Gandhi to include in the letter a discussion of why the two movements are not equivalent?

6. **Infer** Identify Gandhi's purpose, or reason for writing this letter. What specific goals does he hope to achieve?

PERFORMANCE TASK

Writing Activity: Analysis Overall, how would you evaluate the strength of Gandhi's argument?

- Write a one-paragraph analysis of his claims, reasons, evidence, and rhetoric, providing examples from the text of the letter.

- Then, discuss in a second paragraph why you think this argument failed to persuade the Viceroy to change the conditions imposed on the Indian people or even to respond to Gandhi.

Analyzing the Text

COMMON CORE RI 1, RI 3, RI 4, RI 5, RI 6, RI 8

Possible answers:

1. *Gandhi says the British people are not "worse than any other people on earth," and he claims "many Englishmen as dearest friends." These statements may not cause the Viceroy to feel as if Gandhi is judging him personally because Gandhi separates the laws from the people who enforce them.*

2. *Gandhi's central claim is that British rule in India should end. He cites the Indian peoples' poverty, exploitation, political serfdom, and spiritual degradation as reasons in support of his claim.*

3. *Gandhi acknowledges his audience, makes his claim, provides reasons for his claim, and then proposes at least two solutions for the problem. This order of ideas is effective because it is logical while not being adversarial.*

4. *Gandhi uses the word* curse *early in the letter, and he uses the word* conversion *midway through the letter. These word choices are significant because one has a negative connotation and one has a positive connotation. Their placement shows a progression from the negative to the positive.*

5. *Gandhi states that the two movements share the same goal, but not the same means for attaining the goal. Gandhi includes this point because he wants to distinguish himself from the party of violence and make it clear that he favors only nonviolence—a point that he hopes will be persuasive to his audience.*

6. *Gandhi wants to end British rule and help the Indian people. He is willing to consider different options for achieving this goal—conference with the Viceroy or nonviolent protest—but he is not willing to compromise the goal nor his commitment to nonviolence.*

Assign this performance task.

PERFORMANCE TASK

COMMON CORE W 2, W 9

Writing Activity: Analysis Have students use the following questions to prepare outlines before they begin drafting their paragraphs.

- Is Gandhi's claim clear and reasonable? Are his reasons clear and logical?
- Does Gandhi's evidence support his claim and reasons? Is his rhetoric persuasive?
- Why might the letter have failed to persuade the Viceroy?

PRACTICE & APPLY

Critical Vocabulary

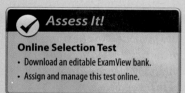COMMON CORE RI 4, L 5b

Answers: 1. *A sandwich covered with mold is unpalatable because it is unpleasant or unacceptable to eat.* **2.** *A sterile beaker of distilled water is unadulterated because it is pure and untainted.* **3.** *A race winner thanking his coach shows humility because the winner does not emphasize superiority over the other contestants.* **4.** *A career criminal robbing people's homes is iniquitous because he or she shows no remorse and is motivated by greed.* **5.** *A passport is peremptory because it is required.*

Vocabulary Strategy: Denotations and Connotations

Students' responses to all items should follow the format of the sample answer.

Sample answer:

I *feared* the growling, barking dog in my neighbor's yard.

I *dreaded* the days I had to walk to school.

While both words mean "to be frightened or scared," dreaded has the connotation of deep fear or anxiety about a future situation.

✓ **Assess It!**

Online Selection Test
- Download an editable ExamView bank.
- Assign and manage this test online.

Critical Vocabulary

COMMON CORE RI 4, L 5b

unpalatable   unadulterated   humility   iniquitous   peremptory

Practice and Apply For each Critical Vocabulary word, choose which of the two situations best fits the word's meaning. Explain why your choice is the best response.

1. **unpalatable**
   a. a sandwich covered with mold
   b. a sandwich too large to eat

2. **unadulterated**
   a. a sterile beaker of distilled water
   b. a precise mixture of water and iodine

3. **humility**
   a. a race winner pumping his fist in the air
   b. a race winner thanking his coach

4. **iniquitous**
   a. a hungry person stealing an apple
   b. a career criminal robbing people's homes

5. **peremptory**
   a. a passport carried by a traveler to China
   b. a map of Beijing bought by a tourist

Vocabulary Strategy: Denotations and Connotations

To persuade his audience, Gandhi uses words with strong **connotations**, or associated meanings and emotions. For example, he uses the Critical Vocabulary word *iniquitous*, which has a negative connotation of something that is not only wrong but also immoral. How would the meaning of the sentence change if the word *unjust* were used instead? *Unjust* has a **denotation,** or dictionary meaning , similar to that of *iniquitous*, but it carries a less immoral connotation. As you read an argument, consider the rhetorical effect of words with strong connotations.

Practice and Apply Analyze the nuances presented by each pair of words with similar denotations. Note that the boldfaced words are from the letter. Use each word in a sentence, and then explain the connotation of each word.

feared/**dreaded** (line 2)   unpleasant/**unpalatable** (line 15)

weakened/**degraded** (line 22)   hunger/**starvation** (line 25)

silent/**dumb** (line 36)   wrong/**sinful** (line 45)

Strategies for Annotation   ✏ 🗏 *Annotate it!*

Denotations and Connotations   COMMON CORE L 5b

Encourage students to use their eBook annotation tools to do the following:
- Highlight in green the boldfaced word as it is used in Gandhi's letter.
- On a note, rewrite the sentence and replace the boldfaced word with a synonym.
- Highlight the synonym in yellow.
- With a partner, discuss the effect of connotation on Gandhi's meaning and rhetoric.

has degraded us spiritually. Lacking inward strength, we have

It has sapped . . . has weakened us spiritually.

CLOSE READ

Background Have students read the background information. Tell them that the titles of the other parts of the film series are *The Making of the Mahatma* and *The Road to Freedom*. *The Rise to Fame* is the second installment. The series is largely chronological, following Gandhi from his early years to his life as a public figure to his final years.

AS YOU VIEW Direct students to use the As You View prompt to focus their viewing. Remind students to write down any questions they generate during viewing.

Analyze Accounts in Different Mediums

COMMON CORE RI 1, RI 7

Point out that the letter to Lord Irwin is a primary source written in Gandhi's own words. A primary source is produced by someone who participates in an event. A primary source may be a letter, a diary, or a photograph. The documentary was produced after Gandhi's death and is therefore a secondary source of information. A secondary source is produced by someone who studied or learned about an event, but did not participate in it. Secondary sources include documentaries, biographies, histories, and analyses.

Ⓐ CITE TEXT EVIDENCE Ask students to identify which details about the events leading to and including the Salt March are emphasized in the documentary and in the letter to Lord Irwin. *(Both accounts include Gandhi's reasoning for choosing the salt tax as a point of protest. However, the letter emphasizes the coming protest, while the film emphasizes the march itself and Gandhi's legacy.)* Ask students to discuss whether they agree with Gandhi regarding the symbolic importance of the salt tax.

Ⓑ ASK STUDENTS to compare and contrast Gandhi's character in each account. *(In the letter, Gandhi shows himself to be a thoughtful, focused, empathetic, and humble man. In the documentary, viewers learn not how Gandhi viewed or presented himself, but about his effect on others, both those who knew him and those who came after him. Although Gandhi was admired for his humility and perhaps criticized for his old-fashioned ways, it is clear that many Indians revered him then and now.)*

COLLABORATIVE DISCUSSION Have student pairs use Venn diagrams to compare and contrast additional elements in the letter and the film clip. Have volunteers share ideas with the class.

---

from Gandhi: The Rise to Fame

Documentary Film by BBC

Background *In 2009, the British Broadcasting Corporation (BBC) aired a three-part documentary series on the life and legacy of Mohandas Gandhi. In it, British-born journalist Mishal Husain retraces Gandhi's steps, interviews those who knew him personally, and provides context for historical footage and photos. Husain's heritage is Pakistani, but her grandfather served in the Indian army before partition, the division of the former British colony into the independent nations of India and Pakistan.*

AS YOU VIEW Identify points of comparison between the letter and film. Write down any questions you generate during viewing.

©BBC Motion Gallery

COLLABORATIVE DISCUSSION With a partner, discuss common elements in the letter and film clip, supporting your ideas with evidence from both.

SCAFFOLDING FOR ELL STUDENTS

Analyze Accounts in Different Mediums To help students comprehend and analyze the documentary, have them fill in a viewing guide that includes the following elements:

- summary of the film clip
- one cause for and one effect of Gandhi's Salt March
- questions they had while viewing

ASK STUDENTS what they learned from the letter that they did not learn from the film. Then ask what they learned from the film that they did not learn from the letter.

PRACTICE & APPLY

Analyze Accounts in Different Mediums

COMMON CORE RI 7

Have partners analyze the letter and the film clip with regard to point of view, purpose, and the relationship between the purpose and the medium. Have students use this analysis to evaluate the strengths and weaknesses of the two mediums. *(Gandhi's point of view toward the British is to condemn the actions without condemning the people; Husain's point of view toward Gandhi is one of admiration. Gandhi's purpose is to persuade; Husain's purpose is to inform as well as entertain. Gandhi chooses the written medium because it is formal; Husain chooses the film medium because she hopes to resurrect the spirit of Gandhi's nonviolent efforts to achieve civil rights and freedom. Written text is powerful because it is structured, rhetorical, and may be reread, but it isn't visual. Film is powerful because it is visual and can be more emotional than writing, but it also can be fleeting.)*

Analyzing Text and Media

COMMON CORE RI 1, RI 2, RI 3, RI 4, RI 6, RI 7, RI 8

Possible answers:

1. *The narrator's tone is admiring of Gandhi. She says that Gandhi's "instincts were often spot on." Her word choice, which includes an idiom, supports her purposes to inform and to entertain.*

2. *The purposes of a biography are to inform and to entertain. The purpose of an argument is to persuade. A biographer can use chronology, narration, and archival images to describe a person and encourage viewers to enjoy the process of "getting to know" the subject. However, the writer of an argument must rely on structure and rhetoric to achieve his or her purpose.*

3. *Both mediums justify the salt issue as a point of protest; both discuss nonviolence and include interaction between Gandhi and Lord Irwin.*

4. *The film emphasizes the Salt March and its aftermath. The film and the letter work together to help the audience understand Gandhi's appeal as a national leader and his impact on Indian history.*

Analyze Accounts in Different Mediums

COMMON CORE RI 7

The narrator of this documentary, Mishal Husain, discusses Gandhi's rise to fame from his beginnings as a lawyer through his emergence as a powerful figure in Indian politics. Factual information about important people and events can be presented in a variety of media, including written biographies, documentary films, and multimedia websites. Each medium has particular strengths and weaknesses. In addition, each person who creates an account in any medium does so from a certain point of view and with a certain purpose. This person's purpose may even drive the choice of medium—for example, video would be the best choice of medium for someone who wanted to emphasize a political leader's speaking skills and personality. To get the most comprehensive picture of a person or event, choose a variety of media sources, and think about the kinds of information that are included, omitted, and emphasized in each account.

Analyzing Text and Media

COMMON CORE RI 1, RI 2, RI 3, RI 4, RI 6, RI 7, RI 8, SL 1

Cite Text Evidence Support your responses with evidence from the selections.

1. **Interpret** Describe the narrator's tone and word choice, providing examples from the video. What can you infer from those word choices about the purpose of this documentary?

2. **Evaluate** In this film, the history of Gandhi's rise to fame is documented in chronological order with the use of present-day narration and commentary interspersed with some supporting archival images. Why is this an effective way to organize a biography but not an argument?

3. **Compare** Which arguments or ideas are apparent in both the letter and the film?

4. **Synthesize** What ideas and events are emphasized in the film? How do the film and letter work together to create a fuller picture of Gandhi than either could alone?

PERFORMANCE TASK

Speaking Activity: Debate Which communicates Gandhi's ideas more effectively, the letter or the film? Decide by participating in a debate.

- Form teams of two to three students each, with half defending the letter as more effective and half defending the film clip. Each team should gather evidence from both the letter and the film to support its position.

- Follow the rules for debating on page R14. Afterward, write a brief evaluation of which side presented a more compelling case.

Assign this performance task.

PERFORMANCE TASK

COMMON CORE SL 1

Speaking Activity: Debate Ask students to prepare charts with headings like the ones below to help them gather evidence for the debate.

Key Idea	How to Best Communicate Idea	Why This Communication Is Effective	How Other Medium Is Less Effective

Synthesize Sources

W 7, L 3a

TEACH

Review with students the criteria for evaluating source material to determine reliability:

- Are the author, publisher, and any reviewers recognized experts in the field?
- What is the purpose of the source? Are multiple perspectives on the issue addressed? What information might be missing from the discussion?
- Is the source current or outdated?
- Where is the source published—in a professionally screened library database or on the Internet?
- How does this source relate to your subject and purpose?

Explain that when students research a subject, it is best to consult multiple sources. This practice will allow students to identify information that is common among sources and information that may be tied to one point of view, information that may be biased, or undocumented information. Have students review the information that is common between Gandhi's letter and the BBC documentary. Then have students review information that is different. Help students understand that some of the differences are related to the time at which each source was created. For example, Gandhi could not know the outcome of the Salt March at the time he composed the letter.

PRACTICE AND APPLY

Provide students with this research question:

"Why was the Salt March important?"

In addition to Gandhi's letter and the BBC documentary, have students locate one additional reliable source. Remind students to use the evaluation questions noted above to determine reliability.

Have students identify information that is common to all three sources and information that is different. Ask them to identify and evaluate the reasons behind the differences.

Then have students compose written answers to the research question using material from all three sources. Help students document their sources correctly, following a style manual such as the *MLA Handbook*.

Analyze Accounts in Different Mediums

RI 7

RETEACH

Review the terms *documentary, medium, point of view,* and *purpose*. Then provide scaffolding for a comparison of the two accounts.

- Have students reread the letter to note which parts they find most striking, memorable, or persuasive. In pairs, have them discuss whether these parts could be communicated as effectively through video.
- Then have students watch the film clip again, noting the parts that make the strongest impression on them. As with the letter, have them discuss in pairs whether the same effect could have been achieved in print.
- Finally, have students make a chart reflecting their analyses. The chart should list what is emphasized in each source, what features of the medium are used to emphasize the details listed, and their conclusion about whether the same details could be treated as effectively in the other medium.

 LEVEL UP TUTORIALS Assign the following *Level Up* tutorial: **Primary and Secondary Sources**

CLOSE READING APPLICATION

Students can apply the skill to a current event as reported in a printed source such as a newspaper and on a television broadcast. Have them work independently to identify point of view and purpose for each, as well as the effect of the medium. Ask students which details are emphasized in each account.

The Briefcase

Short Story by Rebecca Makkai

Why This Text?

Students regularly encounter short stories in textbooks, in periodicals, and in their personal reading. This lesson explores how Rebecca Makkai develops her character through his thoughts, his actions, and his interactions with others. Through the behavior of the character, the reader comes to understand the theme.

Key Learning Objective: The student will be able to analyze interactions between character and theme in a short story.

Common Core Standards

RL 1 Cite textual evidence.
RL 2 Determine a theme and analyze its development.
RL 3 Analyze how complex characters develop, interact, and advance the plot.
RL 4 Analyze the impact of word choice on tone.
RL 5 Analyze how an author's choices create mystery, tension, or surprise.
W 4 Produce writing in which the organization and style are appropriate to task, purpose, and audience.
L 2a Use a semicolon to link two or more closely related independent clauses.

Text Complexity Rubric

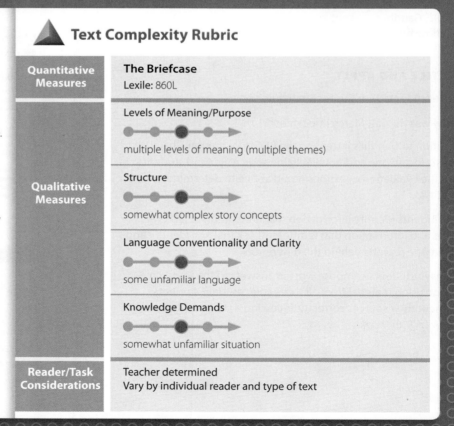

Quantitative Measures	**The Briefcase** Lexile: 860L
Qualitative Measures	**Levels of Meaning/Purpose** multiple levels of meaning (multiple themes)
	Structure somewhat complex story concepts
	Language Conventionality and Clarity some unfamiliar language
	Knowledge Demands somewhat unfamiliar situation
Reader/Task Considerations	Teacher determined Vary by individual reader and type of text

TEACH

CLOSE READ

Background Have students read the background about political prisoners. Tell students that people's sense of identity changes as different life events affect them and shape their sense of who they are. This has happened with some political prisoners in history who eventually rose to positions of power. The most famous may be Nelson Mandela, who was the first black president of South Africa. Prior to that, Mandela spent 27 years in prison for trying to end apartheid, that nation's oppressive racial policy.

AS YOU READ Direct students to use the As You Read statement to focus their reading. Remind students to note any questions they have as they read.

Analyze Character and Theme (LINES 1–8)

Explain to students that writers often use a character's thoughts to help the reader understand the character. Have students reread the opening paragraph and consider what it says about the character.

A CITE TEXT EVIDENCE Ask students to describe the character's state of mind and to cite text evidence that supports their answers. *(He is reflective. He understands "this all happened before." He thinks of "other chains of men on other islands of the Earth," and he concludes that, "since there have been men there have been prisoners.")*

Analyze Tone (LINES 12–13)
COMMON CORE RL 4

Explain that an author's choice of words and sentence structure help to create **tone,** or author's attitude.

B ASK STUDENTS to examine the sentence in lines 12–13. What does this sentence reveal and what tone do the words and structure create? *(Makkai repeats the same idea, using different phrases to note that the chef is thin from starvation. ["His hand was starved, his wrist was thin, his body was cold."] The details are brief, and they are strung together. The structure echoes the marching of the prisoners. Both the words and sentence structure create a somber, matter-of-fact tone.)*

Background *The protagonist of "The Briefcase" is a political prisoner in an unnamed country, a man who has been arrested for associating with the wrong people. Political prisoners are detained, imprisoned, and sometimes executed, without benefit of trial or jury, due to political associations or beliefs that conflict with those of the people in power. Such detentions happen all over the world under regimes that hold absolute power over the people and the press. In this story, author* **Rebecca Makkai** *(b. 1978) innovates the universality of political imprisonment through the use of basic astronomy.*

The Briefcase

Short Story by Rebecca Makkai

AS YOU READ Pay attention to details that reveal something about the chef's character. Write down any questions you generate during reading.

A He thought how strange that a political prisoner, marched through town in a line, chained to the man behind and chained to the man ahead, should take comfort in the fact that all this had happened before. He thought of other chains of men on other islands of the Earth, and he thought how since there have been men there have been prisoners. He thought of mankind as a line of miserable monkeys chained at the wrist, dragging each other back into the ground.

In the early morning of December first the sun was finally warming
10 them all, enough that they could walk faster. With his left hand, he adjusted the loop of steel that cuffed his right hand to the line of doomed men. His hand was starved, his wrist was thin, his body was cold: the cuff slipped off. In one beat of the heart he looked **B** back to the man behind him and forward to the man limping ahead, and knew that neither saw his naked, red wrist; each saw

Image Credits: (bg) JPL-Caltech/University of Virginia/NASA ; (t) ©Ulf Andersen/Getty Images (l) ©Oliver Burston/Ikon Images/Getty Images; (r) S. Willner (Harvard-Smithsonian Center for Astrophysics)/JPL-Caltech/NASA

SCAFFOLDING FOR ELL STUDENTS

Understand Time Sequence The action of this story covers more than a year, but the passing of time is not always obvious. In addition, there are flashbacks and some scenes that take place at no specific time. This may be confusing to some students.

Throughout the reading of the selection, work with students by having them look for clue words such as *before, here, now,* and *after,* which may signal a shift in time. Point out the breaks in the text that also indicate shifts in time.

ASK STUDENTS what date the story begins and what shift in time occurs at line 19. Have students identify the clue words or phrase. *("December first" [line 9]; the story goes back in time; clue phrase, "Before the war…")*

Analyze Character

 COMMON CORE RL 3

(LINES 23–27)

Point out that we learn about the chef is through his actions, both past and present.

C **ASK STUDENTS** to describe the chef's past and present actions. *(The chef once prepared rich foods, but now he is in a situation where he is going hungry.)*

Analyze Theme (LINES 31–38) **COMMON CORE** RL 2

Tell students the idea of identity will be explored in the story. Readers do not know the name of the chef; he's only known as a prisoner and a chef.

D **ASK STUDENTS** whether the writer gives readers the name of the professor and how the identity of the professor changes in this scene. *(no; from professor to prisoner)* Then ask how the chef's identity changes. *(from prisoner to escapee)*

Analyze Character and Theme (LINES 56–60) **COMMON CORE** RL 1, RL 2, RL 3

Tell students that writers may compare one character with another and that these comparisons could reveal a **theme,** or message about life.

E **CITE TEXT EVIDENCE** Have students identify the ways in which the chef is different from the professor. *(He is not scholarly. He only knows science for things like calculating baking times at different elevations or the "evaporation rate of alcohol." His knowledge of biology is limited to preparing meat and understanding bread yeast [line 59].)* Then have students continue to look for comparisons between the chef and the professor in order to identify a theme of the story.

> **CRITICAL VOCABULARY**
>
> **flailing**: Makkai compares the papers flying out of the briefcase to doves thrashing about in the alley.
>
> **ASK STUDENTS** why they think the chef chased down the flailing papers. *(to keep someone from catching him or because they might have value)*

only his own mother weeping in a kitchen, his own love on a bed in white sheets and sunlight.

He walked in step with them to the end of the block.

Before the war this man had been a chef, and his one crime was 20 feeding the people who sat at his tables in small clouds of smoke and talked politics. He served them the wine that fueled their underground newspaper, their aborted revolution. And after the night his restaurant disappeared in fire, he had run and hidden and gone without food — he who had roasted ducks until the meat jumped from the bone, he who had evaporated three bottles of wine into one pot of cream soup, he who had peeled the skin from small pumpkins with a twist of his hand.

And here was his hand, twisted free of the chain, and here he was running and crawling, until he was through a doorway. It was 30 a building of empty classrooms — part of the university he had never attended. He watched from the bottom corner of a second-story window as the young soldiers stopped the line, counted 199 men, shouted to each other, shouted at the men in the panicked voices of children who barely filled the shoulders of their uniforms. One soldier, a bigger one, a louder one, stopped a man walking by. A man in a suit, with a briefcase, a beard — some sort of professor. The soldiers stripped him of his coat, his shirt, his leather case, cuffed him to the chain. They marched again. And as soon as they were past — no, not that soon; many minutes later, when he had the 40 stomach — the chef ran down to the street and collected the man's briefcase, coat and shirt.

In the alley, the chef sat against a wall and buttoned the professor's shirt over his own ribs. When he opened the briefcase, papers flew out, a thousand doves **flailing** against the walls of the alley. The chef ran after them all, stopped them with his feet and arms, herded them back into the case. Pages of numbers, of arrows and notes and hand-drawn star maps. Here were business cards: a professor of physics. Envelopes showed his name and address — information that might have been useful in some other lifetime, one 50 where the chef could ring the bell of this man's house and explain to his wife about empty chains, empty wrists, empty classrooms. Here were graded papers, a fall syllabus, the typed draft of an exam. The question at the end, a good one: "Using modern astronomical data, construct, to the best of your ability, a proof that the sun actually revolves around the Earth."

The chef knew nothing of physics. He understood chemistry only insofar as it related to the baking time of bread at various elevations or the evaporation rate of alcohol. His knowledge of biology was limited to the deboning of chickens and the behavior

flail
(flāl) *v.* to thrash or wave about wildly.

APPLYING ACADEMIC VOCABULARY

incentive	innovate

As you discuss Makkai's story, incorporate the following Collection 6 academic vocabulary words: *incentive* and *innovate.* As you explore the theme of the story, ask students to consider how the professor's question **innovates** astronomy instruction and what the chef's **incentive** is for answering it.

60　of *Saccharomyces cerevisiae*, common bread yeast. And what did
he know at all of moving bodies and gravity? He knew this: he had
moved from his line of men, creating a vacuum — one that had
sucked the good professor in to fill the void.

　　The chef sat on his bed in the widow K——'s basement and felt,
in the cool leather of the briefcase, a second vacuum: here was a
vacated life. Here were salary receipts, travel records, train tickets,
a small address book. And these belonged to a man whose name
was not blackened like his own, a man whose life was not hunted.
If he wanted to live through the next year, the chef would have to
70　learn this life and fill it — and oddly, this felt not like a robbery but
an apology, a way to put the world back in balance. The professor
would not die, because he himself would become the professor, and
he would live.

　　Surely he could not teach at the university; surely he could not
slip into the man's bed unnoticed. But what was in this leather case,
it seemed, had been left for him to use. These addresses of friends;
this card of identification; this riddle about the **inversion** of the
universe.

　　Five cities east, he now gave his name as the professor's, and grew
80　out his beard so it would match the photograph on the card he now
carried in his pocket. The two men did not, anymore, look entirely
dissimilar. To the first name in the address book, the chef had
written a typed letter: "Am in trouble and have fled the city. Tell my
dear wife I am safe, but for her safety do not tell her where I am. If
you are able to help a poor old man, send money to the following
post box . . . I hope to remain your friend, Professor
T——."

　　He had to write this about the wife; how could he ask these
men for money if she held a funeral? And what of it, if she kept her
90　happiness another few months, another year?

　　The next twenty-six letters were similar in nature, and money
arrived now in brown envelopes and white ones. The bills came
wrapped in notes — (Was his life in danger? Did he have his
health?) — and with the money he paid another widow for another
basement, and he bought weak cigarettes. He sat on café chairs and
drew pictures of the universe, showed stars and planets looping
each other in light. He felt, perhaps, that if he used the other papers
in the briefcase, he must also make use of the question. Or perhaps
he felt that if he could answer it, he could put the universe back
100　together. Or perhaps it was something to fill his empty days.

　　He wrote in his small notebook: "The light of my cigarette is
a fire like the sun. From where I sit, all the universe is **equidistant**

inversion
(ĭn-vûr′zhən) *n.*
reversal or upside-
down placement.

equidistant
(ē′kwĭ-dĭs′tənt) *adj.* at
equal distance from.

WHEN STUDENTS STRUGGLE . . .

Makkai's sentence structure may be difficult to follow. She uses colons, semicolons, and dashes to create long and complicated sentences.

Read aloud the sentence in lines 64–66. Point out the colon and discuss how it allows the reader to pause and notice the thought that comes after it. This second clause clarifies the chef's thoughts about the briefcase.

Read aloud lines 74–75 and point out the semicolon. Have students explain how the two clauses, joined by the semicolon, are related. *(They both talk about when pretending to be the professor wouldn't work.)*

Repeat this process to guide students through other complicated sentences.

CLOSE READ

Analyze Character

COMMON CORE　RL 1, RL 3

(LINES 65–78, 80-90)

Remind students that one way readers learn about characters is through their **motivations,** or reasons for behaving as they do.

F **CITE TEXT EVIDENCE** Ask students how the chef feels about stealing the professor's identity, citing text evidence that supports their answers. *(The chef feels justified. In line 69–70, he says he has to do it; in line 71 he describes stealing his identity as an "apology," and a way to put the world in balance; he says his actions will keep the professor alive [lines 72–74]; he believes the briefcase was left for him to take [lines 75–76].)*

Tell students that a character's actions may reveal more about the character than his or her words.

G **ASK STUDENTS** what the chef does to adopt the professor's identity. *(He moves to a new town; he grows a beard; he asks the professor's friends for money; he has them tell his wife that he is safe.)* Then ask students the reason the chef gives for wanting the professor's wife to believe he is alive. *(To keep her happy. If she believes the professor is alive, the chef will keep getting money.)*

CRITICAL VOCABULARY

inversion: The riddle reverses an idea about the universe.

ASK STUDENTS to identify the idea about astronomy in this riddle and what the inversion of this idea is. *(The original idea is that the Earth revolves around the sun; the inversion of this is the idea that the sun revolves around Earth.)*

equidistant: The chef says that everything in the universe is an equal distance from his cigarette.

ASK STUDENTS to discuss how all the universe could be equidistant from a spot on Earth. *(The chef may be thinking broadly or metaphorically that everything is far away from him.)*

Analyze Character and Theme (LINES 103–118)

COMMON CORE RL 1, RL 2, RL 3

Encourage students to continue to look for comparisons of the chef and the professor.

H **ASK STUDENTS** whether the chef was a good student and why he left school. *(Yes, he was good at languages and math; his mother made him quit.)* Have them describe the direct comparisons Makkai makes between the chef and the professor and why these comparisons are important to understanding the chef. *(The professor had years of study and books, while the chef had years of cooking; the chef's hand is used to using kitchen tools rather than using a pen. The chef equates himself to the professor because at this point in his life, instead of his hands smelling like leeks, his hands now "smelled of ink.")*

Remind students that a story's theme can often be revealed through its characters. Point out that in this section of the story, the chef and the professor share more similarities than differences.

I **CITE TEXT EVIDENCE** Ask students to cite text evidence that shows how the chef's character is changing and how this change might relate to the theme. *(The chef is starting to think of himself as the professor. He uses the language of logic [lines 103–106]; he has the "hands of the professor" and as such he is "now the professor" [lines 117–118]. The chef is assuming a new identity.)*

CRITICAL VOCABULARY

transpire: Makkai writes that the professor's students all want to know what happened to him.

ASK STUDENTS to summarize what transpired as the professor walked down the street. *(He was captured by guards to take the chef's place as a prisoner.)*

from my cigarette. Ergo,[1] my cigarette is the center of the universe. My cigarette is on Earth. Ergo, the Earth is the center of the universe. If all heavenly bodies move, they must therefore move in relation to the Earth, and in relation to my cigarette."

His hand ached. These words were the most he had written since school, which had ended for him at age sixteen. He had been a smart boy, even talented in languages and mathematics, 110 but his mother knew these were no way to make a living. He was not blessed, like the professor, with years of scholarship and quiet offices and leather books. He was blessed instead with chicken stocks and herbs and sherry. Thirty years had passed since his last day of school, and his hand was accustomed now to wooden spoon, mandoline, peeling knife, rolling pin.

Today, his hands smelled of ink, when for thirty years they had smelled of leeks. They were the hands of the professor; ergo, he was now the professor.

He had written to friends A through L, and now he saved the rest 120 and wrote instead to students. Here in the briefcase's outermost pocket were class rosters from the past two years; letters addressed to those young men care of the university were sure to reach them. The amounts they sent were smaller, the notes that accompanied them more inquisitive. What exactly had **transpired**? Could they come to the city and meet him?

The post box, of course, was in a different city than the one where he stayed. He arrived at the post office just before closing,

transpire
(trăn-spīr´) *v.* to happen or occur.

---

[1] **Ergo (ûr´gō):** the Latin equivalent of "therefore."

Image Credits: ©Mat Denney/Flickr/Getty Images

and came only once every two or three weeks. He always looked through the window first to check that the lobby was empty. If it

130 was not, he would leave and come again another day. Surely one of these days, a friend of the professor would be waiting there for him. He prepared a story, that he was the honored professor's assistant, that he could not reveal the man's location but would certainly pass on your kindest regards, sir.

If the Earth moved, all it would take for a man to travel its distance would be a strong balloon. Rise twenty feet above, and wait for the Earth to turn under you; you would be home again in a day. But this was not true, and a man could not escape his spot on the Earth but to run along the surface. Ergo, the Earth was still. Ergo, the sun

140 was the moving body of the two.

No, he did not believe it. He wanted only to know who this professor was, this man who would teach his students the laws of the universe, then ask them to prove as true what was false.

On the wall of the café: plate-sized canvas, delicate oils of an apple, half-peeled. Signed, below, by a girl he had known in school. The price was more than a month of groceries, and so he did not buy it, but for weeks he read his news under the apple and drank his coffee. Staining his fingers in cheap black ink were the signal fires of the world, the distress sirens, the dispatches from the trenches

150 and hospitals and abattoirs[2] of the war; but here, on the wall, a sign from another world. He had known this girl as well as any other: had spoken with her every day, but had not made love to her; had gone to her home one winter holiday, but knew nothing of her life since then. And here, a clue, perfect and round and unfathomable. After all this time: apple.

After he finished the news, he worked at the proof and saw in the coil of green-edged skin some model of spiraling, of expansion. The stars were at one time part of the Earth, until the hand of God peeled them away, leaving us in the dark. They do not revolve

160 around us: they escape in widening circles. The Milky Way is the edge of this peel.

Outside the café window, a beggar screeched his bow against a defeated violin. A different kind of case, open on the ground, this one collecting the pennies of the more compassionate passers-by. The café owner shooed him away, and the chef sighed in guilty relief that he would not have to pass, on the way out, his double.

After eight months in the new city, the chef stopped buying his newspapers on the street by the café and began instead to read the year-old news the widow gave him for his fires. Here, fourteen

---

[2] **abattoirs** (ăb´ə-twärs´): slaughterhouses.

TO CHALLENGE STUDENTS . . .

Exploring Themes After they have read the story, ask students what role women play in the chef's life. Makkai writes brief but telling scenes about the chef's relationships with his landlady and his lover. The story climaxes in the confrontation between the chef and the professor's wife.

Have students work in small groups to discuss the importance of women in the story. Have them consider what we learn about the chef through his relationships. Are there ways in which the women highlight different parts of his personality? Tell them to think about how the female characters relate to the theme of identity. Why does the chef feel so strongly attracted to the professor's wife? Ask students to present their ideas to the rest of the class.

CLOSE READ

Analyze Character and Theme (LINES 135–143, 147–157, 162–166)

COMMON CORE RL 1, RL 2, RL 3

Explain that one way writers develop their characters is by having them repeat their actions. Point out that the chef returns to the professor's test question several times throughout story.

J ASK STUDENTS how the chef's analysis of the test question in lines 135–140 is different from his approach on the previous page and how his analysis relates to his own situation. *(The analysis here is somewhat more practical; the chef wants to escape, and his analysis considers flying away in a balloon.)* Then ask students to explain the significance of asking the students to "prove as true what was false." *(The chef is pretending to be the professor and wants his lie to be true.)*

Remind students that character is developed through action.

K CITE TEXT EVIDENCE Point out that by this point in the story, the chef has settled into a regular routine. Have students cite evidence from the text that describes examples of this routine and what this routine says about the chef. *(The chef goes to the same café every day [line 147]; he sits under the painting of the apple and reads newspapers [lines 147–148]; he works on the professor's proof [lines 156–157]. The routine indicates that he is now more comfortable in his new life.)*

Explain to students that writers also develop their characters by sharing the characters' thoughts.

L CITE TEXT EVIDENCE Have students identify the chef's thoughts about the beggar. *(The chef feels both relieved and "guilty" when the beggar is "shooed" away. The chef does not want "to pass" him on the way out.)* Then ask why the chef might feel guilty about passing the beggar and how his guilt relates to the theme of identity. *(The chef sees himself in the beggar, opening a case and "collecting the pennies" from others.)*

Analyze Character and Theme (LINES 167–180, 181–187, 194–203)

COMMON CORE RL 1, RL 2, RL 3

Encourage students to examine the chef's actions.

M **ASK STUDENTS** to describe the progression of the chef's reading habits. *(He stops reading the daily papers; then, he reads papers that are a year old [167–170]; then, he reads papers that are five years old [171–172]; and finally, he turns to "history books.")* Then ask students what the chef reads when he runs out of newspapers and what this pattern of behavior reveals about him. *(He is uncomfortable with what is happening in the present; he doesn't feel safe in the present.)*

Explain to students that writers reveal what characters are like by how they interact with other characters. These interactions might also reveal a theme.

N **CITE TEXT EVIDENCE** Ask students to identify the professor's theory that the chef shares with his lover. *(Stars "circled the Earth, along with the sun.")* Then, remind students about the theme of identity and ask what the chef means when he tells his lover that she might be the only one to understand the theory. *(He knows he has taken the professor's identity and that his lover is part of the lie. ["The universe has been folded inside out."])*

Remind students that writers develop characters by revealing characters' thoughts.

O **CITE TEXT EVIDENCE** Have students review lines 194–203 and cite text evidence that explains the chef's ideas about time and space. *(The chef thinks that all time is the same [lines 194–196: "The years do not pass"; "years pile on like blankets, existing at once"]; all space is the same [lines 202–203: "This city is all cities at all times."])* Then ask students to relate the theme of identity to the chef's thoughts, "I run by standing still." *(The chef understands that in order for him to "run" or to escape and to remain free, he must "stand still" and continue his life as the professor.)*

---

170 months ago: Minister P—— of the Interior predicts war. One day he found that in a box near the widow's furnace were papers three, four, five years old. Pages were missing, edges eaten. He took his fragments of yellowed paper to the café and read the beginnings and ends of opinions and letters. He read reports from what used to be his country's borders.

When he had finished the last paper of the box, he began to read the widow's history books. The Americas, before Columbus; the oceans, before the British; the Romans, before their fall.

180 History was safer than the news, because there was no question of how it would end.

He took a lover in the city and told her he was a professor of physics. He showed her the stars in the sky and explained that they circled the Earth, along with the sun.

That's not true at all, she said. You tease because you think I'm just a silly girl.

No, he said and touched her neck, You are the only one who might understand. The universe has been folded inside out.

A full year had passed, and he paid the widow in coins. He wrote to friends M through Z. I have been in hiding for a year, he wrote. Tell
190 my dear wife I have my health. May time and history forgive us all.

A year had passed, but so had many years passed for many men. And after all what was a year, if the Earth did not circle the sun?

The Earth does not circle the sun, he wrote. Ergo: The years do not pass. The Earth, being stationary, does not erase the past nor escape towards the future. Rather, the years pile on like blankets, existing at once. The year is 1848; the year is 1789; the year is 1956.

If the Earth hangs still in space, does it spin? If the Earth were to spin, the space I occupy I will therefore vacate in an instant. This
200 city will leave its spot, and the city to the west will usurp its place. Ergo, this city is all cities at all times. This is Kabul; this is Dresden; this is Johannesburg.[3]

I run by standing still.

At the post office, he collects his envelopes of money. He has learned from the notes of concerned colleagues and students and friends that the professor suffered from infections of the inner ear that often threw off his balance. He has learned of the professor's wife, A——, whose father died the year they married. He has learned that he has a young son. Rather, the professor has a son.

---

[3] **Kabul . . . Dresden . . . Johannesburg:** cities in Afghanistan, Germany, and South Africa, respectively.

SCAFFOLDING FOR ELL STUDENTS

Understand Dialogue Students may have difficulty identifying spoken language without the use of quotation marks. To guide students' identification of dialogue, project lines 184–187 and invite volunteers to mark up the lines.

- Underline clue words that indicate who is speaking.
- Highlight in yellow the words that the lover speaks.
- Highlight in green the words that the chef speaks.

210 　At each visit to the post office, he fears he will forget the combination. It is an old lock, and complicated: F1, clockwise to B3, back to A6, forward again to J3. He must shake the little latch before it opens. More than forgetting, perhaps what he fears is that he will be denied access — that the little box will one day recognize him behind his thick and convincing beard, will decide he has no right of entry.

　One night, asleep with his head on his lover's leg, he dreams that a letter has arrived from the professor himself. They freed me at the end of the march, it says, and I crawled my way home. My 220 hands are bloody and my knees are worn through, and I want my briefcase back.

　In his dream, the chef takes the case and runs west. If the professor takes it back, there will be no name left for the chef, no place on the Earth. The moment his fingers leave the leather loop of the handle, he will fall off the planet.

He sits in a wooden chair on the lawn behind the widow's house. Inside, he hears her washing dishes. In exchange for the room, he cooks all her meals. It is March, and the cold makes the hairs rise from his arms, but the sun warms the arm beneath them. He 230 thinks, The tragedy of a moving sun is that it leaves us each day. Hence the Aztec sacrifices, the ancient rites of the eclipse. If the sun so willingly leaves us, each morning it returns is a stay of execution, an undeserved gift.

　Whereas: If it is we who turn, how can we so **flagrantly** leave behind that which has warmed us and given us light? If we are moving, then each turn is a turn away. Each revolution a revolt.

The money comes less often, and even old friends who used to write monthly now send only rare, apologetic notes, a few small bills. Things are more difficult now, their letters say. No one understood 240 when he first ran away, but now it is clear: After they finished with the artists, the journalists, the fighters, they came for the professors. How wise he was, to leave when he did. Some letters come back unopened, with a black stamp.

　Life is harder here, too. Half the shops are closed. His lover has left him. The little café is filled with soldiers. The beggar with the violin has disappeared, and the chef fears him dead.

　One afternoon, he enters the post office two minutes before closing. The lobby is empty but for the postman and his broom.

　The mailbox is empty as well, and he turns to leave but hears 250 the voice of the postman behind him. You are the good Professor T——, no? I have something for you in the back.

　Yes, he says, I am the professor. And it feels as if this is true, and he will have no guilt over the professor's signature when the

flagrantly
(flā´grənt-lē) *adv.*
in a blatantly or
conspicuously
offensive manner.

WHEN STUDENTS STRUGGLE . . .

Help students examine the chef's inner dialogue in order to better understand his character. Review the professor's exam question earlier in the story (lines 53–55). Make sure students understand that the professor is asking his students to prove something that isn't true.

Have students reread lines 230–236. Discuss how this passage relates to the professor's question. (*The passage assumes the sun revolves around the Earth.*) Discuss the meaning of "Aztec sacrifices" and "stay of execution." Have students suggest how this passage relates to the chef's circumstances. (*He feels grateful for escaping his own execution; he feels sad for the loss of his old life; he believes people aren't grateful enough for the good things they have.*)

CLOSE READ

Analyze Character and Theme (LINES 217–225)

COMMON CORE RL 1, RL 2, RL 3

Point out that in fiction, theme is usually not stated directly but can be inferred from a character's thoughts or actions.

P CITE TEXT EVIDENCE Have students review lines 217–225 and cite text evidence that explains the chef's state of mind in his dream as well as the significance of the briefcase. Ask students how the chef's dream relates to the story's theme. (*Upon learning that the professor is free ["They freed me at the end of March"] and has returned home ["I crawled my way home"], the chef takes the briefcase and runs away ["the chef takes the case and runs west"]. The briefcase is the source of the chef's identity. Without it, he will no longer have an identity. ["The moment his fingers leave the leather loop…he will fall off the planet."] This relates to the importance of identity and how tenuous the chef's identity is.*)

Analyze Language (LINES 237–246)

COMMON CORE RL 1, RL 4

Remind students that writers use language to create a specific tone.

Q CITE TEXT EVIDENCE Have students review lines 237–246 and identify the words and phrases and the sentence structure that convey the author's tone of despair. (*The chef is receiving fewer letters with "a few small bills." "Some letters come back unopened," implying that those people are gone. Many of the "shops have closed," and the chef has lost his lover.*)

CRITICAL VOCABULARY

flagrantly: The chef questions how the Earth can turn away from the sun in such a blatantly offensive way.
ASK STUDENTS to identify what "we" or the Earth flagrantly leaves behind. (*warmth and light from the sun*)

Analyze Character and Theme (LINES 259–275, 277–292)

 COMMON CORE RL 1, RL 2, RL 3

Have students examine the scene between the chef and the professor's wife, the longest interaction in the story.

R **CITE TEXT EVIDENCE** Ask students what motivates the professor's wife's to meet the chef. *(She wants to know what happened to her husband [lines 260–262].)* Ask students to cite the actions and words that show both the wife's state of mind as well as the chef's. *(The professor's wife is confused; she says she doesn't understand [lines 267 and 271]; she asks what the chef has done with the professor [line 274]. The chef is at a loss for words [lines 264–266] and tries to apply logic to the situation. He points out that he has the professor's shirt [line 272].)*

Remind students that motivation, what drives the characters to behave as they do, can reveal theme.

S **CITE TEXT EVIDENCE** Ask students how the chef reacts when the professor's wife says, "Then he is dead." *(He tries to turn away from her but cannot [line 285: "she is a force of gravity"].)* Then ask how the chef's reaction relates to the theme of identity. *(The chef is desperate to keep the professor's identity to prolong his life.)*

box is brought out. He is even wearing the professor's shirt, as loose again over his hungry ribs as it was the day he slipped it on in the alley.

From behind the counter, the postman brings no box, but a woman in a long gray dress, a white handkerchief in her fingers.

She moves towards him, looks at his hands and his shoes and
260 his face. Forgive me for coming, she says, and the postman pulls the cover down over his window and vanishes. She says, No one would tell me anything, only that my husband had his health. And then a student gave me the number of the box and the name of the city.

He begins to say, You are the widow. But why would he say this? What proof is there that the professor is dead? Only that it must be; that it follows logically.

She says, I don't understand what has happened.

He begins to say, I am the good professor's assistant, madam —
but then what next? She would ask questions he has no way to
270 answer.

I don't understand, she says again.

All he can say is, This is his shirt. He holds out an arm so she can see the gaping sleeve.

She says, What have you done with him? She has a calm voice and wet, brown eyes. He feels he has seen her before, in the streets of the old city. Perhaps he served her a meal, a bottle of wine. Perhaps, in another lifetime, she was the center of his universe.

This is his beard, he says.

She begins to cry into the handkerchief. She says, Then he is
280 dead. He sees now from the quiet of her voice that she must have known this long ago. She has come here only to confirm.

He feels the floor of the post office move beneath him, and he tries to turn his eyes from her, to ground his gaze in something solid: postbox, ceiling tile, window. He finds he cannot turn away. She is a force of gravity in her long gray dress.

No, he says. No, no, no, no, no, I am right here.

No, he does not believe it, but he knows that if he had time, he could prove it. And he must, because he is the only piece of the professor left alive. The woman does not see how she is murdering
290 her husband, right here in the post office lobby. He whispers to her: Let me go home with you. I'll be a father to your son, and I'll warm your bed, and I'll keep you safe.

He wraps his hands around her small, cold wrists, but she pulls loose. She might be the most beautiful woman he has ever seen.

As if from far away, he hears her call to the postmaster to send for the police.

His head is light, and he feels he might float away from the post office forever. It is an act of will not to fly off, but to hold tight to

TO CHALLENGE STUDENTS . . .

Explore Theme How else does the author bring up the theme of unknown or uncertain identity in the story? Remind students that they have already explored the theme of identity through the character development in the story. However, other elements of the story relate back to the same theme. Students may have noticed that the setting (time, place, historical context) is also unknown. Have students work in small groups to discuss the elements of the story, such as setting, and how they convey theme more deeply.

the Earth and wait. If the police aren't too busy to come, he feels
300 confident he can prove to them that he is the professor. He has the
papers, after all — and in the **havoc** of war, what else will they have
the time to look for?

She is backing away from him on steady feet, and he feels it like
a peeling off of skin.

If not the police, perhaps he'll convince a city judge. The
witnesses who would denounce him are mostly gone or killed,
and the others would fear to come before the law. If the city judge
will not listen, he can prove it to the high court. One day he might
convince the professor's own child. He feels certain that somewhere
310 down the line, someone will believe him.

havoc
(hăv´ək) *n.*
destructive disorder
or chaos.

COLLABORATIVE DISCUSSION With a partner, discuss your impression
of the chef. Explain whether you think he is resourceful or simply
dishonest. Cite specific evidence from the story to support your ideas.

CLOSE READ

Analyze Character and Theme (LINES 299–310)

COMMON CORE RL 1, RL 2, RL 3

Remind students that one way we learn about characters and how they may have changed throughout the story is through their thoughts.

T **CITE TEXT EVIDENCE** Ask students to cite evidence that explains why the chef thinks he can convince those in authority that he is the professor and why he is so desperate to prove that he is the professor. *(The chef has the professor's papers [lines 300–301]; anyone who would prove otherwise is gone or too afraid to go to court [lines 306–307]. The chef is desperate to keep the identity.)* Have students explain why the chef feels the wife's backing away from him is "like a peeling off of skin" (lines 303–304). *(As the professor's wife backs away, she is removing the skin— or identity—of the professor.)*

CRITICAL VOCABULARY

havoc: The war has resulted in chaos and destruction.

ASK STUDENTS why no one would be able to check on the chef's identity in the midst of havoc. *(Records may have been destroyed, or those that do exist may be in dangerous places.)*

COLLABORATIVE DISCUSSION Have students pair up and sum up the chef's motivations or reasons for his actions. Remind students to address specific actions the chef takes throughout the story. Remind students to consider how the chef interacts with other characters. Then have students share their conclusions with the class as a whole. Accept all reasonable responses.

ASK STUDENTS to share any questions they generated in the course of reading and discussing the selection.

Analyze Character and Theme

COMMON CORE RL 2, RL 3

Help students understand the relationship between *action* and *motivation*. **Action** is what a character does; **motivation** is his or her reasons for those actions. Explain that a character's motivations are the driving force behind the plot and provide insight into theme.

Discuss with students the chef's action of taking the professor's briefcase and assuming his identity. Ask students to explain the chef's initial motivation for taking the briefcase. (*He needed a new identity to survive; he believed impersonating the professor was a way of keeping him alive; he justified his action by believing the briefcase was left behind for him to use.*) Ask students what these multiple motivations tell the reader about the chef. (*He is willing to steal and lie to remain alive.*) Discuss with students how the chef's motivations for keeping the professor's identity may have changed. (*The chef began to believe his own lie, and the motivations became about keeping that lie alive and believable.*)

Explain to students that **theme** is the central idea of a story. Readers can determine the theme by following the actions and motivations of the main character. Ask students what the chef's assumption of the professor's identity tells them about the chef. Have students use their answers to identify a theme of the story.

Analyze Character and Theme

COMMON CORE RL 2, RL 3

Characters are the people who experience the events in a story. Like real people, they display certain qualities and develop and change over time. Readers come to understand characters through their thoughts, actions, dialogue, and interactions with others. Their **motivations,** or reasons for doing what they do, advance the plot of a story and reveal its theme.

In this story, only the character of the chef is fully developed, and we learn much about him through his interactions with and observations of other minor characters. For example, consider the beggar outside the café. What does the chef think about the beggar? What does this reveal about his character?

Theme is the central idea of a story or the insight about life that the author wants to convey. Themes may be universal, such as "Crime does not pay" or "Love conquers all," or they may be more specific to the story. An author might state a theme directly, but most often readers must infer theme, relying on character development and unfolding events to make an educated guess about what message the author wants to convey.

Use these key elements to analyze the chef's character and determine the theme of the story:

The Character's Actions	Think about the chef's actions in the story. What does his assumption of the professor's identity tell you about him?
The Character's Interactions with Others	The chef interacts with others through letters. He also interacts with his landlady, his lover, the post office clerk, and the professor's wife. What does each interaction reveal about his character?
The Character's Thoughts	Throughout the story, the chef is preoccupied with answering the professor's astronomy question. Here are some examples of his thoughts about it. Given his situation, are these thoughts about more than astronomy? • "My cigarette is on Earth. Ergo, the Earth is the center of the universe. If all heavenly bodies move, they must therefore move in relation to the Earth, and in relation to my cigarette." • ". . . a man could not escape his spot on the Earth but to run along the surface. Ergo, the Earth was still. Ergo, the sun was the moving body of the two." • "The Earth does not circle the sun, he wrote. Ergo: The years do not pass. The Earth, being stationary, does not erase the past nor escape towards the future."

Strategies for Annotation ✎ ▤ *Annotate it!*

Analyze Character and Theme

COMMON CORE RL 2, RL 3

Have students use their eBook annotation tools to analyze the text. Ask them to do the following:

- Highlight the chef's actions in yellow.
- Highlight the chef's thoughts in blue.
- Highlight the chef's motivations in green.
- On a note, relate the chef's actions and thoughts to his motivations. Record how this affects the understanding of the character.

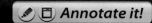

vacated life. If he wanted to live through the next year, the chef would have to learn this life and fill it — and oddly, this felt not like a robbery but an apology, a way to put the world back in balance. The professor would not die, because he himself would become the professor, and he would live.

Analyzing the Text

Cite Text Evidence   Support your responses with evidence from the selection.

1. **Cite Evidence**   What evidence does the author provide that the chef, even after a year in hiding, fears discovery?

2. **Infer**   When the chef first opens the professor's briefcase, the author writes that "papers flew out, a thousand doves flailing against the walls of the alley" (lines 43–44). What might the author want to achieve by comparing the professor's papers to doves? What tone does this image create?

3. **Summarize**   How does the chef justify the theft of the professor's briefcase and identity?

4. **Analyze**   The author compresses a long period of time into a few pages. Instead of providing a comprehensive summary of events in the chef's life during this year, she looks closely at specific moments in time, reminding the reader that eight months, and then a year, have passed. How does this pacing create tension in the story?

5. **Interpret**   In what way is the beggar outside the café the chef's "double" (line 166)? Why does the chef not want to walk past him?

6. **Interpret**   After eight months, the chef prefers to read old newspapers and history books rather than the daily news. What does this choice reveal about the chef's character? How has he changed?

7. **Analyze**   Throughout the story, the author comes back to the astronomy question again and again. What connection can be made between this riddle and the chef's predicament? What incentive does he have to solve the riddle?

8. **Draw Conclusions**   Does the chef ever begin to believe his own lie? Cite evidence from the story to support your answer.

PERFORMANCE TASK

Writing Activity: Personal Letter   Assume the identity of the chef. Write a letter to the professor's son in which you attempt to convince him that you could serve as the boy's father.

1. Gather details from the story that support the chef's idea that he has become the professor.

2. Write a brief letter to the son based on the evidence you have gathered from the text. Address the son using a voice and logic suited to the chef's character, and mention events and relationships of which the chef would be aware.

Assign this performance task.

PERFORMANCE TASK

Writing Activity: Personal Letter   Have students find specific lines and scenes where the chef thinks of himself as the professor. Tell them to pay attention to the *voice* of the chef. Explain that voice consists of the way a character speaks and what he thinks about himself and the world. Have students imagine what the chef thinks about the relationship between the professor and his son. Encourage students to be creative when writing their letters.

PRACTICE & APPLY

Analyzing the Text   RL 1, RL 2, RL 3, RL 4, RL 5

Possible answers:

1. *He fears he won't remember the combination to his box at the post office (lines 210–211); he's afraid that even the box will turn him away (lines 214–215); he dreams about the professor finding him (lines 217–221).*

2. *By comparing the papers to flying doves, the author creates an image of papers flying out of the briefcase and down the alley. It creates a tone of confusion and anxiety, possibly of escape.*

3. *In lines 69–73, the chef's justification is that the act was a kind of apology for trading places with the professor; keeping the professor's identity alive will put the world back in balance.*

4. *This pacing creates tension because the chef's lie has gone on a long time but the threat of discovery is always imminent; it makes the reader wonder which event will lead to the chef being caught.*

5. *The beggar has lost his "real" life and is doing what he must to survive. The chef does not want to walk past him because he sees himself in the beggar and doesn't want to be reminded that he is more like the beggar than the professor.*

6. *The chef is no longer interested in or connected to the modern world. The past is safe because it is predictable (lines 179–180). The chef has settled into his new life and is not interested in time moving forward.*

7. *The astronomy question invites students to prove a theory that isn't true. This relates to the chef because he is living a life that is not true. If he can solve the riddle, then he also has the ability to make his own lie believable. (lines 97–99; lines 116–118).*

8. *The chef does believe his lie. In lines 117–118, he claims to be the professor. In line 209, he thinks of the professor's son as his own son. In line 252, he says he feels it's true that he is the professor. Even in the final paragraph, he thinks people will believe he is the professor.*

PRACTICE & APPLY

Critical Vocabulary COMMON CORE L 2a

Possible answers:

1. *Everyday life was full of confusion and destruction.*

2. *The guards were completely unconcerned because they felt they were above the law, or that they were in a position of absolute authority.*

3. *The sun and the moon are both the same distance from the chef because* equidistant *means "an equal distance"; therefore, everything in the universe is the same distance from the chef.*

4. *The professor's wife hoped to find out what had happened to her husband.*

5. *The professor's test question asks students to prove that the sun revolves around the Earth. This is an inversion because it is the opposite of what is true.*

6. *The professor resisted arrest because he was waving his arms about wildly.*

Language and Style: Semicolons COMMON CORE L 2a

Explain that linking ideas with semicolons affects the tone of Makkai's story. Write the following sentences from the selection on the board and ask students to describe how linking the clauses affects the tone.

The year is 1848; the year is 1789; the year is 1956.

(It connects the ideas as a list; the tone is factual, like something the professor would write.)

He had to write this about the wife; how could he ask these men for money if she held a funeral?

(Linking the clauses shows the chef's thought process.)

Possible answer: Answers will vary. When students have completed their revisions, they should be able to point to two sentences that correctly use semicolons.

Assess It!

Online Selection Test
- Download an editable ExamView bank.
- Assign and manage this test online.

Critical Vocabulary COMMON CORE L 2a

| flail | inversion | equidistant |
| transpire | flagrantly | havoc |

Practice and Apply Answer each question to demonstrate your understanding of the Critical Vocabulary words.

1. The war had created **havoc** in the chef's country. What might you assume everyday life was like for people?

2. The guards **flagrantly** disregarded the law in seizing the professor. How concerned were they that others would find out the professor had been unlawfully arrested?

3. If the chef believes that all things in the universe are **equidistant** from him, is the sun farther from the chef than the moon? Explain your response.

4. The professor's wife tracked down the chef to determine what had **transpired.** What did she hope to find out?

5. When the chef reads the professor's test question, he interprets it as an **inversion** of the universe. Explain why.

6. If the professor's arms were **flailing** when he was seized, did he meekly obey or resist arrest?

Language and Style: Semicolons

Writers use semicolons for three main purposes: to link two independent clauses, to link an independent clause with another clause that begins with a conjunctive adverb (such as *therefore, meanwhile, also,* or *however*), and to separate items in a list when the items already contain commas. Makkai uses semicolons to provide structure and organization in her writing, but she also uses them to influence meaning. Read this sentence from the story:

> Surely he could not teach at the university; surely he could not slip into the man's bed unnoticed.

The author could have separated the two independent clauses with a period, but the two thoughts are closely connected, and Makkai wanted to convey that idea to her readers. Now, read this sentence from the story:

> They were the hands of the professor; ergo, he was now the professor.

In this example, the semicolon links two thoughts, and a conjunctive adverb (*ergo*) shows that the second thought results from the first.

Practice and Apply Look back at the letter you wrote for this selection's Performance Task. Revise your letter to link two independent clauses with semicolons. Then, discuss with a partner how using semicolons helps clarify the meaning of your letter.

Analyze Tone

TEACH

Explain that **tone** is the author's attitude. Tone creates an emotional response in the reader. Recognizing tone helps a reader understand an author's meaning. Review the following elements authors use to create tone.

- **Word choice** conveys more than just information; it can also evoke an emotional response. Makkai writes that the chef's hand was "starved." Ask students to explain how that word is different from "bony." Discuss what emotion is evoked by each word.

- **Figurative language** creates an image in the reader's mind. The chef thinks of mankind as a line of "miserable monkeys." Ask why that is an appropriate image for the chained prisoners.

- **Details,** or a lack of them, indicate what an author wants the reader to experience. Makkai points out when eight months have passed, and then when a year has passed. Ask what effect that has on the reader.

- **Sentence structure** can help the reader understand a character's mental state or create mood in a scene. Makkai creates rhythm by using techniques such as repetition or sentence length. She doesn't use quotation marks when characters speak.

 INTERACTIVE WHITEBOARD LESSON For additional information, refer to the *Interactive Whiteboard Lesson:* **Word Choice and Tone**

COLLABORATIVE DISCUSSION

Have students work in groups to analyze tone in "The Briefcase." Divide the class into four or eight groups, assigning each group one of the elements of tone listed above. Each group should work together to identify examples of how its assigned element develops tone in the story. After compiling examples, they should develop a statement describing the story's tone. Finally, have groups share their understanding of tone in the story during class discussion.

Analyze Character and Theme

RETEACH

Review that the **theme** is the message or messages about life a writer communicates through story. Longer and more complex works of fiction may have multiple themes. A short story often has one main theme. Point out that theme may be interpreted in different ways by different readers.

Tell students that one way theme may be revealed is through a character's preoccupation with an action, idea, or concept. In "The Briefcase," the chef often revisits the professor's exam question. Each time, his approach or logic to solving the question is different. These variations give the reader insight into the chef's character as well as the story's theme.

Have students review lines 101–106 and summarize the chef's explanation of the question. *(The Earth is at the center of the universe; he uses his cigarette to represent the Earth.)*

Now have students review lines 156–161 and explain how the chef's understanding of the question has changed. *(Now he sees the entire universe spiraling away from Earth.)* Ask what insight this gives the reader into the chef. *(He feels less confident; he isn't in control.)*

Have students analyze additional places the chef explores the professor's exam question. *(lines 194–203, 229–236)* Tell them to use their insights to identify the theme of the story. *(Sample answer: Events in our lives affect our sense of who we are.)*

 LEVEL UP TUTORIALS Assign the following *Level Up* tutorial: **Theme**

CLOSE READING APPLICATION

Students can apply the skill to another short story. Have students work independently to read a different story in this textbook. Have them analyze the characters' thoughts and actions and how they relate to the theme. Ask students to identify a theme of the story and cite text evidence to support their interpretation.

Bile

Short Story by Christine Lee Zilka

Why This Text

Students sometimes find it difficult to infer the theme of a story. "Bile" provides an opportunity to analyze character development in order to infer the story's theme. With the help of the close-reading questions, students will analyze how the characters interact and develop. This close reading will lead students to determine the theme, or central idea, of "Bile."

Background Have students read the background and the information about the author. Introduce the selection by telling students that Korea was divided into two countries after the end of World War II in 1945. Prior to that, Korea had been ruled by Japan. Just 5 years after the nation was divided, the Korean War began, in 1950. The father in this story has survived the horrors of the Korean war and started a new life and family in America.

AS YOU READ Ask students to pay attention for clues to the story's underlying message. How soon into the story can they begin to identify the theme?

Common Core Support

- cite strong and thorough textual evidence
- determine the theme of a text and analyze its development
- analyze how complex characters develop over the course of a text
- determine the meaning of words and phrases as they are used in a text

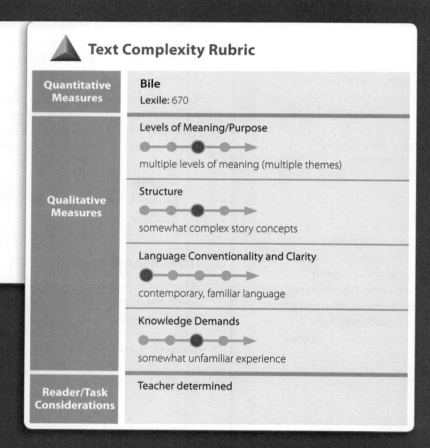

Text Complexity Rubric

Quantitative Measures	**Bile** Lexile: 670
Qualitative Measures	Levels of Meaning/Purpose — multiple levels of meaning (multiple themes)
	Structure — somewhat complex story concepts
	Language Conventionality and Clarity — contemporary, familiar language
	Knowledge Demands — somewhat unfamiliar experience
Reader/Task Considerations	Teacher determined

Strategies for CLOSE READING

Analyze Theme and Character

Students should read this story carefully all the way through. Close-reading questions at the bottom of the page will help them focus on a thorough analysis of the characters which will help them determine the theme. As they read, students should jot down comments or questions about the story in the side margins.

WHEN STUDENTS STRUGGLE . . .

To help students determine the story's theme, have them work in small groups to fill out a chart, such as the one shown below, as they analyze the text.

CITE TEXT EVIDENCE For practice in determining a story's theme, ask students to cite evidence of the development of the two main characters, the narrator and her father. Then, have them infer a theme from their analysis of the character development.

FATHER	NARRATOR
He was "restless" after the war.	She feels an "ancestral fear," like her mother and father.
The narrator's father uses bile to feel alive after the war.	She has to "duck out of view," to escape an angry scene.
Suffering is part of his psyche	She is "Hankook sahrahm." It means she identifies with the idea of Korean suffering.
He yells at the family as if an army is chasing them.	She has to choose between the heat outside and the "cool, poisonous house"
He is unhappy that Eugene has separated himself from the family.	She experiences the "cathartic pain of a bee sting."

Inferred Theme: Family relationships can be difficult and suffering can be handed down from one generation to the next.

Background *In June 1950, Communist North Korea invaded South Korea and U.S. President Truman authorized the use of American ground forces to stop the advance. He felt it was necessary to intervene in order to take a stand against Communist aggression. After some early back-and-forth, the fighting stalled and casualties mounted. American officials worked anxiously with North Koreans to end the war. An agreement was finally reached in July 1953. In all, some 2.5 million soldiers and civilians lost their lives during the war.* **Christine Lee Zilka** *explores the repercussions the Korean War has on one American family in the following short story.*

Bile

Short Story by Christine Lee Zilka

CLOSE READ
Notes

1. **READ ▶** As you read lines 1–33, begin to collect and cite text evidence.

   • Underline text that references the war.
   • Circle text describing the family's background.
   • In the margin, explain what the narrator learns about her father in lines 19–22.

Ⓐ Ⓑ W̲hen the Korean War ended in 1953, my father became restless. Korea lay in ruins, but there were no more enemy soldiers and no more bombs to flee. My father had become addicted to war. Without battles, he had no sense of urgency, no sense of drama. He had already survived, and like the rest of the country, he tried to pick up his life where he had left off. But he was not used to peace. He could make no sense of math equations as an engineering student; it all seemed **trivial**.

He made journeys into the countryside where he had grown up, hoping to reconnect himself. On one of his outings, he found a trapper gutting a
10 bear. An idea came to him. He asked the hunter for the gall bladder of the bear.

My father put his tongue to the gall bladder. It tasted like the war. He smiled grimly. He could not fail. H̲e could not turn back, because behind him were the Japanese army, the North Korean army, poverty, and abuse.

trivial:
of little worth or importance

105

---

1. **READ AND CITE TEXT EVIDENCE** Point out that the author begins this story with a reference to the Korean War.

Ⓐ **ASK STUDENTS** to cite evidence describing the family's background. *Students should cite evidence that the father was a soldier in the Korean War (lines 1–3), and evidence that they are traditional Korean Americans (lines 23–27).*

Critical Vocabulary: trivial (line 7) Ask students to compare definitions of *trivial*. Ask them what seemed trivial to the narrator's father. *The narrator's father endured many life-and-death situations in the war. Everyday experiences seemed insignificant.*

bile:
fluid secreted by the liver

He could not rest. This **bile** would be his medicine. He wrapped up the gall bladder and froze it. Whenever he felt he was getting too content, sleeping an hour too much, smiling a second too long, he would hunger for the taste of it, bitter, and clinging to his tongue.

20   As children, we learned that Daddy would have died if he had not had the bile: the bile reminded him of the misery and bitterness of suffering.

What I now realize is that the bitterness stayed inside him and traveled from his tongue, down into his belly, where it now churns.

The narrator's father uses the bile to stay alive; tasting it reminds him of what he has survived in his past.

Tradition runs strong in our family. We are Korean Americans, a strong line of warriors, descended from the Mongols. We are modern Genghis Khans,[1] quick tempered but passionate, with chronicles of suffering living in our veins. We are nomadic, settling in a country that severed our mother country in half, with a tourniquet of barbed wire, swathed in khaki green.

Suffering is so much a part of the Korean psyche that we have given it a word, *Han*. It is a particular suffering, a sense of helplessness against
30   overwhelming odds, a feeling of total abandonment. This word is part of what we call ourselves and our mother country, *Hankook sahrahm*, *Hankook nahrah*; Korean people, Korean land. This Han is silent and noble. It is our code and **mantra**.

[1] **Genghis Khan:** (1162?–1227) Mongol conqueror who united the Mongol tribes and forged an empire from China to Persia.

mantra:
a sound or phrase repeated in the mind

---

2.   ◀ **REREAD**   Reread lines 1–33. In your own words, summarize what you have learned about the narrator's father. Support your answer with explicit textual evidence.

The narrator's father survived the Korean War, but "he was not used to peace." He kept a gall bladder from a bear in his freezer and tasted it every time he "felt he was getting too content." Like many Korean Americans, suffering is part of his psyche.

3.   **READ** ▶   As you read lines 34–85, continue to cite text evidence.

- Underline text that characterizes Eugene or describes his actions.
- In the margin, explain what happens in lines 34–42.
- Circle text that characterizes the other three family members.

> ❝ **I had hard life, nothing to look forward to, just running away.** ❞

C   On our Sunday hikes, my father brings up the rear. My brother Eugene, the Boy Scout, bounds up the hill on light bunny feet. Safe on the hiking trails of the San Gabriel Mountains, I try to enjoy the views beyond the silt of smog, but Father barks at us, that there is an army behind us. We quicken our pace. There are sharp-toothed men who want to kill us. They have
40   shotguns, horsehair hats. They ride bareback, puff on long pipes, smoke opium, stab each other in the back.

Eugene runs up the hill out of earshot. Father, Mother, and I drip with effort, and we push ourselves to each crest out of this ancestral fear.

"Eugene! Wait for us!" I shout. I don't see him anymore, and he doesn't answer. The path bends mercilessly in the chaparral[2] heat.

"Forget about him. He never wait. Stupid boy, never cares about us," says Father.

Mother hits Father on the arm. "Leave him alone. You are bossy, maybe he's running away from you."

Father glares. Mother doubles her pace so that her shoes kick dust back
50   at us over the switchback.

Up ahead, I imagine Eugene's already arrived at the destination, a shady **plateau** of pine trees. He's taking a long sip of water from the water fountain up there, and drinking in the views of Pasadena. He may even see us, a short and irritated snake making its way.

We gather in the kitchen to eat an early lunch. Our bodies, sweaty with the recent Sunday excursion, stick to the vinyl kitchen seats. Father looks straight at Eugene, points his finger and bellows, "You never wait for us!"

Eugene rolls his eyes and says, "Dad, you never give us a break."

D   Father takes a breath and continues. "I am going to tell you about
60   myself, your father. I had hard life, nothing to look forward to, just running away. Eugene, you run to something, like nothing pushing. We go hiking, you go away. You don't wait for your own family? We have to enjoy together!"

Eugene replied, "You were just slow, and I waited for you at the top. What's the big deal?" My brother kicks me in the leg.

I chime in. "Dad, please don't worry so much. It's not so complicated. Eugene just is in better shape. Don't take it so seriously. We get it!" (Please, please do not tell the story again.)

[2] **chaparral:** a dense growth of tangled thorny shrubs.

plateau:
a raised, flat area of land

Their father yells at them on their hike, as if an army is behind them. Eugene runs ahead of the family.

---

2.   **REREAD AND CITE TEXT EVIDENCE**

B ASK STUDENTS to cite evidence to support their summary of the father. *Students should note that he survived the war (lines 1–3), was still affected by it (lines 19–20), and ate bile to cope with his feelings (lines 12–18).*

3.   **READ AND CITE TEXT EVIDENCE**

C ASK STUDENTS to cite text evidence to support their explanations. *Students should state that the father yells "that there is an army behind" them (line 37). They should contrast Eugene, in lines 34–35, with the rest of the family, in lines 41–42.*

Critical Vocabulary: bile   (line 15) Ask students to determine the meaning of *bile* as it is used in the story.

Critical Vocabulary: mantra   (line 33) Ask students to explain which connotations of *mantra* the author intended here.

Critical Vocabulary: plateau   (line 52) Ask students what symbolic meaning *plateau* might have here. *Students should contrast the ease the narrator imagines for Eugene on the flat plateau with the struggle she experiences climbing with the family.*

FOR ELL STUDENTS   Ask volunteers to explain the meaning of the idiom "We get it!" (line 67). If necessary, explain that it means "We understand."

372d Collection 6

synopsis:
a condensed statement or outline

"I gave up my dreams long ago and decided to have children instead. 70 You don't know your father, what I do for you! You know, I have to teach you good lesson, so you will never forget." This sends my father into a **synopsis** of his life. We have it memorized.

"I don't even know if my brother is alive. He fought against the Japanese, and they took everything, burned our house. I was five years old. But our family was a hero family, so our village supported us," says Father. "Then the Korean War came, and my brother, he joined the Communists. Everyone hated us then. We had to burn his pictures. Still, we survived."

So it was with my mother as well. "Your mommy, her family had to leave North Korea. They took only what they could carry. They put the 80 money and gold and jewelry inside their clothes, inside the silk linings. Rich people became poor in one night!"

Then Mother adds, "But we were smart. Instead of eating only one bowl of rice a day, we mixed it with barley, so we ate a little more often. We always ate, even though sometimes we had to sell our clothes. Your grandma's wedding dress, someone else owns it now."

"Eugene, you are going to learn," says Father. He nods at my mother, points at the refrigerator. My mother takes out a recycled plastic Safeway

4. ◄ REREAD   Reread lines 34–85. Explain how Eugene acts differently from the rest of the family. Why is his father so upset? Support your answer with explicit textual evidence.

Eugene bounds up the hill on "bunny feet" while the other three are a "short and irritated snake." His father thinks Eugene's behavior shows a lack of respect or family pride. His father takes the physical distance between Eugene and the rest of the family as something more meaningful.

5. READ ►   As you read lines 86–156, prepare to cite text evidence.
   • Underline text that explains what the gall bladder and its bile represent to the parents.
   • Circle text that shows the children's reactions to the gall bladder in lines 86–115.
   • In the margin, explain what the father tells Eugene about the gall bladder in lines 94–100.

108

It does not send an alarm, but Eugene raises an eyebrow and I lean forward.

bag. We reuse plastic bags often, and it could contain anything, a box of ice cream or a package of dried seaweed. It does not send an alarm, but Eugene 90 raises an eyebrow and I lean forward.

(E) "We have something for you. It will help you like it helped your father." Eugene nods, distracted. "Enough with the story. I get it! I have heard it all before. You had a lousy childhood . . ."

"Don't say that! I don't think you understand. I took the gall bladder of a bear and drank the bile! It reminded me of what I was working away from. I was working so I would have a better future. So I would have a better future than my past. My past is bile! You have to learn about your father. Who you are, you know?"

"You have to be tough, too," comments Mother.
100 "You will learn, too," says Father.

Mother hands the plastic bag to me, and goes to get a plate from the cupboard. The bag hisses open. Inside is a Ziploc bag, and inside it is a piece of flesh. It looks slimy like the innards of Foster Farm chickens. But this is larger than any chicken liver I've ever seen. It is pear-shaped and bruised in tones of blue and gray and brown. It is dying, deflating, defecating on itself. I fully expect it to pulse, but it lies still. It smells like a goat has parked itself in our kitchen.

Father gestures to me. "Open it! Take it out! Put it on the plate!" I take out the Ziploc bag and place it gingerly on the plate. Is this some kind of 110 sick sushi?

"Open it!" snaps Mother.
I recoil. Mother and Father are on some screwed-up Old World kick, and I duck out of view.

"I won't make you drink it like I did. You're not like me. You will taste it, that's all you need to do. But you will learn."

The gall bladder is from a bear. Its bile reminds the father of his past and the struggles he went through.

109

---

4. **REREAD AND CITE TEXT EVIDENCE**

(D) **ASK STUDENTS** to cite text evidence of what upsets the father. *Students should cite evidence from where the father explains himself in lines 59–63, 69, and 73–81.*

5. **READ AND CITE TEXT EVIDENCE**

(E) **ASK STUDENTS** to contrast the parents' and children's thoughts about the gall bladder. *Students should cite evidence that the bile reminds the parents of a difficult past and the desire to work toward a better future (lines 91, 95–97, 99). They should cite text evidence that the bile does not represent anything worthwhile to the children (lines 89–90, 92, 111, 112–113).*

Critical Vocabulary: synopsis (line 72) Ask students to determine the meaning of *synopsis* as it is used here.

WHEN STUDENTS STRUGGLE . . .

To help students compare and contrast the narrator and her father, invite them to work in small groups to discuss how lines 94–115 give insight into the two main characters, and the theme of the story.

CITE TEXT EVIDENCE Ask students to cite text evidence of the actions and words of the narrator and her father. Then ask them to discuss the theme of the story. At this point, what do they think is the author's message?

FOR ELL STUDENTS Draw students' attention to the phrase "Old World kick" (line 112). Ask them what "Old World" might refer to in this story. *It probably means Korea, in the past.* Ask if anyone knows the idiomatic usage of the word *kick* in this context. *It means "an obsessive interest."*

I can only tell you the before and the after, because I did not watch them feed Eugene the bile.

I leave the room. I hear my mother unwrap the gall bladder and snag it with chopsticks. I hear Eugene's footsteps, my father's commands, the rush 120 of water from the faucet. I imagine the bile as it fills Eugene's body with poison and drains his face of all the pink flesh, leaving it pinched and brittle.

In the hallway outside the kitchen, I am surrounded by childhood awards and family pictures: Father smokes thin white cigarettes, leaning against a white tree trunk with dark gray leaves. He is wearing black pants and a white undershirt. He is lean and tanned. His shoulders are held back at attention, and his skin is **taut**, his eyes open wide. His gaze rests on something soft and gentle. He is at the point of remembering . . .

taut:
tightly drawn

F
There's a picture of me at Disneyland, holding an ice cream cone. My 130 father has no pictures of himself as a child, and maybe that furthers the distance between us, because we have no proof that he was ever a child. He was born a jaw-clenching, wide-eyed man who drank bile.

Eugene brushes past me in the hall. "Move," he says.

I move. "Hey."

He looks up and past me.

"Never mind," I say. There are no words of healing.

In this way, we inherit suffering. But the bile does not strengthen Eugene. It flows within him, as it did within my father, but it does not give him strength and resolve. Only resentment.

140 Long after the gallbladder has become a solid rock of ice next to the ice cream, Father asks me, "Should you taste the bile, too?"

I want to shout, "No!" but I don't. I want to tell him that I think this is sick and perverted, but I don't. I know what I have to say. Like my father, I know how to survive.

I know the answer to this. My father coached me a million times.

"I'm a Hankook sahrahm. I understand why I need this bile, because I already have this bile."

Father nods. He walks out of the kitchen, his feet squeaking against the linoleum.

150 He leaves a wake of anger in his path, and my mother and I sponge it up. We don't want him to return and refuel; it's easier when he does not see what he does to us, even though I think he should. I sit on the stool and stare out the windows into the cul de sac.

Mother scurries around, washing dishes. "You know your father, he really lives just for you. He really loves you, but it comes out all wrong," she apologizes. I stare at her Han figure.

110

G H
I walk into the backyard and stare at the wall, covered in honeysuckle. The scent is sweet, and the drunken bees lumber slowly through the vines. The sun beats against me, and my plastic sandals mold against my feet and 160 stick slightly to the concrete path as they make "smuck-smuck" sounds on the patio pavers.

I've walked into a fireplace and I just want a little relief. I wonder what would happen if I could disappear. I wonder how mad my father would be. The neighbors' wall looms just ahead.

I drag one of the backyard benches over to the wall, and I sit in its shade. I cannot stay sitting for long. I stand on the bench to look over the wall into the neighbors' backyard. The Andersons are away on vacation, and we are on neighborhood watch.

Inside the house, I hear my father yelling at Eugene. Doors slam. My 170 mother makes kitchen noises, the clattering of dishes on countertop tile and porcelain sink. All this, amidst the bees and heat. I can either go inside the cool, poisonous house or melt outside.

My legs twitch. I've been standing still, stretched over the wall, and I ache. I have also been holding my breath. I let out a desperate exhalation. The Andersons' lot is on a higher elevation than ours; it would not be a long

She has to choose between the heat outside and the anger inside.

6. **REREAD** Reread lines 116–156. Summarize the narrator's response to her father's anger and his behavior. Support your answer with explicit textual evidence.

The narrator walks away from the angry scene. At first, she is reflective ("My father has no pictures of himself as a child . . ."). She tries to understand him. She is sensitive to her brother and knows tasting the bile has filled him with resentment, not strength. She avoids her father's rage by uniting herself with him ("I'm a Hankook sahrahm. I understand why I need this bile, because I already have this bile.").

7. **READ** As you read lines 157–184, continue to cite text evidence.
• In the margin, explain the narrator's conflict in lines 162–172.
• Underline text describing the narrator's desires.
• Circle text that describes a change in the narrator in lines 179–184.

111

Critical Vocabulary: taut (line 127) Ask students to determine the meaning of *taut* as it is used here. Why is the father's skin *taut* in the picture? *Students should understand that the picture is from when the father was much younger.*

6. **REREAD AND CITE TEXT EVIDENCE**

F **ASK STUDENTS** to read aloud and discuss their response with a partner. After their discussions, allow students to rewrite their response and add more textual evidence. *Students should cite evidence that the narrator becomes reflective about her father (lines 129–132), that she is sensitive to her brother (lines 137–139), and that she allies herself with her father to avoid the bile (lines 146–147).*

7. **READ AND CITE TEXT EVIDENCE**

G **ASK STUDENTS** to describe the narrator's experience outside. *Students should explain the narrator's conflict: outside it is hot, but inside it is angry (lines 171–172). They should cite evidence of her desire to disappear (lines 162–163), of the bee sting (lines 179–181), and evidence of how the pain is cathartic (lines 181–184).*

CLOSE READ
Notes

fall from the wall. I climb the wall slowly, so as not to anger the venomous bees, but I'm stung before I swing my leg over the top and fall into the Andersons' yard.

I limp to one of the lounge chairs and sit down. There's a welt on my leg
180 with a stinger pulsating in the middle of it. I pull it out, but the pain is still there. A dark part of me wells up and receives that pain. Out of my numbness arises the **cathartic** pain of a bee sting. It loosens the knot in my belly. I can breathe a little now. If I focus on the pain enough, the knot travels a little up my throat.

cathartic:
purifying or cleansing

---

8. ◀ REREAD Reread lines 157–161. What do you think the honeysuckle and the bees represent? Support your answer with explicit textual evidence.

Although the honeysuckle's "scent is sweet," it is full of bees. The sweetness of the honeysuckle might represent an escape that can only be achieved with a measure of hurt, a bee sting.

SHORT RESPONSE

Cite Text Evidence How do parallels between the characterizations of the narrator and the father point to a theme of the story? Review your reading notes, and **cite text evidence** in your response.

When the narrator experiences "cathartic pain," it parallels her father's experience of drinking bile. Whereas her father had the horrors of war in his past, the narrator wants to escape her dysfunctional, angry home, a "cool, poisonous house," symbolized by the sting of a bee. The theme of the story is the difficulty of family relationships and how suffering can be passed from generation to generation: "In this way we inherit suffering."

112

---

8.   REREAD AND CITE TEXT EVIDENCE

(H) **ASK STUDENTS** to discuss their response with a partner. *Answers will vary. Students may think the honeysuckle's "scent is sweet" so it represents an escape. However, it is full of bees, so the escape comes at a price.*

Critical Vocabulary: cathartic (line 182) Ask students to explain how the word *cathartic* ties the narrator to her father.

SHORT RESPONSE

Cite Text Evidence Student responses will vary, but they should cite evidence from the story to support their responses. Students should:

- analyze character interactions between the narrator and her father.
- determine a theme from the character development in the text.
- cite text evidence to support their response.

TO CHALLENGE STUDENTS . . .

For more context and a first-hand view of an American soldier's experience in the Korean War, students can view the video *Korea Vet Recalls War* in their eBooks.

ASK STUDENTS what was difficult for American and South Korean soldiers during the Korean War. In what significant way would the narrator's father's experience have been different from Sherman Pratt's? *Students should make the point that the fictional character would have been fighting in his own country.*

DIG DEEPER

With the class, return to Question 6, Reread. Have students share their responses.

ASK STUDENTS to discuss the narrator's reflections on her father throughout lines 116–156.

- What does the narrator do while her parents feed Eugene bile? *She leaves the room, but still listens. She imagines Eugene's response to the bile. She looks at family photos (lines 118–132).*
- How does the narrator describe the next exchange she has with her brother? *In line 136 she says "there are no words of healing."*
- What does the narrator say that she and her brother inherit? *She says they inherit suffering (line 137).*
- How does the narrator avoid Eugene's fate? *She gives her father a coached answer: "I understand why I need this bile, because I already have this bile" (lines 146–147).*
- What theme can be inferred from the narrator's reflections? *The story has a message that relates to pain in families.*

ASK STUDENTS to return to their Short Response answer and revise it based on the class discussion.

Cloudy Day

Poem by Jimmy Santiago Baca

Why This Text?

Students read poetry on their own and in class. Poetry offers readers the opportunity to relate to ideas, words, and feelings in unique ways. This lesson explores a poem's shift in tone and how that shift is key to the poem's theme.

View It!

Professional Development Podcast:

Text-Dependent Analysis

Key Learning Objective: The student will analyze how a poem's shift in tone contributes to its theme.

COMMON CORE Common Core Standards

RL 1 Cite textual evidence.

RL 2 Determine a theme and analyze its development.

RL 3 Analyze how complex characters develop, interact, and advance the plot.

RL 4 Analyze the impact of word choice on tone.

RL 5 Analyze an author's choices concerning how to structure a text.

SL 1a Come to discussions prepared.

SL 1c Propel conversations; incorporate others in discussion; clarify, verify, or challenge ideas.

SL 1d Respond to diverse perspectives; qualify their own views and make new connections.

L 1b Use various types of phrases.

L 5b Analyze nuances in the meaning of words with similar denotations.

▲ Text Complexity Rubric

Quantitative Measures	**Cloudy Day** **N/A**
Qualitative Measures	**Levels of Meaning/Purpose** single level of complex meaning
	Structure free verse, no particular patterns
	Language Conventionality and Clarity figurative, less accessible language
	Knowledge Demands moderately complex theme
Reader/Task Considerations	Teacher determined Vary by individual reader and type of text

Biography Have students read Baca's biography. Explain that Baca learned to read while in prison. There he realized his passion for poetry and began writing. A year after he was released, he published his first book of poems. Baca has dedicated his life to writing and teaching others, particularly those who are struggling with hardships and are working to overcome them.

AS YOU READ Direct students to use the As You Read note to focus their reading.

Analyze Tone (LINES 1–5, 7–12)　COMMON CORE RL 1, RL 4

Explain to students that **tone** is the poet's attitude toward a subject. Poets often communicate tone through their choice of words and details.

Ⓐ CITE TEXT EVIDENCE Have students identify words or phrases in the first stanza that reveal tone. *("wind crashes," "windows clunk," "iron frames," "seethes," "frightened cat," "empty spaces")* Ask students how the speaker feels about his situation based on this evidence. *(angry, frightened, closed-in, trapped)*

Tell students that writers often choose words because of their **connotations,** or the emotional responses associated with them. Since connotations can be positive or negative, they can provide clues to the tone of a poem.

Ⓑ CITE TEXT EVIDENCE Ask students what words in lines 7–12 have negative connotations. What feelings do these words convey? *("huddled," "haunches," "vigilant"; the words convey feelings of being trapped)*

Determine Figurative Meanings (LINES 1–12)　COMMON CORE RL 1, RL 4

Explain that poets often use **personification,** giving animals or objects human qualities. Personification often gives clues about the poem's tone.

Ⓒ CITE TEXT EVIDENCE Ask students what is being personified in lines 1–12. *(wind)* How do the wind's human-like qualities affect the speaker's attitude toward life in prison? *(The wind seething like a "frightened cat" shows the feeling of imprisonment, but the wind carrying "our words / over the fence" hints at a feeling of freedom.)*

Jimmy Santiago Baca (b. 1952) *was born in Santa Fe, New Mexico. Abandoned by his parents, Baca had a difficult childhood. In his early twenties, he was arrested and subsequently spent over five years in prison. Though locked up, Baca realized the liberating power of language when he began to read and write poetry. Baca has since written several volumes of poetry, essays, memoirs, and a screenplay. "Cloudy Day" first appeared in* Immigrants in Our Own Land, *Baca's first book of poetry, which was based on his time in prison.*

Cloudy Day

Poem by Jimmy Santiago Baca

AS YOU READ Notice the details that tell you about the author of this autobiographical poem. Write down any questions you generate during reading.

It is windy today. A wall of wind crashes against,　Ⓐ
windows clunk against, iron frames
as wind swings past broken glass
and seethes, like a frightened cat
5　in empty spaces of the cellblock.

In the exercise yard
we sat huddled in our prison jackets,　Ⓑ
on our haunches[1] against the fence,
and the wind carried our words
10　over the fence,
while the vigilant guard on the tower
held his cap at the sudden gust.

Ⓒ

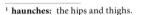

---
[1] **haunches:** the hips and thighs.

SCAFFOLDING FOR ELL STUDENTS

Reading Comprehension: Imagery Read aloud the two stanzas on this page, taking exaggerated pauses. Have students make note of any words they do not understand as they listen. After each pause, ask students to describe the mental image they have. Encourage several students to respond each time so as to share ideas. Then clarify words from the poem they don't understand.

Analyze Theme and Tone (LINES 13–23, 36–46)

COMMON CORE RL 1, RL 2, RL 3, RL 4

Remind students that the **theme** of a work is the message about life the writer wants to share. Writers develop the theme over the course of the work. Since a writer may not directly state the theme, readers can infer it, or make an educated guess, by noticing repeated ideas and the writer's tone toward them.

 ASK STUDENTS to identify what image recurs throughout the poem. *(the wind and its effects)* How do the wind and the speaker's attitude toward the wind change in stanzas 1–4? *(In the first stanza, the wind crashes and seethes; in stanza 2, the wind carries their words out of the prison yard; and in stanzas 3 and 4, the wind blows in his face and plays like a flute.)*

Explain that a writer's tone can change as the work progresses and the characters and events change.

E **CITE TEXT EVIDENCE** Ask students to summarize lines 36–46 and identify the tone, citing examples that support their responses. *(The speaker reflects on how he has seen imprisonment negatively affect the human spirit and how, despite that, he has held on to love and joy. The tone is one of hope and freedom ["I have everything, everything"].)*

Remind students that a writer's tone, particularly a tone that changes, can contribute to a work's theme.

F **ASK STUDENTS** how the tone has changed from the beginning to the end of the poem. *(The tone has changed from fear and powerlessness to empowerment and freedom.)* How do this shift in tone and the speaker's words in line 46 relate to the poem's theme? *(Despite the relentless bleakness of life in prison, the speaker has learned that he has the strength to maintain a spirit of hope and gratitude.)*

COLLABORATIVE DISCUSSION Have student pairs discuss possible incentives for Baca to write about his imprisonment. Share ideas as a class.

D

> I could see the main tower from where I sat,
> and the wind in my face
> 15 gave me the feeling I could grasp
> the tower like a cornstalk,
> and snap it from its roots of rock.
>
> The wind plays it like a flute,
> this hollow shoot of rock.
> 20 The brim girded² with barbwire
> with a guard sitting there also,
> listening intently to the sounds
> as clouds cover the sun.
>
> I thought of the day I was coming to prison,
> 25 in the back seat of a police car,
> hands and ankles chained, the policeman pointed,
>   "See that big water tank? The big
>   silver one out there, sticking up?
>   That's the prison."
>
> 30 And here I am, I cannot believe it.
> Sometimes it is such a dream, a dream,
> where I stand up in the face of the wind,
> like now, it blows at my jacket,
> and my eyelids flick a little bit,
> 35 while I stare disbelieving. . . .

E

> The third day of spring,
> and four years later, I can tell you,
> how a man can endure, how a man
> can become so cruel, how he can die
> 40 or become so cold. I can tell you this,
> I have seen it every day, every day,
> and still I am strong enough to love you,
> love myself and feel good;
> even as the earth shakes and trembles,
> 45 and I have not a thing to my name,
> I feel as if I have everything, everything.

COLLABORATIVE DISCUSSION With a partner, discuss your impression of the poem's speaker. Explain what incentive Baca might have had to write a poem about his imprisonment. Cite specific evidence from the text to support your ideas.

---

² **girded:** encircled, surrounded.

WHEN STUDENTS STRUGGLE . . .

Explain to students that similes and metaphors are types of figurative language that compare two things or ideas. **Similes** use the words *like* or *as*; **metaphors** do not. Figurative language communicates ideas beyond the literal meaning of the words and can make descriptions and unfamiliar ideas easier to understand. Recognizing figurative language can help students better understand the ideas in a poem.

Point out the simile in lines 15–16. Ask students what is being compared. *(tower and cornstalk)* Have them explain what they visualize and how the simile helps them understand how the speaker feels. *(He feels that he has the power to uproot the prison tower as easily as he could uproot a cornstalk.)* Encourage students to identify other examples of figurative language in the poem and the ideas the comparisons convey.

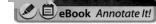

Analyze Theme and Tone

 COMMON CORE RL 2, RL 4

Tone is a writer's attitude toward his or her subject and audience. Writers convey tone through word choice and details. Sometimes, the tone of a work shifts as the author's attitude toward the subject matter changes to create a comprehensive view of the subject. For example, Baca creates an image of crouching, fearful animals early in this poem. Think about the tone this image implies. Then, consider how Baca uses language in the last stanza to express a very different tone.

A selection's tone contributes to its **theme**, or the underlying message the author wants to convey. Use these questions to analyze tone and theme in "Cloudy Day":

- How does the poet feel about his subject matter at the poem's beginning?
- How does the poet feel about his subject matter at the end of the poem?
- What does the shift in tone say about the speaker? What does it say about the nature of people?

Analyzing the Text

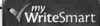 COMMON CORE RL 1, RL 2, RL 3, RL 4, RL 5, SL 1a

Cite Text Evidence   Support your responses with evidence from the selection.

1. **Infer** What words in lines 1–5 have strong connotations? How do these connotations affect the tone of the poem?

2. **Cite Evidence** What evidence does the poet provide in lines 13–17 about how the speaker feels? How do these lines contrast with the first two stanzas of the poem?

3. **Analyze** Lines 24–29 contain a flashback to four years earlier when the author arrived in prison. What purpose does the flashback serve?

4. **Interpret** How do the speaker's descriptions of and feelings about the wind change as the poem progresses? How does this shift show a change in the tone of the poem?

5. **Evaluate** What theme emerges by the end of the poem? How does Baca use contrasts to help build this theme?

 myWriteSmart

PERFORMANCE TASK

Speaking Activity: Discussion Consider the poet's use of imagery and repetition.

1. Make a list of details from the poem that appeal to any of your five senses, and label them as expressing either confinement or freedom. Also, list examples of repeated phrases or ideas in the poem, and label them the same way.

2. Bring your notes to a group discussion, and use them to analyze the themes of the poem.

3. At the end of the discussion, write a summary of how the discussion extended or challenged your ideas about the poem's theme.

Cloudy Day   **375**

Assign this performance task.   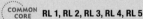 myWriteSmart

PERFORMANCE TASK

COMMON CORE SL 1a

Speaking Activity: Discussion Suggest that students create a chart like this one in which to record notes about imagery and repetition.

Sensory Details/Repeated Phrases or Ideas	Examples from Poem	Confinement or Freedom?

 PRACTICE & APPLY

Analyze Theme and Tone

COMMON CORE RL 2, RL 4

Review the terms *tone* and *theme* and how the tone at the beginning of the poem differs from the tone at the end. Then discuss the questions about how the poet feels about his subject matter at the beginning and end of the poem and what this shift says about human nature. *(The poet is disillusioned and powerless at the beginning of the poem, yet hopeful and empowered at the end. This shift in tone says that humans are resilient—they can be sad, but there is always hope. Also, hope and love can conquer despair and anger.)*

Analyzing the Text

COMMON CORE RL 1, RL 2, RL 3, RL 4, RL 5

Possible answers:

1. *The words "cellblock," "iron frames" and "seethes" have strong negative connotations. These words affect the tone of the poem because the wind and the place seem bleaker and colder. The tone is sad and desolate.*

2. *The speaker feels empowered in lines 13–17 because he thinks he can rip the tower out of the ground like a cornstalk. In the first two stanzas, the wind is powerful, not the people.*

3. *The flashback helps to show how the speaker has changed since the beginning of his prison term, when his situation was most difficult and hopeless.*

4. *The descriptions of and feelings about the wind at the beginning of the poem show that the wind is harsh, cold, unforgiving, and uncontrollable. By the end of the poem, the speaker can "stand up in the face of the wind," as it only makes his "eyelids flick a little bit."*

5. *The theme of freedom and power emerge by the end of the poem. Baca uses the wind to show how weak and trapped he is, but by the end of the poem, the speaker can stand up to the wind.*

Cloudy Day   **375**

Language and Style: Prepositional Phrases

Remind students that a preposition is always followed by a word or group of words that serves as its object. The preposition, its object, and modifiers of the object are called the prepositional phrase. Prepositional phrases may be used as adjectives or adverbs. Tell students that the prepositions in the chart are only some examples. Provide students with a list of additional prepositions and use them to create a prepositional phrase. *(against the wall, above the building, under the desk)*

Possible answers:

Students' answers will vary. Once students have completed their poems, they should be able to point to several examples of prepositional phrases. Have student pairs exchange their poems to identify the prepositional phrases and to confirm correct parallel structure.

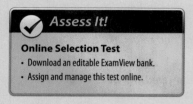

> ✓ ***Assess It!***
>
> **Online Selection Test**
> • Download an editable ExamView bank.
> • Assign and manage this test online.

Language and Style: Prepositional Phrases

Prepositions are words that show relationships between a noun or pronoun and another word in the sentence. The words *in, against,* and *over* are examples of prepositions. Prepositions are used in a phrase called a **prepositional phrase,** which includes the preposition plus a noun object. In his poem "Cloudy Day," Baca uses prepositional phrases to add detail and to create imagery. He also uses them to create rhythm and tone by employing prepositional phrases with parallel structure.

> Reread lines 7–10 from the poem:
>
> **we sat huddled in our prison jackets,**
> **on our haunches against the fence,**
> **and the wind carried our words**
> **over the fence,**

> The author could instead have written the lines this way:
>
> **we sat huddled**
> **and the wind carried our words**

This example lacks the detail of the first. Without the detail, the tone of the poem is more difficult to convey. This example also lacks rhythm. In lines 7–10, the author uses two prepositional phrases of equivalent lengths that end with the words *the fence.* The result is a parallel structure that creates rhythm and makes the poem more enjoyable to read.

Here are some other common prepositions:

Common Prepositions	
Preposition	**Example from the Poem**
in	in the exercise yard
of	of the cellblock
to	to the sounds
at	at my jacket
from	from where I sat

Practice and Apply Write a short poem on the topic of your choice. Use several prepositional phrases to add detail as well as rhythm through parallel structure.

Analyze Author's Choices: Text Structure

COMMON CORE

RL 5

TEACH

Explain to students that the structure of a literary work is the way it is put together. In poetry, structure refers to the arrangement of words and lines to produce a desired effect.

A common structural unit in a poem is the stanza, a group of lines that form a unit. Baca arranges his poem into seven stanzas. A stanza is sometimes characterized by a common pattern of meter, rhyme, and number of lines. However, Baca's stanzas do not display such characteristics. His poem is an example of **free verse.**

COLLABORATIVE DISCUSSION

Ask a student to read the first stanza aloud and identify if Baca uses a set rhythm or rhyme scheme. Discuss why he might have chosen to not use a specific style or form of poetry. Ask how not using a rhyme scheme or rhythm affects the poem. *(It sounds more like the way people talk every day.)* How does it make the speaker more realistic? *(If the poem were formal, the situation and speaker might seem unrealistic and the emotions might seem false.)*

Display the fifth stanza, and ask students what is different about its structure. *(It includes dialogue.)* Display the last stanza and ask students what is different about its structure. *(It is much longer than the other stanzas.)* Ask why Baca might have chosen to end the poem with such a long stanza. How does it help the reader understand the theme? *(The last stanza describes the speaker's inner life, which helps him overcome the physical hardships he faces. This stanza may be longer because it reveals the fully developed theme.)*

Vocabulary Strategy: Denotations and Connotations

COMMON CORE

L 5b

TEACH

Remind students that while the **denotations,** or dictionary meanings, of two words may be similar, their **connotations,** or associated attitudes and feelings, may be different. Writers, including poets, select words with specific connotations in order to relate deeper meanings.

Display the following sentence: "The tired runner was happy when she saw the finish line and happier when she crossed it." Underline *tired, happy, saw,* and *happier.* Then ask students to replace the underlined words with synonyms that have different connotations that convey deeper meanings and feelings. Have volunteers share their new sentences with the class and discuss the differences in connotation between the sentences. *(Sample sentence: The exhausted runner was elated when she glimpsed the finish line and overwhelmed when she crossed it.)*

Refer to the poem *Cloudy Day* to further demonstrate the difference between denotation and connotation. For example, in line 2, the poet says "A wall of wind crashes." A synonymous phrase might be "A gust of wind hits." This synonymous phrase doesn't convey the attitude of power that the writer feels the wind has at that point in the poem. The words *wall* and *crashes* associate more closely with an impact than do the words *gust* and *hits.*

PRACTICE AND APPLY

Have students review the notes they made about the details Baca uses to appeal to the senses in preparation for this selection's Performance Task. Ask students to select two or three of these examples. Then have students revise the details with synonymous words or phrases, and discuss how the revisions may change the meaning and tone of the poem.

 WORD SHARP Have students complete the following *WordSharp: Interactive Vocabulary Tutorial:* **Denotative and Connotative Meanings**

Respond in Discussions

TEACH

Before students begin work on the Performance Task, review how to participate in collaborative discussions.

- Set a clear purpose for the discussion.
- Pose and respond to questions to fully explore the theme of the discussion.
- Pose and respond to questions that expand the discussion by relating to broader themes or larger ideas without straying from the purpose of the discussion.
- Participate in the discussion and encourage others to do so by asking direct questions and by inviting opinions.
- Clarify points being made.
- Justify your own views.
- Challenge ideas and conclusions in a supportive, nonthreatening way.
- Respond thoughtfully and respectfully to differing points of view.
- Summarize points, noting areas of agreement and disagreement.
- Be willing to qualify or change your views based on evidence and reasoning presented during the discussion.

 INTERACTIVE LESSON Have students complete the tutorials in this lesson: **Participating in Collaborative Discussions**

PRACTICE AND APPLY

Have students use the guidelines above as they discuss Baca's use of imagery and repetition in the Performance Task. Remind them to use examples from the charts they created in preparation for this discussion. Encourage students to be open to other points of view, to clarify points that are unclear, and to challenge ideas that need to be verified.

Analyze Theme and Tone

RETEACH

Project *Cloudy Day* onto a whiteboard. Read the first two stanzas aloud and ask students to describe the images they visualize. *(wind blowing through broken-down prison; prisoners crouched against wall in exercise yard, passing time)* Explain that these images express the poet's attitude, or tone, toward the subject of the poem. Underline some words in these stanzas that indicate Baca's attitude. *(wind crashes, windows clunk, broken glass, seethes, frightened cat, sat huddled, vigilant guard)* Describe the tone as one of despair and powerlessness.

Have students repeat this exercise using the last stanza. Then have them describe how the tone has changed. *(It has changed from despair and powerlessness to hope, love, and empowerment.)*

Finally, relate this shift in tone to the poem's theme, or message. Ask students how the speaker's attitude changes during the poem and what this change says about people.

 LEVEL UP TUTORIALS Assign the following *Level Up* tutorial: **Tone**

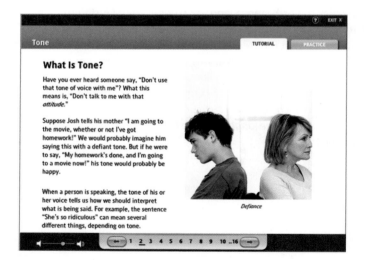

PRACTICE AND APPLY

Students can apply these skills to another poem. Have them work independently to identify images and language that convey the poet's tone in the poem. Ask students whether the tone remains the same or changes during the poem. Have them consider how the speaker's attitude relates to the poem's theme.

Write an Argument

COMMON CORE

W 1a–e Write arguments to support claims in an analysis.

W 9a–b Draw evidence from literary or informational texts.

The texts in this collection explore the struggle for freedom experienced in various contexts around the world and ways in which people fight to overcome oppression. Look back at the texts in this collection, including the anchor text, "Letter from Birmingham Jail," and consider this question: What constitutes true freedom? Synthesize your ideas about the texts by writing an argument about the meaning of freedom.

An effective argument

- makes a persuasive claim about what constitutes freedom
- develops the claim with valid reasons and relevant evidence from "Letter from Birmingham Jail" and two other texts from the collection
- anticipates counterclaims and addresses them with well-supported counterarguments
- uses transitions to link reasons and textual evidence to the claim
- includes a logically structured body
- has a satisfying conclusion that effectively summarizes the claim
- demonstrates appropriate, clear use of language, maintaining a formal tone through the use of standard English

PLAN

Make a Claim Consider the texts you have read in this collection and the ideas presented by each writer regarding oppression and what constitutes true freedom. Does the meaning of freedom vary from person to person and culture to culture, or is it possible to identify characteristics of freedom that apply to many cultures and contexts? Write a claim that clearly and concisely states your position on the meaning of freedom. Remember that you will need to provide sufficient evidence from the texts to convince your audience of your position.

*my*Notebook

Use the annotation tools in your eBook to find evidence that supports your ideas about freedom. Save each piece of evidence to your notebook.

ACADEMIC VOCABULARY

As you build your argument about freedom, be sure to use these words.

comprehensive
equivalent
incentive
innovate
media

WRITE AN ARGUMENT

COMMON CORE W 1a-e, W 9a-b

Introduce students to the Performance Task by reading the introductory paragraph with them and reviewing the criteria for an effective argument. Explain that their completed arguments should contain a developed persuasive claim that is strongly supported by textual evidence and counterarguments that address and logically refute the most likely counterclaims.

PLAN

MAKE A CLAIM

View It!

Professional Development Podcast:

Teaching Argument

As students shape the claim they will be making, remind them that their thesis should be detailed and debatable. They must pick a strong position and build a case for why their side of the argument is true. Their statements cannot be so simple or so obvious that no one would argue against them. Then once students have decided what point they will develop and argue, they can start thinking of reasons people might disagree with this point and use that as a guide when doing their research.

PERFORMANCE TASK

PLAN

GET ORGANIZED

Although students should always begin their essays by establishing firmly and clearly what position they will be taking, they have several options for how they might structure their subsequent points and evidence. They might alternate back and forth between introducing one of their views on a topic and then addressing a potential opposing view. They might order their arguments from strongest to weakest to second strongest or from second strongest to weakest to strongest. Point out that placing the weakest argument in the middle helps a writer begin and end on a forceful and compelling note.

PRODUCE

DRAFT YOUR ESSAY

Remind students that however they choose to order their examples and the arguments they are making, they should use transitions to move the audience from point to point. For example, phrases such as "to begin with," "secondly," "in addition," and "furthermore" help indicate that an argument is moving to the next point.

Gather Evidence Review the texts from this collection. Focus on the anchor text and two other selections that have information you can cite to support your position.

- Reread "Letter from Birmingham Jail," taking notes on the true meaning of freedom as presented by Martin Luther King Jr.
- Choose two other texts from the collection, noting relevant ideas about freedom in those texts as well.
- Think about potential **counterclaims,** or claims that oppose your position. Search for additional evidence to support the arguments you will make to refute those counterclaims.
- Pay attention to specific details, examples, and quotations as you gather evidence from all three texts.

Get Organized Organize your notes in an outline. Be sure to integrate any new information gathered from the additional sources.

- Begin with a claim that states your position on the meaning of freedom.
- Outline several reasons that support your claim.
- Provide textual evidence such as details, examples, or quotations for each claim.
- Write down at least one likely counterclaim, and develop a counterargument for it. Include specific reasons and evidence to support your counterargument.
- Jot down ideas for a comprehensive conclusion that synthesizes your ideas in a final summary.

PRODUCE

Draft Your Essay Write a draft of your essay, following your outline. As you write your first draft, consider your purpose and audience. Who is going to read your essay? Which of your ideas will be the most persuasive to your readers? Your tone and word choices should be appealing and targeted toward them.

- Introduce your claim. Present your argument in a memorable way that will grab the attention of your readers.
- Present your reasons, evidence, and counterarguments in logically ordered paragraphs.
- Explain how the evidence from the texts supports your ideas about the meaning of freedom.
- Include transitions to connect your reasons and evidence to your claim.

myWriteSmart

Write your rough draft in *my*WriteSmart. Focus on getting your ideas down, rather than perfecting your choice of language.

- Use formal language and a respectful tone appropriate for an academic context.
- Write a conclusion that summarizes your position. You might include powerful quotation or a call to action that encourages your readers to promote freedom as you have defined it.

REVISE

Improve Your Draft Refer to the chart on the following page to review the characteristics of an effective argument. Ask yourself these questions as you revise:

- Does my the introduction to my argument sound strong, confident, and persuasive?
- Have I provided sufficient evidence to support claims and counterarguments?
- Is my essay cohesive? Do I need additional transitions to make connections clear?
- Have I used a formal style of English and an objective tone?
- Does my conclusion follow logically from the body of my essay and provide an effective summary of my argument?

PRESENT

Exchange Essays When your final draft is completed, exchange essays with a partner. Read your partner's argument and provide feedback. Do you understand your partner's position? Did your partner successfully persuade you? Be sure to point out aspects of the essay that are particularly strong, as well as areas that could be improved.

myWriteSmart

Have your partner or a group of peers review your draft in myWriteSmart. Ask your reviewers to note any reasons that do not support the claim or that lack sufficient evidence.

REVISE

IMPROVE YOUR DRAFT

When revising, students should check bigger issues like whether the logic of their arguments holds up before dealing with smaller ones like editing their word choices to use more persuasive terms. Caution them to check their arguments to make sure they are not relying on stereotypes, resorting to unsupported emotional appeals, or overgeneralizing.

PRESENT

EXCHANGE ESSAYS

If time permits, let students share their papers with two partners, pairing each student first with a fellow student who took a similar position on the issue and next with a fellow student who took an opposing view. Have students compare the evidence and examples they used to support their arguments and evaluate the strength of the points each side is making.

PERFORMANCE TASK

IDEAS AND EVIDENCE

Have students look at the chart and identify how they did on the Performance Task in the Ideas and Evidence category. Ask them to consider how well they anticipated and addressed counterclaims. Have students list any counterclaims they overlooked along with a few sentences refuting each one.

COLLECTION 6 TASK
ARGUMENTATIVE ESSAY

	Ideas and Evidence	Organization	Language
ADVANCED	• The introduction is memorable and persuasive; the claim clearly states a position on the topic. • Valid reasons and relevant evidence from the texts convincingly support the claim. • Counterclaims are anticipated and effectively addressed with counterarguments. • The concluding section effectively summarizes the claim.	• The reasons and textual evidence are organized consistently and logically throughout the argument. • Varied transitions logically connect reasons and textual evidence to the writer's claim.	• The writing reflects a formal style and an objective, controlled tone. • Sentence beginnings, lengths, and structures vary and have a rhythmic flow. • Spelling, capitalization, and punctuation are correct. • Grammar and usage are correct.
COMPETENT	• The introduction states a clear position on an issue. • Most reasons and evidence from the texts support the writer's claim. • Counterclaims are anticipated, but the counterarguments need to be developed more. • The concluding section restates the claim.	• The organization of reasons and textual evidence is generally clear. • Transitions usually connect reasons and textual evidence to the writer's claim.	• The style is mostly formal, but the tone is occasionally subjective. • Sentence beginnings, lengths, and structures vary somewhat. • Spelling, capitalization, or punctuation mistakes occur but are not distracting. • Grammatical and usage errors occur but do not interfere with the writer's message.
LIMITED	• The introduction is ordinary; the claim identifies an issue, but the writer's position is not clearly stated. • The reasons and evidence from the texts are not always logical or relevant. • Counterclaims are anticipated but not addressed logically. • The concluding section includes an incomplete summary of the claim.	• The organization of reasons and textual evidence is logical in some places, but it often doesn't follow a pattern. • Many more transitions are needed to connect reasons and textual evidence to the writer's position.	• The style is informal in many places, and the tone is often dismissive of other viewpoints. • Sentence structures barely vary, and some fragments or run-on sentences are present. • Spelling, capitalization, and punctuation are often incorrect. • Grammar and usage are incorrect in many places, causing some confusion.
EMERGING	• The introduction is missing. • Significant supporting reasons and evidence from the texts are missing. • Counterclaims are not addressed. • The concluding section is missing.	• An organizational strategy is not evident; reasons and evidence are presented randomly. • Transitions are not used, making the argument difficult to understand.	• The style is inappropriate, and the tone is disrespectful. • Many fragments and run-on sentences make the writing hard to follow. • Spelling and capitalization are often incorrect, and punctuation is missing. • Many grammatical and usage errors change the meaning of the writer's ideas.

TEACHER NOTE:
The page numbers to the left indicate pages in the Student Edition. Except for the two entries below, the page numbers in the Student Edition and the Teacher's Edition correspond.

Writing Arguments

Many of the Performance Tasks in this book ask you to craft an argument in which you support your ideas with text evidence. Any argument you write should include the following sections and characteristics.

Introduce Your Claim

Clearly state your **claim**—the point your argument makes. As needed, provide context or background information to help readers understand your position. Note the most common opposing views as a way to distinguish and clarify your ideas. From the very beginning, make it clear for readers why your claim is strong; consider providing an overview of your reasons or a quotation that emphasizes your view in your introduction.

EXAMPLES

Vague claim: We need more lunch choices.	**Precise claim:** Our school district should allow fast-food restaurants to offer nutritious menu items in the school cafeteria.
Not distinguished from opposing view: There are plenty of people who consider fast food bad.	**Distinguished from opposing view:** While some people consider all fast food unhealthful, the facts say differently.
Confusing relation-ship of ideas: Teens need more choices. Fast food is enjoyed by people of all ages.	**Clear relationship of ideas:** Access to healthful fast-food lunch choices will improve student morale and provide revenue to the school.

Develop Your Claim

The body of your argument must provide strong, logical reasons for your claim and must support those reasons with relevant evidence. A **reason** tells why your claim is valid; **evidence** provides specific examples that illustrate a reason. In the process of developing your claim you should also refute **counterclaims**, or opposing views, with equally strong reasons and evidence. To demonstrate that you have thoroughly considered your view, provide a well-rounded look at both the strengths and limitations of both your claim and opposing claims. The goal is not to undercut your argument, but rather to answer your readers' potential objections to it. Be sure, too, to consider how much your audience may already know about your topic in order to avoid boring or confusing your readers.

EXAMPLES

Claim lacking reasons: Fast-food menu items would be a good thing because students would enjoy them.	**Claim developed by reasons:** Among the benefits of offering fast-food menu choices are a potential increase in student morale and increased cafeteria revenue for the school.
Omission of limitations: The boring old people opposed to this idea deny that there is virtually no downside to the plan.	**Fair discussion of limitations:** We should not dismiss nutritional concerns. Plans for offering fast food options should investigate healthful possibilities.
Inattention to audience's knowledge: Information about minimum daily nutri-tional requirements, chemical additives, and cholesterol-increasing foods is a critical aspect of the plan.	**Awareness of audience's knowledge:** Readers unfamiliar with fast-food menu options may be surprised to learn that many fast food restaurants now offer nutritionally balanced, low-fat items.

Link Ideas

Even the strongest reasons and evidence will fail to sway readers if it is unclear how the reasons relate to the central claim of an argument. Make the connections clear for your readers, using not only transitional words and phrases, but also using clauses and even entire sentences as a bridge between ideas you have already discussed and ideas you are introducing.

EXAMPLES

Transitional word linking claim and reason: Students who buy their lunch from the cafeteria bring hundreds of dollars into the school each day. <u>Consequently,</u> well-chosen offerings of fast-food items would be an important source of revenue for the school.

Transitional phrase linking reason and evidence: Providing fast-food menu items would improve student morale. <u>In fact,</u> the school district's chief dietitian comments that "more healthful options would address students' complaints about boring lunches."

Transitional clause linking claim and counterclaim: The benefits of offering these menu options are clear. <u>Those opposed to the plan, though, would say otherwise:</u> They feel that there is too much potential for school-sponsored poor nutrition.

Use Appropriate Style and Tone

An effective argument is most often written in a direct and formal style. The style and tone you choose in an argument should not be an afterthought; the way you express your argument can either drive home your ideas or detract from them. Even as you argue in favor of your viewpoint, take care to remain objective in tone. Avoid using loaded language when discussing opposing claims.

EXAMPLES

Informal style: Offering fast-food menu options will be way cool.	**Formal style:** Because expanding the lunch menu provides a range of benefits, it is logical for the school district to approve the plan.
Biased tone: It doesn't make any sense to be against this plan.	**Objective tone:** Arguments opposing this plan have been refuted by evidence from many sources.
Inattention to conventions: We need to make this dream a reality!	**Attention to conventions:** This proposal, which will greatly benefit our school, deserves school district attention.

Conclude Your Argument

Your conclusion may range from a sentence to a full paragraph, but it must wrap up your argument in a satisfying way; a conclusion that sounds tacked-on helps your argument no more than providing no conclusion at all. A strong conclusion is a logical extension of the argument you have presented. It carries forth your ideas through an inference, question, quotation, or challenge.

EXAMPLES

Inference: Building lifelong healthful eating habits begins at school.

Question: Who doesn't want to have the choice of carefully selected fast-food menu items?

Quotation: As the sophomore class president points out, "The school district and cafeteria manager can promote student engagement and improve morale by providing new lunch menu choices."

Challenge: Menu options of this type make the difference between an average school cafeteria and a truly responsive one.

Writing Informative Essays

COMMON CORE

Many of the Performance Tasks in this book ask you to write informational or explanatory texts in which you present a topic and examine it thoughtfully, through a well-organized analysis of relevant content. Any informative or explanatory text that you create should include the following parts and features.

Introduce Your Topic

Develop a strong **thesis statement.** That is, clearly state your topic and the organizational framework through which you will connect or distinguish elements of your topic. For example, you might state that your text will compare ideas, examine causes and effects, or explore a problem and its solutions.

EXAMPLE

Topic: *Urban Sprawl*
Sample Thesis Statements
Compare-contrast: The statistics on suburban growth currently and two decades ago reveal the extent of urban sprawl in our community.
Cause-effect: A problem now for more than 50 years, urban sprawl affects the health of both cities and rural areas.
Problem-solution: Our city faces a growing problem with urban sprawl, but through strategic city planning we can manage the issue.

Clarifying the organizational framework up front will help you organize the body of your text, suggest headings you can use to guide your readers, and help you identify graphics that you may need to clarify information. For example, if you analyze causes and effects of urban sprawl, you might create a chart like the one shown to guide your writing. Each row will constitute a separate paragraph.

Overall cause: urban sprawl	**Overall effects:** • damages city's economic and human resources • endangers farmland
Cause: suburbs grow	**Effects:** • population loss in city • loss of jobs in city • brain drain from city
Cause: brain drain from city	**Effect:** decline in school quality in city
Cause: redirection of resources to suburbs	**Effect:** decline in urban centers

Develop Your Topic

In the body of your essay, flesh out the organizational framework you established in your introduction with strong supporting paragraphs. Include only support directly relevant to your topic. Don't rely only on a single source, and make sure the sources you do use are reputable and current. The following table illustrates types of support you might use to develop aspects of your topic. It also shows how transitions link text sections, create cohesion, and clarify the relationships among ideas.

Types of Support	Uses of Transitions
Statistics: One effect of urban sprawl is the loss of farmland; for example, 332,800 acres of farmland in Texas were lost to suburban development between 1992 and 1997.	*One effect* signals the shift from the introduction to the body text in a cause-and-effect essay. *For example* introduces the statistical support for the effect being cited.
Concrete details: Cities also experience a "brain drain"; consequently, the quality of city schools declines.	*Consequently* transitions the reader from a cause to its effect in a cause-and-effect essay.
Facts and examples: Turn to legislation in the city of Portland, Oregon, if you want to see "smart growth" that preserves farmland and expands downtown housing options.	The entire transitional sentence introduces the part of a cause-and-effect essay that summarizes the positive effects of urban sprawl.

You can't always include all of the information you'd like to in a short essay, but you can plan to point readers directly to useful **multimedia links** either in the body or at the end of your essay.

Use Appropriate Style and Tone

Use formal English to establish your credibility as a source of information. To project authority, use the language of the domain, or field, that you are writing about. However, be sure to define unfamiliar terms to avoid using jargon your audience may not know. Provide extended definitions when your audience is likely to have limited knowledge of the topic.

Using quotations from reputable sources can also give your text authority; be sure to credit the source of quoted material. In general, keep the tone objective, avoiding slang or biased expressions.

Informal, jargon-filled, biased language: Portland, Oregon, a very cool city out there on the edge of the continent, has put a cap on exploding suburbs.

Extended definition in formal style and objective tone: One good example of an urban area that has applied the ideas of smart growth is Portland, Oregon; the city has curbed urban sprawl through legislation, community activism, and efficient city growth.

Conclude Your Essay

Wrap up your essay with a concluding statement or section that sums up or extends the information in your essay.

EXAMPLES

Articulate implications: Urban sprawl threatens cities and rural areas, robbing urban communities of population and resources and gobbling up farmland for development.

Emphasize significance: With the country's population increasing, the loss of prime farmland to strip malls and apartment complexes is a serious problem that will affect our nation's economy for decades to come.

Writing Narratives

When you are writing a fictional tale, an autobiographical incident, or a firsthand biography, you write in the narrative mode. That means telling a story with a beginning, a climax, and a conclusion. Though there are important differences between fictional and nonfiction narratives, you will use similar processes to develop them.

Identify a Problem, Situation, or Observation

For a nonfiction narrative, dig into your memory bank for a problem you dealt with or an observation you've made about your life. For fiction, try to invent a problem or situation that can unfold in interesting ways.

EXAMPLES

Problem (nonfiction)	Last year I wanted overcome my fear of public speaking.
Situation (fiction)	A high-school tennis player is anxious about asking a classmate for a date.

Establish a Point of View

Decide who will tell your story. If you are writing a reflective essay about an important experience or person in your own life, you will be the narrator of the events you relate. If you are writing a work of fiction, you can choose to create a first-person narrator or tell the story from the third-person point of view. In that case, the narrator can focus on one character or reveal the thoughts and feelings of all the characters. The examples below show the differences between a first- and third-person narrator.

First-person narrator (nonfiction example)	Standing up to give a speech to my classmates shouldn't have made my hands shake and my stomach turn somersaults, but it did last year.
Third-person narrator (fiction example)	After English class, Carlos asked Peter if he had asked Maggie out on a date yet. It was all Peter could do to respond calmly. He really wanted to blurt out—to scream out—that everyone should just let him ask her out when he was good and ready.

Gather Details

To make real or imaginary experiences come alive on the page, you will need to use narrative techniques like description and dialogue. The questions in the left column in the chart below can help you search your memory or imagination for the details that will form the basis of your narrative. You don't have to respond in full sentences, but try to capture the sights, sounds, and feelings that bring your narrative to life.

Who, What, When, Where?	Narrative Techniques
People: Who are the people or characters involved in the experience? What did they look like? What did they do? What did they say?	**Description:** Peter's friend Carlos, also on the tennis team and friend to Peter since Carlos transferred to the high school least year. **Dialogue:** Carlos said, "You should just ask her out, Peter. If you don't, someone else probably will." Peter replied sharply, "I'm just waiting for the right moment, okay?"
Experience: What led up to or caused the event? What is the main event in the experience? What happened as a result of the event?	**Description:** Peter liked Maggie but was too shy to ask her out on a date. He had a jumpy feeling in his stomach, tight muscles, and insomnia. He was grumpy and short-tempered, so his mother suggested he try a yoga class at school. He resisted trying new things like yoga. After falling asleep in class and being stopped by the hall monitor, Peter ended up in the gym, where the yoga class was just beginning. And there was Maggie, right next to the spot where he placed his yoga mat. She smiled at him.

continued

Who, What, When, Where?	Narrative Techniques
Places: When and where did the events take place? What were the sights, sounds, and smells of this place?	**Description:** Spring of ninth grade: It was the first year of high school and everyone felt both confident and insecure at the same time. Spring meant tennis tournaments on brisk, sunny days and first thoughts about the dances that would end the year.

Sequence Events

Before you begin writing, list the key events of the experience or story in **chronological,** or time, order. Place a star next to the point of highest tension—for example, the point at which a key decision determines the outcome of events. In fiction, this point is called the **climax,** but a gripping nonfiction narrative will also have a climactic event.

To build **suspense**—the uncertainty a reader feels about what will happen next—you'll want to think about the pacing or rhythm of your narrative. Consider disrupting the chronological order of events by beginning at the end, then going back in time to earlier events. Or, interrupt the forward progression or flow of events with a **flashback,** which takes the reader to an earlier point in the narrative.

Another way to build suspense is with multiple plot lines. For example, in the fictional narrative, Peter's anxiety about asking Maggie for a date involves a second plot line in which he has to overcome his hesitancy about trying something new and taking yoga. Both plot lines intersect when Peter goes to yoga class, and as a result ends up next to Maggie, who smiles at him.

Use Vivid Language

As you revise, make an effort to use vivid language. Use precise words and phrases to describe feelings and actions. Use telling details to show, rather than directly state, what a character is like. Use **sensory language** that lets readers see, feel, hear, smell, and taste what you or your characters experienced.

First Draft	Revision
Peter could barely stay awake in class.	Peter floated in a half-wakeful state through his next four classes. [telling details]
Peter went down to the kitchen.	The stairs groaned tiredly under Peter's steps. He also groaned tiredly as he plopped down at the kitchen table. [precise words and phrases]
He had no appetite at lunch.	At lunch, Peter found his stomach was too knotted to let him eat. [sensory details]

Conclude Your Story

At the conclusion of the narrative, you or your narrator will reflect on the meaning of the events. The conclusion should follow logically from the climactic moment of the narrative. The narrator of a personal narrative usually reflects on the significance of the experience—the lessons learned or the legacy left. A fictional narrative will end with the resolution of the conflict described over the course of the story.

EXAMPLE

Peter breathed in. He dared to look around. Maggie was right next to him. He choked a little and coughed. She glanced over and smiled warmly. Peter smiled back and took his first deep breath in days. Maybe yoga wasn't such a bad idea after all.

SEQUENCE EVENTS
Remind students to write legibly as they develop their lists of key events.

Conducting Research

Some Performance Tasks in this book will require you to complete research projects related to the texts you've read in the collections. Whether the topic is stated in a Performance Task or is one you generate, the following information will guide you through your research project.

Focus Your Research and Formulate a Question

Some topics for a research project can be effectively covered in three pages; others require an entire book for a thorough treatment. Begin by developing a topic that is neither too narrow nor too broad for the time frame of the assignment. Also, check your school and local libraries and databases to help you determine how to choose your topic. If there's too little information, you'll need to broaden your focus; if there's too much, you'll need to limit it.

With a topic in hand, formulate a research question; it will keep you on track as you conduct your research. A good research question cannot be answered in a single word and should be open-ended. It should require investigation. You can also develop related research questions to explore your topic in more depth.

EXAMPLES

Possible topics about Julius Caesar, the Roman emperor	• Famous assassinations in history—too broad • Popularity of soothsayers in Roman times—too narrow • Historical figures—fact or fiction?
Possible research question	What was the real Julius Caesar like?
Related questions	• How much of *Julius Caesar,* Shakespeare's play, based on historical fact? • How did historians of Caesar's time describe him?

Locate and Evaluate Sources

To find answers to your research question, you'll need to investigate primary and secondary sources, whether in print or digital formats. **Primary sources** contain original, firsthand information, such as diaries, autobiographies, interviews, speeches, and eyewitness accounts. **Secondary sources** provide other people's versions of primary sources in encyclopedias, newspaper and magazine articles, biographies, and documentaries.

Your search for sources begins at the library and on the World Wide Web. Use **advanced search features** to help you find things quickly. For example, add a minus sign (-) before a word that should not appear in your results or use an asterisk (*) in place of unknown words. List the name of and location of each possible source, adding comments about its potential usefulness. Assessing, or evaluating, your sources is an important step in the research process. Your goal is to use sources that are **credible,** or reliable and trustworthy.

Criteria for Assessing Sources	
Relevance: It covers the target aspect of my topic.	• How will the source be useful in answering my specific research question?
Accuracy: It includes information that can be verified by more than one authoritative source.	• Is the information up-to-date? Are the facts accurate? How can I verify them? • What qualifies the author to write about this topic? Is he or she an authority?
Objectivity: It presents multiple viewpoints on the topic.	• What, if any, biases can I detect? Does the writer favor one view of the topic?

Incorporate and Cite Source Material

When you draft your research project, you'll need to include material from your sources. This material can be direct quotations, summaries, or paraphrases of the original source material. Two well-known style manuals provide information on how to cite a range of print and digital sources: the *MLA Handbook for Writers of Research Papers* (published by the Modern Language Association) and Kate L. Turabian's *A Manual for Writers* (published by The University of Chicago Press). Both style manuals provide a wealth of information about conducting, formatting, drafting, and presenting your research, including guidelines for citing sources within the text (called parenthetical citations) and preparing the list of Works Cited, as well as correct use of the mechanics of writing. Your teacher will indicate which style manual you should use. The following examples use the format in the *MLA Handbook*.

EXAMPLES

Direct quotation [The writer is citing the description given by Roman historian Suetonius.]	In his biographical text *The Lives of the Caesars,* the Roman historian Suetonius describes Caesar as "tall of stature, with a fair complexion, shapely limbs, a somewhat full face, and keen black eyes" (45).
Summary [The writer is summarizing the conclusion in an article about Roman government.]	Rome's republican government was made up of consuls, praetors, a senate, and people's assemblies. The position of dictator was temporary and only used during emergencies.
Paraphrase [The writer is paraphrasing, or stating in his own words, material from an article about the nature of Rome's government during Caesar's time.]	During Caesar's time, Rome was a republic. Two consuls with equal authority were the leaders. Senators suggested laws, and general assemblies voted on whether to approve the suggestions. The position of dictator was used only when there were serious outbreaks of lawlessness.

Any material from sources must be completely documented, or you will commit **plagiarism,** the unauthorized use of someone else's words or ideas. Plagiarism is not honest. As you take notes for your research project, be sure to keep complete information about your sources so that you can cite them correctly in the body of your paper. This applies to all sources, whether print or digital. Having complete information will also enable you to prepare the list of Works Cited. The list of Works Cited, which concludes your research project, provides author, title, and publication information for both print and digital sources. The following section shows the *MLA Handbook's* Works Cited citation formats for a variety of sources.

INCORPORATE AND CITE SOURCE MATERIAL
Remind students to write legibly as they take notes.

MLA Citation Guidelines

Today, you can find free Web sites that generate ready-made citations for research papers, using the information you provide. Although using such sites can save you some time, always check your citations carefully before you turn in your final paper. If you are following MLA style, use these guidelines to evaluate and finalize your work.

Books

One author

Schanzer, Ernest. *The Problem Plays of Shakespeare.* New York: Schocken, 1965.

Two authors or editors

McIver, Bruce, and Ruth Stevenson, eds. *Teaching Shakespeare: Critics in the Classroom.* Newark: U of Delaware Press, 1994. Print.

Three authors

Bennett, Josephine W., Oscar Cargill, and Vernon Hall, Jr., eds. *Studies in the English Renaissance Drama.* New York: New York UP, 1959. Print.

Four or more authors

The abbreviation et al. means "and others." Use et al. instead of listing all the authors.

Wells, Stanley, et al. *The Complete Works of William Shakespeare.* New York: Oxford UP, 1986. Print.

No author given

Elizabethan Literature. New York: Capital, 1957. Print.

An author and a translator

Suetonius. *Lives of the Caesars.* Trans. Catherine Edwards. New York: Oxford UP, 2000. Print.

An author, a translator, and an editor

Moretti, Salvatore. *Essays on Julius Caesar.* Trans. Jonathan Walsh. Ed. Louis Kind. New York: Devonshire, 1962. Print.

Parts of Books

An introduction, a preface, a foreword, or an afterword written by someone other than the author(s) of a work

Heminge, John, and Henry Condell. Preface. *Dramatic Works of Shakespeare.* Edinburgh: William Peterson, 1883. Print.

A poem, a short story, an essay, or a chapter in a collection of works by one author

Roe, John. " 'Character' in Plutarch and Shakespeare: Brutus, Julius Caesar, and Mark Antony." *Shakespeare and the Classics.* Ed. Charles Martindale and A. B. Taylor. New York: Cambridge, 2004. Print.

A novel or a play in an anthology

Shakespeare, William. *The Tragedy of Julius Caesar.* Ed. John Jowett. *William Shakespeare: The Complete Works.* Ed. Stanley Wells and Gary Taylor. Compact ed. Oxford: Clarendon, 1988. 599–626. Print.

Magazines, Newspapers, and Encyclopedias

An article in a newspaper

Weber, Bruce. "Power Play: "Friends, Generals and Captains of Industry, Lend Me Your Ears.'" *New York Times* 31 Jan. 2005: B1+. Print.

An article in a magazine

Tynan, William. "Cleopatra." *Time* 24 May 1999: 37–38. Print.

An article in an encyclopedia

"Julius Caesar." *Encyclopaedia Britannica.* 2004 ed. Print.

Miscellaneous Print and Nonprint Sources

An interview

Covington, Nigel. Personal Interview. 1 Feb. 2011.

A video recording

Julius Caesar. Lions Gate, 2000. DVD.

Electronic Publications

A CD-ROM

"Antony, Mark." *Britannica Student Encyclopedia.* 2004 ed. Chicago: Encyclopaedia Britannica, 2004. CD-ROM.

A document from an Internet site

Entries for online sources should contain as much of the information shown as available.

Author or compiler | Title or description of document
Vernon, Jennifer. | "Ides of March Marked Murder of Julius Caesar."

Title of Internet site | Site sponsor | Date of Internet site
National Geographic News. | Natl. Geographic Soc. | 12 Mar. 2004.

Medium of publication | Date of access
Web. | 18 May 2011.

Participating in a Collaborative Discussion

Often, class activities, including the Performance Tasks in this book, will require you to work collaboratively with classmates. Whether your group will analyze a work of literature or try to solve a community problem, use the following guidelines to ensure a productive discussion.

Prepare for the Discussion

A productive discussion is one in which all the participants bring useful information and ideas to share. If your group will discuss a short story the class read, first reread and annotate a copy of the story. Your annotations will help you quickly locate evidence to support your points. Participants in a discussion about an important issue should first research the issue and bring notes or information sources that will help guide the group. If you disagree with a point made by another group member, your case will be stronger if you back it up with specific evidence from your sources.

EXAMPLES

Disagreeing without evidence: I don't think Shakespeare is relevant today because nobody talks like that.

Providing evidence for disagreement: I disagree about Shakespeare's relevance because his language is so hard for modern kids to understand. For example, in *Macbeth,* Banquo tells the witches, "My noble partner / You greet with present grace and great prediction / Of noble having and of royal hope, / That he seems rapt withal." Who can figure that out? Maybe if it said, "My friend here is so stunned about what you've said— that he's been promoted and will one day be king—that he seems like he's in a trance," kids today would find it relevant. An idea that's this simple shouldn't be so complicated to unravel.

Set Ground Rules

The rules your group needs will depend on what your group is expected to accomplish. A discussion of themes in a poem will be unlikely to produce a single consensus; however, a discussion aimed at developing a solution to a problem should result in one strong proposal that all group members support. Answer the following questions to set ground rules that fit your group's purpose:

- What will this group produce? A range of ideas, a single decision, a plan of action, or something else?

- How much time is available? How much of that time should be allotted to each part of our discussion (presenting ideas, summarizing or voting on final ideas, creating a product such as a written analysis or speech)?

- What roles need to be assigned within the group? Do we need a leader, a note-taker, a timekeeper, or other specific roles?

- What is the best way to synthesize our group's ideas? Should we take a vote, list group members as "for" or "against" in a chart, or use some other method to reach consensus or sum up the results of the discussion?

Move the Discussion Forward

Everyone in the group should be actively involved in synthesizing ideas. To make sure this happens, ask questions that draw out ideas, especially from less-talkative members of the group. If an idea or statement is confusing, try to paraphrase it, or ask the speaker to explain more about it. If you disagree with a statement, say so politely and explain in detail why you disagree.

SAMPLE DISCUSSION

JACK: How about you, Ella? Do you think Shakespeare is relevant to today's teenagers? The rest of us say he is.	*Question draws out quiet member*
ELLA: Well, I don't know. I see how people refer to Shakespeare all the time in movies and commercials and things, but he talks so much about rich, important people with servants and power. That doesn't have anything to do with me or my friends.	*Response relates discussion to larger ideas*
DANTE: But don't people in power have some of the same problems regular people do? I mean, everybody wants love and respect, right?	*Question challenges Ella's conclusion*
ELLA: Sure, but then why not have Macbeth be a regular guy scheming to get the woman he loves or his boss's approval or something? Why does everybody have to be royalty?	*Response elaborates on ideas*
VIVIAN: So you mean that people's struggles are different depending on their class? I can see that, but Shakespeare's plays were really popular with the common people in his time, so it seems like people can identify with his characters despite their differences.	*Paraphrases idea and challenges it further based on evidence*

Respond to Ideas

In a diverse group, everyone may have a different perspective on the topic of discussion, and that's a good thing. Consider what everyone has to say, and don't resist changing your view if other group members provide convincing evidence for theirs. If, instead, you feel more strongly than ever about your view,

don't hesitate to say so and provide reasons related to what those with opposing views have said. Before wrapping up the discussion, try to sum up the points on which your group agrees and disagrees.

SAMPLE DISCUSSION

VIVIAN: OK, we just have a few more minutes. What does everybody think? Do we want to take a vote?	*Vivian and Jack try to summarize points of agreement*
JACK: Sure. I think the three positions are YES, NO, and YES, BUT. . . . Does that sound right?	
DANTE: Yeah, let's make a chart of these. I still say YES, Shakespeare is relevant today. No BUT about it, because realistic characters are at the core.	*Dante maintains his position*
ELLA: And I say YES, BUT. You've convinced me that he talks about some universal experiences and emotions, but I still think that the status of the characters and the difficulty of the language present a big barrier for a lot of readers today.	*Ella and Jack qualify their views based on what they have heard*
JACK: That makes sense. I'm changing my position from solid YES to YES, BUT. I don't think the status is such a big deal because people can always imagine themselves being rich and powerful, but his language is really challenging.	
VIVIAN: I'm with Dante. I think the characters outweigh any barriers. Modern interpretations and movies of Shakespeare's plays will always be popular.	*Vivian supports her position by making a new connection.*

Debating an Issue

SL 1a–d, SL 3, SL 4

COMMON CORE

The selection and collection Performance Tasks in this book will direct you to engage in debates about issues relating to the selections you are reading. Use the guidelines that follow to have a productive and balanced argument about both sides of an issue.

The Structure of a Formal Debate

A debate is a balanced argument discussing opposing sides of an issue. In a debate, two teams compete to win the support of the audience. In a **formal debate,** two teams, each with three members, present their arguments on a given proposition or policy statement. One team argues for the proposition or statement and the other team argues against it. Each debater must consider the proposition closely and must research both sides of it. To argue convincingly either for or against a proposition, a debater must be familiar with both sides of the issue.

Plan the Debate

The purpose of a debate is to allow participants and audience members to consider both sides of an issue. Use these planning suggestions to hold a balanced and productive debate:

- **Identify Debate Teams** Form groups of six members based on the issues that the Performance Tasks include. Three members of the team will argue for the **affirmative** side of the issue—that is, they support the issue. The other three members will argue for the **negative** side of the issue—that is, they do not support the issue.
- **Appoint a Moderator** The moderator will present the topic and goals of the debate, keep track of the time, and introduce and thank the participants.
- **Research and Prepare Notes** Search the texts you've read as well as print and online sources for valid reasons and evidence to support your team's claim. As with a written argument, be sure to anticipate possible

opposing claims and compile evidence to counter those claims. You will use notes from your research during the debate.

- **Assign Debate Roles** One team member will introduce the team's claim and supporting evidence. Another team member will respond to questions and opposing claims in an exchange with a member of the opposing team. The last member will present a strong closing argument.

Hold the Debate

A formal debate is not a shouting match—rather, a well-run debate is an excellent forum for participants to express their viewpoints, build on others' ideas, and have a thoughtful, well-reasoned exchange of ideas. The moderator will begin by stating the topic or issue and introducing the participants. Participants should follow the moderator's instructions concerning whose turn it is to speak and how much time each speaker has.

FORMAL DEBATE FORMAT

SPEAKER	ROLE	TIME
Affirmative Speaker 1	Present the claim and supporting evidence for the affirmative ("pro") side of the argument.	5 minutes
Negative Speaker 1	Ask probing questions that will prompt the other team to address flaws in the argument.	3 minutes

continued

SPEAKER	ROLE	TIME
Affirmative Speaker 2	Respond to the questions posed by the opposing team and counter any concerns.	3 minutes
Negative Speaker 2	Present the claim and supporting evidence for the negative ("con") side of the argument.	5 minutes
Affirmative Speaker 3	Summarize the claim and evidence for the affirmative side and explain why your reasoning is more valid.	3 minutes
Negative Speaker 3	Summarize the claim and evidence for the negative side and explain why your reasoning is more valid.	3 minutes

Evaluate the Debate

Use the following guidelines to evaluate a team in a debate:

- Did the team prove that a significant problem does or does not exist? How thorough was the team's analysis of the problem?
- How did the team convince you that the proposition is or is not the best solution to the problem?
- How effectively did the team present reasons and evidence, including evidence from texts, to support the proposition?
- How effectively did the team **rebut,** or respond to, arguments made by the opposing team?
- Did the speakers maintain eye contact and speak at an appropriate rate and volume?
- Did the speakers observe proper debate etiquette—that is, did they follow the moderator's instructions, stay within their allotted time limits, and treat their opponents respectfully?

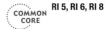
Reading Arguments

An argument expresses a position on an issue or problem and supports it with reasons and evidence. Being able to analyze and evaluate arguments will help you distinguish between claims you should accept and those you should not.

Analyzing an Argument

A sound argument should appeal to reason. However, arguments are often used in texts that contain other types of persuasive devices. An argument includes the following elements:

- A **claim** is the writer's position on an issue or central idea.
- **Support** is any material that serves to prove a claim. In an argument, support usually consists of reasons and evidence.
- **Reasons** are declarations made to justify an action, a decision, or a belief—for example, "The reason I think we'll be late is that we can't get to the appointment in five minutes."
- **Evidence** is the specific references, quotations, facts, examples, and opinions that support a claim. Evidence may also consist of statistics, reports of personal experience, or the views of experts.
- A **counterargument** or counterclaim is an argument against a position. A good argument anticipates the opposition's objections and provides counterarguments to disprove or answer them.

Claim	I should be allowed to work a part-time job on weekends.
Reason	Expenses connected with school and activities exceed what I can earn by doing chores.
Evidence	Field trips, uniforms, and transportation cost about $150 a month. I earn about $80 a month now.
Counter-argument	I know you think my schoolwork will suffer, but I've always done my homework, and I want stay on the honor roll.

Read the following editorial, and use a chart like the one that follows it to identify the claim, reason, evidence, and counterargument.

Extracurricular Sports Should Satisfy State Physical Education Requirement

Track, football, soccer, baseball, basketball, and other sports attract dedicated student athletes who often practice every day after school and then participate in weekend games. Should these students be forced to give up an elective class period to take a required physical education class? In order to meet the state's physical education (P.E.) course requirements, that is exactly what Whitman High School asks them to do. I believe that this policy doesn't make any sense. Instead, the Montgomery County public schools should exempt student athletes from taking P.E. classes.

First of all, participating in an extracurricular sport meets the objectives of the state's course requirements. Those objectives are to promote fitness and improve athletic skill, according to the Whitman course catalog. Involvement in either a varsity or a club sport for one season already makes a student fit and athletically skilled.

A second reason to change the policy is that the physical education requirement forces students to give up an elective class period. High school students can generally choose only eight elective courses from dozens of class offerings. By eliminating the P.E. requirement for student athletes, the county would give students more freedom in selecting their courses.

Finally, exposing students to different sports is one goal of the P.E. requirement, but this objective alone is not important enough to

---

PRACTICE AND APPLY

Students should create a chart like the one on page R16. The chart should include details similar to the ones below. Remind students to write legibly as they create their charts.

Possible answers:

Claim: Montgomery County public schools should exempt student athletes from taking P.E. classes.

Reason: Students involved in sports are forced to give up an elective course in order to meet the state's physical education requirements.

Evidence: Participating in extracurricular sports meets the objectives of the state's course requirements.

Reason: Student athletes must unnecessarily give up an elective class to complete the P.E. requirement

Evidence: According to the Whitman High School course catalog, the objective of P.E. class is to promote fitness and improve athletic skill. Involvement in a varsity or club sport for one season already makes a student fit and athletically skilled.

Counterargument: Exposing students to different sports is also one goal of the P.E. requirement, but this objective alone is not important enough to require students to take P.E. class. Students seldom take P.E. as seriously as they would an extracurricular sport and they don't appreciate the different sports they sample in class.

continued

require students to take P.E. class. Students seldom take P.E. class as seriously as they would an extracurricular sport, so students do not always appreciate sports they sample in P.E. class.

Varsity and club sports require a great deal of time and effort from athletes. The county should recognize that team sports encourage physical activity more effectively than P.E. class. It is more important for student athletes to become well-rounded academically by taking electives than to take P.E. class.

Recognizing Persuasive Techniques

Arguments typically rely on more than just the logical appeal of an argument to be convincing. They also depend on **persuasive techniques**—devices that can sway you to adopt a position or take an action.

This chart explains several ways a writer may attempt to sway you to adopt his or her position. Learn to recognize these techniques, and you are less likely to be influenced by them.

Persuasive Technique	Example
Appeals by Association	
Bandwagon appeal Suggests that a person should believe or do something because "everyone else" does	Be where it's at—shop the Magnificent Mall.
Testimonial Relies on endorsements from well-known people or satisfied customers	Golf champion Links Lorimer uses Gofar clubs. Shouldn't you?
Snob appeal Taps into people's desire to be special or part of an elite group	Dine at the elite Plaza Inn, where you will be treated like royalty.
Transfer Links a product, candidate, or cause to a positive emotion or idea	One spray of Woodsy air freshener and you'll find inner peace.
Appeal to loyalty Relies on people's affiliation with a particular group	Support the Tatum Tigers by wearing the new Win-Team windbreaker.

Emotional Appeals	
Appeals to pity, fear, or vanity Use strong feelings, rather than facts, to persuade	Don't these abandoned animals deserve a chance? Adopt a pet today.

Word Choice	
Glittering generality Makes a generalization that includes a word or phrase with positive connotations, such as *freedom* or *honor*, to promote a product or idea	Hop on a Swiftee moped and experience pure freedom.

Practice and Apply

Identify the persuasive techniques used in this model.

The True Holiday Spirit

The holiday season is almost upon us, and caring people everywhere are opening their hearts and wallets to those who are less fortunate. Charity and community service show democracy in action, and Mayor Adam Miner's actions are setting a good example for village residents. For the last three years, he has volunteered once a week at the local Meals for the Many program. Busing tables, serving soup, and helping wash dishes has made him aware of how fortunate he is and how important it is to share that good fortune. In his Thanksgiving address last week, he urged citizens, "Make this holiday—and all the days that follow—a time of true giving. Join your friends and neighbors in serving others today."

Analyzing Logic and Reasoning

When you evaluate an argument, you need to look closely at the writer's logic and reasoning. To do this, it is helpful to identify the type of reasoning the writer is using.

 COMMON CORE RI 6

PRACTICE AND APPLY

Possible answers:
Appeals by association: bandwagon appeal: "Join your friends and neighbors in serving others today."
Emotional appeals: appeal to pity, fear, vanity: "caring people everywhere are opening their hearts and wallets to those who are less fortunate"; "how important it is to share that good fortune"; "Make this holiday—and all the days that follow—a time of true giving."
Word choice: glittering generality: "Charity and community service show democracy in action, and Mayor Adam Miner's actions are setting a good example for village residents."

The Inductive Mode of Reasoning

When a writer leads from specific evidence to a general principle or generalization, that writer is using **inductive reasoning.** Here is an example of inductive reasoning:

> #### Specific Facts
>
> **Fact 1:** Fewer than 100 Arizona agave century plants remain in existence.
>
> **Fact 2:** Over the last three generations, there has been a 50 percent reduction in the number of African elephants.
>
> **Fact 3:** Only 50 Hawaiian crows are left in the world.
>
> #### Generalization
>
> Extinction is a problem facing many classes of living things.

Strategies for Determining the Soundness of Inductive Arguments

Ask yourself the following questions to evaluate an inductive argument:

- **Is the evidence valid and sufficient support for the conclusion?** Inaccurate facts lead to inaccurate conclusions.
- **Does the conclusion follow logically from the evidence?** From the facts listed in the previous example, the conclusion that extinction is a problem facing *all* living things would be too broad a generalization.
- **Is the evidence drawn from a large enough sample?** Even though there are only three facts listed above, the sample is large enough to support the claim. If you wanted to support the conclusion that extinction is a problem facing all classes of living things, the sample would not be large enough.

The Deductive Mode of Reasoning

When a writer arrives at a conclusion by applying a general principle to a specific situation, the writer is using **deductive reasoning.** Here's an example:

Regular exercise improves academic performance.	General principle or premise
▼	
Stefan has started a running program.	Specific situation
▼	
Stefan's grades may improve.	Specific conclusion

Strategies for Determining the Soundness of Deductive Arguments

Ask yourself the following questions to evaluate a deductive argument:

- **Is the general principle stated, or is it implied?** Note that writers often use deductive reasoning in an argument without stating the general principle. They just assume that readers will recognize and agree with the principle. You may want to identify the general principle for yourself.
- **Is the general principle sound?** Don't just assume the general principle is sound. Ask yourself whether it is really true.
- **Is the conclusion valid?** To be valid, a conclusion in a deductive argument must follow logically from the general principle and the specific situation.

This chart shows two conclusions drawn from the same general principle:

All government offices were closed last Monday.	
Accurate Deduction	**Inaccurate Deduction**
West Post Office is a government office; therefore, West Post Office was closed last Monday.	Soon-Lin's Spa was closed last Monday; therefore, Soon-Lin's Spa is a government office.

Soon-Lin might have closed her spa because there would be fewer customers in town when government offices were closed—or for another reason entirely.

Practice and Apply

Identify the mode of reasoning used in the following paragraph.

A large part of the U.S. population is overweight or obese. There are various weight-loss plans to follow. Fads come and go, but a definite way to lose weight is through a combination of diet and exercise. Because she wants to feel better and have more energy to play with her nephews, Consuelo recently decided to lose some weight. She has cut back on sugary and fatty foods and goes to the gym twice a week. Soon she'll be able to keep up with her nephews no matter how fast they run.

Identifying Faulty Reasoning

Sometimes an argument at first appears to make sense but isn't valid because it is based on a fallacy. A **fallacy** is an error in logic. Learn to recognize these common rhetorical and logical fallacies:

Type of Fallacy	Definition	Example
Circular reasoning	Supporting a statement by simply repeating it in different words	Wearing a bicycle helmet should be required because **cyclists should use protective headgear.**
Either/or fallacy	A statement that suggests that there are only two choices available in a situation that really offers more than two options	**Either** you eat a balanced diet, **or** you'll die before you're 50.
Oversimplification	An explanation of a complex situation or problem as if it were much simpler than it is	Shared interests lead to a **successful relationship**.
Overgeneralization	A generalization that is too broad. You can often recognize overgeneralizations by the use of words such as *all, everyone, every time, anything, no one,* and *none.*	**Everyone** wants to go to college.
Stereotyping	A dangerous type of overgeneralization. Stereotypes are broad statements about people on the basis of their gender, ethnicity, race, or political, social, professional, or religious group.	**Teenagers** just don't care about future generations.
Personal attack or name-calling	An attempt to discredit an idea by attacking the person or group associated with it. Candidates often engage in name-calling during political campaigns.	**Mr. Edmonds drives a beat-up car and never mows his lawn**, so you shouldn't take music lessons from him.
Evading the issue	Refuting an objection with arguments and evidence that do not address its central point	I know I didn't clean up my room, **but that gave me more time to study and improve my grades.**

COMMON CORE RI 8

PRACTICE AND APPLY

Answer:
Deductive reasoning. The writer begins with a general premise about reaching a healthy weight (that diet and exercise work in combination) and applies it to a specific situation (Consuelo's wish to feel healthier) to reach a specific conclusion (that if Consuelo exercises more and makes healthier food choices she'll reach a healthy weight).

Type of Fallacy	Definition	Example
Non sequitur	A statement that uses irrelevant "proof" to support a claim. A non sequitur is sometimes used to win an argument by diverting the reader's attention to proof that can't be challenged.	I'll probably flunk the driving test. **I was late for school today.**
False causation	The mistake of assuming that because one event occurred after another event in time, the first event caused the second one to occur	Marc wore his new goggles in the swim meet and **as a result won with his best time ever.**
False analogy	A comparison that doesn't hold up because of a critical difference between the two subjects	I bet my little brother will be a great skier when he grows up **because he loves playing on the slide.**
Hasty generalization	A conclusion drawn from too little evidence or from evidence that is biased	**I got sick after eating at the pizzeria,** so Italian food must be bad for me.
Commonly held opinions	An argument that is deemed correct just because everyone else supposedly thinks it is correct	**Everyone knows** that cats make better pets than dogs.
Appeal to pity	An argument that uses pity to make you feel sorry for someone	I couldn't finish my homework **because my dog was sick.**

Practice and Apply

Look for examples of logical fallacies in the following argument. Identify each one and explain why you identified it as such.

Everyone agrees that running is the best form of exercise. All you need is a good pair of shoes and you're ready to hit the road. I've run a mile twice this week, so I should know. As a result, I've slept better and my tone on the clarinet has improved. When you run, your heart beats faster because your pulse rate increases. That means that your cells get more oxygen, which is the second most common gas in the earth's atmosphere. You also get to enjoy the beauty of the world around you as you build up your stamina. So if you don't want to be a hopeless couch potato, get going and run for your life!

Evaluating Arguments

Learning how to evaluate arguments and identify bias will help you become more selective when doing research and also help you improve your own reasoning and arguing skills. **Bias** is an inclination for or against a particular opinion or viewpoint. A writer may reveal a strongly positive or negative opinion on an issue by presenting only one way of looking at it or by heavily weighting the evidence on one side of the argument. Additionally, the presence of either of the following is often a sign of bias:

Loaded language consists of words with strongly positive or negative connotations that are intended to influence a reader's attitude.

EXAMPLE:

People who mistreat animals are subhuman and deserve to be locked up for life. (*Subhuman* and *locked up* have negative connotations.)

Propaganda is any form of communication that is so distorted that it conveys false or misleading information. Some politicians create and distribute propaganda. Many logical fallacies, such as name-calling, the either/or fallacy, and false causation, are often used in propaganda. The following example shows

COMMON CORE RI 8

PRACTICE AND APPLY

Possible answers:
Overgeneralization: "Everyone agrees that running is the best form of exercise."
Explanation: The writer uses words such as "everyone" and "best" to make an overly broad generalization about how people feel about running.
Oversimplification: "All you need is a good pair of shoes and you're ready to hit the road." Explanation: The writer makes the idea of running a simple matter that does not take into account other factors.
Non Sequitur: "I've run a mile twice this week, so I should know." Explanation: The statement does not provide sufficient evidence or proof to support the claim.
False causation: "As a result, I've slept better and my tone on the clarinet has improved." Explanation: The writer makes the assumption that one event has caused the others but does not take into account other possible causes.
Circular reasoning: "When you run, your heart beats faster because your pulse rate increases." Explanation: The writer simply restates the idea using different words.
Non Sequitur: ". . . oxygen, which is the second most common gas in the earth's atmosphere. You also get to enjoy the beauty of the world around you." Explanation: The statements do not address the real topic.
Hasty generalization: ". . . if you don't want to be a hopeless couch potato." Explanation: The statement draws the conclusion that people who do not run will become couch potatoes (sedentary and overweight), but it is not based on adequate or appropriate evidence.

R20 Student Resources

R20 Student Resources

an oversimplification. The writer uses one fact to support a particular point of view but omits another fact that does not support that viewpoint.

EXAMPLE:

Since we moved to the city, our gas and electric bills have gone down. (The writer does not include the fact that the move occurred in the spring, when the demand for heat or air conditioning is low anyway.)

Strategies for Evaluating Evidence

It is important to have a set of standards by which you can evaluate persuasive texts. Use the questions below to help you critically assess facts and opinions that are presented as evidence.

- **Are the facts presented verifiable?** Facts can be proved by eyewitness accounts, authoritative sources such as encyclopedias and almanacs, experts, or research.
- **Are the opinions presented well-informed?** Any opinions offered should be supported by facts, be based on research or eyewitness accounts, or be the opinions of experts on the topic.
- **Is the evidence thorough?** Thorough evidence leaves no reasonable questions unanswered. If a choice is offered, background for making the choice should be provided. Any shifts in perspective in arguments should be explained and supported.
- **Is the evidence biased?** Be alert to evidence that contains loaded language and other signs of bias.
- **Is the evidence authoritative?** The people, groups, or organizations that provided the evidence should have credentials that verify their credibility.
- **Is it important that the evidence be current?** Where timeliness is crucial, as in the areas of medicine and technology, the evidence should reflect the latest developments in the areas.

Practice and Apply

Read the argument below. Identify facts, opinions, and elements of bias.

> Are you tired of listening to people talking on their cell phones? I think those disgusting machines should be banned. Using the dumb things while driving or riding a bicycle distracts the user and creates a serious hazard. The phones also give off energy frequencies that can cause cancer. Cell phone users in a German study, for example, were three times more likely to develop eye cancer than people in the control group. Another study done in Sweden showed that people who used cell phones for ten years or more increased their risk of brain cancer by 77 percent. Although other researchers found no connection between cell phones and cancer, those studies stink. People should wise up and stop harming themselves and bothering everybody else.

Strategies for Determining a Strong Argument

To decide whether an argument is strong, make sure that all or most of the following statements are true:

- The argument presents a claim or thesis.
- The claim is connected to its support by a general principle that most readers would readily agree with.

   Valid general principle: *It is the job of a school to provide a well-rounded physical education program.*

   Invalid general principle: *It is the job of a school to produce healthy, physically fit people.*

- The reasons make sense.
- The reasons are presented in a logical and effective order.
- The claim and all reasons are adequately supported by sound evidence.
- The evidence is adequate, accurate, and appropriate.
- The logic is sound. There are no instances of faulty reasoning.

COMMON CORE RI 8

PRACTICE AND APPLY
Possible answers:
Facts: "Cell phone users in a German study, for example, were three times more likely to develop eye cancer than people in the control group"; "Another study done in Sweden showed that people who used cell phones for ten years or more increased their risk of brain cancer by 77 percent."
Opinions: "I think those disgusting machines should be banned"; "People should wise up and stop harming themselves and bothering everybody else."
Elements of bias: "I think those disgusting machines should be banned"; "Although other researchers found no connection between cell phones and cancer, those studies stink"; choosing to quote only studies that claim cell phones cause cancer.

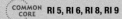

PRACTICE AND APPLY

Students' responses will vary, but they should evaluate the strength of the claim, the evidence supporting the claim, and the counterclaims.

Possible answer: Overall, the speech presents a fairly strong argument. Roosevelt delineates a four-part claim based on the general principle that all people deserve freedom. Two of the four parts of the claim are supported by reasons and evidence drawn from specific world events. A counterargument is hinted at: "That is no vision of a distant millennium." A few rhetorical statements, such as "Freedom means the supremacy of human rights everywhere" and "Our strength is our unity of purpose" are overly broad and lacking in support.

Practice and Apply

Use the preceding criteria to evaluate the strength of the following excerpt from a seminal speech by President Franklin Roosevelt, often called the "Four Freedoms" speech:

In the future days, which we seek to make secure, we look forward to a world founded upon four essential human freedoms.

The first is freedom of speech and expression—everywhere in the world.

The second is freedom of every person to worship God in his own way—everywhere in the world.

The third is freedom from want, which, translated into world terms, means economic understandings which will secure to every nation a healthy peacetime life for its inhabitants—everywhere in the world.

The fourth is freedom from fear, which, translated into world terms, means a world-wide reduction of armaments to such a point and in such a thorough fashion that no nation will be in a position to commit an act of physical aggression against any neighbor—anywhere in the world.

That is no vision of a distant millennium. It is a definite basis for a kind of world attainable in our own time and generation. That kind of world is the very antithesis of the so-called "new order" of tyranny which the dictators seek to create with the crash of a bomb.

To that new order we oppose the greater conception—the moral order. A good society is able to face schemes of world domination and foreign revolutions alike without fear.

Since the beginning of our American history we have been engaged in change, in a perpetual, peaceful revolution, a revolution which goes on steadily, quietly, adjusting itself to changing conditions without the concentration camp or the quicklime in the ditch. The world order which we seek is the cooperation of free countries, working together in a friendly, civilized society.

This nation has placed its destiny in the hands and heads and hearts of its millions of free men and women, and its faith in freedom under the guidance of God. Freedom means the supremacy of human rights everywhere. Our support goes to those who struggle to gain those rights and keep them. Our strength is our unity of purpose.

To that high concept there can be no end save victory.

Grammar

L 1a–b, L 2a–b, L3
COMMON CORE

Writing that has many mistakes can confuse or even annoy a reader. For example, a business letter with a punctuation error might lead to miscommunication and delay a reply, or an essay that includes a sentence fragment might earn its writer a lower grade. Paying attention to grammar, punctuation, and capitalization rules can make your writing clearer and easier to read.

Quick Reference Parts of Speech

Part of Speech	Function	Examples
Noun	names a person, a place, a thing, an idea, a quality, or an action	
Common	serves as a general name, or a name common to an entire group	boat, anchor, water, sky
Proper	names a specific person, place, or thing	Nile River, Acapulco, Swahili
Singular	refers to a single person, place, thing, or idea	map, berry, deer, mouse
Plural	refers to more than one person, place, thing, or idea	maps, berries, deer, mice
Concrete	names something that can be perceived by the senses	stone, crate, wall, knife
Abstract	names something that cannot be perceived by the senses	courage, caution, tyranny, importance
Compound	expresses a single idea through a combination of two or more words	toothbrush, sister-in-law, South Carolina
Collective	refers to a group of people or things	herd, family, team, staff
Possessive	shows who or what owns something	Kenya's, Les's, women's, waitresses'
Pronoun	takes the place of a noun or another pronoun	
Personal	refers to the person making a statement, the person(s) being addressed, or the person(s) or thing(s) the statement is about	I, me, my, mine, we, us, our, ours, you, your, yours, she, he, it, her, him, hers, his, its, they, them, their, theirs
Reflexive	follows a verb or preposition and refers to a preceding noun or pronoun	myself, yourself, herself, himself, itself, ourselves, yourselves, themselves
Intensive	emphasizes a noun or another pronoun	(same as reflexives)
Demonstrative	points to one or more specific persons or things	this, that, these, those

continued

Part of Speech	Function	Examples
Interrogative	signals a question	who, whom, whose, which, what
Indefinite	refers to one or more persons or things not specifically mentioned	both, all, most, many, anyone, everybody, several, none, some
Relative	introduces an adjective clause by relating it to a word in the clause	who, whom, whose, which, that
Reciprocal	expresses a mutual action or relationship	each other, one another
Verb	expresses an action, a condition, or a state of being	
Action	tells what the subject does or did, physically or mentally	run, reaches, listened, consider, decides, dreamed
Linking	connects the subject to something that identifies or describes it	am, is, are, was, were, sound, taste, appear, feel, become, remain, seem
Auxiliary	precedes the main verb in a verb phrase	be, have, do, can, could, will, would, may, might
Transitive	directs the action toward someone or something; always has an object	Mom **broke** the plate.
Intransitive	does not direct the action toward someone or something; does not have an object	The plate **broke**.
Adjective	modifies a noun or pronoun	**frightened** man, **two** epics, **enough** time
Adverb	modifies a verb, an adjective, or another adverb	walked **fast**, **really** funny, **far** away
Preposition	relates one word to another word	at, by, for, from, in, of, on, to, with
Conjunction	joins words or word groups	
Coordinating	joins words or word groups used the same way	and, but, or, for, so, yet, nor
Correlative	used as a pair to join words or word groups used the same way	both . . . and, either . . . or, neither . . . nor
Subordinating	introduces a clause that cannot stand by itself as a complete sentence	although, after, as, before, because, when, if, unless
Interjection	expresses emotion	whew, yikes, uh-oh

Quick Reference: The Sentence and Its Parts

The diagrams that follow will give you a brief review of the essentials of a sentence and some of its parts.

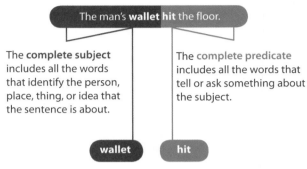

The man's **wallet hit** the floor.

The **complete subject** includes all the words that identify the person, place, thing, or idea that the sentence is about.

The complete predicate includes all the words that tell or ask something about the subject.

wallet

hit

The **simple subject** tells exactly whom or what the sentence is about. It may be one word or a group of words, but it does not include modifiers.

The simple predicate, or verb, tells what the subject does or is. It may be one word or several, but it does not include modifiers.

Every word in a sentence is part of a complete subject or a complete predicate.

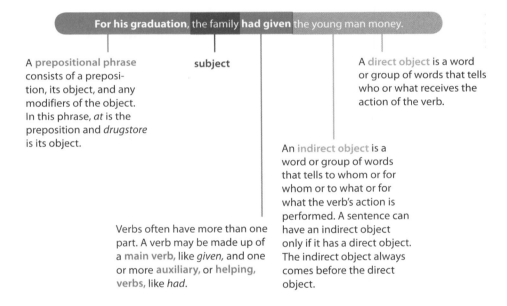

For his graduation, the family **had given** the young man money.

A prepositional phrase consists of a preposition, its object, and any modifiers of the object. In this phrase, *at* is the preposition and *drugstore* is its object.

subject

A direct object is a word or group of words that tells who or what receives the action of the verb.

An indirect object is a word or group of words that tells to whom or for whom or to what or for what the verb's action is performed. A sentence can have an indirect object only if it has a direct object. The indirect object always comes before the direct object.

Verbs often have more than one part. A verb may be made up of a main verb, like *given*, and one or more auxiliary, or helping, verbs, like *had*.

Quick Reference: Punctuation

Part of Speech	Function	Examples
End Marks period, question mark, exclamation point	ends a sentence	The games begin today. Who is your favorite contestant? What a play Jamie made!
period	follows an initial or abbreviation **Exception:** postal abbreviations of states	Prof. Ted Bakerman, D. H. Lawrence, P.M., A.D., oz., ft., Blvd., St. , NE (Nebraska), NV (Nevada)

period	follows a number or letter in an outline	I. Volcanoes
		  A. Central-vent
		    1. Shield

Comma	separates parts of a compound sentence	I have never disliked poetry, but now I really love it.
	separates items in a series	She is brave, loyal, and kind.
	separates adjectives of equal rank that modify the same noun	The slow, easy route is best.
	sets off a term of address	O Wind, if winter comes . . . Come to the front, children.
	sets off a parenthetical expression	Hard workers, as you know, don't quit. I'm not a quitter, believe me.
	sets off an introductory word, phrase, or dependent clause	Yes, I forgot my key. At the beginning of the day, I feel fresh. While she was out, I was here. Having finished my chores, I went out.
	sets off a nonrestrictive phrase or clause and contrasting expressions	Ed Pawn, the captain of the chess team, won. Marla, who was sick, finished last. The two leading runners, sprinting toward the finish line, finished in a tie.
	sets off parts of dates and addresses	Send it by August 18, 2010, to Cherry Jubilee, Inc., 21 Vernona St., Oakland, Minnesota.
	follows the salutation and closing of a letter	Dear Jim, Sincerely yours,
	separates words to avoid confusion	By noon, time had run out. What the minister does, does matter. While cooking, Jim burned his hand.
Semicolon	separates items that contain commas in a series	We invited my sister, Jan; her boyfriend, Don; my uncle Jack; and Mary Dodd.

continued

Part of Speech	Function	Examples
	separates parts of a compound sentence that are not joined by a coordinating conjunction	The last shall be first; the first shall be last. I read the Bible; however, I have not memorized it.
	separates parts of a compound sentence when the parts contain commas	After I ran out of money, I called my parents; but only my sister was home, unfortunately.
Colon	introduces a list	Those we wrote were the following: Dana, John, and Will.
	introduces a long quotation	Susan B. Anthony said: "Woman must not depend upon the protection of man. . . ."
	follows the salutation of a business letter	To Whom It May Concern: Dear Ms. Costa:
	separates certain numbers	1:28 P.M. Genesis 2:5
Dash	indicates an abrupt break in thought and adds emphasis to parenthetical information	I was thinking of my mother—who is arriving tomorrow—just as you walked in.
Parentheses	enclose less important material	Throughout her life (though some might think otherwise), she worked hard. The temperature on this July day (would you believe it?) is 65 degrees!
Hyphen	joins parts of a compound adjective before a noun	She lives in a first-floor apartment.
	joins part of a compound with *all-, ex-, self-,* or *-elect*	The president-elect is well respected.
	joins part of a compound number (to ninety-nine)	Today I turn twenty-one.
	joins part of a fraction	My cup is one-third full.
	joins a prefix to a word beginning with a capital letter	Is this a pre-Bronze Age artifact? Caesar had a bad day in mid-March.
	indicates that a word is divided at the end of a line	Finding the right title has been a challenge for the committee.
Apostrophe	used with *s* to form the possessive of a noun or an indefinite pronoun	my friend's book, my friends' books, anyone's guess, somebody else's problem
	replaces one or more omitted letters in a contraction or numbers in a date	don't (omitted *o*), he'd (omitted *woul*), the class of '99 (omitted *19*)

continued

Part of Speech	Function	Examples
	used with *s* to form the plural of a letter	I had two A's on my report card.
Quotation Marks	set off a speaker's exact words	Sara said, "I'm finally ready." "I'm ready," Sara said, "finally." Did Sara say, "I'm ready"? Sara said, "I'm ready!"
	set off the title of a story, an article, a short poem, an essay, a song, or a chapter	We read Hansberry's "On Summer" and Alvarez's "Exile."
	indicate sarcasm or irony	Oh, she's an "expert," all right.
Ellipses	replace material omitted from a quotation	"Neither slavery nor involuntary servitude . . . shall exist within the United States. . . ."
Italics	indicate the title of a book, a play, a magazine, a long poem, an opera, a film, or a TV series, or the name of a ship	*The Mists of Avalon, Julius Caesar, Newsweek, Paradise Lost, La Bohème, Twilight, Glee,* USS *John F. Kennedy*

Quick Reference: Capitalization

Category	Examples
People and Titles	
Names and initials of people	Alice Walker, E. B. White
Titles used before or in place of names	Professor Holmes, Senator Long
Deities and members of religious groups	Jesus, Allah, Buddha, Zeus, Baptists, Roman Catholics
Names of ethnic and national groups	Hispanics, Jews, African Americans
Geographical Names	
Cities, states, countries, continents	Charleston, Nevada, France, Asia
Regions, bodies of water, mountains	the Midwest, Lake Michigan, Mount Everest
Geographic features, parks	Continental Divide, Everglades, Yellowstone
Streets and roads, planets	361 South Twenty-third Street, Miller Avenue, Jupiter, Saturn
Organizations, Events, Etc.	
Companies, organizations, teams	Monsanto, the Elks, Chicago Bulls
Buildings, bridges, monuments	the Alamo, Golden Gate Bridge, Lincoln Memorial
Documents, awards	the Constitution, World Cup

continued

Category	Examples
Special named events	Super Bowl, World Series
Government bodies, historical periods and events	the Supreme Court, Congress, the Middle Ages, Boston Tea Party
Days and months, holidays	Tuesday, October, Thanksgiving, Valentine's Day
Specific cars, boats, trains, planes	Cadillac, Titanic, Orient Express
Proper Adjectives	
Adjectives formed from proper nouns	Doppler effect, Mexican music, Elizabethan age, Midwestern town
First Words and the Pronoun *I*	
First word in a sentence or quotation	This is it. He said, "Let's go."
First word of sentence in parentheses that is not within another sentence	The spelling rules are covered in another section. (Consult that section for more information.)
First words in the salutation and closing of a letter	Dear Madam, Very truly yours,
First word in each line of most poetry Personal pronoun *I*	Then am I A happy fly If I live Or if I die.
First word, last word, and all important words in a title	*A Tale of Two Cities*, "The World Is Too Much with Us"

Grammar Handbook

1 Nouns

A **noun** is a word used to name a person, a place, a thing, an idea, a quality, or an action. Nouns can be classified in several ways.

1.1 COMMON NOUNS

Common nouns are general names, common to entire groups.

1.2 PROPER NOUNS

Proper nouns name specific, one-of-a-kind things.

Common	Proper
motor, tree, time, children	Bradbury, Eastern Standard Time, Maine

1.3 SINGULAR AND PLURAL NOUNS

A noun may take a singular or a plural form, depending on whether it names a single person, place, thing, or idea or more than one. Make sure you use appropriate spellings when forming plurals.

Singular	Plural
rocket, sky, life	rockets, skies, lives

1.4 POSSESSIVE NOUNS

A **possessive noun** shows who or what owns something.

2 Pronouns

A **pronoun** is a word that is used in place of a noun or another pronoun. The word or word group to which the pronoun refers is called its **antecedent.**

2.1 PERSONAL PRONOUNS

Personal pronouns change their form to express person, number, gender, and case. The forms of these pronouns are shown in the following chart.

	Nominative	Objective	Possessive
Singular			
First Person	I	me	my, mine
Second Person	you	you	your, yours
Third Person	she, he, it	her, him, it	her, hers, his, its
Plural			
First Person	we	us	our, ours
Second Person	you	you	your, yours
Third Person	they	them	their, theirs

2.2 AGREEMENT WITH ANTECEDENT

Pronouns should agree with their antecedents in number, gender, and person.

If an antecedent is singular, use a singular pronoun.

EXAMPLE: *Malcolm* waved as *he boarded the bus to the airport.*

If an antecedent is plural, use a plural pronoun.

EXAMPLES:
Malcolm and *Hal* shared a sandwich as *they* waited to board the plane.
Delores and *Arnetta* rode *their* bikes to the park.

The gender of a pronoun must be the same as the gender of its antecedent.

EXAMPLES:
William will give *his* performance tonight.
Marla played *her* trumpet.

The person of the pronoun must be the same as the person of its antecedent. As the chart in Section 2.1 shows, a pronoun can be in first-, second-, or third-person form.

EXAMPLE: *You classical music fans still have time to buy your tickets.*

Practice and Apply

Rewrite each sentence so that the under-lined pronoun agrees with its antecedent.

1. "The Lottery" tells about a small town and his strange custom.
2. Mr. Summers keeps the box so the villagers can use them each year.
3. Each of the men draws for their family.
4. The people of the town take its chances in the drawing.
5. After the other slips are shown, Tessie is forced to reveal theirs.

2.3 PRONOUN CASE

Personal pronouns change form to show how they function in sentences. Different functions are shown by different **cases: nominative, objective,** and **possessive.** For examples, see Section 2.1.

A **nominative pronoun** is used as a subject or a predicate nominative in a sentence.

An **objective pronoun** is used as a direct object, an indirect object, or the object of a preposition.

SUBJECT   OBJECT   OBJECT OF PREPOSITION

She brought him to us.

A **possessive pronoun** shows ownership. The pronouns *mine, yours, hers, his, its, ours,* and *theirs* can be used in place of nouns.

EXAMPLE: *This horse is mine.*

The pronouns *my, your, her, his, its, our,* and *their* are used before nouns.

EXAMPLE: *This is my book.*

WATCH OUT! Don't confuse the possessive pronouns *its* and *their* with the contractions *it's* and *they're.*

TIP To decide which pronoun to use in a comparison, such as "He runs faster than (*I* or *me*)," fill in the missing word(s): *He runs faster than I do.*

Practice and Apply

Replace the underlined words in each sentence with an appropriate pronoun and identify the pronoun as a nominative, an objective, or a possessive pronoun.

1. Shakespeare was the famous play-wright who ever lived.
2. *Macbeth* is one of Shakespeare's most powerful tragedies.
3. Macbeth and Lady Macbeth are two of the main characters.
4. Macbeth causes the murders of Duncan and Banquo.
5. Duncan's sons are the rightful heirs to the throne.

2.4 REFLEXIVE AND INTENSIVE PRONOUNS

These pronouns are formed by adding –*self* or –*selves* to certain personal pronouns. Their forms are the same, and they differ only in how they are used.

A **reflexive pronoun** follows a verb or preposition and reflects back on an earlier noun or pronoun.

EXAMPLES:
He likes himself too much.
Kiyoko treated herself to dessert.

Intensive pronouns intensify or emphasize the nouns or pronouns to which they refer.

EXAMPLES:
The merchants themselves enjoyed sampling the foods.
You did it yourself.

WATCH OUT! Avoid using *hisself* or *theirselves.* Standard English does not include these forms.

NONSTANDARD: *The children sang theirselves to sleep.*

STANDARD: *The children sang themselves to sleep.*

COMMON CORE L1

PRACTICE AND APPLY

Remind students to write legibly as they compose their responses to the Practice and Apply activities.
Answers:

1. *"The Lottery" tells about a small town and its strange custom.*
2. *Mr. Summers keeps the box so the villagers can use it each year.*
3. *Each of the men draws for his family.*
4. *The people of the town take their chances in the drawing.*
5. *After the other slips are shown, Tessie is forced to reveal hers.*

PRACTICE AND APPLY

Answers:

1. *he; nominative*
2. *his; possessive*
3. *they; nominative*
4. *them; objective*
5. *they; nominative*

2.5 RECIPROCAL PRONOUNS

Reciprocal pronouns express mutual actions or relationships between the members they represent. Reciprocal pronouns also take the possessive forms **each other's** and **one another's.**

> EXAMPLES:
>
> *The children exchanged gifts with one another.*
>
> *Sean and Julie laughed at each other's jokes.*

2.6 DEMONSTRATIVE PRONOUNS

Demonstrative pronouns point out things and persons near and far.

	Singular	Plural
Near	this	these
Far	that	those

2.7 INDEFINITE PRONOUNS

Indefinite pronouns do not refer to specific persons or things and usually have no antecedents. The chart shows some commonly used indefinite pronouns.

Singular	Plural	Singular or Plural	
another	both	all	most
anybody	few	any	none
no one	many	more	some
neither	several		

TIP Indefinite pronouns that end in *–one,* *–body,* or *–thing* are always singular.

> INCORRECT: *Everyone brought their clarinet.*
>
> CORRECT: *Everyone brought his or her clarinet.*

If the indefinite pronoun might refer to either a male or a female, *his* or *her* may be used, or the sentence may be rewritten.

> EXAMPLES:
>
> *Did everybody play his or her part well?*
> *Did all the students play their parts well?*

2.8 INTERROGATIVE PRONOUNS

An **interrogative pronoun** tells a reader or listener that a question is coming. The interrogative pronouns are *who, whom, whose, which,* and *what.*

> EXAMPLES:
>
> *Who wrote that song?*
> *From whom did you get the answer?*

TIP *Who* is used as a subject; *whom,* as an object. To decide which pronoun you need to use in a question, change the question to a statement.

> QUESTION: *(Who/Whom) are you speaking to?*
>
> STATEMENT: *You are speaking to (?).*

Since the verb has a subject (*you*), the needed word must be the object form, *whom.*

> EXAMPLE: *Whom are you speaking to?*

WATCH OUT! A special problem arises when you use an interrupter, such as *do you think,* within a question.

> EXAMPLE: *(Who/Whom) do you think is the better singer?*

If you eliminate the interrupter, it is clear that the word you need is *who.*

2.9 RELATIVE PRONOUNS

Relative pronouns relate, or connect, adjective clauses to the words they modify in sentences. The noun or pronoun that a relative clause modifies is the antecedent of the relative pronoun.

Here are the relative pronouns and their uses:

Replaces	Subject	Object	Possessive
Person	who	whom	whose
Thing	which	which	whose
Thing/Person	that	that	whose

Often short sentences with related ideas can be combined by using a relative pronoun to create a more effective sentence.

SHORT SENTENCE: *Joan Aiken decided to become a writer at an early age.*

RELATED SENTENCE: *Joan Aiken's father was a poet.*

COMBINED SENTENCE: *Joan Aiken, whose father was a poet, decided to become a writer at an early age.*

Practice and Apply

Write the correct form of each incorrect pronoun.

1. Whom has read "By the Waters of Babylon"?
2. Stephen Vincent Benét, which is a famous American author, wrote the story.
3. In "By the Waters of Babylon," him who touches the metal in the Dead Places must be a priest or son of a priest.
4. The narrator's father hisself is a priest.
5. When the narrator sees a heap of broken stones, he cautiously approaches them stones.

2.10 PRONOUN REFERENCE PROBLEMS

The referent of a pronoun should always be clear. Avoid problems by rewriting sentences.

An **indefinite reference** occurs when the pronoun *it, you,* or *they* does not clearly refer to a specific antecedent.

UNCLEAR: *In the article, it claims that the new Pink Blur CD is terrific.*

CLEAR: *The article claims that the new Pink Blur CD is terrific.*

A **general reference** occurs when the pronoun *it, this, that, which,* or *such* is used to refer to a general idea rather than a specific antecedent.

UNCLEAR: *Trudy practices the guitar every day. This has improved her playing.*

CLEAR: *Trudy practices the guitar every day. Practicing has improved her playing.*

Ambiguous means "having more than one possible meaning." An **ambiguous reference** occurs when a pronoun could refer to two or more antecedents.

UNCLEAR: *Jeb talked to Max while he listened to music.*

CLEAR: *While Jeb listened to music, he talked to Max.*

Practice and Apply

Rewrite the following sentences to correct indefinite, ambiguous, and general pronoun references.

1. In the story "To Build A Fire," it tells about a man trying to survive in extremely cold conditions.
2. The man almost steps in a trap. This makes him use the dog to test the trail's safety.
3. An old-timer in the story tells the miner that running will make his feet freeze faster.
4. Snow from a tree falls and puts out the man's fire. This makes him panic.

3 Verbs

A **verb** is a word that expresses an action, a condition, or a state of being.

3.1 ACTION VERBS

Action verbs express mental or physical activity.

EXAMPLE: *You hit the target.*

3.2 LINKING VERBS

Linking verbs join subjects with words or phrases that rename or describe them.

EXAMPLE: *She is our queen.*

3.3 PRINCIPAL PARTS

Action and linking verbs typically have four principal parts, which are used to form verb tenses. The principal parts are the **present,** the **present participle,** the **past,** and the **past participle.**

Action verbs and some linking verbs also fall into two categories: regular and irregular. A **regular verb** is a verb that forms its past and past participle by adding *–ed* or *–d* to the present form.

PRACTICE AND APPLY

Answers:

1. *Who has read "By the Waters of Babylon"?*
2. *Stephen Vincent Benét, who is a famous American author, wrote the story.*
3. *In "By the Waters of Babylon," he who touches the metal in the Dead Places must be a priest or a son of a priest.*
4. *The narrator's father himself is a priest.*
5. *When the narrator sees a heap of broken stones, he cautiously approaches those stones.*

PRACTICE AND APPLY

Possible answers:

1. *The story "To Build a Fire" tells about a man trying to survive in extremely cold conditions.*
2. *The man almost steps in a trap. After this close call, he decides to use the dog to test the trail's safety.*
3. *An old-timer in the story tells the miner that running will make the miner's feet freeze faster.*
4. *Snow from a tree falls and puts out the man's fire. The incident makes him panic.*

Present	Present Participle	Past	Past Participle
perform	(is) performing	performed	(has) performed
hope	(is) hoping	hoped	(has) hoped
stop	(is) stopping	stopped	(has) stopped
marry	(is) marrying	married	(has) married

An **irregular verb** forms its past and past participle in some other way besides adding *–ed* or *–d* to the present form.

Present	Present Participle	Past	Past Participle
bring	(is) bringing	brought	(has) brought
swim	(is) swimming	swam	(has) swum
steal	(is) stealing	stole	(has) stolen
grow	(is) growing	grew	(has) grown

3.4 VERB TENSE

The **tense** of a verb indicates the time of the action or state of being. An action or state of being can occur in the present, the past, or the future. There are six tenses, each expressing a different range of time.

The **present tense** expresses an action or state that is happening at the present time, occurs regularly, or is constant or generally true. Use the present part.

NOW: *This soup tastes delicious.*

REGULAR: *I make vegetable soup often.*

GENERAL: *Crops require sun, rain, and rich soil.*

The **past tense** expresses an action that began and ended in the past. Use the past part.

EXAMPLE: *The diver bought a shark cage.*

The **future tense** expresses an action or state that will occur. Use *shall* or *will* with the present part.

EXAMPLE: *The shark will destroy this cage.*

The **present perfect tense** expresses an action or state that (1) was completed at an indefinite time in the past or (2) began in the past and continues into the present. Use *have* or *has* with the past participle.

EXAMPLE: *The diver has used shark cages before.*

The **past perfect tense** expresses an action in the past that came before another action in the past. Use *had* with the past participle.

EXAMPLE: *He had looked everywhere for a cage.*

The **future perfect tense** expresses an action in the future that will be completed before another action in the future. Use *shall have* or *will have* with the past participle.

EXAMPLE: *Before the day ends, the shark will have destroyed three cages.*

TIP A past-tense form of an irregular verb is not used with an auxiliary verb, but a past-participle main irregular verb is always used with an auxiliary verb.

INCORRECT: *I have saw her somewhere before.*

CORRECT: *I have seen her somewhere before.*

INCORRECT: *I seen her somewhere before.*

3.5 PROGRESSIVE FORMS

The progressive forms of the six tenses show ongoing actions. Use forms of *be* with the present participles of verbs.

PRESENT PROGRESSIVE: *We are dancing.*

PAST PROGRESSIVE: *We were dancing yesterday.*

FUTURE PROGRESSIVE: *We will be dancing on Friday.*

PRESENT PERFECT PROGRESSIVE: *We have been dancing once a week.*

PAST PERFECT PROGRESSIVE: *We had been dancing for a long time.*

FUTURE PERFECT PROGRESSIVE: *We will have been dancing partners for six months next week.*

WATCH OUT! Do not shift from tense to tense needlessly. Watch out for these special cases.

- In most compound sentences and in sentences with compound predicates, keep the tenses the same.

  INCORRECT: *I keyed in the password, but I get an error message.*

  CORRECT: *I keyed in the password, but I got an error message.*

- If one past action happened before another, do shift tenses.

  INCORRECT: *They wished they started earlier.*

  CORRECT: *They wished they had started earlier.*

Practice and Apply

Rewrite each sentence, using a form of the verb in parentheses. Identify each form that you use.

1. In his stories, Franz Kafka (show) the struggles of people against faceless bureacracy.
2. Kafka (write) "The Metamorphosis."
3. In the story, Gregor (know) both of his parents' concerns well.
4. The chief clerk (visit) the house.
5. Struggling with difficulties, Gregor (unlock) the door.
6. The story (reflect) how Gregor approaches even bizarre events by focusing on work.

Rewrite each sentence to correct an error in tense.

7. Gregor wants to communicate with his family and tried to talk to them through the door.
8. The clerk is angry and gave Gregor a stern warning.
9. Gregor's parents and sister had not knew what happened to him.
10. Gregor's mother have fainted at the sight of him.

3.6 ACTIVE AND PASSIVE VOICE

The voice of a verb tells whether its subject performs or receives the action expressed by the verb. When the subject performs the action, the verb is in the **active voice.** When the subject is the receiver of the action, the verb is in the **passive voice.**

Compare these two sentences:

ACTIVE: *Her sunglasses hid her face.*

PASSIVE: *Her face was hidden by her sunglasses.*

To form the passive voice, use a form of *be* with the past participle of the verb.

WATCH OUT! Use the passive voice sparingly. It can make writing awkward and less direct.

AWKWARD: *She was given the handmade quilts by her mother.*

BETTER: *Her mother gave her the handmade quilts.*

There are occasions when you will choose to use the passive voice because

- you want to emphasize the receiver: **The king was shot.**
- the doer is unknown: **My books were stolen.**
- the doer is unimportant: **French is spoken here.**

4 Modifiers

Modifiers are words or groups of words that change or limit the meanings of other words. Adjectives and adverbs are common modifiers.

4.1 ADJECTIVES

Adjectives modify nouns and pronouns by telling which one, what kind, how many, or how much.

WHICH ONE: *this, that, these, those*

EXAMPLE: *These tomatoes have grown quickly.*

WHAT KIND: *tiny, impressive, bold, rotten*

EXAMPLE: *The bold officer stood in front of the crowd.*

 COMMON CORE L1

PRACTICE AND APPLY

Before students begin the activity, note that actions taking place within the story's present time should use the present tense verb.

Answers:

1. *In his stories, Franz Kafka showed the struggles of people against faceless bureaucracy. (past tense)*
2. *Kafka wrote "The Metamorphosis." (past tense)*
3. *In the story, Gregor knows both of his parents' concerns well. (present tense)*
4. *The chief clerk visits the house. (present tense)*
5. *Struggling with difficulties, Gregor unlocks the door. (present tense)*
6. *The story reflects how Gregor approaches even bizarre events by focusing on work. (present tense)*
7. *Gregor wants to communicate with his family and tries to talk to them through the door.*
8. *The clerk is angry and gives Gregor a stern warning.*
9. *Gregor's parents and sister do not know what has happened to him.*
10. *Gregor's mother faints at the sight of him.*

HOW MANY: *some, few, ten, none, both, each*

EXAMPLE: *Some diners had sweet potatoes.*

HOW MUCH: *more, less, enough, plenty*

EXAMPLE: *There was enough chicken to serve everyone.*

4.2 PREDICATE ADJECTIVES

Most adjectives come before the nouns they modify, as in the preceding examples. A **predicate adjective,** however, follows a linking verb and describes the subject.

EXAMPLE: *My friends are very intelligent.*

Be especially careful to use adjectives (not adverbs) after such linking verbs as *look, feel, grow, taste,* and *smell.*

EXAMPLE: *The weather grows cold.*

4.3 ADVERBS

Adverbs modify verbs, adjectives, and other adverbs by telling where, when, how, or to what extent.

WHERE: *The children played outside.*

WHEN: *The author spoke yesterday.*

HOW: *We walked slowly behind the leader.*

TO WHAT EXTENT: *He worked very hard.*

Adverbs may occur in many places in sentences, both before and after the words they modify.

EXAMPLES:

Suddenly the wind shifted.

The wind suddenly shifted.

The wind shifted suddenly.

4.4 ADJECTIVE OR ADVERB?

Many adverbs are formed by adding *–ly* to adjectives.

EXAMPLES:

sweet, sweetly; gentle, gently

However, *–ly* added to a noun will usually yield an adjective.

EXAMPLES:

friend, friendly; woman, womanly

4.5 COMPARISON OF MODIFIERS

Modifiers can be used to compare two or more things. The form of a modifier shows the degree of comparison. Both adjectives and adverbs have **comparative** and **superlative** forms.

The **comparative form** is used to compare two things, groups, or actions.

EXAMPLES:

His emperor's chariots are faster than mine.

Brutus' speech was more effective than Cassius' speech.

The **superlative form** is used to compare more than two things, groups, or actions.

EXAMPLES:

The emperor's chariots are the fastest.

Antony's speech was the most effective of all.

4.6 REGULAR COMPARISONS

Most one-syllable and some two-syllable adjectives and adverbs have comparatives and superlatives formed by adding *–er* and *–est.* All three-syllable and most two-syllable modifiers have comparatives and superlatives formed with *more* or *most.*

Modifier	Comparative	Superlative
tall	taller	tallest
kind	kinder	kindest
droopy	droopier	droopiest
expensive	more expensive	most expensive
wasteful	more wasteful	most wasteful

WATCH OUT! Note that spelling changes must sometimes be made to form the comparatives and superlatives of modifiers.

EXAMPLES:

friendly, friendlier (Change *y* to *i* and add the ending.)

sad, sadder (Double the final consonant and add the ending.)

4.7 IRREGULAR COMPARISONS

Some commonly used modifiers have irregular comparative and superlative forms. They are listed in the following chart:

Modifier	Comparative	Superlative
good	better	best
bad	worse	worst
far	farther *or* further	farthest *or* furthest
little	less *or* lesser	least
many	more	most
well	better	best
much	more	most

4.8 PROBLEMS WITH MODIFIERS

Study the tips that follow to avoid common mistakes:

Farther* and *Further Use *farther* for distances; use *further* for everything else.

Double Comparisons Make a comparison by using *–er/–est* or by using *more/most*. Using *–er* with *more* or using *–est* with *most* is incorrect.

> INCORRECT: *I like her more better than she likes me.*

> CORRECT: *I like her better than she likes me.*

Illogical Comparisons An illogical or confusing comparison results when two unrelated things are compared or when something is compared with itself. The word *other* or the word *else* should be used when comparing an individual member to the rest of a group.

> ILLOGICAL: *The narrator was more curious about the war than any student in his class.* (implies that the narrator isn't a student in the class)

> LOGICAL: *The narrator was more curious about the war than any other student in his class.* (identifies that the narrator is a student)

Bad* vs. *Badly *Bad,* always an adjective, is used before a noun or after a linking verb. *Badly,* always an adverb, never modifies a noun. Be sure to use the right form after a linking verb.

> INCORRECT: *Ed felt badly after his team lost.*

> CORRECT: *Ed felt bad after his team lost.*

Good* vs. *Well *Good* is always an adjective. It is used before a noun or after a linking verb. *Well* is often an adverb meaning "expertly" or "properly." *Well* can also be used as an adjective after a linking verb when it means "in good health."

> INCORRECT: *Helen writes very good.*

> CORRECT: *Helen writes very well.*

> CORRECT: *Yesterday I felt bad; today I feel well.*

Double Negatives If you add a negative word to a sentence that is already negative, the result will be an error known as a double negative. When using *not* or *–n't* with a verb, use *any–* words, such as *anybody* or *anything,* rather than *no–* words, such as *nobody* or *nothing,* later in the sentence.

> INCORRECT: *I don't have no money.*

> CORRECT: *I don't have any money.*

Using *hardly, barely,* or *scarcely* after a negative word is also incorrect.

> INCORRECT: *They couldn't barely see two feet ahead.*

> CORRECT: *They could barely see two feet ahead.*

Misplaced Modifiers Sometimes a modifier is placed so far away from the word it modifies that the intended meaning of the sentence is unclear. Prepositional phrases and participial phrases are often misplaced. Place modifiers as close as possible to the words they modify.

> MISPLACED: *The ranger explained how to find ducks in her office.* (The ducks were not in the ranger's office.)

> CLEARER: *In her office, the ranger explained how to find ducks.*

PRACTICE AND APPLY

Answers:

1. *most powerful*
2. *any*
3. *could*
4. *well*

PRACTICE AND APPLY

Answers:

1. *Soldiers hidden by trees marched toward Macbeth's castle.*
2. *Angry at the witches, Macbeth realized his many mistakes.*
3. *correct*
4. *Reckless ambition, striving for success at any cost, is a key theme in Macbeth.*

Dangling Modifiers Sometimes a modifier doesn't appear to modify any word in a sentence. Most dangling modifiers are participial phrases or infinitive phrases.

> DANGLING: *Coming home with groceries, our parrot said, "Hello!"*

> CLEARER: *Coming home with groceries, we heard our parrot say, "Hello!"*

Practice and Apply

Choose the correct word or words from each pair in parentheses.

1. The play *Julius Caesar* is about the death of the (powerfulest, most powerful) emperor of Roman times.
2. The emperor didn't pay (no, any) attention to the soothsayer who warned him about the ides of March.
3. Caesar (could, couldn't) hardly know what lay in store for him.
4. He thought Brutus loved him (well, good).

Practice and Apply

Rewrite each sentence that contains a misplaced or dangling modifier. Write "correct" if the sentence is written correctly.

1. Soldiers marched toward Macbeth's castle hidden by trees.
2. Angry at the witches, his many mistakes became clear to Macbeth.
3. Weary of struggling for power, Macbeth called for his armor.
4. Reckless ambition is a key theme in *Macbeth,* striving for success at any cost.

5 The Sentence and Its Parts

A **sentence** is a group of words used to express a complete thought. A complete sentence has a subject and a predicate.

5.1 KINDS OF SENTENCES

There are four basic types of sentences:

Type	Definition	Example
Declarative	states a fact, a wish, an intent, or a feeling	I read White's essay last night.
Interrogative	asks a question	Did you like the essay?
Imperative	gives a command or direction	Read this paragraph aloud.
Exclamatory	expresses strong feeling or excitement	I wish I had thought of that!

5.2 COMPOUND SUBJECTS AND PREDICATES

A compound subject consists of two or more subjects that share the same verb. They are typically joined by the coordinating conjunction *and* or *or.*

> EXAMPLE: *Ray and Joe write about families.*

A compound predicate consists of two or more predicates that share the same subject. They too are typically joined by a coordinating conjunction, usually *and, but,* or *or.*

> EXAMPLE: *The father in the poem "Those Winter Sundays" got up early and dressed in the dark.*

5.3 COMPLEMENTS

A **complement** is a word or group of words that completes the meaning of the sentence. Some sentences contain only a subject and a verb. Most sentences, however, require additional words placed after the verb to complete the meaning of the sentence. There are three kinds of complements: direct objects, indirect objects, and subject complements.

Direct objects are words or word groups that receive the action of action verbs. A direct object answers the question *what* or *whom*.

EXAMPLES:

The students asked many questions.
(Asked what?)

The teacher quickly answered the students.
(Answered whom?)

Indirect objects tell to whom or what or for whom or what the actions of verbs are performed. Indirect objects come before direct objects. In the examples that follow, the indirect objects are highlighted.

EXAMPLES:

My sister usually gave her friends good advice. (Gave to whom?)

Her brother sent the store a heavy package. (Sent to what?)

Subject complements come after linking verbs and identify or describe the subjects. A subject complement that names or identifies a subject is called a **predicate nominative.** Predicate nominatives include **predicate nouns** and **predicate pronouns.**

EXAMPLES:

My friends are very hard workers.

The best writer in the class is she.

A subject complement that describes a subject is called a **predicate adjective.**

EXAMPLE: *The pianist appeared very energetic.*

6 Phrases

A **phrase** is a group of related words that does not contain a subject and a predicate but functions in a sentence as a single part of speech.

6.1 NOUN PHRASE

A **noun phrase** includes a noun and the modifiers that distinguish it. Modifiers might come before or after the noun.

EXAMPLES:

The world-class pianist received many accolades after her performance.

The pianist who played at Carnegie Hall was famous for tackling challenging pieces.

In these examples, the noun *pianist* is modified by *world-class* and *who played at Carnegie Hall.* The noun and its modifiers form the noun phrase.

Practice and Apply

Add a modifier to at least one noun in each sentence to create a noun phrase.

1. The song was a hit.
2. My teacher gives a pop quiz every week.
3. A fence borders the edge of campus.
4. The museum was inspiring.
5. The restaurant is known for its cuisine.

6.2 VERB PHRASES

A **verb phrase** consists of at least one main verb and one or more helping verbs. A helping verb (also called an auxiliary verb) helps the main verb express action or state of being.

Besides all forms of the verb *be,* some common helping verbs are *can, could, did, do, does, had, have, may, might, must, shall, should, will,* and *would.*

EXAMPLE: *The veterinarian should consider an expansion of his practice.*

Sometimes the parts of a verb phrase are interrupted by other parts of speech.

EXAMPLE: *The veterinarian had recently been considering an expansion of his practice.*

The word *not* is an adverb. It is never part of a verb phrase, even when it is joined to a verb as the contraction *–n't.*

EXAMPLES:

The dog should not have bitten the boy.

The dog shouldn't have bitten the boy.

COMMON CORE L 1b

PRACTICE AND APPLY

Possible answers:

1. *The catchy song with clever lyrics was an instant hit.*
2. *My demanding Latin teacher gives a pop quiz every week.*
3. *An intimidating fence topped with barbed wire borders the edge of campus.*
4. *The newly remodeled modern art museum was inspiring.*
5. *The restaurant, often surrounded by lines of waiting customers, is known for its Asian fusion cuisine.*

PRACTICE AND APPLY

Possible answers:

1. *She should look both ways before crossing the street.*
2. *The Ruiz family has visited Hawaii every summer.*
3. *The chef will always taste his food before serving it.*
4. *The tree had grown to be 30 feet tall.*
5. *The journey may take a month to complete.*

PRACTICE AND APPLY

Possible answers:

1. *At 6:00 every morning, Mrs. Bowen reads the newspaper. (adverb)*
2. *I watched a spider climb up the railing. (adverb)*
3. *Everyone in the bleachers was cheering. (adjective)*
4. *Until it got too hot, the children played hopscotch. (adverb)*
5. *Hundreds of stunned passersby stared. (adjective)*

Practice and Apply

Rewrite each sentence to include a helping verb.

1. She looks both ways before crossing the street.
2. The Ruiz family visited Hawaii every summer.
3. The chef always tastes his food before serving it.
4. The tree grew to be 30 feet tall.
5. The journey takes a month to complete.

6.3 PREPOSITIONAL PHRASES

A **prepositional phrase** is a phrase that consists of a preposition, its object, and any modifiers of the object. Prepositional phrases that modify nouns or pronouns are called **adjective phrases.** Prepositional phrases that modify verbs, adjectives, or adverbs are **adverb phrases.**

> ADJECTIVE PHRASE: *The central character of the story is a villain.*

> ADVERB PHRASE: *He reveals his nature in the first scene.*

Remember that adjectives modify nouns by telling which one, what kind, how much, or how many. Adverbs modify verbs, adjectives, and other adverbs by telling where, when, how, or to what extent. The same is true of prepositional phrases that act as adjective phrases or adverb phrases.

Practice and Apply

Provide a prepositional phrase to complete each of the following sentences. After the sentence, identify the phrase as an adjective phrase or an adverb phrase.

1. _____ Mrs. Bowen reads the newspaper.
2. I watched a spider climb _____.
3. Everyone _____ was cheering.
4. _____ the children played hopscotch.
5. Hundreds _____ stared.

6.4 APPPOSITIVES AND APPOSITIVE PHRASES

An **appositive** is a noun or pronoun that identifies or renames another noun or pronoun. An **appositive phrase** includes an appositive and modifiers of it.

An appositive can be either **essential** or **nonessential.** An **essential appositive** provides information that is needed to identify what is referred to by the preceding noun or pronoun.

> EXAMPLE: *This poem was written by author Walt Whitman.*

A **nonessential appositive** adds extra information about a noun or pronoun whose meaning is already clear. Nonessential appositives and appositive phrases are set off with commas.

> EXAMPLE: *He wrote this poem, a sad remembrance of war, about an artilleryman.*

7 Verbals and Verbal Phrases

A **verbal** is a verb form that is used as a noun, an adjective, or an adverb. A **verbal phrase** consists of a verbal along with its modifiers and complements. There are three kinds of verbals: **infinitives, participles,** and **gerunds.**

7.1 INFINITIVES AND INFINITIVE PHRASES

An **infinitive** is a verb form that usually begins with *to* and functions as a noun, an adjective, or an adverb. An **infinitive phrase** consists of an infinitive plus its modifiers and complements. The examples that follow show several uses of infinitive phrases.

> NOUN: *To know her is my only desire.* (subject)

> *I'm planning to walk with you.* (direct object)

> *Her goal was to promote women's rights.* (predicate nominative)

> ADJECTIVE: *We saw his need to be loved.* (adjective modifying *need*)

> ADVERB: *She wrote to voice her opinions.* (adverb modifying *wrote*)

Because *to*, the sign of the infinitive, precedes infinitives, it is usually easy to recognize them. However, sometimes *to* may be omitted.

> EXAMPLE: *Let no one dare [to] enter this shrine.*

7.2 PARTICIPLES AND PARTICIPIAL PHRASES

A **participle** is a verb form that functions as an adjective. Like adjectives, participles modify nouns and pronouns. Most participles are present-participle forms, ending in *–ing*, or past-participle forms ending in *–ed* or *–en*. In these examples, the participles are highlighted.

> MODIFYING A NOUN: *The smiling man ate another dumpling.*
>
> MODIFYING A PRONOUN: *Ignored, she slipped out of the room unnoticed.*

Participial phrases are participles with all their modifiers and complements.

> MODIFYING A NOUN: *Visiting gardens, butterflies flit among the flowers.*
>
> MODIFYING A PRONOUN: *Driven by instinct, they use the flowers as meal stops.*

Practice and Apply

Identify the participial phrases and participles that are used as adjectives in the following sentences, and indicate the word each phrase modifies.

1. Aided by good weather and clear skies, the sailors sailed into port a day early.
2. Searching through old clothes in a trunk, Ricardo found a map showing the location of buried treasure.
3. I would love to see it blooming: it must be quite a sight!
4. The cat hissed at the dog barking in the yard next door.
5. Waxing his car in the driveway, Joe overheard a bit of song from an open window nearby.

7.3 DANGLING AND MISPLACED PARTICIPLES

A participle or participial phrase should be placed as close as possible to the word that it modifies. Otherwise the meaning of the sentence may not be clear.

> MISPLACED: *The boys were looking for squirrels searching the trees.*
>
> CLEARER: *The boys searching the trees were looking for squirrels.*

A participle or participial phrase that does not clearly modify anything in a sentence is called a **dangling participle.** A dangling participle causes confusion because it appears to modify a word that it cannot sensibly modify. Correct a dangling participle by providing a word for the participle to modify.

> DANGLING: *Running like the wind, my hat fell off.* (The hat wasn't running.)
>
> CLEARER: *Running like the wind, I lost my hat.*

7.4 GERUNDS AND GERUND PHRASES

A **gerund** is a verb form ending in *–ing* that functions as a noun. A gerund may perform any function that a noun performs.

> SUBJECT: *Running is my favorite pastime.*
>
> DIRECT OBJECT: *I truly love running.*
>
> INDIRECT OBJECT: *You should give running a try.*
>
> SUBJECT COMPLEMENT: *My deepest passion is running.*
>
> OBJECT OF PREPOSITION: *Her love of running keeps her strong.*

Gerund phrases are gerunds with all their modifiers and complements.

> SUBJECT: *Wishing on a star never got me far.*
>
> OBJECT OF PREPOSITION: *I will finish before leaving the office.*
>
> APPOSITIVE: *Her avocation, flying airplanes, finally led to full-time employment.*

COMMON CORE L 1b

PRACTICE AND APPLY

Answers:

1. *"aided by good weather and clear skies"; modifies "sailors"*
2. *"searching through old clothes in a trunk"; modifies "Ricardo"*
3. *"blooming"; modifies "it"*
4. *"barking in the yard next door"; modifies "dog"*
5. *"Waxing his car in the driveway"; modifies "Joe"*

PRACTICE AND APPLY

Possible answers:

1. *The sun hovering with anticipation on the horizon, Dexter waited for his date to arrive.*

2. *The road never seemed to end, the center stripe stretching into the distance beyond sight.*

3. *An awards banquet having been scheduled at the last minute, Maria prepared a feast.*

4. *The heat of the day finally relenting, the sun set beyond the sparkling lake.*

5. *School vacation having just ended, the test was more difficult than we expected.*

PRACTICE AND APPLY

Possible answers:

1. *Last year, Katrina and her family moved to St. Louis, excited about this new adventure.*

2. *At a highway rest stop, her pet cat, a black-and-white ball of energy named Rocket, escaped.*

3. *The family searched desperately to locate their beloved pet.*

4. *Feeling hopeless after hours of fruitless searching, they had to keep going.*

5. *Katrina's cat tracked them all the way to their new home, the mystery of how Rocket knew where to find them never having been solved.*

7.5 ABSOLUTE PHRASES

An **absolute phrase** is a noun or pronoun, its participle, and any modifiers. It modifies an entire clause, rather than just one word.

> EXAMPLE: *The backyard filled with lightning bugs, the children shouted with delight.*

In this example, *The backyard filled with lightning bugs* is an absolute phrase that modifies the sentence *the children shouted with delight*. The noun *backyard* is modified by the participle *filled* and by the prepositional phrase *with lightning bugs*. Notice that a comma separates the absolute phrase from the sentence.

Practice and Apply

Add an absolute phrase to modify each sentence.
1. Dexter waited for his date to arrive.
2. The road never seemed to end.
3. Maria prepared a feast.
4. The sun set beyond the sparkling lake.
5. The test was more difficult than we expected.

Practice and Apply

Rewrite each sentence, adding the type of phrase shown in parentheses.
1. Last year, Katrina and her family moved to St. Louis. (participial phrase)
2. At a highway rest stop, her pet cat escaped. (appositive phrase)
3. The family searched desperately. (infinitive phrase)
4. They had to keep going. (gerund phrase)
5. Katrina's cat tracked them all the way to their new home. (absolute phrase)

8 Clauses

A **clause** is a group of words that contains a subject and a verb. There are two kinds of clauses: independent clauses and subordinate clauses.

8.1 INDEPENDENT AND SUBORDINATE CLAUSES

An **independent clause** can stand alone as a sentence, as the word *independent* suggests.

> INDEPENDENT CLAUSE: *Emily Dickinson did not wish her poems to be published.*

A sentence may contain more than one independent clause.

> EXAMPLE: *Emily Dickinson did not wish her poems to be published, but seven were published during her lifetime.*

In the preceding example, the coordinating conjunction *but* joins two independent clauses.

Two independent clauses can also be joined with a **conjunctive adverb,** such as *consequently, finally, furthermore, however, moreover,* or *nevertheless.* To separate the two independent clauses, a semicolon is often used before the conjunctive adverb.

> EXAMPLE: *The painter decided to take up sculpture;* **however,** *his studio was not big enough for large projects.*

A **subordinate clause ,** or **dependent clause,** cannot stand alone as a sentence. It is subordinate to, or dependent on, an independent clause.

> EXAMPLE: *Emily Dickinson did not wish her poems to be published, although she shared them with friends.*

The highlighted clause cannot stand by itself.

Practice and Apply

Identify each italicized clause in the following sentences as independent or subordinate (dependent). Explain your responses.

1. I heard that one of the guests *who spoke at the ceremony* was Barbara Jordan.
2. *Whenever I think of Barbara Jordan,* I imagine her as she looks in a picture taken at my mother's college graduation in 1986.
3. According to my mother, *Jordan spoke eloquently about the importance of values in our society.*
4. *When Jordan began her public service career in 1966,* she became the first African American woman to serve in the Texas legislature.
5. Two years after the speech, *Jordan decided that she would retire from national politics.*

8.2 ADJECTIVE CLAUSES

An **adjective clause,** or **relative clause,** is a subordinate clause used as an adjective. It usually follows the noun or pronoun it modifies.

> EXAMPLE: *Robert Frost wrote about birch tree branches that boys swing on.*

Adjective clauses are typically introduced by the relative pronoun *who, whom, whose, which,* or *that.*

> EXAMPLES:
> *One song that we like became our theme song. Emily Dickinson, whose poems have touched many, lived a very quiet life.*

An adjective clause can be either restrictive or nonrestrictive. A **restrictive adjective clause** provides information that is necessary to identify the preceding noun or pronoun.

> EXAMPLE: *The candidate whom we selected promised to serve us well.*

A **nonessential adjective clause** adds additional information about a noun or pronoun whose meaning is already clear.

Nonrestrictive clauses are set off with commas.

> EXAMPLE: *Brookhaven National Laboratory, which employs Mr. Davis, is in Upton, New York.*

TIP The relative pronouns *whom, which,* and *that* may sometimes be omitted when they are objects in adjective clauses.

> EXAMPLE: *Frost is a writer [whom] millions enjoy.*

Practice and Apply

Revise the following sentences by substituting an adjective clause (relative clause) for each italicized adjective. Add specific details to make your sentences interesting.

1. As I ran on the track, a *large* dog approached me.
2. The *international* artist received many awards.
3. The four students discussed the *annual* tournament.
4. After the party, the caterer made himself a *delicious* cup of tea.
5. Angela and her classmates excitedly entered the *old* theater.

8.3 ADVERB CLAUSES

An **adverb clause** is a subordinate clause that is used to modify a verb, an adjective, or an adverb. It is introduced by a subordinating conjunction.

Adverb clauses typically occur at the beginning or end of sentences.

> MODIFYING A VERB: *When we need you, we will call.*

> MODIFYING AN ADVERB: *I'll stay here where there is shelter from the rain.*

> MODIFYING AN ADJECTIVE: *Roman felt as good as he had ever felt.*

 L 1b

PRACTICE AND APPLY

Answers:

1. *subordinate; cannot stand alone*
2. *subordinate; cannot stand alone*
3. *independent; is a complete sentence by itself*
4. *subordinate; cannot stand alone*
5. *independent; is a complete sentence by itself*

PRACTICE AND APPLY

Possible answers:

1. *As I ran on the track, a dog that was the size of a small pony approached me.*
2. *The artist, who was from Barcelona but had worked in Israel and Denmark, received many awards.*
3. *The four students discussed the tournament, which was held every year on the day that Daylight Savings Time began.*
4. *After the party, the caterer made himself a cup of tea that was flavored with cinnamon and cloves.*
5. *Angela and her classmates excitedly entered the theater, which had stood for nearly a century and hosted now-legendary performers.*

PRACTICE AND APPLY

Answers:

1. *adverb clause: "While the others worked inside the house"; subordinating conjunction: "While"*

2. *adverb clause: "Because the house had been vacant for so long"; subordinating conjunction: "Because"*

3. *adverb clause: "as if it hadn't been cut in months"; subordinating conjunction: "as"*

4. *adverb clause: "while Lou and I weeded the flower beds"; subordinating conjunction: "while"*

5. *adverb clause: "since the weeds were extremely thick"; subordinating conjunction: "since"*

PRACTICE AND APPLY

Answers:

1. *"that we would play at half time this week"; direct object*

2. *"what we would be playing during the half-time show"; direct object*

3. *"What we can never predict"; subject*

4. *"whoever is asked to play each selection"; indirect object*

5. *"what we think of his sometimes unusual choices"; object of a preposition*

PRACTICE AND APPLY

Possible answers:

1. *Ms. Nguyen is a scientist who works at the local university.*

2. *She has invented many things that are useful to everyone.*

3. *She works wherever her interests send her.*

4. *She does her best thinking at night when it is quiet.*

5. *She should invent a better backpack that will benefit all students.*

Practice and Apply

Identify the adverb clause and subordinating conjuction in each of the following sentences.

1. While the others worked inside the house, Ruth, Lou, and I worked in the yard.
2. Because the house had been vacant for so long, the lawn and gardens were overgrown.
3. The grass in the front looked as if it hadn't been cut in months.
4. Ruth began mowing the lawn while Lou and I weeded the flower beds.
5. We decided to borrow some tools since the weeds were extremely thick.

8.4 NOUN CLAUSES

A **noun clause** is a subordinate clause that is used as a noun. A noun clause may be used as a subject, a direct object, an indirect object, a predicate nominative, or the object of a preposition. Noun clauses are introduced either by pronouns, such as *that, what, who, whoever, which*, and *whose*, or by subordinating conjunctions, such as *how, when, where, why*, and *whether*.

TIP Because the same words may introduce adjective and noun clauses, you need to consider how a clause functions within its sentence. To determine whether a clause is a noun clause, try substituting *something* or *someone* for the clause. If you can do it, it is probably a noun clause.

> **EXAMPLES:** *I know whose woods these are.* ("I know *something*." The clause is a noun clause, direct object of the verb *know*.) *Give a copy to whoever wants one.* ("Give a copy to *someone*." The clause is a noun clause, object of the preposition *to*.)

Practice and Apply

Identify the noun clause in each sentence. Then, tell how each clause is used: as a subject, a predicate nominative, a direct object, an indirect object, or an object of a preposition.

1. Mr. Perkins, the band director, announced that we would play at half time this week.
2. Mr. Perkins did not tell us, however, what we would be playing during the half-time show.
3. What we can never predict is whether he will choose a familiar march or a show tune.
4. He always gives whoever is asked to play each selection a chance to express an opinion about it.
5. He is genuinely interested in what we think of his sometimes unusual choices.

Practice and Apply

Add descriptive details to each sentence by writing the type of clause indicated in parentheses.

1. Ms. Nguyen is a scientist. (adjective clause)
2. She has invented many things. (adjective clause)
3. She works. (adverb clause)
4. She does her best thinking at night. (adverb clause)
5. She should invent a better backpack. (adjective clause)

9 The Structure of Sentences

When classified by their structure, there are four kinds of sentences: simple, compound, complex, and compound-complex.

9.1 SIMPLE SENTENCES

A **simple sentence** is a sentence that has one independent clause and no subordinate clauses.

The fact that such a sentence is called simple does not mean that it is uncomplicated. Various parts of simple sentences may be compound, and simple sentences may contain grammatical structures such as appositive and verbal phrases.

> **EXAMPLES:**
> *Mark Twain, an unsuccessful gold miner, wrote many successful satires and tall tales.* (appositive and compound direct object)
> *Pablo Neruda, drawn to writing poetry at an early age, won celebrity at age 20.* (participial and gerund phrases)

9.2 COMPOUND SENTENCES

A **compound sentence** consists of two or more independent clauses. The clauses in compound sentences are joined with commas and coordinating conjunctions (*and, but, or, nor, yet, for, so*) or with semicolons. Like simple sentences, compound sentences do not contain any subordinate clauses.

> **EXAMPLES:**
> *I enjoyed Bradbury's story "The Utterly Perfect Murder," and I want to read more of his stories.*
> *Amy Lowell's poem "The Taxi" has powerful images; however, it does not use the word "taxi" anywhere in it.*

WATCH OUT! Do not confuse compound sentences with simple sentences that have compound parts.

> **EXAMPLE:** *A subcommittee drafted a document and immediately presented it to the entire group.* (Here *and* joins parts of a compound predicate, not a compound sentence.)

9.3 COMPLEX SENTENCES

A **complex sentence** consists of one independent clause and one or more subordinate clauses. Each subordinate clause can be used as a noun or as a modifier. If it is used as a modifier, a subordinate clause usually modifies a word in the independent clause, and the independent clause can stand alone. However, when a subordinate clause is a noun clause, it is a part of the independent clause; the two cannot be separated.

> **MODIFIER:** *One should not complain unless one has a better solution.*

> **NOUN CLAUSE:** *We sketched pictures of whomever we wished.* (The noun clause is the object of the preposition *of* and cannot be separated from the rest of the sentence.)

9.4 COMPOUND-COMPLEX SENTENCES

A **compound-complex sentence** contains two or more independent clauses and one or more subordinate clauses. Compound-complex sentences are both compound and complex. If you start with a compound sentence, all you need to do to form a compound-complex sentence is add a subordinate clause.

> **COMPOUND:** *All the students knew the answer, yet they were too shy to volunteer.*

> **COMPOUND-COMPLEX:** *All the students knew the answer that their teacher expected, yet they were too shy to volunteer.*

9.5 PARALLEL STRUCTURE

When you write sentences, make sure that coordinate parts are equivalent, or **parallel,** in structure.

> **NOT PARALLEL:** *Erin loved basketball and to play hockey.* (*Basketball* is a noun; *to play hockey* is a phrase.)

> **PARALLEL:** *Erin loved basketball and hockey.* (*Basketball* and *hockey* are both nouns.)

> **NOT PARALLEL:** *He wanted to rent an apartment, a new car, and traveling around the country.* (*To rent* is an infinitive, *car* is a noun, and *traveling* is a gerund.)

> **PARALLEL:** *He wanted to rent an apartment, to drive a new car, and to travel around the country.* (*To rent, to drive,* and *to travel* are all infinitives.)

🔟 Writing Complete Sentences

Remember, a sentence is a group of words that expresses a complete thought. In formal writing, try to avoid both sentence fragments and run-on sentences.

10.1 CORRECTING FRAGMENTS

A **sentence fragment** is a group of words that is only part of a sentence. It does not express a complete thought and may be confusing to a reader or listener. A sentence fragment may be lacking a subject, a predicate, or both.

FRAGMENT: *Waited for the boat to arrive.* (no subject)

CORRECTED: *We waited for the boat to arrive.*

FRAGMENT: *People of various races, ages, and creeds.* (no predicate)

CORRECTED: *People of various races, ages, and creeds gathered together.*

FRAGMENT: *Near the old cottage.* (neither subject nor predicate)

CORRECTED: *The burial ground is near the old cottage.*

In your writing, fragments may be a result of haste or incorrect punctuation. Sometimes fixing a fragment will be a matter of attaching it to a preceding or following sentence.

FRAGMENT: *We saw the two girls. Waiting for the bus to arrive.*

CORRECTED: *We saw the two girls waiting for the bus to arrive.*

10.2 CORRECTING RUN-ON SENTENCES

A **run-on sentence** is made up of two or more sentences written as though they were one. Some run-ons have no punctuation within them. Others may have only commas where conjunctions or stronger punctuation marks are necessary. Use your judgment in correcting run-on sentences, as you have choices. You can make a run-on two sentences if the thoughts are not closely connected. If the thoughts are closely related, you can keep the run-on as one sentence by adding a semicolon or a conjunction.

RUN-ON: *We found a place for the picnic by a small pond it was three miles from the village.*

MAKE TWO SENTENCES: *We found a place for the picnic by a small pond. It was three miles from the village.*

RUN-ON: *We found a place for the picnic by a small pond it was perfect.*

USE A SEMICOLON: *We found a place for the picnic by a small pond near the village; it was perfect.*

ADD A CONJUNCTION: *We found a place for the picnic by a small pond, and it was perfect.*

WATCH OUT! When you form compound sentences, make sure you use appropriate punctuation: use a comma before a coordinating conjunction, and use a semicolon when there is no coordinating conjunction. A very common mistake is to use a comma alone instead of a comma and a conjunction. This error is called a **comma splice.**

INCORRECT: *He finished the apprenticeship, he left the village.*

CORRECT: *He finished the apprenticeship, and he left the village.*

11 Subject-Verb Agreement

The subject and verb in a clause must agree in number. Agreement means that if the subject is singular, the verb is also singular, and if the subject is plural, the verb is also plural.

11.1 BASIC AGREEMENT

Fortunately, agreement between subjects and verbs in English is usually simple. Most verbs show the difference between singular and plural only in the third person of the present tense. In the present tense, the third-person plural form does not change, but the third-person singular form ends in *–s.*

Present-Tense Verb Forms	
Singular	**Plural**
I jog	we jog
you jog	you jog
she, he, it jogs	they jog

11.2 AGREEMENT WITH *BE*

The verb *be* presents special problems in agreement, because this verb does not follow the usual verb patterns.

Forms of *Be*			
Present Tense		**Past Tense**	
Singular	**Plural**	**Singular**	**Plural**
I am	we are	I was	we were
you are	you are	you were	you were
she, he, it is	they are	she, he, it was	they were

11.3 WORDS BETWEEN SUBJECT AND VERB

A verb agrees only with its subject. When words come between a subject and a verb, ignore them when considering proper agreement. Identify the subject, and make sure the verb agrees with it.

> **EXAMPLES:** *A story in the newspapers tells about the 1890s.*
>
> *Dad as well as Mom reads the paper daily*

11.4 AGREEMENT WITH COMPOUND SUBJECTS

Use plural verbs with most compound subjects joined by the word *and*.

> **EXAMPLE:** *My father and his friends play chess every day.*

To confirm that you need a plural verb, you could substitute the plural pronoun *they* for *my father and his friends.*

If a compound subject is thought of as a unit, use a singular verb. Test this by substituting the singular pronoun *it.*

> **EXAMPLE:** *Peanut butter and jelly [it] is my brother's favorite sandwich.*

Use a singular verb with a compound subject that is preceded by *each, every,* or *many a.*

> **EXAMPLE:** *Each novel and short story seems grounded in personal experience.*

When the parts of a compound subject are joined by *or, nor,* or the correlative conjunctions *either . . . or* or *neither . . . nor,* make the verb agree with the noun or pronoun nearest the verb.

> **EXAMPLES:**
> *Cookies or ice cream is my favorite dessert.*
> *Either Cheryl or her friends are being invited.*
> *Neither ice storms nor snow is predicted today.*

11.5 PERSONAL PRONOUNS AS SUBJECTS

When using a personal pronoun as a subject, make sure to match it with the correct form of the verb *be.* (See the chart in Section 11.2.) Note especially that the pronoun *you* takes the forms *are* and *were,* regardless of whether it is singular or plural.

> **WATCH OUT!** *You is* and *you was* are nonstandard forms and should be avoided in writing and speaking. *We was* and *they was* are also forms to be avoided.
>
> **INCORRECT:** *You was helping me.*
> **CORRECT:** *You were helping me.*
> **INCORRECT:** *They was hoping for this.*
> **CORRECT:** *They were hoping for this.*

11.6 INDEFINITE PRONOUNS AS SUBJECTS

Some indefinite pronouns are always singular; some are always plural.

Singular Indefinite Pronouns			
another	either	neither	one
anybody	everbody	nobody	somebody
anyone	everyone	no one	someone
anything	everything	nothing	something
each	much		

L 1b

PRACTICE AND APPLY

Answers:

1. *think*
2. *Is*
3. *was*
4. *are*
5. *was*
6. *were*
7. *enjoys*
8. *was*
9. *was*
10. *were*

EXAMPLES:

Each of the first-time writers was given an award.

Somebody in the bedroom upstairs is sleeping.

Plural Indefinite Pronouns			
both	few	many	several

EXAMPLES:

Many of the books in our library are not in circulation.
Few have been returned recently.

Still other indefinite pronouns may be either singular or plural, depending on the context.

Singular or Plural Indefinite Pronouns		
all	more	none
any	most	some

The number of the indefinite pronoun *any* or *none* often depends on the intended meaning.

EXAMPLES:

Any of these topics has potential for a good article. (any one topic)
Any of these topics have potential for good articles. (all of the many topics)

The indefinite pronouns *all, some, more, most,* and *none* are singular when they refer to quantities or parts of things. They are plural when they refer to numbers of individual things. Context will usually give you a clue.

EXAMPLES:

All of the flour is gone. (referring to a quantity)
All of the flowers are gone. (referring to individual items)

11.7 INVERTED SENTENCES

Problems in agreement often occur in inverted sentences beginning with *here* or *there;* in questions beginning with *how, when, why, where,* or *what;* and in inverted sentences beginning with phrases. Identify the subject—wherever it is—before deciding on the verb.

EXAMPLES:

There clearly are far too many cooks in this kitchen.

What is the correct ingredient for this stew? Far from the embroiled cooks stands the master chef.

Practice and Apply

1. Most scholars (think, thinks) the author of *Le Morte d'Arthur* is Sir Thomas Malory.
2. (Is, Are) the author Syr Thomas Maleore, knight, the same as Sir Thomas Malory?
3. Sir Thomas himself, who lived during the Middle Ages, (was, were) a knight.
4. There (is, are) many knights and ladies in the tales of King Arthur.
5. One of the greatest prose works in the English language, *Le Morte d'Arthur* (was, were) based on French versions that were told earlier.
6. Many legends of King Arthur (was, were) also preserved in Wales.
7. Nearly everyone reading these tales (enjoy, enjoys) the adventures of the knights and ladies.
8. Several times Malory (was, were) put in prison.
9. He spent the last three years of his life in prison; he wrote *Le Morte d'Arthur* while he (was, were) there.
10. These tales featuring King Arthur (was, were) published after Malory's death.

11.8 SENTENCES WITH PREDICATE NOMINATIVES

When a predicate nominative serves as a complement in a sentence, use a verb that agrees with the subject, not the complement.

EXAMPLES:

The tales of King Arthur are a great work of literature. (*Tales* is the subject and it takes the plural verb *are.*)
A great work of literature is the tales of King Arthur. (The subject is the singular noun *work.*)

11.9 *DON'T* AND *DOESN'T* AS AUXILIARY VERBS

The auxiliary verb *doesn't* is used with singular subjects and with the personal pronouns *she, he,* and *it.* The auxiliary verb *don't* is used with plural subjects and with the personal pronouns *I, we, you,* and *they.*

SINGULAR:

She doesn't want to be without her cane.

Doesn't the school provide help?

PLURAL:

They don't know what it's like to be hungry.

Bees don't like these flowers by the door.

11.10 COLLECTIVE NOUNS AS SUBJECTS

Collective nouns are singular nouns that name groups of persons or things. *Team,* for example, is the collective name of a group of individuals. A collective noun takes a singular verb when the group acts as a single unit. It takes a plural verb when the members of the group act separately.

EXAMPLES:

Our team usually wins. (The team as a whole wins.)

Our team vote differently on most issues. (The individual members vote.)

11.11 RELATIVE PRONOUNS AS SUBJECTS

When the relative pronoun *who, which,* or *that* is used as a subject in an adjective clause, the verb in the clause must agree in number with the antecedent of the pronoun.

SINGULAR: *Have you selected **one** of the poems that **is** meaningful to you?*

The antecedent of the relative pronoun *that* is the singular *one;* therefore, *that* is singular and must take the singular verb *is.*

PLURAL: *The younger **redwoods,** which grow in a circle around an older tree, **are** also very tall.*

The antecedent of the relative pronoun *which* is the plural *redwoods.* Therefore, *which* is plural, and it takes the plural verb *grow.*

Vocabulary and Spelling

One key to becoming an independent reader is to develop a toolkit of vocabulary strategies. By learning and practicing the strategies, you'll know what to do when you encounter unfamiliar words while reading. You'll also know how to refine the words you use for different situations—personal, school, and work.

Good spelling is important for communicating your ideas in writing. Learning basic spelling rules and checking your spelling in a dictionary will help you spell words you may not use frequently.

1 Using Context Clues

A word's **context** includes the words, sentences, and paragraphs surrounding it. A word's context can give you important clues about its meaning and help you distinguish between its denotative and connotative meanings.

1.1 GENERAL CONTEXT

Sometimes you need to infer the meaning of an unfamiliar word by reading all the information in a passage.

> On extremely hot days, Mariah *languidly* tends her garden. First she strolls to the yard to water her plants. Then she relaxes under a shady tree.

You can figure out from the context that *languidly* means "in a slow and unenergetic way."

1.2 SPECIFIC CONTEXT CLUES

Sometimes writers help you understand the meanings of words by providing specific clues of the kinds in the chart.

Specific Context Clues		
Type of Clue	**Key Words/Phrases**	**Example**
Definition or **restatement** of the meaning of the word	or, which is, that is, in other words, also known as, also called	A lichen is an example of *symbiosis,* **a relationship in which two species benefit from living closely together.**
Example following an unfamiliar word	such as, like, as if, for example, especially, including	*Prokaryotes,* which **include bacteria,** are among the oldest forms of animal life.
Comparison with a more familiar word or concept	like, also, similarly, in the same way, as, likewise	**Like** his **practical-joker** brother, Abe was a *prankster.*
Contrast with a familiar word or experience	unlike, but, however, although, on the other hand, on the contrary	Most organisms **need oxygen to survive, but** many types of bacteria are *anaerobic.*
Cause-and-effect relationship in which one term is familiar	because, since, when, consequently, as a result, therefore	**Because** they have a system of *membranes*, fish can use their **skin and gill tissue** to adjust to different conditions.

1.3 IDIOMS, SLANG, AND FIGURATIVE LANGUAGE

An **idiom** is an expression whose overall meaning is different from the meaning of the individual words. **Slang** is informal language in which made-up words and ordinary words are used to mean something different from their meanings in formal English. **Figurative language** is language that communicates meaning beyond the literal meaning of words. Use context clues to figure out the meanings of idioms, slang, and figurative language.

Trying to find the ring was like looking for a needle in a haystack. (idiom; conveys idea of "difficulty")
When Brenda couldn't find her ring right away, she went ballistic. (slang; means "became angry")
Mr. Gray has had the same car for over 20 years. Now it is just a rusty tin can. (figurative language; rusty tin can symbolizes the age and condition of the car)

2 Analyzing Word Structure

Many words can be broken into smaller parts. These word parts include base words, roots, prefixes, and suffixes.

2.1 BASE WORDS

A **base word** is a word part that by itself is also a word. Other words or word parts can be added to base words to form new words.

2.2 ROOTS

A **root** is a word part that contains the core meaning of the word. Many English words contain roots that come from older languages such as Greek, Latin, Old English (Anglo-Saxon), and Norse. Knowing the meaning of the word's root can help you determine the word's meaning.

Root	Meaning	Example
anthrop (Greek)	human being	anthropology
hydr (Greek)	water	dehydrate
quer, quest (Latin)	ask, seek	question
pend, pens (Latin)	hang	pendulum
hēadfod (Old English)	head, top	headfirst

2.3 PREFIXES

A **prefix** is a word part attached to the beginning of a word. Most prefixes come from Greek, Latin, or Old English.

Prefix	Meaning	Example
anti–	opposed to	antisocial
de–	down, away from	degrade
sub–	under	submarine

2.4 SUFFIXES

A **suffix** is a word part that appears at the end of a root or base word to form a new word. Some suffixes do not change word meaning. These suffixes are

- added to nouns to change the number of persons or objects
- added to verbs to change the tense
- added to modifiers to change the degree of comparison

Suffixes	Meaning	Example
–s, –es	to change the number of a noun	trunk + s = trunks
–d, –ed, –ing	to change verb tense	sprinkle + d = sprinkled
–er, –est	to change the degree of comparison in modifiers	cold + er = colder icy + est = iciest

Other suffixes can be added to a root or base to change the word's meaning. These suffixes can also determine a word's part of speech.

Suffix	Meaning	Example
–ic	characterized by	sarcastic
–ion	process of	capitalization
–ness	condition of	uneasiness

Strategies for Understanding Unfamiliar Words

- Look for any prefixes or suffixes. Remove them to isolate the base word or the root.
- See if you recognize any elements—prefix, suffix, root, or base —of the word. You may be able to guess its meaning by analyzing one or two elements.
- Consider the way the word is used in the sentence. Use the context and the word parts to make a logical guess about the word's meaning.
- Consult a dictionary to see whether you are correct.

3 Understanding Word Origins

3.1 ETYMOLOGIES

Etymologies show the origin and historical development of a word. When you study a word's history and origin, you can find out when, where, and how the word came to be.

co•ma (kō´mə) *n.*, *pl.* **-mas** A state of deep, often prolonged unconsciousness, usually the result of injury, disease, or poison, in which an individual is incapable of sensing or responding to external stimuli and internal needs. [Greek *kōma*, deep sleep.]

gar•lic (gär´lĭk) *n.* **1.** An onionlike plant of southern Europe having a bulb that breaks into separate cloves with a strong distinctive odor and flavor. **2.** The bulb of this plant. [Middle English, from Old English *gārlēac*: *gār*, spear + *lēac*, leek.]

vin•dic•tive (vĭn-dĭk´tĭv) *adj.*
1. Disposed to seek revenge; revengeful.
2. Marked by or resulting from a desire to hurt; spiteful. (From Latin *vindicta*, vengeance, from *vindex*, *vindic-*, surety, avenger.]

3.2 WORD FAMILIES

Words that have the same root make up a word family and have related meanings. The chart shows a common Greek and a common Latin root. Notice how the meanings of the example words are related to the meanings of their roots.

Latin Root	*spect:* "see"
English	**inspect** look at carefully **respect** look at with esteem **spectator** someone who watches an event

Greek Root	*phil:* "love"
English	**philharmonic** devoted to music **philosophy** love and pursuit of wisdom **philanthropy** love of humankind

3.3 WORDS FROM CLASSICAL MYTHOLOGY

The English language includes many words from classical mythology. You can use your knowledge of Greek, Roman, and Norse myths to understand the origins and meanings of these words. For example, *herculean task* refers to the mythological hero Hercules. Thus *herculean task* probably means "a job that is large or difficult." The chart shows a few common words from mythology.

Greek	Roman	Norse
nemesis	insomnia	Thursday
atlas	fury	berserk
adonis	Saturday	rune
mentor	January	valkyrie

Look up the etymology of each word in the chart and locate the myth associated with it. Use the information from the myth to explain the origin and meaning of each word.

3.4 FOREIGN WORDS

The English language includes words from diverse languages such as French, Dutch, Spanish, Italian, and Chinese. Many of these words retained their original spellings from the source language.

French	Dutch	Spanish	Italian
mirage	cookie	tornado	studio
vague	snoop	bronco	ravioli
beau	hook	salsa	opera

4 Synonyms and Antonyms

4.1 SYNONYMS

A **synonym** is a word with a meaning similar to that of another word. You can find synonyms in a thesaurus or a dictionary. In a dictionary, synonyms are often given as part of the definition of a word. These word pairs are synonyms:

dry/arid   enthralled/fascinated

gaunt/thin   vigorous/strong

4.2 ANTONYMS

An **antonym** is a word with a meaning opposite that of another word. The following word pairs are antonyms:

friend/enemy   absurd/logical

courteous/rude   languid/energetic

5 Denotation and Connotation

5.1 DENOTATION

A word's dictionary meaning is called its **denotation**. For example, the denotation of the word *rascal* is "an unethical, dishonest person."

5.2 CONNOTATION

The images or feelings you connect to a word add a finer shade of meaning, called **connotation.** The connation of a word goes beyond its basic dictionary definition. Writers use connotations of words to communicate positive or negative feelings.

Positive	Neutral	Negative
save	store	hoard
fragrance	smell	stench
display	show	flaunt

Make sure you understand the denotation and connotation of a word when you read it or use it in your writing.

6 Analogies

An **analogy** is a comparison between two things that are similar in some way or share a clear relationship. Analogies are sometimes used in writing when unfamiliar subjects or ideas are explained in terms of familiar ones. Analogies often appear on tests as well, usually in a format like this:

TERRIER : DOG ::   A) rat : fish

                     B) kitten : cat

                     C) trout : fish

                     D) fish : trout

                     E) poodle : collie

Follow these steps to determine the correct answer:

- Read the part in capital letters as "terrier is to dog as. . . . "
- Read the answer choices as "rat is to fish," "kitten is to cat," and so on.
- Ask yourself how the words *terrier* and *dog* are related. (A terrier is a type of dog.)
- Ask yourself which of the choices shows the same relationship. (A kitten is a young cat, but not a specific breed of cat. Therefore, the answer is C.)

 L 4c

PRACTICE AND APPLY

Answers:

Nemesis: Greek; in mythology, Nemesis was the goddess of vengeance or retribution. A person's nemesis is his or her principal opponent, who may impose punishment or cause defeat.

Atlas: Greek; in Greek mythology, Atlas is a Titan who is forced to hold up the world. An atlas, a book of maps, can be said to hold the world.

Adonis: Greek; in Greek mythology, the goddess Aphrodite falls in love with a handsome young man named Adonis, who is killed by a wild boar. An Adonis is a handsome young man.

Mentor: Greek; in the Odyssey, Mentor was Odysseus' wise and loyal advisor and the teacher of Odysseus' son. A mentor acts as a teacher, coach, or experienced advisor.

Insomnia: Latin; in Roman mythology, Somnus was the god of sleep. The prefix in- means "not," so insomnia is the absence of sleep.

Fury: Latin; in Roman mythology, the Furies were goddesses of vengeance. One who feels fury is full of rage or anger.

Saturday: Latin; in Roman mythology, Saturn was an important god. The last day of the week was named Saturn's day.

January: Latin; in Roman mythology, Janus was the god of portals, beginnings, and endings. As the first month of the year, January would have been guarded by Janus.

Thursday: Norse; in Norse mythology, Thor was the god of thunder, war and strength. Thursday (Thor's day) is named for him.

Berserk: Norse; ferocious early Norse warriors were called berserkers. Someone who behaves in a frenzied, furious way is said to have gone berserk.

Rune: Norse; mystical Old Norse poems or songs were known as runes. Today, runes are the characters used by early Scandinavians to write down these poems.

Valkyrie: Norse; in Norse mythology, the Valkyries took the souls of heroes who died in battle to Valhalla, the great hall of the chief god, Odin.

7 Homonyms and Homophones

7.1 HOMONYMS

Homonyms are words that have the same spelling but have different origins and meanings.

I don't want to bore *you with a story about how I had to* bore *through the living room wall.*

Bore can mean "cause a person to lose interest," but an identically spelled word means "to drill a hole."

My dog likes to bark *while it scratches the* bark *on the tree in the backyard.*

Bark can mean "the sound made by a dog." However, another identically spelled word means "the outer covering of a tree." Each word has a different meaning and its own dictionary entry.

Sometimes only one of the meanings of a homonym may be familiar to you. Use context clues to help you figure out the meaning of an unfamiliar word.

7.2 HOMOPHONES

Homophones are words that sound alike but have different meanings and spellings. The following homophones are frequently misused:

it's/its they're/their/there

to/too/two stationary/stationery

Many misused homophones are pronouns and contractions. Whenever you are unsure whether to write *your* or *you're* and *who's* or *whose,* ask yourself whether you mean *you are* and *who is/has*. If you do, write the contraction. For other homophones, such as *scent* and *sent,* use the meaning of the word to help you decide which one to use.

8 Words with Multiple Meanings

Over time, some words have acquired additional meanings that are based on the original meaning.

EXAMPLES: *I was in a hurry, so I* jammed *my clothes into the suitcase. Unfortunately, I* jammed *my finger in the process.*

These two uses of *jam* have different meanings, but both of them have the same origin. You will find all the meanings of this word listed in one entry in the dictionary.

9 Specialized Vocabulary

Specialized vocabulary is special terms suited to a particular domain, field of study or work. For example, science, mathematics, and history all have their own domain-specific, technical or specialized vocabularies. To figure out specialized terms, you can use context clues and reference sources, such as dictionaries on specific subjects, atlases, or manuals.

10 Using Reference Sources

10.1 DICTIONARIES

A **general dictionary** will tell you not only a word's definitions but also its pronunciation, parts of speech, and history and origin. A **specialized dictionary** focuses on terms related to a particular field of study or work. Use a dictionary to check the spelling of any word you are unsure of in your English class and other classes as well.

10.2 THESAURI

A **thesaurus** is a dictionary of synonyms. A thesaurus can be especially helpful when you find yourself using the same modifiers over and over again.

10.3 SYNONYM FINDERS

A **synonym finder** is often included in wordprocessing software. It enables you to highlight a word and be shown a display of its synonyms.

10.4 GLOSSARIES

A **glossary** is a list of specialized terms and their definitions. It is often found in the back of a book and sometimes includes pronunciations. Many textbooks contain glossaries. In fact, this textbook has three glossaries: the **Glossary of Literary and Informational Terms,** the **Glossary of Academic Vocabulary,** and the **Glossary of Critical Vocabulary.** Use these glossaries to help you understand how terms are used in this textbook.

11 Spelling Rules

11.1 WORDS ENDING IN A SILENT *E*

Before adding a suffix beginning with a vowel or *y* to a word ending in a silent *e*, drop the *e* (with some exceptions).

amaze + -ing = amazing

love + -able = lovable

create + -ed = created

nerve + -ous = nervous

Sample exceptions: *change + -able = changeable; courage + -ous = courageous*

When adding a suffix beginning with a consonant to a word ending in a silent **e**, keep the **e** (with some exceptions).

late + -ly = lately

spite + -ful = spiteful

noise + -less = noiseless

state + -ment = statement

Sample exceptions: *truly, ninth, wholly, awful*

When a suffix beginning with *a* or *o* is added to a word with a final silent *e*, the final *e* is usually retained if it is preceded by a soft *c* or a soft *g*.

bridge + -able = bridgeable

peace + -able = peaceable

outrage + -ous = outrageous

advantage + -ous = advantageous

When a suffix beginning with a vowel is added to words ending in *ee* or *oe*, the final, silent *e* is retained.

agree + -ing = agreeing   **free + -ing = freeing**

shoe + -ing = shoeing   **see + -ing = seeing**

11.2 WORDS ENDING IN *Y*

Before adding most suffixes to a word that ends in *y* preceded by a consonant, change the *y* to *i*.

easy + -est = easiest

crazy + -est = craziest

silly + -ness = silliness

marry + -age = marriage

Sample exceptions: *dryness, shyness, slyness.*

However, when you add *–ing*, the *y* does not change.

empty + -ed = emptied but

empty + -ing = emptying

When you add a suffix to a word that ends in *y* preceded by a vowel, the *y* usually does not change.

play + -er = player

employ + -ed = employed

coy + -ness = coyness

pay + -able = payable

11.3 WORDS ENDING IN A CONSONANT

In one-syllable words that end in one consonant preceded by one short vowel, double the final consonant before adding a suffix beginning with a vowel, such as *–ed* or *–ing*. These are sometimes called 1+1+1 words.

dip + -ed = dipped   **set + -ing = setting**

slim + -est = slimmest   **fit + -er = fitter**

The rule does not apply to words of one syllable that end in a consonant preceded by two vowels.

feel + -ing = feeling   **peel + -ed = peeled**

reap + -ed = reaped   **loot + -ed = looted**

In words of more than one syllable, double the final consonant when accent is on the last syllable and remains there once the suffix is added, as in the following examples:

be·gin´ + -ing = be·gin´ ning = beginning

per·mit´ + -ed = per·mit´ ted = permitted

However, do not double the final consonant when the accent is on the final consonant but does not remain there when the suffix is added.

tra´vel + er = tra´vel·er = traveler

mar´ket + er = mar´ket·er = marketer

Do not double the final consonant when the accent is on the first syllable, as in the following examples:

re·fer´ + -ence = ref´er·ence = reference

con·fer´ + -ence = con´fer·ence = conference

11.4 PREFIXES AND SUFFIXES

When adding a prefix to a word, do not change the spelling of the base word. When a prefix creates a double letter, keep both letters.

dis- + approve = disapprove

re- + build = rebuild

ir- + regular = irregular

mis- + spell = misspell

anti- + trust = antitrust

il- + logical = illogical

When adding –ly to a word ending in l, keep both l 's. When adding –ness to a word ending in n, keep both n's.

careful + -ly = carefully

sudden + -ness = suddenness

final + -ly = finally

thin + -ness = thinness

11.5 FORMING PLURAL NOUNS

To form the plural of most nouns, just add –s.

prizes   dreams   circles   stations

For most singular nouns ending in o, add –s.

solos   halos   studios   photos   pianos

For a few nouns ending in o, add –es.

heroes   tomatoes   potatoes   echoes

When the singular noun ends in s, sh, ch, x, or z, add –es.

waitresses   brushes   ditches   axes   buzzes

When a singular noun ends in y with a consonant before it, change the y to i and add –es.

army—armies   candy—candies

baby—babies   diary—diaries

ferry—ferries   conspiracy—conspiracies

When a vowel (a, e, i, o, u) comes before the y, just add –s.

boy—boys   way—ways

array—arrays   alloy—alloys

weekday—weekdays   jockey—jockeys

For most nouns ending in f or fe, change the f to v and add –es or –s.

life—lives   calf—calves   knife—knives

thief—thieves   shelf—shelves   loaf—loaves

However, for some nouns ending in f, add –s to make the plural.

roofs   chiefs   reefs   beliefs

Some nouns have the same form for both singular and plural.

deer   sheep   moose   salmon   trout

For some nouns, the plural is formed in a special way.

man—men   goose—geese

ox—oxen   woman—women

mouse—mice   child—children

For a compound noun written as one word, form the plural by changing the last word in the compound to its plural form.

stepchild—stepchildren   firefly—fireflies

If a compound noun is written as a hyphenated word or as two separate words, change the most important word to the plural form.

brother-in-law—brothers-in-law

life jacket—life jackets

11.6 FORMING POSSESSIVES

If a noun is singular, add 's.

mother—my mother's car

Ross—Ross's desk

Exception: The s after the apostrophe is dropped after *Jesus', Moses',* and certain names in classical mythology *(Zeus')*. These possessive forms can thus be pronounced easily.

If a noun is plural and ends with s, just add an apostrophe.

parents—my parents' car

the Santinis—the Santinis' house

If a noun is plural but does not end in s, add 's.

people—the people's choice

women—the women's coats

11.7 SPECIAL SPELLING PROBLEMS

Only one English word ends in *–sede: supersede.* Three words end in *–ceed: exceed, proceed,* and *succeed.* All other verbs ending in the sound "seed" are spelled with *–cede*.

concede   precede   recede   secede

In words with *ie* or *ei,* when the sound is long *e* (as in *she*), the word is spelled *ie* except after *c* (with some exceptions).

i before *e*	thief	relieve	field
	piece	grieve	pier
except after *c*	conceit	perceive	ceiling
	receive	receipt	
Exceptions:	either	neither	weird
	leisure	seize	

12 Commonly Confused Words

Words	Definitions	Examples
accept/except	The verb *accept* means "to receive or believe"; *except* is usually a preposition meaning "excluding."	**Except** for some of the more extraordinary events, I can **accept** that the *Odyssey* recounts a real journey.
advice/advise	*Advise* is a verb; *advice* is a noun naming that which an *adviser* gives.	I **advise** you to take that job. Whom should I ask for **advice**?
affect/effect	As a verb, *affect* means "to influence." *Effect* as a verb means "to cause." If you want a noun, you will almost always want *effect*.	Did Circe's wine **affect** Odysseus' mind? It did **effect** a change in Odysseus' men. In fact, it had an **effect** on everyone else who drank it.
all ready/already	*All ready* is an adjective meaning "fully ready." *Already* is an adverb meaning "before or by this time."	He was **all ready** to go at noon. I have **already** seen that movie.
allusion/illusion	An *allusion* is an indirect reference to something. An *illusion* is a false picture or idea.	There are many **allusions** to the works of Homer in English literature. The world's apparent flatness is an **illusion**.
among/between	*Between* is used when you are speaking of only two things. *Among* is used for three or more.	**Between** *Hamlet* and *King Lear,* I prefer the latter. Emily Dickinson is **among** my favorite poets.
bring/take	*Bring* is used to denote motion toward a speaker or place. *Take* is used to denote motion away from such a person or place.	**Bring** the books over here, and I will **take** them to the library.

continued

Words	Definitions	Examples
fewer/less	*Fewer* refers to the number of separate, countable units. *Less* refers to bulk quantity.	We have **less** literature and **fewer** selections in this year's curriculum.
leave/let	*Leave* means "to allow something to remain behind." *Let* means "to permit."	The librarian will **leave** some books on display but will not **let** us borrow any.
lie/lay	*Lie* means "to rest or recline." It does not take an object. *Lay* always takes an object.	Rover loves to **lie** in the sun. We always **lay** some bones next to him.
loose/lose	*Loose* (lо̄о̄s) means "free, not restrained"; *lose* (lо̄о̄z) means "to misplace or fail to find."	Who turned the horses **loose**? I hope we won't **lose** any of them.
precede/proceed	*Precede* means "to go or come before." Use *proceed* for other meanings.	Emily Dickinson's poetry **precedes** that of Alice Walker. You may **proceed** to the next section of the test.
than/then	Use *than* in making comparisons; use *then* on all other occasions.	Who can say whether Amy Lowell is a better poet **than** Denise Levertov? I will read Lowell first, and **then** I will read Levertov.
two/too/to	*Two* is the number. *Too* is an adverb meaning "also" or "very." Use *to* before a verb or as a preposition.	Meg had **to** go **to** town, **too**. We had **too** much reading **to** do. **Two** chapters is **too** many.
their/there/ they're	*Their* means "belonging to them." *There* means "in that place." *They're* is the contraction for "they are."	**There** is a movie playing at 9 P.M. **They're** going to see it with me. Sakara and Jessica drove away in **their** car after the movie.

Glossary of Literary and Informational Terms

Act An act is a major division within a play, similar to a chapter in a book. Each act may be further divided into smaller sections, called scenes. Plays can have as many as five acts, or as few as one.

Allegory An allegory is a work with two levels of meaning—a literal one and a symbolic one. In such a work, most of the characters, objects, settings, and events represent abstract qualities. Personification is often used in traditional allegories. As in a fable or a parable, the purpose of an allegory may be to convey truths about life, to teach religious or moral lessons, or to criticize social institutions.

Alliteration Alliteration is the repetition of consonant sounds at the beginning of words. Note the repetition of the *d* sound in this line: The <u>d</u>are<u>d</u>evil <u>d</u>ove into the <u>d</u>eep sea.

See also Consonance.

Allusion An allusion is an indirect reference to a famous person, place, event, or literary work.

Almanac *See* Reference Works.

Analogy An analogy is a point-by-point comparison between two things that are alike in some respect. Often, writers use analogies in nonfiction to explain unfamiliar subjects or ideas in terms of familiar ones.

See also Extended Metaphor; Metaphor; Simile.

Antagonist An antagonist is a principal character or force in opposition to a **protagonist**, or main character. The antagonist is usually another character but sometimes can be a force of nature, a set of circumstances, some aspect of society, or a force within the protagonist.

Archetype An archetype is a pattern in literature that is found in a variety of works from different cultures throughout the ages. An archetype can be a plot, a character, an image, or a setting. For example, the association of death and rebirth with winter and spring is an archetype common to many cultures.

Argument An argument is speech or writing that presents a claim about an issue or problem and supports it with reasons and evidence. An argument often takes into account other points of view, anticipating and answering objections that opponents of the position might raise.

See also Claim; Counterargument; Evidence.

Argumentative Essay *See* Essay.

Aside In drama, an aside is a short speech directed to the audience, or another character, that is not heard by the other characters on stage.

See also Soliloquy.

Assonance Assonance is the repetition of vowel sounds within nonrhyming words. An example of assonance is the repetition of the *u* sound in the following line: I made my <u>u</u>s<u>u</u>al man<u>eu</u>ver on my snowboard.

Assumption An assumption is an opinion or belief that is taken for granted. It can be about a specific situation, a person, or the world in general. Assumptions are often unstated.

Author's Message An author's message is the main idea or theme of a particular work.

See also Main Idea; Theme.

Author's Perspective An author's perspective, or point of view, is a unique combination of ideas, values, feelings, and beliefs that influences the way the writer looks at a topic. **Tone**, or attitude, often reveals an author's perspective.

See also Author's Purpose; Tone.

Author's Position An author's position is his or her opinion on an issue or topic.

See also Claim.

Author's Purpose A writer usually writes for one or more of these purposes: to express thoughts or feelings, to inform or explain, to persuade, to entertain.

See also Author's Perspective.

Autobiography An autobiography is a writer's account of his or her own life. In almost every case, it is told from the first-person point of view. Generally, an autobiography focuses on the most significant events and people in the writer's life over a period of time. Shorter autobiographical narratives include **journals, diaries,** and **letters.** An **autobiographical essay,** another type of short autobiographical work, focuses on a single person or event in the writer's life.

See also Memoir.

Ballad A ballad is a type of narrative poem that tells a story and was originally meant to be sung or recited. Because it tells a story, a ballad has a setting, a plot, and characters. **Traditional ballads** are written in four-line stanzas with regular rhythm and rhyme. **Folk ballads** were composed orally and handed down by word of mouth. These ballads usually tell about ordinary people who have unusual adventures or perform daring deeds. A **literary ballad** is a poem written by a poet in imitation of the form and content of a folk ballad.

Bias Bias is an inclination toward a particular judgment on a topic or issue. A writer often reveals a strongly positive or strongly negative opinion by presenting only one way of looking at an issue or by heavily weighting the evidence. Words with intensely positive or negative connotations are often a signal of a writer's bias.

Bibliography A bibliography is a list of books and other materials related to the topic of a text. Bibliographies can be good sources of works for further study on a subject.

See also Works Consulted.

Biography A biography is the true account of a person's life, written by another person. As such, a biography is usually told from a third-person point of view. The writer of a biography usually researches his or her subject in order to present accurate information. The best biographers strive for honesty and balance in their accounts of their subjects' lives.

Blank Verse Blank verse is unrhymed poetry written in **iambic pentameter.** That is, each line of blank verse has five pairs of syllables. In most pairs, an unstressed syllable is followed by a stressed syllable. The most versatile of poetic forms, blank verse imitates the natural rhythms of English speech. Much of Shakespeare's drama is in blank verse.

See also Iambic Pentameter.

Business Correspondence Business correspondence includes all written business communications, such as business letters, e-mails, and memos. In general, business correspondence is brief, to the point, clear, courteous, and professional.

Cast of Characters In the script of a play, a cast of characters is a list of all the characters in the play, usually in order of appearance. It may include a brief description of each character.

Cause and Effect A cause is an event or action that directly results in another event or action. An effect is the direct or logical outcome of an event or action. Basic **cause-and-effect relationships** include a single cause with a single effect, one cause with multiple effects, multiple causes with a single effect, and a chain of causes and effects. The concept of cause and effect also provides a way of organizing a piece of writing. It helps a writer show the relationships between events or ideas.

Central Idea *See* Main Idea; Theme.

Character Characters are the individuals who participate in the action of a literary work. Like real people, characters display certain qualities, or **character traits;** they develop and change over time; and they usually have **motivations,** or reasons, for their behaviors. Complex characters can have multiple or conflicting motivations.

Main characters: Main characters are the most important characters in literary works. Generally, the plot of a short story focuses on one main character, but a novel may have several main characters.

Minor characters: The less prominent characters in a literary work are known as minor characters. Minor characters support the plot. The story is not centered on them, but they help carry out the action of the story and help the reader learn more about the main character.

Dynamic character: A dynamic character is one who undergoes important changes as a plot unfolds. The changes occur because of his or her actions and experiences in the story. The change is usually internal and may be good or bad. Main characters are usually, though not always, dynamic.

Static character: A static character is one who remains the same throughout a story. The character may experience events and have interactions with other characters, but he or she is not changed because of them.

Round character: A round character is one who is complex and highly developed, having a variety of traits and different sides to his or her personality. Some of the traits may create conflict in the character. Round characters tend to display strengths, weaknesses, and a full range of emotions. The writer provides enough detail for the reader to understand their feelings and emotions.

Flat character: A flat character is one who is not highly developed. A flat character is one-sided: he or she usually has one outstanding trait, characteristic, or role. Flat characters exist mainly to advance the plot, and they display only the traits needed for their limited roles. Minor characters are usually flat characters.

See also Characterization.

Characterization The way a writer creates and develops characters' personalities is known as characterization. There are four basic methods of characterization:

- The writer may make direct comments about a character's personality or nature through the voice of the narrator.
- The writer may describe the character's physical appearance.
- The writer may present the character's own thoughts, speech, and actions.
- The writer may present thoughts, speech, and actions of other characters in response to a character.

See also Character.

Chorus In early Greek tragedy, the chorus commented on the actions of the characters in a drama. In some Elizabethan plays, such as Shakespeare's *Romeo and Juliet,* the role of the chorus is taken by a single actor who serves as a narrator and speaks the lines in the **prologue** (and sometimes in an **epilogue**). The chorus serves to foreshadow or summarize events.

Chronological Order Chronological order is the arrangement of events in their order of occurrence. This type of organization is used in both fictional narratives and in historical writing, biography, and autobiography.

Claim In an argument, a claim is the writer's position on an issue or problem. Although an argument focuses on supporting one claim, a writer may make more than one claim in a work.

See also Argument; Thesis Statement.

Clarify Clarifying is a reading strategy that helps a reader to understand or make clear what he or she is reading. Readers usually clarify by rereading, reading aloud, or discussing.

Classification Classification is a pattern of organization in which objects, ideas, or information is presented in groups, or classes, based on common characteristics.

Cliché A cliché is an overused expression. "Better late than never" and "hard as nails" are common examples. Good writers generally avoid clichés unless they are using them in dialogue to indicate something about characters' personalities.

Climax In a plot, the climax is the point of maximum interest or tension. Usually the climax is a turning point in the story, which occurs after the reader has understood the **conflict** and become emotionally involved with the characters. The climax sometimes, but not always, points to the **resolution** of the conflict.

See also Plot.

Comedy A comedy is a dramatic work that is light and often humorous in tone, usually ending happily with a peaceful resolution of the main conflict. A comedy differs from a farce by having a more believable plot, more realistic characters, and less boisterous behavior.

Comic Relief Comic relief consists of humorous scenes, incidents, or speeches that are included in a serious drama to provide a reduction in emotional intensity. Because comic relief breaks the tension, it allows an audience to prepare emotionally for events to come. Shakespeare often uses this device in his tragedies.

Compare and Contrast To compare and contrast is to identify similarities and differences in two or more subjects. Compare-and-contrast organization can be used to structure a piece of writing, serving as a framework for analyzing the similarities and differences in two or more subjects.

Complex Character *See* Character.

Complication A complication is an additional factor or problem introduced into the rising action of a story to make the conflict more difficult. Often, a plot complication makes it seem as though the main character is getting farther away from the thing he or she wants.

Conclusion A conclusion is a statement of belief based on evidence, experience, and reasoning. A **valid conclusion** is a conclusion that logically follows from the facts or statements upon which it is based. A **deductive conclusion** is one that follows from a particular generalization or premise. An **inductive conclusion** is a broad conclusion or generalization that is reached by arguing from specific facts and examples.

Conflict A conflict is a struggle between opposing forces. Almost every story has a main conflict—a conflict that is the story's focus. An **external conflict** involves a character pitted against an outside force, such as nature, a physical obstacle, or another character. An **internal conflict** is one that occurs within a character.

See also Plot.

Connect Connecting is a reader's process of relating the content of a text to his or her own knowledge and experience.

Connotation A connotation is an attitude or a feeling associated with a word, in contrast to the word's **denotation,** which is its literal, or dictionary, meaning. The connotations of a word may be positive or negative. For example, *enthusiastic* has positive associations, while *rowdy* has negative ones. Connotations of words can have an important influence on style and meaning and are particularly important in poetry.

Consonance Consonance is the repetition of consonant sounds within and at the end of words, as in "lonely afternoon." Consonance is unlike rhyme in that the vowel sounds preceding or following the repeated consonant sounds differ. Consonance is often used together with **alliteration, assonance,** and **rhyme** to create a musical quality, to emphasize certain words, or to unify a poem.

See also Alliteration.

Consumer Documents Consumer documents are printed materials that accompany products and services. They are intended for the buyers or users of the products or services and usually provide information about use, care, operation, or assembly. Some common consumer documents are applications, contracts, warranties, manuals, instructions, package inserts, labels, brochures, and schedules.

Context Clues When you encounter an unfamiliar word, you can often use context clues as aids for understanding. Context clues are the words and phrases surrounding the word that provide hints about the word's meaning.

Controlling Idea *See* Main Idea.

Counterargument A counterargument is an argument made to answer an opposing argument, or **counterclaim.** A good argument anticipates opposing viewpoints and provides counterarguments to refute (disprove) or answer them.

Counterclaim *See* Counterargument.

Couplet A couplet is a rhymed pair of lines. A couplet may be written in any rhythmic pattern, for example:

> Follow your heart's desire
> And good things may transpire.

See also Stanza.

Credibility Credibility refers to the believability or trustworthiness of a source and the information it contains.

Critical Essay *See* Essay.

Critical Review A critical review is an evaluation or critique by a reviewer or critic. Different types of reviews include film reviews, book reviews, music reviews, and art-show reviews.

Critique *See* Critical Review.

Database A database is a collection of information that can be quickly and easily accessed and searched and from which information can be easily retrieved. It is frequently presented in an electronic format.

Debate A debate is basically an argument—but a very structured one that requires a good deal of preparation. In academic settings, debate usually refers to a formal argumentation contest in which two opposing teams defend and attack a proposition.

See also Argument.

Deductive Reasoning Deductive reasoning is a way of thinking that begins with a generalization, presents a specific situation, and then advances with facts and evidence to a logical conclusion. The following passage has a deductive argument embedded in it: "All students in the drama class must attend the play on Thursday. Since Ava is in the class, she had better show up." This deductive argument can be broken down as follows: generalization— all students in the drama class must attend the play on Thursday; specific situation—Ava is a student in the drama class; conclusion—Ava must attend the play.

Denotation *See* Connotation.

Dénouement *See* Falling Action.

Dialect A dialect is a form of language that is spoken in a particular geographic area or by a particular social or ethnic group. A group's dialect is reflected in its pronunciations, vocabulary, expressions, and grammatical structures. Writers use dialects to capture the flavors of locales and to bring characters to life, re-creating the way they actually speak.

Dialogue Dialogue is written conversation between two or more characters. Writers use dialogue to bring characters to life and to give readers insights into the characters' qualities, traits, and reactions to other characters. Realistic, well-paced dialogue also advances the plot of a narrative. In fiction, dialogue is usually set off with quotation marks. In drama, stories are told primarily through dialogue. Playwrights use stage directions to indicate how they intend the dialogue to be interpreted by actors.

Diary A diary is a daily record of a writer's thoughts, experiences, and feelings. As such, it is a type of autobiographical writing. The terms *diary* and *journal* are often used synonymously.

Diction A writer's or speaker's choice of words and way of arranging the words in sentences is called diction. Diction can be broadly characterized as formal or informal. It can also be described as technical or common, abstract or concrete, and literal or figurative. A writer for a science journal would use a more formal, more technical, and possibly more abstract diction than would a writer for the science section of a local newspaper.

See also Style.

Dictionary *See* Reference Works.

Drama Drama is literature in which plots and characters are developed through dialogue and action; in other words, it is literature in play form. Drama is meant to be performed. Stage plays, radio plays, movies, and television programs are types of drama. Most plays are divided into acts, with each act having an emotional peak, or climax. Certain modern plays have only one act. Most plays contain stage directions, which describe settings, lighting, sound effects, the movements and emotions of actors, and the ways in which dialogue should be spoken.

Dramatic Irony *See* Irony.

Dramatic Monologue A dramatic monologue is a lyric poem in which a speaker addresses a silent or absent listener in a moment of high intensity or deep emotion, as if engaged in private conversation. The speaker proceeds without interruption or argument, and the effect on the reader is that of hearing just one side of a conversation. This technique allows the poet to focus on the feelings, personality, and motivations of the speaker.

See also Lyric Poetry; Soliloquy.

Draw Conclusions To draw a conclusion is to make a judgment or arrive at a belief based on evidence, experience, and reasoning.

Dynamic Character *See* Character.

Editorial An editorial is an opinion piece that usually appears on the editorial page of a newspaper or as part of a news broadcast. The editorial section of a newspaper presents opinions rather than objective news reports.

See also Op-Ed Piece.

Either/Or Fallacy An either/or fallacy is a statement that suggests that there are only two possible ways to view a situation or only two options to choose from. In other words, it is a statement that falsely frames a dilemma, giving the impression that no options exist but the two presented —for example, "Either we stop the construction of a new airport, or the surrounding suburbs will become ghost towns."

Elegy An elegy is an extended meditative poem in which the speaker reflects on death— often in tribute to a person who has died recently—or on an equally serious subject. Most elegies are written in formal, dignified language and are serious in tone.

Emotional Appeals Emotional appeals are messages that evoke strong feelings—such as fear, pity, or vanity—in order to persuade instead of using facts and evidence to make a point. An **appeal to fear** is a message that taps into people's fear of losing their safety or security. An **appeal to pity** is a message that taps into people's sympathy and compassion for others to build support for an idea, a cause, or a proposed action. An **appeal to vanity** is a message that attempts to persuade by tapping into people's desire to feel good about themselves.

Encyclopedia *See* Reference Works.

Epic An epic is a long narrative poem on a serious subject, presented in an elevated or formal style. It traces the adventures of a great hero whose actions reflect the ideals and values of a nation or race. Epics address universal concerns, such as good and evil, life and death, and sin and redemption. The *Odyssey* is an epic.

Epic Hero An epic hero is a larger-than-life figure who embodies the ideals of a nation or race. Epic heroes take part in dangerous adventures and accomplish great deeds. Many undertake long, difficult journeys and display great courage and superhuman strength.

Epic Simile An epic simile (also called a Homeric simile) is a long, elaborate comparison that often continues for a number of lines. Homer uses epic similes in the *Odyssey*.

See also Simile.

Epilogue An epilogue is a short addition at the end of a literary work, often dealing with the future of the characters. The concluding speech by Prince Escalus in *Romeo and Juliet* serves as an epilogue.

Epithet An epithet is a brief phrase that points out traits associated with a particular person or thing. In the *Odyssey*, Odysseus is often called "the master strategist."

Essay An essay is a short work of nonfiction that deals with a single subject. Some essays are **formal**—that is, tightly structured and written in an impersonal style. Others are **informal**, with a looser structure and a more personal style. Generally, an **informative** or **expository essay** presents or explains information and ideas. A **personal essay** is typically an informal essay in which the writer expresses his or her thoughts and feelings about a subject, focusing on the meaning of events and issues in his or her own life. In a **reflective essay**, the author makes a connection between a personal observation or experience and a universal idea, such as love, courage, or freedom. A **critical essay** evaluates a situation, a course of action, or a work of art. In an **argumentative** or **persuasive essay**, the author attempts to convince readers to adopt a certain viewpoint or to take a particular stand.

Evaluate To evaluate is to examine something carefully and judge its value or worth. Evaluating is an important skill for gaining insight into what you read. A reader can evaluate the actions of a particular character, for example, or can form an opinion about the value of an entire work.

Evidence Evidence is the specific pieces of information that support a claim. Evidence can take the form of facts, quotations, examples, statistics, or personal experiences, among others.

Exposition Exposition is the first stage of a plot in a typical story. The exposition provides important background information and introduces the setting and the important characters. The conflict the characters face may also be introduced in the exposition, or it may be introduced later, in the rising action.

See also Plot.

Expository Essay *See* Essay.

Extended Metaphor An extended metaphor is a figure of speech that compares two essentially unlike things at some length and in several ways. It does not contain the word *like* or *as*.

See also Metaphor.

External Conflict *See* Conflict.

Fable A fable is a brief tale told to illustrate a moral or teach a lesson. Often the moral of a fable appears in a distinct and memorable statement near the tale's beginning or end.

See also Moral.

Fact versus Opinion A fact is a statement that can be proved or verified. An opinion, on the other hand, is a statement that cannot be proved because it expresses a person's beliefs, feelings, or thoughts.

See also Inference; Generalization.

Fallacy A fallacy is an error in reasoning. Typically, a fallacy is based on an incorrect inference or a misuse of evidence. Some common logical fallacies are circular reasoning, either/or fallacy, oversimplification, overgeneralization, and stereotyping.

See also Either/Or Fallacy, Logical Appeal, Overgeneralization.

Falling Action In a plot, the falling action follows the climax and shows the results of the important action that happened at the climax. Tension eases as the falling action begins; however, the final outcome of the story is not yet fully worked out at this stage. Events in the falling action lead to the **resolution**, or **dénouement**, of the plot.

See also Climax; Plot.

Fantasy Fantasy is a type of fiction that is highly imaginative and portrays events, settings, or characters that are unrealistic. The setting might be a nonexistent world, the plot might involve magic or the supernatural, and the characters might employ superhuman powers.

Farce Farce is a type of exaggerated comedy that features an absurd plot, ridiculous situations, and humorous dialogue. The main purpose of a farce is to keep an audience laughing. The characters are usually stereotypes, or simplified examples of individual traits or qualities. Comic devices typically used in farces include mistaken identity, deception, physical comedy, wordplay—such as puns and double meanings—and exaggeration.

Faulty Reasoning *See* Fallacy.

Feature Article A feature article is a main article in a newspaper or a cover story in a magazine. A feature article is focused more on entertaining than informing. Features are lighter or more general than hard news and tend to be about human interest or lifestyles.

Fiction Fiction is prose writing that consists of imaginary elements. Although fiction can be inspired by actual events and real people, it usually springs from writers' imaginations. The basic elements of fiction are plot, character, setting, and theme. The novel and short story are forms of fiction.

See also Character; Novel; Plot; Setting; Short Story; Theme.

Figurative Language Figurative language is language that communicates meanings beyond the literal meanings of words. In figurative language, words are often used to symbolize ideas and concepts they would not otherwise be associated with. Writers use figurative language to create effects, to emphasize ideas, and to evoke emotions. Simile, metaphor, extended metaphor, hyperbole, and personification are examples of figurative language.

See also Hyperbole; Metaphor; Personification; Simile.

Figure of Speech *See* Figurative Language; Hyperbole; Metaphor; Personification; Simile; Understatement.

First-Person Point of View *See* Point of View.

Flashback A flashback is an account of a conversation, an episode, or an event that happened before the beginning of a story. Often, a flashback interrupts the chronological flow of a story to give the reader information needed to understand a character's present situation. Flashbacks also help create such effects as mystery, tension, or surprise.

Foil A foil is a character who provides a striking contrast to another character. By using a foil, a writer can call attention to certain traits possessed by a main character or simply enhance a character by contrast. In Shakespeare's *Romeo and Juliet*, Mercutio serves as a foil to Romeo.

Foreshadowing Foreshadowing is a writer's use of hints or clues to suggest events that will occur later in a story. The hints and clues might be included in a character's dialogue or behavior, or they might be included in details of description. Foreshadowing creates suspense, mystery, and surprise, and makes readers eager to find out what will happen.

Form Form refers to the principles of arrangement in a poem—the ways in which lines are organized. Form in poetry includes the following elements: the length of lines, the placement of lines, and the grouping of lines into stanzas.

See also Stanza.

Frame Story A frame story exists when a story is told within a narrative setting, or "frame"; it creates a story within a story. This storytelling technique has been used for over one thousand years and was employed in famous works such as *One Thousand and One Arabian Nights* and Geoffrey Chaucer's *The Canterbury Tales*.

Free Verse Free verse is poetry that does not contain regular patterns of rhythm or rhyme. The lines in free verse often flow more naturally than do rhymed, metrical lines and thus achieve a rhythm more like that of everyday speech. Although free verse lacks conventional meter, it may contain various rhythmic and sound effects, such as repetitions of syllables or words. Free verse can be used for a variety of subjects.

See also Meter; Rhyme.

Functional Documents *See* Consumer Documents; Public Documents; Workplace Documents.

Generalization A generalization is a broad statement about a class or category of people, ideas, or things, based on a study of only some of its members.

See also Overgeneralization.

Genre The term *genre* refers to a category in which a work of literature is classified. The major genres in literature are fiction, nonfiction, poetry, and drama.

Government Publications Government publications are documents produced by government organizations. Pamphlets, brochures, and reports are just some of the many forms these publications may take. Government publications can be reliable resources for a wide variety of topics.

Graphic Aid A graphic aid is a visual tool that is printed, handwritten, or drawn. Charts, diagrams, graphs, photographs, and maps can all be graphic aids.

Graphic Organizer A graphic organizer is a "word picture"—that is, a visual illustration of a verbal statement—that helps a reader understand a text. Charts, tables, webs, and diagrams can all be graphic organizers. Graphic organizers and graphic aids can look the same. For example, a table in a science article will not be constructed differently from a table that is a graphic organizer. However, graphic organizers and graphic aids do differ in how they are used. Graphic aids are the visual representations that people encounter when they read informational texts. Graphic organizers are visuals that people construct to help them understand texts or organize information.

Haiku Haiku is a form of Japanese poetry in which 17 syllables are arranged in three lines of 5, 7, and 5 syllables each. The rules of haiku are strict. In addition to the syllabic count, the poet must create a clear picture that will evoke a strong emotional response in the reader. Nature is a particularly important source of inspiration for Japanese haiku poets, and details from nature are often the subjects of their poems.

Hero A hero is a main character or protagonist in a story. In older literary works, heroes tend to be better than ordinary humans. They are typically courageous, strong, honorable, and intelligent. They are protectors of society who hold back the forces of evil and fight to make the world a better place. In modern literature, a hero may simply be the most important character in a story. Such a hero is often an ordinary person with ordinary problems.

Historical Documents Historical documents are writings that have played a significant role in human events or are themselves records of such events. The Declaration of Independence, for example, is a historical document.

Historical Fiction A short story or novel can be classified as historical fiction when the settings and details of the plot include real places and real events of historical importance. Historical figures may appear as major or minor characters. In historical fiction, the setting generally influences the plot in important ways.

Horror Fiction Horror fiction contains strange, mysterious, violent, and often supernatural events that create suspense and terror in the reader. Edgar Allan Poe and Stephen King are famous authors of horror fiction.

How-To Writing A how-to book or article is written to explain how to do something— usually an activity, a sport, or a household project.

Humor In literature, there are three basic types of humor, all of which may involve exaggeration or irony. **Humor of situation** arises out of the plot of a work. It usually involves exaggerated events or situational irony, which arises when something happens that is different from what was expected. **Humor of character** is often based on exaggerated personalities or on characters' failure to recognize their own flaws, a form of dramatic irony. **Humor of language** may include sarcasm, exaggeration, puns, or verbal irony, in which what is said is not what is meant.

See also Irony.

Hyperbole Hyperbole is a figure of speech in which the truth is exaggerated for emphasis or humorous effect.

Iambic Pentameter Iambic pentameter is a metrical pattern of five feet, or units, each of which is made up of two syllables, the first unstressed and the second stressed. Iambic pentameter is the most common meter used in English poetry; it is the meter used in blank verse and in the sonnet. Shakespeare used Iambic pentameter in his plays.

See also Blank Verse; Sonnet.

Idiom An idiom is a common figure of speech whose meaning is different from the literal meaning of its words. For example, the phrase "raining cats and dogs" does not literally mean that cats and dogs are falling from the sky; the expression means "raining heavily."

Imagery Imagery consists of descriptive words and phrases that re-create sensory experiences for the reader. Imagery usually appeals to one or more of the five senses— sight, hearing, smell, taste, and touch—to help the reader imagine exactly what is being described.

Implied Controlling Idea An implied controlling idea is one that is suggested by details rather than stated explicitly.

See also Main Idea.

Implied Main Idea *See* Main Idea.

Index The index of a book is an alphabetized list of important topics and details covered in the book and the page numbers on which they can be found. An index can be used to quickly find specific information about a topic.

Inductive Reasoning Inductive reasoning is the process of logically reasoning from specific observations, examples, and facts to arrive at a general conclusion or principle.

Inference An inference is a logical assumption that is based on observed facts and one's own knowledge and experience.

Informational Nonfiction Informational nonfiction is writing that provides factual information. It often explains ideas or teaches processes. Examples include news reports, science textbooks, software instructions, and lab reports.

Informative Essay *See* Essay.

Internal Conflict *See* Conflict.

Internet The Internet is a global, interconnected system of computer networks that allows for communication through e-mail, listservers, and the World Wide Web. The Internet connects computers and computer users throughout the world.

Interview An interview is a conversation conducted by a writer or reporter in which facts or statements are elicited from another person, recorded, and then broadcast or published.

Irony Irony is a special kind of contrast between appearance and reality—usually one in which reality is the opposite of what it seems. One type of irony is **situational irony,** a contrast between what a reader or character expects and what actually exists or happens. Another type of irony is **dramatic irony,** in which the reader or viewer knows something that a character does not know. **Verbal irony** exists when someone knowingly exaggerates or says one thing and means another.

Journal A journal is a periodical publication issued by a legal, medical, or other professional organization. Alternatively, the term may be used to refer to a diary or daily record.

See also Diary.

Legend A legend is a story handed down from the past, especially one that is popularly believed to be based on historical events. Though legends often incorporate supernatural or magical elements, they claim to be the story of a real human being and are often set in a particular time and place. These characteristics separate a legend from a myth.

See also Myth.

Limited Point of View *See* Point of View.

Line The line is the core unit of a poem. In poetry, line length is an essential element of the poem's meaning and rhythm. **Line breaks,** where a line of poetry ends, may coincide with grammatical units. However, a line break may

also occur in the middle of a grammatical or syntactical unit, creating a meaningful pause or emphasis. Poets use a variety of line breaks to manipulate sense, grammar, and syntax and thereby create a wide range of effects.

Literary Criticism *See* Text Criticism.

Literary Nonfiction Literary nonfiction is nonfiction that is recognized as being of artistic value or that is about literature. Autobiographies, biographies, essays, and eloquent speeches typically fall into this category.

Loaded Language Loaded language consists of words with strongly positive or negative connotations intended to influence a reader's or listener's attitude.

Logical Appeal A logical appeal relies on logic and facts, appealing to people's reasoning or intellect rather than to their values or emotions. Flawed logical appeals—that is, errors in reasoning—are considered logical fallacies.

See also Fallacy.

Logical Argument A logical argument is an argument in which the logical relationship between the support and the claim is sound.

Lyric Poetry A lyric poem is a short poem in which a single speaker expresses personal thoughts and feelings. Most poems other than dramatic and narrative poems are lyric poems. In ancient Greece, lyric poetry was meant to be sung. Modern lyrics are usually not intended for singing, but they are characterized by strong melodic rhythms. Lyric poetry has a variety of forms and covers many subjects, from love and death to everyday experiences.

Magical Realism Magical realism is a literary genre that combines fantastic or magical events with realistic occurrences in a matter-of-fact way to delight or surprise the reader. A famous example of magical realism is Gabriel García Márquez's novel *One Hundred Years of Solitude*.

Main Idea A main idea, or controlling idea, is the most important idea or impression about a topic that a writer or speaker conveys. It can be the central idea of an entire work or of just a paragraph. Often, the main idea of a paragraph is expressed in a topic sentence. However, a main idea may just be implied, or suggested, by details. A main idea and supporting details can serve as a basic pattern of organization in a piece of writing, with the central idea about a topic being supported by details.

Make Inferences *See* Inference.

Memoir A memoir is a form of autobiographical writing in which a writer shares his or her personal experiences and observations of significant events or people. Often informal or even intimate in tone, memoirs usually give readers insight into the impact of historical events on people's lives.

See also Autobiography.

Metaphor A metaphor is a figure of speech that makes a comparison between two things that are basically unlike but have something in common. Unlike similes, metaphors do not contain the word *like* or *as*.

See also Extended Metaphor; Figurative Language; Simile.

Meter Meter is a regular pattern of stressed and unstressed syllables in a poem. The meter of a poem emphasizes the musical quality of the language. Each unit of meter, known as a **foot**, consists of one stressed syllable and one or two unstressed syllables. In representations of meter, a stressed syllable is indicated by the symbol ´; an unstressed syllable, by the symbol ˘. The four basic types of metrical feet are the **iamb**, an unstressed syllable followed by a stressed syllable (˘ ´); the **trochee**, a stressed syllable followed by an unstressed syllable (´ ˘); the **anapest**, two unstressed syllables followed by a stressed syllable (˘ ˘ ´); and the **dactyl**, a stressed syllable followed by two unstressed syllables (´ ˘ ˘).

See also Rhythm.

Mise en Scène *Mise en scène* is a term from the French that refers to the various physical aspects of a dramatic presentation, such as lighting, costumes, scenery, makeup, and props.

Monitor Monitoring is the strategy of checking your comprehension as you are reading and modifying the strategies you are using to suit your needs. Monitoring may include some or all of the following strategies: questioning, clarifying, visualizing, predicting, connecting, and rereading.

Mood In a literary work, mood is the feeling or atmosphere that a writer creates for the reader. Descriptive words, imagery, and figurative language contribute to the mood of a work, as do the sound and rhythm of the language used.

See also Tone.

Moral A moral is a lesson taught in a literary work, such as a fable. For example, the moral "Do not count your chickens before they are hatched" teaches that one should not count on one's fortunes or blessings until they appear.

See also Fable.

Motivation *See* Character.

Myth A myth is a traditional story, usually concerning some superhuman being or unlikely event, that was once widely believed to be true. Frequently, myths were attempts to explain natural phenomena, such as solar and lunar eclipses or the cycle of the seasons. For some peoples, myths were both a kind of science and a religion. In addition, myths served as literature and entertainment, just as they do for modern-day audiences.

Greek mythology forms much of the background in Homer's *Odyssey*. For example, the myth of the judgment of Paris describes events that led to the Trojan War. The goddesses Athena, Hera, and Aphrodite asked a mortal—Paris—to decide which of them was the most beautiful. Paris chose Aphrodite and was rewarded by her with Helen, wife of the Greek king Menelaus.

Narrative Nonfiction Narrative nonfiction is writing that reads much like fiction, except that the characters, setting, and plot are real rather than imaginary. Its purpose is usually to entertain or to express opinions or feelings. Narrative nonfiction includes, but is not limited to, autobiographies, biographies, memoirs, diaries, and journals.

Narrative Poetry Narrative poetry tells a story or recounts events. Like a short story or a novel, a narrative poem has the following elements: plot, characters, setting, and theme.

Narrator The narrator of a story is the character or voice that relates the story's events to the reader.

See also Persona; Point of View.

News Article A news article is a piece of writing that reports on a recent event. In newspapers, news articles are usually written concisely and report the latest news, presenting the most important facts first and then more detailed information. In magazines, news articles are usually more elaborate than those in newspapers because they are written to provide both information and analysis. Also, news articles in magazines do not necessarily present the most important facts first.

Nonfiction Nonfiction is writing that tells about real people, places, and events. Unlike fiction, nonfiction is mainly written to convey factual information, although writers of nonfiction shape information in accordance with their own purposes and attitudes. Nonfiction can be a good source of information, but readers frequently have to examine it carefully in order to detect biases, notice gaps in the information provided, and identify errors in logic. Nonfiction includes a diverse range of writing—newspaper articles, letters, essays, biographies, movie reviews, speeches, true-life adventure stories, advertising, and more.

Novel A novel is an extended work of fiction. Like a short story, a novel is essentially the product of a writer's imagination. Because a novel is considerably longer than a short story, a novelist can develop a wider range of characters and a more complex plot.

Novella A novella is a work of fiction that is longer than a short story but shorter than a novel. A novella differs from a novel in that it concentrates on a limited cast of characters, a relatively short time span, and a single chain of events. The novella is an attempt to combine the compression of the short story with the development of the novel.

Ode An ode is a complex lyric poem that develops a serious and dignified theme. Odes appeal to both the imagination and the intellect, and many commemorate events or praise people or elements of nature.

Omniscient Point of View *See* Point of View.

Onomatopoeia Onomatopoeia is the use of words whose sounds echo their meanings, such as *buzz, whisper, gargle,* and *murmur.* Onomatopoeia as a literary technique goes beyond the use of simple echoic words, however. Skilled writers, especially poets, choose words whose sounds intensify images and suggest meanings.

Op-Ed Piece An op-ed piece is an opinion piece that usually appears opposite ("op") the editorial page of a newspaper. Unlike editorials, op-ed pieces are written and submitted by named writers.

Organization *See* Pattern of Organization.

Overgeneralization An overgeneralization is a generalization that is too broad. You can often recognize overgeneralizations by the appearance of words and phrases such as *all, everyone, every time, any, anything, no one,* and *none.* Consider, for example, this statement: "None of the sanitation workers in our city really care about keeping the environment clean." In all probability, there are many exceptions; the writer can't possibly know the feelings of every sanitation worker in the city.

Overview An overview is a short summary of a story, a speech, or an essay. It orients the reader by providing a preview of the text to come.

Oxymoron An oxymoron is a special kind of concise paradox that brings together two contradictory terms. "Deafening silence" and "original copy" are examples of oxymorons.

Paradox A paradox is a seemingly contradictory or absurd statement that may nonetheless suggest an important truth.

Parallelism Parallelism is the use of similar grammatical constructions to express ideas that are related or equal in importance. Martin Luther King Jr. uses parallelism in his "Letter from Birmingham Jail."

Parallel Plot A parallel plot is a particular type of plot in which two stories of equal importance are told simultaneously. The story moves back and forth between the two plots.

Paraphrase Paraphrasing is the restating of information in one's own words.

See also Summarize.

Parody A parody is an imitation of another work, a type of literature, or a writer's style, usually for the purpose of poking fun. It may serve as an element of a larger work or be a complete work in itself. The purpose of parody may be to ridicule through broad humor, deploying such techniques as exaggeration or the use of inappropriate subject matter. Such techniques may even provide insights into the original work.

Pastoral A pastoral is a poem presenting shepherds in rural settings, usually in an idealized manner. The language and form of a pastoral tends to be formal. English Renaissance poets were drawn to the pastoral as a means of conveying their own emotions and ideas, particularly about love.

Pattern of Organization A pattern of organization is a particular arrangement of ideas and information. Such a pattern may be used to organize an entire composition or a single paragraph within a longer work. The following are the most common patterns of organization: cause-and-effect, chronological order, compare-and-contrast, classification, deductive, inductive, order of importance, problem-solution, sequential, and spatial.

See also Cause and Effect; Chronological Order; Classification; Compare and Contrast; Problem-Solution Order; Sequential Order.

Periodical A periodical is a publication that is issued at regular intervals of more than one day. For example, a periodical may be a weekly, monthly, or quarterly journal or magazine. Newspapers and other daily publications generally are not classified as periodicals.

Persona A persona is a voice that a writer assumes in a particular work. A persona is like a mask worn by the writer, separating his or her identity from that of the speaker or the narrator. It is the persona's voice—not the writer's voice— that narrates a story or speaks in a poem.

See also Narrator; Speaker.

Personal Essay *See* Essay.

Personification Personification is a figure of speech in which human qualities are given to an object, animal, or idea, for example: The night wind sings an eerie song.

See also Figurative Language.

Persuasion Persuasion is the art of swaying others' feelings, beliefs, or actions. Persuasion normally appeals to both the intellect and the emotions of readers. **Persuasive techniques** are the methods used to influence others to adopt certain opinions or beliefs or to act in certain ways. Types of persuasive techniques include emotional appeals, logical appeals, and loaded language. When used properly, persuasive techniques can add depth to writing that's meant to persuade. Persuasive techniques can, however, be misused to cloud factual information, disguise poor reasoning, or unfairly exploit people's emotions in order to shape their opinions.

See also Emotional Appeals; Loaded Language; Logical Appeal.

Persuasive Essay *See* Essay.

Play *See* Drama.

Plot The sequence of events in a story is called the plot. A plot focuses on a central **conflict** or problem faced by the main character. The actions that the characters take to resolve the conflict build toward a climax. In general, it is not long after this point that the conflict is resolved and the story ends. A plot typically develops in five stages: exposition, rising action, climax, falling action, and resolution.

See also Climax; Exposition; Falling Action; Rising Action.

Poetry Poetry is a type of literature in which words are carefully chosen and arranged to create certain effects. Poets use a variety of sound devices, imagery, and figurative language to express emotions and ideas.

See also Alliteration; Assonance; Ballad; Free Verse; Imagery; Meter; Rhyme; Rhythm; Stanza.

Point of View Point of view refers to the method of narration used in a short story, novel, narrative poem, or work of nonfiction. In a work told from a **first-person** point of view, the narrator is a character in the story. In a work told from a **third-person** point of view, the narrative voice is outside the action, not one of the characters. If a story is told from a **third-person omniscient,** or all-knowing, point of view, the narrator sees into the minds of all the characters. If events are related from a **third-person limited** point of view, the narrator tells what only one character thinks, feels, and observes.

See also Narrator.

Predict Predicting is a reading strategy that involves using text clues to make a reasonable guess about what will happen next in a story.

Primary Source *See* Sources.

Prior Knowledge Prior knowledge is the knowledge a reader already possesses about a topic. This information might come from personal experiences, expert accounts, books, films, or other sources.

Problem-Solution Order Problem-solution order is a pattern of organization in which a problem is stated and analyzed and then one or more solutions are proposed and examined. Writers use words and phrases such as *propose, conclude, reason for, problem, answer,* and *solution* to connect ideas and details when writing about problems and solutions.

Procedural Texts Procedural texts are functional texts that were created to communicate instructions, rules, processes, or other detailed, step-by-step information.

See also Consumer Documents; Public Documents; Workplace Documents.

Prologue A prologue is an introductory scene in a drama. Some Elizabethan plays include prologues that comment on the theme or moral point that will be revealed in the play. The prologue is a feature of all Greek drama.

Prop The word *prop*, originally an abbreviation of the word *property*, refers to any physical object that is used in a drama.

Propaganda Propaganda is a form of communication that may use distorted, false,

or misleading information. It usually refers to manipulative political discourse.

Prose Generally, prose refers to all forms of written or spoken expression that are not in verse. The term, therefore, may be used to describe very different forms of writing—short stories as well as essays, for example.

Protagonist A protagonist is the main character in a work of literature—the character who is involved in the central conflict of the story. Usually, the protagonist changes after the central conflict reaches a climax. He or she may be a hero and is usually the one with whom the audience tends to identify.

Public Documents Public documents are documents that were written for the public to provide information that is of public interest or concern. They include government documents, speeches, signs, and rules and regulations.

See also Government Publications.

Pun A pun is a joke that comes from a play on words. It can make use of a word's multiple meanings or of a word's sound.

Quatrain A quatrain is a four-line stanza, or group of lines, in poetry. The most common stanza in English poetry, the quatrain can have a variety of meters and rhyme schemes.

Realistic Fiction Realistic fiction is fiction that is a truthful imitation of ordinary life.

Recurring Theme *See* Theme.

Reference Works General reference works are sources that contain facts and background information on a wide range of subjects. More specific reference works contain in-depth information on a single subject. Most reference works are good sources of reliable information because they have been reviewed by experts. The following are some common reference works: encyclopedias, dictionaries, thesauri, almanacs, atlases, chronologies, biographical dictionaries, and directories.

Reflective Essay *See* Essay.

Refrain A refrain is one or more lines repeated in each stanza of a poem.

See also Stanza.

Repetition Repetition is a technique in which a sound, word, phrase, or line is repeated for emphasis or unity. Repetition often helps to reinforce meaning and create an appealing rhythm. The term includes specific devices associated with both prose and poetry, such as alliteration and parallelism.

See also Alliteration; Parallelism; Sound Devices.

Resolution *See* Falling Action.

Review *See* Critical Review.

Rhetorical Devices Rhetorical devices are techniques writers use to enhance their arguments and communicate more effectively. Rhetorical devices include analogy, parallelism, rhetorical questions, and repetition.

See also Analogy; Repetition; Rhetorical Questions.

Rhetorical Questions Rhetorical questions are those that do not require a reply. Writers use them to suggest that their arguments make the answer obvious or self-evident.

Rhyme Rhyme is the occurrence of similar or identical sounds at the end of two or more words, such as *suite, heat,* and *complete.* Rhyme that occurs within a single line of poetry is **internal rhyme.** Rhyme that occurs at the ends of lines of poetry is called **end rhyme.** End rhyme that is not exact but approximate is called **slant rhyme,** or **off rhyme.** Notice this slant rhyme using the words *care* and *dear:*

> You act like you don't care,
> But I know you do, my dear.

Rhyme Scheme A rhyme scheme is a pattern of end rhymes in a poem. A rhyme scheme is noted by assigning a letter of the alphabet, beginning with *a,* to each line. Lines that rhyme are given the same letter.

Rhythm Rhythm is a pattern of stressed and unstressed syllables in a line of poetry. Poets use rhythm to bring out the musical quality of language, to emphasize ideas, to create moods, to unify works, and to heighten emotional responses. Devices such as alliteration, rhyme, assonance, consonance, and parallelism often contribute to creating rhythm.

See also Meter.

Rising Action Rising action is the stage in a plot in which the conflict develops and story events build toward a climax. During this stage, complications arise that make the conflict more intense. Tension grows as the characters struggle to resolve the conflict.

See also Plot.

Romance A romance refers to any imaginative story concerned with noble heroes, chivalric codes of honor, passionate love, daring deeds, and supernatural events. Writers of romances tend to idealize their heroes as well as the eras in which the heroes live. Medieval romances include stories of kings, knights, and ladies who are motivated by love, religious faith, or simply a desire for adventure.

Sarcasm Sarcasm is a kind of particularly cutting irony. Generally, sarcasm is the taunting use of praise to mean its opposite—that is, to insult someone or something.

Satire Satire is a literary technique in which ideas, customs, behaviors, or institutions are ridiculed for the purpose of improving society. Satire may be gently witty, mildly abrasive, or bitterly critical, and it often involves the use of irony and exaggeration to force readers to see something in a critical light.

Scanning Scanning is the process of searching through writing for a particular fact or piece of information. When you scan, your eyes sweep across a page, looking for key words that may lead you to the information you want.

Scansion Scansion is the notation of stressed and unstressed syllables in poetry. A stressed syllable is indicated by the symbol ´; an unstressed syllable, by the symbol ˘. Using scansion can help you determine the rhythm and meter of a poem.

See also Meter.

Scene In drama, the action is often divided into acts and scenes. Each scene presents an episode of the play's plot and typically occurs at a single place and time.

See also Act.

Scenery Scenery is a painted backdrop or other structures used to create the setting for a play.

Science Fiction Science fiction is fiction in which a writer explores unexpected possibilities of the past or the future, using known scientific data and theories as well as his or her creative imagination. Most science fiction writers create believable worlds, although some create fantasy worlds that have familiar elements.

See also Fantasy.

Screenplay A screenplay is a play written for film.

See also Teleplay.

Script The text of a play, film, or broadcast is called a script.

Secondary Source *See* Sources.

Sensory Details Sensory details are words and phrases that appeal to the reader's senses of sight, hearing, touch, smell, and taste. For example, the sensory detail "a fine film of rain" appeals to the senses of sight and touch. Sensory details stimulate the reader to create images in his or her mind.

See also Imagery.

Sequential Order A pattern of organization that shows the order in which events or actions occur is called sequential order. Writers typically use this pattern of organization to explain steps or stages in a process.

Setting Setting is the time and place of the action of a story.

See also Fiction.

Setting a Purpose The process of establishing specific reasons for reading a text is called setting a purpose.

Short Story A short story is a work of fiction that centers on a single idea and can be read in one sitting. Generally, a short story has one main conflict that involves the characters, keeps the story moving, and stimulates readers' interest.

See also Fiction.

Sidebar A sidebar is additional information set in a box alongside or within a news or feature article. Popular magazines often make use of sidebar information.

Signal Words Signal words are words and phrases that indicate what is to come in a text.

Readers can use signal words to discover a text's pattern of organization and to analyze the relationships among the ideas in the text.

Simile A simile is a figure of speech that makes a comparison between two unlike things, using the word *like* or *as*, for example:

Her blue-eyed stare was like ice.

See also Epic Simile; Figurative Language; Metaphor.

Situational Irony *See* Irony.

Soliloquy In drama, a soliloquy is a speech in which a character speaks his or her thoughts aloud. Generally, the character is on the stage alone, not speaking to other characters and perhaps not even consciously addressing an audience. At the beginning of Act One, Scene 7, of *Macbeth*, Macbeth considers his plans in a long soliloquy. Shakespeare makes use of soliloquies in many of his plays.

See also Aside; Dramatic Monologue.

Sonnet A sonnet is a lyric poem of 14 lines, commonly written in **iambic pentameter.** Sonnets are often classified as Petrarchan or Shakespearean. The Shakespearean, or Elizabethan, sonnet consists of three quatrains, or four-line units, and a final couplet. The typical rhyme scheme is *abab cdcd efef gg*.

See also Iambic Pentameter; Rhyme Scheme.

Sound Devices Sound devices, or uses of words for their auditory effect, can convey meaning and mood or unify a work. Some common sound devices are alliteration, assonance, consonance, meter, onomatopoeia, repetition, rhyme, and rhythm.

See also Alliteration; Assonance; Consonance; Meter; Onomatopoeia; Repetition; Rhyme; Rhythm.

Sources A source is anything that supplies information. **Primary sources** are materials written by people who were present at events, either as participants or as observers. Letters, diaries, autobiographies, speeches, and photographs are primary sources. **Secondary sources** are records of events that were created sometime after the events occurred; the writers were not directly involved or were not present when the events took place. Encyclopedias, textbooks, biographies, most newspaper and magazine articles, and books and articles that interpret or review research are secondary sources.

Spatial Order Spatial order is a pattern of organization that highlights the physical positions or relationships of details or objects. This pattern of organization is typically found in descriptive writing. Writers use words and phrases such as *on the left, to the right, here, over there, above, below, beyond, nearby,* and *in the distance* to indicate the arrangement of details.

Speaker In poetry the speaker is the voice that "talks" to the reader, similar to the narrator in fiction. The speaker is not necessarily the poet.

See also Persona.

Speech A speech is a talk or public address. The purpose of a speech may be to entertain, to explain, to present a claim, to inspire, or any combination of these aims. "I Have a Dream" by Martin Luther King Jr. was written and delivered in order to inspire an audience.

Stage Directions A play typically includes instructions called stage directions, which are usually printed in italic type. They serve as a guide to directors, set and lighting designers, performers, and readers. When stage directions appear within passages of dialogue, parentheses are usually used to set them off from the words spoken by characters.

Stanza A stanza is a group of two or more lines that form a unit in a poem. A stanza is comparable to a paragraph in prose. Each stanza may have the same number of lines, or the number of lines may vary.

See also Couplet; Form; Poetry; Quatrain.

Static Character *See* Character.

Stereotype In literature, a simplified or stock character who conforms to a fixed pattern or is defined by a single trait is known as a stereotype. Such a character does not usually demonstrate the complexity of a real person. Familiar stereotypes in popular literature include the absentminded professor and the busybody.

Stereotyping Stereotyping is a type of overgeneralization. Stereotypes are broad statements made about people on the basis of their gender, ethnicity, race, or political, social, professional, or religious group.

Stream of Consciousness Stream of consciousness is a literary technique developed by modern writers, in which thoughts, feelings, moods, perceptions, and memories are presented as they randomly flow through a character's mind.

Structure Structure is the way in which the parts of a work of literature are put together. In poetry, structure involves the arrangement of words and lines to produce a desired effect. A common structural unit in poetry is the stanza, of which there are numerous types. In prose, structure is the arrangement of larger units or parts of a work. Paragraphs, for example, are basic units in prose, as are chapters in novels and acts in plays. The structure of a poem, short story, novel, play, or nonfictional work usually emphasizes certain important aspects of content.

See also Act; Stanza.

Style Style is the particular way in which a work of literature is written—not *what* is said but *how* it is said. It is the writer's unique way of communicating ideas. Many elements contribute to style, including word choice, sentence structure and length, tone, figurative language, and point of view. A literary style may be described in a variety of ways, such as formal, informal, journalistic, conversational, wordy, ornate, poetic, or dynamic.

Summarize To summarize is to briefly retell, or encapsulate, the main ideas of a piece of writing in one's own words.

See also Paraphrase.

Support Support is any material that serves to prove a claim. In an argument, support typically consists of reasons and evidence. In persuasive texts and speeches, however, support may include appeals to the needs and values of the audience.

Supporting Detail *See* Main Idea.

Surprise Ending A surprise ending is an unexpected plot twist at the end of a story. The surprise may be a sudden turn in the action or a piece of information that gives a different perspective to the entire story.

Suspense Suspense is the excitement or tension that readers feel as they wait to find out how a story ends or a conflict is resolved. Writers create suspense by raising questions in readers' minds about what might happen next. The use of **foreshadowing** and **flashback** are two ways in which writers create suspense.

See also Foreshadowing; Flashback.

Symbol A symbol is a person, a place, an object, or an activity that stands for something beyond itself. For example, a flag is a colored piece of cloth that stands for a country. A white dove is a bird that represents peace.

Synthesize To synthesize information is to take individual pieces of information and combine them with other pieces of information and with prior knowledge or experience to gain a better understanding of a subject or to create a new product or idea.

Tall Tale A tall tale is a humorously exaggerated story about impossible events, often involving the supernatural abilities of the main character. Stories about folk heroes such as Pecos Bill and Paul Bunyan are typical tall tales.

Teleplay A teleplay is a play written for television. In a teleplay, scenes can change quickly and dramatically. The camera can focus the viewer's attention on specific actions. The camera directions in teleplays are much like the stage directions in stage plays.

Text Criticism Text criticism is writing in which literary works, including their various elements, are analyzed, interpreted, evaluated, or compared.

Text Features Text features are design elements that indicate the organizational structure of a text and help make the key ideas and supporting information understandable. Text features include headings, boldface type, italic type, bulleted or numbered lists, sidebars, and graphic aids such as charts, tables, timelines, illustrations, and photographs.

Theme A theme, or central idea, is an underlying message about life or human nature that a writer wants the reader to understand. It is a perception about life or human nature that the writer shares with the reader. In most cases, themes are not stated directly but must be inferred. A theme may imply how a person should live but should not be confused with a **moral.**

Recurring themes are themes found in a variety of works. For example, authors from varying backgrounds might convey similar themes having to do with the importance of family values. **Universal themes** are themes that are found throughout the literature of all time periods. For example, the *Odyssey* contains a universal theme relating to the hero's search for truth, goodness, and honor.

See also Moral.

Thesaurus *See* Reference Works.

Thesis Statement In an argument, a thesis statement is an expression of the claim that the writer or speaker is trying to support. In an essay, a thesis statement is an expression, in one or two sentences, of the main idea or purpose of the piece of writing.

See also Claim.

Third-Person Point of View *See* Point of View.

Tone Tone is the attitude a writer takes takes toward a subject. Unlike mood, which is intended to shape the reader's emotional response, tone reflects the feelings of the writer. A writer communicates tone through choice of words and details. Tone may often be described by a single word, such as *serious, humorous, formal, informal, somber, sarcastic, playful, ironic, bitter,* or *objective*.

See also Author's Perspective; Mood.

Topic Sentence The topic sentence of a paragraph states the paragraph's central idea. All other sentences in the paragraph provide supporting details.

Tragedy A tragedy is a dramatic work that presents the downfall of a dignified character (**tragic hero**) or characters who are involved in historically or socially significant events. The events in a tragic plot are set in motion by a decision that is often an error in judgment (**tragic flaw**) on the part of the hero. Succeeding events are linked in a cause-and-effect relationship and lead inevitably to a disastrous conclusion, usually death. Shakespeare's *Macbeth* is a tragedy.

Tragic Flaw *See* Tragedy.

Tragic Hero *See* Tragedy.

Traits *See* Character.

Turning Point *See* Climax.

Understatement Understatement is a technique of creating emphasis by saying less than is actually or literally true. It is the opposite of **hyperbole**, or exaggeration. One of the primary devices of irony, understatement can be used to develop a humorous effect, to create satire, or to achieve a restrained tone.

See also Hyperbole; Irony.

Universal Theme *See* Theme.

Verbal Irony *See* Irony.

Visualize Visualizing is the process of forming a mental picture based on written or spoken information.

Voice Voice is a writer's unique use of language that allows a reader to "hear" a human personality in the writer's work. Elements of style that contribute to a writer's voice include sentence structure, diction, and tone. Voice can reveal much about the author's personality, beliefs, and attitudes.

Website A website is a collection of "pages" on the World Wide Web that is usually devoted to one specific subject. Pages are linked together and are accessed by clicking hyperlinks or menus, which send the user from page to page within the site. Websites are created by companies, organizations, educational institutions, branches of the government, the military, and individuals.

Word Choice *See* Diction.

Workplace Documents Workplace documents are materials that are produced or used within a work setting, usually to aid in the functioning of the workplace. They include job

applications, office memos, training manuals, job descriptions, and sales reports.

Works Cited A list of works cited lists names of all the works a writer has referred to in his or her text. This list often includes not only books and articles but also nonprint sources.

Works Consulted A list of works consulted names all the works a writer consulted in order to create his or her text. It is not limited just to those works cited in the text.

See also Bibliography.

Using the Glossaries

The following glossaries list the Academic Vocabulary and Critical Vocabulary words found in this book in alphabetical order. Use these glossaries just as you would a dictionary—to determine the meanings, parts of speech, pronunciation, and syllabication of words. (Some technical, foreign, and more obscure words in this book are not listed here but are defined for you in the footnotes that accompany many of the selections.)

Many words in the English language have more than one meaning. These glossaries give the meanings that apply to the words as they are used in this book. Words closely related in form and meaning are listed together in one entry (for instance, *consumption* and *consume*), and the definition is given for the first form.

The following abbreviations are used to identify parts of speech of words:

adj. adjective   *adv.* adverb   *n.* noun   *v.* verb

Each word's pronunciation is given in parentheses. A guide to the pronunciation symbols appears in the Pronunciation Key below. The stress marks in the Pronunciation Key are used to indicate the force given to each syllable in a word. They can also help you determine where words are divided into syllables.

For more information about the words in these glossaries or for information about words not listed here, consult a dictionary.

Pronunciation Key

Symbol	Examples	Symbol	Examples	Symbol	Examples
ă	pat	m	mum	v	valve
ā	pay	n	no, sudden	w	with
ä	father	ng	thing	y	yes
âr	care	ŏ	pot	z	zebra, xylem
b	bib	ō	toe	zh	vision, pleasure, garage
ch	church	ô	caught, paw	ə	about, item, edible, gallop, circus
d	deed, milled	oi	noise		
ĕ	pet	o͝o	took	ər	butter
ē	bee	o͞o	boot		
f	fife, phase, rough	ou	out	**Sounds in Foreign Words**	
g	gag	p	pop	KH	*German* ich, ach; *Scottish* loch
h	hit	r	roar	N	*French*, bon fin
hw	which	s	sauce	œ	*French* feu, œuf; *German* schön
ĭ	pit	sh	ship, dash		
ī	pie, by	t	tight, stopped	ü	*French* tu; *German* über
îr	pier	th	thin		
j	judge	th	this		
k	kick, cat, pique	ŭ	cut		
l	lid, needle*	ûr	urge, term, firm, word, heard		

* In English the consonants *l* and *n* often constitute complete syllables by themselves.

Stress Marks

The relevant emphasis with which the syllables of a word or phrase are spoken, called stress, is indicated in three different ways. The strongest, or primary, stress is marked with a bold mark (´). An intermediate, or secondary, level of stress is marked with a similar but lighter mark (´). The weakest stress is unmarked. Words of one syllable show no stress mark.

Glossary of Academic Vocabulary

abstract (ăb-străkt´) *adj.* apart from physical existence; theoretical rather than concrete.

advocate (ăd´və-kāt´) *v.* to argue for or plead in favor of.

comprehensive (kŏm´prĭ-hĕn´sĭv) *adj.* complete or of sufficient scope to include all aspects.

comprise (kəm-prīz´) *v.* to consist or be made up of.

differentiate (dĭf´ə-rĕn´shē-āt´) *v.* to distinguish or demonstrate the individual qualities of.

discrete (dĭ-skrēt´) *adj.* made up of separate or distinct things or parts.

discriminate (dĭ-skrĭm´ ə-nāt´) *v.* to note clear differences; to separate into categories.

diverse (dĭ-vûrs´) *adj.* made up of elements that are different from each other.

domain (dō-mān´) *n.* a sphere of activity.

enhance (ĕn-hăns´) *tr.v.* to make better, or add to the value or effectiveness.

equivalent (ĭ-kwĭv´ ə-lənt´) *adj.* equal to or similar.

evolve (ĭ-vŏlv´) *v.* to change or develop gradually over time.

explicit (ĭk-splĭs´ĭt) *adj.* clearly stated or expressed.

facilitate (fə-sĭl´ĭ-tāt´) *v.* to make something easier.

incentive (ĭn-sĕn´tĭv) *n.* an inducement or motivation to do something.

incidence (ĭn´sĭ-dəns) *n.* the occurrence or frequency of something.

incorporate (ĭn-kôr´pə-rāt´) *v.* to absorb or make part of a whole.

infer (ĭn-fûr´) *v.* to deduce from evidence or reason.

inhibit (ĭn-hĭb´ ĭt) *v.* to hold back or prevent from acting.

innovate (ĭn´ə-vāt) *v.* to change or develop through new or original methods, processes, or ideas.

intervene (ĭn´ tər-vēn´) *v.* to come between two things, persons, or events.

media (mē´dē-ə) *n.* a means or vehicle for communication.

mode (mōd) *n.* a way or means for expressing or doing something.

orient (ôr´ē-ĕnt´) *v.* to place or align in relation to something else.

perspective (pər-spĕk´tĭv) *n.* a viewpoint from a particular position ; an outlook or standpoint.

priority (prī-ôr´ĭ-tē) *n.* something that is more important or considered more important than another thing.

rational (răsh´ ə-nəl) *adj.* based on logic or sound reasoning.

scope (skōp) *n.* the size or extent of the activity or subject that is involved.

thesis (thē´sĭs) *n.* a statement or premise that is defended by an argument.

ultimate (ŭl´tə-mĭt) *adj.* concluding a process or progression; final.

Glossary of Critical Vocabulary

acuity (ə-kyōō´ĭ-tē) *n.* critical perceptiveness; awareness.

admonition (ăd´mə-nĭsh´ən) *n.* a warning.

annul (ə-nŭl´) *v.* render or declare invalid.

beleaguered (bĭ-lē´gərd) *adj.* troubled with many problems.

benefaction (bĕn´ə-făk´shən) *n.* a gift or assistance.

beneficent (bə-nĕf´ĭ-sənt) *adj.* beneficial; producing good.

botanical (bə-tăn´ĭ-kəl) *adj.* related to plants.

chaotically (kā-ŏt´ĭk-lē) *adv.* disorderedly and unpredictably.

clime (klīm) *n.* climate area.

cognizant (kŏg´nĭ-zənt) *adj.* aware or conscious of.

complacency (kəm-plā´sən-sē) *n.* contented self-satisfaction.

compulsion (kəm-pŭl´shən) *n.* forced obligation.

consecrate (kŏn´sĭ-krāt´) *v.* to make or define as sacred.

consensus (kən-sĕn´səs) *n.* agreement.

contemporary (kən-tĕm´pə-rĕr´ē) *n.* one living at the same time as.

contention (kən-tĕn´shən) *n.* an assertion put forward in argument.

cryptically (krĭp´tĭk-lē) *adv.* in a secretive or mysterious manner.

decisively (dĭ-sī´sĭv-lē) *adv.* in a firm and resolute manner.

defiantly (dĭ-fī´ənt-lē) *adv.* boldly, rebelliously.

denizen (dĕn´ĭ-zən) *n.* a resident.

disseminate (dĭ-sĕm´ə-nāt´) *v.* to spread or circulate widely.

dissenter (dĭ-sĕn´tər) *n.* one who disagrees or refuses to accept.

divisive (dĭ-vī´sĭv) *adj.* causing division or disagreement.

dogma (dôg´mə) *n.* principles or beliefs that an authority insists are true.

enunciate (ĭ-nŭn´sē-āt´) *v.* to articulate or pronounce clearly.

ephemeral (ĭ-fĕm´ər-əl) *n.* a short-lived plant.

equidistant (ē´kwĭ-dĭs´tənt) *adj.* at equal distance from.

flagrantly (flā´grənt-lē) *adv.* in a blatantly or conspicuously offensive manner.

flail (flāl) *v.* to thrash or wave about wildly.

fluent (flōō´ənt) *adj.* able to express oneself clearly and easily.

havoc (hăv´ək) *n.* destructive disorder or chaos.

humility (hyōō-mĭl´ĭ-tē) *n.* modesty; lack of superiority over others.

ideology (ī´dē-ŏl´ə-jē) *n.* a system of doctrines or beliefs.

impetus (ĭm´pĭ-təs) *n.* motivating force or incentive.

implicit (ĭm-plĭs´ĭt) *adj.* understood, but not expressed.

incendiary (ĭn-sĕn´dē-ĕr´ē) *adj.* intended to cause fire; flammable.

iniquitous (ĭ-nĭk´wĭ-təs) *adj.* wicked, evil.

inversion (ĭn-vûr´zhən) *n.* reversal or upside-down placement.

loathe (lō*th*) *v.* to hate or despise.

lucid (lōō´sĭd) *adj.* thinking rationally and clearly.

manifest (măn´ə-fĕst´) *v.* to show or reveal.

moratorium (môr´ə-tôr´ē-əm) *n.* a temporary suspension or agreed-upon delay.

mores (môr´āz´) *n.* established customs and conventions.

obliterate (ə-blĭt´ə-rāt´) *v.* erase completely.

orthodoxy (ôr´thə-dŏk sē) *n.* traditionally accepted codes and customs.

peremptory (pə-rĕmp´tə-rē) *adj.* imperative; required; not able to be denied.

perfunctory (pər-fŭngk´tə-rē) *adj.* done mechanically and without enthusiasm.

petulantly (pĕch´ə-lənt-lē) *adv.* in a grouchy or bad-tempered way.

phantasmagoric (făn-tăz´mə-gôr´ĭk) *adj.* dreamlike or surreal.

plaintively (plān´tĭv-lē) *adv.* sadly or wistfully.

poignant (poin´yənt) *adj.* emotionally moving or stimulating.

pollinate (pŏl´ə-nāt´) *v.* to fertilize.

precarious (prĭ-kâr´ē-əs) *adj.* unsafe or insecure.

precipitate (prĭ-sĭp´ĭ-tāt´) *v.* to cause something to happen rapidly or unexpectedly.

precipitous (prĭ-sĭp´ĭ-təs) *adj.* sudden and rapid.

predecessor (prĕd´ĭ-sĕs´ər) *n.* the person who held a position prior to the current holder.

profusely (prə-fyōōs´lē) *adv.* plentifully, in a freely available way.

prognosticate (prŏg-nŏs´tĭ-kāt´) *v.* to forecast or predict.

propagate (prŏp´ə-gāt´) *v.* to reproduce or extend in quantity.

propensity (prə-pĕn´sĭ-tē) *n.* a tendency to behave in a certain way.

provocation (prŏv´ə-kā´shən) *n.* an action intended to elicit an angered response.

proximity (prŏk-sĭm´ĭ-tē) *n.* nearness.

reaffirmation (rē´ə-fûr mā´ shən) *n.* the act of verifying or endorsing again.

reallocate (rē-ăl´ə-kāt´) *v.* to distribute or apportion again; reassign.

repertoire (rĕp´ər-twär´) *n.* a set of skills, abilities or functions.

resilience (rĭ-zĭl´yəns) *n.* ability to return to a normal state after a change or an injury.

retaliate (rĭ-tăl´ē-āt´) *v.* to respond in kind to having been acted upon, often with harmful intent.

sacrilegious (săk´rə-lĭj´əs) *adj.* grossly irreverent toward what is sacred.

sanctity (săngk´tĭ-tē) *n.* sacredness or ultimate importance.

sate (sāt) *v.* to fully feed or satisfy an appetite.

secluded (sĭ-klōō´dĭd) *adj.* hidden from view.

solace (sŏl´ĭs) *n.* source of relief and comfort.

stimuli (stĭm´yə-lī´) *n.* things that cause a response or reaction.

subordinate (sə-bôr´dn-ĭt) *n.* a person of a lesser rank or under another's authority.

subtleties (sŭt´l-tēz) *n.* fine details or nuances.

transcend (trăn-sĕnd´) *v.* to go beyond or rise above.

translucent (trăns-lōō´sənt) *adj.* semi-transparent; indistinct.

transpire (trăn-spīr´) *v.* to happen or occur.

truncate (trŭng´kāt) *v.* to make shorter.

turbulence (tûr´byə-ləns) *n.* violent, disordered movement.

unadulterated (ŭn´ə-dŭl´tə-rā´tĭd) *adj.* pure and untainted.

unpalatable (ŭn-păl´ə-tə-bəl) *adj.* unpleasant or unacceptable.

usurp (yōō-sûrp´) *v.* to take control of illegally.

vermin (vûr´mĭn) *n.* creatures that are considered destructive, annoying, or repulsive; pests.

vicarious (vī-kâr´ē-əs) *adj.* seen through the imagined interpretations of another.

wizened (wĭz´ənd) *adj.* shrunken and wrinkled.

Index of Skills

Key:

Teacher's Edition page numbers and subject entries are printed in **boldface** type.
Subject entries and page references that apply to both the Student Edition and the Teacher's Edition appear in lightface type.
There is no content from the Close Reader in this index.

A

A&E® (Arts and Entertainment), 171, 213
absolute phrases, **140a**, 300, R42
abstract nouns, R23
Academic Vocabulary, 2, 41, 45, 50, 83, 87, 92, 145, 149, 154, 193, 197, 202, 313, 318, 377. *See also* Glossary of Academic Vocabulary
accept/except, R57
act (in play), R59
action scenes, 144a
action verbs, R24, R33
active voice, R35
activities
   media activity, 144
   speaking activity, 10, 14, 40, 82, 106, 126, 168, 192, 208, 244, 277, 294, 298, 312, 348, 360, 375
   writing activity, 17, 22, 36, 134, 139, 159, 181, 187, 231, 260, 291, 338, 357, 371
adjective clauses, 70, R43
adjective phrases, 128, **140a**, R40
adjectives, R24, R35–R36
   vs. adverbs, R36
   comparatives, R36–R37
   conjunctive, R42
   predicate, R36
   proper, R29
   superlatives, R36–R37
adverbial clauses, 182, R43–R44
adverbial phrases, 128, **140a**, R40
adverbs, R24, R36
   vs. adjectives, R36
   comparatives, R36–R37
   relative, 70
   superlatives, R36–R37
advice/advise, R57
affect/effect, R57
affirmative side, in debates, R14
affixes. *See* prefixes; suffixes
allegory, R59
alliteration, R59
all ready/already, R57
allusion, **205**, **320**, **324**, **326**, **336**, 337, R59
allusion/illusion, R57
ambiguity, 274
ambiguous references, R33
among/between, R57
analogies, **166**, **273**, R53, R59. *See also* metaphors; similes
   false, R20
analysis
   speaking activity, 56
   writing activity, 22, 68, 134, 181, 231, 260, 357
analytical essays
   draft of, 46, 314–315
   elements of effective, 45, 313
   exchanging with partner, 47, 315

organization, 46, 314
Performance Task Evaluation Chart, 48, 316
planning, 313–314
reading aloud, 315
revising, 47, 315
writing, 22, 45–48, 134, 159, 181, 313–316, 338
analyzing
   accounts in different mediums, 213, 319, 359, 360a
   arguments, **203**, **204**, **206**, **207**, 208, **209a**, **230**, **319**, **320**, **321**, **324**, **325**, **326**, **327**, **328**, **329**, **332**, **333**, **334**, **335**, **336**, 337, **340a**, **352**, **353**, R16–R17
   author's choices, 7, **28**, **31**, **32**, **33**, **34**, 35, **71**, **73**, **75**, **78a**, **80**, **93**, **95**, **98**, **119**, **156**, **157**, 158, **160a**, **171**, **172**, **173**, **174**, **175**, **176**, **177**, **178**, **179**, 180, 181, **232**, **234**, **235**, **236**, **237**, **238**, **239**, **254**, **376a**
   author's claim, **61**, **62**, **63**, **65**, **66**, 67, **70a**, 337
   character development, 26, 31
   characters, 3, 4, 5, 6, 7, 8, 71, 94, 102, 113, 117, 121, 216, 217, 219, 220, 221, 222, 223, 224, 227, 228, 230, 233, 235, 236, 239, 240, 242, 245, 246, 249, 250, 261, 262, 263, 264, 265, 266, 267, 268, 269, 270, 271, 272, 273, 274, 275, 276, 278, 279, 280, 281, 282, 283, 284, 285, 286, 287, 288, 289, 290, **292a**, **361**, **362**, **363**, **364**, **365**, **366**, **367**, **368**, **369**, 370, **372a**
   character's motivations, 9, 370
   claims, 67, 337, 356, 357
   complex characters, 106a, 312a
   conclusions, 326
   cultural experience, 300a
   details in text, 30
   development of ideas, 142–143
   evidence, 208, **341**, **342**, **343**, **344**, **346**, **350a**, 356
   figurative meanings, 82a
   film, 13, 141, 142, 293
   historical text, 300a
   idea development, 141, 142, 143, 144a, 161, 163, 164, 165, 166, 170a
   ideas, 167, **184**, **185**, **186**, 187, **188a**, **342**, **343**, **344**, **345**, **346**, 348, **350a**
   idioms, 4, 112
   imagery, 251
   images, 126, 192
   impact of word choice, 12, **18**, **19**, 21, 25, 27, 29, 35, **40a**, 56, **70a**, **98**, 164, 257, **258**, 311
   interpretations of Shakespeare, 301, 302, 303, 304, 305, 308a
   language, 26, 32, 39, 52, 59, 64, 162, 225, 226, 228, 229, 241, 248, 252, 273,

278, 282, 286, 341, 367
media, 13, 14, 141, 144, 294, 360
order, **13**, 14, **129**, **130**, **131**, **132**, 133, **136a**, 143
organization, 129, 130, 132
painting, 191
plot, 278
poetic structure, 156, 157, 160a, 192b
poetry, 40, **59**, 60, 82, 139, 159, 192, **248**, 312, **312b**, 375
point of view, 9, **12a**, 14, **101**, **182a**, **190**, **191**, 356, 360
representations, **293**, 294, **294a**
representations in different mediums, **107**, **108**, **109**, **113**, **114**, **115**, **116**, **118**, **119**, **120**, **123**, **124**, 126, **128a**, **190**, **191**, 192, **192b**, 360
rhetoric, to advance author's point of view, **62**, **63**, 67, 68, **162**, **203**, **204**, **207**, 208, **209a**, **322**, **323**, **326**, **330**, **331**, **334**, **352**, **353**, **355**, 356
seminal documents, 15, 16, 17, **24a**, **325**, **326**, **327**, **328**, **329**, **332**, **334**, **335**, **336**, 337, **340a**
Shakespearean drama, 214–292, 244, 260, 277
Shakespearean references, 306
source material, **295**, **296**, **297**, 298
structure, 14, **60a**, **71**, **73**, **75**, **78a**, **93**, 133, 143, 158, 180, **192b**, **214**, **247**, 348
text, 41, 45, 192, 313, 360
theme, 10, **93**, **94**, **100**, **103**, 181, **215**, **218**, **221**, **222**, **223**, **226**, **230**, **233**, **235**, **239**, **240**, **242**, **246**, **256**, **261**, **262**, **263**, **264**, **265**, **268**, **269**, **271**, **272**, **273**, **274**, **275**, **276**, **280**, **281**, **282**, **283**, **284**, **285**, **286**, **287**, **288**, **289**, 290, **292a**, 337, **340a**, **361**, **362**, **364**, **365**, **366**, **367**, **368**, **369**, 370, **372a**, **374**, 375, **376b**
   time manipulations, 12a
tone, 12, 21, 35, 55, 60, 68, 180, 311, **361**, **372a**, **373**, **374**, 375, **376b**
   use of source material, 108
   word choice, 96, 112, 122, 205, 245, 253
Analyzing Text and Media, 360
Analyzing the Media, 14, **142**, 144, 294
Analyzing the Text, 10, 17, 22, 36, 40, 56, 60, 68, 76, 82, 88, 106, 126, 134, 139, 159, 168, 181, 187, 193, 208, 231, 244, 260, 277, 291, 298, 307, 312, 313, 338, 348, 357, 371, 375
anapest, R69
Anchor Text, 3A, 15A, 51A, 71A, 93A, 107A, 155A, 161A, 210A, 319A
anecdotes, 184
Annotate It!, **9**, 10, **11**, 17, **21**, 22, **23**, **28**, 35, 36, 40, **55**, 56, **57**, 60, **67**, 68, 69, **75**, 76, **77**, **81**, 82, 88, 106, 126, **127**, **133**, 134, **135**, 139, **158**, 159, **167**, 168, **169**, **180**,

181, **182**, 187, **188**, 192, 208, 231, 244, **247**, **255**, 260, 277, **279**, **284**, **290**, 291, 298, **299**, **302**, **306**, 307, **311**, 312, **337**, 338, **339**, **340**, 348, **349**, **356**, 357, **358**, **370**, 371, 375
antagonist, **210**, R59
antecedent, R30
   pronoun agreement with, R30–R31
antonyms, **243**, R53
apostrophe, **240**, **278**, R27
appeals
   by association, R17
   bandwagon, R17
   emotional, R17, R64
   logical, R68
   to loyalty, R17
   to pity, fear, or vanity, R17, R20, R64
   to self-interest, 208
Applying Academic Vocabulary, 5, 20, 26, 34, 53, 62, 65, 73, 80, 97, 104, 130, 141, 163, 179, 184, 189, 204, 207, 235, 242, 250, 253, 259, 272, 304, 321, 325, 342, 346, 353, 362
appositive phrases, R40
appositives, R40
archaic language, 217, 278, 286, 292a, 295
archetypes, R59
argumentative essays, 149–152, 377–380, R64. *See also* arguments
arguments, R59
   analyzing, **203**, **204**, **206**, **207**, 208, **209a**, **230**, **319**, **320**, **321**, **324**, **325**, **326**, **327**, **328**, **329**, **332**, **333**, **334**, **335**, **336**, 337, **340a**, **352**, **353**, 356, R16–R17
   assessing validity of, 22, 67, 208, 356
   claims, **61**, 67, 337, 377, R2
   clarifying own view for, 149
   comparisons in, 332
   conclusions to, 150, **207**, 378–379, R3
   counterarguments, **328**, 337, **340a**, R2, R16
   deductive, R18–R19
   draft of, 150, 378–379
   elements of effective, 149, 377
   evaluating, 22, 68, 208, 337, 356, 357, R20–R22
   evidence in, 17, 68, 208, 356
   examples, 61–66, 203–207, 319–336, 351–355, R22
   exchanging with partner, 151, 379
   false statements and fallacious reasoning in, 22, R19–R20
   gathering evidence for, 378
   inductive, R18
   linking ideas in, R3
   logical, R68
   logic and reasoning in, R17–R19
   organization for, 150, 378
   Performance Task Evaluation Chart, 152, 380

Index of Titles and Authors

Key:

Authors and titles that appear in the Student Edition are in lightface type.
Authors and titles that appear in the Close Reader are in **boldface** type.
Names of authors who appear in both the Student Edition and the Close Reader are lightface. For these authors, Student Edition page references are lightface and Close Reader page references are **boldface**.

Student Edition Acknowledgments

Excerpt from "All Together Now" by Barbara Jordan from *Sesame Street Parents Magazine,* September 1994. Text copyright © 1994 by Barbara Jordan. Reprinted by permission of the Sesame Workshop. All Rights Reserved.

"American Burying Beetle" from *Hope for Animals and Their World* by Jane Goodall with Thane Maynard and Gail Hudson. Text copyright © 2009 by Jane Goodall and Thane Maynard. Reprinted by permission of Hachette Publishing, Inc.

Excerpt from "American Flag Stands for Tolerance" by Ronald J. Allen, from *Chicago Tribune,* June 30, 1989. Text copyright © 1989 by Ronald J. Allen. Reprinted by permission of Ronald J. Allen.

The American Heritage Dictionary of the English Language, Fifth Edition. Text copyright © 2011 by Houghton Mifflin Harcourt. Adapted and reprinted by permission from *The American Heritage Dictionary of the English Language, Fifth Edition.*

"The Briefcase" by Rebecca Makkai from *The New England Review,* vol. 29, no. 2, 2008. Text copyright © 2008 by Rebecca Makkai. Reprinted by permission of Rebecca Makkai and Aragi Inc.

"Called Out" from *Small Wonder* by Barbara Kingsolver. Text copyright © 2002 by Barbara Kingsolver. Reprinted by permission of HarperCollins Publishers and Frances Goldin Literary Agency on behalf of the author.

"Carry" from *The Book of Medicines* by Linda Hogan. Text copyright © 1993 by Linda Hogan. Reprinted by permission of The Permissions Company on behalf of Coffee House Press.

"Cloudy Day" from *Immigrants in Our Own Land* by Jimmy Santiago Baca. Text copyright © 1979 by Jimmy Santiago Baca. Reprinted by permission of New Directions Publishing Corporation.

"Coming to Our Senses" from *Natural History Magazine,* March 2001. Text copyright © 2001 by Natural History Magazine, Inc. Reprinted by permission of Natural History Magazine, Inc.

"5 p.m., Tuesday, August 23, 2005" from *Blood Dazzler* by Patricia Smith. Text copyright © 2008 by Patricia Smith. Reprinted by permission of The Permissions Company on behalf of Coffee House Press.

Excerpt from "Letter from Birmingham Jail" by Martin Luther King Jr. Text copyright © 1963 by Martin Luther King Jr. Text copyright renewed © 1991 by Coretta Scott King. Reprinted by permission of Writers House LLC on behalf of the Estate of Martin Luther King Jr.

"Letter to Viceroy, Lord Irwin" from *Famous Letters of Mahatma Gandhi* by Mohandas Gandhi, edited by R.L. Khipple. Text copyright © 1947 by Mohandas Gandhi. Reprinted by permission of the Navajivan Trust.

"The Lottery" from *The Lottery and Other Stories* by Shirley Jackson. Text copyright © 1948 by Shirley Jackson. Reprinted by permission of Farrar, Straus & Giroux, LLC and A.M. Heath & Co., Ltd.

"The Macbeth Murder Mystery" from *My World and Welcome to It* by James Thurber. Text copyright © 2008 by Rosemary A. Thurber. Originally published in *The New Yorker,* October 2, 1937. Reprinted by arrangement with Rosemary A. Thurber and The Barbara Hogenson Agency, Inc. All rights reserved.

"Magic Island" by Cathy Song from *Making Waves: An Anthology of Writings By and About Asian American Women* edited by Asian Women United of California. Text copyright © 1989 by Asian Women United of California. Reprinted by permission of Copyright Clearance Center on behalf of Beacon Press.

Excerpt from *The Math Instinct* by Keith Devlin. Text copyright © 2005 by Keith Devlin. Reprinted by permission of Perseus Books.

Excerpt from "Metamorphosis" from *Metamorphosis and The Trial* by Franz Kafka, translated by David Wyllie. Text copyright © 2007 by David Wyllie. Reprinted by permission of David Wyllie.

Excerpt from *The Metamorphosis* by Franz Kafka, adapted by Peter Kuper. Copyright © 2003 by Peter Kuper. Reprinted by permission of Crown Publishers, a division of Random House, Inc.

"Musée des Beaux Arts" from *W.H. Auden Collected Poems* by W.H. Auden, edited by Edward Mendelson. Text copyright © 1976 by Edward Mendelson, William Meredith and Monroe K. Spears, executors of the Estate of W.H. Auden. Reprinted by permission of Random House, Inc. and Curtis Brown, Ltd.

"My Life as a Bat" from *Good Bones and Simple Murders* by Margaret Atwood. Text copyright © 1983 by O. W. Toad, Ltd. Reprinted by permission of Doubleday, a division of Random House, Inc. and Phoebe Larmore Agency on behalf of author.

"The Night Face Up" from *End of the Game and Other Stories* by Julio Cortázar, translated by Paul Blackburn. Text copyright © 1963 by Random House, Inc. Reprinted by permission of Random House, Inc. and Agencia Literaria Carmen Balcells S.A. on behalf of author.

Excerpt from *Revolution 2.0* by Wael Ghonim. Text copyright © 2012 by Wael Ghonim. Reprinted by permission of Houghton Mifflin Harcourt and InkWell Management, LLC.

Excerpt from *Simplexity* by Jeffrey Kluger. Text copyright © 2008 by Jeffrey Kluger. Reprinted by permission of Hyperion, an imprint of Buena Vista Books, Inc. All rights reserved.

Excerpt from "Address to the ANC Transvaal Congress, 9/12/53" by Nelson Mandela. Text copyright © 1953 by Nelson Mandela. Reprinted by permission of the Nelson Mandela Foundation.

"We grow accustomed to the Dark" from *The Poems of Emily Dickinson* by Emily Dickinson, edited by Thomas H. Johnson. Text copyright © 1951, 1955, 1979, 1983 by the President and Fellows of Harvard College. Reprinted by permission of the President and Fellows of Harvard College.

"What, of This Goldfish, Would You Wish?" from *Suddenly, A Knock at the Door* by Etgar Keret. Text copyright © 2010 by Etgar Keret. Reprinted by permission of Farrar, Straus and Giroux, LLC and Aitken Alexander Associates, Ltd.

Excerpt from "Why Read Shakespeare?: A Real Question and the Search for a Good Answer" by Michael Mack. Text copyright © 2008 by Michael Mack. Reprinted by permission of Michael Mack.

"Without Title" from *Iron Woman* by Diane Glancy. Text copyright © 1990 by Diane Glancy. Reprinted by permission of The Permissions Company on behalf of New Rivers Press.

Close Reader Acknowledgments